A HISTORY

OF

THE FORESHORE

AND

THE LAW RELATING THERETO.

WITH

A HITHERTO UNPUBLISHED TREATISE BY LORD HALE

LORD HALE'S "DE JURE MARIS,"

AND

HALL'S ESSAY

ON THE

Rights of the Crown in the Sea-shore,

THIRD EDITION.

WITH NOTES, AND AN APPENDIX RELATING TO FISHERIES.

BY

STUART A. MOORE, F.S.A.

OF THE INNER TEMPLE, BARRISTER-AT-LAW.

THE LAWBOOK EXCHANGE, LTD.
Clark, New Jersey

ISBN 978-1-58477-592-8

Lawbook Exchange edition 2006, 2017

The quality of this reprint is equivalent to the quality of the original work.

THE LAWBOOK EXCHANGE, LTD.
33 Terminal Avenue
Clark, New Jersey 07066-1321

Please see our website for a selection of our other publications and fine facsimile reprints of classic works of legal history:
www.lawbookexchange.com

Library of Congress Cataloging-in-Publication Data

Moore, Stuart A. (Stuart Archibald), 1842-1907.
A history of the foreshore and the law relating thereto : with a hitherto unpublished treatise by Lord Hale, Lord Hale's "De jure maris", and Hall's Essay on the rights of the Crown in the seashore / Stuart A. Moore.-- 3rd ed.
p. cm.
Originally published: London : Stevens and Hayes. 1888.
Includes bibliographical references and index.
ISBN 1-58477-592-0 (alk. paper)
1. Crown lands--Law and legislation--England--History. 2. Coastal zone management--Law and legislation--England--History. 3. Fishery law and legislation--England--History. 4. Riparian rights--England--History. I. Title.

KD1102.M66 2005
346.4204'32--dc22
2004025091

Printed in the United States of America on acid-free paper

A HISTORY

OF

THE FORESHORE

AND

THE LAW RELATING THERETO.

WITH

A HITHERTO UNPUBLISHED TREATISE BY LORD HALE

LORD HALE'S "DE JURE MARIS,"

AND

HALL'S ESSAY

ON THE

Rights of the Crown in the Sea-shore,

THIRD EDITION.

WITH NOTES, AND AN APPENDIX RELATING TO FISHERIES.

BY

STUART A. MOORE, F.S.A.

OF THE INNER TEMPLE, BARRISTER-AT-LAW.

LONDON:

STEVENS & HAYNES,

Law Publishers,

BELL YARD, TEMPLE BAR.

1888.

TO

The Honourable

Mr. JUSTICE WILLS

THIS WORK IS BY PERMISSION

Most Respectfully Dedicated

TABLE OF CONTENTS.

HISTORY OF THE FORESHORE.

HALL ON THE SEA-SHORE.

TABLE OF CASES.

N.B.—Figures in thick type indicate the report of the case.

PAGES

INTRODUCTION.

THE sole purpose of the present treatise is to throw light upon the difficult questions which so often arise between the Crown and the subject with regard to the title to the foreshores of this kingdom. I was requested by the publishers to prepare a new edition of Mr. Hall's treatise upon the Sea-shore, which was first published in 1830, and most ably re-edited by Mr. Loveland in 1875. In preparing the work, however, I was so much surprised at the unfairness of the arguments put forth by Mr. Hall, arising, without doubt, from an imperfect knowledge of the true facts relating to the subject (which it is but just to say were not accessible at that time), and at the unquestioned bias in favour of the Crown which is apparent throughout his work, that I induced the publishers to allow me to preface the edition with a brief treatise in which I proposed to controvert some of Mr. Hall's arguments. To do this I had recourse to a large quantity of material relating to foreshores, fisheries, and other manorial rights collected by me during many years from the Public Records and from reported cases. I speedily, however, found that, instead of writing a brief treatise, it would be necessary to set forth these records and cases chronologically, in order that the reader might be fully possessed of the material upon which I have based my arguments. Thus I have been led into writing this History of the Foreshore rather than a brief argumentative treatise. This has been done, I hope in an impartial spirit, with a view of setting forth the true history of the commencement and growth of the theory of the *primâ facie* title of the Crown to the foreshore, from the time of its invention by Mr. Thomas Digges in the reign of Elizabeth. Though fully conscious that the whole of the true facts are by no means as yet ascertained, and that many cases which are collateral to the subject with regard to fisheries and other maritime rights have for want of space been omitted from this volume, I trust that sufficient has been done to shew that the theory of the *primâ facie* title of the Crown is a mere theory of abstract law, a theory of "law taken "for granted," based upon an untrue assumption of a state of facts which *might possibly* have existed, but which is really not in accordance with the true state of facts relating to the matter, so far as they can at the present day be ascertained. I have endeavoured to shew, and I venture to think I have shewn, that the true presumption with regard to the ownership of the foreshore is, and should be, as it clearly was before the time of Queen Elizabeth in England, and down to 1849 in Scotland, that *primâ facie* the manors and estates of the subjects extend to the low-water mark and include the foreshore. This, of course, is precisely the reverse of the presumption which is asked for by the theory which is now vouched as undoubted law. I distinctly wish it to be understood that I do not for one moment suggest that the theory is a theory bad in law, or that it should be overthrown or displaced, and for this reason—that, as we are unable, from the loss of ancient records of the realm, to prove absolutely that the Crown has parted with the whole of the foreshore, we cannot say that no portion of it remains in the Crown as part of the waste dominions of the realm. Of course, if we could prove that absolutely, then there would an end of the theory and the presumption arising from it; but it would have to be proved as a matter of fact, and that cannot be done. What I do contend for—and I think, if this volume be studied, it will be found that I have good grounds for so contending—is, that the theory of the *primâ facie* title is not to be taken, as it has been taken for many years, as a theory of almost irresistible inference in favour of the Crown, for I have proved from records that the true facts shew that the Crown has to a very large extent granted away the foreshore, and that very little, if any, of it really and in fact remains vested in the Crown. But, as the full proof that it has all been granted out cannot be made, although the facts so far as they are proved lead strongly to the presumption that that is the real truth, a doubt is left, as to some portions of the shore, whether they have been granted out or not. This must be admitted; and the moment it is so admitted there appears a foundation for the *primâ facie* theory, and a good and reasonable foundation. The truth or untruth of the theory is, therefore, a question of fact. It amounts to this:—Some undefined portion of the shore may still be vested in the Crown; therefore, as that portion is undefined, and as its situation may be anywhere upon the coast, there is a general presumption that any particular portion of the coast may still be vested in the Crown; and it follows that all cases in dispute must be determined by matters of fact and of evidence as to whether the particular portion of shore in issue is part of the granted, or part of the *possibly* ungranted, shore of the kingdom. Thus the question becomes a question of weighing the probabilities of fact. Now, how should the scales of justice be held in such a case? Clearly by the light of the general knowledge of facts relating to the subject. This must surely be done, for I trust we no longer live in a time when the rights of the prerogative are to be strained, against the private interest of the subject, fairly and unduly, as was done in the times of the Tudor and Stuart Sovereigns. And if this be done, to which side should the scale lean in weighing the probability as to whether acts of modern user are referable to usurpation by the subject or more probably referable to the existence of a grant?

If the theory as heretofore put forth were true, and the Crown had in fact parted with but little of the shore by grant, then it would be fair and just to treat almost all user as probably arising from usurpation; but as now the contrary is shewn, and it is clear that the Crown has parted with by far the greater portion of the foreshore by grant, it follows inevitably that evidence of user by the subject must in justice be referred rather to the presumption of a grant than to any alleged usurpation. Unless we are to cast aside the protection of all Statutes of Limitation and Nullum Tempus Acts, so hardly wrung from the Crown by our forefathers, and the salutary doctrine that all long-continued usage shall be referred, if it possibly can be, to a legal origin, and to hold that no grant can be presumed against the Crown, it is manifestly clear that user by a subject, if reasonably sufficient, must be regarded as evidence of ancient grant, and not as evidence of usurpation. If this should be the result of my labours in compiling this work, I shall have fully succeeded in the object I had in view—viz., to shew the true value of the *primâ facie* theory and the real weight of the presumption which arises upon it. An universal theory such as this is, if unduly pressed, operates unfairly, when it is not absolutely true in fact. It is like the theory that all land in Kent is gavelkind until the contrary is shewn, which is as untrue as that the Crown has never parted with the foreshore. In Kent two-thirds at least of the county is knight-service land, a large but undefined portion has been disgavelled by Acts of Parliament, and a small portion of it is borough English; but by lapse of time and the want of any system of land registry by plan, it is become well-nigh impossible to shew what land is gavelkind and what is not. The theory that all is gavelkind prevails, and gradually all Kent is becoming engavelled. The same process has gone on in the same manner with regard to the foreshore since the time of Queen Elizabeth. It will be seen (chapters x. to xiii.) what vigorous attempts were made by the Tudor and Stuart Sovereigns to regain these lost possessions of the Crown, and to what lengths they went in the arbitrary prosecutions of the claim until they were stopped by the great Revolution. It will be seen how, after a long period of quiescence, the Crown officials, under the inspiration of Mr. Hall, and fully persuaded that all claims to foreshores are based on usurpation (see pp. 592, 597 *et seqq.*), began again to make the same vigorous assertion of the same old claim, though scarcely to the same extent, and how to this day, by the oppressive use of the power of the prerogative to make suits lengthy and expensive, they are gradually getting back into the hands of the Crown portions of the foreshore which have certainly and undoubtedly been granted out (see chapter xxiii.).

It is, I venture to think, clear, from the records set forth in chapters i. to ix., that before the time of Queen Elizabeth no idea of the *primâ facie* theory of the ownership of the *jus privatum* of the foreshore existed in the mind of any man. Bracton was certainly aware that the foreshore was generally in the hands of the subject (see p. 33). King Edward the First and his justices and attorneys never suggested that it was otherwise. Fleta and the other early law-writers make no mention of such a right in the Crown. The statute De Prerogativa Regis is almost evidence to negative the suggestion of its existence. Magna Charta, and the statutes relating to weirs, lead us to the same conclusion. The Crown tacitly admits the right to the *jus privatum* in the shore when claimed by the subject, and the Crown sues for trespasses on the shore, not by right of the prerogative, but as lord of a particular manor (p. 95); and this obtains down to 1562; and then about 1569 Mr. Digges invents the theory, by the treatise set forth in chapter x., based wholly on the Roman Law and an exalted notion of the rights of the prerogative. Then for the first time we have the assertion of the right, and there follow case after case in which the claim was unsuccessfully put forward, until we come to the case of Attorney *v.* Philpott, in 1628 (p. 260 and Appendix I.), in which, for the first time, judgment was given for the Crown by the corrupt judges of King Charles the First under pressure of the King. The abortive result of that judgment is shewn in chapter xiii., and the attempts to recover other portions of foreshore are set forth, shewing the struggle between the King and the subject until, in 1641, the Revolution put an end to the then pending suits (p. 310). During the Commonwealth it would seem that scarcely any attempt was made to set up the Crown title. After the Commonwealth it is revived, and Lord Hale, who appears to have written his treatise somewhere about A.D. 1667, boldly states it to be the law that *primâ facie* the shore is the Crown's (pp. 354, 378), but he only cites in support of the theory the decision in Attorney *v.* Philpott, and the case of the Prior of Tynemouth described in chapter v. Of these two cases he clearly doubts that the Tynemouth case is not a decision in point (pp. 359, 379); and as to the other (Attorney *v.* Philpott), one can only surmise that he was ignorant of what had happened in that case, or that, living in the middle of the reign of Charles II., he dared not omit to notice the one solitary decision in favour of the Crown which appeared upon the records of the realm with which he was so very familiar. Had there been any other decision of the same nature, there can be no doubt that Hale would have discovered it and would have quoted it; nor have my own extensive researches enabled me to find any such case. It is true that he draws a negative inference from Sir Henry Constable's case that the *primâ facie* theory is sound, but (at p. 364) he qualifies it by shewing that the fact was, as has been shewn in this treatise, that the shore had been very generally granted out, for he says that "ordinary experience proves that the foreshore is "most ordinarily parcel of the adjoining land," and (at p. 379) that "it is commonly parcel of the manor adja-"cent." It is evident, from the language throughout both his treatises, that he was conversant with the records set out in this volume, and that he knew as a fact that the foreshore had been almost wholly, if not wholly, granted out throughout the coasts of the kingdom.

See also, per Erle, C.J., Le-strange *v.* Rowe, p. 543, Post.

Lord Hale's statement of the theory has ever since his time been looked upon as "law taken for granted," and the theory has been stated in varying language by judge after judge from that time to the present day (see p. 651), but no judge has ever put it higher than as a *possibility* that the Crown may not have granted the foreshore. It is interesting to compare the forms in which the Crown title is alleged from time to time with the view of the theory taken by the Courts. Digges, at p. 221, avers, in his information against Hammond, that the shore is the King's, and that none can claim it except by special grant. In 1628, in Attorney *v.* Bold (p. 259), the Crown claims the shore without any qualification; and in all the suits in the time of Charles the First the claim is made absolutely in the same manner (see Sir John Banks' speech at pp. 293, 295). In the case of Sutton Pool, in 1662 (p. 314), the claim is again made absolutely; and in all commissions and grants from the time of Elizabeth downwards the Crown deals with the foreshore and salt marsh as if it were absolutely entitled and had never made a grant of them. In 1795, in Attorney *v.* Richards (p. 434), the claim is made absolutely. In 1844, in Attorney *v.* Corporation of London (p. 446), the same absolute claim is set up. In 1849, in the Duke of Beaufort *v.* Swansea (p. 484), we find the Attorney-General arguing "that the foreshore belongs to the Crown, not "as part of the tangible possessions of the Crown, but "by the prerogative," thus going back to Digges' original theory. In 1857, in Attorney *v.* Philipps (p. 510), the claim of the Crown is qualified by the words "subject "nevertheless to such grants by her Majesty or her pre-"decessors as are now in force." In Attorney *v.* Emerson, in 1881, a similar qualification is inserted. In Attorney *v.* Lowther, in 1872, we find the allegation of the title enlarged by stating that the foreshores "have at all times "belonged to the Crown except in so far as they have "been granted out." Thus, by the constant assertion and iteration of the general claim to all the shore, the qualification of the claim has gradually been lost sight of, and we find that there is a prevailing general notion, not only in the lay mind, but also in the legal mind, and most decidedly in the official mind, that it is true as a matter of fact that the Crown has very seldom parted with the foreshore. Nor is this to be wondered at. The constant statement of the rule is very apt to beget a pleasant forgetfulness of the exception. Now, if the rule were in fact true, little harm would come of this mental process; but as we have shewn that the rule is not true in fact, but the reverse of true, a wrong general impression is produced by the constant reiteration of it, and this is what has gradually taken place. If the rule were truly stated upon the facts, it should be stated, to use the language of Lord Hale, that "ordinarily and in common experience the foreshore is "parcel of the adjoining land" except where the Crown *has not granted it.* That would be the true way in which the rule should have been stated from the first, and then naturally it would follow that the general impression would be, as it was in Scotland until 1849, that *primâ facie* the foreshore belonged to the adjoining land. The consequence of this general impression is that the rule as stated prevails; it is thought that the exceptions to it are very rare, and consequcntly, whenever the subject claims the foreshore as his own, he is regarded as a usurper rather than a person having a right. I hope that the statement of the true facts as set forth in this volume may help to remove this erroneous impression, and that in future the claims set up by the subject to foreshore may, in justice, be commonly regarded as most probably founded in right and not as being due to usurpation, and that the evidence brought forward in support of them may be attributed to a legal and not to an illegal origin. In ordinary cases as between subjects the Courts lean most strongly in favour of evidence of long-continued user, notably in the cases of claims to rights of common; and the judges strive by every possible means, by every kind of ingenuity, to discover a legal origin for rights which are so claimed. Now that it has been shewn that there is not only a possible legal origin, but *the strongest probability of an absolutely legal origin*, for the ownership of the foreshore by the subject as against the Crown, it is to be hoped that the principles which have been applied to claims to rights of common and similar rights may in the same way be applied to claims to foreshore.

The case of the Crown with regard to the foreshore has been compared by Lord Hale, and subsequently by Mr. Hall, to the ownership of the lord of a manor in the waste land of the manor; and if there is such an analogy between these cases, surely the same principles should apply. The public, as tenants of the King's great manor of the kingdom, exercise their rights of navigation, fishing, and access over the wastes of the foreshore; the King, as lord of his great manor, grants portions of the waste to individuals, subject always to the rights of the public. The rights of the public need no evidence to support them, for they lie not in grant, but are in the public by the common law. The rights of the commoners in the waste of a manor do lie in grant, and originate in grant, and do require evidence to support them; the rights of the grantees of the wastes of a manor lie also in grant, and require evidence to support them; but both these rights will be supported by the Courts against the lord of the manor upon very slight evidence, those of the commoners especially; and if it were shewn in the case of a manor that it had been a very common practice for centuries to make grants of the soil of the waste in the nature, let us say, of cattle gates, subject perhaps to rights of way by the public, would not a claim to a portion of such waste be regarded as probably founded in one of such grants, and would not the evidence be strained as far as possible to presume the existence of such a grant? It is shewn that in this great manor of the kingdom such grants of the waste foreshore have been very common: and, that being so, it is contended that the evidence should be strained as far as possible in favour of the subject against the Crown. It is shewn that this claim of the Crown was an after-thought, invented for the purpose of getting back that which the Crown had parted with. It was founded in untruth and in injustice, and the too great insistence on it by King Charles I. unquestionably was one of the causes of the great Revolution. If the lord of a manor had granted away his wastes to his tenants in cattle gates, subject only to public rights of way across them, and then his successor in title centuries afterwards had said, "These are the wastes of my manor; "neither I nor my predecessors ever granted them, or "granted only small portions of them; shew me how you "claim to keep possession," it would not require much evidence of possession by his grantees to repel his claim. If, therefore, the analogy as between the case of the Crown as to foreshore and the case of a manor as to its wastes is sound in this respect, why should the Crown stand in a better position than the lord of a manor? The Court would regard the evidence of user by those tenants of the wastes or cattle gates with a most favourable eye; every presumption would be made in favour of them against the lord, especially if he shewed no user except the exercise of the rights of the public; and the case of claimants to foreshore stands exactly in the same position but for one circumstance only—viz., that there is no artificial, untrue theory or presumption of law to help the lord of the manor. Even Sir T. Farrer, in his Memorandum on the duties of the Board of Trade in dealing with the foreshores, admits frankly "that the Crown as a land-"owner ought to be in no better or worse position than "other landowners" (p. 602); and if his view is correct, let us hope that in future the Courts will regard evidence of long-continued user of the foreshore, as against the claim of the Crown, in the same spirit as they regard such evidence in claims between subject and subject.

So far as to the history of the *primâ facie* theory. Let us now examine shortly the facts in relation to it. In the earlier chapters of this work (i. to viii.) I have briefly set forth the result of a very extensive examination of ancient records with a view of shewing the manner in which the foreshore was dealt with, and I think it will follow conclusively from a perusal of those chapters that the theory of the *primâ facie* title had no existence, and the presumption of law down to the time of Queen Elizabeth was that every man's manor extended to the low-water mark. These earlier records shew, especially from the time of Henry III. downwards, the careful manner in which the rights of the Crown were upheld, and the elaborate investigation and inquiry that were constantly made year by year as to usurpations upon the Crown, and encroachments either upon its rights under the *jus publicum* or its possessions under the *jus privatum.* The articles administered to the jurors of the Hundred Rolls (p. 42) and the *Articuli Itineris* shew the anxiety of the Crown to maintain its rights; and yet in the voluminous answers to the inquiries we find not a single presentment of a purpresture or encroachment on the *jus privatum* in the foreshore. This is the more remarkable inasmuch as we find every kind of purpresture on the *jus publicum* of navigation and fishery most carefully presented, and we find purprestures on the soil of the King's highways (p. 97), and on the soil of forests (p. 51), even purprestures so minute as steps standing before houses in the streets (p. 143), accurately returned in all cases. Then we also find (p. 63) presentment of a purpresture upon the foreshore of a manor in the King's hands, and we find (p. 95) the King suing for a trespass on the foreshore, and claiming it as parcel of a manor derived by conveyance from a subject. It cannot, therefore, be suggested that the Crown was not looking after its rights, and it is clear that the presumption of law was that the manor of the subject went to the low-water mark. The Prior of Tynemouth's case, which has hitherto been relied upon as a distinct authority and evidence of the existence of the *primâ facie* claim to the *jus privatum* in the foreshore, has been printed at length, and I venture to think that a consideration of the history of that case will shew that it is not an authority to support the proposition in aid of which it has been cited. In chapter ix. will be found a brief notice of the methods by which the Tudor and Stuart Sovereigns endeavoured to impeach the titles of their subjects to estates throughout the country. While they were attacking titles to valuable estates on the *terra firma*, it is not to be wondered at that they should extend those attacks to possessions below high-water mark. This appears to have been first done in the proceedings with regard to New Romney and Bromhill (pp. 177, 178), in 1561 and 1562, but in those cases the Crown claimed, not in virtue of the prerogative nor of any theory of the *primâ facie* title, but as the lord of the manor. In those cases the defendants appear to have found it desirable to submit, and to take a grant from the Crown ; but, as it is obvious that this method of procedure could only apply to cases in which the sea-coast manors were in the hands of the Crown, it became necessary to invent a means of procedure which should enable the Crown to attack the possession of foreshore and marshes in manors which were not then in the hands of the Crown. This was done by Mr. Thomas Digges in the ingenious treatise which is printed in chapter x., in which he boldly lays claim to all the foreshores and salt marshes in the kingdom to which the subject could not make title by express grant produced *in specie.* This practically meant claiming the whole of the foreshores of the kingdom, for there can be no doubt that express grants of the foreshore in terms were as rare in the time of Queen Elizabeth as they are now. The maxim *Nullum tempus occurrit Regi* was in full force at this period, and therefore, if Mr. Digges' theory could have been established as law, practically the whole foreshore of the kingdom, and indeed the whole of the salt marsh and any portion of the inclosed marsh which could have been shewn to have been anciently overflown by the sea, would have become forfeited to the Crown. But we see that the Courts were not prepared to accept Mr. Digges' theory, and, notwithstanding that it was most energetically put forward by the Crown and its grantees, no judgment in favour of it was ever obtained until the time of Charles the First. On the contrary, we see (p. 223) that in the case of the Queen *v.* Hamond the Court held that the theory was not proved, and that the lands in question *were only averred to belong to the Queen;* and in Sir John Constable's case and Sir Henry Constable's case it was clearly held that the foreshore may be parcel of a manor, and may be so shewn to be parcel by evidence of acts of ownership. These decisions, however, did not deter the Crown from continually asserting its claim to the fullest extent with respect to almost every portion of foreshore and salt marsh in the kingdom. We see that commissions after commissions were issued with a view to recover the shore and marshes, but we cannot discover that the Crown or its grantees succeeded to any great extent; nor was there ever a decision of the Court in favour of Mr. Digges' theory until the case of Attorney *v.* Philpott, in 1628 (p. 260). The history of that case is fully set out, and the decree will be found printed in Appendix I. Now that the true facts regarding it have been discovered, now that we know the circumstances under which the Barons of the Exchequer gave their judgment, now that we know that they were the same judges who gave the decree in Hampden's ship-money case, and that their judgment was abortive and ineffectual, it can scarcely be contended that their decision was in accordance with the law of England, and yet it is the only judgment of any Court that had ever up to that time supported Mr. Digges' theory. But, encouraged by it, the Crown proceeded vigorously against all owners of shore and marsh. The cases noticed at pp. 281 *et seqq.* are but a few of the numerous suits which were proceeding in the reign of Charles the First, and which were all put an end to by the great Revolution. Some idea may be gained of the notions which prevailed with the law officers of the Crown with regard to the prerogative from the remarkable address of the Attorney-General in Rex *v.* Oldsworth (p. 292), which I regret I have not been able to print in full. Sir John Banks' address at p. 295 is remarkable for its ingenuity as well as for the absence of historical knowledge possessed by the learned Attorney, who asserts that the "Mirror" and the "Old Register" were written before the Conquest. In Lord Berkeley's case, in 1638 (p. 306), the prerogative theory received a great shock, for there the Court, in order to construe an ancient grant in general terms, admitted evidence of user to shew that the shore was parcel of the manor. We have not the judgment of the Court in the case; the Crown would not risk it; and, at the desire of the Court and the King's counsel, the defendant at last consented to withdraw a juror. This suit and numerous other similar suits which were pending contributed greatly to the general discontent of the subject, and when the Commons expressed their grievances against the King in the Grand Remonstrance on 1 December 1641, they charged against the King "the taking "away of men's right under colour of the King's title to "land between high and low water marks" (p. 310). Immediately all proceedings in such suits were stayed, and the great Revolution put an end to the attempts to recover the foreshores and marshes for the Crown.

Charles the Second revived the claim, and freely granted the foreshore belonging to the subject all round the kingdom, but apparently with little success. About 1667 Sir Matthew Hale appears to have written his celebrated treatise "De Jure Maris," in which he sets up the *primâ facie* title of the Crown on the authority of the Prior of Tynemouth's case, and Attorney *v.* Philpott, and Sir Henry Constable's case (pp. 345, 379). But, though he sets it up as an abstract proposition of law, he greatly limits the inference to be drawn from it by his statement of the propositions of fact, for he says (pp. 364, 379) "that "ordinary experience proves that it is most ordinarily "parcel of the adjoining land, and that although it is true "that such shore may be, and commonly is, parcel of the "manor adjacent, yet *primâ facie* it is the King's." This statement of Hale's therefore shews that he looked upon the King's title as a title resting upon mere legal theory only, and that he knew that in point of fact the foreshore generally and most ordinarily was then vested in the subject. Hale's statement has been taken in all subsequent cases to have established the theory, and it has been declared *obiter* to be the law by judge after judge in every case down to the present time. It must therefore be taken to be now established as law.

The treatise which is here printed (p. 311) as Sir Matthew Hale's first treatise, and which is in his undoubted handwriting, would seem to be a first draft of the more finished work which was subsequently printed by Hargrave. The earlier part relating to the ports will be found to be almost wholly incorporated and much amplified in his work "De Portubus Maris and of the Customs." The second part of it, at p. 357, would appear to be an argument prepared for the case of Rex *v.* Oldsworth, concerning Sutton Marsh. It is valuable as shewing Hale's contention in a form slightly differing from his argument in the work "De Jure Maris." The long vexed question of the authorship of the tract is now settled, for we have Hale's statement (p. 355) under his own hand that he was present at the trial of the case of the Barons of Barclay. In perusing these works one cannot help being struck with the evidence they contain of the great learning of their author, and of his very large knowledge of records. There can be very little doubt that the documents set out in the earlier part of this work were well known to him; and, if this were so, although he states the *primâ facie* theory in its fullest terms as a theory of law, true doubtless in law and in theory, yet one is not surprised that he should so amply qualify the inference and presumption to be drawn from that theory as to make it clear that commonly and in ordinary experience, as a matter of fact, the foreshore was not generally vested in the King, but in the subject. This he must have known, as Bracton knew it before him, and I think that he would have been very much surprised if he had been told that his dictum would in future ages be construed to mean that *primâ facie* and generally the shore was vested in the Crown, and but seldom and in infrequent cases vested in the subject. Such, however, has been the inference commonly drawn from it within the last fifty years, and such is the view of it clearly taken by the Crown officials (see p. 592). The statement and reiteration of the theory of law has come to be looked upon as a statement of fact.

In the reigns of Charles II. and James II. the efforts of the Crown to regain possession of the foreshores and marshes were continued, but with little success. In the time of William III. these efforts, after two defeats, slackened, and from that time till 1824 scarcely a claim was made, and, indeed, the subject rested in peace until in 1830 there came a re-organization of the office of Woods and Forests, and Lord Morpeth, the First Commissioner, and his officers, inspired by the dictum laid down by Mr. Hall, who published his treatise in 1830, set up the old claim again, not, it is true, to all lands that had ever been overflowed by the sea, but to the foreshores proper between the high and low water marks, and proceeded arbitrarily and without inquiry to deal with the foreshores of the kingdom, as if it were admitted in fact and in law that the whole of these were still vested in the Crown. The proceedings of the Commissioners of Woods, and the subsequent action of the Board of Trade since 1866, will be found fully detailed in chapter xxiii.

Such is the history of the claim of the Crown writ shortly. The cases and documents relating to the foreshore have been analysed in chronological order in this work. These abstracts are necessarily brief, but I have endeavoured to reprint the most important passages of the reported cases which give any dicta relating to the subject. The student, however, is warned that he should not depend upon the extracts here given, but in all cases refer to the original report. The extracts are given to shew the history of the growth of the law as laid down by the Courts, and for the purpose of guiding him to the particular cases which are likely to assist him in any particular inquiry. The Scotch cases noticed in chapter xxii. are not intended to be exhaustive of the law as relating to Scotland ; they are merely inserted to shew the manner in which user of the foreshores is to be considered and construed in cases both in England and in Scotland, for though the *primâ facie* theory was not introduced in Scotland till 1849, the theory there is the same, and the Crown title is to be rebutted by the same class of evidence in both countries.

I have treated briefly in chapter xxiv. of the practice and procedure in suits as to foreshore, and I trust that I have shewn how unfair and unjust is the present method used by the Crown in suits by English information in the Exchequer—a relic of the arbitrary procedure of the "bad old times" of the Stuart Sovereigns, absolutely contrary to the letter and the spirit of the statutes of 21 James I. cap. 2 et 14, which were wrung from the Crown by the Commons to put an end to the oppressions of that most arbitrary of kings—a procedure most oppressive and unjust in every particular, and now, as then, used *in terrorem* to force the subject to re-purchase from the Crown the foreshore which in almost every case must have been for centuries parcel of his ancient inheritance, bought from the Crown by his predecessors in ages past. It is bad enough that this untrue theory of the *primâ facie* title should practically be a standing *quo warranto* against all owners of foreshore, always ready to impeach their titles and to put them to long and expensive suits to establish them; but when the method of procedure is made arbitrary and expensive, and capable of indefinite delay at the pleasure of the Crown officials, it amounts to an absolute denial of justice to the subject. This has been recognised by Parliament (Crown Suits Act, 1855), and a remedy directed to be given; the judges are empowered, and indeed directed, to make rules to assimilate the procedure in suits by English information to the procedure in suits between party and party; but, by whose fault we know not, this has never been done. On the contrary, the utmost care has been taken to preserve the ancient arbitrary, unjust, and, as I venture to think, illegal form of procedure from being included in any of the salutary amendments of the law of procedure that have been made in recent years. It is left to flourish as of old, and it is the one weapon by which the Crown officials are enabled to force the owners of foreshores to compound with the Crown, and to extort large sums of money from them, rather than face the cost, delay, and anxiety of defending an English information to maintain their rights. It is time that a remedy was provided. The power to give such a remedy has been given by Parliament to her Majesty's judges, and it is to be hoped that they will see fit to proceed at once to give effect to the Crown Suits Act, 1855, and to make such rules as shall enable the subject in all cases to try his right, if he have one, fairly, justly, and without excessive delay and cost, for it is not consistent with the honour and dignity of the Crown or the nation that it should be possible, by a form of procedure, to practically deny justice to the subject as completely and as arbitrarily as was done by King James I. or his successors.

I regret that I have been unable in this treatise to refer to and fully consider the numerous cases relating to fisheries in tidal waters, many of which throw light upon the subject before us; but I find myself compelled by the mass of material to confine myself somewhat strictly to the subject immediately under consideration, and to draw a hard-and-fast line, and exclude those cases. They are dealt with in Mr. Hall's treatise and the notes thereto (see *post*, pp. 711 *et seqq.*, and in Appendix II.). I hope at some future time to avail myself of the large collection of material which I have made respecting fisheries in general, and to write a treatise on that subject. Cases respecting nuisances and purprestures upon the *jus publicum* where no question of the title to the *jus privatum* has arisen—*e.g.*, Rex *v.* Ward, 4 A. & E. 406; Rex *v.* Russell, 6 B. & C. 566—I have also found it necessary to exclude. I trust, however, that I have included in this work all, or nearly all, the cases which bear directly on the question of the title to foreshore; but, as I am conscious that some may, notwithstanding a careful research, have escaped me, I shall be very grateful to any kind reader who will call my attention to the omission of any case or record that may help to throw further light upon the subject.

Mr. Hall's essay, with Mr. Loveland's valuable notes, is reprinted as it stood in the last edition. I have added cases to Mr. Loveland's notes, and I have also in my own notes combated some of Mr. Hall's contentions where I think he was mistaken, or has drawn a wrong inference from the facts, or has been led to a wrong conclusion from ignorance of the facts.

My acknowledgments for help are due to friends too numerous to mention, notably to Mr. H. S. Milman, Director of the Society of Antiquaries, who gave me a valuable collection of notes; to Mr. Scargill Bird and Mr. Overend, of the Public Record Office; to Mr. McClymont and Mr. William Wills, of the Inner

Temple; and, lastly, to my clerk, Mr. Inward, for his careful assistance throughout the work and for compiling the Index.

It will be an obvious remark upon this treatise that it is a brief for the subject against the Crown, or against the Crown as representing the public—and so it is. If it were a mere argumentative treatise not founded upon ascertained facts, like the works of Mr. Digges and Mr. Hall, then I should be the first to allow that it might carry but little weight as a mere partisan view of the subject. But I venture to hope it will be found that it is something more. It contains, so far as laborious research has enabled me to discover them, a fair and impartial statement of the facts upon which the arguments and conclusions are drawn, and to those readers who may be inclined to accuse me of too strong a leaning to one side of the question I appeal to consider the facts, and to see for themselves whether the conclusions drawn from them are or are not warranted by those facts. The whole question is one of fact as opposed to a theory which rests for its basis on a presupposition of a possible state of facts which cannot, now that we have the statement of the true facts vouched by records and decided cases, be shewn to be true. It is a counterblast against Mr. Digges and Mr. Hall and the opinions clearly held by Sir T. Farrer and the officials of the Woods and Forests and the Board of Trade. If by this statement of the true history of the foreshore I have succeeded in making it plain that although the theory as applied in some few instances may be quite true, and that the Crown may have in exceptional cases retained the foreshore, yet that by far the larger probability clearly is that in almost every case it has parted with it; and that, therefore, it should be presumed in fact, though not in law, to belong to the subject rather than to the Crown; then I shall hope to see a fairer method of dealing with disputed cases, and true and equal justice dealt out to the owners of foreshore by giving full weight to their acts of ownership when put forward to raise the most probably true presumption that the foreshore is parcel of their manors. On the facts as here set forth I challenge that to be the true assumption of fact, and I think that Lord Hale, notwithstanding that he gives the weight of his authority in support of the theory, knew that the facts were as I have stated, and it must be recollected that it is on Lord Hale's authority, and on *obiter dicta* since the date of his treatise, that the theory rests as a proposition of law.

If the reader should complain that this work is a brief for the subject, let him turn to Mr. Hall's treatise and he will find a brief for the Crown ; but I would ask him to read that treatise by the light of the notes I have added to it, to compare Mr. Hall's arguments with the facts set out in this work, and to judge on which side the probability of truth lies.

I cannot close this Introduction without some remarks upon the very specious suggestion put forward by Mr. Hall (p. 832), and strongly urged in the Memorandum of the Board of Trade (pp. 597–611), that it is desirable and advisable, in the interest of the public at large, that the foreshore should be held to be vested in the Crown in order that the rights of the public under the *jus publicum* may be the better protected. This suggestion, dwelt upon so seriously in the Memorandum, would seem to proceed from a guilty conscience and a shrewd suspicion that the claim of the Crown is of the weakest, not founded in justice and in truth, and most difficult to uphold by legal means against the subject. Why should it be suggested (p. 597) that the Board of Trade, in their dealings, should make it clear that their "principal object is not to assert the proprietary "rights of the Crown to the detriment of frontagers and "others, but to protect the public from private encroach-"ment upon land and sea, which [it is asserted] is the pub-"lic property of the nation" ? and why should it be stated that, by thus pretending, they will "be able to *raise the ques-"tion of title* in a much less invidious way, and with much "greater prospects of success, than could be at present pos-"sible" ? Can it be that it is thought that this title of the

Crown is so shadowy that it cannot be maintained except by deliberately enticing juries and judges to waver from the truth in trying an abstract right by a suggestion that rights of individuals in the foreshore ought to be forfeited because it will be for the benefit of the public? Then it is complained (p. 602) that "the lawyers have cut down "the Statutes of Limitation by allowing juries to presume "a grant," and that "the leaning of Courts and juries is "often in favour of a single concrete human being and "against that abstract or collective entity called the pub-"lic." And it being found difficult to enforce this claim of the Crown in consequence of the upright administration of the law and the honesty of jurymen, it is suggested as a remedy (p. 602) that the Board's endeavour should be to get Courts and juries "to see that they are protect-"ing the public, and to give them fair measure accord-"ingly." Why should the Board of Trade find it (p. 597) "probably prudent to postpone" inquiry as to when and in what place the Crown has parted with its rights? Why is it desirable (p. 611) to postpone bringing in "a "Bill to ascertain, and give facilities for ascertaining, the "Crown's title"? Why is this "a delicate matter, and "must be postponed for some time"? Is it that it is advisable to wait on Providence, and, by pretending not "to assert the proprietary rights of the Crown" except for the pious purpose of protecting the public, to be the better able, so soon as the Board shall "have established a good "character" (p. 601), "*to raise the question of title* in a "much less invidious way, and with much greater pros-"pects of success," so soon as Courts and juries, influenced by the apparently pious and public-spirited intentions of the Board, shall have learnt to lean in favour of "that abstract "and collective entity called the public," and against the right and title of the "concrete human being" to his ancient inheritance in the enjoyment of which he has hitherto been protected by the just administration of the law and the honesty of jurymen? Is there any other explanation of this suggested course of proceeding than that it has been found that this so-called right and title of the Crown is a mere pretence, that cannot now, as it could not in the time of Charles I., be established on a fair trial, and because experience shews that no jury has ever yet been found to uphold it, and the Crown has shrunk from a jury in almost every case (pp. 616, 625)? And is the difficulty to be got over by pretending to protect the rights of the public, and thus indirectly bribing jurymen and influencing courts of justice to uphold this shadowy claim on grounds of expediency, regardless of the law and the facts and the vested interests of a large body of proprietors, contrary to all justice and honesty? Then, again (p. 601), why, if this claim is founded in truth, are the Board of Trade, when they know that "the Crown's title is doubtful, to proceed in "the same way as if it were good," but with greater caution, and "to be more ready to compromise the "question on the principle of reserving to the public their "rights and easements over the soil." What does this mean but attempted extortion?

And then comes the real question. Is it for the benefit of the public that the foreshore should be held to be vested in the Crown? I venture to think that it is not, unless it be intended that all property in the foreshore had better be confiscated and sold, as occasion serves, for the reduction of the National Debt, regardless of the rights of the owners. It is a cardinal principle that the subject can only enjoy the foreshore subject to the rights of the public under the *jus publicum*, and can only use it subject to those rights precisely in the same manner as the Crown could have used it before it was granted, and precisely in the same manner as the Crown could use it if it be forfeited now. The most desirable, the most efficient, and most certain protection to the public is clearly the control of the courts of law; but the Crown is not under that control—the subject is. Who shall control the action of the Board of Trade or the Woods and Forests if foreshores can be turned to valuable account, and they choose to do any act injurious to navigation or derogatory to the enjoyment of a local public—for it is usually a local public, and not the general public, that is injured?[1] Will those departments listen to the complaint of fishermen hindered in their trade, or deprived of their ancient fishing grounds for the benefit of some limited company? Will they hearken to the grievances of some body of Conservators struggling with an unmanageable tidal river to which some erection licensed by them may do incalculable injury? Will Parliament interfere, except in the last resort, to stay their proceedings? *Credat Judæus!* If they choose to dig away the foreshore to the injury of neighbouring landowners, or license the taking of shingle thereon, who shall control them (see Attorney *v.* Tomline, *post*, p. 565). *Quis custodiet ipsos custodes?* But for any such acts done by a subject there is a simple remedy by indictment or injunction. The subject may not inclose the foreshore, nor erect a wharf or pier on it, nor prevent the use of it for navigation nor for fishery (except he have a several fishery), nor do any act in any wise to prevent the public from enjoying all their legal rights thereover. And if he does so, any one may restrain him by simple process, at the slightest cost, and without a doubt as to his success, and in all navigable rivers now there are commissions of conservancy and of fishery, armed with enormous powers to protect the public. But who shall attack the Crown? Take the case of oyster fisheries granted by the Board of Trade. Who listens otherwise than formally, and for the sake of decency, to the grievances of the poor fishermen, who have their lives long got their honest living by anxious toil upon the grounds which are granted away to speculators and company-mongers? This could not be done by the subject. Irreparable mischief is done to these poor men to benefit speculators, and a good return of cash is made in the Board's accounts.

But the Board of Trade Memorandum (p. 599) says that the rights enjoyed by the public are those of navigation, fishing, landing, beaching, walking, *bathing*,

[1] At the present moment it is proposed to close up a large portion of the Solent to make a practising range, and to stop an important navigable channel.

gathering seaweed, &c., and that any interference with them should be reported to the Board by the coast-guard and Customs officers, and that "great care should "be taken to make this point prominent in the circulars "to be addressed to those officers, *so that the public "may see what is the Board's principal object.*" As the law stands, there is no right of bathing, but the question is considered doubtful, and no one ever heard of an owner of foreshore preventing bathing that was carried on in a decent manner. The right of gathering seaweed does not and cannot exist. Are we to suppose that these so-called rights are to be dangled before the eyes of the public with great care, with a view to influence juries, and to show the pious intentions of the Board of Trade previous to their raising the question of title with greater chance of success than is at present possible? I make no accusations against the officials of the Board of Trade, who are most zealous, and properly zealous, in carrying out what they conceive to be their duty in protecting the supposed rights of the Crown and of the public. Let them be judged by their own words as set forth in their Memorandum, and, if it be considered that the course of action therein proposed is consistent with the principles of common honesty and justice, rather than as shewing a desire to attain the object of getting possession as far as possible of the whole of the foreshores by attempting to influence courts of justice and jurymen by a specious but untrue suggestion of general expediency for the benefit of the public, I have no more to say; but that I am driven to the conclusion that we are now to read the ancient theory by the modern doctrine of expediency thus:—*Primâ facie* and of common right the foreshore belongs to the public, and that, as nothing shall be presumed against the majesty of the people, nothing shall be permitted to stand in law against their enjoyment of any man's property. In these latter days it seems to be a growing political doctrine that if a sufficient number of persons sufficiently want any man's property, and sufficiently ask for it, they are to have it, and it would seem to be suggested with regard to the foreshore that this highly desirable result is to be attained, not by sustaining a legal and constitutional claim of right, but by persuading jurymen and judges that, as it is expedient in their own interest, direct or indirect, that owners of foreshore should not be allowed to sustain their titles on the principles of law which have hitherto been universally accepted. They are to be persuaded, by a specious pretence, to lean towards the shadowy claim of the Crown, and unfairly and dishonestly judge of the effect of the evidence brought before them, and to find for the Crown rather than the subject, because it is advisable and expedient that the foreshore should be vested in the Crown for the benefit of the public. Such appears to be the proposition, nor do I think I have unfairly or untruly stated it. Let us compare it with the proposition made to King Charles I. when the same impossibility of getting judges and juries to find for the Crown had put him in the same difficulty as seems to have been felt by the Board of Trade (p. 276). After the abortive result of the judgment in Attorney *v.* Philpott, the "fishing" grantees of the Crown of marshes and foreshores belonging to other people petition the King, and complain that they cannot get possession of the lands granted them, and "this by reason of "the common outcry that your Majesty's title is not likely "to prevail; and the rather because the Barons of your "Majesty's Court of Exchequer have of late appeared very "doubtful in their opinions whether to determine for or "against your Majesty in the question of the said marshes, "which your petitioners do conceive to proceed from the "want of the patronage of some special person of your "Majesty's most honourable Privy Council to countenance "the said matter, and do suppose and hope that the doubts "of the Barons might be removed," and they pray the King to appoint some special person of his Privy Council to take the *care and patronage* of the matter, and to persuade the Barons what the law was, and to find for the Crown; and the King did so. In those days there was no doctrine of expediency for the benefit of the public; the doctrine was that the so-called prerogative of the

Crown should be upheld at any cost, and we see that it was so attempted to be upheld, at the cost of the great Revolution. In these days it would not avail much to appoint some special person of the Privy Council to persuade the judges who now represent the Barons of the Exchequer to find for the Crown contrary to law and justice; but the Crown officials, zealous now, as those "fishing" grantees were then (to use the language of the Grand Remonstrance), to "take away men's right under "colour of the King's title to land between high and low "water mark," are again in the same difficulty. Juries have been found to give honest verdicts; judges, like their predecessors the Barons of the Exchequer, have directed juries to find according to law; and it is again become necessary to ask for the *care and patronage* of some special person; but, alas! in these modern times there is no such special person to be found. The cry, therefore, of the baffled officials, zealously desirous to maintain what they consider the Crown's undoubted right, is no longer for the assistance of some "special person," but takes another form. The rights of the prerogative are not regarded as they were in the time of Charles the First. To the honour of the Crown be it said that they are not now often used to work injustice upon the subject; but the times are changed, and these rights are practically vested in the public. To this "abstract or collective entity called "the public" goes up the cry for help from the Crown officials, and with the same object as the cry of the "fishing" grantees for help to King Charles the First. The "fishing" grantee persuaded the King to misuse the prerogative and coerce the judges in order to obtain his ends; the Crown official to-day suggests to the public that they shall equally work injustice contrary to law for the attainment of the very same object, upon the ground that it is advisable, expedient, and for their own benefit. To further succeed in this long-continued attempt to uphold this untrue theory they must needs have nowadays the *care and patronage* of the public. The historical parallel is, I venture to think, complete; the morality and honesty of the two courses of procedure are very much alike. In both cases the movers of the suggestions are actuated by a perfectly honest belief that what they are asking for is only right and proper ; but in both cases they are mistaken as to the truth of the facts and as to the law. The "fishing" grantees of Charles the First fully believed the claim of the Crown to be undoubted, and that the foreshore and marshes were vested in the Crown as part of the flowers of the prerogative ; and they say so in their petition. In this we know they were mistaken, and the Barons of the Exchequer knew it too. The Crown officials now, misled by Mr. Hall's theories and his ignorance of facts, believe, in the same way, that the title of the Crown is undoubted and indisputable, and that all claimants to foreshore are encroachers and usurpers ; therefore, let neither of these claimants be blamed for their beliefs, but let the reader judge as to the respective morality of the course of proceeding suggested by the "fishing" grantee and that proposed in the Memorandum of the Board of Trade. The "fishing" grantee suggested that the Lords of the Council should persuade the Barons of the Exchequer as to what the law was; the Board of Trade proposes by its method of proceeding to induce the public and the Courts to believe that they are actuated principally, if not solely, by a desire to protect the public from fancied but impossible encroachment by individuals upon their rights, and having thus persuaded the public generally, and in consequence jurymen also, who are members of the public, that it is acting with a view to their general interest and benefit, then it is proposed to "raise the "question of title in a much less invidious way, and with "greater prospect of success than would be at present "possible." King Charles I. put pressure on the judges to warp the law ; the Board of Trade would seem, if we are to judge them by their own Memorandum, desirous of misleading Courts and juries by a doctrine of expediency for the benefit of the public in order to get decision against the rights of the subject. If these be the principles which commend themselves to the official mind, I ask, in conclusion, whether they are the best custodians of the public right, custodians who are practically uncontrollable by the Courts, rather than private individuals who can be readily, quickly, cheaply, and undoubtedly restrained by indictment and injunction from doing any even the slightest act upon the foreshore in derogation of the public rights thereover.

It is scarcely necessary to point out that these last remarks are addressed to the lay, and not to the legal mind; for by no stretch of the wildest imagination can it be supposed that any one would dare to address an argument on the question of such expediency to her Majesty's judges with a view of endeavouring to influence them to regard evidence with a bias or to warp the law in favour of the claim of the Crown.

6 King's Bench Walk, Temple,
November 1888.

A
HISTORY OF THE FORESHORE
AND
THE LAW RELATING THERETO.

HISTORY

OF

THE FORESHORE.

CHAPTER I.

A.D. 765 TO THE END OF THE REIGN OF KING JOHN.

It is evident from a study of the charters of the Anglo-Saxon kings that the territories granted by them extended to the shore of the sea, to the mid-stream of non-tidal rivers, and in the case of tidal rivers *inter fauces terræ*, also to the mid-stream. Most of the Anglo-Saxon charters which have been preserved are grants to monasteries, though some few are made to individuals; and it is a fair inference that those which remain present examples of the ordinary form of grant used in those days, whether made to lay or ecclesiastical persons. The elaborate boundaries which are appended to these charters shew us with much accuracy the extent of the estates granted. In grants of lands lying upon rivers we continually find the description of the boundary in the river is, *e.g.*, "up midne streame by halfen streame"—"into "theie Temise othe mid streame"—"and lang suth on "Temise ad midden streame and long streames be londe "and be stronde eft on Merefleote," &c. These descriptions apply to places situate both on tidal and non-tidal water. When estates are bounded by the sea, the description of the boundaries is not often completed on the sea side, but starts from the sea and passes inland and then returns to it, leaving the sea boundary as a thing well known—viz., to the low-water mark.

Cart. Sax. i. 82, ed. Birch. The grant of Pagham, Sussex, to Bishop Wilford in A.D. 680 sets out the bounds "primitus ab Wedringmuthe, per "illum portum ad locum quæ dicitur Holan Horan "fleot —— ab illo loco in fisc mere et sic in Brynesfleot "sicque dirigitur *in mare.*"

Ibid. i. 99. The adjoining land of Selsey, granted to Bishop Wilford in A.D. 683, has a boundary distinctly including the foreshore to sea-ward "ab introitu portus qui appellatur "Wyndernge *post retractum mare* in cumeneshora; sic "versus occidentalem plagam juxta mare usque Rumbruge "in ante juxta litus maris usque Chenestone; inde in ante "juxta littus usque Heremuthe; et inde versus septen-"trionalem plagam in longum fluvii usque Wialesflet; "sursum usque quo Brimesdik exit; inde versus orientem "in longum prædicti fossati in Woflet; inde versus ori-"entem in longum fluvii; et sic versus australem plagam "usque Wuderingmuthe." There is another grant of Selsey by Brithelm in A.D. 957, "cum omnibus ad se rite per-"tinentibus campis pascuis pratis silvis *capturis piscium.*"

Ibid. i. 177. Battersea (co. Surrey) was granted to St. Peter's, Westminster, in A.D. 693, and is bounded "into thære Tæmese oth "midne streame andlang streames eft into heah Efre" (River Effra). Cearn (co. Somerset?), granted to Winchester in

Ibid. i. 229. 738, is bounded "*Ærest of sæ* uppon Hængestes rieg —— "of earnes hlince æft *ut on sæ.*" Lydd, in Dengey Marsh

Ibid. i. 302. (Kent), is bounded "mare in oriente et aquilone, et ab "austro terra regis ad Wi ubi nominant Denge Merse," &c. And later on we shall see that the "terra regis ad Wi" was granted to Battle Abbey with the shore. Hastings and Pevensey were granted to the abbey of Saint Denis in

Ibid. i. 351. France in A.D. 788 by Duke Berthwald as "meæ possessionis "portus qui sunt in eadem vicinitate super mare Hastinges "et-Pævenisel cum salinis et omni integritate sua." Halling (Kent), granted to Rochester between A.D. 765 and 791 as "Hallingas cum omnibus scilicet ad eam pertinentibus "rebus juxta terminos indigenis certissimos cum campis "silvis pratis paludibus piscationibus venationibus aucupa-"tionibus libenter tenendam et possidendam," is bounded "usque in flumen Medewæge." Gambleworth (Kent) was granted by King Edmund, in A.D. 946, to Ordhelm and Alfwold, and is bounded: "suth fealcing rip *oth sæ* —— thonne thæs biscopes mearc on north healfe and on east healfe *ut on sæ*." Rainham (Kent) was granted to Canterbury "cum campis pascuis pratibus silvis "saltibus piscuosis ac maritimis fretibus paludibus valli-"busque dulcis salsuginesque salisque stationibus coctio-"nesque et cum cunctis fructibus interius exteriusque vel "aliunde usquam ad eas rite vel unquam pertinentibus," &c. Graveney (near Faversham), Cassingburn, and Elmanstude were acquired by the Archbishop of Canterbury, A.D. 811, "cum undique legitimis limitibus rite ad eas pertinentibus "campis silvis pratis pascuis paludibus *litoribus* liberas ab "omni seculari servitio," &c. Graveney and Cassingburn are confirmed to the Archbishop by another charter in A.D. 812. Graveney is described as bounded by the River Swale and the River Medway. Cassingburn, which appears to be near Lympne, in Romney Marsh, is described as "an ivelet"—"ad id insuper addito illo litore "foris maritimo cum pristinis terminibus cunctis ad eam "usquam rite pertinentibus. Dei gratia quoque Rex "Coenulf has prædictas terrulas verbi gratia æt Grafonæa "atque iterum æt Casingburnam litoreque illo cum om-"nibus undecumque legitimis limitibus campis salsuges "pascuis silvis pratibus paludibus *litoribus piscuosis* seu "cunctis aliunde usibus quibusquilibet *maritimisque fructi-"bus* &c. donabo," &c. Hallow, on the River Severn, given to the Bishop of Worcester in 816, is bounded "of Pærlega "in Saferna stream. This synd tha lond gemara in "Halheogan on thest half Sæferne." Calbourn, in the Isle of Wight, was granted to the see of Winchester, in 826, by King Eabyrth with these words, "Volo etiam ut hæc "terra libera semper sit, cum locis montanis ac silvis "pratis et pascuis et campis atque cum omnibus ad me "pertinentibus rebus." It is described by its boundaries as

Cod. Dip. 407.

Cart. Sax. i. 467.

Ibid. i. 469. Nat. MSS. No. 6.

Cart. Sax. i. 477.

Ibid. i. 496.

"Ærest of sæ up on Æstede —— thanon on Cathelbur-"nam and lang Cathelburnam ut on north sæ." Yantlet (Kent) was granted to Rochester, A.D. 779. "Insuper "adiciam mariscum pertinentem ad aridam et ad aquæ "ripam Iaenlede habentem quasi quinquaginta jugerum." Brakelesham and Earnlea (Sussex) were granted to Bishop Ælfred "cum omnibus utensilibus quæ infra terminos "ejusdem juris continentur tam in notis causis quam "ignotis in modicis et magnis, *terra et mari* humido et "sicco," &c.

Cod. Dip. 135.

Ibid. 403.

Tidenham, on the Severn (Gloucester), was granted to the monastery of St. Peter's, Bath, A.D. 956, "cum omnibus "quæ ad eundem locum jure pertinere dinoscuntur tam in "magnis quam in modicis rebus campis pascuis pratis "silvis capturis piscium," and the boundaries are "of "Wegemutham to iwes heafthen —— on Twyford; of "Twyford on æstege pul ut innam Sæfern." Fuller boundaries of Tidenham are given in vol. iii. p. 450 of the Codex Diplomaticus, entitled "Divisiones et consuetu-"dines de Dyddanhamme," and shew that there were on the Severn and the Wye very numerous "cytwæras" and "hæcweras," which are fixed engines locally known as "putchers," still used at Tidenham. Mr. Seebohm ("English Village Communities," p. 150) has most learnedly discussed this document, and shews that the manor extends to the mid-stream, as do all the manors in the estuary of the Severn.

Ibid. 452.

Hale, de Jure Maris, p. 35.

In A.D. 785 Offa of Mercia granted to the monks of Thorney "quandam particulam terræ, id est, casatorum, "ubi solicoli clamare suescunt, et Ældenham, cum omnibus "aptis usibus pratis pascuis piscariis silvis silvarum densi-"tatibus cunctisque necessariis utilitatibus." The bounds are first "up from Colne River to the end of the long "hedge —— so again into Colne River by mid-stream." In A.D. 936 King Athelstan granted to the church of Exeter "aliquam ruris particulam, id est, unum mansam "ubi ignostici vocitant Toppesham." The boundaries are set out "First from Toppesor up along the Exe to the "nearer Team pool; thence up along the Exe; then

Nat. MSS. ii. 2.

Ibid. 14.

"from the Exe to the small lake; from the lake again "on Exe; then up along the Exe to the upper Team "pool; thence along Exe stream to the pool; up from "the pool to the old highway, &c. —— along the dike "out to Clyst; along the stream again to Toppesor."

In A.D. 938 King Athelstan granted to the monastery of St. Mary at Exeter "unum cassatum in loco ubi ab "incolis vocitatur Toppisham." The bounds are first "from Toppesor up the Exe to the nearer breeding pool, "then from the Exe to the small lake, from the lake "again to the Exe, then up along the Exe to the upper "breeding pool, then up Exe stream to the pool, up from "the pool to the old highway to Dyra's Tree, then south "to Wynford, up stream to Wyndeliscombe midward up "to the pear-tree, then along the dyke to the way, east "along the way to the corner of the dyke, along the dyke "out to Clyst, along the stream again into Toppesor." Nat. MSS. ii.

King Athelstan granted to the Archbishop of York "quandam non modicam telluris particulam quam solicolæ "'Agemundennes' vocitant," the bounds of which are "Primitus autem mare; sursum in Cocur usque ad fontem "illius fluminis; ab illo fonti directum in alium fontem "qui dicitur Saxonicè Dulashope; sic per decensum "rivuli in Hoddon ipso dirigamine in Ribbel; et sic *in* "*illo flumine per dimidium alveum iterum recursus in* "*mare.*" Dugd. Mon. viii. 1176.

In A.D. 949 King Edred granted to the church of Canterbury the monastery of Reculver "cum omnibus ad "hoc rite pertinentibus sive litorum sive camporum "agrorum saltuumve sicut inferius territoria promul-"gantur." The bounds are "First on the north side and "on the west from Yfinga ho *out on the sea*, so forth by "the sand as far as Northmouth, from Northmouth to "Macanbrook, then to Ærneway, from Ærneway to Æn-"flæde mouth, from Ænflæde mouth to Marksflæde mouth, "—— to Goathay westward, then to Yfingho, and *so out* "*on the sea.*" Nat. MSS. 15.

In A.D. 957 King Eadwig granted to one Lyfing land at Battersea of which the bounds are "first at High Ibid. ii. 3.

"Efre —— thence north into Thames by midstream, by "half stream again to High Efre."

Cod. Dip. 568. There is a charter of King Edgar, A.D. 971, granting to Ethelwold "ruris portionem at Baruwe [Barrow-on-"Humber] quam olim S. Cedda ante paganorum vasta-"tionum possederat," the bounds of which are set out "Ærest up of Humber and langes there ealdan dic —— "swa andlang mæredic eft ut on Humbre."

Ibid. 579. By another charter, A.D. 972, King Edgar granted lands to Westminster Abbey as "ruris quandam particulam "quinis ab accolis æstimatam mansiunculis ad ecclesiam "beati Petri Apostoli, quæ sita est in nominatissimo loco "qui dicitur Westmynster." The boundaries are set out, "Ærest up of Temese andlang Meorfleotes to Pollen-"stocce —— and lang suth on Temese on midden streame, "and lang streames be lande and be strande eft on "Merfleote."

Ibid. 624. A charter of King Ethelred, A.D. 980, grants to the monks of Winchester "quandam ruris particulam, vii "videlicet cassatos, loco qui noto nuncupatur vocabulo "Hamanfunta," the boundaries of which are "Ærest thær "Ocærburna uttseyt on sæ; thæt upp anlang Ocærburnan "to halegan mærsce eastewеardan —— utt on Limburnan, "thonnæ andlang Limburnan utt on sæ."

Ibid. 554. King Ethelred in A.D. 986 granted to Wenoth, his Min-"ister, ruris quandam particulam vulgariter Lyteltun nomi-"natam" (Littleton on Severn, Gloucester), the boundaries whereof are "Imprimis de Ludepole juxta Severne usque "Colpuylle; —— et ab eodem fossato usque Rishammes "puylle; et per Rishammes puylle directa usque Lude "puylle; et ab eodem loco usque Severne; et sic per "Severne iterum usque Colpuylle."

Ibid. 688. Another charter of King Ethelred's, dated A.D. 995, granted to Rochester "quandam ruris portionem duobis "locis sitam, sex quidem mansas quas Cantuarii syx su-"lunga nominare solent, illo scilicet in loco cui jamdudum "gentis ejusdem indigenæ vocuabulum Wuldaham indi-"derunt" (Wouldham on the Medway). The boundaries are towards the river, "thonne west thonnon be burhhæma

" mearce ut andlang Medwæge be middeweardun stream " oth thara hiwena land to Hrofceastre."

Ethelred also grants to the monastery of St. Peter at Stoneham (Hants) " quandam partitiunculam cujusdam " ruris octo scilicet mansas in loco qui Stanham appellatur " æt Westun." The boundaries of Westun are " Ærest up " of Icenan [Itchen] on rican ford —— on thone beorh ; " of tham beorge on gerihte utt an sæ." Cod. Dip. 713.

King Eadred in A.D. 948 granted to his Minister, Ælfric, " xj mansas in illo loco ubi jamdudum solicoli " illius regionis nomen imposuerunt æt Stoce —— cum " omnibus utensilibus quæ Deus cœlorum in ipso telluris " gramine creavit tam in notis causis et ignotis in modicis " et in magnis, campis pascuis pratis silvis silvarumque " densitatibus donans donabo libertatem." The boundaries are " Ærest of sæ ofer thone stanhricg on thonæ " easteran weg —— thonon suth on tha ealdan dic ; and " lang dic *ut on sæ;* thonon utt on *Solentan west on midne* " *stream* oth hit cymeth upp thær mon ær onfeng." Ibid. 1163.

In A.D. 980 Ethelred granted to the church of Winchester Celcesora ad capturas piscium inibi conficiendas," and says that Bishop Ethelwold gave "*pro hoc litore* capturæ piscium apto et pro supradicta exiguæ telluris particula auream pretiosi ponderis armillam." The boundaries are " Ærest of Solentam on burnan —— on Bradanfleot " andlang Bradanesfleote *ut on sæ.*" Ibid. 626.

King Edred, A.D. 948, granted part of the Isle of Purbeck to the monastery of Shaftesbury. This charter gives the bounds " on the schort mannes polwerth *ut on sæ* " —— *of sæ* an arne stan tor of thane tor on thane clif," &c. We shall see later that the abbot had wreck and the shore of these lands. Dugd. Mon. ii. 478.

King Eadwy in A.D. 956 granted to his Minister, Ædelsig, land at Heglingdig " æt East Stoce cum omnibus ad se " rite pertinentibus campis pascuis pratis silvis." The boundaries are " of ceanninga *utt on sæ.*" Cod. Dip. 1193.

King Eadgar in A.D. 961 granted to one Athulf "x mansas " in illo loco ubi jam dudum solicolæ illius regionis nomen " imposuerunt æt Chenelmstune —— cum omnibus ad se Ibid. 1231.

"rite pertinentibus campis pascuis pratis silvis." The boundaries are "Ærest on thære hwitan flodan neah "Mælan beorge thonon north to Yferlea —— to thære "hwitan dic; wast andlang dic æft to thære hwitan "flodan."

Cod. Dip. 1284. King Ethelred in A.D. 988 granted to one Atsere "quandam ruris portionem in illo loco qui ab incolis Wike "nuncupatur prope videlicet insulam de Portland —— cum "omnibus ad se rite pertinentibus." The boundaries are "Ærest from thære westsæ in Saggelord —— of Ellen-"stubbe on thære æstsæ." This is Wyke Regis, in Dorset.

Ibid. 1296. King Ethelred in A.D. 1002 granted to one Godwin "x mansas qui ab incolis Hæseleia [Hessle, York] æt than "nytheran tunc nuncupatur vocabulo cum omnibus ad se "rite pertinentibus campis pascuis pratis aquarumque "cursibus." The boundaries are "Ærest on roppan forda "thæt andlang wicgan dic thæt hit sticath on Wearraford; "swa andlang mores oth thene bradan herepath; thæt "on thæra æcera heafada thæt hit sticath on Humbra; "andlang Humbra thæt on roppan broc foron ongean "stangedelf; andlang ropan broces on hafocgelad eft and "lang roppan broces thæt hit cimth on roppan ford thær "hit ær onfeng."

Ibid. 1301. King Ethelred in A.D. 1005 granted to one Eadsig "unam mansam in illo loco ubi Anglica appellatione "dicitur æt Fleote cum omnibus quæ ad ipsum locum per-"tinere dinoscuntur tam in magnis quam in minimis rebus "campis pascuis pratis silvis." The boundaries are "Ærest up of thære sæ on Scypcumb up thonne on "Scypcumb on thære bydelæcer sutheweardne; of tham "bydelæcere up on thæt slæd be suthan Dyrnanleage on "gerihte to Berhamme up thonne on Berham suth-"weardne on thæne hricgweg; of tham hricgwege north "on readan weg ufeweardne; of readan wege north and "lang hricges on bitun liege; of bitun liege west and "lang weges on gerihte to Crymelhamme, up on tha dic "on thone herpoth; west thonne herpoth of Cumbweges "heafod; adune thanne on Cumbweg on horegan ford; "of horegan forde adune on stræm on nytheran Stanford;

"of nytheran Stanforda north be thæs yrthlandes foton on "gerihte to litegan hlosstede; of litegan hlosstede on "hreodmæde lace on Axan; of Axan eft *ut on sæ;* and "seo mædræden benithan dic betweonan cealdan lace und "cullig."

There exists a charter of King Knut, dated A.D. 1023, made to the church of Canterbury, whereby he grants to them "portum de Sandwic et omnes exitus ejusdem aquæ "ab utraque portu fluminis *cujuscumque terra sit* a Piper-"næsse usque ad Mearcesfleote ita ut natante nave in "flumine cum plenum fuerit quam longius de navi potest "securis parvula quam Angli vocant taper-eax super "terram projici, ministri ecclesiæ Christi rectitudines ac-"cipiant, nullusque omnino homo habet aliquam con-"suetudinem in eodem portu exceptis monachis æcclesiæ "Christi. Eorum autem est navicula et transfretatio "portus et theolonium omnium navium cujuscumque sit et "undecumque veniat quæ ad prædictum portum et ad "Sandwic venerint. Si quid autem in magno mari extra "portum quantum mare plus se retraxerit, et adhuc "statura unius hominis tenentis lignum quod Angli "nominant spreot et tendentis ante se quantum potest "monachorum est. Quicquid etiam ex hac parte medie-"tatis maris inventum et dilatum ad Sandwic fuerit sive "sit vestimentum sive rete arma ferrum aurum argentum, "medietas monachorum erit, alia pars remanebit inven-"toribus." There is also a Saxon version of the charter, which is clearly a grant of the franchise of a port, a ferry, and wreck, and is the earliest instance we have of the grant of the latter franchise. Kemble marks the charter as being of doubtful authenticity, but gives no grounds for his suspicions.

Cod. Dip. 737.

In A.D. 1042 King Edward granted to the church of Westminster "the vill of Leosne with all things that "thereto belong in wood and in field, in meadow and in "water, and in all other things."

Nat. MSS. ii. 9.

In A.D. 1044 King Edward the Confessor granted to Bishop Leofric and the church of Exeter "quoddam rus in "villa quæ incolis regionis illius vocitatur Doflisc [Dawlish]

Ibid. ii. 12.

"cum omnibus ad se rite pertinentibus." The boundaries are: "First at Teignmouth up along the fleets to Cramp "Start and so back again by the Salterns in the street on "the west side of Saint Michael's Church, and so straight "on to Redstone, from the stone south out on to the sea "(on thæ sæ) so west by the sea to Teignmouth."

Cod. Dip. 785. There is a charter of King Edward, dated between 1044 and 1047 (marked as doubtful by Kemble), which grants to the abbey of St. Benet Hulme, North Walsham, South Walsham, Waxtonesham, Winterton, and other lands in Norfolk and Suffolk, and further grants to the Abbot, "wrek in mari et in litore maris et in portubus maris," and that he shall have it "in mari et in portubus maris in "mariscis et in aqua et extra aquam—et in omnibus "locis."

Ibid. 809. King Edward the Confessor in 1060 granted to Ramsey Abbey a charter, marked as doubtful by Kemble, by which he gives them large possessions, and *inter alia* "Brancester cum omnibus ad se pertinentibus, et cum omni "maris projectu quod nos Anglice ship wrec appellamus." Also "Ringested cum omnibus ad se pertinentibus, et cum "omni maris ejectu quod shipwrec appellamus." He further grants them divers liberties and quittances, "et cum "omnibus quæcumque maris procellosis tempestatibus in "aquam vel in terram eorum ejecta fuerint quod Anglice "shipwreck promulgatur est onomate."

In the reign of King Edward the Confessor, the various churches and monasteries appear to have begun to obtain general charters of liberties and privileges to be used by them in their lands as soc and sac, infangthef, hamsokne, toll, &c. &c. They are described by Kemble, Codex Dip. i., xliii., who remarks that he does not find an instance of such grants which he can regard as genuine before the time of Edward the Confessor. He thinks that the rights now begun to be specified did in fact exist in earlier times, and accounts for the rare mention of them on the supposition that they were so inherent in the possession of the land as not to require particularization. The earliest he prints is a charter of King Edward the Confessor to St. Augustine's, Canterbury. It is in the form of a writ addressed to Earl Godwin and all his thegns in Kent, informing them that he has granted to St. Augustine's soc and sac, toll and theam, &c., "*on stronde and on stræme.*"

There is a charter of King Edward the Confessor to Ramsey Abbey, which Kemble regards as genuine, and which grants to them soc and sac and other liberties "and tha sæ "upwarp on eallan thingen at Bramcæstre and at Ryng- "stede swa wel and swa freolice swa ic hit meseolf betst "habbe bi tha sæ rune ahwær in Engelande and ealle tha "gerihte tha ic meseolf ær ahte." He also grants that the Abbot shall have soc and sac, &c., be lande and be strande, by wood and by field, &c., in all his lands. The Latin version of the charter granted is as follows: "et shipbriche "et se upwarp in omnibus rebus apud Bramcestre et "apud Ringstede ita bene et libere sicut ipse ea melius et "liberius habeo in littore marino alicubi in Anglia om- "nesque rectitudines et jura quæ ibi ego ipse unquam "habui." Cod. Dip. 853.

The Confessor granted to Westminster Abbey the manor of Stanes, with meadows, eyots, waters, and weirs, and all things by land and strand. He also granted to Urk, his huscarl, that he should have "his strand eall forne "gen hys agen land ofee eal wel and freolice *upp of sæ* and "*ut on sæ* and eall thæt to his strande gedryven hys." This is a grant of foreshore and wreck. Urk granted his land to Abbotsbury Monastery. The grant was confirmed by King Edward the Confessor (Cod. Dip. 841). The monastery had confirmation of the land and of the right to wreck from King William I. Ibid. 855. Ibid. 871.

In A.D. 1066, King Edward the Confessor granted to St. Peter's, Westminster, a charter in the following terms:— "I have given him in all his lands sac and soc, tol and "them, infangthef and flymenefermthe, grithbrice and "hamsocne, and foresteal and all other rights *in tide and out* "*of tide,* within borough and without borough, on street and "off street, as full and as free as they first stood myself in "hand. And I will not permit that any man have any Nat. MSS. ii. 16.

"authority over his land, nor over his men by *strand nor* "*by land*, nor in woods nor in fields, except the Abbot "and the Brotherhood for the minster's need."

King Edward the Confessor made extensive confirmations of lands to the Church in the fullest terms, and by a charter to Westminster Abbey in 1066 he confirms all their manors "cum omnibus ad se rite pertinentibus," and grants that "omnia quæ ad locum ipsum pertinent sint "omnino libera, cellæ, æcclesiæ, cimeteria, terræ, pascuæ, "silvæ, venationes, aquæ, piscationes, cum redditibus ser-"vitiis debitis &c. &c., et omnibus quæcunque scriptis et "testimonio bonorum hominum remorari potuerunt quæ a "regibus concessa vel concedanda sunt," and also soc and sac in land and water, and toll, &c.

Dugd.Mon. i. 293.

By another charter he grants that they shall have all privileges in their lands "in terra et in aqua, in aquis, in "piscariis, in molendinis et in omnibus suis appendiciis," &c. The Confessor granted to St. Benet Hulme, in Norfolk, various lands, and also "wreccum in mari et in littore "maris ac in portubus maris;" and the charter is confirmed by similar grants by King Stephen and the Empress Matilda and subsequent Sovereigns. Ely, Ramsey, St. Benet Hulme, St. Edmond's Bury, St. Paul's London, and other ecclesiastical establishments had similar confirmations.

Cod. Dip. 825.

Cart. Antiq. O. 1. D. D. 24. Dugd.Mon. iii. 83.

After the Conquest King William I. made very extensive confirmations of Church lands, and granted privileges to be held "in terra et mari, on stronde and on streame," recognising the rights of the owners of manors to shore. The following charter to the Archbishop of Canterbury will serve as a fair example of these confirmations:—"Willielmus Rex Angliæ, Episcopis Comitibus proceribus "vicecomitibus ceterisque fidelibus suis, Francis et Anglis, "salutem. Sciatis me dedisse Anselmo Archiepiscopo "Archiepiscopatum Cantuariensem ecclesiæ cum omnibus "libertatibus et dignitatibus ad Archiepiscopatum Cantua-"riensem pertinentibus et sak et sok, *on stronde and on* "*streame*, on woden and on felden, tolnes and teames, "gridbrech, hamsokne, forstalles, and infangenestheves,

Cart. Antiq. F. 17. MS. Cott. Galba, E. iv.

"and flemene fremthe, et omnes alias libertates *in terra et* "*mari* super suos homines infra burgos et extra et super "tot theines quot ecclesiæ Christi concessit Edwardus Rex "cognatus meus. Volo etiam ut monachi ecclesiæ Christi "Cantuariensis similiter habeant in omnibus terris et tene-"mentis suis omnes prædictas libertates *in terra et mari*, *in* "*aquis* et viis et in omnibus aliis locis quæ ad eos pertinent "in tantum et tam pleniter sicut proprii ministri mei "exquirere debent. Portus etiam de Sandwico et omnes "exitus et consuetudines eis concedo et confirmo quas "Odo Baiocensis Episcopus et Cantiæ Comes eis conces-"sit et carta sua confirmavit. Et nolo pati ut aliquis "hominum se intromittat de omnibus rebus quæ ad eos "pertinent nisi ipsi et ministri eorum quibus ipsi comittere "voluerint, nec Francus nec Anglus. Testibus Willielmo "Episcopo Dunelmensi et Gundulpho Episcopo Roffensi "et Eudone Dapifero."

Such confirmations are numerous. We find them made to Christchurch Canterbury, to St. Augustine's Canterbury, to Rochester, Abbotsbury, Winchester, Durham, Malmesbury, Westminster, Whitby, Ely, Gloucester, Worcester, and Ramsey, to which abbey wreck in Brancester and Ringstead are confirmed. To St. Peter's Monastery, Abbotsbury, the lands are confirmed together with the right of wreck as they had held it in the time of King Edward the Confessor. To Battle Abbey the Conqueror granted Dengey Marsh with the right to wreck there and royal fish; and also to Abbotsbury. To the monks of Durham the Conqueror gave *wreck in terris suis*.

Cart. Antiq. Dd. 5. Pat. 52 Hen. III. m. 21.

Cart. Antiq. G. 1. Rymer, Fœdera, i. pp. 1, 4.

William Rufus made many similar confirmations, as did his successors. Most of these grants recognise the right of the owners of manors "by land and by strand," and one charter granted to the Bishop of London, giving him all liberties "by land by strande, on tyde and off tyde, "and wreck of the sea," was successfully pleaded by the Bishop in 52 Henry III. when he was challenged for taking wreck at Clacton and Walton, in Essex. Wreck was allowed to the Bishop on the same charter in 7 Henry V. These grants of liberties by the early

Charter Roll, 54 Hen. III. m. 14.

Dugd.Mon. i. 237.

Norman kings, as we shall see, were in later times frequently pleaded in aid of claims to wreck taken within the manors of the Church and of other persons, and allowed by the justices in eyre. The claimants say they take wreck by virtue of the liberties granted to them *in the lands* or *in their fee*, and it is evident that it was well understood that a man's fee was taken to extend to the low-water mark.

These early grants and confirmations are for the most part silent as to any specific grant of shore as belonging to any manor, but we have seen that an estate which is granted "cum omnibus ad se rite pertinentibus" in many cases is shewn by its boundaries to include the bed of the river, tidal or non-tidal, to mid-stream; that in the cases of Stoke Selsey and Dawlish the boundaries actually set out the shore as parcel of the estate; and that in other cases of lands adjoining the sea the boundaries are stated to be "ut on sæ" at either extremity of the estate, no perambulation being given on the sea side of the estate because it was common knowledge that the estate included the shore. These later cases, however, it may be argued, are doubtful, and may well mean that "ut on "sæ" means only the land to high-water mark; but when we come to later documents which illustrate the nature and effect of those early grants, we find confirmations by King Edward the Confessor and the early Norman kings of lands "in terra et mari, on stronde and "streame," &c., and later still we come to another class of documents that throw still further light upon the older grants—viz., the grants of the royal franchise of wreck of the sea, and the proceedings against owners of manors adjoining the sea-coast in respect of their claims to have this franchise, from which it will appear that the shore was admitted to be parcel of such manors.

It is clear from the before-mentioned charters, which have been selected only as examples, that the grant of an estate or manor in Saxon times, "cum omnibus ad se "rite pertinentibus," passed the shore of the sea and the shore and bed of tidal and non-tidal rivers. There is no suggestion of any reservation to the Crown, and it is evident that the shore was treated as parcel of the estate or manor. Nor is there any reason whatever to suppose that any change took place after the Norman accession, for we have a charter of King William the Conqueror granting the manor of Holacumb to Bishop Leofric and the church of Exeter in exactly the same manner as the grants of Saxon kings. It grants the land with its appurtenances, and the boundaries given at the end of the charter shew that those appurtenances included the shore. The grant is dated A.D. 1069, and conveys "Holacumb "tam in magnis quam in modicis rebus ad se rite per- "tinentibus videlicet agris silvis pratis pascuis cultis et "incultis exitibus et redditibus." The bounds are first to Cramp Start, from Cramp Start to Flowhead, —— so upon the Down to Thwart Dyke, so to the *land shore* of Dawlish down to Ariet's Stone, and so *along the strand* to Cramp Start.

Nat. MSS. ii. 16.

That these Saxon estates were in their nature manors is now well recognised. Coke, in his "Compleat Copy- "holder," sec. ii., says of them: "The Saxons (who held "England in subjection immediately before the coming "of the Normans) were unacquainted with these manors, "yet in effect they had manors in those days, in circum- "stances peradventure something varying, in substance "surely nothing differing from our manors at this day; they "wanted neither demesnes nor services, the two material "causes of a manor." There is no pretence for suggesting that any change took place in the nature or extent of the Saxon estates when they were transferred to their Norman proprietors. Domesday Book shews clearly that they passed entire, and as the Saxon tenant held them. In almost every case in that record the Saxon tenant is shewn, and the estate is valued as it was in the time of King Edward, as it was when the grantee took it, and as it stood at the time of the survey.

The want of any Chartularium Anglo-Normannicum prevents us from shewing the terms of the charters by which the earlier Norman kings granted out their manors, but I do not doubt that if those valuable charters could be discovered and collected, we should find that the grants were made in the same form and manner as in the instance above quoted. Domesday Book, which is rather a rate-book than a survey, returns only the profitable portions of an estate, and, though weirs and fisheries, salinæ, &c., are often returned with great accuracy, nothing appears in relation to waste land nor to any portion of the manors described which did not render a taxable profit.

The few charters of early Norman kings which remain shew that those kings, like their Saxon predecessors, granted lands, together with the foreshore as parcel thereof, without actually specifying it in the charter, and also granted lands with the foreshore, describing it in terms in the grant. They also recognised the right of their subjects to hold foreshore as parcel of their lands by virtue of ancient grant confirming to them liberties "on stronde "and on streame, on land and on sea," and they further confirmed grants of lands comprising the foreshores which had been granted to monasteries by their subjects' private grant. The following charter of King William I. grants a manor to the Abbot of St. Augustine's together with the shore:—

MS. Cott. Claud. D. x. 197.

See Placita Anglo-Normannica, p. 63.

"Willelmus Dei gratia Rex Anglorum Archiepiscopis, " Episcopis, Abbatibus, Comitibus, Vicecomitibus, et omni- " bus fidelibus totius Anglie salutem. Sciatis quia volo et " precipio super amicitiam meam ut nullus a modo aliquid " reclamet in Eastanores (in insula de Thanet), sed Wido " Abbas de Sancto Augustino et fratres loci ejusdem libere " et quiete terram illam et *totum littus usque in medietatem* " *aquæ* habeant, sine calumpnia aliqua quia ita direationa- " tum est inter homines meos de Lundonia et homines " Abbatis in tempore meo coram justicia mea apud " Eastanores. Testantibus W. Episcopo de Auphelmo, et " R. Bigot apud Wyndeshore."

There is also a charter of King William I. whereby he confirms a grant made by William de Percy to the monks of Whitby of their land at Whitby, in which the bounds of the manor are set out "a portu Witebiensi *totam* "*marinam*[1] usque ad Blawic et inde de —— usque Horse- "croft et usque Tordisiam et usque in mare et per marinam "ad Witebi." This grant of Percy's is not mentioned in the charter of King William I., but he grants to them all liberties and free customs which the royal power can best give to any church "*super omnes terras suas adquisitas* "*vel adquirendas*," and ordains that no Minister of his shall intromit "infra terminos suos nec de aquis eorum in portu "de Wyteby vel alibi nec de aliqua re quæ pertinet ad "ecclesiam."

King William II. granted to the abbey of St. Mary, York, the site of the abbey, "a Galmon usque ad filum "aquæ Usiæ." Dugd.Mon. iii. 547.

Reginald Earl of Cornwall, the natural son of King Henry I., granted the monks of Tavistock wreck, except of whale and ships entire, in their lands in the Isles of Scilly between 1140 and 1175. They had their lands there by a previous grant of King Henry I. This wreck was afterwards claimed by prescription and was allowed in 30 Edward I. Ibid. ii. 501.

King Henry I. granted to Ramsey Abbey a confirmation of their lands "*in aquis et mariscis in wreck maris in* "*mari et litore.*" Ibid. ii. 563.

Henry I. also confirmed to the abbey of Wymondham the manor of Hapesburgh (Norfolk), which had been given to that abbey by William de Albini, by the description of "totum manerium de Hapesburgh cum omnibus perti- "nentis suis et totum wrec in eadem villa a divisa quæ "est inter villam de Eccles et de Hapesburg juxta mare "in longum versus occidentem usque ad divisam inter "hundredum de Hapesburg et Tunstede." The Abbot's right to his foreshore was acknowledged in 5 Richard II.: see *post*. Ibid. iii. 331.

King Stephen confirmed to the Prior of Bridlington (York) his lands in Bridlington, and granted him the port of Bridlington, and "wrecum maris quod aliquo modo in Pat. 2 Hen. IV. p. 1, m. 21.

[1] "Marina" means the shore: see *post*, Hundred Rolls. The wreck is claimed "per totam marinam de Luthesk."

"futurum eveniet seu emergat in omnibus locis inter fos-"satum vocatum Erledyk et Fleynburg." This territory adjoins the lordship of Holderness, where the Earls of Albemarle had the wreck from the Earlsdike to Hull—afterwards the subject of Sir Henry Constable's case.

Dugd. Mon. iii. 557. The priory of St. Bees was founded in the time of King Henry I. by William Meschines, who gave them seven carucates of land, "videlicet quicquid continetur a "Witohona usque ad Cherchel et sicut eadem Cherchel "cadit integre et egre in mare—et decimas piscariarum "mearum de Coupland."

Ibid. iv. 538. King Henry I. confirmed to the priory of St. Martin, Dover, all their lands "in terra et in mari in teolonio," &c. &c. They were lords of the manor of Deal, and established their rights to wreck and toll therein in 7 Edward I.

Ibid. iv. 633. About A.D. 1101–1120, the founder of the priory of Bassela (Monmouth) made a grant to Glastonbury Abbey of the church and tithes of the parish of Bassela, and it sets out the bounds, including the River Ebboth and the shore, with a port and fisheries.

Ibid. v. 633. About A.D. 1180, Res ap Griffith, Prince of South Wales, founded the abbey of Strata Florida, and granted it lands by metes and bounds, including the foreshore—"fossa vero prefata in termino eat usque ad mare, mare "vero usque ad hostium Arch hit in Aber meilyer et *in* "*litore* et in mari ab hostio Arch usque ad hostium Dyron "Coredan et omnem piscaturam," &c. This grant was confirmed by King Edward III. and King Richard II.

Ibid. v. 672. The charters to Conway Abbey by the Welsh Princes make grants of the foreshore—"usque ad mare et ab hinc "per litus usque ad fossam," &c., all of which have been confirmed by the kings of England.

Ibid. vi. 304. About A.D. 1150, Baldwin de Rivers granted lands in Hampshire and the Isle of Wight to the Priory of Christ Church, Twynham, and also the tithe of wreck, "quicquid illud fuerit quod super feodum meum in pa-"rochia eorum evenerit præter de graspeys cujus sinis-"tram noam de jure antiquo habere debent."

Ibid. vi. 310. King Henry II. confirmed to the abbots of St. Osith the manor of Chiche, in Essex, which had been given them by the Bishop of London, with all its appurtenances and the liberties which the Bishop had in the same manor. We shall see that the Bishop had the franchise of wreck.

King Henry I. recognises the rights of the church of Canterbury on the shores of their manors by the following charter :—"Henricus Dei gratia Rex Anglorum, Epis- MS. Tanner, 223.
"copis Comitibus Proceribus vicecomitibus ceterisque suis "fidelibus Francis et Anglis in omnibus comitatibus in "quibus Archiepiscopus Anselmus et monachi ecclesiæ "Christi Cantuariensis terras habent amicabiliter salutem. "Notum vobis facio me concessise eis omnes terras quas "tempore regis Edwardi cognati mei et tempore Willelmi "patris mei habuerunt et sacam et socne *on strande et* "*streame* on wude et felde tolnes et temes et grithbreches "et hamsocne et forestealles et infangenestheofes et fle-"menefermthe super suos homines infra burgos et extra "in tantum et tam pleniter sicut proprii ministri mei ex-"quirere deberent et etiam super tot thegenes quot eis "concessit pater meus ; et nolo ut aliquis homo se intro-"mittat, nisi ipsi et ministri eorum quibus ipsi committere "voluerint, nec Francus nec Anglus : pretereaque ergo con-"cessi Christo has consuetudines pro redemptione animæ "meæ sicut rex Edwardus et pater meus antea fecerunt, "et nolo pati ut aliquis eas infringat si non vult perdere "amicitiam meam. Dominus vos custodiat."

King Henry II. granted to William de Albini the Pat. 1 Edw. III. p. 1, m. 27.
manor of Snetesham, "cum wreck et cum omnibus per-"tinentiis suis." This manor is the subject of the case of Hale, p. 59.
Lestrange *v.* Rowe, in which the foreshore was decided to 4 Fost. & Finl. 1048.
belong to the lord of the manor.

There is a charter of Henry II. to the church of Cart. 55 Hen. III. m. 3.
Tynemouth confirming to them "omnes ecclesias terras "decimas et alias tenuras ad eam pertinentes," and all that Robert Earl of Northumberland and his men reasonably gave to St. Oswin, that they shall hold them in waters and mills and fisheries and pools, within borough and without borough, in all things and places,

with tol and them and soc and sac and infangthef, *and wreck*, quit of all geld and scot and aid, &c.

Dugd.Mon. vii. 1127. The cell of Neddrum (County Down) was founded, about A.D. 1177, by one John de Courcy, who gave to the monks "Duffren totum terram illam quæ fuit Gillanhari, "cum pertinentiis suis in bosco et plano in pratis in *ripis* "in viis et semitis in *aquis dulcibus et salsis in insulis et* "*portubus in piscariis et piscationibus in salinis et in wreke* "*maris ubicunque inventum fuerit in terra prænominata.*"

Ibid. vii. 1128. Theobald Fitz Walter founded the monastery of Arklow as a cell of the Abbey of Furness, and gave to it his demesnes of "Arkelo versus austrum aquæ cum "omnibus pertinentis suis; ita quod neque stagna "neque piscaria in transverso aquæ ibi fieri possit. "Dedi etiam eis *totam marinam* cum omnibus salinis "prædictæ terræ usque ad terram Moricii filii Moricii "cum *wrecca maris* excepta terra et salinis abbatis et "monachorum de Balkinglas," also "insulam de Arkelo "et mediatatem aquæ prædictæ cum piscatione," &c.

Ibid. vii. 1130. Hervey de Montmorency gave to the abbey of Dumbrody (County Wexford) divers lands the boundaries whereof include portions of tidal rivers, "sino aliquo "retinemento in bosco in plano in aquis per terminos suos "in terra *in mari* in *salinis* in piscariis in piscaturis," &c.

Cart. 55 Hen. III. m. 7. There is also a charter of King Richard I., and another of King John, dated 1 March, 5 John, A.D. 1204, by which they grant and confirm to the Prior of Tynemouth all his lands and all his possessions, to wit, the vill of Tynemouth, &c. &c., and the charter proceeds: "hæc omnia "concessimus jam dictis monachis in redditibus et ho- "magiis et pratis et pascuis in nemoribus et turbariis et "omnibus alius rebus ad jam dictas villas et terras perti- "nentibus cum saca et soca *on stronde* and *on streme,*" &c.

Cart. 1 John p. 1, m. 10, No. 65. King John, in his first year, confirmed to the monks of Dereham a piece of land "in greva maris de Wrangle" to make salt-pans, which had been given them by Simon Brito; it is described as lying "super ripam portus de "Rithflet."

Grants and confirmations of fisheries in the sea by King

John are very numerous. In the 6th John, A.D. 1205, the King granted to the Abbot of Beaulieu (Hants) "alveum super quem abbatia fundata est a vado de Hart-"ford cum fluctu maris in ascendendo et descendendo "inter utramque ripam." Here it is to be observed that this spot is within the New Forest, and the adjacent land was part of the King's own possessions not granted out. The charter is the grant made by King John on his foundation of the abbey, and he grants a part of his own possessions in the New Forest—viz., the angle at the east end of it between the Bewley river and Calshot Castle. Therefore this grant cannot be regarded as a grant of foreshore adjacent to the land of a subject, and there is no example of such a grant in any record before the reign of Queen Elizabeth. Cart. Antiq. G. 15. Cart. 2 Edw. III. m. 24.

In the reign of King Richard I., one Richard fitz Roger founded the priory of Lytham, and granted to the monks of Durham, of which place Lytham was a cell, the vill of Lytham (Lancashire), setting out the bounds of it in his charter: "usque in la Pull de ultra Snartsalte "sicut cadit super arenam maris; et sic sequendo versus "austrum in transversum usque in Ribill ad *filum aquæ* "sequendo filum dictæ aquæ usque in mare versus occi-"dentem et sic ad fossam et crucem prædictas; et totum "mariscum inter prædictas divisas cum omnibus insulis "quæ in eo sunt," to hold "in aquis et molendinis in "stagnis et piscariis *in sabulonibus mare retracto* cum om-"nibus," &c. This charter was confirmed by King John and by Edward III. The Prior was challenged for wreck in 20 Edward I., and disclaimed it. The franchise was taken away and granted to the Earl of Lancaster, but the soil remained with the Prior, and is parcel of the manor at the present time. Dugd. Mon. v. 228. Cart. 2 John, No. 2. Cart. 9 Edw. III. m. 65.

King Henry II., and also King Richard I., confirmed to the abbey of Caen and its cell of Frampton "Manerium de "Northam, situm in comitatu Devensire cum omnibus per-"tinentiis suis in terris et aquis et salinis liberum et "quietum de warrecho," and also the manor of Brideton (Dorset), "quietum de wrecco." Dugd. Mon. vii. 1001, 1071.

Dugd. Mon. vii. 1034.

King John gave the manors of Budleigh and Otterton to the monks of Mount St. Michael, and these manors included the port of Ottermouth (Devon).

Cart. 54 Hen. III. m. 12.

By a charter of 25 July, 17 John, A.D. 1215, the King granted and confirmed to St. Mary of Cartmel "totam "terram de Cartmel cum universis pertinentiis suis. Quare "volumus &c. quod habeant et teneant bene et in pace &c. "in aquis et molendinis in stagnis et vivariis *in mari et* "*mariscis in piscariis in salinis* et fabricis in mineris feriis "et omnibus aliis locis in burgo et extra et in omnibus aliis "rebis cum soc et sac tol et them et infangthef et cum "omnibus libertatibus aliis et liberis consuetudinibus," but here it will be observed there is no specific grant of wreck. The shore, however, is manifestly conveyed by this grant, though the wreck is not. In 23 Edward I. the King recovered the wreck from the Prior through this defect in the charter, and granted it to Edmund Earl of Lancaster, his brother. But he only recovered the franchise, and not the soil of the shore, which remained to the Prior as parcel of the manor by force of his grant, and this case shews that although a grant of wreck is very strong evidence of a right to the shore wherever it is taken in right of the manor, still the shore may remain parcel of the manor after the franchise has been taken away.

Close, 5 Hen. VI. p. 2, m. 27.

By a charter dated 28 July, 31 Henry III., A.D. 1247, the King granted and confirmed to the Abbot of Dieulacres "totam terram de Roghal, cum omnibus pertinenciis suis "quam prædicti abbas et monachi prius tenuerunt de "ballio domini Johannis Regis." He also granted "quod "habeant et teneant predictam terram de Roghal cum "omnibus pertinentiis suis et pratis et pasturis moris et "mariscis turbariis aquis et piscariis et molendinis tam in "terra arabili tam alia et *cum omni wrecco maris quocum-* "*que casu contingente.*" Here we have an example of the grant of a manor with the wreck happening thereon.

It appears from an examination of the Pipe Rolls that by the end of the reign of King Henry II. the franchise of wreck must have been granted out in nearly all the manors of the kingdom. The grants of it which remain to us are comparatively few, but the two following examples will shew the nature of them. The first is a grant by King Henry II. to the Abbot of Cerne in the following terms:— "Sciatis me concessisse Abbatiæ de Cerne wreccum per "*omnes terras suas super mare* et bellum et polam et "forum in villa de Cerne cum omnibus libertatibus suis "militibus et libere tenentibus et eorum serviciis faciendo "mihi servicium duorum militum ad scutagium et unum "militem in expeditione." Cart. 54 Hen. III. m. 7.

The second is a grant dated 12 June, 37 Henry III., A.D. 1253, to the monastery of Peterborough, confirming to them all their lands, and granting them wreck "in "omnibus dominicis suis." There is also a charter of King William I. granting to the monks of Durham "quod "ubique aliqua tenementa habent in regno Angliæ habeant "libera cum soc et sac et toll et theam infangthef et "*wrych* quod vocatur wreck." Ibid. m. 8.

William Earl of Pembroke in 7 Henry III., A.D. 1223, confirmed a grant to Tintern Abbey, which includes a large portion of the foreshores of the Wye and Severn and many weirs and fisheries. This grant was confirmed by King Edward I. Dugd. Mon. v. 267. Cart. 33 Edw. I. No. 33.

There is an instance of dealing with the soil on the Scotch side of the Solway in a charter by William de Brus (A.D. 1194–1214) to the abbey of Holmcultram, in which he grants them the fishery of the Esk along the firm land and sea bank next to the *filum aquæ* of the Solway, excepting craspies and royal fish. Duchy of Lanc. Charters, ii. p. 24.

Many more examples of ancient royal grants of manors including the shores might be referred to, but it is conceived that the foregoing instances will suffice.

The examples given are examples of charters which either in absolute terms or by irresistible implication convey the shore; but it must be remembered that by far the greater number of ancient grants convey manors by the general expression of "manerium cum pertinentiis," "terra," or "terra cum pertinentiis," as in the case of the Duke of Beaufort *v.* Swansea (3 Exch. 413), and in general terms only; those which specify the shore as parcel being the exceptions to the rule. But although this latter class of ancient charters do not convey the shore in terms as parcel of the manors passed by them, it is now well settled that the shore may be shewn to have passed by these charters as parcel of the manor by producing evidence of modern user to prove that the shore has been used and treated as parcel of the manor. When we come later on to shew within what manors the franchise of wreck had been granted, we shall endeavour to ascertain the terms of the original grant in each case; and it will appear that in very many cases the original grant will be in general terms only, while the claim to take the wreck is a claim to take it *infra manerium*, or *infra terras suas*, or *infra feodum suum*, and we shall find that such a pleading, which distinctly sets up a claim to the shore as parcel of a manor, is in no case traversed by the Crown.

On consideration of the charters here referred to, and the very numerous instances in which claims to wreck will be found to have been allowed when claimed *infra manerium*, it will appear that the widely prevailing notion that the Crown has scarcely ever parted with the foreshore has no foundation in fact; and as the theory of the *primâ facie* title of the Crown rests entirely upon this assumption —viz., that the Crown has retained the foreshore as part of the waste dominions of the Crown never granted out—it would seem that this theory (the origin of which we shall shew in the time of Elizabeth) is a theory based upon a presumption of fact which is, as regards, at any rate, the greater part of the kingdom, wholly untrue. It is a theory of what might have been, but it is not a theory based upon true facts.

By the end of the reign of King John the Crown had parted with and granted out almost every manor situate upon the sea-coast and the tidal rivers of the kingdom; very few remained in the Crown. The great earldom of Northumberland, which comprised the county, had been given to William de Mowbray by William Rufus, and the Earl had subinfeudated his manors to his tenants along the coast between the Tweed and the Tyne. The monastery of Tynemouth had many ancient possessions on the coast and on the Tyne. The earldom was forfeited, but the under-tenants remained in possession of their manors, and we find them in possession of the foreshore on the north bank of the Tyne and in numerous places within the county of Northumberland. The Crown retained the manor of Bamborough and had the foreshore there. The county of Durham, which extends from the mid-stream of the Tyne to the mid-stream of the Tees, had been given to the see of Durham as a county palatine; the foreshore passed with it, and is claimed by the Ecclesiastical Commissioners, as against the tenants of the bishopric, to this day. The manors from Yarm on the south side of the Tees to Whitby have all been out of the Crown from the time of Domesday. At Whitby the foreshore belonged to the abbot. From Whitby to Flamborough Head the manors were also out of the Crown. From Flamborough to Bridlington, and to the Earl's Dyke, the coast belonged to the Prior of Bridlington; from the Earl's Dyke to the town of Hull extended the seignory of Holderness, granted to Odo Earl of Champaigne (the subject of the cases of Sir John Constable and Sir Henry Constable). From the Humber throughout the coast of Lincolnshire the manors were out of the Crown, and we shall see that the lords of them claimed wreck upon the foreshore by prescription, and their claim to the shore was not challenged by King Edward I. The case was the same throughout the counties of Norfolk and Suffolk. In Essex, the Crown retained no sea-coast possessions. We shall see that the foreshore was claimed by the lords of manors from the Orwell to the Crouch; from the Crouch to Tilbury nearly the whole of the shore was parcel of the manors comprised in the great honor of Raleigh, which had been granted by the Conqueror to Robert Fitz Wymarc, the father of Sweyn Earl of Essex, and over a large proportion of this tract the foreshore has been proved to be parcel of those manors. In the county of Kent, the Church held most of the sea-coast manors by ancient grant; the lords throughout the whole county claimed the foreshore in the time of Edward I., and their claim was unchallenged, although their claim to wreck was sometimes allowed and sometimes disputed. The Crown seems to have had no sea-coast manor in that county at this period. In the county of Sussex, the monastery of Battle, the Bishop of Chichester, the lords of the baronies of Hastings, Lewes, Arundel, and Bramber, had the whole coast-line between them, and they and their under-tenants owning the manors on the coast claimed the shore, and their claim passed unchallenged. In Hampshire, the Crown held the manor of Porchester and the New Forest from Southampton Water to beyond Hurst Castle ; but the priory of Christchurch had the shore for a long extent beyond, to the boundary of Dorset. The Isle of Wight and its foreshores had been granted to the Earls of Devon. In Dorsetshire, the Crown had the Isle of Purbeck and its shores and the town of Bridport ; but the Abbots of Abbotsbury, Milton, and Cerne occupied nearly all the rest of the coasts as part of their manors by ancient grant, and had the shores as parcel thereof ; and we shall see that Edward I. subsequently purchased of the Abbot of Cerne the manor of Melcombe with its shores. In Devonshire, the Abbot of Mount St. Michael had the shore and port at Budleigh Salterton and Ottermouth. The manors in the estuary of the Exe all comprise the shores ; and the case is the same in Kenton, Hollacombe, Dawlish, Teignmouth, and the estuary of the Teign, all those manors being out of the Crown at this time. The manors on the coast from the Teign to the Dart were all out of the Crown. The Dart and its shores were parcel of the barony of Totness. From the Dart to Plymouth the Crown had no lands. The shores of the port of Plymouth and the water of Tamar were parcel of the manor of Trematon, and were held of the lord of that manor and his subinfeudatories. The county of Cornwall had belonged to John Earl of Mortaigne and Earl of Cornwall, and the Earls of Cornwall held the shores of it, and had granted parts of those shores to many of their sub-tenants. The Crown had no sea-coast possessions in North Devon, except at Bideford; the Prior of Frampton had the shores of Northam, and other lords claimed them throughout the county. In Somerset, again, the Crown had no lands on the coast. In Gloucestershire, the Barons of Berkley had the shores and bed of the Severn by ancient grant made to Robert Fitz Hardinge by Henry II.; they established their right in the time of Charles I. The banks of the Wye and the Usk were out of the Crown. Wales was as yet no part of the kingdom. The palatinate of Chester had been granted to Hugh Lupus by the Conqueror; and we shall see that the manors lying on the Dee and Mersey extended to the mid-stream of those rivers. On the north shore of the Mersey, the manors of Bootle, Litherland, Ince, Blundell, and Crosby were out of the Crown, and the foreshore is parcel of those manors to this day. The manors of North Meols, Hesketh, and Penwortham have the foreshore as parcel as far as the Ribble. On the other shore of the Ribble, the foreshore of Lytham is parcel of the manor: see the grant, *ante*, p. 21). The manors of Cartmel, Russal, Aylmundale, and Furness were all out of the Crown, and the foreshore was parcel of them. In Cumberland and Westmoreland, up to the Solway Firth, the Barons of Coupland, Egremont, Burgh, the Abbot of York, and their sub-tenants had all the sea-coast between them. The Crown therefore had parted with almost all the sea-coast by grants to its subjects before the end of the reign of King John.

Now, either it is true or it is not true that the Crown, in parting with the manors adjoining the sea-coast, reserved or did not reserve the *jus privatum* in the foreshore. In the cases in which research enables us to shew the nature of the grant, and in other cases where we have had examination of the evidence of user from which the nature of the grant has been presumed, we find that the shore had passed from the Crown; but no case has been found, and no case can be found, in which it is shewn that in any ancient grant the Crown has specifically or impliedly reserved the *jus privatum* in the shore. When, therefore, we shew that before A.D. 1216 the Crown had practically granted away the whole sea-coast throughout the kingdom, and whenever and wherever we are able to test the nature and extent of the grant so as to ascertain whether the Crown did intend to reserve the *jus privatum*, we find that it did not reserve it, we may fairly infer that the cases we can test are fair examples of the rest; and it follows that we are enabled to draw the conclusion that it is a fair presumption of fact that the Crown did not, and did not intend to, reserve the *jus privatum* of the foreshore in any of its grants of sea-coast manors. That it reserved the *jus publicum* is admitted on all hands, because the *jus publicum* is inalienable. That it parted with the *jus privatum* in every case may fairly be inferred from the cases in which the question can be, and has been, tested; but a further test may be applied by examining the dealing of the Crown with its subjects when they afterwards claimed the shore as parcel of their manors in the proceedings on quo warranto for wreck, when their claims to the shore as parcel of their fees passed unchallenged. If, then, it be accepted, for the sake of the argument, that there is absolutely nothing from which it can be inferred that the Crown did specifically or generally reserve the *jus privatum* in any of its grants made anterior to A.D. 1216, and since it has been shewn that practically the whole coast of the kingdom had been granted out before that date, it follows that the *primâ facie* theory of the Crown's title to all the foreshore is not wholly true, and is not a theory of unavoidable inference. It rests on the assumption that the Crown has not parted with the shores. It has been shewn that the Crown has parted with the whole of the sea-coasts; and it will hereafter be seen that it never challenged the right of the subject to the shore until the reign of Elizabeth, when the theory was invented. It has been shewn in the cases tested that it did grant all the shore; and therefore it becomes a question of fact, in all the cases which still remain to be tested, whether it did or did not grant out the shore by its grants before A.D. 1216. On which side does the weight of presumption lie? On the side of the subject there is case after case to shew that the shore was granted, followed by unchallenged possession to the time of Elizabeth. On the side of the Crown, there is not one single case to shew that the shore was reserved, not one single case to shew that it was intended to be reserved, and not a pretence that it was reserved by any general reservation in right of the prerogative or by the law of the land. The *jus publicum* could not be alienated; the *jus privatum* could.

Looking, therefore, to the fact of the existence of these numerous grants, and comparing them with the later records set out in this treatise, we shall be driven to the conclusion that, instead of it being true that the Crown retained the foreshore when granting out its dominions, it is more probably true that the Crown did actually grant it out by its original grants of almost every manor in the kingdom, and consequently that the theory of the *primâ facie* title is one on which little reliance can be placed, and certainly is not, as it is commonly and usually held to be, a theory of powerful inference as against the presumption of grant raised by the evidence of ownership and occupation which can be produced by the lords of manors to displace it.

CHAPTER II.

THE REIGN OF KING HENRY III.

WE now come to the reign of Henry III., and to the time when the records of the realm are more full and complete. We now have the records of the eyres of the Justices and the returns made to the general Articles of Inquiry into usurpations on the King's rights and illegal exactions which were administered to the jurors of the hundreds in each county by the justices in eyre. Under these articles the justices were charged to inquire whether the King's rights had been usurped or infringed—who had royal liberties, as wreck of the sea, warren, &c., and by what warrant. "Also of all purprestures whatsoever "made upon the King or the royal dignity, by whom they "have been made, and how, and from what time. Also "as to who had taken fines for purprestures made *per* "*terram vel per aquam* which ought to belong to the "King." Such an inquiry was well calculated to discover any usurpations made upon the shore if, as is contended, the shore was regarded as belonging to the King in point of *propriety* as well as in point of jurisdiction; but it is remarkable that we find no case of any return of a purpresture on the King as to the shore in point of ownership and propriety (except in royal manors), although they are frequent as to jurisdiction.

See the Articles in Fleta, lib. i. cap. 20.

One of the earliest returns is dated 5 Henry III., A.D. 1220. It is the roll of Placita Coronæ for the town of Bristol, and, in answer to the inquiry concerning purprestures, the jurors say as follows: "De purpresturis nihil "sciunt. Dicunt tamen quod plures fecerunt kaios super "ripam per antiquam consuetudinem, et villa non est pejo-"rata, *nec dominus Rex aliquod dampnum habet per hoc.* Et

Coram Rege, No. 13, m. 18.

"ideo loquendum. Nec adventus navium per hoc deterio-
"ratur nec vicini dampnum habent, et libertas sua talis est;
"quod bene possunt edificari super aquam *dummodo nullum*
"*de projectis dampnum faciant.*"

We have seen that very numerous grants had been made by the early kings to their subjects of the right to take wreck *within their lands*. The charter of 20 Henry III., A.D. 1236, which regulates the right to wreck, clearly recognises those rights, and confirms them. The text is as follows:—"Si "vero infra prædictum terminum [trium mensium] nullus "veniret ad exigendum catalla illa tunc nostra sint et here- "dum nostrorum nomine wrecci *vel alterius qui libertatem* "*habuerit wreccum habendi.* Si vero de navi periclitata "taliter ut nullus homo vivus evaserit nec alia bestia sicut "prædictum est tunc bona et catalla in navi illa contenta "nostra sint et heredum nostrorum nomine wrecci vel "alterius *ubi navis fuerit periclitata* qui *libertatem* habuerit "wreccum habendi."

Charter Roll 20 Hen. III. m. 4. Rymer, Fœdera, i. p. 1, p. 227.

BRACTON.

Bracton appears to have written his book "De Legibus et Consuetudinibus Angliæ," at some period before the year 1256. As is well known, he took from the Civil Law a considerable proportion of the earlier part of his work. His debt to the Roman Law is ably discussed by Mr. Maitland in his Introduction to the recent edition of Bracton's Note Book, in which he shews that when dealing with high generalities he copies from the Roman Law, but when dealing with concrete matters he draws his authorities from the records of the English courts. Space does not admit a discussion of the question of his authority; the student is referred to the works noted below.[1]

Bracton's Note Book, Introduction, pp. 34-45.

The passages relating to the shore and rivers occur in the Institutes, in Azo, and in Bracton as follows:—

[1] 2 Reeves' Hist. of English Law, 88, 282; Crabb's Hist. of English Law, 157, 158; 1 Blackstone, Comm., 72, and iv. 25; Gould on Waters, s. 47; Bracton's Note Book, ed. Maitland, Introduction, p. 10; Scrutton, Roman Law in England, pp. 79–121.

INST.	AZO.	BRACTON.
II., § 1. Naturali jure communia sunt omnium hæc: aer, aqua profluens et mare, et per hoc litora maris. Nemo igitur ad litus maris accedere prohibetur dum tamen villis et monumentis et ædificiis abstineat, quia non sunt juris gentium sicut est mare	§ 4. Naturali jure communia sunt omnia hæc aer aqua profluens et mare et per hoc littora maris. § 5. Nemo igitur ad litus maris accedere prohibetur dum tamen villis et monumentis et ædificiis abstineat, quia non sunt juris gentium sicut est mare.	I. xii. 5. Naturali jure communia sunt omnia hæc, aqua profluens aer et mare et littora maris quasi maris accessoria. Nemo enim ad littus maris accedere prohibetur dum tamen a villis et ædificiis abstineat, quia littora sunt de jure gentium communia sicut et mare.
	Imo ædificia in mari vel in littore posita ædificantium sunt et ita in hoc casu solum cedit ædificio licet aliud sit secundum regulam. . . . . Est autem littus maris quatenus hybernus fluctus maximus excurrit, et in eo licet retia siccare et ex mari deducere.	Ideo ædificia si in mari sive in littore posita fuerint ædificantium sunt de jure gentium, et ita in hoc casu solum cedit ædificio licet alibi contrarium quia ædificium cedit solo.
§ 2. Flumina autem omnia et portus publica sunt ideoque jus piscandi omnibus commune est in portu fluminibusque.	§ 6. Publica autem sunt omnia flumina et portus, ideoque jus piscandi omnibus est commune in portu fluminibusque.	§ 6. Publica vero sunt omnia flumina et portus Ideoque jus piscandi omnibus commune est in portu et in fluminibus.
§ 3. Est autem littus maris quatenus hybernus fluctus maximus excurrit.		
§ 4. Riparum quoque usus publicus est juris gentium, sicut ipsius fluminis. Itaque naves ad eas applicare, funes arboribus ibi natis religare, onus aliquod in his reponere, cuilibet liberum est sicuti per ipsum flumen navigare: Sed proprietas earum illorum est quorum prædiis hærent: quâ de causâ arbores quoque in iisdem natæ eorundem sunt.	Riparum quoque usus publicus est jure gentium sicut et ipsus fluminis. Itaque naves ad eas applicare funes arboribus ibi natis religare onus aliquod in his reponere cuilibet liberum est sicuti per ipsum flumen navigare. Sed proprietas earum est illorum quorum prædiis adhærent quâ de causâ arbores in iisdem natæ eorundem sunt . . . . quare autem littora non cedant, sicut et ripæ his qui prope possident prædia potest quæri. Sunt autem hæc intelligenda de fluminibus perennibus temporalia enim possunt esse privata.	Riparum autem usus publicus est de jure gentium sicut ipsius fluminis. Itaque naves ad eas applicare, funes arboribus ibi natis religare, onus aliquod in iis reponere, cuivis liberum est sicuti per ipsum flumen navigare: sed proprietas earum est illorum quorum prædiis adhærent et eâdem de causâ arbores in iisdem natæ eorundem sunt: et hæc intelligenda sunt de fluminibus perhennibus quia temporalia possunt esse privata.
§ 5. Litorum quoque usus publicus juris gentium est sicut ipsius maris; et ob id quibuslibet liberum est casam ibi ponere in quam se recipiant, sicut retia siccare et ex mari reducere. Proprietas autem eorum potest intelligi nullius esse, sed ejusdem juris esse cujus mare et quæ subjacent mari terra vel arena,		*N.B.—Bracton omits the last sentence of section 5 of the Institutes.*

It will be noted that sec. 5 of the Institutes, which states that there can be no property in the shores, is wholly omitted by Bracton, and upon this Hall (p. 105) argues that Bracton "did not mean to deny that the owner- "ship (such as it was) rested with the King, asserting only "that the *usus* was common to all, as that of the sea was," and (says Hall) so far he will be found essentially right; but it is submitted that this reasoning is unsound, for Bracton must have been well aware that throughout the kingdom the foreshore in the point of property was in very numerous places vested in the lords of manors, although subject to the *jus publicum*. It has, however, been clearly decided that many of the passages which Bracton took from the Civil Law are inconsistent with, and form no part of, the English Common Law. It is submitted that the passage in Bracton, if it is to be taken as any authority with regard to the English law of the foreshore, must be taken to refer to the *jus publicum*, and not to the *jus privatum*. It is abundantly clear that Bracton had no idea of any general title existing in the Crown to the foreshore of the kingdom, either by virtue of the prerogative, or as based upon any theory that the foreshore at that time remained in the Crown as parcel of the great waste of the realm not granted out.

Blundell *v.* Catterell, 5 B. & Ald. 268, 304; Bagot *v.* Orr, 2 Bos. & P. 472; King *v.* Yardborough, 3 Dow & Cl. 178, 187; Howe *v.* Stawell, Alc. & N. 353; Ball *v.* Herbert, 2 Durn. & E. 253; Acton *v.* Blundell, 12 Mee. & W. 353.

Bracton's treatise, therefore, cannot be cited to shew that in his time the *primâ facie* theory of the Crown's rights had any existence. The two cases in his Note Book, Nos. 1271 and 1272, as to wreck taken by Michael de Bavent and Simon de Petraponte, although they do not specifically shew that Bavent and Petraponte claimed the shore, yet do shew that the ownership of the shore is implied in the language of the entries; and we shall see later that, in a subsequent procedure against their successors in title, the shore was distinctly claimed, and the claim was not traversed by the Crown. It will therefore be seen that Bracton must have been well aware that the property in the foreshore was, at any rate in some cases, vested in the subject, and for that reason he has omitted the passage in the Institutes which avers that the property in it cannot be owned by any one.

The entries in Bracton's Note Book (iii. 279) are taken from the Assize Roll of William de Raleigh in 23 Henry III., A.D. 1239. The language of the entries would seem to suggest that the view taken of the law relating to wreck at that period was that the subject could not have wreck unless he had the land whereon to take it, unless he shewed some specialty by which he had the liberty. It would also seem that there prevailed a doctrine that the franchise of wreck could not be delegated by the Crown's grantee to another subject, and this appears later in the Quo Warranto Rolls of Edward I. Michael de Bavent (who was lord of the manor of Eston) was summoned by quo warranto for taking wreck in the hundred of Blithing, Suffolk. He pleads that he and his ancestors have always had wreck in the same hundred from the Conquest, and that he took wreck in the time of King John; "et quæsitus de quo tenet tenementum suum per "quod clamat libertatem illam," he says he holds of Earl Roger Bigod; and judgment is given against him because he held nothing of the lord the King, nor of any one who could have such a liberty, nor did he shew any specialty by which that right could belong to him, except that he formerly had "gorz," which is not held for wreck. On the same roll, Simon de Petraponte (lord of the manor of Benacre), being summoned in the same manner, says that he holds his land, "per quam clamat libertatem," of Earl Warren, and that he and his ancestors have always had wreck from the Conquest, and that whatever he had of wreck is enrolled by the sheriff and the coroner; but judgment is given against him. Here it will be observed that although the Crown challenges the franchise it does not challenge the soil, and we find that Bavent's successor in title was summoned in 2 Edward II., A.D. 1309, to answer to the King for taking wreck coming ashore on the sea-coast between Benacre and Snodespyk, in the county of Suffolk, to the value of £200. He pleads that "he does "not know what Snodespyk is but if Snodespyk be not

MS. Addit. 12269, f. 191b.

See post, pp. 61, 90. Coram Rege, Mich., 2 Edw. II. roll 35d.

"*his soil* of Eston," he says he took no wreck between Benacre and Snodespyk or elsewhere *in the King's or any other man's soil;* but if Snodespyk be *his soil* of Eston, he claims to have wreck there, and that he and his ancestors have had wreck there time out of mind. He says also that a writ of quo warranto was lately brought against him in the time of King Edward the First relating to wreck and other franchises in Eston, which quo warranto was still pending and undetermined, and he prays judgment whether he shall be obliged to answer here for the same thing. Thereupon it was ordered that a jury should be summoned to try the fact of taking and appropriating wreck between Benacre and Snodespyk. Upon this record it is to be observed that Bavent claims the wreck *upon his soil,* and there is no traverse for the King that it is not his soil; whereas, if the King's attorney had considered, as the Courts now do, that the foreshore of the sea was *primâ facie* in the Crown, there certainly would have been such a traverse on the record. The fact, however, unquestionably is that there was at this period no presumption of title in the King to the foreshore. This is somewhat confirmed by the following case, which, while it challenges the right to royal fish, admits the defendant's title to the soil. It is a plea between the King and the Prior of Holy Trinity, Canterbury, in 26 Henry III., A.D. 1242, "de quadam balena "capta *in terra ipsius Prioris de Appeldre quæ debet esse* "*domini Regis et ad ipsum pertinere.*" The plea is put in respite until the King's coming, because the Abbot's charters were locked up in St. Augustine's Abbey under the seal of Otho the Legate. No result appears, but the admission of the ownership of the foreshore in the Abbot is clear on the face of the record.

Abb. Placit, p. 119. Coram Rege, 26-7 Hen. III.

At this period there are many returns of purprestures against the King in the Placita Coronæ, but they are all purprestures either upon the King's private property or against his prerogative of jurisdiction as purprestures upon highways and against navigation and the like. The following is a remarkable example:—"Concerning "purprestures they say that Peter de Newport, Arch-

Quo Warranto, Essex, M/2/17 m. 52d, 32 Hen. III.

"deacon of London, occupied a certain 'placea' in Barling "[on an arm of the River Crouch] *juxta rivagium domini* "*Regis*, and appropriated it to himself, in which he made "a certain great dike [fossatum], and afterwards built a "house there, where of old time the King's bailiffs were "accustomed to convene the hundred of the King and "hold it there; and they say that ships with all mer- "chandise used to ply there, and likewise all the country "used to assemble in that place to provide for making "the watch for keeping the peace of the lord the King "*cum Warstaf*." The tenement is ordered to be taken into the hand of the lord the King, and the archdeacon is amerced, but on payment of a fine of sixty marks the purpresture is allowed to stand. It does not appear that the place was on the foreshore; indeed, it is clear that part of it could not have been; but it is to be observed that the purpresture complained of was an interference with the public rights and the right of navigation, and not a purpresture upon the King's soil; nor do we find in any of these presentments of purpresture any suggestion that the soil of the foreshore was looked upon as belonging to the King.

Quo Warranto, Essex, M 2 17/5 m. 1d, 32 Hen. III.

On the same roll the right to wreck and royal fish was allowed in a judgment on a quo warranto to the canons of St. Paul's in Walton and to the Bishop of London in Clacton on production of the King's charters granting them those liberties "*by londe* and *by stronde, on tyde* and "*off tyde*."

Fines, Norfolk, Hen. III. No. 981.

In 34 Henry III., A.D. 1250, we find a fine levied in the King's Court, whereby John de Merlay conveys to Isabel de Cressy lands in Runton and Beston, Norfolk, with the waters, fisheries, sea-port, and *litus maris*.

Coram Rege, 37-38 Hen. III. Abb. Plac. p. 133.

It appears from proceedings in the King's Bench in Michaelmas, 37–38 Henry III., that the wreck at Malberthorpe in Lindsey was in the hands of the King, and that the practice was for the sheriff to have the wreck appraised by the oaths of four neighbouring vills, and to deliver it to those vills to answer for it to the King.

Coram Rege Roll, Hil., 38 Hen. III. roll 7.

In 38 Henry III., A.D. 1254, we find a plea between the Abbot of Faversham and his tenants concerning their services, whereby it appears that the demesne in lands, in water, and *in strand* belonged to the Abbot.

On the Placita Coronæ for Norfolk, 41 Henry III., there are numerous presentments by the hundredors as to "who have wreck of the sea they know not by what "warrant," and the sheriff is ordered to summon them to shew their title. Among them, the Abbot of St. Benet Hulme is summoned for "taking wreck which came "ashore *super terram Abbatis*, and it was witnessed that "the same Abbot has wreck of the sea *in feodo suo* "by the King's charters, which he produced and which "testify this."

Quo Warranto Roll, Norfolk, M/2 4/2 m. 24-35.

In the same year there was a suit between Prince Edward and William de Betenovere and others concerning wreck at Codings, which is part of the honor of Hastings, then belonging to Peter of Savoy. An inquisition was ordered to inquire as to some wreck which came ashore in the land of Prince Edward of the manor of Codings, and the jurors were directed to inquire who took it. They say that a ship came ashore "in baronia Edwardi "filii domini Regis apud Codings," and that the wines which were in the ship "jactata per mare tractata fuerunt "in libertatem dicti Edwardi de Codings, et super feodum "suum," and that divers other quantities of wreck came ashore, and they say, "quod hæc omnia salvata fuerunt et "tractata ad certam terram super libertatem et feodum "dicti Edwardi et etiam maeremium de fractura navis." And they say that William de Bestenovere and others came and carried them away "extra baroniam et feodum dicti "Edwardi usque baroniam de Aquila contra defensionem "ballivorum dicti Edwardi." The jurors being asked what right the said Edward has to have that wreck, they say that, in the time of Alice Countess of Augy, a wreck came ashore in the Rape of Hastings, and the Countess's bailiff took it and another wreck in the same Rape; and in the time of the said Edward a tun of wine came ashore at Codings, and Prince Edward's bailiff took it. Judgment is given for the Prince: and because it is shewn that part of the wine and other things "quæ de wrecco applicuerunt super

Tower Assize Rolls, No. 36, m. 25, 47 Hen. III.

"feodum domini Edwardi" are at Pevensey, where no sheriff has entry, it is commanded to William Agylun, who was the steward of Peter de Savoy, of whose liberty Pevensey is, that he distrain the said William de Bestenovere and others to make restitution to the Prince, and the sheriff is ordered to see that the judgment is carried out.

Tower Assize Rolls, No. 36, m. 7, 47 Hen. III.

In 47 Henry III. there was a suit between John de Warren, lord of the barony of Lewes, and Peter of Savoy, lord of the honor at Aquila, as to the right to wreck which came ashore near Seaford, and the boundary of the respective liberties was in dispute. The jury was summoned to inquire "si wreccum maris ab hominibus ipsius "Petri inventum in mari juxtà costeram Sussex inter "Wasbetel et Forhavene ad ipsum Petrum pertineat. Et "si idem Petrus a tempore quo tenuit honorem de Aquila "semper exstitit in seisina de wrecko maris invento infra "prædictas divisas in quocunque feodo inventum fuerit; "absque hoc quod prædictus Johannes vel aliquis ante-"cessorum suorum unquam esset in seisina de aliquo "wrecko invento infra divisas prædictas. Et si octo dolea "vini quæ prædictus Johannes nuper cepit apud Seford et "ad castrum suum de Lewes adduxit inventa fuerint ab "hominibus ipsius Petri infra prædictas divisas sicut præ-"dictus Petrus dicit: vel si wreckum maris inventum "juxtà costeram maris in Seford in feodo et libertate "pertinente ad prædictum castrum ipsius Johannis de "Lewes pertineat sive inventum fuerit ab hominibus suis "propriis sive ab aliis. Et si idem Johannes et omnes "antecessores sui semper habuerunt wreckum maris "inventum in feodo et libertate prædicta tam infra præ-"dictas metas quam alibi juxta costeram maris de Seford. "Et si prædicta dolea vini inventa fuerint in feodo et "libertate quæ pertinet ad prædictum castrum ipsius "Johannis ubi prædictus Petrus nuncquam percipere con-"suevit wreckum maris sicut prædictus Johannes dicit."

The jurors say "quod in portu de Seford stat quædam "petra que vocatur Whasbetel et dicunt quod Petrus de "Sabaudia a petra illa versus occidentem nihil clamare "potest infra libertatem prædicti comitis nec idem comes "ab eadem petra versus orientem nihil clamare potest infra "libertatem prædicti Petri de Sabaudia nisi tantum quan-"tum quidam homo jactare potest quamdam hachiam "de manu dextra, tenendo quamdam partem capillorum "suorum sub aure dextra de manu sinistra ita quod "in jactatione illa remaneat dextrum brachium infra bra-"chium sinistrum. Et dicunt quod prædicta octo dolea "vini applicuerunt apud la Perre contra terram prædicti "comitis. Et quia convictum est quod prædicta vina non "applicuerunt infra libertatem prædicti Petri; immo infra "libertatem prædicti comitis consideratum est quod præ-"dictus comes inde sine die et Petrus in misericordia pro "falso clameo."

In 52 Henry III., A.D. 1268, we find the Earl of Warwick claiming wreck thrown *upon his land* in the manor of Brighton, Sussex.[1] Abb. Plac. p. 170.

In 47 Henry III., A.D. 1263, Peter Serche and others, merchants, and owners of a ship, sued the Earl Warren for taking the ship which they left derelict near the land of the Earl in Sussex, and which came ashore "super ter-"ram prædicti comitis." The Earl claimed that it was wreck "super terram suam de wrecho venientia tanquam "wrechum suum, quod ipsius libertatis suæ contingit," and the claimants release their claim in court. Coram Rege, No. 136, 47 Hen. III. roll 4.

In 54 Henry III., A.D. 1270, we have confirmation of the right to wreck to the Abbot of Cerne, in the vill of Cerne, Dorset; to the Abbot of Shaftesbury in the manor of Kingston, Dorset; to the Abbot of Abbotsbury in all his lands;[2] and to the Abbot and monks of Peterborough in all their lands and all their lordships. Rot. Cart. 54 Hen. III. m. 8.

In 55 Henry III., A.D. 1271, John de Burgh, who was lord of the honor of Raleigh, made a grant to Guy de

1 See Dickens *v.* Shaw, *post*, at which trial this record was not produced.

2 This confirmation was founded on an inquisition (printed in Dugdale, iii. 57), which finds that the abbots of Abbotsbury "semper "hucusque habuerunt omnia per mare apulsa litori pertinentia ad "ipsam abbatiam scilicet wreck."

Rochford of divers marshes in the island of Foulness, Essex, to hold "as well within walls as without, in waters, "*sands, shores*, wreck of the sea ways," &c., and a fine was levied between them in the King's Court in the same year. This grant was the origin of the present manor of Foulness, the court rolls and ministers' accounts of which shew that a large tract of the northern part of the Maplin Sands, lying between the River Crouch and the Maplin Light, is parcel of that manor, and has been immemorially occupied by the lord and the copyhold tenants of the manor, with weirs, kiddels, and other fixed engines, and that the sands in question have been demised by copy of court roll as "sea grounds," "fishing lands," "fishing grounds," "weirs," "kiddells," and "kiddell grounds," and that the wreck has been immemorially taken by the lords. The grant from Guy de Rochford to John de Burgh was confirmed by a charter of King Edward II., notwithstanding that a quo warranto had been brought by King Edward I. against John de Rochford for the wreck (but not for the shore) in 13 Edward I., A.D. 1285, which, like the majority of the quo warrantos issued by Edward I., was adjourned, and never afterwards prosecuted. This manor of Foulness was parcel of the great honor of Raleigh, which belonged to Sweyn, commonly called the Earl of Essex, at the time of Domesday. That honor comprised numerous manors in the south part of Essex, many of which abutted on the sea-coast. The manors of Foulness, Great Wakering, Little Wakering, North Shoebury, South Shoebury, Prittlewell, Hadleigh, Chalkwell Hall (between Prittlewell and Hadleigh), amongst others, were portions of Sweyn's estate, and the foreshores of some of these manors can be shewn to have been parcel of them, and are out of the Crown at the present day, except a small portion of foreshore belonging to the manor of North Shoebury, which the Crown took possession of a few years ago, the lord of that manor not caring to contest the title. The foreshore of the manor of South Shoebury has been recently purchased by the Crown; the lord of the manor of Southchurch owns the foreshore; the foreshore of Prittlewell

Charter of Edw. II.

was the subject of the suit of Scratton *v.* Brown, where the title to the foreshore was proved. The title to the foreshore of Chalkwell Hall was tried in 1856, when the lord of the manor established his claim. The foreshore of the manor of Hadleigh, which extends from the manor of Chalkwell Hall to South Benfleet, belongs to a grantee from the lord of the manor, who proved his title to it in the year 1863, and the right to the fishery and soil was maintained in an action recently tried before Baron Pollock. The title to the foreshores of the manors of Great and Little Wakering is at present at question in the suit of Attorney-General *v.* Emerson. Part of it has been leased to the Crown; the foreshore of the inland creeks of those manors is admitted to have been parcel of the manor; the bailiffs' accounts and court rolls shew extensive acts of ownership over the foreshore similar to those shewn in the records of the manor of Foulness, to the foreshore of which manor it adjoins on the east; and the lords have wreck of the sea within the manor. Although the title to the foreshores in the manors of Wakering and Foulness has not yet been determined, the fact that the foreshore is parcel of the manors of Hadleigh, Chalkwell Hall, Prittlewell, South Church, and South Shoebury, all members of the same honor, tends, it is submitted, to raise the presumption that when the honor of Rochford, or the manors of which it was composed, were granted out by the Crown, the foreshores of those manors were granted as parcels of them.

4 B. & C. 485.

Ex parte Alston, 28 L. T. 337.

Bridges *v.* Highton, Sol. Journ. viii. p. 1, p. 765, 1863-4; 11 L. T. N. S. 653.

Foster *v.* Frost, 1887.

In 56 Henry III., A.D. 1256, Richard King of the Romans brought a suit against Thomas Rocelyn, for taking wreck coming *super terram præfati Regis* in Baketon (Norfolk).

Abb. Plac. 181.

In this reign there are very numerous entries on the records relating to fisheries and weirs in the sea all round the coasts of the kingdom.

CHAPTER III.

THE REIGN OF KING EDWARD I.

WE now come to the important period of King Edward I., a period when the law of the land was thoroughly revised and settled by this great monarch, who, as Mr. Justice Blackstone says, has been "justly styled our English "Justinian, for in his time the law did receive so sudden a "perfection that Sir Matthew Hale does not scruple to "affirm that more was done in the first thirteen years of "his reign to settle and establish the distributive justice "of the kingdom than in all ages since that time put "together." No one can contemplate the Public Records, especially of the earlier part of his reign, without feeling the truth of Mr. Justice Blackstone's words.

Commentaries, iv. 92.

The records of the courts, which in the previous reign are comparatively scanty and brief, suddenly swell into large rolls containing innumerable pleadings and judgments, the perusal of which shews very clearly that the most even-handed justice was meted out to the King's subjects, and that all men, of whatever grade, stood equal before the law. There is a remarkable illustration of this in an assize roll for the county of York of 7 Edward I., A.D. 1279, where one Gilbert de Mapleton, who was the steward, or "senescallus," to Herbert de St. Quintin, the lord of the manor of Brandsburton in Holderness, a baron of large estate, brought an action of assault against his master, to which the said Herbert pleads that, having heard from certain of his "fidedigni" that his steward was criminally intimate with his wife, he pretended to go upon a journey with certain of his retainers, but, returning suddenly, he went to his wife's chamber, when one of her women slammed the door in his face; whereupon one of his

Quo Warranto Roll, M/1/10/1 8 Edw. I. roll 61.

"fidedigni, ira commotus," smote in the door, and there he saw the said Gilbert and his wife playing and kissing upon his wife's bed.[1] Thereupon the said Gilbert attacked his master's man, and was hurt in the scuffle that ensued. Yet, in spite of these circumstances, so equal was the law that this steward, who had been caught in flagrant adultery with his master's wife, dared, in reliance upon the strict administration of the law, to bring his action openly at the assizes for an assault. This is but one example of most numerous entries on the rolls which shew how equally justice was administered at this period.

But, besides enforcing strict justice between subject and subject, the King was keenly alive to encroachments on the prerogative, and to usurpations against the royal dignity; and, as soon as he was safely settled on his throne, on October 11th in the second year of his reign, A.D. 1274, he issued the well-known great commission of inquiry, the return to which is known as the Hundred Rolls. Under this commission he assigned his justices to make inquiry, under oath by jurors, in all counties by a series of articles. Hundred Rolls, ed. Record Commn.

"First, as to what manors the King has in his hands, "as well of ancient demesne as of escheats and perqui-"sites?

"What manors used to be in the hands of his prede-"cessors; who hold them now, and by what warrant; and "at what time, and by whom, and how, they were "alienated?

"Who hold the King's fees; how, and when, and by "whom they were alienated?

"Also concerning other alienations of lands, hundreds "and wapentakes, cities and boroughs, and concerning "ancient suits, services, and customs due to the King and "now withheld?

"Who also other than the King claim to have return "and estreats of writs, and who hold pleas of withernam, "and *who claim to have wreck of the sea*, and *by what war-"rant*, and *other royal liberties*, as gallows, assize of bread

[1] Ipsum Gilbertum decalciatum, osculantes et ludentes et paratos cubicare.

"and ale, and other things which to the Crown belong, "and at what time?

"Concerning those also who have liberties granted to "them by the kings of England, and have used them "otherwise than they ought to have done; how, and from "what time, and in what manner?

"Also concerning liberties granted which hinder com- "mon justice and subvert the royal power, and by whom "they were granted, and from what time?

"Who also have newly appropriated to themselves free "chaces or warrens without warrant, and likewise who of "old time have had such chaces and warrens by grant of "the King, and have exceeded the metes and bounds of "the same, and from what time?

"Also concerning *all purprestures whatsoever made upon* "*the King or the royal dignity*, by whom they were made, "how, and from what time?"

The King also orders inquiries as to the misconduct of his bailiffs and stewards, sheriffs, and other officers, as to any extortions from the people in a long series of articles.

"Also whereas fines for redisseizin or purprestures "made *per terram vel aquam*, for the concealment of "treasure and other such things to the King belong, and "to the sheriff to attach them; who have taken such fines; "from whom, and how much?"

See the articles, Hundred Rolls, p. 13.

These articles are of the most searching kind, and it is clear that the King intended the fullest inquiry to be made concerning even the slightest encroachment on the rights of the Crown. It is most remarkable that in these articles there is no suggestion of any claim by the Crown to the foreshores of the kingdom as a thing which belonged to the Crown of common right, as it is now claimed by the Crown Departments of the Woods and Forests and the Board of Trade. The only articles which touch it are the articles as to the wreck, and the articles concerning purprestures made upon the King or the royal dignity. It is evident that purprestures here mentioned are purprestures made *per terram vel aquam*.

Any encroachment upon the soil of the foreshore is a purpresture against the King if the soil is his in point of propriety, and is a purpresture against the royal dignity if it be in the nature of a public nuisance to the King's subjects either as to their right of navigation or right of way.[1]

Now, it is clear that, if at this period the foreshore of any large proportion of the manors round the coast was remaining in the Crown in point of propriety, we should expect to find in the returns to this commission numerous presentments of encroachments upon that foreshore by lords of manors, by erecting fishing-weirs, building walls, and inclosing the foreshore in many parts of the kingdom. If the modern theory that the Crown had not parted with the foreshore except in very few instances were correct, it is evident that we must have found in the results of this minute inquiry some evidence to confirm this theory. We will therefore carefully consider the presentments made in these returns, and from them it will appear that not one single instance occurs in which it is suggested that the King had then an interest of propriety in the foreshores outside of the royal manors, although he had an interest of jurisdiction over the whole foreshore of the kingdom. The purprestures which are presented by the

Hall on Sea-shore, p. 6.

1 PURPRESTURE.—Purpresture (*pourprestura*, from the Fr. *pourprist*, an inclosure) is when anything is done to the nuisance of the King's demesnes, or the highways, &c., by inclosure, or buildings; endeavouring to make that private which ought to be public: *Glanvil, lib.* 9, *cap.* 11; 1 *Inst.* 38, 272. And when a man takes to himself, or encroaches anything which he ought not, whether it be in lands, franchise, or jurisdiction, it is a purpresture; and some writers mention three sorts of purprestures—one against the King, the second against the lord of the fee, and the third against a neighbour: *Kitchin*, 10; 2 *Inst.* 38. Purpresture in a forest is every encroachment made therein, by building, inclosing, or using any liberty, without lawful warrant to do the same. And if any inclosures are made in forests, they may be laid open, &c.: *Manwood, ch.* 10; *Cro. Jac.* 156. By statute, purprestures or usurpations upon the King shall be reseised, and if any complain thereof, he may be heard, and have right done him: 4 *Edw. I. c.* 4. Purprestures and encroachments are to be inquired of in the sheriff's tourn: *Dalt. Sher.* 393—Jacob's Law Dict.

jurors are every one of them referable to purprestures against the royal dignity, and not to purprestures on the King's soil. When, therefore, we consider these voluminous, minute, and most carefully recorded returns to this most special and solemn inquiry as to infringements on the rights of the Crown, we are driven to the conclusion that the modern theory of the *primâ facie* ownership of the foreshore in point of propriety had no existence in the mind of the great English Justinian nor in the minds of his justices.

THE HUNDRED ROLLS.

The great bulk of these rolls, which are the returns made to the commission above mentioned, have been printed by the Record Commission in two folio volumes, under the title of the Hundred Rolls, but there exist others of them amongst the Public Records which have not been printed. In one of these unprinted rolls we find a fuller reading of the article concerning purprestures, which shews that that inquiry extended into waters and to the sea and ports; it is as follows:—"De purpresturis factis "super domini Regis sive in terra sive in aqua *sive in* "*mari sive in portu* et per quem nil sciunt."

Chap. Ho. Box. 150, No. 24.

The following is a summary of the principal presentments on the Hundred Rolls which relate in any way to the shore:—

Hundred Rolls, p. 56.

In the returns for the county of Cornwall it is presented that the lords of Scilly take wreck in the islands, but that in the tithings of Dutheno, Dregnal, and Cutherton it was taken and valued by the coroner and delivered to the tithings to be answered before the justices, and that Elias de Bray, the late havener of Cornwall, took wreck in the tithing of Alverton before it was appraised by the King's coroner.

The practice of dealing with wreck belonging to the Crown is shewn by the presentment made by the jurors of the town of Bideford, Devon, in which they state that the King has wreck in Bideford, and that when wreck of the sea happens to the lord the King it is estimated by the oath of lawful men before the coroner of the county, and afterwards the price is delivered to the burgesses of the same borough of Bideford, and the said price ought to be delivered to the justices in eyre when they come into Devon by the hands of the said burgesses. They also present that the Prior of Frampton has wreck and toll in his manor of Northam. They also present that William the Conqueror gave the manor to the abbey of Caen (of which Frampton was a cell), and that they have wreck of the sea without view of the coroner by the King's grant. This entry is a strong confirmation of Lord Hale's well-known argument. The Prior also had royal fish by the same grant, and the liberties are allowed him. Hundred Rolls, p. 63. Chap. Ho. Box. 150, No. 4.

The jurors for the manor of Kenton, Devon, say that the bailiffs of the manor have, in the aforesaid manor, wreck of the sea if it happen "super terram manerii," and they always answer for the wreck to their lord.[1]

The Abbot of Buckfast is presented for a purpresture on the great waste in the common moor of the south part of Dartmoor, *ad nocumentum totius patriæ.* This is an instance of a purpresture on the King's soil. Hundred Rolls, p. 75.

The lord of Totness has wreck of the sea from Blackstone without St. Petrox to the bridge of Totness from all time. This presentment shews the extent of the Aqua de Dart, now belonging to the Duchy of Cornwall, the soil of which is vested in the duchy. It was granted by the lords of Totness to one Nicholas de Tewkesbury in Edward I. as Aqua de Dart; it came by forfeiture to the Crown, and was granted to the duchy by the Duchy Charter of 11 Edward III. Ibid. p. 83.

The Earl of Cornwall is presented as having wreck in the manor of Kenton, and that he also holds the *filum aquæ* of Tamar as far as the Mew Stone (situate outside Ibid. p. 89.

1 The language of this paragraph was prophetic: see case of The Pauline, 2 Rob. Adm. 358, where the question was tried between the Admiral and the lord of the manor as to a wreck in this manor of Kenton, whether it happened within the jurisdiction of the Admiral or on the land of the lord of the manor.

Plymouth Sound). This is the water which was parcel of the Castle of Trematon, referred to by Hale in the case of Sutton Pool.

De Jure Maris, c. 4.

Hundred Rolls, p. 101.

The Abbot of St. Edmund claims wreck *super terras suas* in the hundred of Roubiry, Dorset.

Ibid. p. 102.

The Prior of Christchurch, Twyneham, has wreck at Flete, Walter de la Lynde at Sure, and Philip Harang at Langton. The Abbot of Cerne and the Prior of Frampton take wreck on either side of a weir belonging to the borough of Bridport.

Ibid. p. 103.

In the return for the county of York we find the following presentments :—

Ibid. p. 104.

The Bishop of Durham has wreck at Hoveden.

Ibid. p. 106.

See the case of the Port of Hull in Hale, De Portubus, c. 5.

It is presented that the Archbishop of York appropriates to himself the port of Hull—*i.e.*, the River Hull—which used to be the King's port, and free to all persons.

The Archbishop is presented as having wreck at Pattrington, the Abbot of York at Hornsea, and the lord of Pickering in the borough of Scarborough.

Hundred Rolls, p. 107b.

It is also presented that the Abbot of Whitby made a certain purpresture upon the King at Elsicroft and Lichecot. There is nothing to indicate where this was. There are many purprestures by encroachments upon highways, and by making assarts in the forest.

Ibid. p. 120.

Walter de Useflete claims wreck *super terram suam*.

There is an answer to the article "De purpresturis" which shews very clearly how carefully these inquisitions were taken, for the jurors of the city of York say that "many people have made divers minute purprestures, as "in making gutters and steps, which hardly concern the "King, and therefore nothing is here expressed as appears "in the inquisition."

Ibid. p. 122.

Purprestures are presented upon lands in Easingwold and in Sutton, which were royal manors situate inland.

Ibid. p. 128; Inq. p.-m. 1 Edw. I., No. 31.

Peter de Malo Lacu has wreck from Rymeswick to Thordeseye. This was a case of a grant of wreck *inter metas*. It belonged to Peter de Brus, the owner of the wapentake of Langbargh. The franchise extended over the foreshores of numerous manors between Rymeswick on the sea and Yarm, near Stockton, which belonged to the lords of those manors. This is a case of a claim to wreck *inter metas*, and not *infra manerium*, and is exceptional. It justifies the qualification which Hale gives to his argument that "he that hath wreck of the sea *infra* "*manerium*, it is a great presumption that he hath the "soil;" for he says, "*perchance* the shore is parcel of all "such manors."

It is presented that the fishermen of Blaketoft and the fishermen of Weston make their fisheries (fishing engines) *ultra debitas metas in Aqua de Ouse;* and in the same presentment there are numerous mentions of encroachments upon highways. There is no challenge of the right to make the fishing engines so long as they were not prejudicial to the navigation. Hundred Rolls, p. 130.

The men of Scarborough, Peter de Brus, and the Abbot Whitby, the hospitallers of Steynton, Gilbert de Gaunt, and the Earl of Holderness are presented as claiming wreck, and it is charged against Peter de Brus that he takes wreck even when men escape alive from the ship. Ibid. p. 131.

The Abbot of Selby claims wreck at Selby. Ibid. p. 134.

The Archbishop of York, Henry fitz Conan, and the Prior of Drax have fisheries in the Water of Ouse, by which the said water is much narrowed, to the injury of people passing. This is a specimen of the purpresture with respect to nuisance. Ibid. p. 135.

In the returns for the county of Essex we find that the Abbot of Westminster has all royal liberties in the vill of Ferings, and the Abbot of St. Osith likewise, and the Abbot of St. John's Colchester, in Brightlingsea. That the canons of St. Paul have wreck in Frinton, the Earl Marshal in Dovercourt and Wykes, William Francis in Bradfeld, the Abbot of Colchester in Pitsea, Guy de Rochford in Rochford, the Bishop of London in Clacton, Little Bentley, and Aleford; William de Appleford in Aleford, Alice Blund in Wabenasse; and, although there are numerous presentments of purprestures upon highways and commons and the like throughout the returns, we have only the following presentments relating to the water:—

Hundred Rolls, p. 163.

"Stephen Spinects, Henry Maydelote, John de Cock-"ayne, the Prior of Mersy, the Abbot of St. John Col-"chester, John de Moyon, the lord of Langenho, William "de Ripariis, Roger de Cogeshall, John Alcorn, Roger "Godfelaw, and William le Butler, by the weirs which they "have made, have made purprestures in the water of the lord "the King to the prejudice of the lord the King, and the "grievous damage of the borough of Colchester." This is clearly a presentment against the lords of the manors on either side of the River Colne for making weirs to the hindrance of the navigation. No quo warranto appears to have been issued on this presentment with regard to the soil, and the foreshore of that river is at present owned by the riparian proprietors, who get considerable profits from it for oyster layings and the moorings of yachts and vessels.

See post, p. 88.

Hundred Rolls, p. 164.

The jurors of the hundred of Tendring present that "Peter Cresman made a purpresture appropriating to "himself a weir in the sea, by precept of the steward of "the Bishop of London, where a weir never used to be." This is a presentment of a purpresture contrary to the provisions of the Great Charter against the erecting of new weirs in the sea.

Ibid. p. 169.

In the returns for the county of Gloucester we find that the Earl of Gloucester claims wreck in the manor of Thornbury, the Bishop of Worcester in the manor of Henbury, the Earl Marshal at Tudeham and Alfordston, and William de Valencia at a place not specified; the Prior of Great Malvern in Langene, the Earl of Hereford in Harsfeld, and the Prior of Lanthony in the hundred of Dodeston.

See post, case of *Yates v. The Admiral*, 7 Jas. I.

Hundred Rolls, p. 178.

Concerning purprestures, the burgesses of Gloucester present that the Abbot of Tewkesbury raised a certain weir in the Severn, which is called Stanenewere; and the Prior of Lanthony raised a weir in the Severn, which is called Cocaygne Weir, near the Castle of Gloucester. There are also presentments of new weirs contrary to Magna

Charta. Small purprestures are presented throughout these returns; they do not relate to the sea.

In the returns for the county of Huntingdon there are many returns of small purprestures on highways and water-courses; and there are presentments of weirs built upon the river leading from Lynn to Huntingdon, to the hindrance of the passage of ships, to the injury of all the country.

In the county of Kent the following persons are presented as claiming wreck:—The Archbishop of Canterbury, the Prior of Christchurch, and the Abbot of St. Augustine's, the Lord of Kyngeston, the Prior of Dover and St. Margaret's, Gilbert Peche at Westclive and at Lesnes, the Prioress of Sheppy at Minster in Sheppy, the Prior of Christchurch at Leysdon. There are numerous presentments of purprestures on roads and commons, and the Earl of Gloucester is presented for a purpresture upon the King in increasing the Lowy of Tunbridge by 300 acres. But there are none of purprestures upon the foreshore.

In the returns for the county of Lincoln there are many purprestures returned as to ways, roads, ditches, waters, water-courses, &c. The following people are presented as claiming wreck:—The Earl of Lincoln in the wapentake of Bradley; he also claims wreck from the bounds of Tyd as far as Shullestowe, and it contains at least three *leucæ;* William Longspe at Sutton, the heirs of Fulk Dorey in Gedney from the said place called Shullestowe to the bounds between Gedney and Fleet, and it extends for a *leuca.* Thomas de Multon claims wreck in the port of Fleet, Thomas de Holbeach from the port of Fleet as far as Holbeach for a *leuca*, and also from the house of the priors of Pipewell to the gutter of Weston for half a *leuca;* the Prior of Spalding claims wreck from the said gutter of Weston to Peckebrigge, and he took a whale at Spalding. The Earl of Lincoln has wreck in Northcoats *quantum feodum suum se extendit supra mare;* the Abbot of Peterborough has wreck from the vill of Gosberkirk to the vill of Quadhavering; John Earl of Britany has wreck from the town of St. Pol to Dunington, the King has wreck in Algarkirk, the Abbot of Peterborough has wreck in Fiskerton, the Earl of Britany *per totam marinam de Luthesk* from the time of King Henry I. Alan de Coningholm takes wreck from the port of Salfleteby to the port of Marr, and from the port of Marr to the port of Swyne; the Earl of Britany has wreck in Germerthorpe, the Earl of Lincoln in Burton Starer, the Abbot of Selby in Crowe, the Earl of Britany has wreck from Salteney to Wrangeld *super litus maris*, the Abbot of Waltham claims wreck at Wrangel *in toto feodo suo ubi abuttat super mare* from Wolmersty to the ditch of Lek; Henry de Lacy, Earl of Lincoln, has the same liberty within the aforesaid bounds *wheresoever his fee abuts upon the sea;* Henry de Lacy claims wreck from the bound between Malberthorpe and Crusthorpe to Lekeburnedik for a length of two *leucæ;* the Earl of Lincoln claims wreck by the sea-coast from Marsticros to North Stalflet, except in the fee of Croft, from the time of King John, and he also claims the port of Wainfleet; Americ de Rupecanardi claims wreck *in salinus de Croft*, Gilbert de Gaunt claims wreck at Barton on the Humber, the Earl of Lincoln in Halton, and Isabel D'Arcy at Staningburgh.

See post, 43 Eliz.

The presentments for this county are fuller than in most other counties, and for this reason: the return which is printed is the full and complete original return, whereas in most of the other counties only an abbreviation of the original return remains. If, therefore, this return be a fair sample of the original returns for other counties, we see how very minutely and carefully the inquiry of the commissioners was conducted. We see from it that the royal franchise of wreck had at this period been granted out over almost the whole of the foreshore of the county; and that there is not a suggestion in any presentment that the Crown had, or claimed, any interest other than that of jurisdiction in the foreshore. There are very numerous presentments of purprestures, of which the following are interesting:—

Hundred Rolls, p. 272.

Also they say that "the Prior of Spalding has the "fishery of the river of Spalding appropriated to himself,

" and lets the fishery yearly of the water of the said river, " and the sands towards the sea from the place which is " called Wodelode to the gutter of Weston, for 5/6." The question of his title was tried, and the jury find that he had been immemorially seised of that water, and thereupon he was discharged. This case shews that a fishery in an arm of the sea can be prescribed for as against the Crown. We have already seen that the Prior (p. 271) had wreck of the sea from the said gutter of Weston to Peckebrigge for three *leucæ*, and this ownership of a several fishery and the franchise of wreck would seem to shew that he must have been entitled to the shore.

The jurors of the town of Grimsby present that, forty years past and more, the casting up of the sea accumulated sands and stones at the mouth of the Humber, upon which Lord William de Fortibus, then Earl of Albemarle, began to build a certain town which is called Ravensrod, *and it is an island because the sea surrounds it*, and it is a forestalment to the injury and damage of the King's vill of Grimsby and the country round about to the value of one hundred pounds per annum, and that the men of Ravensrod meet ships at sea, and take them to Ravensrod to the injury of Grimsby, and that the said island of Ravensrod from the time of the said Earl William has descended from heir to heir to the present time. There is a note against this entry: " Nothing here, because they " have sued out a writ before the King." On this presentment of purpresture it is to be remarked that the jurors do not charge that Ravensrod belonged to the King by the law of alluvion, but that it is an island, and so would belong to the King. The town remained parcel of the lordship of Holderness for several centuries, and it was here that King Edward IV. landed on his return to England in the eleventh year of his reign. The town has since been swallowed by the sea, the site of it being just within the Spurn Point. Hundred Rolls, p. 292.

Walter Unkle of Cle found a certain fish, which is called "Mereswin," near his fishing-weirs, upon the sand of the sea, and carried it to his house in the demesne fee Ibid. p. 293.

of the lord the King pertaining to the vill of Grimsby, but the bailiffs of the Earl of Lincoln, of the soke of Thoresby, came and carried it away by force at night, in the name of wreck. They afterwards made a fine for the trespass.

Hundred Rolls, pp. 303, 311, 317. There are numerous presentments of purprestures upon rivers by the erection of weirs. The Abbot of Kirksted raised purprestures in five places upon the royal water of Wynne, between the city of Lincoln and St. Botolph, and blocked the course of the water and the King's highway and the transit of ships, to the great peril of persons navigating over his weirs; and there are numerous similar presentments of weirs obstructing navigation, but none of them make any reference to their being purprestures upon
Ibid. p. 373. the soil of the King. There are also many purprestures concerning the taking of toll in ports, and a number of presentments of weirs erected in the course of the Trent, but they are merely presented as nuisances, together with similar presentments of purprestures by walls and encroachments on highways.

Ibid. pp. 363, 386, 395. There are presentments of appropriating several fisheries in the Rivers Welland and Trent, which the jurors allege to have been formerly common to the country, or common to the men of the town, and in some cases they define the limits of the several fisheries.

Ibid. p. 400. There are some further presentments of encroachments upon the highways and of weirs in the Trent as being larger than they ought to be. John Waslin holds a weir of purpresture in the Trent *larger than it ought to be by forty feet.* Rayner de Waterton made a weir in the Trent *larger than it ought to be by* 100 *feet.* Ralph de Cressy raised against the King a weir *in una aqua de communi* called Hydell, to the injury of the country six pence.

These presentments, like the others, shew that the right to erect the weir, and the right to the soil on which it was erected, were not doubted either by jurors or justices, the only question being whether the weir was a nuisance to the navigation, or an encroachment on the public right of fishing in tidal waters. This return for Lincolnshire has marginal notes which shew that the matters presented by the jurors were afterwards inquired of, and in many cases settled, for we have notes of the posteas giving the verdicts of the jury in the cases thus tried; so that it would seem that the King's justices not only took the presentments made by the jury, but inquired into the matter presented, and tried the question by a jury. For example, at p. 340 there is a presentment that divers persons made a purpresture by weirs in the Ancholme to the damage of the country, which has this note against it: "The fishery of Ancholme is not several to the lord the "King; therefore, nothing." At p. 343 the jurors present that Norman D'Arcy pulled down the weir of Roger Waterton in the Trent, and carried away his nets; and against the presentment is the note: "Nihil hic quia non "tangit Regem." There are also frequent disclaimers of the liberties claimed. It is evident, therefore, that the inquiry under this commission must have been most minutely and accurately taken, and yet we have no reference to the claim by the King to the sea-shore as against the lords of manors.

In the returns for the City of London we find that the Abbot of Westminster claims wreck *per Tamisiam;* that William de Munchensy claims wreck by reason of the manor of Swanscomb (Greenhithe). The Archbishop of Canterbury claims wreck at Lambeth. The records relating to the latter manor shew most extensive user by the Archbishop.[1] The Earl of Cornwall claims wreck at Isleworth, and the Abbot of Westminster at Wandsworth. Hundred Rolls, p. 407.

Numerous persons are presented for building weirs in the Thames to the injury of the navigation, and amongst them the Archbishop of Canterbury. It is presented "that "weirs between Staines and Gravesend, and in the water "of Thames and Medway, are, as they [the jurors] "understand, purprestures by reason of the charter of "Henry III., which orders them to be pulled down." At

[1] The title to the foreshore at Lambeth is at present in controversy between the Thames Conservancy and the Ecclesiastical Commissioners.

p. 421 they say that the weirs which are between the City of London and Gravesend are built in prejudice of the lord the King and the City of London, and all the commonalty of England who navigate the water of Thames. It is also presented that the King has in his demesne the City of London with the water of Thames from Yantlet to Stanes. There are many presentments of purprestures upon the rolls, and no challenge of any claim to the soil of the river in anywise.

See Hundred Roll, London, m. 3.

In the return for the county of Norfolk we find that Richard de Snetterthon had wreck in Brunham, William de Calthorpe in Brunham, the Bishop of Ely and the Prior of Lynne in Mersland, the Abbot of Ramsey and Geoffrey de Marisco in Walsoken, Adam de Hakebeche in Hakebeche, William de Tillington in some place not named, the Countess of Arundel in the manor of Snetisham; the Abbot of Ramsey in Brauncestre, Ringstead, and Welle; the Earl of Gloucester has wreck of the sea *contra villatas de Weld et Warham*, but he exceeds his boundary, and no one dares to go to help save the ship on account of the Earl's bailiffs, who, if the ship is lost and the men are dead, have all the profit, and if they escape alive have half the goods. William de Munchensy claims wreck *juxta feodum suum in Holkham*. These two presentments are in an unusual form. John de Vallibus has wreck between the house of Hamo Ketel and Karewell. Roger Bishop of Norwich has wreck in Norwich from Keteswelle to Styvekey.

Thomas de Meynegarin and the heirs of Thomas Fitzwilliam have wreck from Karewell to Autingdesdiches by charter of Edward Earl of Chester. The Earl of Gloucester has wreck in Walsingham between Well and Styvekey. John Earl of Warren has wreck *ex opposito terrarum suarum* in the soke of Gymingham. The heirs of John de Grey have wreck *ex opposito terræ suæ de Syringham*. Robert de Vere Earl of Oxford, Matilda de Philbrick, and the Prior of Beston have wreck in Runcton and Beston. Hugo de Raymes has wreck *ex opposito terræ suæ* in the vill of Overstrand. The Earl Warren has wreck from Grenehowe to Smeden. Thomas Rocelyn took wreck from Bromholm Cross to Hapsburgh without warrant. The Earl of Cornwall takes wreck in Baketon and Caswyk. The Prior of Wymondham has wreck in Hapsburgh. William le Parker and William de Granario have wreck in places not named. William de Ages has wreck in Palling. Oliver de Ingham and the Abbot of Hulm have wreck in Waxtoneham. The bailiff of B. de Somerton takes wreck in his bailiwick of Winterton.

It is presented that the Countess of Arundel, who has wreck at Snetesham, took wreck at Hulm within the liberty of the Abbot of Ramsey, and that the same Countess, who has wreck by the coast of the sea, exceeds the bounds of her liberty, and, by her bailiffs, takes things which are found and taken in the sea by ship or by net which were found a long way off in the sea before they came to the shore. This presentment shews that the distinction between Admiralty droit and wreck was well understood. Thomas Rocelyn has wreck in Walecote; the Earl Warren and the Earl of Cumberland have wreck in the hundred of Tunsted, Thomas Rocelyn in Ridlington, the Bishop of Ely in Tyrinton, and John de Ingelthorp in Tilleneye. Hundred Rolls, p. 522. See Lestrange *v.* Rowe, 4 Foster & Finl. 1048.

There are numerous presentments of purprestures, as in other counties. They are purprestures upon ways and common of pasture, and the appropriation of several fisheries "where it used to be the common water of the "lord the King," and of making weirs "in the common "water of the lord the King." Hundred Rolls, pp. 450, 508, 509, 511, 513, 522, 528, 530, 536.

"The Abbot of Hulme made a purpresture in the "common river of the lord the King, which extends from "Wroxham Bridge to Grabbardes Ferry, claiming the said "water as his several fishery, and not permitting any one "to fish in the same fishery, to the great damage of all the "country, whereas the said water is common to any one, "and ought to be so by reason of the dignity of the lord "the King, whose river it always was." This is the same fishery as is treated of in Hale, ch. 5, when the question of whether the fishery was the several fishery of the Abbot Ibid. p. 504.

was tried in Trinity, 10 Edward II., A.D. 1317, between the King and the Abbot. The Abbot pleaded that, although it was an arm of the sea, it was his own soil, and that he planted weirs in it; and the Abbot was successful. Hale quotes the case to shew that a fishery with weirs is evidence of the right to the very water and soil itself, and it is to be observed that this presentment does not claim the soil for the King, but only the common right of fishing for the public, by *reason of the dignity* of the lord the King. The presentment, therefore, is strictly a presentment of purpresture *contra dignitatem Regis.*

The jurors of the city of Norwich present that the Prior of Norwich appropriated to himself *quoddam Betemay in aqua domini Regis in Norwico quod vocatur Cunte,* which always belonged to the lord the King until the Prior took it, and what now is Betemay was always the water of the lord the King, and that John Chese appropriated two acres of meadow *in aqua domini Regis* next the mill of Westwyke, which the Prior now holds to the prejudice of the King; and there are other similar presentments of purprestures *in aqua domini Regis* by encroachment on the soil of the water. But here it is to be observed that *the King was the lord of the soil of Norwich,* and these purprestures are purprestures upon his private ownership of property; but we find no similar purprestures as to property upon the soil of any manor which was not in the hands of the King.

In the returns for the county of Northumberland we find that Edmund, the King's brother, has wreck in the barony of Staunford; that the Prior of Tynmouth and Alexander de Baliol claim wreck; that the Prior of Tynmouth on one side of the Tyne, and the Prior and the Bishop of Durham on the other side of the Tyne, have wreck of the sea; that the Bishop of Durham has wreck from Glendal as far as his castle of Northam, *per totam ripam maris;* that William Herun has wreck by charter of King Henry III.; that the Bishop of Durham has wreck at Bedlington. The jurors of Newcastle present that the Prior and convent of Tynemouth have erected on one bank of the

Tyne a certain town which is called North Shields, where there used only to be three loges (or shields) for fishermen, in which town they carry on trades whereby the King loses his toll which used to be given in the town of Newcastle, to the grievous damage of the King; and that the Prior has made a market of Tynemouth to the damage of the King. They also say that the Prior of Durham has built the town of South Shields in the same manner. This presentment gave rise to the suit between the town of Newcastle and the Prior in 18 Edward I., A.D. 1290. They also say that the Prior of Durham has built a weir which is called Sandwardyere, "*et stat injuste super filum aquæ de Tyne*," but they know not from what time, nor by what warrant, and it is four perches long. The Prior has another weir called Smeltyere, *quæ stat injuste super filum ejusdem aquæ*, and is four perches long: and another weir which is called Hunghyere, which is twenty perches long, and Peseyere, which is three perches long, and two weirs called Heburnyere and Sneryere. Also that the Bishop of Durham has three weirs called Kirkyere, Greenyere, and Rokeyere, *quæ omnes stant super predictum filum*; and that the Abbot of Newminster has a weir called Hamesyere, *quæ stat injuste super filum*. These presentments are clearly directed against obstructions to the navigation. Under the head of purprestures are returned many encroachments in the town of Newcastle and in the county. There are many purprestures presented as to encroachments on commons and highways. The jurors of the hundred of Tyne and Coket, as to the article of purprestures, say that "the third part of the water of Tyne from "Edwynistre towards the east [this is above Newcastle] "to Tynemouth belongs to the lord the King, in which "water the bishops of Durham have made a purpresture "upon the lord the King, by three fisheries which are "called 'yeris,' so that where they ought to have only "the third part of the water aforesaid they now have the "moiety and more; and the priors of Durham likewise "have made a purpresture, so that where they ought to "have the third part of the water they have the moiety "and more. Likewise Robert de Neville, where he ought "to have the third part of the water, has the moiety and "more; and they say that all those of the bishopric of "Durham who have fisheries on the south side of the "Tyne exceed the third part of the water against the lord "the King." These presentments shew that the Bishop and his feoffees were claiming to the mid-stream of the Tyne both soil and water, and it is well known that the boundaries of the County Palatine of Durham extend to the mid-stream; but it is here to be noticed that there is no presentment of any purpresture on the soil of the river or the foreshore as being the King's soil, though all these weirs stood upon the foreshore.

In the returns for the county of Nottingham it is presented that the Bishop of Lincoln has wreck within the wapentake of Newark, and that the Sub-dean of York claims wreck in his fee of Burton and Bolum. There is a presentment "that Robert de Brus, the lord of Knayf, ap-"propriated to himself a fishery *ultra filum aquæ de Trent*, "where his fee is on one side and the King's soke of Berset-"law on the other side, and that water used to be com-"mon to all tenants of that soke." Also, that Anketin, formerly bailiff of Kirton, newly made a fishery in Bikeres-dike, where his lord has no land on either side, whereby persons wishing to pass are hindered from passing after sunset, but are taken and amerced by the Earl's bailiff; and that the same Anketin removed a certain other fishery in the same water, to the injury of the manor of Gringeley, three years ago.

In the returns for the county of Somerset the jurors present that the lord of Stoke Curcy has wreck; the Abbot of Glastonbury has wreck in the manor of Brent; that Roger Mortimer and Eudo la Zouch hold the vill of Bridgewater and have all royal liberties, except pleas of withernam and wreck of the sea, by grant of King Henry II.; the Bishop of Bath has wreck in the hundred of Winterstoke. The jurors of the hundred of Porbury say that Lord Raymond de Clivedon, Lord Edmund de Broutton, Lord Ralph de Gapuz, Robert de Weston, Stephen de Capenor, John Tilly, William le Bret, Lord

Maurice de Berkley, the Prior of Brymmor, the Earl of Gloucester, "*et universi manentes supra mare*," have wreck, but they know not by what warrant; John de Tregoz has wreck in Burnham, the Earl of Gloucester in the hundred of Harecliff, and Thomas de Berkley in the manor of Bedminster.

In the returns for the county of Suffolk the jurors present that Robert fitz Roger holds the manor of Bliburgh, and has wreck, as his ancestors have had of long time, of the gift of the King, as the jurors believe; the Abbot of Leyston has wreck; the Countess of Gloucester has wreck in Southwold; Hubert de Bavent in Eston, as his ancestors have had long since. Robert de Petrapont has warren at Wrentham Henestede and Benakre and gallows at Benakre, and *warrech maris*, as his ancestors had from the Conquest of England; his liberty extended from Eston to Benakre. Roger de Colevill and Thomas Latimer have wreck from Benakre to Kyrkele. They say that the bailiffs of the Countess of Gloucester in Southwold appropriated and claimed to have warren in Southwold, where they never had it, and that they exceed the metes and bounds of her fee by taking *warrech maris super feodum Roberti filii Rogeri in Walbertiswik* belonging to the manor of Bliburgh, which is held of the King in chief. This entry is a strong confirmation of Hale's theory, for it is clear that the wreck can only be taken upon the foreshore, and here is a disputed boundary of two fees upon the foreshore. They also say that the burgesses of Dunwich likewise exceed the bounds of their liberty by taking *warrech maris* upon the said Robert's fee in Walbertiswik. Royal fish and wreck at Northel' belong to the King. The manor of Luthingland has wreck of the sea from before the time of memory. The Prior of Bromholm has wreck in the vill of Burgh, in the manor of Ludinglond. This manor of Burgh was granted to the priory by King Henry III. The Earl Marshal has wreck of the sea at Walton (Walton cum Trimley, where the foreshore now belongs to Colonel Tomline). Guy Visdelow has wreck in the hundred of Saunford; the Prior of Botley and Ralph

Hundred Rolls, pp. 148, 200. See ante, pp. 33, 34.

Hundred Rolls, p. 200.

Ibid. p. 182.

Attorney *v.* Tomline, 14 Ch. D. 58.

fitz Ralph have wreck in Balders; the Prior of Snape has wreck from Thorpe "usque Ness de Orford" (Orfordness), the Abbot of Leyston from the port of Menesmere to the vill of Thorp; the Earl Marshal has wreck from the port of Newemore to the port of Haulford, and appropriates to himself the ports of Orewell and Goseford, which pertain to the lord the King. The jurors of the town of Dunwich present that Robert Fitz Roger "has wreck of the sea "from the bridge of Walberswik to Southwold, and "appropriates to himself a certain marsh [mariscum] "from the port of Dunwich *infra filum aquæ et maris* to "the bridge of Walberswik, which ought to belong to the "lord the King and the aforesaid town of Dunwich, they "know not by what warrant." This presentment seems to be a presentment relating to foreshore and the bed of the river, and the burgesses of Dunwich, who held that town of the King at fee farm, evidently claimed the port of Dunwich (now swallowed up by the sea) as against the lord of the manor of Bliburgh, of which Walberswik was parcel. Now, upon this presentment a quo warranto was brought against Robert fitz Roger in 14 Edward I., A.D. 1286, but it does not claim this foreshore for the Crown; it is only a claim for wreck of the sea at Walbertiswik, to which Robert appears, and pleads that Walbertiswik is within the manor of Bliburgh, which manor King Henry II. gave to one William de Norwich, his ancestor, to have and to hold to him and his heirs, with sok and sak, and toll and them, and infangenethef, and with all its liberties, free customs, and quittances, with which the same King held it in his demesne; and he produces the charter of Henry II., which witnesses this, and he claims the liberty of wreck by that warrant. The bailiffs of Dunwich say that the King is in seisin of the wreck, and the judgment is "*Ideo nihil de* "*brevi isto ad præsens.*" Now, it is clear that if it had been thought that the King was entitled *primâ facie* to the shore, this writ of quo warranto would not have been issued simply for the liberty of wreck, but would have included the intrusion upon the shore, which is distinctly shewn by the presentment upon which the writ of quo

Hundred Rolls, p. 200.

Ibid. p. 200.

Quo Warranto Rolls, p. 734. See post, p. 92.

warranto is founded. If it be argued that a writ of quo warranto is not an appropriate proceeding for claiming corporeal hereditaments, although it be proper for claiming usurped franchises, the answer is that there are in the Quo Warranto Rolls innumerable writs of quo warranto claiming manors and lands usurped against the Crown.

The jurors of Luthinglond say "that the manor of "Luthinglond used to be in the hands of the King's "father and his ancestors, which manor Devorgilla de "Bailiol now holds by demise of King Henry III., until "some exchange shall be given her for it, and there are "in the same manor two vills, to wit, Gorleston and "Lowestoft, and that the manor has wreck of the sea, "and always used to have it from the time whereof "memory is not; also that the Prior of Bromholm has "wreck in the vill of Burgh in the manor of Luthinglond. "Also that the burgesses of Great Yarmouth in the time "of Henry III. appropriated to themselves a water which "is the mere between the counties of Norfolk and "Suffolk, the moiety of which water belonged to the "manor of Luthinglond in the time of King John and "his ancestors, kings of England, and this appropriation "of the water is to the damage of the lord the King and "his manor of Luthinglond £10 per annum, and this "appropriation was made in the time of King Henry III., "when Roger fitz Osbert held the manor of Luthinglond "at farm, and now the bailiffs of Great Yarmouth take "customs of ships and nets from the marshes [de mariscis], "to wit, Stonere, Fulholm, and Butterdis, which are of the "demesne of the King of Luthinglond." This presentment shews that the King's manor was claimed to extend to the mid-stream of the River Yare, and therefore to include the foreshore; and it is evident that the complaint that the bailiffs of Yarmouth took toll of ships and nets in the marshes belonging to the manor must mean, by the word *marisca*, lands below high-water mark, for they could not take customs of ships or nets above the high-water mark. Here, therefore, is a distinct presentment that the foreshore is parcel of the King's manor, as no

Hundred Rolls, p. 160.

Ibid. p. 169.

See post, p. 91.

doubt it was; but it is to be observed that it is not claimed as a special right of property by virtue of the prerogative, but as parcel of the manor, and therefore, when we find the foreshore of the King's manor treated as parcel thereof, and we find throughout all this exhaustive inquiry no suggestion that the foreshore of any subject's manor belonged to the King in any sense in point of propriety, we are driven to the conclusion that the presumption of law at this period was that the foreshore was parcel of the manor to which it was adjacent, whether that manor was in the hands of the Crown or of the subject. If the presumption had been otherwise, the justices who took this presentment from the jurors would have corrected the presentment, and required them to present that the bailiffs of Yarmouth had made a purpresture upon the King's soil which was his *jure coronæ*, and not upon the soil which was his *ratione manerii*, as parcel of the manor.

The jurors of the hundred of Carlesford say that "Roger, formerly the Earl Marshal, appropriated to him-"self a liberty in the sea at Harwich to the damage of "the King's borough of Ipswich, and appropriated to "himself all the port of Orwell, and there took *prisas suas* "without warrant, and the present Earl likewise makes "and has made a certain weir *ultra portum ibidem*, so that "strange ships cannot cross it except by pilotage." The Earl Marshal was the owner of Harwich, and also of the manor of Walton opposite to it. He was the owner of the foreshore at Walton certainly, and the present owner of that manor (Colonel Tomline) still possesses it; but the Earl seems to have exceeded his liberties, and to have raised a nuisance to the navigation by his weir. The jurors of the hundred of Colneyse make another presentment with regard to this weir, which shews that it was merely presented as a nuisance; they say that the Earl Marshal, lately deceased, made a purpresture upon the lord the King in appropriating to himself "goys," which are called weres, in the port of Orwell, to the prejudice of the lord the King, and that the Earl's bailiffs stop ships wishing to go

Hundred Rolls, p. 197.

with their merchandise to Ipswich, and make the merchants sell their wares at Harwich, to the great injury of Ipswich and the said merchants. The jurors of the hundred of Saunford also present that the men of Harwich hinder the course of the sea (*impediant cursum maris*), and keep back ships and merchandise coming towards Ipswich, to the damage of the King and of the country forty marks per annum. The jurors of the town of Harwich also complain of the Earl's proceedings, and say that the late Earl Marshal made a purpresture *super aquam domini Regis in portu de Orwell*, which is the port of the lord the King and common to all to buy and sell, stretching from the sea to the town of Ipswich; and that the Earl and his men do not permit merchants to ply to the town of Ipswich with their merchandise, compelling them, against their will, to go to Harwich, which is the Earl's town, by which the town of Ipswich is much damaged. These presentments shew very clearly that it was a question of nuisance, and not of soil, which was before the jurors. The purpresture in the King's water is treated as a purpresture against common right, not against any property of the King in the water and port. The jurors of the hundred of Wyleford say that the Earl Marshal appropriated to himself "the liberty of the water in the port of Gosford "outside the bounds and metes of his liberty." The jurors of the vill of Beccles say that John Bigod, the son of Ralph Bigod, makes a purpresture in appropriating to himself *regalem ripam de —— et piscariam ejusdem quæ est brachium maris* from the dike of Philip Geraud to the mill of Dunebert.

Hundred Rolls, p. 200.

Ibid. p. 191.

In the returns for the county of Sussex the jurors return that William de Breuse has wreck *contra portum maris de Shoreham*. Also they say "that John de Camoys, "Nigel de Brooke, Godfrey le Faukener the heir of "William de Wystenestowe, and Hugh de Buscy have "wreck of the sea *contra terras suas de antiqua tenura sed "ea quæ super terras suas applicata fuerint seu inventa*, they "keep for a year and a day, and if any one shall, in the "meantime, reasonably sue for them, they are delivered to

Ibid. p. 201.

"him, saving expenses." This entry shews that the expression used here, and also in some of the Norfolk presentments, of *contra terras suas*, is equivalent to *super terras suas*, as no distinction is drawn between them. It also shews the necessity of keeping wrecked goods for a year. They say that William de Breuse has wreck in the Rape of Bramber, which appears to have included the whole hundred of Wyndham. The Archbishop of Canterbury, the Earl Warren, William de Breuse, and the Bishop of Chichester have wreck in the hundred of Stenyng; Hugh de Buscy has *wreccum maris contra terram suam* in the hundred of Fishergate, and used to have it of old time. The burgesses of Shoreham say that the Earl Warren and his bailiffs take all things which come of wreck *super ripam maris* in the Rape of Lewes, and keep them to their own use, contrary to common right and custom, and do not keep them to be claimed for a year. The Earl Warren was lord of the barony of Lewes. The jurors of the town of Seaford say that the Queen-mother holds the barony of Aquila, and has wreck, and the Earl Warren has wreck in his baronies. The hundred of Burne is in the Queen's hands, and the Queen's bailiff takes wreck. William Bardolf, junior, has wreck of the sea *contra terras suas proprias* in the manor of Berlyng. John de la Ware claims wreck in his manor of Exsete. The jurors of the hundred of Faxberwe say that the Queen-mother has wreck of the sea between La Forhawine and Le Westberle, *per totam costeram maris;* and they say that she has assize of bread and ale in the hundred of Faxberwe *per totam baroniam*, and that she has warren *per totam baroniam de Aquila.* The jurors of the Rape of Lewes say that the Earl Warren has wreck of the sea *ubique contra dominica sua propria.* The Bishop of Chichester likewise *contra libertatem suam habet ubique wreccum maris;* and that John de Burgh and his ancestors used to have wreck, and that the said Earl disseised him. The jurors of the hundred of Bosham say that Lucas de Vivayne claims wreck, and has no warrant for it. The Bishop of Chichester has all liberties in his manor of

Hundred Rolls, p. 202.

Ibid. p. 202.

Ibid. p. 204.

Ibid. p. 206.

Ibid. p. 208.

Ibid. p. 208.

Ibid. p. 212.

Catham, and Roger le Bigod in his manor of Bosham. The jurors of the Rape of Arundel say that the lord of the honor of Arundel claims wreck in the hundred of Palings, and likewise the Bishop of Chichester; and that Henry Tregoz claims wreck in the vill of Garinges. John de Britannia has the Rape of Hastings, and claims wreck in all the barony of Hastings. The Bishop of Chichester, John de Britannia, and William de Northey claim wreck in the hundred of Newenfield and Byxle. The Abbot of Battle and the Bishop of Chichester claim wreck in the hundred of Byxle. The Abbot of Battle has wreck in the hundred of Gesling.

Hundred Rolls, p. 213.

Ibid. p. 217.

Ibid. p. 218.

In the returns for the county of Southampton the jurors for the hundred of Huggescombe say that the Abbot of Abbotsbury has wreck of the sea *supra terram suam*. The Abbot of Binedon has wreck from the time of King John. The Prior of Christchurch has wreck of the sea at Fleet, Walter de la Lynde at Suyre, Philip Harang and Robert fitz Robert at Langton.

Ibid. p. 223.

From the foregoing examples of purprestures presented, it will be seen that this great inquiry was most minutely carried out, and that everything that was a usurpation or a purpresture upon the King was most carefully recorded, and yet we find that there is not a single instance, throughout the whole series of returns, of a purpresture upon the soil of the foreshore of the kingdom as if it were considered as belonging to the King in point of propriety; indeed, almost the only presentment which can be looked upon as referring to a purpresture upon the soil of the foreshore as belonging to the King is that which relates to the manor of Luthinglond, in Suffolk, and in that case the purpresture is presented as being made upon the King's soil *as parcel of the manor*, and not as parcel of the general lordship of the kingdom. In the cases of purprestures on the water and soil at Norwich, the lordship was also in the King's hand. Now, that which was a purpresture upon the King was well understood at the time, as appears by the statute 4 Edw. I. c. 4, the text of which is as follows:—
"De purpresturis seu occupationibus quibuscunque factis

Purprestures or usurpations upon the King's land shall be reseised.

"super dominum Regem, sive in [libertate, aut in aliis,] "concordatum est, quod tempore regis [definitum erat, "et consideratum], quod ubi occupatores superstites [erant, "vel fuerunt,] Rex de plano resumat rem taliter occupatam "de manibus occupantium quod [et in curia domini Regis "de cetero] observetur; et si quis de hujusmodi resump- "tionibus conqueratur, prout justum fuerit audiatur."

It is abundantly clear from these presentments on the Hundred Rolls that the franchise of wreck had been granted out by the King over the greater part of the coasts of the kingdom, but, nevertheless, in some places it was still in the Crown; and we have in the statute 3 Edw. I. c. 4, a declaration of the Common Law with respect to taking wreck—viz., that where a man, a dog, or a cat escape alive out of the ship, the ship and its goods shall not be adjudged wreck, but shall be kept by view of the sheriff, coroner, and King's bailiff, to be delivered to the owner if claimed within a year and a day, but, if not claimed, they shall be answered for to the justices, if the wreck belong to the King, and where the wreck belongeth to another than the King he shall have it in like manner. This is confirmed by the Statute De Officio Coronatoris, 4 Edw. I.

CHAPTER IV.

THE QUO WARRANTO ROLLS.

THE returns to the commission of the Hundred Rolls were mostly made in the third year of the King's reign, but some of them were in the fourth and fifth years. The King now having obtained complete returns of the liberties claimed and the usurpations made against the Crown, we next find the enactment of the Statute of Gloucester, in 6 Edward I., which recites that the prelates, earls, barons, and others of the realm claim to have divers liberties, and that it was agreed that they should use the same liberties until the next coming of the King or his justices into the county, and enacts that the sheriffs shall make proclamation that all persons claiming any liberty shall come before the King or the justices in eyre to shew by what warrant they claim them. The statute refers to the returns of the Hundred Rolls, and orders the justices to hear cases according to the articles which the King has delivered them.

Fleta, who wrote in the time of Edward I., gives an elaborate description (book i. ch. 20) of the articles which are to be inquired for the Crown in the eyre of the justices. They are similar to the articles of the Hundred Rolls, and amongst them we find the following:—Of wreck of the sea, advowsons withheld from the Crown, escheats, &c.; of purprestures upon the King made *in terra in mari et in aqua dulci infra libertatem vel extra;* of new customs raised *in terra in vel aqua;* who raised them, and where; of manors alienated from the Crown, knight's fees, wapentakes, suits, &c.; who claim wreck of the sea, and by what warrant; and other royal liberties, as gallows and assize of bread and ale and other things which pertain to the Crown,

See articles in Statutes, ed. Record Commn. i. 233, and Capitula Escaetriæ, i. 241.

and from what time ; of those who have liberties by the King's grant, and how they have used them ; of liberties granted which hinder common justice and subvert the royal power ; who have appropriated chaces, warrens, &c. ; who, under colour of wreck of the sea, have appropriated goods which ought not to be called wreck ; and innumerable other inquiries of the most minute kind, none of which, except the article " De purpresturis," point in any way to any general claim by the Crown to a right of property in the sea-shore. We have seen, from innumerable returns to this article " De purpresturis," that it relates exclusively to purprestures upon the royal dignity—that is, upon the *jus publicum*, except in cases where the purpresture occurs upon soil which is parcel of a manor in the King's hands, and not upon soil which is parcel of a manor in the hands of a subject.

In ch. 44 Fleta describes the law as to wreck, and shews that, when it is taken upon the sea-shore, it is to be delivered by view of the coroner and the bailiff of the place into the hands of those of the vill in which it came ashore, and must be kept till the eyre of the justices ; and that, if no claimant appear within a day and a year and make out his claim, it remains to the King, or to the lord of the fee if he enjoys that liberty, whereby it appears that it was well understood that wreck coming ashore on a man's fee belonged to him if he had a grant of wreck *infra feodum*, and there is no suggestion that the foreshore of the fee on which it is taken was not parcel of it ; nor is there in Fleta's treatise a single word from which it can be argued that the Crown at this period laid any general claims to the foreshore of the realm.

In book iii. ch. 1, he treats " De rerum acquisitio-" nibus," and in sec. 4 has this passage : " Rerum autem " aliæ sunt corporales ut quæ tangi possunt ; aliæ incor-" porales ut jura et servitutes : aliæ communes ut aer mare " et litus maris : aliæ publicæ ut jus piscandi et applicandi " flumina et portus. Riparum etiam usus publicus est " de jure gentium sicut ipsius fluminis ; ad plus vero se " habet commune quam publicum ad quod unum ad omne "animatum et aliud ad omnem publicum se extendit." In ch. 2 he treats of the doctrine of alluvion and dereliction, but does not assign derelict land to the King; and, treating of islands, sec. 9, "Præterea agris limitatis non "cedit insula ratione vicinitatis in flumine publico imo "concedatur occupanti *vel regi propter suum privilegium;*" but there is no suggestion in the treatise that the King has any general right to the foreshore.

With regard to the Statute of Gloucester, which is often called the first statute of quo warranto, Coke says 2 Inst. 280. that the King, wanting money, was persuaded by ill counsel that the titles of his subjects to franchises were usurped and bad, and that their charters were lost, and that upon the King's proceedings many persons were dispossessed of their long-enjoyed possessions; that thereupon rose great contention, as indeed is mere matter of history, and that the King subsequently provided a remedy.

Under the statute the claimants came in and filed their claims, and quo warrantos were issued in great numbers, founded for the most part upon the returns for the Hundred Rolls. The proceedings upon these writs have been for the greater part printed by the Record Commission in a volume entitled the Quo Warranto Rolls; but the collection is by no means complete. The proceedings extend from 6 Edward I., A.D. 1278, until 21 Edward I., A.D. 1293; in by far the greater number of cases the proceedings are adjourned before the King, and the result of them does not appear, but in Michaelmas, 22–23 Edward I., A.D. 1294, the Coram Rege, Mich., 22-23 Edw. I. roll 3. King in Parliament granted "for the favour of his people, "and on account of the war in Gascony, that all his writs, "as well of quo warranto as of plea of land, should remain "without day at present until he or his heirs should wish "to proceed thereon." The general result of this adjournment was that the proceedings ceased, and that the owners of the liberties and lands in question remained undisturbed in their possession. This great attempt by the Crown to disturb the ancient possessions of the subject, although it was carried on with great vigour, thus signally failed

The proceedings shew the nature of the claims put forward and the pleas by which they were met, and in some few cases the judgment is given. They are here carefully considered with a view to discover whether the Crown at this period set up any general claim to the foreshores of the kingdom or not. It will appear from them that in no case was such a claim set up, but, on the contrary, the language of the pleas shews that it was taken for granted that the shores belonged to the lords of the manor ; and where they plead that they have rights of wreck *super terras suas* there is not a single case of a traverse of such claim to the soil of the foreshore by the King's attorneys, although they exercised every species of ingenuity in order to traverse the titles of the defendants.

Quo Warranto Rolls, p. 184. On the Dorsetshire eyre of 6 Edward I., A.D. 1278, Walter de la Lynde claimed wreck *in terris suis*, and pleaded that all who had the manor of Suere had used this liberty *a tempore*, &c. The King's attorney replies that "he cannot retain these liberties, not having a special "warrant from the King or his ancestors, because such "liberties are so annexed to the Crown of the lord the "King that they cannot belong to the lands or tenements "of any man without special warrant." Judgment is deferred.

Ibid. p. 184. Adam Harang claims wreck in all his lands, and pleads immemorial user. The King's attorney says "that wreck "of the sea is a certain liberty immediately annexed to "the Crown and dignity of the King, so that no one can "have that liberty without special warrant from the King "or his ancestors, and he prays judgment because the "said Adam claims no other liberty nor stray nor waif, "which are liberties of one nature, and as it were one "liberty, nor shews any special warrant therefor, and asks "whether his old occupation suffices to retain the liberty." There is no judgment.

Ibid. p. 182. Philip Harang claims wreck in the manor of Langton Sarnvile by prescription. The King's attorney disputes his title because he does not claim waif, from which the other liberty depends, and is joined and annexed to it, and that he has no specialty. Issue is joined, but no judgment is entered upon the roll.

The Prior of Christchurch claims wreck in his manor of Fleet by gift of Hauwisia de Rivers and confirmation of King John. He produces King John's charter, which grants him the manor of Fleet with all its appurtenances. The King's attorney prays judgment for the King because special mention is not made of wreck either in the gift or the confirmation; that even if Hauwisia had the wreck, she could not grant it to the Prior. There is no judgment. Quo Warranto Rolls, p. 182.

The Abbess of Shafton claims wreck in her manor of Kingstown, and shews a grant from Henry III. confirming wreck in the manor when it shall happen; and she is discharged. Ibid. p. 182.

The Abbot of Middleton claims wreck in his lands by prescription. The King's attorney says that he is not seised of waif and stray, which are immediately annexed to wreck, and that he cannot claim without special warrant. There is no judgment. Ibid. p. 181.

The Abbot of Cerne claimed wreck *per omnes terras super mare* by grant of Henry II. and confirmation of Henry III. The King's attorney alleges that after the confirmation the present King was seised of wreck in the Abbot's lands, and prays that his seisin be adjudged; but the Abbot replies that the keeper of Corfe Castle unjustly took wreck in his lands, and that he tried the question before the justices and was successful; nevertheless the liberty was taken into the King's hands *quo usque*. See Chad *v.* Tilsed, 2 Brod. & Bing. 403.

William le Moigne claims wreck in Bineford and Ogres and elsewhere in his lands. The King's attorney pleads that he shews no special warrant, and asks whether he may have these liberties by prescription. There is no judgment. Quo Warranto Rolls, p. 184.

It appears from the foregoing entries that the contention of the Crown in 6 Edward I., A.D. 1278, was that the franchise of wreck could not be claimed by prescription, but only by grant, and that unless a man had waif and stray as well as wreck it was evidence to suggest that his claim to wreck was founded on usurpation. This contention, however, must have been decided against the Crown, for in the eyre of Kent which took place in 7 Edward I., A.D. 1279, we find numerous entries of judgments in favour of the subject claiming wreck by prescription.

The Abbot of St. Augustine's, Canterbury, claims wreck of the sea *per omnes terras finibus maritimis junctas*, because those lands were given him as the kings who gave them held them, as the charters of King Knut and King Edward the Confessor shew. The jury find for him, and he is discharged. Here we have a further precedent that long possession under a grant of a manor *adeo plene et integre* as the King held will suffice to establish title to foreshore.

Quo Warranto Rolls, p. 348. The Prior of Christchurch claims the port of Sandwich and *wreccum maris ubi acciderit super feodum ecclesiæ suæ* by grant of King Edward, which grants him these liberties *on strond* and *on stream*, *in terra* and *in mari*, and he pleads prescription, and is discharged.

A further quo warranto was brought against him in
Ibid. p. 367. 21 Edward I., A.D. 1293, for claiming wreck, and he claims it in Lyden, which is a member of Estry and Monkton, and its members Brokhende, Goreshende, and Ham, which is a member of Copton, Aylwarton, Appledore, Agene, Elbene, Orgarswike, Billerica, Fayrefelde, and Clive, and he pleads the previous judgment in his favour. It is found that he has immemorially used the liberty, and judgment is given for him.

Ibid. p. 342. Gilbert Peck claims wreck in West Clive by prescription, and is discharged.

Alexander de Baliol claims wreck and sea toll at Whitstable, and also at Richelingewede, by prescription, and is discharged. A further quo warranto was brought
Ibid. p. 359. against him in 21 Edward I., A.D. 1293, for wreck at Whitstable, and he claims wreck in that manor and toll with merchandise at La Craston in the same manor by prescription, and is discharged. By his same plea he claims the liberties of the assize of bread and beer, infangenethef,

See Gann *v.* The Free Fishers of

gallows, and waif in the hundred of Whitstable, but he distinguishes between the hundred and manor, and claims warren, wreck, and toll only in the manor.

Whitstable, post; 11 C. B. N. S. 387; 13 C. B. N. S. 853; 11 H. of L. 192.

The Prior of St. Martin at Dover claims wreck and sea toll in the vill of Deal by prescription, and is discharged.

Quo Warranto Rolls, p. 343.

In the eyre for Sussex in 7 Edward I., A.D. 1279, the Abbot of Fecamp claims wreck in his manor of Brede and in all his lands in this county, and says that Brede belongs to the manor of Stanynges, which Edward the Confessor granted to his predecessor with all royal liberties in the same manor. The King's attorney avers that the manor of Brede is not contained in the charter, and the case is adjourned.

Ibid. p. 749.

John de Warren the Earl of Surrey claims wreck in all his lands and fees throughout the Rape of Lewes by prescription. The King's attorney alleges that he has usurped it, and the jury find for the Earl that he has the *barony* of Lewes and wreck of the sea in all his fees, demesne lands, and hundreds throughout the whole Rape of Lewes, and he is discharged.

Ibid. p. 751.

At this time the honor of Arundel was in the custody of the Crown by reason of the minority of the heir, and the King orders inquiry as to encroachments on the liberties thereof, and amongst other matters as to who had taken wreck of the sea. The jury find that "Walter "le Harpur, lord of the manor of Middleton, took a "porpoise lately thrown up by wreck of the sea *upon his* "*land* of Middleton, usurping and appropriating to him-"self wreck upon his land of Middleton, to the disherison "of the heir of the honor of Arundel, and the damage of "the lord the King, in the custody of the same, of half a "mark, because he ought not to have wreck there. And "because it was found by the same inquisition that the "said Walter took the wreck *at his land* of Middleton, "which is of the honor aforesaid, to the damage of the "King, having the custody of the said heir, of half a mark, "whereas the same wreck ought to belong to the honor, "the said Walter is ordered to satisfy the King for the "said half a mark, and the sheriff is ordered that hence-

Ibid. p. 751.

"forth he shall not permit him to have wreck *in that* "*land.*" This entry is very remarkable, for while it shews clearly that the right to the soil of the foreshore and the right to the franchise of wreck may be distinct and separate rights, it shews that it was admitted on these proceedings, to which the Crown was a party, that the lord of the manor of Middleton had the foreshore as parcel of his manor, although the lord of the honor or barony of Arundel, out of which the manor of Middleton was subinfeudated, had the right to the wreck over that foreshore, and hence arise the following conclusions:—

1. That by the original grant of the honor of Arundel the soil of the foreshore passed with it throughout the honor.

2. That on the subinfeudation of the manor of Middleton by the lord of the honor of Arundel, the foreshore of that manor, formerly parcel of the honor, passed with the manor, as parcel thereof.

3. That the right to wreck, as a franchise originally granted to be taken within the honor, was reserved to the lord of the honor when he subinfeudated the manor and its shore to the lord of Middleton.

4. That, therefore, when we find evidence of ownership of the shore by the lord of a manor subinfeŭdated out of a great honor, although he has not the right to wreck in his manor, he may still be presumed (from evidence of acts of ownership) to have the right to foreshore as parcel of his manor, both as against the lord of the honor and as against the Crown, for here his right to the foreshore is admitted, although he had not the right to wreck.

5. And, therefore, that he that hath *not* wreck of the sea *infra manerium*, it is no *absolute presumption* that he hath not the shore, for he may have it, although another hath the wreck.

6. And further it is to be here noticed that the Crown, whilst making the fullest inquiry before the justices in eyre, John de Reigate and his fellows, although they had before them distinct evidence that the lord of Middleton claimed the foreshore of his manor, did not set up any

primâ facie title in the Crown to challenge that possession.

7. It would therefore seem clear that at this period the presumption of law was, that a manor adjoining the sea was bounded by the low-water mark and not by the high-water mark, subject always to the public rights thereover.

These conclusions are further confirmed by a proceeding in the King's Bench in 9 Edward I., A.D. 1281, wherein the King and Isabella de Mortimer (to whom the King had granted the custody of the honor of Arundel) brought a suit against Luke de Vyencia and Henry de Tregoz for taking wreck at Garynges, Preston, and Codelawe, which the King claims as belonging to the honor and castle of Arundel. Luke pleads that he claims it in Codelawe by prescription. Henry claims it by prescription in Garynges and Preston. The plaintiff sets out title, and issue is joined. The jury find that the defendants only took it *per surreptionem*, and that the plaintiff is entitled. Judgment is given for the plaintiff. There is no issue as to the ownership of the soil of the foreshore, but it is shewn that Garynges, Codelawe, and Preston are all held of the honor of Arundel. The foreshore, therefore, is admitted on this proceeding, to which the King is a party, to have been parcel of those manors, notwithstanding that the wreck belonged to the honor. This case is quoted by Hale, c. 7, as an example that wreck may belong to an honor by prescription. Coram Rege, Trin., 9 Edw. I. roll 20.

Nigel de Brock and Hugh de Buscy claim wreck in Launcing and Kingston by prescription, but the jury find that William de Brus ought to have that wreck when it happens *per costeram maris* in the Rape of Bramber, and Nigel and Hugh are fined for a false claim. Quo Warranto Rolls, p. 754.

John de St. John claims wreck of the sea in his demesne lands and in his fees lying next the sea in this county by prescription. The jury find for him, and he is discharged. Ibid. p. 755.

John de Camoys and Margaret his wife, lord and lady of the manor of Bradewater, claim wreck in their fees adjoining the sea by prescription. The jury find that the wreck pertains to the barony of Bramber, but, because they have not usurped upon the King or his ancestors, they are discharged.

Roger le Bigod Earl of Norfolk claims wreck in his manor of Bosham by prescription, and is discharged.

Quo Warranto Rolls, 756.

Adam de Bavent claims wreck in his manor of Hay by prescription, but the jury find that the lords of the barony of Bramber have always had that liberty there and elsewhere throughout all that barony; and Adam is amerced for a false claim.

Ibid. p. 758.

The Bishop of Chichester claims wreck of the sea *per omnes terras et feoda sua jacentes juxta mare* from the Conquest and by prescription, and is discharged.

Roger de la Warr claims wreck of the sea in his manor of Excete by prescription. The jury find that he is not entitled, and he is fined for a false claim.

Ibid. p. 760.

William de Braose claims the castle and barony of Bramber with its members and its liberties, and all free customs to the same pertaining. He also claims to have the vill and port of Shoreham and the tolls of ships from old time. He also claims to have wreck of the sea by the sea-coast as far as his barony goes. He is discharged.

Quo Warranto Roll, Somerset, M/15 5/2.

In a roll of Placita Coronæ for 8 Edward I., A.D. 1280, for the county of Somerset, the Abbot of Clive claims wreck *per omnes terras suas.* He produces a charter of King Henry III. The jury find that he has taken it, and he is discharged.

John de Tregoz has wreck and waif in his manor of Burnham.

The Abbot of Glastonbury claims wreck in all his lands, the Bishop of Bath at Sarde in the hundred of Winterstoke, Thomas de Berkley in the manor of Bedminster, Robert Walrond in the manor of Wyke and Stoke Curcy.

Quo Warranto Roll, N. York, 1/2 9/ roll 20, 8 Edw. I.

In 8 Edward I., A.D. 1280, the Abbot of Whitby claims wreck of the sea by charter of Henry II., which he produces, and which grants to him *wreccum maris cum alga per totam terram*, and the Abbot sets out a grant to him of his land in Whitby from Alan de Percy, in which the bounds are

described as extending "a portu Witebiensi *totam mari-* See ante, p. 16.
"*nam* usque ad Blawic et inde de —— usque Hersecroft
"et usque Tordisiam et usque in mare et *per marinam* ad
"Witebi." In this case it is clear that the Abbot shews his title to the shore, for "marina" signifies the shore, and is so described in the Hundred Rolls at p. 335, where the Earl of Britany claims wreck *per totam marinam de Luthesk.* The record in the Abbot of Whitby's case is incomplete. The title to this foreshore is at present in litigation between the Crown and the lord of the manor.

In the Quo Warranto Roll for Somersetshire of 8 Edward I., A.D. 1280, in the eyre of Solomon of Rochester and his fellows, John de Tregoz is summoned for taking wreck in Burnham and elsewhere in his lands in that county. He claims it by prescription. The jury find for him, except that he ought not to have wreck of wine or royal fish. The judgment is given for him, except as to the wine and royal fish. Quo Warranto Rolls, p. 688.

John Tifli is summoned for wreck, but disclaims it. Ibid. p. 694.

Roger de Mortimer claims wreck in Bridgwater and his other lands, and a fishery called Kyngswere. He does not appear, and the liberties and fishery are taken into the King's hand; and the case was the same as to the Prior of St. Swithin. Ibid. p. 695.

Matilda the widow of Walter de Waynham claims wreck, except of wine and whale, in her land of Kingston by prescription. The jury find that she and her ancestors from the Conquest had wreck of the sea in their lands next the sea, except of wine and whale, and she is discharged. Ibid. p. 698.

The Prior of Bromholm claims wreck in his lands, but he does not appear, and the liberty is seised into the King's hands.

Stephen de Cappenovere, being challenged for a wreck, disclaims it; as does Simon de Astone.

Thomas de Berkley claims wreck in the manor of Beaminster by prescription. Judgment is not entered up.

The Bishop of Bath is challenged for wreck, but the record is not complete. Ibid. p. 703.

Quo Warranto Rolls, p. 769.

In the Quo Warranto Roll for the county of Southampton, Michaelmas, 8–9 Edward I., A.D. 1280, the Countess of Albemarle claims wreck in her fee in the Isle of Wight by prescription in her ancestors from the time of Richard I. The King's attorney says that when her brother, Baldwin de Insula, was in the custody of Henry III., the King granted the custody to Richard Earl of Cornwall, and that the said Richard appropriated the wreck without the consent of the King; but the jury find that the Countess and her ancestors have immemorially had it, and she is discharged.

Ibid. p. 771.

Robert Aguylon and Margaret his wife claim wreck in the manor of Christchurch. They plead that they hold the manor as the dower of Margaret of the inheritance of Isabella de Fortibus Countess of Albemarle, with all liberties to the same annexed: and, as to wreck, it was claimed that they and their ancestors before the time of Richard I. were in seisin of having wreck in the manor aforesaid, as to the said manor pertaining; and, although the King's attorney alleges that the Earl of Cornwall usurped the wreck when he had the custody of the manor, the jury find that the Countess and her ancestors always had it in the manor *as appertaining to the manor*, and they are discharged.

Quo Warranto Roll, Southampton, M/5/2. 21

On a roll of Placita Coronæ for the county of Southampton, with the same date, there are proceedings as to the purprestures upon the King's soil which are seised and rented to the King. In one case the jury of the hundred are amerced for concealing purprestures in their verdict. One of these is a purpresture on the street at Winchester, and another a purpresture *super solum domini Regis* at Bere within the limits of the forest; but, although purprestures upon the King's soil in point of property are presented and seised, there is no instance of a purpresture upon the foreshore.

Ibid. m. 31d.

There is also a presentment that Isabella de Fortibus the Countess of Albemarle claims wreck wheresoever in her lands in the Isle of Wight, but the jurors also say that John de Insula, Thomas de Enercy, Robert de Glomorgan, Thomas de la Hule, the Abbot of Quarre, and Matilda de

Sheres claim to have the moiety of all wreck coming ashore on their lands (*applicantia ad terras suas*) throughout the whole island on condition that they save the other moiety to the use of the said Countess, the jurors know not by what warrant. From this entry it would appear that the case of the Isle of Wight was similar to the case of the honor of Arundel above mentioned, and that the sub-tenants of the Countess had their land held under her in the island down to the low-water mark; therefore, the landowners of the island may be well entitled to the foreshore, although the right to wreck was in the Countess and afterwards came to the King by the conveyance of the island by King Edward I.

In the roll of the eyre for Yorkshire, before John de Vallibus and his fellows, in 8–9 Edward I., A.D. 1280–81, the Bishop of Durham is challenged for wreck at Ellerker Welleton, Hoveden, and Wakington. He claims by grant of King Egfrid, and confirmation by the Conqueror and King Edward I., and as to wreck he says that he only claims whale, if whale ought to be called wreck, saving to the King the head and tail; the record is incomplete. Quo Warranto Rolls, p. 187.

Gilbert de Gaunt and Richard Malebise, challenged for wreck, say that they do not claim wreck of the sea, but they do claim the whale of the sea when it comes ashore in the port of Filey, saving to the King the head and tail. The King's attorney prays judgment, because they do not claim wreck, and the whale is a royal fish, and only belongs to the King, and prays inquiry whether in times past they have taken wreck or not. The jury find that they and their ancestors have taken whale, saving to the King the head and tail. No judgment is entered up. Ibid. p. 189.

Walter de Fauconburg claims wreck of the sea and the wapentake of Langbargh. He pleads that he has two manors, Rise and Withernwick, in Holderness, but he does not claim wreck in them, as they are in Holderness. As to the wapentake of Langbargh, he only claims the moiety; and, as the other moiety belongs to persons under age, the case is adjourned. Ibid. p. 193.

Quo Warranto Rolls, p. 197. The Archbishop of York is challenged for wreck at Patrington, but there is no plea.

Ibid. p. 200. Gilbert de Gaunt is challenged for wreck at Hunmanby. He pleads that he does not claim wreck, but only whale, "if it ought to be called wreck, saving to the King the "head and the tail," and this by prescription. The jury find that he and his ancestors had the whale from all time, and he is discharged.

Ibid. p. 201. The Abbot of St. Mary, York, is challenged for wreck at Hornsea. He pleads that he has wreck at Hornsea by this warrant: that he has the manor of Hornsea of the gift of Earl Eudo (the lord of Holderness), who came with the Conqueror, which Earl had wreck as appertaining and annexed to the aforesaid manor, and that the abbots of York have always taken it in the aforesaid manor. He also pleads that William II. granted to his predecessors the same liberties and customs which the church of St. Peter, York, and St. John of Beverley have, and he says that the church of St. John of Beverley hath wreck of the sea, and that the custom of the said church is sufficient warrant for him. The jury find that the Abbot and his predecessors have immemorially taken the wreck; and he is discharged. The manor of Hornsea was granted out of the great lordship of Holderness by Eudo de Campania the Earl of Holderness, and the wreck and the foreshore passed with it, and are claimed by the lord of the manor at the present day.

Quo Warranto, Lincolnshire, M 3/2 15, 9 Edw. I. On a roll of Placita Coronæ for Lincolnshire it is presented that the Earl of Lincoln has wreck of the sea at Sutton, and the Prior of Spalding claims it in all his lands wheresoever it comes ashore; that Henry de Lacy has wreck at Thedelthorpe, Tedney, and Gretham; Walter de Tattersal at Sutton; and that a whale came ashore at Wainfleet, *super terram Philippi de Kyme*, which the said Philip took to his own use, wherefor he was amerced. This presentment would seem to shew that, although royal fish was considered to belong to the King, the foreshore was admitted to belong to Philip de Kyme, for it is clear that the whale cannot be taken above high-water mark.

In the roll of the eyre for the county of Lincoln before John de Vallibus and his fellows, in 9 Edward I., A.D. 1281, Thomas de Multon is challenged for wreck of the sea and port from Fleet to Holbeach, but he disclaims the wreck, and the jury find that he never took it. Nothing is said about the port.

Thomas son of Lambert de Multon was challenged for wreck in Multon and Fleet, and he disclaims it. Quo Warranto Rolls, p. 393.

Roger de Lascelles is challenged for wreck in Fulestowe, but this only of whale when it comes ashore, saving to the King the head and the tail by prescription. The King's attorney says that Roger only claims wreck of the sea of whale, and this liberty specially belongs to the crown of the lord the King, and cannot go out of it except by specialty, and he prays judgment whether prescription of time can be sufficient warrant to him when he shews no specialty by which he claims the liberty. The jury say that the said Roger and his ancestors have always had the whale as he claims it. There is no decision. Ibid. p.400.

The Prior of Spalding claims wreck of the sea, saving to the lord the King the head and tail of whale and other royal fish, and this in all his demesne lands within the manors of Pinchbeck, Sutton, Weston, and Spalding by prescription. The King's attorney says that prescription is not sufficient warrant; that specialty is necessary to take the liberty out of the King; and alternatively that if the Court should consider that prescription is a sufficient warrant, then he says that the Prior has not used it. The jury find that he has used it; and he is discharged. Ibid. p.401.

Emeric de Rupecanardi claims wreck "in salinis de "Croft." He claims wreck of the sea of all royal fish coming ashore, saving to the King the head and the tail *prout decet*, and also all wrecked ships. The King's attorney says that the King has no peer nor parcener in those things which merely belong to his crown, and that wreck cannot pass out of the Crown without specialty; but that if the Court shall consider long seisin a sufficient warrant, he prays inquiry as to the user. The said Emeric Ibid p.397; ante, p. 52; post, 43 Eliz.

also claims wreck in Salkesthorpe, Strutthorpe, Thedelthorpe, and in all his lands adjoining by the coast of the sea, but shews no specialty. The King's attorney demurs that prescription is not a sufficient warrant, and prays inquiry as to the user. The jury find the defendant and his ancestors have immemorially been in seisin of all manner of wreck of the sea, to wit, of royal fish, wrecked ship, and of all other things which can be called wreck of the sea; and he is discharged.

These entries shew that it was decided that wreck could be claimed by prescription, and that royal fish would pass under the grant of wreck.

Quo Warranto Rolls, p. 403. William son of Robert de Wyleghby claims wreck at Hoggesthorpe of whale and all royal fish, saving the head and tail for the King. The jury find that he has taken it *ab antiquo*, and that the King has had what belongs to him of right; and he is discharged. It would thus appear that the right to the head and tail of royal fish was reserved to the King, at any rate throughout the county of Lincoln.

Ibid. p. 394. The Abbot of Peterborough claims wreck of the sea in Goseberkirk and Quadhavering. He claims by charter of 15 May, 44 Henry III., A.D. 1260. The record is incomplete.

Ibid. p. 404. The Abbot of Waltham was challenged for wreck of the sea from Walmerstye to the dyke of Leek. He pleads that he has it *per totum feodum suum infra prædictas metas* by prescription, and that King Henry III. confirmed to him all his lands and liberties; and, being asked what kind of wreck he claims, he says as well whale as all other things which can be called wreck. The King's attorney objects that he shews no specialty, and that prescription is no warrant; that the charter of confirmation of King Henry III. cannot avail him, because in it no special mention is made of wreck of the sea, and that wreck cannot pass from the Crown under general words. The case is adjourned, but no judgment entered up.

Ibid. p. 411. Gilbert de Hagham disclaims wreck in Haburgh, and
Ibid. p. 414. Norman D'Arcy in his manor of Stayningburgh.

Ibid. p. 424. Gilbert de Gaunt claims royal fish only in Barton.

John Fitz Nicholas was summoned for taking tronage and pesage *per totum feodum comitis Richmond in Hoyland.* He claims to have tronage and pesage in the markets of Boston, so that if any one tries to avoid payment it is lawful for him to arrest and distrain him by his goods and ships until he paid the custom, "to wit, "from the town of Boston towards the sea as far as a "certain place which is called Norman depe, and on the "other side of Boston in the river called Wyne to a place "called Dockedik, and within the town of Boston *tam in* "*terra quam in aqua in feodo Richmond;*" that his ancestors were enfeoffed by the Earl Conan 200 years ago. The King's attorney says that such a liberty belongs to the Crown; that John shews no specialty from the King or his ancestors, but only from the said Conan, against whom the King would have his recovery if he were alive; and he prays judgment whether Conan's charter is a sufficient warrant. John replies that he stands upon his charter and his long seisin. The jurors find for him that he and his ancestors have taken that custom in all the aforesaid places, that John could only take the custom, and the Earl of Richmond has the fines for not paying. He is discharged. This case goes to shew that the tidal river as well land as water going up to Boston was admitted to be in the fee of Richmond, and in the hands of a subject.

It was presented that Peter Galle made distraints *in portos regios de Salflete* by his bailiffs in the second year of the King, they know not by what warrant, to the damage of the country half a mark. Thereupon comes John Bek, and says that Philip Galle, son and heir of the aforesaid Peter, enfeoffed him of certain lands and tenements in Skyttbrok, together with the aforesaid port, and he says that those things which are the King's and the rights of the King he has always striven to maintain, and prays a jury. The jury say that the land on the north side of the port is the several soil of the aforesaid John Bek, and the land on the south side is the common of the same John, and of all the vill of Salfleteby, and they say that

Quo Warranto Rolls, p. 429.

they never heard nor knew the lord the King nor any of his ancestors ever had anything in the aforesaid port, nor ever took any rent therefor at the aforesaid time ; and he is discharged. This case shews the possession of a port by the subject, together with the soil thereof.

Quo Warranto Rolls, p. 431.

In the roll of the same eyre we find that there was a quo warranto against Henry de Lacy Earl of Lincoln for claiming wreck and other liberties in Keling, Clypston, and Wardburgh, in Nottinghamshire, which is adjourned.

Ibid. p. 442.

A quo warranto against the Bishop of Lincoln for claiming wreck within the wapentake of Newark is also postponed.

Coram Rege Roll, Mich., 9-10 Edw. I., roll 25, Majus Record.

On the Coram Rege Roll, Michaelmas, 9–10 Edward I., A.D. 1281, we find a suit by the Abbot of Cerne against Richard de Ramesham and others for taking wreck—viz., *ligna navalia borda et ferramenta et alia per wrekum maris confluentia super terram ipsius Abbatis in manerio suo de Symondesberwe*. Defendants plead that they did not take wreck coming on the Abbot's land in Symondesberwe, but aver that they took it within their fee of Bridport, and not in the Abbot's manor. The Abbot joins issue, and sets up his title by prescription and charters of confirmation. The jury find that the defendants *venerunt super solum ipsius Abbatis et prædictum wreccum ibidem inventum vi et armis ceperunt*. Judgment is given for the Abbot. The form of the pleading in this case shews that it is impossible to suggest that wreck is taken anywhere but on the foreshore.

Coram Rege Roll, East., 9 Edw. I., Minus Record, roll 3.

In Easter, 9 Edward I., A.D. 1281, the King, having the custody of the heir of Rayner de Gimingham, impleads William de Calthorp and Cecilia his wife for taking custom of all ships coming (*applicantes*) to Bareham Morton for drying nets there. The defendants admit that they took the said customs, but aver that they took them *super feodum suum proprium et super terram propriam applicantibus et pro retibus ibidem desiccandis*, and not on the land of the said heir. The record is incomplete.

Ibid., Majus Record, roll 21. See also Lestrange *v.* Rowe, post, 4 Fost. & Finl. 1048.

In 9 Edward I., A.D. 1281, the lord of Snetesham, in Norfolk, recovered damages against trespassers for taking a whale on the shore of the manor of Snetesham.

On a roll of Placita Coronæ for the county of Essex, dated 13 Edward I., A.D. 1285, the Abbot of Westminster was impleaded for wreck in the manor of Bemfleet. He produced a charter granting it, and the jury found that he had it: the King's attorney *nil dicit*, and his claim was allowed.

[Quo Warranto Roll, Essex, M 2 9/1, m. 14.]

In the same eyre a claim for wreck at West Thurrock is disallowed.

[Ibid., M 2 9/3, m. 66.]

It is presented that the *mariscus vocatus le Rou Sand* is part of the manor of Hadley. This is the sea-ground lying between Canvey Island and the main land, now known as Hadley Ray, and belongs to the grantee of the lord of the manor. It was the subject of the case of Bridges *v.* Highton.

[Ibid. m. 104d.]

[Sol. Jour. 1863, viii. p. 765, 11 L. T. N. S. 653.]

The Bishop of London claimed a wrecked ship at Clacton, and pleads that the wreck came ashore *super terram suam*, and that he is entitled to wreck *in maneriis suis et super terras suas*. There is no decision.

[Quo Warranto Roll, Essex, M 2 9/3, m. 99d.]

Robert Fitz Walter claimed wreck at Burnham from the Conquest. The jury find that he and his ancestors have immemorially had wrecks of the sea *quandocunque et quotienscunque super terras suas applicuerunt.* This refers to the manor of Burnham on the River Crouch and the Raysand near the mouth of that river. It is the same place as is referred to in Hale, ch. 5, where it is shewn, by a record of 50 Edward III., that the Raysand and the fishery, with the weirs to the same pertaining, is parcel of the manor of Burnham. Hale quotes the latter record to shew that where we find a fishery in the sea is a fishery with fixed engines, it is evidence of the right to the very water and soil itself. He does not appear to have been aware of this proceeding as to the wreck, but it is a strong confirmation of his theory that a fishery with fixed engines is evidence of the right to the soil.

[Ibid. m. 71d.]

John de Rochford was summoned for wreck in Rochford, and he pleads that John de Burgh senior gave to his uncle, Guy de Rochford, whose heir he is, all his marshes of Foulness in the hundred of Rochford, as well out-marshes as in-marshes, together with all other marshes, as

[Ibid. roll 54.]

well within walls as without, to have and to hold the aforesaid marshes, with all their appurtenances, *in aquis sabulis litoribus wrecco maris oris semitis fugationibus warennis et omnibus aliis libertatibus prædictis mariscis pertinentibus*, which gift the King confirmed by charter, with a clause, "so long as nothing shall be hurtful to the King or his "heirs." The King's attorney says that, as to wreck, John de Burgh's charter cannot prejudice the King, because if the same John were alive he would have to answer to the King therefor; and also that the King is not prejudiced, because of the saving clause in his confirmation. The case is adjourned. Whether it was ever prosecuted or not we do not know, but the lords of the manor of Foulness have taken wreck there, and made every use of the foreshore that can practically be made of it. Here is distinct claim to the shore of the sea in a proceeding between the Crown and a subject; and yet there is no traverse of the soil, and no suggestion that the foreshore was in the King. The proceeding was before the justices in eyre, and the King's attorney was a party to the suit; and it is therefore inconceivable that the idea of the *primâ facie* title of the Crown as it is now set up existed at this period in the mind of the King, or his justices, or his attorneys. (See *ante*, p. 39.)

Quo Warranto Roll, Essex, M/2/9/3 m. 49b.

The jury of the borough of Colchester present that in the common river (Colne) between Northpoint and Westnasse, which is an arm of the sea, certain weirs have been raised, to the injury of people passing with ships and boats with wine and other victuals and merchandise, and they set out the names of the persons who have raised them —viz., Stephen Spinek, one weir; Henry Maydelote, one weir; Matilda, sister of John de Cokayne, one weir; Roysia Althorn, four weirs; the Prior of Mersea, three weirs; John de Mounviroun, six weirs; the Abbot of St. John, Colchester, one weir; the tenants of the lord of Langenho, two weirs; the heirs of William de Ripariis, three weirs; Roger de Coggeshale, one weir; Roysia atte Lymmine, one weir; to the injury of the borough and the country. These are evidently the descendants of the same people who were presented for the same purprestures on the Hundred Rolls (3 Edward I., A.D. 1275, *ante*, p. 50). They all appear, and say that their ancestors held the aforesaid weirs from time when memory is not, and that they are not to the injury of any one; and the jury find that this is so, and they are discharged. These persons were the lords of the manors abutting on the River Colne, which extends from the town of Colchester to a place called "the metes" at Westnasse, and it would therefore seem to have been admitted that the soil of the Colne was out of the Crown at this period.

See ante, p. 50.

On the same roll there are claims to wreck in Ramsey in Tendring Hundred, and by the Abbot of Waltham in Stanford, and Osbert de Cantilupe at Bradwell.

Coram Rege Roll, Mich., 13 Edw. I. roll 10.

In Michaelmas, 13 Edward I., A.D. 1285, the Prior of Titchfield sued the burgesses of Southampton for breaking down his weir at Cadland on the southern shore of Southampton Water. The burgesses plead that the navigation to the port of the town is obstructed. The jury say that from the time of memory there was not any weir there, but anciently there used to be there "*pali*," whereby they believe that an ancient weir was thrown down for the same reason as now, because it was to the injury of the navigation; and the Prior is amerced.

Quo Warranto Roll, M 4/6 roll 52.

On a roll of Placita Coronæ for the county of Norfolk, in 14 Edward I., A.D. 1286, the Earl of Cornwall claims wreck in Baketon and Kesewik; he claims by descent from his father. It is ordered that the King shall have a writ.

Ibid. m. 57.

Gilbert de Clare Earl of Gloucester claims wreck in Walsingham and Welles.

Ibid. m. 58d.

Peter Roscelyn claims wreck in Walecote; the Prior of Wymondham claims wreck of the sea *per omnes terras suas juxta litus maris in Hapesburgh* (see *ante*, p. 17; *post*, p. 94). William le Granard and William le Parker claim it in Eccles, William de Ages in Palyng, John de Ingham in Waxtonesham. Peter Roscelyn claims under his father, who died seised, and a writ is ordered against him. The Prior of Wymondham comes, and says that King Henry I.

granted to his predecessors wreck of the sea and all things that to wreck pertain in Hapesburgh, and he produces the charter, and says that he and his predecessors have taken wreck whenever it happened to come ashore. The jury find for him, and he is discharged. William le Granard is under age, and the case is postponed. William de Ages claims by prescription from the Conquest. John de Ingham claims as the bailiff of the Abbot of Hulm; the Abbot is subsequently discharged.

Quo Warranto Roll, M 4/6 m. 74d. 2

Robert de Monte Alto claims wreck in the hundred of Smethedon from a place called Fridaysfleet to another called Depedaleston; the Abbot of Ramsey claims it in the vills of Hulm and Brancester.

Ibid. m. 68d.

The Abbot of Hulm claims wreck from Palyng Cross to the bounds of Yarmouth. John de Warren Earl of Surrey claims wreck *ubique in terris suis in soka de Gimingham juxta litus maris.* Henry de Grey claims wreck *super litus maris in terris suis de Shiringham.* William de Warren, Roger de Felbrigg, and the Prior of Beston claim wreck *juxta litus maris* in the vills of Beston and Runton. William Clement claims wreck in his lands *juxta litus maris* in Runton. Hugo de Reynes claims wreck *juxta litus maris* in the vill of Overestrond. Writs are ordered against them all.

Ibid. m. 56d.

The Abbot of Hulm and William Bardolf claim wreck in Scrouteby. John de Vallibus claims wreck in Holte, Claye, Snyterley, and Letheringset; and the Bishop of Norwich in the manor of Marston.

Quo Warranto Rolls, p. 723.

In the same eyre, Guy de Visdelu was summoned for wreck at Shotley. The King's attorney shews that he pleads no specialty. The case is adjourned. Thomas Bavent is summoned for wreck at Eston; he claims it by prescription. The King's attorney says that he cannot have it without specialty; the case is adjourned. Simon de Petraponte claims wreck at Benakre by prescription. This case is also adjourned.

See ante, p. 34.

Quo Warranto Rolls, p. 726.

Robert Fitz Roger claims wreck at Bliburgh. He pleads that King Henry II. granted the manor of Bliburgh to his ancestors, with all liberties which the King had when he had it in his demesne; and he is discharged. See ante, p. 62. This case goes to shew that wreck may pass by such full general words of *adeo plene* in a charter.

The Abbot of Layston claims wreck in Layston, Middleton, and Dersham. He pleads a charter of Henry II. granting the manor of Layston to Ralph de Glanville, who gave it to his abbey, with all liberties and customs to it belonging, and also a confirmation by Henry II., and an ample charter of various liberties by the same King. The King's attorney prays judgment because wreck is not named in the charters. The case is adjourned.

The Prior of Bromholm claimed wreck in Burgh in Ludinglond, and pleads that one Ralph son of Roger de Burgh held the tenement to which these liberties pertained of King Henry III. by serjeanty, and that he granted it to Gilbert de Wesingham, who surrendered it to the King, and the King granted it to Vincent Prior of Bromholm, and his successors, "with all its appurtenances, well and "in peace, and as wholly as the aforesaid Ralph or any of "his predecessors ever held it in demesnes, rents, escheats, "and other things," and he produces the charter, and says that the said Ralph and his heirs had these liberties. The King's attorney takes issue, and the jury find that the said Ralph was seised of the wreck. This is another case shewing that the foreshore and right to wreck will pass under a grant *adeo plene et integre* if there be evidence of user to support the title. We have seen, *ante*, p. 63, that this manor of Burgh is situate within the King's larger manor of Ludinglond, where the King had the foreshore as parcel of the manor; nevertheless, the subinfeudated manor has the foreshore as parcel of it, and here again there is no traverse of the soil on behalf of the King. Quo Warranto Rolls, p. 728.

Richard de Boyland, being challenged for wreck at Southwold, says that he takes it under the title of Matilda Countess of Gloucester. Edmund de Hemgrave was summoned to shew by what warrant he holds the half-hundred of Mutford and claims to have wreck in the same hundred. He comes and says that the manor of Mutford with appurtenances formerly belonged to Goel Ibid. p. 731.

Baldenit, a Norman, and that when he was in seisin of the said manor he held the aforesaid half-hundred and had the wreck as pertaining to the manor, and he says that Henry III. after the forfeiture of the Normans seized the manor and granted it to Thomas de Hemgrave, his grandfather, with all appurtenances, to hold *adeo libere quiete et integre*, as Goel had held it, with all liberties and free customs to that manor pertaining; and because it cannot be denied that the aforesaid Goel had the aforesaid half-hundred and the wreck as it is presented in the half-hundred of Mutford, *as appertaining to the aforesaid manor of Mutford*, therefore he is discharged. Here is a clear case of wreck passing by grant *adeo plene*, and as being a franchise appertaining to a manor.

Henry son of Nicholas, the parson of Stutton, claims wreck by prescription in Stutton. The King's attorney says his user is usurpation. Issue is joined, but there is no record of the result.

Quo Warranto Rolls, p. 734. Ante, p. 62.

Robert fitz Roger is summoned for wreck at Walbertswik. He claims it as within the manor of Bliburgh, given to his ancestor by Henry II. as above set out. The bailiffs of Dunwich say that the King is seisin of the wreck, and the writ appears to have been discharged. The Abbot of Layston claims wreck at Thorp, Misswell, and Mensmere—viz., from the port of Mensmere to the port of Aldmouth—and he says that that place is in his manor of Layston, which Edward II. gave to Ralph de Glanville, with all its liberties and free customs; that Glanville gave it to the abbey, and that Henry II. confirmed the grant, with all liberties and free customs to that manor belonging; and that the said Ralph was in seisin of taking the wreck all over the said place, and the abbots subsequently. The bailiffs of Dunwich say that the King is in seisin of taking the wreck in the said place by his bailiffs of Dunwich as parcel of their fee farm. A foreign jury is ordered, but the result is not entered up.

Quo Warranto Rolls, p. 735.

The Prior of Snape claims wreck from Thorp to Orfordness, and says that the manor of Snape formerly belonged to one William Martell, who was in seisin of taking the wreck appertaining to the aforesaid manor from the time of the Conquest, and that Martell gave the manor to the Abbot of St. John Colchester, to hold as freely as he and his ancestors held it, to found the priory of Snape, which is a cell of the abbey. The King's attorney says that he shews no special warrant for wreck, and the case is adjourned.

Roger Bigod Earl of Norfolk and Marshal of England claims wreck from the port of Newmouth to a place called Bresnes as pertaining to his manor of Holesle, and in the ports of Orwell and of Gosford as appertaining to his manor of Walton by prescription. The King's attorney says that he shews no specialty. The case is adjourned into the Exchequer, and no judgment is entered up. The foreshore is parcel of the manor.

Quo Warranto Rolls, p. 736.

See Att. v. Tomline, 14 Ch. D. 68.

The burgesses of Yarmouth, under the head of purprestures, present a long list of purprestures *super portum*, evidently being wharves built in the river, and among others that John Brown, of Yarmouth, *artavit super aquam super portum de Gernmouth* for a length of 16 feet and a breadth of 18 feet. They also present a number of encroachments upon highways; and thereupon the sheriff is ordered to throw down *quicquid fuerit ad nocumentum*, and those who make the purprestures are fined. In this case the purprestures are manifestly on the foreshore, but still there is no claim on the part of the Crown to the soil on which they are built. The sheriff is simply ordered to remove them as nuisances.

Quo Warranto Roll, Norfolk, M 4/6 2 14 Edw. I. roll 84.

The jurors of the hundred of Dunwich present concerning new customs, and say that William de Helmet takes a custom in the water of the lord the King next his land—viz., for every ship passing *per terram suam* 4*d.*; and that Peter Helmet, Augustine Joce, Robert Colyng, Richard Silknote, Alexander Kerrich, and John Phelipp take the same custom of every ship passing over their land, and this within ten years past. And William Helmet and the others say that they have lands *mari adjacentes*, and that ships passing over them sometimes anchor *juxta terras suas prædictas*, and that the anchors are sometimes fixed and

Quo Warranto Roll, Suffolk, 14 Edw. I. M 5/5. 31

attached *super terras suas*, and that for the easements aforesaid the sailors of their own free will give 4*d.* for every ship, and they do not claim to take any custom otherwise; and because they admit that they have newly taken this custom without the King's licence, and of their own authority, they are ordered not to take it in the future. This presentment was made before Solomon de Rochester and his fellow-justices in eyre. The foreshore was clearly in question, and there is no claim by the Crown.

Quo Warranto Roll, Suffolk, 14 Edw. I. $\frac{M}{5 \cdot 31}/5$ m. 34d.

The Prior of Ely claims wreck at Melton.

Ibid. m. 4d.

The Prior of St. Andrew claims wreck in the hundred of Coleness, Roger Bigod at Walton, and John de Stratton at Naketon.

Quo Warranto Rolls, p. 487.

In the roll of the eyre for Norfolk in 14 Edward I., A.D. 1286, the Prior of Wymondham was challenged for wreck at Hapesburgh. He says that the vills of Hapesburgh and Neland belonged to one William [de Albini] le Botiler, who had this liberty, and that the said William enfeoffed the Prior's predecessor in the aforesaid manors with the aforesaid liberties. Henry I. confirmed his grant, and also granted to the Prior wreck of the sea in the aforesaid vills, and he is discharged.

See ante, pp. 17 and 89; post, under date 5 Rich. II.

Quo Warranto Rolls, p. 488.

Peter Roscelyn, being challenged for wreck in Walcot, says that he has given it up to the King.

Ibid. p. 490.

William de Warren claimed wreck in Dunton and Beston. The case is adjourned.

Robert de Tateshall was summoned for wreck in Babingley. The case is adjourned.

Ibid. p. 491.

William de Ages claimed wreck in Palyng by prescription. The case is adjourned into the Exchequer.

Ibid. p. 492.

Robert Bigod, of Felbridge, claimed wreck in Runton and Beston by prescription. The King's attorney says that he shews no specialty. The case was adjourned into the Exchequer, but, it being shewn that Robert and all his ancestors had had the liberty, he is discharged.

Ibid. p. 494.

Henry de Grey claimed wreck in Shrivingham by prescription. The case is adjourned into the Exchequer.

Coram Rege, East., 14 Edw. I.,

In Easter, 14 Edward I., A.D. 1286, it was adjudged in the King's Bench that Edward Earl of Cornwall ought to have wreck of the sea in the county of Cornwall, because it appeared to the Court that his father, Richard, died seised thereof, and a presentment made against him is discharged. Minus Record, roll 29, Cornwall. Hale, p. 28.

In Easter, 14 Edward I., A.D. 1286, Queen Eleanor sued Hugh Cole and others for a trespass on the water between Melcomb and Weymouth, and in her declaration recites that the moiety of the water of Weye between Weymouth and the King's manor of Melcomb belongs to her manor, of which the Abbot of Cerne *per cartam suam* enfeoffed the King and the Queen, together with the custom of the freight of ships arriving and departing there; and that the King and Queen have had the custom from the time of making of the charter, and the Abbot and his predecessors from before that time were accustomed to have and take it; but the defendants claim the water and custom, and prevent the Queen's tenants of Melcomb from taking *petram in fundo maris juxta Portland* for the repair of their houses, as they had been accustomed, and that they threw a man into the water because he said that the half of the water belonged to the Queen. Writs of capias are ordered. Coram Rege, East., 14 Edw. I., Majus Record, 11.

The defendants plead that they never did the Queen any injury, and pray that it may be inquired of; and Cole says "quod prædicta aqua de Weymouth integre "est comitis Gloucestriæ de quo ipse habet aquam "illam ad voluntatem ipsius comitis. Et quod ipse "comes fuit in seisina de tota prædicta aqua tanquam "pertinente ad manerium suum de Weymouth," taking the customs of ships over the whole water, so that the said Abbot never had anything therein, nor the Queen by the Abbot's feoffment: and as to taking stone "in fundo maris "dicunt quod fundum ubi prædicta petra est fodenda est in "feodo et super tenementum comitis," and that the Abbot and his predecessors only took it by leave of the Earl or his bailiffs; and as to throwing the man into the water, it was done in a fight between the Queen's man and a Weymouth man, and that he was not drowned, &c. The Queen's attorney replies that the Abbot and his predecessors were in seisin, and the King and Queen by the Coram Rege, M., 16 Edw. I., see No. 115, roll 46d.

Abbot's feoffment. Issue is joined, but judgment is not entered up.

In this case we find the Crown claiming foreshore and the bed of the sea under a title derived from a subject—a state of things hardly consistent with the *primâ facie* theory of the Crown's rights as now put forward.

In the eyre for Huntingdon in 14 Edward I., A.D. 1286, the Abbot of Ramsey was summoned for taking wreck or shipbrich, and he appears, and as to shipbrich, which is the same as wreck, he claims it by a charter of Edward the Confessor, in which it is contained that he released to the abbot and monks of Ramsey "omnia que maris procello-"sis tempestatibus in aquam vel in terram eorum ejecta "fuerint quod anglice seupwerk per vulgatum est nomina-"tum," and also by a charter of William the Conqueror, written in English, whereby the King granted to the same abbot and monks, shipbrech, seupworp, and other laws and customs which to the King pertain. The King's attorney prays that the charters should be judged and interpreted as to what liberties they extend to, because they contain general and obscure words, and that they are not confirmed by the present King. The case was adjourned into the Exchequer, and the result does not appear.

Coram Rege, Trin., 15 Edw. I. roll 26d, Kent.

In 15 Edward I., A.D. 1287, there occurred a dispute between the custos of the heir of Thomas de Normanvill, the lord of Kynnarton, in Kent, and the Prior of Christ's Church, Canterbury, as to a ship wrecked at Kynnarton. It was claimed that Normanvill had wreck *in terris suis* de Kynnarton, but the Prior claimed it, although it was not wreck, because one of the crew was saved. "Et quia "noluit rex quod alteruteri partium injuriatur in hac parte, "nec est juris consonum quod naves navicula vel batella "mercandisis vel aliis rebus carcata vel non carcata "per maris intemperiem ad terram sic projecta integra "vel fracta dum tamen unus homo vel unus catus a "periculo illo vivus evadat pro wrekko adjudicatur;" the Prior is summoned to answer. The record is incomplete.

There is a suit in Easter, 15 Edward I., A.D. 1287, in which Henry Flick and Hildebrand de Lubeck, German merchants, sue Adam Cross and others for carrying away their goods wrecked at Blakeney in Norfolk, and cast ashore outside the port of Blakeney, to the value of one thousand pounds. The defendants say that the ship was wrecked before the port of Blakeney, and that the merchants and seamen left it, and that afterwards the merchants who had come ashore after the sea had ebbed found much of their goods *super litus maris apulsa*, and asked the men of the neighbouring towns to help to save them and to carry them ashore, and that they carried the goods to their houses and kept them until the sheriff should hold an inquest. They also say that they dredged in the deep sea for the said goods by agreement, and plead not guilty. They are, however, found guilty, and the merchants recover their goods and damages. This case shews clearly the manner in which wrecked goods are left upon the shore after the ebb.

Coram Rege, East. 15 Edw. I. roll 28.

There is a presentment of an encroachment upon the highway made by the Abbot of Fécamp between the church and the bridge of Brod, in Sussex, 6 perches in length and 2 in breadth, in a place where horses and carts used to pass. It is found that the purpresture is to the injury of no one, and can be arrented to the King, so that the King's highway is large enough for all persons passing, and the jury value it at 3*d.* per annum. It is arrented to the King at 3*d.*, and the Abbot is ordered to answer for the arrears for seven years. This is a solitary example of numerous similar cases, and it serves to shew how minutely purprestures upon the King's soil were scanned by the justices in eyre. Such presentments are frequent, but there is no one throughout the vast mass of records which I have perused which shews a case of renting any portion of the foreshore to the King.

Quo Warranto Roll, Sussex, 16 Edw. I. M 6 11 / 4 roll 48.

On a roll of Placita Coronæ for Sussex in 16 Edward I., A.D. 1288, it is presented that John de Britannia, the Abbot of Fécamp, and the Abbot of Pont Robert claim wreck *ubicunque applicuerit super terras suas;* that the

Quo Warranto Roll, Sussex, M 6 11 / 4.

Bishop of Chichester claims wreck in the manor of Bexley; that William Bardolf and Johanna de Gurney claim it in their demesne lands of Estdene, Birling, and Were; John de Warren Earl of Surrey claims it in his lands in the hundred of Walesborne; the Bishop of Chichester claims it in Preston; Henry de Tregoz claims wreck *applicans in terris suis* in the hundred of Palyng; the Bishop of Chichester claims it *in terris suis applicans* in the hundred of Manwood, Roger Bigod in Bosham, Richard Fitz Alan in Arundel. Wrecked wine came ashore in the hundred of Palyng: the Bishop of Chichester took it in one place, Henry de Tregoz in another, and Isabel de Mortimer in another. The jurors say that the said wine came ashore *upon the lands* of the said Bishop, Henry, and Isabel. Isabel claims it as part of her dower from Richard Fitz Alan, who claims wreck *ubique in terris suis in Rapa de Arundel*, and the jury witness this. Thereupon the King's attorney is ordered to sue. Henry de Tregoz claims by prescription. There is no result. William de Braose claims wreck in the barony of Bramber from the Conquest. John de Warren Earl of Surrey claims wreck in Seaford and also in the hundred of Hameshowe; and the Prior of Lewes claims wreck.

Parlt. Roll, i. 60. In 18 Edward I., A.D. 1290, John de Rochford, who was challenged for wreck in the manor of Foulness in 14 Ante, p. 87. Edward I., A.D. 1286, petitions the King in Parliament that he may not be distrained for fifty-two marks, which are exacted from him for wreck of the sea, until he shall have Ante, p. 39. judgment upon the plea of quo warranto which is pending before the King, and that in the meantime he shall have respite. The rolls of the Exchequer are ordered to be searched, and, if it is as he says, he is ordered to have the said respite. This shews that these quo warrantos were not prosecuted, and that Rochford continued to take the wreck, and that, as all pending quo warrantos were postponed indefinitely in 1294, it would seem probable that judgment was never given against him. The present lord of the manor is in possession of the wreck.

Coram Rege, Hil., There is an inquisition in 19 Edward I., A.D. 1291, which shews that the King had wreck of the sea and royal fish in the Isle of Purbeck, Dorsetshire. 19 Edw. I. roll 24.

In 18 Edward I., A.D. 1290, the King granted in Parliament that all persons who could shew that they had liberties by prescription, and had used them without interruption and had not misused them, should be confirmed in their estate, and that, to spare the costs and expenses of the people of his kingdom, all pleas of quo warranto should be henceforth pleaded and determined before the justices in eyre, and that all pending pleas should be adjourned into their counties until the coming of the justices. Stat. 18 Edw. I. stat. 2.

In the roll of the eyre for Lancashire, before Hugh de Cressy and his fellows, in 20 Edward I., A.D. 1292, the Prior of Durham was challenged for wreck at Lytham. He shews a charter of the Conqueror granting him wreck. The King's attorney replies that no predecessor of the Prior was seised of Lytham at the time of the charter, and prays judgment. The jury find that at the time of the charter the Prior was not seised, but that from before the time of Richard I. the priors had taken wreck, and because the Prior claimed precisely by his charter, and *not by prescription*, the wreck is taken into the King's hands. The Prior afterwards comes and makes a fine for the wreck, and it is granted to him. Quo Warranto Rolls, p. 369. See ante, p. 21.

Nigel Blundell was summoned for wreck in Aylmunesdale. He pleads that he holds the manor and the wreck in the same manor by prescription as appurtenant to the same manor. The King's attorney says that he shews no specialty, and takes issue on the user. The jury say that Henry III. once gave to the father of the said Nicholas a wrecked ship which happened in the said manor, and that no other of his ancestors ever took wreck, and that no wreck happened in the time of the said Nicholas; therefore it is considered that the King shall recover seisin of having wreck in the aforesaid manor when it happens. Quo Warranto Rolls, p. 369.

The Abbot of Furness was summoned for wreck in Furness. He produces a charter of King Stephen when he was Earl of Bologne, granting all the forest of Furness, Ibid. p. 370.

and confirmations by subsequent kings. And as to wreck, he claims it likewise *ab antiquo* in all lands in Furness next the sea except in the manor of Aldingham. The jury find that he has had wreck in the manner he claims it. He is discharged.

Quo Warranto Rolls, p. 373. William de Cauntefeld claims wreck in the manor of Aldingham. He claims the wreck by prescription from the time of the Conquest. The King's attorney denies that he has used the liberty without interruption, and further that he has no special warrant. The jury find for his prescription. The King's attorney prays judgment for the King nevertheless, and the case is adjourned.

Ibid. p. 375. The Abbot of Dieulacres is challenged by quo warranto for the manor of Russal with appurtenances. He sets forth a charter of 28 July, 31 Henry III., A.D. 1247, by which the King granted him the manor of Russal with wreck of the sea, and that the present King confirmed it. He is discharged. There was a separate quo warranto against him for the wreck, which was found in his favour. He claimed it as annexed to the manor, and was successful.

Ibid. p. 377. The Prior of Cartmel was summoned for wreck in Cartmel in Furness. He says that the manor belonged to William le Marischal before the time of King Richard I., See ante, p. 21. and that the said William had wreck in the manor, and that after the time of Richard I. he gave it to the Prior with all its appurtenances and liberties, and that King John and King Henry III. confirmed the grant. The King's attorney says that wreck and waif are royal liberties, and not pertaining to any free tenement, and as the Prior shews no charter of a king whereby wreck and waif were granted him, nor can claim liberties *ab antiquo*, as can the heirs of those who came with the Conqueror, he prays judgment. The jury say that Henry II. had the manor and gave it to William le Marischal, who had it with these liberties, and afterwards Marischal gave it to the predecessor of the Prior, who, and whose successors, have had those liberties. The King's attorney replies that it is not lawful to have the liberty of wreck or waif unless they are specially granted by the King, and as the aforesaid liberties are not contained in the aforesaid charters, which were made within the time of memory, he prays judgment for the King. Judgment is given that because the Prior cannot claim the liberties *ab antiquo*, for that his predecessor purchased the manor in the time of Richard I., and the Prior shews no specialty from any king, the liberties are taken into the King's hand. This case would seem to shew that at this period royal liberties were not assignable, and that they could not be prescribed for *ab antiquo* except by the heirs of the Conqueror's grantees; but there are innumerable cases of prescription which conflict with this decision.

Henry de Lacy the Earl of Lincoln claims wreck of the sea in all his fees in Lancashire, and says that he claims it in the manor of Penwortham with all its members, and in North Meols, and in Widness, and in Stanton, Freckleton, and Warton, by prescription. The jury find for him. The case is adjourned.

Quo Warranto Rolls, p. 381.

William de Botiler claims wreck in Warrington and Layton from the Conquest. The jury find for him, and he is discharged.

Ibid. p. 386.

In a roll of Placita Coronæ for Cumberland in 20 Edward I., A.D. 1292, John de Huddleston disclaims wreck in his land of Milton. Thomas de Multon the lord of Egremont claims wreck in Egremont. The jurors present that Thomas de Multon the lord of the liberty of Coupland and the Abbot of St. Mary York claim to have wreck of the sea in their land. The Abbot says that his predecessors have had wreck in their land, and that he found his church seised thereof; and Thomas de Multon says that he claims to have wreck as well in the Abbot's lands as in his own lands, and that his ancestors from time of memory have always so had it. The Abbot says that Thomas unjustly claims wreck in his, the Abbot's, lands, because Richard de Lucy, the ancestor of Thomas, granted to Simon, his predecessor, and his church that they should have wreck in their aforesaid lands, and he produces the deed, and he says that his predecessors since then have taken wreck. The jury say that

Quo Warranto Roll, Cumb., M/1/24/7.

Quo Warranto Roll, Cumb., 20 Edw. I. No. 22, m. 21d.

the ancestors of Thomas took the wreck as well in the Abbot's lands as in their own lands until the time of William Turnel, formerly abbot; that after the time of Turnel, sometimes Thomas' ancestors and sometimes the abbots took it. They say that the said abbots never had it peacefully until the last eyre, since when the present Abbot has had it peacefully. They say that Richard de Lucy did grant the wreck, that none of the abbots took it until the time of Turnel, which was a long time, although wreck happened in that time; that Thomas and his ancestors took it, without claim by the abbot. And because it was found by the jury that the abbots did not take wreck immediately after the making of the deed, but rather that Richard and his heirs for a long time afterwards took the wreck, so that the abbots did not take it peacefully, but that the present Abbot occupied it; therefore it is considered that the King shall recover against the said Abbot and Thomas the aforesaid wreck in the lands of the Abbot. This seems somewhat strange justice, for if the wreck did not pass out of Richard de Lucy by his grant it remained to his heirs, and it seems strange that it should have been recovered by the Crown; but this case is remarkable as shewing that the land of the Abbot and the land of Thomas included the foreshore, and that no suggestion of a claim is made on behalf of the Crown.

Quo Warranto Rolls, p. 113.

Thomas son of Lambert de Multon was challenged for wreck throughout all the land of Coupland, and he claims it except in Kirkby and Whitehaven in Coupland, and he likewise claims keletol—viz., toll of ships—and toll of merchandise sold in all the ports of Coupland, and to have assize of nets broken in all the waters of Esk, Airt, Eyre, and Caldre, in the water of Derwent from the sea to Thomas Culwen's mill, to wit, if he finds nets of less than four-inch mesh. The jury say that he has had these liberties immemorially except that the amendment of the assize of nets in the water of Derwent belongs to the King, and he is discharged.

Ibid p. 122.

The Abbot of St. Mary York is challenged for wreck

in Kirkby, Whitehaven, Hensingham, Salterge, and Hokwayt. He claims it by prescription, and says that King Henry III., in the fiftieth year of his reign, granted to the Abbot all liberties and free customs that the church of St. Peter of York and the church of St. John of Beverley have. The King's attorney says that as to the wreck it is a royal liberty, and can only be granted by the King, that none can claim it *ab antiquo* but those whose ancestors came with the Conqueror, and that the Abbot has elsewhere in this eyre claimed the wreck of the gift of one Thomas de Lucy in the time of King John. The case is adjourned.

On a roll of Placita Coronæ for Cumberland, 20 Edward I., A.D. 1292, it is presented that the Abbot of Holm Cultram claims wreck throughout the island of Holm Cultram, and in the same eyre the King sues the Abbot for the island of Holm Cultram. The Abbot says that King Henry II. granted to his predecessor "totam in-"sulam de Holm Cultram per rectas divisas suas." King Richard confirmed the gift, and so did King John by a charter which sets out the bounds very minutely, and they shew that the boundary includes the shore. The boundaries go down the brook of Polneuton to the place where Polneuton *cadit in mare et inde per circuitum maris usque ad locum ubi Wathelpol cadit in mare et sic ascendendo per Wathelpol, &c.*, and in the general words of the grant are included *piscariis maritimis et sabulonibus.* The Abbot is also summoned for taking wreck in Holm Cultram, and he claims it under the charter. The King's attorney says the charter does not pass wreck in his demesne lands. The Abbot replies that his predecessors have taken it from before the time of Richard I. without interruption. The jury find that they have taken it since the making of the charter. Nevertheless, judgment is prayed for the King; and because the Abbot claimed by the charter and not by prescription, and it is not contained in the charter that King Henry I. granted wreck to the predecessors of the Abbot, and because wreck is a royal liberty and not of the appurtenances of any tenement, it is considered that the

Quo Warranto Roll, Cumb., 20 Edw. I. No. 22, m. 21d.

King shall recover the wreck. In this case it is clear that the title of the Abbot to the foreshore was admitted.

In the roll of eyre for Yorkshire, before Hugo de Cressingham and his fellows, in 21 Edward I., A.D. 1293, Nicholas de Meynill was summoned to shew by what warrant he claimed free warren in his demesne lands in Wernelton, Greneho, Semere, and Eston, and he shews a charter of King Henry III. The King's attorney says he has abused the liberty, and that he holds the lands of his neighbours inwarrened. He also says that he holds *riparias adjacentes maneriis suis* inwarrened by authority of the said charter, so that no one can take the fish or the fowls of the *ripariæ* without his licence. Meynill replies that he never hindered any one from fishing in the *ripariæ* adjoining his manors, except in his park and close. One of his manors was the manor of Eston on the Tees, and in that manor Meynill's ancestor granted to the abbey of Fountains the right to a weir on the foreshore.

Fountains Chartulary penes. Sir H. Ingleby of Ripley.

Quo Warranto Rolls, p. 209.

Walter de Fauconberge was challenged for taking wreck from Blackshore to Rimeswick, and for holding the moiety of the bailiwick of Langbargh. He claims it as part of the inheritance of his wife, who was a daughter of Peter de Brus lord of the barony of Skelton. The jurors say that he took wreck where the men escaped alive. There is no result.

Ibid. p. 216.

The Abbot of Selby is challenged for wreck in Selby, but he disclaims it at present. The King's attorney says that he used the liberty. The jury say that he did so use it, for he took in the Water of Ouse those things which are wrecked *super feodum suum*, and that he took by the name of wreck all sturgeons taken in those parts in that water by whomsoever they were taken; and they say that the men of the Abbot pursued the men of William de Aton, who had wounded a porpoise to death, and tried to appropriate it to the Abbot, but that during the fight the men of the Bishop of Durham took the porpoise. The Abbot was amerced, and ordered not to take wreck in future; but here it is to be noted that, although he had not the wreck, nevertheless he had the soil of the shore, and it appears by an inquisition (34 Edward I., No. 79) that the Abbot had three weirs in the Water of Ouse at Selby, and in 12 Edward II., A.D. 1318, licence was granted to him to fix a weir "in feodo suo de Selby" (see *post*).

William Constable of Flamborough claims wreck in Flamborough by prescription. There is no result. Quo Warranto Rolls, p. 220.

The Archbishop of York claims wreck at Beverley by prescription, in this form, to wit: "At Beverley, where a "small arm of the sea extends itself, as often as wood or "other chattels are thrown by the water to land within "the liberty of the same Archbishop, when no suit is made "to the Archbishop, he takes it as wreck." He also claims wreck at Pattrington *ab antiquo*. There is no pleading, and no result.

In the roll of the eyre for Northumberland, before Hugh de Cressingham and his fellows, in Hilary, 21 Edward I., A.D. 1293, the Prior of Tynemouth is challenged for wreck in Tynemouth, Wytheleye, Copum, Anebelle, and Hawkslaw. The Prior pleads that all his charters and muniments are before the King, and he says nothing; and afterwards the Prior's attorney says that all the aforesaid liberties are in the King's hands and so were at the time the writ was issued. The Prior is fined because he claimed liberties of which he was not then in seisin. As will presently appear, there was litigation between the Crown and the Prior at this time, which may account for this entry, for the Prior had wreck by grants of Richard I. and King John.

Robert Fitz Roger claimed wreck in Warkworth by prescription. The jury find for him, but no judgment in given.

Edmund the King's brother claims wreck at Newton, Emeldon, Dunstan, and Crawcester, and because the said Edmund did not claim the liberties on the first day of the eyre according to the form of the Statute of Gloucester, and the sheriff witnesses that he made proclamation for claimants of liberties to come in and claim, the liberties are taken into the King's hand, but were afterwards re-granted to him, and he says that the lands belonged formerly to Ibid. p. 603.

Simon de Montfort, who forfeited them, and that King Henry III. granted them to him with these liberties. The record is incomplete.

Quo Warranto Rolls, p. 604. Robert de Brus holds at Hartlepool, in the liberty of the Bishop of Durham, a port of the sea, and takes keelage of ships and boats coming there, and prises of fish.

In the roll of the eyre for Kent, before John de Berwick and his fellows, in Easter, 21 Edward I., A.D. 1293, Robert de Sherland claims wreck of the sea on Sherland by prescription, and is discharged. Ibid. p. 358.

See ante, p. 72. Alexander de Baliol is challenged for wreck at Whitstable, and also at Chilham, Hachfeld, Kyngston, and Ridlingwald. He says that he holds the manor of Whitstable and the hundred of Whitstable, and claims of wreck and toll of merchandise at La Craston in the same manor by prescription. He is discharged. And as to the other manors, he claims wreck and toll of men arriving in his lands, also by prescription, and is discharged.

The master of the Domus Dei of Dover claims wreck in Colreade and La Riviere, and shews a charter of wreck from Henry III.

Quo Warranto Rolls, p. 361. The Prior of Rochester claims wreck in Grain, which is a marsh adjacent to the sea, which he has from the Archbishop of Canterbury in exchange for the manor of Lambeth, and that the Archbishop had wreck and the priors subsequently by prescription, and he is discharged.

Ibid. p. 362. The Abbot of Faversham claims wreck in Faversham by prescription. The jury find for him, and he is discharged.

Ibid. p. 363. The Abbot of Lesnes claims wreck in Lesnes by prescription, and he is discharged.

The Prior of St. Martin Dover disclaims wreck in La Riviere and St. Margaret's.

Ibid. p. 364. William de Say disclaims wreck at Deptford.

The Prioress of Sheppey claims wreck in Sheppey, Gillingham, Grain, and Bobbing by prescription. The jury find that he only has it in Sheppey, and as to that he is discharged.

The Abbot of Battle claims wreck in Wye, Kingsnode, Hawkhurst, Anglingle, Wethynden, and Dengy Marsh, which are members belonging to the manor of Wye, and he sets out the charter of the Conqueror of the manor of Wye, with its members and all liberties and royal customs as fully as the King could grant them, and he is discharged.

William de Laybourne disclaims wreck in Shorne. Quo Warranto Rolls, p. 366.

The Abbot of St. Augustine Canterbury claims wreck in Minster, Stodmarsh, Chistlet, Northborne, Deal, Snaves, Swalecliff, and Plumstead by prescription, and under charters of the Conqueror and of Henry II., which grant him those liberties on strond and on streme. The jury find that he has used them, and he is discharged. Ibid. p. 367.

The Prior of Christchurch Canterbury claims wreck in Lyden, which is a member of Eastry, and in Monkton and its members, Brokhende, Gorshende, and Ham, which is a member of Copton, Eylwarton, Appledore, Agene, Elbene, Augerswyke, Billericay, Fairfield, and Clive. The jury find that he has used the liberty, and he is discharged.

By writ dated 12 July, 21 Edward I., A.D. 1293, the King commands to his justices in eyre in the county of Kent, that in all writs, as well of quo warranto as of right, which shall henceforth happen to be brought before them, or before the King or any of his justices, limitation shall be made in the declarations of the same from the time of King Richard and the subsequent time. This writ appears to have been sent to all the justices in eyre. Ibid. p. 354.

It was probably a concession to the opposition of the subjects to these continual proceedings by quo warranto, which, as is well known, were strenuously resisted, and it seems very probable that judgment was never obtained for the King in by far the greater number of cases, for in the Parliament of Michaelmas, 22–23 Edward I., A.D. 1294, the King granted for the favour of his people, and on account of the then existing war in Gascony, that all his writs, as well of quo warranto as of pleas of land, Ibid. p. 103

should remain without day until the King or his heirs should wish to prosecute them. This practically amounted to a discharge of all the quo warrantos then undetermined; the subjects remained in the possession of their liberties and lands, and in almost every case where we find a quo warranto against the lord of a manor for wreck we find the lord of that manor at the present day in possession of the franchise.

Looking back at this long list of proceedings and presentments by the Crown, its continual assertion of its rights against the subject, these minute and careful examinations and inquiries into purprestures upon the Crown's property and upon the Crown's dignity, made persistently throughout this long reign by the King and his justices and attorneys, it is surprising that we find no one instance of a claim, or a pretence of claim, on the part of the King to any one piece of the foreshore adjacent to the manor of a subject in any one place. It is especially to be noticed, also, that we do find presentments of purprestures upon the soil of the foreshore adjacent to the manors in the hands of the Crown, and that in those cases the claim is made, not, as it would be made in these days, by reason of the *primâ facie* title of the Crown to the whole of the foreshore of the kingdom, but by reason of the foreshore being parcel of the King's manor in his own hand. The case of Melcombe Regis (*ante*, p. 95) shews also that the Crown took the foreshore as parcel of a manor by grant from the subject. When, therefore, we regard this fact, and contrast it with the fact that, throughout all these proceedings in respect of wreck, the title of the subject to the foreshore of his manor is tacitly admitted by the King and by his justices and attorneys, we are driven to the conclusion that the presumption of law at this period was that the manor of the subject was limited, not by the high-water mark, but by the low-water mark, and that the *primâ facie* title of the Crown as it is now put forward by the Crown advisers had no existence at this period, and must have been, as we shall presently see it was, an invention of later day.

It appears that the King recovered the wreck in Lytham against the Prior of Durham, the wreck in Cartmel against the Prior of Cartmel, and the wreck in the manor of Nicholas Blundell in Aylmundale; and by charter dated 24 September, 23 Edward I., A.D. 1295, the King granted all this wreck to Edmund Earl of Lancaster, and thus the wreck has passed into the earldom and afterwards to the Duchy of Lancaster; but the foreshore would appear to remain parcel of the manors of Lytham, Cartmel, and Aylmundale.

See the grant of Lytham, ante, p. 21.

In the roll of the eyre for Cornwall, before John de Berwick and his fellows, in Michaelmas, 30 Edward I., A.D. 1302, the Abbot of Clive was challenged for wreck in all his demesne lands in Pokewill and Tregalston, and he claims it by a charter of Henry III., and is discharged.

Quo Warranto Rolls, p. 108.

The Abbot of Tavistock claims wreck in the Isles of Scilly by prescription. The jurors say that he and his predecessors have had wreck except of gold, whale, and cloths of scarlet and ermine, and that these the abbots have never taken; and he is discharged.

After this date the pleas of quo warranto for the reign of Edward I. are not printed, and there may be many pleas upon the Assize Rolls and Quo Warranto Rolls of later date which are as yet unindexed and not easily consultable.

It appears from a suit in A.D. 1305, between the Prior of Coningshead and the Abbot of Furness, that the Prior claimed the entire water of Ulverston by a grant from William de Lancaster lord of Kendal, who gave to his predecessor all the water on both sides, as far as the flood flows and re-flows, and that he built a weir there, which the Abbot cut, claiming that it was on his side of the water, and in the part belonging to him. No result of the trial appears, but it is clear that the soil of the tidal river was in this case in the subject.

Coram Rege, East., 34 Edw. I. roll 40.

By an inquisition dated 35 Edward I., A.D. 1306, a fishery and wreck of the sea by metes and bounds was found to belong to the lordship of Thorncastle, in Ireland.

Inq. p.-m. 35 Edw. I. 82.

In the Public Records of the reign of Edward I., and especially in the inquisitions post-mortem, there will be found many records shewing that sea fisheries and ports and the soil of the foreshore were parcel of many manors round the coast. Space does not permit of a detailed description of them in this work, but they, together with the records hereinbefore described, go to shew that at any rate a very large proportion of the foreshore of the kingdom, if not the whole of it, except in the King's demesne manors, has been granted out subject to the rights of the public and the jurisdiction of the Crown.

CHAPTER V.

THE CASE OF THE PRIOR OF TYNEMOUTH.

WE have seen that in the Hundred Rolls the Prior of Tynemouth and the Bishop of Durham were presented for having made purprestures upon the King by erecting trading towns at North and South Shields, at the mouth of the Tyne, to the prejudice of the King's town of Newcastle, which at that time was held of the King at fee farm by the burgesses of Newcastle, and was therefore technically the King's town, although it was granted in fee farm. To this town belonged the port of the River Tyne from Hedwin streams above the town to a place called Sparhawk at the mouth of the river. The burgesses held it as part of their fee farm, but only as a franchise, and not in respect of the soil of the port, for we have seen that the Bishop and Prior of Durham and several of his tenants had weirs upon the Durham shore which had been extended to the mid-stream of the river, and were presented as injurious to navigation. A subsequent inquisition taken by commissioners in the time of Edward III. shews that the lords of manors on both sides of the Tyne, including the Prior of Tynemouth, had weirs upon the foreshore. It would appear, therefore, that the port belonging to the corporation of Newcastle was only a franchise, and, although under that franchise they had the right to take anchorage and groundage, this anchorage and groundage was taken in respect of the port as a port due, and is still so taken, and both the Prior of Tynemouth and the Prior of Durham took groundage for ships coming ashore in their respective manors as a soil due. Ante, p. 59.

The priory of Tynemouth was founded by the Saxon King Oswin, and refounded by Waltheof Earl of North- Dugd. Mon. iii. 302.

umberland in 1074, who confirmed to it its possessions, including the manor of Tynemouth, of which South Shields is parcel ; these possessions were confirmed by Aubrey Earl of Northumberland in 1079, and by Robert de Mowbray Earl of Northumberland, who re-founded the priory in 1090, and were again confirmed by King Henry I. and by subsequent kings. King Henry II. confirmed to them all their lands on strond and on stream, and King Richard I., on 4 November, 1 Richard I., A.D. 1189, granted them all their lands with sac and soc over strond and stream and wreck ; and he gave a further charter in similar terms on 13 November, 10 Richard I., A.D. 1198. This charter of Richard I. granting the wreck was inspected and confirmed by a charter dated 19 March, 3 Edward IV., A.D. 1462–3, which explains the meaning of it, and grants " that they shall have wreck " of the sea where the sea flows and re-flows in and over " all their lands," and grants them liberty to build upon their lands within the reflux of the port of Tyne and of the sea ; and the charter is made by the authority of Parliament. King John, by a charter dated 5 February, 5 John, A.D. 1203–4, granted and confirmed to them all their lands and possessions ; to wit, the vill of Tynemouth, with all its appurtenances and other lands, and all things pertaining to those lands on strond and on stream, with divers liberties, including wreck, that they may have them *super omnes terras suas* wheresoever " as fully as our own " ministers could take them to our use," and he commands that none of his officers shall intromit in the said lands. It is clear, therefore, that the title of the Prior was ample enough to include the foreshore, assuming that he shewed exercise of ownership over it.

After the dissolution of the monastery, the manor of Tynemouth, together with North Shields, was leased to the Earl of Northumberland, and subsequently granted to the predecessors in title of the present Duke of Northumberland as fully and freely as the priory had held it.

When the Northumberland Docks at Hay Hole were built under the Tyne Improvement Act, 1852, the rights of the Duke of Northumberland in the shores of the Tyne were saved by section 79 of that Act. A sum of money, £3800, was paid into court for part of the foreshore of the manor of Tynemouth, which was claimed by the Crown against the Duke, but on the Duke's petition, on the opinion of the then Attorney-General and Solicitor-General, the Duke's title was admitted by virtue of the grants to the Prior of Tynemouth, and the money was paid out to him. The Duke's title to the fishery opposite the manor of Tynemouth was established in 1870 in the case of Duke of Northumberland *v.* Houghton. Several tenements in the foreshore are still copyhold of the manor. There can therefore be no question that the Prior of Tynemouth from the earliest times was the owner of the foreshore in the manor of Tynemouth subject to the rights of navigation and the rights of the Corporation of Newcastle as fee farmers under the Crown of the franchise of the port of Newcastle.

L. R. 5 Exch. 127.

The priors of Tynemouth from the time of Henry III. attempted continually to create a market town at North Shields, and in this they were strenuously opposed by the burgesses of Newcastle. The burgesses appear to have laid claim to the soil of the whole of the port to the high-water mark as being the soil of the Crown and parcel of the port, and accordingly, about 18 Edward I., A.D. 1289, they petitioned the King in Parliament, stating that "they "held the town in fee farm of the King, and that the "Prior of Tynemouth hinders merchants from coming "with their merchandises into the Tyne, and will not "allow them to load and discharge in the Tyne unless "they unload at a place called La Sheles, and that this "matter is to the disherison of the King and the destruc- "tion of their town, and that the Prior impleads the "burgesses in the King's Bench, that the King is entitled "to prises of fish and other customs, and that the Prior "has built a town at Shields and makes forestalment "upon the town of Newcastle." A writ is ordered to be issued for the King and the burgesses of Newcastle to make the Prior come to the next Parliament. The pro-

Parly. Petitions, No. 6005.

Rot. Parl. i. 26.

ceedings hereon are printed in the Rolls of Parliament. The burgesses, suing for the lord the King, say that whereas the King has, and ought to have, all the port in the water of Tyne, from the sea to a place which is called Hydewyn streams, so freely that it shall not be lawful for any one to load or discharge any merchandise, nor to make any forestalment of such merchandise by buying and selling the same except within the town of Newcastle, so that the King may take his tolls, prises, and customs, and other things belonging to his lordship; nevertheless the Prior, who has his demesne lands adjacent to the aforesaid water between the sea and the said town, causes merchandise coming there to be loaded and unloaded, buying and selling in his lands aforesaid at his free will, and making a port there where no port formerly was, and also a forestalment of merchandise, to the manifest prejudice of the King and his town; and they say that the Prior takes wreck, when it happens, which specially belongs to the King; and that where the King ought to have certain tolls and customs, the Prior takes them at Shields, and the merchandise comes not to the proper port of Newcastle. And also that the Prior makes bread and sells it to sailors coming there, and holds a market and exercises trade, whereby ships are prevented from coming to Newcastle. They also say that the King has the towage of ships and boats in the water of Tyne between Newcastle and the sea freely over the lands of all lords, but the Prior stops the transit of any one wishing to enter his lands, and compels them to turn aside *et in aquam profundam gradari*, so that they scarcely escape with their lives, and thus they are hindered from bringing goods to Newcastle. Now, here it is clear that the burgesses are claiming a right to the exclusive port and a right to passage for towing over the foreshore; and the language shews that the Prior did not permit the towers to go over the foreshore, but that he drove them into the deep water, and was clearly setting up a claim to stop the right of way over his foreshore, although exercised as part of the right of navigation, but it will be perceived that there is no claim whatever to the soil of the port. The Prior appears, and pleads "that these matters touch only his "free tenement and liberty, and that the writ demands "that he shall answer for certain grievances and injuries "only, no mention being made of free tenement or things "belonging to free tenement; wherefore he deems that he "ought not to answer concerning his free tenement nor for "any liberty belonging to his free tenement without a "special writ." And afterwards the Prior answers, as to wreck of the sea and forestalment of merchandise, that he and his predecessors have had wreck of the sea *infra terram suam*, and that he has forestalled merchandises, viz., victuals and other necessaries for the sustentation of his house, as was lawful for him; then he sets out the charter of 1 Richard I., which grants him his land, with Ante p 20. wreck and liberties *over strond and stream.* And as to founding a new town at Shields, he says he has not founded it newly, but that in the time of his predecessors there were houses upon his own soil where the King has no soil nor free tenement, because the soil and free tenement of his said house extends to the *filum* of the water of Tyne *ultra terram suam ibidem*, between which *filum* and the land of the aforesaid house he has his free fishery for the length of the same land in the same water; and he says he has sold bread and ale and fish to fishermen, and that he holds no market, and that the fishermen are his fishermen, fishing for the maintenance of his house, without paying toll to the lord the King, notwithstanding that the port of the water of Tyne specially and wholly belongs to the lord the King; and as to towage in the water of Tyne, he says that he has never hindered any one exercising that office except in his marsh of Astwick, which was always exempt from such liberty, as he is prepared to prove. The King's attorneys say that the Prior's charter ought not to help him, and that he takes wreck floating in the Tyne and draws it *ad terram suam*, and that this word wreck ought not to be understood *nisi tantum cum in terram dicti Prioris cecederit;* and as to forestalment they say that liberties granted him over strond and stream and forestall ought to be understood to be in his lands within his liberty of Tynemouth, and not in the port of Tyne, and that this word forestall is to be understood as to the hindering or insulting any one *in Regia strata* and not otherwise, as the Prior understands it. And as to the loading and discharging of ships, and the buying of merchandise and victuals, they say that the port belongs only to the King, and the King is injured, for the King is in seisin of the port, and the Prior cannot claim any liberties *extra dominicum suum et terras suas prædictas.* And as to the town of Shields, they say that there were there certain houses in the time of the Prior's predecessors, but that the present Prior has built there twenty-six houses *super solum quod domino Regi esse debet eo quod fluxu et inundatione maris comprehenditur*, and they pray the record of the justices that the Prior has alleged that the King has no soil there nor free tenement, but that it only pertains to the Prior and his house to the *filum* of the water of Tyne, and they say that the Prior *solus est occupator soli domini Regis ibidem et solus ablator commodorum ville ipsius domini Regis prædictæ.* They further charge that the Prior's fishermen pay no tolls: that the Prior detains ships at Shields, and sells bread and victuals to sailors, and that thereby the King loses his prises and customs; and they refer to the presentment in the eyre of John de Vallibus, in 7 Edward I. (*ante*, pp. 58–59), that the Prior had newly erected the town of Shields, and say that these presentments were never discussed nor judgment given upon them. The Prior says the presentment does not affect him, because he was not Prior then, and prays judgment. The Prior ultimately stands upon his charter, whereupon the King orders a writ of *certiorari* as to whether the priors have used the liberties claimed since the making of the charter, and whether they have usurped and purprestured upon the King, and where and at what time and in what manner: and because the Prior has disclaimed a market or port at Tynemouth or Shields, he is forbidden to hold them, and all signs of a market or port are ordered to be destroyed.

The inquisition ordered by the *certiorari* not having been taken by reason of the absence of one of the commissioners, the King, in Trinity term, 19 Edward I., A.D. 1291, ordered Roger de Brabanzon and others to take the inquisition, which they did, and returned it before the King in Parliament on the morrow of the Epiphany, 20 Edward I., A.D. 1292; which inquisition was delivered to Gilbert Thornton and his fellow-justices of the Queen's Bench, to give judgment thereon, and that judgment was thereupon given and recorded. The judgment is entered in Hilary, 20 Edward I., A.D. 1291–2. The pleadings are set out as in the Parliament Roll. The full text of the inquisition and judgment is as follows:— Coram Rege, 20 Edw. I. roll 58.

Among the Records of the Court of Queen's Bench: Coram Rege Roll, Hilary, 20 *Edward I. Roll* 58.

Northumb. — Between the Burgesses of Newcastle and the Prior of Tynemuwe.

It was commanded to the Sheriff of Northumberland that he should make known to the Prior of Tynemuth that he should be before the King in his Parliament from Easter Day in three weeks to make answer to the same lord the King, and to his burgesses of Newcastle-upon-Tyne, upon certain grievances and injuries done, as well to the aforesaid lord the King as to the burgesses aforesaid, by the same Prior as it is said; and further to do therein what the lord the King of his Council should think fit to order. And that he should have there, &c. By pretext of which mandate the aforesaid Prior, and likewise the aforesaid burgesses, have now come here. And the aforesaid burgesses, for the lord the King, say that whereas the same lord the King has, and ought to have, the whole port in the water of Tyne, from the sea to the place which is called Hydewynestremes, so freely that it may not be lawful to any man to lade or unlade any merchandises or wares, nor to make forestall of such merchandises or wares by buying or selling the same, except within the town of Newcastle aforesaid, so that the lord the King may be able to receive his tolls, prises, and customs, and other things belonging to his lordship there; the aforesaid Prior, who Declaration.

has his demesne lands adjacent to the aforesaid water between the sea and the town aforesaid, causes merchandises and wares whatsoever there arriving to be laden and unladen there, buying and selling in his lands aforesaid at his pleasure, making a port there where no port formerly was, and also forestalls of merchandises, to the manifest prejudice of the lord the King and of his town aforesaid. They say also that whereas the lord the King has, and ought to have, his common ovens at Newcastle so freely that bread for sale ought to be baked there and not elsewhere in those parts, and the same lord the King has received, and ought to receive, from every quarter there baked four pence of custom hitherto used; the aforesaid Prior raised a new town at Scheles, between the sea aforesaid and Newcastle, and has there his fishers, bakers, and brewers resident, from whom the same Prior receives by the year thirty-six marks and more: and the lord the King therefore loses by the year of the issues of his bakery aforesaid to the value of ten pounds, and also by the forestall aforesaid at Scheles to the value of twenty pounds. They say also that the aforesaid Prior takes there wreck of the sea when it happens, which specially belongs to the lord the King. They say also that whereas the lord the King takes, and ought to take, by his sheriff aforesaid his prises and customs due to the port of Newcastle aforesaid, that is to say, from every ship of wine two tuns chosen fore and aft, each tun for twenty shillings; from every ship of herrings one hundred herrings, from a ship of haddocks one hundred haddocks for six pence, from every boat of mullet or rayes the best fish for a penny, and such like: the aforesaid Prior makes his buyings and unladings of ships and boats at Sheles and elsewhere, whereby the lord the King does not receive the prises and customs due, for that the merchandises aforesaid do not wholly come to the due port of Newcastle. They say also that the aforesaid Prior has erected four bakehouses at Tynemouth, which William Sauvage, William the Barber, Robert de Bruern, and Adam le Taillur, common bakers hold, rendering therefor by the year to the aforesaid Prior eight marks. And they say that the bread there baked is sold at Sheles to sailors and others resorting there, and who ought to resort to Newcastle and there to buy their victuals to the amendment of the same town. They say also that the aforesaid Prior has a market on the Lord's Day at Tynemouth likewise, which is not distant from Newcastle more than six leagues, and he has there a tumbrel, shambles hired to butchers and others, and he takes there amends of bread and ale without warrant, and they say that all the country, and also even sailors resorting to Sheles with their saleable goods and merchandises, come and expose them there to sale, to the prejudice of the lord the King, who received no toll nor anything else therefor, &c. They say also that the aforesaid Prior has his fellow-monks merchants of fresh hides throughout the country, who, when they have bought them at Preston, cause them to be tanned and lade therewith ships or boats at Sheles, and sell [them], to the great deterioration and impoverishment of the burgesses of the lord the King of Newcastle, who exercise, and have been accustomed to exercise, such office. They say also that whereas the lord the King has, and ought to have, the towage of ships and boats, large and small, in the water of Tyne, ascending towards Newcastle and descending towards the sea, freely through the lands of any lords whomsoever, the aforesaid Prior does not permit persons wishing to make such transit to enter his lands, and when by chance they have entered his lands he compels them to return and to walk in deep water, whence oftentimes they scarcely with life escape. And some merchants with their goods and merchandises, and likewise others who wished to convey firewood and coal and such-like to Newcastle for the amelioration of the same town, by reason of the aforesaid impediment withdraw themselves, to the no small prejudice of the lord the King, who ought to receive in his port there from every boat with oars four pence, and from a smaller boat without oars one penny, where now he receives scarcely anything. And wherefore they say that, besides the damages which the lord the King has sustained and sustains in the premises, the aforesaid town of the same King is deteriorated and has inestimable damage.

Plea.

And the aforesaid Prior says that these premises charged against him concern only free tenement and liberty, and the writ directed to the sheriff aforesaid, whereby he was forewarned to be now here, explains that he should answer concerning certain grievances and injuries only, no mention being made of free tenement or of things belonging to free tenement; wherefore he does not deem that he ought to answer concerning any free tenement of his, or [anything] belonging to his free tenement, upon forewarning only without summons and without a writ of the lord the King in special case, and very greatly against his statute, which wills that no one shall answer concerning his free tenement without writ unless he pleases, &c. And afterwards the same Prior answers, and as to wreck of the sea and forestalling of merchandises he says that the same Prior and his predecessors have had and received wreck of the sea hitherto when it happened, and by buying have made forestalling of merchandises, that is to say, of victuals and other necessaries for the sustenance of his house aforesaid, within his land aforesaid, as it was good and lawful to him by the charter of the Lord Richard the King, grandfather of the lord the King that now is, which he produces in these words:—"RICHARD, by the grace of God King "of England, Duke of Normandy, [and] Aquitaine, Count "of Anjou, to his archbishops, bishops, abbots, earls, barons, "justices, sheriffs, ministers, and all his faithful people, "French and English, in all countries in which Saint "Alban the Martyr has lands, amicably greeting: We "make known to you that we have granted, and by the "present charter confirmed, to God and Saint Alban "and his church of Saint Oswyn of Tynemuth, a cell of "Saint Alban's, and to the monks serving God there, all "their lands and all their men, with sac, sok, overstronde "and streme, in wode and felde, tol and tem, gridbruth, "hamsok, murder, and forestal, danegild, infangenethef "and utfoggenetheff, flemmenesfremeth, blodwyte, wurec, "and they shall have upon all their lands and upon all "their men, wheresoever they shall be, within borough "and without, as much and as fully as our own ministers "ought to exact to our use. And we are not willing "that any man, neither French nor English, shall inter-"meddle concerning their lands nor concerning their men "in any manner, but only they and their ministers to "whom they shall please to commit. Moreover, that we "have granted to God and Saint Alban, and to the "church of Saint Oswyn of Tynemuth, a cell of Saint "Alban's, for the redemption of our soul and [those] of "our parents, all liberties and all free customs which the "royal power can most freely confer on any church, and "we forbid, upon forfeiture to us, that no one shall "presume to infringe them in any manner. We forbid "also that in their lands or houses no minister, that is to "say, sewer or butler, chamberlain or dispenser, porter or "reeve, shall be placed, against their will and assent, in "the time of us or our successors, by the hands of any "prince or justice at any time whatsoever. Witness, B. "Archbishop of Canterbury, and G. elect of York, &c. "Given by the hand of William de Longchamp, our "Chancellor-elect of Ely, on the fourth day of December "in the first year of our reign at Canterbury." And as to the foundation of the new town at Sheles, he says that he has raised no town there newly, for he says that in the times of his predecessors, priors of the house aforesaid, there were houses there upon his own soil, where the lord the King has no soil nor free tenement, for that the soil of the said house and free tenement extends to the *filum* of the water of Tyne, beyond his dry land there, and between which same *filum* of the water and the land aforesaid of the house aforesaid he has his free fishery in length of the same land in the same water. And he says that they and their predecessors have successively constructed houses and mansions there, and at their will let [them] to fishermen and others, who sold bread, ale, and fish to persons resorting there, without making any amends to the lord the King, but only to the same priors.

m. 58d. He says also that he has no market nor bakehouse, nor claims to have, at Scheles. And as to fishermen and buyings of fish there, he says that his predecessors aforesaid in their times had their own fishermen at their will fishing in the water aforesaid for the sustenance of their house aforesaid, without rendering toll or anything therefor to the lord the King, notwithstanding that the port of the water of Tyne specially and wholly appertains to the lord the King. He says also that the same [priors] had [as] their tenants certain men of Scheles with their boats free within their demesne lands. And he says that he and his predecessors aforesaid freely and quietly bought fish, as also other necessaries for the sustenance of their house and family by land and water there, because he says that, although they made such buyings or unladings of fish there from any fishermen whomsoever besides their own fishermen, the same fishermen, when they resorted to the port of Newcastle or elsewhere, paid, and ought to pay, there the toll and custom due as well for the fish so sold as for the fish in the ship or in the boat sent back and resorting to that port. And as to the market of Tynemuth and other things there, he says that he claims no market there, but he well acknowledges that there is a tumbrill there, and that there are bakers and brewers there, and bakehouses of the same Prior hired out, and shambles for exposing saleable things, as bread, flesh, and fish, which are sold in that town as in other country towns of those parts like as they were in the times of the predecessors of the same Prior, and that they have hitherto taken amends. He says also that he has no monks merchants of hides, as it is charged against him. He says, nevertheless, that they lawfully sell the hides of their larders, or otherwise make their profit thereof. But that they never bought hides throughout the country, nor at Scheles laded ships or boats therewith, nor sold [them], he is prepared to prove, &c. He says also, as to towage in the water of Tyne, that he never hindered persons exercising such office in his land adjacent, except in his meadow of Astwyk, which, concerning such like, is, and has been hitherto, free and exempt; and this he is prepared to prove likewise. He says, moreover, that before the making of the said charter, and from the time of the making of the same, which is prior to any liberty granted to the borough of the lord the King of Newcastle, and to the burgesses there, by the lord the King John, his predecessors, priors of the house aforesaid, took and had all the premises in the manner in which he acknowledges them, freely and quietly, without interruption of time, by virtue of the customs [and] liberties granted to him by the charter aforesaid, in land and water, and of which he found his church seised, and wherefore he has hitherto freely and quietly used them, as his predecessors aforesaid used the same in like manner and in the same places; which he is prepared to prove, &c. And he prays judgment as before, whether he ought to answer concerning a thing done by others, and concerning those things of which he found his church seised, by reason of the soil and of the customs and liberties expressed, which are as freely limited as the royal power can most freely confer them on any church without special writ and summons, contrary to the common law, &c.

And William Inge and John de Insula and others who sue for the King say that the aforesaid charter ought not to avail the aforesaid Prior in this case, for they say, as to wreck of the sea, that when ships out of the high sea within the port aforesaid have arrived in the water of Tyne, and there have been wrecked by chance, the aforesaid Prior, with his men and boats, takes the goods of such ships wrecked in that water, floating within that port, and also other goods remaining in such ships, and leads them to his land, and likewise appropriates such ships to himself. And wherefore they say that this Prior who now is at the present time is seised of sixteen tuns of wine in the name of wreck of a certain ship of Peter de Appelbi, burgess of York, lately wrecked in the water aforesaid, and where this word wreck ought not to be

Replication.

in terram. understood save only when it has fallen on the land of the aforesaid Prior. And as to forestalling, they say that whereas divers liberties were granted to the aforesaid house, as "sac, soc, over strond and strem," &c., and "forstall," all this is to be understood in their lands within their liberty of Tynemuth, and not in the port of Tyne. And likewise this word forstall ought to be interpreted and understood to hinder or insult any man in the King's high street, and not in the other manner as the aforesaid Prior understands it. And as to those things also, and as to ladings and unladings of ships and buyings of merchandises and wares, victuals, and other things, they say that, whereas the aforesaid port of Tyne belongs only to the lord the King and not to the aforesaid Prior, nor to any other, as the same Prior well acknowledged, as often as the same Prior has made such ladings or unladings of ships or boats or any buyings there he manifestly injures the lord the King, since the lord the King is in seisin, and always has been, of that port; nor can the aforesaid Prior claim any liberties, nor ought [he to do so], out of his demesne and his lands aforesaid. And as to the town of Sheles, they say that whatever small dwellings may have been there (if there were any) in the times of the predecessors of this Prior, the same Prior who now is in his time has caused to be made there twenty-six houses upon the soil, *which ought to belong to the lord the King, for that it is comprised by the flow and inundation of the sea;* and they pray record of the justices that the aforesaid Prior has now alleged that the lord the King has no soil nor free tenement therein, but that it *merely appertains* to the aforesaid Prior and his house as far as to the *filum* of the water of Tyne. They say also that in those houses at Sheles are dwelling fishermen and brewers, male and female auctioneers [auxionarii et auxionatrices] of bread and ale and other things, so wealthy that all ships and boats by the hundred or two hundred, more or less, with their things and merchandises, crossing over to those parts resort there for the sufficiency of inns and victuals which they find there, and which ought to resort to Newcastle, and

to buy their victuals there, as they have been accustomed to do, for the amelioration of the same town. And wherefore they say that the same Prior alone is *the occupier of the soil of the lord the King there, and the sole abstractor of the profits of the town of the same lord the King aforesaid.* They say also that the same Prior has in Sheles sixteen fishermen or more fishing with great boats in the sea by the year for the purpose of trade, not for the sake of sustenance for his house aforesaid, and from whom the lord the King receives no toll nor his due custom. They say also that when ships or boats greater or smaller arrive there with fish or other merchandises whatsoever, the same Prior comes and his men and others of the country, with horses and horse-loads [summagiis], and they buy of them necessaries for themselves, so, that is to say, that sometimes those ships or boats depart empty or half-laden to other ports than to Newcastle aforesaid, or at least [go] there with the remains of such fish transferred from several boats into one boat or two, and wherefore the lord the King, who receives his due prises and customs by his sheriff at Newcastle, cannot receive [them], except four pence only from a boat with oars and one penny from that which is found without oars; whereas he received as much from every such boat, how many soever they were, when they arrived; and many other things of which no mention is made here, because on a ship being unladen or breaking bulk [attaminata], or a boat of saleable things, the lord the King shall receive his custom from every merchandise being in that ship or boat; and wherefore the same lord the King scarcely receives from the premises a twentieth or thirtieth part of his custom and prise aforesaid. They say also that as to the bakehouses of Tynemouth, they are very injurious to the lord the King and his borough aforesaid, because they say that the aforesaid Prior causes his corn to be delivered abundantly to his farmers thereof m. 59.
to make money thereof for his behoof, whereby the same farmers commonly bake and sell bread at Sheles, and wherewith persons resorting there are sustained who ought and have been accustomed to buy their victuals at

Newcastle; and wherefore they say that the bakers and brewers of Newcastle for the said cause withdraw from that town and dwell at Tynemuth and Scheles, to the damage of the lord the King and of his borough aforesaid of Newcastle. And as the aforesaid Prior has acknowledged that he and his predecessors have hitherto received the amends of bread and ale at Tynemuth and Scheles, whereas the lord the King receives nothing, neither tolls nor other things, from things and merchandises there sold, nor can it be denied that the lord the King manifestly loses his prises and customs due by the buyings of victuals and unladings of ships of the merchandises and things aforesaid made by the aforesaid Prior, whereas the prises and customs of the lord the King ought to be chosen and taken from the best and entire merchandises and saleable things, and these and other the premises are the personal acts of this Prior, although his predecessors used the like, for that every one of the same deeds is personal and injurious in itself as often as it may have been done, and which cannot be denied, nor is an inquisition there necessary; and wherefore they say that he cannot and ought not by the act of another to cover his own injurious acts, they pray judgment thereof for the Lord the King and his borough aforesaid.

Further charge of presentment undetermined.

And afterwards they say that in the eyre of John de Vallibus and his fellows in the county of Northumberland, in the seventh year of the reign of the lord the King Edward that now is, it was presented by the jurors that the Prior of Tynemouth raised a town upon the bank of the water of Tyne at Sheles on the one side of the water, and the Prior of Durham raised another on the other side of the water, where there ought to be no town, but only "loges" in which fishermen could be lodged, and that fishermen sold fish there which ought to be sold at Newcastle, to the great injury of the whole borough, and to the detriment of the prises of the lord the King for his castle because fish and other merchandises, of which the lord the King used to have his prises, and which are now sold there, ought to be sold at the borough of Newcastle where the lord the King has his prises; and that the same Prior likewise caused brewing to be done at Sheles, and had great ships of fishermen where he ought not to have, save boats only, whereby the lord the King loses his prises, and the borough of Newcastle its custom, to the grievous damage of the lord the King and of the borough aforesaid; and likewise that the Prior of Durham on the other side of the water of Tyne caused brewing to be done, and had ships where he ought to have only boats; and that the aforesaid Prior of Tynemuth caused to be baked in his own bakehouse the bread of others, which ought to be baked at the borough of Newcastle, whereby the borough loses its furnage, that is to say, from every quarter four pence, and whereof they vouch to warranty the rolls of purprestures upon the lord the King, made according to the verdict and presentment of good and lawful men chosen for this purpose of the eyre aforesaid; and they say that those presentments have never hitherto been determined, nor discussed, nor brought up for judgment, nor any amends made upon these things. And they pray that these things may be made manifest to the lord the King and his Council, &c.

And the aforesaid Prior says that this presentment, if such there were, which is a certain accusation, ought not to prejudice him, for that at that time when that presentment was made he was not Prior, which he is prepared to prove; nor is he bound without a special writ to answer concerning another's act, and he prays judgment thereof as before, &c. Replication.

Afterwards before the same lord the King and his Council, in the presence of the lord the King, the parties aforesaid came. And the aforesaid burgesses prayed their judgment upon the record and process aforesaid. And the aforesaid Prior prayed, if it pleased the King and his Council, that he should not answer concerning his liberties, of which the same Prior found his church seised at the time when he became Prior, without the writ of the lord the King: and hereupon he likewise Postea.

prays judgment, &c. And forasmuch as the same Prior, by the writ of the lord the King, came before the same lord the King in his court, and personally appeared before the same lord the King to make answer, as well to the same lord the King as to his burgesses aforesaid, upon whatsoever grievances and injuries done to the same lord the King and his burgesses aforesaid, at a certain day, before certain justices for this purpose in his presence named and assigned by the mouth of the same lord the King to hear, plead, and refer before the same lord the King whatsoever grievances and injuries done to the same lord the King or to his burgesses aforesaid, as it has been fully recorded as well by the same lord the King as by the justices appointed for this purpose, he received, and before the same justices willingly, and of his mere right, precisely made answer in the articles above charged against him; and also he freely and without compulsion propounded the charter of the lord the King Richard and other answers for defending and supporting his right; nor also did he precisely hold himself to that answer that he found his church seised, although in certain articles he so excused himself, as it appears by the record aforesaid: it is said to him that he should shew for himself or say something else if he have or know anything which ought to be of advantage to him, &c. And the same Prior says nothing save as above, but he prays that the lord the King, having understood the charter of the lord the King Richard, his progenitor aforesaid, should do what it shall please him to do. And forasmuch as the lord the King wishes to be certified whether the aforesaid Prior and his predecessors, from the time of the making of the aforesaid charter, by that charter continually and without any interruption have fully used the liberties aforesaid, or not, and also whether the aforesaid Prior in his time, or his predecessors since the making of that charter in their times, have usurped or purprested the liberties abovesaid, or any of them, upon the same lord the King or his progenitors, and where, and from whom, and by whom, and from what time, and in what manner; the same lord the King has appointed William de Vescy, Thomas de Normanville, John de Lethegreynes, and Richard Knout, Sheriff of Northumberland, to inquire the truth of all and singular the articles aforesaid contained in this record, so that they may certify the lord the King thereof at his next Parliament after the Feast of Saint Michael. And a day is given to the parties at the same term. Moreover, forasmuch as the aforesaid Prior claims to have no market or port at Tynemuth, nor also at Sheles, as it appears in the record aforesaid, and as in the presence of the lord the King he acknowledged [this], it is inhibited to him that henceforth he shall not hold, nor cause to be held, a market or port in the places aforesaid, but that he shall cause to be thrown down and destroyed all the signs, whatever they may have been, as well of a port as of a market in the places aforesaid. And it is commanded by the same lord the King that it be inquired by his justices aforesaid whether there have been a market or port in the places aforesaid in times past, and from what time, and by whom, and what damages the lord the King has sustained by reason thereof, &c. Afterwards from the day of Holy Trinity in fifteen days, in the twentieth year of the reign of the King that now is, the aforesaid Prior comes, and likewise Richard de Bretvill, who sues for the King. And Sir Roger le Brabanzon, Sir William de Bereford, and Gilbert de Robiry, justices of the same King, have already sent the inquisition made upon the aforesaid articles, which same inquisition can be found among the records of the term of Saint Michael in the nineteenth year ending, of which inquisition the tenor is—

Commission.

Decree to suppress the market at Shields.

INQUISITION taken at Newcastle-upon-Tyne on Thursday, on the morrow of the Assumption of the Blessed Mary, in the nineteenth year of the reign of King Edward, before Roger le Brabanzon, William de Bereford, and Gilbert de Roubiry, justices of the same lord the King appointed for this matter, concerning divers grievances and injuries done to the same lord the King and his

Inquisition.

burgesses of the town aforesaid by the Prior of Tynemouth at Tynemouth and Scheles, and concerning certain liberties which the same Prior claims to have by the charter of the Lord Richard the King, predecessor of the lord the King that now is, according to the articles contained in the record and process thereof, had between the same lord the King and his burgesses aforesaid, and the aforesaid Prior, before the same lord the King and his Council, by the oath of John de Hertwayton, John de Eslington, William de Framlington, Richard Benet, Robert de Throclawe, Roger de Cressewell, Hugh Gobion, Hugh de Eure, Nicholas de Punchardon, Nicholas Vigrous, Adam de Cambhous, and Richard de Scotton, clerk, who say upon their oath that the port in the water of Tyne, from the sea to the place which is called Hydewynestremes, is the free [port] of the lord the King [est domini regis liber], and that no one in that port can, or ought to lade or unlade in that port, neither the aforesaid Prior nor others, before the takers of the prises of the lord the King or his bailiffs be forewarned by the merchants, and have taken the prises of the lord the King, and have given them licence to unlade, and, unless they have licence, either it shall behove the same merchants to proceed further to the town of Newcastle, or to return to sea. And they say that the aforesaid Prior who now is, and his predecessors from the time of the making of the charter of the lord the King Richard, have used to unlade merchandises and goods arriving at Scheles, and to buy, carry, and take away what they would for their own uses, and this sometimes by licence of the takers and bailiffs of the prises of the lord the King and sometimes without licence. But they say expressly that every time when they did the premises without licence they acted unjustly and to the injury of the lord the King. Being asked which of the predecessors of the aforesaid Prior began to do the premises without licence, and at what time, they say that one William de Horton, formerly Prior of Tynemouth, predecessor of the aforesaid Prior, first, and in the time of King Henry, father of the King that now is, soon after the Battle of

Verdict.

Evesham, now twenty years passed, began to do the premises. Being asked concerning the damages which the lord the King had by the cause aforesaid, they say that the Prior who now is has now been Prior for eleven years, and that the damages aforesaid in his time extend to four pounds, and in the times of his predecessors to sixty shillings. They say also that the men and tenants of the aforesaid Prior of Tynemouth and of Sheles, harboured [receptati] by the same Prior at Scheles, lade and unlade merchandises and wares as if they were merchants, according to the quantity of their goods, and so they make a port and forestalling there where no port ought to be made of right, and this from the time when they began to build, to aggregate houses [adunare domos], and to inhabit at Scheles, and according as facilities offered themselves, and they multiplied their goods, to the damage of the lord the King of ten pounds. And from the time when the men of the aforesaid Prior began to inhabit at Scheles there have elapsed (as they believe) only sixty-six years, before which time there were not there but three shields [scalæ] only for the use of fishermen going to sea and returning. Also as to fishermen, bakers, brewers, and bakehouses, they say that at Scheles there are bakers and brewers, who increase from day to day by reason of merchants coming there, who buy fish and ale, and that there are no bakehouses there, but at Tynemouth there are four bakehouses in which saleable bread is baked, and it is sold, as well at Tynemuth as at Sheles, to sailors and other comers, to the prejudice of the lord the King and forestalling of his town of Newcastle. Being asked concerning the time of the erection of the aforesaid bakehouses, and to what person or persons they belong, they say that they have been erected since the last eyre of John de Vallibus and his fellow-justices last itinerant in this county, which was in the seventh year of the reign of the King that now is, and that the aforesaid bakehouses belong to four men, who are named in the complaint in the record aforesaid, who take furnage for those bakehouses, and the Prior

takes from them amends of the assize broken when they have been convicted thereof, who can take no amends of the assize of bread broken, for that he has not the assize, to the damage of the King of ten pounds. Also as to wreck of the sea, they say that the aforesaid Prior and his predecessors have taken "wrek" *in their lands*, and, when they could reach [attingere] the goods of ships broken, floating in the sea, and within the port aforesaid, with boats and other means, *they have drawn them to land* and carried them away, and in this injury is done to the lord the King, for that such wreck does not appertain to another, but only to the lord the King within the port aforesaid. Being asked concerning the time when they took wreck and such goods within the port aforesaid: and to whose hands they came, they say that twenty years past, in the time of the aforesaid William Bernard, Prior, a certain ship laden with wool was wrecked, and of whose
m. 59d. goods there came to the aforesaid priory to the value of ten pounds, to the damage of the King, &c. Also as to the King's prises and customs of wines and herrings and fish, they say that no wine has been unladen there save for the necessities of the same Prior, and in the manner in which it is above said. Concerning herrings, haddocks, and other fish, they say that there are so many fishermen and other men dwelling there that the mariners resorting there and fishermen find such great delivery of their merchandises that they unlade their ships and sell fish, whereby the lord the King has lost and loses his prises and customs, from the time when men began to inhabit there, to the King's damage of sixty shillings. Also as to a market, they say that on Sunday and other feast days many men assemble at Tynemuth because of Saint Oswin and the church, and there they buy victuals and other merchandises which they find there; but they say that there is not there any certain day of market, nor have the Prior or his predecessors held any market there or received any advantage, as toll or other things, which appertain to market. Also as to hides bought and sold, they say that the aforesaid Prior by his fellow-monks has

neither bought nor sold any hides nor laden ships therewith, as it is charged against him. Also as to towage, they say that the lord the King ought to have the towage of ships in the water of Tyne ascending towards Newcastle and descending towards the sea, through the lands of any lords whomsoever, so that the towers should pass through with the least damage and grievance that they could. And they say that the Prior has not hindered such passengers, save in his damage, and where they passed and made a way within his land more than was necessary. Also as to the foundation of the town of Scheles, they say that there are there five score messuages, with necessary houses belonging to the same messuages, and in which messuages men dwell, of which messuages sixteen have been erected in the time of this Prior, and one place prepared for building. And they say that all those messuages are built without [extra] the "flood-mark" in the soil of the same Prior, except one corner of one house, and each of the aforesaid messuages has its quay erected within [infra] the "flood-mark" in the soil of the lord the King. And in the time of William Bernard, immediate predecessor of the Prior that now is, eight messuages were erected. And in the time of Adam de Mepardishale, predecessor of the same William, and in the time of a certain Ralph, predecessor of the aforesaid Adam, that is to say, within twenty-four years last past, fifteen messuages have been erected. And so they say that all the messuages built between the Bourne towards the east and the sea have been erected from the time aforesaid, except three, which were there from time when memory is not, and used to be called "le Scheles," and of which mention is made above. And on the other side of the Bourne towards the west as far as a certain burn [sikettum] there are situate seven messuages, which were built in the time of King Henry and within sixty years last past, and all which are situate in the soil of the same Prior, except a moiety of one house, which is situate beyond [ultra] the "flood-mark," in the King's soil. And on the other side of the burn towards the west there are situate twenty messuages in the soil of the same Prior, and a moiety of three houses of the aforesaid messuages is situate beyond [ultra] the "flood-mark" and upon quays, and they have been built within sixty-six years last past. And all the messuages aforesaid have quays, and some [have] two. And all other messuages which remain of the aforesaid number have been built within the same time, and are in the soil of the same Prior, but they have no quays. And they say that all the quays aforesaid have been purprested upon the lord the King within [infra] the "flood-mark," in the soil of the same lord the King, that is to say, in some places by sixteen feet, and in some places by ten, and in some by eight, and in some by six, and in some more and in some less, as it appears there. And they say that before the aforesaid time, that is to say, sixty-six years, as they believe, there were not there but the aforesaid three shields [scalæ] only, where now the aforesaid five score messuages are built and inhabited. In witness whereof the aforesaid jurors to this present inquisition have affixed their seals. Given the day, year, and place aforesaid. And it is to be known that the aforesaid inquisition was taken by the aforesaid justices before the aforesaid plaint was sent from the King's Council to the justices of the King's Bench.

Postea. AFTERWARDS, from the day of Saint John the Baptist in three weeks, in the twentieth year of the reign of the King that now is, at Newcastle-upon-Tyne, comes Richard de Bretevill, who sues for the King, and likewise the Prior in his own person and also the jurors come. And because it is found by the verdict of the jurors, as it appears in the record above, that the port in the water of Tyne from the sea to the place which is called Hydewynstremes is the King's free port, and that no one can lade or unlade in that port without licence of the King or of his bailiffs, therefore, as to this, it is considered that the aforesaid port shall remain to the lord the King and his heirs free, with its prises, towage, and all liberties belonging to a port, so that [neither] at Tynemouth nor at Scheles ships may be laden or unladen,

Judgment.

[nor] goods or merchandises may henceforth be sold there, within cover nor without [infra coopertum nec extra], and the lord the King shall recover his damages, which are taxed by the jurors at four pounds, by reason of £4. the lading and unlading of ships there by the aforesaid Prior. Also, forasmuch as it has been found, by the verdict of the jurors, that at Tynemuth there are four common bakehouses, in which saleable bread is baked and sold, and whereof the aforesaid Prior takes amends of the assize of bread broken, and the tenants of the bakehouses take furnage; therefore, as to this, it is considered that the lord the King shall recover his damages of five marks, 5 marks. according to the declaration of the verdict of the jurors aforesaid against the aforesaid Prior. And it is said to Richard de Bretevill, who sues for the King, that he shall sue against those who take furnage of the bakehouses aforesaid, and likewise against the men and tenants of the aforesaid Prior of Tynemuth and Scheles who have made, and make, forestalling to the lord the King and his burgesses of the town of Newcastle-upon-Tyne, by ladings, unladings, buyings and sellings, &c. Also as to wreck of the sea, it is considered that the lord the King and his heirs shall henceforth have wreck *in the aforesaid port*, and that he shall recover his chattels belonging to his Crown of the wreck which came to the priory aforesaid, which are taxed by the jurors at ten pounds. £10. Also as to market and fairs, it is considered that there shall not be at Tynemuth nor at Scheles a market nor a fair, and that at Tynemuth or at Scheles exposure of saleable things shall not commonly be made, as in meats, drinks, nor other saleable things whatsoever; nor any forestalling at Tynemuth or at Scheles whereby the lord the King, his heirs, or his burgesses of Newcastle shall be deteriorated in any wise. And it is commanded to Hugh Gobion, Sheriff of Northumberland, that he shall not permit to be at Tynemuth nor at Seles any market, fair, or signs of a market, fair, or port henceforth, &c. And as to quays and other things erected by the aforesaid Prior within [infra] the "flood-mark," in the soil of the

lord the King, it is considered that they be amoved at the costs of the aforesaid Prior and by the view of jurors; and this was commanded to the aforesaid Hugh the Sheriff, and to the present Custos of the aforesaid borough of Newcastle. And the aforesaid Prior in mercy. And it is commanded to the Sheriff of Northumberland, who is present, that he cause to come before the King, from the day of Saint Michael in fifteen days, wheresoever, &c., all the free tenants of Scheles to make answer to the lord the King, &c.

Mercy.

This case is referred to by Hale, "De Jure Maris," ch. 4, where he says that "judgment was given against the "Prior, but not in express terms for the soil, but implicitly." In his draft treatise, printed *post*, he says "but no "particular judgment given, as I remember, as to that "point" (the soil). It is clear that the King's attorneys do claim that the Prior's houses were built upon the soil, which ought to belong to the King because the tide flows and re-flows over it. They do not say that it belongs to the King in right of his crown; but, looking at the nature of the proceedings, they must be held to say that it belongs to the King in right of his port, and it will be noticed in the inquisition that the jurors find that the Prior and his predecessors have taken wreck in *their lands*, but that they have exceeded their liberty and taken wreck floating in the port and *drawn it to their land*, so that it was clear that they acknowledge that the foreshore belonged to, and was part of the land of the Prior. They then carefully distinguish the position of the houses built upon the shore, and say that some of them are *extra*, that is, above the flood-mark, in the soil of the same Prior, but that the quays belonging to the houses are built *infra*, within the flood-mark, in the soil of the lord the King; and they say that these last are purprestured upon the lord the King, within the flood-mark, *in the soil of the said lord the King*, and these are ordered to be removed. And as to the wreck, the judgment is that the Prior shall not have it *in the port;* but there is no judgment that the Prior shall not have it *in his lands*. Therefore it would seem, notwithstanding the language of this record, that it was understood that the property in the foreshore belonged to the Prior, but that, being subject to the right of navigation, it was called the soil of the King, in the same sense that the soil of highways is treated in the presentments of purprestures on the Hundred Rolls and in the Placita Coronæ—viz., that it is the King's in point of jurisdiction, and not in point of property; and that these wharves were purprestures upon the soil of the King's port, as injuries to the port and its franchise and its navigation. And it is to be observed that they are ordered to be thrown down in order to clear the passage and prevent interference with the franchise of the port, and not arrented to the King, as we have seen before purprestures upon highways and forests were arrented. This case—and it is the only one that has been found before the time of Queen Elizabeth—is referred to by Hale, ch. 4, as an authority in support of the *primâ facie* title of the Crown to the foreshore, but he clearly does not think that it entirely supports the proposition. Then it is to be remarked that it does not support the *primâ facie* title of the Crown to foreshore in the manner in which it is claimed now. The claim as now made is based upon the contention that the Crown did not grant out the foreshore when it granted a manor, but that the foreshore remained in the Crown as a separate property as part of the general waste of the kingdom, and not as a reservation out of the grant of a manor. Now, if that were the view taken in the time of Edward I., it is clear that in this case the King's attorneys would have claimed that these purprestures were made upon the soil of the King because it belonged to him in right of his Crown; but what they do claim is this, that it belonged to the King because he was the owner of the water and port, and that the soil on which the purprestures stood was covered with the tide. It would seem, therefore, that, as the soil of the River Tyne was not parcel of the fee farm of the burgesses of Newcastle, and as this suit was brought in the King's name, but in reality by the burgesses to try their right to their franchise of port as part of their fee farm, the soil in point of property was not in issue, but the soil in point of port jurisdiction was in issue. The pleadings and judgment practically admit the property of the foreshore to have been in the Prior. The Prior would seem to have been preventing the towing, and driving the towers off the foreshore; he was making a port to the injury of Newcastle, and using his right to the soil of the foreshore for a purpose which hindered the towage, and thereby injured the port. The purpresture therefore was a purpresture upon the franchise of the port, and not upon the soil of the King in right of his Crown, for that was not set up; nor upon the soil as belonging to and parcel of the port, for we have shewn that the Prior had the soil, and his successor in title has it at this day, and that title is admitted by the Crown.

From this time to the present the Corporation of Newcastle have exercised the right which they established by this judgment, and for centuries past no quay or building upon the foreshore of the Tyne has been permitted to be erected by any lord of a manor except by licence from the corporation; but in no case has the ownership of the soil been in the corporation, except within their own manors and lands. This case, therefore, cannot be cited as an instance of the assertion of the *primâ facie* title of the Crown, as it is now claimed by the Crown advisers. It is the only ancient record which has been discovered that in any way suggests that the soil of foreshore is *de jure* in the Crown; and when we minutely examine the nature of the case, and when we consider the long list of cases given in the preceding part of this treatise, we cannot but remark that, if the pleading in this case really does set up a claim by the Crown to foreshore *jure coronæ*, it is most remarkable that such a claim was not also set up in the numerous instances in which the right to wreck and foreshore has been shewn to have been in dispute between the Crown and the subject.

CHAPTER VI.

THE REIGN OF KING EDWARD II.

KING EDWARD II., like his predecessor, issued many writs of quo warranto against his subjects. Only a small part of the proceedings are printed in the volume of Quo Warranto Rolls; the residue are unindexed and uncalendered. The earliest we have is a suit against Thomas de Bavent for taking wreck between Benakre and Snodespyke, in Suffolk, in the manor of Eston, referred to *ante*, p. 34, where Bavent claims the wreck if it come upon his soil of Eston. Coram Rege Roll, Mich., 2 Edw. II. m. 35d.

In the rolls of the eyre for the islands of Guernsey and Jersey in 2 Edward II., A.D. 1309, the Abbot of Blackland and the Prior of Erme are summoned for claiming wreck in the island of Erme happening there *tam in terra sua quam in aquis domini Regis in costera maris ibidem ajacente.* The Abbot claims by ancient tenure under a charter of Henry II., by which he granted to his predecessor all the island, with its appurtenances, with all liberties and free customs, and avers that he and all his predecessors have taken wreck. No judgment is entered up. The form of the writ in this case shews that it was admitted that the foreshore of the island was in the Abbot. Quo Warranto Rolls, p. 823.

Nicholas de Cheny and his brother Philip were summoned for claiming the fourth part of the wreck happening *in dominicis terris et aquis domini Regis juxta castrum Regis et alibi in terris ipsius domini Regis et aquis suis et terris tenentium suorum per totam costeram insulæ de Guernsey que non sunt de feodo vel dominio ipsorum Nicholai et Philippi,* and for claiming royal fish by whomsoever taken *in aquis domini Regis ubicumque* coming Ibid. p. 824.

ashore in the aforesaid island. Nicholas and Philip say that Nicholas alone holds the tenements to which the wreck pertains, and these tenements were formerly Robert Earl of Mortaine's, who gave them to Baldwin de Vere, from whose heir Nicholas' father, William, bought them; and he says that the said Earl and Baldwin, and all who held those tenements, have always taken the wreck. The King's attorney says that Nicholas' father was not in seisin. The jury say that the Earl and Baldwin and the said William used to take the wreck in their demesne lands, and afterwards, while the mother of Nicholas held the tenements, there was a dispute between the King's bailiff of the island and the bailiffs of the Abbot of Mount St. Michael and those of the mother of the said Nicholas; and an agreement was made between them to settle the disputes concerning the limits and bounds of their lands where wreck happened. The Abbot was to take wreck happening in his demesne lands at Wale and Lyho, because the Abbot had more land on the sea-coast where wreck happens than any other person; and concerning all the rest of the wreck happening throughout all the island except in the demesne lands of Matthew de Saumareys, equal partition was to be made, half to go to the King and half to be divided between the Abbot and the tenants of the lands which Nicholas now has, saving to the King things anciently excepted, as unwrought gold, silk, &c.; and they say that the wreck has been so partitioned for thirty years. Many adjournments are entered up, but there is no judgment. Here again the right to the soil appears to be admitted.

Quo Warranto Rolls, p. 827.

Matthew de Saumareys and others were summoned for claiming wreck *per totam terram suam de Gerebourgh*. They claim by prescription. The jury find that they have taken it. The judgment is not entered up.

Ibid. p. 828.

The Abbot of St. Michael and the Prior of Wale are summoned for taking wreck *per totam terram suam de Wale et costeram maris contigui*, and for claiming the fourth part of the wreck and royal fish happening *in the lands of the King and his tenants, which are not of their fee;* also for claiming wreck in the island of Jetho. The Abbot disclaims royal fish, except whale and porpoise; and as to wreck, he says that King Edward I., before he was King, made inquiry concerning wreck, and confirmed it to him by charter dated 2 November, 44 Henry III., A.D. 1259, he being lord of the islands at the time. He sets out the charter, which recites the inquisition, stating that of old custom the Abbot was entitled to the fourth part of the wreck in all places in the island, as well of that wreck which by itself and without any aid comes *ad litus maris* as of that which is drawn *ad litus maris*, and that *intus Wale et Lyho et Jetho* he has all the wreck *et omnes aventuras maris* except gold, silk, &c.; and that in the island of Jersey he has wreck *per totam terram suam*. The charter confirms these liberties. The King's attorney prays an inquisition concerning the wreck, and avers that the King was deceived in the aforesaid inquisition. The jurors set out the agreement above mentioned, and the case is adjourned until the Abbot's death, and no decision is entered up.

In this case the right to the shore is admitted, and the inquisition shews very clearly that wreck is taken upon the foreshore.

Peter de Saumareys was summoned for claiming wreck *per totam terram suam* in the parishes of St. Clement and St. Elerius in the island of Jersey. Philip de Carteret was summoned for taking wreck *per totam terram suam* in the parish of St. Owen, William de Augreys in his land in the parish of Holy Trinity, John de Carteret in the parish of St. Owen, and Philip Leveske in the fee which was formerly of Nicholas de Winchilsea. They all claim by prescription. No judgment is entered up. Quo Warranto Rolls, p. 831.

Philip de Carteret and Geoffrey his brother are summoned for claiming wreck *in feodo Paynelli*. They say that Thomas Paynel was a Norman whose lands escheated to the Crown, that King Edward I. granted his lands to their father, and they claim the wreck as pertaining to the said tenements, and that Paynel and his ancestors had it by prescription. The King's attorney Ibid. p. 832.

says that wreck is not named in the charter. No judgment is entered up.

Quo Warranto Rolls, p. 834. The Abbot of Mount St. Michael is challenged for wreck *per totum feodum suum de Nigromonte.* He claims the wreck by prescription and the confirmation by Prince Edward before mentioned. No judgment is entered up; the proceedings appear to have ceased on the Abbot's death.

Ibid. p. 836. Drogo de Barentin is challenged for taking wreck in his land in the parish of St. Martin. He claims it by prescription; there is no judgment.

Ibid. p. 839. Philip de Cheney was summoned for taking wreck *per totam terram suam* in the parishes of St. Saviour, St. John, and St. Owen. As to the parish of St. John, he says that is within Paynel's land, and granted to his father; his land in St. Owen was an escheat, and granted to his father by Henry II., and he claims by prescription. As to St. Saviour's, he bought it of Eustace de Grenville, whose ancestors always had wreck. The King's attorney says that wreck did not pass by the grants, nor by the purchase. There is no decision.

From these entries it is clear that the Crown only claimed the foreshore opposite to its own lands in the Channel Islands.

The commission to the justices who heard these proceedings is printed at p. 840, and it recites as follows:—"Whereas we are given to understand that divers *lands* "*and tenements*, with homages and services, advowsons of "churches and chapels, escheats, wreck of the sea, warrens, "chaces, customs of mackerel, parks of congers, and other "divers liberties which belong to us, and of right ought to "belong, in our islands of Guernsey, Jersey, Sark, and "Alderney, have been unduly usurped and detained, and "that other divers subtractions of our liberties and rights "in those parts and *purprestures* are made there to our "manifest prejudice and disherison, we assign you to "inquire concerning them," &c.; and there are writs to the bailiffs of the islands to aid and assist the justices. Now, this commission requires the justices to inquire concerning lands and tenements usurped and purprestures made; and yet we have the fullest admissions on the records that the foreshore belonged to the subject everywhere, except in the King's own land, and we have a statement as to the wreck taken by the subject *super terram suam* that it either comes *per se ad litus maris* or is drawn *ad litus maris*. It is clear, therefore, that the Crown at this period did not set up a claim to the foreshore as it now does, and that wreck came ashore upon the foreshore.

An inquisition taken in 3 Edward II., A.D. 1310, shews that the Abbot of Middleton had wreck in the manors of Holworth and Ringstead, and the island of St. Helena, in the county of Dorset. In the same year Robert Fitz Payne complained to the King that by reason of his manor of Stoke Courcy, Somerset, he has wreck of the sea by prescription between Lyllestok and Mackespol, and that certain evil-doers have plundered a ship wrecked on the coast of the sea at Laverkesonde, within those bounds, and thereupon a commission was ordered to inquire.

Inq. a. q. d. 3 Edw. II. 79.

Pat. 3 Edw. II. 18d.

On 2 September, 6 Edward II., A.D. 1312, a writ was issued to inquire concerning purprestures made upon the the King in his town and port of Scarborough. The inquisition returned thereto sets forth many small purprestures upon the highways by doorways, steps, and walls, and states that many persons have built their houses over the street so low that men cannot pass under, and that others have placed dung-heaps upon the King's soil in the port so that it is so obstructed and narrowed that ships cannot come in there as they used to do. The town and port belonged to the King, and here we find a most minute inquiry as to purprestures upon the King's soil. Now, what was going on at Scarborough may be fairly assumed to have been going on in other places which did not belong to the King, but still we find no record of any presentment of purprestures in the foreshore in respect of soil anywhere but in the King's own manors.

Inq. a. q. d. 6 Edw. II. 120.

On the roll of the eyre for Kent in Michaelmas, 6

Quo Warranto Rolls, p. 311. Edward II., A.D. 1313, John de Segrave was summoned for claiming wreck in his demesne lands of Folkestone and Terlingham. He claims by prescription. The jury find for him, and he is discharged.

Ibid. p. 312. The Abbot of Lesness claims wreck in Lesness *si forte in terra ipsius evenerit.* He claims by a charter of King John, and he is discharged.

Ibid. p. 314. The Prioress of Sheppey claims wreck in her manor of Sheppey. It is found that it was allowed in the last eyre, and she is discharged.

Ibid. p. 315. Robert de Shirelond claims wreck in his manor of Shirelond by prescription and allowance in the last eyre, and he is discharged.

The Abbot of Faversham claims wreck in Faversham by prescription and allowance in the last eyre, and he is discharged.

Ibid. p. 318. The Abbot of St. Augustine, Canterbury, claims wreck in his manors of Minster, Chistlet, Stodmarsh, Northburn, Deal, Snaves, Swalclive, Plumstead, and Seasaltre by grant of King Edward the Confessor and confirmation of subsequent kings, whereby he has liberties *in terra et in aqua, on stronde and on streme,* and he is discharged.

Ibid. p. 320. The Prior of Rochester claims wreck in his marsh of Grain by allowance in the last eyre, and he is discharged.

Ibid. p. 321. Bartholomew de Badlesmere claims wreck in Whitstable, Kingston, Ridlingwell, and Hatfield, and toll of merchandises at La Grayston in the manor of Whitstable. There is no decision. (See *ante*, p. 74.)

Ibid. p. 325. The Prior of Christchurch, Canterbury, claims wreck in Lyden and other places, as in the previous eyre (*ante*, p. 74), and he is discharged.

Ibid. p. 333. The Abbot of Battle has wreck allowed him in Wye and Dengy Marsh, with its members, as in the previous eyre.

Ibid. p. 325. Nicholas de Criol claims wreck and toll of fish in Walmer by prescription, and he is discharged.

Cart. 3 Edw. III. No. 11. Dugd. Mon. v. 66. On 16 April, 6 Edward II., A.D. 1313, the King granted the manor of Baketon (Norfolk) to the Prior of Bromholm with wreck of the sea.

In 7 Edward II., A.D. 1314, the manor of Great Cotes, in Lincolnshire, was confirmed to John de Sandall, with the wreck of the sea. Cart. 7 Edw. II. 36.

In 8 Edward II., A.D. 1315, a royal fish called a craspeys having come ashore at Abbotsbury, in Dorsetshire, the Abbot petitioned the King, and alleged that he was entitled to wreck *et quicquid per mare ad terram ejusdem Abbatis in Abbotsbury apulsum fuerit vel projectum*, and claimed the craspeys. A jury was ordered to inquire, and they find that the Abbot had always taken royal fish by virtue of the King's charter. They say that wreck and craspeys and whatsoever is thrown upon the shore by the sea upon the land of the Abbot ought to belong to him. Inq. a. q. d. 8 Edw. II. 181.

In Trinity term, 10 Edward II., A.D. 1317, occurs the suit between the Abbot of St. Benet Hulme and John Idayne and others for a trespass on the Abbot's several fishery at Hoveton St. John and Wroxham, Norfolk, which is referred to by Hale (ch. 5) as an example of a several fishery with fixed engines carrying the right to the water and the soil in an arm of the sea. The suit was a simple action of trespass upon the several fishery of the Abbot between Wroxham Bridge and a place called Blakedam. The Abbot recovered £200 damages, but during the plea comes the King's attorney, Gilbert Langelye, "quem "Rex assignavit ad negotia sua prosequenda," and says for the King that the river is an arm of the sea, which extends itself into the salt sea, and is the salt river of the lord the King, flowing and re-flowing, where ships and boats come and ply out of the great sea, loaded and unloaded quietly, without giving toll or custom to any one, and is a common fishery to all; that when any man is drowned by accident there, the coroner's office is not held, because it is an arm of the sea; and he says that it was presented in the last eyre that the Abbot's predecessor made a purpresture upon the King in the river aforesaid by planting weirs in the same and appropriating to himself the aforesaid fishery to hold as several, and that it was considered that those weirs should be amoved and that the said Coram Rege, T., 10 Edw. II. 83.

water should remain a common fishery, and prays a stay of proceedings till the return of that record. And afterwards (says Hale) a *procedendo* was obtained, and, issue being joined, it was found for the Abbot, and judgment and execution given against the defendants for damages, viz., £200.

Pat. 12 Edw. II., p. 1, m. 3.

On 20 January, 12 Edward II., A.D. 1318–19, after an inquiry *ad quod damnum*, licence was given to the Abbot of Selby to fix a weir across the water of Ouse *in feodo suo de Selby* of a length of forty feet, so that the weir does not stretch as far as the *filum aquæ* and that a passage is left for boats. This licence was necessary in consequence of the statute prohibiting new weirs. The right to wreck was taken from the Abbot, but the soil remained to him. See *ante*, p. 104.

Ibid. m. 13d.

On 16 December, 12 Edward II., A.D. 1318–19, a commission of oyer and terminer was issued to inquire into a question of plundering of wreck belonging to Robert de Monte Alto driven ashore at Wigenhale, Snetesham, Hecham, Hunstanton, Thornham, and Tichewell *super solum ipsius Roberti*. Subsequently, in Hilary, 13 Edward II., A.D. 1319–20, Robert de Monte Alto sued John Bird and others for taking wreck *super solum ipsius Roberti per maris in temperiem projectum*, viz., gold and money to the value of a thousand pounds at Wigenhale, Snetesham, Hecham, Hunstanton, Thornham, and Tichewell, in Norfolk. Robert claims by prescription that he and his ancestors had wreck of the sea on their lands on the sea-coast, and declares that the defendants took the wreck. The defendants deny. The jury find that they did take the wreck *super solum ipsius Roberti*, whereupon the King's attorney intervenes. The case is removed to the King's Bench. The writ of error recites Robert de Monte Alto's claim to take wreck *super solum suum*, and there is no traverse of this claim to the soil, but the writ avers that the King is informed that in the places in which the said Robert asserts that the wreck belongs to him, such wreck, when it happens, belongs to the King in right of his crown. The result of the case does not

Coram Rege, H., 13 Edw. II. 41.

Coram Rege Roll, Easter, 13 Edw. II., roll 50, adjourned to Mich.

appear, but Monte Alto must have been successful, for his successors in title have always had the wreck, and the foreshore was found to belong to him in the case of Lestrange *v.* Rowe, *post.* 4 Fost. & Finl. 1048.

In 11 Edward II., A.D. 1318, we find the Abbot of Hulme suing people for taking wreck belonging to him at Winterton. Coram Rege, M., 11 Edw. II. 23.

In 17 Edward II., A.D. 1324, was passed the statute "De Prerogativa Regis." This statute, which defines what belongs to the prerogative of the Crown, enacts that the King shall have wreck of the sea (*warectum maris*), whales, and sturgeons taken in the sea or elsewhere within the kingdom, *exceptis quibusdam locis privilegiatis per Reges.* It thus recognises the right of the subject to wreck, but it is wholly silent as to any right in the Crown *jure coronæ* to the foreshore generally. It has, moreover, in chapter 15 the following passage respecting the prerogative of the King in the construction of his grants of lands:—"Quando dominus Rex dat vel con-"cedit aliquod manerium vel terram cum pertinentiis, nisi "faciat in carta sua vel scripto expressam mentionem de "feodis militum, advocationibus ecclesiarum et dotibus "cum acciderint, ad predicta manerium vel terram perti-"nentibus, tunc hiis diebus Rex reservat sibi eadem feoda "et advocationes cum dotibus, licet inter alias personas "aliter fuerit observatum."

This statute, therefore, limits the construction of a King's grant in respect of what shall pass as appertaining to or parcel of a manor, viz., in respect of knight's fees, advowsons, and dower, and it may be fairly argued that all other things than these which may be appertaining to or parcel of a manor will pass by the King's grant of the manor. Royal franchises, as wreck, treasure trove, chattels of felons, waifs, estrays, &c., and things which are part of the *flores coronæ* will of course not pass out of the Crown in a grant unless they are mentioned; but foreshore is not one of these, and it may be, and generally is, parcel of a manor. Therefore, as this statute does not except it amongst the things which will not pass as Case of Abbot of Strata Marcella, 9 Rep. 24.

parcel of a manor, it would seem clear that it would pass by the King's grant of a manor, although not specifically mentioned, if it can be shewn to have been parcel of that manor, at any rate before the grant, and it will be presumed to have passed by the grant if the evidence of modern user of it is sufficiently strong and goes back sufficiently far to warrant the presumption that it was parcel of the manor at the time of the grant.

Pat.18Edw. II., p. 1, m. 3d.

In 18 Edward II., A.D. 1325, occurs one of the many commissions to survey weirs in rivers which are injurious to the navigation. It is a commission to survey the weirs in the Trent between Nottingham and Gainsborough. The commission recites that the water of Trent for one perch on either side of the *filum aquæ* ought to be free for ships to pass, and that the riparian proprietors have put weirs across the *filum*, and orders the commissioners to remove those which are situate *ex transverso fili aquæ*, so that the navigation be not impeded. This commission recognises the rights of the proprietors to put weirs on the foreshore provided they do not hinder the navigation.

There are many records during this reign relating to fisheries and weirs in the sea and tidal rivers, but it is beyond the scope of the present treatise to deal with them.

CHAPTER. VII.

THE REIGN OF KING EDWARD III.

ON 15 October, 5 Edward III., A.D. 1331, a writ was issued to John de Tichborne reciting that a whale (ceta) was thrown by the sea on shore at Porchester, which belongs to the King as wreck *ratione dominii nostri ibidem*, and ordering an inquiry as to who took it. The inquisition returns that certain fishermen took a fish called "thurlheved" there. The language of this writ is remarkable, for it claims the wreck by reason of the King's manor, and not in right of his crown, the manor of Porchester being then in the Crown's hand. Inq. a. q. d. 5 Edw. III. 19.

It was found by an inquisition in 5 Edward III., A.D. 1331, that William de Kyme had a whale, which came *super terram suam* in his manor of Croft, in the county of Lincoln. Inq. a. q. d. 5 Edw. III. 70. See post, 43 Eliz.; ante, pp. 52, 83.

In 5 Edward III., A.D. 1330–31, is Sir Henry Neville's case, quoted by Hale (ch. 6, p. 26) as an authority that the shore may be parcel of a manor. It was an action by William Newport of London against Sir Henry de Neville for taking ten lasts of herrings in the vill of Walring, to which the defendant pleads that they were thrown by a storm of the sea out of any one's care *upon his land* in Walring, and that he has the franchise of wreck throughout the vill as appendant to his manor of Walring by prescription, and therefore that the wreck was his proper chattel. Year-book H., 5 Edw. III. 3, plea 11.

Ralph de Camois sued Stephen de Peshale and others for seizing wrecked goods at Brawater, in Sussex. Peshale says that he holds the hamlet of Worthing, which is a member of Brawater, in right of Alina his wife, as parcel of the barony of Bramber, which hamlet is situate upon Coram Rege, T., 5 Edw. III., roll 115.

the sea-coast, where he in right of his wife ought to have wreck as pertaining to his hamlet, and he says that the goods *ex impetu fluctuum maris jactabantur super terram in litore maris infra hameletum predictum* out of a ship which was wrecked off the said coast, and that he kept them as wreck until one of the merchants who escaped from the ship claimed them, and he gave them up to him, but denies taking the plaintiff's goods. The jury, however, found the defendant guilty, and awarded damages sixty-four marks. It would seem that the goods were not legally wreck, but the assertion of the right to the foreshore is unchallenged.

Inq. p.-m. 6 Edw. III., 2nd Nos. 132.

It was found by inquisition in 6 Edward III., A.D. 1331–32, that the port of Ottermouth belonged to the Prior of Mount St. Michael as parcel of the manors of Budleigh and Otterton from time immemorial.

Ibid. 126.

In the same year an inquisition was taken to inquire whether it would be to the damage of the King or of others if he granted to Nicholas Champneys, of Sandwich, permission to inclose and build upon *quandam placeam nostram vacuam juxta portum de Sandwyco vocatam Hosand juxta mare.* The jurors find that the place contains, by estimation, thirty acres of sandy land, which cannot be measured *pro eo quod jacent circumquaque inclusæ aqua maris et pro majori parte superundatæ de eadem aqua ita quod vix de eisdem triginta acris duodecim acræ apparant aridæ.* And they say that if the thirty acres are inclosed they would be worth three shillings yearly, but they can only be inclosed at great cost and labour; and that the place belongs to the lord the King, and that it would be no damage to him or any one else if he granted it to Champneys to inclose. This piece of land is obviously an island, and it is clear that at this period islands were known to be the King's, and if it were worth while to inclose such an island the foreshore must have been of considerable value at this period, and yet there is no claim for it by the King.

Inq. a. q. d. 7 Edw. III., 50.

In 7 Edward III., A.D. 1333, an inquisition was ordered to inquire whether the Abbot of Tintern had increased eight weirs in the River Wye so that boats and ships could not get up to Monmouth; but the right to place the weirs on the soil of the tidal water is not challenged.

The Earl of Lancaster had weirs in the manor of Radley in the River Severn. Close, 10 Edw. III., m. 29.

The Minister's accounts of the Duchy of Cornwall for the reign of Edward III. shew very large receipts for wreck in a great many townships in the county of Cornwall. They also shew in some cases that the wreck was claimed by lords of manors in that county. Hale, c. 5.

John le Ercedekne had wreck in the manor of Ellerky, in Cornwall, and many other lords of manors in that county are entitled to wreck as against the Duke. Inq. p.-m. 13 Edw. III., 2nd Nos. 62.

By charter dated 12 October, 14 Edward III., A.D. 1340, the King granted to John de Cheverestoṇ wreck of the sea in Thorleston, Hewish, Soure, and Saltcombe, in Devonshire.

In 16 Edward III., A.D. 1342, Alice Countess of Lincoln, claiming that she and her ancestors have immemorially had wreck of the sea *infra procinctum manerii sui*, sues divers trespassers for carrying away wreck at Sutton, in Holland, which was thrown by the sea in a ship on land at Sutton by the flux of the sea, and says that because no animal escaped from the ship it ought to belong to her as wreck of the sea pertaining to the said manor *ab antiquo*. She also sues other people for taking a whale at Sutton, as wreck happening in the precinct of her manor thrown on land by the flux of the sea at her manor aforesaid; and the defendants are outlawed. This case was cited in the case of Rex *v.* Oldsworth, in 13 Charles I., *post*. Coram Rege, E., 16 Edw. III. 41, and M., 16 Edw. III. 140.

The lords of the Commote of Iscoid Ughirwern, in Wales, were challenged by quo warranto in 18 Edward III., A.D. 1344, for claiming wreck of whatsoever nature in their aforesaid lordship of Iscoit, but there is no plea nor judgment. Quo Warranto Rolls, p. 819.

In 25 Edward III., A.D. 1351, we have the first of the statutes after Magna Charta concerning weirs erected to Statute 25 Edw. III. c. 4.

the injury of navigation. It recites that the common passage of ships and boats in the great rivers of England are disturbed by the levying of weirs, mills, stanks, stakes, and kiddels, to the great damage of the people, and it is enacted that any such erections which were levied and set up in the time of Edward I., and afterwards, in such rivers, whereby ships and boats be disturbed so that they cannot pass as they were wont, shall be put out and utterly pulled down without being renewed, and writs shall be sent to the sheriffs to inquire and do execution. This statute clearly recognises the rights of the owners of the soil in the great navigable rivers to maintain existing weirs so that they be not hurtful to navigation; and it is manifest that many of these weirs must have existed upon foreshore which is now generally claimed by the Crown, and it is but fair to conclude that the Crown made no such claim at this period, because, had the foreshore belonged to the Crown, the weirs would have been purprestures upon the King's soil, and no Act of Parliament would have been required to abate them.

Coram Rege, 25 Edw. III. 49d.

In 25 Edward III., A.D. 1351, the Bishop of Chichester, as lord of the hundred of Lamanwode, sued Thomas de Hunstan, the lord of the manor of Brigham, in Sussex, for taking a boat as wreck within the vill of Westwighthring. He says that the vill pertains to his manor, and claims the wreck by prescription, and that the boat in question was cast by the force of the sea *infra dominium suum*, and was thrown to land out of any one's possession, and he took it, as was lawful. The Bishop rejoins that the *locus in quo* is in the hundred of Lamanwode, and he, as lord of the hundred, has wreck in the hundred by prescription. The defendant joins issue. The jury find that the defendant has not wreck pertaining to his manor, but that the Bishop and his predecessors have wreck by prescription within the whole hundred, and judgment passes for the Bishop. This is a case of wreck claimed within a hundred, but whether the hundred was originally part of the Bishop's fee or not I have not ascertained. It will be observed that there is no traverse of the defendant's claim to the soil of the foreshore of his manor, and this case further shews that the lord of a manor may be owner of the foreshore although another may have the wreck. In the Year-book Mich., 11 Henry IV., pl. 37, it was said *obiter* by Hankford, J., that wreck cannot be parcel of a hundred; which may be true, but it is possible for the Crown to grant to a subject the right to wreck coming ashore within the limits of a hundred. Usually, however, we find that, when wreck is claimed within a hundred, that hundred is coterminous with an ancient barony. The wreck has been granted within the barony, and, the barony being broken up by subinfeudation, the wreck has come to be reputed as belonging to the hundred on account of the identity of extent of the ancient barony and the hundred. There are instances in the county of Sussex.

In 30 Edward III., A.D. 1356, a ship called the *James*, of Fobbing, laden with wine, was lost at sea, and the wine came ashore in the counties of Suffolk and Essex. A commission was issued to inquire who had taken the wreck. The greater part of it was taken up at sea in boats, but the bailiff of the Earl of Suffolk took two tuns thrown ashore at Orford, the canons of St. Paul's four tuns at Walton, John de Burnham a tun at Frynton, Nicholas de Torlworth at Little Holland, the Bishop of London at Great Clacton, and William de Manny a tun at Dovercourt. Ex. Miscell. 81813.

The lady of the manor of Foulstowe, in Lincolnshire, had wreck of the sea. Inq. p.-m. 31 Edw. III., 2nd Nos. 54.

In 31 Edward III., A.D. 1357, Henry Duke of Lancaster claimed to have the water of Mersey open from a place called Freshpool, to the Duke's fishery of Thelewall *tam in solo alieno quam in solo suo proprio* so largely that he may have passage with a boat without impediment over the *filum* of the said water to go to his fishery and back, at all times of the year, and if any impediment be made to the contrary, it is lawful for him to remove it; and he also claims all royal fish taken or found *infra feodum dominii sui predicti.* Quo Warranto Rolls, Cheshire, 31 Edw. III.

In a report made by the late Mr. Black, in 1865, on the right of the lord of the manor of Tranmere, in Cheshire, to the foreshore of the Mersey, a copy of which will be found in the Inner Temple library, there are printed some proceedings on quo warranto in the county of Cheshire, 27 to 31 Edward III., which shew that the lords of manors abutting on the Mersey and the Dee claimed that their manors extended to the mid-stream of those rivers.

Robert de Hokenhull was summoned for claiming free fishery in the water of Dee *infra bundas de la Wodebank*, to wit, from the bounds of Church Shotwick to the castle of Shotwick, *usque ad filum aquæ*, with all fisheries except for whales, sturgeon, and thurlhead, and wreck of the sea within the said bounds, except treasure and wreck royal. There is no decision in this suit.

The Prior of Birkenhead claimed, within the bounds of the manor of Claghton to the mid-stream of the Mersey, to make all manner of fisheries *in solo suo proprio*, and to receive all profits *in dicto solo suo*, except royal wreck. No judgment was made upon his claim.

Henry de Hoton was summoned for claiming a fishery in the water of Dee and Mersey *infra bundas suas proprias de Hoton et Rothscotwick usque ad filum de prædictis aquis cum omnibus piscariis piscacionibus retibus et naviculis et cum omnibus ingeniis et instrumentis omni tempore anni et omnimodas pisces capere ad opus suum et omnia alia proficua percipere præter wreccum regalem thesaurum whale sturgeon et thurlhead.* He claims by prescription. He also claimed a right of passage in boats. He pleads that as to the right of passage and his fishery, although he claims them as liberties, the right of passage is his at common law, and to fish within one's own bounds is free tenement, and does not fall within a claim of liberty, wherefor there is no need for him to shew any warrant; and thereupon it is adjudged that he be discharged.

There is a quo warranto in a similar form against Robert de Burneston for a fishery in the Dee *infra bundas suas proprias de Hasilwall* to the mid-stream, and to which he pleads in like manner, and is also discharged.

John de Leghton makes a similar claim to the mid-stream of the Dee at Leghton, and on the same plea is also discharged.

John le White claims to the mid-stream of the Dee in Parva Neston and Hargreave, and is discharged on a similar plea.

Mr. Black prints similar claims by the lords of the manors of Poddington, Meols, Pulton in Walley, Seacomb and Lystark, Caldy, Kirkby Walley, and Polton.

From the decisions in the cases above mentioned, it would therefore seem that the justices of Chester were satisfied that the manors in question extended to the mid-stream, and that the right of fishery, although the water was tidal, was a right incident to the ownership of the soil, and was established by a plea of *liberum tenementum* in the same manner that it is established in non-tidal water. It is, however, to be remarked that notwithstanding these decisions, and notwithstanding the claims of the lords on the shores of the Mersey made at this time, the Crown has succeeded in possessing itself of large portions of the foreshore of that river, which it has sold for very considerable sums.

There is an account of wreck collected in the Isle of Wight in 30 Edward III. A.D. 1356. Exch. Q.R. Miscell. 905/15.

In 32 Edward III., A.D. 1358, it was presented that a ship was wrecked to the westward of Portland, and that certain goods came ashore within the lordship of the Abbot of Bynendon at Bexinton. He was summoned by the Crown to shew his title. He says that King Henry III. granted his predecessor wreck of the sea *per totam terram suam de Bexinton* and in his other manors in the county of Dorset, and that King Edward I. on 30 November, 9 Edward I., A.D. 1281, reciting the grant, confirmed it, and granted that he should have wreck of the sea *per totam terram suam de* Bexinton, Chalvedon, Bynindon, Lulleworth, and Brembilcombe. The charters being inspected, it appeared manifestly to Coram Rege, 32 Edw. III., Mich., roll 32.

the Court that King Henry III. had granted to the Abbot wreck *per totam terram suam in maneriis suis in Comitatu Dorset*, and he is discharged.

Inq. a. q. d. 35 Edw. III. 1, John Fitz-walter. Co. Placita, Essex, 54.

In 35 Edward III., A.D. 1361, it was found by inquisition that Sir John Fitz Walter, lord of the manor of Burnham, made a weir in the sea upon le Raysand opposite la Zondes vocatos la Fulnesse towards the east, to the prejudice of the King; and he takes twenty shillings a year profit therefrom, to the damage of the King twenty shillings. This looks like a claim by the Crown to foreshore, but the place was probably almost an island, and is situate at a considerable distance from the manor of Burnham, at the mouth of the River Crouch or Walfleet, in Essex.

Co. Placita, Essex, 54.

It appears that on 1 April, 41 Edward III., A.D. 1367, the King granted to Bartholomew Stygand, one of his mariners, *unam placeam sabulonis vocatam Reysand jacentem in mari juxta Walfleet* to hold for life; but it also appeared that the grant was made during the minority of Walter Fitz Walter, the heir of the manor of Burnham, which was in the King's hand by reason of the minority. In 43 Edward III., A.D. 1369, Fitz Walter petitioned the King in Parliament, stating that the place, with a fishery and certain weirs, was parcel of the manor of Burnham, and this upon inquisition was found to be the fact, the jurors finding that it had immemorially been so, and that Fitz Walter's ancestors always had it until Stygand took possession. The cause was tried in the Chancery, and Fitz Walter established his right in 50 Edward III., A.D. 1376, and it was adjudged that *dicta piscaria cum gurgitibus eidem pertinentibus dicto Waltero liberetur*.

Hale, De Jure, cap. v. p. 21.

Inq. p.-m. 41 Edw. III., 2nd Nos. 50.

In 41 Edward III., A.D. 1367, a dispute again arose between the King, as lord of the manor of Melcomb, and the Corporation of Weymouth as to their respective rights in the port. The King now claimed the Melcombe side of it in right of the Crown, not, as Queen Eleanor did, by feoffment from the Abbot of Cerne (*ante*, p. 95). An inquisition was taken, which finds that the moiety of the water of Weye, between the towns of Melcombe and Weymouth from the *filum aquæ*, and the soil under the water, as well when the sea is at "groundebbe" as at all other times, from time immemorial belonged to the King and his progenitors, *and to the lords of Melcombe;* and that the other half, both soil and water, belonged to Lionel Duke of Clarence as lord of the borough of Weymouth. The claim here in right of the Crown is clearly, however, not intended to be a claim by virtue of the prerogative, but a claim in right of the Crown *as parcel of the manor;* and this is a further instance to shew that the theory of the *primâ facie* title was not dreamed of in those days.

In 41–2 Edward III., A.D. 1367–68, the bailiff of Queen Philippa accounted for wreck taken at Seaford and Barling, in the county of Sussex. Exch. L. T. R., Queen's Lands, Min. Accs., 41-2 Edw. III.

In 41 Edward III., A.D. 1367, it was presented that the Abbot of Peterborough had acquired from Nicholas de Rey 300 acres of marsh in Gosberkirk (Lincoln), and another 300 acres of marsh in Gosberkirk, from the Abbot of Swineshead, after the Statute of Mortmain, and *without the King's licence.* The Abbot pleaded that, by the custom of the country, it is, and was from time immemorial, the custom that all lords having their lands or tenements upon the sea-coast, *particulariter habebunt marettum et sabulonem per fluxus et refluxus maris secundum majus et minus prope tenementa sua projecta;* and he says that he has a manor in the said vill of Gosberkirk, many lands of which are adjacent to the sea-coast, and so he has by the flux and re-flux of the sea about 600 acres *maretti* adjacent to his lands, and by increase of time according to the custom of the country of old time; *absque hoc* that he bought *without licence,* as alleged. The jury find that the custom is as he pleads, and the custom extends to the clergy as well as to laymen, and that he has the manor of old time in right of his church, and that he has all the *marettum* aforesaid by the flux and re-flux of the sea, and by increment of time grown up to his land in the manor aforesaid Coram Rege, E., 41 Edw. III. 28.

adjoining the sea-coast, and that he holds it according to the custom of the country; and thereupon he is discharged. This record is referred to by Hale, ch. 6, p. 29, where it is very incorrectly printed.

Exch. L. T. R., Memda. Roll, T., 43 Edw. III. 13.

In Trinity, 43 Edward III., A.D. 1369, occurs the case of the Abbot of Ramsey, referred to by Hale (ch. 6, p. 28) in illustration of the right of alluvion. The case is as follows:—It was presented by an inquisition taken in 42 Edward III., A.D. 1368, before Edmund Thorp and his fellows—assigned by patent dated 12 May, 41 Edward III., A.D. 1367, to inquire in the counties of Norfolk and Suffolk concerning certain purprestures made upon the King, and concerning wardships, marriages, reliefs, escheats, lands, tenements, rents, profits, and emoluments, belonging or appertaining to the King in the counties aforesaid, concealed, withdrawn, occupied, and unjustly detained from the King—that the Abbot of Ramsey appropriated to himself and his house sixty acres of marsh in Brancestre *without the licence of the King;* and thereupon the Abbot was summoned to shew why the said marsh should not be seised into the King's hands. And the Abbot comes, and says that the marsh ought not to be seised, because he and his predecessors from before the time of memory have held the manor of Brancestre, which is situate next the sea, and there is there a certain marsh, which is sometimes diminished by the influx of the sea and sometimes increased by the deflux of the sea, and that he and his predecessors have held the said marsh as parcel of their manor; *absque hoc* that he appropriated it *without licence* of the King. The King's attorney replies that he did appropriate it. The jury find that he did not appropriate it, but that he held the manor of Brancestre, and the marsh increases and decreases by the influx and deflux of the sea, and is part of the manor; and he is discharged. It is to be observed in these two cases that the King's attorney does not claim the alluvion as part of the foreshore, but charges only that the abbots acquired them without licence, contrary to the Statute of Mortmain.

There is no attempt to set up a title in the King to alluvial land, nor to suggest that this is derelict land, nor is there any claim to foreshore *jure coronæ*. In the first case, the Abbot of Peterborough claims alluvion by the custom of the country; in the second, the Abbot of Ramsey claims it at common law; and from these cases Hale deduces the conclusion that the land gained by gradual alluvion belongs to the adjoining owner, and he distinguishes the cases from the cases of land left derelict.

The Abbot of Bardsey was summoned in 44 Edward III., A.D. 1370, for claiming wreck *in terris suis* in North Wales, and he claims by reason of wreck to have all goods and chattels *in terris suis per costeram maris projecta et inventa et per maris intemperiem periclitata* by prescription. The King's attorney avers that by the conquest of Wales all liberties theretofore used were annulled, and asks whether the Abbot can avail himself of the plea of prescription. The Abbot rejoins that all those of Wales who submitted to the King were confirmed in their possessions by the general proclamation, and that the abbots were only tenants for life and could not forfeit, and he prays judgment whether his title by prescription is not good. The case is adjourned, and the result does not appear by the record. Dugd. Mon iv. 660.

The lord of the manor of Skinnergreen, Yorkshire, had wreck of the sea. Inq. p.-m. 45 Edw. III. 20.

CHAPTER VIII.

RICHARD II. TO PHILIP AND MARY.

FROM the reign of Edward II. downwards the Public Records are very voluminous, and are as yet but imperfectly indexed or calendared. Doubtless they contain much valuable information on the subject before us, but their great bulk makes it impossible to search them, and thus it is that but scanty notices are forthcoming to throw light on the dealings with the foreshore between the reigns of Edward II. and Queen Elizabeth. There exist numerous accounts of bailiffs and ministers of manors in the hands of the Crown, either in its immediate possession, or in its temporary custody by reason of wardship, forfeitures, &c. These will give evidence of the receipt of wreck and user of foreshore and fisheries in many seacoast manors now belonging to private individuals; but it is beyond the scope of this treatise to deal with such records.

Close, 5 Ric. II. 29. Hale, cap. vii. p. 43.

On 26 October, 5 Richard II., A.D. 1381, we find a writ reciting that a whale had come ashore *on the soil* of the alien priory of Mersea (Essex), which was then in the King's hands, which fish, it is said, belongs to the King or to the Prior of that priory of right, and the writ orders the sheriff to send the fish to the treasurer of the King's household as quickly as possible. The language of this writ clearly indicates that the foreshore of the island of Mersea belonged to the priory, notwithstanding that the priory was then in the King's hand.

Orig. 8 Ric. II., roll 117 Tower Privy Seals, 8 Ric. II., p. 7.

On 1 October, 8 Richard II., A.D. 1384, the King leased to John Sewale a certain sand in the sea called Colnebench, abutting upon Merseyeheld, in the county of Essex, for eighty years, with power to make weirs on it. This place is a piece of foreshore at the mouth of the River Colne, opposite the island of Mersea, and the lease would seem to have been made because the priory of Mersea was in the King's hands at the time. Sewale appears to have proceeded to erect weirs upon Colnebench which were injurious to navigation, and accordingly on 14 July, 15 Richard II., A.D. 1391, a commission was issued to inquire whether the lease was injurious to the navigation, and the jury find that Sewale having driven the piles upon the sand with the intention of making weirs, they were injurious to the navigation. Whether the lease was avoided or not has not been ascertained. This lease at first sight looks as though the King was exercising the general right of the Crown to ungranted foreshore, but when we note in the writ respecting the whale that the foreshore at the place in question was the soil of the priory of Mersea, then being in the King's hand, we see that the Crown is not dealing with foreshore *jure coronæ*, but *jure prioratus*, and this case cannot be cited as an instance of the Crown's dealing with foreshore opposite to the manor of a subject which was not in the Crown's hands. It is also to be observed that this case shews that the Crown could not make a grant of foreshore in derogation of the public right of navigation, and that the Crown's interest in foreshore, even in its own manors or those which were in its hands, was limited by, and subject to, the public right of navigation.

On 20 April, 5 Richard II., A.D. 1382, the King sent a writ to the Prior of Wymondham reciting that a ship had been left at sea by its crew for fear of enemies, and had drifted ashore at Hapesburgh (Norfolk), and had come *ad terram infra dominium vestrum apud villam de Hapesburgh*. The Prior had claimed it as wreck; but, it being adjudged by the Court not to be wreck because the crew had escaped alive, the Prior is ordered to give it up on payment of salvage. This writ is a very apt illustration of Hale's theory, that he that hath wreck of the sea *infra manerium* it is a great presumption that he hath the shore; and we have here a clear recognition of the

Close, 5 Ric. II., m. 9.

Prior's right to the shore on which the wreck was taken as being *infra dominium.*

Dugd.Mon. iii. 330. The manor of Hapesburgh was given by William de Albini, in the time of Henry I., to the church of Wymondham by the description of "totum manerium de Hapes-"burgh cum omnibus pertinentiis suis videlicet wreck "tol et theam et omnibus aliis libertatibus et consuetu-"dinibus." The grant was confirmed by King Henry I. by the description of "totum manerium de Hapesburge cum "omnibus pertinentiis suis et totum wrec in eadem villa "a divisa que est inter villam de Eccles et de Hapesburgh "juxta mare in longum versus occidentem usque ad "divisam inter hundredum de Hapesburgh et Tunstede." Here, therefore, we find no specific grant of the shore *eo nomine.* It passes under the charter by the words *manerium cum pertinentiis,* the grant of the wreck *in eadem villa* shewing that the shore had passed as parcel of the manor; and then the writ of 5 Richard II. clearly admits that the shore on which the wreck was taken is parcel of the manor, for it is said to have drifted ashore *ad terram infra dominium vestrum apud villam de Hapesburgh.*

Pat.16 Hen. III., p. 1, m. 8.

Pat. 9 Ric. II., p. 7, m. 37d. On 28 January, 9 Richard II., A.D. 1385–86, a commission was issued to William Botreaux and others to inquire concerning lands and tenements, wardships, forfeitures, escheats, goods and chattels of felons, wreck of the sea and other profits withdrawn, concealed, and detained from the King in the county of Cornwall since his coronation, but we do not find the return. These commissions were frequently issued to make inquiry throughout the country, and if any lands had been usurped against the Crown, or any encroachments made upon the foreshore belonging to the Crown, they would certainly have been discovered and returned; but, though many of these commissions and the returns to them exist, no single instance has been discovered of the return of any purpresture or encroachment upon the foreshore, which must have been the case had the foreshores of the kingdom been regarded as belonging to the King by virtue of the prerogative as waste land of the kingdom not granted out, for every groin and every weir would have been a purpresture, and would have been presented, and it is notorious that the sea-coasts and rivers were at this period studded with weirs and fixed engines.

In the Parliament of 15 Richard II., A.D. 1391, on the prayer of the Commons, it was enacted that all manner of contracts, pleas, and plaints, and all other things done and arising in the bodies of counties, as well by land as by water, and also of wreck of the sea, the Court of the Admiral shall have no manner of cognizance or power or jurisdiction, but they shall be tried, determined, discussed, and remitted by the law of the land, and not by the Admiral or his lieutenant in any wise, saving always to all lords, cities, and boroughs their liberties and franchises.

Rot. Parl. iii. 291a. Statute 15 Ric. II. c. 3.

By statute 1 Henry IV. (c. 12), A.D. 1400, the statute concerning pulling down of weirs of 25 Edward III. is confirmed, and further power is given to survey and correct weirs injurious to navigation; and it is provided that, if the justices order a weir to be abated or amended, *he who hath the freehold* of the same shall thereof do execution, at his own cost, within half a year after notice thereof to him to be made, under a penalty of one hundred marks. This statute therefore recognises the right of the owner of the weir to the soil on which it is built.

There is a grant dated 1 Henry IV., A.D. 1400, to Owen Glendower of many lands in South Wales and North Wales, with wreck of the sea.

Pat. 1 Hen. IV., p. 1, m. 19.

The soil of the estuary called Hadley Ray, in Essex, lying between Canvey Island and the mainland, described as *quoddam wagessum vocatum le Re*, was in the possession of Edmund Duke of York as parcel of the manor of Hadley. The title to this piece of foreshore has been frequently litigated, and was established in the case of Bridges *v.* Highton, and recently in the case of Foster *v.* Frost, tried before Baron Pollock on 28th January 1887. The word "wagessum" appears to be peculiar to the county of Essex; it is a Latinized form of the French word

Inq. 3 Hen. IV. 36.

Sol. Journ. and Reporter, viii. p. 1, p. 765, 1863-4; 11 L. T. N. S. 653.

Court Rolls of Great Wakering.

"vase," mud, and we find it described as *wagessum anglice sea ground.* It occurs in a bailiff's account of the manor of Burnham in the time of Henry IV., where oyster layings are described as *peciæ wagessi, peciæ de la wose, peciæ de la ooze.* It also occurs in the court rolls of the manor of Chalkwell Hall, and is generally found in ancient records relating to oyster layings and foreshore in the county of Essex.

Penes Sir John Mildmay. *Re* Alston's Trusts, Weekly Rep. 24 Nov. 1856, i. p. 2, p. 189; 28 L. T. 337.

The manor of Blithburgh, in Suffolk, was confirmed, in 9 Henry IV., A.D. 1408, to Roger Swillington, with wreck of the sea.

Pat. 9 Hen. IV., p. 2, m. 11.

Hale, in his tract on Admiralty jurisdiction, cites a case in the King's Bench, in which Bartholomew Bourchier brought trespass against divers persons for taking oysters in Sywandsfleet in Tollesbury. The defendants pleaded that it was an arm of the sea and common to all, to which the plaintiff replied that he had a several fishery of oysters, which, as Hale says, cannot be but below low-water mark, and he cites the case to shew that the subject may have a fishery below low-water mark which will be out of the jurisdiction of the Admiral as lying in any arm of the sea *inter fauces terræ,* Tollesbury being situate on the River Blackwater.

Hargrave MS. 93, f. 113. Coram Rege, E., 9 Hen. IV., roll 44.

In 11 Henry IV., A.D. 1410, the Abbot of Cliff brought a writ of trespass against J. Herle for taking goods by force of arms. Herle justified that he was seised of a manor in right of his wife, and that his wife's ancestors had wreck of the sea in the manor by prescription; that a ship was wrecked *upon the same land,* and the plaintiff, as lord of the hundred, wished to carry away the goods, and that the defendant would not suffer it. The plaintiff claimed that all lords of the hundred had had the wreck; the defendant replied that he shewed no grant or allowance in eyre. It was decided that a manor might have wreck by prescription without allowance in eyre. Hankford, J., said: "Wreck cannot be parcel of a hundred." The decision does not appear.

Year Book, Mich., 11 Hen. IV., plea 37.

By statute 1 Henry V. (c. 2) the statutes respecting weirs are confirmed.

The lord of the manor of Mallebergh, in Devon, had wreck of the sea. Inq. 3 Hen. V. 49.

In 7 Henry V., A.D. 1419, a commission was issued to inquire concerning concealments and taking of wreck in the county of Essex, and the Bishop of London is sued by the King for taking wreck at Clacton. The Bishop pleads his title, and sets out charters of Edward the Confessor and William the Conqueror, which grant to the bishops all liberties *by strond and by lond, on tyde and off tyde*, and also letters patent of inspeximus and confirmation of 25 January, 12 Edward II., A.D. 1337–38, whereby King Edward II. confirms to them wreck and royal fish in their lands or waters. The Bishop says that Clacton is part of his bishopric, and that he and his predecessors had had chattels of wreck of the sea *infra eandem villam per mare projecta seu evenientia*, and that the wreck in question was thrown by the sea *super terram ipsius Episcopi apud Clacton*. The judgment is not entered up. Exch. Q. R. Memda., H., 7 Hen. V. 22.

The Abbot of St. Osith is sued for wreck at East Mersea. The King recovered it against him. Ibid. m. 17d.

There was a similar commission issued out of the Exchequer on 18 December, 8 Henry V., A.D. 1420, for the counties of Norfolk and Suffolk, directing the commissioners to make inquiry concerning all usurpations and concealment on the King, and as to lands and tenements, deodands, treasure trove, and wreck of the sea withdrawn, detained, or concealed from the King, and all other concealments in the said counties; and similar commissions appear to have been directed throughout the kingdom. It is evident that the Crown rights were by no means neglected at this period, but we find no instance of any claim to foreshore being made by the Crown. Exch. Miscell. $\frac{819}{2}$.

The lord of Snitterley, in Norfolk, had a port there, and wreck of the sea in Carewell. Inq. p.-m. 9 Hen. V. 58.

The lord of Coatingham, Yorkshire, had wreck of the sea. Inq. p.-m. 3 Hen. VI. 32.

The court rolls of the manor of Bamborough of the time of Henry VI. shew presentments of wreck and royal fish as belonging to that manor. Ancient Miscell. Exch. 23-7 Hen. VI.

Year Book, Mich., 8 Edw. IV., plea 30.

In 8 Edward IV., A.D. 1468, an attempt appears to have been made to set up a custom in the county of Kent for fishermen to dig in the soil and to fix stakes in lands adjoining the sea to dry their nets. The custom was adjudged bad. The case evidently refers to land above high-water mark, but it was said in the course of the case by Choke, J.: "If I have land adjoining the sea "so that the sea ebbs and flows over my land, when it "flows any one may fish in the water which has flowed over "my land, for then it is parcel of the sea, and every man "may fish in the sea of common right; and when the sea "has ebbed, then in this land which was overflowed before, "peradventure the defendant might justify his digging, for "this land is no great profit to me." And thus he expresses a doubt as to whether a prescription to fix stakes on the foreshore might or might not be good; but it is clear from the case that the prescription claimed was to fix stakes above high-water mark, and this was decided to be bad as destructive of the inheritance. The case is cited in Sir Henry Constable's case to shew that the shore may be parcel of a manor.

V. Rep. 106.

Exch. Q. R. Memda., M., 11 Edw. IV. 36.

In 11 Edward IV., A.D. 1471, a writ of *certiorari* issued out of the Exchequer to inquire what liberties Sir Maurice Berkley, Knight, had in his manor of Berkley. The matter in question was his right to the return of writs. The return sets out a grant from Henry II. to Robert Fitzharding of "Berkelai et totum Berkelai Harness "manerium," with all its appendances, fully and wholly as it was in the time of King Henry I., and the charter grants that the said Robert Fitzharding and his heirs shall have the aforesaid manor, and all its appurtenances in churches, in woods, in plains, in feedings, in lands, in waters, in ways and paths, and in pleas, and in all things fully, quietly, and honourably, with toll and theam, and sok and sak, and infangenthef, with all its liberties and free customs, and acquittances which were there in the time of King Henry I. It also sets out a charter from King Richard I. to Robert Fitzharding in the same terms, and another charter by King John to Maurice son of Robert de Berkley, in the same terms. These are the charters under which the Barons of Berkley held the barony of Berkley and the soil of the River Severn, the title to which was tried in 16 Charles I., A.D. 1640, which trial is referred to by Hale (ch. 6), and which will be discussed later on.

By statute 11 Edward IV. (c. 7), the former statutes relating to weirs erected to the injury of navigation were confirmed, and further penalties were enacted upon those who maintained weirs to the injury of navigation; but this statute, like its predecessors, recognises the right of the owners of the weirs, provided they were not a nuisance to the navigation.

In 3 Henry VII., A.D. 1488, wreck in the manor of Filey was confirmed to William Beckwith.

Confirmation Roll, 3 Hen. VII., p. 2, No. 4.

In 14 Henry VII., A.D. 1499, claims of liberties in the county of Chester were made by the lords of the manors, and John Hokenhill of Shotwick claimed a liberty of fishery to the mid-stream of the Dee within the bounds of Church Shotwick and the castle of Shotwick, except whale, sturgeon, and thurlhead, and to have wreck of the sea, and he claimed by prescription. A quo warranto was brought against him in 15 Henry VII., A.D. 1500, to which he appears, and pleads that he and his ancestors have had the fishery within the bounds aforesaid, and by reason of the same do have all things, as well alive as dead, thrown up by the sea within the bounds aforesaid, except treasure and royal wreck. The Prince's attorney demurs that the words of his plea are general and doubtful; whereupon he rejoins that as to having wreck of the sea, it is to have all goods and chattels, as well alive as dead, thrown upon the sea-shore (*ad litus*) within the metes and bounds named in his claim, goods and chattels where any one escapes alive only excepted. No judgment is entered up.

Quo Warranto Roll, Cheshire, 14 Hen. VII.

Robert Grosvenor claims to have the serjeanty of the water of Dee, and to keep open the *filum aquæ* from nets unlawfully placed there, and he also claims a free fishery at Eton, and to fix weirs and to have wreck *super terram suam in Eaton; hoc est quicquid ejectum fuerit de aqua super terram dicti Roberti mortuum infra dominium suum extra cujuscunque possessionem prædictus Robertus illud habebit.* No judgment is entered up.

Thomas Massey of Podington claims a fishery within the bounds of his manor of Podington to the mid-stream of the Dee, and to have all profits except royal wreck and royal fish. There is a similar claim by Thomas Pole for his manor of Pole, and also by the hospital of Denwhall. A writ of quo warranto was issued against Massey, but whether proceedings were taken against the others we do not know, nor does the result appear.

In these cases, as in the cases referred to in the Quo Warranto Rolls of the time of Edward I., we see that there is no attempt to traverse the claim of the lords of the manor to the shore; and it is clear that there was at this time no conception of the theory of the *primâ facie* title of the Crown, nor any such title in the Prince in respect of the palatinate of Chester.

Exch. Miscell. $\frac{820}{45}$.

On 12 October, 13 Henry VIII., A.D. 1521, a commission was issued to inquire in the county of Norfolk concerning concealments, purprestures, encroachments, and usurpations upon the Crown.

Special Comm. 32.

A similar commission was issued for the county of Chester.

Doubtless there were commissions at this time in all counties, but we find no return of any claim to foreshore.

Exch. L. T. R., Memda., T., 1-2 P. & M., roll 6.

In 1–2 Philip and Mary, A.D. 1554, wreck was allowed to the lord of the manor of Stokenham, in Devonshire.

Sp. Com. 67.

On 11 May, 3–4 Philip and Mary, A.D. 1557, a general commission was issued to inquire into all lands concealed and encroachments on the right of the Crown.

CHAPTER IX.

THE REIGN OF QUEEN ELIZABETH.

THUS far, from the earliest times down to the end of the reign of Philip and Mary, we find no trace of any claim by the Crown to the foreshores of the kingdom as part of the rights of the prerogative; on the contrary, all the records which are forthcoming shew that the idea of such a claim did not exist. The Crown itself claimed the foreshore only when it was parcel of its own manor; and when it challenged the right of the subject to wreck of the sea taken upon his lands, that is, upon his foreshore, it tacitly admitted his right to the foreshore, and in no case traversed his claim that the wreck was his by virtue of a grant or prescription to take wreck *upon his lands.* We have seen that commissions were continually issued from the time of Henry III. downwards to make inquiry concerning purprestures, encroachments, and usurpations of the rights of the Crown, but no case is forthcoming to shew that any dealing by the subject with the foreshore opposite his land was ever returned as a purpresture or encroachment upon the rights of the Crown to any interest of property in the foreshore.

During the reign of Henry VIII. the needs of the Crown were supplied by the constant forfeitures of the subjects' estates under attainders for treason, and by the forfeiture of monastic lands throughout the kingdom. In the reign of Edward VI. a further accession to the income of the Crown was made by the forfeiture of the lands of colleges and chantries, but, in consequence of the obscurity of the titles, great difficulty was found in identifying the lands and seizing them into the hands of the Crown. Many lands and possessions were unquestionably concealed which ought to have been forfeited, and accordingly from the time of Philip and Mary downwards the officers of the Exchequer were very active in inquiring into these concealments. This they did by issuing commissions of inquiry, the returns to which stated and specified the lands so said to have been concealed, and upon them processes, by information and otherwise, were issued in great numbers, and many lands recovered to the Crown. A notion seems to have prevailed that usurpations of land against the Crown had been general and widespread, and there seems to have been a disposition on the part of the Crown to challenge almost every man's title. Some idea may be conceived as to the extent to which this was carried on when we find that, in the short reign of Philip and Mary, in the county of York alone upwards of a hundred informations were filed, these being only what are called Latin informations, quite irrespective of other processes by English information, and by quo warranto; and in the reign of Elizabeth there are upwards of seven hundred Latin informations (irrespective of other processes) for the county of York only. Commissions of inquiry as to forfeited or concealed lands were issued year after year in regular succession, and the kingdom was searched from end to end to discover the minutest fragment of land that was concealed, or alleged to be concealed, or the smallest right of the prerogative that was encroached upon, by every process which the ingenuity of the Crown officers and a class of persons known as "title-hunters" could invent. On the accession of James I. (knowing, as we do, what an exalted notion that King had of the rights of the prerogative) one is not surprised to find that the efforts of his officials were redoubled. This searching and careful inquiry into usurpations, or supposed usurpations, of the rights of the Crown not unnaturally brought into existence a class of persons known as "title-hunters," who made a regular profession of gathering information respecting titles in order to discover some flaw in them by which lands might be brought into the net of the Exchequer commissioners with a view to the impeachment of the title on behalf of the Crown, or the extortion of blackmail for a new grant to cure the supposed defect in the title. The manner of proceeding was as follows:—Upon the allegation of the title-hunter that there was a flaw in any particular title or titles, the Exchequer officers issued a commission at the suit of the title-hunter to inquire as to the lands alleged to be concealed, and the commissioners thereupon held an inquiry, which in most cases was a mere farce, and, indeed, seems to have been conducted in the absence of the persons interested, and a return was made that the land in question belonged to the Crown; thereupon the title-hunter procured from the Crown, for valuable consideration paid in money, a grant by patent of the lands in question, with a special power to cause informations and processes to be directed against the persons in possession at the suit of the Crown, and if he could succeed in recovering the lands he was to have them either in fee, at a rent to be ascertained by commission, or for a long term of years. These grants were called "fishing grants." Numbers of these grants exist on the Patent Rolls of the reigns of Elizabeth, James, and Charles I., and they comprehend at least half the lands in the kingdom. As soon as the title-hunter had got his grant, he proceeded to inform the persons in possession of the fact, and to suggest that they should buy his interest under the patent, or otherwise he would file an information against them. Many owners submitted to be blackmailed, although their titles in the majority of instances were indisputable, and took conveyances from these fishing grantees. The greater number set them at defiance, and the grantees did not proceed. In some cases informations were filed, and the owners for the most part succeeded in establishing their titles. Nor was the Crown careful to make the grant to one person only; it frequently happened that the first fishing grantee was unsuccessful in either blackmailing the owner or recovering the land, and then another more enterprising fisherman would take another grant of the same land, and try his fortune, and this frequently occurred; indeed, in some cases, where the owner had compounded with the first fishing grantee, the land would be again granted to another, who would suggest that the first patent was void for some reason or other, and so, as says Morant, "these ravenous gleaners upon "forfeited lands sometimes found game which other "sportsmen had overlooked, and, by fresh prowling grants, "came into what others had before paid for, but had not "particularly enough expressed to them by name." At this period there was no limitation of time against the Crown, and this state of the law opened up a wide field of adventure for these nefarious speculators, who, armed with all the powers of the arbitrary prerogative process, and shadowed by the authority of the Crown, contrived to make insecure every title in the kingdom. This being the state of things, it cannot be suggested that the rights and claims of the Crown stood in any danger of neglect at this period, and we have seen that this process is merely a development of the process of inquiry by commission, and by articles to the justices in eyre, which had been regularly and systematically carried on from the time of Henry III. downwards; but we shall see that, whereas before the time of Elizabeth no suggestion was made that the Crown was entitled by reason of the prerogative to the foreshores of the kingdom generally, shortly after her accession an ingenious lawyer, basing his argument upon the civil law and upon that portion of it which Bracton has incorporated in the earlier and less authoritative part of his work, set up the theory of the *primâ facie* title, and claimed for the Crown in the widest sense, not only the foreshore as between high- and low-water marks, but every piece of land which had at any time been subject to the flux and re-flux of the sea; and these lands, together with the foreshore, were, from the commencement of the reign of Elizabeth downwards, persistently claimed by the Crown throughout the whole kingdom as belonging to it in right of the prerogative, or as waste lands of the kingdom not granted out.

Hist. Essex, ii. 301.

King James I. early in his reign perceived that the

profession of a title-hunter was a lucrative one, and he accordingly, so to speak, took the business into his own hands. Instead of merely issuing commissions of inquiry at the suit of title-hunters, and then making grants of the lands returned, for comparatively small considerations, to these professional title-hunters, he issued a general commission to inquire concerning concealments and defective titles, and gave power to his commissioners to compound with the owners of such lands for the defect of their titles, and authorized the commissioners, "for ready money to be paid in hand," to bargain and sell the King's interest, to the owners, in such possessions the titles to which were conceived to be insufficient or doubtful in law. The recital of his commission is as follows:—"Whereas we are informed that there Pat. 9 Jas. I., p. 17.
"are divers of our loving subjects which of long time have "enjoyed divers manors, lands, tenements, and hereditaments, some by descent and others by purchase, the "which do, and of right ought to, belong to us as our "inheritance, partly by reason of the insufficiency of their "grants, and partly for that they have no grants of the "same from us nor any of our progenitors whereby they "can claim any colour of right thereunto; yet, nevertheless, we have nothing more in our desire than the "common good of our people, and especially in matters "tending to the general quiet and security of them and "their posterities for ever; and in that respect we, preferring their benefit before our own, and desirous to free "them not only from all suits which might arise between "us and them concerning the said manors, lands, and tenements, whereby they might be brought into the hazard "of the loss of their lands and possessions, but also to "give them a gracious and ready means by this our commission to pass the same from us for their good and "behoof, whereby all inconveniences hereafter may be "prevented, but also, by a moderate and temperate "execution of the said commission, they might with "less charges and attendance attain to a convenient "composition with us, and their estates thereby be well

"and sufficiently secured, to the small charge and great "benefit of them and their heirs for ever," &c.

The commission empowers the commissioners to settle values and rates of composition with the owners of the lands; and the King further empowers them to sell "all "derelict lands, salt marshes, fitty grounds, graves, sands, "meols, and salt holmes won, ingained, or left bare and "dry from or by the sea," and to compound with the claimants to them; and he enacts that the patents shall be drawn upon the warrant of the commissioners, and shall pass the Signet and Privy Seal and the Great Seal, and shall be valid against the King and his successors as if they had passed under the sign manual in the usual manner. Under these commissions, which were renewed from time to time, the commissioners drove a thriving business for the King, and grants for the amendments of defective titles were freely issued, the composition money bringing in a very substantial revenue. An instance of one of them occurs on the Patent Roll under date 10 June, 10 James I., A.D. 1614. It is a grant to one Sir John Coppin, who had recently purchased the manors of Great and Little Wakering, in the county of Essex, to which a large tract of the Maplin Sand was alleged to belong. The manors had been conveyed to him by his predecessor in title, with all "waters, ponds, pools, as well "salt as fresh, fishings and fishing crofts, fowlings, lanes, "oyster lanes, kiddels, fleets, creeks, havens, channels, "grounds, lands, and sands overflown with the sea, "out grounds, sea-shores, beacons and sea-marks, and "wreck of the sea." Coppin compounded with the commissioners for £166 13*s.* 4*d.*, and procured a warrant from the commissioners for his grant, which, for his further security, "the King passed his signature," and the patent granted him the manors, with "all marshes, waters, "water-courses, streams, streamlets, fisheries, fishings, void "grounds, wreck of the sea, &c., to the said manors "belonging or heretofore reputed parcel of the same;" and it further specially granted "all and all manner of "marshes, as well fresh as salt, lands sandy, rocky, and

Pat. 10 Jas. I., p. 23, No. 20.

"muddy, lands overflowed, lands subject to the overflow "of the sea, willow lands, lands within the flux and reflux "of the sea, and lands which have been recovered from the "sea or left by the sea, the sea bottom, shores, banks of "the sea, accretions made by the sea, creeks and rivers "whatsoever adjoining or adjacent to the aforesaid manors "and tenements, and other the premises, or to any one or "more of them near or next to the manors and tenements "aforesaid, and other the premises or any one of them "situate, lying, or being between the manors and tene- "ments aforesaid and the high sea, and also all our "beacons and beaconage there, and also wrecks of the "sea thrown up by the sea, or found upon the sea or "upon the sea-shore," as fully as the Kings of England or any of Coppin's predecessors in title held the same, and as fully as they then were in the King's hands; and the King covenants that the letters patent shall be valid against him and his successors, notwithstanding all defects.

By this patent, Coppin, whose manor had been out of the Crown from the time of King Richard I., and whose muniments of title shewed the clearest possible user of this foreshore, sought to clear any defect in his title to it and to finally establish the same; yet, notwithstanding this express grant, the Crown officers, in the case of Attorney *v.* Emerson, now deny the validity of it, and seek to recover the foreshore against the present owner. This case is a fair example of the mode of procedure by the Crown at this period in making profit of its claim to concealments and defects in title. Att. *v.* Emerson. Information.

But King James was not content with carrying on the business of compounding for defective titles; he still made grants to the title-hunters, and they still continued to blackmail the subjects under pretence of concealments, until at last this process of extortion was too burdensome to be borne, and in the twenty-first year of his reign the first statute of limitations was passed, entitled "An Act for the General Quiet of the Subject "against all Pretences of Concealment whatsoever," and 21 Jac. I. c. 2.

thereby it is enacted that the Crown should not sue, impeach, question, or implead any person concerning any manors, lands, tenements, rents, tithes, or hereditaments by reason of any right or title accrued or grown three score years past or more and then *in esse*, unless the lands had been in charge or stood *in super* of record in the Exchequer within three score years. By section 4 it is enacted that the subjects shall hold their lands of the King and other persons to all intents and purposes as the same should or ought of right to have been holden if the estates, rights, and interests *established and made sure* by the present Act had been, before the making of this Act, firm, good, and effectual in law, saving to every person and persons, bodies politic and corporate, their heirs and successors (other than his most excellent Majesty, his heirs and successors, and other than all patentees and grantees of concealments or defective titles, and all and every person or persons claiming from, by, or under them, or any of them, for, in respect, or by reason of any such patents or grants of concealments or defective titles), all such rights, titles, interests, estate, rents, commons, customs, duties, profits, and other claims and demands whatsoever, in or out of the said manors, lands, tenements, tithes, or hereditaments, as they or any of them had, or ought to have had, before the making of this Act, anything in this Act to the contrary notwithstanding. And by section 7 it is provided that no putting in charge nor standing *in super* by colour of any letters patent or grants of concealment, presentments by or by reason of any commission or authority to find out concealments, should be construed as a putting in charge, unless thereupon such lands, upon information or suit upon lawful verdict or demurrer, have been adjudged, ordered, and decreed to his Majesty within the said space of three score years.

This Act practically put an end to title-hunting for land above high-water mark; but the Crown does not appear to have considered itself bound by it in respect to land at any time overflowed by the sea, the position taken by the Crown officials being that no person could by any possibility have a title to such land unless he shewed express grant, it being assumed by them that no such land had ever been granted; and, as we shall see, attempts were made to recover marshes, derelict land, and foreshore down to the time of the Great Rebellion. We will now return to the time of Queen Elizabeth, and trace the proceedings as they appear.

In her reign the rights belonging to the prerogative were claimed in the strictest manner, and we shall see that now for the first time the doctrine was propounded that the Crown was entitled, by virtue of the prerogative *jure coronæ*, to an interest of property, as distinguished from an interest of jurisdiction, in lands overflowed by the sea. In the first six years of the reign, however, the doctrine of the prerogative was not set up.

In 3 Elizabeth, A.D. 1561, an information of intrusion was filed against divers inhabitants of New Romney, in Kent, for entering into 440 acres of marsh lying outside the town and walls of New Romney, and 60 acres of land called the Halrings, "which ought to be in the Queen's "hand *by reason of an exchange* between the Archbishop of "Canterbury and King Henry VIII." The defendants plead not guilty, and say that in 3 Edward VI., A.D. 1549, the jurats and commonalty of New Romney let the land to John Padiham for twenty years from Michaelmas 1553. Issue was joined and a trial ordered, but judgment is not entered up, the roll ending abruptly. In 4 Elizabeth, A.D. 1562, a commission issued to examine witnesses, who speak to the silting up of old channels and the inclosure of the marshes. On 28 November, 5 Elizabeth, A.D. 1562, another special commission was issued to survey the lands in Romney Marsh lately in suit between the Queen and the inhabitants of Romney, and to inquire what rents had been paid to the Queen's predecessor for the same. The jurors of the inquisition described the marsh, all of which appears to be above ordinary high-water mark except a salt marsh bounded by the sea on the south and east; and they say that the rents of these marshes have been paid to the Corporation of New Romney, and that the ex-

Exch. Q. R. Memda., M., 3 Eliz. 186.

Exch. Sp. Com. 1078.

Ibid. 1037.

Ibid 1186.

penses of inclosing them have been borne by the corporation's lessees. In this case the corporation seem to have come to a compromise, and it is particularly to be noted that the Crown was not suing under any claim by virtue of the prerogative, but alleges title apparently as lord of the manor—viz., *by reason of an exchange* between the Archbishop of Canterbury and King Henry VIII. The theory of the *primâ facie* title had not yet been invented.

Pat. 5 Eliz., p. 3. On 28 February, 5 Elizabeth, A.D. 1562-3, one Armigill Wade obtained a grant of the salt marshes, foreshores, and kidell grounds at Broomhill, in Kent, which are described below, they being then the property of Henry Guildford, at a rent of £200 a year. The grant alleges, by way of recital, that they were in the hands of King Henry VIII. *by virtue of an exchange with Sir George Harper.* Here again we see that there is no allegation of the *primâ facie* title of the Crown. The title alleged is an exchange from a subject. Mr. Wade had not invented the theory; that was reserved, as we shall see, for one Mr. Thomas Digges. Wade does not appear to have proceeded on Exch. Sp. Com. 2917. his grant for some years, but on 12 February, 10 Elizabeth, A.D. 1567-8, a commission was issued to survey and measure "the salt and fresh marshes called Washpits "Stoneridge, *Kidell-grounds*, William Finch's Salts, and "the Prior of Christchurch's Salts, in the parishes of "Lydd and Broomhill, in Kent and Sussex," which had been granted to him. The jury on the inquisition returned that "891 acres 3 roods are inclosed, and are in "the tenure of Philip Cockeram and others; that there are "302 acres salt marsh uninclosed; that part of the place "called Stoneridge is neither salt marsh nor fresh, but is a "great stony waste and beach next the *litus maris*, and "of no value; that the Kidell-ground is in Broomhill, and "is a sandy ground upon which the sea flows and re-flows, "on which kidell nets are set to catch fish, and is let to "farm at *7s. 4d.* a year." Wade subsequently conveyed his grant to Richard Smith, who, many years afterwards, filed a bill in the Exchequer against Guildford to recover the lands, but Guildford proceeded against him in Chancery, setting up his title to the premises; whereupon, in Easter, 34 Elizabeth, A.D. 1592, Smith procured an order of the Court of Exchequer enjoining Guildford to stay the proceedings in Chancery until the hearing of the cause in the Exchequer. No result appears, nor is there any further order in the cause in the Exchequer Records. It is probable that the suit was compromised, for we find later on that the rent reserved under the grant to Wade was paid, and was apportioned between the holders of the land on 7 December, 2 James II., A.D. 1686. This suit, it is also to be observed, was not a suit to establish the *primâ facie* title of the Crown, and yet we shall find that Mr. Digges, in the treatise setting up that theory, refers to this case and the case of New Romney as though the Crown had established its claim by virtue of the prerogative, instead of by making title under conveyances from the subject.

Exch. D. & O., East., 34 Eliz., fo. 37.

Exch. D. & O., series iv., xiv. 279, xv. 44.

CHAPTER X.

THE ORIGIN OF THE PRIMÂ FACIE TITLE OF THE CROWN.

WE now come to the first conception of the *primâ facie* theory.

About the tenth or eleventh year of Queen Elizabeth, A.D. 1568–9, one Mr. Thomas Digges[1] wrote a treatise entitled "Proofs of the Queen's Interest in Lands left "by the Sea and the Salt Shores thereof." The earliest MS. of this treatise occurs in the Lansdowne MSS., at the British Museum, No. 105, in a collection of documents

[1] Thomas Digges was the son of Mr. Leonard Digges, of Digges Court, in Barham, Kent, who was a celebrated mathematician and surveyor of lands. Thomas Digges, like his father, was also a mathematician and an engineer. He was also learned in astronomy, and is said to have been greatly esteemed by Dr. John Dee and his contemporaries. We find him in 1572 writing to Lord Burghleigh respecting some astrological observation about a new comet or star which had appeared, in which he says that he had waded deep in the paths of ancient astrology to endeavour to ascertain what its influence might be. In 1577 he was active in promoting a new harbour at Winchelsea. From 1582 to 1585 he was a commissioner for superintending the new harbour at Dover in conjunction with Sir William Wynter and Captain Burrough. On 10 November 1585 he was admitted to the Society of the Inner Temple, being described as Thomas Digges, of Barham, late of Lyon's Inn, gentleman. In the same year he was appointed Muster-Master-General in the Low Countries, which office he held until 1594. He died in 1595, and was buried in the church of St. Mary Aldermanbury. Besides the treatise here set out, he was the author of several works, which are described in a sketch of his life in the "Biographia Britannica," v. 238; in which work there is also a sketch of the lives of his father and of his son, Sir Dudley Digges.

formerly belonging to Lord Burghleigh, nearly all of which are annotated and indorsed by him. His indorsement on this treatise is "Mr. Digges. The Case of Lands left "by y[e] Seas," and Digges himself has indorsed it "Proofs "of her Majesty's Interest in Lands left by the Sea and Salt "Shores thereof. By T. Digges." The handwriting is that of Digges, as appears by comparison of a MS. in the library of the Society of Antiquaries relating to the improvement of Dover Harbour, which is written and signed by him. In the Lansdowne MS., at folio 55, there is a list made by Lord Burghleigh of suits made to the Queen for grants, and among them we find "for encroachments "on sea wastes concealed, Mr. Diggs." There is little doubt, therefore, of the authorship of the tract, and that doubt is wholly dispelled by a report of the argument of Plowden for the defendant in the case of Attorney *v.* Sir John Constable respecting the right to wreck and foreshore in the seignory of Holderness, in which he denies the *dicta* of Digges as follows: "and that which Digges "in his book, and also Robert Carey, say to the contrary "is of no regard, as they rely upon the saying of Bracton "in another part of his book." It is clear, therefore, that Digges is the author of the treatise which is set forth below. His original treatise was subsequently added to by him, and his fuller text, which is here printed, occurs in the Lansdowne MSS., No. 100, article 6. It is also in Digges' handwriting. Many other copies of it exist, and will be found in the MSS. referred to below.[1] There is also a document entitled "Arguments against the

MS. Hargrave, 15, fo. 95b.

1 MS. Cott. Vesp. F., iv. fo. 96: this is in Digges' handwriting. MS. Harl. 4717, fo. 1, temp. Eliz. Hargrave MSS. vol. 5, fo. 96; vol. 10, fo. 62b; vol. 98, art. 5; vol. 168, fo. 265; vol. 282, art. 2; vol. 425, fo. 11b and 47. Lansdowne MSS. 170, art. 5 and 6. MS. in possession of the Earl of Derby. State Papers Domestic, Car. I., vol. 339, No. 1: this copy is addressed to the Bishop of London, the Lord High Treasurer. MS. Harl. 1578, fo. 182: copy temp. Charles I. The treatise is also printed in a volume entitled "Miscellanea Aulica," a copy of which is in the Inner Temple library.

"Queen's Prerogative and Interest in Land left or gained "from the Sea and Arms thereof, with Answers to Every "Objection." This is also most probably Digges' work. It is printed from the Lansdowne MSS. 170, article 7, formerly part of the collection of Sir Julius Cæsar, and the Hargrave MSS. 425.

By this treatise was first invented and set up the claim of the Crown to the foreshore, reclaimed land, salt marsh, and derelict land in right of the prerogative. Mr. Digges boldly affirms that no one can make title to the foreshore or land overflowed by the sea, and says it is a sure maxim in the common law that "whatsoever land there "is within the King's dominion whereunto no man can "justly make property, it is the King's by his preroga- "tive." He admits that some subjects may have it by grant, but "whosoever holds it otherwise than by the "Prince's grant they intrude, and that no continuance of "time or prescription can serve their turn." He lays the claim of the prerogative as being in respect of the King's general ownership of the land of the whole kingdom—viz., that the foreshore is parcel of the great waste of the kingdom not granted out; "the fresh shore [he says] "belongs to the lord of the soil adjoining, the salt shore "to the general lord of all." Thus we see that from its inception until to-day the claim of the *primâ facie* title rests upon one basis—viz., that it is parcel of the waste of the kingdom and has never been *de facto* granted out, and that evidence of user and *longa possessio* avails not to give a title to it unless the grant be shewn. Upon this argument began the struggle between the Crown and the subject which has continued from that period to the present time. But it has been decided that Mr. Digges' argument is unsound in law. It is now settled that the foreshore may be shewn to be parcel of the manor by prescription, and, under the Statutes of Limitation, that possession or enjoyment, such as the subject-matter is capable of, for a period of sixty years displaces the theoretical title invented and first conceived by Mr.

Digges, based, as we have seen by the records set forth in the earlier portion of this treatise, upon an assumption manifestly untrue in point of fact, at any rate as regards by far the greater part of the kingdom, if not the whole of it; and yet we find the officers of the Crown still at this day persistently asserting Mr. Digges' contention, and still assuming that it is true in fact, as well as in theory, that the foreshore has not to any great extent been granted out. Upon Mr. Digges' theory they proceed from day to day, and have done so persistently since 1830, as if the theory were true in fact. When a question arises as to the ownership of a piece of foreshore, they institute no inquiry to see whether it has been granted out; they make no investigation as to whether the true owner can shew a sufficient enjoyment for the requisite statutory period; but they sell it or lease it behind his back, without giving him notice or opportunity to make good his claim; and if he asserts it by taking steps against some trespasser, or by doing any substantial act himself, they call upon him to shew his grant and his evidence; if he produces his grant (supposing him to have one in existence), they question its validity; if he produces his evidence of user, they treat it as usurpation, or endeavour to explain away the effect of it by alleging that his acts and those of his predecessors have been done in the exercise of his and their "rights of water frontage." They proceed against him by the arbitrary and unconstitutional process of information (without any previous inquisition to charge the land to the Crown), and they make him set out his title and discover his documents, and answer interrogatories of the most searching kind; they refuse any discovery of their own documents, and when he has done his utmost to set forth every scrap of information in his power, they arbitrarily amend the information without leave of the Court, and put him again through the same process, and then re-amend, and further re-amend, and further further re-amend the information *ad infinitum* arbitrarily at their own option and without control of the

Att. *v.* Constable. Information.

Att. *v.* Lowther. Amended information.

Att. *v.* Lowther. Att. *v.* Constable.

Court. They keep the suit hanging over his head for years until all his witnesses are dead, for they cannot be ruled on as an ordinary litigant can; and they have it in their power to crush him with costs which he is helpless to avoid, and this wholly and solely upon an allegation of a theory, a theory of fact which is untrue, and which was invented by the ingenuity of Mr. Thomas Digges in the treatise set out below.

Parl. Papers, 26 May 1868, No. 127.

A memorandum by Sir T. H. Farrer, of the Board of Trade, dated 1866, shews the view taken by the Crown officials to have been very much the same as Mr. Digges', though much mitigated by the result of the decisions of the Courts which have intervened since Digges wrote his treatise. Sir Thomas Farrer describes the duties of the Board of Trade with respect to foreshores, and says that the *first* of these duties is to ascertain "in "what parts of the coast the Crown has parted with its "rights, in what parts it is undoubted, and in what parts "the title is doubtful." But, having thus stated the duty, he qualifies it in the following remarkable sentence: "This "which logically ought to be the first thing to be done, it "will probably be prudent to postpone." This, as will be seen, is a mitigation of Mr. Digges' view, but the spirit is the same; and we shall see that as Mr. Digges acted upon his view, so the Board of Trade continue to act in precisely the same arbitrary manner, and their method of inquiry by which they should carry out the first duty which they themselves have set up is the method of Mr. Digges—viz., to assume undoubted ownership of the whole of the foreshore in the Crown, to let inquiry alone, but to file informations.

Having shewn the commencement, the origin, and the invention of the *primâ facie* theory, and having shewn its falsity as a theory based upon true fact, and having further pointed out that it is as full of vitality to-day as it was when Mr. Digges invented it, we here subjoin his tract.

Arguments prooving the Queenes Maties propertye in the Sea Landes, and salt shores thereof, and that no subiect cann lawfully hould eny parte thereof but by the Kinges especiall graunte.[1]

THE Prerogatiue of Princes is sutche, especially in this our natiue soile, that those thinges whiche by the lawe of nature were left in common, are by the lawes of this realme to the prince propre and peculiare: as wracks of the sea, treasure troue, Wayfes and strayes, and sutche like thinges, whereunto no subiect can iustly make propertye. And so lardge is the scope of these princely priuiledges that infinite cases may arrise whiche are not mentioned in the olde bookes of Prerogatiue Royall, and yet are thereto of dewtye appertayninge. As appeereth in the case of mines betweene the Queenes Matie and the Earle of Northumberlande decided in the Chequar Chamber, Where not only the Case then in question but many other were alledged duely appertayninge to the Kinge by Prerogatiue, and yet neuer mentioned in eny bookes of Prerogatiue: For our lawes beinge grownded upon the depth of reson dooe alway resonably attribute the woorthyest thinges to the woorthyest persoonnes, as in Mineralls gould and siluer are accounted Mines Royall, the rest beinge of baser sorte are left to the subiect, onlesse sutche baser Mines happen to bee confused wth the Mines Royall, for then bothe growe to the Prince as due by his Prerogatiue. In lyke sorte reson techeth that as the sea of all waters is the cheefe, and as *Salamon* sayth the fountayne whence all Riuers take theyr *Orriginall*, so the propertye thereof ought unto the cheefe the Kinge himself to bee attributed. For that no subiect cann haue propriety therein the Ciuill lawes plainly

[1] In MS. Lansd. 170, the title is "Arguments provinge that the "Quenes Highnes and her progenitors Kings of England are by the "lawes of the Corone just and lawfull owners of all lands and salte "shores wonne by any person or by any other meane of and oute of "the Seas."

affyrme, makinge a most manifest distinction betweene the sea, and fressh Riuers, and the shore of the one called *Littus*, and the other named *Ripa*, whereuppon I will first intrete and then proceede to euerye particular Questyon that may in this case be mooued.

MS. Lansd. 105, fo. 90, begins here.

Of Ilandes arrising in the sea, and of the salt shore compared wth the fresh.

Of landes risinge in the sea, and of the difference betweene the salt shore and the fresh, the ciuill lawe sayth thus.

Institut li[i] 2[i]. De Rerum Diuisione.

Insula quæ in mari nata est quod raro accidit, occupantis sit, nullius enim esse creditur: at in flumine nata quod frequenter accidit, si quidem mediam partem fluminis tenet, communis est eorum qui ab utraque parte fluminis propè Ripam prædia possident, pro modo latitudinis cuiusque fundi quæ latitudo propê Ripam sit; Quod si alteri parti proximior sit eorum est tantum qui ab ea parte prope ripam prædia possident.

Brittoune Cap. De Purchase.

Thus the ciuill lawes maketh manifest difference betweene Ilandes risinge in the sea, and in riuers, geeuinge the one to the borderers, the other Occupanti, whiche *Brittoune* also in his chapter of purchase expressly confyrmeth.

Cap. 2[o] li 2[i] De acquirendo rerum dominio.

Bracton also in his booke *De legibus et consuetudinibus Angliæ* in the second chapter of his seconde booke entituled *De acquirendo rerum Dominio* affyrmeth the verye same. But explaininge the sense thereof in more playne woordes, where hee speketh of those Ilandes that are thus geeuen occupanti, hee adioyneth thes woords *Et per consequens Regi propter suum Priuilegium.*

Ed. Jurip. i. 72.

Iustinianus De acquirendo rerum dominio.

Againe the ciuill lawes where they compare the salt shore w[ch] they call *Littus* wth the fresh w[ch] they name *Ripa*, they haue these sentences ensuinge.

Littus et Ripa quo ad vsum non differunt.
Littus et Ripa quo ad proprietatem differunt.

And towchinge the salt shore whoo shoold haue interest

therein there are in the ciuill lawes these woordes expressed.

> *Littorum quoque vsus publicus est quemadmodum et Riparum, at proprietas eorum potest intelligi nullius esse, sed eiusdem Juris, cuius est mare, et quæ subiacent mari, Terra, vel Arena.* *Justinianus De rerum diuisione.*

Heereby yt plainly appeereth that no borderer or lord of the soyle adioyninge, may claime eny interest in the salt shore, as they maye in the fressh, consyderinge that although in the vse they are publyck and therein agree, yet as towchinge the propertye they are repugnaunt, And therefore maye necessarily bee inferred that the Prince only hath proprietye in them. For yt is a sure Maxime in the Common Lawe that whatsoever lande there is w^th^in the kinges dominion whereunto no man cann iustly make propertye yt is the kinges by his prerogatiue. But the same maye thus bee manifestly approoued. *Brittoune Cap. de Pur. Bracton Ca. 24° li 2^i^ de acquirendo rerum Dominio.*

The Ciuill lawes whose assertion in this is not to bee disallowed (consyderinge many examples in the Common lawes confyrme the same) affyrme Ilands rysinge in the sea, or grownde, or sande coouered wth the sea, to bee of the same nature, right, and interest, that the salt shore is, But Ilandes arrisinge in the sea are flatly before prooued by *Bracton's* owne woordes to bee the Princes; I affirme and conclude therefore necessarily that the salt shore is the Princes also, *quo ad proprietatem;* for *quo ad vsum*, yt is publyck *Jure gentium*. *The proofe Brittoun of Purchase. Bracton Ca. 24° et 2° li. 2^i^ de acquirendo Rerum Dominio.*

Perchance yt maye bee doughted what the salt shore called *Littus* of the *Ciuilianes* is, and howe farre yt extendeth, whereunto I answere seinge there is no certaine diffinition therof in our lawe we must accept that diffinition wch vniuersally through the whole worlde is allowed, wch ensueth.

> *Est autem littus maris quatenus Hybernus fluctus maximus excurrit.* *De rerum Diuis.*

[1]Whereby yt appeereth that the salt shore, and so con-

[1] In place of this, MS. Lansd. 105 has: "Yt may perchaunce be "replyed Yt were very harde to admitt this diffinition; for then the

sequently the princes sea land, recheth as farre as eny *winter flodd roonneth* by the rigour of lawe, but for mitigation thereof *Bracton* hath these woordes ensuinge.

Bracton Cap. 2º De acquirendo Rerum domino.

Vbi autem Flumen alueum sibi non constituit in agrum meum, sed illum inundauerit, non immutatur species quantum ad proprietatem. Sed vbi flumen abstulit mihi prædium meum per aluei constitutionem, deindê redit ad antiquum alueum, de jure stricto in agro quondam meo nihil possum mihi vendicare: Flumen enim alueum sibi constituendo agrum priuatum facit publicum.[1]

Heereby yt may bee inferred likewyse in the seas, that *Inundation* by rage of floodd taketh not awaye propertye from him that iustly had yt before, onlesse yt have possession thereof, and make his settlinge thereon in sutche sort that the bowndes and lymitts bee defaced. And so yt appeereth the sea surrownding eny mans inheritance, and defacinge the boundes therof, by contynuance of time geeueth the propertye to the Prince: wch is also evidently collected by the 93 case decided in the booke of Assises *Anno* 22º *Ed.* 3^tij where yt is doughted that *Inundation* only by an arme of the sea maye take awaye a mans proprietye in his lande.

Assisarum 22º 93º.

But herevppon arriseth an other question, wheth^r prescription maye serue my toorne to prooue my propertye in the salt shore, whereunto I answere no: and prooue yt thus, The propertye that the Kinge hath in the salt shore yt is *Ratione Priuilegij*, and of the nature and effect of those *Priuilegia Bracton* hath these sentences ensueinge.

Bracton, Cap. 24º De acquirendo rerum dominio. Stamford De Prerogatiua Regis.

Ea vero quæ dicuntur Priuilegia licet pertineant ad Coronam tamen à Corona seperari possunt, sed de gratia ipsius Regis speciali; Cuius gratia et concessio specialis si non interuenerint, tempus à tali petitione Regem non excludit, Nullum enim tempus currit

" rage of a tyde overflowing my grounde should take away the pro-
" priety thereof from mee and geeve yt to the Kinge. This is answered
" in Bracton where he hath these words."

[1] Mr. Digges' extracts from Bracton are much garbled and inverted.

Donationi Regis vel contra eum in hoc casu, cum probatione non egeat: constare enim debet omnibus quod huiusmodi pertinent ad Coronam, nisi sit aliquis qui docere possit ex speciali gratia habita contrarium.

Also in an other place entretinge of priuiledges.

In hoc casu se defendere nemo potest quamuis præ se ferat seisinam longi temporis, In his enim diututurnitas temporis non minuit iniuriam, immò auget: In alijs vero vbi probatio necessaria fuerit currit tempus contra Regem sicut contra quoscunque alios.

Where presedents in our lawe faile *Bracton* hath a very sentence howe wee ought to procede.

Si aliqua noua et inconsueta emerserint et quæ prius vsita non fuerint in Regno, si tamen similia euenerint per similia iudicentur, cum bona sit occasio à similibus procedere ad similia. *Bracton li. 1o. de rerum diuisione.*

Yt appeereth manifestly that the Prince hath greter property in the grownde of his ports and harberoughes, then eny borderer or Lord of the soyle adioyninge to eny fresh riuer hath in the bancks of the sayd riuer; ffor notwthstandinge his propertye euery man maye tye botes, fasten anckers, and cast netts vppon his banck, But no man cann lett faull an ancker vppon the Kings grownd in eny porte wthout leue, And payinge therefore to the Kinges Officers for that purpose by pattent appoyncted. *Anchorage paid in all Portes.*

Agayne yt is against all reson to admitt the Kinge a propertye in Wracks, wch both *Iure Naturali, Gentium,* and *Ciuili,* is geeuen *Occupanti:* and to denye his interest in Ilandes, Shelues, and the salt shore, wch by the same lawes are attributed *Occupanti* also. *Cum de similibus idem sit Iudicium.* *Bracton, Ca. 12o. li. 2i de rerum Diuisione.*

Yf occupation, or ffindinge, might geeue propertye of eny thing yt shoold of sutche as are mooueable, rather then of thinges fixed and constant, as wee may behoulde in fisshes and ffoules, where our lawe (by permission of the prince) alloweth the proprietye *Occupanti,* as the Naturall and Ciuill lawes doothe: But in wracks, wch are not lyuinge thinges, but of more fixed and permanent *Bracton, Cap. 4o. li. 2i. de acquirendo rerum Dominio.*

nature, seinge our lawe will not admit the possession or occupation [of] enye propertye, mutche lesse in lande a thing moste fixed and permanent, yt ought to purchase propertye: And therefore yt is an argument *A Fortiori* that seinge wracks are alotted to o[r] prince by the lawes common, muche more of equitye ought the shore, shelues, etc. in the sea; wherewith agreeth the presedents of former princes grauntes, where they have geeuen mannours wth their appertenances, and then annexed these woordes, *Et totum littus vsque ad medietatem aquæ.* And these presedents are to bee seene in recorde of soondrye princes in diuers places sithins the Conquest, and heerew[th] accordeth the custome and vsadge of the land that straungers paye vnto the prince anckoradge for brekinge of her grounde.

Old Presedents.

18 *Ed.* 3[tij]. Also yf eny man dought of the princes interest in the sea let him consyder the statute in 18. Ed. 3[tij]. where hee licenceth his sea shall bee open to all marchaunts for traffick.

Yt maye be farder alledged a greate noomber in this realme haue of the salt shore, and thinck they haue as good propertye in yt as in enye other of their lande or inheritance.

I answere, true yt is, a greate noomber in this Realme possesse part thereof, and hould yt iustly, for they haue yt by pattent from the prince as they haue wracks faulling against their Lordshippes also, but whosoever hould yt otherwyse then by the princes graunte, they intrude, and in this case *Publicus error non facit legem*, no contynuance of time or prescription can serue their toorne, as yt is before prooued by *Brittoune* and *Bractons* owne woordes *De Priuilegijs*, w[ch] also is alledged and vsed as lawe by M[r] Stamford in his booke of the princes prerogatiue.

Stamford In Prerogatiua Corone.

Thus yt manifestly appeereth that in the salt shore mutche lesse then in wracks cast vppon the salt shore a man maye not prescribe, and this is the cause why wracks by our lawes are adiudged the kings w[ch] by the lawes ciuill were geeven *Occupanti*, ffor that by the lawes ciuill they stande in one predicament, I meane the salt shore, and wracks cast on them, by consequens of reson yt muste followe that by our lawe beinge in one predicament also, are therefore bothe the Kinges.

Thus the premisses well wayed and consydered I maye necessarily conclude, that as in Riuers and fressh shores or bancks called *Ripe*, the Lordes of the soyle adioyninge hould a propertye. So in the greate salt riuer I meane the sea enuirroninge the whole Ilande, and in the salt shores thereof, the greate and cheefe lorde of the whole soyle the Kinge himself only muste haue interest and propertye, and no man ells nether by prescription nor eny other waye, salue only by the Kinges especiall graunte maye claime propertye in them. As concerninge the vse bothe of the fresh and salt shore whiles they remayne shores they are and muste bee publyck *Iure gentium*, But so soone as ether by the w[th]drawinge of the waters from them, or enye other accident, they beecoome to leue the name of shores, the vse of them becoommeth priuate. The fresh shore to the Lorde of the soyle adioyninge, The sault shore to the generall Lorde of all. And as the trees that growe on the bancks of the river bee priuate to the Lorde of the soyle adioyninge, although the vse of those bancks bee common. So the commoditye of grasinge or whatsoeuer frute els the salt shores yeelde, ought to bee priuate to the Kinges vse, although the vse of them in respect of dryeinge Netts, tyinge botes, etc. bee publyck.

[1]So that not only from the lowe watermarck downward but also upwarde to the full sea, so highe as naturally by

[1] This passage is altered in MS. 105: "So that not only the sea land "from the lowe water marke downwarde but also upwarde to the full "sea, which properly is called Littus, and in English the sault shore, "must of necessitye be the Princes, onlesse enye man cann shewe howe "the sea hadd woonne the same from his mannour, and that he hath "notw[th]standinge alwaye kept the boundes thereof, so that at the lowe "water his sayd boundes are to bee seene: for in that case in deede yt "is doughted in the 22[th] of the booke of assizes, whether an arme of the "sea by subite encrease wynninge a mans land, and ouerflowinge the "same shall take away his propertye and interest therein. But onlesse "the boundes be in suche sorte preserued that it bee euident howe farre "his said mannour reached, yt is out of question as well by the same

Bracton Libro 2º. Ca. 24º. Britton Cap. de purchase. Assisarum Cas. 93 ann. 22º.

ordinary course euery mooneth w^th^out rage of the wynde or wether or other rare accident, so farre I saye as the sea hath by sutche his naturall course flowde: so farre extendeth the princes land the wch yf yt bee at eny time amplifyed and incresed by the withdrawinge of the sea, the prince is to receyve the benifyte therof, and the subiect that entereth thereuppon intrudeth, and in this case no prescription cann serue his toorne, because the prince is entituled thereto by the priviledge of his Croune.

Assisarum. Cas. 93. Anno. 22°. The 93 Case in the 22th yeere of the booke of Assises plainly prooueth that yf the sea by litle and litle frett awaye eny mans grownde, and wynne vpon his land by slowe increse and processe of time, that the owner vtterly lost his propertye and interest therein; ffor yt is there concluded that enye fressh riuer in the wch a priuate person hath propertye maye in that sorte gaine soyle to his Lord: Mutche more ought the Kinges riuer the sea or armes thereof to purchase soile to his Lorde by sutche kynde of *Aluvion*, And this moste plainly is approoved by the processe of the same case, where coomminge to subite increase wch may properly bee termed *Inundation* or violent ouerflowinge, yt is resolutely adiudged that no priuate persons riuer can by suche soodayne *Inundation* wynne or gaine his lorde an other mans soyle, but of the sea, or enye arme thereof, the judges leue yt doughtfull. Belyke in respecte of the dignitye and preeminence that the sea hath abooue other priuate waters, or for that the Kinge whoose water yt is ought in all cases to haue a prerogatiue before enye subiect or priuate person, yt were therefore extreme iniurye to barre the Kinges streme that right of gayninge soyle by slowe increse called *Alluuion*, wch the lawes have adiudged due to the streme of eny priuate subiect.

"place of the booke of Assises, as also by the places heeretofore cited "out of Bracton, Britton, and the whole coorse of our Lawe, compared "with the Ciuill, that in the sault shore no man cann purchase pro-"prietye but from or by the Prince." The text in "Misc. Aulica," p. 244, has a marginal note, "Carlisle's Case," *i.e.*, Att. *v.* Philpott, *post*, p. 260.

[Yt is farder to be noted howe in this self same case yt is determined that euerye Riuer that dooth ebbe and flowe, so farre as yt so doothe yt, is an Arme of the sea.] Not in MS. 105.

Yt might perchance seeme vnto some an errour in o^r^ lawe or an abuse, that contrary to the lawes naturall, and ciuill, wee shoold debarre the ffinder or fyrst possessor his proprietye in wracks, tresure troue, and sutche lyke common thinges, wch by the lawes of nature and ciuill is geeuen *Occupanti*, That is to the first possessor as *Brittoun* translateth the same: But yf this bee duely wayed our lawe shall bee founde no waye repugnaunte to those lawes *Naturale*, *Gentium*, or *Ciuile*, ffor that wee attribute wracks, tresure troue, Ilands rising in the sea, or armes thereof, and the salt shore also, *Occupanti*, as they dooe. But wee inferre consequently thereuppon w^th^ *Bracton* the title of the prince, consyderinge the Kinges reche is lardger then a priuate persons, his handes stretcheth through his realme, and therefore is sayd to bee the firste seasour and possessor of eny sutche newe accident, And eny other that shall seeme to finde or possesse the same is to bee taken as an intruder vppon that wch the prince by the prerogative of his dignitye had first seased; In proofe whereof I might produce the case of *Alienation* of goodds by the Kings villane before mannuall seasure, alledged in the case of mines reported by *Mr. Ployden*, and many other in the same case vowched wth infinite other examples and similitudes in o^r^ lawe plainly confyrminge the premisses but in a case so euident these maye suffice.

Justinianus Lib. 2° de Rerum diuisione.

Bracton. Cap 2° li 2^i^. Occupanti. Et per consequens Regi propter suum Priuilegium.

MS. 105 ends here, and only adds late precedents in Kent—the three cases of Romney, Bromhill, and Dover; and then it adds a note of Mr. Chute's case.

Yt maye perchance bee sayd howe generally men that haue possessions adioyninge to the sea syde, vse when the sea is gone to put sheepe and other cattell vppon the salt shore, and so euerye man occupyeth of the same so mutche as lyeth against his grownd, and wynne the same from the sea yf they cann, and this is generally vsed, and therefore lawfull by customee.

Yt maye bee answered that true yt is sutche custoome hath bin vsed, and is yet in use, to the greate decaye of

Publicus error non facit legem. manye good harberoughes and Rodes for shippes. Euen so is yt commonly vsed also yf enye logg of wood, or other wrack of small value, be caste vppon the shore, the Tenaunt adioyninge taketh yt, not that hee hath eny right thereto, the same beinge in deede the Kinges, but that yt maye bee trewly sayd *De minimis non curat Rex*, and therefore for sutche base wracks, and for the salt shore while yt lyeth open to the sea and litle woorthe of yt self, Kinges respect them not. But yf wracks more pretious happen, or that the sea abandon the same sault shore whereby it becoome of value, then is yt no reson that the permission of princes to the subiecte to intrude on trifles shoolde priuiledge them in the rest, The princes right being in deede alyke to bothe.

Custome. And as for Coostome the prince is tyed by oath as well to abolish corrupte and unlawfull Customes, as to mainteyne good and lawfull, I confesse there were certaine priuate custoomes, as gauell kynde, and others, w[ch] were by the prince in this realme permitted, and sutche customes are noted and remayne in Recorde, but this intrudinge on the princes sea landes, and salt shores, is none of them, but vtterly vnlawfull, and therefore to bee abolished and refoormed.

Pollicye. Againe yt will bee sayd although yt were vnlawfull yet were yt in *Pollicye* sufferable, because in sutche sorte by the subiects industrye the lymittes of the realme and *Jurisdiction* of the Prince is enlardged, I answere the *Jurisdiction* of the Prince is nothinge incresed, forasmutche as the princes *Jurisdiction* is as well on the sea as on the lande, but yt were an ill exchandge to lose *Proprietye Jurisdiction.* *Proprietye*, for *Jurisdiction*, where bothe of duetye to the Prince therein are due. Againe these ynninges beeinge as by experience yt is manifest the verye cause of the vtter ruine and decaye of harberoughes, and thereby of *Nauigation*, and so consequently a generall hurte and wekeninge to the Realme, yt is *Pollicye* therefore moste requisyte that the Princes right shoold severely therein bee examined, and that sutche Intrusions shoolde bee more exquisytely poonished, then eny other, for that they doo not only robbe the Prince, but also hurt the whole Realme. In deede I confesse in sutche places where land maye be gayned from the sea w^th^out annoy to eny harberoughe, yf the subiect sewe for Charter from the prince to wynne land, in regard of his trauell and chardges hee maye wth reson craue yt at an easy rate, But for eny man to attempt the same w^th^out Charter yt is as *Bracton* saythe *Grauis presumptio contra Regem, et Dignitatem suam, et est quasi crimen Furti*, and woorthy of greter poonishment then the losinge of that hee hath vniustly intruded on. *Bracton Cap. 3°. De Corona.*

Of Landes swared vpp wth the Soyladge of the sea.

Yt is a question to bee mooved yf the sea breake into my owne lande wch neuer was knowne at eny time to bee parcell of the salt shore, or ouerflown wth salt stremes, whether the same shoold therefore change his proprietye and becoome the princes. Hereto I answere yf the same *Inundation* bee soodaine by force of tempest, and afterward in conueniente time be againe expelled, the owner shall not lose his propertye: But yf yt rest thereon ebbinge and flowinge *Anns et Jours*, the resons before alledged well wayed and the Custoomes of other Coontryes well consydered, where so absolute power to the prince is not assigned as in ours, yt plainly appeerethe I cannot claime yt but by the princes Charter, consyderinge yt is become parte of the sea shore wherein no man maye clayme proprietye but the Prince only.

But if the sea bringe in soyladge, and the same reste thereon in sutche sort that it sware vpp and ryse higher by reson of the sayd sea lande, as in manye places by the sea coast yt happeneth that lowe grownde by the sea soyladge is swared vpp a fadome and more in heigth; there yt cannot bee denyed but that place becoommeth entierly the Princes. For the whole grownde that shoolde bee ploughed or otherwyse manured is entierly the Kinges sea lande. I am not ygnorante that it maye bee obiected howe bothe in the lawes ciuill and o^r^ common lawe also

Bracton Cap. 2° lib. 2i De acquirendo Rerum Dominio.

this is a good ground *Solo cædit quod solo inædificatur*, and theruppon maye inferre that forasmutche as the soyle was mine before the sea cam on yt, therfore all sutche lande as the sea bringeth in shoolde also bee toorned into the nature of the soile. But this reson is esely many wayes confuted: ffor first the Ciuill lawe maketh a manifest difference in this case, betweene the sea and all other thinges, saying ewhere all other thinges are toorned into the nature of the soyle, the sea contrariwyse toorneth the same into his owne nature. And heereof yt coommeth to pas that yf the sea dooe violently breke into my lande, although yt bee my ancient Inheritance, all ffisshermen maye coome on yt and drye their netts and dooe eny other thinge thereon, so long as the sea hath his ordinary course thereon, and I cann haue no action of trespasse because the sea by flowinge on yt hath toorned the same into his owne nature. And this is a ruled case in our lawe.

Agayne wheresoeuer eny thing of the princes coometh to be mixt inseperably wth ought of a subiects, they becoome bothe the princes by prerogatiue, and this is manifest by the case of the mines betweene the Queenes Ma^ty^ and the Erle of Northumberlande, because gold wch is the princes mine was mixt wth copper, the prince hadd the copper also, but I dare bouldly saye, land swared vpp wth the Queenes sea soylage is more inseperably mixt and harder to be seperate then those *Mettaline* substances, and therefore must of necessity bee entierly the princes.

And this is also conuenient in respect of the benefite of the whole Relme, for if eny man haue landes lyeinge nighe the sea coast which may bee bettered by letting in the sea, yt is an esye sute to the prince to haue licence, so as yt bee founde not to annoye enye Harberough or Rode for shippes; but for eny subiect to dooe yt of his owne hedd, as yt is *Gravis præsumptio contra Regem, et Dignitatem eius*, as Bracton sayth, so is yt also moste pernitiouse for this whole estate consyderinge the vtter decaye of Hauens in many partes of the Realme especially in Kent hath growne thereby:

Howe a man may lose his propertye and right in his landes beinge surrownded and possessed of the sea or Armes thereof.

That lerned Judge *Bracton* hath a Chapter in his second booke *De acquirendo rerum Dominio* thus entituled, *Qualiter acquiritur Possessio per Vsucaptionem*, wherein hee plainly sheweth howe enye priuate subiect being free-borne wthout eny title or interest maye (by quyett possession for long time) in lande of an other mans purchase proprietye, and that the right owner by his negligence and sufferance shall in time vtterly lose his right, but in what time the same maye coome to passe hee hath these woordes "*Sed quam longa esse debeat non definitur à Iure sed ex Iusticiariorum discretione*," referringe the limitation thereof to the Iustices discretion as a thinge (at that time) by lawe not determined, belyke for that in seuerall cases seuerall times are alotted. But in sea cases of all other less time for translation of proprietye is requyred, as appeereth by the Case in the Common Lawe where yt is decided that yf a shippe of eny subiect in this lande bee once taken and possessed by an adversarye, and yet after recoouered by an other subiecte from the Aduersarye, the firste hath vtterly lost his propertye in her, although shee were but one daye possessed by the Aduersarye: Againe in landes possessed by an Adversarye I maye for example produce CALES, where manye priuate subiects hauinge Inheritance, theyr landes were violently by the Aduersarye seased, I thinck there is no Lawiar doughteth but that the owners haue so farre lost their propertye therein, that yf yt were gayned or recoouered againe no one of them coold claime propertye in their old possessions, no though they did hazard their liues and reueneewes for the wynninge againe thereof, but that yt shoold wholy rest at the princes disposition, so farre is their interest gone in that land wch by their negligence or sufferance either wilfull or constrayned the Ennemye had once seased and possessed: Nowe for application of this I saye, the sea is an Aduersarye no lesse raginge and implacable then the forenamed, the wch after yt hath once seased on my lande that I haue no hope to remooue yt of, but sufferr yt quietly to possesse the same, I auerr by the former example my propertye in that lande is gone, and whensoeuer after this contynewed possession by mee suffered yt shall departe and leue the same, I muste saye wth Iudge *Bracton, In agro quondam meo nihil possum mihi vendicare*, but howe long the sea shoold possesse yt to take the proprietye from the owner, the Iustices must determine by *Bractons* opinion ; In mooueables a daye sufficethe as is before sayd in the case of a shippe taken on the sea, And for lande in Flanders a yeeres possession of the sea geeueth the land to the Kinge. So that yf eny mans land bee there drowned although yt be by subite increse, yf hee sufferr yt so to remayne wthout endeuour to recouer yt againe one whole yeere yt is theyr princes and at his disposition to lett or geeue to whome hee list.

Also the lawes ciuill *Per Confusionem* alwaye geeue property *Digniori* wch is also ratefyed in our lawe, as appeereth in the case of Mines decided betweene the Queenes Matie and the Erle of Northumberland in the Chequar Chamber, where yt was resolutely adiudged because the Riall mines were confused wth the baser, Copper etc., wherein a priuate subiect maye haue propertye, yett *propter Confusionem* they went bothe *Digniori*, and are altogether the princes: sutche is the lawfull prerogatiue of Riall Dignity. Wherfore I auerr in lyke sorte that yf the sea wynne vppon my land and deface the bowndes, there is confusion wth the princes sea land, and therefore *Vtrumque cedit digniori* by the lawes ciuill, ratefyed by the lawes of this realme, and the prince is iustly entituled to bothe, wherewth agreeth the custome of sutche as by Charter occupye parte of the salt shore for they diligently preserue their bowndes, sayinge yf those their markes goe to sea the land is the princes againe :

And this is the verye case of *Broomehill* in Kent, wch was abowte an 100 yeeres sithins surrownded of the sea in sutche sorte that at springe tydes yt was wholy drowned, and at lowe water nothing but oase and mudd, yet soome Monuments of the Churche and howses still remaine, and dyuers haue evidence of their lande there to shewe, but the bowndes beinge defaced, and thus of the sea so long possessed, the prince is iustly entituled to yt, and at this present leaseth yt out and receyueth rent for yt.

Also the lawe is *quod omnes metæ Forestæ sunt integræ Domino Regi*, and in lyke sorte the bowndes betweene England and Scotland are wholy to the Prince, albeyt the Lord Dacres, Mr. Grey and manye other haue land adioyninge vnto them, so that the seas and their salt shores beinge *Metæ seu muri huius Regni* are entirely the Princes, as is also before prooued: but perhappes a question may bee mooued howe farre this salt shore doothe extend and howe yt is to bee limited.

To this I answere, although by the rigour of the lawe the salt shore dooe reche as farre as the gretest winter ffloodd dooth flowe, yet dooe I suppose the lawe and lawfull custoome of the realme will thus interprete the same, that yt bee taken no farder then the sea by Naturall course not enforced by rage of wether doothe rise. ffor all men that haue possessions by the sea side make walls to fense out the rage of waters, not disturbinge the ordinarye course of the sea: so that those walls maye bee trewly accounted the bowndes of mens possessions, and the residue is left to the sea and parcell of the salt shore, wherein no man may haue proprietye but the Prince or his Assignies; And if the sea by rage of wether dooe breke downe my waules, and sease on my Inheritance, yt shall not for sutche soodaine *Inundation* take my propertye from mee, but that I maye in conuenient time ynne and recoouer the same againe, but yf I sufferr the same to lye subiect to the salt water so long that my waulls and bowndes bee defaced, then is yt out of question the Princes *propter Confusionem* as is aforesaid.

Forasmutche as by the premisses yt is prooued that the sea lande and salt shore so farre as the sea by naturall and ordinarye course hath flowne is the

Princes, yt is requisyte soomwhat to saye of the naturall ordinarye, and unnaturall extraordinarye courses of the sea howe they differr.

Iohannes de Sacro bosco lib. de sphæra.

And towchinge the naturall course of the sea yt is to bee noted that as there is euerye daye twoo ebbes and two flooddes, so is there also euerye Mooneth twoo coorses of greate tydes and scant tydes, ffor seuen dayes after the chandge are the greate tydes, wch they call commonly springe tydes. And then the other seuen tydes more that dooe ensue are small tydes, commonly called Neape tydes. And then the next quarter after the full moone are the springe tydes againe, All the last quarter of the moone coome the Neape tydes, wch course of the sea is thus moonethly renewed for euer. And these springe tydes bee as Naturall and ordinarye as the Neape tydes.

But other spring tydes there are wch happen commonly in the springe of the yeere, and likewyse in autumne, soomtime also in the sommer after plentye of rayne, and in the winter by rage of wynde, or wether, or other extraordinary accident, wch rise mutche abooue his naturall and ordinarye course of the seas, and soomtyme ouer flowe the bancks of marshes adioyninge to the sea, as appeereth heere in the Temmes howe soomtime by sutche extraordinarye tydes the medowes are drowned, albeyt the naturall spring tydes that of course coome euerye Mooneth woorck no sutche effect, the one beinge vnnaturall and tempestuous, the other ordinarye and by course of nature, so that these extraordinarye springe tydes drowninge a subiects lande, ought not in equitye, whatsoeuer the rigoure of the lawe bee, to take awaye a mans freehould, but that when the salt water is gone hee hath his land agayne ; but so farre as the sea by naturall course of these ordinarye springe tydes doothe flowe, yt is the salt shore, and propre sea lande, wch none cann challendge but from the Prince.

LATE PRESEDENTS IN KENT.

And in this Princes time wee haue presedents of this case. First at NEWE ROMNEY where the sea left lande and the Townes men possest yt almost twoo hoondred yeeres, And yet they are becoome the Queenes ffarmers and pay her Ma^{ty} rent for yt.

Also at BROOMEHYLL wch was surrownded wth the sea and nowe left againe, and at this present the Queenes Matie receyueth rent therfore.

Also by DOUER certaine houses were built vppon Lande by the sea syde wch in times past was part of the salt shore, for the sea at full water did flowe uppon yt, And nowe the Prince receyuethe rents for these howses, And yt is yeerely gathered by the Surveyo^{r} and payd into the Exchequar.

Also for proofe of the princes interest in riuers flowing from the sea, the Temmes and Conseruation thereof only was not geeuen to the Citye of London, but by their especiall sute the Kinge gave therwthall the grownd and soyle vnder the same, whereuppon yf enye that hath a howse or lande adioyninge dooe make a strande, stayres, or sutche lyke, they pay foorthwth a rent to the Citye of London, howe highe soeuer they bee aboove the lowe water marck, sutche is the Princes interest in all riuers that ebbe and flowe.

There are of these gifts a great noomber in soondry places of Kent wherby menn iustly hould the salt shore by the Princes graunt.

Also in *Magna Carta* yt is expresslie set downe y^{t} the *Justiciarius Itinerarius* shoulde amonge other concealem^{ts} of Lands from the Kinge make especiall enquirie De prepusturis factis super dominum Regem in mari wch is also menconed in *Bracton*, wherebie it is evident that in those daies no man durst intermedle wth the shores of the Sea, or to appropriate any parcell of them to him selfe wthout the King's Charter, but he was for to be presented for an intruder, as is also evident by this case ensuinge of the Abbot of Ramseye.

MS. Lansd. 170, has this passage.

In memõrand Sccij, Dñe Regine nunc Elizabeth, apud Westmonaster, de A° xliij°. Edwardi tertij viz. inter Record de Termino Scte *Trinitatis Rotlo xiij° ex Rem. Thesaurarij ipius domine Regine.*

In that pleadinge the Abbott was charged for intrucõn on certaine Sea Lands viz. *Quod appropriauit sibi et Domui suæ mariscum apud Brancester sine licentia Domini Regis.* This Abbott was faine to come to this Issue. *Absque hoc quod ipse aut aliquis suorum predecessorum appropriauit sibi et domui suæ aliquem mariscum sine licentia Domini* Regis, wherebie it plainelie appeareth that if the iurie had found that he had helde the said Lande *sine licentia Regis* that judgement had past for the Kinge, wherebie it is evidentlie to be concluded as well upon this presedent as by infinit other reasons and arguments that no man ought to encroche on the Sea or shores thereof w^th^out the Kings especiall Licence or Charter.[1]

Arguments against the Queenes Prerogatiue and interest in Land left or gained from the Seaes, and armes thereof wth answeres to euerye obiection.

The first obiection.

THE Seas by the Lawe Civill and also *Jure naturali* are comon, and therefore euerye man at his pleasure maie wime from them what he canne, and take it for his purchase; for that such comon thingse are of comon right geven *occupanti.*

Cicero de Officijs.

Institutionum lib 2 de rerum diuisione.

True it is that Jure naturali the seaes are comon so likewise is the earth and euerye other thinge whatsoever, for as *Cicero* saithe *privatum natura nihil est.* But the Civile Lawes and all suche as comment on them confesse that even as of olde time private men, eyther by first

[1] I trace no rent paid for New Romney or Dover. As to Broomhill, see p. 178. Rent for wharves on the Thames was only paid within the City boundaries. The presentments in eyre were all against encroachments on the *jus publicum* (*ante*, p. 45). The licence in the Ramsey case was licence of mortmain (*ante*, p. 158).

discoverie or antique possession, might purchase propertie in suche particula[r] tenements as theye possessed and by lawe of nature were cōmon, even so maie kings *absolute princes* and *comon* weales doe in the Seas adiacent to their *Territories.* And for example of *Ciuilians* is produced the *Estate Venetian* who haue to them selues vendicate such absolute prerogatiue in the *Adriatike* seas as it is not there lawfull for any to gather amber or other comoditie that those seas yelde, ne yet to make or sell salte of theire seas made but onlie *set marcks* to the use of the state. And in this estate regall of Englande wee see that the King[s] of most auncient times haue in the right of theire crowne helde the seas abowte this Ilande so proper and entire unto them as not onlie whatsoeuer treasure, precious stones or other comodities of any value, the seas shoulde yelde or caste up upon the shores, were and are of dewtie reputed the Princes, but also all wracks whatsoeuer (that almost no prince hathe) are here in respecte of the king's most absolute prerogatiue and right in the seas entirelie adiudged his. Nay it further appeareth that although the Kings of England haue benne content to suffer fishermen *Jure gentium* to enioy to theire owen use such fishe as by theire charges travill and adventure they can in the Englishe Seas take, Yet haue the Kings of England for remembrance of this theire favoure that the memorie of theire propertie in the Seas shoulde not be extinguished, alwaie res(er)ved to them selves the cheif fishe as *Sturgeon Whale* &c. And also to make it manifest y[t] the soile of the seas is also intirelie the King's, no man can let fall any anchore in any roade aboute this Realme but he paiethe for breakinge the King[s] grownde to the officers of the Kinge. Hereof it cometh to passe y[t] the L: Admirall hathe in his pattente *Anchorage, Buyage* &c. So that wee maie necessarielie conclude, that suche manner of purchasinge propertie by occupacion was of auncient time where contries laie wast not inhabited by anie nor w[th]in the limitts of any kings *Territorie.* And also at this daie whosoeuer should by navigacion discouer in the *occidentall oceane seas* anie Island or other wast

Stampford de Prerogatiua Regis.

Bracton, lib 2. de acquirendo rerum dominio, cap. 24.

Anchorage Buoyage.

ground or land beinge hetherto not annexed to any Kings *Territorie* and not inhabited might *Jure naturali* at this daie by such Invention and occupacion iustlie claime

A Maxime. proprietie; but where *Jam diu diuisa sunt rerum dominia* there suche kind of purchase *Jure naturali* cannot hold; and in this Realme of Englande lest of all other, for it is a grounde or maxime in o^r^ lawes that there is no lande w^th^in the King's Dominion, but it is either the land of the Kinge or of the Kings naturall subiecte. And againe there is no lande of any subiect but he holdeth it mediate or immediate of the crowne of Englande, so that there is not lefte w^th^in the Kinge of Englands Dominion anie place to purchase per occupationem, w^ch^ *Bracton* in his booke *de acquirendo rerum Dominio* expresslie reuleth, shewing howe an Ilande risinge in a publicke stream *occupantis est.* And therefore inferreth with these words. *Et per consequens Regi propter priuilegium suum.* And generallie in Wracks treasure troue, and all sutch things as *Jure gentium* are geven *occupanti* by the custome of this realme as *Bracton* saith they are the King's *per priuilegium.* And therefore whatsouer he be, subiecte or other, that shall enter upon anie wastes of or in the seas shores of Englande intrudethe upon the Kinge of Englande's inheritaunce, *Ratione priuilegii,* and suche contempte of the Kinges priuilege is as Bracton saithe *grauis præsumptio contra Coronam et Dignitatem eius est quasi crimen furti.*

Bracton, cap. 2. lib. 2, de acquirendo reru dominio.

Bract. cap. 3, de corona.

The second obiection.

Also *Ex æquitate* the borderers or lande Peers that haue theire possessions lieinge to the sea shore maie claime suche advantage as by the departinge of the seas or other encreasment by the seas maie happen in respecte that theye onlie by the rages of the Seas receive detriment wth soundrie charg^es^ in Scotts Lotts and otherwise to defend and reinforce theire bankes.

This reason woulde debarre the Prince not onlie of these sea left lands but of all wrackes also, for a man maie in like sorte frame his reason thus: the seas by rage of weather have broken into my lands and drowned a thowsande or twoe thowsande of my sheepe or other cattell, and at the same time or some other by like rage throwethe vpp in the same place a shipp or other wrack worth a thowsand or twoe thowsande pounds whereof no owner is knowen, I might therefore by this argument claime this wrack to recompence my damage. But as no suche reason was ever judged availeable to debarre the kinge of his wracke, much lesse ought it in this case for sea lands, consideringe marshe lande is of suche valewe as over and aboue all charges by waie of scotts and lott or otherwise in cleare cōmoditie surmownteth the best vplande respectivelie taken, & by the due observacon of this prerogative, the borderers shall for a surplusage receive this farder benifite that the Queenes tenante lieinge nowe between the sea and him shall quite defraie him of suche charges as he was before put unto in fencinge his lande, and so shall more beneficiallie and wth lesse or moe perill thenceforth enioy the same; And therefore cannot *ex æquitate* (havinge this vndeservede benifite) claime wth any reason these lands of the Queenes and of dutie to the Crowne appertaininge *Ratione priuilegij*. *Argumentum a Simili.*

The thirde obiection.

> Yt is an usaunce and custome cōmonlie vsed that whereas the sea giveth place & leavethe any lande or wast grownde to anie manes freeholde, the same owner or lande peerer occupieth the same, and holdeth it a purchase or perquisite to his lande, and this beinge generallie vsed is therefore lawfull by custome.

As for this obiection of custome it is of all other the wekest, for the Kings of Englande are by othe as well bounde to abolishe corrupte eronious and vnlawfull customes as to upholde good and lawfull customes. Lawfull are well knowene and remayne of Recorde, as in Kent Gavilkinde, in other places Borough Englishe and such like wch by permission of the Prince were and still are allowed. But this kind of Intrusion on Sea lefte Lands *Customes Lawfull & Unlawfull.*

is none suche, but corrupte unlawful and iniurious bothe to the Kinge and also to the whole realme (the rewin of havens that waie proceadinge) and therefore to be abolished and reformed. Further noe such corrupte usage thoughe ioyned wth prescription is available to take awaye the Queenes inheritaunce, being to her Mat^ie^ due *per priuilegium Coronæ* as *Bracton* saith for *Error quamuis publicus non facit legem* where the Kinge is partie, ffor by manie presedents in our Lawe we see between subiecte and subiect, Customes if theye be unreasonable, reiected; much more in this case tendinge bothe to the robbinge of the Kinge and annoyaunce publick of the navie of this Realme. But this error is not indeed so publicke as the intruders will pretende, consideringe that manie haue purchased the Kings Pattent for suche Lands and therebie holde them iustlie and in most places theye kepe perfitt [perfect] bounds of such theire lands and mainetaine wth great dilligence theire sea marks, Insomuch as theye haue it for a vsuall proverbe amonge them that if those theire marks goe to the Sea the Land is the Kings. And this custome of kepinge the bounds & marks to descerne theire owen from the Kings is an honest lawdable custome, but when they shall perceive the Sea to leave more grounde, then to lose there olde marks to steale lande from the Kinge is a fraudulent vsaunce, and not to be permitted; unlesse we wold also permitt men to carry merchandize uncustomed, becawse it is an vsaunce that hath bin accustomablie vsed and secretlie practized almost in all places of this realme. But if this *Error* had bene so publick that thereby borderers might lawfullie haue encroched on the Seas, or any the Kings Streames, and held such soile as the seas had left unto them; what neede men in theire Pattents haue procured and taken beside these words *Manerium cum pertinentijs.* Also theise words *Et totum littus*, as there is to be seene in pattents very auncient even from *William* the Conqueror in divers Kings times, and also pattents that haue besides *Manerium cum pertinentijs* also *cum Accrescentijs Maris*, whereby they thinke to carrey such lands as out of the

Anno 8, Ed. 4, a fortiori.

The errour not publique.

A Graunt of Mannours to the Abbot of St. Augustine in Canterburye.

A Pattent to an auncestor of Sr Thomas

Seas are to theire Manno^r accrewd, or what needed *Romney* towne, wch had so long bin seazed of certaine sea Lands to theire Towne accrued, beinge sued in the Exchequer for intrusion thereon, haue procured the Kings Pattent takinge the said lands from the Prince payinge a Rent perpetuall for the ffee fearme, and givinge for a fyne five hundred Pounds, if any such lawfull custome coulde haue bene found as should haue serued theire tourne. Nay it plainelie appereth that seinge the said towne beinge one of the five Ports, and in that respect endowed wth most ample previleges and immunities havinge so large a scope in the Seas as even to the lowe watter marke and as farre beyonde as any horsman could ride and reche wth a lawnce, wracks and all other comodities was there owene; and yet that notw^thstandinge could not in right hould that land they had so long possessed w^thout the speciall charte^r of the Prince in that behalfe; much less ought any other, hauinge no such preveliges ne yet the like cawse to be favored that a Port Towne hathe, claime or presume to detaine such lands of the Queenes, but rather hold themselves favourablie delt w^thall if they sustaine no further punishment than partinge wth that they haue uniustlie deteyned. And it is to be thought that in all times men haue for such land sought the Kinges Pattent, for in the Isle of *Greyne* and other partes in Kent there is greate number of acres of salts wch the occupio^rs paie unto the Prince for a peny for euerye acre till of late findinge it an easier waie & lesse charge slylie to steale such land, then by sute to the prince dulie to purchase the same, haue benne content to vse it as theire owen, thinkinge either in time it willbe past knowledge or if the worst happen, and that they be taken wth the manniour, yet doubte not for some trifle to purchase it, as latelie the Towne of Hithe hath of my Lord Wentworth passinge theire saltes in his Booke amonge other concealments for no greate rent. Fynallie if under colloure of any such corrupte unlawfull usance it might now be rewled that the borderers might lawfullie enter on such Sea Lands, The Queenes Matie in one place should lose the ffee simple of so much land as is well

Gouylford of the Manner of Iham.

Anno 8 *Reg: Eliz.*

A Fortiori.

Hithe Towne become Tenants to the Queene for the like Land.

wourth, and at this present lette or to be lette for aboue fyve hundred pounds per ann. The thinge I meane is called *Bromehill*, wch beinge recovered from the Seas is (as of duty it ought) in her Ma^ts^ hand.

See p. 178.

The fourth obiection.

Ed. 3, Ann. 22.

Againe the case of a River in the Booke of Assises that by little and little frettinge in longe processe of time may purchase to his owner an other mans soile, will heare be alledged to make for the borderer, because this kinde of Sea Coast landes is by litle and litle and in longe processe of time forsaken and left to the borderer's lands.

That case in the Booke of Assises cannot any way be haled to serue the subiects turne in this case of sea left landes, but flatlie to the contrary, if it be substantially considered: howsoever at the superficial shewe yt may seme otherwise, for that case is of a ryver, this of the Sea; that of a water wherein a subiecte may haue, and is supposed to haue nor in truth can haue property. Further that case of the Assises only sheweth howe a river by continual motion in processe of time may gaine soile to his Lord, but of this watter nowe in question consideringe there is not ne can be any other Lord but the Kinge (as the only Lord of the Englishe Seas), all Land thereby accrewinge must of necessitie by the selfe same case be inferred to be the Kings; ffor in this case is not supposed any watter of a subiects that should by such slowe motion purchase to his Lord land, yea fullie it is by that case approued that if the Sea or any Arme thereof doe by litle and litle in longe time fret, minishe and wynne any subiec^ts^ land, so as the olde bounds be defaced and not to be founde, that the owner hath utterly lost his propertie therein. And the Lord of the Seas must haue the same. For that booke plainly ruleth it that by such slowe encrease or flowinge any private subiects water may purchase to his Lord another subiects land. It were therefore mere sencelesse partialitie to debarre the Kings streame that

This case full wth ye Prince.

prerogatiue that the lawes haue adiudged due to the streame of any subiect, ffor it is to be inferred *a fortiori.* But to remoue all scruple and doubte, it is in the same cased ruled that Armes of the Sea haue such a prerogatiue aboue other Subiects Waters, that albeit the Judge flatlie ruled that a private subjects streame by sodaine encrease or inundacion should not gaine an other subiects Soile, yet of an arme of the Sea the Judge made an exception, leaving it wth a *Quare* as a thinge verie doubtefull whether *Bras du mer* by sodaine inundacion drowninge did not purchase his Lord a subiects soile, and the olde owner to lose his propertie. For these are the words, *En tiel hastiue encresse ne doit nul home perdre son soil si la Riuier ne soit bras du mer.* Such especiall prerogatiue the graue auncient Judges of this Land did knowe the Kings streames ought to haue before the streames of any priuate subiect. Wherein the Civill lawes also seme to concurre, for they say that this marvelous property the sea hath, that whereas all other things geve place to the soile subiect to the same and become of the same propertie; in the sea, saith the Ciuile Lawe, it is contrary, for wheresoever the Sea cometh it turneth the Soile into his own nature and maketh it *Jure gentium* comon: *Et per Consequens*, as *Bracton* saith, by the custome and lawe of this land the Kings. This is also worth the notinge, that any greate river cominge into the seas is by that case ruled to be *Bras' du mer* so farre as it ebbeth and floweth.

A flatt difference ruled in law betwene bras du mer and other riuers.

Bras' du mer 2nd.

The fifth obiection.

> Howsoever the Lawe be, it is good pollicie, consideringe the Case is verie universall and concerneth a multitude of such as haue lands adioyninge to the Sea Coast, to permitt such ordinaunces to the Coasters, as well for that the Kings realme and iurisdiction is thereby enlarged, as also subiects thereby allured to inhabite the frontiers.

This obiection standeth uppon three partes. It concerns a multitude, it enlargeth the Kings Dominions, it peoplethe

the frontieres: whereunto it may be truly answered, the multitude is not so greate that it concernithe, for althoughe the sea invirone the whole Iland yet is it not likely that it hath in all partes abandoned the Shores, and left encrease of Land as it hath upon these Coasts of England that frount *Zeland*, where the Sea hath wthin theise houndred yeres frett away and drowned a greate parte of divers Islands as Zuithenland and Beererlyet, and a greate country by *Keijmerswale*, by the drowninge whereof it may be thought the sea wynninge on that side hath lost on the coasts of *Kent* and *Essex*. But admitt it did concerne a multitude, Is it therefore pollecy to neglect Justice? The like reason might be used in defence of unlawfull transportacons wch is more universall and the multitude five fould greater then of those that practise these intrusions, but bothe the one and the other beinge but priuate benifites and publicke wrongs, they ought in pollecy and justice to be redressed. Neyther is it treuly said that thereby her Majesties Realme and Jurisdiction is enlarged, consideringe the Jurisdiction of her Mat^{y} recheth as well on the Sea as on the Land; but if it were, yet were it slender pollecy for the Prince to leaue propertie for jurisdiction where both of duty to the Kinge doe appertaine; especiallie wthout charter whereby the subiect should occupy the Kings Landes wthout rent paying, and yet holde him selfe no whit the more bound for it. And as for habitation or *peoplinge* of the frontiers, very experience proveth that by sufferance of these lande peeres thus to encroch on the Seas, they kepinge it in theire owen handes and employinge yt wholy to grasinge of bests, neuer encrease one howshould on the coast, but leave thereby the sea side so naked as a man maie see a thousand acres of Land able to norishe twentie howshould and not so much as one little cottage upon them, Whereas contrarywise this land might by the Q. Matie be lett unto such severall Tennants & for such mean rates as in respecte of the easie rents they should pay unto her Matie should build on the coast and replenishe the frontiers wth people. Further these tenaunts of the princes beinge lymitted what and howe much they shall Inne and in what places they shall forbeare, the havens of this Land shall not in such sort hereafter be decaied and destroyed; this lawlesse & licentious Inninge of sea Lands and neglectinge or rather contemninge of the King's prerogative being the only cause of the spoile of so many notable harboroughs, as by the vyage of all sea men on the whole Coast and by the othe of a greate number of persons of discression on the sea coast and by soundrey Commissions hath bene approved. Therefore seing besides the Kings right to this kynd of Sea Lands, it shall also in due pollicy manie wayes benifite the weale publicke, redressinge for the time to come that mischefe of Havens decaie (a matter of noe small momente in this o^r^ land). I thinke there is none of any sounde Judgement that canne or will dislike the severe reformacion of such *Errors* and due execucion of her Mat^ies^ prerogative in that behalfe.

The decay of the hauens caused by encroch-ments on the Seas.

CHAPTER XI.

PROCEEDINGS BY DIGGES.

DIGGES being in negotiation for a grant of concealed wastes, we find a commission issued out of the Exchequer on 4 July, 13 Elizabeth, A.D. 1571, to five commissioners (one of whom is William Digges, Esq.) to inquire according to the following articles:—

Articles to be enquired of on the Queenes Maties behalfe as followethe, viz.:

1. In primis, whether do ye knowe any Mannors, Landes, tenements, Medowes, pastures, fedynges or other heredytaments whatsoever within or adjoyninge to the Countye of Kente at any tyme heretofore covered or surrounded with the salte water or the Sea ye or no, or landes which the sea or salt water hathe lefte drye and forsaken?

2. Item, what ware the names of suche Mannors, Landes, tenements, and other the premisses so surrounded, what do they conteyne by estimation, where do they lye, and howe longe sythens they ware so covered and surrounded?

3. Item, whether do ye knowe any suche Mannors, landes, tenements, and other the premisses so surrounded to be ynned, landed, and recovered from the salte water or Sea, in what place, or places, are the same so ynned or recovered & by what person or persons, and howe longe it is sythens the same was recovered or ynned?

4. Item, in whose tenure or occupacion, possession or holdinge are suche Mannors, lands, tenements, and other the premisses so ynned and recovered, and whether the Quenes Matie hathe bene annswered of thissues and profitts thereof frome the tyme of the recoverye or occupation of

the same hitherto, ye or no, & to whatt yerely value the same be of?

5. Item, what former Charter or Lawfull graunte frome the Prynce any suche Occupyers, possessors, or ynners of the sayde landes, tenements, and other the premisses have whereby to holde, possesse, or occupye any suche Sea lande pertayninge to her Matie her prerogatyve?

6. Item, what Comyssion or Lycense any suche possessors, occupyers, or ynners of the foresayde landes have frome the prynce wherby they myght or maye lawfully ynn, enclose or wynn frome the Seas any kynde of landes, tenements, and other the premisses, and whether theire Lycence or comyssyon, yf they have any, do extende to the inclosinge of the fornamed Landes, &c.

The Return which was delivered to the Exchequer by William Digges on 23rd February, 14 Eliz., A.D. 1571–72.

Wee finde from Nuenden to Apuldoore, & so from there to the sea on ether syde the salt streames and crickes in dyuerse places, lands & tenements heretofore surrounded wth the sea and salt water in the hands and possessions of Thomas Stace yeoman, George Chute gent, Edward Hales gent, Willyam Holmes yeoman, Thomas Thorneton, Robert Gouldinge, Rychard Coovert, and others in sundry places lyinge disparsedly, soome ynned from the seas, but the most commonly overflown wth salt water, and as yet not bearinge grasse, to the yearly value of xxxs̃.

Item wee finde aboute Lydd a waste grounde full of peeble caulled the Ripe, and other land thereto adjoininge heretofore surrounded and coovered with sea and saulte water, and dyvers other landes and tenements uppon the seashore, and crickes of saulte water abowt Rumney and Hide, in thoccupacõn of Thomas Hoonywoode, John Edolf, Thomas Harunden, John Stragee, Rychard Knekchball, and certaine Lands also aboutt Iveychurche & Medley, and other Crickes and Creches of the sea and saultt water, some enclosed from the Sea, soome at Sprynge tydes over flowen the most parte as yet bearinge no grasse, woorth XLs̃ ꝑ annũ.

Item wee finde in dyverse Crickes and Creaches of the sea landes and tenements betweene Hyde and Dover, and abowte the peere of Dover, and from thence betweene yt and Sandwiche, abowt the Ile of Thanet, & abowte the Streame of Sandwiche on ether syde, and abowt Reculver streame and Whitstable dispersedly heere and there certaine places of saulte Marshe heeretofore coovered wth the sea, and yet usually drowned wth salte water; and soome also inclosed, in the possession of Pawle Johnson, Sr Henry Crips, Sergeaunt Looveless, Sergeaunte Manhood, John Fileux, and others, woorth ꝑ annũ XLs̃.

Item we have presented abowt Faversham, Milton, Iles of Hartye, Shepay, and Groyne, and other crickes thereabowt, and on both the sydes of the stream of Rochester and the sea coste in the Hoondred of Hoo, and on Kent side uppon the Arme of the Sea that runneth by Gravesend, a few plotts of small value, heeretofore coovered with sea and sault water, and at many tydes now drowned, woorth by the yeere fyve Nobles.

Dyvers of these foresaid lands have in time past been so covered wth the sea that shypps might and have sayled over them, And as yet for the most partt are commonly at springe tyde surrounded and coovered with salt water. And we cannot learne that the Queenes Matie receyveth any rente for them. And this is as mutche as we can learne by the Juries sworne and soommoned from sundrie parts of the Sheere, whose names are hereunto annexed.

(Signed) THOMAS KEMPE
JOHN GOLDWELL
WILLIAM DIGGES

It will be observed that the commissioners return practically the greater part, if not the whole, of the foreshore and salt marsh in the county of Kent as belonging to the Crown. A comparison of this statement with the charters to Kentish monasteries, and the proceedings as to wreck set forth in the earlier part of this treatise, shews clearly that this return was made purely on the assumption of Digges that no one but the Crown could own land covered by the tide.

Immediately after the issue of this commission, the Queen, by patent dated 25 July, 13 Elizabeth, A.D. 1571, granted to Thomas Digges, and "promised to assure and "assign to the said Thomas Digges and his heirs and "assigns in fee farm, all such and as much of the manors, "lands, tenements, and hereditaments of the same lady the "Queen whatsoever within or adjacent to her county of "Kent theretofore covered by the sea and by the work of "God, or otherwise recovered from the sea, whereof the "issues and profits were not then or after the recovery "thereof were not answered to the same lady the Queen, "or which thenceforth hereafter by the industry or means "of the same Thomas Digges, his heirs or assigns, should "be so recovered, which should be revealed and found out "by the same Thomas Digges, his heirs, executors, ad-"ministrators, or assigns, or any of them, by survey, in-"quisition, information, or otherwise, within the term of "seven years next following: to have and hold to the said "Thomas Digges and his heirs and assigns for ever, "rendering rent for the premises, to be ascertained by "survey, with authority to the said Thomas Digges, with "the consent of the Court of Exchequer, to direct and "appoint any commission or commissions to any one to "whom it shall seem good to him for the due execution "of the premises." This grant is the earliest specimen we have of what are known as "fishing grants," above referred to. Pat. 13 Eliz., p. 9.

This grant to Digges was the first attempt to set up the *primâ facie* title of the Crown to foreshore in a practical manner.

Digges, immediately upon receiving his grant, proceeded to file an information in the Exchequer against George Chute, Edward Cressy, and others, for "50 acres of land "heretofore inundated by the sea lying near Appledore, "whereof part was inclosed twenty years since, and also "for certain lands near the vill of Hydde [Hythe], for- Ex. Q. R. Memda., M., 14 Eliz. 346.

"merly inundated by the sea, containing 50 acres, which "on 14 February, 13 Elizabeth, A.D. 1571, and long before "and after, are, and of right ought to be, in the hands of the "lady the Queen, as in right of her crown of England, "by reason of her prerogative, as in very many records, "rolls, and memoranda of this Exchequer more fully "appears of record."[1] The defendants appear and plead not guilty, and put themselves on the country, and for a plea they say that the barons and inhabitants of Hythe are seised in their demesne as of fee of the said lands adjacent to Hythe, and by indenture dated 20 June, 13 Elizabeth, A.D. 1571, leased them to Edward Cressy for twenty-one years. The Attorney-General confessed the plea, and entered a *nolle prosequi*, and judgment was given for the defendants in Hilary, 15 Elizabeth, A.D. 1572–73. We shall see, however, that Digges procured a new grant; and he subsequently induced the Corporation of Hythe to purchase it from him. The foreshore at Hythe is at present in litigation between the Crown and the corporation.

MS. Lansdowne 105.

In Chute's case we have a memorandum made by Mr. Digges, in which he says:—"The said Chute hath "pleaded for answer how it is a parcel of his manor of "Whoorne: Whereupon, although we might demur in law "and prove, albeit it had once been a parcel of his said "manor, yet an arm of the sea joining the same from his "manor, and so long having possession thereof, his pro- "perty is gone, and the right wholly invested in the "Prince, as well for that her Highness' stream had so "long possession, as also that being confused with other

[1] This allegation referring to the Records of the Exchequer refers to the commission and return set out above, and it was necessary to allege it, because it would seem that if the Attorney-General will make a suggestion for the King to entitle him to any inheritance or freehold without matter of record to induce him to do that, it is void, and all process upon it is void (Dyer 73b). This report does not shew that the Court so decided; but in all informations we find the same allegation of title by record (Coke's Entries, pp. 372, 376, 378, 381). The usual course appears to have been to issue a commission out of the Exchequer and get a return that the land in question belonged to the Crown, and thereupon to found the information.

"her Majesty's sea lands, is by prerogative royal grown "into the same nature; yet forasmuch as it is a thing so "well known to the country that this land had ever been "subject to that arm of the sea till it was (partly by "natural removing of the sea and partly by the borderer's "avarice) gained from the Prince's salt stream (the same "land never being indeed parcel of any man's manor), "we have taken this issue that it is not parcel of his said "manor, and are content to be tried by the country, to "whom the verity of the cause is apparently known." There is no record of the trial, nor of Chute's pleadings thereat, but Chute was clearly successful, and defeated the claim of the Crown as set up by Digges.

Digges filed another information, against Hebblethwait and others, in Trinity, 14 Elizabeth, A.D. 1572, setting forth that a certain waste called the Rype of Lydd beach and Holmstone, being full of pebble stones and sand, together with other lands to the same belonging heretofore, inundated with the sea on 14 February, 13 Elizabeth, A.D. 1571, and long before and afterwards are, and ought to be, in the possession of the Queen, *by reason of her prerogative*, as in the Records of the Exchequer appear, and charges intrusion by the defendants, who appear and plead not guilty; and as to the intrusion, they say that the bailiffs, jurats, and commonalty of the town of Lydd were seised of the said waste land and tenements in their demesne as of fee, and by lease dated 22 July, 13 Elizabeth, let the premises to John Hebblethwaite by the name of all those their lands and grounds called the Rype of Lydd, and all their lands and grounds called Holmstone and back to the same le Rype pertaining and belonging, except a right of pasturage and passage, and except the holme trees and bushes in the Holmstone. The Attorney-General confesses the plea, "and because Thomas Digges, "Esq., upon whose relation the aforesaid information was "exhibited, does not appear, nor shews any evidence for "the maintenance of the information," the Attorney-General enters a *nolle prosequi*, and judgment is given *eant sine die*. These informations are the first that set up the *primâ facie*

Exch.Q. R. Memda., T., 14 Eliz. 97.

title of the Crown as part of the prerogative, and it is to be observed that they were unsuccessful.

Sp. Comm. 1186. On 10 June, 15 Elizabeth, A.D. 1573, Digges sued out a fresh commission to inquire as to salt lands in Kent, in the same form as that above set out. It was returned on the 15 October, 15 Elizabeth, A.D. 1573, and the survey sets out lands at Apledore between high and low water marks; also at Quenton Manor, *alias* Ebney Court, Hythe; Cheyne Court in the parishes of Ivechurch and Medley; and also at Newton and Belgar nigh Lydd. "Item, wee "finde a parcell of land in the occupation of William "Hammond gent, or his assigns, standing west on Rich-"borowe Castle, south and east towards the channel of "Sandwich haven, north on the Mannor of Fleete, the "wch heretofore was surrounded by the natural course of "the sea, and part thereof inned from the sea by the said "William Hammond: There are also betweene the same "and the channell about 30 acres of salts, the wch at the "inninge of the other were verye sea, and are yet usually "drownded at hye tydes, the wch together wth the other "we rate at Vš ꝑ annũ." This last-mentioned piece of shore was the subject of the case of Att. at rel. Digges *v.* Hammond, referred to hereafter.

Pat. 16 Eliz. p. 6, m. 9. By letters patent dated 7 February, 16 Elizabeth, A.D. 1573–74, the Queen, reciting the former grant to Digges of 25 July, 13 Elizabeth, A.D. 1571, and reciting the commission and return of 10 June, 15 Elizabeth, A.D. 1573, above described, grants the whole of those lands to Digges and his heirs, with a proviso that if it was duly proved that any part thereof had been granted out by the Queen's predecessors in fee farm, this patent to be void as to that part. The patent also gives Digges power to embank and inclose the lands.

Dyer 326b. The law with regard to land relinquished by the sea was evidently doubtful at this period, as appears from an anonymous case, reprinted by Dyer, in 15–16 Elizabeth, A.D. 1573. He states that it is a question whether the King shall have it by his prerogative, or the adjoining owner as a perquisite, and inclines to the latter view, citing the Abbot of Ramsay's case, 43 Edward III., *ante*, p. 158, and Digges *v.* Hammond, *post*, pp. 220, 221.

In Michaelmas, 15 Elizabeth, A.D. 1573, an information was filed at the relation of Digges against Will. Holmes, Thomas Stacey, and others to recover *quoddam vastum marinum* lying between Gilforde Marsh and Newenden, on either side of Appledore Stream, Kent, and the New Innings at Appledore and others, marshes and foreshores. The information charges that they were in the Queen's hands at the date of Digges' patent, and long before, by reason of the prerogative. The defendants plead not guilty. Issue is joined. Stacey sets out title under Sir J. Guildford; *absque hoc* that the Queen was seised in right of her crown by reason of the prerogative. On this plea *Curia adv. vult.*, and the case was adjourned till All Souls, 16 Elizabeth, A.D. 1574, when the Attorney-General appears and holds to his information, and prays a jury. Stacey *dicit ut prius*, and prays the like. The case was tried on 29 May, 18 Elizabeth, A.D. 1576, when the jury find that the piece of land in question was within time of memory overflowed by every tide, although it is five miles from the main sea, and that Appledore Stream is *brachium maris;* that the land was inclosed by Sir John Guildford, and is part of the marine waste on the north side of Appledore Stream. And they say if it shall be adjudged by the Court that the marine waste belongs to the Queen by reason of the prerogative, then Stacey has intruded; if otherwise, then he has not intruded. Judgment is not entered up. On 23 April, 22 Elizabeth, A.D. 1580, the Court ordered a hearing of the matter of law on this special verdict, and the order was entered on 3rd June following that the argument was to be heard that day se'nnight, but on the 13th June the Court gave judgment in Hammond's case, and the further prosecution of the suit of Stacey was dropped, and there is no further order on the books of the Court of Exchequer relating to it. But see *post*, p. 251.

Exch. Q.R. Memda., E., 16 Eliz., roll 292, 294.

D. & O., E., 22 Eliz. 360, 370, 376, 384, 388.

Exch. D. & O., 22-27 Eliz.

On 10 October, 15 Elizabeth, A.D. 1573, Digges filed

Exch. Q.R. Memda., M., 15-16 Eliz., roll 445.

an information against Thomas Honywood, William Hamond, and others to recover other parts of the land returned by the commission of 10 June, 15 Elizabeth, A.D. 1573, to which Hamond appeared and pleaded. In the information the Attorney-General charges that, whereas a certain *vastum marinum*, containing by estimation 1000 acres of salt marsh adjoining the salt marshes of Cheney Courte, next the parishes of Ivechurche and Medley, heretofore by the natural course of the sea being entirely overflown, so that the aforesaid 1000 acres of salt marsh were parcel of the shore and waste of the sea [*littoris et vasti marini*], and now are in the occupation of Richard Knatchebull and his assigns; and whereas another parcel of *littoris marini*, containing by estimation sixty acres, lying next Hide, in the county of Kent, bounded towards the south by the same sea, towards the west with the salt marshes of Hide, towards the east with the land of Edward Foxe, Esquire, and towards the north with the land of Thomas Honywood or his assigns; and whereas another parcel of *littoris marini*, containing by estimation 130 acres of land, next Richeborowe Castell, in the county of Kent, bounded towards the east and south with the sea channel called Sandwich Haven, towards the west by Richborow Castle and land adjacent, towards the south with the marshes of Fleet, of which same parcels 100 acres were inclosed from the salt water partly by William Hamond, gent., and partly before and now are wholly in the tenure of the same William Hamond or his assigns; and whereas there is another parcel of the shore or sea waste near Reculver, called Richborow Marsh, containing 500 acres, in the possession of Henry Cripps, knight, and others; also 100 acres *littoris marini adjacens marino de Belgar*, next the parish of Hide (Kent), in the occupation of William Middleton; all which on 13 February, 13 Elizabeth, A.D. 1571, were, or ought to be, in the hands of the Queen as in right of her crown of England by reason of her prerogative, as appears by divers records, &c.: nevertheless the defendants have intruded. Hamond appears and demurs to the information as insufficient in law, and pleads not guilty; and for a plea he says that Thomas Hamond, of Nonington, was seised, and by deed 20 March, 2 Edward VI., A.D. 1548, enfeoffed the said William Hamond. *Absque hoc* that the aforesaid land or any parcel thereof *ever were or are parcel of the sea-shore*, or ought to be in the hands or possession of the lady the Queen, and *absque hoc* that it does not so appear by the records of the Court, except the said information, and that he has not intruded.

The Attorney-General replies generally, and that the said 130 acres *were parcel of the sea-shore.* Issue is joined, and the jury say that Hamond has not intruded, and that the same 130 acres of land *were not and are not parcel of the sea-shore* in the manner and form as the same William Hamond above alleges in his pleading.

The trial in this case took place in Easter, 17 Elizabeth, A.D. 1575, and it is evidently the case referred to by Dyer 326b, who reports that the verdict was solemnly given for Hammond against the Queen; and Coke (4 Inst. 140) reports that "it was adjudged that the land "between the flowing and re-flowing of the sea belonged "to the lord of the manor, as Lord Dyer doth report."

It would appear from the language of the pleadings that the issue in the case was whether the land in question was still part of the open shore; and this record was referred to in the argument of the case of Rex *v.* Oldsworth (*post*) as shewing that there was an admission by Hammond that the sea-shore proper did belong to the Crown by virtue of the prerogative, but that the accreted land did not.

On 21 June, 17 Elizabeth, A.D. 1575, the Attorney-General at the relation of John Nelthrop filed a fresh information against William Hammond for the marsh and foreshore at Richborough, Kent, in which the claim of the Crown is set out for the first time at length, as follows:— Exch. Q. R. Memda., E., 17 Eliz., roll 87.

"Quod cum Domina Regina nunc ratione prærogativæ suæ "proprietatem habeat tam in littoribus maris infra et per "totum regnum Angliæ et in ipsa terra fundo arena et "solo sub eodem mari quam in omnibus terra solo fundo "et arena infra et per totum prædictum regnum quæ aliquo "naturali maris fluxu salsis undis fuere infra tempus "memoriæ hominum absque innaturali et extraordinari "cursu seu impetu ventorum sive tempestatum inundatis "et ratione ejusdem prerogativæ suæ intitulata sit gaudere "et habere et ad usum suum proprium gaudere habere et "retinere debeat omnes ejusmodi terras quæ infra totum "prædictum regnum aliquo naturali maris fluxu seu cursu "salsis aquis fuere inundatas et postea fuerunt vel erunt "relictas sive recuperatas a mare ejusve littoribus aut ab "aliquo membro vel brachio maris ubicumque fuerit infra "regnum suum Angliæ; ita quod nullus ea sive aliquam "earum alicujus parcellam sibi appropriare aut vendicare "possit absque speciali concessu prædictæ Dominæ Reginæ "aut alicujus progenitorum suorum Regum Angliæ proinde "prius obtento et habito." The information charges that there is a piece of marsh containing 120 acres in the tenure of William Hamond, bounded on the east and south by Richborow Haven, on the west by Richborough Castle and lands adjoining it, and on the south with Fleet Marsh, all which was formerly overflowed by the sea, and that Hamond has intruded. Hamond pleads that the information is insufficient, and, as to the intrusion, not guilty, and prays a jury. The record is not entered up.

Baron's Dep., East., 17 Eliz., No. 243.

The depositions of witnesses taken for the Crown exist. They shew that the stream of Appledore had silted up within the memory of the witnesses, and had been inclosed by Sir John Guildford, Sir Henry Goulding, and other landowners. The deponents speak to having navigated over the now inclosed lands, and clearly shew that they had been part of the foreshores within living memory. The defendants' depositions are not forthcoming. The case proceeded, and Hammond pleaded a feoffment to him, whereupon on 26 November, 17 Elizabeth, A.D. 1574, the Court, stating that he had pleaded "a feoffment from an intruder, "traversing only with non intrudit, which amounteth but "to a general issue," ordered him "to plead specially "traversing or answering the special point of the preroga-

Exch. D. & O., vol. 6, fo. 62.

"tive in the information specified," and an injunction was awarded for possession of the land to the Queen's use till the matter in controversy shall be decided. In the following term, however, this injunction was dissolved, and Hammond ordered to keep possession. The suit in the Exchequer, however, continued, and, a second trial being had, a verdict was again given for the defendant. The suit was at last ended by the following remarkable order, made in Trinity, 22 Elizabeth, A.D. 1580:—

Exch. D. & O., Hil., 18 Eliz., 14 Feb.

"It is ordered by the Court in the matter depending "in this Court between the Queenes Matie and William "Hamon upon an information of intrucion agaynst him "at the suyt of Mr Digges for lands surrounded wth the "natural course of the sea, that forasmuch as yt is alledged "by the councell lerned of the sayd Mr Hamond that a "tryal hath bine hade in the same cause & verdicte "given for the def^t^ and also for that the possession "of the lands in question hath bin in the def^t^ or "his assigns this lx yeres, and for that the same lands *is* "*but only averred to belong to the Queenes Highnes*, the sayd "Def^t^ shall plead the generall issue, kepe his posses-"sion, and put in suerties to answer the profytts of the "premises if the tytle fall out agaynst him."

Eccl. D. B., T., 22 Eliz., vol. 6, fo. 390.

This order is evidently drawn up so as to avoid entering judgment against the Crown, and, from the words in italics, it is clear that Digges had failed to prove his theory; he had only averred it. The jury who had tried the case had found against it, but the Court of Exchequer would not directly uphold their finding of fact by declaring the law. They evade the point which they had ordered to be specially brought into issue, and give no judgment upon it, except that it was not proved. It would have been interesting if we had a report of the arguments and the reasons of the judges; but, unfortunately, none exists. The order, however, was final. There is no subsequent order on the records. The prosecution of the information was dropped, and Hammond remained in possession, the Crown being, in truth, really defeated. This ended the attempt of Digges to establish the proposition set up in his treatise. The case of Sir John Constable, which we shall next discuss, had been decided in the previous year, Easter, 21 Elizabeth, A.D. 1579, and affirmed the now well-settled law that the foreshore may be parcel of the manor of a subject.

SIR JOHN CONSTABLE'S CASE.

Anderson, p. 86.

The case of Att. *v.* Sir John Constable occurred in 17 Elizabeth, A.D. 1575. It is partially reported in Anderson, p. 86, who reports only the argument for the Crown. The suit was by information charging that Sir John Constable took wreck of the sea *magis ex opposito manerii et dominii de Holderness.* Constable pleaded that the wreck was found "entre le low water mark & le firme "terre adjoynant a le Manor du Holderness;" that the Duke of Buckingham was seised of the manor, and that he and those whose estates he had, had always had wreck of the sea appurtenant to the manor; that he was attainted, and the manor came to the Crown; that Philip and Mary granted it to the Earl of Westmoreland, with wreck of the sea *infra dictum manerium et alibi ubicumque* in the counties of Lancaster and York to the said manor belonging and appertaining, and that the Earl had conveyed to Constable, who took the wreck between the low-water mark and the bank or firm land, parcel of the manor. Thereupon it was urged that if wreck was appendant to the manor, it passed to the Crown on the attainder, and merged, and that the general words of the patent would not pass it; and also that it was doubtful whether the foreshore was sufficiently pleaded, and that it could not be parcel of the manor nor of the county, for "quant "est floud est parcel del mere que est solement en le Royne "et nemy en ascun subject; car est pur passage pur "chescun, *mes owner de ceo nul si non le Royne*," and for this reason: for it cannot be that one may be proprietor of that which he does not know, and cannot know; for no one knows, of land lying like this, of what he is seised or is proprietor, or how far it extends. If he will make the low-water mark the boundary, then divers absurdities ensue;

for one day he will have land and the next day none; for the sea sometimes comes up to the firm land, sometimes by reason of sands thrown to the shore it is a mile or more or less into the sea, which makes this so uncertain that none can be owner of part who is not owner of the whole; and, therefore, that cannot in reason be part of the manor which has not been a thing of continuance and certainly remaining; for, if so, then it ensues that that which is part to-day is to-morrow no part, for it is in the sea; and that which is in the sea and covered with water to-day, uncovers to-morrow, and so becomes part of the manor, which is inconvenient. And it is not like the case where land is gained to a manor in a long time, which can be known how and when it accrued, for then it is a part; but here for the uncertainty it is not part, and the same reasons serve that it is not part of the county, for it is known by certain metes and bounds, whereas here it cannot be. It was also argued that the patent did not pass the shore.

We find the argument of Plowden for the defendant (which is not reported by Anderson) in a volume of contemporary MS. reports in the Hargrave MSS. No. 15, fo. 95d, the translation of which is as follows:—

"In quo warranto by the Queen against Sir John Con-"stable, who says that the place where, &c., is a manor "which extends into the counties of Lincoln and York, of "which the Duke of Buckingham was seised, and had wreck "appendant thereto, and was in due manner attainted of "high treason, and the attainder found before the escheator "by virtue of his office, wherefore he seized for the King, "and the manor descended to Queen Mary, who granted "it with the appurtenances to Henry Earl of Westmoreland "in fee, and he granted it to the defendant, and by that "warrant he took the wreck.

"PLOWDEN: 'Which he might well so do;' and first "he answers to the exception taken before, that the "attainder is not well pleaded, because the indictment "and all the process is not shewn in certain; and this not-"withstanding it seems good to him to plead that it was "*debito modo attincturæ* generally, without shewing all "the circumstances; for we have shewn that the wreck "is and was appendant, and goes with the manor, and "he who has the manor has title to the wreck by "intendment until the contrary be shewn; then the at-"tainder is only a conveyance of the manor to the King, "which it is not necessary to shew here in certain, because "the manor is not in question, but the wreck which is "appendant to it, and which he who has the manor "by intendment ought to have for that we can aver "conveyance of the manor to the defendant by *que estate*, "without shewing how, whether by lease or feoffment "without shewing deed; for if he has the manor by "disseisin, that is sufficient to justify for wreck appen-"dant. So, if one claim common appendant, tithes, castle "guard, suit of mill, or other such thing, it is sufficient "to convey to him the manor, parsonage appropriate, "castle, or mill, &c., by *que estate*, without shewing how; "or of a corporation, without shewing deed. So 11 "Henry IV. the defendant justifies for wreck because he "was seised of a hundred to which the wreck was ap-"pendant, which estate he had, and adjudged good plea "without shewing deed, and yet the hundred cannot pass "without deed. So, in assize of nuisance, it suffices to con-"vey the land to which the nuisance is done to the plain-"tiff generally, for although he be disseisor, still he shall "have the action. But if the manor had been in demand, "it may well be that he ought to have shewn the certainty "of the attainder, for then the conveyance would have been "necessary and traversable; but when the conveyance is "not of the chose in question, nor of the chose which is of "the substance of the matter, it is not requisite that it "be certain, but may be general: as 34 Henry VI. 48, "the defendant in replevin shews that he recovered "damages against a stranger, and had the land in exe-"cution by *elegit*, and let it to the plaintiff, rendering "rent, by which he avows, and good plea, without "shewing the record and all the matter of the recovery "and execution in certainty, for this is only the conveyance, "and the substance is the lease. So here the principal "matter is the appendancy, and the attainder is but con-"veyance; and if this be not good to plead, still the office "found shews that it was taken before the escheator of the "county of York, and is sufficient title for the King; for the "escheator may find this by virtue of his office, although "it be matter of record, for the book 4 H. 5, where it is "said that he cannot find outlawry or other such matter of "record without writ or certificate of record, is not law as "it seems, for by the statute of 29 Edward I. *de escaetoribus* "it seems to the contrary, and he, by virtue of his office, "could inquire of attainder of all felonies, and of year, day, "and waste, of the profits of temporalties of bishoprics, "and of other such matters, which cannot be without "inquiry of matter of record. And in 3 Edward IV. 25, "all the matter of seisin and attainder of the Earl of "Northumberland is found by the escheator by virtue of "his office, and this is admitted good by all the justices "and serjeants: but the doubt is there, because matter is "found which is against the title of the King.

"As to the matter in law, exception was taken that the "place where the wreck was taken was not certainly (and "as a fact it was certainly enough) expressed, for it was "said that the place where he took it was between the "greensward and the low-water mark. And to take all "this matter, we ought to consider to what place the bounds "of England extend, and then to whom the property of "the sea and of the land under the sea belongs, and to "whom belongs the property of the land between the "greensward and the low-water mark, and within what "county and parish the said soil is. And admitting this "soil to belong to the Queen, whether the defendant can-"not prescribe to have wreck there, and then, whether by "the devolution of this manor and wreck to the hands of "the King the wreck be extinct, and whether by the statute "of 32 Henry VIII., ca. 20, the franchises are not revived. "Firstly, the bounds of England extend to the middle of "the sea adjoining which surrounds the realm; but the "Queen has all the jurisdiction of the sea between France "and this realm by reason of her title to France, and so it "is of Ireland; but in other places, as towards Spain, she "has only the moiety; for there is the same reason con- "cerning the sea as concerning great and public rivers in a "kingdom, and these belong to those who have the land "adjoining, so that every one who has the land bounding "on the rivers shall have, by reason of his soil adjoining, "interest in the said rivers; for Bracton, in his second "book *De acquirendo rerum dominio*, says that an island "made in a fresh river shall belong to those who have the "land adjoining, according to the rate that it is in the "midst of the river, or that it extends more into the "moiety of the river which is next adjoining to their "several soils, so that each one shall have as much of the "island as there is of it in his part of the river, and the "whole if the whole be in his moiety of the river, and then "the island shall be to him a new continent, and shall give "to him interest in the moiety of the remnant of the river: "and Bretton, in his 33rd chapter *De perquisitis*, fo. 86, "says that the property of the river belongs to him who "has the land adjoining, and he says that that which is "thrown to the land by alluvion, which is when the "course of the stream enters there, and by little and "little adds and brings to the land of any one, or by "attraction, that is, when the land by little encroaches on "the soil on one side, and relinquishes as much on the "other side, it shall be in advantage to him to whom "such accession is made; but it is otherwise where the "old course of the stream is changed by sudden violence "and irruption of the water into another soil which he "cannot resist; there he will not lose it, and the other "will gain nothing. The same reason is of the sea and "of the salt water, for in this our Queen has the juris- "diction and governance of all things within the said "bounds of England to the midst and between France "or Ireland and this kingdom, and has all the jurisdiction "of the sea in respect of her title to the land on either side. "This can be understood by 40 Assizes 25, where in "appeal against sixteen (persons) it was said by Chard "that a Norman was master of a ship accompanied with "Englishmen, and they robbed certain Englishmen, and "in the Norman it was adjudged only felony, but in "the Englishmen it was adjudged treason, because they "did it on their lands on the wastes of England; so, if "the servant kill his master, it is treason, and thus it is "by Glanvill, if the homager kill his lord, on account of "the trust reposed in them.

"But although the Queen has jurisdiction in the sea "adjoining her realm, still she has not property in it, nor in "the land under the sea, for it is common to all men, and "she cannot prohibit any one from fishing there, and the "water and the land under it are things of no value, and "the fish are always removable from one place to another. "And also Bracton says, lib. 2, cap. 2: If an island is "born in the sea, which rarely happens, it belongs to the "occupant; and with this Britton agrees; which proves that "the Queen has not property in the sea nor in the land "under it. And that which Digges in his book and also "Robert Carey urged to the contrary is not to be regarded, "for they rely on the saying of Bracton in another place, "that the Queen shall have the island born *propter super-"intendentiam*, and this seems to be understood of a "common river or of an arm of the sea within her realm; "but I marvel much that the Admiral uses in his Court to "hold pleas of robberies and other things done upon the "coast of Spain, which is altogether out of his jurisdiction "and the authority of this kingdom; and I remember that "once Alderman Haywood came into the Chancery and "shewed that, in an assembly of merchants on the coasts of "Burgundy, he was sued and process directed against him "under the seal of England, and yet it was the opinion of "many, amongst whom were Carell, Attorney of the Duchy, "and myself, and we put our hands to it, that he was not "bound to obey this, for he was in the Court of the King of "Burgundy, and although the Queen has the punishment "of any offences done there, still she has not there other "authority.

"Then as to the property of the place between the green-

" sward and the low-water mark, this belongs, as it seems to " me, to him who has the greensward adjoining, and it is " admitted by the Queen, even in her quo warranto, that it " is in the county adjoining, for she demands by what " warrant we took the wreck in such a place within the " county of York. And the statute of 12 Richard II., " chap. 5, Admiralty 1, proves that the ancient law of " the land was that the Admiral ought not to have jurisdic- " tion in this place, but the coroner of the county, and it is " accounted mainland and not of the sea; and 8 Edward IV., " 19, Choke said that if a man have land adjoining to the " sea upon which the sea is accustomed to flow and re-flow, " when the water overflows it any man may fish there, but " when the water is gone away he shall have the land left " dry, and may in this bring trespass. And it seems by the " pleading that this is between the greensward and the low- " water mark, and in 14 Edward III., rot. 432, and in the " Book of Entries, fo. 611, in trespass against an abbot, he " justifies for wreck by prescription in the place over which " the sea flows and re-flows, which is always between the " greensward and the low-water mark, and it was alleged to " be in the parish of A., of which the *visne* was taken to try " the issue as upon prescription; and in the same Book of " Entries, fo. 612, in trespass, the defendant justifies for " wreck as the servant of the King and to his use, and the " abbot claims the wreck in a manor by prescription in the " place in which the sea flows and overflows, which place is to " be understood between the greensward and the low-water " mark, and the wreck is there called flotesome; for there " are three kinds of wrecks, as appears by Bracton, flotsom, " jetsom, and lagan; flotsom is any wreck which is of such " a nature that it will float; jetsom, is anything, but it is " thrown out of the ship which is in danger to lighten it; " lagan is a thing wrecked which is weighty and will sink, " and the practice is to tie cords or other such things for " marks to such weighty things wrecked to find them after- " wards. Also it is used in Sussex and the West country " that fishers pay tithe of their fish taken between the " greensward and the low-water mark, which proves that

This reference is incorrect.

"it is taken to be within the parish adjoining. And in "Norfolk, as I have heard, 500 marks by the year is "made of leases made of this land between the green-"sward and the low-water mark, for they make hedges "there in which they have many fish after the water has "overflowed the land and ebbed back. In 5 Edward III. "a ship laden with herrings was wrecked, which cannot be "in any other place than between the greensward and the "low-water mark, and yet there in replevin avowry is "made for the lord of whom the manor is held as within "his fee, which cannot be if it be not parcel of the manor "and given as parcel of the manor at the commencement; "and 12 Henry IV. 16, wreck 2, in trespass for a ship "taken, the defendant justifies by prescription to have "wreck there, and it is admitted good prescription, and "issue taken upon that, which also proves that the said "place is parcel of the manor in which the wreck is "claimed; and also the statute Ri. 2, cap. 4, by which it "is ordained that if cat, dog, or man escape alive to land "then this shall not be adjudged wreck, for by the statute "it is expressly said that wreck may belong to another "person than the King, and this is good enough by pre-"scription, and 14 Edward II. trespass 236, prescription "is allowed to be good. By these cases it is apparent "that the soil between the greensward and the low-water "mark belongs to him who has the land next adjoining, "and if this land should belong to the Queen, still we "have alleged that the wreck is appendant, and it is not "inconvenient that the defendant may have wreck by "prescription in the soil and frank tenement of the King "as well as estovers or other such *profit à prendre*, and in "the West country they prescribe to have wreck as far "from them as they can see a Humber barrel. Then this "wreck being appendant by prescription in the hands of "the Duke of Buckingham, as it seems to us, is not extinct, "but remained appendant in the hands of the King, and "so passed by the mesne conveyances to the defendant; "for, as it seems, where the King grants such a thing as "was not in him before, as fair, market, chase, or warren, if "this comes to the King afterwards by attainder, the King "will have it, and it shall not be extinct in his person, but "if the King grant anything which was in him before, as "waif, estray, or wreck, if this come to him afterwards, it "shall be extinct, but if such things which were in the "King before are appendant and then come back into the "hands of the King, they are not extinct, but remain "appendant as before. And as to such liberties derived "out of the Crown and being in gross, it is the opinion of "Thrope, 43 Edward III. 22, that it is to be understood "that as to royal liberties derived out of the Crown this "is so. Our case is, if they are appendant they are not "extinct in the Crown. The case in 18 Henry VI. 11, "proves this, where, in action on the case against the "mayor and burgesses of New Windsor, in praying an aid, "there it was held that, by grant of the King of the said "town with appurtenances, the leet passed as appendant, "which could not have been so if it was extinct in the "Crown or in the person of the King; and the reason why "it was not extinct was because it was appendant, for leet "is derived out of the Crown as well as wreck. In our "case, then, if leet appendant be not extinct, but remain in "the hands of the King, the reason is the same of wreck "appendant, &c.; and that the leet is appendant there is "without question, for otherwise it does not pass by the "grant without special words, for the King by his grant "with special words can grant leet to a town, but by his "grant he cannot make leet appendant without prescription "and continuance of time; but such liberties as are not "derived out of the Crown, as fair, market, chase, warren, "park, or the like, if they are forfeited by misuser or non-"user, they shall not be seised into the hands of the King, "but shall be extinct, as the diversity appears 15 Edward "IV. 6, for the King cannot have them in another's soil "and frank tenement no more than he can grant to me to "have such liberties in the soil and frank tenement of "another man."

The argument for the Crown did not satisfy the Court, and judgment was given for Constable in Easter

Term, 21 Elizabeth, a *nolle prosequi* being entered, and *cessat processus versus eum omnino.* The record of the case exists. The information charges that Sir John Constable, without any royal warrant or grant, uses, and claims to have and enjoy, "infra manerium de Holder- "ness et procinctum ejusdem," divers liberties, as view of frankpledge, assize of bread and beer, &c.; and to have "omnimoda wrecca maris in omni loco in mare aut "litore maris ex opposito dominii sive manerii de Holder- "ness inter fluxum et refluxum maris accidentia et con- "tingentia, ac regales pisces in mare aut in litore maris "juxta dominium sive manerium prædictum captos aut "præhensos." To this Constable pleads as to taking the wreck in the sea, or on the sea-shore opposite the manor, that he takes it within the flux and re-flux of the sea "ad "locum vocatum the low-water mark;" and he sets out his title under the Duke of Buckingham, Henry VIII., Edward VI., and Philip and Mary, who granted the manor to the Earl of Westmoreland, who conveyed it to him, and avers that they all had wreck to the low-water mark. He disclaims the wreck beyond the low-water mark, and disclaims royal fish. After many adjourn- ments judgment was given for him, as has been stated. It is clear, notwithstanding the language of the pleadings, that the issue was that the foreshore was parcel of the manor, and that the grant of the wreck was effectual because the foreshore was parcel of the manor, and so it was held, and this was subsequently confirmed in Sir Henry Constable's case in 43 Elizabeth.

Coram Rege Roll, Trin., 27 Eliz., roll 2, Regina.

Coke v. 106.

SIR HENRY CONSTABLE'S CASE.

In Michaelmas, 42 Elizabeth, A.D. 1599, Sir Henry Constable, the lord of the manor and fee of Holderness, brought an action in the Queen's Bench against George Gamble, who was the officer of the Admiral, for taking certain wrecked goods at Barmston, within the fee of Holderness, thrown to land upon the sea-shore there by the sea as goods wrecked. Constable set out a grant of

Ibid. Q. B. Judg- ment Roll, Hil., 42 Eliz., roll 858.

6 February, 4–5 Philip and Mary, A.D. 1557–58, of the manor and fee of Holderness, "with wreck of the sea "happening, arising, and renewing within the precinct "of that manor and fee," and pleaded not guilty. The jury found Constable's title under the grant, and, further, that the manor of Barmston from time immemorial was *infra feodum manerii de Holderness*, and that some of the wrecked goods were wrecked and thrown "upon the "sands then uncovered with water of the manor of "Barmston aforesaid, within the fee of the manor of "Holderness aforesaid, between the flux and re-flux of the "sea, *Anglicè* between the high-water mark and the low-"water mark, in the manor of Barmston, within the fee of "Holderness aforesaid;" and that others of the goods at the time of the trespass complained of were "floating on "the waters of the sea then ebbing in and out of the "sands of the same manor of Barmston, within the fee of "Holderness, between the high and low water marks," and that these last were taken by the defendant as the servant of the Admiral; but whether this was lawfully done or not the jury know not, and pray the advice of the Court; and if it appears to the Court that it was unlawful, they find the defendant guilty, and assess damages at two shillings, and costs at forty shillings; and if to the contrary, then not guilty: and as to the taking of the rest of the goods left high and dry by the ebb, they find the defendant not guilty. The case is reported by Coke, and the argument was whether the floating goods were wreck or not. It was decided that the floating goods were flotsom, and did not pass by the grant of wreck, but that the goods left high and dry on the foreshore did pass as wreck. In the course of the argument it was resolved by the whole Court "that the soil on which the sea flows and ebbs, to wit, "between the high-water mark and low-water mark, may "be parcel of the manor of a subject," but that the Admiral has jurisdiction, when the sea flows, of everything done on the water between high-water mark and low-water mark by the ordinary natural course of the sea;

yet when the sea ebbs the land may belong to a subject, and everything done on the land when the sea is ebbed shall be tried at the common law, for then it is parcel of the county.

This case is generally quoted as the case in which it was decided that the foreshore may be parcel of a manor, but we have seen that the point was really decided previously in Sir John Constable's case, where the issue clearly was whether the foreshore of the manor of Holderness was parcel of that manor or not.

There is a contemporary report of this case in the Lansdowne MS. 1088, fo. 69, from which it appears that Hutton, of Gray's Inn, who was counsel for the plaintiff, said that he was entitled to all goods within the low-water mark, as by the judgment on a quo warranto against Sir John Constable all that which was within the low-water mark is, and was allowed as parcel of the manor. He cites the case of 15–16 Elizabeth, fo. 326, and the Abbot of Ramsey's case, and the case of 17 Elizabeth for Sandwich against the Queen, and says that in truth all that is within the low-water mark is parcel of the manor; and also Peacock *v.* Lacy, 25 Elizabeth, which was a case as to the Admiral's jurisdiction to try a murder committed on the sands at Scarborough, and the Year Book 8 Edward IV. 19, in the case of the City of Bristol *v.* Lord Berkley, as to wreck and flotsom.

MS. Lansdowne 1088, fo. 69.

Dyer, fo. 326; ante, p. 222.

2 Co. 93.

The judgment of Popham, C.J., is set out shortly, and contains the following passage, which is not mentioned by Coke:—"Concerning jurisdiction it is to be considered "that in some places the jurisdiction of the Admiral is "absolute; in others, the jurisdiction of the county is "absolute; and in some places they are mixed. Where "a manor shall be said to extend, and where at one time "any place shall be accounted of the manor, and at "another time not so, those places to which the sea does "not ever ebb are merely in the jurisdiction of the "Admiral, and those places to which the sea does not "ever flow are within the county, governed by the common "law of the realm; and the place which is between is "mixed, for when it is ebb it is parcel of the county, and "when it is flood it belongs to the Admiral; and it is "grown into a proverb, 'The highest flood hath the lowest "'ebb;' and it is the lowest ebb at the highest spring "than at other seasons; and sometimes, by reason of the "wind, the ebb is greater than at other times, as upon the "west coast when the wind is strong in the east, and "all that which becomes uncovered shall be said to be "parcel of the county. The case of Bristol was that they "had flotsom and jetsom in the river and wreck: never- "theless, that which was thrown upon the land upon the "departure of the water shall be accounted within the "manor; and I have seen weirs which at the full sea are "two leagues out in the sea, and had always been "demised by copy of court roll, from the time whereof "memory is not, as parcel of the manor; and at low water "they were clear of the sea, and the copyholder had the "fishery of the river there; but at full sea it is common for "any man to fish there as in the sea, and then neither "the lord nor the copyholder has anything to do there." The report, which is in very bad law French, is a little obscure, and would seem to suggest that Chief Justice Popham thought that the county went to the ebb mark of low-water springs, and the Admiral's jurisdiction *è contra* to the high-water mark at high springs.

Common Roll, T., 43 Eliz., roll 659. Petyt MS. Inner Temple, 518, fo. 94b. See also Barrington MS. x. 93, Inner Temple, Earl of Derby's case, T., 5 Jac. I.

This, however, was clearly the law as understood at this period, for we find that Vincent Brown, the lord of the manor of Croft (Lincoln), on being sued in the Admiralty Court for taking a grampus *infra manerium et super arenas infra metum vocatum the lowest ebbe maris*, got a prohibition from the Court of Common Pleas, on the ground that it was out of the Admiral's jurisdiction, in Trinity, 43 Elizabeth, A.D. 1601.

Chief Justice Popham's definition of what may be parcel of a manor is important, and his *obiter dictum* with regard to copyhold weirs in the sea being evidence of the extent of the manor is valuable in view of the recent judgment of Mr. Justice Cave in Attorney-General *v.* Emerson, now under appeal, who holds that evidence shewing copyhold weirs in the sea is evidence of a right of fishery, and not of soil.

The full text of the report is as follows :—

Hill: 42 [Eliz.] Roll 858, Sir Henrye Constable de Yorkeshire port trespas versus George Gambell et count come P. et M. 6 Feb: a° 4 et 5 grant al Henrye Counte de Westmerland le manor de Holdernes et le fee del ceo, et wrecke del mere deins le precinct del dit manor et fee provenient emergent et renovant, a aver et tenir a luy et ses heires ; et le dit counte 4 Maij 2 Eliz: infeff vn John Constable pere le dit Henry Constable et grant auxi le dit wrecke. Jo: Constable devye 21 Eliz., par que ceo discend al Henrye Constable, qui fuit seisi del dit manor et fee de Holdernes et le wrecke in 10 Novemb: 39 Eliz., que le def: de les biens le pl: scilicet 3 sea mantells, 4 cloakes, et 12 shirts apud Barmpston infra feodum de Holdernes ad terram super littus maris ibidem per mare ut bona wreccata projecta, et quæ ad ipsum Henricum ut bona wreccata pertinere debeant, cepit et ascariavit ad grave damnum. Le def: pled non culp. Et trove fuit par speciall verdit que fuit autiel grant et conveiance del maner de Holdernes et le wrecke come in le count, et que Barmston est deins le fee et precinct de Holder: et que 2 del dits shirts price 12*d.* fuerunt wreccata et projecta super arenas (ad tunc cum aqua salsa minime coopertas) manerii de Barmston infra feodum manerii de Holdernes infra fluxum et refluxum maris, silicet between the highe water and the lowe water marke, et pur un del dits clokes price 2^s, ils trove que ceo fuit floteinge super aquis maris tunc refluentes infra fluxum et refluxum maris, et que le def: comme servant al seignior admirall pur wrecke eux prist ; et si sur tout le matter il soit guilty del trespas, ils assess : domages al 3^s; et pur le residue non culp: Hutton de Greyes Inne argue pur le pl: et que il est intitle al biens deins le lowe water marke: Primes il dit que in quo warranto vers Sir John Constable in 19 Eliz: tout ceo que est deins le lowe water marke est et fuit allowe destre parcell del manor : a ceo auxi il mitt le case 15 et 16 Eliz: 326, ou est question quant le ewe

MS. Lansdowne 1088, fo. 69.

relinquishe grand parte del shore, si le ownor del prochein soile adjoinant al ewe avera ceo, ou nemy, et la le president vouche de 43 del Abbe de Ramsey, qui fuit impleade pur appropriatinge certaine terre a luy sans licence le Roy, et il respond que il avoit terre adjoinant, et le meer relinquishe le terre, et il ceo avoit allowe pur bon plea, et semble la, 17 Eliz: par Sandwich vers le Royne, car revera tout ceo que est deins le lowe water marke est parcell del manor; ceo fuit la cause del case Peacock et Lacye, qui fuit 25 Eliz. ou 2 combatont sur les sands in Scarborough, qui sont ascun foits cover ove le ewe, et ascun foits nemy, et lun tue lauter, et tenus que le Justices de Ass: ne puissont examine ceo matter, mes ceo ne fuit pur ceo que fuit hors de lour jurisdiction, mes quia apres le awardinge de cest commission autre commission fuit agard al certains commissioners par le Admiraltie pur examination de ceo cause, et tenus que ceo repeale le force del 1er commission, et ceo fuit le cause de ceo judgmt; et comment que 8 E. 4, 19, soit que le meer soit commun a touts persons, et que touts persons peuvent pesher la, ceo est quia adonqs quant est overflowe ceo determine destre parcell del manor; et in largument del dit case de Peacocke, vn case fuit remember que fuit inter le citie de Bristow et le seignior Barkleighe, ou le citie avoit wrecke sur le Severne deins le river, et Seignior Barkleigh avoit manor adjoinant a ceo, et wreck auxi deins le manor, et tenus que si wrecke soit ject sur le terre deins le full sea marke que Seignior Barkeleigh ceo auera comment que le river al full sea extend mult pluis al terre al full sea, car quant est ebb poit bien estre discerne, ou le manor se extend; et mitt auxi 22 Ass. 93 que sur le deperture del meere celuy qui ad le terre adjoinant avera le bienfett de ceo, et il cite le liver dentrees trespas in wrecke, que ou issue sum̃ concernant prescription, que avera wrecke en tiel lieu que fuit infra fluxum et refluxum maris, et fuit trie par venire facias al viscount del countye. Gawdye (J.): Si un River decrease de mon terre sensim sine sensu, jeo aver le bienfett de ceo, mes non si soit par sodayne, que poit estre decerne, mes si le meere decrease de mon terre, jeo aver bienfett inde ut-cumque soit. Fenner (J.): Ceo agrea car comme il est de sustayne le damage de overflowinge, issint il doit aver le bienfett del decrease del meere; et in un case que fuit in lescheque fuit tenus accordant; et icy semble que pur les shirts que fuerent ject sur le terre le pl: ad title, car deins le maner; mes pur les cloakes ils fuerent floatsam, et pur ceux celuy qui voile ceux aver doit auer speciall prescription daver floatsam cybien comme wrecke. Popham (C.J.): Come Fener dit pur ceo que fuit ject sur le terre est ove le pl: non pur ceo que fuit floatinge est icy destre considere: 1° le nature de wrecke et que sera dit wrecke, que sera dit floatsam, que jetsam, et que lagan. 2° Concernant jurisdiction est de considerer que in ascun liews le jurisdiction del Admirall est absolute, in autres le jurisdiction del county est absolute, et in ascun liews sont mixt. 3. Ou vn manor sera dit de extendre, et quant al un foits ascum liew sera accompt del manor, et autresfoits nemy; ceux liews a queux le meere nemy unques reflowe sont meerment deins le jurisdiction del Admirall, et ceux liews a quel le meere ne unques flowe sont deins le county, governe par commun justice del Realme; et le lieu qui est meare est mixt, car quant est ebb est parcell del county, quant flud apperteyne al Admirall; est growen al proverb, "The highest flood hath "the lowest ebb," et est pluis lowe ebb al highe springe que al autre temps; et ascum foits par reason del vent le ebb est greinder que al autre temps, come sur le west coast quant le vent est fort al east, et tout ceo que deveigne uncover sera dit parcell del county. Le case de Bristow fuit que ils avoient floatsam et jetsam deins le River et wrecke; tamen ceo que fuit ject sur le terre sur departure del ewe sera accompt deins le manor. Et jeo ay view wears quel al full sea sont 2 leagues deins le meere, et avoient este touts foits demise par copie de Court Roll temps dont memorie come parcel del manor; et al lowe water fuerent cleere del mere, et le copiholder avoit le piscarie del river la; mes al full sea est commun pur chescum home de pisher la comme in le meere, et donqs le seignior ni le copiholder nad riens a faire la. Et le case del judgment in le case de Peacocke et Lacye fuit come ad este remembere, si par cause que le premier comission fuit determine par le 2^{d}, mes semble auterment cleerement que les justices dassise puissont luy arraigne, mes icy le pl: prescribe pur un chose que nest wrecke sur ceo que floate ; et quant a ceo il dit que *jetsam* est ou in le perill de tempest les mariners ject parcell del biens hors del nief descaper le daunger par lighteninge del nief, et cy longe come ceo est sur le meere ceo est jetsam et nemy wrecke. *Floatsam* est ou nief est tout ousterment swallowe par le meere et sinke al bottome, et parcell del biens floate sur le ewe, et ceo nest wrecke tanque ject sur le terre, comment que soit inter le ebb et flood ; et si soit ject issint que ceo touche le terre, si lewe amesna ceo arere est touts foits floatsam. *Lagan* est ceo que sinke et remaine al botome, issint que pur les cloaks quel swime, le pl: nad title, mes le Admirall. Et dit que fuit difference inter wrecke par charter, mes ne dit in quoi ; et dit que si ceo matter ust este bien looked unto, et considerant le temps in que le grant fuit voyd, este dure de faire le graunt del wrecke bon. Et Fenner dit que lagan est mort corps in le meere, et tout ceo que est circa luy ; mes Cooke dit que fuit appell lagan a ligando, scilicet, quant chose sinke al bottome del meere, et est un boy tie al ceo pur que poit estre trove ; et touts les Justices in maner agree que quant chose soit floatinge sur le meere, conceditur inventori tanque soit ject sur le terre ; et lattornye le Royne agrea auxi, ou al meins aver lun moitye : ils touts agrea auxi que ne fuit wrecke tanque soit ject sur le terre, et pur ceo ils touts agrea que pur les cloakes que fuerent floatinge il nad title ; mes ad bon title pur le remnant. Donqs fuit move que inter ea damages fuerent assesse, et ne poit aver iudgment del parte tant, et ceo ils agree auxi. Donqs Hutton voile reles ses damages, et le Court respond : Donqs vous poies aver null iudgment, car in ceo action riens est de recover forsque damages, mes in case ou autre chose præter les damages est destre recovere, les damages bien poient estre relesse ; et ils considerent que judgm^{t} soit enter quod querens nihil capiat per billam nisi melior matteria.—Quære

Notes of the reporter follow.

lintent de Popham si ascum home poit prender ceo que il

appell Jetsam, car in 46 E. 3, 15[a] trespas de bonis asportatis, Def: dit que les biens fuerent jects in le meere par tempest et le def: eux prist, et garda tanque il vient al terre, et donques eux baila al un qui fuit general attornye pur le pl: a garder pur le pl: et a son use, et fuit move que le plea fuit double, lun ou par le breve est suppose que fuerent prise hors del possession le pl: et le barre est que fuerent ject in le meere, sic hors de son possession ; autre le bailment al servant, supposant que il avoit monstre un matter qui exclude le pl: del action, cy bien comme excuse de luy mesme par le delyuerie ex post facto ; et sur ceo le def: demanda judgment del breve, tamen le breve mayntien le plea nient double, et issue fuit joine sur le delyverie, que prove que celuy qui eux trove sur le meere apres que fuerent ject hors par tempest ne eux avera, et a ceo accord Inst. l: 2. tit. 1 : Alia sane. Ou le text dit, Alia sane causa est earum rerum quæ in tempestate levandæ navis causa eijciuntur, hæ enim dominorum permanent, quia palam est eas non eo animo ejici, quod quis eas habere nolit, sed quo magis cum ipsa navi maris periculum effugiat ; qua de causa si quis eas fluctibus expulsas, vel etiam in ipso mari nactus lucrandi animo abstulerit, furtum committit, nec longe videntur discedere ab his quæ de rheda currente dominis non intelligentibus cadunt. Mes in 46 E. 3 appiert que le prisell ne fuit lucrandi animo : quære de his, car a mesme lintent poit estre le case mise par Wilby, 22 E. 3. 16. l. c., que si merchants par doubt de lour enimyes wayvont lour marchandize, et lour niefe in le meere, et les enimyes eux prisont, et auters eux prisont hors del possession les enimyes, ceux quel ont par le maner ne poient eux detayne del premiers owners. Quere si in cest case title doit estre trove par le Admirall al wrecke, ou si le ley intend que il ad ceo de iure communi, et si sic le graunt de wrecke perhaps voile estre voyd pur le Royne, quant est un autre Admirall a cest temps, come in case Sir Tho: Vavasor, Butler de London, ou fuit Butler Anglie devant.

In 20 Elizabeth, A.D. 1578, a special commission was Sp. Com. 2289.

issued to inquire concerning wreck of the sea in the manor of Bishopston, Sussex.

Throughout the reign of Elizabeth numerous commissions were issued out of the Exchequer to inquire concerning concealed lands, derelict lands, and lands gained from the sea, the claim of the Crown to such lands being pushed to the uttermost.

Exch.Dep., E., 23 Eliz. 11. Hoo *v.* Wroth.

In 23 Elizabeth, A.D. 1581, there was a suit respecting the Denes gained from the sea at Lowestoft, in the manor of Gunton.

Barons' Dep., H., 23 Eliz. 616, 617. Ex. Dep., 23-24 Eliz. 11. Sp. Com. 2165. Exch.Dep., M., 27-28 Eliz. 15.

The Queen brought a suit for lands in Stepney Marsh, called "the New Inned Marsh," and in the same year for a wharf at Maidstone.

Also for salt marshes in Kirkton and Falkenham, Suffolk.

There was also a suit relating to marshes recovered from the sea in Alderton and Bordesey, Suffolk.

Barons' Dep.,Mich., 32-33 Eliz., 965. Queen *v.* Crochay, St. Kath. Dock.

During this reign attempts were made to recover newly inclosed marshes in Bawdesey, Sudborn, Hemley, Aldborough, and Orford Haven, in the county of Suffolk; Plumstead and Erith and the Isle of Elmley, in the county of Kent; encroachments on the Thames in the county of Middlesex; Luddenham, Kent; Abergelly, Denbigh; West Ham, Essex; Oozyland, called Burlands, Somerset; Poplar, Middlesex; Kettleburgh, Rendlesham, and Butley, Suffolk; Whitehaven, Ditchfield, and the River Esk, Cumberland; lands embanked on the Ouse in Norfolk; lands bordering on the Severn near Rodney and Minsterworth; and, indeed, inquiry was made throughout the kingdom with a view of asserting the Crown's *primâ facie* title. These commissions of inquiry were sued out by the title hunters. So far as we can trace, very few actual proceedings to recover the lands returned were set on foot, and there appears to be no decree or judgment in favour of the Crown in any one case. There is no report of such a case, and, had it occurred, it is quite certain that we should have found some reference to it in the cases of Sir John Constable and Sir Henry Constable and in the elaborate judgment of the Barons of the

Exchequer in the case of Att. *v.* Philpott in 8 Charles I., *post*, p. 260.

In the reign of James I. the Crown was very active in endeavouring to get possession of lands gained from the sea and derelict lands. As has been already stated, commission after commission was issued, to inquire concerning them, and attempts appear to have been made to recover them by commissions out of the Exchequer, and by making fishing grants of them. We find records shewing such attempts in the following places amongst others :—Great Grimsby (Yorkshire), Cheney Court (Kent), Holbeach (Lincoln), Sarfleet (Lincoln), Gosberkirk (Lincoln), Slimbridge on the Severn, Tetney (Lincoln) and throughout the county of Lincoln, Hornsea (York) and throughout the county of York, Suttonfleet and Gedney (Lincoln), Ivychurch, Lydd, and Medley (Kent), Bardney (Lincoln), East Smithfield (Middlesex), the Isle of Thanet, the Isle of Oxney and Tilbury Hope (Kent), Tirrington (Norfolk), Holland Fen (Lincoln), Tydd St. Mary's, Holbeach, Molton, and Wigtoft (Lincoln), Kirton and Framton (Lincoln), Surfleet and Friskney (Lincoln), Wotton-under-Edge, North Wibley, Stancombe Wick, and Newport (Gloucester), Romney Marsh and Appledore (Kent).

In 11 James I., A.D. 1613, there was a commission to survey all derelict lands, marshes, fens, &c., adjoining the realm of England and the dominions of the same. Sp. Com. 4063.

Amongst the MSS. of Sir Julius Cæsar we find the following treatise, entitled "A Discourse of Wreck of the "Sea," by a Mr. John Talbot, written in 1605, which serves to shew the view taken of the King's rights of wreck at that time. When it is compared with the undoubted rights established by the records set out before in this treatise, it shews the ignorance of the author of records and facts, and the then prevailing notion that the King had been usurped upon generally throughout the realm. To-day we have given up this notion about the wreck, but the Crown officers cling tenaciously to the same idea about the foreshore. MS. Lansd. 144, fo. 23.

Observacions touchinge the Kings Prerogative to Wreck of Sea.

Prescription. Bract. lib. 3, tract. 2, cap. 3, nu. 7.

IT hath bene held, that *wreccum maris, grossus piscis, et aliæ res que Dominum non habent* shold be the Kings by his prerogative, and that no other man might challenge or have any right therin though he had land nigh the sea shore, *nisi de wrecco habendo speciali gauderet privilegio, quamvis pro se pretenderet longi temporis prescriptionem, quia diuturnitas temporis in hoc casu non minuit injuriam, sed auget, nec in isto casu currit tempus contra Regem.* Wherunto Britton also agreeth, fol. 26. 85. as Stamford reporteth, super Prerog. Regis, cap. 11.

Idem. lib. 2, c. 5, nu. 7.

An. 4 Edw. I.

The Statute de officio Coronatoris hath these wordes concerninge wreck of the sea. Whersoever it be found, if any laye handes on it he shall be attached by sufficient pledges, &c.

17 Edw. II. c. 11, Prer. Reg.

Rex habebit wreccum maris per totum Regnum Angliæ, ballenas, sturgiones captos in mari seu alibi infra Regnum, exceptis quibusdam locis privilegiatis per Reges ;

by w[ch] wordes the Kinges grant is argued, w[th]out w[ch] no place can be priviledged.

11 Hen. IV. 16.

In an action of trespass brought by the Lord of a Hundred against the Lord of a Manor w[th]in the same Hundred, for a boat wrecked in the said manor, Hankford vrged that neither the one nor the other shold have the said boat without shewinge of *grant of allowance* in eire.

And yet in the same case the issue was joyned upon prescription and allowed per Curiam, that a man may prescribe in wreck and have it soe without charter. And Broke quoteth another case to the same effect in his Abr. Prescription, p. 60.

9 Hen. VII. 20.

By which opinion (the lawe beinge altered) the Kinge receivith this prejudice, that wheras before, the waye and entrance into the right to wreck of sea was strayt and of some difficultie, inasmuch as it may be supposed that everie man had not meanes to obteyne grant therof, and that the Kinge wold not pass his right therin to everie one that wold crave it, but onlie to persons and places of speciall favour, nowe the sayd waye and entrance is made patent and easy to everie man that hath landes nigh the sea, if the lord, steward, and tenants can kepe their owne counsell till the tyme limited for prescription be run out.

The soile that is betwene the high water marke and the lowe water marke, is that which is called *Littus maris*. *Littus Maris.* Which by the Civill Lawe (as to the nature thereof) is said to be *ejusdem juris cujus est mare et quæ subjacet mari terra vel arena*. Instit. De rer. divis. & riparum. And (as to the propertie therof) it is said, *quod in nullius adhuc dominium pervenit, sed est relictum, ut sit commune, secundum jus naturale primævum*. Hereunto Bracton agreeth where he saith, *quod littora maris sunt de jure gentium communia sicut et mare, et quod nemo ad littus maris accedere prohibetur, et quod littora maris sunt quasi maris accessoria*. Lib. 1, cap. 1, nu. 5. Touchinge which seashoar, it semeth that it shall reteyne the nature though it incrocheth upon the soile of privatt men. For it is sayd, that though by inundacion a man shall not loose his soile, yet if it be by an arme of the sea (much more by the sea) he shall loose his soile, especially if such inundacion be not in a rage or 22 Assis. casu 93. *per vehementes tempestates, sed per ordinarios fluctus maximos qui vocantur springtides, et fiunt bis quolibet mense*, and that by such flowinge of the sea the limitts of the ground surrounded (by metes and bounds) be utterlie defaced; whereunto the Civill Lawe agreeth. Dyer, fo. 326.

Touchinge wreckes found upon the shoare, Bracton saith, "*Quicquid ex naufragio ad terram pervenerit, erit Domini "Regis, et non alterius sine speciali privilegio: Et ita demum "wreccum erit Domini Regis si res in littore maris inveni- "antur, vel tam prope littus ut constare poterit in veritate "quod in littore essent applicandæ.*" Lib. 3, tract. 2, cap. 3, nu. 5. And it semeth there by him that it is most properlie said to be wreck when it is cast upon the shoare, and not before.

The Statute forbiddeth any man to laye hands on wreck *wheresoever* it be found. De offic. Coronat.

And it semeth that the Kinge by his prerogative is to have wreck found *in mari vel alibi*, &c. 17 Edw. II. c. 2, Prerog. Regis.

Especially upon the shoare, *quia nullius est. Et si sit* Bract. lib. 3, tract. 2, cap. 3, nu. 5. *nullius, tunc erit Domini Regis propter suum privilegium.* 8 Hen. IV. 2. Broke, Prerogat., p. 12. And Gascoyn held that all the goodes in Ingland wherin no man hath propertie shall be adjudged to the Kinge by his prerogative, *quod nullus negavit. Et eadem lex dicitur de terris.*

E contrario. Tr. 43 Eliz. It is said that in an action of trespass brought by Sir Henry Constable *v.* Gamboll in the Kinges Bench, the reverend Judges there agreed, That the land which is betwene the high and lowe water marke is parcell of the manor adjoyninge.

Also that when any wreck at an ebb is relinquished upon the shoar betwene the said two markes, it is for the Lord of the Manor (havinge wreck to his manor) and not to the Kinge or his Admirall, except it be flotinge betwene the said markes.

And the practice of officers of divers Corporacions, and stewardes of manors next the sea, is to charge the juries of the Corporacion or manor to inquire of all wrecks found at sea and first landed in the Corporacion or manor (upon supposicion that the propertie shold accrewe by the landinge and not by the first apprehension or seasure). At least to inquire of all wrecks found so nigh the shoar as a man may adventure to ryde with a horse of xviij. hand high and reach with a speare of xviij. foot longe, affirminge the Lord's soile to extend so farr.

Trin., 43 Eliz. Bye the said resolucion of the reverend Judges, the Kinges Majesty hath lost all that which is properlie called wreck (if it be true that Bracton sayth), and indeed more then half of wreckes, for where one wreck is found and seised in the sea, fyve are found and taken on the shoare.

And if the sayd practise of officers of Corporacions and stewardes of manors wer established for lawe, it wold fall out that the Kinge shold have wreck onlie in his owne manors, except it wer found *longius in mari;* and as to such wrecks, Bracton saith, that in case the same be so far on the sea as that by wynde and wether the same may as well fall with a foreyn shoar as with the coast of Ingland, *Tunc erunt inventoris et non Domini Regis, quia Rex in hoc casu privilegium inde habere non potest magis quam privata persona, propter incertum rei eventum.* Lib. 3 de Coron., cap. 3, nu. 5.

In Michaelmas, 7 James I., A.D. 1609, it was decided by Coke and Foster that if lands be overflowed by the sea even for forty years, and the owner can still know their position by metes and bounds or marks, he shall not lose his property in them. 2 Rolle Abr. 169; Hale, ch. 4.

In 7 James I., A.D. 1609, a dispute arose between the Earl of Worcester, as Lord Marcher of the lordship of Chepstow, and Thomas Sadler, Esq., lord of the manor of Hembury on the Severn, respecting the right to take seaweed on the shore at Hembury. The Earl claims to have *wrecca maris ejecta flotson jetson lagan*, &c., within the boundaries of his lordship, from King's Road near Bristoll to Welsh Road, a long extent over the Severn. The lord of Hembury had let the seaweed for many years. The Earl brought a suit in the Admiralty Court against the lessee, who applied to the Court of Common Pleas for a prohibition, on the ground that the seaweed and sea oare were wreck, and were triable in the county and not in the Admiralty Court, and it was granted him. The Earl afterwards brought another suit against John Smith and others to establish his right to a wrecked ship as against the Admiral, and it was decreed in the Exchequer, on 5 February, 13 James I., A.D. 1615, that, as lord of the lordship of Strugoil *alias* Chepstow, he was entitled to all wreck within the bounds above set out. This case shews the right to wreck as distinct from the ownership of the shore, for the lord of Hembury clearly had the shore, while the Earl was entitled to the wreck; but whether Hembury was a subinfeudation of the lordship of Chepstow has not been ascertained. Common Roll, M., 7 Jas. I., roll 1456. See Brooke Ab., 529, 533, tit. Admiralty.

In the case of the Royal Piscarie of the Banne, in Michaelmas, 8 James I., A.D. 1610, the question was whether the fishery of the river, which was tidal and navigable, belonged to the Crown as a separate hereditament parcel of the ancient inheritance of the Crown, or had passed to the Crown's grantee of an adjoining manor by general words in his grant. The fishery was shewn by Pipe Rolls and surveys to have been parcel of the ancient inheritance of the Crown, and to have been in charge as a Davis 55.

several fishery, and granted to the City of London in fee farm; but for 200 years the profit had been taken by Irish lords of adjacent lands, who had intruded on the Crown possessions in Ulster down to 1 James I., A.D. 1603. In the argument for the Crown we find the right of the prerogative to the soil of the sea urged strongly as follows:—

"Secondly, there are two kinds of rivers, navigable and "not navigable; every navigable river as high as the sea "flows and re-flows in it is a royal river, and the fishery of "it is also a royal fishery, and appertains to the King by "his prerogative; but in every other river not navigable, "and in the fishery of such river, the owners of the land "on either side of the water have interest of common "right. The reason why the King has interest in such "navigable river as high as the sea flows and re-flows in it "is because such river partakes of the nature of the sea, "and is called an arm of the sea as far as it flows: *22 Ass.* "p. 93, 8 *E.* 2 *Fitz. Corone*, 399. The sea is only under "the dominion of the King as it is said 6 *R.* 2 *Fitz. Pro-* "*tection*, 46. The sea is of the ligeance of the King as "of his crown of England, but it is also his proper inherit- "ance, and therefore the King shall have the land which "is gained out of the sea: *Dyer*, 15 *Eliz.* 326*b*; 22 *Ass.* "p. 93.

The case in Dyer hardly supports this proposition.

"Also the King shall have the great fish in the sea, "whales and sturgeons, &c., which are fishes royal, and no "subject may have them without especial grant of the "King: *Prerogativa Regis, cap.* 11; *Stanford*, 37, 38; "*Bracton, lib.* 3, *cap.* 3, 39 *E.* 3, 35*a*; and the King shall "have wild swans as *volatilia regalia* upon the sea and "the arms of it: *The case of swans in the seventh part of* "*the report of Lord Coke.* So wreck of the sea is a royal "perquisite: 5 *Coke*, 107, *Sir Henry Constable's case.* And "upon this reason before the statute of 18 Edward III. no "subject could pass over the sea without special licence of "the King, but there it is enacted that the sea shall be "open to all merchants; and all ports and havens, which "are the gates and doors of the kingdom, belong to the

"King because he is *custos totius regni; and Fitzherbert* "*Nat. Brev.* 113*a*: The King ought of right to save and "defend his kingdom as well against the sea as against "his enemies. And that the King has the same prerogative "and interest in the arms of the sea and navigable rivers "as high as the sea flows and re-flows in them as he has "in the high sea is manifest by many authorities and "records."

It was further argued that the King's power of removing purprestures in rivers shewed that he had the soil of the river. Upon the argument it was resolved by the Court that the River Banne as far as the sea flows and re-flows in it is a royal river, and the salmon fishery there a royal fishery, which belongs to the King as a several fishery, and not to those who have the soil on either side of the water; but it was agreed that in inland rivers not navigable the fishery belonged to the riparian owner. It was also resolved that no part of the fishery of the Banne passed by the grant of land adjoining by the general words of *all fisheries*, for it is a royal fishery, not appurtenant to land, but a fishery in gross, and parcel of the inheritance of the Crown by itself; and general words in the King's grant will not pass such special royalty, which belongs to the Crown by the prerogative, as royal mines, royal amercements, royal escheats, will not pass by general words of all mines, amercements, and escheats.

This case would seem at first sight to establish the proposition that a royal fishery in a navigable river and the soil of it belonged to the King by virtue of the prerogative as one of the flowers of the crown; but the facts, so far as we can ascertain from the report, indicate that the fishery of the Banne was an ancient several fishery in gross and an ancient separate hereditament, distinct from the adjoining land, which had been in charge to the Crown as a separate hereditament part of the inheritance of the Crown in ancient times until the possession had been usurped by the intruding riparian owners; and the decision of the case does not support the proposition that it belonged to the Crown by reason of the prerogative, but only that it was an ancient fishery in gross, parcel of the Crown's possessions held in severalty by the Crown, and that the grant of adjoining land with general words of fisheries did not pass a riparian fishery, because the presumption that the fishery was ever parcel of the riparian land was rebutted by the fact that the Crown had held this fishery as a separate hereditament distinct from the riparian land.

The argument that the King has the soil of navigable rivers because he has the power of removing purprestures is hardly tenable if we examine the nature of these presentments as set out in the preceding part of this treatise, where they are shewn to be exclusively purprestures upon the *jus publicum*. Hale disputes the authority of this celebrated case.

See also D. of Devonshire *v.* Neill, 2 L. R. Ir. at pp. 171–2.

Pat. 18 Jas. I., p. 1 and p. 21.

In 18 James I., the King made fishing grants of a marsh at Pagham, Sussex, the beach at Lancing and at Bradwater, and wharfs at Rotherhithe and Shoreham.

Brading Haven, in the Isle of Wight, was claimed; and, indeed, it would seem that no scrap of land which had ever been inned from the sea escaped the searching inquiries of King James' commissioners and title hunters.

The claim of the Crown at this time extended to the high-water mark at spring tides. It would appear to have been strenuously resisted by the landowners, and, although many people compounded with the King's fishing grantees or took grants direct from the Crown, the great majority resisted, and successfully resisted, the attempt to extend the rights of the prerogative. So far, however, as we can ascertain, there is no case during this reign of a suit between the Crown and the subject in respect of foreshore properly so called. The dispute appears to have been as to marshes gained from the sea, and these would presumably be above the ordinary high-water mark; and it seems to have been assumed that foreshore within the ordinary high-water mark belonged absolutely to the Crown without question. This, however, was disputed by the lords of manors, who claimed the foreshore proper as well as the salt marsh above ordinary high-water mark as parcel of their manors. The Crown evidently claimed that, if the sea overflows land which had been formerly recovered and held by the subject, the overflowing of the sea gave title to the Crown, but it was decided in Michaelmas, 7 James I., that when the sea swallowed up land, if the owner could shew by reasonable marks and bounds the extent of the original land, he lost not his property, although it might have been overflowed for forty years; but it would seem to have been held that if he could not shew such bounds, the Crown's title accrued.

Rolle Ab. ii. 169.

Hale, cap. 4, p. 15.

Dyer 226b.

There is no judgment or decree in any case in favour of the Crown's claims so far as we can ascertain. Had there been one, it would certainly have been referred to in later cases. Baron Trevor, in his judgment in Rex *v.* Oldsworth, *post*, p. 303, refers to a case upon an information in Easter, 16 James I., roll 292, in which he says a verdict was found against the King, and says, "But that is "nothing, for it is false." The reference is a bad one, and the case has not been discovered; but the reference is probably Easter, 16 Elizabeth, roll 292, which is the case of Attorney *v.* Stacey and others (*ante*, p. 219), which seems, therefore, to have been decided against the Crown.

CHAPTER XII.

CALLIS ON SEWERS.

SERJEANT CALLIS delivered his well-known lectures on the Statute of Sewers, 23 Hen. VIII. cap. 5, in August 1622, and, in illustrating the law as he understood it, he puts what appears to be a supposititious case as follows: —" A. leases to B. a manor on the sea-coast for years " which hath *incrementum et decrementum maris* in the " county of Chester and the city there, remainder to C. " in fee. Livery is given and taken by attornies at full " sea within the view; the sea then leaves one hundred " acres of land with the shore divided in part from the " continent by a navigable haven; the lease expired, C. " enters, the Prince ejects him, and the King seizes this " relinquished ground." " My opinion is," says Callis, " that the King hath a part, the Prince a part, and the " subject a part of this ground."

He then proceeds to argue that livery within the view will pass the land covered with the sea as parcel of the manor, citing Brooke, title View, iii. 101, and a case in 28 Henry VIII. He then treats of the King's ownership of the sea, and says that the King has therein these powers and properties, viz.:

1. Imperium Regale.
2. Potestatem legalem.
3. Proprietatem tam soli quam aquæ.
4. Possessionem et proficuum tam reale quam personale.

He refers to the Admiral's charter; the Statute De Prerogativa Regis; Sir Henry Constable's case; statutes 18 Edw. III., 28 Hen. VIII. cap. 15, 31 Hen. VI. cap. 4; the case of the fishery of the Banne; Bracton, lib. 2, cap. 12; and states that he has proved the King full lord and owner of the seas.

He then treats of islands, shewing that islands belong to the King. He then considers the question of new gained grounds as follows:—"Now occasion and time "gives me fit opportunity to treat of grounds which be "newly gained from the seas. If, as I have formerly "declared, the grounds be the King's when they be "covered with waters, it must needs be held an in-"fallible ground that they be also the King's when the "waters have left them dry; and when the waters had "their being on the same, the whole profit then arising did "appertain to the King; yet I have known in some coun-"tries where the frontagers have claimed those grounds so "left by pretended custom of frontagers; and some pro-"bable reason might be shewn wherefore they should have "the same, for as their ground was nearest the sea, and so "next to the charge to repair the defence and next to the "loss where any overflow happened, it might therefore "seem reasonable that as they were put to the greatest "charge and in peril of the loss of their lands, that so, if "lands were left by the sea affront them, these lands might "accrue unto them as a reciprocal consideration for "their charge and loss: but I take it that *of late* the law "hath in these cases been oftentimes ruled for the King "against the subject; for at Croft, in the county of "Lincoln, 1600 acres were gained from the sea affront "the manor of Sir Valentine Browne there, yet he was "put to obtain a grant from the King thereof; and one "Bushey, of Skegness, claimed grounds left by the sea by "the said pretended custom of frontage, but they were de-"creed against him in the Court of Wards in 12 Jac. I., "in which case I was counsel,[1] for it were inconvenient that

[1] Mr. Callis is unfortunate in his illustration. Bushey, of Skegness, was a freeholder holding under Sir Valentine Browne as lord of the manor of Croft, and upon a traverse of an inquisition taken after Bushey's death, in which Bushey was found to have died seised of 300 acres of reclaimed land, Sir Valentine Browne recovered the reclaimed land *as lord of the manor* as against Bushey's heir. See Court of

"the subject should have frontage and yet no bounds pre-"scribed thereto; so that 10,000 acres might be left to front "a man's manor, which were not fit a subject should have "this large inheritance by pretence of such allowed custom. "And I suppose I may herein say in this case, as Mr. "Plowden doth of his 'Silver Mines,' that it is incon-"venient a subject should have the silver mines in his "grounds, for so might he become richer than the King; "so it is not fitting that the subject should have the "grounds left by the sea when so much may happen to "be left as the King's own lands in the realm come to; "and so, because *nimium se exaltat in prerogativam Regis*, "I am of opinion that the new gained grounds from the "sea appertain to the King as a royal escheat, and not to "the subject." Callis then argues (p. 26) that subjects may have personal profits arising from the sea by custom and prescription, as to have free fishery, &c., flotson, jetson, wreck, toll and custom, and the game of swans; and he says, "In Sir Henry Constable's case it is taken and *re-"ceived for law* that a subject's manor may extend to the "low-water mark by prescription; and, seeing all these a "subject may have in and on the sea," he asks: "Where-"fore, then, should he not have all the grounds left by the "sea by prescription?" And to that he answers "that he "cannot have claim in anything by prescription and custom "but that which lieth in use, which is the life of them "both; but lands and grounds which have always been "sea could not be nor lie in use, and therefore they "cannot be claimed, nor the same can be bounded out

Wards Decree Books, 12 James I., vol. 92, fo. 474, 574, and 635. Callis is also mistaken in saying that Sir Valentine Browne was forced to take a grant from the King, the fact being that by patent 7 James I., p. 7, 22 November, lands left relicted by the sea in Croft, Skegness, and Winthorp were granted to Thomas Earl of Exeter and others, and described as "lately in the occupation of Valentine Browne;" the probability being that this grant was a "fishing" grant, and that Browne had set the grantees at defiance and remained in possession, for, in the proceeding against Bushey, Browne does not claim by virtue of the grant, but *as lord of the manor*. If Callis's authority be judged by the instances he quotes, it is not of much weight.

"by prescription or custom; yet lands between the high-"water mark and low-water mark and the bounds thereof "may be prescribed to belong to or to be parcel of the "manor, because in every twelve hours or in every day "they lie dry, and so a subject all that time may have use "of them, and so of all the rest of the said things, but in "that which never lay in use no custom or prescription "could take hold of; inasmuch that, in my opinion, no "prescription or custom can fetch lands further than the "low-water mark."

Callis then discusses the law as to derelict lands, stating that the marshes in Lincolnshire and Norfolk, being overflown every day, are not accounted derelict lands, and he cites Dyer 326b and the Abbot of Ramsey's case, 43 Edward III., and on his supposititious case he decides that the island left belonged to the King, and the ground left between the haven and the ancient shore belonged to the Prince as Earl of Chester, having *Jura Regalia et Escaeta Regalia* within his palatinate, and that the shore, because of prescription, appertained to C., the subject, as parcel of his manor. "My tenets, therefore, be these," says Callis:

"1. That the subject may have the grounds of the sea to "low-water mark, and that no custom can extend the "ownership of a subject further.

"2. That a subject cannot have the ground to the low-"water mark but by custom and prescription, and I take "it that it is very disputable whether grounds before they "be relinquished by the sea may be gained by charter and "grant from the Crown. I suppose they may.

"3. That the words *incrementum et decrementum maris* "are fully described by the said record of 43 Edward III. "of the Abbot of Ramsey: that is, that if the decrease of "the sea by little and unperceivable means, and grown "only in long tract of time, whereby some addition is "made to the frontager's grounds, these by these words "may appertain to the subject; and herein the said words "have no other operation: but lands left to the shore by "great quantities, and by sudden occasion and perceivable "means, accrue wholly to the King.

"4. That the increase of the said county palatine, for "the causes aforesaid, doth appertain to the Prince as Earl "of Chester."

In treating of the shore, Callis holds that, in point of property and ownership, "it is the King's as lord of the "seas; but as Sir Henry Constable's case is, a subject may "have the same as belonging to his manor by prescrip-"tion." He distinguishes between the Roman Law, which holds the sea-shore to be common to all, and the Common Law, which says that the King has the property in it and the people the necessary use, and further that a subject may have the property, subject to the necessary use, by prescription.

In summing up his arguments in the fifth lecture, p. 220, he says that "the dominion and empire of the "sea, the legal power of administration of justice, the "property, profit, and possession thereof, doth appertain "to the King, and that these profits were of two kinds: "1. real, 2. personal. The real profits were the grounds "relinquished by the sea, which were always such grounds "as had been always before covered with waters: but "shores and such grounds which *alternis vicibus* were wet "and dry were not accounted relinquished grounds, and "that relinquished grounds belonged to the King; but "the shore and casual drowned grounds might belong to "a subject. The personal profits of the sea do consist of "wreck, flotson, jetson, ligan, and great fishes which are "due to the King by the royal prerogative of his crown; "but subjects may have the inheritance of the first four by "prescription, and of the last by charter from the King." He then states that new islands belong to the King, and that the shore extends from the lowest ebb to the highest flood; that the King had the property thereof *de jure*, though a subject might have it *ex perquisito*, and the people have there their *usum necessarium*.

It would seem, therefore, that it was taken as settled law in 1622 that the foreshore might be parcel of a manor—that alluvion belonged to the subject, and dere-lict land to the King—that new islands were the King's

—that the *jus publicum* on the foreshore was paramount both to the King's ownership and the subject's ownership thereof. The tidal limit of the foreshore was evidently matter of doubt, and Callis's definition has been overruled. He alleges that wreck, flotson, &c., may be claimed by prescription, but that royal fish can only be claimed by charter. The cases on the Quo Warranto Rolls in the earlier part of this treatise shew that in this last dictum Callis is incorrect.

CHAPTER XIII.

THE REIGN OF KING CHARLES I.

AFTER the accession of King Charles I., it is matter of history that the rights of the prerogative were pushed forward in the most illegal manner. As regards the sea-shore, commissions and fishing grants were made of almost every piece of land on the coast whereon the sea had ever flowed.

Sp. Com. 5629. On 13 February, 1 Charles I., A.D. 1625–26, a commission was issued to survey all ports, creeks, lakes, and land which theretofore were surrounded and overflown with the sea near Hemsworth, Langston, the Isle of Hayling, a marsh called Drayton Marsh, the town of Wymering, the Isle of Portsea, the castle of Porchester, the port of Portsmouth, Fareham Haven, the town of Gosport, Hasleworth Castle, a place called Browndown Beacon, the town of Lymington, Boulderbrigg Bridge, Starklake adjoining the beach of Hurst Castle, and between Lymington and Hurst Castle, and to inquire whether they might be recovered from the overflowing of the sea. The commissioners return a survey, with maps and plans, shewing the foreshore between Hemsworth and Hurst Castle; and by patent dated 14 July, 4 Charles I., A.D. 1628, the King, reciting the inquisition, grants these overflowed and oozie lands by particular description to Mary Wandesford and William Wandesford. The grant, which is printed at the end of the case of Attorney-General *v.* Parmenter, 10 Price 378, comprises practically the whole of the foreshore of the county of Southampton and a great part of the Isle of Wight. It is remarkable, however, that the King had already in 3 Charles I., A.D. 1627, granted the greater part of the same lands to Robert Tipper, a notorious title

Pat. 4 Chas. I., p. 18.

Pat. 3 Chas. I., p. 31.

hunter, who it must be presumed surrendered his grant. The Wandesfords attempted to inclose some parts of this foreshore, and much litigation arose between them and the landowners. Some portions they did inclose, and these are said to be held under their title at the present time.

Under this grant an information was filed in 4 Charles I., A.D. 1628, against Bold, Browning, and others for the foreshores and marshes of Wymering and Portsea. In this information the Attorney-General, Sir Robert Heath, alleges that "the King and his predecessors, Kings and "Queens of England, have from time immemorial been "seised in right of the crown of England of and in all "those marsh grounds, lands, and shelves as usually were "overflown by the sea, or whereon the sea did flow and "re-flow, in or near Wymering and Portsea, in the county "of Southampton." This is the form of the claim, and nothing can be wider or more comprehensive. The defendants claim the lands as parcel of the manors of Portsea and Wymering. The result of the case does not appear, but it was probably dropped by the Crown, and a fresh information was filed in 12 Charles I., A.D. 1236, in the case of Att. *v.* Rigges, *post*, p. 290, when the defendant appears to have succeeded. Exch. B. & A. Suht., Car. I., No. 19.

In 5 Charles I., A.D. 1629, the King granted to Robert Killigrew and others "all marshes and surrounded grounds "adjoining the sea and the sea-shore" in numerous places in the counties of Kent, Lincoln, Norfolk, Sussex, and Carmarthen, and commissions were issued to inquire as to the surrounded lands and oozy lands throughout the kingdom. Pat. 5 Chas. I., p. 16.

In Michaelmas, 7 Charles I., A.D. 1631, the Attorney-General filed an information against Stevens and others respecting houses built upon the shore at Cowes, in the Isle of Wight. The Attorney-General in the information recites that "the King is, or ought to be, lawfully seised "in his demesne as of fee in right of his crown of Eng- "land of and in a certain beach cast up by the sea or "other waste ground in or near West Cowes, in the Isle of "Wight, which of late was part of the King's sea and used Exch. B. & A., Southton, Chas. I. 42.

"to be overflown therewith, and was below the flood mark, "and was part of the sea strand, and common for the resort "of all the King's people." He charges that the defendants have intruded thereon and built houses for which they pay no rent to the King. He then recites a commission of inquiry, which shews that some of the houses were built on the foreshore, and avers that this building is a wrong and hindrance to his Majesty, *being the lawful owner and proprietor of the aforesaid beach or waste ground.* He prays a subpœna, and that the defendants shall set out their profits and account for mesne profits. Here we have the claim of the Crown at its fullest, and it is the same claim which is made at the present day. The question raised by this information was finally decided against the Crown in 17 Charles II. in the case of Att. at rel. Wandesford *v.* Stephens, *post*, p. 317.

Pat. 2 Chas. I., p. 24.

On 9 October in the second year of his reign, A.D. 1627, the King granted to Daniel Lea and others certain houses and wharves built upon Wapping Wall, between Limehouse and Shadwell, upon land taken out of the River Thames. This grant was assigned to the Earl of Carlisle, and gave rise to a long litigation with the owners of those houses.

Exch. B. & A., London and Middx., Car. I., No. 103.

In 3 Charles I., A.D. 1628, the Attorney-General at the relation of the Earl of Carlisle filed an information against Serjeant Brampston and John Stepkin to recover part of the Hermitage Wharf at Wapping. The wharf was built upon land called St. Katherine's Marsh, or Wapping Marsh, which being overflowed by the Thames in 26 Henry VIII., the King leased it to Cornelius Vanderbilt with a view to the recovery of it. Vanderbilt agreed with the owners of the overflowed lands to have half of them for himself and they to take the other half. The marsh was inclosed by a great bank or wall, and the agreement for division confirmed by an Act of Parliament in 35 Henry VIII. The Attorney-General in his information charges that the King was the owner of the bank or wall, and that mariners and poor men who attended ships petitioned Queen Elizabeth and King James and the Lord

Admiral that they might erect houses upon the banks of the river adjoining the said wall, and that they were so erected partly on the wall and partly on the shore and soil of the river, and that the tenants and owners of the marsh grounds inclosed afterwards pretended that they were owners of the wall. To this information Serjeant Brampston answered that he was only a trustee for Stepkin. Stepkin answers that his father was owner of the wharf in question (Hermitage Wharf), built upon the wall and foreland of the marsh, which he held of the King in common socage, and that he had other messuages adjoining, which he held of the Earl of Cleveland as of his manor of Stepney. He pleads a possession of upwards of sixty years, and charges that the Crown had been out of possession, and that the premises had not stood *in super* as of record in the language of the statute against pretences of concealment, 21 Jac. I. cap. 16.

On 20 November 1628 we find Sir Thomas Townsend, John Hay, and Robert Alsopp, the Earl of Carlisle's agents, writing to him about his affairs, and in their letter they say: "For the matter of Wapping we find stronge "opposicion; but the cause will come to heareing the nexte "Terme to lead on the reste, which wee hope will goe "very successively on, and the rather *when some of the* "*Barrons have receaved direcions from the Kinge to take* "*it into their better care by way of furtherance, which his* "*Majestie by good meanes wilbe forthwith sollicited to doe.*" State Papers, Dom., Chas. I. cxxi. 21.

On 19 December 1628 Robert Alsopp writes to the Earl of Carlisle: "Your Wapping business goes with great "honour and hope for your lordship, and is set down to be "heard in the beginning of the next term, as last time. "It is and shall be accomodated with all conveniences for "the good effect thereof, which I have no cause to fear." Ibid. cxxii. 59.

The case proceeded until 5 February, 4 Charles I., A.D. 1628–29, when there occurs an order respecting examination of witnesses. The case then appears to have been dropped, for there is no further order, and a new information was filed by the Attorney-General.

The new information was filed in Michaelmas, 5 Charles

2 Anstruther 607. Exch. D. & O., series 3, E., 8 Chas. I., fo. 66b. Sp. Com. 5359.

I., A.D. 1629, against Philpott, Stepkin, and others in respect of houses and wharves erected on the soil of the Thames at Wapping Wall, in the manor of Stepney. It claims the Thames as being an arm of the sea and a navigable royal port, and that the King and his progenitors have always been seised of the soil under the water of the river between the high and low water marks, and of all walls, banks, and common sewers leading along by the soil of the said river from Hermitage Wharf to Dickeshore in Limehouse; that the defendants had intruded on it by building wharves, houses, and docks on the shore, which belonged to the Crown, and were a nuisance to the river. The information claims the rents and profits of the wharves, houses, and docks, and prays for an order to abate them as purprestures. The defendants set out their several titles, but only shew short titles, and in some cases a licence from the Admiral. There is no manorial title set up at all, and, in short, there was no real defence made. The defendants appear to have relied upon their possession and the weakness of the claim of the Crown.

Exch. Decree Books, 7 Chas. I. 36. Memda. Q. R., E., 8 Chas. I. 25.

The Court on 27 November, 7 Charles I., A.D. 1631, decreed that the soil and ground between the ancient wall called Thames Wall or Wapping Wall belonged to the King as parcel of the port of London and his inheritance of the crown of England, and that the encroachments ought to be removed or arrented to the King at his pleasure *for the improvement of the King's revenues;* in short, the foreshore was decreed to the Crown under the claim by virtue of the prerogative; and this is the earliest decree which affirms the doctrine of the *primâ facie* title.

This case appears to have been heard in Trinity, 5 Charles I., A.D. 1629, and subsequently in Michaelmas, 7 Charles I., A.D. 1631. We find a contemporary report of it in the Hargrave MS. No. 30 at fo. 266, which is as follows :—

In Scacc., Le case de Stepney.

"Nota, that upon English information exhibited by "the Attorney-General for the King against divers in "Stepney who have built houses as it was pretended on "the River of Thames, and have encroached land from "the river: Walter, Chief Baron, delivered this for law: "i. That *primâ facie* and of common right those who have "land adjoining to the said river, or any river which ebbs "and flows, shall have all the land to the low-water mark, "and it shall be intended to belong to those who have "the land upon each side. ii. Those who have land ad-"joining to a river which does not ebb and flow, to wit, "a fresh river, shall have the land to the middle of the "river, so that if the water leave any part, that is their "land; and if an island ariseth in the middle of it, it "shall be between them. iii. If land is surrounded and "has remained so surrounded for such a long time that "the marks are not known, the King shall have this if "it be regained, because there is no other person who "could challenge it, and that which no other person hath "a right to pertaineth to the King. iv. But out of this "general rule are excepted the ports of the realm, for they "belong to the King, and in them the King shall have "the land to the high-water mark, and in them the King "shall have the benefit of anchorage. And after the "death of Walter, to wit, in Michaelmas term, 7 Charles I., "A.D. 1631, this cause after divers hearings was decreed "by Davenport, Chief Baron, Denham, Trevor, and "Weston, Barons, and then the case was put in this "manner. The River of Thames did flow and re-flow "ordinarily and at usual tides to and from such a wall: "and without that wall into the river divers houses of the "defendants, and of divers others not parties to the suit, "have been erected of late times. And it was decreed by "all the Barons *unica voce* that the houses of the de-"fendants which were erected without the wall into the "river, and all others erected without the wall into the "river, are purprestures, and that the said houses shall be "arrented or demolished as it pleases the King, and that a "commission shall be awarded in execution of this decree "to divers good men named by the Court for to set out "all the said purprestures and encroachments upon the "river without the said wall into the said river, although "there were divers others, as appears by the proofs, the

22 Assise, tit. barre, plea 302.

"builders of which or the pretended owners of them are "not parties to this suit. And the reasons ensue: The "main and capital question at this time made in this case "was:—Whether all these houses so erected within the "natural course of the River of Thames heretofore within "the bounds whereunto that river did heretofore flow and "from thence re-flow at ordinary tides (for as to spring "tides or extraordinary tides this is no rule) be not pur-"prestures or no? and it was decreed by all that they were. "Then ensues another question:—If they are purprestures, "what shall be done with them? It was said that it had "been agreed without doubt that the port of this navigable "river belongs to the King; and Denham, Baron, said that "all the soil of this river, as far as it floweth and re-floweth "at ordinary tides, or did heretofore flow and re-flow at "such ordinary tides, is parcel of the river, and belongs to "the King, for it is an arm of the sea (but query concern-"ing this, for more than that it is within the port), and "what was gained from the foot of the wall into the river "is purpresture upon the land of the King: *vide* Davis' "Reports, fo. 56. The King has interest in a navigable "river as high as the sea flows and re-flows in it, and the "reason is, because such river partakes of the nature "of the sea, and is called an arm of the sea as high "as it flows, and the King has the sole interest in the "soil of such rivers. And there are two sorts of rivers: "i. navigable, and this is royal and public; ii. not "navigable, as inland rivers. And Davenport, Chief "Baron, said: If an island riseth in the sea, it does not "belong to the occupier, but to the King; and he said "that it had been adjudged that there shall be no "occupant in the case of the King by outrunning the "King's officers, or by their neglect, &c. And he said "that *littus maris* belongs to the King, but *ripa maris* "acknowledges a lord; but still they are for public use "to fasten boats to: *vide* in the said Davis' Reports, fo. 57, "Of purprestures. And that this may be as well in royal

St. 8 E. 3, De nusance en royall

"waters as in royal ways, *vide* Glanvil, lib. 9, cap. 11, Of "purprestures; and *vide* Britton, fo. 28 and 29, What are "purprestures and what are nuisances. And these are to "be ousted at the cost of the purpresturers; others are "sufferable, which shall be taken into our hands, and "according to the discretion of the Treasurer and Barons "of our Exchequer be arrented at fee farm; and *vide* "7 Eliz. di. 240, in a case of purpresture in a forest. "But Davenport, Chief Baron: For the wall itself, being "an upright wall, which is not usual towards the river, "he will not press this that this belongs to the King, "although in forest all the metes, &c., pertain to the King; "and so in point of the boundaries between this realm and "the realm of Scotland; but he leaves this without prejudice "of either side; and decreed against certain [particular] "men, the now defendants, for any particular houses proved "to be erected within the wall into the river, that they shall "be demolished or arrented at pleasure, &c. And because "by the proof it appears that there are divers other houses "of divers other men not made parties with the defendants, "which are also erected within the wall into the river, it "was also decreed that all are purprestures which are "encroached from the foot of the wall into the river; for "this is encroachment upon the port of the King, the "great port, that of London, but sufferable or to be "demolished at the pleasure of the King. It was also "decreed that a commission shall be awarded to certain "persons named by the Court in execution of this decree, "and that the said commissioners upon their view shall "set out what is encroached from the said foot of the "wall south into the river; which commission is only for "executing their decree, and upon its return the Court "will decree. Notwithstanding, it was much opposed, and "prayed that this Court would only establish the possession, and leave the parties to their trial at law. But "afterwards Davenport, Chief Baron, was of another mind, "and said *he would not take away the freehold of any man* "*upon a certificate*."

chemin: lon s'ra rent al roy, et lon abate; tit. Assise, pl. 447.

It is evident from this report that the Court was not agreed in upholding the *primâ facie* theory generally. The Chief Baron Walter, whose great learning and integrity were well known, and who was (says Foss) too independent and too honest to suit the royal will, and who, in consequence of his opposition to the King, was at last prohibited from sitting (that is, within a year after he gave this judgment, as here reported), was clearly not prepared to support the doctrine of the *primâ facie* title. Whether his disgrace had anything to do with his decision in this case we know not, but the coincidence of dates is remarkable. His successor, Chief Baron Davenport, was a strong supporter of the King, and his judgment in the case of Hampden respecting the "ship-money" caused him at last to be impeached by the House of Lords on 6 July 1641. Baron Denman opposed the decision in the ship-money case, but agreed with the rest of the Barons for the sake of conformity. He died shortly afterwards. Baron Trevor was a supporter of the King, and was afterwards impeached for joining in the judgment as to the ship-money. Baron Weston was also a supporter of the King, and was also impeached. It would seem, therefore, without disrespect to the memories of the learned judges who finally decided this case, that they were strongly biassed in favour of the general rights of the prerogative; and when we see that they gave their decision as a matter of law, and refused to accede to the prayer that the parties might have a trial by a jury, we cannot but conclude that the decision in this case, having regard to the time and the circumstances under which it was given, is a very doubtful authority for the propositions of law which it lays down; and yet this case, and the case of the Prior of Tynemouth, *ante*, p. 111, are the only two cases quoted by Hale in support of the doctrine of the *primâ facie* title of the Crown. Even in this case we see that Chief Baron Davenport hesitated to finally decide the question, declaring that he would not take away the freehold of any man upon a certificate, and we shall see that the freehold was not taken away, and that the decree was never enforced, for the owners of the houses resisted it to the utmost, and resisted it successfully.

After the return of the inquiry by the commissioners,

and upon the certificate made by them, the encroachments were ordered to be seized into the King's hand, and the Court confirmed the certificate by decree dated 8 May, 8 Charles I., A.D. 1632. Exch. D. & O., series 3, xii. 66b, 101.

On 2 June 1632 an exemplification of the decree was served upon the tenants of the wharves, and possession was demanded for the King, "*which was peremptorily denied* "by them;" whereupon, on the motion of the Recorder of the City of London, the defendants were ordered to shew cause why injunctions should not go; and accordingly, on 6 June, 8 Charles I., A.D. 1632, there is an order for an injunction to the sheriff to remove the tenants out of possession, and to put and continue his Majesty and his assigns in possession. Ibid. xi. 236.

This appears to have been done with regard to nine houses only, which were in the occupation of the defendants in the suit, and the tenants attorned to the King and paid the rents to the Earl of Carlisle's agents. The Earl of Carlisle died in 1636, and, being indebted to the King, his patent was surrendered; and soon after a new information was filed, at the suit of the King, against Stepkyn and others, and the Earl of Cleveland, who was lord of the manor of Stepney, within which Wapping Wall is situate, and against a large number of his tenants, for the same kind of encroachments. This suit dragged on until 20 June, 16 Charles I., A.D. 1640, when the Revolution supervening, it was dropped. Ibid. xxvii. 67, 410, 448; xxviii. 3, 13; xxvi. 102; xxvii. 45, 61.

We find among the State Papers of the year 1637 the following statement, evidently drawn up and presented to the King, which shews that his Majesty took a personal interest in this suit, and the conduct of it:— State Papers, Dom., 1637, ccclxxvii. 100.

> Informations for your Majestie concerning the incroachments and purprestures upon the River of Thames, near Wapping, Shadwell, Ratcliffe, and Lymehouse, in the Countie of Midlesex, belonging to your Majestie.

Upon the first suite in the Exchequer Chamber exhibited by your Majesty's Attorney on your Majesty's behalfe, but by the prosecucion of the late Earl of Carlile, in the seaventh yeare of your reigne there was a decree for your Majestie against the then Deffendants, which were nine in number.

The Court by that decree did declare in the first place, that whatsoever is incroached upon the River of Thames betweene the high water and lowe water marke, appertaines to your Majestie either to bee arrented or abated at your pleasure.

But because it did not appeare where the bounds of the River were, by an exact measure, to reduce that to a certainty it was further ordred that a commission should goe to certaine Commissioners named by the Courte, whoe upon their viewe, and by testimonie offered to them, should survey, set downe, and describe, where the auncient wall went, which was aunciently called by the name of the Thames Wall, or Wapping Wall, and what houses, buildings, wharffes, docks, or parts of houses, building, wharffes, and docks have bene builded, made, or erected on the south side of the said wall, or on the south side of the place where the said wall ancientlie went, and that those Commissioners should seise into your Majesty's hands all the houses, buildings, wharffes, and docks betweene the said wall and water.

In prosecucion hereof a commission doth issue.

The Commissioners viewe the place and informe themselues of the truth of the fact, and returne their certificate, that the streete nowe called Wapping Streete is the verie place where the ancient wall called the Thames Wall, or Wapping Wall, went, That the houses, buildings, wharffes, and docks built and erected by the nyne deffendants doe all stand betweene the ancient wall, or streete, on the north, and the River of Thames on the south, (except foure feete only towards the streete) and make a perticuler, and an exact descripcion howe many feete by measure everie one of the nine deffendants have incroached upon the soyle of the River, and that they have seised soe much into your hands according to the commission.

This being returned, the Courte at the next heareing of

the cause confirme this certificate, and make that parte of theire decree, and all this appeares by the decree under the seale of the Courte.

It hath since byn conceived by the Court that this decree should not bynde those whoe had the inheritance and not parties to the former suite.

Let that bee admitted, yet the reason of the former decree is the same still against those that have the inheritance, as it was against the parties.

It hath beene objected that the certificate, being made onlie by Commissioners upon viewe or proofes before them, doth not conclude the parties, except the Court had heard proofes, and adjudged it according to the certificate.

To this, it is answered, the Courte upon heareing the certificate, and councell of both sides, confirmed it by decree, and it is not necessarie nor usuall for that or any other Courte to have newe proofes in that kind after publicacion and heareing, but such Commissioners certificate, being only to ascertaine boundes is usually decreed, and being decreed, is as bynding as if it had beene upon proofes.

But it hath beene said, the decree establisheth no more to your Majestie then what was betweene the wall and the River, but the wall must bee extended to the foote of the wall, for that is part of the wall, and from that uttermost part of the wall doth the River beginne.

The answeare to that hath bene thus.

1. The incroachment hath beene declared to bee betweene the high water and lowe water marke, and the high water marke was alwaies to the toppe of the wall and not to the foote.

2. The ancient wall was where the streete now is, and from thence the River is, and alwaies hath beene, accoumpted.

3. If it should be accompted otherwise, then the River of Thames would bee much straightened, for the foote of the wall runs out on that side of the River in some places thirtie, in some places fortie foote, where at a high water, boates and vessells doe alwaies goe and lye at anckor.

4. And this interpretacion would bee expressely con-

trarie to the certificate of the Commissioners, and by consequence contrarie to the decree, which hath confirmed that certificate.

5. Lastlie admitt that the wall to the foote thereof southward were the soyle of the subject, yet to fill that up, or erecte buildings or wharffes thereupon, so farre as the high water marke anciently went must needs bee a purpresture upon the said River.

> If your Majestie shall in your wisdome thinke this to bee reason, because in the time of much weightier affaires your Majestie cannot intend to heare it yourselfe, your Majestie may bee moved to recomend the reheareing thereof to three or foure of your Lords, they calling the Barons of the Exchequer and some of your Majesty's Councell at Lawe to their assistance, they to setle it, or report to your Majesty their opinions.

The King's advisers here had clearly no intention of having the matter tried at law—the verdict of a jury would have been too dangerous.

It would appear that Gregory Philpott, one of the tenants who remained in possession and attorned to the King's grantee, was the tenant of the defendant Peter Stepkin, and accordingly Stepkin, the ousted owner, brought an action in the Common Pleas against him for the rents of the houses lately decreed for the Crown; and that a number of the other landlords of tenants who had attorned did likewise. Thereupon application was made to the Court of Exchequer by the Attorney-General to stay these suits pending the decision of the information against the Earl of Cleveland and others; but on 25 June, 15 Charles I., A.D. 1639, the application was refused and the suits allowed to proceed, and on 12 May, 16 Charles I., A.D. 1640, they were still proceeding; but after this date we have no further trace of them in the records of the Court of Exchequer.

The following petition to the King from the ousted tenants tells the tale very faithfully:—

To the Kings most Excellent Majestie. The humble peticion of Ralph Wilson, Niclas Walker, William Colombine, William Evans, Christopher Fothergill and William Hunt, for and on the behalfe of themselfes and many others severall poore Tenants of your Highnes at Wappinge.

State Papers, Dom., Car. I. cccciii. 97. 26 Oct 1639.

In all humbleness

Shewing unto your Majesty, That whereas many hundreds of howses, wharffs, and docks have beene erected and made within the memorie of man, and are now continued, by incroachment upon the soyle of the north side of your highness River of Tames betweene the ancient high wather marke and low wather marke of the said River, all alonge eastwards from a wharffe called Lewins Wharffe, at or neere the west ende of Wappinge, to Shadwell, and so to Ratcliff, and then to Lyme Howse, and then to Dickshoare, which doe wholly belonge unto your Majesty as in right of your Crowne of England, as may be manifested as well by matter of record as by other good testimony; and to make the same the better appeare, an information being heretofore exhibited in the Exchequer Chamber on your Majesty's behalfe by your Highnes' then Attorney Generall against severall persons as intruders upon nyne severall howses, wharffes, and docks, with their appurtenances, being severall parcells of the said incroachments and lying dispersedly in the severall places aforesaid, a decree upon solempne and many dayes hearing past thereupon for your Majesty above 8 yeares since, and the same have beene ever since enjoyed by your Majesty and your assignes accordingly: And thereupon your poore subjects holdinge severall other howses in Wappinge aforesaid, other parcells of the said incroachments, did attorne tennants to your Majesty without further suite, and have layed out all their estates in building and bettering your said howses, and have ever since payed their rents for the same to such as demaunded the same under your Majesty's title:

Neverthelesse may it please your Majesty that one John Stepkin and Charles Stepkin, gentlemen, and others, pretending title to your subjects' said howses, and takeing notice that the late Erle of Carlile, who was fee farmer of the said incroachments to your Majesty and defended your Majesty's said title, is lately deceased, and that since his decease the same being resumed into your Majesty's own hands is not so well defended as formerly, and knowing that your poore subjects are not able to pay their rents and defend your Majesty's title themselves, have lately brought severall actions of ejectment at law against some of your said subjects, and recovered severall judgments by defaut thereupon against them, without making any defence, and sithence have turned some of them out of dores into the streets, leaving them harborles, and compellinge others of them to enter into bond to leave the possession thereof at Michaelmas next, and have and doe now say in a tanteinge and jereinge manner to your said subjects, "You attorned tenants to the Kinge, how doth hee now defende you?" and taking incoradgment thereby, have brought and doe threaten many other accions against your subjects, whereby they, their wifes, and children are like to perish and be utterly undone.

> In tender consideration whereof, and forasmuch as herein your Majesty in point of proffitt is concerned many wise and your subjects in their whole estates; Your poore subjects therefore most humbly implore your Majesty's grace and favour herein, that your Majesty's title may bee preserved, their possessions restored, and further suite prevented. And they, as by their duty and allegiance they are bound, shall dayly pray for the continuance of your Highnes prosperous, longe, and happy raigne.

The orders made on this petition are as follow:—

At the Court at Whitehall, 26 October 1639. His Majestie, taking the case of theise poore petitioners into His Princelie consideration, and calling to minde that hee had not long since made a former reference to the Lord Keeper, Lord Treasurer, Lord Privy Seale, and Lord Cottington or any three of them to take into their consideration, both this case in particular concerning Wapping, and the improoving of the marishes and surrounded grounds in generall, as matters of importance, and much concerning His Majestie in His immediate proffit, Hath commanded me to signifie His pleasure, that the Lordes aforenamed, with all convenient speed, calling to them Mr. Attorney and Solicitor Generall, and such others of His Counsell at law, as their Lordships shall think fitt, doe advise together what they think fittest to bee done in their owne judgment both for the Petitioners' reliefe, and for His Majesty's owne service; and when they have so done, that then they appoint a convenient tyme to conferre with the Barons of the Exchequer, upon which conference such finall resolution may bee taken as may bee most agreable with the Kinges justice, His honor and proffitt, and the quiett of the Petitioners, for whose peace His Majesty requires their Lordshipps speciall care in the meane tyme as farr as in justice may bee done. And His Majesty's further pleasure is that their Lordshipps acquaint His Majesty how they find the true state of the busines to stand, before they conclude upon any finall resolution.

FRAN: WINDEBANK.

His Majestie haveing receaved informacion that his tytle to the howses, wharffes, docks, and yards incroached upon the River of Thames on the north side of the said River at or neere Wapping, Shadwell, Ratcliff, and Lymehouse, hath long depended in his Court of Exchequer, which first concerned the late Earle of Carlile, and now concernes His Majestie immediately, the Patent granted to the said Earle being surrendered back to His Majestie, and that severall Orders and Decrees have beene had thereupon, one decreing that all the soyle betweene the high wather and lowe wather marke doth belong to His Majestie in right of His Crowne of England, and that all howses, wharffes, and docks built thereupon ought to be abated or arrented at His Majesty's pleasure, and another Decree for 9 severall howses whereof His Majesty and his assignes have possession, whereupon the Inhabitans of those 9

State Papers, Dom., Car. I. cccciii. 154. 22 Feb. 1639-40.

howses have turned tenants to His Majesty, and paid severall fines and rents, and that by their example many others of the Inhabitants of the aforesaid places being in that same estate have likewise become tenants to His Majestie, who are now turned out by suites at Common Law, notwithstanding that there are Informacions dependinge in the said Courte, and thereupon they have peticioned His Majesty for their reliefe: His Majestie, holding it a matter of greate consequence unto him both in the particular case and in the president thereof, is therfore resolved that speciall care shalbe taken for recovery of his right and settling thereof, as farre as in justice may bee. And hath commanded mee to signifie the same; That the Lord Keeper, Lord Treasurer, the Earle of Dorset, Lord Privy Seale, the Lord Lieutenant of Ireland, the Lord Cottington, and the two Principall Secretaries of State, or any 4 or 3 of them, shall have the care and protection of this busines, and calling unto them Mr. Atturney and Mr. Solicitor Generall, and such other of His Majesty's Counsell at law, as they shall thinke fitt, shall examine the Peticions and Informations hereunto annexed, and informe themselfes fully of all things which they conceave necessary for His Majesty's service in this case, and of all the former proceedings therein; *and also at such tymes as they shall thinke fitt shall call to them the Barons of the Exchequer and conferre with them*, to the end that their Lordshipps, understanding the true state thereof, may waite upon His Majestie and deliver unto him their opinions of what hath already past, and what they thinke fitt to bee done for the future; wherupon His Majesty will give such further directions as in his wisedome hee shall find to bee fitt; and in the meane time they are to give such directions for the proceeding or not proceeding therein as they shall thinke fitt.

Added in the margin with a caret.

FRAN: WINDEBANK.

At the Court at Whitehall, 22 February 1639.

On the same day, 22 February 1639–40, the following petition was presented. It is remarkable for a significant alteration in its text made after the petition had been copied into the Book of Petitions.

> To the King's most excellent Majesty. The humble peticion of James Earle of Carlile, Sir James Hay, Knight, Archibald Hay, Esquire, Trustees for the estate of the late Earle of Carlile, and of the Trustees for the estate of Sir Peregrin Barty and Sir Phillip Slandon, Knights, deceased, Sir George Theobalds, Knight, John van Haesdonck, gentleman, and divers others who are interested and have contracted for divers parcells and quantities of marish grounds.

State Papers, Dom., Car. I. cccciii. 151. 22 Feb. 1639.

Shewing that wheras the marshes and marish grounds lying betwixt the flowing and reflowing of the tides of the sea within your kingdome of England and Dominion of Wales have beene esteemed and reputed to bee parcell of and belonging to your Majesty's prerogative royall, as well in this your Realme of England as in your Kingdomes of Scottland and Ireland, as in some cases hath bin adjudged in law for your Majesty; and in confidence of your Majesty's undoubted right and title to the said marshes, your Petitioners and sundry others of your Majesty's loyall subjects have beene encouradged to contract and bargaine with your Majesty for divers and sundry of the said marish grounds, and accordingly have paid divers and great summes of monny unto your Majesty for the same; and have further not onely beene at great costes, charges and expenses of monney in and about the imbanking and gaining of divers of the said marshes from the sea, but also for and about suites at law touching the recovery of possession and enjoyment of the said marshes from the disturbance of many perverse and obstinate people who molest and withould your Petitioners from the quiet use and possession of the said marshes, notwithstanding your Majesties grant of Letters Patent of the said marshes, and of your Majesty's command declared under your Privy Signet unto all Justices of the Peace, Mayors, Sheriffes, Bayliffs, Constables, and all other your subjects for their ayde and assistance towards your Petitioners quiet use and enjoyement of the same; all which have beene produced, read, and shewed unto them, but have taken no effect by reason of the common outcry, that your Majesty's title is not likely to prevail, [1]*and the rather because the Barons of your Majesties Court of Exchequer have of late appeared very doubtfull in their opinions, whether to determine for or against your Majesty in the question of the said marshes, which your Petitioners doe conceive to proceed for want of the patronage of some speciall person of your Majesty's most honorable Privy Counsell to countenance the said matter; and doe suppose and hope that the doubtes of the Barons might bee removed*, if the beginning, progresse and increase of the said marshes from the nature, quality and effects of the flowing and reflowing of the sea at ordinary and high spring tides, and the certain proofes and proper markes whereby the said marshes may bee distinctly knowen to differ from all upland grounds thereunto adjacent, were clearely sett forth and declared, as being the ground worcke and foundacion of your Majesties undoubted right and title vnto the said marshes. For the just preservacion whereof, and to the ende your Petitioners for the reasons before alledged may bee accepted into your gracious consideracion, and that they may not spill nor spend money to their exhaustion and insupportable detriment in a question of so great moment and consequence of proffit to your Majesty, and yet so uncertaine and doubtfull to your petitioners:

Your petitioners most humbly pray, That your Majesty wilbe graciously pleased to command some speciall person of your Majesties most honorable Privy Counsell, whome your Majesty shall thinke meete to take the care *and patronage* of this matter, and to peruse, read, and consider what your Petitioners have digested of and concerning the

[1] The passage in italics was copied in the book from the original petition, but the book has been altered to read as follows:—"and it is "become very doubtful in their opinions whether the matter in "question of the said marshes wilbe determined for or against your "Majesty, which said doubtes your Petitioners doe conceive and hope "that the doubtes thereof may be removed."

nature, quality, and effects of the flowing and reflowing of the sea, and of the true origine and increment of salt marshes, and of the certain and undoubted signes, proofes, and markes whereby they may bee knowen to differ and bee distinguished from all upland and naturall ground, for to informe first your Majesty and your most honorable Privy Counsell of the truth of the matter; and then that your Majesty will vouchsafe to require all and every of your honorable Judges of your Bench, Common Pleas, and Exchequer to meet with your most honorable Privy Councell and others whom your Majesty shall appoint thereunto, and that att the said meeting the matter before mencioned may bee thoroughly and fully consulted of, argued, debated, and considered, and such conclusions and resolucions of opinions produced, as to their grave judgements may best sorte. Wherein it is hoped, that no tract of tyme or habit of usurpacions shalbe admitted in evidence to blott, extinguish, determine, or prejudice what was originally your Majesty's right and chief flower of your prerogative by infallible proofes of demonstration. And that your Majesty wilbe pleased soone after to receive an accompt of the consultacion and resolucion of the said Judges, and the same to bee decreed to the full satisfaction of your Majesty and all your subjects interested therein, and that accordingly the cases of your humble petitioners may bee received into the bosome of your Majesties clemency and most gracious considerations.

And your Petitioners, &c.

On this petition the following order was made :—

At the Court at Whitehall: 22 February 1639. His Majesty's pleasure is that the Lord Privy Seale, the Earle of Dorsett, the Lord Lieutenant of Ireland, the Lord Cottington, and Mr. Secretary Windebank, or any two or more of them, shall take the care *and patronage* on His Majesty's behalf of the marshes, and consider what the Petitioners have digested concerning the same, and certifie His Majestie from time to tyme their proceedings therein,

Words in italics struck out after the copy was made.

and cause all such things to bee putt in execution as His Majestie shall please to order upon such certificates.

FRAN: WINDEBANK.

The alterations in these entries, evidently made to get rid of the reference to the *patronage* of the King, are very significant.

Exch. of Pleas, Enrolments, H., 14 Chas. I. 71; T., 15 Chas. I. 14, 16; T., 16 Chas. I. 47.

The defendants to the Wapping information, who were owners of the tenements on the shore, proceeded not only in the Common Pleas, but in the Exchequer of Pleas, and got judgments in ejectment against the tenants who had attorned to the Crown; and it is clear, therefore, that, although the Crown did, by a very curious process and after very grievous doubts even in the minds of judges subservient to the King, at last get a judgment of the Court (but not the verdict of a jury) in favour of the *primâ facie* title of the Crown, it was unable to sustain it in fact, and that the unhappy tenants who attorned to the King after the decree were ruthlessly treated by the real owners of the property: they were turned into the street harbourless, and were openly taunted that the King did not defend them.

Serjeant Mereweather in his speech refers to this case, and shews that it was never relied upon subsequently, and is of most doubtful authority; and yet this case and that of the Prior of Tynemouth in 20 Edward I. are the two cases on which Hale relies as supporting the doctrine of the *primâ facie* title of the Crown to the foreshore.

2 Keble 759.

We find it, however, once referred to, in the case of Whitaker *v.* Wise, in 23 Charles II., A.D. 1671, where one of the judges is reported to have said that in Trinity, 6 (*sic*) Charles I., in this case it was adjudged, contrary to Sir Henry Constable's case, that the foreshore is in the Crown only.

Serjeant Mereweather in particular states that in the case of Johnson *v.* Barrett in 1647, in which Hale was counsel and was supporting the prerogative claim, Hale does not refer to Philpot's case, which he would certainly have done if he had considered it an authority which would have been acceptable to or was binding on the Court.

There can therefore be little doubt that this decision of the Court of Exchequer was ineffectual to practically support the *primâ facie* title. Although the case has been subsequently relied upon, it has been relied upon by the judges in ignorance of the true facts of it, and it is submitted that it is a more than doubtful authority in support of the *primâ facie* theory. 2 Anstruther 607, 616.

We have seen that, shortly before the decree, the King was to send directions to the Barons "to take it into their "better care by way of furtherance," and that Lord Carlisle's agents had great hopes of success; the question of the *primâ facie* title, therefore, was an open and doubtful one, and it would seem that there was no kind of precedent or decision to guide the Court in the determination of the question.

The report in the Hargrave MSS. shews that Chief Baron Walter did not believe in the *primâ facie* theory. The decision of the other Barons is, that the erections on the shore were purprestures—not purprestures on the *jus publicum* only, but purprestures on the *jus privatum*; and the main authorities on which they rely are the case of the fishery of the Banne (which is a decision only as to fishery, and not as to soil), and the cases relating to purprestures upon the *jus publicum* and purprestures on the soil of a forest. The procedure by commission and certificate was, to say the least, unusual; and even Chief Baron Davenport, after the judgment, when the defendants claimed a trial at law, doubted its legality and "was of "another mind, and said he would not take away the "freehold of any man upon a certificate." The judgment was given by the judges who gave the judgment in the ship-money case, and it is submitted that it is of no greater authority than that celebrated and unconstitutional decision. Davis, fo. 56.

The Earl of Carlisle dying in 1631, the King took up the case himself. We have seen the statement of the case and the advice tendered him, either to try the case himself, or appoint three or four of his lords and the Barons of the Exchequer and the King's counsel at law to settle it.

It appears, by the order of 26 October 1639, that the

King did appoint the Lord Keeper, the Lord Treasurer, Lord Privy Seal, and Lord Cottington to consider the matter with the assistance of the law officers, but specially required them to *consult him* before they concluded upon any final resolution.

The King's personal interest is further shewn from the order of 22 February 1639–40, which states that "His "Majesty, holding it a matter of great consequence unto "him both in the particular case and in the precedent "thereof, is therefore resolved that special care should be "taken for recovering of his right and settling thereof as "far as in justice may be," and appoints the Lord Keeper, Lord Treasurer, the Earl of Dorset, Lord Privy Seal, Lord Lieutenant of Ireland, Lord Cottington, and the two principal Secretaries of State to have the care and protection of this business, and, with the assistance of the law officers and the Barons of the Exchequer, to give their opinions to the King as to what has already passed and what they think fit to be done for the future, whereupon his Majesty will give such further directions as in his wisdom he shall find to be fit. But a curious light is thrown on the question by the petition which follows, and which shews without doubt that the law which had been laid down as to the *primâ facie* title was greatly doubted, and that the common outcry was that it was not likely to prevail, because "the Barons of the Exchequer were very doubtful in their "opinions whether to determine for or against the Crown "on the question," which the petitioners conceive "to pro-"ceed for want of the patronage of some special person of "the Privy Council to countenance the matter, and they "suppose and hope that the doubts of the Barons might "be removed," and they pray the King to appoint one of his Privy Councillors to take the care and patronage of this matter. And also they pray that the King would command the judges of the Bench, Common Pleas, and Exchequer to meet the Privy Council and consult upon the matter. And they hope that "no tract of time or "habit of usurpations shall be admitted in evidence to blot, "extinguish, determine, or prejudice what was originally "your Majesty's right and chief flower of your prerogative "by infallible proofs of demonstration, and that your "Majesty will have the same decreed." To this the King consented, and did appoint a committee, so that we see that the most strenuous efforts were made by the King and his councillors, even by putting pressure upon the subservient judges, to get a new decree to support the previous one, which had become abortive, and which was even at that time held to be of no authority, but all without avail: jury after jury found verdicts in ejectment against the tenants who had attorned to the King under the decree of 1632; the judges of the Court of Exchequer themselves dared not grant prohibition to the suits that were brought; the King's information lingered on in the Exchequer until 16 Charles I., A.D. 1641, and then we find the framers of the Grand Remonstrance complaining that men's rights are taken away under colour of the King's title to land between high and low water marks.

This suit and a number of similar suits that were pending were all dropped, and the Revolution came to sweep away the many abuses of the rights of the prerogative which had been attempted by King Charles I. The judges who gave the abortive judgment were impeached by the House of Lords, and this, the only judgment which supported the theory of the *primâ facie* title, was swept away with the rest of the abuses of the time.

In 8 Charles I., A.D. 1632, there is a return made of a Sp. Com. piece of foreshore in the Tyne known as Jarrow Slake, 5274, 5275. which was claimed by the Crown as lying between high and low water mark. This, however, the Crown never recovered; it belonged to the Dean and Chapter of Durham, and is held by the Ecclesiastical Commissioners at the present time. There are in this reign innumerable returns of this kind; the claim of the Crown was pushed to the uttermost, and strenuously resisted, the defendants almost invariably claiming the lands returned as parcel of their manors.

In 9 Charles I., A.D. 1633, commenced the series of Exch. B. & A., Linc., Car. I. suits relating to lands gained from the sea in the Wash in

120. Att. v. Irby. Lincolnshire and Norfolk, at Moulton, Tidd St. Mary's, Gedney, Sutton, &c. The defendants were Sir Anthony Irby, Erasmus Amy, William Wike, Michael Oldsworth, and others, the lords of the manors opposite which the marshes and foreshore in question lay. The records of the proceedings are very voluminous, and shew that the suits dragged on till the 16th year of Charles I., A.D. 1641, when the passage in the Grand Remonstrance seems to have induced the Crown to cease from prosecuting them, and on the outbreak of the Revolution they were dropped altogether. Some of them were revived in the time of the Commonwealth, but they were unsuccessful in dispossessing the lords of the manors. In the time of Charles II. new grants were made of some of the lands, and the Crown appears to have been successful in one case in 23 Charles II., Whitaker *v.* Wise: see *post.*

See Rex *v.* Oldsworth, post, p. 292 et seqq.

2 Keble 759.

In Easter, 9 Charles I., A.D. 1634, the Attorney-General filed an information against Sir John Strangways to recover a piece of reclaimed land containing six thousand acres known as the Fleet, near Weymouth. The information recites that "Whereas His Majesty and his predecessors "during the time whereof the memory of man is not to "the contrary were seised in their demesne as of fee in "right of the Crown of England of and in a certain great "parcel of land covered with salt water, and lying and "being under the flowing and re-flowing of the sea in a "bay or creek of the sea adjoining on the one part, "towards the lands unto or near Wyke, Melcombe Regis, "Fleet, West Checkerell, Langton, and Abbotsbury, or "some of them, in the county of Dorset, and of the other "part divided from the high sea by a beach or firm bank "of sand or ground, which parcel of land is commonly "called or known by the name of the Fleet and contains "about six thousand acres, in which there was anciently "claimed a fishing by the Abbot of Abbotsbury, which "fishing came to King Henry VIII. and has descended to "his Majesty," and that Sir John Strangways, "by colour "of some grant of fishing in the premises or of some of the "demesne lands of the said abbey adjoining, pretends a

See case of Swans, 7 Coke 86.

"right to the soil and inheritance of the said parcel of "land, and has intruded upon it and drained it and made "it firm land," and he claims it for the Crown.

We have here another form of the Crown claim. The prosecution of this case appears to have ceased, for there is no order relating to it in the Exchequer Order Books, nor is there any trace that the Crown got into possession or that the defendant compromised.

In a treatise by Lord Hale on Admiralty jurisdiction, in the Hargrave MSS. 93, fo. 222, he sets out an inquisition dated 13 October, 6 Edward VI., A.D. 1552 (which he says was lent to him by Sir John Strangways), which was held under the Admiralty jurisdiction upon the shore at Abbotsbury, before the Lieutenant of the Admiral, to inquire whether the Fleet was within the Admiral's jurisdiction. The jury say that the soil and land of the same water called le Fleet and the same water are, and from time of memory were, the several land, soil, and water of the abbots of Abbotsbury; and, remarking on the document, Hale says "that the Fleet was in truth a current "of salt sea water, and yet the proper and private interest "of the said water and fishery thereof did belong to the "Abbot; that this place, though an arm, creek, or fleet of "the sea, was not within the jurisdiction of the Admiral; "that upon the high seas or upon the fleets, currents, or "arms thereof, where a particular person or corporation "hath not the particular or private interest or property, "every subject hath a common right of fishery, but yet in "a creek or fleet of the sea a subject may by custom or "prescription have a private interest or property exclusive "of others, or of that common right of fishery which "others might otherwise have had therein."

MS. Hargrave 93, fo. 222.

We have seen before that the abbots of Abbotsbury had wreck *super terras suas*. We have seen that the possessions of the abbots of Abbotsbury came to them in Saxon times, and that the foreshore was recognised as part of those possessions by a charter of Edward the Confessor to the Abbot's grantor (*ante*, p. 11), and it is probable that Sir John Strangways may have set up the

Abbot's ancient title to wreck and shore in answer to this information. Whether the theory maintained by Hale (who was a student of Lincoln's Inn at this period), that "he "that hath wreck of the sea *infra manerium* it is a great "presumption that he hath the shore," was put forward at this time, and whether it was originated by Hale or not, we cannot tell; still, it is a singular fact that the Crown should at this time have begun to feel the difficulty of succeeding in suits respecting foreshore against the persons who were entitled to wreck, for in 11 Charles I., A.D. 1635–6, it issued innumerable quo warrantos against claimants of wreck. They are not all indexed or accessible, but we find them in the following places:—Harwich, Essex; Minster, Kent; Anderley, Boston, Failsthorpe, Great Grimsby, North Coats, Mounby Chapel, Kidby, Holtest, Ingoldmels, Saltfleteby, Thursthorpe, Lincolnshire; Tynemouth, Blackborn, Blyth, Northumberland; Dunwich, Bawdesey, Ipswich, Layton, Sisewell, Southwold, Sudborne, Thorpe, Suffolk; Scarborough, Whitby, Flamborough, Holderness, Yorkshire; and in the barony of Berkeley on the Severn, in Gloucestershire; and doubtless many others were issued.

Sp. Com. 6016.

In the same year commissions were sent to every coast county to inquire concerning lands overflowed by the sea, to which full returns were made. In that for the county of Devon, which is an example, the foreshores of the Rivers Taw and Torridge at Barnstable, Braunton, Bideford; the foreshores of the Exe at Clist, Topsham, Kenton, Powderham, and Exminster; and, indeed, almost every piece of marsh in the county is set out.

Exch. Q. R. Memda., Trin., 11 Chas. I., roll 102.

The proceeding against George Lord Berkeley was for using divers liberties without warrant in the barony of Berkeley and many other places, including Slimbridge, in Gloucestershire, and for claiming a several fishery in the Severn, and royal fish and wreck, flotson, jetson, and lagon, from Shepperton Ferry to the east end of Arlingham. Lord Berkeley pleaded immemorial user, and set out a great number of charters from the time of Henry II. downward to his predecessors. The Attorney-General confessed the plea, and judgment was given for Lord Berkeley.

This proceeding as to wreck in the barony of Berkeley is noticeable, because we find that at this period the Crown was actively engaged in suits against the owners of reclaimed land and foreshore on the banks of the Severn, which lie within the barony of Berkeley.

It appears from a report of a case of an information of intrusion, in 11 Charles I., A.D. 1636, against Sir Henry Appleton, William Sheldon, and Giles Vandeputt for lands gained from the sea (in Canvey Island, in Essex), that the Attorney-General alleged seisin in King James and his predecessors, and the defendants wished to plead the general issue and retain their possession under statute 21 Jac. I. c. 16, and cited a case of intrusion on land at Goldborough, not lying on the sea. This the Attorney-General opposed, and drew a distinction between land situated inland and land gained from the sea, arguing that there could not be possession of such land so long as it was washed by the sea, for by chance at ebb water some few sheep may be upon it, but this he alleged was no possession. The point does not seem to have been precisely decided, but Chief Baron Davenport decided in favour of the Crown, because the affidavit produced did not sufficiently prove that the King had been out of possession. It is clear from this case that the Crown was still claiming up to the high-water mark of spring tides, and was also endeavouring to avoid the effect of the statute of James, which gave the subject a right to an issue. This is not to be wondered at when we find that the Crown had never succeeded in establishing a claim when the case had been taken to a jury, and, so far as we can ascertain, there never has been a verdict for the Crown in support of the *primâ facie* title except in cases of derelict lands and cases of purprestures upon the public right of navigation. In the case of Attorney *v.* Jones in 1863, the verdict found for the Crown in the first trial was reversed upon a second trial.

Hargrave MS. 30, fo. 269b.

In Michaelmas, 12 Charles I., A.D. 1636, the Attorney-General filed an information against Isaac Bromwich, Thomas Lloyd, John Gage, and others, claiming land formerly part of the bed of the Severn. The information recites that "Whereas the River of Seaverne running and "being between the Counties of Gloucester and Worcester "on the one side and the Counties of Monmouth and "Hereford on the other side is a royal and navigable "river, whereunto the sea as far as the Port and City of "Bristol, the Cities of Gloucester and Worcester, and "upwards hath flowed and reflowed, and doth usually and "ordinarily flow and reflow, which said River of Seaverne "is and always hath been accounted an arm of the sea, "upon which river shippers, merchants, and others, with "all manner of ships, boats, and other vessels coming to "and from the Port of Bristol, Cities of Gloucester and "Worcester, the town of Shrewsbury, and other parts of "this kingdom, being upon the said river, have time out "of mind freely sailed and passed for the ventinge of "their goods, commodities, and merchandises, by means "whereof great traffic and store of shipping always have "been brought from foreign parts and divers places of "this kingdom to the said Port of Bristol and the cities, "towns, and places aforesaid, and other commodities "returned from thence, whereby that part of the kingdom "hath been commodiously and advantagiously supplied "with all provisions; and that all ships, vessels, barques, "and boats, from time to time, at their coming up and "down the said river to and from the said Cities of "Gloucester and Worcester, have usually rid, and were "tyed and anchored as occasion was given upon the soyle "and bancks of the said River of Seaverne; and further "sheweth that the King's Majesty, and his progenitors, "Kings and Queens of England, is and always have been "seised in right of his and their Crown of England of "and in all the soil of the said River of Seavern, not only "under and within the low water mark, but also as far as "the sea or river ever did or now doth ebb and flow." The Attorney-General charges that a parcel of ground containing forty-seven acres in or near the parishes of Saule and Freathorne, and another parcel containing thirty acres in or near the parish of Frampton, between

Exch. Dep. M., 13 Chas. I. 30; H., 14-15 Chas. I. 14.

the sea and the city of Gloucester, were within forty years and before parcel of the soil and under the water of the river at the low-water mark when the water was run out to the lowest re-flux at the lowest neap tide, and that at low water ships and boats passed up and down the channel over the soil of the Severn and of the said parcels; that, the channel having of late years altered its course, the said parcels, being left dry, have become firm ground and borne grass; that by an inquisition taken at Stroud, Gloucester, on 26 September, 8 Charles I., A.D. 1632, it was found that the forty-seven acres in Saule adjoining Saule Warth "are his Majesty's soil, and that "the same until forty years past had been parcel of the "great and common bankery of Severn, and covered with "the water thereof where the sea until then, by all the time "whereof the memory of man is not to the contrary, had "used to ebb and flow, over which there had been till then "a common ship sailing and a common passage of ships, "barques, and boats for all the subjects of this realm as in "the high sea; that the same had since become dry; that "his Majesty and his ancestors had been from all the time "whereof, &c., seised of the said bankery and of the lands "covered with the water thereof as far as the passage was "used to be made by shipping from the sea." He then recites a similar finding for the thirty acres in Frampton, and avers that the commissioners seized the same into his Majesty's hand. He alleges that the defendants, having got possession of certain deeds which do manifest his Majesty's title to the said parcels, have entered into the same, and received the rents thereof, and have embanked part of the said new gained grounds, and thereby straitened the said river and the current thereof, which is a great purpresture to the said river and hindrance to the passage of the boats and ships thereupon.

There exist the answers of Thomas Lloyd, John Gage, and others of the defendants. The defendants say that since the pretended inquisition was taken the Attorney-General filed an information in 8 Charles I., A.D. 1632, against these defendants and against Bromwich and others for a supposed unlawful entry into the two parcels, and, issue being joined, a trial was had at the Bar of this Court in Michaelmas, 9 Charles I., A.D. 1633, by a substantial jury of Gloucester, who, being sworn and empanelled, and being, after full evidence given, ready to yield up their verdict, it pleased Mr. Noye, his Majesty's then Attorney-General, for prevention of a verdict against his Majesty's pretended title, to withdraw one of the jurors. They further say that having put in their several pleas to the said inquisition and traversed the same, and issue being thereupon joined with the defendant John Gage, afterwards in Easter term, 11 Charles I., A.D. 1635, Sir John Banks then being Attorney-General, a trial was likewise thereupon had at the Bar of this Court by another substantial jury of the county of Gloucester; upon which trial a verdict was then given by the said jury against his Majesty, and judgment was thereupon had and entered accordingly. They also say that before the said information of intrusion, Erasmus Finch, his Majesty's lessee of the lands, and now the prosecutor of this cause, as these defendants believe, exhibited an English bill against Lloyd, Gage, and others for recovery of the said lands by and under a former inquisition, and that the defendants answered, and the said suit is yet depending undetermined: by all which it may appear how these defendants have been sued, molested, and impleaded several ways and several times for one and the same matter, and that the matter of the present bill now exhibited against them, being grounded upon the said inquisition of 26 September, 8 Charles I., A.D. 1632, hath been already tried and determined. They deny the King's right to the soil of the river, and say that the soil and ground of the river in the several counties aforesaid, but especially within the parishes or villages of Saule, Fretherne, and Frampton, and so in other places and parishes adjoining and near thereabouts, is, so far forth as unto the middle of the channel or current of the said river, the soil and ground of the several lords of those manors which adjoin unto the said river so far as the same manors extend respectively. And that these several lords respectively have for and in respect of their said manors usually had the benefit and royalty of the several fishing in, through, and over so much of the said river as aforesaid.

They say that Gage and Mary his wife are seised of the manor of Fretherne in right of Mary, and claim to mid-stream, as also all the waste ground formerly left or relinquished by the course and current of the river; that Lloyd is seised of the manor of Sawle, and makes a similar claim; that the forty-seven acres is part of Sawle Warth, which is common land; and as to the thirty acres, all the defendants except Lloyd disclaim any right to it. Lloyd says it is the inheritance of several persons, is partly adjoining the river, and was formerly purchased from the lord of Frampton. Bromwich answers separately, and, after a denial of the statements in the bill, as in the previous answer, he says that he holds twelve acres, which he supposes to be parcel of the thirty acres, but has not interfered with the banks. The plaintiffs replied.

These causes came to a hearing on 10 November, 14 Charles I., A.D. 1638, when the Crown was defeated and the information dismissed. The decree is as follows:—

"Whereas in the cause depending in this Court by "English bill between Erasmus Finch, plaintiff, and John "Gage, Thomas Lloyd, and others defendants, touching "certain parcels of land lying near the River Severn, "supposed to be forsaken and recovered from the said "river; it was, by an order made 13 October this term, "ordered by the Court that all the depositions taken in "the cause should be published, except cause should be "shewed as this day: Now, upon the motion of Mr. Len-"thall, informing the Court on the defendants' behalf that "the said plaintiff's bill was exhibited against them above "six years sithence, and that the plaintiff did never pro-"ceed in the said cause until Easter term last, and then "he served the defendants to reply, and that thereupon "the plaintiff examined some witnesses in town, but never "took forth any commission, and that the defendant had "examined no witnesses as yet; further informing that

See Exch. D. & O., series 3, xiv. 26; xiii. 125, 154; xiv. 200; xvi. 389; xx. 189, 487.

"there had been two several commissions awarded forth of "this Court for to entitle the King to the said lands in "question, whereupon, inquisitions being taken, the de-"fendants appeared and pleaded, and after issue taken "upon one of the defendant's pleas, a trial was had at the "Bar of this Court, and after evidence given on both sides "a juror was withdrawn by Noye, Attorney-General; "and that afterwards, upon an information of intrusion "brought by the said Attorney-General touching the said "lands, another trial was had at the Bar, wherein a verdict "passed against the King; and that after all this the said "Finch procured the now Attorney-General to exhibit an "English information in the Exchequer Chamber against "the said defendants touching the said lands, whereunto "the said defendants appeared and answered, and after "witnesses were examined, the said cause came to a hear-"ing in Hilary term last, and after hearing of the same "the said cause was dismissed *sine die*; and therefore it was "humbly desired on the defendants' behalf that the said "defendants might be dismissed this Court from the said "plaintiff's bill: Whereupon it is this day ordered by the "Court that the plaintiff shall on this day senight shew "cause why the said defendants should not be dismissed "the said plaintiff's bill, and in the mean time publication "to stay." No further proceeding appears.

Exch. B. & A., Car. I., Southton, 106.

In Hilary, 12 Charles I., A.D. 1636–37, the Attorney-General filed an information against Robert Riggs and others respecting a salt marsh in Wymering called Hulsey Marsh. The information recites as follows:—"Whereas the "King's most excellent Majesty now is and ever since his "happy coming to the Crown of England hath been law-"fully seised in his demesne as of fee, in right of his said "Crown of England, of and in all and singular lands, "grounds, void grounds, shores, creeks, bays, inlets, banks, "ouzie ground, fittie ground, glibses, breaches, salt "marshes and marsh ground, wastes of the sea, sands, "watercourses, lakes, floods, rifes, towns, islands, castles, "hamlets and other hereditaments and places within the "realm of England and dominion of Wales, and other his

"Majesty's dominions which heretofore have been or now "are overflowed and surrounded with the sea by any "spring tides of and from the sea of its own natural "course, and which do lie between the high and low water "marks of the sea, or which are or shall be banked, "fenced, gained and recovered from the sea, or otherwise "are or shall be forsaken or left bare by the sea, or which "do lie between or are subject to the flowing and reflow- "ing of the sea." The information then recites a commission of 13 February, 1 Charles I., A.D. 1625–26, to Sir Thomas Fanshawe to survey lands overflown and surrounded by the sea in the county of Southampton, and the return to the inquisition and survey, and avers that Hulsey Marsh was overflown by the sea at spring tide, and lies between the high and low water marks. The land had been granted to Lady Wandesford, who was inclosing it, and the defendant claimed it as parcel of the manor of Wymering under a grant of Edward I. to John le Butler. An order made on 29 June, 13 Charles I., A.D. 1637, states that the point was as to whether the marsh lay between the high and low water marks, and a plan was ordered to be made and witnesses examined to shew how far the ordinary spring tides did go before the embankment was begun, and on 20 May, 14 Charles I., A.D. 1638, the defendant was ordered to appear to a Latin information, and the case to be tried at Bar. As to whether it was tried or not the records of the Exchequer are silent, but if it was it would seem that the verdict was for the defendant, for had it been for the plaintiff the case would have proceeded to judgment, and the Exchequer officers would most certainly have entered up judgment if it had been for the Crown.

Sp. Com. 5636. Exch. Dep. 13 Chas. I., T. 8. Exch. D. & O., Car. I., series 3, xix. 395, xx. 465, xxi. 49 and 63, xxii. 402, xxiii. 60; series 4, iv. 308.

We thus see that at this period the Crown was claiming to the high-water mark of spring tides, but Hale tells us that it was ruled in the case of an information prosecuted by one Van Haesdanke against Mr. Whitford, in the Exchequer Chamber, that the limit of the *litus maris* and the King's title was confined to the ordinary tides, and that it was also so ruled in the King's Bench in

Easter, 15 Charles I., A.D. 1639, in Sir Edward Heron's case.

In Hilary, 12 Charles I., occurred the case of the King *v.* Oldsworth, in respect of relicted land in Sutton Marsh, which is fully described in Hale (ch. 6), in which it was held that land *relicted*, in contradistinction to alluvion or land *projected*, by the sea could not be prescribed for as parcel of a manor, and judgment passed for the King; but it seems doubtful whether he got possession in fact, for we find special commissions issued respecting Sutton Marsh in 14 and 16 Charles I., A.D. 1638 and 1640.

See post, pp. 312, 352.

Sp. Com. 5438, 5440, 5443.

MS. Hargrave 425, fo. 34.

A note of the argument for the Crown in Attorney *v.* Michael Oldsworth and others is extant. It is signed "Ri: Keble." It is the case referred to by Hale, ch. 6, and was an information of intrusion filed in Trinity, 11 Charles I., A.D. 1635, to recover 7000 acres of marsh called Sutton Marsh, lying next Sutton, which were parcel of the sea-shore and left derelict by the sea. King James I., on 9 December 1613, granted them to Peter Aston and others, and afterwards in 11 Charles I., A.D. 1635, the patent was surrendered.

The defendant Oldsworth pleaded that the land was parcel of the sea-shore and parcel of the manor of Sutton, and that the custom of the country was that owners of lands have *marettum et sabulonem*, the alluvion and increment of their lands; and he sets out a grant of the manor under the seal of the Duchy of Lancaster, dated 10 January, 6 Charles I., A.D. 1630–31. Upon this the Attorney-General demurred in law, and excepted to the pleadings, arguing that seisin of the shore had not been alleged in the King before the grant of the manor, &c.; that the custom of the country was the law of the land, and must be pleaded as the law, and not as a custom; that the custom does not exist; and under the pretended custom to have *marettum et sabulonem*, which is only gravel, stone, and sand together, he will have clear another thing, viz., 7000 acres of marsh. The argument rests almost entirely on Bracton and the Civil Law. As to the argument arising from the taking of royal fish, he suggests that sturgeon frequently go up above the tide limit, as above London Bridge, and up Stratford River in Hertfordshire, and that one was lately taken at Hertford Mill, miles above the high-water mark. "And for that a "man may prescribe to have wreck or royal fishes between "the high water and low water mark, it doth not therefore "followe that that place is parte of that man's manor or "soyle or of the county, but it may be some place known, "and neither of all those" (carefully, like Hall, avoiding the point that the wreck is taken *infra manerium*). He argues that the custom is local, and does not bind the King, and does not extend to land "relict," although it may to land "project." He then extols the King and his prerogative, quoting Coke, that the kings of England have by the laws of England as great prerogatives as any king in the world; stating also that the law of England is the law of God; that the King cannot die, nor be impotent, nor err, nor be deceived; that his throne is as the throne of God; that he is vicar of Christ, &c. He argues further on the custom that it cannot affect the King: "Noe more shall "this custome as I conceive, for this diminution of the "royall estate, it were diminution of the honour of the "law that it should not be stronger to preserve an estate "vested in the Kinge then a custom to pull it out of the "Crown. Noe; I conceive it easier to writhe Hercules "his club out of his hand then one land out of the Kings: "for power and revenue are the very Crowne itself." This kind of argument was successful, and the Crown got judgment, but it could hardly be recommended to the Attorney-General as a precedent in these days.

Besides the report of the case in Hale, ch. 6, which appears to be a report of a judgment in the Exchequer in Hilary, 12 Charles I., A.D. 1636–37, there is a full report of a further hearing of the same case in the Exchequer Chamber in Trinity, 13 Charles I., A.D. 1637, which is entitled "The King against Sir Cornelius Vermuyden, "William Wild, L. George, Michael Oldsworth, and "others." This report is found in the Lansdowne MSS. 1081, fo. 178. The facts set out are similar to those described by Hale, and the issue clearly was whether the 7000 acres of marsh were land left by alluvion or land left by reliction. The defendants claimed under a grant of the manor of Sutton made under the seal of the Duchy of Lancaster, and their case was that the land was left by alluvion. Lenthall argued for the defendants that the land was alluvion formed by the flux and re-flux of the sea, which by little and little had thrown up gravel and such kind of slimy stuff which by continuance of time had become firm ground, and he argued that alluvion could belong to the Duchy because the Duchy had *jura regalia*, and shewed that the Duchy had leased many portions of the foreshore from precedents out of the Duchy Records. He cites Sir Henry Constable's case to shew that the foreshore may be parcel of a manor, and a case in 11 Henry VII., in Lincolnshire, of an information for taking royal fish, where the defendants pleaded that they took it within the limits of the vill, and judgment was given against the King. Also a case in 31 Edward I., roll 32, of a grant of wreck *in omnibus terris maritimis*, which was held to be good, and upon which Lenthall argues that "this does not "oust any jurisdiction which the King has in the sea, for "it was held to be soil and no part of the sea, for it is not "inconvenient to have an interest in the land if it be not "the King's waste." And he argued that all grants of wreck in England would be to no purpose if it be the law that where there is a little piece of land between the manor and the sea, that this wreck cannot belong to the lord of the manor, and that he cannot have the benefit of it. There is a note in the report that it was held by all the Court that prescription is good for wreck if the shore is shewn to be parcel of the waste, for this supposes a grant, and a grant of the manor *cum incrementis*. He cites a case in the King's Bench, Hilary, 27 Edward III. roll 11, in which it was found by inquisition that the Earl of Huntingdon was entitled to sturgeon and royal fish in right of his lordship in the salt and fresh water abutting to his manor, and he cites the Abbot of Peterborough's case in 41 Edward III. Also the case of an information

The reference is wrong.

Ante, p. 157.

against the Countess of Lincoln for taking sturgeon and wreck by reason of her manor, in which judgment was given for her in the King's Bench in Michaelmas, 16 Ante, p. 151.
Edward III., roll 140. He also cites the case of the Abbot of Ramsey in 43 Edward III., and Sir John Ante, p. 158.
Constable's case in 17 Elizabeth. Ante, p. 224.

Sir John Banks, the King's Attorney-General, argued for the Crown, and the principal points of his argument are set out here, because it shews what was the contention of the Crown at this period, and upon what authority it was founded. It is as follows:—

"First, he conceived that the King is seised of the "British seas and the soil thereof in right of his crown, "and this he said he would endeavour to prove by autho-"rity and reason. And he answers to the objections made "against him, that in the Book of the Mirror of Justice, "*which was written before the time of William the Con-"queror*, it is said, cap. i., fo. 8, that the sovereignty of "the land, sea, forests, and chief parks belongs to the "King *jure coronæ;* and also that all seignories and "lands were at first in the Crown, and afterwards the "King granted them to lords and other men. Then, if "they cannot shew a grant from the King of the sea and "the soil of it, certainly this remains in the King. In "Britton, another ancient book, cap. 3, fo. 83, it is speci-"fied that some things are more common, as the sea for "navigation, some things less common, as fishing upon the "sea; but this does not prove that the soil is common, "but only the fishing, when that remains part of the sea. "Fleta says: 'Some things are common, as the sea-shores, "'others private, as fishing in the sea,' these shewing greater "commodity in the sea than on the land, viz., fishing "and navigation; but to have the soil of the sea, which "is permanent, this shews nothing, because the soil of "the sea belongs to the King. Bracton, lib. 2, fo. 8, who "wrote in the time of Henry III., does not conclude "that the soil belongs to any subject, but to the contrary, "for he says that *bona inventaria fuerunt communia*, but "now he says that these belong to the King *propter privi-*

"*legium suum.* And in the same book, cap. 3, fo. 120, he "says that wreck of the sea, great fish, and *alia animalia* "*vagrantia* belong to the King *propter privilegium*, and "also, fo. 170, he says that these things are inquirable "before the justices in eyre. So that those things which "are *nullius in bonis* belong to the King; and also those "things to which no man can make title. The law is "the same of islands and the soil of the sea." He cites a grant of Holly Land, by Richard I., of *omnia et singula bona in et super littora maris et inter fluxum et refluxum maris*, and says that "in a famous record in 27 Edward I., "in the Tower, where the people of many nations were "before the commissioners touching the dominion of the "sea, there it was agreed and held that the dominion of "the sea pertained to the King from the time of memory, "and there it was also held that power, dominion, and "jurisdiction thereon belonged to the Admiral. And "the King, by many ancient grants, has given the custody "and guardianship of the sea to others," citing records, 8 Henry III., 9 Henry III., 15 Henry III., 22 Edward I. m. 8, and 23 Edward I.: "these shewing that the King "has perfect ownership in the soil. In the Old Register, "*which was written before the Conquest*, fo. 25 and 26, it "appears that the King can take a man into his protec-"tion as well by sea as by land. . . . . The King is called "the keeper of the peace as well by sea as by land. "Glanvill, who wrote in the time of Henry II., lib. 9, "cap. 11, says that purprestures made upon the sea or "any arm of it belong to the King at first, so that, for all "purposes, the King is seised of the sea in right of his "crown. In 6 Richard II., protect. 46, the sea is called part "of the inheritance of the King; and by the record of Ante, p. 111. "20 Edward I., the Prior of Tynemouth's case, it was "held that the soil of the place, which was an arm of the "sea, belonged to the King, and not to the Bishop of "Durham [*sic*], who was the next lord adjoining to it; "then *a fortiori* all the rest of the sea belongs to him: "*vide* 2 Edward III. 12. In 12 Assize it is a query "whether there shall be apportionment of rent when the

" sea overflows the land. It is clear that if enemies to the " realm gain a part, there shall be apportionment; now the " sea is like an enemy, so it seems to me there shall be " apportionment. In 22 Assize 92 it is said that where " there is a lord of a river, and the river gains upon the " bank of another by little and little, the lord of the river " shall have it, and if it be so in the case of a lord, *a for-* " *tiori* in the case of the King. Those of Ireland are " ruled by the same laws as we, saving as to any particular " statutes; and it appears, by resolution of all the Court in " the eighth entry in Sir John Davis's Reports, that the " sea is the inheritance of the King, and all navigable " rivers belong to the King, and where the sea ebbs and " flows the King shall have the soil; and in Dyer 26b there " was a query as to whom the soil gained by the sea shall " belong: still, it was resolved for the King, as appears " in Michaelmas, 16 Elizabeth, roll 445, in the Exchequer, " in an information against William Hamon for intruding " into the King's land gained by the sea; the issue was, " that it was not part of the shore, or taken from the sea, " admitting that, if it was, this belonged to the King, " and so it was found by verdict. And in the book of " 43 Edward III., cited by Dyer 326b, issue was whether " an abbot had purchased this land without licence; and " it was found that he had not; and as it was pleaded " that this land was gained by the sea, and so found; " yet this was not pertinent nor pursuant to the issue. " And in 41 Edward III., the Abbot of Peterborough's " case, which has been objected against the King, there " was a custom *de consuetudine patriæ*, as in our case; but " the issue was whether the lands were purchased with- " out licence, and so it was found, and also the custom of " the country; but this was not material: firstly, because " it was not the point in issue; secondly, that no excep- " tion was taken to it; and thirdly, that the jurors are not " judges in such a case, for it is matter in law." Here objection was taken that by Sir Henry Constable's case the lord of the manor may have the land between the high and low water mark.

Banne Fishery, Davis 55.

Ante, p. 220.

Ante, p. 158.

Ante, p. 157.

To this the Attorney-General answered: "This case is "only one, and still it may be that it is not impossible, "because it might have passed by grant to him at first; "but Coke 107 there says that the sea is of the allegiance "of the King, and he shall have the profits in and upon it. Ante, p.260. "In Philpot's case, lately resolved in this Court, where the "question was upon an information whether the soil "between high and low water mark belongs to the King "*jure coronæ*, it was resolved *una voce* that it did belong, "and *a fortiori* the soil of the body of the sea belongs to "the King if an arm of it belongs to him: *vide* Institutes, "260. An infant born on the sea is a subject, and Dyer "127, the King is lord of the narrow seas. In Selden's "Mare Clausum, lib. 21, 24, fo. 253, 254, there his inten-"tion appears that the soil of the sea belongs to the King, "and he calls the sea *sacrum patrimonium domini Regis.*" He puts the following reasons:—

"Firstly: because this kingdom is an island, and is "surrounded by the sea, and is bounded by the sea.

"Secondly: the second reason is because no subject can "make title to the soil, for all the soil of this kingdom "pertains to the King, unless it passes from the King by "grant;" and he cites Bracton, and the Doctor and Student, and 8 Henry IV. 2b, that unclaimed goods belong to the King in law, and the case is the same for lands.

Thirdly: He gives as a third reason that all the profits of the sea belong to the King, and therefore the soil itself; and that anchorage is due to the King, which shews that the soil belongs to the King, and that anchorage was demised in 5 Henry V., in the Pipe Office.

Fourthly: He cites the case of the royal mines, and says that in 1 Richard II. "the King let salt marsh in "Sussex for two lives as lands gained from the sea;" that anchorage was demised in 2 Richard II. and 8 Richard II.; that in several reigns of the kings grants had been made of salt marshes, as in Abergenny, Portsmouth, Yorkshire, Gloucestershire, Essex, Sussex, Norfolk, Kent; and that copperas stone thrown by the sea upon the land belongs to the King, and has been let by him.

Fifthly: "If the meadow of a common person be over-"flown by the water, and afterwards become dry, without "question the subject shall have it again; now, the ocean "is the great mead of the King, and the King shall have "the same privilege as a subject."

Sixthly: "The King has the soil of navigable rivers, "and of ports, which are called the gates of the realm, and "for the same reason that the arms of the sea belong to "the King the body shall belong also."

Seventhly: He argues that if the King regain Calais, the subject who had lands at first shall not have them again, although he has evidence to shew for them; so lands gained by the sea are like lands gained by the enemy, as in 7 Edward IV.

Eighthly: "The subject and lord of a manor may take "the sea-shore by grant, as in the cases of 5 Edward III. Ante, p. 149.
"3, and 29 Edward III. 5.

"It has been objected that where waif and stray and "royal fish may be claimed by prescription, Coke, 5 Rep. "107, draws an inference out of these books that the soil "belongs to the subject; but the answer is: firstly, that it "is only Lord Coke's inference; and, secondly, that these "things may be thrown *above* the high-water mark, or that "they were granted at first, and then it would be good." To another objection he replies that the Duke of Lancaster has no grant of lands gained by the sea, and has *jura regalia* only in the County Palatine. He argues that the custom of the country cannot prevail against the King; that custom may gain a freehold in profits out of the land of the subject, but not the land itself, and *a fortiori* in the case of the King, and that all lands first came from the King, and no land can be gained from him except by matter of record; that time runs not against the King, and that the statute of limitation does not bind him, and he cites Boswell's case, 6 Rep. 49, to shew that usurpation gains nothing against the King, and 35 Henry VI. "Custom does not bind the King for his goods, nor *a* "*fortiori* for his lands." He further argues that the custom alleged as the custom of the country for the lords to take alluvion cannot be alleged as a local custom, but must be alleged as the common law, and that the custom is uncertain, because it alleges that all lords of manors may have it, and this must mean lords mediate and immediate, and lords for term of life or years, and then they cannot prescribe; and he cites Gateward's case, and concludes by shewing that the defendants have not shewn seisin in the King before their grant.

The MS. report then gives the judgment delivered for the King by Baron Weston, who, after discussing certain objections to the information, says: "The case is that the "King being seised of the manor of Sutton, in Lincolnshire, "in right of the Duchy of Lancaster, outside the County "Palatine, adjacent to the sea, and certain lands are left "by the sea next the manor—whether the King shall be "seised of these in right of his crown? Bracton, Britton, "and Justinian say that an island left by the sea belongs "to no one in point of property, but goes to the occupant, "and that the sea is free as for passage or fishing *jure gen-* "*tium;* and what has been quoted out of Selden seems "all against them [the defendants]. . . . . As to fishing, "none will admit that the sea is free for every foreigner to "fish there. And Sir Henry Constable's case, cited by "them, that prescription lies for land between high and "low water mark, makes for them, for if it lies in pre- "scription it lies in property, for there ought to be some "person against whom the prescription ought to be, and "against the sea, or another nation or subject, it does not "lie, as is apparent; then it ought to lie against the King, "and this plainly shews that, if such prescription was not, "the King is to have the property. In 6 Charles I. in "the Exchequer Chamber, concerning lands in Wapping, "it was decreed and agreed that the lands in the Thames "between high and low water mark belong to the King; "to this it was answered for the defendants that this is "part of the port of London; and if it be admitted that "the lands in the port pertain to the King, by the same "reasoning the lands outside belong to him, for the King "can increase or diminish the ports at his pleasure; and

Lansd. MS. 1081, fo. 193.

"also there is no land adjacent to the sea but it is in one "port or another. To the objection that the King ought "not to be entitled to anything but by matter of record, "the answer is generally yes; but not always, as in 3 "Reports, Dowtie's case, fo. 10, and 4 Reports, Le "Cominalty de Sadlers. This difference is taken, when "possession is *plena* and when *vacua*, as if the tenant of "the King die without heir, or if the ancestor of the King "die seised, the law throws the possession into the King "without office, because the freehold cannot be in sus-"pense; the law is the same of chattels, as treasure trove, "lagon, flotsam, jetsam, &c. . . . .

"And as to the case in 15–16 Elizabeth, Dyer [326b], Ante, p. 220. "it is only a doubt, but many authorities accord with "it, as Trinity, 43 Edward III., roll 30, the Abbot Ante, p. 158. "of Ramsey's case, which is no authority for the de-"fendants, for the judgment was only given upon "presentment, and not upon information. And as to "Hamon's case, 15–16 Elizabeth, entered in the Memo- Ante, p. 220. "randa of the Exchequer, 16 Elizabeth, roll 445, the title "of Hamon there was that William Hamon enfeoffed him, "*absque hoc* that it was relict by the sea, and upon this "judgment was given for him; and if such an issue had "been taken in our case, without doubt the same judg-"ment would have been given.

"On the point whether the custom may prevail against "the King in such a case, negatively; the custom may be "good if it be pleaded and applied as in 30 Edward III. "28, but as it is pleaded in our case it is bad, for custom "ought to be reasonable and used from time whereof, &c." He decides that the custom is bad for uncertainty, for the custom is alleged *prope* or nigh unto a place, and not *ad locum*. "It is objected that these defects were in the "Abbot of Peterborough's case, and still judgment went "against the King; but the answer is, that there was "more in that than appears, for the power and favour of "the Abbot had great force with the Court, and there also "*scire facias* was sued against the Abbot upon a present-"ment in the time of his predecessor, and no charge was "made against the successor, so that he had no reason to "answer at all; and there also the King's counsel did not "demur, but took an issue, which was found against the "King, and afterwards would not move in arrest of judg- "ment; so that I do not see any reason why judgment "ought to have been given for the Abbot, and I say the "same in this case; and upon that I conclude that judg- "ment ought to be given for the King."

Baron Trevor argued for the King also: "The first "point: that the King has such land *jure coronæ:* As the "King is supreme upon the land, so he is upon the sea; ". . . . and all the land at first was derived out of the "Crown, and the case is the same in all commonwealths in "foreign nations. Also the King, by his prerogative, has all "things of excellency, as royal mines, so the sea being the "chiefest and most excellent of waters (for, as it is said, "all inferior rivers flow and re-flow to the sea), for the "same reason the King shall have it: and as the fresh "shore is called *ripa*, so the salt shore is called *littus;* and "this shore as to its use is common, as Justinian says in "the chapter *De rerum dominio;* and especially in our law "it is laid down that the thing to which none claim pro- "perty is in the King. *Vide* Bracton *De Rerum divisione* "*et rerum dominio*, and Britton *De perquisitione.* In 12 "Henry VIII. 21 it is said that our law is consonant "with the law of God, with which accords Com. 304; and "Lyttleton says that the King is said to possess all things "which belong to the villan, and as the care of the com- "monwealth and the sea belong to the King, it is reason- "able to give the sea to him, it being in no other.

"Secondly, the question is of the large extent the sea- "shore contains: this extends as far as the natural and "ordinary course, but not the forced course of the water: "and the natural course of the sea contains the diurnal "and monthly spring tides; but those tides caused by "tempest, or the autumn tides, &c., extend not to our case. "And if the sea, by reason of breach of its banks, overflow "the adjacent lands, this does not give any title to the "King; but if it continue upon the land so long that no "mark of it may appear, it is otherwise. *Vide* Magna "Charta, cap. 16; 18 Henry VIII. c. 15.

"Thirdly: The question whether custom shall prevail "against the King, negatively. For as the land was in "the King when it was parcel of the sea; now, when it is "made parcel of the dry land, it shall not be taken from "him: and the reason is, because the King shall be pre-"ferred in such case. *Vide* Bracton, lib. 2, cap. i.; Doctor and "Student, cap. 8, fo. 22; Barre, 9 and 285. If enemies "possess a ship for a day, it is lost. . . . . And Sir Henry "Constable's case makes nothing against us, for there it is "only (it may be) *per Curiam*. In Sir John Davis' Reports "it is said that the sea is the inheritance of the King. In "Easter, 16 James I., roll 292, upon an information special "verdict was given, but that is nothing, for it is false. "The precedents of grants by the King in Romney Marsh "and Broomhill prove our case that these lands belong to "the King. . . . .

This should be 16 Eliz.: ante, p. 219.

Ante, pp. 177-179, 201.

"Fourthly: The King never had these lands in right of "his duchy, for a grant of such privileges was never made "to him, and, even if it was, in our case it is not pleaded; "and so I conceive that judgment ought to be given for "the King."

The arguments for the Crown in this case, it will be seen, rest mainly on the Roman Law. We are a little startled at Sir John Banks' assertion that the Mirror and the Old Register were written before the Conquest. He is also driven to contend that the shore cannot pass unless the grantee produce the grant, and he has to call in aid the authorities which support the *jus publicum* to uphold his argument in favour of the *jus privatum*. He avoids the effect of Hamond's case by saying that it was admitted that if the shore in question in that case had not been gained from the sea, but had still remained open, it was the King's; but there is no authority for this statement. The effect of Sir Henry Constable's case he does not attempt to grapple with, but says that it is only one, and that he might have had the shore by grant. He relies mainly on Philpott's case, the history of which we have already shewn, but he fails to get any direct authority out of Selden. His reference to the grants of salt marshes are to the fishing grants, which we have previously discussed, and the argument arising from the claim of wreck by prescription he dismisses as being only Lord Coke's inference, and by suggesting that wreck and royal fish may be thrown above the high-water mark. Although we have seen that these things can only be taken upon the shore, Sir John Banks's argument is still put forward, and was used in the case of the Attorney-General *v.* Emerson, before Mr. Justice Mathew and Mr. Justice Cave in 1887.

Barons Weston and Trevor, who gave the judgment, were, as we have seen, creatures of the King. Weston rests his judgment mainly on Philpott's case, but he practically confirms the doctrine of Sir Henry Constable's case, using it to shew that, unless there is prescription in favour of the lord of the manor, the property must be in the King. He adopts the Attorney-General's view of Hamond's case, but avoids the result of the Abbot of Peterborough's case, on the suggestion that the Abbot was favoured by the Court. Baron Trevor goes wholly for the King. His authorities are the Roman Law and Bracton, but he is clearly wrong in holding that the foreshore extends to the limit of the spring tides.

Exch. D. & O., series 3, xix. 368, xxi. 7, xxii. 79, 119b.

See post, p. 312.

The case was heard upon demurrer, and judgment given on 10 November, 13 Charles I., A.D. 1637. The cause, however, was not finally settled by the judgment, but dragged on till the Revolution, the last order being made on 13 October, 16 Charles I., A.D. 1640, and the Crown, so far as we can discover, never got into possession, but the King seems to have granted the land to the Earl of Lennox, who, after the Restoration, as Duke of Richmond, leased it to one Whitaker, who brought ejectment to recover the land. The case, Whitaker *v.* Wise, is reported very briefly in Keble 759, and resulted in a verdict for the plaintiff, on the authority apparently of Philpott's case.

Exch. D. & O., series 3, vol. 19, fo. 3b.

In the Exchequer Order Book for 1637, we find the following order to deposit Selden's "Mare Clausum" in the Exchequer:—

"Whereas Sr Willim Beecher, Kt, one of the clerks of "his mats most honorable pryvy councill, did this daye "deliver in Court to the Lord Treasurer, Chauncillor, and "Barons of the Courte, a booke lately published by John "Selden, Esqr, entituled 'Mare clausum seu de dominio "'maris,' to be kept in this Courte as a faithfull and "stronge evidence for the undoubted right of the Crowne "of England to the Dominion of the Bryttishe seas, which "saide booke the said Clerke of the Councill did deliver "according to an order in that behalf made by the King's "most excellent matie and the Lords of His Higness "privy councell at Whitehall, the third of Aprill last past, "a coppie of which said order is alsoe delivered with the "said booke: It is, therefore, nowe ordered by the said "Lord Treasurer, Chauncillor, and Barons that the "said booke bee receaved by his Maties Remembrancer "of this Courte, and by him kypt of record amonge "the Records of the Courte as his Maties evidence. "And as well the said order of the third of Aprill before "mentioned as this present order to bee inrolled upon "Record."

Special commissions were running in every county at this time, and we have one in 13 Charles I., A.D. 1637, for the county of Essex, which returns as concealments part of the very marshes in Great and Little Wakering which were part of the demesnes of those manors, and which had been confirmed to Coppin by the patent above described (p. 174). These, however, were never recovered, but the instance will serve to shew the arbitrary manner in which these inquiries were conducted.

In Hilary, 13 Charles I., A.D. 1637-38, we find an information by the Attorney-General against Grove and others for marsh lands in the Isle of Grain (Kent). The information sets out the bounds of the lands, and describes them as abutting on the King's channel, "all which pre-"mises [the Attorney-General avers] were heretofore part "of the sea, and therewith by the salt water thereof, by "all time whereof there is no memory of man to the "contrary, covered, and which by all that time were

Exch. B. & A., Kent, Chas. I. 208.

"within the flux and re-flux of the sea and the salt "water thereof, and between high-water and low-water "marks, until about ten years last past, within which "time by dereliction and going back of the sea, or "casting up of great banks of sand, gravel, silt, soil, "and other matter, whereby they have had their increase "and growth, and the raising of walls and banks and "other inclosures thereupon, the said several parcels of "marishes and marish ground are become bare and dry "land, and have been recovered, inned, and gained from "the sea, being yet of the nature, quality, and condition of "deserted lands, by means and occasion whereof the soil "of the said marishes and marish ground and of every of "them doth appertain to our said Sovereign Lord the "King, and His Majesty was, is, and ought to be seised "thereof in his demesne as of fee in right of his crown of "England, and also ought to have, receive, and take the "rents, issues, and profits thereof." The Attorney charges intrusion and combination against the premises, and refers to several inquisitions remaining in the Court. The defendants answer and say they have been immemorially seised, and deny that the lands are between the flux and re-flux of the sea.

See also Exch.Dep., Easter, 13 Chas. I. 30; M., 13 Chas. I. 9.

Here we have (notwithstanding the previous decision as to high-water mark referred to by Hale) the claim of the Crown stated in its fullest extent, following the decision of Baron Trevor that it extends to the limit of the spring tides.

About 12 Charles I. was commenced the suit against Mr. John Smith, farmer of the Lord Berkeley, concerning 300 acres of land near Slimbridge on the Severn. The suit was by the Attorney-General at the relation of Sir Sackville Crowe, and is fully reported by Hale (ch. 6), who says he was thoroughly acquainted with the case, and attended at the bar at the trial. The information was founded on a commission dated 21 July, 13 Charles I., A.D. 1637, to the Bishop of Llandaff and others to inquire what dry, sandy, muddy, slimy, or oozy grounds or lands within the sea or the King's royal and navigable rivers, and

Sp. Com. 6029.

the flood or tides thereof, in the counties of Gloucester and Monmouth, have been inned and won by reason of the flux, re-flux, or deserting of the sea, or alteration of the force of tides, eddies, currents, or former channels of the sea, or any royal or navigable rivers aforesaid, and also what lands had been reclaimed that were formerly overflowed and left dry at low-water mark, and who have held them, and what have been concealed, &c. The inquisition was taken on 6 September, 13 Charles I., A.D. 1637, and the jurors return the new inclosed grounds at Slimbridge, containing 300 acres; also Dumble's new-gained ground containing 30 acres formerly part of the foreshore and the new-gained grounds in Arlingham, also formerly part of the foreshore.

According to Hale, the information set forth that the Severn was an arm of the sea flowing and re-flowing with salt water, and was part of the ports of Gloucester and Bristol, and that the river had left about 300 acres of ground near Slimbridge, and therefore they belonged to the King by his prerogative. There exist the depositions taken on the part of the King. They are dated 5 September, 13 Charles I., A.D. 1637. The deponents for the Crown testify that the land in question was formerly overflowed by the tide, and was slimy ground for many years, and that they have been recovered from the sea or Severn during the witnesses' memory and within sixty years; that they are bounded on the north-east end with Frampton, south-west on the length thereof with Cheosloagers Pill, on the west and north-west with the Severn, and on the south-east with Slimbridge Wharf, and that they were embanked from the flood tide or waters of the sea or Severn by Mr. Smith, servant to Lord Berkeley, and others. Other witnesses say that they were sandy, sleddy, or muddy ground overflowed twice in every twenty-four hours with the tides at the lowest neap tides, and there can be no doubt upon the evidence that they were parcel of the foreshore.

Exch. Dep. Miscell. 510, 583, 1233, 1375.

On 1 May, 14 Charles I., A.D. 1638, Lord Berkeley having appeared, and the defendants having pleaded not

Exch. D. & O., series 3, xxii. 379.

guilty, are ordered to shew cause why the cause should not be tried at bar. The defendants, having shewn possession for twenty years, were permitted to plead the general issue, and on 5 May, 14 Charles I., A.D. 1638, on the motion of the Attorney-General, the cause was ordered to be tried at bar.

Exch. D. & O., series 3, xxv. 75d.

On 2 June following there is an order to amend the panel in consequence of a misdescription of a juror.

Ibid. xxiv. 14.

The trial took place at bar, and Hale reports it. It was proved for the King that the lands were newly gained from the Severn, and that the very channel of the river within the time of memory ran in the very place where the land in question lay, and that the Severn had deserted it, and the channel ran about a mile towards the west. The defendant set out the title of the Barons of Berkeley from the time of Henry II. These charters have been described *ante*, p. 166, and they pass the great manor of Berkeley with its appurtenances as fully and freely as it existed in the hand of King Henry I. It is to be observed that in the charter there are no special words to carry the soil. The defendant then said that the Severn to the *filum aquæ* was time out of memory parcel of the manor, and that the *filum aquæ* of the river was the common boundary of the manors on either side. Upon this it was insisted for the Crown that the river being an arm of the sea, it lay not in prescription to be part of a manor; but the Court overruled that exception, and admitted that even such a river, though it be the King's in point of interest *primâ facie*, yet it may, by prescription and usage time out of mind, be parcel of a manor. The defendant thereupon went to his proofs, and insisted on very many badges of property or ownership—viz., that the lords of the manors had taken royal fish opposite to their manor to the *filum aquæ;* that they had all wrecks cast between high and low water mark; that the lords of the manors adjacent had ancient rocks or fishing places and weirs or such as were of that nature within the very channel; that they had granted and leased these fishing places by court roll and had taken rent for them; that by common tradition and reputation the manors on either side of the Severn were bounded one against another by the *filum aquæ*, and divers ancient depositions were produced wherein it was accordingly sworn by very many ancient witnesses; and he shewed that increases happening by reliction of the river were constantly enjoyed by the lords adjacent. Before the defendant had gone half through his evidence the Court and the King's Attorney-General (Sir John Banks) and the rest of the King's counsel were so well satisfied with the defendant's title that they moved the defendant to consent to withdraw a juror, which though he were very unwilling, yet at the earnest desire of the Court and of the King's counsel he did agree thereunto.

This case, which was tried in Trinity term, 14 Charles I., A.D. 1638, shews conclusively that the foreshore and even the sea bottom may be parcel of a manor, and that the *primâ facie* title of the Crown may be rebutted by evidence of acts of ownership such as were shewn by Lord Berkeley. It also shews that an ancient grant of a manor without any general words of shore may be construed as against the Crown as passing the foreshore as parcel of the manor.

At this time there were informations pending respecting derelict lands in many places—as Brading Haven in the Isle of Wight, foreshore at Whitstable, marshes near Titchwell in Norfolk, Surfleet Marsh in Lincolnshire, in Sir Edward Heron's case referred to by Hale (p. 26), marshes at Thedelthorpe and Saltfleteby, Lincolnshire, and other places.

The case of Attorney-General *v.* Sir Samuel Rolle, Sir Richard Buller, and Sir Thomas Arundel, in 16 Charles I., was a suit by English information in respect of the foreshore of some manor in Cornwall, but as the pleadings have been lost from the file, and the depositions are also missing, and the decree is not entered up, we cannot tell to what place it relates, but Hale reports that in this case it was decreed in Easter, 16 Charles I., A.D. 1640, that the foreshore may be parcel of a manor.

Exch. D. & O., series 3, xx. 418; xxii. 315, 416; xxiii. 444, 451; xxiv. 234; xxv. 163, 300.

It having been established by these cases that the foreshore may be parcel of a manor, and that the *primâ facie* title of the Crown may be rebutted by evidence of acts of ownership of the foreshore in question, such acts shewing such user as the foreshore is capable of, notwithstanding that in the grant of the manor there were no apt words to convey the foreshore, the officers of the Crown seemed to consider that the *primâ facie* title of the Crown could no longer be used to impugn the ancient title and possession of the subject, and after this we find that very few informations were attempted to be filed.

The struggle against the King's unwarrantable use of the prerogative was now absorbing the attention of all persons in the realm; the Great Rebellion was on the eve of breaking out, and on 1 December 1641 the Grand Remonstrance was presented. Article 26 of this memorable document charges against the King "the taking away "of men's right under colour of the King's title to land "between high and low water marks;" and in article 43 it is charged "that the Chancery, Exchequer Chamber, "Court of Wards, and other English Courts have been "grievous in exceeding their jurisdiction;" and again by article 47, "that the Common Law Courts, seeing all "men more inclined to such justice there where it may "be fitted to their own desires, are known frequently to "forsake the rules of the common law and strain beyond "their bounds upon pretence of equity to do injustice." In the following year the Civil War broke out, and the King raised his standard at Nottingham on 25 August 1642. Thus it will be seen that the attempt to enforce the *primâ facie* title of the Crown was one of the causes of the Great Rebellion.

The judges who were not subservient to the King, and who must have watched the energetic but unsuccessful efforts of the Crown to uphold the *primâ facie* title, appear to have come to the conclusion that it was not founded in law and truth. This is very evident from the
Aleyn 10. case of Johnson *v.* Barrett, in which Hale, as counsel, upheld the Crown's right, but was defeated. The case

was tried in Easter, 22 Charles I., A.D. 1646, in the King's Bench, before Rolle, C.J., who had been appointed by the Parliament. The report in Aleyn is as follows:—

"In an action of trespass for carrying away soil and "timber, &c., upon trial at the bar, the question arose upon "a key that was erected in Yarmouth, and destroyed by "the bailiffs and burgesses of the town; and Rolle said "that if it were erected between the high-water mark and "low-water mark, then it belonged to him that had the "land adjoyning. But HALE *did earnestly affirm the con-"trary; viz., that it belonged to the King of common right.* "But it was clearly agreed that if it were erected *beneath* "*the low-water mark*, then it belonged to the King. It "was likewise agreed that an intruder upon the King's "possession might have an action of trespass against a "stranger; but he could not make a lease whereupon the "lessee might maintain an *ejectione firmæ*."[1] Aleyn does not report the result, but it was probably in favour of the plaintiff, for we find that in Trinity, 1650, an information was filed by the Attorney-General on behalf of the Corporation of Yarmouth against Thomas Barrett and others for building a quay in Yarmouth Harbour, but in it there is no allegation of the *primâ facie* title. The allegation is in the form that we find before the time of Elizabeth—viz., that it is injurious to the navigation. The defendants built salt works and wharves and quays on the Suffolk side of the harbour. The object of the suit was to prevent them setting up an opposition harbour to that of Yarmouth. The allegation is that the customs are evaded, and the *channel narrowed and straightened, and navigation made dangerous to ships in the ebb tyde.* The defendants claim that the

Exch. B. & A., Commonwealth, Norfolk, 3.

[1] Serjeant Mereweather in his speech (p. xcvii) calls attention to this case, and remarks that the doctrine of the *primâ facie* title is overruled by it, and that Hale did not refer to the case of Attorney *v.* Philpott as an authority in favour of the Crown. This is highly probable. The decision in that case had evidently been resisted successfully, and the fact must have been common knowledge. Hale, therefore, would have been rash to have quoted it to a Parliamentary judge within five years of the Grand Remonstrance; but the report is meagre, and no one can say whether he did refer to it or not.

erections complained of are on their own soil, and are not nuisances, and it is quite clear that they extended over the foreshore.

Later on in the Commonwealth, however, the claim of the State to derelict land appears to have been revived. In 1658 and 1659 the Attorney-General, at the relation of grantees from the Crown, appears to have revived the suits relating to lands gained from the sea in Wainfleet, Gedney, and Sutton Marshes in the Wash, in Lincolnshire. It appears that Gedney Marshes had been granted on 23 August, 12 Charles I., A.D. 1636, to Sir Edward Dymock and Sir Henry Wootton, the patent being founded on a return to a commission issued in 1629, which found that these marshes were lands left derelict by the sea. The defendants William Wise and Michael Oldsworth, who were the lords of the manors, claimed them as parcel of their manors, and as lands accreted to them, and that their manors extend to the middle channel of the "Long "Washes." They demur to the information that the commission did but find the King's title, and they deny the prerogative right, and plead the custom of the county, referring to the Abbot of Peterborough's case in 41 Edward III. These proceedings must have been either dropped or resulted adversely to the Crown, for we find a commission issued to inquire of concealed salt marshes in Gedney in 8 William and Mary: see *post*.

Exch. B. & A., Lincoln, Commonwealth, 206 and 215. Exch. Dep. 1659, Easter, 3. Sp. Com. 6097, 6130, 6084. Ante, p. 304.

The Protector in the latter part of the Interregnum issued a commission to inquire what lands were derelict between the castles of Deal and Sandown in Kent in the manor of Court Ash. We have only the articles of inquiry, the commission and return being lost. The claim here set up was resisted successfully, and, after many futile attempts to enforce it, was finally disposed of in favour of the lord of the manor in the reign of William III.: see *post*.

Sp. Com. 6084.

On the Restoration, the Crown officers of the Exchequer promptly returned to their old practices, and there are throughout the reign numerous commissions to inquire as to concealments and derelict lands, and lands gained from the sea or royal rivers, and many proceedings under them against the owners of foreshore and reclaimed land. They seem to have disregarded the decision that the King's *primâ facie* title only extended to the high-water mark of ordinary tides, and to have steadfastly claimed as of old all land which had ever been overflown by the spring tide. The Crown also asserted its claim to the whole of the foreshore of the kingdom in the widest manner by making grants and leases of foreshore over large tracts of country.

In August 1661 a lease was made to the Duke of Richmond and others of all waste and oozie grounds in the county of Dorset. In October 1662 there is a grant to the Earl of Bath of wreck, seaweed, sand and sandy ground, pit coal, amber, amber-grice, fishing, fishes, royal lastage and ballastage of ships in Bideford (Devon), Widmouth, Woolston, Stratton, Stratton Kirkhampton, Woodford, North Leigh, and Mitchelmorton (Cornwall). Signet Book, 1661.

In June 1664 there is a grant to Elizabeth Countess of Peterborough of derelict lands.

In January 1664–65 we find a lease to Dr. Quartermaine and Robert Alkham of 300 acres of land lately gained from the sea, called Gatecombe Haven, in the Island of Portsea, for ninety-nine years, at the rent of fourpence an acre: see *post*.

In August 1665 there was a grant to Sir John Buller and others of all the foreshores of the Shannon, and in February 1665–66 another grant to Sir John Denham of lands in the island of Selsey, for which he is to pay fourpence an acre when they are embanked.

We find a petition from Richard Alchorne and others concerning the taking of seaweed, tangle, sand, gravel, and stones to be gotten as ballast on the sea-shore between high and low water marks, which appear to have been granted by patent to one David Halsall, and a proclamation relating to the taking of it was issued. We also find in the Privy Council Registers in 1662 that Viscount Devereux was claiming wreck at Orfordness, and the Earl of Anglesea in his manor of Llanstephan, Carmarthen. Privy Council Register, 20 March 1662, fo. 351.

In 13 Charles II., A.D. 1661, there was an information by the Attorney-General against John Edmunds and others concerning foreshore called Copnor Grounds, in the Isle of Portsea.

See Wightwick, p. 208.

In Easter, 14 Charles II., A.D. 1662, occurred the suit relating to Sutton Pool, near Plymouth, referred to by Hale, De Portubus (ch. 4, p. 57; *post*, pp. 350, 352). It is an information by the Attorney-General against Oliver Ceeley and others for making encroachments on the soil by wharves and buildings erected below high-water mark. The information recites that "whereas our Sovereign Lord King Charles "that now is during all the time of His Majesty's reign "over England hitherto hath been and still is seised in "his demesne as of fee *in right of His Crown of England* "of and in the ground and soil of the coasts and shores "of the seas of and belonging to his Kingdom of England, "and of and in the ground and soil of all and every the "ports, havens, arms of the sea, creeks, pools, and navigable "rivers thereof into which the sea doth ebb and flow *or* "*hath used to ebb and flow*, and in particular of and in the "ground and soil of all that pool, haven, creek, and arm of "the sea commonly called Sutton Pool, near unto the port "and town of Plymouth, and of the fishery, wreck of the "sea, wharfage, tolls," &c. The Attorney charges that the defendants have intruded. The defendants answer that they do not know that the King is seised, and set up title as part of the manor of Sutton Prior. In this information it will be observed that the Crown claims under the general prerogative, and not as owner of the soil in right of the Duchy of Cornwall as parcel of the castle of Trematon. The case was tried at bar, and a verdict was given for the Crown; and it was declared by Hale, C.J., and the other Barons that they were fully satisfied that all the soil of Sutton Pool within the flux and re-flux of the sea at ordinary tides is the King's. It is clear that Hale meant "the King's as lord of the manor of Trematon," for he shews in his treatise De Portubus, ch. 4, p. 56, that Sutton Pool was parcel of that manor, which had formerly belonged to Roger de Valletort, who gave it to Richard, King of the Romans and Earl of Cornwall, and thus it came to the Duchy; and he says that it passed to the

Exch. B. & A., Chas. II., Cornwall, 49.

Wightwick 210; see also Exch. Dep., 15 Chas. II. 36; Exch. Dep., Miscell., 333; Exch. Dep., H., 15-16 Chas. II. 16; Exch. Decree Book, M., 16 Chas. II., fo. 41;

Duchy as parcel of the manor of Trematon. Referring to this case he says that the Crown shewed evidence of ownership as parcel of the manor by the Duchy accounts and records, and that it was decreed to the Crown as parcel of the manor, but if that were so the original information must have been amended. In his draft treatise he quotes the case as an example to shew that although *primâ facie* both the franchise and the soil of ports belong to the King, yet a subject may have them : and he says "that the King's "very title to the Port of Plymouth, both in point of fran-"chise and in point of propriety or dominion of the soil, "is under the conveyance of Vautort, who was a subject." In the report in Wightwick, p. 211, Wood, B., calls attention to this claim in right of the prerogative to foreshore which had come to the Crown as parcel of a manor, and observes that in a subsequent proceeding to establish the same title in 1744 the claim was laid in respect of the right of the Duchy. This case is an example of the continued attempt of the Crown to uphold Mr. Digges' doctrine ; it is true that it obtained a verdict ; a verdict not supporting Mr. Digges' doctrine, but directly controverting it, for the verdict was grounded upon evidence which shewed that the Crown was entitled, not by the prerogative, but under a grant of foreshore made to the Crown by a subject.

Exch.Dep., Miscell. 1085; Exch. Dep., E., 26 Geo. II. 6.

See case of manor of Melcombe, purchased from Abbot of Cerne, ante, p. 95.

It is clear that Lord Hale had very little faith in the truth of the theory of the *primâ facie* title of the Crown, and that he knew how ineffectual had been the continual attempts to support the arguments of Digges, for in his interesting tract entitled "Considerations touching the "amendment and alteration of laws," printed in Hargrave's Tracts, p. 277, he has the following remarkable passage: "Touching lands left by the sea, we find very "many and very troublesome suits ; the subject vexed "that projectors may make advantage, and the King "bears the undeserved odium of it, and *in conclusion* "*gains nothing else by it ;* and yet it is possible that vast "improvements may be gotten from the sea in course of "time which yet may be encroached by the adjacent "owners. I think it may be a just and profitable law "that those that have been in possession of shores and "relicted lands for forty years last past should quietly "enjoy them without question, and that there should be "set up posts and marks round about the kingdom for "the discrimination of what is now held from what shall "be afterwards acquired, to the end that what lies without "the extent of those bounds may unquestionably be the "King's, excepting only such salt rivers where the subject "hath by grant or prescription the river itself, and conse- "quently the fluvialia incrementa."

It will be seen that Lord Hale was well aware of the oppressive nature of the Crown's claim. His just and wise suggestion, it need hardly be said, has not been carried out, and although Sir Thomas Farrer has laid it down that it is the first duty of the Board of Trade to ascertain where the foreshore has been granted out, he qualifies his statement by suggesting that this is a thing which it will be probably prudent to postpone; and now again, after a lapse of 200 years, we find the Crown officials setting up Mr. Digges' untrue theory more vigorously and more arbitrarily, and unfortunately more successfully, than ever was done by the Stuart Sovereigns or their patentees, or, as Hale calls them, their projectors. And here we may notice that no single case appears before the middle of the reign of Charles II., notwithstanding the innumerable suits brought by the Crown and its grantees from the time of Digges downwards, in which the Crown was successful when the issue went to a jury. The case of Attorney *v.* Philpot is not an authority to support the *primâ facie* title, as has been shewn, and it was not decided on the verdict of a jury. We find no other, and had there been one it would have assuredly been cited; on the other hand, we have verdicts against the Crown on the point throughout the period.

Bulstrode *v.* Hall and Stephen, 1 Siderfin 148.

In the case of Bulstrode *v.* Hall, in Trinity, 15 Charles II., A.D. 1663, which was an action in ejectment for houses built between the wall of the Isle of Dogs and the River Thames, and the matter in evidence was whether the place where the houses were built was parcel of the manor of Stepney, or parcel of the King's waste or of the River Thames, and if it was parcel of the waste or of the River Thames, the King had granted it to the City of London; but *semble* that the place was parcel of Stepney manor, which was the inheritance of Lord Cleveland; and in this case it was affirmed and not denied that the soil of all rivers, as far as the flux and re-flux of the sea goes, is in the King, and not in the lords of manors *without prescription*, referring to 2 Rolle 170, 5 Coke 107.

In Trinity, 16 Charles II., A.D. 1664, the Attorney-General filed an information against one Jolly, of Padstow, claiming the soil of the port of Padstow by the prerogative, and averring that Jolly had pulled down part of a quay on the foreshore and claimed anchorage and moorage, pretending that the land within the full sea mark was his. Defendant answers that he is unacquainted with the King's right to the ports, creeks, and havens within the full sea mark of the aforesaid place. And thereupon exception was taken by the Attorney-General that he does not set up title to the land within the full sea mark. Exch. B. & A., Cornwall, Chas. II. 44.

A return to a special commission in 16 Charles II., A.D. 1664, shews that derelict marshes in Drumburgh, Easton, and Brough, in the county of Cumberland, are extra-parochial. Sp. Com. 6186.

In 15 Charles II., A.D. 1663, commenced the suit brought by Lady Wandesford (who claimed, under the grant made to the Wandesford family in 4 Charles I. above mentioned, the foreshores of the county of Southampton and the Isle of Wight) against Richard Stevens and others, which is referred to by Hale (ch. 4), and in which it was again decided that the King's title was limited by the ordinary high-water mark. The depositions in the case shew the *locus* to have been on the foreshore. On 9 February 1664–65 a trial at bar was ordered, when a verdict was found for the defendant, and on 20 June, 18 Charles II., A.D. 1666, the information was dismissed. Ante, p. 260. Exch. Dep., E., 16 Chas. II. 19; T., 16 Chas. II. 1. Exch. Decrees, E., 17 Chas. II., fo. 63 and 137.

This case is the latest in point of date which Hale quotes. It may therefore be fairly assumed that he wrote his treatise about this time. It is, accordingly, here inserted.

CHAPTER XIV.

SIR MATTHEW HALE'S FIRST TREATISE.

THE first treatise here printed is from an original MS., in the undoubted handwriting of Sir Matthew Hale, preserved in MS. Hargrave No. 98. It is evidently the original draft of the works "De Jure Maris," "De Portubus Maris," and "Concerning the Customs," which were published by Hargrave in 1786. It treats shortly of all the subjects of Hale's work, but in a much more abbreviated form and in somewhat different language. It shews Hale's work as he first conceived it, and he must have put it aside when he wrote more fully the work which Mr. Hargrave printed. That the printed work, equally with this MS., is from the hand of Hale there can now be no kind of doubt, for this MS. contains, in Hale's own handwriting, the well-known passage describing the suit between the King and Lord Berkeley, at which he says he was present, and thus we have Hale's testimony under his own hand that he wrote the work which has been printed. In some notes upon the MS. initialled by Hargrave, he states that he received it as a present from Mr. Beardsworth, and that the handwriting is clearly Lord Hale's, and further that he was not possessed of the MS. until after he had printed Lord Hale's treatise.[1]

[1] The following are Mr. Hargrave's notes on the outside sheet of the MS.:—"Received as a present from Mr. Beardsworth.—F. H." "The handwriting is Lord Hale's, as I conclude from a comparison "with various MSS. known to be Lord Hale's, which I have seen.— "F. H." "I am clear that the handwriting is Lord Hale's.—F. H." "This outside cover to be preserved in the bindings." "I was not "possessed of this MS. till the treatise by Lord Hale on the same "subject, published by me in my first volume of Law Tracts, was "wholly printed.—F. H." See Preface to the 8vo edition, p. 5.

A NARRATIUE LEGALL AND HISTORICALL TOUCHINGE THE CUSTOMES. [BY SIR MATTHEW HALE.]

Caput primum.

CONCERNINGE THE PORTS THEYR NATURES AND ORIGINALLS.

BEFORE I come to treate of custumes and theyr kindes and originalls, it may bee conuenient to premise somethinge concerninge the ports, theyr natures and kindes and originalls, partly bycause it hath somewhat of relation to the customes of merchandizes exported and imported, and partly bycause there seemes to bee somewhat of the consideration for which some customes are taken in the Kinges interest in the ports and his care of them.

For the better explication of the nature of the ports and what they are, there are these termes to bee explained, vizt. a rode, a hauen, a port, and a creeke :

A rode is an open place in the sea, which yet in respect of its scituation, the protection by the adjacent shore, the conuenience of the channell or deepe where it is, is neuertheles a conuenient place for shipps to ride with safety, as Douer Rode, Hungrode, Kirkly rode, and the like, which, though they are at a reasonable distance from the shore, are safe in respect of theyr scituation for rideinge of shipps at anchor or otherwise.

A Hauen is a part of the sea within certaine neckes or cinctures of land, which are yet more safe for the rideinge or anchoringe of shipps, wherby they are protected almost on euery side from the violence of the windes, and not farre of from the conuenience of the port, as Milford Hauen, Plymouth Hauen, Falmouth Hauen, and the like; wherof some are larger, some straiter, some purely made up by nature, some made or at lest helped by art.

A port is an agregate thinge, partly naturall, vizt. the contiguity of the sea or some creeke therof, or, some nauigable riuer, wherby vessells may haue accesse to vnlade, and partly artificiall, vizt. keyes and landinge places and howses and receptacles for mariners and merchandizes, as the port of London, of Douer, of Southhampton, Bristoll, &c., wherin though the denomination bee from the town or city, which is as it were *caput portus*, yet the port itself is a thinge of larger extent, and takes in sometymes a greate tract of water or nauigable riuers; as the port of London includes all the riuer of Thames down below Grauesend, the port of Bristoll includes the channel of Seuerne vp to Gloucester and down to Kingrode and Hungrode.

If a thinge bee alledged to bee done in *portu de Blakeney*, the visne shal come *de vicineto portus*, 7 *H.* 6, 22. But yet if the *venire facias* bee *de vicineto de Blackney*, it hath been held good; bycause though the port may bee more extensiue, yet it doth not appeare to the Court that it is so.

Creekes are of two kindes, vizt.: i. such as are really members of ports, or small landinge places within the extent therof; or ii. such places as though in theyr own nature are as much ports as others, yet are comonly called creekes, bycause the Kinge hath no fixed custome officers there; but the custome house and custome office is held at the *caput portus*. Thus Mynhead was formerly a creeke of the port of Bridgewater; Dartmouth, Barnstaple, and Ilifordcome, creekes of the port of Exeter; and though ships come not vp to Exeter nor farther then Toppesham, yet Exeter is the *caput portus* and giues the denomination of the port, though aunciently Toppesham was the port. And so is at this day Grauesend indeed not so much a creeke as a member of the port of London.

And this shal serue for the explication of termes; so that vpon the whole matter a port in ordinary appellation is nothing else but a town, city, or village contiguous to the sea or some nauigable river appointed for the arrival, ladinge, and vnladeinge of shipps; a kinde of sea market, though it doth and may include within the extent of its denomination many other towns or places contiguous to the sea, creekes, or nauigable riuers, nay part of the ocean; for at this day, though the town of Great Yarmouth is a town lyinge 4 miles within the land, yet it, the port of Yarmouth, conteines the whole riuer and the mouth of it down to the sea; and also Kirkly roade that lyes many miles without the points of the land which is by the Kinge's charter annexed vnto and made part of that port.

So that in truth as a city or borough or colledge denote an artificiall aggregate nature or franchis, so doth a port denote a place not only where shipps naturally may but civilly and legally may come and vnlade and relade. And thus much shal suffice touchinge the general nature of a port.

I shall now discend to the examination how and in what

manner and by what meanes a port may bee legally created or constituted.

A port, as is before sayd, is a franchis or liberty, as a markett or faire is, and may bee acquired by the same meanes, vizt.:

i. By prescription or vsage immemoriall; and thus are most of the ports of England.

ii. By the creation or institution of the Kinge; for *portus* and *portatica* are amonge the *regalia* not only in this kingdome, but generally in all kingdomes and states.

And they may bee *de nouo* created by two meanes, vizt. by proclamation where the Kinge erects a port in his own demesne, so that there is no grauntee of it: and thus the Kinge may and doth erect fayres or marketts in his own demesne. The tenor of the proclamation is to this effect: *Rex Vicecomiti, salutem: Quia volumus quod sit de cætero portus maris et applicatio navium apud S. in comitatu tuo, tibi præcipimus quod proclamari facias per totam ballivam tuam quod de cætero sit portus maris et applicatio navium cum bonis et mercandisis suis apud S. prædictum, quodque omnes mercatores et alij cum navibus bonis et mercandisis suis licite venire, et ibidem bona et catalla sua in naues suas onerare, et ab eisdem exonerare, sine impedimento nostri hæredum vel successorum nostrorum, saluis nobis subsidiis et custumis et aliis inde nobis debitis, etc.*

When the liberty of a port is created and att the same time transferred to another, this is done by charter, sometymes general, sometymes speciall, wherof herafter; and most ordinarily there goes out a proclamation writt to the Sherif to giue notice of it to the people, as herafter shal also appeare.

If a man hath a port by graunt or prescription, it may bee considerable whither the Kinge cannot erect or create another port neare it to the damage of it, as in case of a market, faire, or ferry; or whether in this case, inasmuch as the ports of the kingdome are the gates of the kingdome, and of so greate use for the commerce and trade of the kingdome, and so not of the same nature with other petty franchises, whither the Kinge may not erect a port *de novo* contiguous to that port hee hath so graunted, though it bee to the private nusance of it.

But if the Kinge haue the liberty of an auncient port, and hee erects another port, possibly upon the same river, and graunts it over in fee ferme, and graunts farther that the application of ships shall be there *et non alibi;* this is good, for nobodyes interest is concerned but the Kinges, which he may derogate from by his own graunt, and though consequentially it may bee a prejudice to the country, bycause it restraines the liberty they had of accesse to the former port.

This was the case of John de Britannia Earle of Richmond:

The Kinge Edward I. was seised of the port of Great Yarmouth and of the mannor of Little Yarmouth and Gorleston, to which mannor there had been comonly vsed arrivall of shipps and vnladinge of merchandizes; and this mannor lyes between Greate Yarmouth and the sea upon the same river, though on the other side.

Kinge H. 3^d^ beinge thus seised of the mannor of Little Yarmouth graunted it at will to John de Britannia Earle of Richmond:

Afterward the same Kinge E. 1, by his charter dated graunted to the Burgesses of Greate Yarmouth and theyr successors *quod omnia mercandisæ et mercimonia quæcunque sive sint de piscible sive de aliis rebus quibuscunque, quæ infra dictum portum dictæ villæ Magnæ Jernemuthæ in nauibus aut batellis seu alio modo adduci seu deferri contigerit, ut ibidem negotietur de eisdem licite et aperte, apud eandem villam de Magna Jernemutha et non alibi infra portum prædictum discarcentur et ibidem vendantur absque aliquo forstallamento vel abrochiamento vel aliquo alio impedimento.*

After this the same Kinge graunted the mannor of Little Yarmouth and Gorleston unto John de Britannia and the heyres of his body with all faires and markets and all franchises as fully and freely as John de Baylol held it, which John held these mannors with this arrivall of shipps.

The charter of Greate Yarmouth in the tyme of Kinge E. 2 against this graunt made subsequently to John de Britannia: For that liberty of arrivall of ships in Little Yarmouth was in the Kinge at the tyme of the graunt made to Greate Yarmouth, and hee might justly derogate from his own interest; But if the interest had been graunted out to John de Britannia befor this exclusive graunt made to Greate Yarmouth, then the Kinge could not by his subsequent graunt exclude the arrival of shipps at the mannor of Little Yarmouth by an exclusive clause of *non alibi:* though hee might haue settled a concurrent port as it seemes in Greate Yarmouth.

John de Britannia, not satisfyed with the former judgement,

petitioned in the Parlement, *Rot. Parl.* 8 *E.* 2, *m.* 6, and after that in the Parlement of 1 E. 3, to haue the charter of Greate Yarmouth repealed, bycause graunted without any writt of *ad quod damnum*, and to the prejudice of the Kinge and the county, which is debated in the Yeare Booke 2 E. 3, 7. But hee obtained not.

After many disputes this busines was ended by the award of the Kinge and his Councell, which is entred *Rot. Pat.* 5 *E.* 3, *pt ja*, *m.* 2, which was to this effect:

i. That the port of Yarmouth was but one port, and that it belonged to the town of Greate Yarmouth.

ii. That all customable goods comeinge into the port shal bee brought to Great Yarmouth and there vnladed and sold, and not elsewhere, except the proper shipps of the men of Gorleston and Little Yarmouth.

iii. That the shipps belonginge properly to Little Yarmouth and Gorleston laden with customable goods shal come up to Greate Yarmouth and pay theyr custom, which beinge ther payd, they may go with theyr ships and goods to Little Yarmouth and Gorleston, and sell or dispose the same there.

iv. That yet they may if they please sell theyr goods at Great Yarmouth.

v. That al ships laden with herringe or goods uncustomable comeinge within the port of Yarmouth shal vnlade and sell those goods at Greate Yarmouth *et non alibi*, except the proper shipps of Gorleston and Little Yarmouth laden with herringe or other uncustomable goods, and those may unlade and sell at Gorleston and Little Yarmouth.

vi. That the men of Gorleston and Little Yarmouth shall not own other men's shippinge upon paine of forfeiture. *V.* stat. 9 Edw. III. c. 1.

Upon this record and proceedinge these thinges are to bee plainly collected:—

1. That the liberty of arrivall of shipps may by usage bee appendant or incident to a mannor even in the Kinges hands.

2. That this liberty will passe by the graunt of the mannor with relative words *in tam amplis modo et forma, &c.*

3. That by usage a right of such arrivage may bee acquired even to the tenants and occupyers of a mannor with theyr own ships and vessels, for it is but a kinde of easement. And this appears here bycause that interest that was in John de Britannia could not at all bee looked upon, for it was derived under the Kinges pro-

visue to the graunt to Great Yarmouth: But it was the interest of the *homines* and *tenentes* of Gorleston and Little Yarmouth that was prejudiced by the general inhibition of vnladinge elsewhere then at Greate Yarmouth, and it is that interest which is saved and provided for by this wise and just ordinance.

4. That even the proper ships and goods customable of the men of Little Yarmouth and Gorleston were, notwithstandinge theyr usage of landinge at home, subjected to passe up to Great Yarmouth, which was the *caput portus*, in order to the satisfaction of the Kinges customes.

5. That the *tenentes* and *inhabitantes* of Gorleston and Little Yarmouth could not alledge a custom or clame a priviledge for strangers ships to arrive and unlade there against the speciall inhibition of the charter; for this would have been a franchis, and not acquirable but by charter or prescription, which the *homines* and *inhabitantes* had not power nor capacity to claime.

6. But if John de Britannia had had a graunt of a port and free arrival of ships precedent to the graunt of those of Greate Yarmouth, or if hee had had a port by prescription, this had been a right of a franchis lodged in him, and in that case, though possibly the King might have erected a kinde of concurrent port, yet hee could not have excluded the arrivage of strangers ships at his port.

7. But even in that case, for the accomodation of the Kinges customes, that they might bee the better answered, the Kinge, as it seemes, might have appointed them to bringe up theyr goods to the principall port to have been entred and payd theyr customes, though not to unlade and sell there, but with liberty to unlade and sell at the small port: But this may bee doubtful. To solve this difficulty, it is therfor provided, by the stat. of 1 El. cap. 11, that the Queen might assign the ports and keyes where goods should bee landed. See the statute.

Thus farre wee have examined what may bee done for the erection of a port by the Kinge. But regularly no subject, though haveinge a palatine jurisdiction, can within this kingdom erect a port, though by title of prescription or charter hee may have a port: as shal bee sayd.

And therfor at this day if a man have land adjoininge to the sea, and shipps unlade theyre goods upon his land without any title of usage or prescription enablinge of them, the owner may take amends for the trespasse. But if hee sett formall and constant rates upon those that land, this is fineable: first, bycause it is a kinde of accrochment of a port; 2, because it is *nova consuetudo levata*, which was an article inquirable in the Eyer: and so it was resolved.

It appeares *Claus.* 11 *H.* 3, *m.* 3, that the Kinge had graunted to the Earle of Penbroch a kinde of restrained liberty of port or arrivage of shipps, vizt. *Rex concessit et licentiam dedit Willelmo Comiti Mariscallo quod naves de dominica terra sua cum mercandizis in eis contentis libere expedite et sine impedimento veniant ad portum suum de Rosse, et ibidem morentur et inde recedant, dum tamen aliæ naves de terra domini Regis et naves de aliis terris venientes in Hiberniam eant et veniant ad portum de Waterford; Mandatum est G. de Mariscis quod naves de terra ipsius Comitis ad portum suum venire permittat et alias naves ad portum de Waterford.*

The Earle of Penbroch, beinge a greate man and havinge this bottome, did therupon, by his own authority or the incrochment of merchants, use this as a comon port: And therupon *Claus.* 20 *H.* 3, *m.* 4 *dorso*, there issued another writt directed to the *Justiciariis Hiberniæ* to this effect: *Cum villa nostra de Waterford sicut audivimus plurimum deteriorata est per applicationem navium, quæ omisso portu ejusdem villæ apud Ros et Insulam in terra G. Mariscalli Comitis Penbrochiæ: Mandaverimus eidem Comiti quod nullæ naves in terra sua prædicta applicare debeant nisi illæ solummodo qui sunt de terra sua propria: et hoc de permissione nostra prohiberi faciatis, quod naves aliquæ nisi naves hominum suorum de terra sua propria de cætero non applicent apud Ros nec apud Insulam, per quod prædicta villa nostra damnum incurrat; quod nisi facere voluerit, id per vos fieri faceremus. Et ideo vobis mandamus quod ea clamari faciatis et firmiter inhiberi, ne aliqua navis quæ non sit de propria terra ejusdem Comitis apud Ros vel Insulam applicare decætero presumat, super forisfacturam nostram; sed magistri et marinarii tendent et accedent cum navibus suis et mercandizis usque Waterford, si voluerint ibidem negotiari, sicut se ipsos voluerint indemnes servare.*

Which auncient record, though it concerne Ireland, yet is truly declarative of the law of England, that a subject may not accroch a port or application of ships without a lawfull prescription or warrant from the Kinges charter, nor yet farther then that charter warrants him, vizt. if the charter extend but to a limitted port hee may not enlarge it. This is againe reinforced by another mandat, P. 19 E. 1, m. 15.

It is true by mediation afterwards it seemes that port or the conditions therof were inlarged by the Kinges award, *quod vide P.* 50 *E.* 3, *rot.* 19, *Hibernia, Coram Rege in Thesauraria:*

To this wee may add the famous case of the Burgesses of Newcastle and Prior of Tinmuth, which is entred amonge the *Placita Parliamenti* 20 *E.* 1, *and in the Kinges Bench, Hill.* 20 *E.* 1, *Coram Rege, rot.* 19; wherein the Burgesses for the Kinge do complaine that, *Cum dominus Rex habeat et habere debeat totum portum in aqua de Tyne a mare usque ad locum qui dicitur Hydewin stremes ita libere quod non liceat alicui carcare nec discarcare mercandizas aliquas seu denarratas, nec forstallum facere de huiusmodi mercandizis vel denarratis, emendo vel vendendo illam nisi infra villam de Novo Castro prædicto; ita quod dominus Rex tolneta sua prisas et custumas et alia ad dominium suum spectantia percipere possit; prædictus Prior, qui habet dominicas terras suas prædictæ aquæ adjacentes inter mare et villam prædictam, carcare et discarcare facit ibidem mercandizas et denarratas quascunque ibidem applicantes, emendo et vendendo in terris suis prædictis pro voluntate sua, faciendo ibi portum, vbi nullus portus prius fuit, et etiam forstallum mercandizarum in prejudicium domini Regis.* And that hee hath built a town at Sheles, and hath fishermen, bakers, bruers, and there they entertain the mariners, sell provisions to them, een to the damage of the Kinges port of Newcastle. The Prior as to some points charged justifyes, and claymes the propriety of the soil *usque filum aquæ de Tyne* accordinge to the extent of his lands, *and upon those there were several inquiryes directed, but appear not in that record to bee determined.* But as to any market or port disclaimes; wherupon *inhibitum est ei ne mercatum vel portum in locis prædictis teneat, immo quod omnimoda signa quæcunque fuerint tam portus quam mercati in locis prædictis prosternere faciat et diruere.* But afterwards in 20 *E.* 1, *rot.* 59, *Northumbria;* Judgment entred, vizt.: *quod dominus Rex habebit totum portum maris a mari ad locum qui dicitur Hydewinstremes, et quod nullus in portu illo possit carcare vel discarcare sine licentia domini Regis vel ballivorum suorum, et quod portus ille remaneat domino Regi et heredibus suis libere, cum prisis et towagio et omnibus libertatibus ad portum spectantibus, ita quod neque apud Sheles neque apud Tinmuth naves carcentur, et wreccum maris, etc.*

By all which and much more it is apparant that a port is a franchis in which the Kinge hath an interest, and cannot bee sett up without a lawful title derived from the Crown by charter or prescription.

And thus much concerninge the makeinge of ports and the authority by which it may or may not bee done: now let us see how they may bee unmade or destroyed.

Regularly a port is a place that is *juris publici*, wherin all men have somewhat of interest, as in publique or common wayes, or rivers that are navigable, or comon passages for boates: And therfor it seemes that unles a port become totally unusefull by accident, as beinge sanded or stopt up by the sea: it cannot bee abolished without an Act of Parlement. Wee have some instances wherin it was done by Parlement, vizt.:

Rot. Parl. 11 H. 6, n. 38, the port of Melcomb is annulled, and the port established at Poole.

And thus much of the nature and manner of constitution of ports, and how and by whome.

Caput secundum.

CONCERNINGE THE SEVERAL INTERESTS IN THE PORTS OF THE KINGDOM; AND FIRST OF THE JUS REGIUM.

There is a threefold interest in the ports of the kingdom, vizt.: i. *Jus regium*, or prerogative, ii. *Jus publicum*, iii. *Jus privatum*.

The *jus regium* or prerogative intereste is that right which peculiarly belonges to the Kinge as the supreme magistrate, and this is uncomunicable to any subject, though otherwise endued with *jura regalia*, as a count palatine, which is a right of manageinge and orderinge of ports for the publique safety and good of the kingdome: it is part of those incommunicable *jura summi imperii* which are lodged in the supreme power, and these are of three kindes in order and respect to three greate importances, vizt.: 1. in respect of the safety of the kingdom, 2. in respect of the commerce and trade of the kingdome, 3. in respect of the revenue of the Crown or his customes.

I. As to the first of these, vizt. the *jus regium*, as it relates to the safety of the kingdome, which is a power, 1. of shuttinge the ports in reference to the safety, 2. a power for the gardinge and defendinge of the ports against foren enemyes or invasions;

I shal only consider the former, bycause the latter is comon both to ports and other places adjoininge to the coasts, and comes under the extent of the auncient and usuall writt or proclamacion called *Costeræ defensio:*

The shuttinge of the ports in order to the preservation of the peace or safety of the nation is of two kindes. 1. The shuttinge out of persons or thinges prejudiciall or that in probability might bee prejudiciall to the kingdome; the exclusion of forein enemyes and spyes in tyme of hostility. 2. The exclusion of any forren soveraigne prince unles he come with the leave and safe conduct of the Kinge of England, though a prince in amity, as was done in the tyme of H. 3, when the Emperor came to visit the Kinge. 3. The exclusion of those thinges that might bee prejudiciall to the peace of the kingdome and the bringers of them, *ne quis importet intra hoc regnum Angliæ prejudicialia paci regni vel juri regis:* as seditious pamphlets, and hertofor the popes bulls, breves, interdictions, or excommunications. And proclamations of this sort were frequent, and the violators thereof punished.

ii. The shuttinge in of persons and thinges in tymes especially of hostility that might bee assistinge or advantagious to the enemy: so that this breakes into these two parts, vizt. the inhibition of persons passinge out of ports, and the inhibition of thinges.

1. For persons: By the Comon Law all persons might passe the seas without the Kinges licence unles prohibited, but by the statute of 5 R. 2, there was a general prohibition of all but noblemen, merchants, and the Kinges soldiers to passe the seas without licence, and thus it continued till it was repealed 4 Jac. cap. 24. But though at Comon Law every man might freely passe the seas, yet when they were under an inhibition, they might not; and these inhibitions were of two kindes: generall, which ordinarily happened in tyme of hostility to prevent intelligence to bee exported, and sometimes the better to discover spyes, and sometymes to prevent carrying supplyes to the enemye; and sometymes these inhibitions extended generally to all the ports and al persons not to passe without the Kinges licence, as *Claus.* 10 *H.* 3, *m.* 27 *dorso; Claus.* 11 *H.* 3, *m.* 25 *dorso; Claus.* 3 *E.* 3, *m.* 9 *dors.* And sometymes all ports were prohibited but one or som few, as Douer, *Claus.* 3 *E.* 3, *m.* 26 *dors.*, *v. Dy.* 265, 296. And these general prohibitions as longe as they were in tymes of publique danger, and carryed the reason

of themselves with them, were quietly borne; but when they grew to bee devises to gett mony for licences, they were complained of in Parlement, and prayed *que le mere soit overt* as well in reference to persons as merchandizes. *Rot. Parl.* 18 *E.* 3, *n.* 10; 20 *E.* 3, *n.* 8; 25 *E.* 3, *n.* 22.

So that at this day, the stat. of 5 R. 2 being repealed, there lyes no restraint upon any mans passinge the seas but what was at Comon Law either by this generall prohibition or by the particular inhibition by the writt *De securitate invenienda ne quis exeat regno, de quo vide Fitzh. fol.* 85.

ii. That of thinges: thus in tymes especially of publique hostility, the exportation of armes, bowes, arrowes, etc., and thinges of that nature which might advantage an enemy, were inhibited. But of this wee shal see more under the next consideration.

II. The second relation or respect of this *jus regium* or *imperii* is in relation to trade and commerce: wherin wee will examine what *de facto* hath been done and what *de jure* may bee done by the Kinges prerogative merely in relation to commerce. And this hath a double respect: 1. to merchandises imported, 2. to merchandises exported.

1. In reference to merchandises imported *de facto*, as sometymes ther have been such kinde of inhibitions, sometymes totally and sometymes as in reference to some particular ports; but as these have not been warranted by law, so these inhibitions have proved utterly uneffectuall to the end designed, bycause such an inhibition could not induce any forfeiture, and therfor wee shal see in all tymes the recourse hath been to inhibit them by Act of Parlement: *vide the case of monopolyes*, 10 *Rep.* accordingly resolved; and accordingly resolved in the case of Southampton cited by Sir Ed. Cook, *magna carta, cap.* 30; the graunt that no merchant stranger should land any malmeseyes in any port but Southampton upon payment of treble custome, though this did not take away the whole liberty of comerce, yet adjudged void, and a spetiall Act of Parlement passed for the settlinge of it. For the great charter, cap. 30, the stat. of 2 *E.* 3, *cap.* 9, 9 *E.* 3, *cap.* 1, 25 *E.* 3, *cap.* 2, and divers other statutes are against such exclusion or inhibitions.

2. In reference to merchandises exported, wee will see what *de facto* was done in former tymes and how the law stands at this day.

We find auinciently instances of these two kindes tendinge to the restriction of exportation, vizt., 1. generall inhibitions of the exportation of some sorts of goods, 2. particular ports assigned for the exportation of some sort of goods and others restrained.

1. Touching generall inhibitions of exportation of some sort of goods, and this done only by the Kinges prerogative. *Claus.* 38 *E.* 3, *m.* 29, a prohibition of exportation of horses, falcons, wollen or linnen thred, bowes, arrowes, bow strings, and other armes under paine of seisure of the goods and ships wherin they were laden. *Claus.* 41 *E.* 3, *m.* 24 *dors.*, an inhibition of exportation of horses, beasts, armes, bowes, arrowes, upon paine of imprisonment. *Claus.* 43 *E.* 3, *m.* 3 *dorso*, a prohibition of exportation of corne, gold, silver, bowes, armes, and arrowes *sub forisfactura omnium terrarum et bonorum tam emptorum quam venditorum*. *Claus.* 45 *E.* 3, *m.* 4 *dors.*, *Claus.* 10 *E.* 2, *m.* 13, prohibitions of exportation of corne, victuall, and timber. And there were many tymes proceedinges in the Courts at Westminster, especially in the Exchequer, for attempts against these proclamacons, and sometymes in the Kinges bench: *v. H.* 1 *E.* 2, *Coram Rege, rot.* 38, a proceedinge against such as exported horses, armes, mony, and plate against the proclamation of Kinge Ed. 1st.

But these proclamations had but small effect: for though there were added clauses of forfeiture, yet they were but *in terrorem;* for by the law a proclamation cannot induce a forfeiture, as hath been often resolved, though the exportation in the particular case might possibly bee prohibited: And besides unles it were in reference only to armes and in tyme of hostility, such prohibitions of exportations were in truth against the law unles prohibited by special Acts of Parlement. And therfor for the supply of these defects, and to make an effectuall prohibition in these cases, particular Acts of Parlement were passed for the prohibitinge of exportation of these and the like comodityes, as 1 *E.* 4, *cap.* 5, of horses; 1 *et* 2 *Ph. et M. cap.* 5, of corn; 9 *E.* 3, *cap.* 9, of gold and silver; 25 *H.* 8, *cap.* 2, of victualls; and the like of other thinges, 26 *H.* 8, *cap.* 10.

Somewhat suitable to these prohibitions of exportation by proclamation were those proclamations for the increase of navigation, that the ships of aliens should not bee freited with English comodityes till the English ships were laden, *Claus.* 41 *E.* 3, *m.* 25; but that proved ineffectual, and for the very same reason. And therfor it was provided by Acts of Parlement, vizt. 14 *R.* 2, *cap.* 6, that English merchants should freit only English vessels; but this provoked foren princes to do the like, and was found inconvenient to trade, and therfor repealed by the *stat. of* 1 *Eliz. cap.* 13. But now againe renewed in substance by the last Act of Navigation. And thus much touchinge general restrictions of exportation.

2. I come to particular; vizt. the limittes of particular ports for the exportation or market of particular comodityes, as, namely, of wooll, and such were the staples, which were settled upon these three accounts: 1. to keep the vent and trade of wool under a regulation; 2. that the Kinges great custome, which principally arose upon wool, might bee the more certainly answered; 3. that there might be a more certaine returne of bullion for the wool exported accordinge to the auncient statutes.

This beinge the ground of the settling of staples and particular ports for the exportation of wool, the progresse of these staples was thus:—

Rot. Pat. 6 *E.* 2, *p.* 2, *m.* 5: the Kinge by his commission comitted to the merchants of England power to nominate places for the staple, and imposed penaltyes upon them that did not submitt to it; and this seemes to bee the first basis or foote of these staples.

Claus. 13 *E.* 2, *m.* 1 *dorso:* Upon the disobedience of this constitution of the staple strict commissions issued to inquire of the offenders.

Pat. 2 *E.* 3, *m.* 24: The ordinances of the staple are reproclaimed and the places for them settled.

But this beinge conceived against the greate charter and other statutes, especially as to merchants strangers, who by the then late statute of 2 E. 3, cap. 9, to have free trade, all staples, both in England and beyond the sea, were dissolved and decryed. And when afterwards it was found that certain merchants beyond the seas intended to sett up by a kinde of combination a staple at Bruges, they were inhibited by proclamation grounded upon that statute.

Pat. 6 *E.* 3, *m.* 20 *dors.:* But notwithstandinge all this, and though not only the stat. of 2 E. 3, cap. 9, were against it; but divers other new lawes that fixed and established the liberty of trade, especially merchants aliens, viz., 9 *E.* 3, *cap.* 2, 25 *E.* 3, *cap.* 2: the usefulnes and convenience of staples beinge found, they were again erected by proclamation both on this side and beyond the sea: wherof wee finde frequent mention in the Parlement Rolls, vizt. 17 *E.* 3, 22 *E.* 3, 25 *E.* 3. But the foundations of these staples were too weake, and wanted the strenth of an Act of Parlement to settle them against the force of those lawes that were contrary to them; and so, though they were usefull, yet they did not the busines ontill the greate statute of the staple, 27 *E.* 3, *cap.* 1, settled them upon a sure foote. And greate priviledges and advantages were allowed to the merchants by the same Act, possibly as a recompence for the constitution. How the staples succeeded or vanished afterward is not greatly pertinent to this discourse. By what hath been shewn it appeares the power of shuttinge the ports in reference to trade could not bee well done by law without an Act of Parlement. It is true that *de facto* it hath been semely done; and when it was but rarely done, and upon emergent occasions that seemed to justify the necessity of such restraints, it was not much opposed or contested; but when it began to bee too frequent or trou[ble]-some or unnecessary, then people complained, and the Kinges Councell never thought it safe or prudent to insist upon the validity of such inhibitions or restrictions, but they were, as there was just occasion, settled by Parlement, and so rendred effectuall and unquestionable.

III. The third relation of the *jus regium* is in reference to his customes and subsidyes ariseing upon merchandises exported or imported. And this right may bee of two kindes: 1, the limitation of places wher goods shall bee exported that should answere the Kinges customes; 2, the limitation or appointment of evidences to make out that the Kinges dutyes are satisfyed.

1. Touchinge the limittinge of spetiall ports for the transportation of goods that so the Kinge might bee the better answered his customes: this indeed hath been attempted by the Kinges, as wee see aboue in the case of the staples. And *Claus.* 5 *E.* 3, *parte j*[a], *m.* 12 *dorso*, there issued a spetiall proclamation that wools, out of which the greate custome then issued, should not bee transported but in certaine particular ports ther mentioned, *ubi sigillum nostrum quod dicitur cokett et tronum nostrum deputentur*, vizt. Newcastle, Kingston upon Hull, St. Butolfs, Lynn, Yarmouth, and Ipswich, London, Southampton, Chichester, Melcomb, Exeter, Hartlepole, Sandwich.

This seemed hard, for though the original power of instituteinge ports is lodged in the Crown, yet, when the ports are settled, the subject hath an interest in them: and upon the same account as all the rest of the ports might bee stopped up, on the same authority the greatest part of these might bee stopped: And hence wee finde, *Rot. Parl.* 6 *H.* 4, *n.* 54, when the Kinge had restrained the shippinge of wooles at Ipswich, the merchants complained that it was to the greate disease and destruction of the merchants and the danger of the losse of theyr woolls, and also in diminution of of the Kinges customes. It was therupon answered, *soit le passage de laines quires et peux lanuites ovesqe le tronage de leines cibien a Gipwic comme a Gernemuth in assay tanqe le prochein Parlement*, so that the greiuance was not wholly releiued, but respitted.

But the truth is the hold that was upon the subject in that case was this. If the goods were not cocketted they were seiseable by the searcher, and the cockett not beinge there, they could not bee cocketted; which, though it were a damage, yet it was not readily releivable. But little feare ther could bee of great inconvenience to the subject by this meanes; for if this restraint were an inconvenience to trade, it would quickly inconvenience the Kinge in his customes, which probably hee would not occasion.

But to avoid all question now by the statute of 1 Eliz. cap. 11, it is enacted that no ship bee laden or unladed but in some open place or assigned by the Queenes Commission in the ports of London, Southampton, Bristoll, Chester, and Newcastle, and in some open key or wharf in all other ports, havens, creekes, or roads (Hull excepted) where a customer controller and searcher had been by ten yeares last resident or should bee resident.

This did sett open all the ports where there had been a customer controller and searcher within ten yeares; wherby all considerable ports were free, bycause in such ports there had been customers within ten yeares; so that this did put little inconvenience upon the merchant.

Thus much concerninge limittinge of ports in order to the payment of customes. There were other restraints upon merchandises in reference to the Kinges customes and the security of theyr payments, vizt.:

1. For native or inland goods, The cockett.

2. For forrein goods, certificates now called letts, passes, or transire.

These, though they were not direct restrainte of ports, yet they were consequentially such, for without these the goods laden aboard were and at this day are subject to bee seised.

1. The cockett, which was a small warrant under the seale appointed by the Kinge for the same use for the passinge of goods custumable, and hence is that frequent mention in auncient records of *bona* or *mercandisæ* seised *quia non cockettata*. They were auncientiy made in the Kinges name, and that use continues still for leather; and they were made in Latin: the conclusion of the cocket in Latin was auncientiy *quo quietus est*, which being writt short, *quo quiet*, gave the name of *cockett.* But for other goods the cocket is made in the name of the collector and controller.

These cocketts were and are of two sorts, vizt., generall or absolute cocketts when goods custumable were to bee transported beyond the seas: this cockett was a testimoniall of the payment of the customes and a warrant for the searcher to cleare them:

Coast cocketts which wer graunted upon sendinge of customable goods from one port to another; in which case no custome was due, but bycause beinge abroad at sea, they might possibly carry them to other countryes, and so defet the Kinge of his customs, the merchant was to give bonds to unlade them at the port appointed, and upon a certificate therof to bee discharged of his bond.

The cocket is nothinge but a warrant under the Kinges seale testifyinge the payment of the custome. Where the goods were not customable goods there was no cockett needful, nor used; and therfore when all the goods customable outward were wools, woolfells, and leather, vizt., the greate custome, the cocket was only for these goods and no other: and this appeares abundantly by the old accompts in the pipe of E. 1 and E. 2 tyme; at which tyme the Kinge was answered the profitts of the seal of the cockett, which was in som ports 2^{d} for every merchant, in some ports 2^{d} ob., in some ports, as Exeter 4^{d}. The collector of the greate customes answered it thus, vizt.: *Et de x^{s} de exitibus sigilli quod dicitur cocket prædictarum lanarum, pellium et coriorum vizt. de quolibet mercatore lanas pelles seu coria exeuntia in aliqua nave in portu de Lynne 2^{d}*; and sometyme 2^{d} ob., as appeares in all the collectors accounts of the tyme of E. 1 and E. 2. But sometymes there was nothinge answered of the profitts of this seale, *quia clericus qui facit contra rotulum et facit literas de warranto solutionis* *dictæ custumæ et scribens rotulos ejusdem custumæ illam recipit pro labore:*

And therfor it seemes the cockett began with the customes outwards, and extended no farther then such goods as were customable, which was auinciently only wools, woolfells, and leather outwards. And therefor it was a mistake in the late tymes that though goods were not chargeable with subsidy or custome, they were yet liable to forfeiture or seisure *quia non cockettatæ:* Wheras all those auncient records that speake of seisure of goods *non cockettatæ* add also *nec custumalia;* for the cocket was only the certificat or warrant to the officers below stayres, as the searchers, to acquaint them the customes due were payd.

But indeed when other goods came by Act of Parlement to bee charged with customes or subsidyes outward, the cockett extended and was requisite for such goods so chargeable. The tenor of the cocket is as followeth, vizt.[1]

2. Certificates: and this is grounded upon the statute of 3 H. 7, cap. 7, wherby it is enacted that goods brought into one port and ther entred and then carryed to another port within the realme (in which case the merchant was not to pay customes a second tyme), that the customer of the port where they were first entred and customes payd shal make certificate therof, and of the particular discriptions of the merchandises, to the end they may bee veiwed and examined by the customer of the 2d port; and that if any goods shal bee discharged or sold other then at the port where they were first entered without such certificate they are forfeit.

This Act was made for the benefit of the merchant, that he should not bee twise charged for custome or troubled when hee had once payd, and partly for the Kinges benefit, that men might not escape without customes at both places by false or uncertain certificates. But it seemes plaine that if the goods are once landed and sold at the first port, though they bee after sent by water to another port, nay, if sent beyond sea, the merchant is not bound to have any certificate, but they may bee sent of by cockett: for the intent of that statute was to supply the inconvenience when they were transported in the same vessel, and under pretence of payment of custome before, would escape custom free: but if once they were landed and sold, they are now become inland

[1] But Hale does not give it.

goods; and if the custom were not payd before, they were forfeited by the landinge, and so the Kinge secured of his duty.

And thus much concerninge the *jus imperii* or *regium* of ports, and the several lawes that abridge the extent of the prerogative in reference to them: And this right belonges to the Kinge, although in point of franchis or propriety they may in particular belonge to a subject; for they are *ostia regni* and the avenues of trade of the Kinges realme, and in these respects are so farre forth as by law they are subjecte to the *jus regium.*

Caput tertium.

CONCERNINGE THE JUS PUBLICUM OF PORTS.

The ports of the kingdome are like the comon roades or highwayes of the kingdome, wherin every man hath an interest for his use and convenience, though possibly in point of propriety they may belong to another: And therfor

i. They ought not to bee obstructed or shutt to the prejudice of trade, wherof at large in the precedent chapter.

ii. They ought to bee carefully repayred and made serviceable for the ends they are instituted.

iii. They ought to bee rescued from all publique or comon nusances.

The former of the three hath been sufficiently opened, vizt. when and in what cases the ports may bee shut and when not. I will now consider of the other two thinges.

And first in generall by the lawes of England in all thinges of publique interest which concern all, and not any one particular person, the law hath transferred the care and provision for such publique matters to the Kinge, and hee doth *sustinere personam vindicis et tutoris jurium publicorum*, as highwayes, navigable rivers, and the like, although the particular interest of franchise or propriety may possibly belonge to a private person; and therfor al suits and proceedinges in such cases are *pro domino Rege:*

I. Therfor as to the care of repayre of ports, this is in a special manner left to the Kinges care and power.

And therfor hee may by his prerogative impose a publique taxe upon all comers to any haven for the necessary safegard and repayres therof: these two sorts of taxes.

1. Murage: for the wallinge in of a port; that so it may bee safe against invasion of forren enemyes, vizt. reasonable sums for a reasonable tyme of all shipps and carriages comeinge therunto for the repayreinge of a decayed wall or buildinge for the safegard and defence of the place and goods of merchants thither brought.

2. Kaiage or wharfage; for the repayre of an old key or wharf or makeinge of a new, if need require, for the landinge of goods, vizt., a reasonable sum of mony for reasonable tymes of al ships and vessels comeinge within the port. And frequent instances have been of both. And these kinde of tolls are agreable to law, for 1. the subject is not forced to come thither by any externall injunction, but only for his own convenience; 2. hee hath *quid pro quo,* though it may bee not in present yet in a short tyme his safety and convenience and accomodation.

II. The second consideration is touchinge nusances done to ports, and they are of two kindes.

> 1. Such as respect the port merely, as a place of publique use and convenience: such are obstructions of the passage and accesse of shipps or vessels.
>
> 2. Such as concerne it in some more restrained respect; as possibly as it is a franchis, a forstall, etc.: of both these shortly.

For the former of these are of divers sorts; the chokeinge up of a port with castinge filth into it: this some tyme prohibited. *Claus.* 46 *E.* 3, *m.* 14 *d.*, command to the Mayor, Sherifs, and Aldermen of London to interpose some effectual meanes *ne cirpi fimi fimaria et alia nociva in rivum Thamisiæ nullatenus jactentur sed abinde amoveantur in emendationem portus London:* and at other tymes punished by fines: sometymes amoved by the partyes damnifyed. Thus *Mich.* 13–14 *E.* 1, *Coram Rege, rot.* 10: In trespass by the Abbot of Tichfeud against the burgesses of Southampton *eo qd diripuerunt gurgitem suum apud Cadelond:* the Burgesses justify *quia gurges prædicta levata fuit ad nocumentum domini Regis et villæ Suthamptoniæ et quod batelli et naves impediuntur quo minus venire non possunt ad portum villæ:* and the Jury accordingly found it, and judgment for the Defendants. Sometymes they are amoved and the offences punished by the judgements of the Kinges Courts.

If they are out of the bodyes of countyes, then these nuisances are presented, punished, and amoved by the Court of Admiralty; and these nuisances are part of the articles of theyr inquiryes. If they are within bodyes of countyes, then they may bee indited and the offenders punished and the nuisances amoved in the Kinges ordinary courts of law. The Kinges Bench may upon presentments in leetes or hundreds, and this was ordinary.

Speciall provisions are made by Acts of Parlement for the avoidinge nuisances in some ports: *v. statutes* 23 *H.* 8, *cap.* 8, 27 *H.* 8, *cap.* 23, for the anoyances in the ports of Devon and Cornewall: 27 *H.* 8, *cap.* 18, for the annoyances of the port of London.

V. 34 H. 8, cap. 9, for sewers.

Generally that which stopps the port or chokes it up, as castinge out of filth or ballast or otherwise, obstructs the passage of ships or vessels, as weares, gurgites, piles, fills or makes the passage dangerous, as fixinge of piles, or layinge in of anchors without buoyes or markes, or stoppinge up a channel or rode, or turninge of it another way, to the prejudice of the arrivall of ships, are *primâ facie* nusances. And bycause the people are interested in ports as *jura publica*, the Kinge can not licence a makeinge or continuinge of a nuisance in a port more then in a highway.

And therfor if there bee a trench leadinge to a port from an arme of the sea for passage of boates or vessels, though that trench bee in a greate measure sanded up and rendred unusefull, yet *the very owner of the soyle* can not obstruct the old trench and make a new without the Kinges licence, nor yet by the Kinges licence, unles upon a writt of *ad quod damnum* it bee found not to bee a damage to the people, *Regist.* 252, for the Prior and Convent of Christ Church, Canterbury.

Though the straitninge of a port bee *primâ facie* a nusance, yet it is not every straitninge of a port that is a nusance; for in some cases the straitninge of a port is a convenience to it, and indeed it is not possible that there can bee any port unles there bee a straitning of the port, not only below the high water marke, but also below the low water marke; for without such a straitninge there could bee no keyes nor wharfs for the landing of goods immediatly out of the ships: and if every straitninge of the water of a port should bee *eo ipso* a nusance, the Kinge could not licence the makeinge of wharfs and keyes for the convenience of merchandise, which would destroy half the ports in England. Nusance, therfor, or not nusance, is a question of fact; and such the straitninge of a port may bee that it may bee a nuisance, as if howses or wharfs bee built in the very deepe where ships vsually have ridden, etc.; or it may bee no nusance, as if it only bee made upon the shallow where ships cannot ride, or if the key for receit of wares immediatly out of shipps cannot bee made without penninge in or restraninge the flush of the water and divers other instances.

And what is sayd concerninge nuisances in ports may bee sayd likewise and applyed to navigable or comon rivers, either parcell of a port or leadinge to it, or servinge for the usuall passage of boates; for they are in nature of comon highwayes, in which all the Kinges people have a liberty of passage: frequent instances are of that kinde.

H. 50 *E.* 3, *rot.* 23, *Linc. B. Regis*, the Abbot of Burgh fixinge pales in his port in the river of Trent without beken or withe, to the damage of vessels passinge that way: the piles are amoved by judgement. The like for nusances in the Water of Ouse, *Hill.* 23 *E.* 3, *B. Regis*, *rot.* 61; in the water of Leigh, *T.* 28 *E.* 3, *B. Regis*, *rot.* 29, 19 *Ass.* 6; in Severn *H.* 21 *E.* 1; and generally in al publique rivers, *Stat. magn. car. cap.* 23, *M.* 18–19 *E.* 1, *B. Rs.*, *Michis.* 36 *E.* 3, *B. Rs. rot.* 65, *Rot. Parl.* 14 *R.* 2, *n.* 34, *etc.*

2. I come to the second sort of nusance, which immediatly indeed concernes the port or its franchis; but consequently do redound not only to the damage of the Kinge in respect of his customes, but to the prejudice of the people; for the ports themselves, beinge either neglected or forstalled, doth introduce a decay of the ports and likewise a prejudice to trade: And upon this accompt the forestallinge of a port and all thinges that immediatly conduce therunto come under the notion of comon nusances.

1. Forestallinge by sea or without unladinge, but only *in transitu: v. Rot. Parl.* 8 *E.* 2, *m.* 16, a prohibition *ne naves vendant bona particulatim antequam veniant ad portum de Hull:* but this prohibition suspended bycause to the prejudice of the Archbishopp's port at Beverley.

2. Buildinge of keyes or havens or publique Brewhowses or victuallinge howses between the Kinges port and the sea: this is a nusance to the port, bycause it withdrawes the resort of mariners and merchants to the *caput portus*, and so wastes and decayes the port and gives opurtunity of stealinge the Kinges

customes: and therefor such interlopeinge buildinges between the port and the sea have been ordered to be abated, or at lest turned to other uses.

The case of Newcastle before mentioned makes this appeare. The judgement against the Prior of Tinmuth is entered *H.* 20 *E.* 1, *rot.* 59, *Northumb. B. Rs.* *T.* 11 *Car. in Camera Scaccarii*, upon the complaint of the city and port of Bristoll against Morgan, that had erected houses of receit at Crockhampill, a decree was made for the demolishinge therof for the same reasons. *Lib. Dec.*

But how ever it happened, the execution of the decree hath not obtained, for the houses stand to this day: possibly the owners made some composition, which might bee made in this case with all the partyes interested.

Wherin this difference is to bee observed: When a nuisance concernes immediatly al men, as the obstruction of a port, the makeinge of a weare in a publique river; this can neither bee licenced nor dispenced with, though the Kinge and the owner of the soil of the river should consent therunto, bycaus it is immediatly a comon nusance, and all are directly or immediatly concerned in it.

But where the nusance is only by consequence to the publique, but immediatly to the franchis or the fermor therof and to the Kinge ther, the Kinge and the owners of the franchis or fermors thereof may dispence with it, as in the case of buildinge howses between the port and the sea.

Capitulum quartum.

CONCERNINGE THE JUS PRIVATUM, OR PRIVATE INTEREST OF PORTS.

I come to the third right that may bee found in every port of the kingdome, vizt., the *jus privatum*, or the profittable interests of ports.

And all these three former rights, vizt. the *jus regium*, the *jus publicum*, and the *jus privatum*, are to bee found in every port of this nation, though sometymes the *jus privatum*, at lest as to some points of them, may bee found in the hands of subjects, as shal bee shewn:

This *jus privatum* is of two kindes: vizt., the right of a port in respect of the franchis of it, or the right of a port in respect of the soyle of it: for these two bee of severall natures.

I. The right of franchis or liberty: for as a market or faire is a liberty or franchis distinct from the soyle wherin it is held or kept; so the right of a port is distinct and of another nature from the soyle itself wherin it is kept or held.

Every port imported in it the liberty of a market, both for the sale of merchandise, shipt and unshipt, and also for furnishinge of victualls for the marriners. *Pat.* 14 *E.* 1, *m.* 22.—*Rex omnibus ad quos, etc. Quia accepimus per inquisitionem quam fieri fecimus, etc. Quod homines et mercatores nostri de Ravensrod bene et sufficientur possunt invenire omno tempore anni omnibus et singulis ad villam illam confluentibus bonum panem et bonam cervisiam secundum assisam nostram inde provisam.*

50 *E.* 3.—*Et hoc parati sunt facere et nulli deeste et quod extranei in prædicta villa de Ravensrod non residentes cupiditate ducti panem et cervisiam in navibus ad vendendum ibidem ducunt in ipsorum hominum et mercatorum nostrorum dispendium non modicum et status sui et villæ prædictæ deterioracionem et contra consuetudinem hujusmodi villarum super mare scituatarum; nos indemnitati hominum et mercatorum nostrorum provideri volentes in hac parte, concessimus eis quod nullus extraneus panem vel cervisiam in portu vel in mari juxta prædictam villam de Ravensrode contra voluntatem hominum et mercatorum nostrorum prædictorum vendere presumat: et ideo vobis mandamus quod aliter contra voluntatem hominum et mercatorum prædictorum quantum in vobis est fieri non permittatis.*

This right of franchise, as all other franchises, is originally in the Crown, and flowes from it, as marketts, faires, warrens, ferryes, and the like; for, as I have before sayd, every port of the sea hath somewhat of the nature of a comon markett, and more, for they are the *ostia regni* for the arrivage of shipps, as well of subjects as strangers, and the unladinge and reladeinge of theyr goods, and thence they are distributed as well into the kingdome as into foren ports. For *portus maris* doth as much designe a liberty as *mercatum* or *feria*, and much more. There are certaine perquisits or casualtyes belonging to the lord or owner of this franchis, but they are so intermingled and of such a mixed nature with those profitts that result from the ownership of the soyle that they will best be considered afterwards.

Only the Kinge in respect of his customes had a particular incident profitt or perquisite in all ports, vizt. *Tronagium*.

This tronage, consistinge of a beame, weights, and scales, was to the end those merchandises that answered the Kinge customes by weight might there bee weighed at theyr importacion and exportacion.

And bycause that at first only wooles answered customes, and answered them by weight, therfor it was called *tronagium lanorum*. But afterwards, as other customes came to bee answered by weight, as the customes of haverdupois of aliens, and afterwards the subsidy of poundage, these thinges came also to bee weighed at the Kinges beame.

And not only so, but bycause there were divers occasions between merchant and mariner for the weighinge of theyr goods as they were laden or unladen, and the Kinges beame and troner beinge ready at hand, they made use therof when the Kinges busines was done, which increased the officers profitt, but not the Kinges, which was only relative to those goods that were weighed in reference to the Kinges duty; and that only auncientiy in reference to wools, which were the original ground of institutinge this Tronage.

The *Tronum Regis*, or Kinges beame, and weight and scales were auncientiy in the custody of the collector of the customes, and when hee gave an accompt of the profitts of the greate Custome hee also under that gave an accompt of the profitts of Tronage, as is plainly to bee seen in the accompts of the Customers in the severall yeares of Kinge E. 1, Edw. 2, Edw. 3, remaininge with the Clerke of the Pipe, which I have carefully perused.

The profitts of Tronage, as likewise of the cockett, or Kinges seale, were in some ports more, in some lesse; but ordinarily in those auncient times they did not exceed 2^{d} ob. for every merchant that weighed his woole. The manner how it was answered was after the Customer had given his account of the greate Custome, then followed the accompts of the Cockett and of the Tronage, vizt.: *Et respondet de* 5^{li} *de exitibus de cocketto*; and sometymes *De exitibus sigilli quod dicitur Cockett dictarum lanarum vizt. de quolibet mercatore lanas pelles lanutas vel coria habente exeuntia de portu prædicto in aliqua nave.*

Et respondet de 5^{l} *provenientibus de Tronagio prædictorum lanorum per idem tempus vizt. de quolibet sacco integro* 2^{d} *ob.*

This was the usuall rate in the tymes of Ed. 1, Edw. 2[d], as appeares in the accounts of the Collectors of Lynne, London, Boston, etc.; but in some ports they answered by the sacke, as in Chester *de quolibet sacco lanæ unum quadrantem.*

But when the Tronage was fermed or graunted, as many tymes it was, then the entry was *non respondet quia J. cui Rex comisit custodiam plumbi pesagii averi ponderis et Trohagi reddendo Regi per annum certum redditum officium illud exercet et proficua inde reciepit.*

Although this bee in the Kinges hands a profitt taken in the port, yet it is not immediatly by reason or in respect of the port, but in respect of his customes; and therfor it seemes it cannot bee claymed by a subject by prescription, bycause it seemes to have commenced with the greate customs in the tyme of Kinge Ed. 1, *quod quære, tamen vide postea.*

But certainly by the general grant of the port to any subject the tronage did not passe unles it were particularly mencioned, vizt. *unacum tronagio;* bycause it is in its use and originall collaterall to the port.

But the beame to weigh the goods of subjects without reference to the Kinges customes, as, namely, of thinges not customable, might possibly have been incident to a port by prescription and passed by the general graunt of the port. But yet that must needes now signify nothing, bycaus all goods imported and exported are now subject to tonnage or poundage, and therefore incidently to bee weighed by the Kinges officer relateinge to his customes.

But of this enough. As to those perquisits of ports of other natures wee shal see in what followes.

II. The second private or particular interest is that of the interest of the soyle. And that is of two kindes.

1. The soyle adjacent to the water or the shore or the houses therupon built, the city or town which is called the port: and of this *there is little question but the propriety may even with the same right belonge to a subject as the interest of any inland mannor or town or demesnes:* though in most of the auncient ports the Kinge tooke so much care that hee preserved to himself a comon wharf or key where his custome house was kept.

And in reference to this interest of the soil contiguous to the water there are these and such as these usually due to the owners:—

Crenage, wharfage, mesurage. Rot. Parl. 50 E. 3, n. 163.

Morage for ships, terrage, wharfage. Towage of comon right: any person may take amends for towinge of boates through his ground, but that amends must bee reasonable: this appears by the stat. of 19 H. 7, cap. 18, where there is a spetiall proviso for the savinge of this liberty of the owners of lands adjacent to the river of Severne.

But though this bee a comon right incident to the owners of the soyl, yet in as much as it is for the publique good that such convenience for the passage of vessels in ports and navigable rivers, by custome a right may bee acquired to mariners, vizt. a liberty of towage of shipps: this appeares by the greate case of the port of Newcastle so often before cited; amonge which this is one right that is assessed to belonge to the Kinge and his port, vizt. *quod cum dominus Rex debeat habere Towagium navium et battellorum majorum et minorum in aqua de Tyne ascendendo versus Novum Castrum et discendendo versus mare libere per terras dominorum quorumcunque; prædictus Prior non permittit hujusmodi transitum volentes terras suas ingredi et cum forte terras suas ingressi fuerint compellit eos reverti et in aquam profundam gradari, etc.* Judgment is accordingly given against the Pryor in affirmation of this custome. And the statute of 23 H. 8, cap. 12, where the like liberty of Towage upon the river of Severne is affirmed, and the exactors of anythinge as a toll or gratuity for the same punished. V. ye Towage in Trent, Pat. 6 R. 2, p. 1, m. 23.

For though these passengers bee not corporate, yet in as much as it is but an easement, and an easement for the benefitt of the comon wealth, it is a servitude that is acquirable to them by custome, like that in the booke of 8 *E.* 4, 18, the custome of Kent for fishermen to dry theyr netts upon the shore, though the soyle of others.

And what is sayd for Towage may bee for morage of ships to the adjacent shore, though of comon right it bee not due, yet it may by usage or custome, as in the case of Towage.

2. The soyl of the sea water, creeke, or arme of the sea wheron ships do or may ride in the port:

Prima facie, all lands covered with the sea at low water or at comon tydes do belonge to the Kinge and are part of his demesnes; as is agreed in 5 *Rep.*, *Constable's case*: But the land overflowed with salt water at extraordinary tydes happeninge by greate windes or floods, or by the greate springe tydes wch happen in the springe and fall, *yea or at certaine periods of the age of the moon*, do not belonge to the Kinge, but are in point of propriety as other lands.

And as these lands covered with salt water belonge to the Kinge *prima facie*, so much more if they ly within ports. This was solemnely decreed *in Cam. Scaccarii P.* 8 *Car.*, *the Kinge against Philpot and others* for lands in Wappinge within the port of London, and the record of the case of Newcastle before cited.

The profitts that comonly arise in ports are of so mixed a nature that it is hard to determine in all cases what are such as arise *ratione soli* and what are those that are *ratione libertatis* or franchesiæ; for in some ports they follow one consideration, in some another.

The makeinge of Ballast shores for the castinge out of Ballast between the high water and low water marke by the Kinges licence or graunt is a fruit of his propriety of soyle as is used in the port of Newcastle.[1]

The takeinge up of ballast for shipps within the precinct of the Kinges port by the King's licence or graunt is a fruit of his propriety of soyle, as is used in the Port of London by the Governors of the Trinity House by the Kinges charter dated [*sic*] . The arentations of incrochments or purprestures between the high water and low water marke, which, though an incrochment upon the Kinges soyle, yet possibly may not bee comon nusances; for then they could neither be licenced nor arented, but must bee demolished, as is before shewen:

Fishinge within the port, and rents or dutyes payd for the same by fishermen there, as in Plymouth, Thames, and other places. Thus it appeares *Communia, Mich.* 3 *E.* 3, in *Scaccario.* The constable of London took usually of London fishermen in Thames 6^s^ 8^d^ per annum, of all forreners 8^s^ per annum, and accompted for it at the Exchequer *de consuetudine antiqua.*

Ancorage, or a certaine toll for castinge of Anchors within the

[1] Here Hale is mistaken as to the fact. The Corporation of Newcastle have always granted the licence to erect the ballast shore, but the soil on which it is erected is invariably the property of the lord of the manor in which the ballast key is situate. The owners of the ballast key and the owners of the franchise of the port shared between them the dues payable for landing the ballast. This appears from the records of the Corporation of Newcastle.

port, is ordinarily an evidence and fruit of ownership, as shal bee shewen; but yet sometymes it growes as a fruit barely of the franchis, for in some cases the Kinge hath ancorage between high water and low water marke, vizt. when the sea flowes, and yet the propriety of the soyle at the reflux of the sea belongs by usage to the subject, as is usuall to bee found in many places and precincts within many ports in Devonshire, though the port bee the Kinges.

There are divers other rights which various customes in several ports have given to the owner of the port either in point of franchis or point of propriety, or both, or at lest havinge theyr rise or originall from them, or some of them; as in the port of Plymmouth, busselage, measurage, etc., belonginge to the Kinge in respect of that port, whereof the Havenor gave yeerely an account to the Crown. In the port of Exeter certain small dutyes called petty customes belonginge to the Kinge and to the mayor and cominalty, as his fee fermers, and in his right: in the port of Newcastle the Kinge auncienty gathered by the hands of his Sherif, vizt. besides his prisage of wines, divers port dutyes, vizt. of every ship laden with herringes 100 herringes without payinge anythinge for them; of every ship laden with hadoks 100 haddocks for 6^{d}; of every ship laden with mullett, the best fish for a penny; which were called *prisæ antiquæ:* besides the bakeinge of bread and biskett for the marriners at his own ovens, *furnagium:* all which appeare in the record above cited between the Burgesses of Newcastle and the Prior of Tinmouth. And the like prizes or port dutyes of the like nature were used to bee taken in some other ports, especially where the Kinge had a castle for the protection of the port, as in the port of Southampton, *T.* 18 *E.* 3, *in Scaccario:* of wool, wyne, fish, and salt in the port of London, the Constable of the Tower, it seemes, auncientiy had of every boat laden with smelts 100 smelts for a penny, and a certain proportion of ladinges of red herringes, spratts: *vide Communia, M.* 3 *E.* 3, *in Scaccario.* The like kinde of prises were taken by the Constable of the Castle of Bristoll, as appeares.

Many of which prises are now antiquated bycause possibly some of them might bee encrochments and others lost and forgotten in length of time, or disused bycause they became more troublesome to collect then was answered by the value of the collection.

And thus much shall serve in general concerninge the *Jus privatum* of a port, consistinge in point of franchis or in point of propriety of the soyle, or both; and those port dutyes that arise by it or in respect of it.

Capitulum Quintum.

CONCERNINGE THE TRANSLATION OF THE FRANCHIS OR PROPRIETY OF A PORT TO A SUBJECT.[1]

Wee have before stated it that *prima facie* the private interest of the ports of this kingdome, both in reference to the franchis itself and also in respect of the propriety of the soyle that lyes under the water of the sea, even to the ordinary extent of the flux of the sea, and the soyl not only below the low water marke, but between the high water and low water marke, doth belonge to the Kinge, and are part of the wast demesnes of his Crown. And this holds regularly true, not only in the vast ocean, but even in navigable rivers, creekes, and ports wher the sea flowes and reflowes: and with this agrees 22 *Ass.* 93, 5 *Rep.*, *Constable's case.* But though this bee true *prima facie*, yet a port of the sea may belonge to a subject both in point of franchise and also in point of propriety; and that by the very same wayes or meanes whereby a faire or a market in point of franchis, or the shore between the high water or low water marke out of a port, may belonge to a subject. Let us consider both these.

[1] This note, added as a memorandum merely by Hale, occurs in the margin here:—Fishinge in the sea, vizt. *in mari nostro prope Jernemuth*, liberty graunted to the Hollanders to fish ther, *Pat.* 23 *E.* 1, *m.* 6. *v.* restraints of fishinge by proclamacion upon the sea, *Rot. Parl.* 3 *H.* 5, *pars* 1, *n.* 33. But untill such inhibition it is free for every subject to fish there: The like in any arme of the sea, yet by speciall custom a private person may have a several fishinge in an arme of the sea or river that flowes and reflowes. *T.* 10 *E.* 2, *rot.* 83, *Norf.*, ad ge [*sic*] in the case of the Abbot of S[t] Benetts for a several fishery below Wroxam bridge to Blackdam in Norfolk, and *P.* 34 *E.* 1, *B. Rs. rot.* 14, *Lanc.*, for the Prior of Coningshed for several fishinge graunted him by the Earle of Lancaster as lord of the mannor of Kendall, who graunted *aquam et piscariam de Ulverston ex utraque parte quantum impetus maris fluit et refluit*, and *T.* 4 *E.* 1, *rot.* 4, *B. R. Suff.*, wher the Prior of Stoke makes title to the several fishinge in aqua de Sturmer, called piscaria maris de Sturmer.

I. In point of franchise a port may belonge to a subject just as a faire or market or warren : and this :—

1. By graunt or charter, when the Kinge doth particularly and by precise words graunt it, though in auncient tyme the graunts were not so particular.

> 1 *pars*, *Pat.* 1 *E.* 3, *m.* 27, an exemplification of a graunt made by Henry I. to William de Albiny, wherby hee graunts the mannor of Snetsham and the two hundreds of Snetsham *cum pertinentiis suis et misteria de Lynn cum medietate fori et tholneti et cum cæteris consuetudinibus et portum cum applicatione navium et les —— et viam ipsius aquæ et transitum cum omnibus querelis.*

Sometymes the graunts are only *una cum portu maris:*

And as thus the franchis of a port may bee acquired by graunt, so it may bee by usage or prescription, which is a sufficient title to this as to any other franchis of a faire, market, or the like, which lyes in prescription, as wee shal see by very many instances, some wherof are such as follow :—

The Earles Palatine of Chester and the Prince as Earle of Chester had the franchis of the port of Liverpole, and it may bee also all the rest of the ports within that County Palatin belonginge to him in right of that County Palatin of Chester : and hee had likewise prisage of wynes. This appeares *Claus.* 40 *E.* 3, *m.* 22, *pro Stephano Ward*, who was discharged of prisage in Leverpole, havinge payd it before in London.

The Bishop of Durrham had the port of Hartlepole as belonginge to his County Palatine, and claymed to have prisage of wines there, *Communia*, *Trin.* 6 *E.* 3, *in Scaccario.* This port was formerly Robert de Brus, and came by escheate to the Bishopp of Durham, and the record tells us that Robertus de Brus *habet mercatum et feriam apud Hertelpol et portum maris et habet ibidem keelagium et prisam piscis.*

The Earle of Cornwall, as it seemes, had many ports in Cornwall as belonginge to that Earledom. But this earldom had somewhat of a palatine jurisdiction.

Let us come to cases of a lower nature, where subjects, though they had no palatine county or jurisdiction, yet had *portus maris :*

The Archbishop of Yorke brought a suit against the Burgesses of Kingston upon Hull for hindringe him to take and use his tolls and libertyes *infra totam aquam suam de Hull juxta Kingston super Hull in quodam loco vocat Amor usque stremes de Humber;* and amonge the rest for hindringe his ministers to measure corne etc., *per bussellum Archiepiscopi ad hoc antiquitus deputatum capiendo pro qualibet nave navicula seu batella hujusmodi mercandizas deferentes, cum sic fuerint mensurati, quatuor denarios;* And for hindringe ships to unlade, etc. The Defendants plede that they hold the borough in fee ferme by graunt of the Kinge and the place where, etc., is parcell of the borough, and pray ayd of the Kinge. The Archbishop counterpledes the ayd, and alledgeth that the place where is no parcell of the extent of theyr borough. The Mayor and Burgesses rejoine *quod Archiepiscopus Eboracensis est dominus villæ de Beverlaco ad quam quidem villam pertinebat et aliquo tempore pertinebat applicatio battellorum et aliorum hujusmodi minutorum vasorum; et de hiis Archiepiscopus cepit custumas tolnetas etc.; quia fuit dominus soli ex utraqe parte aquæ; et quod naves applicabant ad quendam locum vocat Gronale;* and that the Kinge exchanged lands with the Abbot of Meux for a certain Town called Wyke, *et ibidem edificavit quandam villam ibidem et vocavit eam Kingston, infra quam villam est quidam cursus aquæ qui vocatur Sayrcrike et est bunda inter dictam villam et villam de Dripoole; quem quidem cursum aquæ idem dominus Rex avus etc. ad meliorationem ejusdem villæ fecit elargari per obstructionem et remotionem paludum clayarum et pontium in eodem cursu existentium, et ibidem quendam portum fecit, et ad opus suum cepit diversas custumas et alia proficua de diversis mercandisis in eodem portu provenientibus, et postmodum per cartam suam fecit prædictam villam in liberum burgum et homines ejusdem ville liberos burgenses, et eis concessit diversas libertates, et quod prædictus cursus aquæ et prædictus portus sunt pertinentes ad burgum prædictum ac parcella ejusdem, et sunt idem locus ubi archiepiscopus queritur terras prædictas sibi fieri.* And bycaus the Archbishopp tooke divers tolls of merchands there in prejudice of the port, they justify the hindringe of him, and travers the hindringe of him in any other place.

There was no tryal, but upon this record as the original of the port of Kingston upon Hull appeares, so it is admitted that the Archbishopp had a smal port at Beverley.

But see after, when wee come to the custom of prisage, that the Archbishopp did enjoy somewhat of prisage in this port: this record is *Mich.* 44 *E.* 3, *B. Rs. Eborum, rot.* 24:

Again, the Port of Toppsham did aunciently belonge to the

Earles of Devon. And judgement was accordingly given for the Countess against the Mayor and Burgesses of Exon: and the Earles of Devon had not only the franchis of the port, but the very interest of the soyle and the fishinge in that port. *Escaet* 12 *E.* 1, *n.* 1, *portus et piscaria et mariscus de Toppesham spectat Regi, M.* 2 *et* 3 *E.* 1.

M. 2 *et* 3 *E.* 1^mi^, *rot.* 16, *Devon. Juratores dicunt quod Baldwinus de Ripariis quondam Comes Devoniæ et omnes antecessores sui a conquestu Angliæ et similiter Amicia Comitissa Devoniæ quæ manerium de Toppesham tenet in dotem fuerunt in seisina quod mercatores ad prædictum portum venientes pro voluntate sua poterunt ad dictum portum de Toppesham naves suas applicare et mercandisas suas ibidem exonerare et per particulas et in grosso vendere et ibidem pernoctare et cibaria sua emere: Ideo consideratum est quod mercatores decætero pro voluntate sua possunt ad prædictum portum applicare et exonerare etc. et cives in misericordia.*

It appeares amonge the charters of the Dutchy of Cornewal remaininge in the receit that Rogerus de Valletorta gave to Richard the Kinge of the Romans and to the heyres of his body *Castrum de Trematon et* 59 *feoda militum in Cornubia et Devonia ad idem Castrum pertinentia ac etiam manerium de Trematon et villam de S. cum aqua. Claus.* 17 *E.* 3, 2, *m.* 14, *Sutton cum aqua et portu spectat ad Castrum de Trematon.*

The ports of Saltash and of Plimouth, formerly called Sutton, were parcel of this mannor of Trematon, and the profitts of that port are to this day accounted for as parcell of the mannor of Trematon, for, by the death of Richard without issue, the Earledom of Cornewall, and also the Castle and Mannor of Trematon, came to the Crown, and were afterward by the charter of the Duchy, 11 E. 3, settled upon the Kinges eldest sonne etc. and to this day the *Aqua de Pola*, or Sutton Pool, which is the very body of the port of Plymouth, is part of the possessions of the Dutchy of Cornewall, and accordingly, upon a longe evidence upon a tryall at the barre, recovered, *M.* 16 *Car.* 2, upon an informacion of intrusion, as part of the mannor of Trematon.[1] And under the accounts of that mannor the profitts of busselage, ancorage,

[1] See pp. 314–352, and see the information in Wightwick, pp. 208–210; the Crown claimed by virtue of the prerogative.

fishinge, and all other port dutyes were constantly accounted for and answered; so that the Kinges very title to the port of Plymouth, both in point of franchis and in point of propriety or dominion of the soyle, is under the conveyance of Vautort, who was a subject:

One more shal suffice: The Earle Warren Earle of Surry had auncienlty the port of Poole; and ancorage and other port dutyes as belonginge to it. *P.* 10 *E.* 3, *B. Rs. rot.* 73, *Dorset.*

To this wee may add the case of the Earle of Richmond befor cited, who had a port at Little Yarmouth and Gorleston; the case of the Earle of Penbroch, who had a port at Rosse, under the qualifications above expressed, and many more of the like nature. Only, as is befor observed, when a subject hath the franchis of a markett or ferry, the Kinge cannot graunt a markett or ferry to another person or create one by proclamacion so neare that it may bee a damage to the former markett or ferry in the hands of a subject; yet in the case of a port of the sea, bycause that is a fran-of a more publique concernement, both to the Kinge in respect of his customes and to the realme in respect of safegard and comerce here; though the subject hath a port, yet the Kinge may, as it seemes, erect another port neare to the former, so it bee not within the precincts of the extent of the subjects port; as appeares in the case of Hull, and is more then intimated in the case of John de Britannia.

But then it must bee only a concurrent liberty, not exclusive of that liberty of a port formerly lawfully settled in a subject by graunt or prescription: and thus much for the interest of franchis acquirable by a subject in a port:

II. Touchinge the interest of propriety of the soyle of the land covered with salt water: this though *prima facie*, as is sayd before, belonges to the Kinge, yet it is acquirable by a subject not only by charter, wherof there can bee no doubt, but by usage, custome, or prescription: And this will appeare by these ensuinge stepps and degrees.

1. It is plaine that the shore covered at ordinary tydes with the salt water, lyinge out of a port, may beelonge to a subject, and bee part of his mannor: this is agreed in Sir Henry Constable's case, and therof there is little question.

M. 23 *E.* 3, *B. Rs. rot.* 26, *Lincoln.* The Abbot of Petreborough, questioned for acquiringe 300 acres *maretti in Gosberkirke, licentia regia non obtenta.* The Defendant pleded, *quod per consuetudinem patriæ est et a tempore quo etc. usitatum fuit quod omnes et singuli domini maneria terras seu tenementa super costeram maris habentes particulariter habebunt marettum vel sabulonem per fluxus et refluxus maris secundum magis et minus prope tenementa sua projecta ; et dicit quod habet quoddam manerium in eadem villa unde plures terræ sunt adjacentes costeræ maris et sic habet per fluxus et refluxus maris circiter* 300 *acras maretti terras suas adjacentes et per temporis incrementum secundem patriæ consuetudinem : etc. ; Absque hoc quod perquisivit etc. ;* and so issue is joined, but it continued neare twenty year by divers adjournements before it was tryed. But afterwards, *P.* 41 *E.* 3, *B. Rs. rot.* 29, *Lincoln :* verdict and judgement is given for the Defendent.

Note that this doth not only extend to the shore, vizt. between the high water and low water marke, but the insensible increases *per alluvionem*, or as here *per projectionem.*

But as it is pleded it doth not extend to an acquisition *per* Ante,p.292. *relictionem maris.* And therfore in the case of Sutton Marsh, *in Scaccario* about 10 Car., where the information was for lands *relicta per mare*, a title made either to the shore or to the *projectionem maris* doth not answer the information ; and therfor in that case judgement was given for the Kinge upon a demurrer.

2. As the subject may have the right of a shore of the sea as parcell of his mannor, so hee may have the right of the shore within the precincts of a port, if hee bee owner of the port in point of franchis : this will bee plaine by what followes.

3. A subject, beinge owner of the franchis of a port by prescription, may by the same title bee owner of the soyl of the haven within that port, not only between the high water and low water marke, but even of the very soyl within the points of the land, though constantly covered with salt water : this is evident by the case of Plymouth, above cited, wherin Vautort was not only Lord of the Town or ports of Sutton Vantort, and also of Claus. 17 E. 2, m. 14 et 18. Saltash, but of the very water and soyle within the points or extremityes of that port called in the record *aqua de Esse ;* and the bounds of that water as they are bounded upon the record are to the very extremity of the points of that port or haven, all the water *inter fauces terre ;* and under that title the Kinge hath Ante, pp. 314, 350. it as parcell of his mannor of Trematon unto this day, beinge longe since annexed to the Duchy of Cornwall.

4. A subject, though hee hath not the port in point of franchis, as in the case befor, may by usage or custome have the shore between high water and lowater marke parcell of his mannor, though within a port; and this is apparant *de facto* in many greate ports of the sea, as Plymouth, and divers others. Many lords that have mannors borderinge upon the haven within the port have by longe and constant usage had the shore there and disposal of sand and kilp, and also wrecks happeninge there as wrecks within theyr mannor, but this will bee more plaine by what followes.

5. A subject that hath not the franchis of the port, yet hee may by usage and prescription have the very soyl and channel of a navigable river, creeke, or channel wherin the sea flowes and reflowes, nay though it bee constantly salt water at low water: And this shal bee made out by divers evidences, and the reason is bycause those in respect of theyr nature are as well acquirable in point of propriety as any other fresh river.

The rivers of Weigh in Monmouthshire, Medwey, Humber, and divers others are armes of the sea; yet there are very many Lords adjacent that have auncient weares and fishinges by prescription, wherby they acquired a kinde of private propriety in them: *v. Pat.* 12 *E.* 2, *pars* 1, *m.* 3, *in Ouze; Fine* 2 *E.* 1, *m.* 1, *and* 7 *Rep. case* —— *de Abbotsbury fleete.*[1] Cf. p. 387.

The river of Severne is a greate river, an arme of the sea, wherin the water flowes and reflowes up above Gloucester, and it is in part of the port of Bristoll and in parcell of the Creeke of Gloucester, yet from Gloucester down to Aust, and to the very mouth of Aven, the Lords of the mannors adjacent have the propriety of the soyl *usque filum aquæ* as parcell of theyr mannors: on the west syde, Minsterworth, Westbury, Aure, Radley, Lydney: on the east side, Elmore, Slimbergh, Barclay, Hull, Auste: and Cf. p. 388.

[1] These notes occur in the margin:—Reyesant beinge a fishinge place in a creeke of the sea belonginge to Burnham, yet it was found to bee parcell of the Mannor of Burnham: *T.* 50 *E.* 3, *B. Rs. rot.* 2, *Rex.* The Abbot of Selby had improvements in the river of Ouze: *Pat.* 12 *E.* 2, *pars* 1, *m.* 3. The lords adjacent had theyr fishings in the River Tese: *Pat.* 32 *E.* 3, *p.* 1, *m.* 15 *dors.* The like in the River Twede: *Fines* 2 *E.* 3, *m.* 1. The like frequently in Severn: *Pat.* 2 *E.* 4, *pars* 3ª, *m.* 16; *Pat.* 32 *E.* 3, *pars* 2, *m.* 15 *dorso.* For the Abbot of Pershore in the river of Trent: *Pat.* 18 *E.* 2, *pars* 1, *m.* 3 *dorso; Pat.* 43 *H.* 3, *m.* *dorso.*

they graunt rocks and fishinge places in the very middle of the streme by copy of Court Roll; and the *filum aquæ*, though it often change by the unrulines of the river, is the comon boundery of the adjacent mannors on either syde: and to this day the rocks called Radleyes weare and Garrons weare are parcell of the mannor of Radly, parcell of the Dutchy of Lancaster; though they ly in the midst of the river, as appeares by infinite records; *v. Claus.* 10 *E.* 3, *m.* 29, an allowance of timber claymed by prescription by the Earle of Lancaster in the forrest of Deane *pro reparacione gurgitum suorum manerii de Radley.*

Cf. p. 382. There is a notable record *Claus.* 18 *H.* 3, *m.* 21, *vizt. Quia dominus Rex accepit per inquisitionem quam fieri precepit quod illa pars terræ quam vtraque villata de Slimberg et Aure sibi vindicant eo quod aqua Sabrinæ eam occupavit super campum de Slimbridg versus campum de Aure, et postea processu temporis eam rejecit ad campum de Slimberge antequam sic rejecta esset per aquam Sabrinæ de jure perinet ad eadem villam de Slimbridge et in parte fuit terra arabilis et in parte pastura ad eandem villam de Slimbridge pertinentem per divisam fossati quod vocatur Hedgwood; Dominus Rex precipit Vicecomiti Gloucestriæ quod eædem villatæ de Slimberge plenam seisinam de prædicta parte terræ sine dilatione habere faciat. Teste Rege apud Gloucestriam* 24 *die Maii.*

By this record it doth appeare that the former owner had his lands againe accordinge to the auncient boundery, notwithstandinge it was once gained by the Severn and thrown to the other syde. The Kinge claymed nothinge by reason of this, but the two Townes adjacent, and the Kinge beinge but six miles of, vizt. at Gloucester, decided the controversy.

But most certainly at this day, and for al tyme wherof the memory of man is not, the *filum aquæ Sabrinæ*, or the middle of the streeme or channel at low water, is the constant boundery of the mannors on every syde, let it change its course as often as it will and as much as it will.

And all this that I have sayd was admitted upon a greate tryall upon an information in the Chequer prosequuted by Sir Sackvile Crow against the Lord Barclay for a great quantity of land in Slimbridge called the "New gained grounds," which was proved to have beene within twenty yeares or therabouts the very channel wher the river did run: and upon the evidence it was admitted both by the Court and Kinges Councell that such a navigable river, though within a port, might bee parcell of a subjects mannor. And bycause the evidence to prove the fact that it was so was so stronge, the Kinges atturny moved a juror might bee withdrawn: and though the defendant was very unwillinge, but desyred to have a verdict, yet, at the mediation of the Court, a juror was withdrawn: *and this I know, for I was present and acquainted with the whole busines;* and ever since that busines hath rested in quiet, and the lands are still to this day enjoyed by the Lord Berclay and his fermers, beinge worth above 300^{l} per annum.

And to this purpose may bee added that writt of *ad quod damnum, Register* 252. A trench or creeke *aquæ ducit a brachio maris versus villam de R. quæ est in solo ipsorum Abbatis et Conventus Christi Cantuariensis per quam naves et batelli ad villam prædictam venire solebant,* yet the propriety therof belonginge to the monastery.[1]

But notwithstandinge this private propriety of the soyl of any creeke or navigable river within a port or leadinge to it may belonge to a subject; yet these thinges must bee remembred.

1. That this private propriety doth not take away nor can abate the *jus franchesiæ*, or the right of franchis of the port, if it bee in the Kinge or in any other person then him that hath the propriety of the soyle.

2. That it doth not deminish nor take away the *jus regium* in the port, as it is one of the gates of the Kingdome and a place wherin his customes and revenue is concerned.

3. That it doth not take away the *jus publicum* of a port, but it ought to bee free and safe for accesse of merchants, and all publique nuisances to shipps or navigation in these ports, though they belonge to a subject in point of propriety and also in point of franchis, as where there is a comon highway over my soyl, my private property in the soyl cannot inable mee to do a nuisance to the damage of the people; and if I do, I am punishable at the Kinges suit, who is *vindex et defensor jurium publicorum:*

And therfor the conclusion that the reporter makes in the case of the piscary of Ban in Sir John Davys reports *is somewhat too* Ante, p. 247;
strayte; as if a subject could not by usage or custome have an post, p. 388.

[1] This note occurs in the margin:—Againe though regularly as befor the fishinge as well in an arme of the sea as in the sea itself regularly and *prima facie* belonges to the King as a perquisite.

interest in a publique or royall streame, must not bee construed that hee cannot; but that if hee claym it by charter, it must have spetiall words; and if by usage, it must bee very good proof and evidence to make it out: *and as his conclusion is a little too strayt, so his reason is strained too farre*, vizt. bycause they are called the Kings stremes, therfor a subject cannot have a property in them, is as wide in consequence; for they are not called the Kinges streames so much in reference to propriety as in reference to the comon use of them, as the Kinges highway is so called, though the propriety of the soyl bee in a subject. And so though the subject hath the propriety of the soyl of a river, whether fresh or salt, yet if it bee a river for the comon portage of boates or vessells, it is *hault streame le Roy*, and any nuisance comitted there shal bee punished at the Kinges suit, as in case of a nuisance in a highway. And in the inditement it is and must bee stiled *alta via regia*, though the propriety of the soyle belonge to a subject: *v. St.* 25 *H.* 8, *cap.* 10.

Capitulum Sextium.

CONCERNINGE PORT DUTYES.

This hath been touched before incidently in relation to the Franchis and soyle of ports. But now I shal proceed with it distinctly and *ex proposito*. These *portatica*, or port dutyes, are of several sorts.

1. Some arise incidently to the customes or subsidyes due to the Crown: as the cocket and Tronage.

2. Some arise in respect of the shore or land adjacent to the port: as morage, terrage, wharfage, cranage, busselage, towage, etc.

3. Some arise by reason of the interest of the haven itself wherin the ships are, either in respect of the franchis or soyl, or both; for they are sometymes in relation to one, sometymes to the other, sometymes to both; and these are of two kindes, vizt.:—

The more comon and usuall: such are ancorage, keelage.

The more spetiall: which are varyed in ports according to prescription, as busselage, measurage, prises, and tolls of various sorts.

For the port dutyes incident to the customes.

1. Cockett: the whole history of it, 50 *E.* 3, 63.

Tronage: the whole history of that, 50 *E.* 3, 63.

Other dutyes paid there, vizt. chalkinge, mensurage, wharfage, 1[d] a diem, ibidem.

Cranage:

port dutyes, petit customes. Exon:
in Hull, 33 H. 8, cap. 33.

[Here the treatise breaks off, Hale having noted the following references :—]

Exon portus 31 H. 8, cap. 4; 3 Jac. 12.

Le mere soit overt, parl. 1 H. 5, n. 41; 22 *E.* 3, 8; 25 *E.* 3, 22; 18 *E.* 3, n. 10.

Staple R 21 R. 2, n. 89, 82.

The MS. then goes on with the following treatise, also by Hale, which from internal evidence appears to have been drawn up as an argument in the case of Rex *v.* Oldsworth as to Sutton Marsh, for at p. 361 he speaks of it as "*this* Sutton Marsh." Although it repeats many of the arguments used in the preceding treatise, it has been thought best to print it as it occurs, in order that no word of the learned author on the subject of the shore should be lost. Ante, p. 292.

CONCERNINGE THE RIGHT OF THE KINGE TO THE SHORE ETC.

1. As to ports, havens, and creekes, the Kinge hath a three fold right:

I. First of jurisdiction, which is clere:

II. Of priviledge or franchise; which is the reason that as no market may bee erected upon he [*sic*], so no place may bee imployed as a port without the Kinges graunt: Thus in 18 et 20 E. 1, the Prior of Tinmuth, havinge erected a Towne wherin hee used the liberty of a port, was by judicial proces in Parlement compelled *ut omnia signa portus amoveretur.* John of Bretain, his patent for a port at Jernemuth, 2 *E.* 3, 7, *les ports sont al Roi per Claver:*

III. Of interest or propriety in the soile of the haven. This is accordinge to the use likewise of other countryes, that *portus maris sunt inter regalia tam quoad jurisdictionem quam quoad dominium et proprietatem.* And this likewise appeares by the custome Griphiander de Insulis, cap. 11, s. 42; cap. 25, s. 60.

of ancorage payd, as I am informed, for the breach of the Kinges soil if cast within the haven.

IV. *Jus alluvionis maritimæ sive maritima incrementa*, bee it *per alluvionem quæ sit successive etc.* or *per recessum vel refluxum maris*, by the positive lawes of our land regularly belonge to the Kinge and are part of his prerogative: *Littus maris* is by Justinian defined to be *quatenus hibernus fluctus maximus excurrit*, which is somewhat too generall, bycause questionles the extraordinary tydes may outgo the shore: But by others thus: *est totus ille locus vadosus et sabulosus inter aggeres et mare qui modo ab æstu maris occupatur, modo ab ejusdem recessu denudatur:* which agrees with our occupation and use, as appeares in Sir H. Constable's case, 5 *Rep.* 107. Alluvion is described likewise to bee *incrementum terræ ab aqua ita latenter adjectum ut intelligi non potest quantum quoquo temporis momento adjiciatur.*

Lib. 2 de rerum divisione.

Grip. de Ins., cap. 10, s. 39.

Grip., cap. 18, s. 16.

Recessus maris is usually taken for an unusual retyringe of the sea, from the usuall low water mark: Now that these do by the law regularly belonge to the Kinge appeares:—

I. Bycause the sea, at lest so much therof as adjoines nearer to our cost then to any other foren cost: as it is within the Kinges jurisdiction, which amongest other evidences therof appears by the booke 6 *R.* 2, *protection* 46, wher Belknap affirmes the sea to bee of the ligeance of the Kinge as of his Crown of England, so likewise it is the Kinges in propriety as his roiall waste, and therfor hee hath those *bona caduca* or *vacantia*, as *floatsam* etc., partly in respect of the right of property which hee hath in the soyle underneath the water; and therfor questionles the Ilands neare adjoininge to our cost are parcell of the Kinges inheritance, as beinge part of that greate royal wast covered with the British Ocean: and no more evident right can there bee of ownership or propriety then to bee master of comon right of such profits as any way the sea adjoininge yeelds.

II. It is cleare that *littus relictum* and the ground acquired *per recessum maris* are within this realme, and therfor of comon right must belong to the Crown, unles by some investiture from the Crowne or by some other sufficient title it bee mainteined against the Kinges right: for by our law there is *nullum bonum vel hereditas vacans*, and that is the reason that the Kinge, who, as the civilians speak, *fungitur vice populi*, hath all those goods that are *vacantia* or *caduca* as a part of his regality, and therby prevents any title to bee gained *per occupationem vel vacuæ possessionis adeptionem:* This is evidently proved.

1. By the practise of other countryes: v. *Grip. de Insulis cap.* 11, *per totum: et cap.* 18, *maritima incrementa ad regalia pertinent*, and gives many instances in Upper and Lower Germany: v. *Grotius de Jure Belli, l.* 2, *cap.* 8. *Fluvialia incrementa fluminis publici de jure communi populi sunt aut ejus qui jure populi utitur.*

2. By our owne authorityes: Bracton, speakinge only of an Iland that *in flumine publico nata conceditur occupanti ideoque Regi propter suum privilegium*, comes not home to the point, for *Insulæ et alluvionis eadem est ratio*, as shall appeare: But the severall records herafter mentioned, wherin the Kinge is excluded by reason of some spetial custome or accident, prove that of comon right it is the Kinges: In 18 E. 1, in the Parlement Booke, fol. 8, in the proces against the Prior of Tinmuth, who claimed to have the land *usque ad filum aquæ de Tine*, the Kings prosequutors replyed *quod ipse Prior qui nunc est tempore suo ibidem fieri fecit viginti sex domos super solum quod domino Regi esse debet eo quod fluxu et inundatione maris comprehenditur et petunt record justiciariorum quod prefatus Prior jam allegavit quod dominus Rex nullum habet solum nec liberum tenementum sed quod mere pertinet ad prædictum Priorem et domum suam usque ad filum aquæ de Tine: But no particular judgment as I remember given as to that point:*

3. In the Kinges case *termini sunt integre domino Regi:* thus it holds in a forest, much more in a dominion.

As touchinge the shore:—

III. *Littus maris* may bee to the low water marke parcell of a mannor; this appeares resolved in Sir H. Constable's case, 5 Rep. 107; or parcell of a parish, *Rast. Entryes*, 684, *in casu Archiepiscopi Cant.;* so it may belonge to a subject: and so it is clerely admitted 8 *E.* 4, 19, *per Choke.*

IV. Lands yeelded *per recessum vel alluvionem maris vel alicujus inde brachii* may by custome or prescription belonge unto a subject havinge lands abuttinge upon the sea, and such custome or prescription is good:

1. The first reason therof is grounded upon the rule of the Civile Law: By them there is a difference between *insula nata in mari vel flumine publico et jus alluvionis:* the former *conceditur occupanti;* the latter is as a perquisite, *et sine nova possessionis* Grip. de
apprehensione is presently and in a moment annexed in propriety Ins., cap.

18; in fine, s. 104. to the adjacent soile, bee it the Kinges or a subjects: Thus—*Justinian, libro* 2—*Quod si naturali alveo in universum derelicto ad aliam partem fluere cœperit, prior quidem alveus eorum est qui prope ripam ejus prædia possident:* yet with this difference, *ubi agri sunt limitati vel certa mensura comprehensi non ibi spectat ad agrum jus alluvionis sed populo vel principi etc. ubi autem non sunt limitati sed ad mare vel flumen usque pertingunt;* there by the auncient Roman law, and likewise by the practise of other countryes, *jus alluvionis agrum contiguum possidenti spectat, Grot. de Jure Belli, lib.* 2, *cap.* 8, *s.* 14: so that it appeares that it is no custome or prescription contrary to law, for it is in part countenanced by the Civil Law, *from whom Bracton borrowes much of his learninge in this particular: and only thwarted by our own positive lawes, which may be qualifyed or restrained by custome,* and the rule is true in both Grip., cap. 11, s. 60. lawes *consuetudo multum valet in augendis vel minuendis regalibus:* therfor these the lands which with us have no other bounds but the sea have theyr enlargements and abridgements by the sea or arme therof.

2. Although that a man cannot make title to land in gross by prescription or custom, as Brook rightly observes upon the case of 8 H. 6, 16, yet as an incident as in case of an office, or to prescribe it as a perquisite or additament or parcell of another thinge; so a man may prescribe in it, and therfor by the same reason that prescription for weif, stray, or wreck are good, by the same reason here, for they are only prerogatives grounded upon mere matter in fact, and so ly in prescription or custome.

3. It carryes with it a reasonable ground or presumption of a lawfull commencement.

1. Bycause the subject shal bee at prejudice *per maris influxum*, and therfor it is reason hee should have benefit *per defluxum:*

2. The subject is or may by reason therof bee bound to the maintenance of the banks: for although that the care and supervision for the defence of the sea walls belonge to the Kinge, yet the burden therof and the danger of the neglect belonges to the borderer: and there was the same power at comon law of the Kinges Commissioner of Sewers as ther hath been since the Statutes, as appeares by theyr commissions *et per Rot. Parl.* 8 *E.* 2, *m.* 23. This was the reason why the auncient Romans permitted by theyr lawes the *jus alluvionis* and *ripæ relictæ* to belonge to the adjoininge borderers *ut inde ad ripæ defensionem melius provocentur.*

Now for cases as to this particular: *P.* 41 *E.* 3, *rot.* 28, *Coram Rege,* where the plea that *consuetudo patriæ* is so, and allowed, and judgment given for the Abbot of Petreborough for lands in Gosberkirk in Lincolneshire: the case of the Abbot of Ramsey, *T.* 43 *E.* 3, *rot.* 13, *in Scaccario, cited Dyer* 327, where without any plea of any custom yet *quia quandoque mariscus minoratur quandoque majoratur etc.* Judgement for the Abbot upon a verdict: the like 15 El:

I finde in the Hundred Roll of Grimsby in Lincolnshire about 3 Edward I., a presentment *quod* 40 *annis elapsis et amplius de jactione maris accumulavit arenam et lapides per quam accumulacionem dominus Willelmus le Fort tunc Comes Albemarle incepit edificiare quandam villam que vocatur Ravensrod, et est insula eo quod mare eam circuit et est forestallum ad nocumentum et dampnum villatæ Regis de Grimbsby et patriæ quolibet anno* 100*l. Sed quia in manu Regis nihil. Item sciendum est quod dicta Insula de Ravensrode a tempore dicti Willelmi Comitis decessit de herede in heredem de manu ad manum usque ad tempus Regis nunc. Nihil hic quia sequitur per breve coram Rege:* Upon which I collect that this might be purprise upon the Kinge bycause it was an Iland and separate: *separata est ratio:* But when I come to the presentments of purprises upon the Kinge in the Hundred Roll of Kirketon, within which *this Sutton Marsh* and other marshes lye, of which there is likewise mention made in the roll to other purposes; yet when they come to this article; *qui in super de novo appropriarunt:—Nihil sciunt,* which proves that the *jus alluvionis* belonges by the custom there to the next adjoining soile.

Ante, p. 53; post, pp. 365, 383.

Now as concerninge armes of the sea which are defined to bee so high as the water ebbs and flowes, 22 *Ass.* 93. I conceive 1. *Quoad Jurisdictionem* they may bee *intra corpus Comitatus* where a man can see from one syde to the other. 8 *E.* 2, *Bacon* 399, and therfor within the Coroners jurisdiction as to some purposes:

2. By the Civil Law if any river eates up my whole ground by desertinge his channel and yet returnes againe to his owne course, I have lost my land, and it goes to the benefit of him that *in extremo fluxu fluminis* had his ground adjacent next the river. *Justin. ubi supra:* otherwise if it were only an inundacion which doth not *mutare speciem:* and although that without speciall custom *per alluvionem marina maris vel brachii maris ad regem spectat:* 22 *Ass.:* [93] Yet if that I can prove that I lost thus much ground *per influxum maris vel brachii inde,* I shal have it againe if, *per re-*

cessum vel alvei mutationem, the sea yeelds up my old soile: *Claus.* 18 *H.* 3, *m.* 22, *pro villata de Slinebreg.* An excellent record.

CONCERNINGE MARSHES ETC.

1. Concerninge ports, havens, and creekes, the Kinge by our law hath in them a threefold right: 1. A right of jurisdiction, which is clere; 2. A right of franchis or priviledge: it is a kinde of sea merket, and therfore none may erect a port in his owne soil without the Kinges graunt: In a plee against the Prior of Tinmuth, began 18 E. 1, who had erected a port in his owne land, judgement was after given against him *quod omnia signa portus amoveret:* 2 E. 3, 7, in the case of John de Britannia *les ports sont al Roi, per Claver*, and may by him bee made any where, so that it bee not to the prejudice of a former grauntee; 3. The right of property or interest in the very soile: and this agrees likewise with foren practise, that *portus sunt inter regalia tam quoad dominium et proprietatem quam quoad jurisdictionem: in quibus anchoras injicere sine consensu principis non licet*, which agrees with our custome of anchorage paid to the Kinge or owners of ports.

In libro Parl. E. 1.

Grip. de Insulis, cap. 11, s. 42. Ibidem, cap. 25, s. 60.

2. *Jus alluvionis sive recessus maris sive brachii inde et maritima incrementa* regularly without any other sufficient title made to some other belonge to the Kinge *jure regiæ prerogativæ. Alluvio* is described to bee *incrementum terre ab aqua ita latenter adjectum ut intelligi non potest quantum quoquo temporis momento adjiciatur:* And therefor they say it is *probatu difficilimus: Recessus maris* I take to bee the retyre of the sea from the usuall *low water mark:* my reasons for this are:—

Griph. de Insulis, cap. 18, s. 16.

1. Bycause as the Kinge hath right of jurisdiction or dominion of so much at lest of the sea as adjoines to the Brittish coast nearer then to any forren coast: which appeares by *Belknap*, 6 *R.* 2, *protection* 46; so as soone as any matter of profitt happens upon or by reason of the said sea capable of propriety, it doth presently belonge to the Kinge unles some other better title doth interpose: such are wrecks, floatsam, etc. *Insulæ natæ in mari*, etc.; therfor though the Kinge cannot have propriety in the water, yet when any thinge therin emergeth that it is capable of propriety it is the Kinges as aforesaid: The sea is the Kinges royal wast *de communi jure.* But to leave that doubtfull question whither the soil of the sea be the Kinges *aqua marina adhuc coopertum.*

2. It is certein that those *maritima incrementa* bee ther *per*

alluvionem, wherby ther is a contiguity or annexation of the soil to the soile, or *per insulæ nascentiam* they belonge to and are part of the realme of England, and therfor if no man hath title to them so that they are *vacantia* and *nullius in bonis*, it is by evident reason the Kinges presently, for hee hath such a preventinge right that hee doth prevent all right to bee gained against him *per vacuæ possessionis adeptionem* or occupancee: if it beelonge to any other, it cannot bee but by a title derived from the Kinge, as by investiture or graunt; or elce by a presumption of such derivation from the Kinge, as prescription or custome, for all land within the realme is the Kinges or held of him. But what shal bee sayd a title hic postea:—

3. This is confirmed likewise by practise of foren countryes; vide Griph. de Insulis, cap. 11, *per totum*, where he shewes many instances in severall countryes; and a received right in Germany that *maritima incrementa sive per alluvionem recessum maris vel insularia sunt inter regalia: v. Grotium de Bello et pace, l.* 2, *cap.* 8, where hee in a manner concludes that *insulæ et fluvialia incrementa sunt de patrimonio publico: populi scilicet vel ejus qui vice populi fungitur.* Idem, cap. 18,

4. As by the records herafter mentioned the subjects do make theyr title to the *jus alluvionis vel maritimi incrementi*, so by the manner of theyr plees they admitt that were it not for theyr speciall titles the Kinge (*cujus titulum est de jure communi fundatum super hujusmodi incrementa*) would have title; therfor I finde in the proceedinge against the abovementioned Prior of Tinmouth for erectinge a new towne called Sheles as a purpresture to the Kinge and his port of Newcastle; the Prior there claimes to have the freehold *usque ad filum aquæ de Tyne;* to which the prosequutors reply *quod ipse Prior qui nunc est ibidem fieri fecit* 26 *domos super solum quod domino regi esse debet eo quod fluxu et inundatione maris continetur et petunt recordum Justiciari quod prefatus Prior jam allegavit quod dominus Rex ibi nullum habet solum nec liberum tenementum sed quod mere spectat ad prædictum Priorem et domum suam usque ad filum aquæ de Tine;* although *I do not remember that any judgement as to that particular is given against the Prior;* which yet proves the Kinges claim in those dayes. Lib. ple. 18 E. 1, fol. 8.

3. As to the shore, it is by Justinian described to bee *quatenus hibernus fluctus maximus excurrit:* or as Griph. de Insulis, cap. 10, s. 39; *est totus ille locus vadosus et sabulosus inter aggeres et* De rer. divis. equidem.

mare qui modo ab estu maris occupatur modo ab ejus recessu denudatur: This although it bee *quoad usum commune,* yet it is capable of propriety: and therupon

Post, p. 394. 1. I conceive that *littus maris* may questionles belonge to and bee parcell of a subjects mannor, which is the point resolved in Sir H. Constable's case, 5 Rep. 107, agreed clerely by Choke, 8 E. 4, 19, and so in manner allowed by pledinge, *Rest. Entryes,* 634, *in casu Archiepiscopi Cantuariensis.*

2. The cases above and likewise ordinary experience prove that it is most ordinaryly parcell of the adjoyning land:

3. Yet I conceive that unles speciall usage makes for the subjects title, it doth of comon right and *prima facie* belonge to the Kinge, which is strongely proved: 1. bycause *bona non dicuntur wreccata* befor they are *relicta vel projecta super terram vel arenam;* the Kinge presently therby acquires title, and by comon presumption are wrecced upon the shore: 2. bycause as in forests so espetially in dominions *termini sunt integre Regi;* the shore is as it were part of the ocean, which is *terminus* though not *jurisdictionis,* yet perchance *proprietatis:* And this agrees with foren practise that *ripatica et littora inter Regalia sunt:* And in most places where the subject by prescription hath wreck, hee hath comonly the shore, on which it hath a kinde of dependance; Thus, if my memory much faile mee not, the Earles of Cornewall have aunciently had by prescription *bona wreccata per totum Comitatum;* therfor the right of the shore there belonges to him and his tenants as an usuall concomitant.

4. Lands gained *per recessum maris vel alluvionem* may belonge to the subject (otherwise then by investiture from the Kinge) and to the lands next adjoininge, upon two grounds.

By custome or prescription; wherin wee must somewhat observe Insula. the rule of the civil and imperiall law as a direction: By them there is a difference between *insula nata in mari;* for that *sit ejus cujus est flumen etc.,* and bycause they admitt not a right of ownership in the sea, *conceditur occupanti: Just. de rerum divisione s. insula.* But in as much as we contend that the Kinge hath at lest a right of jurisdiction and prerogative (if not of estate and propriety) in the adjoining sea and armes therof, we say that the Kinges prerogative prevents any occupation. And thus Bracton, lib. 2, cap. 2, speakes only of an Island *quod sit Regis propter privi-* Ante, p. 53; post, p. 383. *legium:* Thus I finde in the Hundred Roll of Grimsby, 3 E. 1, a presentment *quod* 40 *annis elapsis et amplius de jactione mare accumulavit arenam et lapides per quam accumulationem dominus Willelmus le Fort tunc Comes Albemarle incepit edificare quandam villam que vocatur Ravensrod ad nocumentum et est insula etc.*, and that this had passed *de herede in heredem de manu in manum usque ad tempus Regis nunc:* But that it was then in the Kinges hands, which I collect to be bycause, it beinge an Iland, it did belonge to the Kinge and could not be claimed by prescription, *quia separatim separata est ratio:* it had no contiguity to the shore :[1] But when the Civile Law comes to *jus alluvionis*, there it gives it wholly to the next adjoininge land *pro longitudine etc. Just. de rerum divisione* § *preterea :* yet with this difference, where *agri* are *limitati vel certa mensura comprehensi ibi non cadit jus alluvionis proximum prædium possidenti.* But where *agri non sunt limitati nec certa mensura comprehensi sed dicuntur ad flumen vel mare usque pertingere* there *flumen vel mare* may abridge or increase that land *et habet jus alluvionis:* This is affirmed likewise by Grotius, *ubi supra*, and gives the reason excellently thus; *Sed populus ut aliis ita et proxima prædia possidentibus jus alluvionis concedere potest et concessisse haud dubie videtur si agri illi ea ex parte non alium finem quam naturalem, id est, flumen ipsum habeant:* And with us the Kinge *fungitur vice populi:* So that by this there is a faire colour or countenance for such a custome by the admission of foren law; and therfor wher by our usage and comon practise the subjects mannor hath no other bound but the sea or arme therof there, as his title is good against the state beyond the sea, so good against the Kinge here *quoad jus alluvionis vel littoris relicti:*

Inst. li. de rerum divisione, § quod si naturali.

For farther maintenance of this custome or prescription.

1. It is a thinge that lyes in custome or prescription: 1. those prerogatives which are merely founded upon matter in fact, although they are high regalityes, yet are prescribable, as wrecke, waifes, etc. But such as the Kinges title cometh unto by matter of record, etc., they must be claimed by graunt *in casu Abbatis de Strata Marcella:* this is acquired merely by matter in pais, and therfor may be claimed by usage: the rule of the civilians is good and true likewise with us, that *consuetudo multum valet in augendis vel minuendis regalibus:* for as the Kinge is entitled merely *jure*

9 Rep. 24.

[1] It was in the King's hand, after the death of the heiress of the Earls of Albemarle, as part of the seigniory of Holderness.—ED.

positivo, and bycaus non else hath a better title, so may this *jus positivus* bee abridged by a prescription or custom alledged and proved against the Kinge, the subject matter being *res prescriptibilis:*

See post, p. 391.

2. It is a coherent incident or parcell, and so claimed: and therfor, although Brook rightly observes upon the case 8 H. 6, 16, that a man can never make title to land by prescription as a thinge in grosse, yet as an incident (as unto an office) or as a parcell, as of my mannor, or *ratione alterius rei*, a man may make title to it by prescription or custome: and this *recessus vel alluvio marina*, it is annexed, it is called by the civilians an accessory acquired *ratione vicinitatis et ideo possessio alluvionis sine nova apprehensione agri conjuncti domino accedit non item Insulæ:*

Grip. de Ins., cap. 18, § 138.

3. It carryes with it a reasonablenes, 1. of proportion; as the adjoininge lands are liable to loose *per eluvionem vel influxum maris*, therfor reason to gaine *per refluxum vel recessum:* 2. The adjoininge lands are liable for the defence of the sea walls most comonly: and those of that level were at comōn law (befor any Commission of Sewers grounded upon statute) equally compellable for the defence of the sea walls even by the seisure of theyr lands as it seemes, *Rot. Parl.* 8 *E.* 2, *m.* 23, as now they are: This was the reason why by the Roman law *in agris non limitatis* the adjoininge land had *jus alluvionis ut a necessitate ripæ muniendæ populus liberetur atque id onus incrementum vindicanti imponeretur:*

Grip. de Insulis, cap. 27, § 27.

For the authorityes the only case that I know as to the point of custom is the Abbot of Petresborough case, *P.* 41 *E.* 3, *rot.* 28, where *per consuetudinem patriæ quod domini maneriorum terras seu tenementa super costeram maris habentes particulariter habebunt marettum et sabulonem per fluxus et refluxus maris secundum majus et minus prope tenementa sua projecta:* and therupon a verdict and judgement for the Abbot: 16 El. Dy. 327.

And in the perusall of the Hundred Roll of Kirketon de anno 3 E. 1, within which are divers marshes mencioned to bee likewise in the same roll, as 240 acres of marsh in Sutton and Algerkerk belonginge to the Abbot of Crowland, 240 acres of marsh belonginge to the Abbot of Swineshead, 6 acres of marsh of the sea in Wiberton, etc., yet when that article of the Crown *qui in super de novo appropriarunt nihil sciunt:* surely, had not custom tooke place, some presentment of incrochment of such marishes would have beene made, as there is befor for Grimsby.

See post, p. 399.

Concerninge the right of deserted lands, I take it regularly to be true that *terra relicta est ejusdem juris cum aqua relinquente:* therfor where the water itself is *juris privati* there the *alveus* or channel, the banck, the Ilands, the increase any way happeninge, is likewise *juris privati.* Where the water is *juris publici* ther likewise is the increase happeninge therby *juris publici:* this of comon right: Therfor, 1. I conceive that by the auncient civill law there was not admitted to bee right of ownership or propriety in the sea-shore or Ilands of the sea, although the bancks of publique rivers were admitted to bee publique *quoad usum: sed proprietas earum illorum est quorum prediis haberent:*

As to ports, havens, and creeks of the sea, they are regularly the Kinges, 1. in point of jurisdiction; 2. in point of franchis or liberty (which is the reason that none may levy a port without the Kinges charter), 2 *E.* 3, 8, *in John of Bretanns case: Parl.* 18 *E.* 1, *fol.* 8, *in casu Prioris de Tinmuth;* where a port erected in prejudice of the Kinges port was demolished; 3. in point of ownership or propriety of the soile; which is one of the reasons of the custom of ancorage due to the Kinge within a port: Therfor I conceive that the soile of the creeks, ports, and havens for receit of ships are of comon right *integre domino Regi:* and this accords with the usage in other countryes: *flumina publica.* Grip., cap. 11, § 42.

2. As touchinge the right of the sea shore and *jus alluvionis et maritima sive fluvialia incrementa:* I conceive that by the comon positive law of this Kingedom they belonge to the Kinge as a part of his prerogative: my reasons are these as well in propriety as jurisdictions.

1. The narrow seas, or at lest so much therof as adjoines to the English shore, is within the Kinges jurisdiction or roialty, 6 *R.* 2, *protect.* 46, etc.: and likewise in right of propriety; for although the use of the sea be comon, yet the propriety therof belonges to the Kinge as a royal wast: which is the reason that as well all the *bona vacantia* upon the seas belonge to the Kinge as the right of his admirall jurisdiction, so likewise ilands in the sea, which although by civil law *fiunt occupantis,* yet in our law they are annexed in point of interest to the crowne, who is therof presently in possession, and so prevents any right to bee acquired *per occupationem.*

2. All rights to any land in this kingdom depends upon mediate or immediate tenure of the Kinge: therfor this *jus acquisitum per*

alluvionem, if it bee not otherwise derived out of him by some sufficient title, it is part of his waste and inheritance.

With this agrees our records. *Casus Prioris de Tinmuth*, 18 *E.* 1; *Bracton*. The practise in other countryes, wher *littus maris et fluvialia incrementa* are now *inter regalia:*

Termini sunt integre domino Regi:

Ante, p. 364; post, p. 394.

3. I conceive that the *littus maris*, which is so much as is between the high water and low water mark, *est littus maris quatenus fluctus hibernus maximus excurrit:* this may bee parcell of a mannor, *Sir H. Constable's case*, or parcell of a parish: *Rast. entryes*, 634.

4. I conceive that *terræ per maris vel fluminis publici alluvionem* may belonge by usage unto a private mans soil adjoininge, wherin I conceive

1. That the enquiry will bee all one for an arme of the sea which flowes and reflowes as with the maine, which shal bee the next enquiry:

2. It is to bee observed that by the Civil Law it hath beene usually taken 1. a difference between *insula nata in mare* and *jus alluvionis*—the former they say *acquiritur occupanti;* the 2d, bee it by the sea or by any other river *proxime fundum possidenti* as a perquisite *idque sive nova possessionis apprehensione:* with this difference; where theyr *agri* were *limitati*, which, as some conceive, was that it was bounded out by a set quantity of acres or by speciall limits other then the river or sea, *ibi jus alluvionis populo acquiritur;* wher they were bounded only with the sea, ther it had *jus alluvionis:* This beinge theyr law, I conceive that such a custome is good.

1. Bycause it is only a positive law that entitles the Kinge to this increase, and therfor a custome or prescription may as well acquire it to the subject, especially havinge more color and aid from the civil law then the Kinges right; and although by our law title cannot be made to land immediatly by prescription, yet I may make title to land *ratione alterius*, as of an office or of my land; and so by the greatest civilians it is called an incident:

2. It may have a supposition of a good commencement by the Kinges, and therfore, beinge acquired but by matter in fact, may as well bee challenged by prescription as wreck and weif; and in some auncient graunts it is graunted *una cum maritimo incremento* or *usque ad filum aquæ.*

3. The maintenance of the sea bancks, which I finde why it was accounted by the civil law to bee of no value, vizt. theyr *fluvialia incrementa*, bycause it would but countervail theyr charge in defence.

4. They are at prejudice by the losse, therfor should have benefit by the gaine.

The Abby of Ramseyes case: *aliquando minoratur*.

The Abbot of Petreboroughs case.

The presentment in the Hundred Roll 3 E. 1.

The enjoyment by William Earle of Albemarle, 8 E. 4.

AS TO PUBLIQUE RIVERS.

1. *Quoad jurisdictionem sunt intra corpus Comitatum*, 8 *E*. 2, *Corone*, 399, by the auncient law:

2. *Quoad proprietatem* they agree in all points with the sea.

3. If there bee an increase it belonges by the civil law to the next adjoiner; by our law it may so belonge in salt waters; it doth in fresh waters.

CHAPTER XV.

HALE "DE JURE MARIS."

HALE'S completed work, as edited by Hargrave, is here reprinted. The editor has not been able to discover the original MS. Copies of the work occur in MSS. Hargrave No. 97; MS. Addit. Brit. Mus. 30228, formerly belonging to Lord Lansdowne, being copies made in the eighteenth century.

There is also a valuable treatise on Admiralty Jurisdiction by Hale in MS. Hargrave No. 93, but space is wanting for its publication in this work.

Of the authorship of the work there can no longer be any doubt; a comparison of it with the draft treatise printed above shews that it is an amplification of that draft, which is without any doubt in Hale's own handwriting, and the statement that he was present at the time of Lord Berkely's case occurs in the draft treatise at p. 355 *ante*, and in the printed work at p. 404.

A TREATISE DE JURE MARIS ET BRACHIORUM EJUSDEM. BY LORD CHIEF-JUSTICE HALE.

CAP. I.

Concerning the interest of fresh rivers.

FRESH rivers of what kind soever, do of common right belong to the owners of the soil adjacent; so that the owners of the one side have, of common right, the propriety of the soil, and consequently the right of fishing, *usque filum aquæ;* and the owners of the other side the right of soil or ownership and fishing unto the *filum aquæ* on their side. And if a man be owner of the land of both sides, in common presumption he is owner of the whole river, and hath the right of fishing according to the extent of his land in length. With this agrees the common experience.

Vide Mich. 18–19 *Ed.* 1, *B. R. Rot. Nott.* in an assize by Robert Baker against Hugh Hercy for hindering his fishing in the water of Idell.

Juratores dicunt, quod prædictus Hugo non tenet prædictam piscariam in separali suo, simul cum Roberto Mortayn; quia dicunt, quod omnes, qui tenent terras abuttantes super aquam illam, in ea piscantur pro voluntate sua usque filum aquæ, sicut illi de Grenely ex parte orientali, et illi de Stratford ex parte occidentali. Dicunt etiam, quod quædam pars villæ de Stratford est de feodo de Lancastria, abuttans se super aquam prædictam, et ipsi de feodo illo piscantur usque filum aquæ. Hugo in Misericordia.

And so it was accordingly agreed upon evidence, *Tr.* 2 *Jac. B. R. Owen et Dunch, Vide* 8 H. 7, 5, 22 Ass. 93. Rastall's Entries, 666, *et sæpius alibi.*

But special usage may alter that common presumption; for one man may have the river, and others the soil adjacent; or one man may have the river and soil thereof, and another the free or several fishing in that river.

If a fresh river between the lands of two lords or owners do insensibly gain on one or the other side; it is held, 22 Ass. 93, that the propriety continues as before in the river. But if it be done sensibly and suddenly, then the ownership of the soil remains according to the former bounds. As if the river running between the lands of A and B, leaves his course, and sensibly makes his channel entirely in the lands of A, the whole river belongs to A; *aqua cedit solo:* and so it is, though if the alteration be by insensible degrees, but there be other known boundaries as stakes or extent of land. 22 Ass. pl. 93. And though the book make a question, whether it hold the same law in the case of the sea or the arms of it, yet certainly the law will be all one, as we shall have occasion to shew in the ensuing discourse.

But yet special custom may alter the case in great rivers. For instance, the river of Severn, which is a wild river, yet, by the common custom used below Gloucester bridge, it is the common boundary of the manors of either side, what course soever the river takes; viz. the *filum aquæ* is the common mark or boundary, though it borrow great quantities of land, sometimes of one side, sometimes of the other, and gives them to the opposite shore.

Though fresh rivers are in point of propriety as before *primâ facie* of a private interest; yet as well fresh rivers as salt, or such as flow and reflow, may be under these two servitudes, or affected with them; viz. one of prerogative belonging to the king, and another of publick interest, or belonging to the people in general.

Of these in the ensuing chapters.

CAP. II.

Of the right of prerogative in private or fresh rivers.

THE king by an ancient right of prerogative hath had a certain interest in many fresh rivers, even where the sea doth not flow or reflow, as well as in salt or arms of the sea; and those are these which follow.

1st. A *right of franchise* or *privilege*, that no man may set up a common ferry for all passengers, without a prescription time out of mind, or a charter from the king. He may make a ferry for his own use or the use of his family, but not for the common use of all the king's subjects passing that way; because it doth in consequent tend to a common charge, and is become a thing of publick interest and use, and every man for his passage pays a toll, which is a common charge, and every ferry ought to be under a publick regulation; viz. that it give attendance at due times, keep a boat in due order, and take but reasonable toll; for if he fail in these, he is fineable. And hence it is, that if a common bridge be broken, whereby there is no passage but by a boat or ferry, it hath been anciently practised in the Exchequer to compel that ferryman, that ferries over people for profit without a charter from the king or a lawful prescription, to accompt for the benefit above his reasonable pains and charge. *Communia Paschæ*, 20 E. 3, *in Scaccario*. *Vide Claus*. 36 E. 3, *m*. 10. The bridge called Heckbeth bridge [Nottingham] being in decay, neither was it well known who should repair it; the king grants a temporary ferry and certain particular rates for passengers, appoints the profits to be taken in the first place for defraying of the charge of the barge and bargemen; and if it can appear who is by tenure to repair it, then surplusage of the profits of the ferry to be answered to the king; and if that cannot be known, then *charitatis intuitu* the king allows it to the repair of the bridge.

And this, that is said in reference to a fresh or private river, holds place much more in a publick river or arm of the sea; and therefore it need not be repeated when we come to that subject.

2dly. An *interest*, as I may call it, of *pleasure* or recreation. Before the statute of *Magna Charta, cap.* 16, it was frequent for the king to put as well fresh as salt rivers *in defenso* for his recreation; that is, to bar fishing or fowling in a river till the king had taken his pleasure or advantage of the writ or precept *de defensione riparia*, which anciently was directed to the sheriff to prohibit riviation in any rivers in his bailiwick. But by that statute it is enacted, *quòd nullæ ripariæ defendantur de cætero, nisi illæ quæ fuerunt in defenso tempore Henrici regis avi nostri, et per eadem loca et per eosdem terminos, sicut esse consueverunt tempore suo.*

Riviare—To have a liberty in a river of fishing and fowling: Jacob. Law Dict.

After this statute the *Ripariorum defensiones* ran thus, as appears *Claus.* 20 *H.* 3, *m.* 3 *dorso. Claus.* 22 *H.* 3, *m.* 2 *dorso, et sæpius alibi.*

Rex Vicecomiti Wigorniæ salutem. Præcipimus tibi, quod sine dilatione clamari facias et firmiter prohiberi ex parte nostrâ, ut nullus de cætero eat ad riviandum in ripariis nostris in ballivâ tuâ, quæ in defenso fuerunt tempore Henrici regis avi nostri; et scire facias omnibus de comitatu tuo, qui ab antiquo facere debent pontes ad riparias illas, quod provideant sibi de pontibus illis, ita quod prompti sint et parati in adventu nostro quando eis scire faciemus.

And thus it was written to most counties.

But because this left the country in a great uncertainty in the writs of 22 H. 3, so afterwards it mentioned some one particular river.

Et *in alijs riparijs in ballivâ tuâ, quæ in defenso esse consueverunt tempore Henrici regis avi nostri;*

As Avon in Worcestershire, Bladen in Oxfordshire, Mules in Surrey, &c.

This hath been long disused; for it created a great trouble to the country; and little benefit or addition of pleasure to the king.

Close 24 Hen. III., m. 1d; 25 Hen. III., m. 4d; 26 Hen. III., p. 1, m. 14. And see Neill *v.* Duke of Devonshire, 8 App. Cas. pp. 177, 178. Duke of Devonshire *v.* Pattinson, 20 Q. B. D. 263.

3rdly. An *interest of jurisdiction; viz.* in reference to common nuisances in or by rivers; as where the sewers were not kept, which gave the rise to the commission of Sewers, as well for fresh rivers as for salt. *Vide* Stat. 23 H. 8, cap. 5. The commission thereby enacted recites this part of the king's jurisdiction, viz.

"We therefore, for that by reason of our royal dignity and "prerogative royal we are bound to provide for the safety and "preservation of our realm," &c.

And another part of the king's jurisdiction in reformation of nuisances, is, to reform and punish nuisances in all rivers, whether fresh or salt, that are a common passage, not only for ships and greater vessels, but also for smaller, as barges or boats; to reform the obstructions or annoyances that are therein to such common passage: for as the common highways on the land are for the common land passage, so these kind of rivers, whether fresh or salt, that bear boats or barges, are highways by water; and as the highways by land are called *altæ viæ regiæ* so these publick rivers for publick passage are called *fluvii regales*, and *haut streames le Roy;* not in reference to the propriety of the river, but to the publick use; all things of publick safety and convenience being in a special manner under the king's care, supervision, and protection. And therefore the report in Sir John Davys, of the piscary of Banne, mistakes the reason of those books, that call these *streames le roy*, as if they were so called in respect of propriety, as 19 Ass. 6, Dy. 11, for they are called so, because they are of publick use, and under the king's special care and protection, whether the soil be his or not.

And this leads me to the third chapter.

CAP. III.

Concerning publick streams.

THERE be some streams or rivers, that are private not only in propriety or ownership, but also in use, as little streams and rivers that are not a common passage for the king's people. Again, there be other rivers, as well fresh as salt, that are of common or publick use for carriage of boats and lighters. And these, whether they are fresh or salt, whether they flow and reflow or not, are *primâ facie publici juris*, common highways for man or goods or both from one inland town to another. Thus the rivers of Wey, of Severn, of Thames, and divers others, as well above the bridges and ports as below, as well above the flowings of the sea as below, and as well where they are become to be of private propriety as in what parts they are of the king's propriety, are publick rivers *juris publici*. And therefore all nuisances and impediments of passages of boats and vessels, though in the private soil of any person, may be punished by indictments, and removed; and this was the reason of the statute of *Magna Charta, cap.* 23.

Omnes kidelli deponantur per Thamisiam et Medwayam, et per totam Angliam nisi per costeram maris.

These kinds of nuisances were such, as hindered or obstructed the passage of boats, as wears, piles, choaking up the passage with filth, diverting of the river by cutts or trenches, decay of the banks, or the like.

And they were reformed:

Sometimes by indictments or presentments in the leets, sessions of the peace, oyer and terminer, or before justices of assize.

Oftentimes in the king's bench; as *Hil.* 50 *E.* 3, *B. R. Rot.* 23, for nuisances in the river of Trent; *H.* 23 *E.* 3, *B. R. Rot.* 61, in the river Ouse; *H.* 21 *E.* 1, in the river Severn; *Tr.* 28 *E.* 3, *Rot.* 29, in the river Leigh; and generally in all other rivers within the bodies of counties, which had common passage of boats or barges, whether the water were fresh or salt, the king's or a subject's, *Rot. Parliamenti* 14 *R.* 2, *n.* 34, *Mich.* 36 *E.* 3, *B. R. Rot.* 65, *Mich.* 18–19 *E.* 1, *B. R.*, and infinite more.

Sometimes by special commission; as for the river of Leigh, 19 Ass. 6.

And sometimes by the parties, that were prejudiced by such nuisance, without any process of law.

More of this we shall see when we come to consider of common nuisances in havens and ports.

But if any person at his own charge makes his own private stream to be passable for boats or barges, either by making of locks or cutts, or drawing together other streams; and hereby that river, which was his own in point of propriety become now capable of carriage of vessels; yet this seems not to make it *juris publici*, and he may pull it down again, or apply it to his own private use. For it is not hereby made to be *juris publici*, unless it were done at a common charge, or by a publick authority, or that by long continuance of time it hath been freely devoted to a publick use. And so it seems also to be, if he that makes such a new river or passage doth it by way of recompence or compensation for some other publick stream that he hath stopped for his own conveniency; as in the case of the Abbot of St. Austin's Canterbury, mentioned in the Register. So likewise if he purchaseth the king's charter to take a reasonable toll for the passage of the king's subjects, and puts it in use, these seem to be devoting and as it were consecrating of it to the common use. As he, that by an *ad quod damnum*, and licence thereupon obtained, changeth a way, and sets out another in his own land; this new way is thereupon become *juris publici*, as well as a way by prescription. For no man can take a settled or constant toll even in his own private land for a common passage without the king's licence.

CAP. IV.

Concerning the king's interest in salt waters, the sea and its arms, and the soil thereof: and first, of the right of fishing there.

THUS much concerning fresh waters or inland rivers, which, though they empty themselves mediately into the sea, are not called arms of the sea, either in respect of the distance or smallness of them.

We come now to consider the sea and its arms: and first, concerning the sea itself.

The sea is either that which lies within the body of a county or without.

That arm or branch of the sea which lies within the *fauces terræ*, where a man may reasonably discerne between shore and shore, is or at least may be within the body of a county, and therefore within the jurisdiction of the sheriff or coroner. 8 E. 2, *Corone*, 399.

The part of the sea which lies not within the body of a county, is called the main sea or ocean.

The narrow sea, adjoining to the coast of England, is part of the wast and demesnes and dominions of the king of England, whether it lie within the body of any county or not.

This is abundantly proved by that learned treatise of Master Selden called *Mare Clausum;* and therefore I shall say nothing therein, but refer the reader thither.

In this sea the king of England hath a double right, viz. a right of jurisdiction which he ordinarily exerciseth by his admiral, and a right of propriety or ownership. The latter is that which I shall meddle with.

The king's right of propriety or ownership in the sea and soil thereof is evidenced principally in these things that follow.

Ist. The right of fishing in this sea and the creeks and arms thereof is originally lodged in the crown, as the right of depasturing is originally lodged in the owner of the wast whereof he is lord, or as the right of fishing belongs to him that is the owner of a private or inland river. I shall not give many instances of this, because they are abundantly done to my hand in the book I formerly cited.

Pat. 23 *E.* 1, *m.* 6. The king grants liberty to the Hollanders to fish *in mari nostro prope Jernemuth.*

Rot. Parliamenti 3 *H.* 5, *pars* 1, *n.* 33. The king by proclamation made a general inhibition of fishing upon the coasts of Ireland to the prejudice of the English. Desired to be recalled, but was not.

Rot. Parl. 8 *H.* 5, *n.* 6.

Item pri le Commons, que come nostre Seigneur le Roy et ses noble progeniteurs de tout temps ont estre Seigneurs de le mere, et ore per le grace de Dieu est si venus, que nostre Seigneur le Roy est Seigneur de costs de ambe parties de le mere d'ordeiner sur touts estrangers passants permy le dit mere tiel imposition al oeps nostre Seigneur le Roy apprendre que a luy semble reasonable pur le salve gard del dit mere.

Responsio, "*Le Roy s'avisera.*"

But though the king is the owner of this greât wast, and as a consequent of his propriety hath the primary right of fishing in the sea and the creeks and arms thereof; yet the common people of England have regularly a liberty of fishing in the sea or creeks or arms thereof, as a publick common of piscary, and may not without injury to their right be restrained of it, unless in such places or creeks or navigable rivers, where either the king or some particular subject hath gained a propriety exclusive of that common liberty.

Mich. 19 *E.* 3, *B. R. Rot.* 127, *Lincoln.* The commonalty of Grimsby impleaded the fishermen of Ole, which is within five miles of Grimsby, for lading and unlading their fish and other victuals at Ole;

Custumâ non solutâ, quæ est debita dictæ villæ Grimsby juxta cartas regis contra prohibitionem regis.

The defendants plead,

Quòd ipsi sunt liberi tenentes in hamletto de Thrusco, qui est infra præcinctum villæ de Ole, et quòd ipsi tanquam piscatores juxta costeram maris à tempore quo, &c. usi sunt piscari cum retibus et battellis suis, et pisces captos ad terram apud Thrusco et alibi in partibus ibidem venditioni exponere, absque hoc quòd blada victualia bona aut mercimonia carcarunt aut discarcarunt aut venditioni exposuerunt. Ideo veniat jurata.

Vide Statutum 2 *E.* 6, *cap.* 6. 5 *El. cap.* 5. *Bracton, lib.* 2, *cap.* 12. *Jus piscandi omnibus commune in portu et in fluminibus.* It must be taken to be rivers that are arms of the sea, and *primo intuitu;* for *de facto* there doth fall out in many ports and arms of the sea an exclusion of publick fishing by prescription or custom.

IId. The next evidence of the king's right and propriety in the sea and the arms thereof is his right of propriety to

The shore; and
The *Maritima Incrementa.*

(1.) The shore is that ground that is between the ordinary high-water and low-water mark. This doth *primâ facie* and of common right belong to the king, both in the shore of the sea and the shore of the arms of the sea.

And herein there will be these things examinable.

1st. What shall be said the shore, or *littus maris.*

2nd. What shall be said an arm or creek of the sea.

3d. What evidence there is of the king's propriety thereof.

1. For the first of these it is certain, that that which the sea overflows, either at high-spring tides or at extraordinary tides, comes not as to this purpose under the denomination of *littus maris;* and consequently the king's title is not of that large extent, but only to land that is usually overflowed at ordinary tides. And so I have known it ruled in the Exchequer-chamber in the case of Vanhaesdanke on prosecution by information against Mr. Whiting, about 12 *Car.* 1, for lands in —— in the county of Norfolk, and accordingly ruled 15 *Car. B. R.* Sir Edward Heron's case, and *Pasch.* 17 *Car.* 2, *in Scaccario,* upon evidence between the Lady Wandsford's Lessee and Stephens, in an *ejectione firmæ* for the town of Cowes in the isle of Wight. That therefore I call the shore, that is between the common high-water and low-water mark, and no more.

MS. 97 has "that oaze land."

Ante, p. 317.

2. For the second, that is called an arm of the sea where the sea flows and reflows, and so far only as the sea so flows and reflows; so that the river of Thames above Kingston and the river of Severn above Tewkesbury, &c. though there they are publick rivers, yet are not arms of the sea. But it seems, that, although the water be fresh at high water, yet the denomination of an arm of the sea continues, if it flow and reflow as in Thames above the bridge.

22 *Ass.* 93. Nota *que chescun ew, que flow et reflow, est appel bras de mere cy tantavint come il flow.*

3. For the third, it is admitted, that *de jure communi* between the high-water and low-water mark doth *primâ facie* belong to the king, 5 Rep. 107. Constable's case. Dy. 326. Although it is true, that such shore may be and commonly is parcel of the manor adjacent, and so may be belonging to a subject, as shall be shewn, yet *primâ facie* it is the king's.

And as the shore of the sea doth *primâ facie* belong to the king, Cf. p. 364. viz. between the ordinary high-water and low-water mark, so the shore of an arm of the sea between the high-water and low-water mark belongs *primâ facie* to the king, though it may also belong to a subject, as shall be shewn in the next chapter.

In the case between the town of Newcastle and the prior of Ante, p. 111. Tinmouth, 20 E. 1, which is afterwards, in the Second Part, chapter the 6th, more fully recited; one of the charges against the prior is, that he had built houses at Sheles upon the river of Tyne between the high-water and low-water mark. The prior pleads that it was built on his own soil.

Ubi dominus rex nullum habet solum, neque liberum tenementum, eo quòd solum dictæ domus et liberum tenementum extendit se usque ad filum aquæ Tyne, ultra terram suam siccam, et inter quod quidem filum aquæ et terram prædictam domus prædicta habet piscariam suam liberam in longitudinem terræ ejusdem in eâdem aquâ.

The king's attorney replied,

Quòd, qualescumque mansiunculæ ibidem fuerunt temporibus prædecessorum prioris, idem prior, qui nunc est, tempore suo fieri fecit ibidem 26 *domus super solum quod domino regi esse debet, eo quòd fluxu et inundatione maris comprehenditur.*

Afterwards judgment was given against the prior, but not in express terms for the soil, but implicitly. See the judgment afterwards in the Second Part, 6th chapter.

And consonant to this there was a decree *Paschæ* 8 *Car.* 1, in Ante, p. 260 et seqq. the Exchequer, entered in the Book of Orders of that term, fol. 66, whereby it was decreed, that the soil and ground lying between Wapping-wall and the river of Thames is parcel of the port of London; and therefore and for that the same lies between the high-water and low-water marks of the river of Thames, all the houses built between the Hermitage-wharfe unto Dickshore eastward, and between the old wall or Wapping-wall on the north and the river of Thames on the south, are decreed to the king; and the same were accordingly by commission seized into the king's hands.

The title of the bill or information was laid, viz. 1st. That the river of Thames flowed and reflowed. 2d. That consequently it was an arm of the sea. 3d. That it was the king's river. 4th. That it was the king's port.—And upon all these it was concluded, that the land between the high-water and low-water mark was the king's land, and accordingly decreed.

And this shall suffice for the king's right in the shore of the sea, or rivers that are arms of the sea, viz. the land lying between the high-water and the low-water mark at ordinary tides.

(2.) The king hath a title to *maritima incrementa*, or increase of land by the sea; and this is of three kinds, viz. 1. Increase *per projectionem vel alluvionem*. 2. Increase *per relictionem vel desertionem*. 3. *Per insulæ productionem*.

1. The increase *per alluvionem* is, when the sea by casting up sand and earth doth by degrees increase the land, and shut itself out further than the ancient bounds went; and this is usual. The reason why this belongs to the crown is, because in truth the soil, where there is now dry land, was formerly part of the very *fundus maris*, and consequently belonged to the king. But indeed if such alluvion be so insensible, that it cannot be by any means found that the sea was there, *idem est non esse et non apparere;* the land thus increased belongs as a perquisite to the owner of the land adjacent.

MS. 97, "sand and oare."

2. The increase *per relictionem*, or recess of the sea. This doth *de jure communi* belong to the king; for as the sea is parcel of the wast or demesne, so of necessity the land that lies under it, and therefore it belongs to the king when left by the sea; and so also it regularly holds in lands deserted by a river, that is an arm of the sea or a creek of the sea *primâ facie*, especially if the creek or river be part of a port.

Claus. 10 *E.* 3, *m.* 18. Upon an inquisition finding that half an acre in the suburbs of Canterbury,

> *Crevit in cursu ripæ Cantuariæ per alluvionem et diluvionem dictæ ripæ*,

this half acre was seized into the king's hands, but it is true, it was afterwards restored to the Abbot of St. Austin's; because by another inquisition it was found,

Quòd non est solum nostrum, nec accrevit per alluvionem et diluvionem dictæ ripæ, sed extitit solum abbatis, &c. à tempore cujus memoria, &c.

Car. primi, Upon an information against Oldsworth and others for that which is now called Sutton Marsh, that 300 acres of land was *relictum per mare*, and that the defendants had intruded into it; the defendants pleaded specially, and entitled themselves by prescription to the lands project by the sea; and upon a demurrer adjudged against them. That 1st, by the prescription or title made to lands project, which is *jus alluvionis*, no answer is given to the title of the information for lands relict, for these were of several natures. 2d, It was held, that it lies not in prescription to claim lands relict *per mare;* for so if the channel between us and France should dry up, a man might prescribe for it, which is unreasonable; for Ante, p. 292.

Nihil prescribitur nisi quod possidetur.

But this hath some exceptions, besides these that follow in the ensuing chapter. Cf. ante, p. 366.

If a subject hath had by prescription the propriety of a certain tract, or creek, or navigable river, or arm of the sea, even while it is covered with water, by certain known metes or extents; this, though it should be relicted, the subject will have the propriety in the soil relicted. For he had it before, though covered with water; and although the sea is a fluid thing, yet the *terra* or *solum subiectum* is fixed; and by force of a clear and evident usage a subject may have the propriety of a private river; though the acquest of the former be more difficult, and requires a very good evidence to make it out, as shall be said in the ensuing chapter.

If a subject hath land adjoining the sea, and the violence of the sea swallow it up, but so that yet there be reasonable marks to continue the notice of it; or though the marks be defaced; yet if by situation and extent of quantity, and bounding upon the firm land, the same can be known, though the sea leave this land again, or it be by art or industry regained, the subject doth not lose his propriety: and accordingly it was held by Cooke and Foster, *M.* 7 *Jac. C. B.* though the inundation continue forty years.

If the marks remain or continue, or extent can reasonably be certain, the case is clear.—Vide Dy. 326.—22 Ass. 93. See for this a notable case in the case of an overflowing by the Thames, which is an arm of the sea, *Rot. Parliamenti* 8 *E.* 2, *m.* 23, *pro Willielmo Burnello.* Philip Burnell, father of William, being seized of the manor of Hacchesham near Greenwich, died his heir within age during his minority.

Aqua Thamissæ magnam partem terræ et prati manerij prædicti ac aliarum terrarum contiguarum superundavit:

The bishop of Bath and Wells, by agreement with the king, was to stop the breach at his own charges, and was to hold the land for seven years to reimburse his charges. This he did, and the land was regained, and the bishop held the land for his seven years, and three years over them. Burnell desired relief for his land in Parliament against the Bishop. The answer was,

Sequatur versus episcopum ad communem legem;

which would not have been, if the king had been intituled by the inundation.

P. 18 *E.* 2, *Rot.* 174, *B. R.*, upon the like account a considerable quantity of marsh ground, containing 100 acres, parcel of the manor of Stebunhith, was regained from the Thames, and enjoyed accordingly. I think it is the same that is now called Stepney Marsh, or at least some part of the manor now built upon and contiguous to the Thames. The record is worth the reading, but long.

Claus. 18 *H.* 3, *m.* 21, *pro Villata de Slimberge* in Gloucestershire.

Cf. p. 354. *Rex Vicecomiti, &c. Quia accepimus per inquisitionem, quam fieri precipimus, quòd illa pars terræ, quam utraque villata de Slimberge et Aure sibi vendicant, eo quòd aqua Sabrinæ eam occupavit super campum de Slimberge versus campum de Aure, et postea processu temporis eam rejecit ad campum de Slimberge, antequam sic rejecta esset per aquam Sabrinæ; de jure pertinuit ad villam de Slimberge, et in parte fuit terra arabilis, et in parte pastura, ad eandem villam de Slimberge pertinens per divisam fossati, quod vocatur Hedgewood: precipimus tibi, quòd eidem villatæ de Slimberge plenam seisinam de prædictâ parte terræ habere facias. Teste Rege apud Gloucesteriam.*

The river of Severn had gained upon Slimberge so much, that its channel ran over part of Slimberge lands, and lost part thereof unto the other side, and then threw it back again to Slimberge. It shall not belong to Aure. Neither was it at all claimed by the king, though Severn in that place be an arm of the sea. But it was restored to Slimberge as before.

But the truth is, that there the *maritima incrementa* of that river belong to the barons of Barclay, as shall be shewn. Yet the propriety of the soil was not lost to the owners that had it before.

And the truth is also, that river, which is a wild unruly river, and many times shifts its channel, especially in that flat between Slimberge and Aure, is the common boundary between the manors of either side, viz. the *filum aquæ*, or middle of the stream. And this is the custom of the manors contiguous to that river from Gloucester down to Aure, which was not taken notice of in that record. Yet it serves for this purpose to shew, that the king gained not the propriety against the town by such inundation.

It is true, here were the old bounds or marks continuing, viz. the Hedgewood. But suppose the inundation of the sea deface the marks and boundaries, yet if the certain extent or contents from the land not overflown can be evidenced, though the bounds be defaced, yet it shall be returned to the owner, according to those quantities and extents that it formerly had. Only if any man be at the charge of inning of it, it seems by a decree of Sewers he may hold it till he be reimbursed his charges, as was done in the case of Burnell before alledged. But if it be freely left again by the reflux and recess of the sea, the owner may have his land as before, if he can make it out where and what it was; for he cannot lose his propriety of the soil, though it be for a time become part of the sea, and within the admiral jurisdiction while it so continues.

3. The third sort of maritime increase are islands arising *de novo* in the king's seas, or the king's arms thereof. These upon the same account and reason *primâ facie* and of common right belong to the king; for they are part of that soil of the sea, that belonged before in point of propriety to the king; for when islands *de novo* arise, it is either by the recess or sinking of the water, or else by the exaggeration of sand and slubb, which in process of time grow firm land invironed with water; and thus some places have arisen, and their original recorded, as about Ravensend in Yorkshire. Ante, pp. 63, 361, 365.

And thus much of the king's right of propriety which he hath in the sea, and also *primâ facie* and in common presumption in the ports and creeks and arms of the sea.

CAP. V.

The right which a subject may have in the creeks or arms of the sea, and how it may be acquired.

ALTHOUGH the king hath *primâ facie* this right in the arms and creeks of the sea *communi jure*, and in common presumption, yet a subject may have such a right.

And this he may have two ways.

1st. By the king's charter or grant; and this is without question. The king may grant fishing within a creek of the sea, or in some known precinct that hath known bounds, though within the main sea. He may also grant that very interest itself, viz. a navigable river that is an arm of the sea, the water and soil thereof. He may also grant a manor *cum littore maris eidem adjacente;* and the shore itself will pass, though in gross and not parcel of the manor. He may also grant a manor or land contiguous to the sea, *unà cum maritimis incrementis*, and that will pass that *jus alluvionis*, whereof Ante, p. 21. before. *Vide Cartæ Antiquæ, G.* 15, Grant 6, *Johannis* to the abbott *de Bello loco, viz. alveum super quem abbatia fundata est à vado de Hartford cum fluctu maris in ascendendo et descendendo inter utramque ripam.*

Ante, p. 16. *Vide ibidem, I.* 17, *Carta Willielmi primi abbati sancti Augustini de totâ terrâ Estanore et totum littus usque medietatem aquæ.*

Ante, p. 9. *Vide ibidem, Carta Knuti monachis sancti Augustini de terrâ insulâ Thanet, tam in terrâ quàm in mari et littore.*

Vide ibidem, F. 17. A grant by king William the first to the monks of Trinity, Canterbury, of divers liberties in their possessions *in terrâ et in mari.*

Ante, p. 12. *Vide Cartæ Antiquæ, O.* 1. A grant by Edward the Confessor to the abbey of Hulm, *videlicet, wreccum in mari et in littore maris et in portubus maris. Cartæ Antiquæ, D. D.* 24.

But it seems the grant of *incrementa maritima* will not pass lands that often happen to be relict by the sea; because that is not so properly *maritimum incrementum.* And besides, the soil itself under the water is actually the king's, and cannot pass from him by such an incertain grant as *maritima incrementa;* but it must pass a present interest.

But if the king will grant land adjacent to the sea, *unà cum mille acris terræ aquâ maris coopertis eædem terræ secundum consuetudinem, &c. adjacentibus;* such a grant, as it may be penned, will pass the soil itself; and if there shall be a recess of the sea leaving such a quantity of land, it will belong to the grantee.

2d. The second right is that which is acquired or acquirable to a subject by custom or prescription; and I think it very clear, that the subject may by custom and usage or prescription have the true propriety and interest of many of these several maritime interests, which we have before stated to be *primâ facie* belonging to the king. I will go over them particularly, and set down which of these interests are acquirable by usage or prescription by a subject.

A subject may by prescription have the interest of fishing in an arm of the sea, in a creek or port of the sea, or in a certain precinct or extent lying within the sea: and these not only free fishing, but several fishing.

Fishing may be of two kinds ordinarily, viz. the fishing with the net, which may be either as a liberty without the soil, or as a liberty arising by reason of and in concomitance with the soil, or interest or propriety of it; or otherwise it is a local fishing, that ariseth by and from the propriety of the soil. Such are *gurgites*, weares, fishing-places, *borachiæ*, *stachiæ*, &c. which are the very soil itself, and so frequently agreed in our books. And such as these a subject may have by usage either in gross, as many religious houses had; or as parcel of or appendant to their manors, as both corporations and others have had; and this not only in navigable rivers and arms of the sea, but in creeks and ports and havens, yea and in certain known limits in the open sea contiguous to the shore.

And these kinds of fishing are not only for small sea fish, as herrings, sprats, pilchers, &c. but for great fish, as salmons, which, though they are great fish, are not royal fish, as the report of Sir John Davys in the case of the fishing of Banne would intimate. And not only for smaller fish, and salmons, but even royal fish, as whale, sturgion, porpoise, which, though they are royal fish, and *primâ facie* and of common right do belong to the king, yet a subject may prescribe even for these as appurtenant to his manor, as is unquestionably agreed by our books.

Now for precedents touching such rights of fishing in the sea and arms and creeks thereof belonging by usage to subjects, the most whereof will appear to be by reason of the propriety of the very water and soil wherein the fishing is, and some of them even within the ports of the sea.

P. 4 *E.* 1, *B. R. Surrey.*—The prior of Stoke brings trespass for the fishing in *aquâ de Sturmer* against Hamon Clever.—The defendant justified, *quòd piscavit in communi aquâ ipsius Hamonis ex parte comitatûs Suffolchiæ, ubi ipse et antecessores sui semper solebant piscare.*—The prior *dicit, quod Michael avus ipsius Hamonis dedit totum jus, quod dicebat se habere in piscariâ maris de le Sturmer Deo et sancto Johanni de Stoke, &c.*

Ante, p. 109. *P.* 34 *E.* 1, *B. R. Rot.* 14, *Kancia.—Prior de Coningshed implacitat abbatem de Furneys pro prostratione gurgitis in aquâ de Ulverstone.* The defendant justified; because each end of the wear was fastened upon the abbot's land. The abbot replied, *quòd Willielmus de Lancaster dominus de Kendal dedit prædecessori domûs suæ prædictæ aquam et piscariam ex utrâque parte ejusdem quantum impetus maris fluit et refluit.*

Vide Rastall's Entries, trespass in piscary, pl. 4. Prescription pur several fishing *in aquâ maritimâ fluente et refluente in seisonabili tempore cum* 7 *stallis separatis separalis piscariæ fixis pro retibus.*

P. 35 *E.* 1, *B. R. rot.* 18, *Suffolchia.—Willielmus Braham implacitat Riccardum S. et* 7 *alios pro piscatione in separali piscariâ suâ apud Braham. Defendens dicit, quòd prædicta piscaria est quoddam brachium maris et communis piscaria eorundem et aliorum, et non separalis piscaria. Ideo veniat jurata.*

Whereby it is admitted, though *primâ facie* an arm of the sea be in point of propriety the king's, and *primâ facie* it is common for every subject to fish there, yet a subject may have by usage a several fishing there, exclusive of that common liberty which otherwise of common right belongs to all the king's subjects.

Ante, p. 145. *Trin.* 10 *E.* 2, *B. R. Rot.* 83, *Norfolchiæ.* The abbot of St. Benedict Hulm impleads divers for fishing *in ripariâ, quæ se extendit à ponte de Wroxam usque quandam lacum vocatam Blackdam.*—Pending the suit the king's attorney came in, and alledged for the king, *quòd prædicta riparia est brachium maris, quæ se extendit in salsum mare, et est riparia domini regis salsa fluens et refluens, ubi naves et battelli veniunt et applicant extra magnum mare carcati et discarcati quietè absque tolneto seu custumâ alicui dando, et est communis piscaria quibuscumque; et dicit, quòd presentatum fuit in ultimo iitnere coram Solomone de Roffa et socijs suis justiciarijs itinerantibus in comitatu isto, quod prædecessor prædicti abbatis fecit purpresturam super dominum regem in ripariâ prædictâ, gurgites plantando in eâdem et appropriando sibi prædictam piscariam tenendo tanquam separalem; per quod consideratum fuit, quòd gurgites illæ amoverentur, et quòd prædicta aqua remaneret communis piscaria. Et petit, quòd non procedatur ad aliquam inquisitionem inde capiendam, quousque præfati justiciarij super recordo et processu prædictis certiorentur.* Thereupon search is granted, and the record certified. And afterwards a *procedendo* was obtained; and issue being joiued, it was found for the abbot, and judgment and execution given against the defendants for the damages, viz. £200.

Upon which record these things are observable.

1st. That *de communi jure* the right of such arms of the sea belongs to the king.

2d. That yet in such arms of the sea the subjects in general have *primâ facie* a common of fishing, as in the main sea.

3d. That yet a subject may have a separate right of fishing, exclusive of the king and of the common right of the subject.

4th. That in this case the right of the abbot to have a several fishing was not a bare right of liberty or *profit à prendre;* but the right of the very water and soil itself, for he made weares in it.

Escætria, 12 *E.* 1, *n.* 1. The earls of Devon had not only the port of Toppesham, *de quo infra;* but the record tells us, that *portus et piscaria et mariscus de Topsham spectat Amiciæ comitissæ Devon.*

Mich. 13–14 *E.* 1, *B. R. rot.* 10. The abbot of Tichfeud impleaded the burgesses of Southampton, *quòd diripuerunt gurgitem suam apud Cadeland. Burgenses respondent, quòd ipsa gurges levata fuit ad nocumentum domini regis et villæ Southampton, et quòd batelli et naves impediuntur, quo minus venire non possunt ad portum villæ prædictæ. Juratores dicunt, quòd à tempore quo, &c. non fuit ibi aliqua gurges, sed antiquitùs solebant stare pali, per quod credunt, quòd tunc fuit prostrata gurges eâdem occasione quâ modo, eo quòd fuit ad nocumentum transeuntium.* Ante, p. 89.

Upon which record these things are observable.

1st. That a subject may by prescription have a wear in the sea, and consequently have an interest below the low-water mark; for probably weares be such. Cf. p. 353.

2dly. That, yet if it be a nuisance to the passage of ships, it may be abated.

Ante, p. 283. 7th *Rep.* 15. It appears, that the abbot of Abbotsbury before dissolution had not only a game of swans, but the fishing, yea and the soil of an arm or creek of the sea called a meere or fleete, *in quam mare fluit et refluit;* and it came to the king by the dissolution of the monastery.

Ante, pp. 353, 354. And in many considerable arms of the sea that were navigable rivers, and flowed and reflowed with salt water, divers persons had weares and local fishing sluices. As for instance, in the river of Severn the earls of Lancaster had certain weares called Radley weares, part of his manor of Radley. *Clause* 10 *E.* 3, *m.* 29. The like for others in the river of Tese, *Patentes* 32 *E.* 3, *pars* 1, *m.* 15 *dorso in Twede, fines* 2 *E.* 3, *m.* 1, *in Trent. Pat.* 18 *E.* 2, *pars* 1, *m.* 3 *dorso. Pat.* 43 *H.* 3, *m. dorso in Severn. Pat.* 2 *E.* 4, *pars* 3, *m.* 15 *dorso. Pat.* 32 *E.* 3, *pars* 2, *m.* 15 *dorso in Ouse. Pat.* 12 *E.* 2, *pars* 1, *m.* 3.

Ante, p. 156. *Trin.* 50 *E.* 3, *B. R. rot.* 2, *Essex. Walterus filius Walteri monstrat domino regi, quòd cùm piscaria vocata le Reysand ab antiquo ut parcella manerij sui de Burnham appendebat, dominus rex per cartam suam eam concessit durante minore ætate suâ cuidam Bartholomeo Stigoune, qui prædictam piscariam detinet ad præjudicium et exhæredationem dicti Walteri.* And thereupon a *scire facias* awarded. The defendant prayed aid of the king; and after a *procedendo* they plead to issue, and the jury find, that *dicta piscaria est parcella manerij prædicti. Ideo consideratum est, quòd prædicta piscaria, cum gurgitibus eidem pertinentibus, dicto Waltero liberentur.*

Infinite more of this kind might be produced. I shall add no more here; but in the subsequent parts of this and the next chapter some other instances of this nature will occur, which be applicable to the prescription of the right of fishing in navigable rivers; and I have added the more, because there are certain Ante, pp. 247, 355. glances and intimations in the case of the piscary of Banne, in Sir John Davys's reports, as if the fishing in these kinds of royal rivers, were not acquirable but by special charter, which is certainly untrue; for they are acquirable by prescription or usage, as well as royal fish may be.

It is true, that by the statute of *Magna Charta, cap.* 23, *Omnes kidelli deponantur de cetero penitùs per Thamisiam et Medwayam per totam Angliam, nisi per costeram maris.*

And this statute was seconded with others that were more effectual, viz. 25 E. 3, cap. 4. 1 H. 4, 12. 12 E. 4, cap. 7.

And by force of these statutes, weares, that were prejudicial to the passage of vessels, were to be pulled down; and accordingly it was done in many places. But that did no way disaffirm the propriety, but only removed the annoyance, which, as before is shewn, was not to be allowed in an inland river, if it be a common passage.

The exception of weares upon the sea-coasts, and likewise frequent examples, some whereof are before mentioned, make it appear that there might be such private interests not only in point of liberty, but in point of propriety, on the sea-coast and below the low-water mark; for such were regularly all weares.[1] But as by the statutes of 25 E. 3, cap. 4—45 E. 3, cap. 2—1 H. 4, 12—4 H. 4, cap. 11, and other statutes, the erection of new weares and inhancing of old is provided against in navigable rivers; and by other statutes particular provision is made against weares new or old erected in particular ports (as in the port of Newcastle, by the statute of the 21 H. 8, cap. 18; in the port of Southampton, by the statutes of 11 H. 7, cap. 5; 14 H. 8, cap. 13; in the rivers of Ouse and Humber, by the statute of 23 H. 8, cap. 18; in the river and port of Exeter, by the statute of 31 H. 8, cap. 4; in the river of Thames, by the statutes of 4 H. 7, cap. 15; 27 H. 8, cap. 18; 3 Jac. cap. 20, and divers others); so by the statute of 3 Jac. cap. 12, all new weares erected upon the sea-shore, or in any haven harbour or creek, or within five miles of the mouth of any haven or creek, are prohibited under a penalty. But in all these statutes, though they prohibit the thing, yet they do admit, that there may be such an interest lodged in a subject, not only in navigable rivers, but even in the ports of the sea itself contiguous to the shore, though below the low-water mark, whereby a subject may not only have a liberty but also a right or propriety of soil. But yet this, that I have said, must be taken with this allay, which I have in part premised.

1st. That this interest or right in the subject must be so used as it may not occasion a common annoyance to passage of ships or boats; for that is prohibited by the common law, and these several statutes before mentioned, viz. erecting new weares, inhancing old, fixing of pikes or stakes, and the like, in order to fishing: for the *jus privatum*, that is acquired to the subject either by patent or prescription, must not prejudice the *jus publicum*,

[1] Weirs are situate both above and below low-water mark.—ED.

wherewith public rivers or arms of the sea are affected for public use.

2d. That the fishing, that a subject hath in this or any other private or public river, or creek fresh or salt, is subject to the laws for the conservation of fish and fry, which are many.

And this gives me an occasion to divert to the examination of those commissions, that have been granted in common rivers, commonly called commissions of conservancy or water-bailiffs; which commissions have of late time especially been granted in all the great rivers in England, and [under which the patentees] have exercised a jurisdiction irregularly enough and to the damage of the people, and under the disguise of a publick good have filled their own purses with the money exacted from the people. Therefore touching their office,

1st. The office of a water-baillie or *scrutator* is a bare ministerial officer, which the king doth or may appoint in those rivers or places that are his in franchise or interest. And his business was, to look to the king's rights, as his wrecks, his flotson, jetson, water-strays, royal fishes. And he had no jurisdiction at all *quâ talis;* but his office was only ministerial, to receive and account for the casualties belonging to the king upon publick or great rivers, which did or in common presumption might belong to the crown. Such was that office of searcher, *scrutator*, or baillie of the river of Severn *usque ad pontem Wigorniæ. Pat.* 27 *H.* 6, *parte* 2, *m.* 20. *Pat.* 8 *E.* 4, *parte* 1, *m.* 22.

2d. The office of conservator of rivers and fish in rivers; and of these patents of conservancy we find mention in the statute 1 Eliz. cap. 17. And by a grant made to the city of London, and confirmed by the parliament of 17 R. 2, cap. 9, the conservancy of the river of Thames from Stainsbridge down to Medway is granted to the mayor of London.

This office of conservancy is of two kinds, or rather there are or may be two branches thereof.

1st. The conservancy in order to nuisances in rivers. This is grounded upon the statute of 1 H. 4, cap. 12, whereby it is enacted, that there shall be commissions granted to survey and keep the waters and great rivers, and to correct and amend the defaults. And this for Thames is annexed to the mayor of London also by the statutes of 4 H. 7, cap. 15; 27 H. 8, cap. 18.

2d. The conservancy in order to fishing. And this is that which is mentioned in the statute of 1 Eliz. cap. 17. And this is grounded upon the stat. of Westminster 2, cap. 47, which enacted, That the waters of Humber, Owse, Trent, Dove, Aire, Darwent, Wherf, Nidd, Ore, Swale, Tese, Tyne, Eden, *et omnes aliæ aquæ in regno, in quibus salmones capiuntur, ponantur in defenso, &c. Et in partibus ubi hujusmodi ripariæ fuerint, assignentur conservatores istius statuti, qui ad hoc jurati sæpius videant et inquirant de hujusmodi transgressoribus. Et in primâ transgressione puniantur per combustionem retium, &c.* By the stat. 13 R. 2, cap. 19, the former statute is confirmed, and the river of Thames added; and the rivers of Lone, Wyre, Merse and Ribbell, and all other waters in the county of Lancaster be put in defence as to the taking of salmons, &c. and in parts where such rivers are, there shall be assigned and sworn good and sufficient conservators of this statute, as of the statute of Westminster.

But neither of these statutes extended to any rivers but such wherein salmon be. And inasmuch as such a commission could not be without the warrant of an act of parliament, as is observed truly by my Lord Coke upon the statute of Westminster 2, cap. 47, consequently their commission cannot extend further than that act warrants, viz. to none but to those that are particularly named, or at least wherein salmon are.

By the statute of 17 R. 2, cap. 9, the justices of the peace are appointed conservators of these statutes, except only as to the conservancy of the river of Thames and Medway annexed to the mayor of London.

By the stat. of 1 Eliz. cap. 17, there is a farther and more extensive provision against the destruction of other fish as well as salmon; and it limits, that the lord admiral, the mayor of London, lords of leets, &c. and all other persons, &c. which by grant or other lawful ways or means lawfully have the conservation or preservation of any rivers, shall have power within the precincts of their lawful jurisdiction to inquire of, by the oaths of twelve men, and to hear and determine such offences.

This indeed doth enlarge the power of these conservators in respect of the offences, but not in respect of the limit of their jurisdiction.

Upon all this it follows,

1st. That these commissioners of conservancy have no power in reference to fishing, but in such places where salmons are or the rivers mentioned in the acts, though in those rivers they have jurisdiction as to other fish as well as salmon; and that the conservators have no power except in reference to nuisances in common or public rivers, and not in private nuisances between party and party.

2d. Consequently, not in the small rivers that fall into those rivers; for such small rivers as they, are not named in the acts of Westminster 2, nor 13 R. 2, and they have not any salmons in them, and so not within their jurisdiction.

3d. But yet in those rivers particularly named in the statutes of Westminster 2, and 13 R. 2, or in such rivers where salmons are, they have power to inquire of all offences contrary to the statute of 1 Eliz. because committed within the precinct of their jurisdiction.

4th. But then they must not convict nor fine men barely upon a presentment without a tryall; for such conviction without tryall is against law in any case, but a leete or swanmote court.

And therefore all those offences that are against the statute of 1 Eliz. within small rivers, are only punishable by the leete, or by the justices of the peace at their sessions, who are general conservators by the statute of 17 R. 2, cap. 9, and not before these conservators by commission, except as to the offences in Thames, which are inquirable by the mayor of London.

And thus much by the way concerning conservatorships and water-baillies; and also concerning the right of fishing in the sea or arms thereof belonging to a subject, either by grant or prescription, either as a liberty or in respect of ownership of soil.

CAP. VI.

Concerning the ownership or propriety which a subject may have in the sea-shore and maritime increments, &c.

I COME now to those other parts of propriety which a subject may have by prescription or usage, viz. the sea-shore and maritime increases; which, though we have before stated to belong *primâ facie* to the king, yet they may belong to the subject in point of propriety, not only by charter or grant, whereof there can be but little doubt, but also by prescription or usage.

I. The shore of the sea.

There seem to be three sorts of shores, or *littora marina*, according to the various tides, viz.

(1st.) The high spring tides, which are the fluxes of the sea at those tides that happen at the two equinoxials; and certainly this doth not *de jure communi* belong to the crown. For such spring tides many times overflow ancient meadows and salt marshes, which yet unquestionably belong to the subject. And this is admitted of all hands.

(2d.) The spring tides, which happen twice every month at full and change of the moon; and the shore in question is by some opinion not denominated by these tides neither, but the lands overflowed with these fluxes ordinarily belong to the subject *primâ facie*, unless the king hath a prescription to the contrary. And the reason seems to be, because for the most part the lands covered with these fluxes are dry and mainorable; for at other tides the sea doth not cover them; and therefore touching these shores some hold, that common right speaks for the subject, unless there be an usage to entitle the crown; for this is not properly *littus maris*. And therefore it hath been held, that where the king makes his title to land as *littus maris*, or *parcella littoris marini*, it is not sufficient for him to make it appear to be overflowed at spring tides of this kind. *P.* 8 *Car.* 1, *in Camerâ Scaccarii*, in the case of Vanhesdanke for lands in Norfolk; and so I have heard it was held, *P.* 15 *Car.* 1 *B. R. Sir Edw. Heron's case, &* *Tr.* 17 *Car.* 2, in the case of the lady Wandesford, for a town Ante, p. 317. called the Cowes in the Isle of Wight, *in Scaccario*.

(3d.) Ordinary tides, or nepe tides, which happen between the full and change of the moon; and this is that which is properly *littus maris*, sometimes called *marettum*, sometimes *warettum*. And touching this kind of shore, viz. that which is covered by the ordinary flux of the sea, is the business of our present enquiry.

1st. This may belong to a subject. The statute of 7 Jac. 1 cap. 18, supposeth it; for it provides, that those of Cornwall and Devon may fetch sea-sand for the bettering of their lands and shall not be hindered by those that have their lands adjoining to the sea-coasts, which appears by the statute they could not formerly. *Vide Cartæ Antiquæ D. D. n.* 24, the charter of Alan de Percy to the monks Ante, p. 16. of Whitby, and the bounds thereof, viz. *totam marinam à portâ de Whitby usque Blowick, &c. et usque Terdiso, et usque in mare, et per marinam in Whitby*, confirmed by king Henry I. And the bounds of that abbey's possessions take in many creeks of the sea, yet are given by a subject, viz. Derwent, Muse, Esk, &c.

2d. It may not only belong to a subject in gross, which possibly may suppose a grant before time of memory, but it may be parcel of a manor. And thus it is agreed 5 Reports, 107, in Sir Henry Constable's case, and the book of 5 E. 3, 3, cited accordingly. And according to this was the resolution cited Dyer 316, to be between Ante, p. 219. Hammond and Digges, *P.* 17 *Eliz.* And accordingly it was decreed in the Exchequer-chamber, *P.* 16 *Car.* 1 *inter l'* Attorney General Ante, p. 309. *et* sir Samuel Roll, sir Richard Buller, and sir Thomas Arundell, *per omnes barones.* And the evidences to prove this fact are commonly these; constant and usual fetching gravel and sea-weed and sea-sand between the high-water and low-water mark, and licensing others so to do; inclosing and imbanking against the sea, and enjoyment of what is so inned; enjoyment of wrecks happening upon the sand; presentment and punishment of purprestures there in the court of a manor; and such like.

And as it may be parcel of a manor, so it may be parcel of a vill or parish; and the evidence for that will be usual, perambulations, common reputation, known metes and divisions, and the like. And upon this account the parson of Sutton about 14 Car. had a verdict for the tithes of Sutton-Marsh in Lincolnshire, upon a long and a great evidence; though it appeared, that within time of memory it was the mere shore of the sea covered at ordinary tides, and without the old sea-bank.

Ante, pp. 343, 344, 347, 352, 353, 355, 364, 365.

3d. It may not only be parcel of a manor, but *de facto* it many times is so; and perchance it is parcel almost of all such manors as by prescription have royal fish or wrecks of the sea within their manor. For, for the most part, wrecks and royal fish are not, nor indeed cannot be well left above the high-water mark, unless it be at such extraordinary tides as overflow the land: but these are perquisites, which happen between the high-water and low-water mark; for the sea withdrawing at the ebb leaves the wrecks upon the shore, and also those greater fish which come under the denomination of royal fish. He therefore that hath wreck of the sea or royal fish by prescription *infra manerium*, it is a great presumption, that the shore is part of the manor, as otherwise he could not have Ante, p. 149. them. And consonant to this is the pleading of Sir Henry Nevill's case, 5 E. 3, 3, and Rastall's Entries 634, transcribed out of the record *M.* 14 *E.* 1, *Rot.* 432, where an abbot, prescribing for wreck belonging to his manor, doth it in this form: *Ipseque et omnes prædecessores sui abbates monasterii prædicti et domini ejusdem*

Wrong reference given by Rastall.

manerii, per totum tempus prædictum, habuerunt, et habere consueverunt, ratione manerii prædicti, omnimoda bona wreccata super mare et ut wreccum super terram projecta per costeram maris in quodam loquo ubi mare secundùm cursum suum pro tempore fluxit et refluxit à quodam loco vocato M. in parochiâ de L. &c. And in the following plea, an abbot prescribes to have *wreccum maris infra præcinctum manerii sive dominii sui projectum et flotesan maris infra præcinctum manerii deveniens, quòdque prædictum dolium vini fuit wreccum maris per mare projectum super littus maris apud S. infra præcinctum manerii sive dominii illius.*

And with this agrees the Register 102. Yet I find the earl of Cornwall had *wreccum maris per comitatum Cornubiæ;* and thereupon being questioned for wreck, adjudged, *quòd eat sine die. P.* 14 *E.* 1, *minus B. R. Rot.* 6, *Cornubia.* But that was in a contest between the king and him; for possibly the inferior lords might have it by usage against the earl. Ante, p. 94.

Thus much shall suffice concerning the shore or space between the high-water and low-water mark, which may belong to a subject and be parcel of his manor.

II. Let us now come to the *maritima incrementa*, viz.

Alluvio maris;
Recessus maris; et
Insula maris.

(1st.) For the *jus alluvionis*, which is an increase of the land abjoining by the projection of the sea casting up and adding sand and slubb to the adjoining land, whereby it is increased, and for the most part by insensible degrees, Bracton, *lib.* 2, *cap.* 2, writes thus: *Item quod per alluvionem agro tuo flumen adjecit, jure gentium tibi acquiritur. Est autem alluvio latens incrementum. Et per alluvionem adjici dicitur, quod ita paulatim adjicitur, quòd intelligere non possis quo momento temporis adjiciatur, &c. Si autem non sit latens incrementum, contrarium erit, ut ecce vis fluminis partem aliquam ex tuo prædio detraxit, et vicini prædio appulit, certum est eam tuam permanere, &c.* But Bracton follows the civil law in this and some other following places. And yet even according to this, the common law doth regularly hold at this day between party and party. But it is doubted in case of an arm of the sea, 22 Ass. 93.

This *jus alluvionis*, as I have before said, is *de jure communi* by the law of England the king's, viz. if by any marks or measures it can be known what is so gained; for if the gain be so insensible and indiscernible by any limits or marks that it cannot be known, *idem est non esse et non apparere*, as well in maritime increases as in the increases by inland rivers.

But yet custom may in this case give this *jus alluvionis* to the land whereunto it accrues.

This is made out very plainly by these ensuing records.

Ante, p. 158. *Communia Trin.* 43 *E.* 3, *Rot.* 13, *in Scaccario*, which is that very record which is cited by Dyer 326, out of the book of Ramsey.—Process went out against the abbot of Ramsey *ad ostendendam causam, quare* 60 *acræ marisci in manum regis non debent sesiri, quas abbas appropriavit sibi et domui suæ sine licentiâ regis, super quâdam generali commissione de terris à rege concelatis et detentis. Abbas respondit, quòd ipse tenet manerium de Brancaster, quod scituatum est juxta mare, et quod est ibidem quidam mariscus, qui aliquando per influxus maris minoratur, aliquando per defluxus maris augetur, absque hoc quòd appropriavit sibi prout per præsentationem prædictum supponitur.* And issue joined and verdict given for the abbot by *Nisi prius* before one of the barons. *Et judicium quòd eat sine die, salvo semper jure regis.*

Though there were a verdict upon the issue, whether *appropriavit* or not, yet it is plain, that the title stood upon that which the abbot alledged by way of increment. And note, here is no custom at all alledged; but it seems he relied upon the common right of his case, that as he suffered the loss so he should enjoy the benefit, even by the bare common law in case of alluvion.

Ante, p. 351. *M.* 23 *E.* 3, *B. R. Rot.* 26, *Lincolnia.*—The abbot of Peterborough was questioned at the king's suit for acquiring from Nicholas de Rey 30 *acras marisci in Gosberkirke licentiâ regis non obtentâ.* The abbot pleaded, *quòd consuetudo patriæ est et à tempore quo, memoria non extitit quòd omnes et singuli domini, maneria terras seu tenementa super costeram maris habentes, particulariter habebunt marettum et sabulonem per fluxus et refluxus maris secundùm majus et minus prope tenementa sua projecta. Et sic dicit, quòd ipse habet quoddam manerium in eâdem villâ de Gosberkirke, unde plures terræ ejusdem manerii sunt adjacentes costeræ maris, et sic habet ipse per fluxus et refluxus maris circiter* 600 *acras maretti terras suas adjacentes, et per temporis incrementum secundùm patriæ consuetudinem de antiquo; et absque hoc quòd ipse aliquem marrettum de prædicto Nicholao perquisivit, &c.* And upon issue joined, it depended many years before the issue was tried. But afterwards, *P.* 41 *E.* 3, *B. R. Rot.* 28, *Lincolnia, Rex* viz. verdict and judgment was given, *quòd, secundùm consuetudinem patriæ, domini maneriorum prope mare adjacentium, habebunt marettum et sabulonem per fluxus et refluxus maris per temporis incrementum ad terras suas costeræ maris adjacentes projecta, &c. Ideo abbas sine die.*

Observe,

1st. Here is custom laid, and he relies not barely upon the case without it.

2d. In this case it was *per incrementum temporis* and *per mare projecta.* It is not a sudden reliction or *recessus maris,* as I shall have occasion to mention hereafter. And though there is no *alluvio* without some kind of reliction, for the sea shuts out itself; yet the denomination is taken from that which predominates. It is an acquest *per projectionem* or *alluvionem,* not *per recessum* or *relictionem.*

3d. That such an acquisition lies in custom and prescription; and it hath a reasonable intendment, because these secret and gradual increases of the land adjoining *cedunt solo tanquam majus principali;* and so by custom it becomes as a perquisite to the land, as it doth in all cases of this nature by the civil law.

(2d.) Now as touching the accession of land *per recessum maris,* or a sudden retreat of the sea, such there have been in many ages. Sometimes the ocean, especially the narrow sea lying between us and France and the Netherlands, leaves the English shore in a great considerable measure; possibly by reason of some superundation on the other eastern shore, or by some other reason we know not.

This accession of land, in this eminent and sudden manner by the recess of the sea, doth not come under the former title of *alluvio,* or increase *per projectionem;* and therefore, if an information of intrusion be laid for so much land relict *per mare,* it is no good defence against the king to make title *per consuetudinem patriæ* to the *marettum,* or *sabulonem per mare projectum;* for it is an acquest of another nature. And this was accordingly adjudged, *H.* 12 *Car.* 1 *Rot.* 48, in the case of the king against Oldsworth and others for Sutton Marsh, *in Scaccario.* And in that case it was likewise held and adjudged, that lands acquired *per relictionem maris* are not prescribable, as part of a manor or as belonging to

Ante, p. 292.

the subject; for that were to prescribe, in effect, that the narrow seas to the coasts of France or Denmark were part of a manor. In that case the information plea and judgment were in substance as followeth, viz.

Quod cùm 7000 *acræ marisci salsi vocati Sutton Marsh, jacentes et existentes juxta Sutton Long in comitatu prædicto, videlicet, inter Sutton Long et mare ad refluxum ejusdem, fuissent parcella littoris marini, ac ad refluxus maris naturalis et ordinarios aquis salsis et marinis inundatæ: cùmque eædem* 7000 *acræ marisci salsi nuper à mari, unde inundatæ fuissent, fuissent relictæ.* Then the information sets forth a grant by king James under the great seal to Peter Ashton and others, and a regrant by them by deed inrolled to the king, and that Michael Oldsworth, &c. intruded. The defendant Oldsworth came in; and as to part pleaded as tenant, viz. *quòd bene et verum est, quòd prædictæ* 7000 *acræ marisci salsi vocati Sutton Marsh, jacentes et existentes juxta Sutton Long, viz. inter Sutton Long et mare ad refluxum ejusdem, fuerunt parcella littoris marini, et ad refluxus maris naturales et ordinarios aquis salsis inundatæ et à mari relictæ prout per informationem.* But he further saith, the king was seized in right of the duchy of the manor of Sutton, *et quòd plures terræ dicti manerii ante relictionem dictæ costeræ maris adjacebant; et quod consuetudo patriæ est et à tempore quo, &c. quòd domini maneriorum, terrarum, seu tenementorum super costeram maris adjacentium, particulariter habebunt marettum et sabulonem per fluxum et refluxum maris secundùm majus et minus prope terras seu tenementa sua projectum sive relictum: quodque et prædictæ* 7000 *acræ marisci salsi ad terram prædictam parcellam manerii de Sutton adjacent, et per fluxus et refluxus maris relictæ fuerunt à mari, et projectæ ad terram prædictam parcellam manerii de Sutton prædicti, ratione cujus relictionis prædictæ dominus rex fuit seisitus, &c. de prædictis* 7000 *acris in jure ducatûs, &c.* And then he entitles himself by a grant under the duchy seal, and traverseth what he had not confessed. Upon this there was a demurrer and judgment for the king, upon solemn argument; and principally upon this reason, that custom cannot entitle the subject to relicted lands, or make it part of a manor: and it differed from the case of the abbot of Peterborough before cited; for there it was only *project*, but here *relict* is added to the plea, that it might answer the information; though the plea in the abbot of Peterborough's case was the precedent by which the plea was drawn, and with which it agreed, saving that addition of *relict*.

And yet the true reason of it is, because the soil under the water must needs be of the same propriety as it is when it is covered with water. If the soil of the sea, while it is covered with water, be the king's, it cannot become the subject's because the water hath left it. But in the case of *alluvio maris*, it is otherwise; because the accession and addition of the land by the sea to the dry land gradually is a kind of perquisite, and an accession to the land; and therefore, in case of private rivers, it seems by the very course of the common law, such a gradual increase *cedit solo adjacenti*; and though it may be doubtful whether it be so *ex jure communi* in case of the king, yet doubtless it gives a reasonableness and facility for such right of *alluvio* to be acquired by custom; for though in every acquest *per alluvionem* there be a reliction or rather exclusion of the sea, yet it is not a recess of the sea, nor properly a reliction. Cf. pp. 363, 400.

But this is to be carried along with us in the case of *recessus* or *relictio maris vel brachii ejusdem*; that where the land, as it stood covered with water, did by particular usage or prescription belong to a subject, there the *recessus maris*, so far as the subject's particular interest went while it was covered with water, so far the *recessus maris vel brachii ejusdem* belongs to the same subject. Cf. ante, p. 366.

The king of England hath the propriety as well as the jurisdiction of the narrow seas; for he is in a capacity of acquiring the narrow and adjacent sea to his dominion by a kind of possession which is not compatible to a subject; and accordingly regularly the king hath that propriety in the sea: but a subject hath not nor indeed cannot have that property in the sea, through a whole tract of it, that the king hath; because without a regular power he cannot possibly possess it. But though a subject cannot acquire the interest of the narrow seas, yet he may by usage and prescription acquire an interest in so much of the sea as he may reasonably possess, viz. of a *districtus maris*, a place in the sea between such points, or a particular part contiguous to the shore, or of a port or creek or arm of the sea. These may be prescribed by a subject because they may be possessed by a subject, and prescribed in point of interest both of the water, and the soil itself covered with the water within such a precinct; for these are mainorable, and may be entirely possessed by a subject.

The civilians tell us truly, *nihil præscribitur nisi quod possidetur*. The king may prescribe the propriety of the narrow seas, because he may possess them by his navies and power. A subject cannot. But a subject may possess a navigable river, or creek or arm of the sea; because these may lie within the extent of his possession and acquest.

The consequence of this is; that the soil relinquished by such arms of the sea, ports, or creeks; nay, though they should be wholly dried or stopped up; yet such soil would belong to the owner or proprietor of that arm of the sea, or river, or creek: for here is not any new acquest by the reliction; but the soil covered with water was the subject's before, and also the water itself that covered it; and it is so now that it is dried up, or hath relinquished his channel or part of it.

And such an acquest of a propriety in an arm or creek of the sea may be as well within the precinct of a port, as without; and that, though the king or some other subject hath the port in point of franchise or privilege. For though the soil of all creeks and navigable rivers, especially within ports, do *primâ facie* belong to the king in point of propriety as well as in point of franchise, yet the subject may have so great and clear a possession of the soil lying under the water of that port, that it may belong to a subject in point of interest or propriety of the soil, though he have or have not the port in point of franchise: and consequently, if the sea should relinquish the channel or creek or arm of the sea within such a port, it might and would belong to that subject, that had the propriety of the soil and water before it were so relicted.

And this is an exception out of that generality, possibly, that *terræ relictæ per mare* may not be prescribed. But a certain creek, arm of the sea, or *districtus maris*, may be prescribed in point of interest; and, by way of consequence or concomitance, the land relicted there, according to the extent of such a precinct as was so prescribed, will belong to the former owner of such *districtus maris*. But otherwise it would be, if such prescription before the reliction extended only to a liberty, or *profit à prendre*, or jurisdiction only within that precinct; as liberty of free fishing, admiral jurisdiction, or the jurisdiction of a leet or hundred or other court; for such may extend to an arm of the sea, as appears by 8 E. 2, *Corone;* for these are not any acquests of the interest of the water and soil, but leave it as it found it.

Therefore the discovery of the extent of the prescription or usage, whether it extend to the soil or not, rests upon such evidences of fact as may justly satisfy the court and jury concerning the interest of the soil.

That which I have to say concerning creeks or havens or arms of the sea, and the propriety of them, will be contained in these following assertions.

1st. That a subject may, by usage or prescription, be owner or proprietor of such an arm of the sea, creek, or particular portion of the sea contiguous to the shore, as is not a public port or haven; and consequently, if that part be left dry *per recessum vel obstructionem maris*, that will belong to that subject, that had that antecedent propriety when it was covered with water.

This will appear by the review of those cases that are in the precedent chapter concerning the right of fishing in the sea, many of which instances make it appear, that there may be a right of propriety in the soil *aquâ coopertâ*, and the right of fishing resulting not as a *profit à prendre*, but upon the very right of the soil itself. And those instances, that follow in this chapter, will farther make out the propriety of the soil of such places as these compatible to a subject.

2d. That a subject having a port of the sea may have, and indeed in common experience and presumption hath, the very soil covered with the water; for though it is true, the franchise of a port is a differing thing from the propriety of the soil of a port, and so the franchise of a port may be in a subject, and the propriety of the soil may be in the king or in some other, yet in ordinary usage and presumption they go together.

If the king at this day grant *portum maris de S.* the king having the port in point of interest as well as in point of franchise, it may be doubtful whether at this day it carries the soil, or only the franchise; because it is not to be taken by implication. But surely, if it were an ancient grant, and *usage had gone along with it*, that the grantee held also the soil, this grant might be effectual to pass both; for both are included in it.

And so if by prescription or custom a man hath *portum maris de S.* in ordinary presumption he hath not only the franchise, but the very water and soil within the port; for a *portus maris* is *quid aggregatum*, as a manor; and such a prescription may carry the soil as well as the franchise; and though this doth not always hold, yet most times it doth.

The Editor's experience does not confirm this.

Escaetria 12 *E.* 1, *n.* 1, *Portus et piscaria et mariscus de Topsham spectant ad Amiciam comitissam Devon.* She had not only the franchise of the port, but the soil of the port, and the fishing and salt-marsh adjoining. *Vide infra*, when we come to the right of ports.

And *vide infra, par.* 2, *cap.* 4, the case of the port of Plymouth, parcel of the manor of Trematon, wherein it will appear, that a subject, as he may be owner of a port in point of franchise, so he may be owner of the very soil of the haven in point of propriety. And see in the same chapter concerning the port of Poole. The earl of Surrey was owner of it in point of propriety as well as franchise, and had the anchorage of ships there, which seems to be ordinarily a perquisite in respect to the soil.

3d. That a man who is not owner of a port in point of franchise, but the franchise of the port belonging to the king, yet such a subject may by usage have the very propriety of a creek or arm of the sea parcel of that port, and of the soil thereof; and may have upon that account the increases of land that happen by the recess of the water of that arm of the sea.

Register, 252. The prior of Christ Church *Canturiæ* petitions the king, *quòd cùm quædam antiqua trenchea, quæ se ducit à brachio maris vocata A. versus villam de B. quæ est in solo ipsorum prioris et conventûs, per sabulones et arenam maris jam de novo taliter sit obstructa, quòd naves per trencheam illam usque ad dictam villam de B. venire nequeunt, ut solebant; et quædam alia trenchea, ducens ab eodem brachio maris usque ad eandem villam de B. jam vi maritimâ facta existit, per quam naves et batelli à mari usque ad villam illam commodè et sine impedimento poterunt transire.* An *ad quod damnum* issues to inquire, *si sit ad damnum vel præjudicium nostri aut aliorum, seu nocumentum dictæ villæ de B. si eis licentiam concedamus, quòd ipsi dictam antiquam trencheam omnino obstruere et commodum suum inde facere possint.*

Here the common passage for ships to a town admitted in point of propriety to belong to the prior, and that they may make profit of the soil being stopt up.

Ante, p. 306. *In Scaccario Car.* —— upon the prosecution of Sir Sackville Crow, there was an information against Mr. John Smith, farmer of the lord Barclay, setting forth, that the river of Severn was an arm of the sea, flowing and reflowing with salt water, and was part of the ports of Gloucester and Bristol, and that the river had left about 300 acres of ground near Slimbridge, and therefore they belonged to the king by his prerogative.

Upon not guilty pleaded, the tryall was at the exchequer bar, by a very substantial jury of gentry and others of great value.

Upon the evidence it did appear by unquestionable proof, that the Severn in the place in question was an arm of the sea, flowed and reflowed with salt water, was within and part of the ports of Bristol and Gloucester, and that within time of memory these were lands newly gained and inned from the Severn; and that the very channel of the river did within time of memory run in that very place where the land in question lies; and that the Severn had deserted it, and the channel did then run above a mile towards the west.

On the other side, the defendant claiming under the title of the lord Barclay alledged these matters, whereupon to ground his defence, viz.

1st. That the barons of Barclay were from the time of Henry the second owners of the great manor of Barclay.

2d. That the river of the Severn *usque filum aquæ* was time out of memory parcel of that manor.

3d. That by the constant custom of that country, the *filum aquæ* of the river of Severn was the common boundary of the manors on either side of the river.

When the state of the evidence was opened, it was insisted upon, that the river in question was an arm of the sea, a royal river, and a member of the king's port, and therefore lay not in prescription to be part of a manor. But the court overruled that exception; and admitted, that even such a river, though it be the king's in point of interest *primâ facie*, yet it may be by prescription and usage time out of mind parcel of a manor.

Thereupon the defendant went to his proofs, and insisted upon very many badges of property or ownership; as, namely,

That the lords of the manors adjacent to this river, and particularly those of that manor, had all royal fish taken within the river opposite to their manor *usque filum aquæ:*

That they had the sole right of salmon fishing:

That they had all wrecks cast between high-water and low-water mark:

That the lords of the manors adjacent had ancient rocks or fishing-places, and weares, or such as were of that nature, within the very channel:

That they had from time to time granted these fishing-places, some by lease, some by copy of court roll at their several manors, by the names of rocks, weares, staches, boraches, putts; and that they were constantly enjoyed, and rent paid by those copy-holders and lease-holders:

That by common tradition and reputation, the manors on either side Severn were bounded one against another by the *filum aquæ*, and divers ancient depositions produced, wherein it was accordingly sworn by very many ancient witnesses:

That the increases happening by the reliction of the river were constantly enjoyed by the lords adjacent.

evidences, MS. 97.

These and many other badges were opened, and were most effectually made good by most authentical evidences and witnesses. But before the defendant had gone through one-half of his evidence, the court and the king's attorney-general Sir John Banks, and the rest of the king's counsel, were so well satisfied with the defendant's title, that they moved the defendant to consent to withdraw a juror, which though he were very unwilling, yet at the earnest desire of the court and the king's counsel he did agree thereunto.

So that matter rested in peace, and the lands being of the yearly value of two hundred pounds and better, are enjoyed by the lord Barclay and his farmers quietly and without the least pretence of question to this day. This I know; for I was thoroughly acquainted with this case, and attended at the bar at the tryall.

This great and solemn tryall for the right of a royal river, in a port and part of it, doth fully prove that which I have to say touching this matter.

But though the subject may thus have the propriety of a navigable river part of a port, yet these cautions are to be added, viz.

1st. That the king hath yet a right of empire or government over it, in reference to the safety of the kingdom and to his customs, it being a member of a port, *prout inferiùs dicitur*.

2d. That the people have a publick interest, a *jus publicum*, of passage and repassage with their goods by water, and must not be obstructed by nuisances or impeached by exactions, as shall be shewn when we come to consider of ports. For the *jus privatum* of the owner or proprietor is charged with and subject to that *jus publicum* which belongs to the king's subjects; as the soil of an highway is, which though in point of property it may be a private man's freehold, yet it is charged with a publick interest of the people, which may not be prejudiced or damnified.

(3d.) As touching islands arising in the sea, or in the arms or creeks or havens thereof, the same rule holds, which is before observed touching acquests by the reliction or recess of the sea, or such arms or creeks thereof. Of common right and *primâ facie*, it is true, they belong to the crown, but where the interest of such *districtus maris*, or arm of the sea or creek or haven, doth in point of propriety belong to a subject, either by charter or prescription, the islands that happen within the precincts of such private propriety of a subject, will belong to the subject according to the limits and extents of such propriety. And therefore if the west side of such an arm of the sea belong to a manor of the west side, and an island happen to arise on the west side of the *filum aquæ* invironed with the water, the propriety of such island will entirely belong to the lord of that manor of the west side; and if the east side of such an arm of the sea belong to a manor of the east side *usque filum aquæ*, and an island happen between the east side of the river and the *filum aquæ*, it will belong to the lord on the east side; and if the *filum aquæ* divide itself, and one part take the east and the other the west, and leave an island in the middle between both the *fila*, the one half will belong to the one lord, and the other to the other. But this is to be understood of islands that are newly made; for if a part of an arm of the sea by a new recess from his ancient channel incompass the land of another man, his propriety continues unaltered. And with these diversities agrees the law at this day, and Bracton, *lib.* 2, *cap.* 2, and the very texts of the civil law. *Vide Digest, lib.* 41, *de acquirendo rerum dominio, legibus* 7, 12, 21, 29, 30, 38, 50, 56, 65, *et ibidem, lib.* 43, *tit.* 12, *de fluminibus, l.* 1, § 6. *Vide Bracton ubi supra. Habet etiam locum hæc species accessionis in insulâ natâ in flumine, quæ, si mediam partem fluminis teneat, communis eorum est, qui pro indiviso ab utrâque parte fluminis prope ripam prædia possident, &c.* For the propriety of such a new accrued island follows the propriety of the soil, before it came to be produced.

And thus much shall suffice to have been said concerning these *incrementa maritima*, and how they may in point of propriety belong to a subject. It remains, that a few words be said touching some other prerogatives, that have a cognation with this matter we are about, viz.

Wreck of the Sea; and
Royal Fishes;

which shall be the business of the next chapter.

CAP. VII.

Concerning the prerogative and franchise of wreck and its kinds, and royal fish.

As touching wreck of the sea, in the first place, it is sometimes called *wreccum maris*, sometimes *warettum*, which is sometimes in records applied to the accession of lands by alluvion. The record of the abbot of Peterborough, cited in the former chapter, is, *domini habuerunt warettum et sabulonem*. Though I have used the word *warettum*, in the old French it is called wreck, and sometimes *varech*.

The kinds of it are two, viz.

1st. Such as is called properly so, the goods cast upon the land or shore.

2d. Improper for goods that are a kind of sea-waifs or stray, *flotson*, *jetson*, and *lagon*.—Of both these briefly.

I. Touching wreck of the sea. It is not properly wreck, till it be cast upon the shore or land; and therefore by the statute of 15 R. 2, cap. 3, wreck of the sea is declared to be determinable by the laws of the land, and not before the admiral in any wise; and it was one of the articles anciently within the inquiry and jurisdiction of the coroner. *Vide* stat. 4 E. 1, *officium coronatoris*, viz. concerning wreck of the sea, wheresoever found; and if any lay hands on it he shall be attached by sufficient pledges, and the price of the wreck shall be valued and delivered to the towns. This power was annexed to the coroner by the statute of 3 E. 1, called Westminster 1. And therefore as long as the goods are floating upon the sea, they are not wreck; and according is the resolution 5 Reports, sir Henry Constable's case.

But all goods cast upon the shore are not therefore *ipso facto* wrecked so as to entitle the king or lord of a liberty to them; but it must have these qualities, viz.

1st. It must be such goods or ship that is wrecked or perished

at sea. For if the goods were taken by pirates, and then they come or be brought or left upon English ground by any means, they are not wreck to be forfeit, but provision is made for restitution to the merchant by the statute of 27 E. 3, cap. 13. And upon this account it seems, that resolution of the judges is grounded, which is cited in the comment upon Westminster 1, cap. 4, viz. that if enemies or pirates take a ship, and take out all the passengers and goods, and turn the hull to the sea, and it is cast upon the land, though no living thing come in her, she is not wrecked so as to give the forfeiture. Yet though the law may be such, the case, that is cited, warrants it not, which is *Clause* 5 *R.* 2, *m.* 24; for Ante.p.161.
there the mariners got all to land in Norfolk in the long-boat, and left the ship to the enemies, and so within the following rule.

2d. Though the ship or goods be wrecked and cast upon the shore, yet if any living thing escape alive to land out of the ship, it is not such a wreck as gives a forfeiture. And this was the ancient law before the statute of Westminster 1, cap. 4, as is resolved and made evident by the resolution of Constable's case, *ubi supra*, and the lord Coke's comment upon that statute; for though the common law give the king *bona wreccata*, as shall be shewn; yet, because it was *lex odiosa* to add affliction to the afflicted, it was bound up with as many limits and circumstances and to as narrow a compass as might be.

3d. That these goods be cast upon the shore or land, and not brought thither in a ship or vessel. *Vide inter placita* Gersey 2 et 3 E. 2. A ship was broken at sea; and the goods floating in the high sea, certain mariners took them up and put them on shipboard, and they came with their ship into the land of Geffry Carteret, who by charter had wreck of the sea; and before he seized, the vessel went to the shore of the abbot of Chirburgh, who had likewise wreck. The goods being seized by the king's officer, these two interpleaded for the goods as wreck.

Et Willielmus le Mareis, qui sequitur pro domino rege, dicit, quòd nullus eorum petere possit bona prædicta ut wreccum; quia dicit, quòd ea tantùmmodo sunt wreccum, quæ fluctus maris projiciunt ad terram, vel infra portum, aut tam prope terram, quòd a stantibus in terrâ possunt perpendi, et sic ducantur vel trahantur ad portum; sed quæ reperta sunt in alto mari, unde certum non existit, quòd fluctus maris ea vellent projicere, si non per laborem marinellorum levantium à mari, et ponantur in navi vel batello, et sic in vasi ducantur ad terram et non tangunt terram alicujus pertrahentium, nec alio modo non possunt dici wreccum, sed tantùmmodo de adventuris maris, de quibus nullus potest aliquid clamare, nisi salvatores et dominus rex, vel ille, cui rex concesserit libertatem percipiendi hujusmodi adventuras. Et petit judicium pro domino rege, et prædicti, &c. non dedicere possunt. Consideratum est, quòd prædicta vina remaneant domino regi, et prædicti Petrus et alij in misericordiâ pro falso clamore. Postea prædicta vina de prædictis doliis concessa sunt prædicto priori pro 60s. de quibus solvit prædictis salvatoribus 40s. pro parte suâ, et de 20s. residuis respondet regi.

This, though it were a proceeding in Gersey, who were heretofore and yet are guided by the customs of Normandy, yet even, these customs as to the point of wreck are very near if not altogether the same with those of England, as appears by the 17th chapter of the *Grand Custumier, de Varech.* And this resolution above cited is consonant to that of sir Henry Constable's case, 5 Reports, though differing in terms and names.

And thus much of the nature of wreck, and this by the laws of England is forfeit; and the propriety of the first owner is, by the seizure of the king, or his officer, or lord of the liberty having this franchise, wholly divested.

But if goods are cast upon the shore, though they have not all these properties, they may be seized by the king, or the lord that hath the liberty of wreck, and lawfully detained, till the right owner come and claim them, and make it appear that they are his; and the common law allowed him a year and a day for the making his claim. And therefore as to this also the statute of Westminster 1, cap. 4, was but an affirmance of the common law, as it seems; for the very same time is allowed for the claim of goods so seized by the *Custumier* of Normandy.

And the time, from whence the year and the day is to be accompted, is from the time of the seizure, as appears by the comment upon that statute; and if not claimed within that time, they were lost.

But if there were a seizure by persons that had no right to seize, the elapse of the year and the day, as it is conceived, did not bar the right owners.

The statute of the 27 Ed. 3, cap. 13, provides more expedition for the restitution of the merchant, where the goods are not lawful wreck; but it seems the generality of that statute takes not away the loss of the goods by non-claim by a year and day after seizure.

35 H. 6, 27. If goods of a common person be seized as wreck, if he claim not in a year and day, they are lost; but if the king's goods were wrecked, he need not claim.

And *nota*, this claim is available only where the goods are cast upon the shore, but they are not a legal wreck, as perchance some living thing escaped to the land. But where the goods are a legal wreck, this claim signifies nothing; for the goods are *ipso facto* forfeit by being wreck and seized; for the provision of the statute of 3 E. 1 as to the claim and proof within the year and day refers only to such goods as are cast upon the shore, but are not lawful wreck.

But yet in such case, where the goods are not wreck in law, the merchant must allow salvage, or the charge that the taker up of the goods is at for their saving. *Pat.* 14 *E.* 4, *m.* 12 *dorso.*

Thus much for the nature of wreck. Now concerning the propriety of it.

The statute of *Prerogativa Regis*, cap. 11, tells us to whom wreck doth of common right belong in England. *Rex habebit wreccum maris per totum regnum, balenas et sturgiones captas in mari vel alibi infra regnum, exceptis quibusdam privilegiatis locis per regem.*

This was the common law before this statute; and this statute as to this point, and most if not all other points of prerogative in that statute called *Prerogativa Regis*, is but declarative of the common law, and rather a repetition or collection of the king's prerogatives than any enacting law.

And the same was the prerogative of the duchy of Normandy, as appears in the *Grand Custumier, cap. de Varech.*

See Spelman *in Glossario*, title *wreck*, several charters mentioned by king William the first, yea and by Edward the Confessor, of *wreck* and *jactura maris.*

King R. 1 in the second year of his reign released wreck through all England, as the same author cites it out of Hoveden. But his successors resumed the prerogative again, and that before the statute of 17 E. 2, called *Prerogativa Regis;* and frequent instances thereof are long before that statute in the times of E. 1, H. 3, and king John.

But though wreck of the sea doth *de jure communi* belong to the king, yet it may belong to a subject.

1st. By charter; and this is without question.

2d. By prescription; and although this was doubted in the time of Bracton, yet the law is settled and unquestionable at this day.

Ante, p. 77, Hale is wrong in his topography. He gives the reference to the roll as "Essex."

Sometime wreck hath belonged to an honour by prescription; as to the honour of Arundel, though the *caput baroniæ* were in the county of Sussex; being another county from the place where the wreck arose. *T.* 9 *E.* 1, *B. R. Rot.* 20, *Sussex.*

Sometime to the owner of a county. The lords of all counties palatines regularly had *wreccum maris* within their counties palatines, as part of their *jura regalia.* But yet inferior lords might prescribe for wreck belonging to their several manors within a county palatine. The earl of Cornwall, which though it were not a county palatine it had many royalties belonging to it, had *wreccum maris per totum comitatum Cornubiæ,* viz. as against the king, though particular lords might prescribe for it against the earl. *P.* 14 *E.* 1, *B. R. Rot.* 6 & 29, *Cornubiæ.*

Ante, pp. 94, 364.

And thus much concerning wreck, and the right of it.

II. Somewhat is fit to be mentioned concerning *flotson, jetson,* and *lagon.*

These are not wreck of the sea, but of another nature; neither do they pass by the grant of *wreccum maris,* as is resolved in that case of sir Henry Constable, and the case of the 3 E. 2, where they are stiled *adventuræ maris.*

And as they are of another nature, so they are of another cognizance or jurisdiction, viz. the admiral jurisdiction.

The right of flotson, jetson, and lagon, and other sea-estrayes, if they are taken up in the wide ocean, they belong to the taker of them, if the owner cannot be known.

But if they be taken up within the narrow seas, that do belong to the king, or in any haven port or creek or arm of the sea, they do *primâ facie* and of common right belong to the king, in case where the ship perisheth, or the owner cannot be known; which is also one of the resolutions of sir Henry Constable's case. But if the owner can be known, he ought to have his goods again; for the casting them overboard is not a loss of his propriety.

Although the right of these adventures of the sea within the king's seas belongs to him, where the owner cannot be known, yet the king hath little advantage of it; for by the custom of the English seas, the one moiety of what is so gained belongs to him that saves it. And accordingly the custom is recited in a letter by the king of England to the French king, *Claus.* 7 *E.* 3, *parte* 1, *membrana* 23 *dorso*, to satisfy him of the usage, that if the merchant's goods, that are floating in the sea, be saved, though the merchant made out his property, yet the goods were usually divided, the one moiety to the merchant, and the other moiety to them that save them for salvage. But it seems by the statute of 27 E. 3, cap. 13, that hard custom was mitigated as to the merchant; and a reasonable amends allowed for salvage, according to the expence pains or adventure of them that saved it. But whether anything hath altered that custom as to the king, I find not.

The other moiety of these *bona vacantia* taken upon the narrow seas was anciently, and I think at this day, taken by the admiral as his fee; which yet he takes in *jure regis.*

And this appears by the old articles of the admiralty entered in the black book of that court, wherein, though there be many extravagant articles, that no way belong to their jurisdiction, yet those that concern these things in question are good evidence what the usage was.

Among which this was one: *Item soit inquise de touts neifes vesseux et bateux, que sont troves waife sur le mere, dont l'admiral ne ad sa part à lui due d'office, c'est à dire la moiety.*

And again: *Item soit inquise de touts ceux, que ont trove sur le mere flotesan tonne ou pipe de vyne ou doyle ou bales de madder drape coffres ou autres choses dont l'admiral ne ad sa part à lui due d'office.*

And thus much for the *jus commune* of these *adventuræ maris.*

But yet a subject may be entitled to these, as he may be entitled to wreck, viz.

1st. By charter.

2d. By prescription. And that is agred in that case of sir Henry Constable, viz. that a man may have flotson, &c. by prescription between the high-water and low-water mark. Some of the west country prescribe to have it as far as they can see a Humber barrell. And much more may be had by prescription in an arm of the sea; and accordingly the barons of Barclay have ever had it in the river Severn, of the east side of the *filum aquæ*, over against their barony of Barclay.

These liberties of wreck, flotson, jetson, and lagon, and that also of royal fish, may be parcel of or belonging to an hundred. But enough of this.

Now touching royal fish, therefore called so, because of common right such fish, if taken within the seas parcel of the dominion and crown of England, or in any creeks or arms thereof, they belong to the crown; but if taken in the wide sea, or out of the precinct of the seas belonging to the crown of England, they belong to the taker. 39 E. 3, 35, *per* Belknap.

Touching the kind of these fishes that are called royal fish, there seem to be but three, viz. sturgeon, porpoise, and *balæna*, Ante, p. 160. which is usually rendered a whale. *Claus.* 5 *R.* 2, *m.* 29, *de pisce vocato* whale *jam noviter ad terram in solo prioris de Merse alienigenæ in manu regis existente ad opus regis deferendo.*

But because they may be great fish that come under no known denomination, we find the claim of such under the name of *piscis regius*, or sometime *grand pisce*, without any certain denomination. *Vide Claus.* 20 *H.* 3, *m.* 3 *dorso.* A controversy between the king's bailiff and the prior of St. Swithen *de quôdam pisce regio* claimed by each without any distinct name. The prior procures the king's bailiff to be thereupon excommunicated, and the king commands his absolution. But salmon or lamprey are not royal fish.

By the common right of the king's prerogative these belong to the king, if taken within his seas or the arms thereof.

Ante, pp. 81, 82, 83. Anciently the entire sturgeon belonged not to the king; but only the head and the tail of the whale, according to Bracton, cited by Stamford upon this chapter of the prerogative.

According to the custom used in the admiralty, these great fish, if taken in the salt water within the king's seas, they were divided, and a moiety was allowed to the taker, the other moiety to the admiral in right of the king: one of the articles of the admiralty above cited being, *Item soit enquise de ceux, que ont prise ou trove sur le mere whales, balens, sturgeon, porpoise, ou grampise, dont l'admiral n'a sa part pur le roy, c'est à scavoire la moitie.*

Where observe these two things:

1st. That these royal fish extended to other than whale and sturgeon, viz. to porpoise, and *grampise*, or great fish.

2d. The admiral is to be answered for the king the moiety, which seems to expound Bracton as to the division of the whale. The king had the head, and the queen the tail, which countervailed a moiety; and the taker had the body, which countervailed the other moiety.

Thus much for the right of the king to these royal fish.

A subject might and may unquestionably have this franchise or royal perquisite.

1st. By grant.

2d. By prescription within the shore between the high-water and low-water mark, or in a certain distinct *districtus maris*, or in a port or creek or arm of the sea; and this may be had in gross, or as appurtenant to an honour manor or hundred, as appears by infinite precedents and examples and books of the law.

And this shall suffice concerning the rights of the sea and the creeks thereof according to the laws of England, as far forth as it is necessary to be known in order to what follows, viz. the havens ports and creeks of the sea within the dominion of the crown of England, which shall be the business of the second part of this discourse, as a necessary *præcognitum* to the customs and right thereof according to the laws of Eng.and.

The following note by Francis Hargrave is prefixed to the "*De* "*Jure Maris et Brachiorum ejusdem*," first printed in Hargrave's Collection of Law Tracts, 1787.

[The manuscript, from which this treatise is printed (MS. Hargrave, No. 97), was part of the valuable present to the editor from GEORGE HARDINGE, Esquire, Sollicitor-General to the Queen; for which acknowledgement is made in the preface to this volume. There cannot be the least doubt of its being written by lord chief-justice HALE; though it is not in his hand-writing, but appears to be a fair copy by some transcriber. The contents agree with the article No. 20 and 21 in the list of lord chief-justice HALE's manuscripts at the end of his life by bishop BURNET.]

CHAPTER XVI.

A.D. 1666 TO THE END OF THE REIGN OF CHARLES II.

Poulson's Hist. of Holderness, ii. 464.

ABOUT the year 1666 a large island, afterwards known as Sunk Island, arose on the north side of the River Humber, and was leased on 18 December 1688 to Anthony Gilby, being described as containing 3500 acres of drowned ground. It was an unquestioned island, severed from the main land by a low-water channel, and has been gradually inclosed and embanked, and the accretions to it between the island and the shore added to it by process of time have now extended and been inclosed until it is annexed to the main land. It is a clear instance of the unquestioned right of the Crown to islands rising in the sea. The subsequent history of the gradual inclosure of the island under leases from the Crown down to 1802 is set out in the 2nd Report of the Surveyor-General of the Land Revenue, p. 62. The island was still an island in 1841, for, on the renewal of divers leases of parts of it in that year, the lessees were bound to contribute to the cost of cleansing the *north channel* there, which cut it off from the main land. See plan shewing north channel in the Commissioner of Woods' Report, xxv. 50. See also the twenty-eighth Report, p. 6.

Report of the Surveyor-General, 1797-1809, Inner Temple Library.

Com. of Woods' Rep. xix. 24.

2 Keble 294.

In Michaelmas, 19 Charles II., A.D. 1667, in the case of Kirby dem. Killigrew and Prodger *v.* Gibbs, on a trial at bar in the King's Bench, the Court agreed that the lord may have lands between high and low water mark as belonging to his manor by grant or prescription, but by common intendment in a royal river it belongs to the King till the contrary appear, but by grant of lands by particular names, as Lady Croft, &c., such lands will not pass without shewing *such profits as were proper to be taken thereof* were taken by the grantee. These cases related to shore at Bermondsey. The report has this note:—The high-water mark is as far as is overflowed *by neape or ordinary tides.* Killigrew, who was a title-hunter by profession, was the lessee from the Crown of encroachments made upon the Thames in the parishes of Redriff and St. Mary Magdalene, Surrey. He assigned his lease to Prodger, who applied for a renewal of it in 1684. It would appear from the report that the defendant claimed merely as a freeholder and frontager, and not under any lord of a manor.

In May 1666 the King granted to the governors of Sutton Hospital Mersea fleet and Great Ditch, Middle Ditch, and Poldam, otherwise Thornhill Fleet, in Essex. Signet Books, May 1666.

In 1669 the Earl of Bath and others petitioned the King for a grant of all lands overflowed by the sea in the counties of Denbigh and Flint, with all mines and minerals which shall be found there; and in the same year Lady Dacre petitioned for a lease of the marsh lands of Pevensey. Home Office Entry Book, 33, p. 17. Ibid. 91.

On 24 March, 21 Charles II., the King granted to Sir John Lowther, Bart., 150 acres of land between high and low water mark near Whitehaven, in Cumberland.

In Easter, 23 Charles II., A.D. 1671, in the case of Whitaker *v.* Wise and Lady Newburgh, ejectment was brought under a lease granted to the Duke of Richmond of Sutton Marsh, in Lincolnshire. The plaintiff claimed by a grant under the Great Seal of derelict land; the defendant, under a grant under the Duchy Seal as parcel of the manor of Sutton, the land being within high and low water mark. Sir Henry Constable's case was cited, but Moreton, J., said that in Trinity, 6 Charles I., in the Exchequer, between the Earl of Carlisle and Stepkins, it was adjudged, contrary to Sir Henry Constable's case, that such lands are in the Crown only. It was said by the plaintiff's counsel, and agreed by Twisden, J., that the Court inclined against a recovery and execution in a writ of intrusion, 21 Jac. I. cap. 14; the defendant could not

Whitaker *v.* Wise, 2 Keble 759, B. R.

This is a mistake for 8 Chas. I.: see ante, p. 260.

allege that these were not gained lands from the sea, and verdict for the plaintiff as *derelict* lands.

There appears to have been an attempt to get a new trial on the ground of the plaintiff having entertained and fed the jury; but, it being shewn that this took place after they were agreed, the application was refused. This case, so imperfectly reported, refers to the same lands as the case of Rex *v.* Oldsworth, *ante*, p. 292. The Crown, therefore, would not seem to have got possession after the decision of that case, and only seems to have got a verdict in this case upon the ruling of the judges that Sir Henry Constable's case was reversed in the case of Att. *v.* Philpott. Whether the Duke of Richmond ever got possession we know not.

2 Keble 767.

In Easter, 24 Charles II., A.D. 1672, the Attorney-General filed an information of intrusion against Palgrave and others for 500 acres of marsh called Kelling and Salthouse Marshes, Oby Marsh, Runham Marsh, East and West Summerton Marsh, Martham Marsh, and Repps Marsh, in the county of Norfolk, "all which marshes [the "Attorney alleges] were heretofore surrounded and over-"flowed with the sea water, and are now derelicted "grounds, and of late times recovered from the sea, and "lie between the ancient high and low water marks." The King had let them by Exchequer patent dated 20 March, 23 Charles II., A.D. 1670–71, to Sir John Poyntz, at whose relation the information was filed. One of the defendants, Clippesby Guyton, claims Oby Marsh as parcel of the manor of Oby. He sets out a sixty years' title, and cites the statute of 21 Jac. I. cap. 2, against pretences of concealment. This suit seems to have been dropped, as no order relating to it occurs in the Exchequer Order Books down to Easter, 27 Charles II., A.D. 1676.

Exch. B. & A., Norfolk, Chas. II. 218.

Exch. D. & O., 24 to 27 Chas. II.

In January 1674 the King made a grant to one James Herbert of the sole and several fishing and dredging, as well for oysters as other fishes, of what nature soever, within the great water, river, or arm of the sea called the East Grounds, lying, flowing, or extending into the several parishes of Milton, Iwade, Emley, Minster, Tongue, and

Pat. 26 Chas. II., p. 9, No. 12. Signet Index, Jan. 1674.

Eastchurch, or any of them, in the county of Kent or hundred of Milton, with prohibition to all others to fish therein. This grant includes the greater part, if not the whole, of the River Swale; and it appears by the case of Wenman *v.* Mackenzie that the fishery at Emley Island was parcel of the manor of Milton. 5 E. & B. 447; 3 Q. B. 1307.

In the same year there is a lease for sixty-one years to Edward Villiers and Richard Brett of the privilege of laying and keeping oysters in the channels, creeks, and oyster lanes belonging to the Lord High Admiral and Lord Warden of the Cinque Ports upon the coasts of Essex and Kent; but this lease has a laudable exception of all the rights and privileges of the lord or lords of any manor or manors adjacent to any of the said creeks or shores. Signet Index, Feb. 1674-5.

In Trinity, 28 Charles II., A.D. 1676, in the case of the Attorney-General against Sir Edward Farmer, King James I. granted to J. S. the manor of Holbeach, in Lincolnshire, and certain particular marsh lands bordering on the sea, and further granted him "all soil, ground, sand, "and marsh land contiguous to the premises now over-"flown, or which *hereafter* should be recovered from the "sea." After the grant, 100 acres became derelict; the question was whether they belonged to the King or the patentee. It was argued that the King should have it, because the King had not those 100 acres since become derelict, and that he could not grant that which was not in him to grant, and that the lands which the King has by his prerogative cannot pass by general words, but must be expressly named, and that the extent of land granted was indefinite. It was argued for the defendant that the soil of the sea was in the King, and that he could grant it, and that subjects are capable of holding a property in the sea. Levinz reports that Montague, C.B., with the advice of the Chief Justices of the King's Bench and Common Pleas, held that nothing passed by the general words, and the patent as to the 100 acres which became derelict after the grant was void; but it is to be observed that the argument that the King had not the land in him 2 Levinz 172; Sir T. Raymond 241; 2 Mod. 106.

to grant was untrue, for he has the soil of the sea by his prerogative, and may grant it to a subject.[1] In the report in Modern it is said that no judgment was given. It appears, however, that a case was agreed upon by counsel, but the judges disagreed and made no order, leaving the Attorney-General to proceed as he pleased. The three reports are very unsatisfactory, but it would seem that no real decision was come to on the point.

Exch. Decrees, series 4, xii. 373; 17 May, 29 Chas. II.

In 30 Charles II., A.D. 1678, a grant was made of all derelict lands near Bridgewater, Somersetshire.

Pat. 30 Chas. II., p. 31. Sp. Com. 6444.

In the same year Sir John Lowther having erected a quay at Whitehaven without the King's licence, it was ordered to be suppressed, and thereupon Lowther appears to have got a grant of 150 acres of land between high and low water mark near Whitehaven, with all the rocks thereupon, extending east to west 200 yards, and north to south about two miles.

Exch. Dec. Bk., T., 30 Chas. II., fo. 224b. Exch. Q. R. Memda., E., 31 Chas. II., rot. 102; T., 32 Chas. II., rot. 38. Signet Bks. 1678-79.

In January, 33 Charles II., A.D. 1681–82, the King granted to Samuel Keck and Robert Heiton all houses, docks, wharves, quays, and premises encroached, lying upon, and taken out of the north side of the River Thames in the parishes of St. Mary Matfellon, otherwise Whitechapel, Stepney, and St. Paul's Shadwell. This appears to be the same property as the subject of the case of Attorney *v.* Philpott, *ante*, p. 260, and this was probably an attempt to raise the question afresh.

Signet Bk., Jan. 1681-82.

In Hilary, 34 Charles II., A.D. 1682, the lord of the manor of Mitching, in Sussex, claimed to have the best anchor and cable out of any ship wrecked *super fundum et solum manerii* although the seamen were saved from the wreck; but it was held a void custom, as being without consideration. There was a similar claim in the manor of Birling, Sussex, in Trinity, 3 William and Mary: Simpson *v.* Bithwood.

3 Levinz 85, Geere *v.* Berkanshaw.

3 Levinz 308.

On 28 August, 36 Charles II., A.D. 1684, one Edward Progers, who had purchased a lease, granted to Sir Robert

S. P. Dom. Ent. Bk. 71, fo. 13.

1 Many cases shew that oyster grounds, which are below low-water mark, pass by grant: *ante*, pp. 154, 155, 156, 164. See case of Sutton Pool, *ante*, p. 314. Hale's first treatise, *ante*, pp. 343, 352.

Killigrew for forty-one years, of encroachments on the Thames in the parishes of Redriffe and St. Mary Magdalen, Surrey, petitioned for an additional term of thirty-two years to his lease. (See *ante*, Killigrew *v*. Gibbs, p. 414.)

Down to the end of the reign of Charles II. commissions were constantly issued to discover derelict lands, and, as we have seen, the King insisted on the right of the prerogative to the foreshore even to a greater extent than had been done by his father. The results of these many commissions and grants have not been discovered, but we find no trace of any decision in favour of the Crown, and it would seem that the grants were "fishing grants" of the same description as those described at p. 169, *ante*. We see that many persons admitted the claim of the Crown, or did not care to fight it; but we also find that it was resisted in most cases, and successfully resisted.

CHAPTER XVII.

THE REIGNS OF KING JAMES II. AND WILLIAM III.

IN the reign of James II. one is not surprised to find that the same exalted notion of the rights of the prerogative obtained. In June, 1 James II., A.D. 1685, the King made a grant to Henry Hillyard, Esq., of all those lands and grounds sometime heretofore derelict and left by the sea adjoining the manors and lordships of Marsh Chapel and Northcoats, Lincoln, commonly called the "Fifties "or Fitties," lying between the said lordships and the sea there at low water, at a rent of £5. This land was the subject of the suit of Rex *v.* Lord Yarborough in 1824, in which the Crown was defeated.

Signet Index, June 1685.

See also Exch. Dep., E., 11 Will. III. 22; T., 11 Will. III. 6.

In 1 James II., A.D. 1685, disputes arose between the Bishop of Durham and some of his tenants as to the right of the Bishop in respect of the palatinate to the foreshore of the Tees, Wear, Tyne, Blythe, Camois, and Holy Island.

Sir Thomas Haselrig, as owner of the monastery of Monk Wearmouth, Durham, claimed to be seised "of the "soil of the River Wear to the *filum aquæ* as far as his "land extended on the north side of the river, and to be "entitled to the priviledges of beaconage, anchorage, "plankage, and wharfage, and the laying of ballast on "the shore there for building quays for the better laying "of ships, vessels, and boats there;" but the Court of Exchequer held that the privileges of beaconage, anchorage, and plankage were privileges properly belonging to a royal port, and that Haselrig was incapacitated from holding the same, and his bill was dismissed as to them. With regard to wharfage and ballast shore, a trial was ordered—(1) As to whether the wharf in question was erected on the plaintiff's freehold; (2) As to how far the

Exch. Dep., M., 1 Jas. II. 37. Exch. Decrees, Hil., 2 Jas. II. 68b; T., 2 Jas. II. 95. Exch. Dep., T., 4 Jas. II. 14.

See Hale, ante, pp. 345, 346.

plaintiff's soil extended into the river; (3) Whether plaintiff and his predecessors had taken the ballast on the wharf in question time out of mind. A verdict was found that the soil did not extend to the *filum aquæ*, but only to the low-water mark; that the wharf was on the freehold of the plaintiff; and that he and his predecessors had been immemorially accustomed to take ballast there. Accordingly, it was decreed on 18 June 1688 that plaintiff should enjoy his soil and ground and wharf as his freehold, and might take ballast. A second trial was had, and a similar verdict returned, and final judgment was given on 12 November 1688 to the same effect as the former judgment.

In 2 James II., A.D. 1686, there was an information by the Attorney-General against Hugh Spicer and others respecting their rights in the port of Topsham and Exmouth Bar, Starcross, Dawlish, and Teignmouth, and the manor of Kenton, as to the right of the copyhold tenants of Kenton to dig ballast within the port. This suit dragged on to the publication of the depositions in Easter, 4 James II., A.D. 1688, after which it was dropped. The foreshore in the manor of Kenton and at Starcross belongs to the Earl of Devon. See case of the *Pauline*, *post*, p. 481.

Exch.Dep., E., 2 Jas. II. 30; E., 4 Jas. II. 33; T., 2 Jas. II. 9.

Exch. D. & O., E., 4 Jas. II., to Hil., 6 Will. III.

Exeter *v.* Devon, L.R. 10 Eq. 232.

An information was also filed against Rothwell and others concerning Friskney Marshes, Lincolnshire.

Exch. B. & A., Lincoln, Jas. II. 40.

In 3 James II., A.D. 1687, informations were filed against several persons for intrusions upon the shore of Rotherhithe.

Exch. Q. R. Infns., &c., Eliz. to Anne, portf. i. 455, 456, 457, 458.

In Hilary, 3–4 James II., A.D. 1687–88, informations were filed to recover derelict lands in the Isle of Grain; the manor of Gillingham, Kent; the Isle of Selsey, in Hampshire; lands at Deal claimed by the Archbishop of Canterbury; and at Wapping, Deptford, Bermondsey, and Rotherhithe.

Exch. Dep., Hil., 3-4 Jas. II. 22.

There was an information against Spooner and others for derelict lands in Friskney, Lincolnshire.

Exch. Dep. E., 4 Jas. II. 34.

In November, 4 James II., A.D. 1688, the King leased for thirty-one years, at a rent of twenty shillings, to William Smith the sole licence and privilege upon any soil belong-

1688. Signet Index, Nov. 1688.

ing to his Majesty between high and low water mark in England and Wales, except the county of Kent, to take any stones useful for making copperas, and to erect sheds for that purpose on the sands, shores, or waste grounds adjoining.

Throughout the reign commissions had been issued to all parts of the country to inquire concerning derelicted and concealed lands, and the last of them was a commission issued on 8 June, 4 James II., A.D. 1688, viz., about six months before the end of his reign, to Mark Ryder, Marmaduke Gibbs, and others, to inquire of derelict lands in Kent and Essex, being lands within sixty years last past uncovered by the water which ought to have come to the King in right of his crown of England, but are concealed, withdrawn, and unjustly detained. The commissioners proceeded to make the inquisition, but it appears that, instead of making it before a jury properly empanelled, they simply took the depositions of witnesses *ex parte* on behalf of the King, and made their return accordingly into the Exchequer. On the depositions of these witnesses, the commissioners return as belonging to the Crown the foreshore and fishery and reclaimed land in Deal Valley, numerous several fisheries in Hadley, Canvey Island, Hadley Creek, Bemfleet Ray, Pitsea Island Creek, Tottenham Creek, and the marshes in South Bemfleet, Leigh, Vange Hall, Foulness, and in particular they return 150 acres of marsh in the manor of Little Wakering and nine acres of marsh in Great Wakering. They say that Haven Gore Marsh was inned within five years; New England Marsh, in Little Wakering, within fifteen years; Keymarsh, Nasewick Marsh, and the Island of Foulness were then being embanked; that Yokfleet Creek, Waterfleet Creek, the Haven, and Layland Creek are fishing places. All these last-mentioned marshes and fisheries in Wakering and Foulness are parcels of the manors of Wakering and Foulness, and never belonged to the Crown; they are not claimed by the Crown at the present day, although the foreshore of the manors of Great and Little Wakering are at present in dispute in the case of Attorney *v.* Emerson,

Exch. Q. R. Memda., M., 4 Jas. II., rot. 79. Exch. Dep., Miscell., 695-700. Sp. Com. 6675. Petty Bag, Concealments, ble. 5, No. 3.

and it is admitted by the Crown that Yokfleet Creek, Waterfleet Creek, and the Haven are parcels of those manors.

A piece of land near Deal Castle, commonly called the sea valley or beach, containing by estimation twelve acres, lying between Deal Castle and Sandown Castle, having been returned by this inquisition, one George Watson obtained a grant of this land in March 1688–89, and in Trinity, 3 William and Mary, A.D. 1691, the Attorney-General, at the relation of Watson, filed an information against Richard Godkin and the Archbishop of Canterbury to recover the land. The defendants claimed part of the land as part of Chamberlain Fee, and the Archbishop claimed other part as part of the waste of the manors of Deal and Deal Prebend. The Archbishop in a demurrer says it was found by a former inquisition on 1 April, 14 Charles II., A.D. 1662, that the land in question belonged to the King, but that nothing was done under it; that in 4 James II., A.D. 1687, some person, desiring to obtain a grant, sued out another commission (that above described), and that the commissioners examined a few witnesses *ex parte* on behalf of the King, without any jury being empanelled to inquire concerning the said lands; but Watson got a grant, and the tenants of the lands, apprehending that they were likely to be disturbed in their possession, on 6 February, 1 William III., A.D. 1689–90, moved the Court of Chancery, and complained of the undue execution of the last commission, and prayed that it might be quashed. The relator appeared and defended the motion, but the Court declared that the execution and return of the said commission was unjust and illegal, and a great violation of the right of the subject, and a wrong to the said tenants, and ordered the said return to be damned, cancelled, and suppressed, and taken off the file. The inquisition, however, remains in the Exchequer Records, and is also enrolled on the Memoranda Roll.

Exch. B. & A., Kent, T., 3 Will. and Mary, 93. Exch. Dep., E., 6 Will. and Mary, No. 36.

The relator afterwards returned to the commission of 14 Charles II., and obtained a grant, dated 7 July, 2 William and Mary, A.D. 1690, of the land in question.

The Archbishop pleads the statute of 21 Jac. I. cap. 14, and says that the matter should be tried at common law.

Exch. Decrees Book, H., 6 Will. III., fo. 249.

The decree was made on 22 February, 6 William III., A.D. 1694–95. It appears that the case was referred to Sir John Somers, Lord Keeper; Sir John Holt, Chief Justice of the King's Bench; and Sir George Ireby, Chief Justice of the Common Pleas, who made their award in favour of the Archbishop: that the land was waste of the manors of Deal and Deal Prebend, and the King had no title to it, either on pretence of its being derelict or waste belonging to the Crown. The Attorney-General opposed the confirmation of the award because the Archbishop was dead, but the Court ordered its confirmation, and granted an injunction to quiet the possession.

It appears from the Signet Book of September 1691 that King James II. had granted to one Philip Ford all wrecks from Landguard Fort, near Harwich, to the North Foreland, and thence to the Scillies and round to Barnstaple Bar; and the same grant was made to Thomas Neale in September 1691, but this can only refer to floating wreck as Admiralty droits, unless it was intended to impeach the titles of the landowners to wreck.

Exch. Orders, 7 Will. III. 385.

In 7 William III., A.D. 1695, an injunction was granted to restrain the erection of a pier at Parton, near Whitehaven.

Sp. Com. 6775, 6872.

In 2 & 3 William and Mary, A.D. 1690, commissions were issued to inquire as to derelict lands near Plymouth, and on the coast of the Dee in the hundred of Wirrall, Chester.

Exch. B. & A., Ebor, Will. III. 111. Sp. Com. 6863. Exch. Dep., M., 7 Will. III. 33; M., 9 Will. III. 44. Petty Bag, Concealments, ble. 5, No. 3. Exch. Decrees Book, series 4, xvii. 148.

On 27 March 1696 an information was filed against Fairfax and others, tenants of the Bishop of Durham, for an intrusion into derelict lands adjoining the River Humber, in South Cave, Ellerker, and Brownfleet, Yorkshire, the lands having been left derelict by a change in the channel of the river. It was founded on the return to a commission in 2 William and Mary, A.D. 1690, that a quantity of land formerly overflowed by the sea had been left derelict by a change in the channel of the Humber. The Bishop claims the soil of the River Humber as parcel of the manor of Hoveden, and other defendants claim other parts as parcel of manors. A trial at bar was ordered in the case, when a verdict was returned for the defendants, but on 27 June, 12 William III., A.D. 1700, the information was dismissed with costs.

In 8 William III., A.D. 1696, commissions were issued to inquire into derelict lands at Lancing, Shoreham, Pevensey, Bexhill, and Newhaven, in the county of Sussex, and Horsey Island, Sidlesham, Pagham, Selsey, Fayley, Farlington, Porchester, Milford, Bewley, Hamble, Thorley, Isle of Kingston, Elinge, and Hayling Island, in the county of Southampton. Sp. Com. 6856. Exch.Q. R. Memda., H., 8 Will. III. 64. Sp. Com. 6847, 6848. Petty Bag Concealments, ble. 5, Nos. 4 and 5.

Upon one of these commissions, in February, 8 William III., A.D. 1696, a grant was made to Matthew Weston, of London, of derelict land in the parishes of Sidlesham, Selsey, and Pagham, in Sussex, and Hayling Island, in the parishes of Failey and Wymering, "all which "lands are left by the sea, and not in the possession of, "nor claimed nor owned by, any person or persons, but "do of right belong to the Crown, and were seized into "his Majesty's hand by virtue of a commission for that "purpose issued." Whether any attempt was made by the grantees to get possession we know not; but the same land appears to have been let again in 1805 and 1837, and was not then embanked. See *post*. Signet Office Docket, Feb. 1696

Commissions were also issued as to derelict lands and salt marshes at Gedney, in Lincolnshire. Petty Bag, Concealments, ble 5, No. 1.

This, so far as we can discover, was (with one exception in 1722) the last attempt made to assert the title of the Crown to derelict land or foreshore until comparatively recent times, but the Crown officers then appear to have turned their attention to the question of wreck of the sea, and in Michaelmas, 8 William III., A.D. 1696, an information was filed against Peter Aclam for taking wreck at Hornsea, Yorkshire. Defendant sets out his title from the Abbots of St. Mary York, who, as we have seen before, had wreck of the sea in Hornsea. The case proceeded as far as the publication of depositions, but no decree appears ever to have been made. Exch. B. & A., York, 182. Ante, p. 82.

Exch. B. & A., York, Will. & Mary, 178. Similar informations were filed for wreck, flotson, and jetson in the manors of Marsk and Kirkleatham, in Yorkshire; the manor of Eccles, near Attleborough, and the towns of Palyng and Hapsburgh, in Norfolk; also in the manors of Bromholm, Keswick, and Baketon, Norfolk. The cases of Marsk and Kirkleatham were never prosecuted to a decision, and in the case of Bromholm the depositions shew that the shore of the manor was parcel thereof, and that there was no attempt by the Attorney-General to set up the *primâ facie* title of the Crown. The lord of the manor must in this have succeeded. See Wygon *v.* Branthwaite, below.

Ante, p. 161. Exch. Dep., M., 9 Will. III., 34.

Ibid. 58. There was also an information against the bailiff and judge of the Admiralty Court in Great Yarmouth touching Admiralty droits taken up at sea.

Exch. B. & A., York, 116. In Hilary, 5 William and Mary, A.D. 1693–94, the Attorney-General filed an information against Viscount Dunbar, the lord of the seigniory of Holderness, for wreck, flotsom, jetsom, &c., to which he answered, setting out his title, and claiming the wreck happening within the high and low water marks within the manor; and he made a further answer, setting out the names of numerous townships within the seigniory in which he had taken wreck. The case proceeded to the further publication of depositions on 11 February, 9 William III., A.D. 1697–98, but the Crown never proceeded to judgment, and the lord of Holderness is entitled to the wreck at the present time.

Exch. Ord. Books, T., 8 Will. III., fo. 32b; T., 9 Will. III., fo. 175b; M., 9 Will. III., fo. 194; H., 1697, fo. 225.

1 Ld. Raymond 473; Holt 758; 12 Mod. 259. In Trinity, 11 William III., A.D. 1699, in the case of Wygon *v.* Branthwaite, it was decided by Holt, C.J., in a case in Suffolk, that where the Abbey of Bromholm had wreck and was dissolved, and the King granted the office of Admiral to Lord Lisle, with all wreck thereto belonging while the abbey was in the Crown's hands, the wreck did not go to the Admiral as part of his office, because the wreck was appertaining to the manor by prescription, and passed to the King's grantee of the manor.

Petty Bag, Concealments, ble. 5, No. 7. In 4 Anne, A.D. 1705, a commission issued to inquire as to reclaimed lands throughout the county of Lincoln, but nothing appears to have been done under it.

CHAPTER XVIII.

QUEEN ANNE TO A.D. 1795.

ALTHOUGH the Crown appears to have given up the attempt to recover derelict land, we now find records of suits between private persons with regard both to foreshore and to wreck, but we do not find any attempt on the part of the Attorney-General to intervene in these suits, as is his practice at the present day. There are several such suits during the reigns of Anne and George I. and George II. relating to rights of wreck and foreshore in Dunwich, Thorpness, and Minsmere, Suffolk; St. Peter's, East Hale, and Bradwell, Essex; Holbeach, Lincolnshire; Flamborough, Frimsthorp, Awbourn, Welsthorp, Helderthorpe, Bridlington Key, and Sowerby, Yorkshire; Padstow, Cornwall; Langenhoe, Essex; Stonehall, in the parish of Frampton, Lincolnshire; Bosham, Sussex; Hatfield and Thorne, Yorkshire.

There was an information filed against the lord of the manor of Ihame or Higham, near Winchelsea, in 1722, for salt marsh and foreshores there, and in the manors of Pett and Mersham, Sussex. It appears by the depositions of the witnesses that the lord of the manor had always taken wreck and anchorage, and that the land was accreted ground. The suit does not appear to have been pushed to a decision.

Exch.Dep., M., 9 Geo. I. 36; Att. *v.* Short.

About the year 1724 large accretion began to arise in the Humber opposite to the manor of Little Humber, parcel of the seigniory of Holderness, which was called Cherry Cob Sand. This was claimed by the Crown as an island, and it was alleged that it was severed from the main land by a low-water channel. This contention was disputed by Mr. Constable, the lord of the seigniory of

Holderness, who asserted that Cherry Cob Sand was an accretion to the foreshore of his seigniory and to his manor of Little Humber, parcel of that seigniory, and that it belonged to him, because he was entitled to the foreshore to the low-water mark. Negotiations were carried on between the Surveyor-General of the Treasury and Mr. Constable from 1724 down to 1762, when at last an information was filed against Constable, claiming the Cherry Cob Sand as an island. To this Constable answered that it was parcel of the manor of Little Humber, parcel of the seigniory of Holderness. The Crown evidence was all directed to shewing that Cherry Cob Sand was an island, and that there was formerly a navigable channel between it and the main land, but in Trinity, 1762, leave was given to the Attorney-General to amend the information by altering the word "island" to the word "sand."

Papers in the possession of Sir Talbot Constable. Exch.Q. R. Memda., E., 2 Geo. III., rolls 144, 165; ibid. H., 4 Geo. III. 134; Exch. Dep., H., 2 Geo. III. 1 Exch. B. & A., York, Geo. III. 44. Exch. Orders, T., 1762, 140.

On 4 June 1763, on the motion of the Attorney-General, the cause was ordered to be tried by a special jury of the county of York. Defendant was allowed to withdraw his special plea and plead the general issue. At the trial the real question was whether the land was an island or not; no attempt appears to have been made by the Crown to challenge Mr. Constable's right to foreshore. The verdict passed for Mr. Constable at the assizes in July 1763, and in Hilary, 4 George III., A.D. 1764, a fresh information was filed. This, however, was not pressed to a trial, and the dispute was settled by an Act of Parliament in 1766, whereby a small portion of the sand was given to the governors of Saltagh Hospital, who appear to have been the promoters of the suits on behalf of the Crown, and the remainder was assigned to Mr. Constable, with a general saving of his rights as lord of the seigniory of Holderness.

Ibid. 1763, 24.

Brief in possession of Sir T. Constable.

Throughout these proceedings Mr. Constable's title to the foreshore of the seigniory of Holderness was in no way challenged by the Crown, it being evidently considered that his title had been established in Sir John Constable's case and Sir Henry Constable's case. The title is again in litigation with the Crown in the pending suit of Attorney-General *v.* Constable.

In 1754 occurs the case of Attorney-General *v.* Mayor of Plymouth. The original information was filed in Hilary, 17 George II., A.D. 1744, by the Attorney-General of the Prince of Wales and Robert Hewer against the corporation, but abated by the death of Hewer, and was revived in Trinity, 20–21 George II., A.D. 1747, but was again abated in 1751 by the death of the Prince of Wales, and again revived in Trinity, 25 George II., A.D. 1752, on behalf of the Crown. To the bill of revivor the defendants demurred. The demurrer was overruled, and the case was heard in 1754. The information was to recover part of Sutton Pool, near Plymouth. It was not disputed that this part of the Duchy of Cornwall was part of the inheritance of the Crown. It was proved that King Charles II. had leased Sutton Pool to Lord Arundel on 27 February, 13 Charles II., A.D. 1660–61, for thirty-one years, and had made a reversionary lease in 28 Charles II., A.D. 1676, for fifteen years, and a further reversionary lease for thirteen years was made on 10 June, 3 William and Mary, A.D. 1691, to Edward Treganna and Peter Courtenay; this lease expired in 1719. It was not disputed that these leases were made, nor was the general right of the Crown denied, the main fact in issue being whether the defendants were or were not in possession of any of the premises within high-water mark, and whether they had made a title under the Statute of Concealments, 21 James I. cap. 2, but it was decided that the statute had not run, and judgment passed for the Crown. In this case the title was not in dispute. It had been settled by the previous suit, described at p. 314.

Wightwick 134.

In Trinity, 28–29 George II., A.D. 1755, occurred the case of Biddulph *v.* Ather. The plaintiff claimed, as lord of the manor of Lancing, Sussex, a wreck cast ashore on the manor, and that he was entitled by prescription to all wreck of the sea thrown upon that manor. He proved by court rolls and parol evidence that the lords of Lancing had taken wreck uninterruptedly from 1663. The

Biddulph *v.* Ather, 2 Wilson 23.

defendant, as bailiff of the Duke of Norfolk, had seized the wreck and claimed that the Duke was entitled to all wreck thrown upon any lands lying within the rape or barony or honour of Bramber, within which the manor of Lancing lies. For the defendant it was proved that, in 7 Edward I., Adam de Bavent had claimed a wreck in his manor of Hay by prescription, and it was found by the jury that he had not the wreck, but that the barons of Bramber had it throughout all their barony; and he was amerced for his false claim. It was also proved that it was presented Ante, p. 77. that Nigel de Brooke and Hugh de Buscy claimed wreck in their manors of Lancing and Kingston, near Shoreham, by prescription, and on that presentment it was found that the lord of Bramber had the wreck on the sea-coast of the rape of Bramber; and they were amerced for a false claim. Also that, in 7 Edward III., John de Mowbray, the lord of the honour of Bramber, recovered damages against John Odrich and others for carrying away wrecks cast upon lands at Hone, Worthing, Lancing, Pende, Shoreham, and Kingston, within the honour of Bramber, and it was insisted that these records cut off the head of the plaintiff's prescription. The judge held that the records were not conclusive, but were matter of evidence to be left to the jury, and, unless the said records were conclusive, he thought that the verdict was agreeable to the evidence, which was for the plaintiff, damages £50.

On a motion for a new trial it was insisted that the records were conclusive, but it was resolved by the whole Court that neither these two allowances in eyre nor the judgment in trespass were conclusive; and some of the judges doubted whether they were any evidence at all; but all agreed that usage for the plaintiff for ninety-two years last past was much stronger proof of the plaintiff's right, and the whole was fit to be left to the jury, and they all said the jury and judge had both done right. They also appear to have said that the records were no more conclusive than an inquisition post-mortem or a verdict (in many cases) touching the same matter, which is often *res inter alios acta*, as in the action of trespass by Mowbray; it might perhaps be brought by the person then in possession against persons who were mere wrongdoers, for anything that appears. The report is not very full, but it would seem that the plaintiff's possession, even if the wreck did belong to the lords of Bramber in the time of Edward I. and Edward III., raised a presumption of a grant from them to the plaintiff's predecessors.

By statute 9 George III. cap. 16, A.D. 1768, commonly called the "Nullum Tempus Act," the Statute of Concealment of 21 James I., cap. 2, was recited and confirmed; and by section 8 it is further provided that nothing in the Act shall extend or be prejudicial to the right, title, or claim of any person or persons in or to any manors, lands, tenements, or hereditaments by virtue of or under any grant or letters patent from his Majesty or his ancestors or predecessors passed before 1 January 1769, so that such right, title, or claim be prosecuted with effect by bill, plaint, information, or other suit or proceeding in some of his Majesty's courts of record at Westminster within the space of one year from 1 January 1769; and by section 10 it is provided, as in the previous Act, that no putting in charge nor standing *in super* by colour of any letters patent, grants of concealments, inquisitions, &c., shall be so construed unless the Crown has had judgment on some information and suit within sixty years next before issuing or commencing of every such action, bill, plaint, information, commission, or other suit or proceedings as shall at any times hereafter be filed, issued, or commenced for recovering the same.

These statutes not only bar the remedy of the Crown after the expiration of the period of limitation, or negative and exclude the right and title of the Crown, but affirm and establish the estate of the subject. Lord Ellenborough, indeed, said that the statute of 9 George III. does not give a title. It only takes away the right of the Crown, or those claiming from the Crown, against such as have held an adverse possession against it for sixty years. But Lord Coke, in his commentary on 21 James I. cap. 2, which in terms is similar to, or rather the same in this

Brown, Law of Limitation, 566.

Goodtitle *v.* Baldwin, 11 East 488.

3 Inst. 188.

respect as, the statute of 9 George III. cap. 16, says distinctly that the statute not only excludes negatively the right and title of the Crown, but also establishes affirmatively the estate of the subject.

Tuthill *v.* Rogers, 1 Jo. & Lat. 36.

Under these statutes, therefore, it is clear that an owner of foreshore may make a title against the Crown by evidence of user sufficient to shew that the foreshore is parcel of his manor, and that he has been in possession of his manor, with its appurtenances, for sixty years, or, where he is not lord of the manor, by shewing such evidence of user of the foreshore in question as will shew such possession of that foreshore, having regard to its nature and situation, as it is capable of.

Lord Advocate *v.* Young, 12 App. Cas. 544.

By statute 48 George III. cap. 47, the provisions of the Act of 9 George III. cap. 16, were extended to Ireland.

Stat. 48 Geo. III. c. 47, A.D. 1808. See 39 & 40 Vict. c. 37.

After the accession of William and Mary, the attempts of the Crown and its grantees to recover derelict lands, foreshore, and wreck from the subject appear to have been wholly unsuccessful. The suit against the Archbishop of Canterbury for the lands at Deal was decided against the Crown in 1695. The Bishop of Durham defeated the Crown in 1713. The commissions issued to inquire concerning concealed lands down to 1698 appear to have produced no fruit. The informations with respect to wreck between 1693 and 1696 did not succeed, and were all abandoned. The commission as to derelict lands in Lincolnshire in 1705 brought nothing to the Crown. The information respecting marshes and foreshore at Higham, Kent, in 1722, was not prosecuted. In Constable's case, as to Cherry Cob Sand, between 1724 and 1763, no attempt was made to claim the foreshore. In 1705 the Crown made a lease of the Middle Sands and the Holm, near South Cave and Brownfleet, in the Humber, to one Henry Worthington, with a view to a reclamation, but this was never carried out. Leases were made of overflowed lands in Gatcombe Haven, Sidlesham, Pagham, and Selsey, Hants, in 1773 and 1776, but we do not find that the lessees ever got possession. Sunk Island remained in the Crown, and was leased to the family of

Woods and Forests Reports, 1787, Appx. pp. 43, 48, 50, 58

Gilby in 1771, but with this exception there is, in the return of lands belonging to the Crown made by the Commissioners of Woods and Forests in their Report of 1787, no reference to any foreshore or derelict land as being in the Crown's possession at that time. The subject was no longer vexed with commissions of concealments, but was allowed to remain in quiet possession of the foreshore down to the end of the eighteenth century.

We then find the Crown beginning to re-assert its claims, but in doing so it no longer asserts the *jus privatum* simply, but puts forward the *jus publicum* as well as the *jus privatum*, and attacks acts upon the foreshore as purprestures rather than as encroachments; but it is to be observed that in the first case of this kind it was distinctly held that *primâ facie* the right to the foreshore is in the Crown. Att.-Gen. *v.* Richards, 2 Anst. 603.

CHAPTER XIX.

A.D. 1795 TO A.D. 1829.

IN Trinity, 35 George III., A.D. 1795, an information was filed against one Richards with respect to a wharf at Gosport, and in this case the Attorney-General lays no claim to the foreshore in point of property, but only in point of jurisdiction. The information states that by the royal prerogative "the sea and sea-coasts as far as the sea "flows and re-flows between the high and low water marks "and all the ports and havens of the kingdom belong to "his Majesty, and ought to be preserved for the use of his "Majesty's vessels and others, and that his Majesty has "the right of *superintendency over them for their preserva-* "*tion*," and that the defendants in 1774 erected a wharf or quay and two docks on the foreshore so as to prevent boats and vessels from sailing over that spot or mooring there, and also to endanger further damage to the harbour by preventing the free current of the water to carry off the mud. The information prayed that the defendants might be restrained from making any further erections; that those made might be abated, and the harbour restored to its ancient situation. The defendants claimed the soil under the grant of 14 July, 4 Charles I., A.D. 1628, to Lady Wandesford, and also pleaded possession for sixty years, but they were unable to trace back their title to the Wandesfords and so bring the grant into them. It was admitted that the defendants had had possession of a piece of mud land adjoining the piece in question for upwards of sixty years; that the ground in question had never been recovered from the sea till the erections complained of by the bill, which were made after notice of intention to dispute the right; that the defendants

Att.-Gen. *v.* Richards, 2 Anst. 603.

Ante, p. 258.

had had possession by keeping floats of timber moored there for some time before; and it was proved that the embankment was prejudicial to the harbour and the navigation.

The Attorney-General in his argument said that the King had the foreshore as a *jus privatum*, which he might grant away; but he also had it as a *jus publicum* vested in the King for the use of his subjects, and that this was inalienable; that where there was an invasion of the *jus privatum* it was a purpresture by encroachment on the soil; where the *jus publicum* was violated it was a nuisance, and he cited Attorney-General *v.* Philpott, 8 Charles I., Ante, p. 260. respecting a purpresture abated in the Thames, and laid the case upon nuisance. He argued that the grant to Wandesford was bad because the King was only seised of the *jus publicum*, and there was no possession of the soil under the *jus privatum*, and the right to enjoy it, being only a possibility when it should be recovered from the sea, could not be granted to a subject, citing Attorney- Ante, p. 417. General *v.* Sir Edward Farmer (2 Levinz 171, Sir T. Raymond 241). He also argued that the grant was made for the purpose of embanking, and that this was not done, and the land not reduced into possession, and that even if the land passed to the grantee he had thrown it open to the public use, and the King had acquired a new right in it by the possession of his subjects, and he shewed that the defendants did not deduce title from the patentee. In the judgment Macdonald, C.B., said: "It is clear that "the right to the soil between high and low water mark "is *primâ facie* in the Crown; then the onus of proving an "adverse title is thrown upon the defendants," and he held that the *locus in quo* was not included in the grant; that the grant was intended to operate to bring the lands into cultivation as a condition of it; that the grantees, if they ever had title, had abandoned it, because the Crown had been in possession by its subjects, and it had been open as a public passage from 1629. Judgment passed that the soil was the property of the Crown, and the nuisance was ordered to be abated.

In this case, as we have seen, the grant relied upon by the defendants was an invalid and arbitrary grant by the Crown, and this case is wholly distinguishable from the case where foreshore is claimed as parcel of a manor; although the case strongly supports the doctrine of the *primâ facie* title of the Crown, it fully admits that that title may be displaced by evidence of user for which a lawful origin may be presumed.

Att.-Gen. *v.* Parmeter, 10 Price 378.

The case of Attorney *v.* Parmeter, which was decided in 1811, was a suit by information apparently in respect of another wharf and timber-ground on the shore at Gosport. In the information the Attorney proceeded on the question of nuisance, and alleged that the grant to Wandesford above mentioned was void and of no effect to pass the soil; that no one had been in possession under the grant until the erections complained of, but that the Crown and its subjects had been in possession by the exercise of acts of navigation over the shore; that if the land had been well granted, yet the grant could not extend to deprive the Crown and its subjects of the rights of navigation, nor authorize the erection of the buildings in question; that it was a nuisance, and tended to choke up the harbour; that the erections were all subsequent to the year 1784; and that even if the defendants had been in possession for sixty years, nevertheless the erections might be abated as a common nuisance. The defendants in their answer admitted the prerogative right of the Crown to the sea-shore, and that the Crown had the right of superintendency, but alleged that the buildings were not a nuisance; that they had been in possession; and that the land on which the buildings were erected was above the high water of neap tides. They set up the grant to Wandesford, and, after referring to the statute 9 George III. cap. 16, they set out a conveyance to them of the year 1784, and averred that they believed that their grantors derived their title from the Wandesfords, but this they did not prove. Macdonald, C.B., gave the judgment of the Court, and found that the erections were a nuisance; and on the question of the validity of the grant to pass the *locus in quo*, said: "But it is either "within the grant or it is not; if it is within the grant, I "think it may be easily shewn that the grant is good for "nothing. It is perfectly clear that all the soil under the "salt water between high-water mark and low-water mark "is the property of the Crown; such property has cer-"tainly been (as it may be) communicated in a great "many instances to the subject, but that is always sub-"servient to the public right of the King's subjects gene-"rally. It is compared by Lord Hale, with his usual "simplicity, to the case of a highway; the private right "of the Crown may be disposed of, but the public right of "the subject cannot, even if it be within this grant. . . . . "Now, I take it that nothing can be clearer than that the "King can in no degree affect the public right of the "subject passing and repassing upon the salt water; he "cannot affect that by anything which can be done by "him. Lord Hale lays down clearly that ports, creeks, "and havens are the subjects of the public right; in none "of these places, therefore, can the public right be waived, "although there might be a grant of the soil; but such "grant must be considered as subject to that public right "which cannot be disturbed." He then discusses the Wandesford grant, and the commission and inquisition on which it is founded, and shews that the grant is larger than is warranted by the commission; that the grant was made on condition that the land should be reclaimed, and this he holds was to have been done within a reasonable time, and he shews that it had never been acted upon for a century and a half, and says: "It is most manifestly "clear either that the grant was never acted upon at all, "or we must presume that it was surrendered, if ever the "grantees did avail themselves of it." And he held, upon the ground of the existence of a nuisance, the illegality of any grant affecting the *jus publicum* between high and low water mark, and the great length of time and no fruit having come of the grant; that the grant could be of no avail whatever; and consequently made the same decree for the abatement of the nuisance as in the case of

Attorney-General *v.* Richards, grounded upon the illegality of the grant itself.

Parmeter *v.* Att.-Gen. (Sir Vicary Gibbs), 10 Price 412.

The case was appealed to the House of Lords, and was decided in 1813. The appellants set forth the Wandesford grant, and the conveyance to them of 1784, and alleged that it appeared from their deeds that their grantors derived their title from Dame Mary Wandesford, and alleged divers acts of ownership on the *locus in quo;* also that the neap tides did not cover the place where the erections were made, and that no injury was done to the harbour; that the grant included the land; that it had never been abandoned and was not void; and they relied on the statute of 9 George III. cap. 16. The appellants' case further stated the effect of the evidence, and that the cause was first argued principally upon the question of nuisance, upon which the Court did not deliver any opinion, but ordered the case to be re-argued as to the validity and effect of the grant, and that the Court, by its decree on 23 December 1811, decreed that the right to the soil was in the Crown, and ordered the works to be abated. They finally stated that the judgment was formed without regard to the question of nuisance, the only ground on which any relief was sought by the information, but upon one of these two grounds, viz., that the grant was against the *jus publicum*, and therefore, or for some other reason, void; or that the land claimed was not comprised in the grant. They averred that the case differed from Attorney-General *v.* Richards, because the present defendants claim title from Dame Mary Wandesford; that owners of other property under the grant were entitled to be heard as to its validity, and that it cannot be repealed without a writ of *scire facias*. The respondent insisted that the decree of the Court of Exchequer ought to be affirmed, first, because the grant was absolutely void *ab initio* and of no effect; secondly, that if it had been good it had been abandoned; thirdly, that the *locus in quo* was not comprised in the grant; fourthly, that the erection was a nuisance. A long discussion took place upon the validity of the grant, and a very learned argument was made to uphold the enormous stretch of the prerogative which had been made by Charles I. in granting it; but the House of Lords decided that the grant was void as to the particular *locus in quo* only, and the judgment was affirmed, Lord Eldon stating (according to Price): "But I am anxious to say this, and this only, that as I "conceive that where there has been a possession for "sixty years under this grant nobody can be removed, "so I desire not to be understood to imply one way or "the other what may be the effect of these letters patent "with respect to any one part of the land which this "instrument covers, except the soil on which these build-"ings are erected. It is my judgment, that on the cir-"cumstances now before your lordships there is matter "sufficient to put in issue on this record the question "of the validity of this grant; that, looking to these "letters patent, with respect to this soil, I am of opinion "that the Court of Exchequer have stated a proposition, "true in law, that the title is in his Majesty. I give no "opinion as to the effect of any use that has been made "of the land."

In Dow, Lord Eldon is reported to have said: "There "appeared no other way here of making good the appel-"lants' title but by shewing sufficient possession. In "this case there was no sufficient possession, for the "Crown had still remained in possession for upwards of "150 years, which created a presumption against its own "grant. If there had been possession under the appellants' "title for sixty years there would have been an adverse "possession against the Crown; but they could shew "nothing more than nineteen or twenty years." The decree of the Court of Exchequer was accordingly affirmed on the ground of non-user at this particular place, merely without reference to the general question as to the validity of the grant or the right under it to other places.

1 Dow H. of L. 316, 13 Feb. 1813.

In 1801 occurred the case of Bagot *v.* Orr. It was an action of trespass for carrying away shell fish and shells on the foreshore of the manor of Keysham, in Morecambe

Bagot *v.* Orr, 2 Bos. & P. 472.

Bay. The defendants pleaded the common law right to fish, and asserted that they took the fish and the shells in the exercise of that right, and that they did not take the soil, the plaintiff's right to the soil being admitted. It was argued for the defendants that the ownership of the foreshore would not exclude the public right to fish, and it was also argued that the statute 7 James I. cap. 18, as to the taking of sand in Devon and Cornwall, was a full recognition of the right of the subject to use the shore of the sea in every way in which it could be serviceable to him, and that it proves that his right is not confined to the privilege of taking shell fish left on the shore by the ebbing of the tides, but they may also take the fish shells, and even the sand of the shore. For the plaintiff it was argued that the statute of James proved precisely the contrary, and, admitting the right to fish, that shell fish and fish shells were part of the manor of Keysham; that the King might grant the shore to a subject, reserving or not, as he pleases, a general right of shore to all his subjects. The plaintiff ought not to be called upon to prescribe for a right of fishery over that which is admitted to be his own, for when once it is established that the *locus in quo* belongs to the plaintiff it must be presumed to be exclusively his, unless some inconsistent right is set up by the defendant. (Here, however, arises a fallacy, for the common law right would survive, notwithstanding the grant of the shore, unless the franchise of a several fishery had specially been granted.) The Court were of opinion that if the plaintiff had it in his power to have abridged the common law right of the subject to take sea fish, he should have replied that matter specially, and that, not having done so, the defendant must succeed upon his plea as far as related to the taking of fish; but observed that, as no authority had been cited to support his claim to take shells, they should pause before they established a general right of that kind. Thereupon the defendant struck out his plea as to fish shells. No judgment appears to have been given as to the right to take fish shells, and the Court evidently leaned against such a claim.

Warren *v.* Matthews, 6 Mod. 73; 1 Salk. 357; 1 Mod. 105. Ward *v.* Creswell, Willes 265; 16 Viner's Abr. 364.

See Le-strange *v.* Rowe, post, p. 542. Duchess of Sutherland *v.* Watson, post, p. 578.

See Howe *v.* Stawell, post, p. 464.

On 18 March 1799 the Commissioner of Woods let to James Kelsey and others the Ham oyster ground, situate below the low-water mark at the east end of the Isle of Sheppey, Kent, for thirty years, at a rent of £10. A similar lease was made by the Crown in 1812 to Haridge and others, of the Leigh Swatch, near Southend, Essex, for an oyster ground. In 1805 a lease was proposed to be granted to Lord Selsey of mud lands in the parishes of Sidlesham, Pagham, and Selsey for thirty-one years, at a rental of £72, with a view to a reclamation, but it does not appear to have been carried out. A further lease of the same derelict land was granted on 16 June 1837 to William Wadman at a rent of £200, the consideration for the lease being the embanking of the land.

Surveyor-Gen.'s 2nd Rep., p. 68.

Crown Leases, Exch.

Surveyor-Gen.'s 3rd Rep., p. 134.

Comr. of Woods' 15th Rep., p. 30.

By statute 48 Geo. III. cap. 75, A.D. 1808, it was enacted that bodies cast on shore within the lands of a parish shall be buried by the churchwardens and overseers in the churchyard at the costs of the parish, and when cast ashore in an extra-parochial place, it shall be done by the constable or headborough in the same manner. A fee of five shillings is to be paid to the finder of the body or bodies, who shall give notice to the churchwardens or constables within six hours after finding the same, and the finder, if he does not give such notice within six hours, is made liable to a penalty of £5. The churchwardens and constables are to be reimbursed these charges by the county treasurer. By section 13 it is enacted that when lords of manors entitled to wreck have been accustomed to pay a small fee for burying these bodies (such payments having been adduced as evidence of the right to wreck at trials), they may continue to pay the same fee to the churchwardens, to be applied in part discharge of the expenses. The Act is still in force, except the last section, s. 14.

In the statute 54 Geo. III. cap. 159, A.D. 1814, for the regulation of ports and harbours, which gives power to the Admiralty to lay buoys and do other acts therein, there is the following special saving clause of the rights of property of all lords of manors to any ports, harbours,

See Nicholson *v.* Williams, post, p. 550. havens, roads, roadsteads, sounds, channels, creeks, bays, or navigable rivers of the United Kingdom, or to the banks, shores, or sides thereof:—

Proviso for right of property, &c. "XXVIII. Provided always, and be it further enacted, "That nothing in this Act contained shall extend, or be "construed to extend, to prejudice, diminish, abridge, alter, "or take away any right of property, privilege, or jurisdic- "tion, or any powers of conservancy held, possessed, used, "exercised, or enjoyed by any body corporate or politic, or "by any lord or lords, lady or ladies, of any manor or "manors, or any person or persons whatsoever, in, to, upon, "or over any of the ports, harbours, havens, roads, road- "steads, sounds, channels, creeks, bays, or navigable rivers "of the United Kingdom, or to the banks, shores, or sides Proviso for local Acts. "thereof, or to repeal any of the provisions contained in "any Act or Acts of Parliament which may have been "passed for the regulation of any river, port, or harbour in "the United Kingdom, or the shipping frequenting the same, "except such Acts and provisions as are expressly repealed "by this present Act; but that such respective rights of "property, privileges, jurisdictions, and powers of conser- "vancy shall be respectively and exclusively enjoyed in as "full, ample, and beneficial a manner in every respect, to "all intents and purposes, as if this Act had never been "made; anything herein contained to the contrary notwith- "standing."

Att.-Gen. of Prince of Wales *v.* Sir John St. Aubyn, Wightwick 167. In 1811 occurred the case of the Attorney-General of the Prince of Wales *v.* Sir John St. Aubyn. This was an information at the relation of Benjamin Tucker to recover certain houses and a quay built on the foreshore of the River Tamar, and the information prayed that the defendants might set out their title and deeds, and that the inheritance might be established in the Prince. It was demurred that the Prince had no right to proceed by his Attorney-General by English information; but this was overruled, it being shewn that the Prince had so proceeded in the case of Sutton Pool in 1754, in the case of the Attorney-General *v.* the Inhabitants of Oving, in Michaelmas, 4 James I., and other cases, Wood, B., *dissentiente.*

The Duchy claimed the premises as parcel of the manor of Trematon. Sir John St. Aubyn claimed them as parcel of the manor of Stoke Damarel. The result of the case does not appear in the report, which is devoted to the question of the right of the Prince to sue by information.

In 1813 occurred the case of the King *v.* Ellis, which was a question whether the lessee of the fishings of Halves and Halfendoles, belonging to the manor of Radley, in the county of Gloucester, being a manor within certain limits on the River Severn, and of all royal fishes taken within the said limits (put and wheel fishing excepted), was rateable to the poor in respect of such fisheries. The ground for the rate was that the fishery carried the soil, it being contended, on the other hand, that the fishery was a fishery unconnected with the soil. Lord Ellenborough in his judgment referred to the case of the Barons of Berkley, cited by Lord Hale as evidencing the custom of the manors on the Severn, that they extended to the *filum aquæ*, and considered that the language of the grant of "the Halves "and Halfendoles with the fishings due and accustomed "in the Severn," and the language of a subsequent indenture leasing the one-fourth part of "all those fishings "of the Halves and Halfendoles, and of the fishing with "the appurtenances to the Halves and Halfendoles, due "and accustomed within the River Severn, from a certain "bay or pill within the manor or lordship of Rodley, in "the county aforesaid, commonly called Newnham's Pill, "unto a certain place in the lordship of Rodley aforesaid, "opposite to Epney's Weir, and also a fourth part of all "royal fishes to be taken between the said bay or pill and "the said place opposite to Epney's Weir as aforesaid," appeared distinctly to shew that these Halves and Halfendoles were in the nature of land or some local limit within which the fishery connected with the soil was to be exercised. "I cannot consider it," he says, "otherwise than as "a grant of something territorial." "There are also these "further words: 'all royal fishes there to be taken.' The "like expressions occur in the second grant, from all "which an argument has been drawn from Lord Hale's

King *v.* Ellis, 1 M. & S. 152.

"treatise, who speaks of it as a great presumption that the "shore is parcel of all such manors as by prescription have "royal fish, otherwise they could not have them; and it "is argued here that the grant of the one thing leads to a "necessary implication of a grant of the other, by which "alone the thing can be conveniently exercised. *Such is "the argument, and it is certainly one of powerful influence.*"

Bayley, J., in his judgment, says: "It is stated by "Lord Hale that a fishery may be either unconnected "with the soil or connected with it; I should doubt very "much if the grant of a fishery would convey the soil and "everything underneath it, such as all minerals, though I "can conceive that it may pass so much of the soil as is "connected with the fishery." The rate was upheld on the ground that the soil passed.

Att.-Gen. *v.* Johnson, 2 Wilson Ch. Cas. 87. Rex *v.* Ld. Grosvenor, 2 Starkie 511.

In 1819 Earl Grosvenor erected a wharf at Millbank, under a lease from the Corporation of London as owners of the soil by grant of the Crown, and an information was filed to abate it as a nuisance, and to restrain him from proceeding until the hearing of an indictment in the King's Bench. Evidence was given that it was a hindrance to the navigation. The title to the soil was not in question in the case. The Lord Chancellor in giving judgment remarked that the information rested simply on the ground that the wharf was a nuisance, and he laid down "that the "Crown has not the right, either itself to use its title to "the soil between high and low water mark as a nuisance, "or to place upon that soil what will be a nuisance to "the Crown's subjects; if the Crown had not such a right "it could not give it to the City of London, nor could the "City transfer it to other persons." He took it to be clear that *primâ facie* the subject has a right to use that which may be called a water highway, and which *primâ facie* includes the water between high and low water mark when it covers the soil, and that those who think proper to inclose that soil are *primâ facie* bound to shew that they can take it away without injury to the subject, and said that "there ought to have been an *ad quod damnum*." On the hearing of the indictment it was held that a corporation, being conservators and owners of the soil between high and low water mark, cannot authorize a lessee to erect a wharf there which produces inconvenience to the public in the use of the river for the purposes of navigation, and further "it is proper to presume that if "any person meditates an alteration in a public highway "or in any other subject-matter which is a public right, "the legitimate course of proceeding is by means of an "inquiry before the sheriff, in order to ascertain whether "the change will operate to the prejudice of the public, "and if he does not the onus is on him to make it out."

In 1821 occurred the case of Blundell *v.* Caterall, in which it was decided by Abbot, C.J., Bayley, J., and Holroyd, J. (Best, J., *dissentiente*), that the public have no common law right of bathing in the sea, and as incident thereto of crossing the sea-shore on foot, or with bathing machines for that purpose. The place in dispute was the shore of the manor of Great Crosby, near Liverpool, and the title to the shore was admitted. It was contended, on the authority of Bracton and the Civil Law, that the common law right to bathe exists, and was evidenced by the universal practice of the whole realm. The learned judgments delivered in this case are important as shewing that the King's interest in the foreshore was an interest limited by the rights of the public, and that the grantee of the Crown can only have such limited interest as the Crown had. Mr. Justice Holroyd in his judgment compares the passage in Bracton, taken from Justinian, with the common law, and shews that it is not consistent with it, and discusses the rights of the King's subjects to the use of the shore for the purposes of navigation, trade, commerce, intercourse, and fishery as of common right, distinguishing them from particular rights, which may be claimed by custom in particular localities, and shews that as the King has only a right to the soil of the foreshore subject to the *jus publicum*, he cannot license an erection thereon which shall be a common nuisance, and that his grantee is in the same position; but where a purpresture is made upon the King's soil, he may either demolish it or

Blundell *v.* Caterall, 5 B. & Ald. 268.

arrent it or seize it at his pleasure, provided no mischief or injury arises therefrom to public rights ; but he holds that evidence to prove the shore parcel of a manor disproves the general right of all the King's subjects on the shore, at least when and where it is not covered with water, and concludes that the right claimed cannot exist at common law, because it is unsupported either by usage or custom. Bayley, J., in his judgment, lays down that the foreshore and the property in it is *primâ facie* in the King. It may by grant or prescription belong to a subject, but, until the contrary is shewn, the presumption is that it belongs to the King ; and he holds that the King cannot make a grant in derogation of the rights of the public ; and he holds that the right claimed cannot exist, "as it is "not confined to any particular place, and, if it exists at "all, must exist upon every part of the sea-shore. Every "private building, then, erected on the sea-shore, and even "wharves and quays, would be an obstruction to the right "claimed, and of course abateable or indictable, and such "a case has never happened." Abbot, C.J., decides against the right, as no mention is found of it in any book, ancient or modern. He decides that the passage in Bracton is not conformable to the law of England, and, as there is no general right to unlade merchandise on the shore, there can be no right to traverse the shore with carriages or otherwise for the purpose of unlading. He points out that if the right existed, embankments, wharves, and improvements on the shore could not be made ; and, with regard to the argument advanced that persons have always walked, ridden, or driven on the sea-shore without hindrance of lords of manors, he remarks "that many of "those persons who reside in the vicinity of wastes and "commons walk or ride in all directions over them for "their health and recreation, yet no one ever thought that "any right existed in favour of this enjoyment, or that "any justification could be pleaded to an action at the "suit of the owner of the soil." Best, J. (*dissentiente*), held in favour of the defendant, arguing that the present state of the shore shewed the manner in which the Crown must have used it. Some parts of it were held exclusively by the Crown for the purposes of fisheries, harbours, warehouses, &c., but the greatest part was left open as a common highway between the sea and the land; this is the state in which it continues to this day, and in which, on account of its general sterility, it must ever continue; from the state of the greatest part has arisen the general rule, and the state of the portions exclusively occupied has occasioned the exceptions, and he lays it down that the claim of the public to a right of way over the beach stands on the general law, and a person who will dispute this public right in any particular part of it must establish his right to do so by shewing, first, that the King had an exclusive possession of that part, and that a right to such exclusive possession has been conveyed to the Crown from such person. He holds that the King had the right of soil in the shore in general, but that the public had a right of way over it, and that the King's grantee can only have it subject to the same right. He lays it down that the universal practice of England shews the right of way over the sea-shore to be a common law right. He discusses the passages in Bracton, but says that he does not say that the whole of the passage is now good law, but that it was all good law at the time he wrote, and all of it that is adapted to the present state of things is good law now, and he gives his judgment on the ground of general expediency and principles of public policy.

In the same year 1821 occurred the case of Chad *v.* Tilsed, in which Sir Charles Chad, the owner of the island of Brownsea, in Dorsetshire, which had formerly belonged to the Abbey of Cerne, brought an action for trespass against Tilsed for fishing on the foreshore of the island. The defendant pleaded not guilty, licence, and the common law right of fishing in tidal water. At the trial a grant of Henry II. in 1154 to the Abbot of Cerne of wreck "by "all their lands upon the sea" was produced, which was confirmed by *inspeximus* by Henry VIII. in 1509. Also a grant in 26 Henry VIII. to the Earl of Oxford of the island of Brownsea surrounded with water, and the shores

Chad *v.* Tilsed, 5 Moore 192; 2 Brod. & Bing. 403.

thereof, lately belonging to the monastery of Cerne, together with wreck of the sea as fully as the late Abbot enjoyed it. It was also proved that St. Andrew's Bay, the *locus in quo*, was left nearly dry at low water; that the plaintiff's predecessor in title had about fifty years ago embanked it, using the seaweed, mud, and gravel within the bank; the embankment had been broken, and still remained so, and that the plaintiff's predecessor had treated the place as his property and had claimed and taken wrecks. For the defendant two of Charles II.'s fishing grants were given in evidence—viz., a grant of 13 Charles II., A.D. 1661, to the Duke of Richmond of the waste and boggy ground in St. Andrew's Bay provided he should reclaim it within five years, and another similar grant in 17 Charles II., A.D. 1665, to Charles Giffard—but it appeared that nothing had ever been done under the grants. The jury found for the plaintiff. On a motion for a new trial it was urged that the place was an arm of the sea, and that there was evidence that the public had fished without interruption; that there was no evidence to shew that the Abbots of Cerne or their successors had the *locus in quo* in severalty, and that the grant of wreck did not convey any right to the soil. The grant to the Earl of Oxford only conveyed the island of Brownsea surrounded with water, and not the water surrounding the island. It excluded the soil and only granted the wreck, which the abbots had had. Also that the grants by Charles II. shewed that the foreshore was in the Crown. Dallas, C.J., in his judgment, agreed that the case must rest upon one or both of two grounds, that is to say, either on the documentary evidence, which consisted of the grants produced at the trial, or on continual user, which presupposes the existence of a grant. Also that, "when a grant has been produced, no usage, "however long, can alter or countervail the terms of such "grant, for what is done under usurpation cannot constitute a legal usage," and he lays down the rule of construction as follows:—"The fundamental rule laid down is "that when an ancient grant contains general words, the "best exposition of it is by constant and uninterrupted "usage; unless, therefore, an usage and enjoyment for forty "years can be shewn to have originated in usurpation, it "is evidence from which usage anterior to that time may "be presumed; here the modern usage as connected with "the ancient affords a strong exposition of the meaning "of the original grant of Henry II. The general rule is "that if the language of the grant be obscure or its con-"struction doubtful, general usage may be resorted to to "expound, although not to control or contradict, the instru-"ment, and such usage is a strong practical exposition of "the meaning of the parties. Ancient grants, therefore, "are to be construed by evidence of subsequent usage, "however general such grants may be, reducing it to a "mere question of fact as to the mode of right which has "been generally and usually exercised," and, construing the grant of the island and its shores by the evidence of user, he refused the rule. As to the question of the grant of wreck not conveying the soil, he remarked that it must not be confined to such wrecks only as float in the water, but those which rest and remain on the soil after the receding of the tide. Burrough, J., pointed out that the evidence confirmed the grants of wreck to the abbots "throughout their lands upon the sea," and shewed that the wrecks had been left upon the foreshore and there taken, and this, he says, is a strong fact to shew that the Crown intended to grant the land in question in the first instance under the words of "all their lands upon the "sea." [It would have been more accurate to say that the Crown had *previously* granted the foreshore, and acknowledged its grant by granting wreck to be taken upon the land.] He held that the grants of Charles II. were of no weight, because they were not acted upon, and other persons were in possession under the older grants. The other judges concurred. Rule discharged.

In 1822 we have the case of Attorney-General against Burridge, in which the Crown raised the question of the title to the foreshores of the borough of Portsmouth. This was an information in respect of a wharf and timber

Att.-Gen. *v.* Burridge, 10 Price 350.

pond erected in a species of natural dock, called the Camber, in Portsmouth Harbour. The information claimed the soil of the shore for the Crown, and the right of superintendence, and charged that the wharf was a nuisance, and that it had been erected in defiance of a notice not to do so. The information averred that the defendants claimed under grants to the Corporation of Portsmouth. The Attorney-General charged that such grants were void, and of no force or effect to pass the soil. Also, that they had been abandoned, and that the *locus in quo* is not, and could not be, included in such grants. He also charged that defendants had not been in possession for sixty years, and could not avail themselves of the Statute of Limitation. The defendants set out a charter of 13 Charles I., A.D. 1637, to the Corporation of Portsmouth of groundage and anchorage of vessels in the haven of the borough, and a grant of the borough with confirmation of former grants, under which the defendants set up a title in the corporation to the foreshore of the haven or harbour within the town and borough, and claimed under a lease from the corporation of the mud land in question. It was contended for the Crown—first, that the Crown had no right to grant the land; secondly, that it had not been granted; thirdly, that the defendants had no right to use it as they had done; and fourthly, that it was a nuisance. On the part of the defendants it was contended that they had the right to the possession of the soil, and that the erection was not a nuisance. Richard, C.B., in his judgment, said: "I am "enabled to premise, for there can be no doubt of it, that "the law with respect to the general rights of the Crown "is clear, and that it is admitted on all sides. It is a "doctrine of ancient establishment that the shore between "high and low water marks belongs *primâ facie* to the "King, and it is clear that the lands in question are "between the ordinary high and low water marks, and "consequently *primâ facie* belong to the King; but it is "equally clear that the King may grant his private right "therein to his subjects. It is upon such a grant that "the defendant in this suit mainly relies, and such a title "it is clearly incumbent on him to prove against the "King. The subject may acquire a right of property in "these mud lands by grant, charter, or prescription, and "the first question is whether the defendant has in this case "established his title by either of those means of acquiring "the right of possession, and shewn that the right has "been taken out of the King and transferred to him. It "is incumbent on the defendant to prove that case." He further says that the defendant having the onus of proof on him, "his evidence consists of acts of ownership inconsistent with the right of possession being in the Crown; "but he must go further, and shew that the right is in "him;" but he did not decide the point, and directed an issue. On the question of nuisance, he says that the Crown has no doubt a right to abate a nuisance notwithstanding it be on the lands of the subject. In discussing the law as laid down in Hale, he considered this part of the case was proper to be referred to a jury, and directed an issue accordingly. The case was never proceeded with from 1822 until 1869, when a new information was filed against the Corporation of Portsmouth. See post, p. 555.

In Burridge's case the corporation appear to have claimed the whole of the foreshores of Portsmouth Harbour. This claim, however, was too large, and in the subsequent suit the corporation restricted their claim to the foreshore adjacent to the borough only.

In 1822 occurred the case of Dickens *v.* Shaw. This was an action for trespass by the lord of the manor of Brighton against the defendant for digging sand on the sea-shore. The defendant pleaded not guilty, putting it upon the plaintiff to prove his title to the *locus in quo*. The plaintiff succeeded in proving the right of the lord to wreck, but he was unsuccessful in shewing any act of ownership upon the shore, and it appeared from his own evidence that "sand, stones, &c., had been immemorially "dug and carried away by all mankind that pleased, "without interruption or payment;" but an Act of Parliament passed for the appointment of certain commis- Dickens *v.* Shaw, Hall on Sea-shore, ed. 1875, Appendix.

sioners, 50 George III. cap. 38, A.D. 1810, was put in which had a saving clause that the said Act should not extend to enable the commissioners to authorize the putting of any bathing machines upon the shore, to dig away any sand, rock, &c., without the consent of the lords of the manor of Brighthelmstone, or the consent of any person or persons who, by reason of property in the soil or otherwise, may legally be entitled to prohibit or prevent the same; but it appeared that no rent was paid to the lord of the manor for bathing machines. Park, J., in summing up, mentioned the Act of Parliament to the jury, and told them the foreshore was *primâ facie* in the King; "at the same time it was not only possible, but "was often proved to be the case, that grants have been "made by the King of this soil to his subjects." He shewed that the bailiff of the manor in seventeen years had taken three small topmasts as wreck, but his evidence shewed that other people had been in the habit of carting away the soil without his permission. The court rolls of the manor were produced to shew presentments of taking wreck. This was practically the whole of the evidence for the plaintiff, and the jury found for the defendant. On a motion for a new trial, Mr. Justice Park being dissatisfied with the verdict, the case was argued at length; but it appearing that the only evidence of acts of ownership by the lord being the taking wreck, and that other acts had been done by the public on the shore without interference by the lord, the Court refused the rule. Bayley, J., in his judgment, says: "*Primâ facie* "the lord of the manor is entitled up to high-water mark, "for between high and low water mark the right is *primâ* "*facie* in the Crown; and the Crown has likewise the "right to wreck. The right of wreck and the right of "soil being both in the Crown, the Crown may grant both "the one and the other to one and the same individual; "or it may grant the soil without the wreck; or it may "grant the wreck without granting the right to soil." He then points out that in forming a judgment "whether in "any particular spot, as in the boundary of any particular "manor, there has been a grant to any and what particular extent, the proper thing is to look to the exercise, "and see how the lord of the manor has from time to "time acted." "The right of the Crown is not in general "for any beneficial interest to the Crown itself, but for "securing to the public certain privileges in the spot "between high and low water mark." He admits that the right to wreck is proved, but points out that there are other rights which may be exercised, and one of them is getting stones; and this had been exercised against the lords by persons who did it as if they had been claiming a right.

Holroyd, J., says that "It is true that Lord Hale "instances wreck as one species of right which tends to "shew a right to the soil. In one place in his treatise "'De Jure Maris' he intimates that if it were otherwise "the party could not get down to take the wreck. I think "it may be evidence of ownership, particularly *if coupled* "*with other acts of enjoyment of the right of soil.* Where "the Crown grants the right of wreck it is probable the "Crown grants the right of soil also; but if the Crown "grant the right of wreck alone, by that grant the party "would have a right to come and take the wreck as incidental to the grant, otherwise the grant of a right would "not be a grant of anything whatever. Everything necessary for the enjoyment of a right passes incidentally with "the grant." "The circumstance of any person who chose "getting sand, and their manner of conducting themselves, "evidently thinking they had a right to do it, is evidence "to shew that the right was in the Crown, and not in the "lord of the manor, who may be presumed to have been "present and looking after his right, not personally, but "by his reeve or bailiff, or some other person whose business it was to look after his property. If the right is in "the Crown, the Crown is more likely not to be looking "after this, which though it may have been beneficial to "the public, yet is a sort of property which the Crown would "be less likely to interfere with and take away the right "from the subject who is likely to derive a benefit from it."

Best, J., concurred, thinking the case made for the lord of the manor was extremely weak. He holds that the right to the soil is in the King at common law, and that the King would permit these things to be done if they were not injurious to navigation.

Exch. B. & A., Northumberland, Geo. IV. No. 39.

On 10 June 1823 the Attorney-General filed an information against William Clark and Thomas Taylor, lessees of the Duke of Northumberland of a wharf and stage at Whitley Colliery, in the parish of Tynemouth, erected on the foreshore. In the information the Attorney claims that the foreshore of the kingdom belongs to the Crown, and that the King has the right of superintendence over the same for the safety of the realm and the benefit of commerce, &c., and that all obstructions thereon should be abated, and he proceeded entirely on the question of nuisance, and laid no claim to the soil. The defendant set up that the soil was part of the manor of Teignmouth and belonged to the Duke of Northumberland. The result of this proceeding does not appear.

Exch. Ord. Bks., 1823-33; Exch. Decrees Bks., 1823-41.

The King *v.* Comrs. of Pagham Level, 2 Mann. & Ry. 468.

In 1823 occurred the case of the King against the Commissioners of Pagham Level, in which it was decided that persons occupying lands adjoining the sea may erect groins and such defences as are necessary for the preservation of their own lands, although such erections may render it necessary for their neighbours to do the like.

Comrs. of Woods' 5th Rep.

On 27 November 1824 the Commissioners of Woods sold to Francis Robinson and another the Crown interests in a piece of woodland at Newhaven, Sussex, containing 3 acres 1 rood 14 perches, for £45.

Rex *v.* Ld. Yarborough, 1 Dow & Cl. 178; 3 B. & C. 91; 4 Dowl.&Ry. 790; 5 Bing. 163.

Petty Bag, Concealments, ble. 5, No. 8.

In 1824 occurred the case of Rex *v.* Lord Yarborough. This was an information to recover 453 acres of land adjoining the manor of North Thoresby-cum-Northcoats, in Lincolnshire, which had formerly been covered by the sea. In this case the ancient practice of issuing a commission and taking an inquisition was resorted to. The inquisition was returned on 12 November 1818 into the Office of the Petty Bag, and it was found that the land in question had, in times past, been covered with the sea, but had been for several years *left* by the sea, and was not covered except at high tides; but that it was still unoccupied, although the herbage had been from time to time eaten by cattle and sheep belonging to tenants or occupiers of land situate within the parish or lordship of Northcoats. The inquisition further states that the commissioners had seized it into the King's hand. The defendant traversed the inquisition, and said he was seised of the manor of North Thoresby-cum-Northcoats, and the demesne lands thereof, and that the piece of land in question had by slow, gradual, and imperceptible projection, alluvion, subsidence, and accretion of ooze, soil, sand, and matter been slowly, gradually, and by imperceptible increase in long time cast up, deposited, and settled by and from the flux and re-flux of the tide and waves of the sea in, upon, and against the outside and extremity of the demesne lands of the same manor, and had become parcel of them. The Attorney-General took issue that the land was *left* by the sea. The jury found for the defendant, and a rule for a new trial was argued. The land in question was 450 acres of salt marsh called "Fittees," and it was proved that it was formed by the deposit cast up by the Humber. The sea had receded as much as 150 yards in twenty-six years, but the recession had been gradual. The case was argued on the cases of alluvion quoted by Hale—viz., the Abbot of Ramsey's case, *ante*, p. 158; the Abbot of Peterborough's case, *ante*, p. 157; Digges *v.* Hammond, *ante*, p. 219. Abbot, C.J., delivered the judgment of the Court, and, holding that the increase was imperceptible, refused a rule for a new trial.

The case went to the House of Lords, when it was contended for the Crown that the judgment of the Court of King's Bench ought to be reversed—first, because the land was gained by alluvion, which, by the law of England, belongs of common right, by virtue of his prerogative, to the King; secondly, because the right of the subject so gained does not appear on this record to be supported by the allegation of any custom, or by the allegation that there has been any alternate ingress or regress by the sea upon the land in question, or any other legal ground in

1 Dow & Cl. 178; 5 Bing. 163.

opposition to the claim of the Crown; thirdly, because the title of the Crown, as found by the inquisition, remains without answer, and the King is therefore entitled to judgment upon this record notwithstanding the issues found for the defendant. For the defendant it was contended that the judgment ought to be affirmed—first, because the land, being gained by gradual accretion, is the property of the defendant by the common law; secondly, because, inasmuch as the King hath not any common law right or title to the land in question, it was not necessary for the defendant to state any custom or prescription; thirdly, because the traverse filed by the defendant is sufficient to bar the supposed right of the King. The case was tried in the presence of eleven judges. Best, C.J., delivered their opinion "that there is no local "custom on the subject, but the judges are unanimously "of opinion that, by the general custom of the realm, "lands gained gradually and imperceptibly from the sea "by alluvion or projection belong to the owner of the "adjoining demesne lands, and not to the Crown. When "the sea retreats suddenly and leaves a tract of land "uncovered, that land belongs to the Crown; but it is "otherwise with lands gained gradually and impercep-"tibly by alluvion or projection;" and he cites Bracton and Hale, the cases of the Abbot of Ramsey, Digges *v.* Hammond, the Abbot of Peterborough, Rex *v.* Oldsworth, as cited by Hale. The judgment of the Court below was affirmed.

Thus ended the long-continued attempt by the Crown to get possession of accretions in front of the manor of Northcoats, which had been attempted from time to time from the reign of James I.

6th Rep. Comrs. of Woods, p. 8.

It appears from the Sixth Report of the Commissioners of Woods that this case was taken by the Crown as a test case. Upon the decision against the Crown the Commissioners remark: "This decision is of great importance, "not only as it regards the claim in question, *but as* "*setting at rest similar claims, to the extent of many thou-* "*sand acres in different parts of the kingdom;* and although "the investigation has terminated unfavourably to the "Crown, and has been attended with considerable ex-"pense, we felt that we could not, consistently with our "duty, relinquish a claim of so much importance, and "concerning which great difference of opinion appeared "to have been entertained by the most eminent law "authorities, until the question had received the most "ample discussion and been decided by the highest legal "tribunal in the kingdom."

In 1824 an action of trespass was brought by Mr. Scratton, lord of the manors of Middleton Hall and Prittlewell Priory, in Essex, against one Brown, a cement-maker, for taking stones on the foreshore belonging to him. The defendant justified under a conveyance from the plaintiff's predecessor of "sea grounds, shores, oyster "layings, and fisheries called Middleton Hall and Prittle-"well Priory shores or sea grounds, with liberty to fish, "dredge, and lay oysters thereon, and from thence to take "and carry away the same, which said sea grounds, oyster "layings, shores, and fisheries did extend from the south "at low-water mark to the north at high-water mark, and "abutting west towards Leigh upon the lands or sea "grounds of E. Tyrrell, Esq., called Chalkwell Hall, and "towards the east upon the sea or oyster grounds of "Thomas Drew, Esq., and which contain in the whole "800 acres of land covered with water, or thereabouts, as "the same are beaconed and marked out, saving to the "lord of the manor wrecks of the sea, royal fish, flotson, "jetson, and lagon," &c. At the trial, Graham, B., held that the deed did not convey the soil, but only the right of fishing. The jury found a verdict for the plaintiff. On the motion for a new trial, the question turned on the construction of the words in the deed, and it was held that the soil passed, and that the additional words of "oyster fishery" did not limit the grant, but defined it. Littledale, J., says that upon the construction of the deed it is clear that if the words *sea grounds* had stood alone the soil would have passed under them; sea ground is either ground bordering on the sea or covered with the

Scratton *v.* Brown, 4 B. & C. 485; 6 Dowl. & Ry. 536.

sea ; the word *ground* itself is sufficient to pass the soil, and the word *sea* annexed to it only shews where it is situate. The next words, *oyster layings*, would not of themselves pass the soil, but the word *shores* unconnected with other words would pass the soil. "Then as to the "word *fisheries*, it is said that the word *oyster* must be "coupled ; but I do not know why they are to be con-"nected together. It may indeed be said that the word "*fishery* is unnecessary, for, if the soil passed, the fishery "passed also, but that is not so ; a fishery in a river would "pass by the conveyance of the adjoining land, because "of common right it might be incident to the soil, but in "this case it was absolutely necessary to grant the fishery, "for the grant of the soil would not be sufficient to con-"vey a peculiar privilege to fish between high and low "water mark, because all the King's subjects would have "a right to fish there unless a particular person was "entitled to it by specific grant or prescription." Bayley, J., said: "The word 'shore' is quite inconsistent with the "idea of an easement, for it passes the soil itself; nay, it "is the soil itself" (6 Dowl. & Ry. at p. 546).

It appeared from the case that the sea had encroached, and it was held that there may be a movable freehold ; the encroachment, having been imperceptible, followed the law of accretion, and belonged to the grantee of the sea ground. This foreshore has recently been sold by the lord of the manor to the Southend Local Board.

Petty Bag, Concealments, ble. 5, No. 9.

In 1826 the Crown laid claim to a portion of the foreshore of the borough of Hastings, which had been reclaimed from the sea and built upon, and a commission issued to inquire as to its extent. A return was made (with plan annexed), which finds that it belonged to the Crown, and that the houses had been erected without the King's licence. The land in question had been claimed, partly under a lease from the Earl of Chichester as lord of the rape of Hastings, and partly through the Corporation of Hastings under a grant to them by Queen Elizabeth of the "Stone Beach ;" but on the inquisition taken on 6 December 1827 the land was found to have been formerly

Mace *v.* Philcox, 33 L. J. C. P. 124; 10 Jur. N. S. 680. Ivall *v.* Corp. of Hastings, covered by the sea, and to be situate outside the bounds of any manor or manors, and unoccupied till within sixty years past. No attempt was made to traverse the inquisition, and no opposition was made to the claims of the Crown. The Crown seized the premises, and compounded with the occupiers. An attempt was made to recover some land at Rye in the same manner, which seems to have failed. A Mr. Miller, solicitor, of Lincoln's Inn, was the "title hunter" for the Crown in these two cases.

L. R. 19 Eq. pp. 562-565. Rep. of Comrs. of Woods, vi. 8; vii. 57, with a plan.

In the case of Lopes *v.* Andrew, in 1826, which was a case of trespass on the foreshore of the River Tavy, in Cornwall, the plaintiff was lord of the manor, and the defendant claimed under the *primâ facie* right of the Duchy of Cornwall to the foreshore by the parliamentary charter of 11 Edward III. to the Duchy. The evidence of user was contradictory. It was argued for the defendant that under the Duchy charter the foreshore was inalienable. The learned judge charged the jury that "the "land between high and low water mark belonged *primâ* "*facie* to the Crown, but that evidence of enjoyment by "the owner of the adjoining manor would justify the pre-"sumption of a grant from the Crown, and that although "the spot in question appeared to fall within the terms of "the parliamentary grant to the Black Prince, and there-"fore to be inalienable, yet the jury were at liberty to "presume a statute granting the land between high and "low water mark to some former owner of the plaintiff's "manor." There was a verdict for the plaintiff, and, on a motion to set it aside, it was held that the direction of the learned judge was correct in point of law. [It would perhaps have been a more correct direction to have told the jury that they were at liberty to presume a grant from the Crown to the lord of the manor before the creation of the Duchy, which was most probably the true fact, as the foreshore must have been parcel of the manor before *Quia Emptores*, and therefore long before 11 Edward III.]

Lopes *v.* Andrew, 3 Mann. & Ry. 329.

In 1828, in the case of Fitzpatrick *v.* Robinson and others, an action was brought for a trespass to a quay situate on the foreshore of the town of Cove, in Ireland.

Fitzpatrick *v.* Robinson & others, 1 Hud. & Br. 585.

The plaintiff, who was the lessee of Lord Middleton, proved that Lord Middleton was seised of part of the town of Cove, and of the beach and shore of the river on which the quay was built to the low-water mark, and that he and his predecessors had received keelage for vessels lying on the shore, and that the quay was erected by the plaintiff on part of the shore let to him on 25 October 1815. The defendants pleaded that the *locus in quo* was part of the beach of a public navigable river, and was a common highway, and insisted that the beach was dedicated to the public, and shewed user of it by the public; but Bushe, C.J., citing Abbot, C.J., in Blundell *v.* Caterall, held that an user by the public of an open strand or waste does not necessarily lead to the inference that the owner of the soil has abandoned his right to it or given it to the public.

5 B. & A. 315.

Benest *v.* Pipon, 1 Knapp P. C. 60.

In 1829, in the case of Benest *v.* Pipon, which was a suit with respect to cutting "vraic" or sea ware on L'Isle Percée, in the parish of St. Brelades, Jersey, it was held that the lord of a manor cannot establish a claim to the exclusive right of cutting seaweed or rocks *below* low-water mark, except by a grant from the King, or by such long undisturbed enjoyment of it as to constitute a title by prescription. The possession necessary to constitute a title by prescription must be uninterrupted and peaceable, both according to the law of England, the Civil Law, and those of France, Normandy, and Jersey.

CHAPTER XX.

A.D. 1830 TO A.D. 1866.

AFTER the passing of the Crown Lands Management Act, 1829 (10 Geo. IV. cap. 50), the Commissioners of Woods and Forests began actively to revive the claims of the Crown to foreshore, which had practically laid dormant for upwards of a century. In doing so they appear to have approached the question in the same spirit as Mr. Digges and the Stuart Sovereigns; they seem to have assumed that the foreshore was wholly in the Crown and had never been granted out, and that it could not be held by the subject unless he could shew an express grant of it. A review of these proceedings from 1830 downwards will be found hereafter. The Commissioners of Woods, in this revival of the Crown's claims, had for their guide Mr. Hall, who published his work on the Sea-shore in 1830. Mr. Hall's bias was altogether in favour of the Crown, and his work is evidently written with intent to support the Crown's claim by every argument that could be made to uphold it. Although he was, unlike Lord Hale, certainly ignorant of the true facts, he disputes Lord Hale's dicta wherever they tend to favour the subject, and misquotes, or imperfectly quotes, his words to make them suit his own arguments. He denies the authorship of "De Jure Maris," and his bias is very clearly shewn by the fact that when Hale's dictum favours the Crown he quotes it as Lord Hale's; but, wherever the dictum favours the subject, we read: "in the treatise "ascribed to Lord Hale." Mr. Hall's work is printed at the end of this treatise; the Editor's notes to it will shew the manner in which Mr. Hall has treated Lord Hale's text and attempted to pervert his arguments.

Comrs. of Woods' Reps. vii. 32; viii. 24.

On 17 December 1830 the Commissioners of Woods sold to Robert Vyner, Esq., the lord of the manor of Bidston, Cheshire, the foreshore and soil of Wallasey Pool, in the Mersey, containing fifty-four acres. Mr. Vyner took this grant to confirm his title, and claimed under this grant and as parcel of his manor in the suit of Vyner *v.* Mersey Dock Board, *post*, p. 540.

In 1829–33 the Commissioners of Woods sold a large tract of foreshore at the mouth of the River Dee, in the parish of Hollywell, to several persons. This was foreshore parcel of the manor of Englefield, which was then in the possession of the Crown.

Alcock *v.* Cook, 5 Bing. 340; 2 M.& Pay. 625; but see G. E. Ry. *v.* Horner, 9 App. Cas. 940.

In 1829, in the case of Alcock *v.* Cook, which was an action for trover for wreck at Sutton, Lincolnshire, the question was whether a grant by the Crown is or is not void when it grants in possession that of which the Crown had only the reversion. It appeared that King James I. in 12 James I., A.D. 1614, had made a lease to one Livingstone, *inter alia*, of wrecks in the honour of Bolingbroke for a term of thirty-one years, and that Charles I. in 6 Charles I., A.D. 1630, pending the lease, had made a grant (which did not recite the lease) of the manor of Gretham, within the honour of Bolingbroke, within which manor Sutton was supposed to lie, with a full grant of liberties *adeo plene* as any previous possessor had held it, but not mentioning wreck *nominatim*. The question was whether, as the King had granted the lease of this property, and had not recited that lease in the grant of the fee in perpetuity, the latter grant was not by the common law of England altogether void. "We," said Best, C.J., "are of opinion that it was altogether void. "We take it to be a principle of the common law of this "country that, if the King makes a grant which cannot "take effect in the manner in which it ought to take "effect according to its terms, we must conclude that the "King has been deceived in that grant, and therefore that "the grant is void," and he cites the case of the Earl of Rutland and the case of Alton Woods, and says that the doctrine of these two cases, which is confirmed by several

8 Rep. 57a.
1 Rep. 26.

others, has become the settled law of the land. "If the "King is deceived in his grant, the grant is altogether "void; and it appearing by decided cases that the King is "deceived in his grant when he grants that which he "cannot give according to the terms of his grant, and it "appearing also at the time that the grant of 6 Charles I. "was executed the property granted was already in the "possession of Livingstone under a lease for years, and "that that lease had several years to run, the grant of 6 "Charles I. is altogether void."[1]

In Hilary 10–11 George III., A.D. 1830, the Attorney-General filed an information against Bolton and others respecting the foreshores of the Hull and Humber at Hull. Exch.Q.R., File of Informations, 32 Geo. II., 6 Vict.

In 1832 occurred the case of Lowe *v.* Govett. It was an action for trespass. It appeared that by an Act of Parliament, 42 George III. cap. 32, a company was empowered to embank a tract of land called the Lairie, in Lipson Bay, near Plymouth, adjoining the defendant's estate, called Lipson Ground. The company, in cutting a drain, appear to have encroached on the Lipson Ground Estate above the high-water mark of ordinary tides, and it was argued that the Crown's right extended to the high-water mark of spring tides, but as the language of the Act of Parliament described the land to be granted as being "daily "overflowed by the sea," and as the company could only take what was in the Crown, "that is," said Littledale, J., Lowe *v.* Govett, 3 B. & Ad. 863.

[1] As to the validity and construction of Crown grants, see also Mayor of Kingston *v.* Horner, Cowp. 102; Gledstanes *v.* Earl of Sandwich, 5 Scott N. R. 689, 12 L. J. C. P. 41; Regina *v.* Kempe, 1 Lord Raym. 49; Parmeter *v.* Gibbs, 10 Price 412; Att.-Gen. *v.* Parmeter, 10 Price 378, 1 Dow 316, 323; Chad *v.* Tilsed, 2 B. & B. 403, 5 Moo. 185; Gray *v.* Bond, 2 B. & B. 667, 5 Moo. 527; Att.-Gen. *v.* Hanmer, 27 L. J. Ch. 837, 4 Jur. N. S. 751; Att.-Gen. *v.* Ewelme Hospital, 17 Beav. 366, 36 L. J. Ch. 846; Lord *v.* Commr. of Sydney, 12 Moo. P. C. C. 473; Baird *v.* Fortune, 4 Macq. H. of L. Cas. 127, 5 L. T. 2, 10 W. R. 2; Duke of Beaufort *v.* Swansea, 3 Exch. 413; Duke of Somerset *v.* Fogwell, 5 B. & C. 875; Feather *v.* Regina, 6 B. & S. 283, S. C. 35 L. J. Q. B. 204, 12 L. T. N. S. 114; R. *v.* London, Mayor of, 1 Cr. M. & R. 12; R. *v.* 49 Casks of Brandy, 3 Hagg. Adm. 271; Dyer 77; Cro. Car. 143; 5 Rep. 94; Moore 293; 12 Rep. 46; 1 Mod. 195; 10 Rep. 109; Bl. Com. lib. ii. p. 1.

"the ground between high and low water mark," judgment was given for the defendant, Park, J., remarking that, as the land in question was above the ordinary high-water mark, the plaintiffs could not entitle themselves under the Crown.

Att.-Gen. *v.* Mainwaring and Jones, House of Commons Returns, 1858, 314.

In 1833 an information of intrusion was filed in the Exchequer by the Attorney-General against Mainwaring and Jones to establish the right of the Crown to 278 acres of land called Lach Eyes, formerly overflowed by the tide, situate near the city of Chester, on the River Dee. The case was tried on 25 August 1835 before Lord Abinger and a special jury, when a verdict was found for the Crown. The land was sold to the Marquis of Westminster for £7500. There is no report of this case, but it seems to have been a suit either for derelict land or for an island in the River Dee.

Howe *v.* Stawell, Alcock & Nap. 348.

In 1833 occurred the case of Howe *v.* Stawell. It was an action for trespass for taking seaweed and sea oare, and wrack commonly called oareweed, in the plaintiff's close, called Glannaverne Strand. The defendant pleaded the general issue, and that the closes were part of the sea-shore where the subject had a right to pass and re-pass and take oareweed and seaweed deposited by the flux of the sea. The plaintiff took issue, and denied the alleged right. The defendant demurred, and the case was argued on the demurrer. The plaintiff's title to the shore was admitted. The defendant relied on the case of Bagot *v.* Orr, *ante*, p. 439, arguing that the ownership of the soil is vested in the King of common right, but he holds it only as a trustee for the public privileges, and his grantee can only take it subject to the same rights, citing Davis 57, Callis on Sewers 17–18, and Hale, and Dickens *v.* Shaw, and Year Book 18 Edward IV. 19. Blundell *v.* Caterall was attempted to be distinguished, and Benest *v.* Pipon was cited as an authority. For the plaintiff it was insisted that there was no such common law right in the public. "Such an unqualified right is at variance with legal prin- "ciple and analogy, with the rights of private property "which are admitted on the pleading, and with all adjudi-

"cated cases. The only common law rights pertaining to "the sea are the rights of piscary and the rights of navi-"gation, which exist for the benefit of the commonwealth "as incident to commerce and the public subsistence." The judgment of Holroyd, J., in Blundell *v.* Caterall was cited to shew that the passage in Bracton adopted from the Civil Law was inconsistent with the principles of common law. With regard to Dickens *v.* Shaw, it was said that it merely decides that a right to wreck will not alone confer a title by presumption or construction of law to the ownership of the soil of the shore as against the Crown; and Best, J., in that case says that, while the right is in the King, it is to be presumed that he would permit those things to be done (viz., the taking of sand and other products from the shore) if they were not injurious to the navigation, thus referring the enjoyment by the public to the acquiescence of the Crown, and not to the common law right. Jebb, J., delivered the judgment of the Court, and held against the common law right set up. He says: "Now we cannot find any authority or precedent "for this, which is in effect a proposition amounting to this, "that the right to enter upon the sea-shore and to take "seaweed thereon is co-extensive with the right of fish-"ing when the shore is covered with water, or of entering "upon the shore when the water has left it and taking "fish that may have been left and remaining there. But "there is not only no decision to this effect, but whatever "is to be found upon the subject in books of authority "seems against such a right," and he cites the passage in Hale respecting the fetching of gravel and seaweed and sea sand from the foreshore by the lords of manors, and says that the passage furnishes a strong presumption against the existence of the right. On the authority of Mr. Justice Holroyd's judgment in Blundell *v.* Caterall, he holds that the doctrine of Bracton is not consistent with the common law, and that the statute of 7 James I., cap. 18, as to taking sand in Devon and Cornwall, tends to shew the non-existence of any such common law right in all the King's subjects. "This being a claim of right in "derogation of, and as a qualification of, the King's general "right, it ought not to be allowed without some decision, "or some authority, or some reason drawn from some "decision or authority in favour of it." "That the King "has the soil of the shore from high to low water mark, "as well as beyond that mark, is clear from the authority "of Hale, Callis 39, and Davis 53. These prerogatives "[waif, flotsam, wreck, &c.] are qualified or adapted to the "public benefit by the clearly allowed common right of "the King's subjects to fish in the sea, or arms or creeks "thereof, as a public common of piscary (subject to ex-"ception in case of exclusive rights), and this liberty "seems to extend to the taking of shell fish left on the "sea-shore upon the re-flux of the tide between high and "low water mark (Bagot *v.* Orr, 2 Bos. & P. 472), upon "the same reason—viz., that the taking of fish is for the "immediate sustentation of man, a reason which does "not apply to the liberty of taking seaweed; a liberty "which may in many situations and under many circum-"stances be very reasonable and beneficial, and which "may be established by local custom, but can be legally "claimed for all the King's subjects, or any portion of "them, by virtue of such local custom, and not as being "part of the common law." The language of the concluding words of the judgment, as printed, is not quite clear, but it is evident the decision is that a claim to take seaweed cannot exist in the public, and can only be claimed by a local custom, not by the public, but by some ascertained and limited class who could be capable in law of having it.

2 Y. & C. Exch. 61.

In 1836 occurred the case of Perrott *v.* Bryant, in which it was decided that perches or oyster layings on the foreshore of the parish of Oystermouth were not extra-parochial, and were liable to tithe by custom, Alderson, B., being of opinion that the fact that these perches had never been rated to the poor was not at all a strong circumstance to rebut the presumption of parochialty shewn by evidence of perambulations of the parish, and evidence that the tithes had been paid on them for sixty years without dispute.

In 1836, in the case of the King *v.* 49 Casks of Brandy, William John Banks, Esq., the lord of the manor of Corfe Castle, in the Isle of Purbeck, laid a claim to wrecked brandy taken up within three miles of his manor. He set out an inquisition of 4 Richard II., A.D. 1380, inquiring into the King's rights in the Isle of Purbeck, in which the boundary of the island and manor was set out, and it was stated that the King was entitled to wrecks of the sea, royal fish, and prisage of wine; he further shewed that by patent dated 15 January, 32 Henry VIII., A.D. 1540–41, the King granted to his consort, Queen Catherine, the hundreds of Rowborough and Haslar, which comprehended the Isle of Purbeck, with wreck of the sea, flotson, jetson, lagon, and royal fish; that Queen Elizabeth in 14 Elizabeth, A.D. 1572, granted the castle and manor of Corfe and the Isle of Purbeck, with wrecks of the sea, to Sir Christopher Hatton, and further granted to him that the said manor should be exempt from the jurisdiction of the Admiral, and that he and his heirs should be Admirals within the said castle, lordship, and manor of Corfe and Isle of Purbeck, and the precincts and liberties of the same, as well by water as by land, and upon the high sea flowing to or adjoining the aforesaid island or any part thereof, and of and over all ports, creeks, rivers, arms of the sea, and other waters and places whatsoever being within the aforesaid island. He also shewed that on a quo warranto in 16 Charles II., A.D. 1664, against Sir Ralph Banks, for the liberties granted to him, the said liberties were allowed by the Court. 3 Hagg. 257.

In 1834 wrecked casks were taken up, some floating and some aground, and Banks claimed them all as being within the limits of his liberty and estate. The Admiralty Proctor replied that the boundaries of the manor do not extend to the sea, but must be construed to refer to the foreshore only; that there had been no exercise of the office of Admiral which had been granted. The judge (Sir John Nichols) said, "By the general law all goods "found afloat and derelict on the high sea belong as "droits to the Crown in its office of Admiral," and held that the claimant must clearly make out his claim. He doubted how far the Crown had the power of granting away rights and perquisites which had always belonged to a high office of state. Considering the principles upon which such a grant should be construed, he cited Blackstone ii. 347: "The King's grant shall not enure to any "other intent than that which is precisely expressed in the grant." Also Lord Stowell in the case of the *Rebecca* (1 Rob. 230): "All grants from the Crown are to be "strictly construed against the grantee, contrary to the "usual policy of the law in the consideration of grants, "and upon this just ground, that, the prerogatives, rights, "and emoluments of the Crown being conferred upon it "for great purposes and for the public use, it shall not be "intended that such prerogatives, rights, and emoluments "are diminished by any grant beyond what such grant, by "necessary and unavoidable construction, shall take away. "This was on a question as between the King and the "Lord Admiral, and it was there held that the Lord "Admiral had these droits in preference to the King "himself. That is the principle upon which the grant to "Sir Christopher Hatton is to be construed." He decided that the goods picked up on the high sea—that is, not within any land jurisdiction—belong to the office of Admiral, and those which were found within the limits of the Isle of Purbeck are wreck of the sea and belong to the claimant. He also decided that the casks picked up outside the low-water mark, but within three miles of the shore, were afloat on the high sea beyond low-water mark, not in the body of any county or the limits of the Isle of Purbeck, and consequently belonged to the Admiralty; that those which were afloat between high and low water marks, but being afloat and never having even touched the ground, had not become wreck of the sea, and those which had been found on the ground, the tide being out, were wreck of the sea; that those which were found on the ground, though still moved by the waves, the sea at one time surrounding them and at another leaving them dry, were doubtful, but ought to be considered wreck of the sea, because they had struck the ground.

In 1837, in the case of the King *v.* Two Casks of Tallow, the lords of the manors of Caistor Pastons and Caistor Bardolfs, Norfolk, claimed two casks of tallow under a title to wreck by prescription. The casks had been taken to the custom-house at Great Yarmouth as having been found derelict flotson, jetson, or ligan. It was argued for the Admiralty that the casks were secured before they were grounded on the beach within the manors, and that they did not become grounded on the beach or shore till after the act of salving the same had commenced by the salvors, who were obliged to go into the sea for that purpose, it being after low water; and to this it was rejoined that the casks had grounded before the act of salving the same commenced—that it was not low water, but at least half flood, at the time. Sir John Nichols decided that *wreccum maris* is not such in a legal acceptation until it comes ashore, and that the lord of a manor as grantee of the Crown can have no claim beyond low-water mark. If the article be found floating, it belongs to the sea—it is not *wreccum maris*, but flotsom; if it become fixed to the land, although there may be some tide remaining round it, it may be considered as *wreccum maris*, but it having merely touched the ground and being again floating about, its character will depend upon its state at the time it was seized and secured into possession; whether, for instance, the person who seized it as salvor was in a boat or wading or swimming. "I cannot agree," he says, "to the proposition that things having once "touched the ground, thereby necessarily become the "property of the lord of the manor. What might be the "law in the case of things having become fixed on the "shore, and afterwards the sea leaving them and then "returning, may be a question hereafter, but it is one that "does not arise at present in this case," and he adjudged the casks in question to be Admiralty droits.

The King *v.* Two Casks of Tallow, 3 Hagg. 294.

On the last point, see *post*, the *Pauline*, p. 481.

Re Hull and Selby Railway, 5 M. & W. 327.

In 1839, the River Humber having encroached upon and washed away certain growths above the foreshore of the Humber formerly the property of Henry Broadley, a railway was made upon the foreshore, which had formerly been growths above the high-water mark, and the purchase-money paid into court was claimed by Broadley and by the Crown. Broadley did not claim to be entitled to the foreshore, but to the land which had been encroached upon by the river; but judgment was given for the Crown on the converse of the principle laid down in Rex *v.* Lord Yarborough, viz., "that in all cases of gradual accretion "which cannot be ascertained from day to day, the land so "gained goes to the person to whom the land belongs to "which the accretion is added, and *vice versâ;*" therefore gradual accretion gives the soil to the landowner, gradual decretion gives it to the Crown.

House of Commons Returns, 3 June 1858, 314.

Besides the action against Mr. Broadley, the Crown proceeded against a number of other frontagers, and altogether recovered £3185 *6s. 7d.* by their submissions to the continued suits of the Crown. The cases were pure questions of alluvion and dereliction, and the defendants did not claim under any manorial title.

Marwood *v.* Harewood, privately printed.

In 1841 Mr. Marwood, the successor in title to Peter de Brus, the lord of the wapentake of Langbargh, claimed a portion of the bed of the River Tees, near Middlesborough, which had become dry by a diversion of the river made under the powers of an Act of Parliament. He claimed it as land left derelict, and as belonging to him under a grant of King John of "the wapentake of "Langbargh with its appurtenances," under which grant he and his predecessors had claimed wreck between Yarm and Rimeswick. See *ante*, pp. 48, 81.

He produced a record of a proceeding upon a quo warranto by the Attorney-General (Sir Francis Bacon) against Sir Henry Bellasis, the owner of the wapentake in the time of James the First, to which Bellasis pleaded, and claimed wreck, anchorage, flotson, jetson, and other very extensive franchises and rights throughout the wapentake, but did not claim the foreshore or bed of the

Tees. On this plea the Attorney-General entered a *nolle prosequi*.[1]

The case turned upon a conflict of evidence of user brought forward to shew who was the owner of this portion of the bed of the Tees. The evidence of the plaintiff was slight, that for the defendant was strong, and the jury found a verdict for the defendant. Mr. Justice Maule, in summing up to the jury, set forth the *primâ facie* title, and said that the land was in the Crown unless the Crown had granted it to somebody. "The Crown "formerly had a more unrestrained power of making "such grants than it has now, and such grants were "extremely common; and a very large portion of the "actual sea-shore, and a still greater portion of that "constructive sea-shore which belongs to the banks or "beds of tidal rivers, is really in private subjects, deriving "their title originally from the Crown; some of them "before the time of King John, and some after, but from "such early times one cannot tell when; only they have "it, and it is possible they may have it lawfully, and it "never could be considered unlawful unless the contrary "is shewn. Such rights do exist derived from the Crown "in ancient times, and they exist more (it is natural they "should) with respect to rivers which are inland, though "they are also portions of the sea in the sense I have "mentioned—that is, the tide flows into them; and with "respect to such rivers as this, it is not very unlikely— "one would think it a likely thing—that a portion of the "soil, half of the soil of a river like this, should be "granted to the owner of the soil on the banks, and not "to a stranger. It is more likely that should be the case

[1] There are strong grounds for believing that this proceeding was collusive, for, in point of fact, Bellasis was at the time only entitled to a moiety of the wapentake. Having, however, got this judgment in his favour, Bellasis began to claim all the shore of the wapentake, extending over about forty miles, and endeavoured to make the lords of the manors within it take leases of the seaweed, anchorage, &c., from him; some of them did so, others resisted his claim, others repudiated the leases after they were granted, and at last Bellasis gave up the contest.—ED.

"than portions of the bed of the open sea—more incon-"venience would result from the owners not having that "right, and more convenience from their having it. Again, "it would be more worth their while to apply for it, and "afford cogent reasons to the Crown for granting it to "them, than the beach of the open sea, which might not "be worth purchasing; and I think, when you are con-"sidering, in an equivocal and doubtful case, what was "and what was not in the Crown at a given time, and "what the Crown did or did not part with, you may "fairly enough look at the subject which it is alleged the "Crown had, and which it is alleged the Crown parted "with."

He then discussed the nature of the plaintiff's evidence, and shewed that the grant of "the wapentake with its "appurtenances" did not necessarily comprehend all the land which the Crown might have in the place, and shewed that, although it was admitted that the land generally within the bounds of the wapentake did not pass by the grant, it was argued that, whatever land was remaining in the Crown at the time of the grant did so pass, and he held that the evidence tended to shew a grant of franchises rather than of land, especially observing that Bellasis had made no claim to the foreshore in his plea to the quo warranto. In speaking of the user, he said: "Suppose a man carries away seaweed—that is "user; or takes wreck upon the land—that is user;" and held that the evidence of taking anchorage and wreck does not necessarily shew a right to the soil, and pointed out that Mr. Marwood had shewn no evidence of user on the spot in question.

The defendant having shewn substantial user, the verdict passed for him.

Calmady *v.* Rowe, 9 C. B. 861.

In 1844 occurred the case of Calmady *v.* Rowe. It was an action of trespass on the foreshore in the parish of Wembury, Devon, by taking seaweed and oareweed. The defendants pleaded not guilty, that the close was not the plaintiff's close, that the close was the close of the Queen in right of her crown, and that the defendants were the

Queen's licensees. The plaintiff took issue on the first two pleas, and replied that the defendants were not the Crown's licensees. The plaintiff was lord of the manor of Langdon, which had been granted to Vincent and Richard Calmady, his ancestors, in 1564. The grant recited a lease by the Crown, 17 August, 4–5 Philip and Mary, A.D. 1557, to John Wynslande, of the manor, with all its rights, members, and appurtenances, with all wastes and full general words, but no word of wreck or shore, and granted to Calmady the reversion of the premises, together with wastes, rocks, islands, and the ground and soil thereof, ways flooded by the sea, waters, watercourses, passages for water, piscaries, fishing pools, stew-ponds, &c., shipwrecks, wrecks of the sea to the said manor belonging, as fully as all predecessors had had them. Evidence was given to shew that the plaintiff and those under whom he claimed had for at least forty years been in the habit of taking, by themselves or by their tenants, from the shore, between high and low water mark, sand and oareweed for manure and stones for the repair of the fences of the manor and the boathouse which stood upon the beach above high-water mark; that the plaintiff's tenants had been in the habit of laying nets between high and low water mark fixed to iron stanchions driven into the soil; and that no person other than the tenants of the manor had, without the lord's permission, taken sand or seaweed. Evidence was also given that wreck had on three or four occasions been taken by the plaintiff upon the *locus in quo* and applied to his own use. A presentment of the boundary of the manor, which stated that the royalty of the owner of Langdon extended as far south as a lumber cask may be seen, was rejected by the judge (Pattison, J.), on the ground that this was not a question of boundary. A presentment for taking stones on the shore was also rejected, on the ground that it did not appear that any fine had been imposed.

On the part of the defendants it was conceded that the plaintiff had sufficiently shewn a right to take sand, stones, and seaweed from the shore between high and low water mark, and also a right of wreck and several fishery; but these, it was insisted, were in the nature of easements only, and proved no right to the soil of the sea-shore, especially in the absence of any specific grant of the *litus maris*. And it was contended that the plaintiff was bound to shew his right with the same degree of strictness as if the question had arisen between himself and the Crown upon a writ of intrusion. No evidence was offered for the defendants.

The judge, in leaving the case to the jury, observed that "the grant of Elizabeth certainly contains no word "which necessarily implies a conveyance of the soil of the "shore; the word *funda* has not, I conceive, this meaning." He then cites Hale at length, and says: "Lord Hale's "doctrine as to the presumption arising from the grant of "wreck may be a little questionable. I do not, however, "think that it is *essential*, in order to shew the lord's right "to the sea-shore, that *litus maris* should be expressly "mentioned; such right may be inferred from long and "uninterrupted enjoyment independently of the particular "words that are found in the grant. As to this the "evidence is all one way; the presentments made at the "courts of the manor I did not consider to be admissible "evidence, because they did not appear to have been "followed by punishment of the purprestures. It is to be "observed that no evidence whatever was given of any "strangers having at any time come to take sand or sea-"weed from the shore of the place in question in assertion "of any right in contradiction to, or in repudiation of, the "exclusive right claimed by the plaintiff. It is, however, "for you to say whether, from the evidence which has "been laid before you, you can satisfactorily arrive at the "conclusion that the sea-shore was granted by the Crown "to the ancestors of Mr. Calmady—that is to say, that the "sea-shore was parcel of the manor." The jury returned a verdict for the plaintiff.

On a motion for a new trial, on the ground of misdirection and that the verdict was not warranted by the evidence, it was argued for the defendants that although the plaintiff had the right to wreck, his grant did not convey the soil, and that it did not follow that, because wreck of the sea was granted, the soil of the sea-shore was intended to pass also; that the case was unlike the case of trespass upon an inland close; and that the plaintiff ought to prove his title just as if the Crown had been a party, seeing that the rights of the Crown in respect of the sea-shore are merely ancillary to the convenience and rights of the public; and that plaintiff ought to prove his title as if he were seeking to establish it against the Crown. It was attempted to shew that Lord Hale's dictum as to "he that hath wreck of the sea," &c., was qualified by the case of Dickens *v.* Shaw, which was quoted at length. But Maule, J., remarked, "In that case "there was no evidence of any grant of wreck within "the manor." The statute of 7 James I. cap. 18, was also cited, but upon that Maule remarked, "No private "rights are interfered with by that statute."

Tindal, C.J., in his judgment, remarks that the grant under which the plaintiff claimed was long anterior to the statute, and that the statute was not intended to deprive third persons of any rights legally vested in them. "I "think there was abundant evidence in this case to warrant "the jury in the conclusion at which they arrived. The "grant of Queen Elizabeth gave the right of wreck, which, "according to Lord Hale, affords strong ground for pre-"suming that the soil between high and low water mark "is intended to be passed by it;[1] and there was, besides, a "considerable body of evidence of acts done by the plain-"tiff and those under whom he claimed that raised a "strong and almost irresistible presumption that they "were owners of the soil. As to the direction of the "learned judge, I see no ground for quarrelling with it. "The objection seems to be that, having read certain pas-"sages from a treatise that has generally been esteemed "as of authority upon this subject, and very commonly "ascribed to Lord Hale, my brother Pattison gave too

[1] That is, the soil was parcel of the manor before the grant, and the grant of the wreck was of wreck to be taken on that soil.

"much weight to it, and omitted to notice a case which "my brother Channell suggests to have somewhat abridged "the doctrine of that very learned judge. I cannot, how- "ever, perceive any impropriety in the mode in which the "case was left to the jury. I therefore think that there "is no ground for a rule."

Coltman, J.: "I am of the same opinion. The case of "Dickens *v.* Shaw certainly does not to any material extent "contravene the authority of Lord Hale. The observa- "tions of the learned judges in that case must be taken "with reference to the particular circumstances therein "proved."

Maule, J., concurred. "It cannot be denied that the "defendants were wrongdoers in taking seaweed from the "*locus in quo* whether the soil belonged to the Crown or "to a subject. It is said that the learned judge, in leaving "the case to the jury, laid too much stress upon the grant "and enjoyment of wreck to and by the plaintiff and his "ancestors. It appeared that Queen Elizabeth, in the "year 1564, granted the manor in question, together with "wreck of the sea, several fishery, and other extensive "rights; and there was evidence that wreck had on several "occasions been taken by the plaintiff. That, coupled "with the other evidence given in the cause, is, to my "mind, conclusive to shew that the soil of the sea-shore "was granted to those under whom the plaintiff claims. "The plaintiff seems to me to have made out as complete "a case of ownership as can well be conceived."

Cresswell, J.: "I am of the same opinion. It is no "ground for granting a new trial that the judge thought "this or that piece of evidence more or less material. I "think there was no misdirection, and that the evidence "of acts of ownership fully justified the conclusion to "which the jury came."

8 Beav. 370; 14 L. J. Ch. 305; 1 H. of L. 440; 12 Beav. 8, 171, 217; 2 Ha. & Tw. 1.

In 1844 the Attorney-General filed an information in Chancery against the Corporation of London, which sets out "that by the royal prerogative the ground and soil of "the coasts and shores of the sea round this kingdom, "and of every port, haven, and arm of the sea, creek, pool, "and navigable river thereof into which the sea ebbs and "flows, and also the shore lying between high-water mark "and low-water mark at ordinary tides, belong to her "Majesty, who has also a right of empire or government "over the navigable rivers of this kingdom," and charges that the Crown was seised of the Thames, and the corporation were by prescription or grant conservators, but they did not in virtue of such office take or acquire any estate or interest in the ground and soil of the bed or shore between high and low water marks of the said river. The information further charged that the corporation claimed the soil and gave licences to embank it, and particularly licensed William Cubitt to embank it opposite to the Isle of Dogs, and had also given a licence to embank a portion of it at Rotherhithe, and that these embankments would be injurious to the navigation and hurtful to the river, and were common nuisances, and ought to be abated. The information prayed discovery of the corporation documents, that the rights of the Crown might be declared, the claim of the Corporation declared null and void, an injunction, and abatement of the embankments.

The corporation appeared, and demurred to the information except as to the nuisances, and as to those they answered that they were not nuisances. The Master of the Rolls overruled the demurrer. Against this order the corporation appealed.

The question turned upon whether an information of this character might be maintained by the Crown in the Court of Chancery without any transfer of any new power from the Court of Exchequer to the Court of Chancery, and it was held that it could. The facts of the case were not gone into, the question before the Court being as to whether the Crown was entitled to discovery.

The case was heard in Chancery on 8 December 1849, when Mr. Serjeant Merewether made his learned address on behalf of the corporation. 2 Ha. & Tw. 1.

He contended that the *primâ facie* right of the Crown as claimed in the information did not exist; that there was

no sound authority for it; and that, though it had been asserted by learned judges on the Bench, such assertions were merely *obiter dicta* and opinion, and if this opinion, though so long entertained, was wrong, it must be abandoned, citing Bodenham *v.* Hill (7 M. & W. 274) and the observation of Lord Denman in Regina *v.* O'Connell (11 Cl. & Fin. 155) that "a large portion of that "legal opinion which has passed current for law falls "within the description of law taken for granted." He then proceeds to review the ancient authorities to shew that the idea of the *primâ facie* title was not conceived before the time of the Stuarts. He does not seem to have been aware of Mr. Digges' treatise. He refers to the Saxon charters, the Saxon laws, Domesday Book, the laws of William the Conqueror and Henry I., Glanvill, Magna Charta, and upon this he remarks that kidells and weirs upon the sea-coast were expressly exempted from it, from which he argues that the sea-shore was in the ownership of private individuals. He disputes the authority of Lord Hale's treatise, and refers to the case of Slimbridge in the time of Henry III., quoted by Hale. He discusses Bracton, Britton, the statute De Extenta
Ante, p. 89. Manerii (4 Edward I.), the case of the Abbot of Tichfield as to the weir at Cadland, and upon this he argues that it shews that at this period the owner of the adjoining land was entitled to follow the sea. He discusses the Prior of
Ante, p. 111. Tynemouth's case, and shews that that proceeding was founded solely on the ground of nuisance. He refers to the Year Books and the Rolls of Parliament, Statham, and Fitzherbert, and remarks upon the absence of any mention of such a right in the Crown. He cites the
Ante, p. 145. Abbot of Hulme's case in 10 Edward II., the statute De
Ante, p. 149. Prerogativa Regis, the Mirror, Sir Henry Neville's case (5 Edward III.), the case of the Abbot of Saint Augustine,
Ante, p. 157. the Book of Assizes 22 Edward III., the Abbot of Peter-
Ante, p. 156. borough's case, the case of the weirs at Burnham (50
Ante, p. 158. Edward III.), the statutes relating to weirs, the Abbot of
Ante, p. 219. Ramsey's case (43 Edward III.), Digges *v.* Hammond (17
Ante, p. 166. Elizabeth), the Year Book 8 Edward IV., cases of Sir

John Constable and Sir Henry Constable, and then proceeds to shew by the time of James I. the doctrine had been introduced. He further cites the Banne Fishery case and Callis, remarking that the authorities he quotes do not support his proposition. He refers to the Wandesford grant of 4 Charles I., A.D. 1629, shewing that it was invalid from the first. He refers to Attorney *v.* Philpott, Ante, p. 260. and states that it was never acted upon and was not to be relied on, to which the Solicitor-General says, "It is very possible." Serjeant Merewether evidently was not aware of the true history of the case. He refers to the dictum of Moreton, J., in Whittaker *v.* Wise, and argues that it Ante, pp. 304, 415. was a reporter's note, and that Philpott's case was repudiated. He refers to Johnson *v.* Barrett, Bulstrode *v.* Hall, the case of Sutton Pool, and Rowe *v.* Brenton. As to the Abridgements of Statham, Fitzherbert, and Rolle, he says that they are all of them free from the assertion of this prerogative right, but that Comyns, Bacon, and Viner in their Abridgements all state it, but that the authorities that they quote do not support it. He says that Blackstone's authorities do not support him. He cites Butler's notes on Coke upon Littleton, the saving clause of the Act of 54 George III. cap. 159, Lord Grosvenor's case, Blundell *v.* Caterall, Chad *v.* Tilsed, Dickens *v.* Shaw, Scratton *v.* Brown, Benest *v.* Pipon, Rex *v.* Ward, and Duke of Beaufort *v.* Swansea, and he sums up his argument by stating "that up to the period when the Stuarts succeeded to the "throne there is not the slightest pretence or shadow of "a case or document or record to shew that any such "prerogative existed, and that from that period precedents ought to be taken with the utmost caution; and "[he continues] I am justified in saying so by the words "of Mr. Baron Wood's judgment in one of those cases to "which I referred your lordship.[1] I say, therefore, that

Rex *v.* Ward, 4 Ad. & E. 384.

[1] "I must say I have not much veneration for precedents taken "from the arbitrary reigns of those monarchs, and I hope I shall not "see such precedents revived in this reign; if they do take a temporary "root they will soon be eradicated" (per Wood, B., in Attorney *v.* St. Aubyn, Wightwick 187).

"from that period precedents must be looked at with sus-"picion; not but that there might be in those days "decisions sound in law, quoted from time to time, acted "upon and dealt with as law, and which, whatever the "times were, would be regarded as authority; but if you "find at such a period only a text author suggesting this "doctrine, without any authority quoted for it, the matter "loosely mooted, a sort of *obiter* argument by counsel on "the one side and the other, followed up by such a case "as the one I have referred to (Attorney *v.* Philpott), not "finding that case afterwards quoted except to be re-"pudiated by the statement that it was contrary to "Constable's case (Whittaker *v.* Wise), charters granted by "the Crown at that same time (there was that of the De "Wandesfords, to which I have alluded, and one also "relating to part of the shore of Dorset (Chad *v.* Tilsed), "both, however, held to be void)—how this doctrine, now "revived, can be supported merely on the authority of "text authors and the *obiter dicta* of learned judges mis-"led by the treatise published under the name of Lord "Hale, but not, I think, rightly so, I must confess I am at "a great loss to understand."

He challenges the Attorney-General to quote a single case in support of the doctrine, and submits that there is no ground in law for this prerogative right, and that it cannot be maintained.[1]

The Court decided against the corporation, and held the answer insufficient, and granted discovery. The case dragged on till 18 December 1856, when an agreement was come to, and an arrangement was subsequently made between the corporation and the Crown, by which a grant was made on 1 March 1857 of all the estate and interest of the Crown in the bed and soil of the Thames within the flux and reflux of the tide, and all encroachments, embankments, and inclosures therefrom and thereupon, except in front of, or adjacent to, any Crown or Government property. This agreement and grant were confirmed by

[1] The speech will be found printed in the last edition of Hall on the Sea-shore.

the Thames Conservancy Act, 1857, in consideration of £5000, with a third of the proceeds of all sales and grants of foreshore thereafter to be made. This conveyance only passes such interest as the Crown had in the Thames, and owners of foreshore by antecedent ancient title are not affected by it.

In this case the claim of the corporation would appear to have been ill founded, for the corporation were never anything but conservators, and conservancy carries no right to the soil, and, although in some cases it may possibly be that the conservator may have the soil, it will be found that he has it, not by virtue of his title as conservator, but that he holds it under some other distinct and separate grant. (Hale, pp. 353, 390, 401.) When the corporation were challenged as to the conservancy in 3 James I., they laid no claim to the soil, but established their title to the conservancy. (Coke's Entries, p. 353.)

By statute 8 & 9 Vict. cap. 99, A.D. 1845, power was given to the Commissioners of Woods to lease the "estate, "right, title, and interest" of the Crown of and in any portions of the shore of the sea or any arms thereof, or of navigable rivers, or lands derelict or gained, or what hereinafter may become derelict or to be gained, from the sea or any arms thereof, or navigable rivers, for ninety-nine years. The Act has no saving clause, but, as its power is limited to letting the Crown "interest" only in the foreshore, the title of the subject is unaffected by it.

In 1845 occurred the case of the *Pauline*, in the Admiralty Court. (The *Pauline*, Robinson Ad. Rep. 359.) It appears that the *Pauline* was wrecked on the Pole Sand, near the Warren, at the mouth of the River Exe, and was claimed by the Admiralty, and also by the Earl of Devon as lord of the manor of Kenton, as wreck. It appeared that the Admiral's men and the Earl's men took possession about the same time, and that they went aboard the wreck, in boats which floated. It was admitted that the *locus in quo* was within the low-water mark and within the manor. Dr. Lushington decided against the lord of the manor, because the ship was within the Admiralty jurisdiction at the time of the capture, viz., lying on land covered with water;

but decided in favour of the lord of the manor in respect of some casks which actually came on shore, on the authority of the case of the Two Casks of Tallow (*ante*, p. 469).

Duke of Beaufort *v.* Swansea, 3 Exch. 413.

In 1849 occurred the case of the Duke of Beaufort *v.* the Corporation of Swansea, in the Exchequer. This was an action for trespass upon the plaintiff's close at Swansea, and for erecting thereon certain seats. The defendants pleaded not guilty, and that the close was not the close of the plaintiff. It appeared that the seats were erected on a ballast bank on the foreshore, and the plaintiff claimed it as parcel of the seigniory of Gower, which had been granted to his predecessor in title, William de Braose, in 4 John, by the name of "Terra "de Gower," with all liberties, free customs, and appurtenances to the same belonging. That charter was confirmed by King Edward I. with the addition of all manner of jurisdiction and all royal liberties and free customs which Gilbert de Clare, son of Richard de Clare, heretofore Earl of Gloucester and Hereford, had in his land of Glamorgan. Subsequent confirmations were produced, but no grant which conveyed the shore in terms, nor any grant of the right to wreck *infra manerium;* but evidence was given of many acts of ownership in modern times. The judge (Williams, J.) told the jury that the plaintiff's case, was that he was entitled to the ground between high and low water mark as part of his seigniory of Gower; that the plaintiff relied, first, upon documentary evidence, and that he (the judge) was of opinion that the documentary evidence did not necessarily carry a right to the ground in question, and that they (the jury) must look at all the evidence in the case, and say whether they thought that either by grant or by prescription the property had passed from the Crown to those whose estate the Duke now had, and he put a question to the jury: "Is the land between high and low water mark part of "the seigniory of Gower?" The jury found this question in the affirmative, and the verdict was entered for the plaintiff, with leave to move. On the application for a new trial, it was argued, against the rule, that the word "terra" used in the grant was formerly used as the ordinary term of a grant of an extensive territory, and that it was equivalent to the words "honor," "baronia," and "feodum," and it was the same as "manerium," "dominium," and "baronia;" that a grant of the manor of Swansea would have beyond doubt included the sea-shore—that is to say, it would have been open to shew by parol evidence what the seaward boundaries of the manor of Swansea were; the word "manerium" would include the sea-shore, provided it be shewn that the sea-shore is parcel of the manor. If the grant of a manor would pass the sea-shore, the grant of a seigniory, which is a great manor or a great honour or a great lordship, would also pass it. Lord Hale was cited, and Sir Henry Constable's case, to shew that the sea-shore may be parcel of a manor; also the case of the castle of Trematon as to Sutton Pool. It was further argued that "the sea-shore is parcel of the solid soil of the "county. It does not belong to the King as a "prerogative franchise, but, as Lord Hale puts it, to "the various waste domains of the Crown. There is "a presumption of law in favour of the Crown, but it is "a presumption only. There is nothing mystic in the "term sea-shore; the presumption of law is that the "sea-shore is not parcel of a manor, and, not being so, it "is like other unappropriated land, which by the original "right of the Crown is vested in it as part of the soil of "England which the Crown has not parted with. But "the instant that the sea-shore is shewn by evidence to "be within the ambit of the manor, the presumption is "changed in favour of the lord of the manor; the waste "on the sea-shore is as much the property of the lord "of the manor as any other piece of inland waste." As to the construction of the grants, Chad *v.* Tilsed was cited, where it was laid down that where a grant of remote antiquity contains general words, the best exposition of such a grant is long usage under it. Here Baron Parke intervened, as follows:—"That is 7 East 199.

"agreeable to what Lord Ellenborough says in Weld *v.* "Hornby, that however general the words of the ancient "deeds may be, they are to be construed, as Lord Coke "says, by evidence of the manner in which the thing "has always been possessed and used. If this were not "so, there would be no mode of shewing whether the "thing granted was parcel of the manor or not." The Attorney-General, for the rule, argued that the foreshore belongs to the Crown, *not as part of the tangible possessions of the Crown, but by prerogative.* If that be true, it is clear that it could only be granted by express words, upon which Parke, B., said, "If any portion of the sea-"shore would pass by the word 'terra,' cadit quæstio." Alderson, B.: "It lies upon you to prove, not that it "might not have passed, but that it could not have "passed." The Attorney-General further argued that, between subject and subject, the term "terra" might be sufficient, or, indeed, the word "manerium," or "dominium;" but he said that the question is different with respect to the Crown. He admitted that where the lord of the manor is found in the exercise of the right of wreck, it is strong evidence that the Crown has granted the shore, but, he said, it is only evidence; it does not prove that the word "manor" could pass the shore. The Court held that the direction of the learned judge was quite correct. Pollock, C.B.: "The question is, whether "the direction given by the learned judge is a proper "mode of directing the jury. It appears to me to be "unobjectionable. In substance it is this:—There is a "grant of the seigniory of Gower. What is the seigniory "of Gower? The learned judge says, You cannot define "the seigniory of Gower merely from those words; you "cannot say that the spot which the plaintiff claims is his, "as being part of the seigniory of Gower, merely from those "words; but if, by usage which is of so long standing "that we may presume it to be contemporaneous with the "grant itself, the sea-shore in question has always been "considered to be part of the seigniory of Gower, and you "will take the grant and usage together; or, in the

See Perrott *v.* Bryant, 2 Y. & C. Exch. 61; ante, p. 466.

"language of the learned judge, 'looking at all the "'evidence in the cause'—not the documentary evidence "alone (which, he expressly tells the jury, does not "necessarily carry the right of the Crown), but, looking "at the grant, coupled with the usage, you are to form "your own opinion. I think that the direction is perfectly "correct."

Parke, B.: "I am of the same opinion. I think the "learned judge was perfectly correct in all he said to "the jury upon this subject. This is a grant in the time "of King John of 'Terra de Gower.' It does not purport "to create for the first time a new manor or franchise, but "to convey whatever belonged to the 'Terra de Gower' "at that time. The word 'terra' may embrace, as appears "from the authorities cited by Mr. James, as much as the "word 'manor' may. The authorities are clear that the "sea-shore may be parcel of the manor; as such it was "taken by Lord Hale and by Lord Coke in Sir Henry "Constable's case. In Hargrave's Law Tracts, p. 12, he "gives the same rule that in point of practice the sea-"shore is taken and treated as part of the adjoining "manor. By a grant of the manor everything would "pass which is parcel of the manor. The only question "is whether, it being uncertain how much constituted the "'Terra de Gower' at the time in the reign of King John, "modern usage may be made use of as evidence to shew "what was comprised within the limits of the manor; that "is, what was the boundary of the manor both upon the "land side and the sea side. Unquestionably, if evidence "may be given to shew what was the boundary of the "manor upon the sea side, the evidence here shews that, "in point of fact, the manor in the hands of the Crown, "and possibly in the hands of a subject before, was "actually bounded by the then line of demarcation, viz., "the low-water mark. All modern usage to that effect "is evidence to shew what was the meaning of the grant. "I have no doubt that all ancient documents where a "question arises as to what passed by a particular grant "can be explained by modern usage. I think the jury

Ante, pp. 351, 353, 359, 364, 368, 392, et seq.

"were properly instructed in this case to inquire from "modern usage whether the limit of the 'Terra de "'Gower' was or was not the low-water mark of the "sea-shore."

Alderson, B., and Rolfe, B., concurred.

On the question of construction of grants of manors, and as to what could pass thereby, see the case of Attorney *v.* Ewelme Hospital, decided in 1853.

17 Beav. 366.

House of Commons Returns, 1858, 314.

In 1845 an information was filed against William Chambers and others to establish the right of the Crown to the shores of the River Bury and Lougher, adjacent to the parish of Llanelly, in co. Carmarthen, and to mines thereunder. The proceedings are fully described in the Return here referred to.

Earl Cawdor claimed the whole of the foreshore as part of the lordship of Kidwelly; Chambers claimed under an alleged grant from the Crown by virtue of acts of ownership; other defendants claimed as frontagers.

In 1852 issues were directed to be tried, and in 1853 an agreement was come to respecting Earl Cawdor's rights, whereby the Crown and Earl Cawdor shared the proceeds. The case dragged on till 1854 against Chambers, when judgment was delivered by the Lord Chancellor.

Att.-Gen. *v.* Chambers, 4 De G. M. & G. 206; 23 L. J. Ch. 662; 11 Jur. 779.

The information claimed the shore by the prerogative and the coal mines thereunder, and especially that the foreshore extended to the medium line of high-water mark between neap and spring tides, but the defendants contended that the neap tide was the limit, and that the Crown's case did not embrace any alluvion of gradual formation. In this case it was finally decided, upon the advice of the judges (Alderson, B., and Maule, J.), that "the average of the medium tides in each quarter of a "lunar evolution during the year gives the limit, in the "absence of all usage, to the rights of the Crown on the "sea-shore." Although it was argued for the Crown that the right extended to the highest tide, the judges decided upon the authority of Hale and the cases quoted by him, and thus the arbitrary claim of the prerogative which was first set up by Digges in 1565, and which was so energetically used by the Stuart Sovereigns notwithstanding the decisions of the Court of Exchequer in the cases cited by Hale, was at last finally set at rest, and the Crown's *primâ facie* title was limited to the ordinary high-water mark.

On 29 April 1859 the case was again heard before the Lord Chancellor on the question whether the right of the Crown was affected by alterations in the high-water mark made by *artificial* causes arising out of operations connected with smelting works, the working of a colliery, and the construction of a railway. The Crown contended that these works, which were encroachments, caused an artificial accretion to be added to the mainland, and the question turned on the distinction between the gradual accretion of the sea-shore by natural and artificial causes. The Lord Chancellor, observing that the point was a new one and not decided by authority, and as, in the present state of the evidence, it was impossible for him to direct the inquiry as to what was the original medium line of high-water, considered it necessary to direct issues to be tried to decide—first, whether, by the direct or indirect operation of the acts, and by what acts, of the defendants or others, the natural high-water mark on the the lands of the defendants had been varied, and, if so, to what extent; secondly, whether the variation, if any, had been slow and imperceptible, or otherwise; and thirdly, whether there were any marks or boundaries by which the former natural line of high water could now be ascertained. He does not appear to have given any decision as to whether the change in the natural high-water mark brought about by artificial causes would conclude the limit of the Crown title or not.

Wenman *v.* Mackenzie, 5 Ell. & Bl. 447; 25 L. J. Q. B. 44.

In 1855 occurred the case of Wenman *v.* Mackenzie. This was an action by the lady of the manor of Milton, Kent, for a trespass on her several fishery in the River Swale, which surrounds the Isle of Elmley, the foreshore of which was claimed as parcel of the manor of Milton. The defendant claimed under a Mr. Gipps, who was owner of part of the island of Elmley, and the action was to try the right to the soil between Gipps and Wenman. The case, as reported, turns on the admissibility of certain evidence. Lady Wenman appears to have established her title under a grant of the manor to her predecessor by King Charles I.

Macnamara *v.* Higgins, 4 Ir. C. L. 326.

The case of Macnamara *v.* Higgins, in 1854, was an action for taking sand on the sea-shore at Ballyellery, Ireland. The defendants pleaded that the land was not the plaintiff's, and that there was a custom for occupiers of land in the barony of Corconroe to take sand for manure from the foreshore. Lefroy, C.J., held that the custom was bad as a *profit a prendre in alieno solo*, and that there is no distinction in such a case between the foreshore vested in the Crown and the foreshore vested in a subject. It was argued for the defendant that the statute of 7 James I. as to taking sand in Devon and Cornwall was a statute declaratory of the common law right; but it was held that it was an enacting statute, and not declaratory.

House of Commons Returns, 1858, 314.

In 1851 an information was filed against the Corporation of Liverpool to compel them to purchase the foreshore of the Mersey between Birkenhead and Monksferry. The corporation succumbed, and paid the Crown £4000 for seven and a half acres of foreshore.

Ibid.

In 1852 an information was filed against Lord Mostyn to establish the claim of the Crown to coal and culm under that part of the estuary of the Dee which lies opposite to the vill or manor of Mostyn, in co. Flint. This information was founded on an inquisition taken in 3 William and Mary, by which it was returned that a large quantity of marshes and sands on the western bank of the estuary of the Dee, extending from near the city of Chester beyond Mostyn to the mouth of the estuary, belonged to the King and Queen in right of the Crown. A lease had been made of the mines in question. The Crown officers applied to Lord Mostyn's solicitors for a statement of the nature of his claim; that application not being complied with, the information was filed. Lord Mostyn claimed by a grant, anterior to the inquisition, in which the foreshore was not granted in express terms, but he claimed the shore as parcel of the manor of Mostyn. Affidavits were filed. The opinion of Sir Alexander Cockburn, Sir Richard Bethell, Mr. James, and Mr. Hanson was taken for the Crown. They thought that the evidence in support of the *primâ facie* title, and particularly the lease of the mines in question, would not have much weight with the jury in counterbalancing the defendant's evidence, and thereupon the suit was discontinued.

In 1852 an information was filed against Robert Waite and another for erecting a shed or house at Castleton, in the Isle of Portland, on land formerly below high-water mark, but reclaimed by artificial means. The building was a nuisance to navigation. The defendants submitted. In this case the Crown was owner of the manor.

By statute 16 & 17 Victoria, cap. 56, s. 5, A.D. 1853, power was given to the Commissioners of Woods, with the consent of the Crown by sign manual, and of the Treasury by warrant, to compromise and settle disputed claims by the Crown. The necessity for these consents is now dispensed with by statute 29 & 30 Victoria, cap. 62, s. 11.

By the Merchant Shipping Act, 1854, the control and management of wrecks was transferred to the Board of Trade. Receivers of wreck were appointed, and their duties were set out by the Act. By section 454, where the lord of a manor claims wreck, he is to give notice to the receiver of his claim, and make proof of the validity of his title to the satisfaction of the receiver, who is thereupon to give notice to such lord of the manor of any wreck coming ashore within the limits of his manor. Shortly after the passing of this Act the Board of Trade appointed Mr. O'Dowd to make inquiry as to the titles to wreck and the limits of them round the coasts. The lords of manors were required to send in their claims and proofs, and Mr. O'Dowd settled the limits within which they were entitled to wreck. The titles to wreck having been adjudicated on and admitted by Mr. O'Dowd, and the limits within which such wreck was found to belong to the lords of manors having been settled, the

Stat. 17-18 Vict. c. 104, part 8.

receivers of wreck were instructed to pay over to the persons so entitled the proceeds of unclaimed wreck sold in accordance with the provisions of the Act, which is done by the receiver of wreck in each port, notice being sent by the receiver on a printed form, stating the nature of the wreck, the place where it came ashore, and the amount of the proceeds of the sale. The lord of the manor may claim either the wreck or the proceeds of it. Further provisions were made by 25 & 26 Victoria, cap. 63. By section 52 of that Act it is provided that upon delivery of the wreck, or the proceeds of it, the receiver shall be discharged from all liability, but such delivery shall not affect the title to such wreck as between third parties, nor shall prejudice or affect any question concerning the title to the soil in which the wreck may have been found. It is also provided that, if the wreck be not claimed within a year, the proceeds shall go to the Crown, or the Duchies of Lancaster and Cornwall, as the case may be.

House of Commons Returns, 1858, 314.

In 1854 an information was filed against Lord Vivian to enforce an agreement to purchase for £1000 the interest of the Crown and the Duchy of Cornwall in a portion of the shore of the River Truro adjoining Lord Vivian's estate of Newham. Lord Vivian submitted, and does not appear to have contested the Crown's claim.

Ibid.

In 1855 an information was filed against Viscount Falmouth claiming minerals under the foreshore in the Botallack Mine, in the parish of St. Just, Cornwall. This suit was compromised, under the advice of the Attorney- and Solicitor-General, by Lord Falmouth taking a lease whereby he receives a third of the royalties. In the same year a return was made to an Exchequer commission, certifying that the lands called Frater Lake, in Portsmouth Harbour, belonged to the Crown; but whether any action was taken upon it we know not.

Petty Bag, Concealments, ble. 5, No. 10.

House of Commons Returns, 1858, 314.

In 1856 the Crown proceeded against James Bailey for taking shingle from the beach under the East Cliff at Dover. The defendant, who was in needy circumstances, expressed his contrition, and paid one shilling as an acknowledgment of the trespass.

In 1857 the Attorney-General proceeded in the county court against William Knight for taking stones on the shore near Littlehampton. The defendant was ordered to pay five shillings damages. These proceedings were commenced on the representation of a body of landed proprietors whose lands were likely to be injured by the taking of the stones.

House of Commons Returns, 1858, 314.

In the same year an information was filed against the South Wales Railway Company to recover the value of land taken by the railway in Milford Haven below high-water mark. The defendants submitted, and the value of the land was paid to the Crown.

In 1843, 1844, and 1847 the Crown, by submission and arrangement, recovered lands formerly part of the bed of the Clyde which had become reclaimed by the operation of the Clyde Trustees.

In 1856, after proceedings, the Crown's interest in another portion of the bed of the Clyde was sold for £4000.

In March 1855 the Commissioners of Woods and Forests conveyed to the Eastern Counties Railway a piece of land which was part of an oyster ground known as Chalkwell Ooze, opposite to the manor of Chalkwell Hall, between Leigh and Southend, in Essex, for a sum of £300, which was paid into court under the Lands Clauses Act. The sum was claimed by the trustees under the will of William Alston, who was the grantee of the lord of the manor of Chalkwell Hall, alleging that the foreshore in question was parcel of the manor. It was shewn that William Alston had purchased the shore as an oyster ground, between 1809 and 1814, from the lord of the manor, and that it was bounded on the south by a creek called Leigh Swatch, which had been leased by the Crown for an oyster fishery, and described as being bounded by the manor of Chalkwell Hall. The court rolls of the manor of Chalkwell Hall were produced, and they shewed evidence of acts of ownership upon the shore, and grants of pieces of "wagessum," or foreshore (see *ante*, p. 163), and modern usage was proved. The case was heard

Ex parte Alston, 28 L. T. 337.

before Vice-Chancellor Wood, who said that there were two ways of displacing the *primâ facie* title of the Crown—the one being a clear grant from the Crown of a manor with words expressing a grant of the land in question, and the deduction of the title under that grant; and the other being a clear title under the Nullum Tempus Act, in opposition to the rights of the Crown, viz., on clear and distinct acts of ownership exercised without interruption during a period of sixty years. He held that, as to rights of this description, it had been settled, by a series of decisions for some years past, that where, by an ancient grant of a manor adjoining the sea-coast, the limits of the manor are not defined, modern usage is admissible in evidence to shew that the sea-shore lying between high and low water mark is parcel of that manor, and he cited the case of Duke of Beaufort *v.* Swansea, and said it was plain, on the evidence, that this manor had since the time of Edward III. been a manor in the possession of those from whom the petitioners claim. He discussed the entries in the court rolls, in which grants of "wagessum" and "mussel ooze" were frequent. He remarked that the word "wagessum" had not been explained, and he had consulted many glossaries, and the Deputy-Keeper of the Records and another gentleman in the Tower, but had been unable to obtain any result. He said that the case turned upon the meaning of the word wagessum or mussel ooze, and that it was clear it was not a grant of a mere right of fishing, but a grant of so many acres, to which a person is admitted in the ordinary course of the court roll; and although it would be very unsatisfactory to determine the case upon this particular word, as being applicable to the piece of land claimed, yet, looking to the evidence as afforded by the court rolls, and by leases of the ooze from 1766, there was quite sufficient, without this, to shew that this piece of land was part of the manor in question. Then as to the acts of ownership, these were all consistent with documentary evidence and very distinct, especially as regarded the erection, in 1832, of a stage across this very piece of land—one of those acts of obstruction of which the Crown was at all times extremely jealous—and the officers of the Crown had for many years very distinct knowledge of this locality, and it must therefore be assumed that their attention had been called to it. As to sending the case to a jury, his honour said he was clearly not justified in doing so, as such a course would clearly be contrary to the spirit of the Lands Clauses Act, the Alston family being strictly in possession of the land, and therefore strictly within the 79th clause, and he held that the petitioners were entitled.

This manor of Chalkwell Hall was parcel of the great honour of Raleigh, as were the manors of Prittlewell Hall referred to in the case of Scratton *v.* Brown, *ante*, p. 457, the manor of Foulness, see *ante*, pp. 39, 87, 98, the manors of Shoebury, the manors of Great and Little Wakering, and the manor of Hadley, extending over the coast of Essex from Canvey Island to the River Crouch, the whole of which tract of foreshore is parcel of the adjoining manors.

The Vice-Chancellor's judgment is as follows:—"In "this case the question arises on the petition, or rather "two petitions, presented by the Alston family, claiming "to be paid a certain sum of money which had been "awarded by the arbitrator in respect of certain lands "taken by the Eastern Counties Railway Company, and "which the petitioners insist were their lands; but the "title to which lands in the petitioners the company dis-"pute, and, not being satisfied with the title, they have "paid the money in question into court under the 76th "section of the Lands Clauses Act, which provides for "cases where the title is in dispute or a good title not "shewn. The main question, in truth, between the parties "is this: whether or not the Alstons are entitled to the "soil and freehold of this land, or whether the soil and "freehold is not in the Crown, and the Alstons only en-"titled to an easement in it as to the exercise of various "rights over the particular soil in question, which exercise "the company attribute to their right in respect of an "easement, and not to their right in respect of ownership.

"As to that, there is no doubt whatever in the case. It "was insisted, in the first instance, for the petitioners that "under a section in the Lands Clauses Act, which provides, "and most wholesomely provides, that, where any parties "are in possession of property which may be required for "the purpose of a railway, they shall be deemed to be "the persons *primâ facie* entitled, until the contrary be "shewn, throwing thereby the onus on all those who may "claim to set up a title, to establish that claim in the first "instance, since otherwise persons who are brought to a "compulsory sale of a portion of their property would be "exposed to have the whole title to their estates called in "question in a manner which they would not be subjected "to except for the public convenience where it was re-"quired for the passing of a railway Act. It was insisted "that, under those clauses, the petitioners were entitled to "say, 'We are in possession of this land, and, consequently, "'we are to be deemed to be the owners until the contrary "'be shewn on the part of those who claim, as the railway "'company have done throughout, by grant under the "'Crown.' The answer to that, in the first place, was, "that it would not be very convenient to try the question "in that form, because one of the questions actually in "dispute was as to whether or not there was a possession "of the land as distinguished from the possession of an "easement; but, independently of that, and assuming the "possession of the land to be in the Alstons, yet, on the "clear *primâ facie* right of the Crown—viz., the undis-"puted right of the Crown to all the land between high "and low water mark until the contrary title be shewn in "a subject—it is clear that an answer must be given to the "claim of the company, who claim under a grant from the "Crown; and the question which had to be tried was "whether or not, in truth, the soil and freehold were in "the Alstons, or whether this *primâ facie* right of the "Crown was displaced, the onus imposed by the Act of "Parliament being shifted on the Crown, the grant from "the Crown being produced of the land in question, and "the *primâ facie* right of the Crown therefore being thus "set up. With regard to rights of this description, which "have been called in question frequently of late years, "upon which actions have been tried, and the various "proceedings taken frequently within the last twenty "years, independently of the two clear modes of proving "a title, the one being a clear grant from the Crown of a "manor, with words expressing a grant of the land in "question, and the deduction of the title under that grant, "and the other being a clear title under the Nullum "Tempus Act, in opposition to the rights of the Crown— "viz., on clear and distinct acts of ownership exercised "without interruption during a period of sixty years. "There is also a course open to those who claim a title, "as subjects, in land of this description, which course is "pointed out by the deliberate decision of the full Court "on a motion for a new trial in the case of the Duke "of Beaufort *v.* the Corporation of Swansea, where the "learned judges laid down as the principle to guide the "jury in their verdict, that they were entitled to look both "at the documentary evidence and at acts of recent "ownership; which words clearly import acts of owner-"ship within sixty years, because a continued ownership "during sixty years would have rendered any other title "unnecessary. They may look at the acts of recent "ownership and the documentary evidence together, and "on those two circumstances may form their opinion. An "objection was taken to the ruling of the learned judge "in that case at Nisi Prius; that objection was disposed "of in favour of the successful claimant against the Crown, "and the Court decided that that was the correct mode of "laying a case of this description before a jury. There-"fore what I have now to look at is this, whether, in truth, "on the documentary evidence and acts of ownership "taken together in this case, I am satisfied that the title "of the Alstons to the land in question can be maintained; "and I have come to the conclusion that it can. The "documentary evidence appears to me to be really of a "very strong description in itself. I have not before me, "at starting, either any grant by the Crown, as there was "in the case of the Duke of Beaufort *v.* Corporation of "Swansea, by the general words of a manor, so as to leave "open the question what the manor included; but I have "before me a case perfectly analogous to that, because it "is conceded on all hands that this has been a manor "from the time of Edward the Third; and it seems then "to have been in the occupation of one of the priories, or "one of the religious houses, and from that time down-"ward has continuously been a manor, where a grant has "been found, and that either a manor, if it were a royal "manor, must have been granted, or, if it were not a "royal manor, it must have been created prior to the "statute of Quia Emptores, and that must be taken as a "matter established beyond all doubt or dispute. In fact, "there is no ground suggested, or no argument to the "contrary, that this manor has, from the time of Edward "the Third, been in the possession of those through whom "the petitioners claim. The question, then, that I have "to try is similar to that which arose in the case of "the Duke of Beaufort, namely, whether the evidence "of documents and the acts of ownership satisfy me that "this manor includes a particular portion of the land in "question. Now, a portion of the land in question may "be best described—and I prefer taking that description "as the one which can be best complained of by those "who resist the claim of the Messrs. Alston—from the "lease, first, down to the conveyance in 1814, which "exactly followed it, of that portion of the water, as to "which I shall have more to say presently, called the "Leigh Swatch, and which is the undisputed property of "the Crown, or was until the sale of it, and in the grant-"ing of which the particular land in question is pointed "out well by the name of Chalkwell Ouze in the demise of "Leigh Swatch, which is in 1785, by the Crown to "Thomas Harridge and others. The grant there is, 'All "'that piece or parcel of ground covered with water, being "'the soil or bed of a certain creek commonly called or "'known by the name of Leigh Swatch, near the town of "'Leigh, in the county of Essex, abutting northwards on

"'Chalkwell Ouze, and southward on Canvey Spit,' and "other places. Therefore, the land had at that time, to "the knowledge of the Crown, required that description, "by which it appears to be the best known, of Chalkwell "Ouze. In the grant of 1814 to Messrs. Alston, the "boundaries are described in an exactly similar manner, "and I will not therefore repeat it. The question is, "whether or not this Chalkwell Ouze was a part of the "manor. It appeared to me, I confess, from the first, that "the evidence was extremely strong on the part of the "plaintiffs to shew that, as regarded all the documentary "evidence, this had ever been treated as a portion of the "manor; but, in the first instance, we must look to the "court rolls, if it is only on acconnt of a word which "nobody has yet explained. I am sorry to say that I "have not got any further in the investigation as far as "external evidence is concerned. I think there is some "strong internal evidence in the documents as to the "meaning of the word; but as to the external evidence I "have not been able to ascertain the meaning of a word "of frequent occurrence here, namely, 'wagessi.' I have "had the assistance of a gentleman of very considerable "eminence, Mr. Devon, in this case; I have also con-"sulted the various glossaries, as I believe had been "done before by the parties in the case without effect. I "have also referred to the learned Assistant-Keeper of the "Records, who is entirely ignorant of any such word ever "having been used. I have also consulted another gentle-"man of considerable ability in the Tower, and the only "suggestion I have been able to obtain is, that it is a mis-"copy of some other word, which I cannot well adopt on "any sound principles to lead me to a decision, more "especially regard being had to the constant and frequent "repetition of the word; it can hardly be supposed to "have been so often miswritten in the anterior documents "as to have been miscopied in this copy about the time of "Elizabeth. The court rolls which I have before me are "not the original rolls, but a copy of the rolls made in "1615, which would be in the time of James, and which "is certified by the person making the copy as being a "correct copy of what was on the original rolls, and must "be taken to be the best evidence of those rolls that can "be procured. The original rolls appear to have been "lost, and there are no other means of ascertaining what "the original rolls consisted of. Now, we find in those "rolls, in the first place, indisputable grants, with a copy "of the court rolls, of 'mussell ouze,' and that there is no "question occurred very early—several as early as 1434. "That is the first of them I find, and it is numbered 9 in "those portions of the extracts handed in to the Court, "and which I here read from the translation: 'The jurors "'present that Julian Stretys, who held of the lord for life "'two acres land of muskelwoze, died since the last court, "'and the said two acres of muskelwoze were seized into "'the hands of the lord.' Then No. 10, which follows, is "also in the same year, 1434: 'Also it was commanded that "'John Baldwin, who held of the lord ten and a half acres of "'muskelwoze for the term of life,' &c. Then it proceeds "to direct what shall be done. Therefore it is perfectly "clear that at that very remote period—and those entries "continued down to a late period—there were constant "grants of this 'mussell ouze.' The term 'ouze' is a term "used in the latest grants of the Crown, and 'chalkwell "'ouze' appears to be the right designation of this land. "It appears to abound in mussels, which, of course, would "not be found, as everybody knows, inland. I have no "question, therefore, that this was a portion of the 'ouze' "which was so constantly granted by the title of 'mussell "'ouze,' and so held by that title of the lord of the manor. "Clearly, therefore, as far as the documentary evidence is "concerned, it was part of the manor; the word 'wages-"'sum' appears to mean a large extent of land. There "are more frequent grants and large grants; many of "them are repetitions, and many of them are simply re-"grants of the same land; but still there are a sufficient "number of grants of very considerable quantities both "of 'mussell ouze' and of 'wagessum,' and much more "of the 'wagessum.' As far as the description of the "'wagessum' goes, it is described in one or two places as "being bounded by the Goldstone channel and the "channel of the Leigh—and there are also one or two "descriptions of it where it is represented as being "bounded by the 'wadium.' There is an entry as to "Johannes Roll, but I do not think it is one of those "which have been copied; it is an entry in the year 1575. "Johannes Roll is admitted to some 'wagessum.' Then "in describing the abutments, it is described as abutting "on one side of the 'wadium' of William Forman. I "have not found certainly the word 'wadium,' but I have "found in one of the numerous glossaries which I have "had to look into, namely, Romaine's, the word 'waide' "described, as one would naturally suppose it might be "from the derivation of the word, in this way: he puts "the Latin word 'vadium,' which would be the more "proper, and he describes the word 'waide' to mean a "creek or bank of sand. But the matter does not seem "to me to rest there; there is one entry which appears to "be a genuine entry and an actual interpretation of the "word, and it is in the year 1568. I had not noticed it "before when the case was being argued, but I have been "comparing it with the original document put in of the "10 Elizabeth, and in the margin it is 'Sweetes ouze,' "and very plainly written in the original which I have "before me. This is a translation of it: 'It was found in "'the rolls of this court, there holden on Thursday, the "'8th day of May, in the 20th year of King Henry, that "'the then lord of this manor granted out of his hands to "'John Sweete, four acres of wagessi lying on the side "'called the Goldstone Channel between the wagessi of "'the late John Spodell on the west side, and the wagessi "'of Mylton Hall on the other.' Then it is headed in "the margin 'Sweetes ouze.' It seems to be the contem- "poraneous interpretation of what the word is, and, in the "absence of any better, would be a very strong con- "firmation of the other passages in which one has always "found it to be included, and which would have "led me to consider it the interpretation of the "word. However, as I said before, I was anxious not to "determine this case with a word unknown if I could "possibly help it; but it does not appear to me that the "case turns upon the word 'wagessum,' because there is a "clear and distinct grant of so many acres of 'mussell "'ouze,' about which there is no dispute, and there is also "a grant of a fishing hatch. It is not a mere grant of a "right of fishing, but a grant of so many acres to which "a person is admitted according to the ordinary course of "the court roll. But the term 'mussell ouze' comes so "frequently that it appears to me to be of more value "than any of those terms I have mentioned. I am now "only looking to the petitioners' evidence. I shall com-"ment presently upon what the respondents say on the "documentary evidence. After this the petitioners take "up the case from 1766. I observe up to this time all "the old grants have a copy of the court roll, and that, I "think, is important to observe, because, when it comes "to be demised by way of lease, the property stood in a "different position and no longer formed a portion of the "manor, which explains the entry in the early fine in "which there is a particular mention of this land. In "1766 Chalkwell Ouze was demised by the lord of the "manor for twenty-one years to Harridge, with this "description: 'all that the wash, ouze, and sea grounds "'abutting from high-water mark,' and so on, describing "it. There is no question about it. It is not like the "case of Scratton *v.* Brown, where the words used were "far more definite. It is demised as 'the wash, ouze, or "'sea ground.' Those are the terms in the demise, and, "as far as they go, there can be no question that those "persons took the demise and paid a considerable rent for "this property so demised to them; contemporaneously "with this there was going on a continual demise of the "swatch to some persons from the Crown, and ultimately "to Mr. Alston. From the year 1809 to 1814 he seems "to have been dealing in treaty, sometimes acquiring one "portion of the property, and at other times another; "the definite period is not certain till 1814, and he then "becomes the purchaser of the part held under those de-"mises, and held under the lord of the manor, and the "purchaser also of part of Leigh Swatch, which was held "under demises from the Crown. And here would seem "to be a continued series of acts on the part of third "parties—paying their money down, coming into the "lord's court, paying their fine and thereupon accepting "the leases, paying the money to the lord in respect of "those lands, treating him as the owner, and in every way "dealing with this property, as far as all the documentary "evidence is concerned, as if it formed part and parcel of "the manor. The leases, of course, might not be conclu-"sive as to its being part of the manor, but when you "have the old grants of 'mussell ouze' in the manor courts, "I can have no hesitation in saying that there were "persons dealing on the faith of its being part of the "manor for about 400 years last past. Then it is said, "in answer to this, that you are to look to the fine levied "in the time of Charles II., which does not describe any "land which would answer the description. If the land "were out in copyhold grants it would not be described, "but what would be described would be the lord's "domain, and there would be a fine of the lord's "domain lands, and you would not expect to find in "any fine a passing of the part which was copyhold or "held out upon copy of court roll on the part of the "different tenants. When the property becomes severed "from the copyhold lands on its being no longer demis-"able according to the will of the lord, having been "granted out for terms of years, then it is that you do "find leases at a later date which do mention and specify "this property. There was a later fine levied on the 18th "of June 1778, and there it is described as 'the manor "'of Chalkwell,' and the lands or grounds commonly "called 'Ouze.' Then there was a deed referring to the "manor of Chalkwell, with the messuages, barns, gardens "and orchards, and 200 acres of land. I see it is only "generally described, although there is land enough to "cover it. It is simply 200 acres of land, and nothing

" more describing it. The deed uses that expression 'the " 'manor of Chalkwell.' I took it down at the time of the " argument, and I have it in my note-book: 'manor of " 'Chalkwell and the grounds commonly called Ouze.' " That was added in 1788, leading to the uses of the " fine, but it is not mentioned apparently of any other. " The 200 acres of land would be sufficient to cover it. " The whole of the copyhold land would naturally pass " under the description of the manor, and it would be a " proper description by which it should pass; but when " you have severed it in this way, it would not pass unless " you had a sufficient quantity of land to pass to have it " in this fine. It appears that there is a sufficient quantity " for that purpose, and therefore I do not see, either in the " one or the other fine, any reason for saying that there is " to be an assumption against this mass of documentary " evidence, which clearly speaks of considerable sums of " money being paid from time to time, the original copy-" hold fees, but afterwards considerable sums of money in " respect of the leases by persons on the faith of this being " an actual portion of the manor and the actual property " of the lord, leased by the lord, and which can be traced, " as it seems to me, from the grant by court roll up to " the time of his making it by lease. There is a gap " of about 150 years between the dates of the differ-" ent documents, but I do not think anything arises " upon that, unless there is some evidence to disconnect " that which certainly, in its description, is plainly and " clearly connected. Nobody can disconnect 'mussell " 'ouze' in the old grants, 400 years back, from the ouze " or oyster grounds granted by these modern deeds, except " by shewing some more modern evidence of a separation " between those two which would dislocate the connection " between those descriptions of property. This, of course, " is all the documentary evidence simply of what is, and " what is not, parcel of the manor; and the Crown, I " apprehend, could not be bound by this alone if there " were no acts of ownership—by which acts of ownership, " according to the case I have before me, the title would "be made out. These modern acts of ownership are "exceedingly clear and distinct; nothing can be more "precise. I have evidence of that since Mr. Alston became "possessed of the property. I do not rely much upon the "separation of the manor, though I think that is not alto-"gether to be disregarded—it would go to a jury with "the other circumstances; but it does appear in evidence "at a very early period that separations were made from "those portions of the ouze and from other portions of the "ouze on the right and left, and the witnesses speak of "that as being intended for a separation of the manor. "The answer to which was this, that if the stone that was "put to make this separation was put on Canvey Spit, "which, according to the whole of the case, as far as any "evidence has been given by the petitioners, would be "beyond the boundaries of the manor, there is no doubt "it weakens that evidence. At the same time the witness "who went to put down those stakes to separate the "boundaries, now nearly thirty years ago, found old "stakes, and he put down the new stakes in the position "where the old ones were. Therefore, for whatever time "the old stakes had been there, there was a separation "drawn on the part of the respondents, who claim through "the Crown. It might be simply a separation of the "boundary for the purpose of separating the fishery, which "was distinct from the grant of the land itself, and to "mark out the several boundaries at which this free fishery "might possibly exist. It may be that these are not very "strong acts of ownership, although, under other circum-"stances, the mere running of stakes into the soil is of "itself a dealing and treating with the soil which would "tend to shew the ownership to be in the party who "asserts that right. But here you have later acts, not by "any means so very recent, none of them later than 1833, "some of them as early as 1825: for I think in 1825 "you had an action for trespass brought in respect of a "person who trespassed on this property, and the party "yielded in that action of trespass so brought. But you "had much more than that; you had in the year 1832, "which was at the time when all this dispute arose, which "was some twenty years ago—you had a lease made, and "a stage erected across this very piece of land, and there "was a distinct occupation of it, a right which no person "could possibly have unless he had a right in the soil, and "you have another person taking that lease, and consent- "ing to pay a rent of £40 a year for it for a considerable "number of years. That was a lease for twenty or thirty "years. That is a distinct and open act of ownership, "and one, be it observed, of which the Crown, represented "by that portion of its officers who take this species of "property under their peculiar care, the Admiralty, is ex- "ceedingly jealous. It is very well known, from many "applications to Parliament, that there is an excessive "jealousy on the part of the Crown in allowing any "obstruction to be erected which will impede the navi- "gation of the River Thames. It is a matter as to which "the Crown entered into a considerable dispute with the "Corporation of London as to the right of the corpora- "tion to grant licences for the erection of obstructions "which, in the judgment of the Crown, might in any way "affect or impede the navigation. Then it is said, again, "that this is not property to which the attention of the "Crown, or of its officers, has been directed. But long "before 1814, as far back as 1783, we have it in these "documents that the Crown was granting leases of Leigh "Swatch, and describing it as bounded by Chalkwell "Ouze, and when the attention of its officers must have "been called both to the ouze and to the swatch. It is "impossible to say that this is a locality to which the "Crown would not, through its officers, have had its "attention distinctly called from the separate lease in "1783 down to the actual sale in 1814, which must have "led them to pay necessarily, from the nature of the case, "very considerable attention to it. We find in the grant "of 1814 that it grants the bed and water of the swatch "from low-water mark, with its banks on each side; "which it was supposed might have some effect; but I "think that the throwing in of those additional words "cannot be held to have any effect against the other de- "scription of the property, which describes it as abutting "on Chalkwell Ouze—as something distinct from Chalk- "well Ouze. The Crown, in making the grant, pays its "attention to the fishery, and says that it shall be carried "on, and makes it a condition of the grant that the oyster "fishery shall be carried on; and one thing that was done "was, that the oysters were laid on this very land, "which may be an easement, but which continual occu- "pying of a definite portion of the land apparently "has been exercised as a right of occupation inde- "pendently of, and adversely to, all the comers except "the Crown. Then, the Crown being so circumstanced, "I find that for more than twenty years preceding "the taking of this land the Crown has allowed this stage "to be erected, and the Crown has allowed this right "to be exercised in an open and apparent manner, "and I find that act quite consistent with the whole "of the documentary evidence which I have before "me in the case, establishing this as part and parcel of "the manor. Further than that there is the fact of the "digging of the stones, which is not altogether to be "disregarded. It is not so plain and so manifest as the "erecting of the stage, but it is still a right of some "importance, because the very case, Scratton *v.* Brown, "which arose on that right shews the valuable nature of "this cement property. I have no reason, therefore, to "suppose that the Crown would be asleep as to its rights "in that respect. Alston is clearly proved to have dug, "through his servants, with a pickaxe those stones for "cement that lay on the shore, and to have put them up "together, and to have sold them. Now, the thing that I "rely on by far the most is the modern usage, and that "right which he exercised of erecting this stage, which is a "plain and palpable defiance of the right of the Crown, if I "may say so, if any such right existed. It was said, how- "ever, by Mr. Rolt in the portion of his argument which "he first addressed to me, that, however you might suppose "the manor to be bounded—and there are considerable "authorities in the books to shew that manors are very "commonly bounded, and numerous cases occurred to "shew it, and it has been laid down by the *dicta* of the "judges, that it is more common than not to find manors "bounded by high and low water mark, including the "shore down to low-water mark where they adjoin the "sea-shore—yet Mr. Rolt said, 'How can you predicate "'that of a manor thus situated, and how do you predicate "'the ownership of the ouze as appertaining to a manor "'when you find that it is not a claim to low-water mark, "'but a claim only down to this Leigh Swatch, where the "'low-water mark in the River Thames extends consider- "'ably to the other side of the swatch?' It does not "appear to me that there is any solid foundation for that "argument. The swatch is a piece of water which to a "certain extent is the boundary of the low-water mark; "that is to say, the water is never lower than the bed of "the swatch at that particular portion, and it does not "get below the bed of the swatch because the swatch "itself intervenes and is of itself navigable for small "craft, whatever it may be for large ones; and the ouze "there is the natural and defined boundary which that "river or that swatch or boundary of the river appears "to have presented at all times to this particular land, "and the reason, no doubt, why manors adjoining to the "sea have been held to be so commonly bounded by the "sea itself is that it is a natural boundary—a piece of "land actually belonging to the Crown, but which may or "may not be granted by the lord—the sea being the "physical boundary. In this particular case I have a "physical boundary quite as well defined in this Leigh "Swatch, constantly existing with regard to the property "on the other side, and which has acquired a definite "name. I began by saying that the Crown itself recog- "nises the definite character of this boundary as being "called and known by the one single name of Chalkwell "Ouze; that is a name derived evidently from the pro- "perty which adjoined it, and is quite sufficiently definite "for the Court to be led to the presumption, corrobo-

"rated by every entry in court rolls; and there are "numerous entries in the court rolls, and confirmed by "all the subsequent transactions, of persons dealing on "the faith of it with those who held as lords of the "manor; and confirmed still more, as I think, by those "open acts of ownership which have been submitted to "by the Crown, without dispute, during the last twenty-"three years. This is the way in which the case appears "to present itself, and if this had been an ordinary case, "it appears to me, as it is an important right, that it is one "in which the parties ought not to be bound without "having the decision of a jury; but it does not appear "to me, looking at the Act of Parliament, and the object "of the Legislature in passing that clause which gives a "*primâ facie* right to the owners of land who are in "possession, that I should be at all justified in sending "this matter to a jury if, in my view of the case, I "came to the conclusion that the evidence was sufficient "to support the title of the occupier. I find him to be "strictly in possession by means of this stage at the time "the property was taken, and strictly, therefore, within "the benefit of that clause by which it is provided that "he shall be deemed to be in possession till the contrary "is shewn. The *primâ facie* evidence obliged him to "rebut that evidence, but, at the same time, to say that a "person who happens to hold a very small portion of "land that is required to be taken in consequence of a "railway passing through his property is to be put to "try his right before a jury unless there be some-"thing beyond mere doubt thrown upon it, I think it "would be entirely contrary to the whole spirit of this Act "of Parliament. I am not concluding any of the other "rights here that I have before me, or concluding the "right of anybody to anything at all excepting the sum "of £300 in question, which is the only right I can here "possibly determine by this order. It appears to me "that I ought not to hesitate to make an order unless I "were of opinion that a contrary title was in truth clearly "shewn as against those occupiers."

Doe dem. Rajah Sub-krish *v.* East India Co., 10 Moo. P. C. C. 140.

In 1856 the English law relating to foreshore and alluvion was decided to be applicable to India, and the East India Company, as representing the Indian Government, are entitled to the foreshore, the owners of adjacent soil being entitled to land formed by gradual accretion.

Att.-Gen. *v.* Chamberlaine and others, 4 K. & J. 292.

In August 1856 an information in Chancery was filed by the Attorney-General against George John Chamberlaine and others to establish the right of the Crown to part of the foreshore of a creek or pool forming an inlet of the River Mersey, called Tranmere Pool, part of which had been inclosed and built upon by the defendants. The claim of the Crown was to the inclosed parts as well as to that left open. The defendants set up a title to the whole under a grant from the lord of the manor of Tranmere as parcel of that manor, and also insisted that part of the land alleged to be reclaimed was never subject to the flow and re-flow of the tide. On motion for decree, the question arose as to the form of decree, and as to the issues to be tried. On the part of the Crown it was proposed to try—(1) the title of the Crown to the whole of the foreshore, inclosed or uninclosed; (2) whether the Queen was seised of any portion of the shore; and (3) whether the Queen's right to any portion was barred by adverse possession of the defendants. And it was further proposed, in case of a verdict for the Crown upon either the first or second issue and also upon the third issue, that it should be referred to an engineer to report what portion had been embanked within the ordinary high-water mark within sixty years before the filing of the information. It was objected by the defendants that it lay upon the Crown to shew how far the ordinary high-water mark extended before the issues were tried, because the defendants denied encroachment. The Solicitor-General argued that the inquiry as to how far the high-water mark went was properly matter for inquiry and not for a jury, and relied upon the case of Attorney-General *v.* St. Aubyn (Wightwick 167) and Attorney-General *v.* Philpott. (An abstract of the decree is printed in the note: see *ante*, p. 442.) Counsel for the defendants said that the proposed course might seriously prejudice the defendants. "The case for the defendants must be made "out by evidence either from an actual grant or from acts "of ownership from which a grant must be presumed; but "until the Crown has pointed out how much it claims as "foreshore, how can the defendants know within what "limits it will be material for them to prove acts of "ownership? Very possibly the defendants will not "be able to prove acts of ownership between the present "high and low water marks, while they may be able to "prove such acts between the old high and low water "marks, but to make such evidence material it must "first be ascertained what the Crown will be content to "treat as ancient high-water mark; otherwise the whole of "the defendants' evidence may be rejected at the trial as "relating to ground which the Crown disclaims. Besides, "the defendants may be still further prejudiced if the "onus of shewing what is foreshore is to lie with them "and not with the Crown, for, by admitting the soil on "which they prove acts of ownership to have been part of "the foreshore, in the event of their evidence proving "insufficient to warrant the presumption of a grant they "will have proved the case of the Crown, and admitted "possibly against themselves that the ancient foreshore "extended farther inland than the Crown would ever "have thought of extending its claim." The Vice-Chancellor (Sir W. Page Wood), while admitting the difficulty in which the defendants were placed, held that, as they had denied the title of the Crown generally, the Crown had the right to try which title was the stronger in the first instance, and directed the issues to be tried before the inquiry was made.

In this case the evidence for the defendants to shew that the shore was parcel of the manor appears to have been strong. A report on the documentary part of it was made by Mr. Black, and a print of that report exists in the Inner Temple Library. After the Vice-Chancellor's judgment, the case was compromised by the advice of the law officers. The defendants took a grant of the interests of the Crown in the land claimed by them, and the interest in an adjoining parcel was conveyed to a Mr. Orred, the whole consideration paid to the Crown being £110, the costs incurred by the Crown in the litigation amounting to £559.

H. of C. Returns, 1860, 464.

Att. *v.* Phillips, ibid.

On 31 December 1857 the Attorney-General filed an information in Chancery against Sir Thomas Phillips for erecting a pier upon foreshore opposite to land belonging to him within the Crown manor of Liswenny and Libeneth, upon the River Usk, in the county of Monmouth. The information lays the claim of the Crown in the following form:—"The sea adjoining the coasts of this kingdom, and "all arms, estuaries, creeks, havens, and ports of the sea, "and all navigable rivers within these realms, where and so "far as the tide flows and re-flows, and the land or ground "at or in the bottom or bed thereof respectively, as also "the shores, banks, and strands thereof respectively, "below high-water mark at ordinary tides, and the soil "of the same, together with all profits arising therefrom, "belong of common right to her Majesty the Queen, and "have at all times so belonged to her and her royal pre-"decessors, kings and queens of this realm, in right of "their crown, *subject nevertheless to such grants by her "Majesty or her predecessors as are now in force.*"

Sir Thomas Phillips, by his answer, submitted to the Court the question as to whether the Crown was entitled by the prerogative generally as claimed in the information, and whether the foreshore of the kingdom generally had at all times belonged to the Crown, and whether or not it has so belonged subject only to such grants by her Majesty and her predecessors as are now in force; and in the second and third paragraphs of his answer he says as follows:—

"2. But I say that I have been advised, and I submit, "that the land and soil between high-water mark and low-"water mark upon the sea-shore or upon the banks of "tidal rivers in England, hereinafter called the 'foreshore,' "does not belong to the Crown as a mere prerogative "franchise, but that the same may belong, and often does "belong, to a subject, and that the seisin of a title to the "foreshore may be established in the same manner as the "seisin of a title to any other land. For although, in the "absence of any evidence of ownership in a subject, the "title to the foreshore may *primâ facie* be in the Crown, "yet such foreshore would then belong to the Crown as "any other waste land, or land without any owner, or un-"appropriated land, which is presumed to have originally "belonged to the Crown, and which the Crown has not "parted with. But such *primâ facie* title may be displaced "by the common and usual evidence of title shewing the "ownership thereof to be in a subject, and in order to "shew a title to the foreshore in a subject it is not neces-"sary to shew a grant of a licence to use the same. But "evidence of ownership may be adduced to shew that the "foreshore passed by a grant of the manor or of other "lands within the manor of which such foreshore is parcel, "or that a right to the same has been otherwise acquired "and (amongst others) the following things and rights "are, and always have been, considered as strong evidence "that the foreshore is parcel of the manors wherein such "rights are enjoyed—namely, the right to an enjoyment of "wrecks within the manor, the possession of a right to "make weirs and fishing places, and the right to fix stake "nets, and to take the sand upon and from the foreshore "within the manor, and the enjoyment of anchorage. "And such things and rights are held to be the very soil "itself, and, in fact, the foreshore is parcel almost of all "such manors as by prescription have wrecks of the sea "within their manor.

"3. And I say that I have been advised, and I submit, "that, even if with regard to other parts of England the "title to the foreshore is *primâ facie* in the Crown, with "regard to the county of Monmouth and other parts in "England and Wales, formerly lordships marchers, the title "to the foreshore is *primâ facie* in the lords of the manors "formerly lords marchers. For the lords marchers be-"came entitled to their lordships marchers by grants "made to them from time to time by the kings of Eng-"land of such counties in Wales as they should win from "the Welshmen, to be held by them and their heirs of the "kings of England as lands purchased by conquest. And "the lords marchers in their several lordships marchers "exercised a kind of feudal sovereignty, and enjoyed in "as ample mannner as the King himself all such royal "rights and prerogatives as were necessary for the due "execution of the laws in their respective lordships "marchers, and, like the lords of counties palatine, they "uniformly had 'wreccum maris' within their lordships "marchers as part of their *jura regalia;* and it was not "until the reign of King Henry the Eighth that the "dominion of Wales (which then included that district "now called the county of Monmouth) was incorporated "with and annexed to the realm of England."

He then alleges that, by statute 27 Henry VIII. cap. 26, it was enacted that divers lordships marchers (within which the foreshore was situate) were incorporated into the shire of Monmouth; and that it was further enacted that the lords marchers should have all liberties, wreck of the sea, wharfage, and customs of strangers as they had in times past as though such privileges were granted unto them by the King by point of charter, and that the statute 1 & 2 Philip and Mary, cap. 15, confirmed these privileges.

Sir Thomas Phillips then proceeds:—

"6. And I say that when lords marchers have claimed "the rights and privileges formerly enjoyed by lords "marchers, and reserved to them by the said statutes, "such claims have been always allowed; and as evidence "thereof I say that in Michaelmas, 9 Elizabeth, 1566, an "information of quo warranto was brought against William "Earl of Pembroke in respect of certain liberties or fran-"chises enjoyed by him within his lordships in the county "of Monmouth, and amongst others in the lordship of "Wentlooge hereinafter mentioned, and in defence thereto "the said Earl pleaded that the said lordships were lord-"ships marchers, and he pleaded the benefit of the said "statutes, and the grant to him as Sir William Herbert "by King Edward VI. of the said lordships, and judgment "was given in his favour. And, as evidence thereof, I "further say that in Michaelmas, 33–34 Elizabeth, 1591, "an information of quo warranto was brought against "Thomas Cornwall, of Burford, Esq., in respect of certain "franchises and liberties enjoyed by him within his lord-"ships in the county of Hereford, and in defence thereto "he pleaded the benefit of the said statutes, and that the "said lordships were lordships marchers, and judgment was "given in his favour."

He further says that the pleadings in these cases are set forth in Coke's Entries, and referred to by him in 4 Inst., and that "further in 8 James I., 1610, the Earl of "Worcester filed his bill in the Exchequer against Ed-"mund Smith and others for infringing his title to wreck "of the sea in his lordship of Chepstow, which was a lord-"ship marcher, and extended to the River Severn and the "River Wye; and in the said suit the right of the said Earl "to wreck of the sea in his said lordship as a lordship "marcher was admitted, and a decree was made in his "favour."

Sir Thomas Phillips sets out his title at great length, claiming under a previous lord of the manor by convey-ances made before the Crown purchased the manor in 1832.

The information was amended on 11 November 1858, and the answer thereto was filed on 19 January 1859. A supplemental answer was subsequently filed, and then, upon the opinion of the law officers, the suit was ordered to be discontinued, and on 15 August 1859 an order was obtained by the informant by which the information was dismissed, the Crown paying the defendant's costs, taxed at £358.

On 28 July 1858, at the Ipswich Assizes, an action of trespass was tried between the Duke of Hamilton and Clark for taking coprolites from the foreshore of the manor of Walton-cum-Trimley. The manor rolls were put in evidence, and it was shewn that, from 1739, moneys had been paid to the Duke's account for wreck, for groundage of vessels, for salvage, for licence to take shingle. Leases were produced for the right to take stone for cement, and a verdict was found for the plaintiff.

Stat. 21-22 Vict. c. 109. In 1858 the Cornwall Submarine Mines Act, 1858, was passed to settle a dispute between the Crown and the Duchy of Cornwall respecting title to minerals lying under the foreshore of the county of Cornwall and under the sea adjacent below the low-water mark. The question had been referred to Sir John Patteson, who awarded the mines under the foreshore to the Duchy and those under the sea to the Crown. This Act, however, relates only to the respective titles of the Duchy and the Crown, and it is expressly recited that the reference to Sir John Patteson was not intended to apply to or affect any claim or title of any person claiming any mines or minerals adversely both to the Crown and the Duchy. By section 9 the rights of all persons are saved. A question subsequently arose as to the respective rights of the Crown and the Duchy in lands within estuaries *inter fauces terræ*, which was referred to Sir John Coleridge, and decided substantially in favour of the Duchy.

Reg. *v.* Keyn, L. R. 2 Ex. D. at pp. 121, 155-158, and 199-202.

At the Exeter Assizes on 30 July 1858 Lord Clinton established a right to the foreshore of part of the River Exe against a trespasser named Beevis.

Queen *v.* Musson, 8 Ell. & Bl. 900. In 1858, in the case of the Queen *v.* Musson, it was decided that the foreshore may form part of a parish coming down to the shore, but there is no *primâ facie* presumption that it does so ; and in the absence of evidence that it does form part of the parish, it must be taken to be not part of it. The case was in respect of the Wellington Pier at Great Yarmouth. The land below high-water mark upon which the pier was built was conveyed to the company by the Commissioners of Woods and Forests. The rest of the pier was built on the waste of the borough of Great Yarmouth. Lord Campbell : "It is clear that "the foreshore here is *primâ facie* in the Crown, though it "may be proved to be in a subject, and so the spot is "*primâ facie* extra-parochial, though it may be shewn to "be in a parish; the burden of proof lies on those "alleging it to be in a parish." Weightman, J.: "There "is abundant authority that such land is within the county, "and may be in a manor, and may be in a parish; but "there is no presumption of law that it is within either; it "requires evidence to shew that it is part of the parish."

In 1858, in the case of Attorney-General *v.* Hanmer, it was held that coals under the foreshore passed under the word "waste" in a grant, and that the word "waste" is a sufficient description of the soil between high and low water mark. This was an information filed in February 1856 by the then Attorney-General, on behalf of her Majesty, against Sir John Hanmer, Bart., and, as amended, against certain other persons, for the purpose of having the question decided whether the grant of certain letters patent, dated in the 12th year of the reign of King Charles I., passed to the grantees thereunder the coals and mines of coal within the manor or lordship of Englefield, in the county of Flint, under the shore or estuary of the River Dee, between high and low water mark, and under any part of such shore called the White Sand.

Att. *v.* Hanmer, 4 De G. & J. 208; 31 L. T. 379; 27 L. J. N. S. Ch. 837; 4 Jur. N. S. 751; 6 W. R. 804.

The Crown in 1636–37, being entitled to the said manor or lordship of Englefield, by the letters patent above mentioned granted to Francis Braddock and Christopher Kingscote (through whom the defendant Sir J. Hanmer claimed), their heirs and assigns, for ever (among other hereditaments), "all those coals and mines "of coals found or to be found beneath the commons, "waste lands, or marish grounds [infra communias, terras "vastas, sive mariscos] within the *dominium* or lordship of "Englefield, in the county of Flint, with full liberty, power, "and authority to dig, sink, and find pits, and to open the "said mines in all convenient places within the said "commons, waste lands, and marish grounds, to acquire "coal within the *dominium* aforesaid." The said letters patent contained a clause expressly granting that they were to be construed strictly towards the King and his heirs, and most strictly and beneficially for the said grantees, their heirs and assigns, as well in all courts as elsewhere within the kingdom of England.

Manors on the Dee seem to extend to the *filum aquæ*: see ante, pp. 154, 155, 167.

It was admitted by the Attorney-General, on behalf of the Crown, that the manor or lordship of Englefield extended to the middle of the channel of the estuary of the River Dee; and the question was whether the space within the manor between high and low water marks was comprehended within the terms "commons, waste lands, "and marish grounds within the *dominium* or lordship of "Englefield" so as to entitle the defendants to the coals found under that space.

The letters patent are fully set out below.

Watson, B., said: "This is an information, at the suit "of the Attorney-General, praying that the right of her "Majesty to the coals under a part of the sea-shore or "estuary of the River Dee between high and low-water "mark, called White Sand, may be established and de- "clared, and that it may be declared that the grant in "certain letters patent did not comprise the coal under "White Sand at the time of the grant of the said letters "patent. The Crown, as lord of the manor of Englefield, "in the county of Flint, was entitled to the land lying "between high and low water mark, called White Sand, "as within and parcel of the said manor of Englefield, "and to the coal thereunder. By letters patent bearing "date in the February of the 12th of Charles I., "A.D. 1636–37, his Majesty made a grant of coal "within land of this manor (amongst many other "manors, lands, and franchises) to Francis Braddock and "Christopher Kingscote, in fee, in these words:—'Necnon "'omnes illos carbones et mineras carbonum, inventos aut "'inveniendòs infra communias, terras vastas, sive maris- "'cos, intra dominium de Englefield, in comitatu nostro "'Flint, cum plenâ libertate, potestate, et authoritate, "'fodere, deprimere, et experire puteos, et aperire dictas "'mineras in omnibus locis convenientibus, intra dictas "'communias, terras vastas, et mariscos, ad acquirendum "'carbones infra dominium prædictum per particulare "'inde nominatos fuisse dimissos Dominæ Dorotheæ "'Hanmer viduæ, nuper uxori Johannis Hanmer, militis "'et baronetti, defuncti; et esse annualis reditûs sive "'valoris quadraginta solidorum, ac parcella terrarum et "'possessionum nuper comitis Castriæ.' The letters "patent contained an exception and a provision, of "which the following is a copy:—'Except always, "'nevertheless, out of this, and to ourselves, our heirs "'and successors, wholly reserved all arrears of rents for "'the said premises now due and depending; and also "'all advowsons, donations, free dispositions, and rights of "'patronage of rectories, churches, vicarages, chapels, and "'other ecclesiastical benefices whatsoever to the premises, "'or to any or either of them, in anywise belonging, ap- "'pertaining, incident, or appendant; and all knights' "'fees, wards, and marriages of the premises, and all "'services for or in respect of the same; and also "'except all royal mines of gold and silver within or "'upon the premises being or to be found, and all pre- "'rogatives to the same mines belonging. And further, "'we will and by these presents for ourselves, our heirs "'and successors, do grant to the aforesaid Francis Brad- "'dock and Christopher Kingscote, their heirs and assigns, "'that these our letters patent, or the enrolment thereof, "'shall be in and by all things firm, valid, good, sufficient, "'and effectual in the law, and shall be expounded and "'construed strictly towards and against us, our heirs and "'successors, and most strictly and beneficially for the "'aforesaid Francis Braddock and Christopher Kingscote, "'their heirs and assigns, as well in all our courts as else- "'where wheresoever within our kingdom of England, "'without any confirmations, licences, or tolerations to "'be procured and obtained from us, our heirs and suc- "'cessors; notwithstanding the ill naming or not naming, "'or the wrong reciting or not reciting, the aforesaid "'manors, granges, messuages, lands, tenements, and "'hereditaments, and other the premises above by these "'presents before granted or mentioned to be granted, or "'any part or parcel thereof; and notwithstanding the

" 'not finding or ill finding of any office or offices, or in-
" 'quisition or inquisitions, of the premises, or of any
" 'parcel thereof, by which our title ought to be found
" 'before the making of these our letters patent, and not-
" 'withstanding any defect or defects in not reciting or
" 'ill reciting any demise or grant, demises or grants, gift
" 'or gifts, of or concerning the premises, or of or concern-
" 'ing any part or parcel thereof, or any of the profits
" 'thereof, being of record or not of record, heretofore
" 'made, and notwithstanding the ill naming, or not
" 'rightly naming, or not naming any city, town, hamlet,
" 'place, parish, or county in which the premises, or any
" 'parcel thereof, are or be; and notwithstanding any de-
" 'fect or defects in wrong naming, or not naming, or not
" 'rightly naming of any tenant, farmer, or occupier of the
" 'premises, or of any parcel thereof; and notwithstanding
" 'any variation, discrepancy, or difference in any matter,
" 'name, or form between these our letters patent and any
" 'particular certificate or survey of the premises, or of any
" 'parcel thereof, heretofore made, or between these our
" 'letters patent or any other letters patent of the pre-
" 'mises, or any parcel thereof, heretofore made, or be-
" 'tween these our letters patent and any record or
" 'records, account or accounts, in anywise touching
" 'concerning the premises aforesaid, or any parcel
" 'thereof; and notwithstanding any defect or defects in
" 'not mentioning, or not rightly or ill mentioning, the
" 'true yearly value of the premises, or of any part
" 'thereof, or the true yearly rents reserved out of, in,
" 'or upon the premises, or any parcel thereof, specified
" 'in any particular survey or account heretofore made or
" 'hereafter to be made of the premises, or any or either
" 'of them; and notwithstanding that the same premises
" 'or any the profits thereof are, or at any time have
" 'been, of greater yearly value than specified in these
" 'letters patent or any particulars of the premises; and
" 'notwithstanding that of the estate or title of us or any
" 'of our progenitors to have the same premises, or any
" 'part thereof, or of the manner or ways in which

"'the same premises came to our hands, or to "'the hands of any of our progenitors, or of any "'part thereof, mention be not made, or true or right "'mention be not made, in these letters patent; and "'notwithstanding the statute made in Parliament in "'the 18th year of Lord Henry the Sixth, formerly "'King of England; and notwithstanding the statute "'made in Parliament in the 1st year of the reign of "'Lord Henry the Fourth, late King of England; and "'notwithstanding any defects in not naming or not "'rightly naming the nature, kind, species, quantity, or "'quality of the premises, or of any parcel of them, or "'of any person or persons who before us was or were "'seised of the premises, or of any one or more thereof, "'or any estate tail or other estate made to us or any of "'our progenitors or ancestors, or any indenture or annex-"'ation by our late most dear father (of happy memory), "'or any other of our progenitors or ancestors, late Kings "'and Queens of England, before now made, or any con-"'vention, agreement, or covenant concerning the same "'premises, or any part thereof, in anywise notwith-"'standing; and notwithstanding that the same pre-"'mises by our said father before our accession to "'our crown were in any way, or as to any part "'thereof, granted to us and our heirs, kings of "'England, or to us and our heirs male, kings of Eng-"'land, or to us and any other person whomsoever; and "'notwithstanding that of any other grant of the premises, "'or any parcel thereof, mention is not made, or true "'mention is not made, by these presents; and notwith-"'standing that the premises or either of them are or "'were formerly parcel of or annexed to any castle or "'honour, or were heretofore, or are now, annexed or "'united to any castle or honour; and notwithstanding "'any other cause or matter whatsoever. Also we by "'these presents do grant to the aforesaid Francis "'Braddock and Christopher Kingscote, their heirs and "'assigns, that they may or shall have these letters "'patent as well under our Great Seal of England as

" 'under the seal of our Duchy of Lancaster and the seal " 'of our county palatine of Lancaster and the seal of " 'our counties palatine of Chester and Flint, made and " 'sealed in due manner without fine into our hanaper, " 'etc.' The demise to Lady Hanmer in 1625, mentioned in the letters patent, is only important as being " of the same coal-mines, and the lease is in English and " translated into Latin in the letters patent. The operative words are: 'All those coals and coal-mines found " 'or to be found within the commons, waste grounds, or " 'marshes within the said lordship of Englefield, in the " 'county of Flint, with full liberty, power, and authority " 'to dig and search for, and sink pits, and open the said " 'mines in all places convenient within the said commons, " 'waste grounds, and marshes for getting of coal within " 'the lordship aforesaid.' The question turns on the " true construction of the letters patent; and that question is whether the coals under the foreshore or land " between high and low water marks called White Sand " passed under these letters patent. The Crown contended " that the coals did not pass. The defendants asserted " the affirmative. It is not a grant from the Crown " of its prerogative right to the foreshore, but a grant " of coals within and parcel of the manor of Englefield. " In order to ascertain the effect of this deed it is " necessary to inquire first, Are there apt words to pass " the coals under White Sand? The words of the grant " are, 'All coals under the commons, waste grounds, or " 'marshes.' It is not necessary here to put a construction " on the words 'commons' or 'marshes,' for it appears " to me to be clear that the word 'waste' is sufficient to " pass the foreshore or the coals thereunder. The word " 'waste' means desolate or uncultivated ground, land " unoccupied, or that lies in commons. This is the plain " and common acceptation of the word, and undoubtedly " land between high and low water mark falls within this " signification. It lies open, desolate, unoccupied, uncultivated; and so Bayley, J., in delivering his judgment in " Scratton *v.* Brown, calls the land between high and low "water mark 'waste.' Again, in descriptions of lands or "manors, the terms 'lord's waste' or 'waste of the manor' "are well known. The large open common within and "parcel of the manor over which rights of common or "other commonable rights are exercised are 'wastes' "of the manor; moors, also, are strips of unoccupied "land within the manor. The right to strips of "land by the side of highways is not unfrequently "the subject of litigation between the adjoining land-"owners and the lord claiming them as wastes of the manor. "The true meaning of wastes, or waste lands, or waste "grounds of the manor is the open, uncultivated, and "unoccupied lands parcel of the manor, or open lands "parcel of the manor other than the demesne lands of "the manor. Lord Hale says that the main sea is the "waste and demesne of the kings of England, and the "King is the owner of that great waste, the sea. It is "therefore impossible to say that, as the sea-shore is waste, "that word 'waste' is not an apt word to pass the coals "under this foreshore, being parcel of the manor; and as "the foreshore is waste, and waste of the manor, it seems "that there is no more appropriate word in a grant like "the present. It was argued on the part of the Crown "that the proper description of the foreshore is 'littus "'maris, marina, or warrena,' and no doubt that is so; "but it is equally clear the Crown might alienate the "foreshore by other words if it were the apparent inten-"tion to be collected from the grant itself, or in an ancient "grant construed by user (the Duke of Beaufort *v.* "Mayor of Swansea; Calmady *v.* Rowe). This is not a "grant by the Crown of its prerogative right, but a grant "by the lord of the manor of the coals under the wastes "of the manor. Certainly, very different words might be "sufficient in dealing with the wastes of a manor than in "a direct grant from the Crown. The words in these "letters patent being sufficient to pass these coals, a "second question arises—viz., Is it to be collected from the "letters patent that it was the intention of the grantors "that the coals under this foreshore should pass? This "intention is to be collected from the letters patent. At "the time of the grant, the coals under the copyholds as "demesne lands (Viner's Abridgement, 'Manors,' c. 2), "and also all the coals under the waste grounds of the "manor, were vested in the Crown, as lord of the manor "of Englefield, as parcel of that manor. The Crown then "grants all the coal and coal-mines found or to be found "within the common, waste grounds, or marshes, without "any exception, which would pass any coal to be found "in any part of the manor under commons, waste ground, "or marshes. There is a power to enter such lands, and "'to get' or 'for getting' coals within the lordship. These "last words would not enlarge the extent of the grant so "as to render it a grant of coal not under the commons, "wastes, or marshes, but it shews that the right to get "coals was to be co-extensive with the manor. There is "nothing to be collected from the letters patent to shew "that the grant should not extend to coals under ground "between high and low water mark, and no reason can "be assigned why it should be so. On the other hand, "it would seem strange that the Crown should retain these "coals where the power of getting them would be most "difficult and expensive, if not impossible, and the extent "of the coals granted on the part of the grantee would "shift as the sea receded from or encroached upon the "land (Rex *v.* Lord Yarborough, 3 B. & C. 91; Scratton "*v.* Brown, 4 B. & C. 435). Considering that the Crown "did not reserve or except out of this general grant, it is "abundantly clear that it was the intention of the Crown "to pass the coal under the foreshore. It was contended "on the part of the Crown that the words of the grant "ought to be read, 'all coals under commons, whether "'waste grounds or marshes,' and that the grant was "accordingly to be confined to lands over which common-"able rights were or might be exercised. Indeed, one of "the counsel for the Crown urged that we were to find "the interpretation of this grant in the words of the "Statute of Merton, which is confined to approvement by "the lord against common of pasture only—not against "other common rights. Supposing such a construction "to be adopted, it is putting too narrow a construction "on the word 'commons,' for that word means as often "lands where rights of common are exercised as common "uninclosed open land where there are no commonable "rights. Taking the word in this confined sense, over "land between high and low water mark easements and "privileges are exercised in many manors bordering on "the sea in many parts of England; thus, freeholders by "prescription, and copyholders as against the lord by "custom, have a right to get seaweed for manure for their "lands, to get stone and sand from the foreshore to "repair their buildings and walls. Public ways pass "over it, and it would be a valid custom for the "inhabitants of a villa within the manor to bathe in the "sea and go over the foreshore. These rights are analo-"gous to, although not strictly speaking, commonable "rights (see judgment of Holroyd, J., in Blundell *v.* "Caterall, 5 B. & Ald. 289). But the true answer to "this and other arguments urged on the part of the "Crown is that on these letters patent full effect must be "given to all the words, and in doing so the true con-"struction of this grant is that the coals under the "common, the coals under the waste grounds, and the "coals under the marshes within and parcel of the manor "pass thereby. To hold otherwise would be to depart "from the rule of construction expressed in the letters "patent, that the deed should be construed most favour-"ably to the grantee. The case of Doe d. Marwood *v.* "Lord Harewood[1] was cited for the Crown, where Maule, "J., held, upon a charter produced in that case, that by "commons and waste places the King did not grant

[1] In the case of Doe d. Marwood *v.* Harewood the grant was of the wapentake of Langburgh with appurtenances. It was contended that the grant passed the whole of the foreshore of the wapentake, which comprises nearly the whole North Riding of Yorkshire, because the lords of the wapentake had wreck of the sea within it (*ante*, p. 470). No user of soil being shewn for the plaintiff, the judge held that the soil of a part of the Tees which had been diverted did not pass by the grant. The report was privately printed in 1842.

"the soil of the foreshore between high and low water "mark in the River Tees; which was quite clear from the "context, as the grant was of an easement over that land, "which negatived the intention that the soil itself should "pass. It does not seem consequential reasoning that "because in one deed the intention shewed the land "between high and low water mark did not pass, there- "fore such words would not pass coal under the sea- "shore, being waste of the manor, in any other deed. I "do not consider it necessary to go through any of the "documents, such as modern Inclosure Acts for inclosing "land with herbage, and other documents adverted to in "the argument, as they throw no light on the mode of "construing this grant—certainly none in favour of the "Crown. I have not adverted to the parol evidence of "user, as I think the letters patent prove the right on the "part of the defendant. I am therefore of opinion that "the coals under the White Sand did pass, because there "are apt words and a clear intention on the face of the "letters patent leading to that conclusion."

The Vice-Chancellor (after stating his obligations to Watson, B., for the opinion he had delivered in the case) said that "that opinion seemed to him a perfectly sound "view of the construction of the instrument which had "been referred to. The question for decision was "extremely short. It was whether or not by the word "'waste' there was a sufficient description of the soil "between high and low water mark. There were facts "which had been admitted on the part of the Crown "which, when duly considered, really seemed to make the "case reasonably clear. It was admitted that the lord- "ship of Englefield extended to the middle of the channel "of the estuary of the Dee. It was admitted that the "soil between high and low water mark was parcel of the "manor. Being necessarily uncultivated land, in ordinary "language it would be fairly described as 'waste.' Bayley, "J., speaking in court and using the language of a judge "to describe the soil between high and low water mark, "called it waste. That being so, it seemed inevitable "that the conclusion to be arrived at was that the Crown, "in granting the right to work for coal and the coal-mines "under the 'waste' of this lordship without words "excepting the soil between high and low water mark, "must be considered to have passed the right to work for "coal under the soil between high and low water mark. "But supposing the question were doubtful. Supposing "that on a narrow view of the language of the grant, and "putting a strict construction upon it, a doubt were raised; "still the Crown had declared that if there should be a "doubt that doubt should be resolved against the Crown. "Therefore the duty of the Court in this case seemed to "be a very plain one, and, as he (the Vice-Chancellor) had "ascertained the opinion of Watson, B., he was now "enabled to dispose of the case finally so far as he was "concerned. This information must be dismissed. It "was to be regretted that it had been filed. The bounty "of the Crown had been extended to this family, and it "was much to be regretted that the advisers of the Crown "in later times, considering the language of the grant and "the ample terms in which the bounty of the Crown was "expressed, should have deemed it expedient that this "expensive litigation should be commenced. The question "must, however, be decided against the Crown, and the "only consideration which remained was as to who ought "to bear the costs of the litigation. Some time ago he "took occasion to observe that the rule which used to "prevail at law with reference to the costs of the Crown, "by which it used to be held that the Crown ought "neither to pay nor receive costs, did not prevail in this "court. That was so decided in the case of the Attorney-"General *v.* the Earl of Ashburnham, where the Crown "was entitled to receive costs. In the case of Kane *v.* "Reynolds, in Sm. & Giff. Reports, he took occasion to "observe that such a rule did not prevail in equity, and it "was desirable that it should not prevail, for nothing "could be more contrary to justice than that the Crown "in its own court should have the means of conducting a "litigation on terms, with reference to the expenses of it, "more favourably than those on which it could be con-"ducted by any subject of the Crown. Therefore he "had come to the conclusion that justice required that, as "this claim had been urged in an expensive litigation, and "failed, the ordinary rule should be applied which pre-"vailed in this court—namely, that where litigation was "instituted and property was claimed, and the claim was "found to be unrighteous, and one which ought not to pre-"vail, the claim failing, the claimant must pay the costs. "He thought, therefore, that this information must be dis-"missed, with costs."

Donegall *v.* Templemore, 9 Ir. C. L. Rep. 374.

In 1858, in the case of the Marquess of Donegall *v.* Lord Templemore, ejectment was brought for quays, called Bute's Quay and Gigg's Quay, on the foreshore of the River Lagon, and mud lands in front of them. The defendant purchased of the Corporation of Belfast. The question turned upon the construction of a grant, there being conflicting evidence of user, and as to the limits of the River Lagon, the fishing in which and, as was alleged, the soil of it having been granted in 1620 to Lord Donegall's ancestors. It was held that evidence of modern user is admissible to explain the meaning of an ancient grant.

McCannon *v.* Sinclair, 2 Ell. & Ell. 53.

In 1859, in the case of McCannon *v.* Sinclair, it was decided that, when a parish comes down as far as the bank of a river, there is a *primâ facie* presumption that the parish extends as far as the middle of the river. This was the case of the Commercial Dock pier at Rotherhithe, but Lord Campbell drew a distinction between this case and that of Regina *v.* Musson—viz., that here the parish abutted on the *river*, and that in Regina *v.* Musson it abutted on the *sea*.

Queen *v.* Gee, 1 Ell. & Ell. 1068.

In 1860, in the case of the Queen *v.* Gee, it was decided that, where the sea-shore forms the boundary of a parish, the portion of the shore between the high-water mark of ordinary spring tides and that of medium tides is within the limits of the parish.

Embleton *v.* Brown, 3 Ell. & Ell. 234.

In 1860, in the case of Embleton *v.* Brown, it was decided that the part of the sea-shore comprised between the high and low water mark forms part of the body of the adjoining county, the justices of which, and not the Admiralty, have jurisdiction to take cognizance of offences there committed, whether or not committed when the shore is covered with water. The case arose upon information in respect of an attempt to take salmon trout in the Stell fishery, in the township of Amwell, belonging to the Duke of Northumberland, which was situate upon the foreshore of an arm of the sea.

In 1860 an information was filed against John Munby to remove the defendant from the possession of a booth on the sea-shore at Cleethorpe, in Lincolnshire. Defendant paid the costs and acknowledged his trespass, and removed the booth. The site of the booth and other foreshore have been leased to an adjoining landowner. House of Commons Returns, 1860, No. 464.

In the same year the Crown proceeded against several poor persons for taking sand from the foreshore at Paignton, Devon. The defendants were fined. The object of the proceedings was to prevent injury to the frontage. Ibid.

There appears to have been no limitation of time as to the Duchy foreshore in Cornwall until, in 1860, an Act, 23 & 24 Victoria, cap. 53, was passed for the limitation of acts and suits by the Duke of Cornwall in relation to real property. This Act, after reciting that the Duchy Manor Act, 7 & 8 Victoria, cap. 105, did not extend to the foreshore and beds of navigable rivers and ports in the Duchy, enacts that all the provisions of the Statute of Limitations, 9 George III. cap. 16, shall apply to the Duke of Cornwall, subject to sections 72 and 75 of the Act of 7 & 8 Victoria. Stat. 23-24 Vict. c. 53.

In 1861 an Act was passed confirming the Act of 9 George III. cap. 16, for quieting possessions and titles against the Crown, and for confirming the Act of 7 & 8 Victoria, cap. 105, for quieting titles in the county of Cornwall against the Duchy of Cornwall, and another Act of 23 & 24 Victoria, cap. 53, for the limitation of actions by the Duke of Cornwall. By the Act it is enacted that the Crown shall not sue after sixty years by reason of lands having been in charge, &c. By section 2 it is enacted that Stat. 24-25 Vict. c. 62.

this Act shall apply to actions by the Duke of Cornwall and to the provisions of 7 & 8 Victoria, cap. 105, and 23 & 24 Victoria, cap. 53. Section 3 of the Act is as follows:—"The Queen's Majesty, her predecessors and successors, "shall not be held, deemed, or taken, for the purposes "of the said Act of the ninth year of King George the "Third, to have been answered the rents, revenues, issues, "or profits of any lands, manors, tenements, rents, tithes, "or hereditaments which shall have been held or enjoyed, "or of which the rents, revenues, issues, or profits shall "have been taken, by any other persons or person by the "space of sixty years next before the filing, issuing, or "commencing of any such action, suit, bill, plaint, infor-"mation, commission, or other suit or proceeding for "recovering the same or in respect thereof, as in the "said Act is mentioned, by reason only of the same "lands, manors, tenements, rents, tithes, or hereditaments "having been part or parcel of any honour or manor or "other hereditaments of which the rents, revenues, issues, "or profits shall have been answered to her Majesty or "her predecessors or successors, or some other person "under whom her Majesty hath or lawfully claimeth, or "shall hereafter have or lawfully claim as aforesaid, or "of any honour, manor, or other hereditaments which "shall have been duly in charge to her Majesty, her pre-"decessors or successors, or stood insuper of record as "aforesaid."

Free Fishers of Whitstable *v.* Gann, and Gann *v.* Johnson, 11 C. B. N. S. 387; 13 C. B. N. S. 853; 11 H. of L. 192.

In 1861 occurred the cases of the Whitstable fishermen with respect to the claims of the Company of Free Fishers (who were the owners of oyster beds lying below the low-water mark, under a title from the lord of the manor, as parcel of the manor of Whitstable) to a prescriptive toll of one shilling for anchorage on the soil below low-water mark. In the first trial of Gann *v.* Johnson they were successful, the Court (Erle, C.J., Williams, J., and Byles, J.) holding that they had established their title to the soil, and that the Crown had power to grant

11 C. B. N. S. at p. 413.

them the right to the toll. Erle, C.J., held "that the "soil of the sea-shore for three miles from the beach is "vested in the Crown, and I am not aware of any rule of "law which prevents the Crown from granting to a subject "that which is vested in itself; and if the Crown did "grant the soil of the shore in question, it may well be "that the right of taking an anchorage toll of one shilling "was granted with it. Considering the nature of the "property—an oystery fishery—it seems to me that there "is the strongest possible presumption that the soil would "be granted, and the right to the shilling compensation "for anchoring there likewise. Nothing has been cited "to shew that such a grant could not be made; and "many of the passages cited from Hale go to shew that "a district or arm of the sea, or the soil of a navigable "river, may be vested in a subject; and it is most clearly "for the interest of the subject that a grant should be "made for the sustenance of a profitable fishery. There "is no authority against it, and the case of the Duke of "Somerset *v.* Fogwell (5 B. & C. 875) is an authority "to shew that, where the terms of the grant under which "the claim is made are unknown, the owner of a several "fishery may be presumed to be the owner of the soil. "Now, the existence of this fishery time out of mind is "recited in the Act of 1793. There is nothing to shew "that at the time of the original grant the soil was not "granted. The nature of the grant would render it "necessary that the soil should be granted, and I think "we are bound to infer, from the usage, that the toll was "granted in respect of the use of the soil—there is "nothing to shew that the law prohibits the enforcement "of such a toll by the owners of the soil, and there is "authority to shew that such a claim may be lawfully "made."

Williams, J.: "I am entirely of the same opinion. I "do not propose to add anything to what the Lord Chief "Justice has said upon the general points of the case. I "will merely say a word as to the proposition contended "for by Mr. Hawkins, that there could not be a legal "right in a subject to claim a toll or due for dropping an "anchor on a spot which is always covered by the sea.

"It is said that no amount of usage can establish such a "claim, because it could not by possibility have a legal "origin. That certainly is an argument which, but for "the history of our law, would be a forcible one. It is "said that the public have an unquestionable right to "navigate at their free will and pleasure in all navigable "rivers or arms of the sea; and that, if they have that "right, as incident thereto, to drop their anchors there. "The same argument may be, and has been, urged as to "several fisheries claimed in navigable rivers where the "tide flows and re-flows. The right of fishing in a navi-"gable river or an arm of the sea *primâ facie* belongs to the "public at large. But before Magna Charta the monarchs "of this realm sometimes thought themselves entitled to "abridge the rights of the public in this respect; and "that was the origin of the monopoly of several "fisheries. Since Magna Charta that can no longer "be done. As to the power of the Crown to transfer to "a subject the property in the sea-shore there can be no "doubt. This is distinctly laid down in the passage "cited by Mr. Denman from Hale 'De Portubus Maris,' p. "72, where it is said: 'As touching the first of these, "'the right of the lord to the port, we have before shewn "'that, though of common right the King is *primâ facie* "'owner and lord of every public sea-port, yet a subject "'may by charter or prescription be lord or owner of it.' "That seems to shew that by a grant in early times it "may have happened that the soil of this marine manor, "as it has been called, may have been transferred by the "Crown to a subject, from whom the fishery company "derive their title in the manner shewn by the evidence. "It does not, however, follow, because a part of the soil of "the sea-shore has by grant of the Crown become vested "in a subject, that therefore the right to take a toll for "anchorage is acquired. The conveyance or transfer of "the soil from the Crown to a subject superinduces this "consequence, that the owner may prevent the public "from using his soil without his permission; but the right "to demand and enforce a toll for its use does not neces-

"sarily follow. Toll is a matter of royal grant. That "is the reason of the passage from Hale to which I "referred in the course of the argument, where it is said: "'The ownership of propriety is, where the King, or a "'subject by charter or prescription, is the owner of the "'soil of a creek or haven where ships may safely arrive "'and come to shore. This interest of propriety may, as "'hath been shewn, belong to a subject. But he hath "'not thereby the franchise of a port; neither can he so "'use or employ it, unless he hath had that liberty time "'out of mind, or by the King's charter. Indeed, he may "'bring thither for his own private use his own boats and "'vessels, to carry off and bring in his own goods that "'are not customable, as fish, &c., but he may not use it "'as a public port, or admit foreigners, unless in case of "'necessity, nor take toll or anchorage there, for that is "'fineable, either by presentment or in a quo warranto, as "'hath been shewn.' That is to say, that although a "subject may be the owner of the soil of a port or an arm "of the sea, and may prevent others from anchoring "therein, yet he cannot without a royal grant or charter "demand toll or anchorage there—which clearly assumes "that if he had a royal grant he might take anchorage. "That is an express authority to shew that the claim of "the owners of the soil in this case may have had a legal "origin; and, if so, it seems to me that there was abun-"dant evidence of an exercise of the claim for anchorage "here to warrant the presumption that it had a legal "origin."

Byles, J.: "I am of the same opinion, and I have very "little to add to that which has fallen from my lord and "my brother Williams; but I cannot help saying that I "see no reason for casting any doubt upon the existence "of this very valuable right. Whether the *locus in quo* "was a part of a navigable river or an arm of the sea, in "either case it was originally vested in the Sovereign. It "is plain, from the deeds which were in evidence, that it "is now a portion of the manor of Whitstable; and, if so, "it must have been granted by the Crown to the lord of "the manor at some very early time, before the statute of "Quia Emptores, in 1290. The Crown cannot at this "day create a manor; it can exist only by prescription. "This portion, then, of this ancient manor having come "to the hands of the Whitstable Fishery Company in the "manner shewn by the subsequent conveyances, let us "see how they have exercised their rights of ownership. "They have used the soil for the formation of oyster "beds; and they have as far back as living memory goes, "and farther, demanded and exacted payment of a toll of "1*s.* from all vessels found anchoring within their fishery. "That being so, they are the owners of the soil, with the "right to receive a toll for anchorage there. It is said "that the right to the anchorage was lost by the severance "of the fishery from the terrestrial part of the manor in "1793. But that cannot be so; a manor cannot be "divided by act of the parties in respect of the services "due to the lord; but a division of the soil of the manor "in no way interferes with the enjoyment of the rights "incident to the use of the soil. As to the right to "demand the anchorage I have nothing to add. And as "to the right to enforce it by distress, the passage cited "from Gilbert on Distress seems to me to be a strong "authority to shew that it may be so enforced. The "right to anchorage is closely connected with the owner-"ship of the soil, and, unless it could be enforced by "distress, it would be next to impossible to enforce it at "all, and the right would be valueless. If, then, such a "right can exist by prescription, three instances are given "in the evidence of its having been exercised, and its "exercise acquiesced in."

The case was appealed to the Exchequer Chamber, when the decision was unanimously affirmed. Mellor, J., in delivering the judgment of the Court, observed: "It was "argued that although the bed of the sea where the claim "arose was at one time the property of the Crown, and "might possibly have been granted to a subject before "Magna Charta, yet that it could only have been lawfully "granted subject to the paramount right of navigation, of

" which anchorage is a necessary incident, unless it could " be shewn that the grantee has a consideration for the " grant, and had afforded some countervailing advantage " to the Crown for the benefit of the public." Upon this argument he decides "that before Magna Charta the King " could have granted, not only the shore of the sea to a " subject, but also the bed of the sea itself, in what Hale " calls *districtus maris*. There may be, and we think " there is, a distinction between the shore, or *litus maris*, " and the bed of the sea with reference to the modes in " which a subject may have acquired proprietary rights " therein, as well as in the nature and extent of the rights " so acquired. It may, we think, be admitted that there " is a paramount right of navigation in the sea, and that " any grant by the Crown of any portion of the bed of " the sea, or of the soil of the arms of the sea, or of " navigable rivers, must be subject to this paramount right " (Williams *v.* Wilcox, 8 Ad. & E. 328, 3 Nev. & P. 606; " the Mayor of Colchester *v.* Brooke, 7 Q. B. 373; the " Mayor of Nottingham *v.* Lambert, Willes 111); and, " although a subject may by prescription have a weir in " the sea, yet, if it be a nuisance to the passage of ships, " it may be abated. 'The people have a public interest, " 'a *jus publicum*, of passage and re-passage with their " 'goods by water, and must not be obstructed by " 'nuisances, or impeached by exactions': Hale 'De Jure " 'Maris,' 36. And the law as to this right of navigation " is laid down by Holroyd, J., in Blundell *v.* Caterall, in " these terms: 'By the common law, all the King's sub- " 'jects have in general a right of passage over the sea " 'with their ships, boats, and other vessels, for the purposes " 'of navigation, trade, and intercourse, and also in navi- " 'gable rivers; and they have also *primâ facie* a common " 'of fishery there; but they may be excluded from the " 'latter right, though not now by charter, at least by im- " 'memorial custom or prescription. These rights are " 'noticed by Lord Hale; but, whatever further rights, if " 'any, they may have in the sea or in navigable rivers, it is " 'a very different question whether they have, or how far

" 'they have, independently of necessity or usage, public " 'rights upon the shore (that is to say, between the high " 'and low water mark) when it is not sea or covered " 'with water, and especially when it has from time im- " 'memorial been, or has since become, private property.' " Now, although in this passage the reference to the rights " of the public in the shore is confined to the point " between high and low water mark, and where it is not " sea, still it gives, we think, the rule with reference to the " right of anchorage as an incident to navigation in such " portions of the bed of the sea as have been granted to " a subject.

" Any person navigating a vessel may, if compelled by " reasonable necessity arising from stress of weather, or " similar cause, drop his anchor in any part of the bed of " the sea; but we do not think that such a right is incon- " sistent with a claim to an anchorage due in any case in " which a navigator, of his own will, and without necessity, " anchors in the bed of a *districtus maris* like that in " question. It is true that, in the anonymous case re- " ported in the note to p. 517 of 1 Campbell, Wood, B., " is said to have directed the jury that 'a navigable river " 'is a public highway, and all persons have a right to " 'come there in ships, and to unload, moor, and stay " 'there as long as they please. Nevertheless, if they " 'abuse that right so as to work a private injury, they " 'will be liable to an action.'

" This certainly appears to be inaccurately expressed if " it means that the right to unload or to moor in a navi- " gable river is absolute and independent of any licence or " compensation in respect thereof.

"Anchorage is defined by Lord Hale—'De Portubus " 'Maris,' 74—to be 'a prestation or toll for every anchor " 'cast there; and sometimes though there be no anchor. " 'And this doth, in truth, properly and *primâ facie* arise " 'from and in respect of the propriety in the soil, and is " 'an evidence of it; but yet is not so always, but grows " 'due in respect of the franchise.'

" In the Mayor of Colchester *v.* Brooke, 7 Q. B. 355,

"Coltman, J., in directing the jury, is reported to have "said: 'It may be law, according to the ancient custom "'of the place, that a party may be liable, if he takes the "'ground, to make a reasonable payment to the owner of "'the soil. If the ground belongs to these parties, they "'very properly enforced payment if a vessel took ground, "'such payment being sanctioned by ancient custom.'

"If the authorities establish, as we think they do, that "the soil in the bed of the sea, in a creek or haven, arm "of the sea, or *districtus maris* might have been granted "to a subject, it seems to follow that any dropping of "an anchor not occasioned by reasonable necessity, but "voluntarily, in the bed of the sea so granted would en-"title the owner to compensation for the breaking of his "soil. If that be so, what objection is there in principle "to that compensation being fixed, and determined, and "made uniform by custom or grant, as in the case of "stallage or piccage in a market, to which all the public "have a right to resort, but, if they require to erect stalls, "must make compensation to the owner of the soil? See "the Mayor of Northampton *v.* Ward, 1 Wils. 114; "Comyn's Digest, Market.

"Toll paid to the owner of a port is perhaps not strictly "analogous to the due claimed by the plaintiffs, inasmuch "as the duty of repair may be deemed to be a considera-"tion for it. So, in the case of toll-thorough, which is a "sum demanded for passage on a highway, to support "which a consideration is necessary. But toll-traverse, "which is a sum demanded for passage over the private "soil of another, appears to be a claim of the same "character with that demanded in the present case. In "the case of the Mayor of Nottingham *v.* Lambert, Willes "111, the judgment of the Court is based on this distinc-"tion; and accordingly a prescription to take toll for "passing along the navigable River Trent through the "manor of Nottingham was held bad,—'For how can a "'duty be imposed on all the subjects of England only "'for enjoying that privilege which is their inherent birth-"'right, and which every subject had a right to before?

"'If, indeed, they receive any particular benefit, as going "'over a bridge, coming into a quay, wharf, port, or the "'like, this indeed may alter the case; but then this must "'be particularly shewn.'

"Had the claim under consideration been in respect of "passage over the *locus in quo*, it is clear that the pre- "scription could not have been supported; but it appears "to us that the defendant did receive a particular benefit "by anchoring there, and that there is nothing unreason- "able or against common right in sustaining the prescrip- "tion in the present case. We think that, after so long "a period of enjoyment, it is the duty of the Court to hold "it valid, unless we can see some valid reason against it, "either upon principle or authority.

"We are, therefore, of opinion that the plaintiffs are "entitled to the customary payment, and that the judg- "ment of the Court below was right, and must be "affirmed."

11 H. of L. Cas. 192.

The case went to the House of Lords, where, after a learned argument, the judgment was reversed, it being held "that this claim interferes with the free enjoyment "of the right of navigation subject to which the original "grant must be taken to have been made, and it cannot "be supported on the ground of ownership of the soil, and, "while it was admitted that such a toll might be payable "in a port which was repaired by the owner, there was no "evidence to shew there was a port at Whitstable, or that "the public had any advantage as a consideration for the "toll."

Whitstable Fishers *v.* Forman, L. R. 2 C. P. 688, 36 L. J. C. P. 273, 16 L.T. 747, 15 W. R. 1133; L.R. 3 C.P. 578, 37 L.J. C.P. 305, 18 L. T. 734, 16 W. R. 1019; L. R. 4 H. of L. 266, 21 L. T. 804.

The question was subsequently tried in Whitstable Fishers *v.* Forman, on a case stated, in which the history of the manor from the time of Domesday downwards was set out, and it was shewn that the lords had been entitled to tolls by prescription, and that the Whitstable Company maintained buoys and beacons which were an aid to the navigation, and, as there was evidence that the buoys and beacons had been maintained as far back as living memory extends, the Court thought that it ought to presume that they had existed from time immemorial, and the anchorage dues, having been received during this period, ought to be referred to a legal origin if it can be done; and it was held that the maintenance of the buoys and beacons, taken in connection with the ownership of the soil of the anchorage ground and the benefit to the public therefrom, afforded a sufficient consideration to support the plaintiffs' claim to the anchorage dues.

In 1863 occurred the case of Attorney-General against Jones. This was an information by the Crown claiming a piece of land about 80 yards in length and 40 yards in width on the foreshore adjacent to the village of Cemmaes, in the parish of Llanbadrig, in the county of Anglesea, which was claimed in right of the Crown "as in "and by very many records of this Exchequer appears on "record." The information charged intrusion and the building of a pier. It appears to have been a Latin information, to which the defendant pleaded that the Crown was not possessed. At the trial before Keating, J., at the Cheshire Assizes, 1862, the defendant gave in evidence an inquisition of 9 Edward I. concerning the laws and customs of Wales and the laws of Howel Dda, and it was contended that by virtue of the Statute of Rudland, 12 Edward I., and the 27 Henry VIII. cap. 26, s. 31, these laws are still in force in the county of Anglesea. Among these laws in the Venedotian Code of Howel Dda is the following:—"Whoever possesses land "upon the margin of the shore owns as much of the beach "as the breadth of his land; and he may make a weir "or other things thereon if he will; but if the sea throw "any things upon the land or upon that beach they "belong to the King, for the sea is a pack horse to the "King." It was proved that the defendant was the owner of the adjoining land. He also produced an extent of the county of Anglesea, 26 Edward III., A.D. 1352, in which the manor of Cemmaes was mentioned, and evidence was adduced to shew that it extended to the sea-shore of the place in question. Also a grant of the manor in 7 James I., A.D. 1609, to an ancestor of the present lord.

Att. *v.* Jones, 2 Hurl. & C. 347; 33 L. J. Ex. 249; 1 L.T. 955.

In this grant were mentioned fisheries, fishings, wrecks of the sea, and all other rights, jurisdictions, franchises, liberties, privileges, profits, and commodities. Formerly there was an island rock, which was blasted when the present pier was built, and the defendant had used some of the stones for building the pier; beyond the pier was a weir. The defendant adduced evidence to prove that the lord of the manor had prevented people taking sand from the shore near the pier, and on one occasion he had taken wreck; but it appeared by evidence in reply that the public were accustomed to take sand from the sea-shore, and the surveyor of highways had taken stones for their repair—that, on the inquiry as to wreck in 1857 under the Merchant Shipping Act, the lord of the manor had put in a claim, but offered no evidence. The judge directed the jury that the presumption of law that the sea-shore between high and low water mark belonged to the Crown extended to Wales, and that the right of the Crown was not affected by the statutes of 12 Edward I. and 27 Henry VIII. cap. 26; that although the grant of James I. of the manor of Cemmaes gave the right to wreck, it did not in terms give any right to the sea-shore between high and low water mark; that the question for their consideration was whether, upon the evidence of acts of user, they were satisfied that the *primâ facie* title of the Crown was displaced by title in the defendant or the lord of the manor. The jury gave a verdict for the Crown, and stated that they found, first, that the site of the rock belonged to the defendant and the sea-shore to the Crown; secondly, that there was no evidence that the lord of the manor ever took or claimed wreck. A rule for a new trial was obtained, on the ground that the learned judge misdirected the jury in directing them that there was no evidence of a grant of the sea-shore by the Crown, and in directing them that the ancient laws of Wales did not apply to this case. The Attorney-General shewed cause, and argued that there was no evidence to rebut the *primâ facie* title; that the common law right of the Crown was not affected by the Welsh laws, which were not now the law of Anglesea; and that the grant of James did not convey the foreshore, citing Attorney-General *v.* Chambers. For the defendant it was argued that the word "manor" would include the shore, and that the judge ought to have told the jury that the foreshore may be parcel of the manor, and that the words of the grant were sufficiently large to include the shore; and he should have left it to them to say whether the evidence of user, coupled with the grant, satisfied them that the foreshore was parcel of the manor, citing Duke of Beaufort *v.* Swansea and Calmady *v.* Rowe. It was also argued that the laws of Howel Dda were still the laws of the county of Anglesea. The Attorney-General, in reply, referred to Dickens *v.* Shaw. Bramwell, B., gave the judgment of the Court, and held that "the judge should have coupled the evidence of "ownership with the grant, and have told the jury that "although the grant did not necessarily pass the shore "between high and low water mark, yet that it might do "so, and that whether it did or not they were to determine "upon consideration of all the other evidence." He directed a new trial. No judgment was given as to the Welsh laws. The case was again tried before Channell, B., at the Cheshire Summer Assizes, 1862, when additional evidence of user was adduced on the part of the defendant, and the learned baron having directed the jury in accordance with the above judgment, they found a verdict for the defendant. The Attorney-General obtained a rule *nisi* for a new trial, on the ground of misdirection—first, that there was no evidence which ought to have been left to the jury to shew that the *locus in quo* was within and parcel of the manor of Cemmaes; secondly, that there was no evidence which ought to have been left to the jury to shew that there had been any possession of the *locus in quo* adverse to the Crown for sixty years before the filing of the information so as to bar the title of the Crown under 9 George III. cap. 16; thirdly, that the learned judge misdirected the jury as to the construction of the grant of James I., and also that the verdict was against the weight of evidence; but the rule was discharged.

In this case it will be observed that, although there was evidence that the public took sand on the foreshore, the evidence of other acts of ownership, coupled with the grant, established the title of the lord of the manor notwithstanding considerable user by the public.

House of Commons Returns, 1863, No. 42; 1864, No. 3.

In 1862 an information was filed against the Sittingbourne and Sheerness Railway Company for specific performance of an agreement to purchase lands belonging to the Crown above the high-water mark, and also in respect of a pier erected on the foreshore of the West Swale at Queenborough, Kent. After answer, by the advice of the law officers the claim to the foreshore was given up by the Crown, the specific performance of the agreement as to the land above high-water mark being decreed.

Ibid.

In 1862 an information was filed against the Swanage Pier Company in respect to the foreshore, but, after answer, the Crown proceedings were stayed, and the Crown paid the defendants' costs.

Vyner *v.* Mersey Docks, 14 C. B. N. S. 753.

Comrs. of Woods' Rep., xxii. 31.

In 1863 occurred the case of Vyner *v.* the Mersey Docks and Harbour Board, in which the plaintiff, who was the lord of the manor of Bidston, in Cheshire, had on 17 December 1830 procured a grant from the Commissioners of Woods of 54 acres of foreshore in Wallasey Pool, a creek of the River Mersey, for £3000. Subsequently, in 1854, the Commissioners of Woods conveyed the bed and shores of the said pool to the Mersey Docks and Harbour Board, and the second grant comprehended the land conveyed by the first grant. It was contended that the defendants had acquired title against the plaintiff either under several Acts of Parliament, or by the grant of 1854, or by the acquiescence of the plaintiff. The plaintiff's claim was founded, first, on length of possession; secondly, upon his rights as lord of the manor of Bidston, and he gave evidence to shew that the foreshore was parcel of that manor; and, thirdly, under the grant of 1830, by which he got in the Crown's claim. It was held that the conveyance of 1854 could not divest the estate which had vested in the plaintiff under the grant of 1830, and that the subsequent Acts of Parliament created no statutable title either in the Dock Commissioners or the defendants.

Erle, C.J.: "If the land had been before conveyed "from the Queen as it had been in 1830 to the plaintiff, "the agreement of 1844 and the indenture of 1854 can "have no effect; that which has been before granted "cannot pass again by a subsequent grant from the "same grantor unless an Act of Parliament has intervened, and given that which otherwise would be con"trary to all the common principles of law."

Constable *v.* Nicholson, 14 C. B. N. S. 230; 32 L. J. C. P. 240; 11 W. R. 698.

In 1863 occurred the case of Constable *v.* Nicholson. It was an action of trespass for taking sand, stone, ballast, and seaweed on the foreshore of the seigniory of Holderness, in the townships of Owthorn and Withernsea. The defendants set up a right in the inhabitants of the townships to take gravel, &c., for the cultivation and improvement of their land and for the necessary repair of the highway of the parish. It was held that the pleas were bad, for that so far as they were capable of being construed as justified under a custom, such custom would be void, being a claim of a *profit a prendre in alieno solo*, which can only exist by grant or by prescription; and if the claim were founded on prescription, it would be equally bad, inasmuch as it was a claim by persons who, not being a corporation, were incapable of taking by grant, and not being claimed in a *que estate*.

Willes, J.: "As far as the right is claimed by custom, "if any such exist it is clearly bad; the distinction is well "established that by custom you may claim an easement "to be enjoyed over the land of another, but you cannot "claim a profit out of the land," and he cited Bailey *v.* Stephens, 12 C. B. N. S. 91.[1]

[1] See also Oxenden *v.* Palmer, 2 B. & Ad. 852; Padwick *v.* Knight, 22 L. J. N. S. Exch. 198, 7 Exch. 854; Howe *v.* Stawell, Al. & Nap. 348; Hamilton *v.* Att. for Ireland, 5 L. R. Ir. 555; Race *v.* Ward, 4 E. & B. 702; Blewet *v.* Tregoning, 3 A. & E. 690; Lord Rivers *v.* Adams, 3 Ex. D. 361; Chilton *v.* Corporation of London, L. R. 7 Ch. D. 735; Bland *v.* Lipscombe, 24 L. J. N. S. Q. B. 25, 135; Mayor of Lynn *v.* Taylor, 3 Lev. 160; Hamerton *v.* Honey, 24 W. R. 603; Goodman *v.* Mayor of Saltash, 7 App. Cas. 633; De la Warr *v.*

15 C. B. N. S. 600; 33 L. J. C. P. 124; 10 Jur. N. S. 680; 9 L.T. 766; 12 W. R. 670.

In the case of Mace *v.* Philcox, in 1864, it was held that, a piece of the shore at Hastings having been let by the Crown to the plaintiff, the defendant, a bathing-machine keeper (who claimed under a licence from the local authority), had no right to place the machine upon any part of the beach, which was private property. A distinction was drawn here as to the right of the public to bathe and their right to use the shore. Erle, C.J.: "I "take it to be clear that the usage of bathing along the "shore gives no right to the persons availing themselves "of it to place machines there, whether drawn by horses "or by means of a capstan." Commenting on Blundell *v.* Caterall, he said (p. 611), "If you can lawfully get to "the sea-shore, I apprehend you may lawfully bathe there."

Lestrange *v.* Rowe, 4 Fost. & Finl. 1048.

In 1866 occurred the case of Lestrange *v.* Rowe. This was an action of trespass for taking shingle, sand, seaweed, and mussels from the shore of the hundred of Smetheden and manor of Snettisham (Norfolk), and trespass to a several fishery. The defendant denied the fishery, and pleaded the public right and leave and licence. Evidence was given of a grant of the manor, with general words of groundage, anchorage, and wreck of the sea. Wreck had been taken, jetties run out, persons had been prosecuted for taking mussels, and licences to take mussels and shingles were shewn, entries of payments for them, and presentments on court rolls against persons who had taken wreck. Erle, C.J., in summing up the case to the jury, directed them that the place was on the foreshore in front of the manor, and that the act of the defendant was a clear trespass, to whomsoever the land belonged; but the plaintiff's title is denied, and he goes on to say:

"And I should tell you that by the law of England "the soil between high and low water mark, that which "is left dry by the ebb of the tide and which is covered "by the full tide, is presumed to be in the Crown unless "the Crown at some time or other parted with it. There

Miles, 17 Ch. D. 585; Neill *v.* Duke of Devonshire, 8 App. Cas. 135; Baird *v.* Fortune, 7 Jur. N. S. 926.

"are some manors that remain in the Crown—that are the "property of the Crown—as in Cornwall; but I take it "that, in the great majority of cases, the right to the "foreshore between high and low water mark is in the "lord of the manor. Whether that is so in the majority "of cases is not closely pertinent to the issue you have to "decide, because the issue you have to decide is whether "the foreshore in front of the manor of Snettisham is "shewn upon this evidence to be in the lord of the manor. "If there had been a grant from the Crown directly of "the foreshore in front of this manor, there would be an "end of this inquiry; but the grant is of the manor of "Snettisham with a great many general words, and "among the general words there is the grant of anchor-"age, groundage, and wreck of the sea. It is a grant of "the manor *with the appurtenances*, and there is a strong "presumption in law that by the grant of a manor with "those terms annexed the soil of the sea-shore was "intended to pass. In a great number of cases juries "have been told that the grant of those three rights, or "either of them, is some evidence for the jury that the soil "between high and low water mark was intended to pass. "One reason is, that in respect of anchorage there is what "we in law consider to be a direct interference with the "soil—letting go an anchor that penetrates into the soil "and alters the surface; but that is not conclusive. Again, "if you grant the right of groundage in any of the ways in "which the ground may be required for purposes of navi-"gation—in particular, if it is a district where the tide "goes out and the vessel lies between high and low water "mark—there would be the use of the soil for the ship "that is to ground, and the person who is to have the "payment for that groundage is presumed to have a right "to the soil. If it was law I should so lay it down, but "I say it is a presumption. Again, in respect of the right "of wreck—things thrown up by the sea, coming with the "rise of the tide and left upon the shore when the tide "goes out—the person who has the grant of the wreck of "the sea must go down upon the shore to collect that

Ante, pp. 19, 57, 90, 146, 348.

"wreck, and therefore it is that that has been taken to be "very good evidence on which the jury is justified in pre- "suming that the Crown, in granting a manor with those "additional rights, intended to grant the foreshore of the "manor wherever those rights were to be exercised.

"In the case of Calmady *v.* Rowe, 6 C. B. 861, where "there was a grant of wreck and anchorage only, and the "judge left to the jury that which I am stating now, that "it was good presumptive evidence on which the jury "might act, and the jury acting upon it, the Court had to "consider if that was the proper way of laying down the "law, and there held that it was a correct statement "of the law, and a correct interpretation of the effect of "that charter.

"With regard to many matters of fact in common life "the jury may well be supreme judges, and, in my "opinion, there never was a more salutary part of our law "than making them supreme judges as to what they "consider the proper inference from the evidence brought "before them in matters of ordinary life, mercantile "transactions, and the course of business; but when the "matter that is offered them in evidence is something in "the nature of these royal grants, the courts of law, for "many centuries, have been in the habit of putting an "interpretation upon them; and though the line of demar- "cation between where the province of the judge ends "and the province of the jury begins ought to be clearly "marked, and although the effect of these presumptions "is for the jury, not for the judge, still it is one of those "presumptions as to which, if I was upon the jury, I "should consider that the judge was much more likely to "have a clear notion of the legal effect according to the "laws and customs of England than if he interpreted the "oral evidence of witnesses before him on any of the "more common transactions of life.

"There has been a uniform course of decision on this "subject. The right to the foreshore has been discussed "many times, and the law has been constantly laid down, "as far as I know, and maintained to be rightly laid down, "that the grant of a manor with anchorage, groundage, "and wreck is good presumptive evidence, for the reasons "I have given, on which the jury may find that the soil "of the foreshore is in the party to whom that manor "belongs. It may well be that there was reason for that "interpretation, and it may well be that the lord of the "manor might have the right of the soil subject to a "great many privileges and rights on the part of the "subject, and also clogged with duties in many respects "towards the subject; but there is very sound ground and "reason for letting that property be in the management "of some one who may have, as in this case, very great "interests at stake in having the shore maintained and "kept up. The operative grant in this case was in the "early part of the reign of King James I., who granted "to Cary this manor of Snettisham, and he granted it "with the fullest words, to this effect: 'I grant the manor "'of Snettisham,' and, among other things, 'I grant the "'wreck of the sea, anchorage, and groundage, and all "'other privileges which are belonging to the manor, and "'all to be held by him in the same manner as it had "'been held in former times.'

"Now, that is the documentary part of the case.

"Then we come to the oral evidence which has been "produced before you—evidence by acts of ownership.

"Now, when you come to look at the weight of acts of "ownership over any close which may be in question, the "nature of the close is of the essence of the matter before "the jury. If it is arable land, who takes the crops? If "pasture land, who turns cattle upon it? If it is wood-"land, who cuts the trees and carries them away? But "when you come to the sea-shore that is between high "and low water mark, the acts of ownership must be "limited to the matters that are upon the sea-shore—"matters of profit for persons to take away. It cannot be "inclosed; there is no such thing as a crop growing upon "it; and it must be for the most part that which the sea "throws up—that which can be used by those who have "occasion to go upon the soil. Almost the only matters "that I know of are connected with taking wreck. Now, "how has there been a user in that respect on this manor? "There is a local agent, who gives an account of a wreck "in his time thirty years ago. The Mayor of Lynn also "gives evidence of accounting for wrecks to the lord of "the manor afterwards, at a more recent time. Then we "are told that thirteen years ago jetties were run out for "one hundred yards, beginning from the top of the bank "and running out into the sea. No doubt that is not so "direct an exercise of an act of ownership as the taking "such profit as the land affords, but is good evidence for "the jury to attend to, and it may be considered that you "cannot have jetties to run out upon the land of another "without the leave of that person, unless it is on acount "of the sea breaking in, and you stop it, under those "privileges that arise in the case of emergency. Such a "right as building constructions to stand for a great "many years, to maintain the shore in a general way, is a "right that I have not known to be exercised under the "powers for stopping out the sea. I do not say that it "might not be exercised, if the sea could not be otherwise "kept out, by an ordinary freeholder; but this, to my "mind, is good piece of evidence to the jury—that Mr. "Lestrange employed a man to put these jetties down, "running them out to that distance to maintain the shore "for his own benefit and the benefit of every one whose "lands would be washed over if the sea came in.

"Then there is evidence of what, to my mind, was a "very strong act of ownership in respect to the taking of "mussels, and that was in the action by the plaintiff. If "a man gave notice to Mr. Lestrange that he disputed "his right, and sent a horse and cart to take the mussels "away, and Mr. Lestrange did not bring an action "against him, it would be strong evidence indeed that he "had not the right; but, on the other hand, it is a very "strong piece of evidence that a person was sued by the "plaintiff in an action of trespass for taking the mussels, "and that, when the law was to be brought in force against "him, he paid £5, and agreed to pay a royalty to Mr.

"Lestrange for all the cartloads of mussels that he should "take away.

"Then there are entries in the books of payments to the "lord for shingle, and licences granted by the lord, &c. "There is no counter evidence, that I see. Then it "appears that from the books of deceased stewards there "were many entries for wreck—so far a considerable "exercise of the rights of ownership. The court rolls "of the manor are produced, shewing that persons were "presented as defaulters against the lord of the manor "who took away wreck without leave of the lord. They "were ordered to give up the wreck to the lord, and were "ordered to pay a penalty.

"That is the case for the plaintiff; and there is nothing "to be said against it on the other side that I am "aware of."

In 1865 an information was filed against the Herne Bay Fishery Company to establish the title of the Crown to about six square miles of land forming part of the bed of the sea near Herne Bay. The defendants submitted, and took a lease from the Crown. House of Commons Returns, 1869, No. 4.

In 1886, in the case of the Ipswich Dock Commissioners against the Overseers of St. Peter's, it was decided that an estuary or arm of the sea is *primâ facie* extra-parochial, but this presumption may be rebutted. The place in question was a wet dock built in the River Orwell partly on the foreshore and partly in the channel. Evidence of parish perambulations shewed that the parish extended to high-water mark; but, on the other hand, there was evidence that lands had been reclaimed out of other parts of the river, and had been rated to the poor for more than fifty years without opposition. The Court, attaching more weight to those acts which raise a question of money value than to the evidence of reputation of perambulations, drew the conclusion that the bounds of the parishes abutting on the Orwell go down the middle of the channel. Ipswich *v.* St. Peter's, 7 B. & S. 310.

In the same year, in the case of the Trustees of the Duke of Bridgewater *v.* Bootle, the question arose Bridgewater Trustees *v.* Bootle, ibid. 348.

whether land on which docks had been constructed on the foreshore of the Mersey was rateable to the township of Bootle for a highway rate. It was held that the presumption was that the land was not within the township of Bootle, and that it was not within a district maintaining its own highways within statute 5 & 6 William IV. cap. 60, s. 5. And it was further held, with respect to the presumption of extra-parochiality, that there is no distinction between the sea-shore and the shore of a tidal river. There is no presumption that the foreshore is parochial, and the onus lies upon those who say it is to prove it; and in this case they did not do so. (See also Blackpool Pier *v.* Tylde Union, 46 L. J. M. C. 189.)

CHAPTER XXI.

A.D. 1866 TO A.D. 1888.

By the Crown Lands Act, 1866 (29 & 30 Victoria, cap. 62), the management of the foreshore and bed of the sea and of every channel, creek, bay, estuary, and of every navigable river as far up the same as the tide flows, was transferred from the Commissioners of Woods and Forests to the Board of Trade, except such portions thereof in relation to which any instrument had been, before 1 January 1867, made or executed by the Commissioners of Woods, and except the foreshores of the Thames, Tees, and county palatine of Durham, and also except foreshore adjacent to any Crown lands, and except as to mines under the foreshore. By section 25 it is provided that the powers and rights of the Crown over the foreshore shall not be extended by the Act, but, as between the Crown and all other persons, such powers and rights shall continue as the same existed before the passing of the Act. Powers of arbitration between the Crown and the subject are given by sections 26 and 29; and there is a general saving of rights. By this Act the greater part of the foreshore is placed under the control of the Board of Trade, but the Commissioners of Woods retain the management of a considerable portion which had previously been dealt with by them. Under this Act the Board of Trade have actively dealt with the foreshore, and, although they appear to be fully aware that the claim of the Crown cannot be set up as arbitrarily and confidently as it was set up by their predecessors, the Commissioners of Woods and Forests, yet whether the title of the Crown be doubtful or not, they act in all cases as if the Crown's title were indisputable in every case. A review of their proceedings will be found in a subsequent chapter.

Nicholson v. Williams, L. R. 6 Q. B. 632; 40 L. J. M. C. 159; 19 W. R. 973.

In 1871 occurred the case of Nicholson *v.* Williams. The respondent was convicted of unlawfully taking shingle from the shores and banks of the port of Kingston-upon-Hull, whereby the said port was, and is, in danger of being damaged, contrary to 54 George III. cap. 159. It was a prosecution by the Board of Trade against the agent of Sir Talbot Constable, the lord of the seigniory of Holderness, who was receiving a revenue of about £1200 a year from the sale of gravel from his foreshores. By 54 George III. cap. 159, s. 14, it is enacted that, in order to prevent damage being done to the shores or banks of the ports, harbours, or havens of this kingdom, no person shall take any ballast or shingle from the shores or banks, or any portion of the shores or banks, of any port, harbour, or haven from which the Commissioners for executing the office of Lord High Admiral shall find it necessary, for the protection of such port, harbour, or haven, or the works thereof, by order to prohibit the taking of such ballast, &c. See the saving clause at p. 441, *ante*. By 25 & 26 Victoria, cap. 69, s. 16, the powers vested in the Admiralty were transferred to the Board of Trade; the Board of Trade accordingly made orders preventing the removal of shingle; the defendant took the shingle by order of Sir Clifford Constable, the lord of the seigniory of Holderness, at a place outside the harbour of the Humber, but within the limits of the customs port of Hull, which had been extended to Bridlington. Lush, J., in delivering the judgment of the Court, reviewed the Acts, and said: "It is "therefore clear that the jurisdiction of the Board of Trade "to prohibit the taking of shingle extends *not over the* "*whole coast of the kingdom*, but only over such portions "thereof as are *within the ambit of a port, harbour, or haven;* "whatever is done beyond those limits is left to be dealt with "at common law, but *within those limits* the jurisdiction of "the Board to prohibit the public from taking shingle or "ballast is absolute and without appeal. On the other "hand, it is equally clear that their jurisdiction is not limited "to ports or havens for which regulations have been made "under the earlier sections of the Act of 54 George III. cap.

"159; the enactment applies, as the object and purport of "it require that it should apply, to *every port, harbour, and* "*haven in the kingdom.*" He then discusses the nature of ports, and shews that their limits are appointed from time to time by the Crown, and he holds that the powers of the Board of Trade extend to the limits of the port as defined for fiscal and customs purposes. Thus, in effect, the learned judge contradicts his own judgment, for he does not seem to have been aware that the whole of the coasts of the kingdom have from the earliest times been entirely divided up into various royal ports for customs purposes, and that the limits of those ports have always comprehended between them the whole of the coast; that, though those ports have been from time to time subdivided or aggregated by Royal Commissions and under Acts of Parliament; there never was a time when any portion of the shore of the kingdom was outside the limits of a royal port, and therefore what he says at p. 640 of the judgment, that "whatever is done in the way of taking shingle *outside the* "*ambit of a port, harbour, or haven* is not within the jurisdiction of the Board of Trade," is simply a nullity, for there is no such portion, nor ever was. It is submitted, therefore, that the words "port, harbour, or haven" in the Act of 54 George III. should be read as meaning ports, havens, and harbours in the physical sense, and of harbours for the purposes of navigation and mooring of ships; and a careful perusal of the rest of the Act, and a consideration of the purposes for which it was passed, greatly strengthen this view. The saving clause of the Act, which saves all the rights of lords of manors, does not appear to have been referred to, and, on the whole, it is submitted that the decision is highly unsatisfactory, and by no means conclusive to empower the Board of Trade arbitrarily and without appeal to prevent the lords of manors holding the foreshore from removing ballast or shingle from their lands on the open sea-coast in places where such digging can have no effect upon the physical condition of any haven, and it is to be greatly doubted whether the saving clause of the Act of 54 George III. does not

See Surveys of Ports in Exch.Q. R. Memda., and Special Commn.; also Customs Accounts.

entirely preserve the rights of lords of manors even in the ports.

But see Att.-Gen. *v.* Tomline, L.R. 12 Ch. D. 58.

In the case of the Queen *v.* Clinton, in 1869, it was held that drifted and ungathered seaweed cast on the shore between high and low water mark of him who has exclusively the ownership of the said shore is not the subject of larceny.

4 I. R. C. L. 6. See also Reg. *v.* Justices of Dublin, 5 I. R. C. L. 548.

Healy *v.* Thorn, 4 I. R. C. L. 495.

In 1870 occurred the case of Healy *v.* Thorn. It was an action of trespass for taking seaweed on the foreshore of Shennick Island, co. Dublin. The plaintiff shewed that he and his predecessors had let the island and received rent as far back as 1811, and had had exclusive use of the seaweed. He made title under a grant from the Crown of 30 June 1605 of the priory of Holmpatrick, together with several islands, with wreck of the sea, &c., *adeo plene* as the priors had it. The defendant claimed a right in the public to take the seaweed, and argued that the patent did not pass the shore, putting forward the arguments of Hall that to obtain title to sea-shore by lapse of time there must be exclusive possession, as by embankment. It was held that the words of the grant, explained by the evidence of user, were sufficient to pass the shore, and that, if no grant had been produced, the acts of ownership were sufficient to raise the presumption of a lost grant. Also that the public has no right to take seaweed on the foreshore, citing Howe *v.* Stawell.

Corp. of Hastings *v.* Ivall. L. R. 19 Eq. 558; 22 W. R. 724.

In 1874 occurred the case of the Corporation of Hastings *v.* Ivall. This was a suit by the Corporation of Hastings for the purpose of preventing the deposit of earth on the sea-shore at Hastings. It appeared that by letters patent 14 February, 31 Elizabeth, the Queen granted to the Corporation of Hastings, amongst other things "all that her parcel of land and her hereditaments "called the 'Stone Beach,' with the appurtenances in "Hastings." Under this grant the corporation claimed the whole of the foreshore. The defendant set up the title of the Crown. It appeared, from the evidence, that, although the corporation had exercised many acts of ownership over the shore, the Crown had laid claim to it, and had actually granted portions of it, and the grantees were in possession, and the title was then in dispute between the Crown and the corporation; but Vice-Chancellor Malins held that the corporation were in possession, and that the possessory title by persons claiming foreshore was sufficient against a trespasser, without producing evidence to displace the title of the Crown, and that, in a suit against a trespasser by persons claiming title to foreshore and giving evidence of acts of ownership in support of their title, it is not open to the defendant to prove any acts of ownership by the Crown except such as can be shewn to have been done with the knowledge of the plaintiffs. The Vice-Chancellor, referring to the evidence of acts by the Crown, said: "But, however strong those "transactions may be as shewing an admission by the "corporation of a title in the Crown, I am of opinion "that they cannot be set up by the defendant as against "the plaintiffs, who are clearly shewn to be in possession "of the whole beach, and by virtue of such possession, "whether rightful or wrongful, are, as against the Crown, "entitled to restrain the unlawful proceedings of the de-"fendant. It is impossible, in my opinion, for a trespasser "on an estate to justify his trespass by shewing that the "person in possession, who seeks to restrain the trespass, "has at a former period, either by word or act, admitted "that some other person than himself was entitled to the "estate. Notwithstanding those admissions or acts of the "plaintiffs, it is clear that they are in possession of that "part of the beach upon which the defendant has "deposited the rubbish or earth, and such possession, "whether the right to it was acquired under the charter "of Elizabeth or otherwise, entitles them to restrain the "proceedings of a wrongdoer."

In 1874 occurred the case of Brew *v.* Haren. This was an action for taking seaweed in Ireland. The plaintiff was the owner of lands adjoining the sea-shore under a grant of James II., which granted them with general words of "all and singular lands, tenements, &c., to the premises, "or any part thereof, incident or appendant, or accepted,

Brew *v.* Haren, 9 I. R. C. L. 29.

"reputed, or known as parts parcel of the same, &c." He adduced evidence of convictions, and an action against a trespasser which was put to arbitration and awarded in his favour, and shewed divers acts of ownership by taking seaweed and licensing others to do so. The defendant produced evidence with a view of shewing that there was a public right to take seaweed. It was held that the general words were capable of passing the sea-shore adjoining the lands specifically granted, and that the acts of ownership were admissible to prove it. In this case there was no grant of any manor, but merely of lands, and it was here held that the foreshore may be parcel of "lands" as well as parcel of a manor, and that this may be proved by evidence of acts of ownership.

Lee *v.* Brown, 2 Mod. 69; Freem. 207; Pollexfen 410.

In 1874, in the case of Mulholland *v.* Killen, it was held that evidence by the plaintiff of acts of ownership by taking seaweed on the foreshore of Carlingford Lough established the title to the foreshore, although no grant from the Crown was shewn, the Crown never having interfered. It was again held, following Howe *v.* Stawell, that there is no common law right in the public to take seaweed, &c., from the shore.

Mulholland *v.* Killen, Ir. Rep. 9 Eq. 471.

In 1875 occurred the case of Wyse *v.* Leahy. This was an action of trespass on a piece of foreshore at Rostellan, co. Cork, by taking seaweed. The plaintiff held under a patent of 1709 granting the slob land of Rostellan to the Earl of Inchiquin, and under a conveyance from the Landed Estates Court, and he shewed extensive user of the shore, convictions of trespassers, &c. The defendant denied the title and possession, and set up a right in the public to take the seaweed, and shewed acts by the public. Lawson, J., directed the jury that foreshore was *primâ facie* in the Crown; but if the owner of the adjoining lands proved that he was in possession of it, and exercised acts of ownership over it, excluding all other persons, a jury was at liberty from such user either to construe the patent as including the shore or to presume a grant from the Crown. The jury found for the plaintiff. On application for a new trial, on the ground that the verdict was

Wyse *v.* Leahy, Ir. Rep. 9 C. L. 384.

against the weight of evidence, the verdict was upheld, Morris, J., remarking, on the evidence brought forward to shew acts of user by the public: "The usual attempt "was made by the defendant to set up trespasses as "evidence of public user, and the usual number of pleas "were pleaded relying on such user. These were all nega-"tived by the jury; the plaintiff has been in possession "since 1839, and the defendant is a mere trespasser."

In the case of the Attorney-General *v.* the Corporation of Portsmouth, in 1870, an information was filed to establish the title of the Crown to the bed and soil and foreshores of Portsmouth Harbour, which had been claimed by the Corporation of Portsmouth. The question arose in consequence of the extension of the old dockyard on the north side and the building of the new steam basin. The defendants claimed the whole of the foreshore adjacent to the borough except the site of the ancient dockyard, which was in the possession of the Crown. They claimed it as part of the land of the borough under a charter of King Henry III. granting to the men of Portsmouth the town or borough in fee farm, and by later confirmations and charters to the time of King Charles I. These charters did not expressly pass the foreshore, but defendants rested their case upon evidence of acts of ownership exercised by them and their predecessors upon the foreshore, which they averred were sufficient to raise the presumption that the foreshore had passed as parcel of the town or borough by these grants from the Crown. The defendants also relied upon a charter of Charles I. granting to them anchorage and groundage in the *port* of the borough and the members of the same, claiming that the grant of this anchorage and groundage was a due arising from the ownership of the soil; but in this they were clearly wrong, as anchorage and groundage in a *port* are port dues, and not soil dues (see Bishop of Durham *v.* Haselrig, *ante*, p. 420). In the course of the argument Baron Cleasby said that his idea was that anchorage has no connection with the foreshore, and by itself would not afford the slightest presumption of any grant. By this

Att.-Gen. *v.* Portsmouth (not reported).

contention the corporation prejudiced their case, for the anchorage was taken over the whole harbour, and at first they claimed the soil of it, but gave up the claim, and reduced it to the foreshore of the borough or town. A special case was stated, and the cause was heard on 19 April 1877 before Baron Cleasby and Baron Pollock. The evidence of user was conflicting, there being user by the Crown as well as user by the corporation, and the whole question was whether the evidence raised the presumption of a grant, or whether it was to be taken as evidence of usurpation. In the portion of the foreshore to the southward of the dockyard the evidence for the corporation was very strong. It was found that the natural dock called Camber had been in possession of the corporation for 200 years, and that the Crown had leased and purchased pieces of foreshore from the corporation and its lessees in other parts to the southward of the dockyard; but to the northward of the dockyard the evidence of user by the corporation was slight, and it was also shewn that in that portion the Crown had exercised acts of ownership which had not been disputed by the corporation.

Baron Cleasby, delivering the judgment of the Court of Exchequer, held the language of the charters granting the borough or town was clearly sufficient to include the soil of the foreshore within the borough if evidence of enjoyment under the charters was shewn, citing Duke of Beaufort *v.* Swansea, 3 Exch. 413. He held that the Crown could grant the ownership of the foreshore, but that it could not in any way by doing so affect the *jus publicum*, citing Hale, ch. 6; and, with regard to the evidence of acts of ownership in the southern part of the foreshore, held that they were admissible in evidence as to the title to the foreshore generally. Remarking on the fact that the Crown had asserted no claim since the case of Attorney *v.* Burridge in 1822, and the fact that the Crown had purchased portions of foreshore from the corporation, he held that "the Crown did grant, not by general words, but "by a sufficient description, all the land that was in its

Jones *v.* Williams, 2 M. & W. 331; Lord Donegall *v.* Lord Templemore, 9 Ir. C. L. R. 374, 1 Ir. Eq. 442.

"own hands at the time of the grant down to low-water "mark; that the evidence for the corporation was sufficient to displace the *primâ facie* title of the Crown, and "outweigh the other evidence on the part of the Crown." The case went to the Court of Appeal, and judgment was given on 18 May 1878, reversing the judgment of the Court of Exchequer.

Lord Justice Cotton, delivering the judgment of the Court, said: "The Crown is entitled by its prerogative to "the foreshore on all the coasts of England and in all "inlets of the sea, unless and except so far as any subject "can establish title to any portion thereof either by "proving a grant thereof made by the Crown, or facts from "which such a grant may be presumed, or by proving "possession for the period necessary to establish a title "against the Crown. The burden of proof, therefore, is on "the defendants, and, unless they make out a title, judg-"ment must be for the Crown." It was held that the charters were sufficient to pass, and did pass, land, "but a "grant by the Crown of a town will not, even when the "place in question abuts on the sea, carry the foreshore "unless the grantee can establish, by acts of ownership "or other sufficient evidence, that the foreshore claimed "is part of the town lands; if this be established, the "grant of a town will, like a grant of a manor, carry the "foreshore. A grant of land abutting on the sea does not "carry the adjoining foreshore, and it still remains for the "corporation to establish that the foreshore within the "limits of the claim is parcel of the town." He proceeds to allude to the strong evidence of acts of ownership on the foreshore to the south of the dockyard, the non-prosecution of the information in Attorney *v.* Burridge, and the acquiescence of the Crown, and says: "If the question were "as to the foreshore south of the dockyard, we should be "of opinion that there is evidence on behalf of the corpo-"ration, as regards this portion of the foreshore, sufficient "to establish their title thereto, either as raising a pre-"sumption of some grant other than that of Henry III., "or as shewing that it was parcel of the town lands; but "the royal dockyard lies within the limits of the foreshore "which the corporation contend passed by the charter of "Henry III. We have no clear statement of the pro- "gressive growth of the dockyard, but large portions of "the existing dockyard are constructed on what was "originally foreshore, and that was done without any "licence or grant from the corporation, and without any "objection on their part, though large extensions on the "foreshore were made after the question as to the title of "Crown and corporation had been raised in the case of "Attorney-General *v.* Burridge. . . . . The acts of owner- "ship on the part of the Crown over the foreshore adjacent "to the dockyard afford strong evidence to shew that this "part at least of the foreshore was not granted to the "corporation by the charter of Henry III., and, as this is "interposed between the portion of the foreshore to which "this information relates and the foreshore south of the "dockyard, it breaks the continuity of the foreshore, and "prevents the acts of ownership of the corporation on the "portion of the foreshore south of the dockyard being "evidence which can maintain their claim to the foreshore "now in question" (thus reversing the judgment of the Court of Exchequer). He then considers the acts of ownership on the portions of the foreshore north of the dockyard, and considers them insufficient to support the claim, especially as considerable acts were done upon that portion by the Crown between 1843 and 1862 without objection by the corporation. "The result, therefore, is "that both the Crown, the grantor, and the grantees "under the charter of Henry III. have exercised acts of "ownership over the portion of foreshore now in question. "This, in consequence of the acts of the Crown in relation "to the foreshore adjacent to the dockyard, cannot be "considered as continuous with the foreshore to the south "of the dockyard, and, unless the corporation can shew, by "their evidence, that it was parcel of the town granted "by the charter of Henry III., remains in the Crown. In "our opinion, the acts of ownership proved by the corpo- "ration are not, having regard to the acts of ownership

See Att.-Gen. *v.* Portsmouth, 25 W. R. 559.

"proved on behalf of the Crown, sufficient to establish "this, and the burden of proof is on the corporation. "The title, therefore, of the Crown must prevail, and, in "our opinion, the Crown is entitled to all the foreshore "north of the dockyard except those portions to which a "title has been acquired by adverse possession, or which "are in the possession of grantees of the Crown. The "different result at which this Court and the Exchequer "Division have arrived is explained by this: that that "Court, for reasons which to us are not satisfactory, did "did not attach much importance to the acts of the "Crown on the dockyard foreshore, and, while it dealt "with the evidence as if the title claimed by the defend-"ants was to the entire foreshore within the limits of the "borough, treated the acts of ownership exercised by the "corporation over the foreshore south of the dockyard as "strong evidence in support of their title to foreshore "separated by the dockyard where these acts were done. "We may mention that we have not overlooked the grant "to the corporation, contained in the charter of Charles "the First, of groundage and anchorage, which was much "relied on by the counsel for the defendants. This might "be some evidence in support of a claim to the soil of the "inlet [the entire harbour] both above and below low-"water mark throughout the limits of the borough, but is "not, in our opinion, evidence that the corporation are "entitled to a portion of the foreshore."

Lord Bramwell concurred in the judgment, and said: "I "entirely agree in the law, and that the defendants, there-"fore, might be entitled on the documents and materials "shewn, but whether they are entitled or not is a question "of fact. Their title-deeds, charters, and other things do "not inevitably shew that the foreshore was granted to "them; therefore it is a question of fact to shew what "they are entitled to either by those deeds or otherwise, "and therefore the burden of proof is upon them. The "presumption is that the foreshore belongs to the Crown, "and the corporation have to make out that the title is "vested in them." He holds that the corporation could not make out a title to the harbour as a whole, and they must make out in some way a title to the part claimed; "they must make out that there is some distinctive part, "I do not mean separate by metes and bounds, but that "there is some peculiarity about it which separated it "from the *corpus*, if I may use such an expression of the "harbour, and they must shew that they are entitled to "it. Well, they do so; they shew that what would be "called the *terra firma* part of the borough extends from "the Clarence Esplanade Pier to the northern boundary "of the borough, and they shew also that they are "riparian owners all along except as to some particular "part." He then proceeds to say that they have a strong case as to the part southward of the dockyard, "and if "the question were whether they were entitled to those "parts, or possibly to parts of the foreshore adjacent "thereto, I should say they had made out a very strong "case. But then comes this difficulty. Between this por-"tion and the northern part, which is now in controversy, "there is the dockyard, the dockyard being nearly as "wide, calculating along the coast, as the parts southward "of it are; then, as to the dockyard, it is clear to me "that the title is not now in the corporation. Of course "it may have been an encroachment by the Crown, but "we ought to attribute everything to a lawful origin "rather than to an unlawful one, if we possibly can; and "therefore it seems to me, upon this evidence, that we "ought to say that a good title is shewn by the corpora-"tion to that which is to the southward of the dockyard, "but that no title is shewn in the corporation, and that, "on the contrary, a good title is shewn in the Crown, *in* "*accordance with the presumption*, as to the dockyard. "The consequence of that is, as it seems to me, that this "distinctive piece was cut in two . . . . and it seems to "me that this case ought to be considered, and really "must be considered, with reference to what is proved "with respect to the area—that is to say, the area "coloured blue" (the piece northward of the dockyard); and he held that evidence of ownership of the southern part was not evidence as to the whole, because of the interruption of continuity made by the dockyard. He was also of opinion that the acts of ownership shewn by the corporation were encroachments, and that, considering the nature of the property, the Crown had exercised such acts of ownership as it very well could; and he was of opinion that the corporation had not displaced the title of the Crown. "I am of opinion it "has not done so, and I wish merely to make this "remark in addition, that the opinion I express on the "present occasion is really not what one may call a "technical opinion; it is not an opinion that I consider I "ought to come to in point of law; but I really do as a "matter of fact, putting myself in the place of a juryman "as much as one possibly can—I do not believe that the "corporation is entitled to this foreshore. I do not "believe that it ever belonged to them as a matter of "absolute fact, and that, so far as they have exercised "their rights of ownership upon it, they have been tres-"passers and encroachers."

In this case, it will be seen, there was a very great conflict in the evidence of user. The Crown had undoubted evidence of very ancient and very extensive ownership of a large portion of the foreshore of the borough of Portsmouth. The corporation, on the other hand, had the most cogent evidence of their ownership of the southern portion of the foreshore, which lay opposite the ancient town itself. The origin of title to the dockyard was altogether unknown. The foreshore to the north of the dockyard, until comparatively recent times, had been a useless waste. The evidence of user with respect to it, both by the corporation and by the Crown, was all comparatively modern, and the Crown had exercised very considerable user over it, extending over a number of years, without objection by the corporation. The whole question was as to the weight of the evidence in respect to the northern part; and, assuming that the Lords Justices were correct in their view that the principles laid down in Jones *v.* Williams were inapplicable to the case, and there-

See Lord Bramwell's conclusion above.

fore threw the weight of the evidence of user by the corporation to the southward of the dockyard out of the scale, the balance of evidence as to the northern part was distinctly in favour of the Crown, and the onus being on the corporation to rebut the presumption of the *primâ facie* title, the evidence, taken as a whole, pointed to the presumption of a lost grant to the corporation of the portion to the southward of the dockyard and opposite to the ancient inhabited part of the borough alone, or to a grant of the whole foreshore of the borough with a reservation to the Crown of the site of the dockyard and the foreshore to the north of it. The case was not carried farther: the corporation retained the southern portion, the Crown recovered the northern portion.

This case is important as extending the dictum in Sir Henry Constable's case, that the foreshore may be parcel of a manor; for it is laid down that the foreshore may also be parcel of a borough or town, and that, although there may be no words in the charters apt to convey the foreshore, evidence of user is admissible to shew that the foreshore is parcel of the borough, and that, in a suit by the Crown, the *primâ facie* theory is to be rebutted by evidence of user on the part of the defendants.

Stackpool *v.* the Queen, Ir. 9 Eq. 619.

In 1875, in the case of Stackpool *v.* the Queen, where a log of wood was found floating in the sea near the shore, and was drawn on a rock by a person wading into the water, and another log, having been cast high and dry on the beach, was marked by the grantee of wreck, and was by the next tide swept out to sea and there taken while floating, it was held that both were Admiralty droits.

Stat. 39-40 Vict. c. 37.

By the Nullum Tempus Act, Ireland, 1876, the provisions of 24 & 25 Victoria, cap. 62, were extended to Ireland, and this Act is to be read with the Act of 48 George III. cap. 47.

Mayor of Penrhyn *v.* Holm, L. R. 2 Ex. D. 328; 46 L. J. Ex. 506;

In 1877 occurred the case of Mayor of Penrhyn *v.* Holm. This was an action for trespass and ejectment against the defendant, who had taken possession of a piece of the foreshore of Penrhyn Harbour, in the county of

Cornwall. The corporation claimed the foreshore under 37 L. T.
a conveyance from the Ecclesiastical Commissioners. 133; 25 W. R. 498.
The title of the Ecclesiastical Commissioners was twofold: they claimed, first, as grantees of the foreshore under a conveyance from the Duke of Cornwall dated 18 July 1865, which purported to convey the rights of the Duke of Cornwall to the foreshore in question; and, secondly, they claimed as successors to the see of Exeter, and thus as lords of the manor of Penrhyn. The report states that the second of these claims depended on various charters from the Crown to the Bishops of Exeter, but the consideration of their *derivative title* became immaterial. [This statement is not strictly accurate. I was concerned in the case, and the fact was that the Bishops' title was the superior title, but the Ecclesiastical Commissioners had been induced to compound for and get in the claim of the *primâ facie* title set up by the Duchy, and the corporation thought it undesirable to go to the expense of proving the ancient charters to the Bishops of Exeter, which were in general terms, and the acts of ownership by the bishops and their lessees under those charters, which would have enabled them to set up the superior title, more especially as the manor had for a long series of years been in lease to the Dukes of Leeds and their predecessors, and it would have been necessary to produce the Duke's muniments to shew the user necessary to construe the ancient grants.] The claim through the Duke of Cornwall arose under the Duchy charter of 11 Edward III., which has the force of an Act of Parliament, and grants to the Duchy the profits of ports, wreck of the sea, and royal fish in the county of Cornwall [but this charter was long subsequent to the commencement of the title to the Bishops of Exeter]. A dispute arose between the Crown and the Duchy as to their respective rights *primâ facie* to the foreshores of the county of Cornwall, which was finally settled by 20 & 21 Victoria, cap. 109, whereby mines and minerals under the foreshores in Cornwall are vested in the Duchy as part of the soil and territorial possessions of the Duchy. The defendant set up no title

in himself, and the judge directed a verdict for the plaintiffs, with leave to move on the ground that the plaintiffs had failed to make out their title.

Kingdon, Q.C., for the defendant, moved accordingly. He contended that the charter of Edward III. had only conveyed to the Duke of Cornwall the manors named in it, and the rights appurtenant to them, and the royal prerogatives in relation to them, and that it was not intended to pass all the prerogatives of the Crown within the county. The grant of a manor with wreck of the sea may pass the foreshore attached to that manor (Attorney-General *v.* Jones, 2 H. & C. 347, 33 L. J. Ex. 249), but cannot do more. The statute 21 & 22 Victoria, cap. 109, goes no farther, and must be construed as applying only to the manors named in the charter, and the words in the statute shewing that the Duke of Cornwall held the minerals "as part of the soil" confirm this view.

For the plaintiffs it was argued that the words relating to the prerogatives of the Crown in the charter are perfectly general, and cannot be cut down as suggested. The statute is declaratory, and puts a wide construction on the charter, declaring that the foreshore belongs to the Duke of Cornwall "as part of the soil and territorial possessions of the Duchy." This construction is confirmed by the fact that the statute gives rights of access to the Crown to work the mines below low-water mark, which would not have been necessary had the foreshore been vested in the Crown.

It was held that, although under the general words of the Duchy charter of 11 Edward III., which grants to the Duke all the profits of ports within the county of Cornwall, together with wreck of the sea and royal fish belonging to the Crown, a question might be raised whether they could have the effect of passing the whole foreshore of the Duchy, and, if the question turned wholly on the construction of this charter, there might be a difficulty; that difficulty was got rid of by the Act of 21 & 22 Victoria, cap. 109, whereby the interest of the Crown in the foreshore in Cornwall was conveyed to the

Duke. It was also held that the plaintiffs resting on the *primâ facie* case, and the defendant having no answer, the action was maintainable. "The decision rests upon this: "the *primâ facie* title to the foreshore is everywhere in the "Crown. The effect of the charter and the Act of Parlia-"ment is to transfer the [*primâ facie*] title to the Duke of "Cornwall of the foreshore in the county of Cornwall. "The plaintiffs claim under the Duchy of Cornwall, and "therefore establish a *primâ facie* case, and the defendant "has no answer. Resting, therefore, on the *primâ facie* "case, the consequence is that the action was maintain-"able."

In 1879 occurred the case of Attorney-General *v.* Tomline. This was an information by the Crown and an action by the War Department against Colonel Tomline, the lord of the manor of Felixstowe Priory, to restrain the defendant from taking shingle and sand from the beach so as to endanger certain land, which formed the site of a martello tower known as the U. tower, near the mouth of the River Deben. The defendant, as lord of the manor, claimed to be entitled to the foreshore. The shingle and the beach protected the site of the tower, and was the only barrier which prevented the sea from encroaching on it. The defendant had sold a very large quantity of shingle from the beach, the natural barrier was in danger of being destroyed, and, if that were done, the site of the tower would be liable to be washed away. The defendant denied the title of the Crown to the site of the tower, and claimed that the land was part of the waste of his manor, that the shingle was taken by him in the exercise of his proprietary rights as owner of the foreshore. He denied that any danger existed to the tower in consequence of his acts. For the Crown it was argued that the defendant was not entitled to use his property in such a way as to injure the property of the Crown; putting the right of the Crown simply as that of a landowner (though without abandoning any right which it may have by virtue of its prerogative), if there is a natural bank of a river or the sea, the owner of it has no

Att.-Gen. *v.* Tomline, L. R. 12 Ch. D. 214.

right to take it away so as to cause water to flow on his neighbour's land, citing Smith *v.* Fletcher. The Crown in this case sued as owner of the land. It was contended for the defendant that the owner of the foreshore is entitled, in the legitimate use of his property, to sell the shingle for profit and take it away, and that the taking of shingle was a legitimate and natural use of his land.

L. R. 7 Ex. 305; 9 Ex. 64; 2 App. Cas. 781.

Fry, J., reviewed the evidence as to the effect of the removal of the shingle, and held that danger had been created, and that, if the removal was continued, the danger would increase, and granted the injunction. He also held that the taking of shingle was a natural user of the land, and it would seem that the owner of foreshore in removing shingle therefrom for the purposes of sale is using his land in a natural, not in a non-natural, way, and would not, therefore, be, on this ground, responsible to a neighbouring landowner for the damage resulting from a consequent overflow of the sea; but the judgment was given for the Crown that it is part of the prerogative and it is the duty of the Crown to preserve the realm from the inroads of the sea, and a subject is, therefore, not entitled to destroy a natural barrier against the sea. "There is, in my judgment, a prerogative and a duty in "the Crown which is inconsistent with the alleged right of "the defendant, and imports such a right in a private "person as the Crown now insists upon, that prerogative "and duty being the obligation, and with it the right, to "protect the land from the inundation of the water, for the "benefit, not of one person in particular, but of the whole "commonwealth, which is interested in the protection and "preservation of the land alike from foreign enemies and "from the water which surrounds our islands;" and he cites the statute 6 Henry VI. cap. 5, relating to commissions of sewers; statute 23 Henry VIII. cap. 5; the case of the Isle of Ely, 10 Coke 141a; Henley *v.* Mayor of Lyme, 5 Bing. 91 and 109; and Hudson *v.* Tabor, 2 Q. B. D. 290; and says: "I come, therefore, to the "conclusion that there exists in the Crown this prerogative "right and duty, a duty, of course, to its subjects of which

P. 230.

"the law must take cognizance, although the law does not "enforce the performance. And if this prerogative and "right exist in the Crown, it seems to me impossible to "suppose that the subject can have the right to do that "which the defendant claims to do; it would be absurd "that the subject should be at liberty to destroy that "which the Crown is bound to protect. I hold, therefore, "that there is in the Crown the prerogative and duty to "which I have referred, and a right in every one of her "Majesty's subjects to have that duty performed (though, "of course, the duty is not one which the Courts can "enforce), and consequently there is an obligation on "every person possessed of a sea-bank to do nothing "inconsistent with the protection of the land in this "country from the inroads of the sea; that right, it "appears to me, the defendant has violated; and, as the "result, I must grant the injunction which is prayed."

The case was appealed. For the appellant it was argued that he used his land in a legitimate way, and that he was under no liability to protect his neighbour from the sea, citing Hudson *v.* Tabor; that the plaintiff can get no assistance from joining the Attorney-General in the action; and that an individual who has no right of action cannot invoke the royal prerogative to assist him. For the Crown it was said that the duty which lies on the Crown to protect the realm from the sea, renders the act of the defendant, by which the natural barrier against the sea is interfered with, a wrong (the case of the Isle of Ely, 10 Rep. 141a). If the foreshore were in the possession of the Crown, as originally it must have been, it would be a violation of duty in the Crown to remove the bank, and the defendant cannot do what the Crown could not do.

Att.-Gen. *v.* Tomline, L. R. 14 Ch. D. 58; 49 L. J. Ch. 377; 42 L. T. 880; 28 W. R. 870; 44 J. P. 617.

Lord Justice James affirmed the judgment upon the grounds given by the learned judge below, and held that when all the land was the land of the Crown, as all the land in the country was, or is presumed in point of law to have been, at one time, beyond all question it would have been wrong on the part of the Crown wilfully to have removed this barrier. When the land was transmitted by grant to a subject, the subject could not do that which would have been a wrongful act on the part of the Crown if the land had remained in the possession of the Crown, and that where there is such a natural protection—a barrier against the encroachments and inroads of the sea—any person who wilfully removes that natural barrier so as to occasion damage to his neighbour would be guilty of a nuisance, and, if a nuisance, it would be one which would give a right of action to the person who suffered from it, and he distinguished the cases of Smith *v.* Kenrick and Chasemore *v.* Richards, shewing that there was no analogy between them and the present one.

7 C. B. 515; 2 H. & M. 181; 7 H. L.Cas. 349.

2 Q. B. D. 290; 46 L. J. Q. B. 463; 36 L. T. 492; 25 W. R. 740.

Lord Justice Brett concurred, and shewed that although the case of Hudson *v.* Tabor is a binding authority to shew that there is no obligation upon the defendant to keep up the bank if the sea wore it away or broke through it, yet, although he is not bound to keep the sea out, he must not do an act which would let the sea in; and that as there was a duty in the Crown not to break through the bank, that duty gives rise to a correlative right on the part of the subject; the subject has a right to have that bank in that place or a corresponding bank.

Lord Justice Cotton also concurred, holding that, as the foreshore came into the hands of the defendant subject to an obligation not to break through it, it was not a natural use of the land if he breaks through the obligation or duty attaching to the land, so as to cause injury to his neighbours. He agrees with the second ground above set out, and says: "Theoretically, for the purpose of considering how the matter legally stands, all land must "be considered as having been derived from the Crown, "and the question arises, What were the obligations of the "Crown as regards this land now vested in the defendant? "This is material, because, where land is vested in the "Crown subject to public uses, the grantee of the Crown "must take it subject to all the obligations to which the "land was subject when in the hands of the Crown. The "Crown holds the bed of a navigable river or the shore "of the sea between high and low water mark subject to "the right of navigation, and the grantee of the Crown "can never do anything to interfere with the navigation; "and if a grant were made for the purpose of enabling "the grantee to do that which would interfere with the "navigation, that would be a void grant, because it would "be a grant which the Crown could not make, having "regard to the fact that it held the land for the benefit of "the public—that is, subject to the public right of naviga-"tion. What, then, was the right and duty of the Crown as "regards this land when it was in the hands of the Crown? "The duty and obligation of the Crown was to protect the "land from the incursions of the sea, and, if there is land "vested in the Crown which is a natural barrier against "the sea, in my opinion the public have a right to say "that the Crown shall not deal with that in such a way "as to deprive the realm of that natural barrier against "the sea, and a grantee of the Crown can stand in no "better position than the Crown itself would do." He then points out that although the right cannot be enforced against the Crown, because the Crown is not amenable to the jurisdiction of the Court, yet when once you get the land into the hands of a subject who is liable to the jurisdiction of the Court, any other subject who suffers a special injury from the user of the land can, by action, insist on the land not being used in contravention of a public right. "In my opinion, the land of the "defendant, when vested in the Crown, was held by the "Crown for the public purpose of protecting the land "from the sea; the land could not be granted free and "discharged from that duty; and the defendant, or those "through whom he claims, as they theoretically take from "the Crown, must hold the land subject to that duty, and "cannot be allowed to use the land in such a way as to "destroy the natural barrier against the sea."

Hamilton *v.* Att. for Ireland, 5 L. R. Ir. 555.

In 1881 occurred the case of Hamilton *v.* Attorney for Ireland, which was a suit to establish the plaintiff's title to foreshore after the prosecution of several actions for taking seaweed on the foreshore by a number of defendants, who alleged that the foreshore was in the Crown, and attempted to justify the taking as a right at common law. The Attorney-General was made a defendant to protect the rights of the Crown, but he made no claim on behalf of the Crown. It appeared that King James I. had granted to the plaintiff's predecessor the site of an ancient priory, and certain lands adjoining the sea-shore belonging to the priory, with waters, wastes, fisheries, wreck, flotsom, jetsom, &c., but the grant did not expressly grant the shore. There was considerable evidence of user by the plaintiff and his predecessors, and there was also evidence of adverse user by the public for many years. It was held by Vice-Chancellor Chatterton that the language of the patent was capable of passing the sea-shore between high and low water mark, and, when coupled with adequate evidence of ownership, was sufficient to confer on the grantee a title to the shore. It was also held that acts of ownership in one part were evidence of possession in other parts of the shore. It was proved that various persons had for many years taken seaweed and gravel and quarried stones from the sea-shore, such acts not being referable to any alleged ownership of soil, but it was held that, in the absence of the Crown, these acts by the public could not be relied upon as evidence to displace the title to the sea-shore derived under the patent. It was also held (following Howe *v.* Stawell and Macnamara *v.* Higgins, 4 Ir. C. L. 326) that there is not any common law right in the public to enter on the sea-shore to take away seaweed left by the tide.

Howe *v.* Stawell, Al. & Nap. 348; Mulholland *v.* Killen, I. R. 9 Eq. 471; Healy *v.* Thorne,

It was further held that the evidence of taking seaweed by the public, acting in no corporate capacity, cannot be proof of title to the shore in them, for these acts are taking a profit *in alieno solo*, and there is no common law right to dig soil or take seaweed, and that these acts do not shew that the Crown is owner of the foreshore. The Crown is, in respect of *profit a prendre* in the soil of the sea-shore, in no different position from a private owner. "If there had been such a common law

"right for the public to take seaweed, &c., such acts 4 I. R.C. L.
"proved by the defendant would be important evidence 495; Macnamara v.
"on the question of ownership of the soil; but this is not Higgins, 4 I. R. C. L.
"so." 326.

The case of Attorney-General *v.* Reeve, in 1885, was Att. *v.* an information against the lord of the manor of Lowes- Reeve, 1 Times L. toft to recover a considerable accretion to the shore, R. 675. which appears to have been caused by the works at Lowestoft Harbour. The defendant claimed it as part of the waste of the manor of Lowestoft, and as alluvion gradually and imperceptibly accreted in contradistinction to derelict land, but admitted the Crown's claim to the foreshore. Evidence was given shewing the growth of the land from year to year; the sea sometimes encroached and sometimes receded, but the gradual growth was clearly perceptible. It was held by Lord Coleridge, C.J., and Pollock, B., that, where accretions of land on the sea-shore are shewn to have been perceptible by marks and measures as they took place, such accretions belong to the Crown, and not to the adjacent owner. The case turned almost wholly upon the oral evidence, and the defendant appears to have increased his difficulties by giving up his claim to the foreshore, which was certainly part of his manor.

In 1885, in the case of Daly *v.* Murray, evidence of Daly *v.* user by taking seaweed, &c., licensing others, and prosecu- Murray, 17 L. R. Ir. ting others for taking it, was held to be sufficient to main- 185. tain the title to foreshore at Evagh and Lisvady, co. Cork, under a patent of Charles II., containing only general words, and not specifically granting the foreshore; and it was also held that evidence for the defendant of user by the public, asserting that it was done by leave and licence of the Crown, cannot avail to displace the title. In this case the Attorney-General was made a defendant, and filed a formal answer claiming the rights of the Crown, whatever they may be. The defendant denied that the patent passed the foreshore, and alleged that they had done the acts complained of as licensees of the Crown.

Stat. 48-49 Vict. c. 79. By the Crown Lands Act, 1885, the powers of leasing the foreshore given by the Act of 10 George IV. cap. 50, s. 22, are extended, and power is given to the Commissioners of Woods and the Board of Trade, when an order under the Sea Fisheries Act, 1868, has been made for an oyster or mussel fishery on any part of the sea-shore which is under their management, to make a lease not exceeding sixty years of such shore.

CHAPTER XXII.

SCOTCH CASES, A.D. 1813 TO A.D. 1887.

THE author does not venture to encroach on the province of the Scotch lawyer with regard to the law of foreshore in Scotland, but as it seems to him that there has been the same encroachment by the Crown on the rights of the subject in Scotland by an application, within the present century only, of the *primâ facie* theory of the prerogative right to the *jus privatum* in the shore as there has been in England, and as the principles upon which the subject is enabled by evidence of user to rebut the presumption in favour of the Crown appear now to be held to be the same in Scotland as in England, he has thought fit to refer to a few of the numerous Scotch cases which serve to illustrate the manner in which the subject may establish his right against the Crown, or the Crown prevail against the subject. Being wholly ignorant as to the law of Scotland, he leaves the subject to the abler hands of his brethren of the Scotch Bar, merely premising that it seems to him that the ancient law on this subject in Scotland has, like the ancient law in England, been overridden by the prerogative theory, and that in very modern times, by English judges imbued with the theory of Mr. Digges and the dictum of Lord Hale. The general result of the cases seems (subject to correction) to be that in Scotland, as between subject and subject, proof of ownership of the adjoining land suffices to shew title to the shore; but in cases between the Crown and a subject, by the presumption of the *primâ facie* title, in order to oust the claim of the Crown the subject must shew acts of ownership on the shore in precisely the same manner as in England. With regard to the nature and *quantum* of the user necessary to be shewn in order to rebut the claim of the Crown, no general rule is laid down, or can be laid down; but it would seem, from the remarks of Lord Fitzgerald, that less evidence of user will suffice in Scotland than in England or Ireland, though upon what principle of justice (seeing that the issue in both countries is the same—viz., as to whether the Crown has made the grant of the shore or not) it is very difficult to discover, except that the theory of the *primâ facie* title is of older acceptance in England than in Scotland. In England it was first conceived in 1568; it was in doubt, and strenuously resisted, till 1670, but has been accepted since that date, on somewhat doubtful authority, as unquestioned law: in Scotland it seems only to have been advanced in 1849.

Lord Advocate *v.* Young, 12 App. Cas. 544.

The law with regard to foreshore in Scotland differs from that in England; in Scotland the law appears to be, or rather to have been, what it was in England before Mr. Digges invented his theory. It is thus stated by Bell, who follows Stair and Erskine:—"It [the sea-shore] is "not, as in England, held to be the property reserved to "the Sovereign, but presumed to be granted as part and "pertinent of the adjacent land under the burden of the "Crown's right as trustee for public uses."

Smith *v.* Earl of Stair, 6 Bell's App. Cas. 487.

Stair, 189; Erskine, 221 b, 357, 358 *note*; Bell, 642, 647.

"The shore, so far as capable of appropriation, may in "England be part of the manor of a subject. In Scotland it may be conveyed by royal grant, subject to the "public use, and grants of the adjacent land are under "that implied burden. If the sea or the sea-shore be the "boundary of any man's property, the grant is construed "to include the shore to the ebb mark, and to extend or "recede with the waters, the shore or what is covered "at ordinary high water being still subject to the use of "the public. It has also been permitted to such owner "to prevent by artificial operations the encroachment of "the sea, and even by such means to gain by encroachment on the sea. Whether these decisions are to be "entirely approved of, or whether the strict construction "to which royal grants are subject should not lead to a

Bell, 643.

"different conclusion, may be doubted. But, at all events, "the grantee who gains by embankment in such cases "must hold the shore as still subject to the public uses. "It has been held that there is no substantial difference "between a grant of land as bounded by the sea and as "bounded by the sea-shore, and that the shore is given in "each case subject to public use. But, after a grant so "bounded, nothing remains in the Crown but the public "trust, and no one can, by subsequent grant or otherwise, "be allowed to interpose between the grantee and the "shore."

"A right to the shore includes by implication sea-greens "which are occasionally covered by the water, rocky "islands also occasionally covered, with their seaweed, "&c. In England the original right of the Crown com- "prehends everything but imperceptible additions." Bell, 644.

"The taking of kelp on the shore, the convenience of "bathing, &c., are not understood to be uses necessary "for the public, and inalienable: but seem to go with "the express or implied grant, provided the primary "[navigation] and secondary [fishing] public uses are left "uninjured." Ibid. 647.

In Campbell *v.* Brown, in 1813, Lord Glenlee laid down the settled rule of the law of Scotland as follows: —"When a landowner is bounded by the sea, it is true "he has a bounding charter. But it is a boundary "movable and fluctuating *suâ naturâ;* and when the "sea recedes, he must be entitled to preserve it as his "boundary. The shore is indeed still *publici juris;* but "when the sea goes back, the shore advances, and the "proprietor is entitled to follow the water to the point to "which it may naturally retire or be artificially embanked." Campbell *v.* Brown, 18 Nov. 1813, Fac. Coll. at p. 447.

In 1837, in Macalister *v.* Campbell, the proprietor of land adjoining the sea brought an action against trespassers who took seaweed from the shores. The defendants alleged that the plaintiff's title-deeds did not shew that the shore passed to him; but it was held that in Scotland, when the proprietor of an estate is infeft "with parts, "pendicles, and pertinents," although his titles do not Macalister *v.* Campbell, 15 D. B. & M. Sess. Cas. 490.

describe his estate as bounded by the sea, yet nevertheless, when the estate is *de facto* and notoriously situated next to, or surrounded by, the sea, the grant must be held to have included the sea-shore, Lord Gillies saying: "In such a case it would be a very serious matter indeed "if this Court were to hold that the shore was reserved "out of the grant whenever it is not expressly inserted in "it. I see no warrant for so construing a grant of land on "the sea-coast." "I hold, therefore, that the conveyance "of an estate which is notoriously bounded by the sea "conveys the shore as effectually as if the words 'bounded "'by the sea' were in the charter. And, considering the "great value of sea wreck to properties lying along the "coast, it would be a very serious matter to cast a doubt "upon this dictum, as I think it is probable that the titles "of many of the largest proprietors may contain no words "whatever expressly stating that the sea is their boundary, "which is nevertheless notoriously the fact."

The law as here laid down clearly suggests that in Scotland the presumption of ownership of the foreshore is in favour of the adjoining owner, whether his titles describe his estate as "bounded by the sea" or not. There does not appear to have been any presumption that the Crown is *primâ facie* entitled. This is precisely the state of things which existed in England before the time of Queen Elizabeth, but the law laid down by Lord Gillies has been materially altered by later decisions, and the theory of Mr. Ante, p. 260. Digges and the dictum of Lord Hale have been made to apply to Scotland in a manner that Lord Hale could never have contemplated, for it can hardly be suggested that he intended to treat of the law of Scotland in his treatise.

Smith *v.* Earl of Stair, 6 Bell's App. Cas. 487.

In the case of Smith *v.* the Earl of Stair, in the House of Lords, in 1849, the question was as to a purpresture on the shore opposite the barony of Duddingstone, near Portobello, in Scotland, and it was decided that in Scotland the Crown has a right to prevent, by interdict, any encroachment by the proprietors of ground adjoining the sea-shore upon the enjoyment of the shore by the lieges for the purposes of passage or of relaxation when they shew no user nor exclusive possession of the shore. Lord Brougham, in his judgment, refers as follows to Hale "De "Jure Maris":—"It is a posthumous treatise, but it is of "high authority. Its authority cannot be impeached, and "its authority must not be understood in any way to be "doubted by us, either as to its being Lord Hale's, which "the profession and Parliament, in which it has been "frequently cited in debates, as well as before courts of "law, have never doubted (I state that because it was "disputed at the bar); nor, secondly, can we dispute the "high authority of that work of Lord Hale's from its own "intrinsic merits, and from the venerable authority of the "author." At this time the law as to the limit of the fore-shore with respect to the tide was not settled, and the House of Lords declined to express an opinion on the subject. Lord Campbell said: "Notwithstanding some "loose dicta to the contrary, there can be no doubt that, "*by the law of Scotland, as by the law of England*, the soil "of the sea-shore is presumed to belong to the Crown by "virtue of the prerogative, although it may have been "alienated subject to any easements which the public "may have over it."[1] It appeared that the encroachment made was above the ordinary high-water mark, and it would seem that, although Mr. Smith had a charter of the barony of Duddingstone *cum alga fucoque maritimis*, lie, wrack, wath, waive, &c., he did not shew any user of the shore in question. Lord Campbell further said: "Al-"though I have examined the authorities which have been "cited at the bar, I studiously abstain from giving any "opinion as to the evidence, either by grant or by enjoy-"ment, which is required to shew that the sea-shore, which "*primâ facie* belongs to the Crown, has become vested in "a subject; but I may venture to say that, whatever may "be the effect of the grant of a barony described to be "upon the sea-shore, *there is no foundation in law for the*

[1] This dictum was followed in Gamell *v.* Lord Advocate, 3 Macq. H. of L. 419, at p. 457.

"*position that the simple grant of a piece of land will pass* "*the sea-shore by which it happens to be bounded.*"

Lord Advocate and Commrs. of Woods *v.* Hamilton, 1 Macq. H. of L. 46.

In the case of Lord Advocate *v.* Hamilton, in 1852, with respect to the title to part of the *alveus* of the Clyde, Lord St. Leonards laid it down that "beyond all "doubt the soil and bed of a river (we are now speaking "of navigable rivers only) belong to the Crown;" and Lord Brougham said: "We generally speak of the soil of "a navigable river as being in the Crown, not only in "Scotland, but in England. This case does not require "that we should dispose of that question either way, but "it is fit, as it has been argued, that we should state our "opinion."

Duchess of Sutherland *v.* Watson, 6 Ct. of Sess. Cas. 3rd ser. 199.

The case of the Duchess of Sutherland *v.* Watson, in 1868, was an action for taking mussels from mussel scalps in Cromartie Bay. Lord Neave held that "the "foreshore is in the Crown as a patrimonial right of pro-"perty subject to public rights. Mussel scalps are *partes* "*soli* because, although the mussel has powers of loco-"motion, and uses them in early life, when it once settles "down and fixes its domicile it seems to do so *animo re-*"*manendi*, and, becoming part of the soil, it is a trespass "to take it. Mussel scalps are the subject of exclusive "grant by the Crown to an individual. The Crown may "grant the right of using these scalps and taking the "mussels from them in two ways. It may give the *solum* "and *fundus* of the sea as a feudal estate, and, if it does "so, it gives the scalps along with it. They would pass as "accessories, and it would be trespass to remove them, as "it would be to remove sea-waie and other plants, but the "Crown may retain the soil and grant the privilege of "enjoyment of the ground still vested in the Crown, which "it would have given as an accessory of the property "if it had given out the whole property. I do not see "any objection in principle to that course. It will be "a different kind of estate in point of form. It may be "a perpetual privilege, but it will be as good a grant "or right as the other, though in a different category of "law. It will be a perpetual licence granted out by the

"Crown." It was held in this case that the soil did not pass by the title, and that the fishery was one of the *regalia minora*.

There is no case analogous to this decision in England. The whole current of authority, from Hale downwards, has an opposite tendency: see Lestrange *v.* Rowe, *ante*, p. 542; Scratton *v.* Brown, *ante*, p. 457; *In re* Alston's Estate, *ante*, p. 491. The suggestion of a possible grant of mussel fishery unconnected with the soil seems to have arisen in the judge's mind by analogy to the law of Scotland, which gives salmon fishings on the coast to the Crown as one of the *regalia minora*—a state of the law which does not exist in England. But see Rex *v.* Ellis, 1 M. & S. at p. 663, per Bayley, J.

Agnew *v.* Lord Advocate and Commrs. of Woods and Forests, 11 Ct. of Sess. Cas. 3rd ser. 309.

In 1873 occurred the case of Agnew *v.* the Lord Advocate and the Commissioners of Woods and Forests. This was a question between the Crown and a subject as to the right to the foreshore of lands in the barony of Lochnaw, in Wigtownshire, Scotland, and from this case it appears that the *primâ facie* title of the Crown to foreshore in Scotland may be rebutted by the same kind of evidence of acts of ownership as avails to rebut it in England. The appellant was able to shew user of the foreshore by taking of sand, &c., boring for coal, taking of wrack and sea-ware, and leasing it, and that the possession had been exclusive of any possession on the part of others. It was held, in a question between the Crown and a vassal—first, that, when an estate on the sea-shore, whether barony or not, is held under a Crown charter which does not by express grant or specific boundary extend the right of the vassal beyond high-water mark, there is no presumption that the foreshore is appurtenant to the land; *but*, secondly, that in such a case the charter may be shewn to include the foreshore by such long-continued possession thereof as can only be ascribed to a right of property, and it was said that the taking of sea-ware for making kelp is a right of property, and not of servitude. "The Crown has a right of property "in the foreshore, not as one of the *regalia minora*, but "as a portion of the *solum* of the country, and may alienate "the same subject to the burden of certain public uses "which attaches to it, whether held in property by the "Crown or by a subject. The right of the public to use "the foreshore for the purposes of navigation is vested in "the Crown as one of the *regalia minora*." In this case the Crown was defeated.

Lord Advocate *v.* Lord Blantyre, 4 App. Cas. 770.

In 1879 occurred the case of the Lord Advocate and the Trustees of the Clyde Navigation *v.* Lord Blantyre and his son. This was a claim by the Crown to the foreshore of the River Clyde *ex adverso* Lord Blantyre's barony of Erskine, and the Trustees of the Clyde Navigation insisted that the property in the ground was vested in them by Acts of Parliament. Lord Blantyre claimed the ground as "pertinents" to his adjoining lands, but subject to any rights of navigation or other rights which the public might have over the same, and also subject to any statutory rights conferred upon the Trustees of the Clyde Navigation. Lord Blantyre's lands extended for about five miles, and the foreshore in question was about 750 acres. Lord Blantyre and his son claimed, first, in virtue of their title to the barony alone; secondly, in respect to their titles coupled with acts of possession exercised from time immemorial by them and their predecessors upon the foreshore. The acts of possession relied upon by them were, the pasturing of cattle on the sea-greens, the regular cutting of weeds and seaweeds, the taking of sand and stones for building purposes, and the granting permission to others to do so; they had also by legal process repeatedly prevented persons from removing sand and stones without their permission, and had excluded the public from the foreshore; in fact, it was alleged that they had used or permitted its use, and that on both sides of the river, *for all purposes for which ground of this description can be used.* There was no controversy with regard to any rights of or incident to navigation, or with regard to any of the other rights of the public in connection with the shore of the navigable river. At the trial in the court below, Lord Curriehill, the Lord Ordinary, traced the barony title of Lord Blantyre, and said: "There is no longer any doubt, if such ever existed, "that the foreshore of the sea and of navigable rivers, "though belonging to the Crown subject to certain public "uses connected with the navigation and the like, are never-"theless alienable by the Crown subject to such public "uses. Such alienation may be made by express grant, "or by a conveyance of land expressing the boundary to "be the sea or river, or by a grant 'with parts and per-"'tinents' silent as to boundaries, but explained by pos-"session to include the foreshore, and a grant of barony "followed by possession has the like effect, but the "pursuer (Lord Blantyre) maintains that, in virtue of his "barony title *alone*, the foreshore and banks of the Clyde "belong to him as 'pertinents' of the barony, and that "the grant of barony entitles him, *without proving any* "*possession*, to follow the Clyde and appropriate its fore-"shores and banks, subject always to the right of the public "and of the Clyde Trustees." This question the Lord Advocate considers as settled in the case of Agnew *v.* Lord Advocate (21 January 1873; 11 Macpherson 309). "In that case the Court decided that the pursuer, Sir A. "Agnew, whose title was a barony title in which no "boundaries were specified, had right to the foreshore of "his lands, which were *de facto* bounded by the sea, in "virtue of his titles and of the possession which had "followed, but the judges were unanimous in holding, "although they did not make it matter of judgment, that "without the proof of possession they could not have "sustained the barony title alone as a sufficient title to the "foreshore. The Lord Justice Clerk stated it to be his "clear opinion that as Sir Andrew Agnew's title 'contained "'no specific description of the component part of the lands "'conveyed, and as no specific boundary of the barony or "'lands is expressed in them, the extent of the barony and "'lands can only be determined by the state of possession.' "The other judges expressed similar views, and although "an appeal was presented against the judgment to the "House of Lords by the Lord Advocate, it was abandoned, "and the opinion of the Court must therefore be held as "an authoritative statement of the law. This being so, "I am of opinion that the pursuers' claim to the property "of the foreshore as belonging to them in virtue of their "titles alone cannot be sustained."

Lord Curriehill then discussed the evidence of the acts of ownership by Lord Blantyre and his predecessors, which were very extensive, and are fully described at p. 774 of the report. He shewed that the acts were acts of possession and not of servitude, and could only be attributed to the exercise of a right of property, and held that the pursuers had made out their claim to the property in the foreshore. He discussed the powers of the Clyde Trustees and their alleged acts of possession, and shewed that they were only acts made lawful by the powers conferred upon them, and not acts of ownership, and said: "It is in vain, therefore, for the defenders to "maintain that any acts done by the Clyde Trustees "during the last hundred years upon these foreshores "have been of such a character as to prevent the posses- "sion which Lord Blantyre and his predecessors are "proved to have exercised from time immemorial from "having the character of exclusive possession as pro- "prietors. And on this branch of the case I am of "opinion, not only that the defenders have failed to "prove any acts of possession inconsistent with the full "right of property being in Lord Blantyre, but that the "pursuers have succeeded in proving acts of possession of "a character, and extending over a length of time, suffi- "cient to establish in them the property of the foreshores "of the Clyde *ex adverso* of all their lands on both sides "of that river as belonging to them in property as per- "tinents of these lands under their title thereto. It may "be the case that no positive acts of possession have been "exercised by Lord Blantyre and his predecessors upon "every yard of the shore fronting the river, *but on ground of* "*such extent it is obvious that minute proof of such posses-* "*sion could not be expected.* I think the proof establishes "that Lord Blantyre has substantially possessed the whole "foreshores as his property from time immemorial."

Lord Blackburn, in his judgment, refers to the judgment of Lord Mure, in which it is decided that the shore is capable of being transferred to a private proprietor, and that a Crown title, and especially a barony title, followed by possession, will confer the right, but that a barony title without specific description, and not followed by possession, will not confer the right; and that where an estate is on the sea-shore held by titles which do not by express grant or specific boundary extend the right of the proprietor beyond high-water mark, there is no presumption that the foreshore is a pertinent of the land, citing Agnew *v.* Lord Advocate. Lord Blackburn observed that it was admitted that the law as laid down by Lord Mure was an accurate statement of the law of Scotland, and that, consequently, the question was whether Lord Blantyre's title, taken in connection with the proof of possession which has been had of the foreshore, is sufficient to entitle him. He then reviews shortly the evidence of acts of ownership, and says: "Every act shewn "to have been done on any part of that tract by the "barons or their agents, which was not lawful unless the "barons were owners of that spot on which it was done, "is evidence that they were in possession as owners of "that spot on which it was done. No one such act is "conclusive, and the weight of each act as evidence "depends on the circumstances; one very important "circumstance as to the weight being whether the act "was such, and so done, that those who were interested "in disputing the ownership would be aware of it. And "all that tends to prove possession as owners of parts of "the tract tends to prove ownership of the whole tract, "provided there is such a common character of locality as "would raise a reasonable inference that if the barons "possessed one part as owners they possessed the whole, "the weight depending on the nature of the tract, what "kind of possession could be had of it, and what the kind "of possession proved was. This is what is very clearly "explained by Lord Wensleydale (then Baron Parke) in "Jones *v.* Williams, 2 M. & W. 326, at p. 331. And as "the weight of evidence depends on rules of common-"sense, I apprehend that this is as much the law in a "Scotch as in an English court. And the weight of the "aggregate of many such pieces of evidence taken to-"gether is very much greater than the sum of the weight "of each such piece of evidence taken separately.

"Now, in the present case, there is a great volume of "evidence of almost every kind of act of ownership. "Some of them are, if they stood alone, not of great "weight. Some are very weighty indeed. That which "makes most impression on my mind is that wherever "throughout this whole tract any part of the foreshore "has been elevated by the deposit of rubbish or soil so "as to be raised above the level of the tide and turned "into dry land, the land from which the water has been "excluded has been taken possession of by the barons of "Erskine. I do not attach so much weight to acts of "this sort done recently, one may say almost *post litem* "*motam*, but I attach very much weight to what has "been done both before the forty years and during the "earlier part of the forty years, during which time every-"body, including the Clyde Trustees, seems to have as-"sumed that the foreshore was the property of the "barons of Erskine. It was argued that, as the barons "had an unquestionable right as riparian proprietors to "have access to the water at high tide, even though the "foreshore was still the property of the Crown, the Clyde "Trustees, when depositing mud and shingle on the fore-"shore so as to shut them off from such access, did what, "if not authorized by the statutes, would be an injury; if "authorized, a matter for which they were entitled to "compensation. That is true, but there was nothing to "justify the Clyde Trustees or any one else in making "compensation to the barons for this injury by giving "them the foreshore if it was the property of the Crown. "If it was the property of the barons, they were entitled "to it, and it is perfectly intelligible that they did not ask "for compensation from the Clyde Trustees for doing that "to their land which was really an improvement to it.

"I may say that I think any evidence tending to shew "that the Clyde Trustees acted as owners of this tract, or "of any parts of it, would, in my mind, have been relevant "as shewing that they were, and consequently that the "barons of Erskine were not, in possession, but, as far as I "can perceive, every act done by the Clyde Trustees is "attributable to their statutable powers. The same "remarks apply to the less important question whether "the evidence proves that the owners of Glenarbuck have "been for forty years in possession as owners of the fore-"shore *ex adverso* that smaller property."

Lord Hatherley, in his judgment, further reviews the acts of ownership by Lord Blantyre and the acts of the Clyde Trustees, and shews that the acts of the latter were not attributable to the ownership of the soil, and says: "In all cases where there is such a grant as this, extend- P. 798. "ing for several miles along a river, it is necessary for "your lordships to consider anxiously what the exact "nature of the acts of ownership is. Now, it is not merely "one corner or one field which is shewn to have been used "as pasture for the cattle for two or three days, owing to "some accidental occurrence, in connection with their "going to a fair or the like; such casual exercises of the "right are not the matter here in question. There seems "to have been a regular exercise on the part of the "respondent of the right of pasturing cattle in the manner "described in the evidence, just like any other proprietor "on his own field; and this was a valuable right. So "with the right of taking sea-ware. It appears from the "evidence that, owing to some alterations which were "made in the River Clyde some years ago, the stones "became nearly bare and the sea-ware ceased to be "collected. But, as I understand the evidence, so long as "there was any ware worth collecting, it was collected "by the tenants of the respondents. In short, as Lord "Curriehill says in the judgment which has already been "referred to so often, all the rights that possibly could be "exercised were exercised by the respondent, either from "time immemorial or for forty years, and thereby he ful-

"filled all the requisites of the Agnew case, should that "case ultimately be held, and at present I see no reason "why it should not be held, to be sound law. The "respondent, therefore, escapes from the stringency of that "case by complying with the conditions which it imposes, "namely, by shewing that he had held possession of, as it "appears to me, sufficiently large portions of the shore "immediately in front of his lands to justify your lord-"ships in coming to the conclusion that he is entitled to "what he claims. It appears not to have been partial "exercise at one particular spot or at one particular time, "but a general exercise, as often as he or his tenants "thought fit, of the right to do what they conceived them-"selves justified in doing by virtue of the title acquired by "him." The appeal was dismissed, and Lord Blantyre's title confirmed.

Lord Advocate *v.* Lord Lovat, 5 App. Cas. at p. 288.

In 1880, in the case of the Lord Advocate *v.* Lord Lovat, which was a case to determine the extent of certain salmon fisheries belonging *ex adverso* to certain baronies in Scotland, the principles upon which acts of possession are to be considered when called in aid to define the extent of an ancient grant were discussed, and Lord O'Hagan said: "As to possession, it must be considered in every "case with reference to the peculiar circumstances. The "acts implying possession in one case may be wholly inad-"equate to prove it in another. The character and value "of the property, the suitable and natural mode of using "it, the course of conduct which the proprietor might "reasonably be expected to follow with a due regard to "his own interests—all these things, greatly varying as "they must under various conditions, are to be taken into "account in determining the sufficiency of a possession; "the dealing with a river requiring activity and vigilance "for the realization of profit from its fisheries may fail to "give reliable evidence of this which might be satisfactory "if the stream were unproductive and incapable of com-"pensating for larger effort and expenditure. Again, in a "case like the present it is not necessary, for proving the "possession of a fishery, that the claimant of a baronial "title should shew the exercise of his right in every "portion of the river capable of yielding fish. I adopt "the opinion of the Lord Ordinary on the point: 'I do "'not,' he says, 'mean to express or indicate any opinion "'to the effect that, where a right to fish salmon depends "'upon a barony title followed by possession, it is necessary "'that the party pleading prescription should prove that "'he has regularly fished in the proper manner every part "'and stream in the river in which a salmon might be "'expected to be caught. It would be enough, in my "'opinion, were it proved that he substantially fished over "'the whole river within his bounds in the appropriate "'manner and regularly and continually within the year "'throughout the prescriptive period. I would be slow to "'hold that if he fished certain parts regularly, and others "'only occasionally or not at all, he had failed to establish "'a right to fish in the whole.'"

Lord Blackburn cites Lord Gifford's opinion, in which he observes that the fishing was conducted by cruives fixed at a particular spot, and he says: "Practically, the result "was that Lord Lovat, by means of these cruives, could "take all the salmon he wanted below the falls instead of "going up above them; as expressed in argument, he took "his crop of salmon at that point, but the crop he took "there was that of the whole river; that, whether legal or "not, is perfect possession of the whole river;" and with this Lord Blackburn and Lord Cairns agreed.

Lord Blantyre *v.* Clyde Navigation Trustees, 6 App. Cas. 273.

In 1881, in the case of Lord Blantyre *v.* the Clyde Navigation Trustees, Lord Blantyre, who had established his title to the foreshore of the Clyde subject to the rights of the public and the rights conferred on the Trustees by Acts of Parliament, sought to restrain the Trustees from dredging the channel of the river within part of the foreshore in question under the powers of their Acts; but it was held, affirming the decision of the Court below, that the Clyde Navigation Trustees, being empowered by sections 76 and 84 of 21 & 22 Victoria, cap. 149, to dredge the bed of the River Clyde to a depth of 17 feet, cannot be interdicted from dredging ground which has been declared the property of the riparian owners subject to any right which the public may have over it, and subject also to any rights conferred on the Trustees by their Acts of Parliament.

Lord Advocate *v.* Young, 12 App. Cas. 544.

In the case of the Lord Advocate *v.* Young, in 1887, the pursuer brought an action to establish his title against the defenders and the Crown to the foreshore of the sea *ex adverso* the lands of Colinswell Park, on the shore of the Firth of Forth, near Burntisland. He claimed under a grant of feu made to his ancestor in 1804, which describes the property granted as land "bounded by the "sea," but he did not endeavour to shew that the grantor had an express title from the Crown. He shewed that his predecessor in 1827 built a wall on part of the shore; that he and his predecessors had taken stones and sand; and that they and their tenants had exclusively exercised the right since 1825 of daily carting seaweed for manure. On the other hand, it was shewn that, in 1857, 1875, and 1882, stone and clay had been taken for harbour works at Burntisland; that the villagers carried away the drift sea-ware in creels; and that the public bathed, gathered sea-shells, and shot wild fowl. It was argued for the Crown that the acts done were insufficient in weight to support title, and that the acts of ownership must be such as to warn the Crown to protect its rights; that the Crown cannot be divested by acts of possession not different from those which the public are doing; and that, if the Crown has tolerated possession by the public, the presumption of an implied grant of the shore is negatived. For the pursuer it was argued that, in the law of Scotland, where property is described as being "bounded "by the sea," the sea means the sea at low water; that the acts of ownership shewn presumed a Crown title in the pursuer's predecessors; that the character of possession was such as the subject-matter would admit of; the foreshore cannot be absolutely private, nor can possession of every part be taken; the possession proved was what would reasonably be expected—viz., such ordinary possession and beneficial enjoyment as a proprietor would exercise in dealing with the sea-shore as his own property. Lord

Watson, in his judgment, laid down the principles upon which evidence of acts of ownership must be regarded as follows:—"It is, in my opinion, practically impossible "to lay down any precise rule in regard to the character "and amount of possession necessary in order to give a "riparian proprietor a prescriptive right to foreshore. "Each case must depend upon its own circumstances. "The beneficial enjoyment of which the foreshore admits, "consistently with the rights of navigators and of the "general public, is an exceedingly variable quantity. I "think it may be safely affirmed that, in cases where the "sea-shore admits of an appreciable and reasonable amount "of beneficial possession consistently with these rights, "the riparian proprietor must be held to have had posses-"sion within the meaning of the Act of 1617, cap. 12, if "he has had all the beneficial uses of the foreshore which "would naturally have been enjoyed by the direct grantee "of the Crown. In estimating the character and extent "of his possession, it must always be kept in view that "possession of the foreshore in its natural state can never "be, in the strict sense of the term, exclusive. The pro-"prietor cannot exclude the public from it at any time; "and it is practically impossible to prevent occasional "encroachments on his right, because the cost of preven-"tive measures would be altogether disproportionate to the "value of the subject.

"Upon the question of fact raised by the evidence in "this case, I have come to the same conclusion with the "Second Division of the Court, and the reasons by which "I have been influenced are very clearly stated in the "judgment of Lord Young. I think the appropriation of "part of the sea-shore since 1827, and the exclusive "exercise of the right of taking drift sea-ware by the "respondent and his predecessors, constitute such posses-"sion as might have been expected if they had been the "grantees of the Crown, and are therefore, taken *per se*, "sufficient to fortify the respondents' title against the "claim now made by the Crown."

13 Ct. of Sess. Cas. 4th ser. at p. 324.

With respect to the argument that acts of possession

were shewn to have been done upon the foreshore by the public, he says: "The only difficulty which I have felt in "considering this case has been in regard to what is some-"times referred to as *contraria possessio*, but is better "described as *concurrent possession* by members of the "public who have no grant or licence from the Crown. "I attach not the slightest weight to the fact that some "old women carried off sea-ware in creels for the purpose "of manuring their gardens, which were not upon the "lands of Colinswell. The removal of clay and stones "from the foreshore which is proved to have taken place "at three several periods is a very different matter. "These were in no proper sense the acts of the Crown; "but acts of that description, although done without title, "tend to derogate from the possession of the riparian pro-"prietor, and, if carried far enough, will deprive his pos-"session of that exclusive character which is necessary in "order to establish a prescriptive right. After careful con-"sideration of the evidence bearing upon these acts, I am "satisfied that they were neither of such extent, nor of such "duration in point of time, as to affect the quality of the "possession had by the respondent and his predecessors. "It seems to be proved that these encroachments by the "public (for in any view they were acts of encroachment) "were not known to the proprietors of Colinswell; but I "do not think the respondent would have benefited by "their ignorance if the acts had been more marked in "character or longer continued."

Lord Fitzgerald concurred, remarking that "by posses-"sion is meant possession of that character of which the "thing is capable;" but he said: "If the appeal had "related to similar rights either in England or in Ireland, "I would have hesitated much before reaching a conclu-"sion favourable to the pursuer."

Lord Halsbury and Lord Macnaghten concurred in Lord Watson's judgment, and the appeal was dismissed.

It is submitted that the suggestion of Lord Fitzgerald, that evidence of user must be regarded from a different point of view when brought forward to establish title to foreshore in Scotland and in England or Ireland, does not rest upon sound foundation. It has been shewn that the *primâ facie* theory of the Crown's title rests upon the same basis in England as in Scotland, the only distinction being that it was set up in England in the time of Elizabeth, and imported into the law of England, on the authority of Lord Hale, in the time of Charles the Second, whereas it first obtained in Scotland in 1849, upon the dictum of Lord Campbell in Smith *v.* the Earl of Stair. As the theory of the Crown's title is precisely the same both in England and in Scotland, it would seem naturally to follow that the principles with regard to the construction of the evidence necessary to displace the *primâ facie* right must be the same in both countries, and, if this be so, there is no foundation for Lord Fitzgerald's doubt. The principles, therefore, upon which evidence of user should be construed, as set forth in these Scotch cases, are, it is submitted, the principles upon which such evidence must be construed with regard to the foreshores of the whole of the United Kingdom.

CHAPTER XXIII.

LEASES AND SALES OF FORESHORE BY THE CROWN, A.D. 1830 TO A.D. 1887.

Stat. 10 Geo. IV. c. 50.

BEFORE the passing of the Crown Lands (General Management) Act, 1829, the claim of the Crown to the foreshore had not been very vigorously prosecuted; but under that Act a new set of Commissioners of Woods and Forests was appointed, with Lord Morpeth as the Chief Commissioner, and the rights of the Crown began to be more carefully looked after. Accordingly we find that, between 1830 and 1857, the Commissioners of Woods and Forests, acting on the same principle as the Stuart Sovereigns—viz., that the foreshores of the kingdom are *de facto* and *de jure* vested in the Crown—made grants and leases and took acknowledgments for divers pieces of the foreshores of the kingdom in various places, a list of which is given below. These transactions appear to have been done without any consideration as to whether the foreshore really belonged to the Crown or not.

House of Commons Returns, 1858, No. 374.

The view taken of the prerogative right by the Crown officials is shewn by the evidence given before the Select Committee on the Woods and Forests in 1848 and 1849. It is clearly derived from Mr. Hall's treatise, which was published in 1830, in which he holds that no subject can make title to the foreshore except he shew a specific grant, or, if he set up title by evidence of user, he must shew the same exclusive user as if the land were on the *terra firma*. This dictum, it is hardly necessary to remark, has been completely overthrown by subsequent decisions, and is not to be upheld by any antecedent authority. Viscount Morpeth, the First Commissioner of Woods, at question 322 says that he hopes for a large increase in the Crown revenue from the foreshore, "because the Crown has lately been "pushing with vigour its claims to property on the fore-"shore of rivers and the sea." He admits that the Crown's right to foreshore is the subject of litigation in the Thames, and that litigation is threatened on the Mersey and the Tay.

House of Commons Returns, 1858, No. 314. Settled by compromise.

Question 327: "Has any decision been come to as yet "in favour of the rights of the Crown to the foreshore of "rivers?—The right has been repeatedly admitted, and the "Crown has received the purchase-money for the property "that it has assigned."

Q. 328 [Earl of Lincoln]. "In fact, whenever litiga-"tion has taken place and the rights of the Crown have "been disputed, has it not been on the ground that the "Crown has at some antecedent period alienated its rights "by grant or by sale?—Certainly; I am not aware of one "adverse decision to the claim of the Crown to the pro-"perty between high and low water mark."

Q. 329. "Has the general right of the Crown ever been "disputed by any of those litigant parties apart from the "question of antecedent alienation?—I believe not."

Mr. Jonathan Thompson, the Crown Receiver of the Northern Counties, gave the following evidence, which shews that his very clear view was the same as that of Mr. Digges:—

Q. 1306. "Are there any claims made adverse to the "claim of the Crown to the foreshore of rivers?—In every "case, and that is a very important question, and it is a "question that requires a settlement, I think, because in "every case you meet with opposition in making the claim, "more or less, because it is not clearly defined how far "the Crown's rights extend on the foreshore of the rivers, "nor even upon the sea-shore."

Q. 1307 [Sir R. H. Inglis]. "Is it not rather a ques-"tion how far the Crown has surrendered the original "and inherent right?—In some cases the Crown has, but "then the parties who claim exemption from the Crown's "claim must produce a specific grant from the Crown, by "which the Crown has granted down to low-water mark "all the foreshore or all the sea-shore; down to low-water "mark *they must shew a specific grant, otherwise the right* "*of the Crown is decidedly to be sustained*, and we have "sustained it in many cases; in one case it was sustained "against Lord Lonsdale in Lancashire on the Cumberland "side of the Duddon.

Q. 1308 [Mr. Locke]. "Is that where the tide flows?— "Yes."

Q. 1309. "Does it make any difference as to these "rivers when the tide does not flow?—Certainly; we have "no claim where the tide does not flow."

Q. 1310 [Chairman]. "You think it would be of con- "sequence that these claims should be clearly defined?— "Yes, and if such a thing as an inquiry or visitation of "the Crown's fee farm rents were undertaken, the rights "upon the sea-shore or on the shore of navigable rivers "might be looked to at the same time."

Q. 1311 [Sir R. H. Inglis]. "Could they ever be "decided except by a court of law?—Perhaps not, but "an opinion might be given that would guide one before "one went into a court of law."

Q. 1312 [Earl of Lincoln]. "Or it might be possible "at the same expense, if an Act of Parliament were "required, to give the person who should make those "inquiries a power of arbitrating in the same way as power "has been given by Act of Parliament in the case of "adverse claims between the Prince of Wales and the "inhabitants of Cornwall with respect to the Duchy in "that county?—Certainly; that would simplify matters "very much."

Q. 1313. "And avoid all subsequent appeal to a court "of law?—Yes."

Q. 1314 [Chairman]. "Have there been any extensive "sales in your district since you have been appointed?— "None except one, and that not an extensive one, only to "the amount of £65."

House of Commons Return, 3 June

Between 1830 and 1857 the Commissioners of Woods leased or granted or dealt with lands at Egremont, New Brighton, Tranmere Pool, and Seacomb, on the Mersey,

Cheshire; Uplyme, Devon; the foreshore adjacent to the parishes of Kenton Dawlish and East Teignmouth, West Leigh and Bideford, Devon; the Isle of Portland, the manor of Colway at Lyme Regis, Stanton St. Gabriel, Dorset; Sutton Bridge, Lincolnshire; Ferriby Sands on the Humber, Lincolnshire and Yorkshire; Woolwich, Kent; Shadwell, Middlesex; Fairlight, Sussex; lands on the Humber taken by the Hull and Selby Railway Company, foreshores at Hull and Hinderwell, Yorkshire; the Menai Straits, Anglesea; Penmaenmawr and the shore from Penmaenrhos to Little Orme's Head and other places in Carnarvonshire; foreshore near Llandulas River and at Llandrillo in Rhos, Denbighshire; the River Vorid, and at Northop on the Dee, Flintshire; the River Mordac at Merioneth; lands in Scotland and in the Isle of Man; the estuary of the Dudden, Cumberland; the foreshores of Powderham and Kenton on the Exe (which clearly belong to the Earl of Devon), Blackstone Marsh on the River Plim near Saltran; foreshores at Appledore, Northam, Heanton, Punchardon, Braunton, West Leigh, and Bideford, and Fremington, Instow, Tavistock, and Bishop's Tawton, Topsham and Laymouth Creek, at Lynton, Devon; Leigh and Prittlewell, Benfleet, West Ham, Rainham and Hornchurch, Tilbury and Dovercourt, Essex. The foreshores at Leigh and Prittlewell were sold to the Eastern Counties Railway Company, but the lord of the manor of Chalkwell Hall established his title to them in the case of *Ex parte* Alston. Also, lands at Dibden and Fawley on Southampton Water and between Hurst Castle and Keyhaven, and between Fraterlake and Bedenham Creek in Portsmouth Harbour, and on the River Hamble at Bursledon, Hants; on the Medway at Rochester and the East Cliff at Dover, Kent; at Great Grimsby, at the site of the docks of the Manchester, Sheffield, and Lincolnshire Railway on the Humber; at Fulham and Putney; at Wells and Great Yarmouth, Norfolk; at Lowestoft, Suffolk; Rye Harbour, Sussex; Betham, Cartmel, and Haversham, and on the River Kent, Westmoreland; at Middlesborough, Hull, and Kilnsea Clays, Yorkshire; the

1858, No. 314.

Ante, p. 491.

foreshore at Hull granted to William Travis is the subject of the pending suit of Attorney-General *v.* Constable. They have also dealt with a number of other places in Wales, Scotland, Ireland, and the Isle of Man.

House of Commons Returns, 1860, No. 464; 1861, 547.

Further returns of dealing with the foreshores were made in 1860 and 1861, which are of the same nature, and shew the same disregard of the claims of the subject, as the previous one; in short, it may be taken that the Commissioners of Woods and Forests have claimed to deal with, and do deal with, the whole of the foreshores of the kingdom as though they were the unquestionable fee simple property of the Crown, and on the apparent assumption that the Crown has never granted the foreshore in any part of the kingdom. They do not appear to make the least inquiry as to whether the foreshore has been granted or not.

H. of L. Returns, 1869, No 4.

There is a further return of the Crown's dealings with the foreshore from 1863 to 1866, which is of the same character as its predecessors.

H. of L. Papers, 1867, 127.

By the Crown Lands Act, 1886 (29 & 30 Victoria, cap. 62) the management of the greater part of the foreshore was transferred from the Woods and Forests to the Board of Trade, and a Memorandum was prepared by Sir T. Farrer as to the Board of Trade's dealings with the foreshores and bed of the sea. This Memorandum shews the view then taken of the subject by the officers of the Board of Trade. It is inserted here as it is full of interesting suggestions that may help to guide owners of foreshore either in approaching the Board with a view of making a compromise for the Crown's claim or in resisting the Board's attack, which, it will be observed, is to be made just as vigorously when the Crown doubts its right as when it is confident in the justice of its claim. The papers in the Appendix to this Memorandum are omitted. The italics are the Editor's—not Sir T. Farrer's.

MEMORANDUM AS TO BOARD OF TRADE'S DEALINGS WITH FORESHORE AND BED OF THE SEA.

BOARD OF TRADE, *December* 1866.

THE duties of the Board of Trade with respect to foreshores and bed of the sea may be conveniently divided under the following heads:—

1. To ascertain in what parts of the coast the Crown has parted with its rights, in what parts its rights are undoubted, and in what parts the title is doubtful.
2. To prevent encroachments on the foreshore.
3. To watch Bills which may contain enactments affecting the foreshore.
4. To sell or lease or license the use of the soil where expedient so to do.

1. *Ascertaining Title.*

This, which logically ought to be the first thing done, it will probably be prudent to postpone.

The Office of Woods will give us as complete a statement as can be furnished of the present state of the title all round the coast; but this must necessarily be very imperfect. They can give us those cases in which the Crown has undoubtedly conveyed away its rights, but their knowledge must be very imperfect of the titles set up by innumerable claimants, especially as regards the claims which virtually rest upon user.

I have no doubt that in the end we shall have to do something to ascertain or determine these rights; but with the present prejudice against the Crown, it would be unwise to stir the question now. If we can, in the course of our dealings, make it clear that our principal object is *not to assert the proprietary rights of the Crown* to the detriment of frontagers and others, but to protect the public from private encroachment upon land and sea which is the public property of the nation, *we shall be able to raise the question of title in a much less invidious way and with much greater prospects of success than would be at present possible.*

It is, however, to be remembered that every day which passes without an assertion of the Crown's rights is telling against those rights. In many places acts of ownership, or apparent ownership, are going on, and we either do not know of them or cannot prevent them. The law seems to have decided, absurdly enough, that whilst the statutory period in case of actual and complete adverse possession sufficient to give a title as against the Crown is 60 years, yet that enjoyment for a much shorter period and of a much more limited kind may be enough to justify a jury in finding that an original grant from the Crown is to be presumed. Thus a man may have been in possession of land in the Regent's Park for 59 years, and have built upon it and used it as his own without disturbance during the whole of that time, and yet if he defends his occupation on the ground that he has acquired a title by adverse possession, he may be turned out in the 60th year. But if he has taken shingle from a beach during a much shorter time, it seems doubtful whether it might not be presumed as against the public that the Crown at some unknown period made him a grant of the soil. Moreover, it has been held that modern user is admissible to explain an ancient grant (in general terms) of a manor or territory, and to shew that the shore on which acts of ownership have been exercised was in fact part of the property granted, although not in express terms included in the description in the grant.

In considering the subject of the Crown's title to foreshore and bed of the sea, it is to be remembered that this title is not usually an absolute title to the exclusive enjoyment of the soil, and that the Crown cannot ordinarily convey such title. Its title is subject to various rights on the part of the public, *e.g.*, rights of fishing and of navigation, and in particular places and according to local customs, to other public rights. The public right of bathing has been denied by a court of law, but the decision has been questioned by high authorities, and may be considered doubtful.

Whatever may have been the principles which the Office of Woods, guided by their statutes, have been compelled to pursue, there can be no doubt that it should be the policy of the Board of Trade, so far as the law will permit, to admit and even encourage, and perhaps in some cases to enforce, such rights, whether over the soil which still remains in the Crown, or over those parts of it which have been granted away to private persons. Indeed, it is with a view to the protection of such rights rather than with a view to revenue that it is desirable to maintain the title of the Crown. This subject is further adverted to below.

2. *Preventing Encroachments.*

These may be going on at all times and in all places. They may be of various kinds; *e.g.*

1. Encroachments by constructing works, docks, walls, piers, drains, &c. &c., on or in the foreshore or bed of the sea.

2. Taking of gravel or other materials from the foreshore or bed of the sea.

3. Excluding the public from walking, bathing, boating, landing, fishing, &c.

4. Other acts of ownership, or claims to ownership of various kinds which it is impossible to define.

Means of obtaining notice.

Of these acts some may be injurious to navigation or other public rights; whilst others may have little or no effect as against the public, except as evidence against the title to the Crown. But whatever they may be, it is desirable that they should be brought at once to the notice of the Board of Trade, in order that it may judge whether or not it is desirable to take steps to prevent or to qualify them. For this purpose we should issue a circular through the Board of Customs and the Coast Guard to all their officers directing them to report any of the above cases at once to this Board.

In doing so these officers should describe the nature of the act, should give us, if necessary, a plan, and should inform us, if they can, whether the act is done under the claim of a proprietary title or not. They should also be carefully instructed to state whether the act interferes with any *right* hitherto enjoyed by the public, such as that of navigation, fishing, landing, beaching, walking, *bathing, gathering seaweed, &c.* Great care should be taken to make this point prominent in the circular, so that the public may see that it is our principal object.

Cases where encroachment is not injurious.

The course to be adopted on receiving notice of such encroachment must differ according to the circumstances. The act may not be injurious to the rights hitherto enjoyed by the public, and may only be objectionable on the ground that it tends to establish a title adverse to that of the Crown, and may thus help to prevent the Board of Trade from asserting that title in subsequent instances. In such cases we may be placed in great difficulty, especially if the act itself is useful, and if the title of the Crown is doubtful. We shall have no public support in protecting a mere title which does not appear to be of any immediate public advantage. And we shall be not unnaturally found fault with if we interpose obstacles to the execution of a really useful work. In such cases we must endeavour, as well as we can, to encourage the work, and at the same time get the parties to make some acknowledgment which may reserve the Crown's rights. Again, the act may or may not be injurious, but the pecuniary value, present or future, of the title affected by it, may be such as to make it important on this ground to assert the rights of the Crown. These are the cases of which I am most afraid. We cannot give way, and we shall fight at great disadvantage. It is impossible to lay down beforehand any precise rule for all such cases, and we must be guided by circumstances. But our object must be to get the parties making the encroachment to purchase or take a lease. The mode in which this may be done is considered below, under Heading No. 4.

Cases where encroachment is injurious.

In another class of cases we shall see at once that the act is immediately injurious to the public, and that there is reason to interfere, not only on the ground of its affecting title, but because it tends more or less directly to deprive the public of some existing right or enjoyment. In such cases the Crown may clearly have no title, or it may have a good title, or it may be doubtful whether it has a title or not.

In the first of these cases we shall have no better *locus standi* for interference than we have at present, and we shall find ourselves in the same difficulty as we were in before the foreshores were transferred to us.

We are now often called on by persons locally interested in the navigation or otherwise to prevent some inclosure, to preserve some beaching ground, to stop the taking of shingle, &c. &c.; and we are placed in great difficulty because we have not, except in the case of Local and Private Acts, any special or summary powers for enforcing the public rights. We can in fact do nothing more than any individual may do. If there is a case for it the Attorney-General may file an information for an injunction or bring an indictment for a nuisance. But it is always a serious question whether such proceedings are worth the expense, and whether the Government should undertake them. This is a difficulty which I think must sooner or later be met by legislation, giving both to the Board of Trade and to Local Harbour

Authorities more summary remedies than at present exist. Various Bills have been drawn at various times both at the Admiralty and the Board of Trade for this purpose, but they have never been proceeded with, and it will probably be wise now to defer any attempt to deal with this part of the subject till we have more experience of the foreshore question.

The law on this part of the question is well stated in the annexed memorandum by Mr. Thring, written at a time when he was consolidating the Admiralty Statutes.

It will be observed that he there proposes that the title of the Crown to the foreshore should be made subservient to the above purposes. This course we propose to adopt, but it will not help us where the Crown has parted with its title.

In the second case, viz., where the title of the Crown is clearly good, we shall be bound to take some steps to put a stop to the injurious encroachment. But what these steps may be will depend upon its nature.

In some cases we must require it to be stopped altogether; in others we may be content with a modification. From our present experience I believe that a simple requisition from the Board of Trade, charged as it is with the duty of protecting the public, and now armed with a title to the soil, will, in many cases, be sufficient. If this is not acceded to we may have to go to law, and in such a case, I fear that the remedy, as the law as at present stands, may be troublesome and expensive. I do not doubt that legislation on this point will be necessary hereafter, *but it is better to defer it till we have more experience*, and *have established a good character.*

Lastly, in cases where the Crown's title is doubtful *we must act in the same way as if it were good, except that we must do so with greater caution, and be more ready to compromise the question on the principle of reserving to the public their rights and easements over the soil.*

3. *Watching Bills which contain Enactments affecting Title to Foreshore.*

This will be a laborious business every Session.

The memorandum from the Office of Woods, a copy of which is annexed, shews what has hitherto been found necessary. I trust it may not be found as formidable as it looks in the list.

Bills containing alterations of the general law.

The title of the Crown being peculiar, it seems to have been thought necessary to examine not only Bills which specially affect those parts of the soil of the United Kingdom which belong to the Crown, but all Bills which alter the Law of Evidence or of real property. I have some doubts whether we ought to trouble ourselves about these Bills. If any alteration of the general law is desirable I see no reason why it should not apply to the Crown's titles as well as to other titles. The Crown as a landowner ought to be in no better or worse position than other landowners. At present it is nominally in a better position, practically it is in a worse. Its title is ousted by adverse possession of 60 years instead of 21. On the other hand it has no one to look after its rights; *and the lawyers have practically altered the Statutes of Limitation applicable to the Crown by the fiction of allowing a jury to presume a grant.* It is accused of oppression if it brings actions against individuals; and the leaning of courts and juries is often in favour of a single concrete human being and against that abstract or collective entity called the public. Our endeavour should be not to reserve questionable legal privileges, but *to endeavour to get courts and juries to see that we are protecting the public and to give to us fair measure accordingly.*

I think, therefore, we may let Bills affecting the law generally alone, or at any rate we may trust to the watchfulness of the Office of Woods, who will still for the sake of the remaining Crown property be obliged to see to them as before.

Fisheries Bills may also now be practically let alone. The Oyster and Mussel Fisheries Act, 1866 (29 & 30 Vict. c. 85), provides Provisional Orders for persons anxious to obtain fishery grants.

The remainder of the Bills under consideration, viz.: Bills specially affecting foreshore and bed of the sea, we shall have carefully to examine. They may be divided into two classes:

(*a.*) Those which authorize the construction of some work on the soil.

(*b.*) Those which, without authorizing any work on the foreshore or bed of the sea, either directly or by implication affect the title to it.

Bills for constructing some works on

(*a.*) In the former case we already examine the Bills and plans in order to see that they do not injuriously affect navigation, and we must continue to do so. In the course of this examination we may do all that is required to protect title. In the case of Railway Bills, or of Harbour and Dock Bills, and of Provisional Orders for Harbours and Docks, we shall have to see "that the "Railways Clauses Consolidation Act, 1845, the Railways Clauses "Act, 1863, and the Harbours, Docks, and Piers Clauses Act, "1847," are properly incorporated. When this is done there are clauses referred to in the margin, which coupled with section 5 of "The Harbours Transfer Act, 1862," provide that the plans shall not be carried out without the consent of the Board of Trade, nor except according to such working plans as the Board of Trade may approve; and which also give certain other powers for the protection of the public. These clauses will probably give us ample power to make provision when the working plans are submitted to the Board of Trade both for the protection of public rights, of navigation, &c., and of the Crown's title; and we have only to see that the clauses in question are properly incorporated and not impaired by other provisions.

the foreshore. 8 Vict. c. 20, s. 17. 26 & 27 Vict. c. 92, ss. 13 to 19. 10 Vict. c. 27, s. 12. 25 & 26 Vict. c. 69.

Of course the above observations do not apply to the case of a work which is essentially objectionable, and the objections to which cannot be removed, such as reclamation schemes which would destroy an important harbour. These we must oppose *in toto*, if and so far as we can.

In cases where works are contemplated, and the above Acts are not incorporated, *e.g.* in the case of Drainage Acts, our course will be to require the insertion in the Bill of clauses similar to those in the Consolidation Acts.

There is, however, one case unprovided for by these clauses, viz., that of land on the shore to be reclaimed by the proposed works. For the disposal of such land, and for the reservation of due compensation to the Exchequer, special provision must be made in each case.

Bills which affect title without construction of works.

(*b.*) In the second class of Bills, viz., those which affect the title of the Crown without proposing to construct works, we must examine the Bills and require such alterations as may be necessary in the clauses, and also, if it is proposed to take foreshore, add a clause such as is now always inserted, to the effect that it shall not be taken without our consent.

I fear this may cause a good deal of labour, as will be seen by looking at the subjoined list of Bills. It would be facilitated if the standing order which now requires the deposit with the Board of Trade of railway and navigation Bills were extended to all Bills which in any way affect the title to foreshore; and it would be still better if in any general Consolidation Act we could get clauses introduced saving the Crown's rights in all cases of reclamation of land, and in all cases where it is proposed to affect the title of the Crown.

Whatever we do, this watching private Bills is a most harassing and unsatisfactory business. After all our work we do not know what is done with any Bill in its progress through the House. It is impossible to watch it at every stage, and we have no control whatever over it in either House.

4. *The selling, leasing, or licensing the use of Foreshore.*

The class of cases will be threefold.

(*a.*) Cases arising under private Acts or Provisional Orders.

(*b.*) Cases of persons making encroachments as above mentioned who are stopped by the Board of Trade, and only allowed to proceed on condition of purchasing or acknowledging title.

(*c.*) Cases where parties apply to the Board of Trade for leave to purchase.

Cases under Acts or Provisional Orders.

(*a.*) In the first of these cases it is, in general at any rate, to be assumed that the use of the foreshore is required for some purpose of public utility; and there can therefore be no question as to the propriety of the Crown parting with its rights upon such conditions as may be contained in the Act or Order and upon such further conditions, if any, as the Board of Trade, by the special Act or Order, may be empowered to impose for the protection of the public. The only questions will be what those conditions should be, and what should be the terms of sale or lease. The special conditions will of course depend on the circumstances of each case. We may have to require facilities of access to the shore, to beaching ground for fishermen, and many other things which it is impossible to detail.

Experience shews that the easiest plan of settling such questions is in ordinary cases to allow the Bill to pass with such provisions as are contained in the clauses above referred to, giving to the Board of Trade ample control over the execution of the works; and then to settle details afterwards when the works are to be commenced. This relieves the office, as well as the agents and engineers, in the busy part of the Session; it postpones the questions of detail till a time when all parties have a more complete knowledge of the case; and it prevents unnecessary labour on abortive schemes.

In the same way it will be well as a general rule *to postpone the terms of lease or sale till after the Act has passed*, relying on the various clauses I have referred to above.

The question of the terms of sale or lease is the same in the case of sales or leases under private Acts as in other cases, and is considered below.

Cases not under Acts or Provisional Orders.

(*b.*), (*c.*) In the second and third class of cases mentioned above there is no presumption that the intended use of the shore is beneficial, and the first question we shall have to ascertain is, whether the grant of the soil or liberty to use it shall be made at all.

For this purpose we must, as above suggested in the case of an encroachment, first of all make the following inquiries:—

1. What is the work or use of the soil which is contemplated?
2. What are the present rights or enjoyments of the public over it, and how far will what is proposed interfere with them?[1]

For this purpose we must have a form of letter to the applicant, and another for the officer of Coast Guard or Customs on the spot. And if any serious question appear to be raised, we must be prepared to send some one down to make special inquiry.

Supposing it proves that what is proposed can be done (with or without modification) so as not to prejudice public rights or enjoyments, we may enter on the question of terms of purchase. But when these are settled and the purchase is to be completed, we ought to insist on the insertion of stipulations similar to those contained in the Railways Clauses Acts, viz., to the effect that no work shall be executed on the land conveyed or leased unless plans are first submitted to and approved by the Board of Trade; and that in case of any works when constructed becoming nuisances or dangerous, the Board of Trade shall have power to remove and charge the expense against the grantee.

The above suggestions have reference to the protection of the public, and though their tendency will be to diminish the value

[1] Might it not be well to inquire whether it belongs to anybody? —ED.

of the soil and the purchase-money of what we sell, *we must be most careful to put them prominently forward.*

There is one other point on which we should be careful. The frontager, though he may have no legal title, has certainly a considerable interest in the foreshore, and we must take care that he is heard, and that we do not hastily or wantonly authorize works on the foreshore which will be detrimental to him. For this purpose it will be right to require every intending purchaser and lessee to give notice to the frontager. And it may often, if not generally, be found both just and expedient to give him the right of pre-emption. In cases where the title to the foreshore is in dispute between the Crown and the frontager, it may often prove desirable to compromise this question by a settlement, which, whilst preserving to the frontager the enjoyment of his own estate, shall prevent either party from excluding the public from the shore.

Terms of sale or lease.

It remains to consider the question of the terms and form of selling or leasing, and the following observations on this point have reference to all the three classes of cases we are considering under this heading.

A great deal of the prejudice which exists upon this subject has arisen from the fact that the Office of Woods has been bound to get the best possible price; and it is not unnaturally alleged that they have been ready to sacrifice important public rights if they could only get high prices.

The matter is essentially a difficult one even for a department which is not bound to look only, or principally, to price.

In our hands the property in question is simply the property of the public,—the whole proceeds go to the Exchequer; and strictly speaking it may seem that there is no reason why the public should not make the most of their property and sell it for the highest price they can get, just like any other landowner.

Where the Crown has granted away its rights over foreshore, *e.g.*, at Liverpool, the Corporation of Liverpool and neighbouring landowners have sold them for enormous sums. Why should not the Crown, which is the original grantor, do the same? Any grant to a corporation, a company, or an individual, of foreshore at less than its market value is a gift to that particular party out of the Exchequer of a sum of money equivalent to the difference between the market value and the price at which he gets it.

If we could act strictly on this view our course would be clear. But we should find ourselves in serious difficulties. The argument assumes *that the title of the Crown is clear*, that the courts of law and the public will support us in enforcing it; it assumes, finally, and the assumption is fatally erroneous, that the pecuniary interest of the public in the foreshore is its most important interest.

In a country crowded as England is, where the preservation of every open space is of the highest importance for the public health and enjoyment; in a maritime country, where facilities for navigation, for fishing, boating, beaching, landing, and shipping are essential to our trade and to the well-doing of our maritime population—it is of the greatest moment that the control of the public and of the Government over the bed of the sea and over the strip of common which lies between land and open sea should be preserved so that it may be used for the furtherance of the important interests above referred to, and so that nothing may be done with it which is inconsistent with those interests. To sell it to private persons because a high price is offered, without reference to these interests, would be as absurd as it would be to sell Dover pier or to inclose or build in the London parks. It is with this view that I have suggested the various precautions mentioned in the earlier part of this memorandum, and with the same view we must be prepared to forego in many cases the prices which, if we were private landowners, we might insist on demanding.

We have, therefore, to act on very mixed considerations. We have to consider the actual existing value of the soil; the value of it to the purchaser when used for his purposes; the use he intends to make of it, and how far that use is beneficial to the public; and finally the restrictions we have to place on that use in order to prevent injury to the public.

It is obvious that with such a state of things we can lay down no specific rules concerning the terms we shall demand. But the following are principles which, so far as the law permits, I think we may try to apply to the cases as they arise. Proposed principles.

1. The proposed work may be one occupying but little space, may be of obvious public utility, and may yet be one in which there is no direct pecuniary return. Of this nature are culverts made through or over the beach for the purpose of draining a

town; groynes for the purpose of maintaining a public road; hards or landing places open to the public without payment; rifle butts erected on the shore, &c. &c.

In such cases we ought, I think, to be satisfied to give a licence to use the soil either without any payment at all, or with such a nominal payment only as will, coupled with the requisite acknowledgment, reserve the title to the soil.

2. The work may be one taking up little of the shore, and be one of obvious utility, but for the use of which rates are demanded and from which there may consequently be a revenue. Of this nature are the piers at watering places, now so common; the numerous jetties and landing places, and even small harbours constructed by proprietors and others for the improvement of their properties and for the benefit of fishermen, &c. In these cases also I think we may be liberal. Little is taken from the public by the work, and much convenience is given to them by it. It is true that the public benefited is a local public, but local publics are numerous, and there is something of a general character in these outlets of the kingdom. Some small payment should probably be made as an acknowledgment, but it should be small. And when it is found possible to take it in the shape of a royalty on profits actually made, so much the better.

3. The work may be one occupying a large quantity of foreshore, and with a view to an important commercial undertaking, *e.g.*, a railway, or a dock, or a harbour for shipping. In this case we shall probably require a careful survey and valuation, and must act accordingly. To what extent the prospective value, arising perhaps from the work itself, is to be taken into consideration is very hard to say, and much will probably depend on the circumstances of each case. Whenever it is possible to take the payment in the shape of a royalty on profits it will be desirable to do so. Possibly a distinction may be made between the case of a company working for profit and a public trust; but this is doubtful.

4. The work may be a land reclamation scheme. In this case, as it is an undertaking simply with a view to make the land itself more valuable, I think we are entitled to a fair share of profit corresponding to the corpus which we give up. There must of course be a valuation in each case. We must not take a share of the land reclaimed, for we shall be bad landowners; but possibly

we may take a payment proportioned to the value of the land reclaimed.

5. The work may be any oyster or mussel fishery. In this case we may probably take a small royalty on the produce. A licence to use the soil would probably be sufficient in this case.

But assuming these principles, vague as they are, to be correct, we must see what the law allows us to do. We have at present under the Act of last session the same powers, and the same powers only, which the Office of Woods have had, and we are limited by the same restrictions. Legal difficulties.

Their Acts have been purposely framed so as to prevent their parting with land at less than its value. Mr. Trevor has prepared a note of the effect of these Acts, which is appended to this memorandum, as is also the opinion of Mr. Reilly on the same subject. The general result is as follows:

We have not under these Acts any express power to give a licence to use the soil. Our consent must be given in the shape of a lease or deed of sale. We have no power to make a lease or sale without receiving a sufficient rent or consideration, and it is obvious that according to the spirit of these Acts this rent or consideration ought to represent the full value. Leases must not be for more than 31 years, except in the case of land upon which docks, embankments, &c., are to be made, in which case they may be for 99 years. No sale, unless the purchase-money is under £100, and no lease can be made without a Treasury warrant; but the warrant may be granted for a class of cases. No sale or lease can be made without a previous survey or valuation, except in cases where the value cannot be ascertained by survey, or when the value is known to be so inconsiderable as not to be worth the expense of survey.

If these provisions are to be strictly acted upon in the spirit in which they appear to have been conceived; if we are to put the parties to the expense of a survey whenever the property will bear it; if we are in all cases to ask full value and to require the Treasury sanction, it will be impossible to act on the principles I have indicated above as essential to the successful working of the Act of last session; and, sooner or later, we must amend it, by getting rid of the necessity for surveys, and by obtaining powers to grant licences to use the soil and power to arrange disputes as to title on the footing of reserving public rights and enjoyments. Probable legislation.

Observe the difficulty we are in, and the danger to the title we are supposed to protect. Suppose an encroachment to be brought to our notice, *e.g.*, a pier built by a frontager. The soil occupied is of small importance in point of money to the Crown, the work is in itself useful, but it will certainly be used hereafter as an evidence of title against the Crown. If we can say to the proprietor, "Take a licence from us or lease at a nominal rent "and acknowledge the Crown's title," the difficulty would probably be at an end. But if under the present law we must say to him, "You cannot build your pier without a lease or deed of "purchase, and in order to get it we must send down a surveyor, "and you must pay his expenses and the lawyer's bill, as well as "the price he chooses to put on the land," of course he will resist if he can, and we, if we go into court, shall do so with a prejudice against us. Our alternative would be to let the matter entirely alone, and allow the title of the Crown and the future rights of the public to be silently, but not the less effectually defeated.

It is true that the following enactments, viz., 10 Geo. IV. cap. 50, s. 60, enabling the Treasury to grant their consent for a class of cases instead of in each individual case; the same Act, s. 62, dispensing with the necessity of a survey in cases where the land is obviously not worth a survey; 16 & 17 Vict. c. 56, s. 5, giving power, with consent of certain authorities, to compromise and settle disputed claims; and 29 & 30 Vict. c. 62, s. 11, dispensing with the necessity of any consent to compromises,—may, if liberally construed and acted upon, enable the Board of Trade to escape from these difficulties in some cases. But the whole scope and purport of the Acts concerning the Crown property is to prevent sales and leases at less than the real value; and if we are to act on a different principle it is desirable, if not necessary, to have the distinct sanction of Parliament.

There is one special class of cases in which we may perhaps avoid the above difficulties, viz., the case of Provisional Orders, either for fisheries or for piers. In these cases we might, if the Treasury will consent, introduce into each order a clause enabling the Board of Trade to grant a lease or licence to use the soil if, and so far as it belongs to the Crown, on such terms as they may think fit. These orders being confirmed by the confirming Act will become law, and we shall be enabled to act properly in the most pressing class of cases.

As regards other cases, it will probably be well to wait a little before introducing any Bill. We shall know better what we want after some little experience.

The above memorandum contains all the points on the subject of foreshores of which I can think at the present moment; others will suggest themselves in the course of practice.

There can be little doubt that we shall have sooner or later to bring in a Bill or Bills for the following purposes:

1. To ascertain, or give facilities for ascertaining, the Crown's title. *This will be a delicate matter and must be postponed for some time.*
2. To enable the Board of Trade more effectually and summarily to protect navigation and other public interests.
3. To give the Board of Trade express powers to compromise disputed titles to the soil on the footing of reserving the rights and enjoyments of the public.
4. To enable the Board of Trade to deal more liberally with the title of the Crown in the case of works of public utility.

31st December 1866. T. H. FARRER.

It is to be noted, from the tone of this Memorandum, that the decisions of the Courts between 1848 and 1866 had sadly altered the official view of the law. We have no longer the high prerogative notions of Lord Morpeth, Mr. Thompson, and Mr. Digges as to the certainty of the Crown's title. Sir T. Farrer deplores the practice of the judges in allowing juries to find against the Crown under a plea of lost grants based on evidence of user, but feels obliged, sadly and sorrowfully, to bow to their decisions and to suggest the course to be pursued by the Crown officials to get over the awkward difficulty. Nevertheless, we cannot peruse this Memorandum without seeing that its author evidently thinks that the whole of the foreshore is really vested in the Crown, and the policy he plainly advocates is to treat every claimant as a usurper. He clearly believed that the Crown had not in fact parted with the foreshore except in very few cases, and he manifestly directs the Board of Trade officials to proceed on that assumption, and they do so without regard to the rights of any one. It will, however, hardly be thought that the courses he does suggest are very consistent with the honour and dignity of the Crown.

House of Commons Returns, 1872, No. 61; 1877, No. 127; 1882, No. 122; 1887, No. 100.

The Board of Trade has made returns of sales and leases of the foreshore from 1 January 1867 to 31 December 1886. These dealings are very extensive, and consist of leases, sales, licences to lay telegraph cables, to build piers, to make oyster fisheries, to lay groins and protections against the sea on the foreshore, which is a right which every owner of land has at common law. For the most part the considerations received are comparatively small. There has evidently not been the slightest attempt to inquire whether the foreshore belonged to any one or whether it was claimed by any one. The grants have been made clearly behind the backs of the owners, and, indeed, in some cases licences have been granted to do acts upon the foreshore when the title to it was still in litigation undetermined between the Crown and the lord of the manor, and this without any notice being given to the claimant.

Rex *v.* Commrs. of Pagham Level, 8 B. & C. 355.

In the return of 1872 there are printed the forms used by the Board of Trade in dealing with ordinary applications for the rights and interests of the Crown in foreshore. The first form is addressed to the applicant, who is precisely asked what uses the public have made of the foreshore, and who are the owners and occupiers of the land adjacent. The second is to the officer of the coastguard, asking the same questions. The third is to the harbour authority, asking them to make any observations upon the application; but there is not one word of suggestion of any kind of inquiry as to whether any person is, or claims to be, owner of the foreshore. There is, however, another form not printed in this return—viz., a form in which the officers of the coastguard return the particulars of any act or encroachment done upon the shore. In that form the coastguard officer is directed to state whether the act is done under a claim of proprietary title or not; but in the forms relating to an application to lease or purchase foreshore there is no suggestion that such an inquiry should be made. It is evident that the Board of Trade has accepted Sir T. Farrer's definition of its duties, and very prudently postpones, and persistently postpones, any inquiry as to whether the Crown has parted with its rights, and that that which Sir T. Farrer said was "logically the first thing to be done," the officers of the Board find that it is most "prudent to postpone," and to treat it as the last, the very last, thing to be done. The litigation which has occurred since 1866 confirms this view. No inquiry is made. The Board of Trade officials will sell to any applicant the Crown's title in any piece of foreshore round the kingdom, even if it be notorious that it is claimed and owned by the subject. They do not inquire whether the Crown's title is doubtful, but, if it is doubtful, in the words of Sir T. Farrer they "act in the "same way as if it were good," but they do not accept his advice "to do so with greater caution," and to be more ready to compromise for the good of the public. They treat all claimants to foreshore as usurpers upon the Crown, and upon the slightest shew of resistance resort to the arbitrary process of equity information. If the claimant be poor, he not unnaturally submits; if he be rich, they trust to their power of prolonging the litigation, which they can, without control of the Courts, prolong indefinitely, and so endeavour to deter him from upholding his just rights by the fear of the annoyance and expense, which, in the present state of the Crown procedure, he is utterly unable to escape, and from which the Courts would seem to have no power to protect him. They no longer send out a commission to make inquiry and to return the lands as belonging to the Crown. That inconvenient safeguard of the subject is dispensed with—whether legally or not is uncertain. On such an inquiry the subject could make his title good and defeat the Crown, or be defeated, at comparatively slight cost and with scarcely any delay. That does not suit the officers of the Board. The stronger weapon of equity information, under which it is somewhat difficult to get the case to a jury, is the procedure they prefer, and they use it without scruple.

Crown Suits Act, 1865 (28-29 Vict. c. 104), s. 52.

CHAPTER XXIV.

ON PROCEDURE.

SPACE does not permit of a treatise on the mode of procedure by English information, which is the method now almost invariably employed by the Crown in the cases relating to foreshore, but the following remarks are made with a view of shewing the manner in which the Crown officials deal with the subject. Procedure by English information on the equity side of the Exchequer has the inestimable advantage, as at present used, of making it difficult for the owner of foreshore to have the facts which shew the acts of ownership, which either expound his grant or raise for him the presumption of a lost grant, speedily tried by the proper tribunal to decide such matters, a jury, or on a special case stated under the Crown Suits Act, 1859, s. 10. We have already seen how King Charles I. found juries unmanageable and judges not to be persuaded to find for the Crown, and how Sir Thomas Farrer complains that the judges permit juries to presume lost grants. Now, it is to be observed—

i. That it is the fact that one scarcely ever finds (and I speak from a very large experience) an instance of a grant which conveys the shore in terms;

ii. That the title to the shore in almost every manor in the kingdom depends upon grants made long anterior to the time of John (see pp. 24, 25);

iii. That the records of the realm are almost wholly lost before that period;

iv. That when manors which anciently comprised the foreshore as parcel thereof came back into the Crown by escheat or forfeiture, in the time of the Tudor or Stuart

Sovereigns, and were again granted out, they were invariably re-granted to the subject to hold "as fully, freely, and "wholly, and in as ample manner and form," as they were held by the persons by whom they were forfeited, and by all their predecessors in title who had ever had or held them, and "as fully, freely, and wholly, and in as ample "manner and form, as the King or any of his predecessors "or progenitors ever had or held them," and "as fully "and wholly as they had come into the hands of the "King by reason of any escheat, attainder, forfeiture," &c., and this without any reservation or exception of the foreshore in any one single case. Grants, therefore, or rather re-grants, by the Tudor and Stuart Sovereigns were nothing more, in fact, than conveyances of the manors, with every parcel belonging to them, precisely as they were held under the original ancient grant, the great majority of such ancient grants being as old as the Conquest.

This being so, and it can be proved up to the hilt, it is clear that the title to foreshore in almost every case must depend, and does depend, upon the presumption of a lost grant, or upon the construction of a grant in simple form, as "terra de Gower," "manerium cum pertinentiis" (see *ante*, p. 23), "Berkelai Harness manerium cum pertinentiis," (*ante*, p. 166 and p. 306). In the great majority of cases, however, the ancient grant is not to be found, and the case rests upon evidence of user.

Duke of Beaufort *v.* Swansea, 3 Exch. 413.

It follows, therefore, that in almost every case the issue to be tried between the Crown and the subject with respect to foreshore is an issue of fact which should properly be tried by a jury. The subject has on such a trial the fairest means of displacing the presumption invented by Mr. Digges, decreed by the judges who decided against Hampden, treated as an axiom by Hale on the authority of that case alone, and upheld by *obiter dicta* as law taken for granted from that time to the present. The title of the subject, whether he have a grant *in specie* or whether he can merely shew possession, depends wholly and solely upon the construction of the acts of ownership which he can prove, and the construction of such evidence is for the jury, and for

See Hale, ante, p. 401.

the jury alone (and I say it without a suggestion of disrespect to her Majesty's judges), the legal mind has been so misled by *obiter dicta*, and the constant and persistent reiteration of the theory that the Crown has seldom or never parted with the foreshore, that it is not so fit as an independent jury, aided by the proper direction of the judge, to consider the weight and effect of the evidence of acts of ownership in cases of this description. How often one reads in reports, how often one hears in court, the remark of the judge, "Putting myself, so far as I possibly "can, in the position of a juryman"! In any case it is clear that the subject ought to have a right to have an issue of this kind, an issue of fact, and purely of fact, tried by a jury, if he so wishes it; but from this constitutional method of trial, from the very commencement of this assertion of the Crown's *primâ facie* title, the Crown has almost invariably shrunk, and its officers have had good reason to do so. From the time that Digges first attempted to recover the marsh and foreshore from Hammond in 17 Elizabeth, A.D. 1574, until the present day, so far as I can discover, no jury has been found (with one exception) to give a verdict for the Crown against evidence of user on the part of the subject. In the exception mentioned, on a second trial the verdict was against the Crown. One is therefore not surprised that Sir Thomas Farrer objects to trial by jury between the Crown and the subject, nor that the Crown elects in almost every case to proceed by English information.

Ante, p. 544.

Att.-Gen. *v.* Jones, ante, p. 537.

The ground of equity usually alleged in informations with regard to foreshore is that the defendants have encroached and have confused the boundaries. This gives a ground for discovery. It was formerly the practice on the equity side of the Court of Exchequer to have every question of law and fact which was reducible to an issue tried by a Latin information and a jury. "It is "open to the Court, upon the hearing of an English information, to send any questions that may arise upon the "title to a trial at law." That was the usual course. "If

Att.-Gen. *v.* St. Aubyn, Wightwick pp. 228, 229, per Graham, B.

Ibid. p. 264, per Macdonald, C.B.

Ibid. p. 181, argument.

"a matter of law, particularly a *legal title*, should occur, a "jury is called in, and the rest of the matter remains with "the Court." "Where the King gives the Court to be "informed that an intrusion has been committed upon his "land, although no matter of mere equitable jurisdiction "were stated, yet the informations have been retained and "a trial at law directed if the case required it; but in no "instance has the information been dismissed on the "ground that it might be better disposed of and adjudged "at law than it could be in a court of equity." But although upon the older authorities it would appear that it is incumbent on the Court, so soon as the question in the case appears to be a matter of law and fact, to direct the case to be tried by a Latin information and by a jury (the Judicature Acts not applying to proceedings on the equity side of the Exchequer), yet it is a question not free from doubt, and the later authorities shew that the directing of an issue by a court of equity is a matter for the discretion of the Court.

Wightwick p. 265, per Macdonald, C.B.

See Att.-Gen. *v.* Molesworth, Hil., 3 Chas. I., cited by Wood, B., Wightwick 207.

Att.-Gen. *v.* Constable, 4 Ex. D. 172; Att.-Gen. *v.* Emerson, 10 Q. B. D. 191.

The Crown Suits Act, 1865, part II., which regulates proceedings by English information, is silent as to this point of practice. The Rules of 1866 under that Act are equally silent. Fowler's "Practice in the Exchequer in "Equity," published in 1817, the latest book of practice in these matters, seems to shew (ii. 164) that it was the regular practice to try all facts by a jury. Speaking of decrees, Fowler says: "The decree may be either final "or interlocutory: final, where it decides absolutely upon "the right; and interlocutory where a party is to shew "cause against it, or where, by the intervention of a jury, "a fact is to be tried to inform the conscience of the Court, "or a reference is made to the master upon matters to be "reported to the Court for its future decision." At p. 194 he treats of issues as part of the usual practice. Between subject and subject it would seem (Fowler, i. 301) that the fact that the plaintiff bringing in a bill in equity to establish his title to land or a several fishery, had not first established his title at law is a good ground of demurrer, and it is difficult to see why the case should be different

See Att.-Gen. *v.* Parsons, 2 M. & W. 24.

between the Crown and a subject. It seems, however, to be now established that in the practice in the equity side of the Exchequer the directing of an issue is a matter for the discretion of the Court.

Bullen *v.* Michel, 2 Price 466, A.D. 1816.

Lord Eldon, in the House of Lords, says: "I take it to "be quite clear that a court of equity in cases of this "sort [bill for tithes on the equity side of the Exchequer], "as well with respect to all cases where matters of fact "are in question, has a right itself to determine upon the "fact without the intervention of a jury. I very readily "admit that the exercise of its judicial discretion will in "many cases make it its duty to call for the assistance of "the verdict of a jury, but I can never admit that, if the "evidence which is before a court of equity is satisfactory "upon the fact, a court of equity is bound to send any "such case to a jury, and that is a doctrine which I con- "ceive to be as clear in matters of tithe as it is with "respect to any other matters of fact."

Att.-Gen. *v.* Burridge, 10 Price 350.

In Attorney-General *v.* Burridge, in 1822, with regard to the foreshore at Portsmouth, Richards, C.B., said that he was unable to satisfy his conscience as to the equity between the right of the Crown and the claim of the defendant. He came to the conclusion that he must have further assistance, and directed an issue. This issue was never tried, and when the question of the title was again raised, in Attorney-General *v.* Portsmouth, in 1870, on an information of intrusion, a formal verdict was found for the Crown, subject to a special case to find the facts. It would seem, therefore, that the directing of an issue in cases by English information is a matter purely in the discretion of the Court, and, if we assume that in the circumstances of any particular case an equity information for foreshore will lie, and cannot be successfully demurred to, the result is that the subject is practically denied the *right* to have the issue, which is in fact the only issue which can truly be raised, tried by a jury. The issue almost invariably is: Is the foreshore parcel of his manor, or not, by construction of an actual grant or by presumption of a lost one? Wood, B., in his judgment in Attorney-General *v.* St. Aubyn, took a strong view of this point. At p. 180 he says: "Where there are "legal rights there is no occasion to come into a court "of equity; the courts of common law can give relief. "My idea is that the proper information is an informa-"tion of intrusion at common law, and that the persons "in possession have a right to retain the possession till "the title of the Crown is found. If the Crown can "come here and, by filing a bill of this kind [an English "bill], compel a person to disclose his title, there will "be an end of the benefit of the statute of 21 James I. "cap. 14, and the subject will be deprived of his trial by "jury." The case was an equity information filed by the Prince of Wales as Duke of Cornwall to recover encroachments upon the foreshore of the Tamar as parcel of the manor of Trematon, the title to the foreshore of Sutton Pool as parcel of that manor having been decreed to the Duchy in a previous suit, the question being whether the Prince or the Crown had a right to proceed in such a case by English information. "I take it," he says (p. 185), "to be a clear and settled principle of a court "of equity that you shall not have relief in equity where "you have a legal remedy, or at least not until the right "has been established in a court of law." Several precedents of the reigns of James I., Charles I., and Charles II. having been cited, he remarks that not one since the Revolution was forthcoming, and says: "I must say I "have not much veneration for precedents taken from the "arbitrary reigns of those monarchs, and I hope I shall "not see such precedents revived in the present reign, or "that, if they do take a temporary root, they will soon be "eradicated. James the First, in the last Parliament he "held, was under the necessity, in order to get a subsidy "from his subjects, to pass some beneficial laws to relieve "them from the oppressive exertions of his prerogative, "and among others an Act which I think is extremely "material in the consideration of this case, and I will state "it: it is entitled 'An Act to admit the Subject to plead "'the General Issue in Informations of Intrusion brought

Wightwick, p. 180.

Ibid. p. 197.

21 Jac. I. c. 14.

" 'on the behalf of the King's Majesty, and retain his Posses- " 'sion till Trial.' Before this Act of Parliament, the ancient " course of the Exchequer had been, that if, in an informa- " tion of intrusion into lands or tenements, the defendant " had pleaded not guilty, he was to lose his possession; 4 Inst. 116. " Lord Coke states that to be the practice; he might at " any time have pleaded his title specially, but if he pleaded " the general issue, immediately on that plea a writ issued " to turn him out of possession, and to seize the premises " into the hands of the King; and therefore to relieve the " subject against the special pleading of his title, and to " permit him to plead the general issue, and retain his " possession, this Act was made. It recites, that the King " by his prerogative may enforce the subject in informa- " tions of intrusion to a special pleading of his title, and " that, being willing to remit a part of his ancient and " regal power, out of his gracious disposition to his subjects, " and at their humble suit, it is enacted, 'that where the " 'King, and those from whom he claims, and all others " 'claiming under the same title, have been out of posses- " 'sion twenty years, or not received the profits within " 'twenty years, before the information of intrusion, the " 'defendant may, if he thinks fit, plead the general issue, " 'and not be pressed to plead specially, and shall retain " 'the possession, until the title be tried, found or adjudged " 'for the King;' then follows a proviso, which shews the " anxiety of the Legislature to prevent any evasion of this " Act; and that provides, 'that where an information of " 'intrusion may fitly and aptly be brought on the King's " 'behalf, no *scire facias* shall be brought whereunto the " 'subject shall be forced to a special pleading, and be " 'deprived of the grace intended by that Act.' Can it " have been at that time understood by the Legislature that " there was any proceeding by English bill that could " avoid this Act of Parliament? Most undoubtedly not. " Their idea was, that there could be a proceeding only by " information of intrusion, or perhaps (by reference to the " Prince's case) by *scire facias;* and as these were the " only things that existed, they provide that to informa-

"tions of intrusion you shall plead the general issue, and "not set out your title; and that no proceeding by *scire* "*facias* shall be devised to oblige the subject to set out "his title: had they any idea that the King's Attorney-"General might come into a court of equity and oblige "a man on oath to set out his title? It is quite im-"possible."

"Now, let me suppose that the Attorney-General of "James the First, after this Act had passed, whereby "the King remits part of his ancient and regal power by "releasing the subject from the special pleading of his "title, and from being pressed to plead specially, had "turned short round, and said, 'I will evade this Act of "'Parliament; I have nothing to do but to go into the "'equity side of the Exchequer by English bill, and I "'shall get rid of this Act of Parliament; I will not only "'oblige the subject there especially to plead his title, "'but I will make him set it out on his oath also; and "'not only so, but he shall produce all his title-deeds and "'writings, that I may inspect them, and try if I cannot "'pick holes in them.' Could such an abominable eva-"sion have been endured even in the arbitrary reign of "James the First? and more especially when you see "so much care taken to prevent the subject from being "deprived of the King's grace by any other mode of pro-"ceeding: the Legislature evidently meant that that should "be the course of proceeding. It is evident there was no "other information of intrusion but that on the law side "at the time, nor any mode of proceeding on the equity "side for intrusion unmixed with circumstances of equity. "If there are circumstances of equity, a question of law "may incidentally arise; *but when a question of law does* "*incidentally arise, it must be put into the proper course of* "*proceeding;* therefore I conclude that if this had been "an intrusion into the possessions of the King, the common "law information must have been the course of proceed-"ing, and not this on the equity side; if the Prince is to "stand in the same situation as the King (but which I "think there is no authority for), even in that case

Wightwick, p. 212.

"he must proceed in the same way for an intrusion "into his possessions, as the King must—viz., by law "information of intrusion. What is Lord Coke's definition "of the jurisdiction of this Court of Exchequer Chamber, "before the *Lord Treasurer, Chancellor*, and *Barons* (which "is what I take to be our equity side)? He says their "jurisdiction is as large for matters of equity as the Barons "in the Court of Exchequer have for the benefit of the "King at the common law; evidently pointing out this "distinction, that *where the King's title is matter of equity,* "*he must resort to the equity side; where legal, to the law* "*side;* and it is highly necessary, for the security of "the subject, this distinction should be kept up." He then cites Sir Thomas Walsingham's case, and proceeds: "The Constitution has prescribed specific modes to be "pursued by the Crown before the subject can be dis-"seised or put out of his lands or tenements, in all which "the subject has a right to a trial by jury, *as matter of* "*right, and not as favour of the Court,* in shape of an issue. "The modes that occur are, first, by inquisition, finding "the King's title; the subject may plead to issue, and "try it by a jury. The next, by *scire facias,* the subject "may plead to it, and try it by jury. The next, by *quo* "*warranto,* the subject may plead to it, and try it by "jury. The next, by information of intrusion (which "would be the legal course of proceeding in the present "case, if it were the claim of the Crown), in which "case the subject might plead, and try by a jury; and, "if the Crown had not been in possession within twenty "years, the subject might avail himself of the 21st of "James the First, cap. 14, and might plead the general "issue, and retain possession till the King's title be "found. If you can supersede all these modes by re-"viving this proceeding by English bill; if you can "substitute depositions instead of trial by jury; if you "can make men set out their titles upon oath, and "wring their deeds from them for your inspection—all "those safeguards which our forefathers have been at "all times so anxious to obtain and preserve, and which

4 Inst. 118.

Hardres 49.

Wightwick, p. 214.

"are so essential to the security of the subject, will be "broken down and destroyed."

Referring (p. 223) to the general object of the information, he says: "This proceeding appears to me, I must "say, to be an attempt to introduce an unconstitutional "inquisition to pry into men's titles, and to withdraw "from the cognizance of the common law, and the trials by "jury, that which solely belongs to those tribunals by the "fundamental principles of our Constitution; and are a "few straggling precedents (if they were more to the point "than those cited from the arbitrary reigns of James the "First and Charles the First) sufficient to warrant such "a violation of the constitutional rights of the subject? I "am aware that it may be said (for so it has been urged "in argument) that the Court, if they see any doubt, when "the evidence is taken upon depositions, *may send it to law* "*to be tried;* most undoubtedly they may; but I have no "doubt that those who so argue will also argue that it is "in the discretion of the Court whether they will or will "not send it to law, and *would, in fact, most strenuously* "*oppose it.* In my opinion, it does not depend upon any "discretion of this Court; the subject has a right to come "in the first instance, before he has been harassed and "worn down by the grievous expense and delay of "answers, exceptions, commissions, and depositions, and "to say to this Court, 'There is nothing of equity in this "'claim; the claim is wholly dependent upon the rules of "'the common law, and the facts upon which this claim is "'founded are triable by a jury; and therefore the Court "'ought not to proceed upon it, but dismiss it.' Establish "first that the ground and soil of the Tamar between the "high and the low water mark belongs to you before you "come to this court to ascertain its boundaries or to seek "an account of the rents and profits."

Baron Wood, whose great ability and learning are well known, was, however, overruled, in this particular case in question, by Baron Graham, on the ground that the remedy at law would not be adequate, because by it the Crown could not possibly ascertain how much the shore had been encroached upon without discovery;[1] but he held that, in order to entitle the Crown to come to this court, *the King must shew a case for which he cannot at least have an adequate remedy at law.* Macdonald, C.B., sustained the information, and pointed out that a similar information was filed in the case of Sutton Pool in 1754, and in that case (he said) "two points were made: one, as to the title of "the King; another, as to the injury done to the harbour: "the Court, in the decree, separated these considerations, "and, as to the title, they directed a Latin information, "which was tried at bar, and as to the harbour, a commis- "sion was issued;" but it appears clearly from his judgment that he considered that, whenever a legal title arose, trial by jury was necessary to determine it.

The decision, however (Wood, B., *dissentiente*), practically determines that in a case relating to foreshore an English information will lie whether there are grounds of equity shewn on the face of it or not; but with the distinct qualification that if a legal title shall occur a jury must be called in. A distinction, therefore, would seem to exist between the law as between subject and subject and the law as between the Crown and a subject. The English information of the Crown would appear (if this decision is good law) not to be demurrable whether there is any ground of equity in the information or not, whereas between subject and subject the legal title must be tried first. If this case is sound law, the benefit of the statute of James is, as Baron Wood declares, taken away, and the right of the subject to a jury under that statute is no longer a legal right, but a matter for the discretion of the Court, a matter of favour and grace. Assuming, therefore, that this decision is sound, which, it is submitted, is very doubtful, it would be well to consider what are the precedents and practice which should guide the Court in the exercise of its discretion in granting an issue in cases relating to the title to foreshore. The informations in the

[1] In the particular case the general title of the Duchy to the shore was admitted. The question was as to boundary, and length of possession under the Statute of Limitation.

time of Elizabeth (*ante*, pp. 215–223) were all Latin informations. In the reign of James I. many English informations were filed, and, so far as we can discover, not one of them was pressed to a decision. In the reign of Charles I., with the one exception of the case of Attorney *v.* Philpott, in every suit by English information respecting foreshore the title was ordered to be tried at law or at bar. In the cases of Attorney *v.* Irby, Oldsworth, and others (*ante*, pp. 281, 282), relating to the marshes in Lincolnshire, the titles were all ordered to be tried at law. In the case of Attorney *v.* Appleton and others (*ante*, p. 285) it does not appear whether the information was a Latin or an English one, but it would seem to have been a Latin one, but there the Crown shrunk from the jury.

Exch. D. & O., 3rd ser., vol. xiv. 53; xv. 94; xxiv. 4.

In the case of Attorney *v.* Bromwich and others (p. 285) the case was tried at law. In the case of Attorney *v.* Riggs (*ante*, p. 290) the title was also to be tried at law. The case of Rex *v.* Oldsworth was tried upon demurrer. In the case of Attorney *v.* Smith and Lord Berkeley the defendants, having pleaded the general issue, were ordered to shew cause why a trial at bar should not be ordered, and trial at bar was ordered on motion of the Attorney-General. The case of Attorney *v.* Philpott is the only case at this period in which a trial at law was refused (*ante*, p. 265), but even then Chief Baron Davenport seems afterwards to have felt that the refusal was wrong, for he changed his mind, and said "he would not take away the freehold "of any man upon a certificate," and we see (at p. 269), in the statements submitted to the King regarding the case, that "after the decree it was conceived by the Court "that the judgment would not bind those who had the "inheritance," and it has been shewn that it did not bind them. The case of the Archbishop of Canterbury, in 1694 (*ante*, p. 423), was referred to arbitrators. The Bishop of Durham's case, in 1696 (*ante*, p. 424), was tried at bar. The case of Attorney *v.* Constable, as to Cherry Cob Sand (*ante*, p. 427), was sent to a jury. In the case of Attorney *v.* Richards, in 1795 (*ante*, p. 434), the defendants asked for an issue on the point of nuisance; this was resisted

Ibid. xiii. 125, 154; xvi. 389.

Ibid. xxii. 402; xxiii. 60.

Ibid. xxii. 269; xxiii. 15, 39.

by the Crown, and was refused by Macdonald, C.B., on the ground that the soil was in the Crown, and that Hale holds that "when the King claims and proves a right to the soil, "when a purpresture and nuisance have been committed he "may have a decree to abate it," citing Attorney *v.* Philpott, Bristol *v.* Morgan, Hale de Portubus, p. 81, and the Prior of Tynemouth's case. The case of Attorney *v.* Parmeter, in 1811 (*ante*, p. 436), was heard upon depositions. In Attorney *v.* Burridge, in 1822 (*ante*, p. 449), the judge directed issues, which the Crown never attempted to try. In Attorney *v.* Chambers, in 1845, the Crown compromised soon after issues were ordered to be tried. In Attorney *v.* Lord Mostyn, in 1852, the Crown withdrew its claim before issue was joined. In Attorney *v.* Chamberlaine, in 1856, the Crown strove hard to keep the case from a jury, and, as soon as the issues were ordered, compromised with the defendant. In Attorney *v.* Phillips, in 1857, the Crown withdrew its claim. In Attorney *v.* Jones, in 1863, the Crown proceeded by Latin information and obtained a verdict on a first trial, which was reversed on a new trial, and the Crown has never gone to a jury on a question of foreshore since that date.

Notwithstanding that Baron Wood was in the minority in the decision in the case of Attorney *v.* St. Aubyn, it would seem that his judgment was in the main sound, and we shall see that what he prophesied would happen has now come to pass. It is impossible to suppose that the decision in that case can suffice to override and nullify the effect of the statute of James, under which, said Lord Abinger, the Crown is placed in the position of a subject. The practice of the Court of Exchequer clearly shews that the judges never thought (except in Attorney *v.* Philpott) that they had a right to deprive the subject of the benefit of that statute, for we have seen that in every case (except Attorney *v.* Richards) where questions of fact have arisen they have directed an issue; and it is submitted, looking to the precedents, that at this day the Court is bound to grant an issue wherever a legal title comes in question under a suit by English information. If it were not so,

Att.-Gen. *v.* Parsons, 2 M. & W. 24.

the hardships referred to by Baron Wood must be borne by the subject, and in point of fact in all recent cases the subject has borne them. Under the modern procedure defendants are made "to set out their titles, their deeds "are wrung from them for inspection, and the safeguards "which their forefathers did obtain by the statute of "James, and which are so essential to the security of the "subject," have in recent years, as Baron Wood prophesied, been broken down and destroyed.[1] Of course the great difficulty which a defendant has is to shew his possession for twenty years, because the nature of the foreshore precludes the possibility in almost every case of shewing possession exclusive as of *fact*, in contradistinction to possession exclusive as of *right;* the foreshore is always open to the user of the subject under the *jus publicum*, and the Crown officers have always claimed that the user under the *jus publicum* shews possession in the Crown of the *jus privatum*. Moreover, as there must almost always of necessity be some casual user by the public trespassing by taking sand, &c., precariously on the shore, and doing small acts which do not call for serious action on the part of the owner, the Crown relies upon these to shew that the defendant has not been in possession; but with regard to these latter it has been held, unless they are done by the distinct licence of the Crown, they are not evidence to shew that the Crown has been in possession. Having regard to the language of Lord Watson in Lord Advocate *v.* Young, it would seem that, if an owner of foreshore can shew such possession of the foreshore as that foreshore is reasonably capable of, he is entitled, it is submitted, to avail himself of the statute of James, and either to demand an issue as his legal right, or at least to crave the leave of the Court to plead the general issue before he answers the information, and so to avoid the expense, delay, and vexation of the Crown procedure by English information, the interrogatory, the discovery, the amendment and re-amendment of informations, and all the machinery of that

Wyse *v.* Leahy, ante, p. 554; Hamilton *v.* Att. for Ireland, ante, p. 569; Daly *v.* Murray, ante, p. 571. Lord Advocate *v.* Young, 12 App. Cas. 553, ante, p. 588.

[1] But the practice as to discovery in ordinary suits is greatly changed since Baron Wood's time, A.D. 1811.

weapon of oppression on which the Crown officials now rely to make owners submit to re-purchase from the Crown the foreshore which has belonged to them and their predecessors for centuries, and to which, if they could have a speedy trial at law, they could, at any rate in the great majority of cases, establish their right without any serious delay or extravagant expense.

It is to be noted that, notwithstanding all the recent amendments of procedure by the Judicature Acts, the Crown has been successful in keeping on foot this ancient method of procedure, so oppressive and so unjust to the subject. It is not a procedure dating from remote antiquity. In the time of Edward I. the King sued in the same manner as a subject, by simple suit, and down to the time of Edward III. no procedure of the kind was permitted; from that time to the time of Henry VI. there were constant petitions to Parliament by the Commons praying that the Crown might not be allowed to proceed upon "suggestions" and "informations" given to the King; but in the reigns of Henry VI. and Edward IV. procedure by information gradually became established as a method to be employed by the Crown only. The notorious Empson, in the reign of Edward IV., procured an Act extending it to the Duchy of Lancaster, but that Act was repealed by Henry VII. The oppressive use of the process during the reigns of the Tudor and Stuart Sovereigns has been fully shewn; but by the two statutes of 21 James I. cap. 2 et cap. 14, the Commons at last succeeded in mitigating the effect of this misuse of the prerogative, and the subject has remained under the protection of these statutes until comparatively recent times. But now, in these later days, we see this engine of oppression revived in its full strength, and attempted to be used more arbitrarily and more oppressively than even Charles the First dared to use it. The method of procedure has been carefully excepted out of all recent amendments of the laws of procedure, and the subject is harassed by English informations and pretences of concealment under the *primâ facie* theory as effectively as if the two statutes of James and the Nullum Tempus

Quo Warranto Rolls; Coram Rege Rolls, *passim*; Rolls of Parliament, *passim*.

Att.-Gen. of Duchy of Lancaster *v.* Duke of Devonshire, 14 Q. B. D. 195.

21 Jac. I. c. 2, c. 14.

Acts had never been passed. The rules of procedure on the equity side of the Exchequer are almost unknown; the only book of practice, and it is a very imperfect one, is that of Fowler, published in 1817. The Crown Suits Act of 1865, and the Rules made under it, are certainly not calculated to give any assistance to a defendant in a suit by the Crown. Surely it is time that some steps were taken to place the subject in a just position to try his rights, as against the Crown, by some other method than this almost unknown procedure by English information. Down to 1855 the Crown, if defeated in litigation, was not liable for costs, the subject, on the other hand, not paying costs to the Crown; but this state of things was very inequitable. The Crown could put the subject to unlimited expense with very little cost to itself, and at last, in 1855, this abuse of the prerogative was brought before Parliament, and abolished by the Crown Suits Act, 18-19 Vict. c. 90. 1855. The attention of Parliament having been called to this method of procedure, and the injustice of it to the subject being felt, it was enacted by section 3 of that Act that, "whereas the procedure and practice in informations, suits, and other proceedings instituted by "or on behalf of the Crown in her Majesty's Court of "Exchequer *is dilatory and requires amendment*, and it "is desirable that the same should be assimilated as nearly "as may be with the course of practice and procedure now "in force in actions and suits between subject and subject," the Barons of the Exchequer in England and the Exchequer in Ireland shall have power "to make all such "general rules and orders for the regulation of the pleading and practice in such informations, suits, and other "proceedings, and to frame such writs and forms of proceedings, as to them may seem expedient for the purpose "aforesaid;" but, *mirabile dictu*, no such Rules have ever been made!

By the Crown Suits Act, 1859, s. 10, power was given, 22-23 Vict. c. 21. by consent and order of a judge, to state any question of law in a special case for the opinion of the Court without pleadings. Rules were made under this Act, in which the rights of the subjects to the benefit of the statutes of James were acknowledged; but the Rules are confined to proceedings in the Exchequer at law, and the 143rd rule is, "These Rules shall not be deemed to apply to suits in equity." Thus, again, the ancient oppressive procedure was preserved. As has been before observed, the Crown Suits Acts, 1865, and the Rules made under it, give no assistance to the subject; and it has been decided that the Judicature Acts do not apply to procedure by English information.

Att.-Gen. *v.* Constable, 4 Ex.D, 172; Att.-Gen. *v.* Emerson, 10 Q. B. D. 191.

With regard to recent suits, in the case of Attorney *v.* Portsmouth the defendants were unable to claim the benefit of the statutes of James because the Crown shewed distinct and considerable use of the parts of the foreshore in question within the period of twenty years. This case was by consent tried on a special case. The information was filed in 1869; the case was not heard until 1877.

In the case of Attorney-General *v.* Lowther, as to foreshore on the Tees, the information was filed on 17 September 1872, amended in November 1873, re-amended in 1874, further amended as to parties only till 1877. The question in the case was whether the foreshore was parcel of the manor of Wilton or not. The informations and answers extend to nearly five hundred pages of print. It was proposed to further re-amend the information, when the case was compromised, very advantageously for Mr. Lowther.

In the case of Attorney *v.* Constable, four informations were filed in January 1879, and answered separately at great expense in 1880. An attempt was then made by the defendants to have the informations consolidated, as the issue in the four cases was all the same—viz., whether the foreshore was part of the seigniory of Holderness or not. This was refused; one of the four cases is now being proceeded with, *the Crown reserving its right to proceed with the other three if it should think fit;* the amended information was immediately answered, and the fullest disclosure made of all documents in the defendants' possession. Nothing was done until 1887, when the Crown proceeded to examine a witness before issue was joined. Issue is not yet (June 1888) joined, and it is expected that the information will be further re-amended. The defendants cannot insist on issue being joined, and it is asserted that the Court has no power to rule on the Attorney-General.

In the case of Attorney *v.* Emerson, proceedings commenced in 1880, the information was amended in 1881, and the cause was tried in 1887, but in this case the defendants had a special power to rule the Crown on.

In all these cases the issues were one and the same—viz., Is the foreshore parcel of the manor? It was a question of fact, and of fact only, and might have been tried by a jury or on a special case within twelve months of the dispute arising in each of the cases; but the Crown officials shrink from a jury; they proceed by information, and they do what Baron Wood foresaw they would do; before the subject can have a trial he is "harassed and worn down by the "grievous expense and delay of answers, exceptions, com-"missions, and depositions; when there is nothing of equity "in this claim of the Crown, the claim is wholly dependent "upon the rules of common law, and the facts are triable "by a jury." If, therefore, the procedure in recent cases is a valid procedure, a lawful procedure, it is clear that the subject has lost the benefit of the statutes of James, and Baron Wood's prophecy is fulfilled. If the Crown has a right, and a valid right, before trial to pry into the subject's title, and make him discover his documents, to put him to illimitable expense in tracing his title back, if happily he be able to do so, to the ancient grant upon which his title to foreshore must rest; if it may then take exceptions to his answer at any time it pleases without limitation, and drive him to a hearing of the exceptions; if it may then, after waiting an indefinite time, perhaps for years, arbitrarily amend the information, and again put him through the same process of answers, interrogatories, discovery, and exceptions, and, having waited another few years, re-amend and further re-amend the information *ad infinitum*, as under the present procedure it claims to be at liberty to do, and does do, without control of the Court; if, in short, it may prolong the preliminary steps in the suit until all the defendant's old witnesses are dead, and he is left without the means of shewing his possession within sixty years, without the means of raising the presumption that his grant carried to him the foreshore, then it is submitted, either that Baron Wood was right, and that the majority of the Court were wrong, or, if that be not so, then that it is high time that her Majesty's judges made Rules under the powers given them by the Crown Suits Act, 1855, to amend this procedure, and to assimilate it to the procedure between subject and subject, as directed by that Act. It is by this method of procedure, and by it alone, that the Crown is enabled to force owners of foreshore to re-purchase it from the Crown, and they have done so wherever the owner has not been rich enough to resist their claim: the poorer men give way sooner than risk the cost and vexation of such proceedings; the richer men have almost invariably resisted, and generally with success.

House of Commons Papers, 1858, No. 314; 1860, No. 464; 1861, No. 547.

In the cases of Attorney *v.* Chambers, issues having been directed to be tried between the Crown and Earl Cawdor, the Crown compromised with the Earl. In Attorney *v.* Corporation of London a compromise was effected and confirmed by the Thames Conservancy Act, 1857. In Attorney *v.* Lord Mostyn the Crown withdrew its claim, and the information was dismissed. In Attorney *v.* Sir John Hanmer the Crown was defeated. In Attorney *v.* Chamberlaine issues were ordered to be tried, and then the Crown compromised. In Attorney *v.* Sir Thomas Phillips the information was dismissed. In Attorney *v.* Lowther the Crown came to a compromise. In Attorney *v.* Jones the Crown got a verdict on the first trial, but was defeated on a new trial, and no case as to foreshore has gone to a jury since. Thus we see how the Crown proceeds; the old system of "fishing grants" cannot now be used, but the Commissioners of Woods and the Board of Trade emulate King James I., and proceed to make the subject compound for what they allege to be "defective titles," or no titles at all, just as he did (*ante*, pp. 169–177). He proceeded on the assumption that all possession was usurpation till Parliament was forced to protect the subject by the first Statute of Limitations and the statute respecting informations. These statutes he and his successor ignored in respect of foreshore and marsh land, till the Revolution stopped their proceedings. Gradually the old claims have been revived, and from 1830 till to-day they have been vigorously pushed. Lord Morpeth and his officers in 1849 (*ante*, p. 592) were fully persuaded that no one could hold foreshore without shewing a grant *in specie*, and that no lost grant could be presumed, and in this they follow Hall, who wrote his treatise in 1830. The Nullum Tempus Acts are disregarded. "When the Crown's claim is doubtful, it "is to proceed," says Sir T. Farrer, "as if it were good;" the subject is denied his right to a jury if it can possibly be managed, but the moment a jury is called in to try the question of fact, and there is nothing else to try, the Crown shrinks from the contest, and either gives it up or compounds with the defendant. It is clear, therefore, that it behoves all defendants in informations as to foreshore to stand upon their right to an issue, and to insist that the question of law and fact shall be tried before they are put to the cost, vexation, and delay of answer, interrogatories, discovery, exceptions, and amended, re-amended, and further re-amended informations. The subject must be entitled to try his right by the proper tribunal, the only tribunal by which the question of fact as to whether the foreshore is parcel of his manor or not can rightly be determined. The Courts have never but once (Attorney *v.* Philpott) denied him such right. The jury is his safeguard against the encroachments of the Crown. It is his right by Magna Charta and by the statute of James, and to deprive him of it by an ingenious suggestion of equity for the Crown is a violation of all constitutional privilege. It may be answered that it is not denied him; it lies in the *discretion of the Court* whether he is to have it; but, as Baron Wood says, the Crown "would, in fact, most

21 Jac. I. c. 2, c. 14.

"strenuously oppose it," and he holds that is not a matter of discretion, but a matter of right. Again, if it be not denied him by the present procedure, it is practically denied him, for if he is to answer interrogatories discovering his documents so that the Crown may pick holes in his title on any technicality, and, having found out some blot on his title or imperfection in his evidence, may amend the information to suit its own case; if the Crown is allowed to put him to extravagant expense and inordinate delay until his witnesses are dead and his evidence lost, without control of the Court, *before* the issue of fact can be tried, his right is indeed practically denied him. This cannot be the law, and if it is, then, I repeat, it is high time that her Majesty's judges took steps to put an end to the abuse of this procedure, and this attempt to revive the extortions and iniquities of the reigns of James the First and Charles the First.

It may be answered that as regards discovery a defendant to an equity information is in no worse a position than a defendant to a suit between subject and subject under the Judicature Acts. There could, of course, be very little objection to discovery as regulated by the principles which guide the Courts in ordinary litigation, although the practice would be clearly contrary to the spirit and intention of the statutes of 21 James I. cap. 2 et 14, which were passed for the very purpose of preventing the Crown from prying into men's titles with a view to discover defects in them whereon to issue a "fishing grant," or to file an information on a pretence of concealment, and the subject would have an equivalent advantage of getting discovery from the Crown, which it cannot now do.[1] But the grievance is that the Crown uses the knowledge gained by discovery to delay the suit and keep the defendant from a trial. It amends the information to suit its own case, and then, having seen the defendant's case, it endeavours to overthrow him by taking exceptions to his answer; if it fails in this, it exercises its prerogative in delaying the suit

[1] No person who is concerned against the Crown is permitted to search records at the Land Revenue Office.

indefinitely, and the defendant cannot get to trial, however much he may desire it. The Crown will not join issue, and (it is alleged) cannot be forced to do so, and thus it can prolong the litigation by amended, re-amended, further re-amended, and further further re-amended informations, at terrible cost to the defendant, indefinitely, arbitrarily, and to any extent. Thus the defendant is practically denied his rights, and is kept from a trial till his old witnesses may be dead and his case hopeless, and he has no alternative but to submit to have the price demanded by the Crown for its theoretical right to the foreshore extorted from him, as it had perhaps been more than once extorted from his predecessors by "fishing grants" and pretences of concealments in the arbitrary reigns of Elizabeth and James before Parliament found it necessary to put an end, as it thought, to this process of extortion by those statutes of 21 James I. cap. 2 et 14, which were passed specially for the protection of the subject in cases of this kind.

Assuming that the Crown, in informations for foreshore upon the allegation of its theoretical right and title in law, has a right (while refusing to give discovery) to get discovery from a defendant who has been in possession for twenty years, notwithstanding the statute of 21 James I. cap. 14, it is submitted that, having regard to the circumstances under which that statute was passed, and the purpose for which it was passed, the Crown ought not to be at liberty to practically evade the effect of that statute by delaying justice to the subject as it now does. It has been decided that the Court cannot dismiss the Attorney-General's information, although it is matter of doubt whether, if the Attorney-General does not proceed, the Court may not give judgment for the defendant as if the Attorney-General had confessed the plea.[1] It was alleged by Clarke, B., in 1744, that the Court had done it: "If

[1] King *v.* Musters, Parker 50; Att. *v.* Eyton, 6 Price 85; King *v.* Evans, 6 Price 480; Wall *v.* Att.-General, 11 Price 706; King *v.* Slee, 1 M. & Y. 361; Peto *v.* Att.-General, 1 Y. & J. 509; Regina *v.* Ray, 9 M. & W. 761; Att. *v.* Ray, 11 M. & W. 464.

"the Court could not do it, there have been times when "such a power of keeping the suit hanging over the "defendant might have been made an ill use of."[1] The point, however, is doubtful, and the Courts in recent times have held that they have no power to make an order on the Attorney-General. But if the Court has no power to prevent the Crown from making use of the knowledge which it gains from discovery to prolong the litigation indefinitely and to harass the subject by all this vexatious process (the rules as to the regulation of which are practically unknown), then it is submitted that the subject ought to have the benefit of the statute of James, and to be enabled to refuse discovery "until the title be tried, found, "and adjudged for the King;" if this be not so, then the statute is of no avail, and the Crown is just as able, though by another process, to oppress the subject in these matters as completely and fully as it did before the statute was passed.[2]

Surely, therefore, it is time that some new rules were made. Let the judges make a simple rule to get rid of the exceptions of Order 62, and let proceedings in equity informations be conducted under the Rules of the Judicature Acts. No injustice can be done to the Crown. Time would be granted to the Attorney-General in all cases where it was reasonable and necessary, and then the subject might try the issue between him and the Crown fairly and properly, either before a jury or upon a special case, and without unnecessary cost. It is plain that injustice is done to the subject under the present procedure, and that he is unjustly crushed with costs and delay. In many cases, no doubt, his title may be bad or incapable of proof; but there is no reason that

1 The Court will control the Attorney-General when his privilege is sought to be made use of for the purpose of accomplishing that which between party and party could not be done: Peto *v.* Att.-General, 1 Y. & J. 509, per Macdonald, C.B. See also Cocker *v.* Tempest, 7 M. & W. 502; Reg. *v.* Prosser, 11 Beav. 306, 18 L. J. Ch. 35, 13 Jur. 71; Att. of Prince of Wales *v.* Crossman, 4 H. & C. 568; Campbell's "Lives of the Lord Chancellors," ii. 173.

2 See Att. *v.* Parsons, 2 M. & W. 24; Att. *v.* Brown, 14 M. & W. 300; Att. *v.* Lord Churchill, 8 M. & W. 171.

he should therefore be denied a trial with reasonable speed and without extravagant expense. It is time that this antiquated and almost unknown practice, which has been so carefully preserved through all the salutary amendments made in the law of procedure in modern times, should be swept away. It is used to work injustice. The times have come again when, as Baron Clarke says, "the power of keeping the suit hanging over the defend-"ant has been made an ill use of." Parliament has recognised that, and has declared that it is bad and requires amendment; part of the oppression worked by it as to costs has been abolished, and power is given to the judges to complete the work. It is hoped, therefore, now that the history of the dealings of the Crown with the subject in respect of the foreshore have been fully set out, that her Majesty's judges will lose no time in sweeping away once and for ever this relic of the arbitrary proceedings of the bad old times, which works so much oppression and wrong to the subject, and brings (as Lord Hale said) nothing but undeserved odium upon the Crown.[1]

Crown Suits Act, 1855, s. 3.

[1] "Nulli vendemus nulli negabimus aut differemus justitiam vel rectum" (Magna Carta, cap. 29). "It is required by the common "law that *plena et celeris* justitia fiat partibus, not *plena* alone, nor "*celeris* alone, but both plena et celeris" (Coke, 4 Inst. 67). All writs are "*sine dilatione*" (*ibid.*). "We cannot, nor will not, delay on the strength of our oath" (per Shardelowe, J., 18 Edward III. 54a). By statute 20 Edward III. cap. 2 (repealed by 42 & 43 Victoria, cap. 59), it is enacted that the Barons of the Exchequer "shall do right and reason "to all our subjects great and small, and that they shall deliver the "people reasonably and *without delay* of the business which they have "to do before them *without undue tarrying*, as hath been done in "times past." (See the oath of the barons, Price, "Hist. of Exchequer," p. 48, also chapter 10; and observations on the equity of the Exchequer, Att. *v.* Wall, 11 Price 710.) "The duties of the King's "ministers in his Court of Exchequer have been well described in a "book as old as the reign of King Henry II. to have for object 'ut "'Regis utilitati prospiciant,' qualified by the condition 'salva tamen "'equitate.' The jurisdiction in equity of the Court of Exchequer, it "should be observed, must necessarily, as between Crown and subject, "be always exercised as *against* the King, who can have no equities "there, even his equitable demands being all treated as matter of "right in that court, which was purposely created for the establishment, "protection, and recovery of the rights of the Crown."

CHAPTER XXV.

SUMMARY.

THE ground upon which the *primâ facie* claim of the Crown rests is the allegation that the Crown has seldom or never parted with the foreshore to the subject, but has from the earliest time retained it as part of the waste dominions of the Crown. Here, of course, we speak of the *jus privatum*, or right of property in the foreshore, which the Crown may alienate, in contradistinction to the *jus publicum*, which is inalienable, and survives for the benefit of the public whether the Crown retains the foreshore or grants it to a subject. It is nowhere alleged that the Crown has *never* parted with any portions of the foreshore; it is always admitted that at any rate in some places it has so parted with it. The truth or untruth of the theory, and the relative value and weight of the presumption in favour of the Crown which is based upon it, depend, therefore, on a question of fact. If the records of the realm were perfect from the Conquest, and it could, by reference to them, be proved that before the time of King John, or before the time of Queen Elizabeth, the Crown had actually and *de facto* granted away the whole of the foreshore as parcel of the sea-coast manors, there would be an end of the theory, and of the presumption based upon it; but the earlier records of the realm are lost, and we are unable actually to prove the whole of the true facts; we can only prove some of them. Hitherto, from want of proper research, and from the constant reiteration of the *primâ facie* theory in *obiter dicta* of judges and text writers based upon imperfect knowledge of the facts, an impression has generally prevailed, both in the lay and legal mind, and especially in the official mind, that the

Crown has in fact only parted with a few isolated portions of the foreshore. Now, if that were true in fact, the theory would raise a presumption of very powerful inference in favour of the Crown, and it would be the duty of the Courts to very jealously regard claims made to foreshore, and the evidence upon which they were based; because, if it were true that the Crown had but very seldom parted with it, there would be a large probability that the claim put forward was a claim based rather upon usurpation than upon lost grant, for, if it were true that instances of real grant were few, the chance that the *locus in quo* in the case in question was within one of such grants would be disproportionate to the chance that the place in question was part of the larger portion of the foreshore which the Crown had in fact retained. But now we find that the records which remain clearly shew that instead of the Crown having largely retained the foreshore as part of the waste dominions of the realm, it has in fact parted with it in almost every portion of the coast. This being so, how are we to look upon the theory? We must say:—True it may be the Crown may by possibility have retained the shore (though not a single instance of any specific reservation of it can be shewn); but it is clear from the records, so far as we have them remaining, that by far the larger portion of the foreshore of this kingdom has been granted out and vested in the subject by the grants of Saxon kings and the confirmations and grants of Norman kings in almost every part of the coast. Then, if this be proved, and a claim be made to foreshore, evidenced by long usage and possession, how should the Courts regard it? Clearly not as probably arising from usurpation, but rather as arising from a legal origin by grant, because, the facts assumed upon the theory being reversed, the probabilities are reversed also; and the evidence must be looked upon, not as evidence pointing to probable usurpation, but as evidence pointing by the strongest inference of presumption to lost grant. In short, we are not driven, as is so often the case in questions of the construction of evidence of ancient usage, to search ingeniously to discover a *possible* legal origin for the usage and possession ; for we have ready to our hands, not only a *possible*, but a *highly probable* legal origin ; and it is submitted that, in accordance with the principles of construction of such ancient usages in other cases, the Courts are bound to construe acts of ownership most strongly in favour of the presumption of the *high probability* that the Crown *has* granted the foreshore, rather than in favour of the *bare possibility* that is has *not* done so.

We will now consider what the remnant of the ancient records, so far as we have been able to search them, and that only imperfectly, goes to shew. The evidence of the Saxon charters clearly proves that the foreshore passed by them ; and this is strongly confirmed by the manner in which Edward the Confessor, the Conqueror, and the early Norman kings confirmed privileges to the monasteries in their lands *in terra et mari*, *on strond and on stream*, *on tide and off tide*, shewing that their lands were clearly understood to extend generally over, and to include, the foreshore. We have remaining only some few of these confirmations to ecclesiastical corporations ; that similar ones were made to laymen there can be very little doubt, but they have perished in the lapse of time. Some of the early charters no doubt specifically convey the shore, notably those made by subjects, but the greater number of the charters that remain to us are in general terms. The large majority of the grants of sea-coast manors are wholly lost. We have shewn, however, that by the end of the reign of King John practically all the manors on the sea-coast had been granted out by the Crown. Such of the grants as are in existence shew no reservation of the shore, but the majority are lost ; we are therefore driven to ascertain the nature of them by evidence of the use which has been made of the shore by the grantees of those manors in subsequent ages, in order to see whether they have claimed it as their own, and whether, when they have so claimed it, the Crown has denied their right ; for if, when a claim has been made to the shore as parcel of a fee or parcel of a manor in a suit between the Crown and a subject, the Crown has not

Ante, pp. 1-14.
Ante, pp. 17-21.
Ante, p. 24.

traversed the allegation that the shore is parcel of the subject's manor in any wise, it must be taken that, at any rate so far as that particular manor was concerned, the officers of the Crown were aware that the foreshore had been granted with the manor, and that they admitted that it belonged to the subject. This brings us to the consideration of the claims to wreck of the sea described in the earlier part of this treatise. It will be found that, almost without exception, the claims are made by the claimants to take the wreck *super terram meam—super terram manerii—quantum feodum meum se extendit super mare—in toto feodo meo ubi abuttat super mare—per totam marinam—per totam baroniam—per omnes terras super mare—per omnes terras suas jacentes juxta mare—ubi acciderit super feodum ecclesiæ—per omnes terras suas juxta litus maris* in Hapsburgh—*applicans in terris suis—infra procinctum manerii sui—infra dominium suum*—and by every possible expression to shew that the wreck was claimed to be taken *upon the land* of the claimant. In no case does the Crown challenge this claim to the soil; it is universally admitted; and even where the wreck has been wrongly claimed, and is taken away by order of the Court, the lord of the manor's claim to the soil is not challenged, and he is left in possession of it. It is clear that it was admitted; and when the Prior of Wymondham was ordered to deliver up a derelict ship which had come ashore in his manor, the crew having escaped, the King in his writ says that the ship came *ad terram infra dominium vestrum apud villam Hapsburgh.*[1] As it is clear, therefore, that in the times of

Ante, pp. 75, 77.

Ante, p. 161.

[1] The cases in which the wreck is not claimed as upon the soil of the manor appear to be as follows:—The case of the wapentake of Langburgh (*ante*, pp. 48, 81, 470), where the wreck is claimed *inter metas* from Yarm to Rymeswick, and had been granted to Peter de Brus, the lord of the barony of Skelton, but whose barony did not include all the manors on the sea-coast. Yet, nevertheless, we find that some of these manors have the foreshore as parcel, although the wreck is in other hands. In the case of the lordship marcher of Chepstow (p. 247) there is a claim to wreck *inter metas*, but there also we see that a manor on the coast has the shore as parcel of it. These two cases are the only ones that have been found where the wreck was not claimed as

Edward the First and Edward the Second the Crown admitted, contrary to the theory since invented, that the foreshore was parcel of a considerable number of manors upon the sea-coast, let us consider to what extent over the coast these admissions apply, premising always that, although we have discovered a great many of these proceedings between the Crown and the subject as to wreck, we have by no means discovered all of them, and the probabilities are that many more will be discovered, and also that many which have existed have been lost. We will, however, deal with those which we have, and if we look at them, and compare them with the map of the coast, we find that they cover almost the whole of the sea-coast of Yorkshire and Lincolnshire, that of Norfolk almost without an exception, nearly the entire coast of Suffolk and of Essex, the whole of Kent and Sussex, a large portion of Hampshire, the Isle of Wight, nearly the entire coast of Dorsetshire, by far the greater part of Devonshire, a large proportion of Cornwall and Somersetshire, parts of Wales, almost the whole of Cheshire, Lancashire, Westmoreland, and Cumberland. Durham and Northumberland were early granted to the Earls of Northumberland

granted to be taken *upon* the manor. The following cases at first sight appear to exclude the idea that it was so claimed, but on examination it is found not to be so. A presentment is made (p. 56) that the Earl Warren has wreck *ex opposito terrarum suarum* in the soke of Gymingham, but when he is challenged by quo warranto (p. 90) he claims it *ubique in terris suis in soka de Gymingham juxta litus maris*. Henry de Grey (p. 56) is presented as taking it *ex opposito terræ suæ de Syringham*, but his successor claims it (p. 90) *super litus maris in terris suis de Shiringham;* and the claim to the shore is not traversed. In the presentments for the county of Sussex (p. 65) several persons are presented as taking wreck *contra terras suas*, but on the quo warranto (pp. 77, 78) we find that they claim *per omnes terras et feoda sua jacentes juxta mare*. In Sussex, also, there are claims to wreck in the rapes and hundreds of the county, but these we find to be conterminous with ancient baronies, and the claim is in right of the barony (pp. 67, 75, 76, 77). Therefore, with the exception of the case of the wapentake of Langburgh and the case of Chepstow, all cases of wreck hitherto discovered point to grants of wreck *infra manerium*, and the presumption is that the shore was parcel of those manors on which the wreck was to be taken.

and the Bishops of Durham. In Durham the *regalia* belonged to the bishops, who for the most part retained them in their own hands, but sub-infeudated many of the manors with the foreshores to their tenants. In Northumberland there are several cases as to wreck, and the earls have sub-infeudated the manors with their foreshores in that county to their tenants.

Thus we see that with regard to almost all the coasts of the kingdom the lords of the manors distinctly and unquestionably claimed the foreshore, and that the Crown did not in any way challenge or deny their claim. It must be recollected that at this period the *primâ facie* theory had not been invented. We will next turn to the evidence which exists of the view which the Crown at this period took of its rights over the foreshore. It is clear, from the elaborate inquisition of the Hundred Rolls and the presentments in eyre, that the Crown Officers and Justices were well aware that the *jus privatum* had been alienated to the lords of the manors all round the coast, and that only the *jus publicum* remained vested in the Crown for the benefit of the public. There is no instance of a presentment of a purpresture upon the *jus privatum* except opposite to manors which had remained in the hands of the Crown. The nature of the presentments of encroachment on the *jus publicum* shews that it was admitted and well understood that the *jus privatum* of the foreshore was vested in the subject, and it was only when he exercised his rights in derogation of the *jus publicum* that a presentment was made against him—*e.g.*, as when he made weirs or built wharves upon the shore to the hindrance of navigation: see the case of the Colne (pp. 50, 88), the case of the Orwell (p. 64), and others. Then if we look (p. 75) at the case of the Crown as custos of the honour of Arundel against the lord of the manor of Middleton, we see that the Crown clearly admits that the foreshore of Middleton was parcel of that manor, although in the case in question the Crown was directly interested in denying the fact. Then, again (p. 95), we find the Crown suing for a trespass on the foreshore, not setting up any claim under the *primâ facie* title, but claiming as the lord of a manor under a grant from a subject. The case is the same in the case of Sutton Pool (pp. 314, 350), where the foreshore of the manor of Trematon passed to the Duchy in the time of Henry III. by the grant of a subject. Again, in the case of the Dart, the Water of Dart with its foreshore was parcel of the barony of Totnes, and passed to the Crown in the time of Edward the First by grant from Nicholas de Tewksbury, and afterwards by charter to the Duchy of Cornwall. The justices of Cheshire (p. 154) admit the claims of the lords of the manors on the Dee and Mersey to the mid-stream; King Richard the Second (p. 161) admits that the foreshore is parcel of the manor of Hapsburgh; and, in short, it has been shewn that, notwithstanding the most minute inquisitions as to encroachments upon the property of the Crown from the time of Henry the Third to that of Elizabeth, there is not a trace of any suggestion that the Crown laid any claim to the *jus privatum* of the foreshore, and the Crown sued for foreshore as parcel of a manor, and not in right of the prerogative, down to 5 Elizabeth, A.D. 1562. There can be no doubt that before Mr. Digges invented the *primâ facie* theory, in 1568, the clear presumption of law in England, as in Scotland down to 1849, was that the sea-coast manors extended to the low-water mark. The only case which in any way suggests that the Crown had any claim in respect of the *jus privatum* upon the foreshore is the case of the Prior of Tynemouth (p. 111), but that case has, it is submitted, been clearly shewn to relate to an infringement of the *jus publicum*, and not to a purpresture upon the *jus privatum*, and Hale, notwithstanding that he cites the case (pp. 345, 359, 363) in support of the theory of the *primâ facie* title, clearly doubted whether the judgment was given for the Crown with regard to the soil, for he says (p. 359), "but no parti-"cular judgment given as I remember as to that point." The suit was a suit in the name of the King, but on behalf of the Corporation of Newcastle, who had not the soil of the port, and the suit was properly brought in the

King's name, because it was a suit to suppress a public nuisance in a public port, for, as Hale says (p. 336), "by "the laws of England in all things of public interest "which concern all, and not any one particular person, "the law hath transferred the care and provision for such "public matters to the King, and he doth *sustinere personam vindicis et tutoris jurium publicorum*, as highways, "navigable rivers, and the like, although the particular "interest of franchise or propriety may possibly belong to "a private person; and therefore all suits and proceedings "in such cases are *pro domino Rege*." The suit was in the nature of an indictment for making a purpresture upon a public port, and the King's name was used as the defender of the *jus publicum*, upon which the Prior had encroached by erecting houses and wharves upon the foreshore of his manor, which interfered with the public exercise of the port and the due maintenance of it. These are decreed to be a purpresture; they are said to have been built *super solum quod domini Regi esse debet eo quod fluxu et inundatione maris comprehenditur;* that is. that they have been built upon the soil, which is subject to the *jus publicum* for navigation and passage, which belongs to the King under the *jus publicum*, for the King is acting in this suit as *vindex et tutor jurium publicorum*, and not to the King by reason of the *jus privatum*, for we have shewn that the foreshore belonged to the Prior before the suit, is admitted to belong to him in the suit, and belongs to the Duke of Northumberland, his successor in title, at the present day, subject always to the *jus publicum*, which the Prior, by his act of building the wharves, had interfered with. The judgment, therefore, does not support the *primâ facie* theory of the right of the Crown to the *jus privatum* of the foreshore, but aptly illustrates the power of the Crown to abate purprestures and nuisances upon the *jus publicum* in ports; and this clearly was the opinion of Hale. This is the one solitary case which appears to give any ground for a suggestion that the Crown claimed the *jus privatum* in the foreshore in the time of Edward the First, and it is submitted that, on careful examination

See also p. 355.

of it, it does not support that theory, but, on the contrary, shews there is no foundation for it.

The dictum of Hale (p. 394), "that perchance the fore-"shore is parcel almost of all such manors as by prescrip-"tion have royal fish or wrecks of the sea within their "manors," and the very weighty presumption which arises from such possession, has been a stumbling-block to the supporters of the *primâ facie* title from the time of its first commencement. Mr. Digges (pp. 189, 203, 205, 207) takes the bull by the horns, and argues that wreck being *primâ facie* vested in the Crown, it is evidence that the foreshore belonged to the Crown ; but we must recollect that Mr. Digges held that the subject could only hold foreshore by express grant *in specie*. In the case of Rex *v.* Oldsworth (p. 299), Sir John Banks, the Attorney-General, when discussing Sir Henry Constable's case, was driven to contend that the wreck might be thrown *above* the high-water mark. Hall wilfully misrepresents Lord Hale's meaning, and struggles vigorously to shake the presumption arising from the perception of wreck *infra manerium*. Phear, in his excellent treatise, does not touch the matter. Jerwood tries to avoid the difficulty by the absurd suggestion that *infra* means *below*. That Hale's argument, that it is a great presumption that the shore is parcel of the manors that have wreck of the sea *infra manerium*, is, as Lord Ellenborough said, "an argument "of powerful influence," there can be no doubt ; and now that we have seen to what an extent of coast this argument applies, we are not surprised, knowing, as we do, how well Hale was acquainted with records, that he should have stated his proposition so fully, or that he should say, as he does (at p. 364), after quoting Sir Henry Constable's case and the Archbishop of Canterbury's case, that "the cases above, "*and likewise ordinary experience*, prove that it [the fore-"shore] is most ordinarily parcel of the adjoining land ;" "and in most places where the subject by prescription "hath wreck he hath commonly the shore on which it "hath a kind of dependence : thus, if my memory much "fail me not, the Earls of Cornwall have anciently had by

King *v.* Ellis, 1 M. & S. 662.

"prescription *bona wreccata per totum comitatum;* therefore "the right of the shore there belongs to him and his tenants "as an usual concomitant." And, again (p. 366): "It "[the shore] is a coherent incident or parcel, and so claimed, "and therefore, although Brook rightly observes on the "case 8 Henry VI. 16, that a man can never make title "to land by prescription as a thing in gross, yet as an "incident (as unto an office), *or as parcel of my manor* "or *ratione alterius rei,* a man may make title to it by "prescription or custom." It is clear that Hale was aware of the proceedings as to wreck which have been set out in this treatise, and, now that we have shewn that the lords of the manors almost all round the coast have wreck by prescription within their manors, the powerful inference arising upon Hale's dictum almost conclusively shews that the whole of the foreshore had been granted out by the Crown in fact long before this theory of the *primâ facie* title was invented.

I should have thought it almost unnecessary to prove that wreck and royal fish can only be taken upon the foreshore; the proposition would seem to be self-evident; but, as the advisers of the Crown have even so recently as the case of Attorney *v.* Emerson been driven to follow the lead of Sir John Banks, and to charge in their information that wreck in the manor of Wakering was only taken within the inland waters and not upon the open sea, and that fishery crofts whereon kiddels to catch fish were placed on land *above* the high-water mark, it becomes necessary shortly to shew that wreck and royal fish are taken upon the sea-shore. If the reader will refer to the pages indicated in the note[1] he will find ample evidence to prove that wreck comes on to the foreshore. At p. 95, in particular, he will see that wreck was *super litus maris apulsa.* At p. 150, *ex impetu fluctuum maris jactabantur super terram in litore maris infra hameletum prædictum.* Sir John Constable's case (p. 224) is conclusive on the point, and also Sir Henry Constable's case (p. 233). What is,

[1] Pp. 35, 75, 82, 89, 97, 139, 141, 143, 145, 146, 150, 151, 160, 161, 167, 246, 247; Hale, *ante*, p. 364.

and what is not, wreck is settled by the case of Rex *v.* 49 Casks of Brandy (*ante*, p. 467), and numberless other cases might be cited.

Dickens *v.* Shaw, ante, p. 451.

It has been rightly held that the mere perception of wreck without shewing that the right to it arises in respect of a grant of wreck *infra manerium* is not sufficient of itself to give a title to the shore, and this is obviously accurate, because we have shewn, in the case of the wapentake of Langburgh, that the wreck was clearly granted *inter metas*, and not *infra manerium*, for in that wapentake the manors were not all held of one barony, and there can be no presumption that the wreck was granted *infra baroniam* in such a way as to raise the presumption that the foreshore was parcel of the barony before the grant of the wreck was made. Again, in the case of the lordship of Chepstow (*ante*, p. 247), we find the wreck over a long district of the shore in the hands of one person, and the foreshore of a manor within that district in the hands of another, but whether that district was ever one great barony of which the manor within it was anciently parcel we know not; but, having regard to the arguments in Attorney-General *v.* Phillips, *ante*, p. 511, it probably was. In cases of the baronies in the county of Sussex we have a similar state of things, of which the case of the manor of Middleton (p. 75) is an example; there the King, in right of the honour of Arundel, had the wreck, and the lord of the manor of Middleton, which was a sub-manor of the honour, had the foreshore. The manner in which this state of things arises is as follows:—The King grants the barony or honour, comprising a number of manors over a large district of the coast, and by his grant conveys the entire foreshore of the district, and then grants the wreck to be taken *infra honorem* or *infra baroniam*. The lord of the honour or barony then sub-infeudates the sea-coast manor with the foreshore to his vassal, but retains the right to wreck, and thus one man has the foreshore and another the wreck; and this obtains very generally in the county of Sussex (see pp. 75–77). Thus it will be seen that the rights to

Ante, pp. 48, 81, 470, 641.

foreshore and wreck are not *necessarily* (though they are usually) concomitant. They depend upon separate titles by separate grants, and the weight of the presumption that the shore is parcel of the manor when the lord takes wreck depends wholly upon the question whether the wreck is claimed by a grant which must be presumed to be a distinct grant from the grant of the manor, and to be a grant giving the lord of the manor a right to take the wreck *within* or *upon* the manor. When the grant is of that nature, the presumption that arises is— Hale, p. 364, ante.

i. That the manor was granted together with the foreshore;

ii. That the wreck was granted to be taken *within* and *upon* that manor; and, therefore,

iii. That the foreshore must have been parcel of that manor, because the wreck to be taken can only be taken upon the foreshore.

But the moment it is shewn, as has been done, that the right to the foreshore and the right to the wreck may, either by force of the original grant of the wreck or by the severance of the two rights when in the hands of the subject, be vested in different persons, it becomes impossible to argue that because a man has wreck simply, he therefore has the shore; and this is what was decided in Dickens *v.* Shaw. In that case the presentment, noted at p. 39, that the Earl Warren claimed wreck thrown *upon his land* in the manor of Brighton was not produced, and, indeed, there was but very slight evidence given of taking wreck at all, and there was no evidence of any other user of the shore or interference with acts done there. The judges, therefore, rightly concluded that the evidence was insufficient to raise the presumption of a grant of the shore. It follows, from what has been said, that Hale has quite rightly stated his proposition, for he qualifies it by saying, "*perchance* it is parcel," and it would be wholly wrong to omit such qualification. The Courts, therefore, rightly hold that the right to wreck alone is not evidence of the right to the foreshore, but have laid it down that the right to wreck *coupled with other user of the shore* suffices See case of the manor of Middleton, ante, p. 75.

Ante, pp. 453, 472, 475, 476, 539, 543, 544, 552, 554, 571.

to presume a grant; but with regard to cases, of which so many have been set out in the previous part of this treatise, where the Crown has challenged the right to wreck, and the subject has pleaded that he takes it *upon his fee*, and the Crown has not traversed or challenged the allegation that the shore is parcel of his fee, we have no dictum or decision to shew that such a claim so made, and not traversed, and followed by perception of wreck whenever it happens, down to modern times, is not to be held evidence, even if unsupported by other user, that the soil has passed. It is submitted that in such a case it would be sufficient evidence; but the case is hardly likely to arise, because it almost always happens that the lord of a manor can shew other acts of ownership, as by fishing with fixed engines, taking seaweed and sand, &c. &c., to support his claim. If, therefore, the mere perception of wreck, independent of any record as above specified, *coupled with other user*, is held to be sufficient to presume a grant, *a fortiori* the perception of wreck emphasized by such record of ancient claim to the soil unchallenged by the Crown will, when coupled with other user, necessarily presume a grant. This being so, it follows that, having regard to the numerous instances of claims to wreck *super feodum, infra manerium, super terras*, &c., above set out (assuming that the present lords of those manors can shew other acts of ownership), it is capable of proof that by far the greater portion of the foreshore of this kingdom had passed into the hands of the subjects before the reign of Edward the First; and that, although the original grants, by the loss of the ancient records of the realm and by the lapse of time, have disappeared, the evidence of the records above quoted, coupled with modern usage, will be sufficient to raise the presumption that those grants which are lost did convey the foreshore to the subject. What, then, having regard to these facts, is the weight of the presumption in favour of the *primâ facie* title? It would seem to be reduced to this: There is a presumption under the theory, *not* that only a small portion of the foreshore has been granted out, but a presumption that *scarcely any of the foreshore remains in the Crown.* We have now for the first time brought to light the true facts with regard to this theory. The judges who, from the time of Hale downwards, have asserted and reiterated this doctrine appear to have asserted it as though they believed that it was the fact that scarcely any of the foreshore had been granted out. They have given out their *dicta* always *obiter*, in ignorance of the true facts of the case, for until recent years the records were a closed book. They have asserted it on the faith of Hale, whose authorities are the case of the Prior of Tynemouth and Attorney *v.* Philpott, and who only put it forward as a bare theory of law, and almost says it is not generally true in fact. Can it be supposed for a moment that if those learned judges had known the true facts with regard to these claims to wreck; if they had known the history of the case of Attorney *v.* Philpott, and that it was decided by corrupt judges under pressure from King Charles the First, and was wholly ineffectual; had they known the true history of the Prior of Tynemouth's case, can it for one moment be believed that they would have laid down the law so steadfastly and firmly as they have done, until, by the constant reiteration of this untrue theory, it has come to be generally believed that the Crown did not in the original part with the foreshore, and that the claims to it are in almost every case based upon usurpation and not upon right?[1]

It has, however, been shewn that the grants of Saxon kings passed the shore; that the confirmations by Norman

[1] The principal cases in which the dictum has been laid down are as follows:—A.D. 1667 (p. 414), Kirby *v.* Gibbs, 2 Keble 294; 1671 (p. 415), Whitaker *v.* Wise, 2 Keble 759; 1676 (p. 417), Att. *v.* Farmer, 2 Lev. 172, Sir T. Raym. 241, 2 Mod. 105; 1795, Att. *v.* Richards, per Macdonald, C.B., *obiter*, but Hale and Att. *v.* Philpott were cited by Att.-Gen.; 1811, Att. *v.* Parmeter; 1811, Parmeter *v.* Gibbs, per Lord Eldon, *obiter*; 1819 (p. 444), Rex *v.* Lord Grosvenor; 1821 (p. 445), Blundell *v.* Caterall; 1821 (p. 447), Chad *v.* Tilsed; 1822 (p. 449), Att. *v.* Burridge, per Richards, C.B., *obiter*—"It is a doctrine of ancient "establishment that the shore between the high and low water marks "belongs *primâ facie* to the King, but it is equally clear that the "King may grant his private right therein to his subjects." And this has been followed in all subsequent cases. But see Lestrange *v.* Rowe, *ante*, p. 543, per Erle, C.J.

kings acknowledged that it had passed. At the time of the Conquest the transference of the Saxon estates to the Norman owners brought about no change in the nature and extent of those estates (*ante*, p. 15). We have shewn that in a few grants which remain, made by private individuals in the early Norman period, the shore is conveyed as parcel of the manor. Other grants, whether by the King or by private persons, in general terms are held to pass the shore if modern evidence of user be forthcoming to expound them.

Duke of Beaufort *v.* Swansea, 3 Exch. 413; case of the Barons of Berkley, ante, p. 306; Att.-Gen. *v.* Portsmouth, ante, p. 555.

We have further shewn that the lords of manors upon the sea-coast claimed practically the whole of the foreshore in the reign of Edward the First, and their claim passed unchallenged. Also that the Crown, when it claimed the foreshore, claimed it as parcel of its manors down to 1562, and that no purpresture upon the *jus privatum* was ever presented, except in the King's own manors, down to that period. Then, in 1569, we first come upon the theory that the Crown had scarcely ever parted with the foreshore, and that the subject could not hold it except by the King's express grant. Now, what is the value of the theory, what is the true presumption arising from it, in the face of these facts? There is scarcely a shadow of presumption in favour of the Crown; the presumption is all the other way, and it is submitted that, when the subject sets up the title to foreshore, and produces evidence of it by such acts of ownership as might necessarily have beneficially been exercised by any prudent or reasonable owner of such foreshore, having regard to its situation, nature, and capabilities for profitable use, there is but one presumption which can with reason and justice be made, and that presumption is that these acts of ownership are attributable, and can only be attributable, to a legal origin arising upon a title by a lost grant from one of the ancient kings: and it is submitted that there is practically no presumption that such acts are attributable to usurpation and encroachment. It is to be hoped, therefore, now that the true facts are known, that in cases relating to foreshore the Courts will regard the evidence of acts of user produced by the subject with a more favourable eye, and not treat them, as there has been a strong tendency to treat them, as attributable to usurpation. Whether or not the acts shewn are sufficient of themselves to raise the necessary presumption of a grant will of course be a question of fact to be determined in every case either by the Court, or more properly by a jury, or else by means of a special case stated under section 10 of the Crown Suits Act, 1859. But whatsoever the nature of the acts may be, it is submitted that they must, having regard to the facts now at last brought to light, be looked upon and weighed, not as acts of usurpation, but as acts of ownership.

The general conclusions which result from the cases referred to in this treatise may be briefly stated as follows :—

1. That in theory of law the foreshore and the soil of the sea and the arms thereof were originally, at the time of the Conquest, vested in the Crown as part of the waste dominions of the realm ; this, however, is mere theory, and wholly incapable of being proved in fact ; for in Saxon times questionless the greater part of the foreshore was out of the Crown. The Conquest changed not this state of things otherwise than in theory. The Conqueror confirmed or re-granted the Saxon estates, and re-granted with them the foreshores as parcel thereof, for there is no instance of any such reservation ; it clearly was never contemplated ; subsequent confirmations of liberties and franchises to be exercised " in terra et mari, " on strond and streme, on tyde and off tyde," confirm this view.

2. That, in point of fact, so far as the truth can be ascertained from existing records, the Crown by its ancient grants did pass the foreshore in almost every part of the kingdom to the subject.

3. That Bracton was well aware that this was the fact and purposely omitted the passage in the Institutes which refers to the property in the shore. See p. 33.

4. That there is anterior to the reign of Queen Eliza-

beth not a single record nor any dictum in any treatise on the law which supports the theory of the *primâ facie* title to the *jus privatum* in the foreshore as it was afterwards put forth.

5. That before the reign of Queen Elizabeth it was taken for law that all sea-coast manors and boroughs extended to the low-water mark, whether they were in the hands of the Crown or its subjects.

6. That no instance of an express reservation of the foreshore on a grant by the Crown has been found.

7. That, subject to the exercise of the *jus publicum*—viz., the right of navigation and access, and the right of public fishery when it has not been excluded—the subject may make title to—

a. The foreshore proper—*i.e.*, the soil between the high and low water marks of the medium tides.

b. Accretion by gradual alluvion either to the foreshore when it is in the subject, or to the land above the medium high-water mark when the foreshore is not in the subject, but not to land left derelict by sudden and perceptible reliction by the sea.

c. The soil below low-water mark certainly when situate *inter fauces terræ*, and possibly also upon the open sea, but instances of the latter case are rare.

d. Islands arising in tidal water in cases where the bed and soil of such tidal water were in the subject before the island arose, but not to islands arising in the open sea or tidal rivers where the ownership of the bed has remained in the Crown.

8. That the title of the subject to the foreshore may now be established in any of the following ways:—

a. By modern grant by specific description when it has not been made in derogation of an ancient grant.

b. By ancient grant *in specie* with specific description.

c. By ancient grant in general terms explained by sufficient evidence of modern user.

d. By sufficient evidence of ancient and modern user from which a lost grant may be presumed.

e. By evidence of modern user only sufficient to raise the presumption of a grant.

f. By mediæval grant or re-grant of forfeited or attainted or purchased lands, granting them *adeo plene* and referring back to a former grant, supported by evidence of user.

g. By grant for the amendment of a defective title passing the shore in terms.

h. By evidence of possession under the Statutes of Limitation and Nullum Tempus Acts.

9. That the foreshore and bed of the sea are usually parcel either of a manor or a borough, but may be claimed by a frontager by evidence of user, although he be not a lord of a manor or borough, but presumptively derives his title under such lord. The foreshore may be shewn by evidence of user to be parcel of lands, not being a manor, granted by the Crown with no specific words to pass the foreshore, but only general words explained by the evidence of user to shew that the shore was intended to pass as parcel of the lands so granted.

10. That the owner of the foreshore holds it subject always to the exercise of the *jus publicum*—viz., the rights of public fishery, navigation, access—and, therefore, that evidence of the exercise of these rights by the public does not derogate from his claim.

11. That where, in any case, the public have exercised acts of quasi-ownership, as by trespasses in taking sand, seaweed, stone, &c., from the foreshore without any special licence from the Crown, these acts are not to be construed as acts of adverse possession by the Crown, unless the Crown has given special licence to do them; but evidence of these acts will be taken into consideration as evidence of *contraria possessio*, and will be weighed according to their extent and nature against the weight of the evidence of acts of ownership shewn by the claimant to foreshore, and will be held either to weaken the effect of that evidence or not to affect it according as they have

been constant, uninterrupted, long continued, and important, or trivial and infrequent and not calling for action on the part of the owner of the shore to prevent them.

12. That the owner of foreshore may not use it to the hindrance of navigation nor of public fishery, nor may he dig away the soil of it in such a manner as to expose adjoining land to the inroads or action of the sea; but if the foreshore is washed away by the action of the sea, he is not responsible for the damage which may ensue.

13. That there is at common law no right in the public to dig and carry away sand, stones, seaweed, &c., from the foreshore, whether it remains vested in the Crown or has been granted to a subject.

14. That it is worthy of remark, as shewing the ill-success of the Crown in laying claim to the foreshore from the time of Queen Elizabeth downwards, that, notwithstanding the innumerable commissions of inquiry and returns of foreshore and salt marsh as belonging to the Crown, and the vast numbers of "fishing grants" made upon these returns, we find scarcely an instance in which foreshore or salt marsh is now held by a title under the Crown as an estate separate and distinct from the ownership of the adjoining manors, dating from the period anterior to 1830. Since that date, unquestionably, many such grants of the Crown's "interest" have been made, either to the lords of manors or to individuals, but how far these grants may be held to be valid may be a question in many cases.

With regard to the evidence necessary to support the title to foreshore, it is wholly impossible to lay down any general rules; each case must depend upon its own peculiar circumstances. The nature of the place, the condition of the shore, whether bare, rocky, and unprofitable or sandy and sheltered, or whatever its nature may be, would affect the class of evidence which would be called for as sufficient to establish the title. In many cases the evidence may be ample, in others exceedingly scanty, as where it is a muddy shore, or bare rocky shore, which can only be very slightly used; but it is submitted that the evidence should shew that the owner has done, upon the foreshore in question, practically all such acts as the Crown or its lessees could have done, and might naturally be expected to have done, if the Crown had retained the foreshore in its own possession. There will be a conflict of evidence in almost every case. Acts will be shewn to have been done by members of the public which are not attributable to their rights under the *jus publicum*, as the occasional taking of seaweed in small quantities, digging of sand, gathering of shell-fish, &c.; and in examining this kind of evidence it will be desirable to ascertain whether these acts have been done by the public openly, and as of right, and not by stealth and without the knowledge of the owner, to shew that they have been interfered with from time to time, and that prosecutions have taken place, or that "they have been committed through the absence "of the proprietor, or through his ignorance, partial or "complete, of the acts relied on, or through his neglect or "indifference to them, as not vitally affecting his interest "or position, or as requiring from him, for the purpose "of resistance, effort or expense unjustified by the neces-"sity of the case, or as allowed from kindly or bene-"volent motives to humble people, for a great length of "time."

Neill *v.* Duke of Devonshire, 8 App. Cas. at pp. 153, 156, and 170.

The acts of ownership usually relied upon to shew title to the shore may be classified as follows:—

a. The taking of wreck and royal fish: this franchise, when exercised *infra manerium*, raises a powerful inference that the shore is parcel of the manor. When it has been claimed, upon a quo warranto, to be exercised *infra manerium*, *super feodum*, *super terram*, &c., and the claim to the shore thus set up has not been challenged by the Crown, the inference appears to be irresistible that the foreshore is parcel of the manor within which it has so been claimed. When this franchise has been exercised in such a way as not to raise the presumption that the right to exercise it arises from a grant of wreck to be taken *infra manerium*, the presumption arising is not so strong, and then, in order to shew that the shore is parcel of the manor, user of other kinds must be shewn to raise the presumption of a grant.

b. The exercise of a right of several fishery by weirs and fixed engines upon the shore. Such acts as these Hale considers to be of the highest importance, and, indeed, treats them as conclusive to shew that the soil is parcel of the manor. When these fisheries in sea-coast manors are granted, as is most frequently the case, by copy of court roll, the strongest presumption arises that the soil of the foreshore is parcel of the manor, for the copyholds are parcel of the demesnes, and seisin is delivered of them, and a franchise, which a several fishery must be, if it be not by reason of the soil, is not the subject of tenure, nor can a rent service, and *à fortiori* services and suits, be reserved out of it, nor can livery of seisin be given of it; but of foreshore as parcel of a manor it can. Hale (pp. 385–388) gives several instances and examples of fisheries in tidal waters to shew that the soil was parcel of the fishery and of the manor. The cases of the manor of Burnham and the manor of Radley, cited by him, are in point, for in those manors the fisheries are demised by copy of court roll, and he says that "infinite more of this kind "might be produced." He cites the statutes as to the correction of weirs to shew the existence of this right in the soil. By the statute of 1 Henry IV. cap. 12, *he who hath the freehold* is ordered to abate the weir if it be a nuisance (see p. 163). In Sir Henry Constable's case (*ante*, pp. 236, 239) Popham, C.J., cites a case of copyhold weirs in the sea to shew that the shore may be parcel of the manor; and, indeed, there can now be little doubt that a fishery in tidal water is in fact almost in every case attributable to ownership of the soil, and not to a grant of a particular franchise. The franchise granted is the exclusion of the common law right of fishing. Palles, C.B., in the case of the Duke of Devonshire *v.* Neill (2 L. R. Ir. 132), says: "It appears to me to be beyond dis-"pute that the exclusive right of fishing in tidal waters

Co. Litt. 47a, 142a, 144a; Marshall *v.* Ulleswater Co., 3 B. & S. 732; Callis, 13; Brook, title View, pl. 101; post, p. 706, note (*c*).

"vested in the hands of the Crown is no more than an "incident of the soil over which the waters flowed, as "affected by the exercise of the King's franchise of ex- "cluding the public; and that right can, and generally "does, exist in the subject as an incident of the soil, and "*not as an incorporeal hereditament.*" Of course it may be urged that the Crown may grant the franchise of excluding the public over soil of which it retains the possession. In that case the franchise merely would pass to the grantee. But he could not then demise this franchise in parcels by copy of court roll, reserving rent and services, and making an incorporeal hereditament the subject of tenure, nor could he fix weirs and fixed engines in the soil unless his grant gives him special licence to do so, and no one ever saw such a grant. The idea that a fishery in tidal waters must be an incorporeal hereditament rests mainly upon the report of the case of the Banne Fishery (p. 247), of which Hale exposes the fallacy at pp. 355 and 388. Evidence of the existence, therefore, of a several fishery, especially if worked by fixed engines, and more especially if demised time out of mind by copy of court roll, which raises the presumption that the soil was parcel of the manor from before the statute of *Quia Emptores*, is most important evidence in a claim to foreshore and bed of the sea. In the manors of Chalkwell Hall, Prittlewell Priory, Middleton Hall, Southchurch, Shoebury, Wakering, Foulness, Barling, Packlesham, Burnham, Tollesbury, and other manors in Essex, the foreshore and oyster beds have always been demised by copy of court roll.

c. The taking of anchorage and groundage of vessels upon the foreshore. This evidence is equivocal. When it is taken by the lord of a manor who is not also owner of a port, it is evidence of a claim to the soil; when it is taken by the lord of a manor who is owner of a port, it is referable rather to the franchise of the port than to ownership of the soil.

d. Taking of ballastage. This is a practice frequent in Northumberland and Durham, of taking a due for ballast cast out of ships upon wharves or ballast-shores built upon the foreshore, and is referable only to a claim to the soil of the foreshore.

e. Making erections upon the sea-shore by building wharves, piers, stages, causeways, timber ponds, &c., on the foreshore. These are all acts of ownership on the foreshore.

f. Making inclosures against the sea by embanking and inning of salt marshes and shores. These embankments can sometimes be shewn to have been made below the medium high-water mark, but most generally they are made above that mark and only exclude the extraordinary tides, because it is desirable in building a sea wall to have a footing or "foreland" outside the wall towards the sea to protect the foot of the wall from the action of the waves, and it is evidently less expensive and safer to erect the sea wall on the salt marsh, which is only covered once a fortnight at spring tides, than upon the shore, which is washed by every tide. They are more frequently erected to secure accretions of salt marsh than to resist the erosive action of the sea upon ancient dry land. It may, however, be sometimes shewn that the level of the marsh within the ancient wall is below the level of ordinary high-water mark, although the salt marsh outside the wall may be above such level. In these cases a presumption of some weight arises that when the actual sea wall was built, it was erected on the foreshore and inclosed part of it, and then it is evidence of ownership of the foreshore.

g. The constant and usual fetching of gravel and sea-weed and sea sand between the high and low water mark—licensing others to do so and prosecuting those who do so without licence. These are distinct acts of ownership, and may be proved orally or by bailiffs' accounts. It appears that the fact of certain members of the public having been permitted to take seaweed and sand in small quantities will not affect the title of the claimant to foreshore unless such practices have been long continued, and not interrupted, and of large extent, because they are in any case trespassers either against the Crown or the subject; but such evidence will be taken into account as tending to countervail the evidence of possession shewn by the claimant, and tending to raise a presumption that the shore has not been granted to him, as, if it had, he might have been expected to have prosecuted such trespassers on the property to which he claims to be exclusively entitled. See above, No. 11.

h. Presentment and punishment of purprestures on the shore in the court of a manor. These will appear upon the court rolls, the charge of the fine being shewn upon the margin of the roll opposite the entry of the presentment.

i. The payment of tithes and rates for fisheries upon the shore or arm of the sea anterior to the year 1874 shews that the fishery is incident to the soil, and this, though not strictly evidence of ownership, is evidence of the occupation of the owner or his lessee.

j. The erection of groins and jetties for the sole purpose of protecting the land from the encroachment of the sea. These are acts of ownership on the foreshore, but the weight of them is questionable, as these erections may be attributed to the common law right of the subject to protect his land from the inroads of the sea. Whether such right to erect protections would authorize the going upon the adjoining foreshore and using it for that purpose, however, is very questionable, and such acts, taken in connection with other evidence of user, may be very important. The Crown now exacts a rent for such erections whenever they are put up.

k. In actions between subject and subject the owner of foreshore is only required to shew his possession sufficiently to succeed against a trespasser claiming under no title. The trespasser usually sets up the Crown title, and denies the plaintiff's possession, but the plaintiff is not bound to prove his title if he shews evidence of possession.

It will be seen, therefore, that every case of a claim to the foreshore must in the main depend for success upon a careful and accurate marshalling of the evidence of user. The grant of the manor, borough, or land of which the foreshore is alleged to be parcel will, in almost every case, be found to be inconclusive and doubtful in its language. Ancient grants of foreshore, or of manors or lands including the foreshore in terms, are extremely rare. The grant in almost all cases requires evidence of user to explain its intentions. It has been shewn that almost all the sea-coast manors of the kingdom were out of the Crown before the end of the reign of King John, and that the original grants of manors are for the most part wholly lost. Grants from the Tudor and Stuart Sovereigns of manors which have come into the hands of the Crown by forfeiture and attainder are invariably re-grants of all the parts and parcels of those manors in the same state and condition as they came to the Crown, and are granted *adeo plene* as fully and wholly as previous owners held them ; they are in fact practically mere conveyances of all that came to the Crown by the attainder or forfeiture. Evidence, therefore, derived from records or bailiffs' accounts anterior to those grants is valuable to shew what was parcel of the manor before it came into the Crown, and is evidence to shew what passed by the re-grant. This evidence is procurable usually from court rolls, rentals, bailiffs' accounts, and other manorial records. Such documents are usually to be found in the possession of the lord of the manor, but are not infrequently to be discovered among the muniments of families whose predecessors had been lords of the manor, and who have retained them by mistake when the documents of title have been turned over to the purchasers upon a sale. Not infrequently, especially in the case of manors belonging to monastic institutions, the court rolls and bailiffs' accounts have been kept on one roll for several manors which have been retained by the owner of one manor when he has sold another. Amongst the Public Records, also, much information is to be gathered relating to foreshore in the case of manors which have come into the hands of the Crown by forfeiture, surrender, exchange, escheat, wardship, &c., and valuable ancient bailiffs' and ministers' accounts and other documents are to be found amongst them, and there exists a large mass of accounts of the Crown receivers and ministers, either remaining on the Exchequer Records or enrolled upon the Pipe Rolls, Chancellors' Rolls, and Memoranda of the Exchequer. These evidences of ancient user are extremely valuable as greatly strengthening the effect of modern user as shewn by the oral evidence of ancient witnesses, and it is desirable, in all cases respecting the foreshore, to make every possible inquiry and research to obtain such evidence.

HALL'S ESSAY ON

THE RIGHTS OF THE CROWN

AND THE PRIVILEGES OF THE SUBJECT

IN THE SEA-SHORES OF THE REALM.

THIRD EDITION.

REVISED AND CORRECTED, TOGETHER WITH EXTENSIVE ANNOTATIONS, AND REFERENCES TO THE LATER AUTHORITIES IN ENGLAND, SCOTLAND, IRELAND, AND THE UNITED STATES.

AN ESSAY ON THE RIGHTS OF THE CROWN

IN THE SEA-SHORES OF THE REALM, ETC. (*a*)

Of the King's Title to the British Seas. (*b*)

THE British Seas, sometimes called the Four Seas, are those which encompass the coasts of England, Scotland, and Ireland. To the west they not only include the sea between Great Britain and Ireland, but extend over the Atlantic Ocean, which washes the western coasts of Ireland: this western part of our sea is subdivided; for, so much as runs between England and Ireland is called St. George's Channel, or the Irish Sea; and the sea on the west coast of Scotland is sometimes named the Caledonian, Deucaledonian, or Scottish Sea, and sometimes the North Sea. To the east we have the German Ocean, which is bounded principally by the opposite coasts of Germany, and

The British seas, and the king's title therein.

(*a*) Mr. Hall's essay was first published in 1830. It was re-edited, with notes, by Mr. R. L. Loveland in 1875. Mr. Loveland's edition is now reproduced, with further notes by the present Editor. Mr. Hall's original notes are reprinted as in the original edition. Mr. Loveland's notes are shewn by square brackets. The Editor's further notes are in round brackets, and identified by the word "ED." at the end of each note.

(*b*) (The law with regard to the title of the Crown to the British seas treated of in this chapter has been so seriously altered by the decisions in Reg. *v.* Keyn, L. R. 2 Ex. D. 63, that the Editor refers the reader to that report, and to a valuable discussion of the subject in Mr. Gould's treatise on Waters, sections 1–20, but he has thought it undesirable to vary Mr. Hall's text, having regard to the diversity of the opinions expressed by the judges in Reg. *v.* Keyn. See Territorial Waters Jurisdiction Act, 1878, 41 & 42 Vict. c. 73.—ED.)

the United Provinces (now Belgium); lastly, to the south there is the British Channel, or Sea, which runs along the
[2] French coast, and, comprehending the Bay of Biscay, ends with the northern coast of Spain.(*c*)

Over the British seas, the King of England claims an absolute dominion and ownership, as Lord Paramount, against all the world. Whatever opinions foreign nations may entertain in regard to the validity of such claim, yet the subjects of the King of England do, by the common law of the realm, acknowledge and declare it to be his ancient and indisputable right.(*d*)

This dominion and ownership over the British seas, vested by our law in the King, is not confined to the mere usufruct of the water, and the maritime jurisdiction, but it includes the very *fundum* or soil at the bottom of the sea.

The king's title to the British seas includes both the sea and the land covered by it.

"The sea is the King's proper inheritance,"(*e*) and he is "Lord of the Great Waste," both land and water; "*tam aquæ quam soli*." Selden,(*f*) in his celebrated treatise on the Dominion of the Seas, would seem to contemplate this ownership of the King, as combining both jurisdiction and ownership; the one, indeed, would seem to involve the other, if Selden's doctrine to its full extent be admitted.

There are eminent writers upon natural and upon national law, who have controverted Selden's doctrines, and have denied the King of England's exclusive dominion, and consequently his ownership over the British seas; but however this may be, and probably will ever continue, *vexata quæstio* between such writers, we know that the

(*c*) Hargrave's notes to Co. Litt. 107 b, being a summary of the 1 Ch. 2d Book of Mr. Selden's Mare Clausum. [Woolrych, pp. 4, 5. Jerwood's Dissertation on Rights of Sea-Shore, p. 13.]

(*d*) 1 Roll. Ab. 528, l. 15. 2 Roll. Ab. 168 and 170, lines 42 and 43. 3 Leo. 73. Co. Litt. 107 and 260 b. Callis, 39. 2 Molloy, 207, 9th ed. Black. Com. 264. Hale, De Jure Maris, *ante*, pp. 376, 384, and see the cases cited *post* on the Fisheries, which admit this to be settled law. [Woolrych, p. 433.]

(*e*) Dav. Rep. 57. Callis on Sewers, 39, 41.

(*f*) Mare Clausum, Lib. 2, Ch. 22 and 24. (There is no word in Selden that can be construed as upholding the *primâ facie* title of the Crown to foreshore.—ED.)

writers on the common and municipal law of England, as well as the decisions of our judicial courts, all speak the [3] same language, and appropriate the dominion of the British seas *tam aquæ quam soli*, to the King. (*g*)

It includes all creeks and arms of the sea, and tide-rivers, as far as in the reach of the tides.

This dominion not only extends over the open seas, but also over all *creeks*, *arms of the sea*, *havens*, *ports*, and *tide-rivers*, as far as the reach of the tide, around the coasts of the kingdom. All waters, in short, which communicate with the sea, and are within the *flux* and *reflux* of its tides, are part and parcel of the sea itself, and subject, in all respects, to the like ownership. This is abundantly proved by the cases hereinafter referred to, where the public *right of fishing* in the creeks, arms of the sea, havens, ports, tide-rivers, &c., of the kingdom has been, in many instances, established upon the principle that they are *part of the sea*, and of the King's dominion, and as such, liable to the common law right of the subject to fish therein ; of which right we shall, in a future page, take notice. (*h*)

(*g*) [Angell on Tide Waters, p. 3.]

(*h*) [The soil of the sea, estuaries, and navigable rivers, within the British dominions, was originally in the Crown, and remains so still, except in those cases where it can be proved to have legally passed into the hands of private persons. Phear on Rights of Water, p. 41. See Malcolmson *v.* O'Dea, 10 H. of L. Cases 593 ; R. *v.* Stimpson, 32 L. J. M. C. 208 ; Att.-Gen. *v.* Chambers, per Alderson, B., 4 De G. M. & G. 206, S. C. 23 L. J. Ch. 665 ; Blundell *v.* Caterall, per Bayley, J., 5 B. & Ald. 304 ; Carter *v.* Murcot, 4 Burr. 2164; but subject to the right of passage over them, see Gann *v.* Free Fishers of Whitstable Co., 11 H. of L. Cases 192, S. C. 20 C. B. N. S. 1 and 35 L. J. C. P. 29 ; Colchester, Mayor of, *v.* Brooke, 7 Q. B. 339, S. C. 9 Jur. 1090. In England (where it has not been granted away—ED.) it is held to be the property reserved to the sovereign ; but in Scotland it is presumed to be granted as part and pertinent of the adjacent lands, under the burthen of the Crown's right as trustee for the public uses. Bell on Law of Scotland, 5th edit. 251. See Duchess of Sutherland *v.* Watson, 6 Macph. 199, Jan. 1868. (See Scotch cases, *ante*, p. 573.—ED.) The doubt which seems to have existed, as to the ownership of the soil of navigable rivers (see Williams *v.* Wilcox, 8 Ad. & E. 333), is now set at rest by Lord St. Leonards, in the case of the Lord Advocate *v.* Hamilton, 1 McQueen (H. L.) 46 ; where he advised the House of Lords that, "With respect to the question which "has been mooted as to the rights of the Crown to the alveus or bed [4]

[4] Lord Hale, in the treatise ascribed to him, aptly compares the King's property in the sea and tide-rivers, creeks, &c., to the ownership of lords of manors in the common or waste lands of the manor. The soil and freehold of the

"of a river, it really admits of no dispute; beyond all doubt the soil "and bed of a river (we are now speaking of navigable rivers only) "belongs to the Crown." As to the soil of a lake, see Marshall *v.* Steam Navigation Co., 3 B. & S. 732; Bell's Principles on Law of Scotland, 651; Phear, p. 13. A river is *primâ facie* navigable in which the tide ebbs and flows: Murphy *v.* Ryan, 2 Ir. R. C. L. 143; (Hargreaves *v.* Diddans, 44 L. J. Q. B. 178; Musset *v.* Birch, 35 L. T. N. S. 486; Reece *v.* Miller, 8 Q. B. D. 626—which limits tidality to the flow-back of ordinary tides; Pearce *v.* Scotcher, 9 Q. B. D. 162—ED.;) see also Malcolmson *v.* O'Dea, 10 H. of L. Cases 618, per Willes, J.; Rex *v.* Montague, 4 B. & C. 598; Miles *v.* Rose, 5 Taunton 705; Woolrych on Waters, pp. 40, 411; Schulte's Aquatic Rights, p. 128. This question has occupied the attention of the Courts in America more than in this country, owing to the large rivers there, which are non-tidal, though for many miles navigable; and while some of their Courts have held that tides are necessary to make a river navigable in law, others have held navigability in fact to be navigability in law. See McManus *v.* Carmichael, 3 Iowa 1-52; Middleton *v.* Pritchard, 3 Scam. (Ill.) 510; Rowe *v.* Granite Bridge Corporation, 38 Mass. (21 Pick.) 344, 347; People *v.* Canal Appraisers, 33 New York (6 Tiffany) 461, 500; Pollard's Lessee *v.* Hagan, 4 Miss. (3 How.) 212; Child *v.* Starr, 4 Hill (N.Y.) 369; Den *v.* East New Jersey, 15 Howard U.S. Sup. Ct. Rep. 426; and remarks in Stevens *v.* Paterson and Newark Railway Company, 34 New Jersey Law (5 Vroom) R. 532; Angell on Tide Waters, pp. 38 and 76; Angell on Watercourses, 6th edit. p. 130; Houck on Navigable Rivers, p. 26 *et seq.* (Gould on Waters, sect. 17 *et seqq.*—ED.). The management of the rights and interests, belonging to the Crown, in the shores and bed of the sea, and the rivers of the United Kingdom, as far as the tide flows, was by 29 & 30 Vict. c. 62, s. 7, transferred from the Commissioners of the Woods and Forests to the Board of Trade in the following terms:— "From and immediately after the thirty-first day of December, one "thousand eight hundred and sixty-six, all such parts and rights and "interests as then belong to her Majesty in the right of the Crown of "and in the shore and bed of the sea, and of every channel, creek, "bay, estuary, and of every navigable river of the United Kingdom, as "far up the same as the tide flows (and which are hereinafter for "brevity called the foreshore) except as in this Act provided, shall, "subject to the provisions of this Act, and subject also to such public "and other rights as by law exist in, over, or affecting the foreshore, or "any part thereof, be and the same are hereby transferred from the

waste belong to the lord, but subject to certain rights of [5]
the manorial tenants; such as common of pasture, piscary, turbary, ways, &c., claimed and enjoyed by them, by the custom of the manor, in and out of such waste lands. So the king is lord of the great waste of the sea, subject [6]
to certain beneficial rights and privileges of fishing, navigation, &c., immemorially enjoyed by his subjects therein, by the custom of the realm, which is the common law. (*i*)

Nature of the king's title to the land under the sea.

The title of the King of England to the land or soil *aquâ maris cooperta*, is similar to his ancient title to all the *terra firma* in his dominions, as the first and original proprietor and lord paramount. It is a fundamental principle of our laws of property in land, that all the lands in the realm belonged originally to the King; and, according to the feudal principles of our ancient laws of tenure, the landowners of England are, to this day, *tenants* to the King, holding their lands of him, as their lord paramount.

"management of the Commissioners of the Woods and Forests to, "and thenceforth the same shall be under, the management of the "Board of Trade." And the duties of the Board with respect to the [5]
foreshore and bed of the sea are, *inter alia*, to protect the Crown's rights, to ascertain in what parts of the coast the Crown has parted with its rights, in what parts the rights of the Crown are undoubted, and in what parts the title is doubtful; to prevent encroachments on the foreshore, to protect navigation and other public interests, and to sell, lease, or license the use of and otherwise deal with the soil, where expedient so to do, under the powers contained in 10 Geo. 4, c. 50; 2 & 3 Will. 4, c. 1 and 112; 3 & 4 Will. 4, c. 69; 5 Vict. c. 1; 8 & 9 Vict. c. 99; 14 & 15 Vict. c. 42; 15 & 16 Vict. c. 62; 16 & 17 Vict. c. 56; and 29 & 30 Vict. c. 62. The 10 Geo. 4, c. 50, s. 60, enables the Treasury to grant their consent for a class of cases, instead of in each individual case, and by the 62nd section of the same Act, the necessity of a survey is dispensed with in cases where the land is obviously not worth a survey; the 16 & 17 Vict. c. 56, s. 5, gives power, with the consent of certain authorities, to compromise and settle disputed claims; and the 29 & 30 Vict. c. 62, s. 11, dispenses with the necessity of any consent to compromises. See also Board of Trade Arbitrations, &c., Act, 37 & 38 Vict. c. 40.

(*i*) [See the case of the Ipswich Dock Co. *v.* Overseers of St. Peter's, Ipswich, 7 B. & S. 344, and remarks of Blackburn, J., therein. Angell on Tide Waters, p. 24. De Jure Maris, *ante*, p. 377.]

That part of the land which the King and his ancestors *have never granted out to the subject*, remains to the King, as his *demesnes*, in absolute ownership. (*k*) The *terra firma* of England has become, almost entirely, the property (by grant and tenure) of the subject; but the *terra aquâ maris cooperta* still remains to the King in wide and barren ownership. (*l*)

Grants by the king, of portions of land sea-covered.

Some rare and antique instances (*m*) may indeed be found of actual grants, by Kings of England, of certain portions of land *under the sea*, *i.e.* of both sea and land, to a certain extent. These grants have been made in such places where some creek or bay has afforded the means of exclusive possession. Thus, the tract ascribed to Lord Hale, and before quoted, recites a grant of King Canute "de "terrâ insulæ Thanet, tam in terrâ quam *in mari* et *lit-* "*tore;*" (*n*) and another of William the First, "Abbati
[7] "Sancti Augustini de totâ terrâ Estanore, *et totum littus* "*usque medietatem aquæ;*" and the author of the tract adds, "If the King will grant lands adjacent to the sea, together "with a thousand acres of land covered by the sea adjoin- "ing, such grant will pass the soil itself; and if there should

(*k*) Madd. Formulare Anglicarum, 202.

(*l*) (But if it be shewn that the kings of England have to any large extent granted out this *terra aquæ maris cooperta* in past ages in the same manner that they have granted out the *terra firma*, the presumption here so largely stated is greatly narrowed. It is admitted, with regard to the *terra firma*, that the presumption is that it has been granted; this presumption is a presumption arising from known facts; if, therefore, evidence be brought with regard to the shore that it has been very largely and generally granted, the presumption that it raises in favour of the Crown is much weakened. See *ante*, p. 24. Hale (p. 343) says "there is little question but the propriety [of the "shore] may even with the same right belong to a subject *as the* "*interest of any inland manor or town or demesnes.*" Also, p. 351: "Touchinge the interest of propriety of the soyle of the land covered "with salt water: this, though *prima facie*, as is sayd before, belonges "to the Kinge, yet it is acquirable by a subject not only by charter, "wherof there can bee no doubt, but by usage, custome, or prescrip- "tion."—ED.)

(*m*) (See the previous treatise, pp. 1–29.—ED.)

(*n*) De Jure Maris, *ante*, p. 384.

"be a recess of the sea, leaving such a quantity of dry land, "it will belong to the grantee."(*o*)

Callis,(*p*) in his book on Sewers, says, "I take it, it is "very *disputable* whether grounds, before they be relin-"quished by the sea, may be gained by *charter* and *grant* "from the Crown; *I suppose they may*." But if such grounds could not be gained by *charter* or *grant*, it would seem to follow that they could not be gained by *prescription;* for nothing can be prescribed for, which could not have had a lawful beginning by grant: Callis, however, in the very same place, says, "A subject cannot have the grounds to the *low* "water-mark, *but by* custom or *prescription;*" and he adds, that, "the subject *may* have the grounds of the sea, to "the *low* water-mark, and that no *custom* can extend the "ownership of a subject *further*." (*q*) But he adduces no authority, and there seems no sufficient reason why prescription or custom should not give title, as well to a specific portion of sea, or of a creek or arm of the sea, as of the shore. The true question is, whether *prescription* or *custom* will give title to either. But of this more hereafter.

Having stated the law to be that the king is absolute owner of the ground or soil under the surface of those seas which are within, or parcel of the British dominions (*r*);—let us proceed to distinguish the lines drawn by the law, [8] between the *terra firma*, the *sea-bottom*, and the *sea-shore*.

Distinctions between terra firma, sea-bottom, and sea-shore. Tides and inundations.

The waters of the sea, being liable to fluctuation, sometimes rise above and overflow the land, and at other times retire from and leave the land dry. These fluctuations of the waters are of two different characters; they are either periodical and according to the regular course of natural causes and effects: or, 2ndly, *extraordinary* fluctuations,

(*o*) [De Jure Maris, *ante*, p. 384.]

(*p*) Callis on Sewers, p. 53; [but see Free Fishers of Whitstable *v.* Gann, 11 C. B. N. S. 387, and remarks of Erle, C.J., and Lord Chelmsford in the same case 11 H. L. 218; see also Schulte's Aquatic Rights, 110; Angell on Tide Waters, 286; and the case of Att.-Gen. *v.* Farmen, 2 Levinz 171.]

(*q*) Callis on Sewers, p. 53.

(*r*) (Except where he has granted it to his subjects.—ED.)

such as happen irregularly and rarely. The periodical and regular fluctuations are called the *tides;* and are thus distinguished from extraordinary *inundations*, and *floods*, as well as from sudden and unusual recessions or derelictions of the sea. The manner, extent, and permanency of these changes will be found to govern and determine the ownership of the soil affected; and our inquiry, therefore, will be directed to ascertain how far these changes in the natural character of the *locus in quo* will, in the consideration and judgment of law, alter or affect the pre-existing title.

Sea-bottom.

In legal, as well as common parlance and intendment, the *sea-bottom* is that soil which is "*semper aquâ maris co-*" *operta*," and *never* known to become dry by changes of the surface of the sea.(*s*) But with regard to the "*terra firma*,"

Terra firma.

or dry land, although, in common speech, it imports land wholly exempt from the action of any of the tides, yet it would seem that the legal *terra firma* ranges down to the ordinary high-water mark. In the Roman law the shore extended "quatenus hybernus fluctus maximus excurrit," a boundary line equivalent, as it would seem, to the limits of our high spring tides. But with us it has been long settled, that *that* portion only of the land adjacent to the sea, which is alternately covered and left dry by the *ordinary* flux and

Sea-shore.

reflux of the tides is, in legal intendment, the *sea-shore;* although the word *shore* has often, in common parlance, a

[9] somewhat more extensive meaning,(*t*) taking in all that ex-

(*s*) (Except so much as lies between the low-water mark of ordinary tides and the low-water mark of extraordinary spring tides. This would be part of the sea-bottom according to the law laid down in Att. *v.* Chambers, 4 De G. M. & G. 206.—ED.)

(*t*) Callis, pp. 54 and 55, in his book on Sewers, makes a distinction between *coast* and *shore:* "coast," says he, "certainly contains both "sea and banks; but he tells us, that "shore at every full sea is "covered by the waters." He also quotes the Gospel of St. Matthew, c. 13, v. 2, where our Saviour "went into a boat, and sat, and all the "multitude stood on the *shore;*" and Callis thence learnedly infers, "that the *shore* was the dry-land *quia* they '*stood* thereon,' and it was "a great quantity of ground, for thereon stood a multitude; and it "was near the brink of the water, because they heard Jesus speak

tensive belt of waste ground or strand of sand, shingles, and rock, which encircles the British Isles, liable to the action of *every kind* of tide, and of which a part, next the land, is seldom covered by the water, even at the *highest spring tides.* But, in fact, no more of this unreclaimed tract is, at law, *sea-shore,* than that portion which lies between the *high-water* and *low-water* mark, at *ordinary* tides. (*u*)

The law takes notice of three kinds of tides: (*x*)— [10]

Tides, three kinds of

High spring tides.

1st. The high spring tides, which are the fluxes of

" unto them out of the ship,"—a mode of proving a legal argument, not so much followed now, as in the quaint times in which the learned reader on Sewers lived and argued. We may observe, however, that as it was a *lake,* without tides, on which Jesus embarked, it could not, properly, be said to have a " shore," according to our legal understanding of that term; it had "*ripam,*" but not "*littus.*" [See also Angell on Tide Waters, p. 67.]

(*u*) [This point has been finally decided by the case of the Att.-Gen. *v.* Chambers, 4 De G. M. & G. 206; in which Ld. Ch. Cranworth was assisted by Maule, J., and Alderson, B. "The principle," says his lordship, "which gives the shore to the Crown is, that it is " land not capable of ordinary cultivation or occupation, and so is in the " nature of unappropriated soil. Lord Hale gives as his reason for " thinking, that lands only covered by the high spring tides do not " belong to the Crown, that such lands are for the most part dry and " manoriable; and taking this passage as the only authority at all " capable of guiding us, the reasonable conclusion is, that the Crown's " right is limited to land, which is, for the most part, not dry or manori-" able. The learned judges whose assistance I had in this very ob-" scure question, point out that the limit indicating such land is the " line of the medium high tide between the springs and the neaps; all " land below that line is, more often than not, covered at high water, " and so may justly be said, in the language of Lord Hale, to be " covered by the ordinary flux of the sea. This cannot be said of any " land above that line; and I therefore concur with the able opinion " of the judges, whose valuable assistance I had, in thinking that the [10] " medium line must be treated as bounding the right of the Crown." In Lowe *v.* Govett, 3 B. & Ad. 863, it was held that where land was covered by the high water of the ordinary spring tides, but not by the medium tides, in the absence of proof as to acts of ownership, the soil must be presumed to have belonged to the owner of the adjoining estate, and not to the Crown. As to when goods are said to be " landed," see Harvey *v.* Lyme Regis, Mayor of, L. R. 4 Ex. 260.]

(*x*) [De Jure Maris *ante*, p. 393. See also Smith *v.* Earl of Stair, 6 Bell's App. Cases 487] (Scotch cases, *ante*, p. 576—ED.).

the sea at those tides which happen at the two equinoctials.

Spring tides. 2nd. The spring tides, which happen twice every month at the full and change of the moon.

Neap tides. 3rd. The neap, or ordinary tides, which happen between the full and change of the moon, twice in the twenty-four hours.

In one book (*y*) it is said that the lands overflowed by spring tides are called *sea-greens*, and they have been *supposed* to be *inter regalia* in England; but in Scotland they are private property. (*z*)

As to the soil subject to spring tides. In the marshy districts and fens along the coasts of the sea, creeks, and tide-rivers, the lands which are subject to the action of the *spring* tides, are of considerable extent and value, and by no means so barren and unprofitable as the ordinary sea-shore or strand. These marshes, indeed, are in many places "manoriable," as Lord Hale expresses it,—and the right to embank and enclose them against the effects of the high spring and spring tides, and reduce them to a completely cultivable state, is of no small importance to the lords of adjacent manors, and the owners of the adjacent *terra firma*. In Dyer 326, and 2 Roll. Abr. p. 170, pl. 13, the following quotation is given, "22 lib. Ass. Ca. 93, *de* "*alluvione, accrescentiâ et inundatione maris seu fluminis*
[11] "*subito et extraordinarie per vehementes tempestates, et quando* "*per naturales et ordinarios fluxus maximos* (*viz.* spring "tides) *qui fiunt bis quolibet mense, differentia magna est.*" (*a*) Here, it seems the *spring* tides (fluxus maximos) are termed "naturales et ordinarios," being the same terms as also used for the *neap tides*. They are "natural," and periodical, but certainly not "ordinary," compared with neap tides.

Callis, also, would seem, though incorrectly, to consider *spring* tides as *ordinary* tides. "It is certain," says he,

(*y*) Bell's Scotch Law Dict.

(*z*) (Sea-greens or places in which samphire usually grows are generally situate within the flux of the ordinary tides, and are usually part of the foreshore, but whether they are so part of it or not is a question of evidence in each case.—Ed.)

(*a*) Dyer 326, Roll. Abr. 2, p. 170, l. 43.

"that, at spring tides, the sea useth to overflow the "marshes in Lincolnshire and Norfolk, and returneth "within a short space again; these being *usual* and "*annual*, be not accounted grounds left or gained from "the sea; so, because the marshes and sands in Lincoln-"shire be overflown every twelve hours, and then dry again, "they are not accounted grounds left or gained from the "sea, because the sea hath daily her recourse thereon." (*b*)

But, if the *spring* tides are deemed *ordinary* tides, and the marshes subject to the spring tides are not accounted grounds gained from the sea, then such marshes might seem to be "*partes maris, et marisci*," and to belong to the king. Callis, however, does not expressly so state the law; and the inference afforded by the case in Dyer, (*c*) as will appear by reference, is *contra*, and more in favour of the subject, and against the King's title; for the "*magna differentia*" there alluded to, is this; viz. that all sudden and unusual inundations, which totally deface all the land-marks, will convert such inundated land into sea-bottom and sea-shore, and, as *such*, it will belong to the King; but that the more regular and periodical inundations of the spring tides, do not, by overflowing the lands, change their legal land-marks and ownership, nor, consequently, convert them, for the King's benefit, into sea-bottom or sea-shore; and if they are not sea, or sea-shore, they must be part of the *terra firma* adjoining. Relatively speaking, it would seem that the spring tides, though *periodical*, can scarcely be denominated "*ordi-*"*nary*," when there are other tides which take place daily, and more regularly, viz. the *neap* tides. Besides, the land subject to spring tides, is, for the greater part of the year, dry land. [12]

Spring tides not "ordinary" tides.

Wherefore, as the authorities almost uniformly describe the "shore," as that which lies within the "*ordinary* flux and "reflux of the tides," it would seem to be most correct to consider the soil which is subject to the "high spring tides," and the "spring tides" as part of the adjoining *terra firma*, and belonging to the same title; and that, when such tides

As to soil subject to high spring and spring tides.

(*b*) Callis on Sewers, p. 50. (*c*) See *suprà*.

have ceased to act, the soil returns to the owner of the adjoining land. "That this is law," says Lord Hale, (*d*) "in "regard to *high spring tides*, is admitted on all hands, but "with regard to the *spring tides*, some hold that common "right speaks for the subject; unless the King hath a pre-"scription, or usage, to entitle the Crown; for this is not "properly *littus maris*. And, therefore, it hath been held, "that where the King makes his title to land, as *littus maris*, "or *parcella littoris marini*, it is not sufficient for him to "make it appear to be overflowed by spring tides of this "kind; p. 8, Car. 1, *in Camerâ Scacarii*, in the case of "Vanhaesdanke for lands in Norfolk; and so I have heard "it was held p. —, 15 Car. B. R. Sir Edward Heron's case, "and Trin. 17 Car. 2, in the case of the Lady Wansford for "a town called the Cowes, in the Isle of Wight." He says more decidedly, *ante*, p. 378, "the King's title is only to "lands that are usually overflowed at ordinary tides." Upon

[13] the whole, it may be regarded as good law at this day, that the *terra firma*, and right of the subject, in respect of title and ownership, extends beyond the lines of the *high spring tides* and *spring tides*, and down to the edge of the high-water mark of the *ordinary* or *neap* tides; and that the Scotch and English Law are, in this respect, the same. (*e*)

Terra firma includes land subject to high spring and spring tides.

The shore, or littus.

Below this ordinary high-water mark, down to the low-water mark, *i.e.* between the ordinary high and low water marks, lies the *shore* or *littus maris*. This shore, throughout the coasts of England, as well of the sea, as of creeks and tide-rivers, doth [*primâ facie*] *de jure communi* [and in common presumption] belong to the King [yet the subject may have such a right (*f*)]. (*g*) In this respect, as matter of

Is the King's (*primâ facie*).

(*d*) De Jure Maris, *ante*, p. 393.

(*e*) [See Att.-Gen. *v.* Chambers, 4 De G. M. & G. 206; Lowe *v.* Govett, 3 B. & Ad. 863; Smith *v.* Earl of Stair, 6 Bell App. Cases 487.]

(*f*) (Mr. Hall's method of quotation may be appreciated by noting his omissions added in brackets.—Ed.)

(*g*) (Hale, cap. v.) See pp. 668 and 711 for authorities; most of the cases relating to the king's ownership of the sea, and to the rights of fishing, either expressly or impliedly admit the king's ownership in the *shore*. See particularly the cases of Bagot *v.* Orr, 2 Bos. & Pul. 472;

title, it would seem to be part of the *fundum*, or sea-bottom, which, as before said, belongs also to the King. "Our Common law of England," says Callis, (*h*) "doth "much surpass in reason either the Imperial or the Civil [14] "law, for (by our law) it is said *Rex in ea habet proprie-* "*tatem, sed populus habet usum ibidem necessarium.*" (*i*)

Of the title which a subject or corporate body of subjects may have in a portion of sea-shore or sea.

As all the land of England, whether *terra firma*, sea-shore, or sea-bottom, belonged originally, according to [the theory of] our laws of tenure, to the King; and as the ownership of a subject, in or over any part of it, could only be derived by *grant* from or through the King, it might seem to follow that every claim of the subject, or of a Corporate body of subjects, to any part of the sea-shore, or of the shores of tide-rivers, must be supported by precisely the *same* evidence of *title* as a claim to any inland estate, as against the King's *primâ facie* title. Nor does it appear how the King's right and claim to the sea-shore, or shore of tide-rivers, or any part thereof, can be

Title to any part of the shore must be proved and supported as inland titles are.

Blundell *v.* Caterall, 5 Barn. & Ald. 268, Dav. Rep. 55; and the King *v.* Smith and others, 2 Dougl. 441, as to the shore of tide-rivers. [It was urged in this case, that the river Thames above London Bridge was not "navigable," although it was flowing and reflowing, inasmuch as the tide beyond that limit was occasioned by the pressure and accumulation backward of fresh water; but the distinction attempted was, by Lord Mansfield, pronounced new and inadmissible; it was taken for granted, however, that the water was salt, the case stating that the Thames was navigable. (See Reece *v.* Miller, 8 Q. B. D. 626, where the limit of tidality is the flow-back of ordinary tides.—ED.) In Horne *v.* Mackenzie, 6 Cl. & Fin. 628, the question was, what was to be considered "river" and what "sea," and the direction was "that "the thing to be looked for was the fact of the absence or prevalence "of the fresh water, though strongly impregnated with salt;" this was, however, held to be bad. See as to ownership of shore in America, Commonwealth *v.* Charlestown, 18 Mass. (1 Pick.) R. 180; Chapman *v.* Kimball, 9 Conn. R. 40; Peyroux *v.* Howard, 7 Peters (U.S. Sup. Ct.) R. 324; Rowe *v.* Granite Bridge Corp., 38 Mass. (21 Pick.) 344, 347.] See also the cases of the King *v.* Lord Yarborough, 3 B. & C. 91, and Scratton *v.* Brown, 4 B. & C. 485.

(*h*) Callis on Sewers, 55.

(*i*) (When Mr. Hall wrote, the limit of foreshore had not been settled by Att. *v.* Chambers.—ED.)

rebutted by any other kind of evidence than that which would be called for by our courts of law in a case of *inland title.* It is presumed that the *sea-shore* is legally and technically speaking "*land*," as is the adjacent *terra firma*, in all cases of disputed title between the King and a subject, and between subject and subject. (*j*)

Grants of the sea-shore by the King.

The Kings of England have frequently, and from the most ancient times, exercised their right of ownership in the sea-shore, by making *grants* thereof to the subject, accompanying grants of the *terra firma* adjoining, and by similar forms of grant. Thus the King might grant [the soil and water of a navigable river. He may also grant] a manor (*k*) "cum littore maris adjacente," and the shore itself will pass, though *in gross*, and *not parcel of the manor.* (*l*) He might also grant a manor, or land contiguous to the sea, *cum maritimis incrementis*, and that will pass the "jus alluvionis," *i.e.* land left by the retirement of the sea. Thus King John granted to the Abbot de Bello Loco, "alveum super quem Abbatia fundata est, "à vado de Hartford cum fluctu maris in ascendendo et
[15] "descendendo inter utramque ripam." (*m*) So William I.

(*j*) (But the King's ownership of the shore was ownership *in theory* rather than *in fact*, and differed not from, but was part of, his general ownership of all the *terra firma* of the kingdom. The Saxon estates embraced the foreshore, and when the Conqueror re-granted them he granted the foreshore with them as parcel; and as the King's interest of property in the sea-shore can only be a limited and qualified interest subject to the public rights thereover, so he could only grant out that qualified interest of property, and that alone the subject could take. It would seem, therefore, that it must be competent for the grantee of foreshore to shew his title by evidence of possession of that qualified interest of propriety, and he cannot be bound to shew title against the Crown by evidence of possession, exclusive as of fact, in him as he would be in the case of *terra firma*; for the Crown had not the exclusive possession to grant, and cannot call upon the grantee to shew exclusive possession of that which, from its nature, cannot be exclusively held.—ED.)

(*k*) De Jure Maris, *ante*, p. 384.

(*l*) (He may also grant "terra de G. cum pertinentiis," and the shore will pass as parcel of the manor: Duke of Beaufort *v.* Swansea, 3 Exch. 413. He may also grant the sea-bottom and a *districtus maris* both *inter fauces terræ*, and on the open shore.—ED.)

(*m*) De Jure Maris, *ante*, p. 384.

granted, "Abbati sancti Augustini de totâ terrâ Estanore "et *totum littus* usque medietatem aquæ." (*n*) Such also was the grant of Canute, quoted before; (*o*) and the muniments of title to many manors on the sea-coasts, will probably furnish similar *express* grants of the *littus*, or sea-shore, together with the manors themselves. (*p*) In Sir Henry Constable's case (*q*) it is said, "that it was resolved by the whole Court that the soil on which the sea "flows and ebbs, (*r*) *i.e.* between the high-water mark and "low-water mark, *may* be *parcel* of the manor of a subject." (*s*) Indeed, there is no doubt but that a subject

The shore may be made the subject of express grant (or the grant may be implied from evidence of user).

(*n*) De Jure Maris, p. 384.

(*o*) P. 672, *ante*, and see also 4 Inst. for two other instances. Even Grotius admits that there *may* be private ownership in some creek, or small part of the sea, or tide-river, although he founds such ownership on "primary occupation." Grotius, Mare Lib. ch. 5 and 7.

(*p*) (The ancient grants of manors seldom—indeed, hardly ever—contain express words of the grant of *littus maris;* the general words of ancient grants are usually very scanty, but the shore will pass under them if evidence be forthcoming that it is parcel of the manor. In Sir Henry Constable's case, next quoted, the grant is "Dominium de Holderness," without any word of shore. See also "Manerium de Hapesburg," *ante*, pp. 17, 161, 162. The shore will also pass under the grant of a town or borough: Att.-Gen. *v.* Portsmouth, *ante*, p. 555.—ED.)

(*q*) 5 Co. 107.

(*r*) 2 Roll. Abr. 170; Dyer, 326; Scratton *v.* Brown, 4 B. & C. 485.

(*s*) [Continuous acts of ownership exercised by the grantee upon the sea-shore between high and low water mark may be called in aid to prove the shore to be parcel of a manor: Calmady *v.* Rowe, 6 C. B. 861; and see Att.-Gen. *v.* Jones, 33 L. J. Ex. 249; Walton cum Trimley Manor, *In re*, 28 L. T. N. S. 12, S. C. 21 W. R. 475; Healy *v.* Thorne, 4 Ir. Com. Law R. 495; *In re* Belfast Dock Act, 1 Ir. Eq. R. 128; Le Strange *v.* Rowe, 4 F. & F. 1048; Donegall, Marquis of, *v.* Lord Templemore, 9 Ir. Com. Law Rep. 374. And modern usage is admissible in evidence to shew that such sea-shore was part of the manor; Beaufort, Duke of, *v.* Swansea, Mayor of, 3 Ex. 413; Dickens *v.* Shaw, *ante*, p. 451; also Jerwood, p. 74. Juries may presume an ancient lost grant from the Crown, from long-continued acts of ownership exercised by the adjoining proprietor on the sea-shore: see *In re* Belfast Dock Act, 1 Ir. Eq. R. 128; Att.-Gen. *v.* Chambers, 4 De G. & J. 55; *Re* Alston's Estate, 5 W. R. 189, S. C. 28 L. T. 337; and cases cited in Taylor on Evidence, 6th edit. vol. i. p. 144 *et seq.* (Hamilton *v.* Att. for Ireland, 5 L. R. Ir. 555. Evidence of acts of ownership on parts of the foreshore which were separated and divided from the part in dispute by foreshore admitted to belong to the Crown was held admissible to prove the right to the

may be owner of a portion or tract of shore, by ancient *charter* or *grant* from the Crown. (*t*)

[16] The question whether a title to the sea-shore can be supported by Prescription considered.

But it is also laid down, in the tract ascribed to Lord Hale, as well as by Callis,—that a title to the *soil*, as well at the *bottom* of the sea, as upon the *sea-shore*, may be acquired and possessed by the subject by "*Prescription.*" The doctrine of the Treatise is, that there are *two* ways by which a subject may acquire a right to such soil or shore; 1st. By the King's Charter or Grant. 2nd. By *custom* or *prescription.* (*u*) Callis, (*v*) indeed, goes so far as to say that "a subject *cannot* have the ground to the low-water "mark, *but* by custom and prescription." But in this he is clearly wrong.

As the ownership claimed by a subject to any portion of the sea-shore is in opposition to and in derogation of the King's *primâ facie* title, it will be proper in this place to consider, with attention, the grounds upon which the King's subjects are supposed to found their titles to any part of the sea-shore when claimed by them against the King's ancient right and dominion. Neither good policy, nor public utility will, it is conceived, incline towards the

whole tract of which they formed part: Att. *v.* Portsmouth, 25 W. R. 559; but on appeal the doctrine was held not to apply to that case, because it was held that the tract in question was not continuous: *ante*, p. 555.—ED.) As the shore, says Hale, C.J., *ante*, pp. 359, 368, 379, may be parcel of a manor, so it may be parcel of a vill or parish: see Calmady *v.* Rowe, 6 C. B. 880; but, *primâ facie*, it is extra parochial: see Duke of Bridgwater's Trustees *v.* Bootle, 7 B. &
[16] S. 348, S. C. L. R. 2 Q. B. 4; Ipswich Dock Company *v.* Overseers of St. Peter's, Ipswich, 7 B. & S. 310; R. *v.* Gee, 1 E. & E. 1068; Reg. *v.* Musson, 8 E. & B. 900; but see 31 & 32 Vict. c. 122, s. 27; and further, as to public and private rivers, McCanon *v.* Sinclair, 2 E. & E. 53, S. C. 5 Jur. N. S. 1302; see also Proprietors of Waterloo Bridge *v.* Cull, 5 Jur. 1288; Perrott *v.* Bryant, 2 Y. & C. 61; Rex *v.* Landulph, Inhab. of, 1 Mood. & R. 393. Still the shores of the sea and beds of navigable rivers are part of the adjoining counties, and justices have power to convict persons charged with fishing in such waters, where there is a private right of fishery, Embleton *v.* Brown, 6 Jur. N. S. 1298.]

(*t*) (And such ownership is shewn in rare instances by actual grant of *littus maris*, but most usually by evidence of acts of ownership from which such grant is presumed.—ED.)

(*u*) [See Hale, *ante*, p. 385. See Benest *v.* Pipon, 1 Knapp 60.]

(*v*) Callis, Sewers, 53.

claim of the individual subject; and it may be presumed that, the exclusive ownership of the sea-shore, or of any of the creeks, or arms of the sea, or of the ports or tide-rivers, or any part of them, ought, whenever set up by a subject, to be regarded and construed *stricto jure*,—in [17] favour of the Crown, *pro bono publico.*

It has already been premised, that the *terra firma* of England has become, almost entirely, transferred to and vested in the King's subjects, by grants from him. Without adverting to obsolete modes of tenure, and division of property, it will suffice to explain further that, as against the King, the subject holds his landed estate under two general denominations of title, according to the two most prevailing divisions of landed property, viz. into manors, which are tracts of freehold land, accompanied by peculiar rights and privileges; and naked freeholds, or freehold lands, unaccompanied by any such manorial rights and privileges. *Copyholders* are mere *tenants* of the lord of a manor.

Two principal kinds of tenures, manors and freeholds.

As, however, claims set up to portions of the sea-shore, and to the shores of tide-rivers, are almost invariably made by *lords of manors*, in right of their manors, it will simplify our subject, and answer every useful purpose, if we discuss the question of right and title to the "shore," chiefly with reference to the ownership claimed therein by lords of adjacent manors.

As to the claims of lords of manors to the sea-shore.

We have already shown that any of the King's subjects, whether lords of manors, or not, may have a right and property in portions of the sea-shore by ancient *express grant* from the King. (*x*) With regard to claims founded on grants of manors [where the grant exists], it need only be remarked, that the title to the "shore" will depend wholly upon the construction of the metes and bounds of the grant. Thus, if the boundary be expressed to be "down "to the *sea*" or "bounded on one side by the *sea*," or any similar phrase, it is presumed the ordinary *high-water mark* must be deemed the intended line, and not the low-water mark, for the whole shore is "quasi pars maris;" or, as [18] Bracton expresses it, "quasi maris accessoria." (*y*) But, if

Grants.

(*x*) See p. 684, note (*a*). (*y*) Lib. 1, cap. 2, and lib. 2, cap. 12.

the boundary line be expressed to be "down to the low-"water mark," or extend to any ascertainable line beyond low-water mark, this will be tantamount to a grant of the *sea-shore*. So, if the grant extend to any known and distinct limits within the sea, or tide-river—as "usque filum "aquæ," or "medietatem aquæ," &c. In fact, the land granted, whether situate upon the coast or inland, is co-extensive with the words of grant, and no more. (*z*) (*a*)

(*z*) [A patent of James the First granted the priory of Holmpatrick, and also the four Islands to the priory belonging, to wit the island called Shennick, &c., and the patent used the large general words, granting wreck of the sea, flotsam, jetsam, &c., and all the appurtenances to the priory belonging. It was held that these words, coupled with the proof of enjoyment for 70 years of the foreshore, by letting to tenants to take seaweed, &c., were sufficient evidence to support a finding that the shore passed under the grant, Healy *v.* Thorne, 4 Ir. C. L. R. 495 (see also Hamilton *v.* Att. for Ireland, 5 L. R. Ir. 555. A possessory title in the shore evidenced by acts of ownership is sufficient against a trespasser, and it is not open to the defendant to prove acts of ownership by the Crown, except such as can be shown to have been done with the knowledge of the plaintiffs: Corporation of Hastings *v.* Ivall, L. R. 19 Eq. 558. The shore will pass by general words as parcel of lands or *reputed parcel* of such lands if acts of ownership be shewn: Brew *v.* Haren, I. R. 9 C. L. 29—ED.), and the soil of the shore between high and low water mark may pass under the term "waste" in a grant, Att.-Gen. *v.* Hanmer, 27 L. J. Ch. 837, S. C. 4 Jur. N. S. 751; see Scratton *v.* Brown, 4 B. & C. 485, per Bayley, J., and Att.-Gen. *v.* Jones, 33 L. J. Ex. 249; or "ripa," *In re* Belfast Dock Act, 1 Ir. R. Eq. 128, 139, or "anchor-"age, &c.," see Foreman *v.* Free Fishers of Whitstable, L. R. 4 E. & I. App. 266, L. R. 2 C. P. 688; Le Strange *v.* Rowe, 4 F. & F. 1048, Calmady *v.* Rowe, 6 C. B. 861; also under other terms, Macalister *v.* Campbell, 15 D. B. & M. Session-Court, 490. (The shore also passes by a grant of "Terra de G." when acts of ownership are shewn to prove it parcel of the manor: Duke of Beaufort *v.* Swansea, 3 Exch. 413; Att. *v.* Portsmouth, *ante*, p. 555; Chad *v.* Tilsed, 5 Moore 192, 2 B. & B. 403.—ED.) As between the Crown and the Duchy of Cornwall, all mines between high and low water mark, in the county of Cornwall, are by 21 & 22 Vict. c. 109, vested in the Prince of Wales, as part of the soil and territorial possession of the Duchy, see Phear, p. 49.] (See also Mayor of Penryn *v.* Holms, L. R. 2 Ex. D. 328.—ED.)

(*a*) (Mr. Hall did not admit that the subject could shew title to foreshore otherwise than by express grant. He does not add, as he

If a manor on the coast be granted by the same form of words as it used to grant an inland manor, nothing but *terra firma* would pass by such grant; no part of the "sea-shore" would be included in such grant. (*b*) In a former page (*c*) we are told, that the King might grant a *manor*, "cum littore maris adjacente," and the shore will pass, though in *gross*, and *not parcel of the manor*. So that it is evident a sea-coast manor does not *necessarily*, by reason of its locality, include the *shore* within the *precincts* (*d*). Some grants of manors on the coast may include, *expressly*, not only the "*shore*," but also *wreck*, and *royal fish*, *flotsam*, &c., and a *separate fishery*; others may comprise the shore, but none of these liberties, profits, or franchises; and others may contain all these, or one of these privileges only, and no grant of the shore at all (*e*).

A manor on the sea-coast does not necessarily include the shore.

[19]

It is agreed on all hands that *wreck*, or *royal fish*, are (under the technical denomination of *franchises*) *separate and peculiar species of property*, in the hands of subjects, and

In like manner as it does not necessarily include the regalia of wreck, royal fish, &c.

ought to have done, that the subject may have it by construction of a grant in general terms, and by presumption of a lost grant by evidence of user. Grants of manors, except in Saxon and very early Norman times, never expressly set out the boundaries of manors. What is the boundary of the manor is always a question of evidence outside the description of the parcels of the grant. It is also well established that evidence of acts of ownership are admissible to prove what has passed by a grant. The principles set forth in this passage are not sound. See p. 684, note (*z*).—ED.)

(*b*) (This dictum is also inaccurate. See note (*z*).—ED.)

(*c*) P. 680, *ante*.

(*d*) (Here Mr. Hall has used unfairly the text of Hale, cap. v., who certainly does say that the shore may pass in gross and not as parcel of the manor; but he also distinctly shews that it may also be parcel of a manor. "It may not only be parcel of a manor, but *de facto* it "many times is so; and perchance it is parcel almost of all such "manors as by prescription have royal fish or wrecks of the sea "within their manor," Hale, cap. vi. s. 3, p. 394; and see pp. 359, 364, 366. It is true that a grant of a sea-coast manor does not *necessarily* include the shore, but it may do, and may be proved to do so by evidence of acts of ownership over such shore.—ED.)

(*e*) [See Dickens *v.* Shaw, *ante*, p. 451; Healy *v.* Thorne, 4 Ir. R. C. L. 495. See *post*, p. 755.]

distinct from the property of the soil. If, therefore, one species of property be expressly granted, and another kind clearly omitted, it would seem to be contrary to the ordinary and acknowledged rules of construction to *presume*, or infer, a grant of that *one* which is omitted, *unless* it be *so* essential to the enjoyment of the *other*, as to render the implication or inference, in common sense, *necessary*. It is equally agreed, on all hands, that one man may have the soil of the shore; another man the franchise of wreck; another the liberty, or profit *à prendre*, of a private fishery, &c., and all this may be upon the same line of coast, and on the same spot of shore. "The property in such land" [the shore] "is *primâ facie* in the Crown. It *may*, how- " ever, be in a subject; and *different* rights, in that descrip- " tion of property, may be vested in a subject, *according to* " *the terms of grant*. The King may have granted to a " subject the soil itself, or the privilege of fishing, &c." *Per* Bayley, J., in Scratton *v.* Brown, 4 B. & C. 485.

[20] These rights and titles, therefore, it would seem, are not, in respect of their subject matter, dependent upon each other, or necessarily linked together. The grant of the *sea-shore* down to low-water mark, is one thing; and the grant of *wreck* is *another* thing; nor does it appear ever to have been established that the possession of the franchises of Wreck, or of Royal Fish, by an express grant, *totidem verbis*, conferred also a title to the shore itself. The rule, "*expressum facit cessare tacitum*," applies as strongly to such form of grant, as to any other form.

The ownership of wreck, or separate fishery, does not, *per se*, give title to ownership of the shore.

Neither is it necessary to the full enjoyment of all, or any of these grants of *wreck*, *separalis piscariæ*, &c., that the soil of the shore should accompany them; it is clear that the King, or a subject under him, may retain the soil, subject and without prejudice to such usufructuary rights vested in some other individual. It would seem, therefore, too much to contend that an express grant of any one, or more of these "franchises," will *per se* carry the soil of the "sea-shore;" (*f*) and it should be remembered,

(*f*) ["The privileges of 'wreck' and 'royal fish' have been sepa- "rated from the other incidents, which would attach to ownership of

that the King's grants to a subject are, by the rule of law, to be construed strictly, and in the King's favour, and more by the letter thereof, than a grant from one subject to another; in which case the grant is construed most in favour of the grantee. (*g*) (*h*)

"the shore, and vested in the Crown as distinct incorporeal rights. "This fact is of no importance, while both the property of the shore, "and the ownership of these rights, remain in the hands of the Crown; "but when a subject has established a claim by grant to either of "them, it often requires to be remembered that there is no mere "implication or presumption to carry the other with it." Phear, p. 52. See also Dickens *v.* Shaw, *ante*, p. 451.]

(*g*) In Dav. Rep. 55, it is distinctly laid down that "the grant of the "king passes nothing by implication."—The great case of the fishery of the river Banne, Ireland. In the Duke of Somerset *v.* Fogwell, this doctrine is distinctly recognized by Mr. Justice Bayley, who says, "in "grants from the Crown, nothing passes unless the intention is *mani-* "*fest* that it should pass;" 5 B. & C. 875; Jerwood, 60.

[In Feather *v.* R., 6 B. & S. 283, S. C. 35 L. J. Q. B. 204, and 12 L. T. N. S. 114, Cockburn, C.J., says: "It is established on the best "authority, that in construing grants from the Crown a different rule "of construction prevails from that by which grants from one subject "to another are to be construed. In a grant from one subject to "another, every intendment is to be made against the grantor, and in "favour of the grantee, in order to give full effect to the grant; but in "grants from the Crown, an opposite rule of construction prevails. "Nothing passes except that which is expressed, or which is matter "of necessary and unavoidable intendment, in order to give effect to "the plain and undoubted intention of the grant; and in no species "of grant does this rule of construction more especially obtain than in "grants which emanate from, and operate in derogation of, the pre- "rogative of the Crown;" and he then cites the language of Lord Stowell in the case of the Rebeckah, 1 Ch. Rob. 227, 230. (But see Chad *v.* Tilsed, 5 Moore 192, per Dallas, C.J.; Duke of Beaufort *v.* Swansea, 5 Exch. 413. Nothing passes except that which is expressed or *is matter of necessary and unavoidable intendment*—*e.g.*, by grant of a manor, all that which is *parcel* of that manor passes by unavoidable intendment; what is such parcel is a question of evidence in every case.—ED.)

[The rule in England, that a grant from the Crown is strongly construed against the grantee (Feather *v.* Reg., 6 B. & S. 283; Lord *v.* Commissioners of Sydney, 12 Moore P. C. 496; R. *v.* London, Mayor of, 1 Cr. M. & R. 12; R. *v.* 49 Casks of Brandy, 3 Hag. Adm. R. 271; and Forsyth's Constitutional Law, 175), applies to grants from the United States. "All public grants," says Chan. Manning, "are to be

[21] Enquiry whether a title to any part of the sea-shore can be acquired by "prescription."

Our next enquiry is, whether a Lord of a Manor or any other subject, or a Corporation Sole or Aggregate, may also acquire an ownership in the sea-shore, by *prescription.* The learned writer already quoted (Lord Hale), clearly alludes to that kind of prescription, or usage, which supports such franchises and usufructuary rights, liberties, and

"strictly construed, and nothing passes under them by implication;" La Plaisance Bay Harbour Co. *v.* City of Monroe, Walker's Chan. R. 155; McManus *v.* Carmichael, 3 Iowa 1-53; Haight *v.* Keokuk, City of, 4 Iowa 200; People *v.* Canal Appraisers, 33 N. Y. (6 Tiffany) 461. In Iowa the Supreme Court expressed similar views. An additional reason for the rule mentioned is, that the United States Government holds all the public lands as a mere trustee; see McManus *v.* Carmichael, *supra.*]

(*h*) (The franchise of wreck and royal fish is a franchise distinct and separate from the soil; it is one of the "flores coronæ," and has no relation to the soil or the possession thereof. It has generally been granted out by distinct and separate grants from the grants of manors, but it merges in the prerogative on the forfeiture of a manor (Abbot of Strata Marcella, 9 Rep. 24; Duke of Northumberland *v.* Houghton, L. R. 5 Exch. 131). We constantly find it granted together with the manor, and by the same grant, or, to speak more correctly, re-grant. It is conceded that a grant of wreck *per se* will not carry the shore, and this is obviously correct, because the King may grant it to be taken by the grantee *infra metas* between known limits, either over the soil of the Crown or that of a subject, or both; or he may grant it to be taken *infra wapentachium,* as in the case of the wapentake of Langburgh, Yorkshire (see p. 641), where it was granted to be taken between Yarm and Rymeswick, a district comprehending the whole shore of the North Riding. This form of grant, however, is very exceptional. The grant of wreck generally is *infra manerium suum,* and it is upon this form of grant, which is the usual and common one, that Hale, cap. vi. (p. 394), founds his argument that possession of the franchise *infra manerium* is strong evidence to shew that the shore is parcel of the manor. This argument (which Mr. Hall here suppresses) is as follows :—"It [the "shore] may not only be parcel of a manor, but *de facto* it many "times is so; and perchance it is parcel of all such manors as by "prescription have royal fish and wreck of the sea within their manor. "For, for the most part, wrecks and royal fish are not, nor indeed "cannot, be well left above the high-water mark, unless it be at such "extraordinary tides as overflow the land; but there are perquisites "which happen between high-water and low-water mark; for the sea, "withdrawing at the ebb, leaves the wrecks upon the shore, and also "those greater fish which come under the denomination of royal fish. "*He therefore that hath wreck of the sea or royal fish by prescription*

profits, as were just now mentioned, viz. wreck, royal fish, separate fishery, &c., the immemorial use and enjoyment whereof will, *per se*, support a title to them. (*i*)

[22] It may be concluded from some of our best authorities (*k*) that a title to "*land*" or freeholds corporeal cannot

Prescription gives no title to lands.

"*infra manerium, it is a great presumption that the shore is part of* "*the manor, as otherwise he could not have them.*" In King *v.* Ellis, 1 M. & S. 662, Lord Ellenborough, discussing Hale's argument, says: "It is argued that here the grant of one thing leads to a necessary "implication of the grant of the other, by which alone the thing can "be conveniently exercised. Such is the argument, and certainly it "is one of powerful inference." Hale's argument has been generally accepted and acted upon, with this necessary qualification, that although enjoyment of wreck *per se* gives not presumption of title to the shore on which it is taken, yet if such taking be accompanied by other acts of ownership on the shore, the right to wreck, *coupled with the other user*, raises the presumption of a grant of the shore: Calmady *v.* Rowe, 6 C. B. 61; Lestrange *v.* Rowe, 4 Fost. & Finl. 1048; Healy *v.* Thorne, 4 Ir. C. L. 495. The collection of the profits of wreck was in the hands of the sheriffs, who render their accounts in the Exchequer upon the Pipe Rolls, which extend from the reign of Henry II. downwards. On these rolls, which the Editor has minutely studied, there occur occasional entries of profits of wreck returned to the Crown—*e.g.*, Pipe Roll, 5 Henry II., the sheriff of Devon answers for 21*s.* 10*d.* of wreck; Pipe Roll, 33 Henry II., Cornwall, the sheriff answered for £26 13*s.* 4*d.* of the wreck of a ship wrecked at Scilly; Pipe Roll, 7 Richard I., Norfolk and Suffolk, contains entries of wreck at Paxton and Baketon. The very few cases in which the sheriff returns wreck, and the known existence of numerous grants of wreck anterior to the reign of John, leads strongly to the presumption that before that reign nearly the whole of the Crown's rights to wreck had been granted out. Some part of it, doubtless, did remain in the Crown, as is shewn by subsequent grants by later monarchs, and subsequent entries of receipt, mostly in Devonshire, existing amongst the *placita coronæ* and assize rolls. The Statute of Wreck (stat. 3 Edward I. cap. 4) recognises the right of the subject to wreck *in locis privilegiatis per regem.*—Ed.)

(*i*) See Dickens *v.* Shaw, *ante*, p. 451. (Lord Hale says by "prescription and usage," and gives examples of the usage—viz., exercise of franchises granted to be exercised *infra manerium*, and exercise of acts of ownership, by leasing the shore and taking the profits of it. Mr. Hall's argument as to presumption rests upon a wilful misreading of Hale's text.—Ed.)

(*k*) 2 Roll. Abr. 264, l. 3. Co. Litt. 48 a, 113 b, 114 b, 195 b. Vin. Abr. title Prescription.

be supported by *prescription*. The words of Blackstone are, "no prescription can give a title to lands, and other "corporeal substances, of which more certain evidence (of "title) can be had;" (*l*) and he states this more certain evidence to be "corporeal seizin and inheritance." Now, there are two grounds of title to land:—1st. By *Grant*. 2nd. By what is called *adverse possession*, founded on the *Statutes of Limitation*. A title by "adverse possession," under the *Statutes of Limitation*, is, indeed, sometimes spoken of as held by "prescription;" but at common law, as at present understood, "prescription alone, it is con- "ceived, confers no *title* to freehold land." In the Scotch law, (*m*) *positive* prescription is said to be "the acquisition "of property, by the possessor's continuing his possession "for the time which the law has declared sufficient for "that purpose." *Negative* "is the loss or omission of a "right, by neglecting to follow it forth, or use it during "the whole time limited by the law." (*n*) Erskine's Principles, p. 372. In the French Code it is laid down, "la prescription est un moyen d'acquérir ou de se libérer "par un certain laps de temps, et sous les conditions "detérminées par la loi." And this "moyen d'acquérir" is applied to *lands*, as well as to *incorporeal* rights. But when, in our law, the word is used in its technical sense, it does not correctly apply to a title to freehold lands or corporeal hereditaments. (*o*)

Two grounds of title to lands.
1. Grant.
2. Adverse possession supported by statute law.

(*l*) 2 Blac. Com. cap. 17, 264, and see Doct. and Stu. Dial. i. cap. 8, Finch 132, and see note to Com. Dig. title Franchise, where it is said, "land cannot be claimed by prescription." Hammond's Ed.—The *text* there, from Co. Litt. 114 b, has only relation to a "tenant in "common," and see p. 722, *post*, and accord. Litt. Sect. 310. (But see the text, and also the reasons in the note, and in Blackstone.—ED.)

(*m*) See Ld. Advocate *v.* Graham, 7 D. B. M. 183.

(*n*) [See Napier on Prescription, p. 650. Earl of Fife *v.* Woods and Forests Co., 11 D. B. M. 889, as to whether "negative" runs against the Crown.]

(*o*) (Mr. Hall here uses the word *prescription* in a highly technical sense. (See Phear, p. 68.) He seeks to distinguish prescription from user—*i.e.*, evidence of long-continued acts of ownership from which presumption of a grant arises. Gale on Easements, p. 176, says: "Prescription is described by Mr. Justice Blackstone as meaning at

Adverse possession of land without the aid of statute [23] law, is no *title;* but prescription, as a title to incorporeal rights, is everything without statute law. (*p*) In prescription for a customary privilege, immemorial usage is allowed to raise the presumption of an ancient grant. (*q*) But as to

"common law a mode of acquiring real property where a man could "shew no other title to what he claimed than that he and those under "whom he claimed had immemorially used to enjoy it." It is well settled that a subject may make a title against the Crown to foreshore by evidence of immemorial user—*i.e.*, by prescription presuming a grant; the question which is *not* settled is what *quantum* of user and what *character* of user are sufficient for this purpose. This cannot be settled upon principle, but must depend in every case upon the evidence which is produced: Lord Advocate *v.* Young, 12 App. Cas. 544, and remarks on Scotch cases and evidence, *ante*, pp. 581–591.—Ed.)

(*p*) [See 2 & 3 Will. 4, cap. 71. The right to a given substratum of coal lying under a certain close is a right to land, and cannot be claimed by prescription; but a right to take coal in another's land may be; Wilkinson *v.* Proud, 11 M. & W. 33 see Phear, p. 68, n. It has been held that negative easements are not within the Prescription Act, which only deals with easements which are used in and upon the servient tenement, and are capable of interruption by the owner of the servient tenement. Neither can prescription apply to a right which has been expressly prohibited by statute, unless the grant be presumed to have been made before such statute was passed; nor can such right be claimed against the public, if it directly operate as a nuisance to a public right or franchise. Webb *v.* Bird, 10 C. B. N. S. 268, 31 L. J. C. P. 335; Murgatroyd *v.* Robinson, 7 E. & B. 391, 26 L. J. Q. B. 233.]

(*q*) (So also to shew what passed by ancient grant as parcel: *ante*, p. 681, note (*s*), and p. 684, note (*z*).—Ed.) "The several modes of "establishing an old title by pleading a lost grant, &c., often proved "insufficient to meet cases of real hardship," says Mr. Phear. "For "instance, enjoyment might have been sufficiently long and adverse to "render a disturbance of it most unjust, and yet it might be possible for "the opposing party to defeat the pleas, by showing that its actual com- "mencement was inconsistent with them; or, even if the enjoyment "necessary for supporting the plea were proved, circumstances adverse "to the legal inception of the right might be shown, notwithstanding that "the present enjoyment ought, in all justice, to be entirely unaffected "by them. The statute 2 & 3 Will. 4, c. 71, known as the Prescription "Act, offers a remedy for some of these cases." Phear, p. 83.

[In Shuttleworth *v.* Le Fleming, 19 C. B. N. S. 687, S. C. 34 L. J. C. P. 309. To a declaration in trespass for breaking and entering the plaintiff's close and landing fishing nets there, the defendant, amongst

[24] land, whether there was or was not an ancient grant, is immaterial to the *effect* of the statute; for the statute may

other things, pleaded, that the land was part of the shore of an inland lake, and that he, and all his ancestors, for sixty years before the suit, enjoyed as of right and without interruption a free fishery in the said water, with the right of landing their nets on the shore, &c., and to these pleas the plaintiff demurred. In delivering judgment, Montague Smith, J., said :—"The demurrer raises the question whether the rights "so pleaded to belong to the plaintiff in gross, are within the Prescrip-"tion Act, 2 & 3 Will. 4, c. 71. The construction of the statute on "this point is not free from difficulty; and although the question has

[24] "arisen in the courts, it has not been decided. We are now called "upon to determine it; and upon consideration of all the provisions "of the Act, we are led to the conclusion that rights claimed in gross "are not within it. The fifth section gives the key to the true con-"struction of the Act. It professes to enact forms of pleading appli-"cable to all rights within the Act theretofore claimed to have existed "from time immemorial, which forms it declares shall, in such cases, "be sufficient. Those forms have clearly relation to rights which are "appurtenant to the land, and to such rights only. The whole prin-"ciple of the pleading assumes a dominant tenement, and an enjoy-"ment as of rights by the occupier of it. The proof must, of course, "follow and support the pleading. It is obvious that rights claimed "in gross cannot be so pleaded or proved." See also Gale on Easements, 151.

[By sect. 1 of the Act, claims to right of common and other profits *à prendre* are not to be defeated after thirty years' enjoyment, by showing only that such right was first taken or enjoyed at any time prior to such period; and when such right shall have been so taken for sixty years it shall be deemed absolute and indefeasible, unless it had been taken by consent or agreement.

[And by sect. 2, in cases of claims of right of way or other easements, the periods are twenty and forty years. "It may be remarked," says Mr. Phear, "that in making use of this Act whenever the mere alle-"gation of right, and not immemorial usage, was originally sufficient, "the general issue will render everything under this Act available to "rebut it; but when the allegation of immemorial usage was neces-"sary, the user given by the Act must be alleged, and the general "issue will only traverse that; other defences must be pleaded spe-"cially. It may be added that claims under this Act may be made "in respect of enjoyment by the occupiers of land without alleging the "right of the owner of the fee;" but although by sect. 6 no presumption in favour of the claims is to be derived from a user short of thirty years, the statute does not take from such shorter user its weight as collateral evidence of a grant. Hanmer *v.* Chance, 11 Jur. N. S. 397, S. C. 32 L. J. Ch. 413.]

be a bar to the "best title in the world," and confirm the worst against all presumption.

The common law was peculiarly strict in all questions of title to the freehold, and realty. But upon questions of minor right,—as upon the enjoyment of some petty convenience, or benefit derived from the land,—it was not so strict; such claims, therefore, as a right of way, a right to [25] fish, or a right to dig turf, or a right to pasture cattle, were allowed, upon the proof of a continued acquiescence on the part of the owners of the soil, for a time beyond memory of man. "Not that the Court believes" (as Mr. Butler (*r*) well observes) "that any actual grant of such right once "existed;" but upon the general political principle of quieting possessions. (*s*)

But immemorial usage *alone*, without the aid of statute law, will not, it is conceived, raise a title to land at this time of day; and especially not against the Crown. (*t*) Whatever may have been the "old law," as explained by Bracton, (*u*) and Coke, (*x*) previously to the statute of Merton (20 Hen. 3), yet, from the time of that statute, title to land by length of time of possession, or, as Bracton borrows it from the civil law, "*usucaptio*," has depended upon statute law. Whether, under the feudal system, "usucaptio" was ever a valid ground of title to land, *as between subject and subject*, we need not stop long, in this place, to inquire; our inquiry being into the effect of such act against the Crown. It is said that, previously to the statute of Merton, "what length of time was necessary to "give such right [to land,] was not defined by the law, but "was left to the discretion of the *Justices;*" (*y*) and it would seem to have been fixed by those Justices of whose discretion in this matter we have the earliest record, that no "seizin could be alleged by the demandant in a real

(*r*) See his note Co. Litt. 261 a.

(*s*) Taylor on Evidence, 6 edit. p. 146.

(*t*) (But it raises the presumption of a grant even against the Crown: Att. *v*. Portsmouth, *ante*, p. 555.—ED.)

(*u*) Lib. 2, fo. 51, 52.   (*x*) 1 Inst. 114 b.

(*y*) Reeve's Engl. Law, vol. i. p. 305.

"action, but from the time of Hen. I." This discretion of the Justices has, it is considered, ceased since the stat. of Merton, as regards title to the freehold and inheritance of lands.(z)

[26] It is to be noted, however, that neither the "discretion "of the Justices," anterior to the statute law, nor the statute law itself, for a long period after the stat. of Merton, enabled a subject to make title to land, "by length of "time of possession," *against the Crown.* The maxim "*nullum tempus occurrit Regi*" prevailed, until a period much later than the stat. of Merton.

Against the King, therefore, as it would seem, "prescrip-"tion" or "usucaptio" did not, by our common or feudal law, give title to lands; and, consequently, it is contended, not to lands of the Crown covered by the sea, or upon the sea-shore. (a) It is by the statute law *alone*, without any reference to the "old law" of prescription between subject and subject (whatever that law might have been), that adverse possession will, by lapse of time, prevail against the King's original and paramount title. These statutes are comparatively recent, so far as they affect the Crown; and are not founded upon any principle or right of prescription against the Crown, known to have prevailed in our feudal system of laws prior to those statutes. (b)

Since the statute of Merton, therefore, as regards the law between subject and subject; and both *before* and since *that* and subsequent statutes, as regards the law between the Crown and a subject, there has existed and still exists a sufficiently marked distinction between "prescription" for certain usages or rights, and title to land under the statutes of limitation. Mr. Butler, in his annotations (c) on Co. Litt., has touched upon this part of our subject, but would seem to have adopted the doctrine of Lord Hale, in regard to titles to the "sea-shore," and to have considered such titles

(z) [See Angell on Tide Waters, p. 279; Phear 77.]

(a) [Sed *vide* (*Re* Alston's Estate, *ante*, p. 491; Att. *v.* Portsmouth, *ante*, p. 555—Ed.) Benest *v.* Pipon, 1 Knapp 68.]

(b) [21 Jac. 1, c. 2; 9 Geo. 3, c. 16; and 24 & 25 Vict. c. 62.]

(c) Butler's Notes to Co. Litt. 261 a, n. 205.

as capable of being made good by prescription. He first explains the distinction between titles, founded in *common* [27] *right*, which is an ownership conferred by mere act of law, and titles acquired by the act of the party, and which are in derogation of such common right. "In inquiries," says he, "of this kind, where it is said that a person is entitled "to the right or property in question, by *common right*, but "that it *may* belong to another, it is intended to say, that "the right or property in question is, by common law, "annexed to the particular capacity of the party, or to "some property of which he is owner; yet that it is not so "inseparably or inalienably annexed to this capacity or "ownership, but that the party may transfer it to another. "So that in all these cases, the presumption is in favour of "him to whom the right or property is said to belong by "common right; yet this does not exclude the possibility "of its belonging to another. To another, therefore, it *may* "belong, but if he claim it, he must prove his title to it. "On the other hand, the party to whom it belongs of *com-* "*mon right* is under no obligation of showing his title to it; "to him, in the intendment of the law, it belongs till there "is proof of the contrary. To exemplify this doctrine, the "lord of a manor is lord of the soil of the manor of common "right; (*d*) that is, if it be admitted or proved that he is lord "of the manor, his right to the soil necessarily follows so far "that it is not incumbent on him to produce any proof of "it. He may, therefore, of common right, dig for gravel, "unless it is to the prejudice of his tenants. But this right "is not inseparable or unalienable from the seignory. The "lord may grant it (*i.e.* the right to dig gravel) to the "tenants; to the tenants, therefore, it may belong. But if "they claim it, it is incumbent on them to prove their title "to it. There are two ways of doing this,—one by showing [28]

(*d*) The word "manor" includes the soil, as "*omne majus continet* "*in se minus*,"—yet are they separable. (It may, and generally does, include the foreshore as parcel of the soil of the manor: Duke of Beaufort *v.* Swansea, 3 Exch. 413; Att. *v.* Portsmouth, *ante*, p. 555; Lestrange *v.* Rowe, *ante*, p. 542. It is a question of evidence simply in each case whether it does so include it or not.—Ed.)

"the grant from the lord, the other by *prescription;* that is, "by proving an immemorial usage of it, which, in the eye "of the law, always presupposes a grant. Now, prescrip- "tion is shown by producing repeated and unequivocal "instances of the immemorial usage or exercise of the "right contended for; the tenants, therefore, in the case "we have mentioned, if they cannot produce the original "grant, must, to make out their title to dig for gravel, "produce repeated and unequivocal instances of their hav- "ing done it immemorially. If they do this, they estab- "lish their title to the right in question. But, though the "lord is not called upon in the first instance to prove his "title; yet, when it is claimed by others, he may disprove "their claim by showing he has done acts inconsistent with "it. Thus, if, on the one hand, the tenants can prove, by "repeated instances, that they have exercised the right in "question of digging for gravel, the lord may, on the other "hand, show that in all, or a considerable number of these "instances, the parties have been presented at his court, or "otherwise punished for the acts in question, and this may "destroy the effect of the evidence in their favour, arising "from the instances adduced by them. In the same man- "ner, the lord may show that they have dug only in one "particular spot of the waste, at particular times, or for a "particular purpose; by this he may circumscribe their "right as to the place, time, and manner of its enjoyment. "It should also be observed, that though it is said that pre- "scription presupposes a grant, and non-user presupposes a "release, it is not that, strictly speaking, the courts always, "in these cases, *really believe* that such a grant, or such a "release, is actually executed; but because for the sake of "the general principle of quieting possessions, they will not "permit them to be disturbed by claims long dormant, and
[29] "therefore determine in the same manner as they would "determine if the very instrument of grant or release were "produced," The learned writer then goes on to say (quoting from Lord Hale), "as to the *soil between high and* "*low-water mark* at ordinary tides, this, of common right, "belongs to the King. It *may*, however, belong to a subject

"by grant or *prescription.* Sometimes it is parcel of the "adjacent manor: sometimes of the adjacent vill, or parish: "sometimes it belongs to a subject in gross;" "still, how- "ever," says Mr. Butler, "it belongs of common right to "the King; it is therefore incumbent on the subject to "prove his right. This may be done by producing the "grant. Hale, ib. ch. 4, 5, 6. (*e*) Sir Henry Constable's case, "5 Rep. 107. But as it is part of the possessions of the "Crown, *jure coronæ*, it does not pass by general words, and "therefore to establish a right to it under the grant, it must "contain such words as either *expressly*, or by *necessary* "*implication*, convey the soil. If the grant cannot be pro- "duced, it can *no otherwise* be proved than by 'prescrip- "'tion,' that is, as we observed before, by repeated unequi- "vocal and immemorial *usage*. As to *ports*, there is a "very material and important distinction between the *fran-* "*chise* of a port and the *property of its soil.* As to the "franchise; by the common law, a port is the only place "where a subject is permitted to unlade *customable* goods. "This privilege constitutes what is called the franchise of a "port. To create the franchise of a port is part of the royal "prerogative. *But this does not in anywise affect the pro-* "*perty of the soil.*" "It may be considered as a striking "instance of the respect of the law of England for private "property, that though it entrusts the King with the pre- "rogative of originating ports, and though the use of the "adjacent soil is essentially necessary to the existence of a "port, the law does not permit the King to take any part of [30] "the soil from the owner; so that, if the soil is not the pro- "perty of the King, it is necessary to secure the property of "the shore beforehand, for the purposes of the port. (*f*) The

(*e*) *Ante*, pp. 376, 384, 392.

(*f*) (This, in the Editor's experience, is not the case. The ownership of the soil is not necessary to the exercise of the franchise of a port: in the numerous cases of claims to the soil of the port by the port owners which he has had to investigate, it has almost invariably turned out that they have not the soil, or at any rate not the foreshore, but only the franchise; and although they take duties, groundage, and anchorage, which savour of the soil, they take them as port dues, and not as soil dues. The distinction between such dues and ballastage dues is

"franchise belongs to the King of common right, but by "charter or *prescription*, it may be, and frequently is, the "right of the subject. The soil generally belongs to the "owner of the port; but it is going too far to say that "it belongs to him of common right. The mere grant of a "port would not, in a *modern* charter, (*g*) pass the soil; but "*perhaps* it would be sufficient in an *ancient* charter to pass "it, if no evidence to the contrary could be shown; and it "certainly would be considered as sufficient to pass it in "an ancient charter, if accompanied with the additional "circumstance of immemorial usage." The learned annotator then adds:—"Having thus shown to whom the soil of "the shore and of ports belong by common right, it remains "to state succinctly the nature of the evidence by which "the right to it may be proved to exist in another. (*h*) It "may be done by showing that he, and those under whom "he claims, have immemorially, frequently, and without "restriction to any part of the soil, dug gravel, (*i*) fetched

shewn in an unreported decision of the Court of Exchequer: Haselrig *v.* Bishop of Durham, Exch. Decrees, Michaelmas, 4 James II., No. 10, *ante*, p. 420. The soil of a port *may* be in the owner of the port, but does not pass to him by the grant of the port any more than the soil of foreshore passes by the grant of wreck. In the ports of Newcastle, Hull, Colchester, Ipswich, Southampton, Exeter, &c., the soil of the ports is not in the owners of the ports, except, perhaps, such portion of as is parcel of the boroughs: Att. *v.* Portsmouth, *ante*, p. 555.—ED.)

(*g*) See above, note (*f*).

(*h*) Hale, De Jure Maris, *ante*, pp. 394, 395.

(*i*) Yet copyholders do not acquire a right to the soil by proving an immemorial custom to dig gravel or sand. Why, therefore, should such act, by a lord of a manor, in the shore, raise a title in him, against the king, to the ownership of the shore? (Because such user is evidence of an act done as of right by the lord of the manor, who claims the shore as parcel of the manor, and is part of the natural usage of the shore which may have been granted to him by the Crown. The copyholder can only dig under a custom to have an easement to dig for the use of his ancient tenement, and cannot have a custom to dig and *sell* the gravel. It is also evidence which presumes title in the lord, because he is a person to whom such a grant could have been made. Mere digging by members of the public who have not at common law a right to dig sand on the shore, whether it belong to the Crown or to a subject, is only evidence of a trespass; but digging by the

"away seaweed or sand, or embanked against the sea. If "it be claimed to be part of a manor, the right of common-"age for the cattle of the lord and the tenants; the prose-"cution and punishment of purprestures in the court of a [31] "manor; its being included in the perambulations, *and* "*every other act by which the right to the soil of inland pro-*"*perty is established*, may be given in evidence in support "of it. The right to wreck of the sea, or royal fish by pre-"scription *infra manerium*, is a strong presumption for the "shore's being a parcel of the manor. Lord Hale's expres-"sion is very strong; perchance (says his lordship), the "shore is parcel almost of all such manors as by prescrip-"tion have royal fish or wrecks of the sea within their "manors. But it should be observed, that though wreck is "frequently parcel of a manor, it is a royal franchise, and "belongs of common right to the Crown. But by *grant* "or *prescription* it may, and, in fact, frequently does belong "to a subject, sometimes *in gross*, but *oftener* as *parcel of* "*his manor*, parish, or vill, adjacent to the sea."

Mr.Butler's opinion as to the proofs of title to the ownership of the sea-shore, considered.

Mr. Butler, in the foregoing note, adopts the doctrine of the treatise he quotes, that a title to the soil of the sea-shore may be founded on prescription. He tells us also, that the same evidence which is allowed to establish inland title, *may* be adduced in support of titles to portions of the sea-shore; but he does not say that such evidence, and *no other*, MUST be adduced. On the contrary, we find that *wreck*, *royal fish*, a *separate fishery*, *right of digging sand*, *&c.* are also adduced as good evidence of title to the *land* or soil itself. This, however, it will be admitted, is not evidence which would support a title to inland property. (*k*)

Rights and privileges which do not imply or confer a title to the soil of inland estate.

Common of pasture, of turbary, of piscary estovers, rights of digging brick earth, or marl, and rights of way, in manors, are rights analogous to those of wreck, separate

lord of the manor raises the presumption of a grant of the soil, because he is capable of having taken such a grant: Howe *v.* Stawell, Alc. & Nap. 348; Att. *v.* Tomline, 14 Ch. D. 58.—ED.)

(*k*) (But see *post*, as to the nature of the limited possession which a subject can have in the shore, and Scotch cases, *ante*, pp. 581–591.—ED.)

Analogous privileges in the sea-shore have no greater effect.

[32]

fishery, and digging of sand, &c. on the shore, and yet none of these analogous rights are allowed to give title to the soil. Neither can the form or mode of pleading a title to these incorporeal rights or privileges, be used in pleading a title to land. Wreck, and a right of way, are both founded on the like grounds of title, viz. either *grant* or *prescription*, which prescription is, in substance, evidence or proof of usage, or custom, beyond memory of man, and which usage raises the presumption of an ancient grant of such privileges. (*l*)

The shore is, technically, *land*.

Now, we have it laid down, as before quoted, that a title to land, *i.e.* freehold estate, cannot be founded on "prescription." (*m*) Are we then to conclude that the land or soil on the sea-shore is not, in legal intendment, or consideration, "*land*"? It is apprehended that no distinction whatever exists in legal construction, between the land on the shore, and land in the interior. Accordingly, in Scratton *v.* Brown, (*n*) the "shore" is expressly regarded, by the Court, as "land," in all its technical attributes, as a corporeal hereditament held by tenure, and as a "move-"able freehold." The Court said, "where the grantee has "a freehold in that which the Crown grants, his freehold "shifts as the sea recedes or encroaches."

Acts which are evidences of an inland title are evidences of title to sea-shore.

There can be no difficulty in agreeing with Mr. Butler, that those acts which are evidence of title to inland estates, are equally available to prove a title to the land on the shore. Thus, for instance, if I inclose a piece of waste land in the interior, and cultivate it, this is an act *primâ facie* denoting title; *so*, if I inclose by an embankment a piece of the sea-shore; for these are both actual taking seizin and possession of the land. If I can prove such seizin for a period of sixty years, in regard to such piece of land, whether on the coast or inland, the *statute law* confirms my title to such piece of land. Land on the coast, as well as land in the interior, may equally be acquired by adverse possession, and the statutes of limitation. When possession

(*l*) [See now 2 & 3 Will. 4, c. 71, and *ante*, p. 691, note (*p*).]
(*m*) *Ante*, p. 690. (*n*) 4 B. & C. 485.

of land is taken adversely to the king's ownership, or to the ownership of a subject, the law requires that there should [33] be some manifest act or acts of the party demonstrating an intention to assume the *territorial* ownership of the *locus in quo*. The intrusion or disseizin must be such as the statute may recognize as the substantial territorial acquisition which it (the statute) was intended to act upon and confirm. The statute was not passed for the purpose of confirming a partial ownership in the land; such as a right to dig marl, or to pasture cattle, but the *droit droit*, or absolute ownership. Such, therefore, ought to be the positive and unequivocal nature of the possession taken. There is no difficulty in admitting a title to a *districtus maris*, under an *express* grant from the Crown. But there seems some difficulty in determining what acts shall be considered sufficiently forcible and exclusive to oust the King's ownership in a certain *districtus maris*, still continuing open to the action of the tides. Every attempt of this kind is a *wrong;* and the less intitled to aid from the law, as being a wrong against the Crown. How far certain acts, more equivocal, but less difficult than are required in inland titles, will be held sufficient evidence of *ouster* and possession, in cases of *districti maris*, against the king, is not very clearly settled; but that there *are* acts sufficient to constitute *seizin* at law of certain portions of land covered by the sea, as so much *land*, seems to be allowed by the books. If this be so, it will *à fortiori* be admitted that the *sea-shore* is *land*, and capable of grant and conveyance (for it has been granted and conveyed) from one person to another, like other lands; and it must therefore follow, that such shore is capable of *seizin* in law; and it will also be admitted that portions of the sea-shore are *capable* of being taken such exclusive possession of, as, under the statutes of limitation, will ultimately make a good title. This forcible and exclusive possession of a portion of the sea-shore may be taken adversely to another individual, which is a *disseizen;* or against [34] the King, which is an *intrusion;* and such disseizen or intrusion, may, after sixty years, by virtue of the statutes of limitation, work a good title to the disseizor, or intruder.

The sea-shore capable of seizin, in law.

The sea-shore, therefore, does not seem to be that species of property which, in its nature, requires from the indulgence of the law, a more relaxed, and less certain evidence of title than inland property. There is no necessity for our law to admit other evidence of title to the shore, than it calls for in regard to inland estate. (*o*)

(*o*) (Mr. Hall, in the foregoing paragraphs, endeavours to lay down the broad proposition that no title can be made to the shore against the Crown except by exclusive adverse possession by inclosure and exclusion of all other persons, in precisely the same manner as may be done for the *terra firma*, and argues that advantage cannot be taken of the Statutes of Limitation and the Nullum Tempus Acts, except by evidence of exclusive possession. This argument is not tenable. The Act of 21 Jac. I. cap. 2, enacts that the King shall not impeach or sue any person concerning any manors, lands, tenements, or hereditaments, which have been out of the Crown for sixty years, or have not stood *in super* of record in charge in the Exchequer accounts for sixty years. This is confirmed by 9 George III. cap. 16, and 24 & 25 Vict. cap. 62. There is no suggestion of exclusive possession such as Mr. Hall says is necessary. If the hereditaments have been out of the possession of the Crown, and out of the charge of the Exchequer, and in the possession of other persons, the right of action and claim of the Crown is barred. The word "manors" in these Acts will extend to all that can be shewn to be parcel of those manors. Moreover, as the Crown only grants a limited and qualified ownership to the subject in the foreshore, the grantee cannot, from the necessity of the case, shew more than a limited and qualified user of the subject-matter of his grant. If, therefore, he shews that he has immemorially made such use of the shore in question as that shore is capable of from its nature, situation, and condition, he has shewn that he has used it as amply as the Crown could grant it to him, and as amply as the Crown ever had it in possession. When, therefore, the Crown challenges its grantee for alleged intrusion, averring that it has never granted the foreshore, and claims to regain its original possession, it is submitted that, on the grantee shewing that he has immemorially used the foreshore in the same manner that the Crown could have used it had it not been so granted out, and has had such possessions as from the nature of the shore the Crown could have had, and this for sixty years and upwards, he has rebutted the claim of the Crown and raised in his favour the presumption of a grant to his predecessors, and as the Crown could not have had physical exclusive possession, as by embankment and inclosure (impossible in almost every case), it cannot call upon the grantee to shew such impossible occupation—an occupation which the Crown itself could never have had. Mr. Hall himself says, *post*, p. 706:—"The aw requires the best evidence of the

Lord Coke (*p*) tells us, that "*prescription* is regularly *the* "*mother of things appendant or appurtenant;*"(*q*) and he then proceeds to distinguish between what may, and what may not be appendant or appurtenant; from which an inference is clearly deducible that "*land*" cannot be appendant or appurtenant to *land.* (*r*) "A thing corporeal," says he, "can-

Prescription concerns things appendant or appurtenant.

"right *which the nature of things will allow.*" It cannot require more, for that would be to require an impossibility. See Lord Advocate *v.* Young, 12 App. Cas. 544, *ante*, p. 588.—ED.)

(*p*) Co. Litt. 121 b, 122 a.

(*q*) "Concerning things appendant or appurtenant, two things are im- "plied: first, that prescription (which regularly is the mother thereof) "does not make anything appendant or appurtenant, unless the thing "appendant or appurtenant agree, in quality and nature, to the thing "whereunto it is appendant or appurtenant; as a thing corporeal, can- "not properly be appendant to a thing corporeal, nor a thing incorpo- "real to a thing incorporeal. But things incorporeal, which lie in grant, "as advowsons, villeins, commons, and the like, may be appendant to "things corporeal, as a manor, house, or lands, or things corporeal to "things incorporeal, as lands to an office. But yet, as hath been said, "they must agree in nature and quality, for common of turbary, or es- "tovers, cannot be appendant, or appurtenant to *land*, but to a house, "to be spent there. Secondly, That nothing can be properly appen- "dant or appurtenant to anything, unless the principal or superior "thing be of perpetual subsistence, and continuance; for example, an "advowson, that is said to be appendant to a manor, is *in rei veritate* "appendant to the demesnes of the manor, which are of perpetual sub- "sistence, and not to rents or services, which are subject to extinguish- "ment and destruction." Co. Litt. 121 b, 122 a.

(*r*) It has been expressly decided, that "land cannot be appurtenant "to land." Buszard and others *v.* Capel and another, 8 B. & C. 141. In this case it had been found by a jury, in a special verdict, "that by "indenture, T. B. demised to W. R. J. and G. J. all that wharf next [35] "the river Thames, described by abutments, together with all ways, "paths, passages, *easements*, profits, commodities, and *appurtenances* "whatsoever, to the said wharf belonging; and that by the indenture, "the exclusive *use* of the land of the river Thames, opposite to, and in "front of the wharf, *between high and low-water mark*, as well when "covered with water, as dry, for the accommodation of the tenants of "the wharf, was demised, as *appurtenant* to the wharf,—but that the "land itself between high and low-water mark was not demised." Lord Tenterden, C.J., said, "it is difficult to understand how the *exclusive* "*use* [of the land] could be demised, and the *land* not.—If the mean- "ing of this finding be that the land itself, [*i.e.* between high and low- "water mark, in other words, 'shore or *littus*,'] was demised *as appur-*

[35] not be appendant to a thing corporeal." (*s*) But if the shore be land, then the shore cannot be appendant or appurtenant to adjacent land, or manors, or be prescribed for as such. The phrase "parcel of," signifies "*pars totius*," and denotes that the thing is an integral part, and homogeneous. But if *wreck* be *appendant*, and yet be allowed to carry the shore with it, then the *shore* is in effect appendant, but according to Lord Coke, this cannot be. (*t*) It may be further observed (as marking the distinction between things which may, and things which may not be prescribed for) that *spiritual* persons may, and regularly do *prescribe for tithes*, because they are *incorporeal* hereditaments, when owned by spiritual persons; but *lay impropriators* cannot *prescribe* for tithes because impropriate tithes, in lay hands, are not incorporeal hereditaments, but *real estate*, and of *freehold* quality, and have "the nature and all the incidents of "temporal inheritances, and are sued for and recovered in "the temporal courts in like manner as lands and other "hereditaments. (*u*) Hence a title to lay tithes, can no

Distinction between things which may, and things which may not be prescribed for.

[36] more be made "*by prescription*," than a title to lands. (*x*) The very change from a spiritual to a lay inheritance, at once destroys all title by *prescription*. (*y*)

"*tenant* to the wharfs, that would be a finding that one piece of land "was appurtenant to another, which in point of law cannot be." [An exclusive right of fishing for oysters, may be prescribed for as appendant to land: Hayes *v*. Bridges, 1 Ridg. L. & S. 390.]

(*s*) Co. Litt. 121 b.

(*t*) (It is abundantly clear that land cannot be appurtenant to land, and if foreshore be claimed as appurtenant to a manor or an estate, no doubt such a claim may be bad; but foreshore is not claimed as *appurtenant* to but as *parcel of* the manor, and evidence of user is admissible to shew what is parcel of a manor or estate. It is upon this ground that foreshore has been held to pass by the grant of a manor, not as *appurtenant* to but as *parcel*, and it is manifest that the shore may be parcel of and *pars totius manerii*, and will pass by a grant of the manor if user be shewn to prove that it was so parcel.—Ed.)

(*u*) Toller on Tythes, 16–18.

(*x*) Toller, 18.

(*y*) ["The mode of proof which is technically called prescription," says Mr. Phear, p. 68, "can only be employed to establish rights "originating in a grant, *i.e.* almost exclusively incorporeal rights," and referring to this argument of Hall's, he says, "and for this reason

Usage the essence of prescription.

The essence of a prescriptive right is the *usage*. Proof of the usage, and proof of its having been in use *time out of mind*, are equally necessary. (*z*) The thing claimed is the use, viz. a right to do, or enjoy in future, that which has been, and is proved to have been heretofore time out of mind, done or enjoyed. It is not the claiming one thing, *because* another thing has been used or enjoyed. Proof that a common of pasture, or a road, or the franchise of wreck has been immemorially enjoyed, is confirmatory of my title to enjoy such common, or road, or wreck, in future. This right or privilege is not tangible, but exists only in the eye and contemplation of law. Either the express grant, or the [37] continued and immemorial usage, is the best possible evidence the law can procure of the franchise or privilege claimed, and therefore it rests content with such evidence. (*a*)

" considering it inapplicable to prove a title to the ownership of the " shore itself, he has devoted much space in his excellent treatise to " showing how seldom the questions raised between private claimants " and the public have amounted to questions of actual ownership and " therefore how little there is to support the common dictum, that " such ownership can be established by prescription." "His observa- " tion," continues Mr. Phear, "is very just if the word prescription be " always understood in its narrowest sense, as pointing only to the " quantity of enjoyment requisite for establishing a right; but it will be " found on examining the cases therein referred to, that 'prescription' " was used in them to express merely that the right in question could " not be assailed after long enjoyment, and was not there intended to " specify further, that such enjoyment, either really or constructively " had the immemorial duration which is characteristic of prescription " in its technical sense, and which gives a title, as opposed to the " limited enjoyment which the statutes of limitation rendered protec- " tive of possession. This general employment of the word prescrip- " tion is common enough in our text writers."

[A plea of prescription is supported if the party prove a right more extensive than that pleaded; but the right must be of such a nature that it may comprehend the right pleaded. Coleridge, J., in Bayley *v.* Appleyard, 8 Ad. & Ell. 167, S. C. 3 N. & P. 257.]

(*z*) [See 2 & 3 Will. 4, c. 71, and *ante*, pp. 691, 692.]

(*a*) [In Blewitt *v.* Tregoning, 3 Ad. & Ell. 583, Littledale, J., says :— " If evidence establishes a user as far back as memory goes, and there " does not appear to be any time at which it did not exist, that is proof " of prescription." In Jenkins *v.* Harvey, 1 Cr. M. & R. 894, Alderson, B., says :—" If an uninterrupted usage of upwards of seventy years,

The law requires the very best evidence of the right which the nature of things will allow. Wherefore, if I claim a title to a thing which is tangible, and capable of seizin and manual possession, the law requires proof of such seizin or manual possession, either past or present, or both, as the best evidence that I have made it mine. The reason given (as before said) why land cannot be claimed by prescription is this, that it is a thing capable of more certain evidence of ownership(*b*) than those things which lie in prescription are capable of; viz. of a transfer of the actual possession—*i.e.*, the land itself, from one to another—from the last owner to the present. This actual transfer is called livery of seizin; and prescription never was, and is not now allowed to supply the place of seizin, in questions of titles to things of which seizin can be given.(*c*) Prescription is the allegation

"unanswered by any evidence to the contrary, is not sufficient to "establish a right like the present (receipt of toll for coal imported into "the port), there are innumerable titles which could not be sustained." In Fitzpatrick *v.* Robinson, 1 Hud. & Br. 585, it was held that a user by the public of an open strand or waste, does not necessarily lead to the inference that the owner of the soil has abandoned his right to it and given it to the public; and in Murphy *v.* Ryan, 2 Ir. C. L. R. 143, it was held that the public cannot acquire by immemorial usage any right of fishing in a river in which, though it be navigable, the tide does not ebb and flow; for the word "navigable," used in a legal sense as applied to a river in which the soil *primâ facie* belongs to the Crown, and the fishing to the public, imports that the river is one in which the tide ebbs and flows.]

(*b*) 2 Bl. Com. 264.

(*c*) (But livery of seisin of foreshore as parcel of the manor may be given: Brook, title View, pl. 101. "Sed est auter diversitie concernant "viewe car si un feoffment de B. acre que gist del auter part dun moun-"taine tout hors del viewe la liverey de ceo nest bone sans express "viewe tamen tout voile passer per viewe de parte *et sic in mon case ou* "*part gist south le floud del mere ceo non obstant passe ut parcel del* "*mannor*": Callis, 13.—Ed.) There seems an exception which is given

[37] by Littleton, sect. 310, that "*tenants in common* may be by title of "prescription, as if the one and his ancestors, or they whose estate he "hath in one moietie, have holden in common the same moietie with "the other tenant which hath the other moietie, and with his ancestors, "or with those whose estate he had *undivided* time out of mind." To this Lord Coke subjoins, "but joint tenants cannot be by prescription, "because there is survivor between them, but not between tenants in

and proof of a *usage*, not *occupation*. The shore must be not [38] merely *used*, but so *occupied* as of necessity to involve actual seizin or possession of it. If I prove such usage of it as is tantamount to seizin and exclusive possession, that is, in fact, showing title by *adverse possession*, and not by *prescription*, and it remains to be seen by the statute law whether my possession can be supported. Or, the land may be used as a mere convenience, as for a road, or as a fishing-place; and if I prove such use of a road, or such custom to fish there, to have existed time out of mind, I have proved certain specific rights which the common law allows and confirms to me, without statute law. In such case I have made good my title to a *distinct* species of property from the land itself: why should the law go further, and *that* even against the King, by tacking to it a right to the very soil itself? (*d*) (*e*)

Prescriptive rights are no doubt all founded on *presumptive* evidence, and therefore it is that land cannot be precribed for; *i.e.* presumed in point of title. (*f*). To say that the shore lies in prescription, is placing it on a par, in point of title, with mere easements, which is surely incorrect. (*g*)

As to evidence of boundaries in titles.

As to the evidence to particular *limits* and *boundaries* of

"common." There seems also another exception, Co. Litt. 121, 122, as to lands annexed to an office, which is an incorporeal *hereditament*, to which lands may be appendant or appurtenant, and pass by *deed* of grant of the office only,—but it appears that there must be a "deed, "and secondly, the thing to which the land is appended must be "*ejusdem generis*, *i.e.* an *hereditament*, which franchises, commons, "and liberties are not."

(*d*) Jerwood, 31.

(*e*) (Because if I shew that I have used the thing as amply and fully as the Crown could have granted it to me, and that immemorially and to the exclusion of similar user by others, I have, in fact, shewn that the Crown did grant it to me, and has left me quietly in possession, so far as physical possession is possible, and my possession implies such a grant, and the statutes protect my possession.—ED.)

(*f*) 2 Bl. Com. 264. See p. 682, *ante*.

(*g*) (The shore is never prescribed for as a separate hereditament nor as an easement; it is prescribed for as parcel of a manor, borough, or land, and evidence of user is produced to shew it to be such parcel. —ED.)

estates, it is to be remembered, that in every such enquiry
[39] of metes and bounds, the titles to the *estates* of which some particular spot in question is claimed to be *parcel*, are not disputed, but are admitted to be good, according to the strict rule of evidence of title to lands; the question only refers to and concerns the metes and bounds of the respective estates. But, as against the Crown, *reputation* does not seem admissible in such question. (*h*) (*i*) It has also been refused between two private disputants. (*k*) There is no doubt but that *written* documents, or sixty years' quiet possession, under the statutes of limitation, will prevail over all verbal testimony, or prescriptive—which is presumptive evidence, however strong. Where there is nothing but presumptive evidence on both sides, except that one has positive possession, the Courts of law do no more than refuse to disturb the possession.

The king's title is positive, and by the common law.

Now, as between the King and a subject, in respect of the sea-shore, there can be *presumptive evidence but on one side only*, the King's right is not presumptive, but a legal title of the strictest kind; the common law itself is the King's evidence of title, and no better can exist; and presumptive evidence must necessarily be inferior to it. (*l*) In the absence

(*h*) 2 Roll. Abr. 186, pl. 5, tit. Prerogative.

(*i*) (This dictum is very questionable, but, in cases of proving foreshore to be parcel of the manor, it is very seldom that such evidence will be used alone. The proof is usually made by bailiffs' accounts, the evidence of acts done by servants of the lord, and matters of record.—ED.)

(*k*) See Outram *v.* Morewood, 14 East 331, note. [R. *v.* Inhab. of Bedfordshire, 4 E. & B. 535, 541, 24 L. J. Q. B. 81. See also cases cited in Taylor on Evidence, and Hunt on Boundaries 226 *et seq.* See *post*, pp. 761, 763.]

(*l*) See Jerwood, p. 124. (Mr. Hall's view of the strictness of the legal title of the Crown will, I trust, be reconsidered by the light of the history of that title set forth in this volume. It is now clear, upon the proved facts, that the title by presumption of fact is all the other way. There is presumption in favour of the Crown *upon a theory*; there is presumption in favour of the subject *upon the facts*. It is clear that the Crown never did, and never intended to, reserve the foreshore in any grants anterior to Elizabeth, and all the coast had been granted out long before that date. The statute *de Prærogativa Regis* negatives the presumption of any such reservation. There is no instance of such a reservation in any grant of a manor subsequent to Elizabeth. It

of any grant or documentary title, the only other title to land is, it is conceived, by adverse possession, ratified and confirmed by the statutes of limitation. Can, then, adverse possession, or seizin of the soil of the sea-shore be *legally proved* by mere evidence of a right of wreck, a right of fishery, or the privilege of digging sand? Are these such uses of the land itself as necessarily carry with them the seizin and possession of such land? It is difficult to admit this doctrine. If the *freehold* of the shore were intimately and *essentially* connected with the franchise of wreck, or those other franchises, liberties, or usufructory privileges which are enjoyed thereon, then indeed a title to the one could not be made good without involving with it the title to the other. But if we examine the nature and quality of these franchises, liberties, and privileges, which are noticed by our law, we shall find that they not only do not *necessarily* involve or carry with them the soil of the sea-shore, but that they may, and generally do, actually exist separate and distinct from the ownership of the shore,—as such examination is not foreign to our subject, we will consider these franchises and privileges in their order. (*m*) (*n*)

Adverse possession of the shore may be confirmed by statute law, but not by prescriptive rights to wreck, &c.

[40]

The franchises, liberties, profits, and advantages derivable from the *sea*, may be considered as follows :—

1st. Fishing, (*o*) public and general, or private and several.

Profits. Franchises and liberties derivable from the sea.

follows, therefore, that the true presumption is that the Crown has granted out all the foreshore, and against such a presumption there is only the theory invented by Digges that the Crown had seldom or never done so.—ED.)

(*m*) [See remarks on case of Dickens *v.* Shaw.]

(*n*) (As has been stated before, *ante*, p. 648, the right to franchises does not *per se* carry the shore. The right to the franchise of wreck raises the presumption that the shore is parcel of the manor in which the wreck is taken; but that presumption alone is insufficient; when, however, other acts of ownership of a character affecting the soil are shewn, a further presumption arises, and then this right to the franchise considered with the further presumption arising from the other acts does raise the presumption of title to the shore. See pp. 646, 688.—ED.)

(*o*) Whale, sturgeon, and porpoise, whenever and by whomsoever caught in the British seas, are the property of the Crown by royal prerogative. They each constitute what in our law is called a royal

2nd. The use of the sea for the transportation of merchandise in traffic, and for ports, or for any other purpose of use or enjoyment to which it can be applied.

3rd. The perquisite of what in our law is called Wreck,(*p*) being the unclaimed ships and cargo wrecked on the shore.

[41] And of the shore. The uses and profits of the *shore* are,—1. Fishing ;(*q*) 2. Wreck, and its accompaniments flotsam, &c. ; 3. Egress and regress, and right of Way, for the purpose of navigation, fishing, bathing, and other uses of the sea ; 4. Ports ; 5. The digging and carrying away its soil and materials for building, ballast, manure, &c.

Now, as we have already attributed the absolute ownership of the sea, and sea-shore, to the King, *ab origine*,—it

franchise. Such franchises, however, were formerly granted away by the Crown to a subject; limited within certain districts, as a manor, hundred, &c. In Scotland, salmon seems to have been inter regalia. See Erskine's Principles.

(*p*) Wreck is also a royal franchise, and with the perquisites called flotsam, jetsam, and lagan, was formerly often granted within certain territorial limits to the subject, as within a manor, hundred, &c. 1 Bl. Com. 290.

The above regalia, or royal franchises, are possessed by the Crown, not in respect of the land or soil of the shore, or the ownership of the sea, but by the royal prerogative, in distinct and peculiar ownership.

"[Whenever goods floating on the sea, or stranded below high-water "mark, cease to be either actively or constructively in the possession of [41] "their owner, they *ipso facto* vest in the Crown as wreck ; if they formed "portion of a ship, or its cargo, out of which none of the crew nor any "domestic animal escaped alive, they become immediately the absolute "property of the Crown ; in other cases, the vesting in the Crown is "for temporary protection only until the lapse of a year and a day, "during which time the original owner may come in and revest them "in himself; but at the expiration of that period, without any claim "having been made by the owner, the title of the Crown becomes, as "in the first instance, indefeasible." Phear, p. 99 (note). See authorities cited in Dunwich *v.* Sterry, 1 B. & Ad. 831. "At common law "a distinction is made between wreck which is stranded, and that "which is sunk in the sea or floats on its surface : the first is termed "wreck proper, and the latter bears the name of flotsam, jetsam, or "lagan, according to the circumstances," &c. Phear, p. 99, and see *post*, p. 753, and statutes concerning wreck.]

(*q*) De Jure Maris, *ante*, p. 377.

might be thought that the above perquisites are absolutely his own, and grantable exclusively to any one of his subjects. But according to the acknowledged law of the land, although the King is owner of this great waste, *yet the common people of England have regularly a liberty of fishing in the sea, and creeks and arms thereof, and in navigable rivers within the tides, as a public common of piscary.* (*r*)

[42] Public right of fishing in the sea.

This public or general right of fishing in the sea, claimed by the subject, is a beneficial privilege enjoyed by British subjects, time out of mind. (*s*) Whether, in fact, it was originally a public grant from the King, or whether it was a reservation by the people of such right, when they vested the rest of the property of the sea in him, or whether it be one of those natural and necessary rights which, like the air we breathe, has ever been free and unquestioned in enjoyment, is immaterial; for the conclusion is the same; viz. that such right of fishing has immemorially belonged to, and been enjoyed by the public, and that, in point of title, it is admitted to be held and enjoyed *by common right*, *i.e.* by the common law, and custom of the Realm. (*t*)

(*r*) Lord Fitzwalter's case, 1 Mod. 105. Anonymous, 6 Mod. 73. Warren *v.* Matthews, 1 Salk. 357. Smith *v.* Kemp, 2 Salk. 637. 16 Vin. 354, pl. 1. Ward *v.* Cresswell, C. B. 14 & 15 of Geo. II. Sir J. Davys' Rep. 57. Willes, 265. The great salmon fishery on the River Banne in Ireland. See also Bro. Abr. Prerog. pl. 35, and 6 Bac. Abr. 398. Carter *v.* Murcot, 4 Burr. 2163. Plowd. 315. Bro. Abr. Custom, pl. 46. Fitz. Abr. Barre, pl. 93. Bagot *v.* Orr, 2 Bos. & Pul. 472. Mayor of Orford *v.* Richardson, 4 T. R. 438, and see 7 Comyn Dig. 70. "Jus piscandi omnibus commune est in portu et in fluminibus," Bract. Lib. 2, ch. 1. Here it is observable that Bracton makes no distinction [42] between those parts of rivers which are, and those which are not, within the flux and reflux of the tides. The public right does not seem to extend above the tides. See accord. Lord Fitzwalter's case, per Hale, C.J., 1 Mod. 105. Dav. 57 [and Hall's Profits à Prendre, 307. Murphy *v.* Ryan, 2 Ir. C. L. R. 143. Taylor's Evidence, part 1, cap. 5, p. 133, 6th edit.].

(*s*) [See Sea Fishery Act, 31 & 32 Vict. c. 45.]

(*t*) [" When the soil of the shore, as is generally the case, is in the " Crown, the rights of the public in the sea, and tidal waters, such as " fishing and navigation, &c., are 'natural rights,' accruing to them as " *cestui que trustent* in possession; but that when a private individual " holds the shore, such of these rights as remain to the public have

Navigation.

[43] The use of the sea, *as a great high way*, for the transportation of merchandise, or any other purpose for which its waters can be usefully navigated, is also a liberty or privilege belonging of common right to the people of England, by the same title as the fishery. (*u*)

" become, strictly speaking, 'easements.' However, in the latter case, " the private owner cannot have a more advantageous position than his " grantor the Crown, and must therefore be subject to all public rights, " unless he can prove an immemorial title to exemption. Hence, in all " cases, the rights of the public in the sea and its shore are *primâ facie* " and must be treated as 'natural rights;' while those of a private indi- " vidual, whether his claim extends to territorial possession or not, can " rest upon no other foundation than the strict construction of a grant." Phear, p. 52. See Malcolmson *v.* O'Dea, 10 House of Lords Cases 593; Marshall *v.* Ulleswater Steam Navigation Co., 3 B. & S. 732; Murphy *v.* Ryan, 2 Ir. C. L. R. 143.]

(*u*) [The right of navigation belongs by law to all the subjects of the realm, and is paramount to the right of fishing; where a part of the sea-coast or shore, being the property of the Crown, and giving *jus privatum* to the King, is granted to a subject for uses, or to be enjoyed so as to be detrimental to the *jus publicum* therein, such grant is void as to such parts as are open to such objection, if acted upon so as to effect nuisances by working injury to the public right, or it is a grant which does not divest the Crown, or invest the grantee; Att.-Gen. *v.* Parmeter, 10 Price 378–412. (The Crown has not the right either itself to use its title to the soil between the high and low water marks as a nuisance or to place upon that soil what will be a nuisance to the Crown's subjects. If the Crown had not such a right, it could not give it to the City of London, nor could the City transfer it to other persons: Att. *v.* Johnson, Wils. Ch. Cas. 87; Rex *v.* Lord Grosvenor, 2 Starkie N. P. 511. The right of navigation, however, is not a right of property; it is simply a right of way: Orr-Ewing *v.* Colquhoun, 2 App. Cas. 839.—Ed.) The right to anchor is a necessary part of the right to navigate; this right never could have been interfered with by grant from the Crown, but evidence of mere immemorial usage will not support a claim to dues for anchorage, and it cannot exist merely in respect of the use of the soil, it must be founded on proof that the soil of the claimant was originally within the precincts of a port or harbour, or that some service, or aid to navigation, was rendered by the owner of the soil, who claims the dues. Gann *v.* Free Fishers of Whitstable, 11 House of Lords Cases 192; Whitstable Fishers *v.* Foreman, L. R. 2 C. P. 688, 4 E. & I. App. 266; see as to the public right of navigation, Att.-Gen. *v.* Lonsdale, L. R. 7 Eq. 377; Colchester, Mayor of, *v.* Brooke, 7 Q. B. 339; Williams *v.* Wilcox, 8 Ad. & E. 329; R. *v.* Ward, 4 A. & E. 384; also Williams *v.* Blackwall, 32 L. J. Ex.

But wreck, and royal fish, are royal franchises, belonging [44] exclusively to the King, by the prerogative of the Crown, Wreck and royal fish.

174; Post *v.* Munn, 1 Souths (New Jersey) R. 61; Angell on Tide Waters, p. 80; Houck, 146; Phear, 53; Angell on Watercourses, 554.

[If property be placed in the channel of a public navigable river, so as to create a public nuisance, a person navigating is not justified in damaging such property by running his vessel against it, if he has room to pass without so doing, for an individual cannot abate a nuisance, if he is no otherwise injured by it than as one of the public (Colchester, Mayor of, *v.* Brooke, 7 Q. B. 339; Brown *v.* Perkins, 12 Gray 89, 101–102); and therefore the fact that such property was a nuisance is no excuse for running upon it negligently: and there is no right to erect a weir which shall obstruct part of the stream. Williams *v.* Wilcox, *supra*; see as to other obstructions, Norbury *v.* Kitchen, 15 L. T. N. S. 501; White *v.* Phillips, 33 L. J. C. P. 33; White *v.* Crisp, 10 Ex. 312; Hancock *v.* York Railway Co., 10 C. B. 348; Att.-Gen. *v.* Johnson, 2 Wils. C. C. 87. The liberty of passage on a public navigable river is not suspended, when the tide is too low for vessels to float. The public right in this respect includes all such rights as, with relation to the circumstances of each river, are necessary for the convenient passage of vessels along the channel. It is, therefore, no excess, if a vessel, which cannot reach her place of destination in a [44] single tide, remains aground till the tide serves; although, by custom or agreement, a fine may be payable to the lord of the soil for such grounding. Colchester, Mayor of, *v.* Brooke, 7 Q. B. 339.

[A riparian proprietor has no greater right to use the alveus of a tidal than a non-tidal river, and therefore cannot construct a jetty so as to injure the property of others or interfere with navigation. Att.-Gen. *v.* Lonsdale, L. R. 7 Eq. 377. See also Bickett *v.* Morris, L. R. 1 Sc. App. 47, and Angell on Tide Waters, p. 95.

[In the Att.-Gen. *v.* Terry, L. R. 9 Ch. App. 423, a wharf owner drove piles into the bed of a river extending the wharf so as to occupy 3 feet out of a breadth of about 60 feet available for navigation. It was held that this was such an obstruction as would be restrained at the suit of a municipal corporation empowered by Act of Parliament to remove obstructions.

[In the court below, the Master of the Rolls held that an owner of land at the side of a public navigable river has no right to erect on the bed of the river, for the benefit of his own trade, any structure, whether any actual obstruction to the navigation of the river will or will not be thereby occasioned; and any benefit to his own trade is too remote to be held for the advantage of the public generally, and so to justify the erection. See American cases, Gould *v.* Carter, 9 Humph. (Tenn.) 369; Commonwealth *v.* Bilderback, 2 Pars. (Penn.) 447.

[No amount of collateral benefit, resulting from any manner of obstruction to the local community, can divest it of its character of a

or to individuals, deriving them, as an exclusive private
[45] possession from the Crown. For the present we will confine our view to the *fishery*.

nuisance, an abridgment of the right of navigation can only be justified when the erection is productive of a greater public benefit. R. *v.* Russell, 6 B. & C. 566. This case was a trial by indictment for a nuisance by erecting staiths in a river, and the jury were directed to acquit the defendant if they thought that the abridgment of the right of passage, occasioned by such erections, was for a public purpose, and produced a public benefit, and if the erections were in a reasonable situation, and a reasonable space was left for the passage of vessels on the river. The judge pointed out to the jury that by means of the staiths, coals were supplied at a cheaper rate, and in a better condition than they otherwise would be, which was a public benefit. It was held by Bayley and Holroyd, JJ., that the direction was proper, but Lord Tenterden, C.J., dissented therefrom, he being of opinion that the price and condition of coals were points not properly to be taken into consideration in the question raised by the
[45] indictment, and that the question to have been taken was, whether the navigation and passage of vessels on a navigable river were injured by the erections in question. See R. *v.* Ward, 4 A. & E. 384.

[But it is not necessary that any interruption of, or interference with, the public rights should amount to a nuisance, Reg. *v.* Betts, 16 Q. B. 1022, 19 L. J. Q. B. 501; R. *v.* Ward, 4 A. & E. 384; Gates *v.* Blencoe, 2 Dana (Ken.) 158; that is a question for the jury, Reg. *v.* Randall, Cas. & M. 496; R. *v.* Russell, 3 E. & B. 942. As to the abatement by injunction, &c., where an individual has sustained damage different from and independent of that which is sustained by the rest of the public, see Bridges *v.* Highton, 11 L. T. N. S. 653; Rose v. Groves, 6 Sc. N. R. 653; Edleston *v.* Crossley, 18 L. T. N. S. 15; Norbury *v.* Kitchen, 18 L. T. N. S. 501; Blakemore *v.* Glamorganshire Canal Co., 1 My. & K. 154; Att.-Gen. *v.* Richards, 2 Anst. 603; Att.-Gen. *v.* Cleaver, 18 Ves. 211; Att.-Gen. *v.* Lonsdale, L. R. 7 Eq. 377; and see remarks of Chancellor Kent in 2 John. Ch. 382, and Georgetown *v.* Alexandria Canal Co., 12 Peters (U.S.) 91. By the customary law of Connecticut, a riparian has the right of soil between high and low water mark, so as to enable him to construct wharves; but before the soil had been so reclaimed, the right of fishing on the flats remains common. E. Haven *v.* Hemingway, 7 Connect. R. 186. See Angell on Watercourses, p. 743.

[In Brown *v.* Mallett, 5 C. B. 599, which was an action against an owner of a vessel sunk by accident, for injuries received by another vessel coming in contact therewith, Maule, J., laid down the following principles:—That it is the duty of a person using a navigable river with a vessel of which he is possessed, and has the control and management, to use reasonable skill and care to prevent mischief to

The public right, (*x*) or common of piscary, (*y*) claimed [46] and allowed by the common law to the people of England in the sea, extends, not only over the open sea, but over all bays, creeks, ports, havens, arms of the sea, and tide-rivers, up to the reach of the tide, (*z*) and also, as it would seem, *over and upon the sea-shore itself*, for such kinds of fish as are

Public fishery.

others, and the liability is the same whether his vessel be in motion or stationary, floating or aground, under water or above it, and this liability may be transferred with the transfer of the possession and control to another person, and on the abandonment of such possession, control, and management, the liability also ceases. See also Hamond *v.* Pearson, 1 Campb. 515; but it is also clear from Rex *v.* Watts, 2 Esp. 675—"that from an unavoidable accident producing the wreck "of a vessel, an indictment cannot be preferrred against the owner for "not removing the impediment to navigation which it creates. There "is no reason for throwing on the owner any special share in the con- "sequence of what may be considered as a misfortune, both to him "and to the public." See White *v.* Crisp, 10 Ex. 312; Parrett Navigation Co. *v.* Robins, 10 M. & W. 593; Parnaby *v.* Lancaster Canal Co., 11 A. & E. 223; 19 Geo. 2, c. 22, s. 3; 54 Geo. 3, c. 159, s. 19; and [46] 10 & 11 Vict. c. 27.

[The Board of Trade is enabled, by the various powers contained in the Railways Consolidation Act, 8 & 9 Vict. c. 20, s. 17; the Harbours, Docks, and Piers Clauses Act, 10 Vict. c. 27, s. 12; the Harbours Transfer Act, 25 & 26 Vict. c. 69; and the Railways Clauses Act, 26 & 27 Vict. c. 92, ss. 13 to 19, to protect the foreshore from being injuriously affected by the construction of such works, as to which these statutes refer, and in the case of Bills for all such works, the Board of Trade take care to see that these Acts are incorporated.]

(*x*) In Anonymous, 6 Mod. 73, it is said, that the King's grant could not bar the public of their right to fish, and as it is a rule that nothing can be *prescribed for* which might not have a lawful commencement by *grant*, it would follow, that no such thing as a separate fishery in the sea, or tide-rivers, could exist if this were good authority. (In 6 Mod. 73 the word is "cannot" grant, not "could not." The case cannot be read as referring to ancient grant.—Ed.) But, 6 Mod. 73 is clearly not law, so far as regards *ancient* grants, and was overruled in Carter *v.* Murcot, 4 Burr. 2163. The doctrine of 6 Mod. 73 is also held (as to the sea) in 2 Com. 431, and is supported in a note (see this note cited in p. 723, *post*) to Carter *v.* Murcot. At this day the King cannot, by grant, abridge the general public right, nor has any such right existed in the Crown since Magna Charta.

(*y*) [See Benett *v.* Costar, 8 Taunt. 183, 1 B. & B. 465 S. C.]

(*z*) See the cases cited p. 711, *ante*.

usually caught upon the rocks, and sands of the coast. (*a*) But in some cases, statute law has set bounds to the exercise of this right, in respect of seasons, particular kinds of fish, and manner of fishing. (*b*) There are also other excepted cases; viz. where private individuals, (*c*) or Corporate bodies, claim and enjoy a separate fishery, in some par-
[47] ticular places in derogation and exclusion of the general right. (*d*) (*e*)

This divides the right of fishery into "communis pisca-

(*a*) Bagot *v.* Orr, 2 Bos. & Pul. 472.

(*b*) [See Woolrych, p. 85 *et seq.*]

(*c*) Dav. Rep. 57 a; Carter *v.* Murcot, 4 Burr. 2163; Warren *v.* Matthews, 1 Salk. 357; Hale, De Jure Maris, cap. v.

(*d*) [" This public right is an established principle, and whether the " opinion of those writers, who class this right among the *jura regalia*, " be preferred, or that, on the other hand, of those who hold the right to " be *jus publicum vel commune*, it is nevertheless certain that, *primâ* "*facie*, the liberty in question is general." Woolrych, pp. 76, 85; Angell on Watercourses, p. 73. And where there is reasonable evidence to show that the question of title raised by a defendant is *bonâ fide*, the jurisdiction of magistrates is at end. R. *v.* Stimpson, 32 L. J. M. C. 208; but see Embleton *v.* Brown, 6 Jur. N. S. 1298. " As a public right, belonging to the people, it *primâ facie* vests in " the Crown; but such legal investment does not diminish the right, " or counteract its exertion." Schulte, p. 15.]

(*e*) (These cases are very numerous. The Editor has made a large collection of documents from the public records which shews the existence of several fisheries throughout the rivers and estuaries of the kingdom. The collection, though large, is by no means complete or exhaustive. There is, however, very little doubt that in ancient times, when fish both from fresh and salt water was an exceedingly valuable article of food, the rights of fisheries were jealously watched. Every non-tidal river was covered with several fisheries from the source to the tide, and in nearly all the tidal rivers there existed similar fisheries extending all over the tidal part of the river and far into the estuary, and in many cases they exist upon the open shore of the sea. A list of the places in which records are found of the existence of several fisheries both in tidal and non-tidal waters, with some remarks on this subject, is given in the Appendix II. at the end of this volume. Mr. Hall's remarks would lead the reader to infer that cases of several fisheries in the tidal water were as rare as cases of foreshore in the hands of the subject are according to his contention. The facts are precisely opposed to the inference he endeavours to draw. See the Appendix II.—ED.)

"ria," or the public common of piscary mentioned above, and the *several*, or *private* fishery belonging to particular owners, and excluding all other persons. The *several* fishery is claimed and enjoyed by *prescription*, or *ancient usage*, presupposing a grant, or by express grant from the Crown, anterior to Magna Charta. (*f*) Several or private fishery.

As the public right of fishery cannot be enjoyed without making use of the sea-shore for egress and regress, and for other essential conveniences which the fishery requires in [48] The public fishery includes a right of egress and regress, &c.

(*f*) [In Allen *v.* Donelly, 5 Ir. C. L. Rep. 229, the petitioner claimed an exclusive right of fishing in an arm of the sea, and a public navigable river, and the petitioner prayed that he might be quieted in possession by an injunction. The respondent relied on the general common law right of fishery in the sea, but it was held that the Court had jurisdiction to entertain such a suit, and the petitioner need not be left exclusively to his common law remedy. In O'Neill *v.* Allen, 9 Ir. C. L. R. 132, the plaintiff in support of a claim to a several fishery in the open sea, proved an adventurer's certificate of the year 1666 acts of ownership by parties unconnected with the person found entitled to the fishery by the certificate, were proved from 1668 to 1701. No such act was proved from that date to 1798, but from 1798 to 1857 there was undisturbed user by the O'Neill family, from whom the plaintiff derived. It was held that a several fishery was rightly found, that the granting of a patent subsequently to 1668 might have been presumed; but that 17 & 18 Car. 2, c. 2, rendered such presumption unnecessary. Whether a several fishery is such a franchise as can be lost by non-user was not decided, but if it were, the absence of evidence of user from 1701 to 1799, did not amount to proof of non-user. (It has since been decided that a several fishery cannot be abandoned: Neill *v.* Duke of Devonshire, 8 App. Cas. 151.—ED.) See also Little *v.* Wingfield, 8 Ir. C. L. Rep. 279; and 11 Ir. C. L. Rep. 63; [48] Malcolmson *v.* O'Dea, 10 House of Lords Cases, 593. And, in the United States, the right of fishery may be granted by the States in the navigable waters in their borders, to individuals, provided the free use of the waters for purposes of navigation and commercial intercourse be not interrupted; 1 Kent Com. 489; Rogers *v.* Jones, 1 Wend. 237. An exclusive right, however, must be shown, and if it can be shown, it may be exercised exclusively, though the presumption is against it, unless a prescriptive right, or express legislative grant, can be given in evidence; for such right shall not be presumed, but the contrary, *primâ facie.* Schulte, 70. See Commonwealth *v.* Charlestown, 18 Mass. (1 Pick.) Rep. 180; Storer *v.* Freeman, 6 Mass. R. 435; Delaware and Maryland Railway Co. *v.* Stump, 8 Gill & J. (Md.) 479; Day *v.* Day, 4 Ind. 262. See also Angell on Watercourses, p. 70, 6th edit. (The right need not be absolutely

order to be carried on with effect, the use of the *sea-shore*,(*g*)
[49] for all purposes essential to the enjoyment of the right of fishery, necessarily accompanies such right. But it is quite clear that the public use of the shore, for the public exercise of the fishery, *does not impeach the King' sownership or property in the soil itself* (*nor the ownership of the subject*). (*h*) Wherefore, the King (or his grantee) remains

exclusive; part of the fishery, as for floating fish, may be given up, and the fishery for shell fish retained: Rogers *v.* Allen, 1 Campb. 39; Neill *v.* Duke of Devonshire, 8 App. Cas. 151.—ED.)

(*g*) We do not speak here of the "*ripa*," or bank, which is adjacent *terra firma*, but of the *sea-shore* only. But for all reasonable purposes of safety and convenience in fishing, and navigation, the *ripa*, or immediate *terra firma*, is, by common right, subject to the free egress and regress of the public. Bro. Abr. Tit. Custom, pl. 46. But this does not extend to any *permanent* appropriation of such *ripam*. Nor will it authorise *towing-paths* to be made. Ball *v.* Herbert, 3 T. R. 253. Towing is not navigation, properly so called. But, it seems, towing-paths, and other modes of moving, raising, and securing vessels, and fishing-boats, &c. upon the adjacent *terra firma*, may well be acquired and enjoyed by usage, or prescription, as a local easement, S. C.

[In this case, Kenyon, C.J., said he remembered when the case of Pierse *v.* Lord Fauconberg, 1 Burr. 292, was sent to that Court from the Court of Chancery, and it was then the current opinion in Westminster Hall, that the right of towing depended on usage, without which it could not exist. See Winch *v.* Conservators of Thames, L. R. 7 C. P. 458, S. C. 41 L. J. C. P. 241; Badger *v.* S. Y. R. Co., 1 E. & E. 347; Monmouth Canal Co. *v.* Hill, 4 H. & N. 427; Kinlock *v.* Nevile, 6 M. & W. 795; Hollis *v.* Goldfinch, 1 B. & C. 205; Angell on Watercourses, 6th edit. 740, on Tide Waters, 176; Woolrych, 164; Brown *v.* Chadbourne, 31 Maine 23, 26; Treat *v.* Lord, 42 Maine 552, 563; Ledyard *v.* Ten Eyck, 36 Barb. 102. The supreme Court of Illinois, and that of Tennessee, have, however, decided agreeably to the civil law, that the right of navigation is not
[49] limited to the bare privilege of floating upon the river, but included the right to land, and to fasten to the shore, as the exigencies of navigation may require; and that such was a burthen upon the owner of the land, which he must bear as a part of the public easement. Middleton *v.* Pritchard, 3 Scam. (Ill.) R. 520; Corp. of Memphis *v.* Overton, 3 Yerg. (Tenn.) R. 390.

(*h*) (The words in brackets are not in Mr. Hall's text.—ED.) See Lord Fitzwalter's Case, 1 Mod. 106; Dickens *v.* Shaw, *ante*, p. 451. (Lord Fitzwalter's Case, in 1 Mod. 105, relates to the River Burnham, the soil of which belongs to the lord of the manor of Burnham. The owner of the shore, liable to such use of it by his subjects, as their ancient common of piscary therein, and in the waters around it, naturally calls for; and this would seem to include a public *right of way* to and fro over the sea-shore.

Several fishery.

A *several*, or *private* fishery (*i*) is claimed, not only against the King's original right, but against the general public right of the subject. It may be either in gross, (*k*) *i.e.* an absolute personal right, or privilege attaching to the individual, or Corporate body of individuals (as many Religious Houses formerly had); or it may be appendant or appurtenant to (or parcel of) manors; and *this* (*l*) not only in navigable rivers, and arms of the sea, but in creeks, ports, and havens; and in *certain known limits in the open sea, contiguous to the shore.* In 2 Com. 431, the contrary is held, as to the *sea;* but in 4 T. R. 437, Mayor of Orford *v.* Richardson, where both a *several*, and a *free* fishery were prescribed for, Lord Kenyon said, "there can be no doubt "but that there may be a *prescriptive* right in a subject to [50] "a several fishery in an arm of the sea." (*m*)

In gross.

Or appendant, or appurtenant.

Editor was concerned in a case in which the title was proved. See also a case relating thereto in 50 Edward III., *ante*, p. 156, cited by Hale, cap. v.—ED.)

(*i*) See *post*, further, on this kind of fishery, [and Phear, p. 64.]

(*k*) [Shuttleworth *v.* Le Fleming, 19 C. B. N. S. 687.]

(*l*) De Jure Maris, *ante*, p. 385, [see Hayes *v.* Bridges, 1 Ridg. L. & S. 390; Hamilton *v.* Donegall, Marquis of, 3 Ridg. 311; Rogers *v.* Allen, 1 Camp. 39.]

(*m*) [A several fishery passes under the words "all the salmon "fisheries, pyke, eyle, and other fishings of and in the river," Ashworth *v.* Brown, 7 Ir. Jur. O. S. 315, Q. B.; and a "free fishery" *primâ facie* means a "several fishery," per Willes, J., in Shuttleworth *v.* Le Fleming, 19 C. B. 697. The definition of a several fishery in 13 & 14 Vict. c. 88, s. 1, is "all fisheries lawfully possessed and enjoyed "as such, under any title whatever, being a good and valid title at law, "exclusively of the public, by any person or persons, whether in navi- "gable waters, or in non-navigable, and whether the soil covered by "such waters be vested in such persons or in any other persons." In Holford *v.* Bailey, 13 Q. B. 426, the words "sole and exclusive" were held to be equivalent, at all events after verdict, to a "several fishery." Undisturbed possession of the right for sixty years and upwards is some evidence to entitle the jury to presume a legal grant. Little *v.* Wing-

Fishing modes—
1. By nets, lines, &c.
2. By wears and fixed places.

Fishing, in practice, may be of two kinds, *viz.* 1. with nets, hooks, or other moveable apparatus; 2. or by means

field, 8 Ir. C. L. Rep. 279, also 11 Ir. C. L. R. 63. See also 2 & 3 Will. 4, c. 71, s. 1; evidence of a continuous practice for upwards of sixty years, wholly unresisted, for a corporation to grant licenses to fish in a navigable tidal river, and to obstruct and warn those who fish without a license is sufficient evidence for a jury to conclude that the corporation was owner of a free fishery: Mannall *v.* Fisher, 5 C. B. N. S. 856; see Malcolmson *v.* O'Dea, 10 H. L. Cases 593; O'Neill *v.* Allen, 9 Irish C. L. Rep. 132; Chad *v.* Tilsed, 2 B. & B. 403. But although long exclusive enjoyment of a right to a several fishery in a public navigable river, is sufficient *primâ facie* evidence, upon which to presume that the Crown had granted a separate right before Magna Charta, yet the omission of all mention of the right in any probably true inventory, taken since that period, of all the possessions of the then alleged owner, of that right, or any reasonable ground for considering that the user had not been exclusive, but in common with other persons, may be sufficient to negative such presumption; even if a fishery may pass as appurtenant to land—see Hayes *v.* Bridges, 1 Ridg. L. & S. 390; Hamilton *v.* Donegall, Marquis of, 3 Ridg. 311—it cannot be appendant to a several pasture; Edgar *v.* Special Commissioners for English Fisheries, 23 L. T. N. S. 732, C. P. A corporation which had an immemorial right to an oyster fishery in a navigable river, became in 1740, by the ouster of several of its members, unable to continue, or to carry on the management of the fishery. In 1763, the corporation was re-incorporated by charter, under the old name, and the charter ratified, confirmed and restored all fisheries, &c.
[51] There having been no actual dissolution, the fishery never passed to the Crown; and though the corporation had granted a license to certain persons to dredge, &c., this did not operate as a demise of the fishery, so as to put the corporation out of possession; Colchester, Mayor of, *v.* Brooke, 7 Q. B. 339. And where a several fishery is legally granted before Magna Charta, it does not merge by forfeiture to the Crown: Northumberland, Duke of, *v.* Houghton, L. R. 5 Ex. 127. Where the Crown grants by patent the soil and bottom and a several fishery in a navigable river, and enjoyment under that patent was shown, it was held to be evidence that the Crown was seized in fee at the time of making the grant, but the several fishery must have been created before Magna Charta, if so it can be granted afterwards: Devonshire, Duke of, *v.* Hodnett, 1 Hud. & Bro. 323; as to the law of several fisheries in America, see Houck, p. 137 *et seq.*

[Trespass lies for breaking and entering the "several" or "sole and "exclusive" fishery of one person over the soil of another and disturbing the fish: Holford *v.* Bailey, 13 Q. B. 426, 18 L. J. Q. B. 109, Ex. Cham. If the *locus in quo* is an arm of the sea, and yet a several fishery be claimed, it is not sufficient in answer to such plea, simply to

of wears,(*n*) stakes, or fixed enclosures or fishing places. [51] Now, it is obvious, that the public right of fishing cannot be carried on by the latter modes, since an enclosure by one person excludes others.

As to fishing with nets, &c.

Fishing with nets, hooks, &c. may, according to the treatise De Jure Maris, be "either as a liberty without the "soil; or arise by reason of or in concomitance with the "soil itself, and the proprietorship of it." (*o*) Now, as the public cannot claim the soil under the sea or of the shore itself, the *public* fishing of the subject is a floating liberty [52] of fishery with nets, hooks, &c.; whereas the *several*, or private fishery, may be claimed, either as an individual personal right of fishing with nets, hooks, &c. *in loco*, the soil or shore whereof belongs to the King or to any private

The public fishery is a floating right, with nets, &c., only.

deny the public right, but the plaintiff is bound to set up his exclusive claim in a replication: Crichton *v.* Collery, 19 W. R. 107, Ir. Ex.

[Where a several fishery exists in a tidal river, the waters of which have permanently receded from one channel and flow in another, it cannot be followed from the old to the new channel: Carlisle, Mayor of, *v.* Graham, L. R. 4 Ex. 361, 38 L. J. Ex. 226 S. C.] (Foster *v.* Wright, L. R. 4 C. P. D. 438.—ED).

(*n*) See De Jure Maris, *ante*, pp. 387, 388, for numerous instances of these wears.

(*o*) (The passage in Hale in which he speaks of the interests acquirable by the subject by usage or prescription is as follows:— "Fishing [*i.e.*, several fishery] may be of two kinds ordinarily—viz., "the fishing with the net, which may be either as a liberty without the "soil, or as a liberty arising by reason of, and in concomitance with, "the soil or interest or propriety of it; or otherwise it is a local "fishing that ariseth by and from the propriety of the soil. Such are "gurgites, weares, fishing places, borachiæ, stachiæ, &c., which are the "very soil itself, and so frequently agreed in our books. And such "as these a subject may have by usage, either in grosse, as many "religious houses had, or as *parcell of*, or appendant to, their manors, "as both corporations and others have had; and this not only in "navigable rivers and arms of the sea, but in creeks and ports and "havens; yea, and in certain known limits in the open sea contigu- "ous to the shore." Mr. Hall's extract is most unfairly taken. He conceals the fact that the word "fishing" is used by Hale to mean several fishery, and carefully avoids the latter part of Hale's *dictum*, that the fishery may be *parcel* of the manor: the argument and inference he draws are wholly at variance with the evident meaning of Hale. A fishery, soil and water, may be parcel of a manor: Duke of Devonshire *v.* Pattinson, L. R. 20 Q. B. 272.—ED.)

subject; or it may be claimed as appendant, or appurtenant to the ownership of the adjoining manor, or freehold.

The public fishery and the private are incompatible with each other.

The public fishery and private fishery are incompatible (*p*) with each other. So also is a right to fish with nets, hooks, &c. (moveable machinery) incompatible with a fixed fishery. No fishery with nets, hooks, &c. can be enjoyed by the public, or even by one person, in a place where another enjoys a *private* right to make wears and enclosures; and yet both these kinds of fishing may be enjoyed in waters, the shore and soil of which belong to another; nor can such owner of the soil or shore prevent the other from exercising his paramount right to fish. Thus, all the subjects of the Realm have a right to fish in the sea or any creek thereof, or in a tide-river, the shore and soil of which place of fishing belong to the King, or to the lord of the manor. Or the lord of the manor alone, may have a separate fishery, not only exclusive of his manorial tenants, but also of all other persons; or some other individual may have a separate fishery, exclusive of the lord, and all other persons, or a *free* fishery in common with the lord. (*q*)

Private fishery considered, as giving colour of title to the sea-shore.

As the private or several fishery alone, gives colour of title to the sea-shore, or soil itself, it will be necessary for us to consider this private right more minutely.

(*p*) In the case of Mayor of Orford *v.* Richardson, 4 T. R. 437, Buller, J., said, "one party is to prove that this is an arm of the sea, "in which, *primâ facie*, every subject hath a right to fish; the other "is to establish a prescriptive right *which destroys the general right.*"

(*q*) (But it seems that the public may have the right to fish in an arm of the sea for floating fish, although the owner of the soil may have the concurrent right to fish for ground fish, as oysters, mussels, &c. This is the case in the River Burnham or Wallfleet, in Essex. See Rogers *v.* Allen, 1 Campb. 39, and it arises from the owner of the several fishery having given up his right to the floating fish, and reserved the more valuable right of oyster fishing. Evidence of fishing by the public in a several fishery will not destroy the title to that several fishery. See also Duke of Devonshire *v.* Neill, 8 App. Cas. 135, 2 L. R. Ir. 132. But according to Popham, C.J., in Sir Henry Constable's case, *ante*, pp. 236, 239, the fishery by weirs and fixed engines may belong to the lord of the manor, although at high water the public may fish for floating fish.—Ed.)

That the ownership of the sea-shore, or the soil under the sea to any given distance, should include a right to [53] fish, seems reasonable enough; and, accordingly, the King's general right of ownership to the shore and sea-bottom, doubtless entitles him to fish, in common with his subjects. In like manner, if the King have conferred such ownership of any part of the shore on a subject (as on a lord of a manor), the general right of fishery does not exclude the lord. (*r*) But the mere ownership of the shore, whether possessed by the King, or by a lord of a manor, will not entitle the owner to establish a *separate* fishery, and exclude the public. In fact, the mere ownership of the soil will not, it would seem, confer or include a right to a separate fishery in the sea or tide-rivers, whether by nets and lines, or by wears and enclosures. (*s*) The right to exclude the public can only be supported by prescription, *i.e.* by evidence of immemorial usage. A several and exclusive fishery, immemorially enjoyed by an individual subject, or a corporate body, will exclude the public right. The common law gives stability to a right thus immemorially enjoyed; and although the public may claim a preference, where the usage is doubtful, yet, where the usage is proved to have existed on the side of the individual, and to have been acquiesced in by the public, time out of mind, the public will be excluded, precisely as if such private fishery had been granted by the King himself, to the individual. (*t*)

The ownership of the soil of the shore does not entitle such owner to establish an exclusive fishery.

(*r*) If a man claim to have "communiam piscariam," or "liberam "piscariam," the owner of the soil shall fish there. Co. Litt. 122 a.

(*s*) "In case of a *private river*, the lord's having the soil is good "evidence to prove that he has the right of fishing, and it puts the "proof on them that claim *liberam piscariam;*" "but in case of a "river that flows and reflows, and is an arm of the sea, there, *primâ* "*facie*, it is common to all, and if any will appropriate the privilege to "himself, it lies on his side."—Per Hale, C.J. [in Lord Fitzwalter's case], 1 Mod. 105.

(*t*) In a note to Carter *v.* Murcot, 4 Burr. 2165, the following remarks are made upon the doctrine of separate fisheries. "According "ing to some authorities, every navigable river, as far as the sea flows [54] "and reflows, is an arm of the sea, and it may perhaps not be un-"reasonable to admit such property may be by *prescription*, in some "such navigable river; but in the sea or in such rivers as have free

[54] It seems certain that the *mere ownership* of the soil will not *exclude* the public, or authorise the owner to exclude the public fishery; for no subject can take more than the King had to grant, out of the shore or sea-bottom, and therefore the grantee must have taken his grant, subject to

"communication with the sea, where the catching of fish cannot "diminish the stock, more than it could in the sea, the right which "the subjects confessedly have, to fish there, ought not to be suffered "to be restrained, either by *prescription*, or by the *King's grant;* for "it is a principle incontestable, that all customs, prescriptions, and "royal charters, that are either contrary to reason, or the good of the "commonwealth, are void; and it is apparent that all such restrictions "are against both, and are injurious to the public in hindering a large "supply of fish, as well as a means of livelihood to many particular "persons, without any benefit to the public, or to any but monopolists, "and inhancers of the price of fish; but in rivers not having a free "communication with the sea, the case is quite different; for if the "fishery there is made private property, the same would be preserved, "and produce more, than if all persons were allowed to fish there, for "by that means the breed would be in a manner destroyed, as is the "case in many rivers not supplied by the sea." No modern grant can be made by the King of a separate, or free fishery in the sea, or on the sea-coast, or *in* navigable rivers. Since the time of Henry II. all grants from the Crown of this kind of fishery have been contrary to statute* law, *viz.* Magna Charta, and the Charter of Henry III. and subsequent Acts of Parliament; and therefore, if a grant *be produced,* it must be dated so far back; the consequence is, that these kind of fisheries are always *prescribed for.* An ancient grant was put in, in the case of Warren *v.* Matthews, 1 Salk. 357, and probably others may be found, particularly to ancient Abbeys. (Grants of several fisheries as parcel of, or appurtenant to, manors are extremely common. Specific grants of several fisheries *per se* apart from manors are somewhat rare. Such grants from the Crown are very rare, being made *only* in manors which were at the time of the grant in the hands of the Crown. Many examples exist of grants to abbeys by lords of manors of several fisheries *per se;* but an original grant from the Crown *creating* a several fishery opposite to a manor not being at the time of the grant in the hands of the Crown, the Editor believes does not exist. There are grants from the Crown (but very few) of ancient several fisheries which have been created and held in the Crown's hands until after the adjacent land had been parted with (case of Banne, *ante*, p. 247); but these are not cases of grants *creating* the fisheries.—Ed.)

---

* See 2 Bl. Com. 39.

the public common right of piscary, to which the sea and *sea-shore* were liable, even in the King's hands. Therefore, although the ownership of the soil may afford some colour, or pretext to the claim of the individual to a private or several fishery, yet, unless such owner, and the former owners of such soil, have immemorially excluded the [55] public, by means of a separate fishery, prescribed for, and *proved*, or founded in express ancient grant, the public right will prevail. (*u*)

Nor does an exclusive fishery give title to the soil.

It is not, therefore, the ownership of the soil, but immemorial usage or prescription, and ancient grant, which support the several and exclusive fishery; and if so, then, it seems singular to hold (as Lord Hale seems to do), that a several fishery by means of wears, or fixed stakes, &c., "*is* "*the very soil itself:*" (*x*) *i.e.* that such kind of fishery can, *per se*, be sufficient to confer a title to the soil itself. For, if the ownership of the soil will not confer an exclusive fishery (which in the eye of the law is a *minor* right, and rather an adjunct to the soil), why should the mere right to fish confer a *greater*, and in the eye of the law a more valued right, to land itself, thus making the greater an adjunct to the less? This is reversing the law rule, "*majus* "*dignum continet et trahit ad se minus dignum.*" Why is it not enough to construe it a separate fishery, of the kind proved according to the prescription? Why should the mode of fishing, which is varied according to the kind of fish, their habits and haunts, be construed into an ownership of the soil? A right to catch fish by nets or wears, is still, in either case, no more than a mere right of fishery. Why should the owner of the land around be deprived of the soil where the private fishery *was* once enjoyed by

(*u*) (But since the general right of fishery does not exclude the owner of the soil from fishing, such owner can fish there more advantageously than the public. He is able, by virtue of his ownership, to erect fixed engines on his soil, and fish with kiddels, weirs, bucks, stakes, &c., which the public cannot do, and where he does that he shews ownership of the soil by these acts of user, whether he be entitled to exclude the public generally or not. See Sir H. Constable's case, *ante*, pp. 236, 239.—ED.)

(*x*) De Jure Maris, *ante*, p. 385.

another, but which has ceased, by the permanent drying up of the waters? (*y*) (*z*)

(*y*) Co. Litt. 4 b. [See Marshall *v.* Ulleswater Steam Navigation Co., 3 B. & S. 732, 748, 6 B. & S. 570 S. C., and *post*, p. 738.]

(*z*) (Mr. Hall mistakes the meaning of Lord Hale's words. Lord Hale is describing the various modes of fishing, and states the fishing by weirs and kiddels is a means of fishing exercised by the owner of the soil. It is obvious that such a right could not be exercised by any one else. To fix a weir on the soil would be either a trespass against the owner of the soil or a purpresture upon the Crown. What Lord Hale means is this—that where you find fishing carried on by means of weirs, kiddels, &c., by the lord of a manor, that kind of fishing arises *by reason of the ownership of the soil*, and therefore there is nothing singular in Lord Hale's holding that weirs, kiddels, &c., are the very soil itself. It is clear that he had no doubt upon the point, for he says "and so frequently agreed in our books." Palles, C.B., in Neill *v.* Duke of Devonshire, 2 L. R. Ir. at p. 169, says of a fishery in a tidal river, &c., after citing Hale and other authorities: "It appears to me to be beyond dispute that the exclusive right of "fishing in tidal waters vested in the hands of the Crown is no more "than an incident of the soil over which the waters flowed as affected "by the exercise of the King's franchise of excluding the public; and "that right can and generally does exist in the subject as an incident "to the soil, and not as an incorporeal hereditament," and he points out that a several fishery is not one of the "flores coronæ." It was held by the justices in Chester, in the time of Edward III., that fishery in the tidal water of the Dee and Mersey was an incident of the soil, and belonged to the lord of the manor by common right: *ante*, pp. 153–155. The Editor entirely agrees with the doctrine of Chief Baron Palles. His researches among the Public Records entirely confirm that doctrine. Almost every case of a fishery in tidal waters with which he has met shews that the fishery was carried on by means of fixed engines by the owner of the soil, for that was the usual and natural method of taking the profit of the fishery. See Duke of Devonshire *v.* Neill, 8 App. Cas. at p. 143. In Rex *v.* Ellis, 1 M. & S. 663, Bayley, J., says: "It is stated by Lord Hale that a fishery may "be either unconnected with the soil or may be connected with it. "I should doubt very much if the grant of a fishery would convey the "soil and everything underneath it, such as all the minerals, though "I conceive that it may pass so much of the soil as is connected with "the fishery;" but, as it appeared in the case in question that the owner of the fishery *drove piles into the soil*, he held, following Lord Hale, that the soil was connected with the fishery, agreeing with Lord Ellenborough and the other judges. In Att.-Gen. *v.* Emerson, in 1887, Mr. Justice Cave held that evidence of user of fisheries by "kiddels" on the Maplin Sands raised the presumption of a grant from the Crown

The doctrine that the ownership of the soil affords a presumption in favour of a separate right of *fishery*, does not involve the same consequences of law, as saying, that a separate fishery gives a right to the soil, for *this* involves [56]
the question of title to *land*, and the form or mode of supporting that title. To say that if I prescribe for, and prove a separate fishery, I thereby gain the ownership of the soil, is as much as to hold that I may prescribe for an ownership in the soil; *i.e.* that a title to land, or fee simple estate, may be supported by prescription; a doctrine denied by some of our best authorities. (*a*) . It is also remarkable that, when we get *beyond* reach of the tides, and the river is no longer *pars maris*, the doctrine is, that the ownership of the adjoining land, is good presumptive evidence that such owner has the exclusive right of fishing,—per Lord Hale, C.J., in Lord Fitzwalter's case, 1 Mod. 105;—but as soon as we get *within* the flux and reflux of the tides, the doctrine is reversed, and the ownership of a private fishery, is *said* to be good presumptive evidence of title to the soil itself. This, in itself, seems singular doctrine. (*b*)

A freehold, or title to land, is one right and thing, and a fishery is another, and the rights and titles to these several things are not supported in like manner. A fishery, as

to the lord of the manor "of a right of taking all kinds of fish, "including shell-fish, on the foreshore;" but he cites no authority, nor does he give any example of such a grant in other places. The cases cited as conclusive by Lord Hale, and Lord Selborne's judgment in Duke of Devonshire *v.* Neill, are opposed to this. The case is appealed.—ED.)

(*a*) Co. Litt. 114 b.

(*b*) (Here again is a perversion of Lord Hale's meaning. He distinctly says you may have a several fishery *without* the soil, and you may have one with the soil. He nowhere suggests that a grant of several fishery in the sea does *per se* pass the soil, but that where the lord of the manor has the several fishery, and fishes it by fixed engines, it shews that he has the soil. This is the summing up of his statements. "Now for precedents touching such rights of fishing in the sea "and arms and creeks thereof belonging by usage to subjects, *the* "*most whereof will appear to be* by reason of the propriety of *the* "*very water and soil* wherein the fishing is, and some of them even "within the ports of the sea."—ED.)

well as any other franchise, liberty, profit or easement (as a right of road or way over another man's ground, or a right to pasture cattle on the manorial waste or common) may, as before explained, either be founded on express grant, or prescriptive usage; whereas, a title to land must be founded either on express grant, or on what is called "*adverse possession;*" which is not what our common law intends by "*prescription.*"

Lord Hale's authorities considered as to the fishery giving the soil.

It is remarkable, that the cases of separate fisheries, cited in the treatise ascribed to Lord Hale, p. 387 *et seq.*, by way of authority that a separate fishery carries the soil, do all use the term *piscaria*, which signifies merely a fishery; and not one assumes an ownership of the soil, (*c*)
[57] in virtue of the "piscaria," even where it is claimed as "separalis." In some cases the "piscaria" and the sea-shore are mentioned separately; thus, "the Earls of Devon "had, not only the port of Toppesham, but the record "tells us, that the *Portus* et *Piscaria*, et *mariscus* (*d*) "(marsh) de Toppesham spectant Amiciæ Comitissæ "Devon." (*e*) The only plausible instance adduced by the learned writer to prove that a separate fishery includes the ownership of the soil, does not seem, upon examination, to support such doctrine.

"Trin. 10, Ed. 2. B. R. Rot. 83, Norfolchiæ.—The abbot "of Benedict Hulm, (*f*) impleads divers, for fishing in riparia "quæ se extendit a ponte de Wroxam, usque quendam "locum vocatum Blackdam. Pending the suit, the King's "Attorney came in, and alledged for the King quod "prædicta riparia est brachium maris, quæ se extendit in "salsum mare, et est riparia Domini Regis salsa fluens, ubi "naves, et battelli, veniunt et applicant extra magnum "mare carcati et discarcati quiete, absque tolneta, seu "custuma aliqua dando, et est *communis piscaria* quibus-

(*c*) (This is not true. See note (*k*), p. 730, *post.*—ED.)

(*d*) De Jure Maris, *ante*, p. 387.

(*e*) "Mariscus" will pass the soil. Co. Litt. 4 b. But "Piscaria" will not.

(*f*) Case of the Abbot of Benedict Hulm, quoted from De Jure Maris, *ante*, p. 386.

"cumque; et dicit quod presentatum fuit, in ultimo itinere, "coram Solomone de Roffa, et Sociis Justiciariis itinerantibus in comitatu isto, quod prædecessor prædicti Abbatis "fecit purpresturam super dominum regem in riparia prædicta, gurgites plantando in eadem, et appropriando sibi "prædictam *piscariam tenendo tanquam separalem;* per "quod consideratum fuit, quod gurgites illæ amoverentur, "et quod prædicta aqua remaneret *communis piscaria.* Et "petit quod nunc procedatur ad aliquam inquisitionem "inde capiendam quousque præfati justiciarii super recordo "et processu prædictis certiorentur. Thereupon search [58] "is granted, and the record certified; and afterwards, "a procedendo was obtained; and issue being joined, "it was found for the Abbot, and judgment and execution given against the defendants for the damages; viz. "£200."

"Upon which record," says the learned writer, "these "things are observable:—

"1st. That, *de communi jure*, the right of such arms of "the sea belongs to the King.

"2nd. That yet, in such arms of the sea, the subjects in "general have, *primâ facie*, a common of fishery, as in the "main sea.

"3rd. That yet, a subject may have a separate right of "fishing, exclusive of the King, and of the common right "of the subject.

"4th. That in this case, the right of the Abbot to have "a several fishing, was not a bare right, liberty, or profit "*à prendre;* but the right of the very water, and *soil itself;* "for *he made wears in it.*"

Comments. With deference, however, to such eminent authority, it does not seem very observable, upon this record, that the Abbot *had* the right of the "water, and *soil* itself," *because* he made wears in it. (*g*) Nothing more, in fact, appears, than that the Abbot by making wears, claimed to have *piscariam tanquam separalem* (a private fishery), which, on trial, was allowed against the King, who claimed the fishery in favour

(*g*) [Jerwood, p. 54.]

of all his subjects as an open right. (*h*) That separate [59] fisheries, by means of water-sluices, wears, &c., may, and frequently do, belong to subjects in right of their manors, and as appendant to their manors, &c., there can be no doubt, for these may be prescribed for. That the soil where these separate fisheries are, *may* be "*parcel of*" (*i*) a manor (*i.e.* within the boundaries and *parcel*, as the other lands within the manor are parcel) is also admitted.—In the principal creeks and tide-rivers of England, and in the flat and marshy districts upon the coast, these fisheries, some with, and some without the soil, are not unfrequent. But it does not follow, that because they *may* be good in point of title by prescription, *as fisheries*, they confer also a title to the soil itself, without other evidences. (*k*)

(*h*) P. 34, Ed. I. B. R. Rot. 14 (*ante*, p. 109) Lanc: Prior de Coningshed implacitat Abbatim de Ferneys pro prostratione Gurgitis in aquâ de Ulverstone. Defendant justified, because *each end of the wear* was fastened upon the abbot's land. The abbot replies, quod Wilhelmus de Lancaster Dominus de Kendal dedit prædecessori domus suæ prædictæ *aquam* et *piscariam* (which words carry the soil: Throckmorton *v.* Tracy, Plowden 151—ED.) ex utraque parte ejusdem quantum impetus maris fluxit et refluxit. Here the wear is treated as a mere [59] fishery. Vide Rastall's Entries, trespass in pischary, pl. 4. Prescription for *several fishing*, in aquâ maritimâ fluente et refluente in seizonabili tempore cum 7 stallis separatis *separalis piscariæ fixis pro retibus*. Vide de Jure Maris, *ante*, p. 386.

(*i*) The phrase "*parcel of*" does not seem synonymous with "appendant" or "appurtenant."

(*k*) (Mr. Hall's averment that the cases quoted by Hale do not assume an ownership of the soil is wholly wrong. In the case of the Abbot of Furneys, the Abbot pleads a grant of *aqua et piscaria*, which carries the soil: Throckmorton *v.* Tracy, Plowden 151. In the second case the fishery is described as by *fixed* stalls. The third case is quoted as an instance of Hale's first proposition, that fishing may be a liberty without the soil. The case of St. Benet Hulm is shewn to be a fishery by fixed weirs (*gurgites plantando in eadem*). The Editor has examined the record, from which it appears that the Abbot had been presented for a purpresture on the soil, so that it is clear that it was in issue, and Hale's argument that the Abbot had the "water and "the soil itself, for he made wears in it," is a sound conclusion from the record; for, if the soil was the King's, such fixing of weirs was a purpresture; and had it been any one else's soil it would have been a trespass. In the Earl of Devon's case the soil is in the lord at the

Lord Coke, in his Com. on Litt. 4 b, says, "if a man be "seized of a river, and by deed do grant, 'separalem "'piscariam' in the same, and maketh livery of seizin, "'secundum formam chartæ,' the soil doth *not* pass, for "the grantor may take water there, and *if the river become* "*dry he may take the benefit of the soil;* for there passed "to the grantee but a particular right. For the same "reason, if a man grant '*aquam suam*,' the soil shall *not* "pass, but the pischary within the water passeth. And "land covered with water shall be demanded by the name "of so many acres 'aquâ coopertas,' whereby it appeareth "that they are distinct things." (*l*) (*m*)

There certainly exists a difference of opinion amongst the authorities, as to whether a "*separate* fishery" ***necessarily***, and ***per se***, includes the soil or not. This question is [60] ably considered by Mr. Hargrave in a note to Co. Litt. 122 a, note 7, (*n*) and he concludes in the *negative*. After quoting a passage in 1 Inst. 122, relative to this subject, as follows: "A man may prescribe to have *separalem* piscariam "in such a water, and the owner of the soil shall not fish "there; but if he claim to have *communiam* piscariam, or "*liberam* piscariam, the owner of the soil shall fish there," Mr. Hargrave observes, "According to this passage, owner-"ship of the soil is *not* necessarily included in a several "fishery, and common of fishery and free fishery are the "same thing." He then refers to Judge Blackstone's doc-

Mr. Hargrave's opinion that a separate fishery does not give title to the soil.

present time. The Abbot of Titchfield's case in Southampton Water shews that he fixed weirs in his soil to the injury of the navigation. The case of Radley weirs is in the Severn, where the soil belongs to the lord of the manor: King *v.* Ellis, 1 M. & S. 661; case of the Barons of Barkley, Hale, cap. vi. In the case of the manor of Burnham, the fishery, with the weirs belonging to it, is adjudged to be parcel of the manor, and the present lord is owner of the soil there, and of valuable oyster layings in that river of Burnham or Wallfleet now called the Crouch. The title was established a few years ago at the Essex Assizes in a case in which the Editor was concerned.—Ed.)

(*l*) [See Marshall *v.* Ulleswater Steam Navigation Co., 3 B. & S. 747, per Cockburn, C.J., and *post*, p. 738.]

(*m*) (But if a man grant *aquum et piscarium*, the soil doth pass: Throckmorton *v.* Tracy, Plowden 151.—Ed.)

(*n*) Hargrave's note to Co. Litt. 122 a, note 7.

trine, who lays it down, "that the ownership of soil is essen- "tial to a *several* fishery; and that a *free* fishery differs "both from *several* fishery and *common* of fishery; from the "former, by being confined to a public river, and not "necessarily comprehending the soil: from the latter by "being exclusive." 2 Black. Com. 8 Ed. 39. Mr. Hargrave replies to this: "We doubt whether this distinction may "not be, in a great degree, questionable. 1. In respect to a "several fishery,—where is the inconsistency in granting "the sole right of fishing, with a reservation of the soil, "and its other profits? Bracton expressly takes notice "of such a grant; for his words are, that one may 'servi- "'tutem imponere fundo suo quod quis possit piscari cum "'eo, et ita in communi, vel quod alius per se ex toto.' "Brac. fo. 208 b. There are also numerous other authori- "ties for it; the old books of entries agreeing that one may "prescribe for a *several* fishery against the *owner* of the "soil; to which should be added the three cases of Eliza- "beth, cited by Lord Coke. See Lib. Intrat. 162 b, 163 a, "Rastall's Entr. 597 b, and the books cited under the letter "d, in fol. 4, B, and under m here, and the cases referred to
[61] "under the * on the other side. Nor do we understand "why a *several* piscary should not exist *without* the soil, as "well as a several pasture,(*o*) as to which latter we have "already shown the doctrine to be settled, *supra*, n. 6. "The chief reasons which occur against Lord Coke seem "to be these:—Several writs, never applicable except to "the soil, lie for a piscary; such as a præcipe quod reddat, "monstraverunt de rationabilibus divisis, and trespass, "which latter writ is particularly insisted on by Lord Ch. "J. Holt; Dav. 55 b; Hugh Comm. Orig. Wr. 11 W. Jo. "440; 1 Ventr. 122; 2 Salk. 367; Skinn. 677. Suum "liberum tenementum is a good plea to trespass for fishing "in a several piscary; 17 E. IV. 6; 18 E. IV. 4; 10 H. "VII. 24, 26, 28. The soil will pass, as it is said, by the "grant of a piscary; Plowd. 154. But all these objections

(*o*) [See Melvin *v.* Whiting, 24 Mass. (7 Pick.) 79; Cortelyou *v.* Van Brundt, 2 John. Ch. 357, 362; Ipswich *v.* Brown, Savile 14.]

" may be repelled. The writs relied on will not always lie " for a piscary. Thus, if a præcipe quod reddat is brought " of a piscary in the water of another person, the writ is " bad, and a quod permittat is the proper remedy ; Fitz. " Abr. Briefe, 861 ; F. N. B. 23 i ; and note b of the 4to ed. " Besides, in the cases of actions for trespass in a several " piscary, or at least in some of them, the writ seems in " effect to state a several piscary in the plaintiff's own soil, " which therefore proves nothing as to the sense of several " piscary, without further explanation ; Reg. B. R. Orig. " 95 b ; Carth. 285 ; Skinn. 677. The plea liberum tene- " mentum may be replied to by prescribing for a several " piscary. See the books before cited, as to such a pre- " scription. Though the *grant* of a piscary generally may " *perhaps* pass the soil, yet it will not, if there are any " words to denote a different intention ; as where one " seized of a river grants a several fishery in it, which is " the case put by Lord Coke in another place ; and much [62]
" less will the soil pass when there is an express reserva- " tion of it ; ante 4 b, and n. 2, there. Hence, as it " should seem, the arguments are short of the purpose ; " for, at the utmost, they only prove that a *several* piscary " is presumed to comprehend the soil, till the contrary " appears, which is perfectly consistent with Lord Coke's " position, that they *may* be in different persons, and " *indeed appears to us the true doctrine on the subject*." (*p*) (*q*)

(*p*) In Partheriche *v.* Mason, 2 Chitty's Cases, temp. Mansfield, 661, Lord Kenyon is made to say, " there is no reason why a person may " not have a several fishery in *alieno solo*." But the Report adds, " SED " PER CURIAM, where a man has a several fishery, the presumption is, " that he has the soil ; *that* presumption is conclusive, *if not opposed*." But this was said of a fishery in a river *not within the tides* though navigable. *Within* the tides the presumption *is* always *opposed* by the King's title ; see also Lofft 364 ; [Marshall *v.* Ulleswater Steam Navigation Co., 5 B. & S. 732 ; Hall's Profit à Prendre, p. 310 *et seq.*]

(*q*) (The controversy on this question as to whether or no a several fishery carries with it the right to the soil thereof has been a long and an interesting one, but it is submitted that it has been argued upon unsubstantial and doubtful bases. From the moment that it is admitted that it is possible that there may be a several fishery wholly independent of the soil (see the case of Duke of Somerset

Comments. But the doctrine thus noticed by Mr. Hargrave is not, as applied to the Crown, precisely the same as when applied between subject and subject; nor is it the same when applied to the soil *beyond or above* the flux and reflux of the tides, as when applied to the soil upon the *shores* of the sea and tide-rivers. Admitting that a *several* fishery, in waters *not* subject to the tides, and, therefore, no part of the sea, may, between one subject and another, be made ground of presumption (where there is no proof to the contrary), that the soil goes with it (although from what is before said, p. 53 *et seq.* a presumption of that kind does not seem *necessary*), it may be insisted, that between the *flux* and *reflux* of the tides, every such presumption is against the right of the Crown, and that implication is not to be made against the King. A very modern case would seem to justify this distinction; the case is that of the Duke of Somerset *v.* Fog-

v. Fogwell, discussed in the next paragraph), the question resolves itself into a question of fact, and not of law. During the argument of the case of Duke of Devonshire *v.* Pattinson, 20 Q. B. D. 263, it was put interrogatively by Lord Justice Bowen: "Is it not always a question "of evidence in every case whether a several fishery carries the soil or "not?" It must be a question of fact in each case, and can only be determined by the particular evidence of user produced. If the fishing shewn is mere fishing for floating fish in the tide water to the exclusion of the public, and there is nothing else, a presumption is raised of a grant of several fishery independent of the soil, as in the case first put by Hale. Such a fishery might arise by direct grant from the Crown when owner of the soil, or by grant from a subject being owner of the soil and having a several fishery thereover by the exercise of the prerogative in excluding the public: see Duke of Devonshire *v.* Neill, 2 L. R. Ir. at p. 169, per Palles, C.B. If, however, the fishery is a fishery carried on by fixed engines planted in the soil, then there is a presumption of ownership of the soil wherein those engines are fixed, because they could not be put there without being either a purpresture on the Crown if the soil is the Crown's, or a trespass on the soil if the soil is in a subject. It has been suggested that there might be a grant from the Crown of a liberty to fish with fixed engines, but, speaking from a very extensive experience of royal grants, the Editor declines to believe that such a grant ever was made. He has never seen one or heard of one, and submits that such a grant cannot be presumed without some precedent to shew that it is probable in fact.—ED.

well, (*r*) in which letters patent of the 44th of Eliz. were given in evidence, by which she granted to Edward Seymour, Esq., his heirs and assigns, "all those domain lands "and manors of Berry Pomeroy and Bridgetown Pomeroy, "and the castle of Berry Pomeroy, with all their rights, members, liberties and appurtenances, in the county of Devon, "then lately parcels of the lands, and possessions, and hereditaments of T. Pomeroy, Kt.;" and after making use of general words to pass the lands, &c. and tithes of Berry, her majesty granted "*all waters, fisheries*, &c. to the aforesaid manors, castle, and premises, and to each and every "of them belonging, or appendant, known, accepted, held, "used, or reputed or deemed as part or parcel of the same "premises." There were also produced two fines, one levied in 2 Ed. VI., and the other in 2 and 3 William and Mary, of the manor, &c. "*ac de separali piscariâ de aquâ de* "*Dert.*" It was also proved that the present Duke and his ancestors had, since 1765, regularly received a rent for the *fishery* in the river Dart, which was a navigable and *tide-river*. In the course of the argument, the doctrine of Judge Blackstone "that ownership of the soil is essential to a "several fishery,"—and the contrary doctrine of Lord Coke, before quoted, (*s*) and the argument of Mr. Hargrave in the text, were mentioned and commented on. The question, whether the words of the letters patent, "all waters, fish-"eries, &c." and the words in the fines, "separalis piscaria," carried the *soil*, was not the principal question; but was mooted in reference to the effect of a lease of the "separalis "piscaria" made without deed. If the "separalis piscaria" were a *territorial* hereditament, including the soil, then such lease was good; but if "separalis piscaria" were merely an *incorporeal* hereditament, then a grant by deed was necessary to vest such hereditament in the lessee. In the latter case, an action of trespass brought by the Duke, as plaintiff, was well brought; but if the parol demise was good, then the action should have been brought in the name of the lessee.

[63]

[64]

(*r*) [5 B. & C. 875; Marshall *v.* Ulleswater Steam Navigation Co., 6 B. & S. 570; and see Hall's Profit à Prendre, p. 19, and *post*, p. 738.]

(*s*) See p. 727, *ante*.

The Court decided that the fishery in question was not a *territorial*, but an *incorporeal* hereditament, and required a grant, by deed, to divest it from the Duke. Mr. Justice Bayley, in delivering the judgment of the Court, said, "No "conveyance of the right of fishing, or of the soil, was pro-"duced at the trial, but it appeared not to be an *ordinary* "fishing, resulting to the owner of the adjoining land in re-"spect of the land, *but a fishery in a navigable river, where* "*the tide flows and reflows*, and, therefore, in the nature of a "royal franchise, which Sir William Blackstone calls a *free* "fishery. (*t*) Such a franchise could not be created after "Magna Charta, but there was evidence in this case from "which its existence from time beyond legal memory might "be presumed." Then, after alluding to the words, "sepa-"ralis piscaria" in the fines, and quoting the words of Lord Coke, as just now quoted, (*u*) the learned judge proceeds: "in "the case here put (that from Lord Coke), (*x*) the grant was "made by the owner of the soil, capable of granting it, and "yet a grant 'separalis piscariæ,' followed up by livery, "which properly applies to a thing corporeal, *did not convey* "*the soil*, livery being made secundum, &c. If then a "fishery only is granted, nothing passes but a right to take "the fish, and to use such means as are necessary for that "purpose; which is, in truth, nothing more than a liberty "to fish; the grantee has no property in the water, none "in the soil. And this is a case where the grant is made "between subject and subject, and, consequently, is to be "construed against the grantor, a principle inapplicable to "grants made by the Crown, whereby nothing passes,
[65] "unless the intention that it should pass is manifest." After quoting the case of the river Banne, from Davis 55, in which there was a grant by letters patent from the Crown, of "omnia castra, messuagia, &c. *piscarias, piscari-* "*ones, aquas, aquarium, cursus*, &c.," the learned judge proceeds: "It was held that the fishery of the Banne did not "pass by the grant of the land adjoining, and by general

(*t*) 2 Com. 39. (*u*) P. 727, *ante*.

(*x*) But Lord Coke's case was not between the flux and reflux of the tides, or against the King, which is, therefore, a case *à fortiori*.

"grant of all piscaries, &c.; for that it was a *royal* fishery, "not appurtenant to the land, but a fishery in gross, and "was by itself part of the inheritance of the Crown; and "that general words by the King would not pass such a "special royalty, which belongs to the Crown by preroga- "tive; and it was further agreed, that *the grant of the King* "*passes nothing by implication.* It was contended in argu- "ment, that the owner of a several fishery must be pre- "sumed to be owner of the soil. That *may* be true, where "the terms of the grant under which he claims are un- "known [*i.e.* it is presumed, where he claims by prescrip- "tion]; but when they appear, and are such as convey an "incorporeal hereditament only, the presumption is de- "stroyed." This last remark of the learned Judge may, however, be considered as applied to a case between subject and subject,—not where a subject claims the soil against the *King* in right of a several fishery between the flux and reflux of the tides,—by prescription, or by "a grant, "the terms of which are unknown;"—for to *presume* the owner of such fishery to be owner of the soil, is taking the soil from the Crown, by a presumption not necessary. First, a grant from the Crown is presumed:—but of what? Of a separate fishery. But such grant, if produced, would not carry the soil:—why then should the presumed grant do so?—is it because the terms of it "are unknown"? This would be singular reasoning; for we know that the doubtful terms of an actual grant by the Crown are construed strictly *in favour* of the Crown; and yet we are [66]
told that a grant, the terms of which are so much more doubtful, as to be "unknown," may be construed most *against* the Crown. It is presumed that the words of the learned Judge, as well as of Mr. Hargrave, had reference only to "several fisheries" in waters *not* within the flux and reflux of the tides; and even to that extent they both seem to speak with doubt, using the phrase "may be." (*y*) (*z*)

(*y*) [In Marshall *v.* Ulleswater Steam Navigation Co., 3 B. & S. 732, 748, 6 B. & S. 570, Cockburn, C.J., (*dissentiente*) says: "It is "admitted on all hands that a several fishery may exist independently "of the ownership of the soil in the bed of the water. Why then

With regard to a "free fishery," as distinguished from a "several fishery," Mr. Hargrave remarks, in continuation of the note before quoted, "both parts of the description of a

"should such a fishery be considered as carrying with it, in the "absence of negative proof, the property in the soil? On the contrary, "it seems to me that there is every reason for holding the opposite "way. The use of water for the purpose of fishing is, when the "fishery is united with the ownership of the soil, a right incidental "and accessory to the latter. On a grant of the land, the water and "the incidental and necessary right of fishing would pass with it. If, "then, the intention be to convey the soil, why not convey the land at "once, leaving the accessory to follow? Why grant the accessory "that the principal may pass incidentally? Surely such a proceeding "would be at once illogical and unlawyerlike,—the greater is justly "said to comprehend the less, but this is to make the converse of the "proposition hold good. A grant of land carries with it, as we all "know, the mineral which may be below the surface; but whoever "heard of a grant of the mineral carrying with it the general owner-"ship of the soil? Why should a different principle be applied to the "grant of a fishery,—which may be said to be a grant of that which is "above the surface of the soil, as a grant of the minerals is a grant of "that which is below it? Nor should it be forgotten that the opposite "doctrine involves the startling and manifest absurdity, that should "the water be diverted by natural causes, or become dry, the fishery, "which was the primary and principal object of the grant, would be "gone, and the property in the soil, which only passed incidentally, "and as accessory to the grant of the fishery, would remain." (But read Mr. Justice Weightman's judgment in this case.—ED.) See Paterson's Fishery Laws, 65; and Jackson *v.* Halstead, 5 Cowen (N.Y.) 216.]

(*z*) (This case of Duke of Somerset *v.* Fogwell is an instance of Lord Hale's first proposition, that there may be a grant of a several fishery independent of the soil. The *locus in quo* was in the River Dart, in the tidal part of it, and there was no pretence for setting up a right to the soil, and no evidence of anything but mere fishing. The "Aqua de Darte" was part of the ancient possessions of the barony of Totnes from the time of Domesday, and descended as part of that barony until it was sold to one Nicholas de Tewkesbury, *temp.* Edward I., and by him forfeited to the King. It remained in the Crown till 11 Edward III., A.D. 1337, when it was granted as part of the possessions of the Duchy of Cornwall, and has remained inalienably annexed to the Duchy ever since. The soil of it is in the Duchy, except where the former owners had granted it away. The fishery here must have had its origin in a grant from the Barons of Totnes before the time of Edward I., but there is no suggestion of a grant of the soil by them, and no evidence was produced from which it could be presumed. This

" 'free fishery' seem indisputable, though, for the sake of dis-
" tinction it might be more convenient to appropriate *free* [67]
" *fishery* to the franchise of fishing in *public* rivers, by derivation from the Crown; and though in other countries it " may be so considered, yet, from the language of our " books, it seems as if our law practice had extended this " kind of fishery to all streams, whether private or public, " neither the Register nor other books professing any discrimination. R. 95 b; Fitzh. N. B. 88 g; Fitzh. Abr. " Ass. 422; 4 E. 4, 28, 17 E. 4, 6 b, 7 a; 7 H. 7, 13 b; " Cro. Ch. 554; 1 Ventr. 122; 3 Mod. 97; Carth. 285; " Skinn. 677. Again, it is true that, in one case, the Court " held free fishery to import an exclusive right, equally with " several piscary, chiefly relying on the writs in the Reg. " 95 b, and the 43 E. 3, 24. But then this was only the " opinion of two Judges against one, who strenuously in- " sisted that the word 'libera,' *ex vi termini*, implied " 'common,' and that many judgments and precedents were " founded on Lord Coke's so construing it. Smith *v.* " Kemp, 2 Salk. 637; Carth. 285. That the dissenting " Judge was not only unwarranted in the latter part of his " assertion, appears from two determinations a little before " the case in question. See Upton and Dawkins, 3 Mod. " 97, and Peake and Tucker, cited in Carth. 286, in marg. " We may add to this, the three cases cited by Lord Coke " as of his own time; and that there are passages in other " books which favour his distinction. See Cro. Ch. 554; " 17 E. 4, 6 b, 7 a; 7 H. VII. 13 b."

The phrase "*free fishery*,"(*a*) seems a technical phrase, answering to "*free warren*." Now, one or *more* individuals may have "free warren" in another man's land, and "free " fishery" in a river of the soil of which another individual is owner. In a "free fishery," the owner of the soil is not excluded.(*b*) But in "separalis piscaria" he may be.— [68]

case is an example of the danger of applying the dicta laid down in a case when the *whole* of the facts relating to the property in question do not appear on the face of the report.—ED.)

(*a*) [See Shuttleworth *v.* Le Fleming, 19 C. B. 700, *et ante*, p. 50.]

(*b*) Co. Litt. 122. [See Hall's Profit à Prendre, p. 312; Paterson, 46.]

Distinction between libera, separalis, and communis, piscaria.

Thus "separalis" is opposed to "libera," *tanquam species generalis*, to show that "no one else" (*c*) can share in the fishery. Thus A may prescribe for "libera piscaria," in the *locus in quo*, in common with B;—and B prove that in such place, he, B, has "separalis piscaria,"—which excludes A; yet C may be owner of the soil. But "separalis "piscaria" necessarily excludes C as well as A, whereas "libera piscaria" does not. Thus there is "libera piscaria," "separalis piscaria," and "communis piscaria," which latter is not a *franchise* like the former, but a common right, *sui generis*. But, "libera piscaria" being a "franchise," is, like "free warren," generally found where the soil is in another, and by no means involves, or carries with it the soil. (*d*) It may be further observed that the word "*separalis*" seems to apply peculiarly to that kind of private fishery which is carried on by means of weares, and other artificial fixed apparatus, which being the labour of the individual, cannot be used by others, and like his nets, or the moveable apparatus, are his own property. This mode of fishing was (like the oppressive forest laws) ever obnoxious to our ancestors, but more especially as being obstructions to commerce and navigation. (*e*)

(*c*) See accord. 5 Burr. 2814, per Lord Mansfield, in Seymour *v.* Lord Courtney. In that case, also, the Court declined giving any opinion "whether a person can have a several fishery *without* being owner of "the soil."

(*d*) (In ancient records the universal experience of the Editor is that the words "libera" and "separalis" are used indifferently to mean the same thing, and are found so used indifferently in the evidences of title of almost every fishery. Lord Holt lays it down in Smith *v.* Kemp, Holt 322, that *separalis piscaria* is where the owner has the soil, and *libera piscaria* where he has only the fishing; but in a subsequent case, Holt 323, he says: "It has lately been adjudged that a separate fishery and free fishery are all one." In short, no satisfactory argument can be raised upon the meaning of these words, for they are used so indiscriminately, and where either the one or the other occurs, and the question is whether the soil passes, recourse must be had to the evidence of facts of user to determine the question. The Editor has seen a several pasture described as "*libera et separalis pastura.*"—Ed.)

(*e*) [A "free fishery," *primâ facie*, means "a several fishery," per Willes, J., in Shuttleworth *v.* Le Fleming, 19 C. B. 697. See Melvin *v.* Whiting, 24 Mass. (7 Pick.) R. 79; Freary *v.* Cook, 14 Mass. R. 488. In

From the earliest times, it was no uncommon act of the legislature to destroy these weares and fixed fishing-places, as nuisances to navigation. By Magna Charta it was declared, "omnes kidelli deponantur de cetero penitus per "Thamaesiam et Medwayam per totam Angliam, *nisi per* "*costeram maris*." And this statute was seconded by others that were more effectual, viz. 25 Ed. III. c. 4, 1 H. IV. 12, and 12 Ed. IV. c. 7; and other subsequent statutes, whereby such weares and stake fisheries were abated from time to time; not only in rivers, but *along the sea coasts*. "And, by force of this last statute," says Lord Hale, "weares, which were prejudicial to the passage of vessels, "were to be pulled down; and accordingly it was done, in "many places." (*f*) And he adds, "The exception of weares "upon the *sea-coasts* [in Magna Charta], and likewise fre-"quent examples, some whereof are before mentioned, "*make it appear* that there might be such private interest, "not only in point of *liberty*, but in point of *property*, on "the sea-coast, and below the low-water mark; for such "were regularly all weares. But, as by the statutes of "25 Ed. III. c. 4; 45 Ed. III. c. 2; 1 H. IV. c. 12; "4 H. IV. c. 11; and other statutes, the erecting of new "weares, and 'inhancing' (*g*) of old, is provided against, in [69]

Exclusive and fixed fisheries discountenanced by the law.

Malcolmson *v.* O'Dea, 10 H. of L. Cases 593, Willes, J., says, "Some "discussion took place during the argument as to the proper name of "such a fishery, whether it ought not to have been called in the plead-"ings, following Blackstone, a 'free' instead of a 'several' fishery. "This is more of the confusion which the ambiguous use of the word "'free' has occasioned, from as early as the year book, 7 H. 7 P. "fol. 13, down to the case of Holford *v.* Bailey, 13 Q. B. 444, where it [69] "was clearly shown that the only substantial distinction is between an "exclusive right of fishery, usually called several; sometimes free "(used in 'free warren'), and a right in common with others, usually "called 'common of fishery;' sometimes 'free' (used as in 'free port'). "The fishery in this case is sufficiently described as a several fishery, "which means an exclusive right to fish in a given place, either with "or without the property in the soil."]

(*f*) [De Jure Maris, *ante*, p. 389.]

(*g*) [This is supposed to be a mistranslation of lever, for levying or setting up: per Lord Denman in Williams *v.* Wilcox, 8 A. & E. 335.] (It is no mistranslation: *lever* is to "raise upon" or "inhance."—Ed.)

"navigable rivers; and by other statutes, particular provi-
[70] "sion is made against weares new or old, erected in particular ports, as in the port of Newcastle, by the statute of "21 H. I. c. 18; in the port of Southampton, by the "statutes of 11 H. VII. c. 5; 14 H. VIII. c. 13; in the "rivers Ouse and Humber, by the statute of 23 H. VIII. "c. 18; in the river and port of Exeter, by the statute of "31 H. VIII. c. 4; in the river of Thames, by the statutes "of 4 H. VII. c. 15; 27 H. VIII. c. 18; 3 Jac. c. 20; "and divers others; so, by the statute 3 Jac. c. 12, all new "weares *erected upon the sea-shore*, or in any haven, harbour, "or creek, or within five miles of the mouth of any haven "or creek, are prohibited, under a penalty."(*h*)

[71] It is further observed by the learned writer (Lord Hale) upon the above legislative acts, "that they did *no way dis-*

(*h*) See De Jure Maris, *ante*, p. 389. [All new fixed nets, not legally existing in 1862, are illegal, and any person may destroy them: Williams *v.* Blackwall, 32 L. J. Ex. 174, S. C. 2 H. & C. 33, 9 Jur. N. S. 579, 11 W. R. 621, and 8 L. T. N. S. 252; Moulton *v.* Wilby, 32 L. J. M. C. 164. A weir appurtenant to a fishery, obstructing the whole or part of a navigable river, is legal, if granted by the Crown before the commencement of the reign of Edward I., and such grant may be inferred from evidence of its having existed before that time. If the weir, when so first granted, obstruct the navigation of only a part of the river, it does not become illegal by the stream changing its bed, so that the weir obstructs the only navigable passage remaining. But where the Crown had no right to obstruct the whole passage of a navigable river, it had no right to erect a weir obstructing a part, except subject to the rights of the public; and, therefore, in such a case, the weir would become illegal upon the rest of the river being so choked that there could be no passage elsewhere. Williams *v.* Wilcox, 3 N. & P. 606, 8 A. & E. 314. See Gann *v.* Whitstable Free Fishers, 11 H. L. C. 192, 35 L. J. C. P. 29; Rawstorne *v.* Backhouse, L. R. 3 C. P. 67; Holford *v.* George, L. R. 3 Q. B. 640, London Law Magazine, vol. 28, p. 325. The statute 12 Ed. 4, c. 7, relates to navigable rivers only, and though weirs in navigable rivers are illegal unless they existed before the time of Edward I., such an easement might be acquired in private waters by grant from other riparian owners, or by enjoyment, or by any means by which such rights may be constituted. Rolle *v.* Whyte, L. R. 3 Q. B. 286. See Leconfield *v.* Lonsdale, L. R. 5 C. P. 657; Hall's Profit à Prendre, p. 308; Paterson's Fishery Laws, c. 4; and Jerwood, p. 83. As to salmon fisheries, see 24 & 25 Vict. c. 109; 28 & 29 Vict. c. 121; 36 Vict. c. 13.]

"*affirm the propriety*, but only remove the annoyance; and "though they prohibit the thing, yet they *do admit* that "there may be such an interest lodged in the subject, "though below the low-water mark, whereby a subject "may not only have a liberty, *but a right or propriety of* "*soil*."(*i*)

No inference from the Statutes against weares, &c., that such exclusive fisheries carry the soil. (*j*)

In reply to this, it is to be observed, that it does not appear how these statutes admit *a weare or fishing sluice* to be sufficient evidence of a title to the soil, which is the inference intended by Lord Hale; or that the weare is anything more than a mere fishery. They go no further than admitting the existence of such an interest, franchise, or liberty, as a "separalis piscaria," in a subject, to be exercised by means of weares, &c., so that in the exercise of such right, he be careful not to injure or interrupt other paramount general rights of the public. (*k*) Not only is a separate or private fishery thus restrained; but the ownership of the soil, even in the King himself, cannot be made

(*i*) *Ante*, p. 389. (*j*) [See Jerwood, p. 84.]

(*k*) (This argument involves this: that there may be a grant of a fishery to fish with fixed engines—for weirs are extensive and important structures, and not mere fishing sluices, as Mr. Hall puts them—or a grant of fishery with a licence from the Crown to erect fixed engines in the soil. They could not be fixed of common right, nor in respect of a mere grant of the franchise of fishery without the soil. They would (as has been said) be either purprestures on the Crown, liable to be abated by indictment, or trespasses to the soil if the soil was in another subject. Such grants have never been seen, and the Editor is convinced do not, and never did, exist. The erection of weirs in the soil of the sea or on the foreshore is, as Lord Hale treats it, evidence of an act of ownership by the owner of the soil, and he rightly argues that the statutes for the suppression of nuisances by weirs do recognise the right of owners of the shore to erect them so that they be no hindrance to the right of navigation. If they were mere purprestures, they could be abated without the aid of any Act of Parliament. To put this to a practical test. Take the case of the Tyne, where these statutes were enforced under a royal commission. There were weirs in every manor on the banks, and the lords of the manors are owners of the foreshore from one end of the river to the other. In the port of Exeter the case is the same, and innumerable cases may be shewn in the Thames, Trent, Tees, Ouse, Derwent, and other rivers, and on the sea-coast.—ED.)

a ground for obstructing the subjects in general, in the navigation of the seas or tide-rivers. Whether the obstruction or nuisance be a weare, or a mere wall, it is equally a nuisance, if in prejudice of the *jus publicum;* for, as the learned author truly observes, (*l*) "the *jus privatum*, that "is acquired to the subject by *grant*, *patent*, or *prescrip-* "*tion*, must not prejudice the *jus publicum*, wherewith "public rivers and arms of the sea are affected for public "use."

[72] Weares and fixed fisheries being opposed to the *jus publicum*, to be construed strictly.

The frequent nuisances occasioned by the formation of weares, and fishing sluices (attested by the numerous statutes in force against them), would warrant their being construed *stricto jure*, (*m*) and to include nothing more than the fishery. Nor is it desirable (in a public view) to afford to lords of manors any additional, or easier means of establishing a title to the *soil on the sea-shore*, or the creeks, or arms of the sea, or in the public rivers, than is allowed to them in regard to *terra firma* titles; especially, as such ownership is so capable of being perverted to the public annoyance.

Distinction between several fisheries in places not within the tides, and in the sea and tide-rivers.

There may be a difference, too, very fairly taken, betwixt the grant of a separate fishery, in rivers, streams, and lakes, which are not connected by the tides with the sea, and therefore not subject to the "jus publicum," and the grant of a separate fishery in parts of the sea, creeks, havens, or tide-rivers; which grants, being to the prejudice of public rights and benefits, are, and ought to be, more strictly construed than in cases where there are no public rights to be sacrificed. (*n*)

(*l*) And see Com. Dig. Title Pleader, 3 M. 37.

(*m*) See Dewell *v.* Sanders, Cro. Jac. 491, and Fowler *v.* Sanders, Cro. Jac. 446.

(*n*) (Fisheries in non-tidal waters (except, perhaps, lakes) have their origin exclusively in the possession of the soil, and are not franchise fisheries in *their origin* in any sense. The Crown could not grant a several fishery in non-tidal water unless it was the owner of the river and the soil of the river in which the fishery was so granted. The distinction is clear. In the non-tidal water the owner of the soil makes the grant or continues to hold the fishery and soil as parcel of his manor, whether the manor be in the Crown or not. In the tidal

In Weld *v.* Hornby, (*o*) the question was whether an ancient weare heretofore constructed of wicker work and brush-wood, might be converted into one of stone, and it was decided that it could not. Lord Ellenborough, C.J., said, "The erection of weares across rivers was reprobated in the "earliest periods of our law. They were considered as "public nuisances. The words of Magna Charta (ch. 23) "are, that all weares from henceforth shall be utterly pulled "down by Thames and Medway, and through all Eng-"land, &c. And this was followed up by subsequent acts "(vide 12 Ed. IV. c. 7), treating them as public nuisances, "forbidding the erection of new ones, or enhancing, strait-"ening, or enlarging of those which had aforetime existed. [73] "I remember that the stells erected in the river Eden, by "the late Lord Lonsdale, and the Corporation of Carlisle, "whereby all the fish were stopped in their passage up the "river, were pronounced in this Court, on a motion for a "new trial, to be illegal, and a public nuisance. Now here "it appears that, previous to the erection of this complete "stone weare, there had always been an escape for the fish "through and over the old brushwood weare, in which those "of the stream above had a right; and it was not com-"petent for the defendant to bar them of it by making an "impervious wall of stone through which the fish could not "insinuate themselves, as it is well known they will through

water the Crown might grant the fishery to one and the soil to another, or might grant the soil without the fishery, or the soil and the fishery *uno flatu* to one alone; but in every case it must be a *question* of *evidence* as to what the Crown did grant. It might grant the soil first, and then add the exclusive fishery to the same possession by another grant excluding the public. In that case the grantee would have the qualified property in the soil and the franchise thereover: see *ante*, p. 733, note (*q*). But, as the Crown could grant no such franchise in non-tidal water, the argument here made by Mr. Hall, it is submitted, is fallacious: see Duke of Devonshire *v.* Pattinson, 20 Q. B. D. 263.—ED.)

(*o*) 7 East 195. [As to weirs, see Hamilton *v.* M. of Donegall, 3 Ridg. P. C. 267; Leconfield *v.* Lonsdale, L. R. 5 C. P. 694; D. of Devonshire *v.* Smith, Alc. & Nap. 442; Malcolmson *v.* O'Dea, 10 House of Lords C. 593; D. of Devonshire *v.* Hodnett, 1 H. & Br. 332; Commonwealth *v.* Chapin, 22 Mass. (5 Pick.) 199.]

"a brushwood weare, and over which it is in evidence that "the fish could not pass, except in extraordinary times of "flood. And however twenty years' acquiescence may bind "parties whose private rights only are affected, yet the "public have an interest in the suppression of public "nuisances, though of longer standing. No objection, "however, of this sort can apply to the case, where the "action was commenced within twenty years after the "complete extension of the stone weare across the river, "by which, it is proved, that the plaintiff has been injured. "Then, however general the words of the ancient deeds "may be, they are to be construed, as Lord Coke says, "'by evidence of the manner in which the thing has always "'been possessed and used.'" Nothing is said in this case from which we can infer that the court considered the weare as giving title to the soil. It is treated throughout as a mere fishery.(*p*)

A shore of a manor is often of several miles in extent, whilst the weare may be of but a few yards.

It will hardly be contended, that an express grant of a "piscaria" without more words will pass the whole shore of a manor, which shore *may be of several miles in extent;* and if the express grant of it will not, why should an implied, or presumed grant do so? It is also singular [74] law to hold, that a weare or fishing-place, which may cover only a few yards of shore, should give title to the whole shore, throughout the whole extent of the manor, which may be several miles along the coast, creek, or tide-river.

Now, if we nowhere find a case in point, where the right to the soil on the shore, or under the sea, or an arm thereof, or a tide-river, is *solely* supported on the basis of a prescriptive right of fishery, either separate or common; and, if we find this separate fishery frequently put down by statutes, as nuisances and encroachments on the *jus publicum;*—and that these statutes nowhere notice the separate

(*p*) (As the soil was not in question in this case, and no issue was raised upon it, the inference of Mr. Hall is unwarranted and valueless. The fact remains that there was an ancient weir built into the soil of the river (a non-tidal river), and this is strong evidence to shew the ownership of the soil.—ED.)

fishery, as conferring the soil itself, or otherwise than as a mere "piscaria" and nuisance;—and if we likewise know that fisheries are, in legal title and intendment, mere franchises, and usufructuary liberties or privileges, and are, technically, a distinct species of property and ownership from the soil, and as such, founded either in express ancient grant, or on immemorial usage or prescription; we may be allowed to doubt, whether either an ancient grant of, or a prescription for, any fishery, *eo nomine*, however private, will support a title to the soil itself. (*q*)

An express grant of a separate fishery, and no more words, will not (it is considered) include the soil.

With respect to the express ancient grant, it does not appear how it could be construed to include the soil itself; for suppose the King to have granted, in some creek or arm of the sea, to W. S. the exclusive fishery thereof, by means of weares, stakes, &c., (*r*) without any express words of grant of the soil itself, and the whole creek became suddenly dry land, by the permanent retreat of the waters, it would not be consistent with the received rules of construction, to construe such grant into a grant of the land. (*s*) As well may it be said that the franchise of *free warren*, or even a grant of common of pasture, or of turbary, or a right of way over or in any land, is an absolute disposal of such

(*q*) (This may be true as far as it goes, but fisheries in gross owned separately from the ownership of manors or lands are extremely rare. The title to a fishery is almost always shewn in connection with, or as parcel of, a manor. Weirs, says Lord Selborne, were the means usual in ancient times for appropriating and enjoying several fisheries in tidal waters. Those words meant more than the mere structures projecting into the stream from which the fishermen launched their boats and cast their nets or conducted other fishing operations, and he shews that "quædam piscaria sive le weare" extended three miles in length *ex adverso* the manor in question: Neill *v.* Duke of Devonshire, 8 App. Cas. 143. See also Malcolmson *v.* O'Dea, 10 H. of L. Cas. 619, 620.—ED.)

(*r*) (A grant in these terms was never yet seen.—ED.)

(*s*) (But if the King granted the fishery as "piscaria nostra de A." and it appeared that the grantee had invariably used that fishery by means of fixed engines affixed to the soil, the grant would, it is submitted, be construed as having passed the soil wherein to fix the engines, the user being referred to as evidencing the intention of the Crown in making the grant.—ED.)

[75] land. (*t*) (*u*) It may plausibly be urged that an inclosure by means of a weare, or by stakes, &c., is a virtual appropriation of the soil within it, because no one can make use of it without breaking such inclosure. But in answer to this it may be contended, that the weare or inclosure was made for no other purpose than to catch fish ; *as to the land*, the inclosure was not made *eo intuitu*. It is different from

(*t*) But Lord Coke tells us, "if a man grant to another to dig turves "in his land, and to carry them away at his will and pleasure, the land "shall *not* pass, because but part of the profit is given." Co. Litt. 4 b. Plowd. 154 is contra, and makes it carry the soil ;—but the better opinion is with Coke.

(*u*) (A grant of free warren is invariably (the Editor has seen many hundreds of them) in these terms, that the grantee shall have warren *in omnibus dominicis terris suis*. It presupposes the possession of the soil over which the warren is granted in the grantee. The Crown could not, nor ever did, grant free warren over the soil of another, and a man cannot have warren except in his own lands or in his own lordship : Roll. Abr. ii. 265, l. 53. If, therefore, there is any analogy between grants of free warren and grants of several fishery, the inference is rather that the grant is to the owner of the soil than to a stranger, and it is very questionable whether the Crown would grant several fishery over the soil of another, though it might of course grant it over its own soil. The cases of common of pasture, or turbary, or right of way are the same. Such grants can only come from the owner of the soil. True they pass not the soil to the grantee, but they shew that the soil was in the grantee when the grant was made, and it cannot be suggested that the Crown could grant a right of common over the soil of another. See, as to warren and fishery, Year Book, T., 10 Henry VII. pl. 1 ; Duke of Northumberland *v.* Houghton, L. R. 5 Exch. 127. The inference arising from a grant of free warren *in omnibus dominicis terris suis* is that the grantee has the land whereon the franchise is to be exercised. The inference from a grant of wreck *infra manerium per terras suas*, *super feodum suum*, is precisely the same—viz., that the grantee has the soil whereon the wreck must be taken. If Chief Baron Palles' doctrine is correct (Neill *v.* Duke of Devonshire, 2 L. R. Ir. at p. 169), that a several fishery in tidal water arises from ownership of the soil affected by the exercise of the prerogative in excluding the public from fishing over that soil, then a grant of fishery in tidal water leads up to a presumption that the grantee previously had the soil, but subject to the public right till it was excluded. But in every case it is, and must be, a question of evidence of the nature of the user made of the soil underlying the fishery. See *ante*, p. 733.—Ed.)

an *embankment* made expressly to secure land from the water. If the place where the weare stands should become dry land, the *fishery* is destroyed; and that which was a lawful inclosure for catching fish, may be unlawful when used for asserting a title to grow corn there. The prescription is necessarily gone, when the subject matter of it, and the medium through which it was exercised, is destroyed; when such a prescription, dependent upon the water, has ceased to exist, what is left to support a title to the dry land? The grantor of the franchise or liberty would seem to recover his exclusive dominion again. (*x*) If a weare were placed on the sea-shore, still, on the recess of the tide, the soil within may be of much use for ballastage, or for manure, building materials, &c. (*y*) without injury to the fishery; and what should prevent him, who granted the fishery only, from claiming all the right and uses in the soil that are not inconsistent with his grant, and also the soil itself, when the fishery has ceased to exist by natural causes? Indeed, if the law acknowledge a separate fishery as a distinct species of property, and rank it amongst franchises differing essentially both in title and estate from an inheritance and title to land, it is impossible to admit that the grant in question (which is one only of the many usufructs of the sea or sea-shore) can include the land itself. (*z*)

Distinction between weares and an embankment.

[76]

(*x*) See p. 730, *ante*, and see Co. Litt. 4 b; and see accord. what is said per Bayley, J., in the case Rex *v.* Montague, 4 B. & C. 603, as to the ceasing of rights by natural causes.

(*y*) See p. 730, *ante*, where it is said, that the owner of the soil, though he grant a separate fishery, "may take the water," and also "make profit of the soil when dry." In the case Hollis *v.* Goldfinch, 1 B. & C. 213, the ownership of four *hatches* or *water sluices* made on the banks of a canal was adduced as evidence of title to the soil of the banks; on this evidence Lord Tenterden observes, "It is said that the "demise of the *hatches* imports that they belong to the lessor, and that "if they do so, the bank to which those hatches are affixed must also [76] "belong to him; but that is a conclusion which by no means follows, be- "cause, if they were necessary for the purpose of maintaining the navi- "gation of the river, the undertakers (of the canal) had a right to place "those hatches there, *although they might not be owners of the soil.*"

(*z*) In a case in 1 M. & S. 666, the King *v.* Ellis, Bayley, J., observes, "I should doubt very much if the grant of a fishery would

As to prescription, the rule is, that it presupposes a grant; but no other grant can be presupposed than such as is tantamount to the fishery prescribed for; and if so, a presupposed grant of a separate fishery cannot reasonably go further than the actual grant of such fishery.(*a*)

As to other franchises of wreck, &c.

We will next proceed to consider, in their order, the several other rights, franchises, and uses which arise from or are claimable in respect of the sea and sea-shore; because the learned writer, in the treatise alluded to, in order to establish his doctrine,—that the sea-shore may belong to the subject by "prescription," as well as by charter or grant, —not only quotes the *private fishery*, but various other

[77] And their giving title to the soil.

franchises, rights, and usufructs, the enjoyment of which, by a subject, will, as he concludes, (be evidence from which a grant may be presumed to) support a title to the soil of portions of the sea and sea-shore. Lord Hale says, (*b*) "It may not only belong to a subject, *in gross*, which pos- "sibly may suppose a grant before time of memory, but it "*may* be *parcel* of a manor." "And this," says he, "it is "agreed, 5 Reports, 107, Sir H. Constable's case,(*c*) and

"convey the soil, and everything underneath it, as all the minerals, "though I can conceive that it might pass so much of the soil as is "connected with the fishery." As this was a fishery with *staked nets*, q. Whether the right to drive stakes for that purpose is more than an easement? [See (*ante*, pp. 658, 733, note (*q*).—ED.), Duke of Somerset *v.* Fogwell, 5 B. & C. 875, per Bayley, J., and Hayes *v.* Bridges, 1 Ridg. L. & S 420, per Finucane, J.]

(*a*) (Here again, after much argument, we are brought back face to face with the original proposition, stated at p. 733—viz., that it is a question of evidence in each case whether the soil goes with the fishery. If the user on which the prescription rests shews evidence only of a naked right to fish without fixed engines, a grant is to be presumed of a franchise fishery, as in Duke of Somerset *v.* Fogwell, 5 B. & C. 875, a fishery without the soil; if, on the other hand, the evidence shews fishing by means of weirs and fixed engines, as in Neill *v.* Duke of Devonshire, 8 App. Cas. 153, the presumption arises of a grant of the fishery and the soil. The whole question is matter of fact, and not of law.—ED.)

(*b*) [*Ante*, pp. 393, 394.]

(*c*) (*Ante*, p. 233.) The words of this case are these: "It was "resolved by the whole court that the soil on which the sea flows

"the Book of 5 E. 3, 3, cited accordingly. And accord- [78]
"ing to this was the resolution cited, Dy. 316, to be "between Hammond and Digges, p. 17, Eliz.;—accord- "ingly it was decreed in the Exchequer Chamber, p. 16, "Car. inter. Attorney-General *v.* Sir Sam. Roll, Sir Rd. "Buller, and Sir Thos. Arundell, per omnes Barones. "*And the evidences to prove this fact are commonly these;* "constant and usual fetching gravel, and seaweed, and sea

"and ebbs, sc. between the high and low water mark, *may* be *parcel* "*of the* manor of a subject," and Dyer, 326 b, is cited as accord. 2 Roll. Abr. 170 has also the same words. But this doctrine of Lord Coke may be freely admitted without admitting that "it may be "parcel of the manor" by *prescription;* Lord Coke does not in the above resolution say *that;* the resolution in fact seems to be directed against the doctrine of the civil law writers, who hold that there can be no ownership in the "shore" at all.

The phrase "parcel of," signifies that when the subject has the shore, he has it as *pars totius*,—as he holds the rest of the lands of the manor —and does not in any wise release him from proving it to be "parcel," by the same kind of evidence as is required for the title to all the other parcels of land in the manor. In a note to Carter *v.* Murcot, 4 Burr. 2165, it is said, "in 1 Sid. 149, prescription was admitted to be a title to "the soil of a river, within the flux and reflux of the sea, which is a "consequence from its being allowed in 5 Co. 107. 2 Roll. Abr. 170, "pl. 12, that it may *by prescription* be part of a manor." But the word *prescription* is not to be found either in the resolution in 5 Co. 107, or in 2 Roll. Abr. 170, pl. 12. In Siderfin the words are, "and in this case "it was repeatedly affirmed, and denied by no one, that the soil of all "rivers (cy-haut), where there is fluxum et refluxum, is in the King, "and *by no means* (nemy—) in the lords of manors, sans prescription," and no authority whatever is quoted. Callis also quotes Constable's case as an authority, "that a subject's manor may extend to low-water "mark by *prescription*." See p. 725. Coke, however, upon *his own* authority, and not as giving the resolution of the court—adds (alluding to a case of replevin, Fitz. Replev. 41), "on which I observe three "things. 1. That wreck may be claimed by prescription," [which is admitted.] "2. That forasmuch as a ship cannot be wreck, scil. cast "on the land, but between the high-water and low-water mark, "thence it follows that *that* was parcel of the manor," q.e.d., for according to this doctrine, prescription for a *lesser* thing, a mere franchise, viz. wreck,—gives title to a *greater* thing, viz. land,—and *that* against the King. Besides, the conclusion is a non sequitur, for [78]
wreck may be cast upon the shore, and yet belong to one who has *only* the franchise. [See Jerwood, p. 57.] (But see *ante*, pp. 647–650, 685, 686.—ED.)

"sand between the high-water and low-water mark, and "licensing others so to do; *enclosing* and *embanking* "against the sea, and enjoyment of what is so inned; "enjoyment of *wrecks* happening upon the sands; pre- "sentment and punishment of purprestures there, in the "court of a manor; and such like;" and he adds, "it "not only *may* be parcel of a manor, (*d*) but, *de facto*, it "many times is so; and *perchance* it is parcel of almost "all such manors as, by prescription, have *royal fish*, or "*wrecks* within their manors. For, for the most part, "wrecks and royal fish are not, and indeed cannot be well "left above the high-water mark, unless it be at such "extraordinary tides as overflow the land: but these are "perquisites which happen between the high-water and low- "water mark; for the sea withdrawing at the ebb, leaves "the wrecks upon the shore, (*e*) and also those greater "fish which come under the denomination of royal fish.

Lord Hale's doctrine, that wreck and royal fish raise a presumption of ownership in the shore.

"He, therefore, that hath wrecks of the sea or royal fish, by "prescription *infra manerium*, it is a great presumption that "the shore is part of the manor, or otherwise he could not "have them. And consonant to this is the pleading in Sir "Henry Neville's case, 5 E. 3, 3, and Rastall's Entries, [79] "684, transcribed out of the record, M. 14. E. 1. Rot. 432,

Pleading in Sir Henry Neville's case.

"where an Abbot, prescribing for wreck belonging to his "manor, doth it in this form:—Ipseque et omnes præ- "decessores sui Abbates Monasterii prædicti, et dominii "ejusdem manerii, per totum tempus prædictum, habue- "runt et habere consueverunt, *ratione manerii* prædicti, "omnimodo bona *wreccata* super mare, et ut wreccum "super terram projecta, per *costeram maris*, in quodam "loco, ubi mare, secundum cursum suum pro tempore "fluxit et refluxit, à quodam loco vocato M. in parochiâ "de L. &c." And in the following plea an Abbot prescribes to have "Wreccum maris *infra* (*f*) præcinctum

(*d*) [Calmady *v.* Rowe, 6 C. B. 861; Beaufort, Duke of, *v.* Swansea, 3 Exch. 413.]

(*e*) [See Dickens *v.* Shaw, *ante*, p. 451. Calmady *v.* Rowe, 6 C. B. 861.]

(*f*) Mr. Hargrave, in a note to Co. Litt. 107 A. n. 115, observes upon

"manerii, sive dominii sui projectum, et Flotsan maris "infra præcinctum manerii deveniens; quodque præ-"dictum dolium vini fuit wreccum maris, per mare pro-"jectum, super littus maris apud S. infra precinctum "manerii sive dominii illius."(*g*)

We may collect from the foregoing quotations(*h*) that the learned writer considers not only a separate fishery, by wears, stakes, &c., but also a right to royal fish, to wrecks, to flotsan, jetsan, and ligan, and lastly, a usage to dig and carry away sand, seaweed, &c., or to make embankments and inclosures of portions of the shore, may [80] all be adduced (by prescription) in support of a title to the land or soil of the shore itself. (*i*) He does not say that *all* these are necessary together: we may infer, indeed, from his language, that *all* of them are *not* necessary to raise (the presumption of) an absolute title to the ownership of the sea-shore itself; but he does not inform us whether any one, or more, of them will suffice, or which of them is *essential.*

Comments on such doctrine.

Now, with regard to the franchise of royal fish (which

Royal fish.

this word, that on many occasions it may be of importance thoroughly to understand the phrase *infra*, or, as according to classical style it ought to be, *intra;* and he construes infra quatuor maria to mean intra quatuor maria. In like manner, in the abbot's plea, *infra* was used for *intra*, although infra præcinctum manerii means, according to ordinary construction, *below*, and not *within* the precincts of the manor. Lord Coke uses the word intra, and not infra. "Intra quatuor "maria," within the four seas; "extra quatuor maria," *beyond* the four seas: 260 b, Co. Litt. But in his third Inst. 113, he uses the phrase, "infra corpus comitatus" for "intra corpus comitatus;" and in Constable's case he uses "infra præcinct. manerii" for "intra." (Jerwood, p. 59, has the hardihood to suggest that *infra* means *below* and not *within* the manor. This arises simply from ignorance of mediæval Latin. *Infra* in records is used invariably for within: *infra villam, infra comitatum, infra parochiam*—in all these cases the word means *within.* See the claims of wreck in the early part of the previous treatise, and p. 62, a marsh *infra filum aquæ;* p. 69, *in terra in mari et in aqua dulci infra libertatem vel extra;* p. 84, *infra prædictas metas;* . 133, *extra et infra le floodmark.*—ED.)

(*g*) [De Jure Maris, *ante*, p. 394.]

(*h*) See also Mr. Butler's N. to Co. Litt. 261 A. n. 205.

(*i*) De Jure Maris, *ante*, p. 394.

are whale, sturgeon, and porpoise), this is reckoned by Blackstone (*k*) *inter regalia*, and one of the King's ordinary branches of revenue, and one of the flowers of the Crown. Those fish are claimed on account of "their "superior excellence," according to Blackstone, who vouches for the royal taste, not in right of the sea-shore, but by royal prerogative, and from the most remote antiquity. Whether thrown on shore, or caught in the sea, or on the coast, they are the property of the King, not of the catcher, even in a private fishery. (*l*)

Wreck.

In like manner wreck (when no owner can be found) is part of the King's ordinary revenue, in right of his royal prerogative, and is a flower of the Crown. So also flotsan, jetsan, and ligan, are perquisites of the Crown. These royal rights and franchises are *not* claimed by the Crown as part of or appurtenant to the *ownership* of the sea-shore, nor enjoyed in virtue of such ownership. They belong to the Crown in virtue of the *royal prerogative*. (*m*) They are regarded as "*nullius bona*," and allotted to the [81] King by the law, for want of other ownership. The King might grant them, or any one of them, to a subject, *without any grant of the shore.* (*n*) So, he might grant the wreck to one person, and royal fish to another, and the shore itself to a third person. (*o*) There are not wanting instances where lords of manors on the coast are possessed of, and can prescribe for, *both* these royal franchises, or but *one* of them, and yet have never had or claimed the ownership of the shore itself. (*p*)

Flotsan, &c.

All or any of these rights may and often are held without any right to the shore.

(*k*) Blackstone's Com. vol. i. p. 289, 13th ed.

(*l*) Black. vol. i. p. 290. [See Paterson's Fishery Laws, 24 and 165; Stewart on Fishery Rights, Scot. p. 46.]

(*m*) Bracton, 2 Vent. 188, and 5 Co. 108, Constable's case; Sutton *v*. Buck, 2 Taunt. 311, *et ante*, p. 709.

(*n*) And see Scratton *v*. Brown, 4 B. & C. 485.

(*o*) Anon. 6 Mod. R. 149.

(*p*) [The grantee of "wreck" has a special property in all goods stranded within his liberty, and may maintain trespass against a wrongdoer for taking them away, though such goods were part of a cargo of a ship from which some persons escaped alive to land, and though the owners within the prescribed time claimed and identified them, and before any seizure on behalf of grantee (Dunwich Bailiffs *v*. Sterry, 1

Wreck and royal fish are no part of the realty; they may indeed be prescribed for by the lord of the adjacent manor, and may be and commonly are attached as franchises to the *manors* on the sea coast; but still they are prescribed for on the ground of immemorial usage, or are proved by express grant, and are not claimed in right of (*ratione*) the ownership of the sea-shore. It is nowhere said, nor could it be intended, that a mere grant of so many acres of sea-shore, or sea bottom from the King, would pass, *inclusive*, the royal franchises of wreck and royal fish; and yet these might seem to be more reasonably attached to the shore than the shore attached to them; and if the rule "*accessorium non ducit sed sequitur suum principale*" be applicable at all, it were much more reasonable to hold that the ownership of the soil is evidence of the franchises before mentioned (which, however, it is not) than that these rights, or any of them, are proof of title to the shore. It is difficult to conceive how all or any one of these rights, together or separate, can confer a different title to a different thing, viz. the soil. I may obtain the royal fish from the King, and wreck from another man to whom the King once

These rights are no part of the realty.

[82]

A grant of so much shore by the King, and no more words, will not pass wreck, &c.

B. & Ad. 831); but to constitute wreck the goods must have touched the ground (Pauline, 2 Rob. Adm. R. 358), though they need not have been left dry: Rex *v.* Forty-nine Casks of Brandy, 3 Hag. 257; see also R. *v.* Two Casks of Tallow, *ibid.* 294. But if timber is found without an apparent owner, having broken away from its fastenings and drifted out to sea, it is not "wreck" within 17 & 18 Vict. c. 104, s. 458, so as to entitle the finders to salvage in respect of their services: Palmer *v.* Rouse, 27 L. J. Exch. 137, 3 H. & N. 505 S. C. (See also Stackpoole *v.* the Queen, I. R. 9 Eq. 619.—ED.) "Wreck" will not pass under general words: Alcock *v.* Cooke, 2 M. & P. 625. See further, *ante*, p. 709, and Dickens *v.* Shaw, *ante*, p. 451; Talbot *v.* Lewis, 6 C. & P. 603; the Pauline, 2 Rob. Adm. p. 358; Phear, p. 52, and note in p. 99; Angell, on Tide Waters, 289, &c. Goods thrown on the shore by the violence of the waves are "wreck" within the provisions of 3 & 4 Will. 4, c. 52, s. 50; Legge *v.* Boyd, 1 C. B. 92, S. C. 14 L. J. C. P. 183; see also Barry *v.* Arnaud, 10 A. & E. 646. Disputed title to "wreck" by 17 & 18 Vict. c. 104, s. 472, may be decided by two justices in the same manner in which disputes as to salvage are therein directed to be determined, and by the same Act the Board of Trade has power on behalf of the Crown to purchase rights to wreck, sect. 474.]

granted it; I may *prescribe* for my title to one, and produce an express *grant* of the other, and yet the soil of the shore remain where it was. (*q*) I may prescribe for all these rights, but that is not prescribing for or proving another right; each right must be supported on its own title; nor does it appear why the prescribing for wreck should confer a title to the soil, more than prescribing for wreck should confer a title to a separate fishery, or to royal fish, which clearly it will not do.

Wreck implies egress and regress to get it, but not the right to the shore itself.

As to the observation that "a right to wreck or to royal "fish cannot be well had above high-water mark, for the "sea withdrawing at the ebb, leaves the wreck or royal "fish upon the shore, and consequently that he who hath "wreck of the sea, or royal fish, by prescription, *infra* "*manerium*, it is a *great presumption* that the shore is part "of the manor, as otherwise he could not have them," (*r*)

[83] —it may be replied that this does not seem to be a *necessary* consequence; for wreck, or royal fish, may clearly be granted, *per se, without* the shore; so far as the shore is essential to the enjoyment of the franchise, it will be subject to egress and regress for that purpose; (*s*) nor does it appear what should prevent the grantee from claiming the wreck, or royal fish, although the shore may remain with the King; it is not *necessary*, in order to make the grant of wreck perfect, that more should be conceded than egress and regress.

Now, if it be not *necessary*, that in order to enjoy the wreck, the grantee should be owner of the soil of the shore, no *presumption* necessarily follows that he is such owner. If I have common of pasture upon the waste lands of a manor, I must go upon the waste for the purpose of pasturing my cattle, and yet no presumption of ownership of the soil is raised on that account. The pleadings in Neville's case, (*t*) quoted by the learned writer, do not set

(*q*) See p. 685, *ante*.

(*r*) Constable's case, 5 Co. 108. [De Jure Maris, *ante*, p. 394. R. *v*. Ellis, 1 M. & S. 662. See Calmady *v*. Rowe, 6 C. B. 861, and Beaufort, Duke of, *v*. Swansea, Mayor of, 3 Exch. 418.]

(*s*) 6 Mod. R. 149.

(*t*) 5 E. 3, 3, p. 752, *ante*.

up any title to the shore. Sir H. Neville merely claims wreck, ratione manerii, *i.e.* wreck in right of, or as appurtenant to the *manor*, and passing with the manor into the hands of all owners for the time being of the manor, but nothing is said as asserting a claim to the shore, *ratione wrecci.* (*u*) (*x*)

The abbot's plea considered.

The other authority, of the abbot's plea, (*y*) assumes the wreck and flotsan to be *infra*, or (according to Mr. Hargrave) *intra* præcinctum manerii, and it asserts the "dolium "vini" to have been cast "super littus maris, *apud S.* infra "præcinctum manerii sive dominii illius."(*z*) It may be agreed that the abbot considered the shore as within the precincts; [84] although the next antecedent is the locus in quo, viz. S.—which *locus* the plea states to be *within* the manor. But admitting the plea to intend that the shore, as well as the place S., was within the precincts, yet he was not pre-

(*u*) [Jerwood, pp. 54, 55.]

(*x*) (Mr. Hall here carefully avoids Lord Hale's argument upon the evidence of wreck raising the presumption of an antecedent grant of the shore having been made in the case of the lord of a manor prescribing for wreck. The whole argument turns upon the words *infra manerium.* Hale does not say he that hath wreck of the sea by grant *inter metas* or *infra wapentachium* it is a great presumption that he hath the shore also; he says, he that hath wreck of the sea *infra manerium* it is a great presumption that he hath the shore, as otherwise he could not take it. Hale's argument is clear and incontrovertible, for a grant of wreck *infra manerium* would be valueless and void if the manor stopped at the high-water mark. There are a few cases where it can be shewn that the right to wreck depends on a grant *inter metas* or *infra wapentachium*, and in these cases Hale's argument is of no avail to raise any presumption of antecedent grant of the shore; indeed, the opposite presumption arises—viz., that the shore either remains in the Crown or has been granted to others in their manors within the wapentake or within the bounds between which the wreck is granted. In Sir H. Neville's case, Y. B., Hil., 5 Edward III., plea 11, p. 132 b, 4to edition, replevin was brought against Neville for herrings cast ashore in the vill of Walring, and he pleads that they were thrown "sur nostre terre en Walring, et nous avons franchise "de wreke parmy tout la ville avantdit come appendant a nostre "maner de W." This is clearly a plea of a grant of wreck *infra manerium* as Hale reads it. Comment is unnecessary on Mr. Hall's statement of the case.—ED.)

(*y*) P. 752, *ante*. (*z*) *Ibid.*

scribing for or claiming a title to anything else but wreck and flotsan ; *and he certainly did not claim or prescribe for the shore in virtue of his title to the wreck.* The shore might or might not be his, and within the boundary of his manor ;(*a*) but nothing appears to show *that it was his because the wreck was his ;* or that his prescription for the wreck was *allowed* evidence of a title to the shore ; the shore was not in dispute at all. The form of plea, in both these cases, does not show a title to the shore in right of the wreck. Nor is it *necessary* to show a title to the shore, in order to prove a title to wreck.(*b*)

Case of Barons of Barclay for the soil of the river Severn.

It is proper here to notice a case, which is cited at considerable length in the treatise ascribed to Lord Hale,(*c*) and which appears to be the only case cited by him from which the doctrine now under consideration seems to derive any material support. The learned writer quotes it as a case with the decision of which he was personally familiar.

Ante,p.306.

"In Scaccario, Car. —— upon the prosecution of Sir "Sackville Crow, there was an information against Mr. "John Smith, farmer of the Lord Barclay, setting forth "that the river of the Severn was an arm of the sea, flow-"ing and reflowing with salt water, and was part of the "ports of Gloucester and Bristol, and that the river had "left about 300 acres of ground, near Shinbridge, and "therefore they belonged to the King, by his prerogative.

(*a*) See accord. p. 685, *ante*.

(*b*) (Hale does not put forward this case, as Mr. Hall suggests, to shew that the Abbot claimed the soil because he had the wreck, nor that he claimed the wreck because he had the soil, but that he claimed the wreck because he had the franchise of wreck *infra manerium*, and he justifies the taking by saying that the shore *was* infra *manerium*—*i.e.*, that he had the shore by one title and the wreck *infra manerium* by another. It is to be noticed that there is no traverse to his plea of soil—it was admitted to be his—the question only being whether he had the franchise, or whether that franchise was still in the King. If the defendant in the case had pleaded in modern times, he would have pleaded the King's title to the soil in traverse of the Abbot's allegation, and put the Abbot to proof that the soil was parcel of the manor ; but in those days the doctrine of the King's *primâ facie* title to the foreshore was not invented.—Ed.)

(*c*) De Jure Maris, *ante*, p. 402.

"Upon not guilty pleaded, the trial was at the Exchequer "bar, and by a very substantial jury of gentry and others "of great value."

"Upon the evidence," proceeds his Lordship, "it did [85] "appear, from unquestionable proof, that Severn, in the "place in question, was an arm of the sea, flowed and re-"flowed with salt water; was within and part of the ports "of Bristol and Gloucester; and that within time of "memory these were lands newly gained and inned from "the Severn; and that *the very channel of the river did,* "*within the time of memory, run in that very place where* "*the land in question lies;* and that the Severn had "*deserted it,* and the channel did then run above a mile "towards the west." (*d*)

On the other side, the defendant, claiming under the title of the Lord Barclay, alleged these matters, whereupon to ground his defence, viz.:—

"1st. That the barons of Barclay were, from the time "of Henry the 2d, owners of the great manor of Bar-"clay." Q. e. d.

"2d. That the river of the Severn, usque filum aquæ, "was, time out of memory, *parcel* of that manor."

"3d. That, by the *constant custom of the country,* the "filum aquæ of the river of Severn was the common *boun-* "*dary* of the manors on either side of the river."

"When the state of the evidence was opened, it was "insisted upon that the river in question was an arm of "the sea, a royal river, and a member of the King's port, "and therefore lay *not in prescription to be part of a manor.* "But the Court overruled that exception, and admitted "that even such a river, though it be the King's in point "of interest, *prima facie,* yet it may be by *prescription* and "usage time out of mind parcel of a manor."

(*d*) In Lord Fitzwalter's case, 1 Mod. 106, Hale, C.J., says, "In the "Severn there are particular restraints, as *gurgites,* &c., but the soil "belongs to the lord on either side, and a *special* sort of fishery "belongs to him likewise, but the common sort of fishery is common "to all."—And in some other place the Severn is said to be "an un-"ruly river," often changing its channel.

[86] "Thereupon the defendant went to the proofs, and "insisted upon many *badges* of property or ownership, "as (viz.)"

"That the lords of the manors adjacent to this river, "and particularly those of that manor, had all *royal fish*, "taken within the river opposite to their manors usque "filum aquæ."

"That they had the sole right of salmon fishing."

"That they had all wrecks cast between high-water "and low-water mark."

"That the lords of the manors adjacent had ancient "*rocks* or fishing-places, and *wears*, or such as were of "that nature, within the very channel."

"That they had from time to time granted these fishing-"places, some by lease, some by copy of court roll, at their "several manors, by the names of '*rocks*,' *wears*, *statches*, "*boraches*, *putts*, (*e*) *and that they were constantly enjoyed*, "*and rent paid by those copyholders and leaseholders*."

(*e*) These four last are all *artificial* apparatus for taking the fish, as their names import. Gurges, which is sometimes translated "weare," is a *natural* formation in the river, and, by Lord Coke, is said to be "a deep pit of water, a gors, or gulfe, and consisteth of *water and* "LAND, and by that name the soil shall pass." Co. Litt. 5 b. He takes no notice of "weares," as a fishery, nor of the *other* words in the text. Callis, 255, tells us, that the "kidelli," mentioned in Magna Charta, are "weares," and yet, by stat. 25 Ed. 3, c. 4, "all mills, *weares*, "stanks, stakes, *and kiddels* which were set in the time of King Edward "(grandfather of Edw. 3.), and after, whereby ships and boats were "disturbed, should be *pulled down*." In stat. 12 Henry 4th, weares and fishgarths are mentioned together as nuisances, and in a case Benedict Hall *v.* Mason, quoted by Callis, 262, a weare and fish-guard are put together, and mentioned as "having been letten by the "late Queen (Eliz.) at yearly rents, with the profits of fishing." This weare, which was stated to have been built of *timber and stone*, was demolished as a nuisance. According to Plowd. 154, "by the grant of "a *pool*, the soil *and wear* shall pass, because it is included in the "word; for by one book a formedon lies de *gurgite*." Here the "*soil*" and "*wear*" are distinguished.* Ld. Coke, however, translates "stag-
[87] "num, a pool," and "gurges, a deep pit of water," but says nothing of the weare, which, in fact, may be constructed in a marsh or lake, stag-

* Co. Litt. 5.

"That by common tradition and *reputation* the manors [87]
"on either side Severn were *bounded* one against another
"by the filum aquæ, and divers *ancient depositions* pro-
"duced, wherein it was accordingly *sworn by very many*
"*ancient witnesses*."

"That the increases happening by the reliction of the
"river were constantly enjoyed by the lords adjacent."

"These," says the learned writer, "and many other
"*badges*, were opened, and were most effectually made
"good by most authentical evidences and witnesses. But
"before the defendant had gone through one half of his
"evidence, the Court, and the King's Attorney-General,
"Sir John Banks, and the rest of the King's Counsel, were
"so well satisfied with the defendant's title, that they
"moved the defendant to consent to withdraw a juror,
"which, though he were very unwilling, yet, at the earnest
"desire of the Court and the King's Counsel, he did agree
"thereunto. *So* that matter rested in peace, and the
"lands, being of the yearly value of £200 and better, are
"enjoyed by the Lord Barclay and his farmers, quietly,
"and without the least pretence of question, to this day."

Comments on the case of the Barons of Barclay.

By this report of the case it is made to appear, that the Court declared that the soil of such a river (*i.e.* the Severn, a tide-river and arm of the sea) may, by *prescription* and usage time out of mind, be parcel of a manor. No grant whatever of the soil of the river to the Barons *appears* to have been produced on the trial. The great manor of Barclay, as it would seem, was *admitted* to belong to the Barons; the title to the *manor*, therefore, was not disputed: the true question was, whether such manor com- [88] prised or included within its limits the soil of the river or not. Now this was a mere question of *boundaries* of a manor, the ownership of which was not disputed. This

num (pool), gurges (pit of water), or in the river course, or on the sea-shore. So, the word "sea-grounds" will, it seems, pass a portion of sea-shore.—Scratton *v.* Brown, 4 B. & C. 485, [and see Malcolmson *v.* O'Dea, 10 House of Lords Cases 593.] (See also Neill *v.* Duke of Devonshire, 8 App. Cas. 151, "quædam piscaria sive le weare," meaning a fishery three miles in extent and carrying the soil.—ED.)

manor was *asserted* to extend usque *filum aquæ;* and whether it did or did not extend so far, was the question.(*f*) Two distinct kinds of evidence were adduced to prove a title to the soil; the first kind was that which has been just now controverted; viz. that the Barons, owners of the manor, had immemorially enjoyed the franchises and liberties of wreck, royal fish, and separate fisheries, by wears, borachiæ, &c. The other kind of evidence was such as has, in later times, been admitted to support titles to inland estates; viz. *copyhold grants,* (*g*) *leases,* and taking rents, &c., surveys, records, terriers, and evidence of old witnesses, and ancient depositions to the *boundaries* of the manor.(*h*) These, in the absence of the grant, are admitted as evidence of boundaries to inland estate. But mere reputation, or common tradition, will not alone, it is conceived, be sufficient to support a title to the freehold.(*i*)

(*f*) (The grant of the manor was "Berkelai et totum Berkelai "Harness manerium," with its appendances. There is no word in it, or in any subsequent grant, to carry the soil of the river: *ante*, pp. 166, 284. The evidence was used to construe the grant, and was all admitted for that purpose, and it follows that evidence of taking wreck and royal fish, the erection of fixed engines for fisheries, and granting of copyhold and leasehold interests in them is fit and proper evidence to shew whether the soil of the sea is parcel of a manor. Evidence of reputation also was clearly admitted in this case against the Crown, and is clearly admissible upon an issue as to the boundaries of a manor.—ED.)

(*g*) See 2 T. R. 53; 4 T. R. 514, 669; 10 East 206; 14 East 331; 2 Roll Ab. 186, pl. 5. [Ancient leases are good evidence, showing the ancient state of possession; entries on court rolls of fines and presentments, Walton cum Trimley Manor, 21 W. R. 475, S. C. 28 L. T. N. S. 12; bills and answers in Chancery between parties litigating the title, Malcolmson *v.* O'Dea, 10 House of Lords Cases 593; see also Tisdall *v.* Parnell, 14 Ir. C. L. Rep. 23; verdicts in former actions, and an award, where the party or his predecessors were privy to it, Wenman *v.* Mackenzie, 5 E. & B. 447; Evans *v.* Rees, 10 A. & E. 151; Kinnersley *v.* Orpe, 2 Douglas 517; but an unauthenticated M.S. report of a trial 140 years back, of an action of trespass, and of the charge of the Ld. Ch. Baron (which was received in the Court below) is a document which ought not to be admitted in evidence: Bridges *v.* Highton, 11 L. T. 653.]

(*h*) 1 Maule & Sel. 81, and 687, 689. Doe *v.* Thomas, 14 East 323.

(*i*) See p. 798, *ante*, nor does the question, as to what kind of evidence

So, perhaps, the evidence to the custom of the country, as [89]
to *boundaries*, "affecting a whole district of manors," may have been good evidence in this case. (*k*) The custom, however, of one *manor* is not evidence of the custom of *another*. (*l*)

It is admitted, that a man may be owner of a definite tract of sea, or river, if it be capable of demarcation; but yet the required evidence of the boundary line, (*m*) whether of old *terra firma*, or of land covered with water, is legally and technically stricter than when an easement is claimed by prescription, founded on usage. If it be admitted (as it was in the principal case) that a man is owner of the Great Manor of B. such manor must have its boundaries and limits, both on the land side and on the water; and it is competent for me to prove, by evidence, those limits, and witnesses are in such case admissible evidence. Lord Hale tells us, (cap. 6.) "That the shore may not only be "parcel of a manor, but also of a vill or parish; and the "evidence for that will be, usual *perambulations*, *common* "*reputation*, known *metes and divisions*, and *the like*. (*n*) "Now all this is evidence to *boundaries*; but 'wreck' or "'a fishery' is no evidence to boundaries." (*o*)

shall be admitted to prove the "boundaries of a manor," or that a particular close is part of an estate, appear yet to be fully settled. See [89]
also Phillipp's Evidence, [10th edit. vol. i. p. 170.]

(*k*) R. *v*. Ellis, 1 Maule & Sel. 662, per Ld. Ellenborough.

(*l*) D. of Somerset *v*. France, 1 Strah. 658, and cases cited in Phillipp's Ev. 10th edit. vol. i. p. 497. [Jerwood, p. 48. (Rowe *v*. Brenton, 8 B. & C. 737.—ED.) Anglesea, Marquis of, *v*. Hatherton, Lord, 10 M. & W. 218, S. C. 12 L. J. Exch. 57.]

(*m*) It is the practice to "beacon out" the limits of appropriated portions of shore, or sea-grounds; and these "beacons" are evidences of boundaries. See Scratton *v*. Brown, 4 B. & C. 485, [Calmady *v*. Rowe, 6 C. B. 881.]

(*n*) But see p. 798, *ante*, [and McCannon *v*. Sinclair, 5 Jur. N. S. 1022; Ipswich Dock Commissioners *v*. Overseers of St. Peter's, Ipswich, 7 B. & S. 310. See Perrott *v*. Bryant, 2 Y. & C. 61, *et ante*, p. 681.]

(*o*) (But evidence of the limits within which wreck is taken under a grant of wreck *infra manerium* will be evidence of the extent of that manor, and evidence of the limits of a fishery fished with weirs and fixed engines will also be evidence of the extent of such a territorial fishery.—ED.)

The evidence ought to establish such acts on the part of the claimant and his ancestors, as far back as the statutes of limitation require, as are in their nature the most effec-
[90] tual for acquiring and retaining the *possession* of the land. These acts must be *eo intuitu*, having for their express and manifest object the seizin and possession of it. These acts must also have been *continued* for the time required by the statutes of limitation. At the time the foregoing case was tried, the ancient time of Richard I. was the period of limitation, and it is expressly stated, that the Barons of Barclay had held the manor from the time of Richard I., *nor was this controverted.* The evidence went to prove that, during all the time they were lords of the manor, the Barons had made a series of copyhold grants of various portions of the disputed soil, and leases also, which were overt acts(*p*) of ownership; and the evidence as to boundaries went as far back as living testimony could go.

We are not informed what part of the evidence adduced in this case prevailed most with the Court; we know which would do so in a case of inland title at the present day; and our object is, to separate from this mass of evidence that which was valid from that which was not.

This case, indeed, presents a precedent for those to follow, who, without a grant, have to make good a similar claim; for every kind of evidence (except the "taking "sand") which could give colour of title to the soil was amassed upon the trial; but it does not inform us whether *all* this evidence was *necessary*, or if not all, what part of it was essential in establishing the title to the bed of the river.(*q*) In other cases, therefore, where but one, two, or three of these proofs are adduced, we are left to the principles of the common law to determine whether such proof
[91] be legal evidence or not; as, for instance, whether wreck, or royal fish (and on the sea-coasts these are the most

(*p*) See accord. Rogers and others *v.* Allen, 1 Camp. 309; and see 5 T. R. 412.

(*q*) But see Lord Ellenborough's comments on this case in the King *v.* Ellis, 1 M. & S. 662.

common attributes of manors), will alone, without more substantial evidence, support a title to the sea-shore, or to soil under the sea. (*r*)

With regard to *terra firma*, there is no difficulty as to the nature of the *acts* required to testify seizin and possession. These are such as occupation, and taking possession or seizin, inclosing, letting, (*s*) and taking rent, cultivating and making profit of the soil, land-marks, perambulations, and other acts which savour of *ownership*, *i.e.* which common sense acknowledges as acts of appropriation and occupation, and which naturally flow from continued and exclusive possession; and these acts must have continued for the period required by the statutes of limitation. Nature of the acts required to give title to terra firma.

It may be a question what other acts, besides those just noticed, shall be said to attest an appropriation and personal possession of the soil under the water, in a tract of sea or sea-shore, whilst it continues sea or sea-shore. There must be something in the acts themselves evidencing the "animus habendi, possidendi, et appropriandi,"—not the usufruct of the water merely,—*but of the soil itself under it*. The acts of ownership must not be more appropriate to the *water* than to the *land*. They ought to savour of the land itself, and be the natural result of the personal and exclusive occupation of the soil itself. The animus piscandi, or wreccum capiendi, is not animus solum appropriandi. (*t*) Acts of fishing, continually used, do at last establish a *right* to fish in future; and this is embodied by our law into a "fishery," a technical and distinct species of property and ownership. Why should

(*r*) (It is submitted that this case was not decided in respect of any particular class of evidence, but upon the evidence taken as a whole, and, so taken, it was clearly overwhelming to prove the ownership of the soil. The taking of sand as of right under a title as lord of a manor is cogent evidence to shew ownership of the soil.—ED.)

(*s*) But see Tyrwhitt *v.* Wynn, 2 Barn. & Ald. 554.

(No; but the *animus wreccum capiendi* arises from consciousness of possession of the soil upon which the wreck is to be taken by the force of the grant *infra manerium*.—ED.)

[92] those acts go further? That which those acts savoured most of they were allowed to give a title to, viz. a fishery; and by the same reasoning, that only which savoured most of the soil, ought to give a title to that soil; that which savours most of one kind of property and ownership, can hardly be said to savour most of another kind of property and ownership. The usufruct of the water vanishes with the water,(*u*) and where both usufruct and water are gone, it seems singular to construe such usufructuary right, now no more, into proof of a new species of ownership in the land, and *that* in derogation and to the ousting of the King's original property in such land.(*x*)

Digging for sand, &c.

With regard to the "constant and usual fetching of sea-"sand, sea-weed, and gravel, between the high-water and "low-water mark, and licensing others so to do; and "embanking against the sea, and enjoyment of what is so "inned;" these, it must be admitted, are all acts likely to be done by the owners of the soil; and they afford colour, that he who does these acts is such owner: but these acts *may* be usurpations or intrusions on the King's ownership, and *prima facie* are so.(*y*)

(*u*) See 4 Rep. 88 and Co. Litt. 4 b.

(*x*) (But the user of a fishery with engines fixed in the soil savours of a use of the soil which cannot be without an interest in that soil, and it is well decided that a fishery with weirs carries the soil: Co. Litt. 5 b; Neill *v.* Duke of Devonshire, 8 App. Cas. 151. See *ante*, pp. 722–734, 743.—ED.)

(*y*) [The lord of the manor cannot acquire an exclusive right to cut seaweed below low-water mark, unless by grant from the King, or such long and undisturbed enjoyment, as to give him a title by prescription. The sea is the property of the King and so is the land beneath, except such part as is capable of being occupied without prejudice to navigation, and of which a subject has either a grant from the King, or has exclusively used for so long a time as to confer on him a title by prescription: Benest *v.* Pipon, 1 Knapp Rep. 68. Nor is there at common law a general right in the public of entering on the sea-shore to take seaweed even between high-water and low-water mark: see Howe *v.* Stawell, 1 Alc. & Nap. 348; Healy *v.* Thorne, 4 Ir. C. L. R. 495; (Hamilton *v.* Att. for Ireland, 5 L. R. Ir. 555—ED.;) for Scotch cases see Paterson's Compendium of English and Scotch Law, p. 6. But seaweed thrown up by extraordinary tides belongs to the riparian

As to the right of digging for sand, the authorities [93] show that this may, and often does exist, without conferring any title whatever to the land ; for similar rights are exercised by the tenants in the wastes of a lord's manor, and yet the tenants have no title to the soil ; but such rights are mere profits *à prendre*. (*z*)

A custom to dig sand or seaweed is analogous to the customary right of digging turf, or brick earth, or sand, or coal, or minerals, in the waste lands of a manor, by the customary tenants. Such custom is good, but it does not raise any title to the land ; it is a mere usufructuary liberty, or right of commonage in the lord's waste, supported by express grant, or by usage and prescription. It further appears, that a single individual may possess similar rights,

proprietor upon whose land it is thrown : Lowe *v.* Govett, 3 B. & Ad. 967. In Lord Hale's treatise, *ante*, p. 394, there is only one instance [93] in which seaweed is mentioned, where he says "the shore may be part "and parcel of a manor, and the evidences to prove this fact are "constant and usual fetching of seaweed, &c." "This passage," says Angell, "would seem to indicate that the learned author considered "the public to be, *primâ facie*, entitled to seaweed. For if he had not "so considered it, then the circumstance of its being exclusively "taken by the lord of the manor, could not be received as a proof of "his adverse right of property in the shore."

[In Howe *v.* Stawell, 1 Alc. & Nap. 348, which was an action of trespass for breaking and entering the plaintiff's close, a plea of justification that the close was the sea-shore, and that all the subjects of the King had the right to enter and carry away the seaweed left by the tide, and that the defendant being such subject entered, was held to be bad. (See also Hamilton *v.* Att. for Ireland, 5 L. R. Ir. 555.—Ed.)

[For law in America see Emans *v.* Turnbull, 2 Johns (N.Y.) R. p. 314, Kent, C.J. ; Chapman *v.* Kimball, 9 Connect. R. 38, 3 Kent Com. 522 ; Philips *v.* Rhodes, 48 Mass. (7 Met.) R. 322 ; Moore *v.* Griffin, 9 Shep. (Me.) R. 350 ; Sale *v.* Pratt, 36 Mass. (19 Pick.) R. 191.]

(*z*) (There is no right at common law for any one to take sand or seaweed upon the foreshore : Howe *v.* Stawell, 1 Alc. & Nap. 348 ; Constable *v.* Nicholson, 14 C. B. N. S. 230, 33 L. J. C. P. 240, 11 W. R. 698 ; Hamilton *v.* Att. for Ireland, 5 Ir. L. R. 555. But the digging of sand or shingle on the foreshore by the owner thereof is using his land in a natural way ; such owner, however, may not dig away a natural barrier against the sea, and may be restrained by injunction from so doing : Att. *v.* Tomline, L. R. 12 Ch. D. 214, 14 Ch. D. 58.—Ed.)

exclusive of all others, *in alieno solo.*(*a*) But if this be so,
[94] then it would seem that a custom (local at least) to dig sand or seaweed in the great waste of the shore might be prescribed for (as in the analogous cases), without its conferring a title to the shore itself.(*b*) The statute of 7 James I. c. 18, after reciting or taking notice that, "Whereas "the sea-sand, by *long trial and experience*, hath been found "to be very profitable for the bettering of land, and "especially for the increase of corn and tillage within the "counties of Devon and Cornwall, where the most part of "the inhabitants have not *commonly* used any *other* manure "for the bettering of their arable grounds and pastures; "notwithstanding divers having *lands adjoining* to the "sea-coast there, have of late interrupted the bargemen "and such others as have used of their *free wills and* "*pleasures* to fetch the said sea-sand, to take the same "*under the full sea-mark*, as they have *heretofore used to do*, "unless they make composition with them at such rates as "they themselves set down, though they have very small "or no damage or loss thereby, to the great decay and "hinderance of husbandry and tillage, within the said "counties;"—enacts—"That it shall and may be lawful "to, and for *all persons whatsoever resident and dwelling* "within the said counties of Devon and Cornwall, to fetch "and take sea-sand at all places under the full sea-mark, "where the same is or shall be cast by the sea, for the "bettering of their land, and for the increase of corn and

Statute of 7 Jac. I. c. 18, in favour of taking sand on the shore in Devon and Cornwall.

(*a*) "If a man *grant* to another to dig turves in his land, and to carry "them at his will and pleasure, the land shall not pass, because but "part of the profit is given." Co. Litt. 4 b. So "If a man *prescribe* "or allege a custom to have and enjoy *solam vesturam terræ*, from such "a day to such a day, hereby the *owner of the soil* shall be excluded to "pasture or feed there: so he may *prescribe* to have *separalem pastu-* "*ram*, or *separalem piscariam*, and exclude the *owner of the soil* from "pasturing or fishing there." Co. Litt. 122 a.

(*b*) (It has been decided that no such custom can exist: Howe *v.* Stawell, 1 Alc. & Nap. 348; Constable *v.* Nicholson, 14 C. B. N. S. 240; Hamilton *v.* Att. for Ireland, 5 L. R. Ir. 555; Padwick *v.* Knight, 7 Exch. 854; Oxenden *v.* Palmer, 2 B. & A. 236; Lynn *v.* Taylor, 3 Lev. 160.—ED.)

"tillage, at their wills and pleasures. II. And that it "shall and may be also lawful to and for all bargemen "and boatmen, and all other carriers of sea-sand of the "said counties, that shall fetch or take sand as aforesaid, "*to land and cast* out of their boats and barges such sand "as they shall so fetch or take at *such places* as sand hath "at any time within the space of fifty years last past been "used by such bargemen and boatmen *to be landed and* "*cast;* and also to fetch and carry the same by and through [95] "such ways as now be and by the space of twenty years "last past have been used for the carrying and fetching "thereof, paying for the taking, casting out and landing of "every barge-load, boat-load, or sack of the said sand "*upon the grounds of any man*, such duties as heretofore, "within the said time of fifty years, have been used and "accustomed to be paid for the same, and for passage by "and through the *said ways*, such duties as have usually been "paid by the space of twenty years, and in such manner "and form as the same, within the said several times, "have respectively been used and accustomed to be paid. "And in such places where certain usual duties have not "been paid, but uncertain compositions have from time to "time been made by agreement with the owner of the soil "there, to yield such reasonable compositions as, by "agreement with the said owners, shall from time to "time be made."(*c*)

Comments on the statute.

This statute raises an inference against the presumption that the mere digging of sand, &c. may entitle either lords of manors or others to the *soil* of the sea-shore; for, by this statute, the sea-shore, throughout two of the largest maritime counties in England, is declared to be, and to have been heretofore *commonly* open to the spades and mattocks of all the *inhabitants* of those large counties. Now, if the lords of manors were actually entitled to the sea-shore in this district, the statute was unusually arbitrary, even in that arbitrary reign. (*d*) But the statute does not take notice of any

(*c*) [Jerwood, p. 87.]

(*d*) (The Editor submits that the inference to be drawn is to the contrary of this proposition, for if the inhabitants had the *right* to dig

ownership of the lords of the manors; it states these lords, or rather "owners of lands adjoining," to have interrupted bargemen and others as *had used*, of their free wills and pleasures, to fetch sea-sand, and take the same under the full sea-mark, *as they had theretofore used to do;* (*e*) and without
[96] noticing or regarding any ownership of the lords or others

before the statute, the statute was unnecessary to give them the right. The claim of inhabitants at common law to dig sand and take seaweed even on the lands of the Crown has been held to be bad: Howe *v.* Stawell, 1 Alc. & Nap. 348; Hamilton *v.* Att. for Ireland, 5 L. R. Ir. 555. The fact probably was that the owners of foreshore in Devon and Cornwall had permitted inhabitants to get sand, and this Act turns the permissive use into a right. In the Mayor of Penryn *v.* Best, *ante*, p. 562, it was decided that the charter to the Duchy of Cornwall, 11 Edward III., passed to the Duke all foreshores *then* remaining in the Crown. The Editor was engaged in that case. The manor of Penryn was an ancient manor belonging to the Bishops of Exeter, which had been leased by a succession of leases to the Dukes of Leeds and their predecessors. At the trial the plaintiffs were unable to produce evidence of user of the foreshore by the bishops' lessees, and were compelled to rest their title on a recent conveyance from the Duchy of the foreshore in question. There exists, however, abundant evidence to shew that the lords of manors in Cornwall have title to the foreshore, as against the Crown and the Duchy, by grant anterior to the creation of the Duchy. The statute is not *declaratory*, as Mr. Hall argues, but *enacting*. See Macnamara *v.* Higgins, 4 Ir. C. L. 326; Hamilton *v.* Att. for Ireland, 5 L. R. Ir. 555.—ED.)

[96] (*e*) Lord Hale, *ante*, p. 393, draws the following inference from the statute. He says, "This (the shore) *may* belong to a subject. The "statute 7 James c. 18 supposeth it, for it provides that those of Devon "and Cornwall may fetch sea-sand, for the bettering of their lands, "and shall not be hindered by those who have their lands *adjoining* "*the sea-coast*, which appears by the statute, they *could not formerly*." But the words of the statute expressly state, "That by long *trial and* "*experience* it had been profitable for the bettering of land;" and that "most part of the *inhabitants* had not *commonly* used any other;" and "that they had been of late prevented from doing what they had "been *used* to do at their free wills and pleasures," and "what they "had *heretofore* used to do." So that it appears by the statute that they *could* do so formerly (had done so formerly, but not as of right —ED.). The statute is directed mainly against the owners of "lands "*adjoining to the coast*," and no sound inference is afforded by it, against the King, in favour of the right of the lords of manors of Devon and Cornwall to the sea-shore. [See Calmady *v.* Rowe, 6 C. B. 879.]

in the shore, enacts that *all* persons in the said counties should be at liberty, as theretofore, to take sea-sand at all places under the full sea-mark.

In the case of Bagot *v.* Orr(*f*) it was disputed at the bar, whether this statute was merely *declaratory* of the general right of the subject throughout the coasts of England, or an *enacting* of a *special* and peculiar privilege for the men of Devon and Cornwall, but the Court gave no opinion on the point. There was nothing in the privilege or benefit itself which peculiarly applied to the inhabitants of those counties; it was equally likely to be claimed and used in Sussex or Norfolk, and probably, had the other maritime counties made the same complaint of prevention, the same remedy would have been obtained. It is a right which is most likely to have grown up and been exercised in all maritime districts, immemorially, in like manner as the free fishery has been enjoyed. There are other instances where *general* rights *have* been confirmed to particular places, by special statute.

At all events, it is certain, from the foregoing statute, [97] that such right to dig, &c. may be claimed and enjoyed by thousands who have no ownership in the soil itself; and it also appears that one person may enjoy such right exclusive of all others, even of the admitted owner of the soil himself; and, if so, then such right exercised in the *shore*, does not *necessarily* involve title to such shore. (*g*) In Devon and Cornwall an exclusive right to dig sand or weed on the shore, or to license others so to do, cannot now be set up by lords of manors; nor do the men of those counties stand in need of any licence other than the statute.

Admitting that an exclusive right of digging sand, &c. on the shore, may be exercised by some lords of manors; still it is necessary to *prove* such right, in the first instance, if it is to be used as a ground of title to the shore. Such right can only be proved two manner of ways—1st. by ex-

(*f*) 2 Bos. & Pul. 472.

(*g*) (There is no authority for this proposition. All authority is to the contrary.—ED.)

As to an express grant of right to dig sand, &c.

press grant exclusively to dig, &c. 2nd. By prescription or custom. Now, if we take a manor extending along *several miles* of sea-shore, such shore belonging clearly to the King, and he, by express grant, give to the lord of the manor a right to dig sea-sand, *without more words*, it would be strange to construe this into a grant of the whole of these several miles of sea-shore; and, if so, it would be still more strange to construe a prescriptive right or custom (*i.e.* one grown up by usage and encroachment), more liberally than the King's express grants, and beyond the terms even of the prescription. (*h*) Every argument, indeed, which has been already applied to a several fishery, will equally apply to an exclusive privilege of digging sand, to show that prescription for a mere liberty, profit, or privilege, is no title to land. The shore *may* be subject to a general or to a local right, claimed by others than the owners of the soil, of digging shells or sand, as well as to a right of fishing, or it may *not* be so subject; if no such general or local custom can be established, the ownership of the soil—whether vested in the King, or in a subject by grant from him—is *entire;* but if such custom or usage be established, then one usufruct of the ownership, and no more, is detracted from it. (*i*)

Prescription ought not to have larger effect than an express grant of the right prescribed for would have.

[98]

The lord of a manor claiming such profit *à prendre* out of the shore, might be considered in the same situation, in regard to the King, his lord paramount, as a copyhold tenant is in regard to the lord of the waste of a manor; and therefore, it is conceived, the right to dig gravel, &c. may exist as privilege in the lord, without carrying the ownership of the soil, as well as in a copyholder or freeholder without carrying the soil. If, indeed, such right were *prescribed* for by the lord, as a profit *à prendre* in the shore, the title to the soil of the shore would seem to be excluded by the very terms; for the ownership of the

(*h*) (There never was such a grant. Mr. Hall's argument rests upon a supposition of a state of things that can be shewn never to have existed.—Ed.)

(*i*) (It is clear, upon the authorities before quoted, that no such right can exist.—Ed.)

land is more than a mere privilege, or usage, or profit *à prendre.*(*k*)

Embanking and its evidence of title to the shore.

With regard to the acts of the lord of a manor, or other owner of the old adjoining *terra firma*, in "embanking" against the sea or a tide-river, and enjoying what is so inned, and making grants to do the same, it is impossible, it must be owned, to construe this into a mere profit *à prendre*, like the digging for gravel, &c., for it is a positive and exclusive entry upon and taking possession of the land. Where no *grant* to the lord exists, such an act is an "in-"trusion" upon the King's prima facie title; and looking at such act *per se*, it would seem singular to construe an intrusion upon *one* piece of another man's land into evidence of a right to seize upon other parts of it, and even into evidence of title to that which has not yet been, but is liable to be intruded upon.(*l*)

(*k*) (Such a right is never prescribed for as a *profit à prendre*; as such it has been decided to be bad, and bad also as a custom. Evidence is given of such right to shew acts of ownership by the lord of the manor as a person capable of taking a grant of the shore, and capable of having that right as owner of the shore, for he can have it by no other title. It is submitted that Mr. Hall's argument against the effect of evidence of the taking of sand by the lord of the manor entirely fails; such taking can only be ascribed to ownership of the soil, and is very cogent evidence of such ownership. He cannot take it at common law; he cannot take it by custom; and a grant of liberty to take it is a pure imagination of Mr. Hall's, forced on him by the stress of the argument against him. Such a grant never was seen, and never existed.—ED.)

(*l*) [Every landowner exposed to the inroads of the sea has a right to protect himself, and is justified in erecting such works as are necessary for that purpose: R. *v.* Pagham Commissioners, 8 B. & C. 355. As [99] to embankments on rivers, see R. *v.* Ward, 4 A. & E. 384; Menzies *v.* Breadalbane, 3 Wilson & Shaw 235, S. C. 3 Bligh N. S. 414; R. *v.* Trafford, 1 B. & Ad. 880, S. C. 8 Bingham 204; Angell on Tide Waters, p. 95. But no encroachments can be made on the property of the Crown or its grantee: Todd *v.* Dunlop, 2 Rob. Scot. App. Cas. 333; Smart *v.* Council of Dundee, 8 Bro. Par. Cases 119. The Crown has a title to prevent, by application for interdict, any encroachment, by the proprietors of grounds adjoining the sea-shore, upon the enjoyment of the shore by the lieges for the purpose of passage or relaxation. A proprietor of ground, described by his title as being of a specified extent, and as bounded by the sea-shore, has no

[99] But, in point of fact, the question, in this case, would seem to be one of *boundaries*. The title to the adjacent *terra firma* being admitted to belong to the claimant, the inquiry is directed to the boundary-line sea-ward. Acts of ownership down to the low-water mark are admissible evidence to carry the boundary-line so far. The *law* has fixed the high-water mark as the boundary, unless the contrary be shown; but the contrary *may* be shown.

[100] Thus if a series of "intakings," by the lord of the manor and his predecessors, or their grantees, should be proved, and although anciently and frequently exercised and repeated, should have been uniformly acquiesced in by the crown; and such intakings and grants should be regularly entered upon the court rolls of the manor (accompanied by the jurisdiction of "presentment and punishment of "*purprestures*," (*m*) *i.e.*, of inclosures attempted by others), a

right to enclose that part of the shore, which is covered by the sea only in ordinary spring tides, over which the public has been from time immemorial in the habit of passing, and over which he cannot prove any past use or possession by himself. Smith *v.* Stair, Earl of, 6 Bell's App. Cases 487.

[Where the Crown seeks to recover lands alleged to have been reclaimed from the sea by encroachment or purpresture, if the defendant disputes the Crown's title to the soil, between present high and low water mark, the Court will direct issues to try that right, before inquiring how far in former times the ancient high-water mark extended inland; and this course will be adhered to, notwithstanding the hardship it may impose upon the defendant, who, by admitting the soil, on which he has done acts of ownership, to be part of the foreshore, will in effect have proved the case of the Crown, in the event of his failing to satisfy a jury, that a grant must be presumed. Att.-Gen. *v.* Chamberlaine, 4 K. & J. 292. But if the defendant admits the Crown's title to the soil between present high and low water mark, then, upon an inquiry what is the boundary of the foreshore, the onus would be thrown upon the Crown, of showing that the high-water mark in former times extended further inland than at present. *Ibid.*; see also Lord Westbury's remarks in Bicket *v.* Morris, L. R. 1 H. L. Scot. 60; Att.-Gen. *v.* Lonsdale, Earl of, L. R. 7 Eq. 377; Att.-Gen. *v.* Rees, 4 De G. & J. 55.]

(*m*) Query, whether the proof of jurisdiction to present and punish purprestures on the shore, in the Lord's Court, may not be deemed very decisive evidence of ownership of the shore. Purprestures are unlawful inclosures, and the right to put down and punish them seems

presumption is said to arise in favour of the lord's title to the *whole* shore, down to *low-water* mark, in proportion as these evidences are numerous, extensive, and unequivocal. These acts assert and involve the whole *seizin* and ownership, and not one profit only, like sand-digging. A presumption, therefore, if made at all, must confer a title akin to that involved or assumed by the acts on which it is raised. The *seizin* of the rest of the shore shall, it is said, be *presumed* from the repeated seizin taken of specific parts, so as to carry the boundary-line from that which bounds the *terra firma*, to that which bounds the *shore*. In such case, it is not the lapse of time which raises the presumption, but the acts of the party, and the acquiescence of the *prima facie* owner.

It might, perhaps, be thought that these "intakings" should be left to their own limits, and to stand or fall by their several titles, without adding the whole shore to them. For the principle which dictates these kind of presumptions is, the quieting possessions,—a principle not very applicable to the case in question, where a large extent of shore, never yet reduced to possession, but daily [101]
under the dominion of the sea, is thus presumed to belong to *him* who has neither possession nor grant to plead. But it appears, that this kind of evidence in regard to boundaries is admitted in some cases of *inland* title, as well as in titles to the sea-shore.

The case of Hollis *v.* Goldfinch (*n*) turns partly upon this point. It was there contended, that certain acts of ownership exercised by proprietors of canal shares on *other* parts of the bank of the canal, were evidence of ownership of a particular spot in question. The Court, indeed, there held, that the plaintiff was *not* "at liberty "to go into evidence of the exercise of acts of ownership

strong evidence of ownership in the *locus in quo*. [See Calmady *v.* Rowe, 6 C. B. 86; Beaufort, Duke of, *v.* Swansea, Mayor of, 3 Exch. 413; Le Strange *v.* Rowe, 4 F. & F. 1048; Phear, p. 89.]

(*n*) Hollis *v.* Goldfinch, 1 B. & C. 205. [See Vaughan *v.* De Winton, 15 W. R. 1145; Simpson *v.* Dendy, 8 C. B. N. S. 433; Taylor *v.* Perry, 1 M. & G. 605; Wild *v.* Holt, 9 M. & W. 672.]

"on *other* parts of the bank, but ought to have been "confined to evidence of acts done on the *particular spot* "*in question*." See also Tyrwhitt *v.* Wynn, 2 B. & Ald. 554. But Mr. Justice Bayley's comment, in Hollis *v.* Goldfinch, on another case (Stanley *v.* White, 14 East 332), would seem to draw a distinction as to the cases in which such evidence *aliunde* shall or shall not be admitted. "In all those cases," observes the learned Judge (Bayley), "where evidence of acts done in one spot have been held "admissible, in order to show a right in another spot, a "reasonable probability has been previously made out, "that the whole land had been formerly in one owner, "and had been all subject to one and the same burden. "The decided cases proceed on the ground of *unity of* "*ownership or character* between the spot in question, and "other places with respect to which the acts of ownership "given in evidence are adduced. Now, in the present "case, there was no such unity of ownership or character
[102] "established, *for the acts of ownership* are exercised *on* "*different parts of a bank of a new cut which, in all proba-* "*bility, passed through the lands of many different persons.*" Mr. Justice Best also said, "The question between the "parties in this case was, to whom the right of soil in the "bank belonged? Now how was that question to be "decided? In the first place by title deeds, which must "clearly relate to the *locus in quo*, or no inference what- "ever can be drawn from them. If title deeds cannot be "produced, the next best evidence is possession; but then "it will be the possession of the *locus in quo*. In this "case there was no evidence of possession. The only "other evidence must be acts of ownership: (*o*) now acts "of ownership can only prove that which would be better "proved by title deeds or possession. Acts of ownership

(*o*) *i.e.* Acts of ownership manifesting the animus possidendi, of the *locus* itself, and not a mere *animus* of taking or using some one *particular* profit, or easement. Actu externo opus est, unde *occupatio* potest intelligi. Seld. Mar. Clau. lib. 2, c. 2.—"Usus" et "occupatio" are not the same, as profits *à prendre* show;—the "usus," if it have the import of "occupatio" or "possessio," must imply the usufruct in an absolute exclusive sense.

"when submitted to, are analogous to admissions or "declarations by the party submitting to them, that the "party exercising them has a right so to do, and that he "is therefore the owner of the property upon which they "are exercised. The declaration of A, who is in posses-"sion of land, that B is the owner of that land, is "evidence in favour of B, and against A, as to that par-"ticular portion of land; but it is no evidence that B is "the owner of the adjoining land, which is occupied "by another person, unless, indeed, A and the holders "of the adjoining land all held by one and the same title. "Generally speaking, therefore, acts of ownership sub-"mitted to by the holder of one portion of land cannot "be any evidence that the person exercising them has any "right to the adjoining land. Besides, one landholder [103] "might, from goodnature or other causes, permit acts "which others would refuse; or he might lose his rights "by negligence. It would be extremely hard, therefore, "to construe the implied acknowledgment, arising from "acts of ownership exercised over the lands of A, to be "received as evidence of an acknowledgment of a similar "right over the land of B, who has never submitted to any "acts of the kind."(*p*) The above doctrine of the learned Judge (Bayley) seems to apply strongly to the acts of ownership alluded to in the shore of a manor; and it may be concluded that embankments, and intakings of portions of the shore, immemorially, repeatedly, and uninterruptedly exercised by the lord, or his grantees, will establish a presumption in favour of the lord, against the Crown. But it is not to be forgotten, that as the King's grants are always construed strictly, so presumptions of this kind are only to be admitted against the Crown on strong evidence, more especially in a case in which public utility sides with the Crown, as, indeed, is always assumed.(*q*) (*r*)

The King's grants construed stricto jure.

(*p*) See Stanley *v.* White, 14 East 332; Barnes *v.* Mawson, 1 Maule & Selw. 77; Child *v.* Winwood, 1 Taunt. 208.

(*q*) [Rex *v.* 49 Casks of Brandy, 3 Hag. Adm. R. 271; see also *ante*, p. 686; and Forsyth's Constitutional Law, p. 175, *et ante*, pp. 688 (note), 737, and *post*, 781.]

(*r*) (But this point has now been decided, in Att.-Gen. *v.* Portsmouth, 25 W. R. 559, *ante*, p. 555—viz., that acts of ownership on parts

Conclusion that none of the before-mentioned franchises or uses of the shore will give title to the soil.

If what has been urged be well founded, (*s*) the conclusion to be drawn is,—that neither a fishery, nor a right to wreck, nor the franchise of royal fish, nor, *perhaps*, the usage or custom of digging of sea-weed, shells, or sand, ought to support a claim to the actual freehold and ownership of the soil of any tract of sea, or sea-shore, bounding a manor,—so long as it retains the character of sea-shore,—where presumption arising from the more decisive acts of ownership of intaking and granting the soil itself, and the presentment and punishment of per-
[104] prestures are wanting. All such *franchises* and *liberties* are distinct from the ownership of the soil, both in essence, in title, and in technical character; and the enjoyment of such rights does not, by any *necessary* presumption, involve the seizin and ownership of the soil in which they are exercised. (*t*) And if this be not the case, between sub-

of the foreshore, which were separated and divided from the part in dispute in that case by foreshore admitted to belong to the Crown, are admissible to prove the right to the whole tract of which they formed part. The Court of Appeal did not reverse this doctrine as founded on Jones *v.* Williams, 2 M. & W. 331; Donegall *v.* Templemore, 9 Ir. C. L. Rep. 374, but held that it did not apply to the case in question because the Court considered that the tract of foreshore was not continuous.—ED.)

(*s*) (This begs the whole question.—ED.)

(*t*) (But if it be shewn that the fishery is a fishery carried on by means of fixed engines which, if erected by the owner of the fishery, must either be purprestures on the soil of the Crown or trespasses on the soil of another if the soil be not in the owner of the fishery, and that the right to wreck is a right to take it either by grant or prescription *infra manerium*, and it is proved to be so taken by presentments in the court rolls and receipts upon the accounts of the bailiffs of the manor, and that the digging of sand and taking of seaweed have been done by the lord of the manor as of right; and it be further shewn that there is no common law right, nor any custom valid in law, for the public to take sand or seaweed from the foreshore, even if it be the Crown's; then it is submitted that the case put by Mr. Hall, and the conclusions attempted to be drawn by him, are reversed, and the evidence is evidence of the nature cited by Hale, and is evidence to raise the presumption of a grant of the shore from the Crown; for it is shewn that the grantee is making just such use of the shore in question as the Crown could have done had it retained that shore in its own hands or let it to a lessee.—ED.)

ject and subject, *a fortiori* it ought not to be against the King's ownership and title.(*u*)

It may be here also noted, that Lord Hale himself, in one part of his work (see De Jure Maris, *ante*, p. 398), lays it down as law, that *custom* "cannot entitle the "subject to *relicted* lands, or make such lands part of a "manor." If so, it may, perhaps, be reasonably contended, that the enjoyment of mere customary privileges in the shore cannot "entitle the subject to the lands of such "shore, or make such lands part of the manor."(*v*) (*w*)

(*u*) (But *it is the case* between subject and subject: see Duke of Beaufort *v.* Swansea, 3 Exch. 413, and numerous other cases; and the Editor fails to see, when the question to be determined by this evidence is whether or no the shore has passed as parcel of a manor, that there can be any distinction to be drawn between a presumed grant from one subject to another, when they are capable of granting and taking, and a presumed grant from the Crown to the subject of a matter which the Crown could grant and the subject could take. If the shore could be granted (and of that there is no doubt), the question between the Crown and the subject is, Has it been granted? The evidence of user is admissible to prove or disprove this, and the only question is in each case as to the quantum, the nature, character, and extent of such user, and whether it is sufficient to raise the necessary presumption of grant, having regard to the situation, character, and condition of the shore in question, and having regard to the kind of acts of ownership which could have been exercised actually and physically, and might reasonably have been expected to be exercised by prudent persons whether the Crown had kept possession or had granted the shores to a subject. When the shore is of a profitable nature the user will be large; in rocky shores on the sea-coast it will be slight, and probably only exercised from time to time; but, whatever the user be, if it be user such as the shore in question is capable from its nature of giving opportunity for, it is submitted that such user should displace the *primâ facie* title of the Crown, and it does so: Att.-Gen. *v.* Portsmouth, *ante*, p. 555; *Ex parte* Alston, *ante*, p. 491, &c.; and see *post*, p. 783, note (*i*). To require from the grantee (as Mr. Hall would persuade the Courts they ought to do) evidence of exclusive user of that which, whether it was in the Crown or not, could only be partially and occasionally used is to demand of a man by quo warranto to shew a title to a thing larger than that which could have been ever granted to him; and it is thought that no Court will do this at the present day. —ED.)

(*v*) [See Att.-Gen. *v.* Turner, 2 Mod. 107; Att.-Gen. *v.* Farmen, 2 Lev. 171; Callis, 48, 53.]

(*w*) (As has been repeatedly stated, there are no such things as

Impolicy of favouring individual claims to the sea-shore against the King's rights.

Neither would there seem to be better ground in point of policy than at law for thus taking, by means of presumption alone, the ownership of the sea-shore from the King, and transferring it to individuals, whose private gains and petty profits may create frequent public inconvenience and illiberal extortion. In a commercial country such as England, the free and unrestricted use of the sea-shore is of national importance, and no encouragement ought to be given to claims which have a tendency materially to interfere with the national welfare, and they ought therefore to be treated *stricto jure.*(*x*)

Civil law doctrine as to ownership of the shore.

It is well known, that by the Roman law the sea-shore was common to all, and incapable of ownership, even in the Emperor. "Littorum quoque usus publicus jure gen-"tium est, sicut ipsius maris;—*proprietas* autem eorum "potest intelligi *nullius* esse; sed ejusdem juris esse cujus
[105] "et mare, et quæ subjacent mari, terra vel arena." (*y*) So also, Grotius (*z*) holds, that a man cannot have any property in the shores and sands of the sea; these are all incapable of improvement, and can only be exhausted by the only uses to which they can be applied; viz. of supplying fish and sand. And even our own early law writers did not hesitate to hold *nearly* the same doctrine

Bracton's doctrine.

as part of our own law. "Naturali vero jure," says Bracton, (*a*) "communia sunt omnia hæc,—aqua profluens, "aer et *mare*, et *littora* maris, quasi maris accessoria.

customary privileges on the shore. There is the public right of navigation, and perhaps of way and of bathing, but the latter is doubtful; there is the *primâ facie* public right of fishing; there is the jurisdiction of the Admiral; but there is no privilege of any kind by custom or by common law but these.—ED.)

(*x*) (But where the Crown has granted the shore (always for valuable consideration in past ages), or must by law as it stands be presumed to have so granted, it consorts not with the honour of the Crown nor the dignity of the public to overthrow private titles because the subjects of them happen to have become valuable. Let the titles be tried *stricto jure*, and the balance of justice held fairly between the Crown and the subject as between subject and subject. See Introduction.—ED.)

(*y*) Inst. Lib. 2, tit. 1, sect. 5, lib. ii. sect. 2, c. 3.

(*z*) Grot. de Jur. Bell. ac. Pac.

(*a*) Bracton, lib. ii. fol. 7, sect. 5.

"Nemo enim ad littora maris accedere prohibetur, dum "tamen a villis et ædificiis abstineat, quia littora sunt de "jure gentium communia, sicut et mare." But he does not add the remainder of the sentence from the civil law, viz. "proprietas autem eorum potest intelligi nullius esse," —by which it may be inferred, that he did not mean to deny that the "*ownership*" (such as it was) rested with the King, asserting only that the "*usus*" was common to all, as that of the sea was;—and so far he will be found essentially right;—for the uses to which the sea is applicable, and also common to all, are "navigation" and "fishing,"—and for these uses the shore is acknowledged to be equally applicable and common.(*b*) Other common uses of the shore have been of late claimed on behalf of the public, viz. for the purpose of bathing in the sea,(*c*) and for digging and carrying away sand, shells, stones, and weed, for agricultural and building purposes.(*d*) The value and utility of these rights to the public, entitle them to the fullest consideration before the law is to be deemed settled *against* these enjoyments. It might seem [106] most desirable that the shore should remain vested in the King, whose policy it would be to leave it open to his subjects for useful purposes, and to be, as it were, the trustee thereof for the public use and benefit.

Alienation of Crown lands prohibited.

There was a time when the Crown could grant away to the subject the royal demesnes and landed possessions at pleasure; but now, by statute law,(*e*) such royal grants

(*b*) (But this is scarcely the right conclusion. Surely the omission denotes that the property could be in some one, and, looking at the cases cited in the early part of the preceding treatise, Bracton must have known that this property was commonly vested in the subject. See *ante*, p. 33, as to Bracton's omission.—ED.)

(*c*) Blundell *v.* Caterall, 5 B. & Ald. 268.

(*d*) Bagot *v.* Orr, 2 Bos. & Pul. 472. See these cases fully considered hereafter.

(*e*) [1 Anne, ch. 7, sec. 5. See Doe d. R. *v.* York, Archbishop of, 14 Q. B. 81.

[Although the Crown may not of its own authority part with any portion of its prerogatives, yet, where the Crown has acted under the authority of Parliament, it may part with them: Eduljee Byramjee, *Ex parte*, 5 Moore P. C. C. 294, S. C. 3 Moo. Ind. App. 468.]

are prohibited, and the Crown lands cannot be so aliened. So much, therefore, of the sea-shore as has not been actually aliened by grant, and bestowed on lords of manors and other subjects, still remains vested in the Crown, incapable of alienation. A King of England cannot be insensible of the value of this property, for it concerns, through him, the public advantage; and it is not going too far to say that the Crown ought, upon all occasions, to evince great jealousy in the preservation of this right against the encroachments of particular individuals, and to require the strictest proof of their exclusive ownerships, whensoever claimed. The law itself protects the property of the Crown with greater jealousy and strictness than the property of the subject. The rule, as before stated, being that the King's grants shall be construed *strictly*, and with a leaning in his favour as against the grantee; (*f*) but that, as between subject and subject, the grant shall be construed most in favour of the grantee and against the grantor. But to support a title to the
[107] sea-shore in favour of the subject against the Crown, upon "presumption" drawn from the enjoyment of a prescriptive right,—is to open a wide door to individual claims against Crown lands. The King's right is a *jus publicum*, and it is not the rule of our Courts of Justice to assert or favour the *jus privatum* against the *jus publicum*; on the contrary, the *jus privatum* is to be tried *strictissimo jure*, whenever it offends or may offend against the public good or public rights. (*g*)

An express grant of so much sea-shore from the King, made at a time when such grants were not prohibited by statute law, cannot, of course, be set aside. But, as the other lands of the Crown cannot be taken from the Crown by a claim or presumption founded on prescription, and the sea-shore is as much land of the Crown as any other land in its possession,—there seems to be no better ground for admitting mere prescription to prevail in the one case

(*f*) Bro. Abr. Tit. Patent, pl. 62. [See Jerwood, p. 125, *et ante*, pp. 686, 737, 777.]

(*g*) [See remarks on the case of Dickens *v*. Shaw, *post*.]

than in the other; nor has a single case or decision presented itself wherein the learned writer of the treatise so much referred to has been confirmed in his doctrine, that a title to a prescriptive franchise, liberty, or easement, derivable from the sea or sea-shore, will, by presumption or construction of law, support a title to land; nor can it possibly do so, if the doctrine quoted in a former page (*h*) be law, viz. that prescription alone cannot give title to lands, because of lands more certain evidence of title may be had; viz. by grant;—or by adverse possession during the period prescribed by the statutes of limitation. (*i*)

Public rights construed favourably.

But although it may be deemed an object of no small importance to protect the right of the Crown to the sea-shore, against the encroachments of individuals; yet, where a claim is made on behalf of the *public*, and the King's right is opposed to the general right of the subject, [108] the Courts of Law, which favour liberty, and have an

(*h*) P. 690, *ante*.

(*i*) (Here Mr. Hall again perverts Lord Hale's arguments. It is not Lord Hale's doctrine "that a title to a prescriptive franchise, "liberty, or easement, derivable from the sea-shore, will, by presumption or construction of law, support a title to land" (see pp. 360, 366). Lord Hale argues on a presumption of *fact*, not of *law*, and his argument distinctly is that evidence of the exercise of franchises *within a manor*, which cannot be exercised except upon the supposition that the shore on which they are exercised *must necessarily have been parcel of and within the manor*, is evidence of *fact* to shew that the shore is parcel of the manor, and was parcel thereof at the time of the grant. The cases he quotes entirely support that contention. Mr. Hall admits that an express grant will pass the foreshore, but argues that a grant cannot be presumed against the Crown. The case of Att. *v.* Rolle, and the case of the Barons of Barclay cited by Hale, cap. vi., and the cases hereafter set out, are distinctly to the contrary. In Parmeter *v.* Att.-Gen., 1 Dow House of Lords 316, it was held by Lord Eldon that sixty years' adverse possession of the shore was a title against the Crown. Evidence of enjoyment by the lord of a manor justifies the presumption of a grant from the Crown: Lopes *v.* Andrew, 5 M. & R. 329; Att.-Gen. *v.* Hanmer, 27 L. J. Ch. 837, 4 Jur. N. S. 751; Att. *v.* Jones, 33 L. J. Exch. 249, 2 H. & C. 347; Agnew *v.* Lord Advocate, 11 Ct. of Sess. Cas. 3rd ser. 309; Lord Advocate *v.* Lord Blantyre, 4 App. Cas. 770; Att.-Gen. *v.* Portsmouth, *ante*, p. 555.—ED.)

anxious regard for public rights, and presume the King himself to be personally interested in the public good, will protect the claims of the public to the utmost verge of the law. The *ownership* of the shore, as between the public and the King, has been settled in favour of the King (*primâ facie*—ED.); but, as before observed, this ownership is, and has been immemorially, liable to certain general rights of egress and regress, for fishing, trading, and other uses claimed and used by his subjects. These rights are variously modified, promoted, or restrained by the common law, and by numerous acts of parliament relating to the fisheries, the revenues, and the public safety, but a statement of which is not within the limited scope of our subject. (*k*)

(*k*) (This kind of specious argument, which is to-day put forward very boldly—viz., that the right to the *jus privatum* in the foreshore is now a right vested in the Crown as trustee for the public—is untrue and unfair, and under colour of it the Crown officials, following Mr. Hall, attempt to justify their attacks on private property vested in the subject. According to them, all ownership of the shore by the subject is due to usurpation and encroachment, and they say they are bound to protect the public in its enjoyment and use of the foreshore. See Introduction, and chapter xiii. Now, although it is true that the *jus publicum*, the right of jurisdiction, is vested in the Crown as trustee for the public, it is not true that the *jus privatum*, the interest of property, is so vested except *primâ facie*; and it is not true that ownership of the shore by the subject tends to limit either the rights or enjoyment of the public to which they are entitled at law under the *jus publicum*. The subject is as limited in his ownership as the Crown was before it granted him the shore; he cannot use it in any way so as to derogate from the rights of the public: Rex *v.* Lord Grosvenor, 2 Stark. 511, *ante*, p. 444; Att. *v.* Tomline, *ante*, p. 565. The public receives no injury, nor can receive any injury, from this private ownership of the *jus privatum*. On the contrary, the Crown is far more likely to exclude the public, if money is to be made by selling the foreshore, than the private owner, who, if he encroached, could be attacked at once, where the Crown would be unassailable. See *ante*, chapter xiii.; and see the cases of granting several fisheries by the Board of Trade, excluding the poor fishermen from grounds they have immemorially fished and got their living from, for the benefit of limited companies and other speculators, and, although the validity of these grants is questionable, no one dares raise the question as against the Crown. It is under colour of this argument that private titles to property are attacked; and although the profits,

Let us now proceed to inquire how the law stands with regard to tracts of dry land adjoining the shore which are deserted by the sea, and become *terra firma* by new formation, and usually are interposed between the old *terra firma* and the ordinary high-water mark of the shore. It is for the most part barren and waste, but in some places (particularly in low and marshy districts) capable of pasturage and cultivation. This soil embraces not only that which is always dry, but that also which is subject to high spring tides and extraordinary inundations. It is all deemed land gained from the sea. (*l*)

As to derelict land and alluvion.

Land gained from the sea is of three kinds:

1st. Per alluvionem, alluvion, or land washed up by the sea.

2nd. Per relictionem, derelict land, or land left dry by the shrinking or retirement of the sea.

3rd. Per insulæ productionem, *i.e.* islands and islets gradually or suddenly formed out of the sea, or at the mouths of rivers, &c. (*m*) [109]

The law on this part of the subject is laid down by Blackstone, (*n*) in these words: " As to lands gained from

Alluvion.

and no small ones, are turned over to the reduction of the National Debt, it is not consistent with the honour and dignity of the Crown that ancient titles of undisputed validity should be pushed aside, and the subject harassed with expensive suits, and his property, derived and purchased from the Crown for money, confiscated, on the specious allegation that all this is done for the benefit of the public !—ED.)

(*l*) De Jure Maris, ch. vi. sec. 2 ; *ante*, p. 395 ; and see pp. 675 and 676 *ante*.

(*m*) De Jure Maris, *ante*, pp. 383, 405 ; Callis, 43.

(*n*) 2 Black. Com. 261. [In Att.-Gen. *v.* Chambers, 4 De G. & J. 55, Lord Chelmsford, referring to the passage in Blackstone, says, " I " am not quite satisfied that the principle 'de minimis non curat lex' " is the correct explanation of the rule on this subject ; because, al- " though the additions may be small and insignificant in their progress, " yet, after a lapse of time, by little and little a very large increase may " have taken place which it would not be beneath the law to notice ; " and of which if the party who has the right to it can clearly show that " it formerly belonged to him, he ought not to be deprived. I am " rather disposed to adopt the reason assigned for the rule by Baron " Alderson, in the case of the Hull and Selby Railway Company, 5 M. " & W. 327,—viz. 'That which cannot be perceived in its progress is

"the sea either by *alluvion*, *i.e.* by the washing up of sand "or earth, so as in time to make *terra firma;* or by *dere*-"*liction*, as when the sea shrinks back below the usual
[110] "water mark, in these cases the law is held to be, that if "this gain be by little and little, by small and *imperceptible* "degrees, it shall go to the owner of the land adjoining, for "'de minimis non curat lex;' but if the alluvion or dere-"liction be sudden and considerable, the land shall go to "the King, as lord of the sea." His authorities are, Bracton, lib. ii. c. 2; Callis on Sewers, 48, 53; 2 Roll. Abr. 170; Dy. 326. (*o*)

Derelictions imperceptible.

The words of Bracton are, (*p*) "Item quod per alluvionem "agro tuo flumen adjecit, jure gentium tibi acquiritur. Est "autem alluvio latens incrementum, et per alluvionem adjici "dicitur, quod ita paulatim adjicitur, quod intelligere non "possis quo momento temporis adjiciatur, &c. si autem non "sit latens incrementum, contrarium erit." Lord Hale (*q*) observes upon these words, "Bracton follows the civil law

"'taken to be as if it never had existed at all;' and, as Lord Abinger "said, in the same case, 'The principle,' as to gradual accretion, 'is "'founded on the necessity which exists for some such rule of law for "'the permanent protection and adjustment of property. It must be "'always borne in mind that the owner of lands does not derive benefit "'alone, but may suffer loss from the operation of this rule; for if the "'sea gradually steals upon the land, he loses so much of his property, "'which is thus silently transferred by the law to the proprietor of the "'sea-shore.' If this be the true ground of the rule, it seems difficult "to understand why similar effects, produced by a party's lawful use "of his own land, should be subject to a different law; and still more "so if these effects are the result of operations upon neighbouring lands "of another proprietor; whatever may be the nature and character of "these operations, they ought not to affect a rule which applies to a re-"sult and not to the manner of its production. Of course, an exception "must always be made of cases when the operations upon the party's "own land are not only calculated, but can be shown to have been in-"tended, to produce this gradual acquisition of the sea-shore, however "difficult such proof of intention may be." See Rex *v.* Lord Yarborough, 2 Bligh N. R. 162; Emans *v.* Turnbull, 2 Johns (N.Y.) R. 313; Angell on Tide Waters, p. 250.]

(*o*) And see note to Dyer, 326; [and American case, Municipality No. 2 *v.* Orleans Cotton Press, 18 Louis. R. 122.]

(*p*) Lib. ii. ch. 2.

(*q*) *Ante*, p. 395.

"in this and some other following places; and yet, even "according to this, the common law doth regularly hold "at this day between party and party." And he further observes: "This jus alluvionis is, de jure communi, by the "law of England, the King's; viz. if by any marks or "measures it can be known what is so gained, and if the "gain be so insensible and indiscernible by any limits or "marks, that it cannot be known, idem est non esse et non "apparere, as well in maritime increases as in the increases "by inland rivers." (*r*)

Although the doctrine is laid down by Bracton and Lord Hale upon the word "*alluvio*," yet there is no doubt that Blackstone is right in applying it also to gradual and imperceptible *derelictions* of the waters; in both cases the owner of the soil adjoining is entitled by common law, for the reasons given by these writers; viz. "de minimis non curat "lex,"—"idem est non esse et non apparere;" and because it is in compensation for land either actually or in danger of being lost. (*s*) Blackstone (*t*) says, that the soil so gained by the owner extends to "the USUAL water mark;" he does not explain what is the usual water mark, whether the high or low water mark; but from what is already said, it is clear that the *usual* water mark is the high-water mark. (*u*) (*v*) [111]

Belong to the owner of the adjacent land.

(*r*) [In the Att.-Gen. *v.* Chambers, *supra*, Lord Chelmsford, after quoting this passage, said: "Lord Hale clearly limits the law of "gradual accretions to the cases where the boundaries of the sea-"shore and adjoining land are so undistinguishable, that it is impos-"sible to discover the slow and gradual changes which are from time "to time accruing, and where, at the end of a long period, it is evident "that there has been a considerable gain from the shore, yet the exact "amount of it, from the want of some mark of the original boundary "line, cannot be determined. But where the limits are clear and "defined, and the exact space between these limits and the new high-"water line can be clearly shown, although from day to day, or even from "week to week, the progress of the accretion is not discernible, why "should a rule be applied which is grounded upon a reason which has "no existence in the particular case?" See also Stewart *v.* Greenock Harbour Trustees, 4 Scot. Session Cases, 283, 3rd series.] [111]

(*s*) Callis, 48.

(*t*) Black. vol. 2, p. 261.

(*u*) P. 675, *ante, et seq.*

[The materials accumulated from mining or manufacturing operations

[112] Now, the owner here intended is the absolute owner of *freehold;* it cannot mean a *leaseholder* or *copyholder*, for these are not looked upon by the law in the light of land-*owners.* If, therefore, the lord of the adjoining manor claim at all, he must claim in respect of his freehold, and he has the freehold,—

What ownership of the adjacent land entitles to the alluvion, &c.

1st. Of the demesnes; *i.e.* the freehold lands in his own occupation.

2nd. Of the copyhold tenements; *i.e.* subject to the copyholder's interest.

3rd. Of the waste; *i.e.* subject to the tenant's right of commonage, &c.

(4th. Of the waste beach above high-water mark as waste land parcel of the manor.

upon lands bordering the sea, or upon a public river, where there has been a gradual silting up of rubbish, slate, or other material, either upon the lands where the mines or manufactories are situated, or upon the neighbouring property, would seem to be subject to the ordinary rule, for the title to alluvion arising from artificial causes does not differ, as to the rights of the landowners, from the title to alluvion arising from natural causes, where the artificial causes arise from a fair use of the land adjoining the sea-shore, and not from acts done with a view to the acquisition of the shore: Att.-Gen. *v.* Chambers, 4 De G. & J. 55; Seebkisto *v.* East India Co., 10 Moo. P. C. C. 140. But it has been decided, that the grantee of premises situate on the shore has no right to follow the sea, or take the land acquired from it, where a corporation had a right to the whole territory of the burgh vested in them by charter: see Todd *v.* Dunlop, 2 Rob. Sc. App. 333; Smart *v.* Dundee, Corp. of, 8 Bro. P. C. 199. In America, wherever tide-waters flow, alluvion goes to the proprietor of the adjoining land, as in this country, and upon the same principle: New Orleans *v.*
[112] United States, 10 Peters 717; Banks *v.* Ogden, 2 Wallace 67; Saulet *v.* Sheperd, 4 Wallace 502; Murray *v.* Sermon, 1 Hawks N. C. Rep. 56; Adams *v.* Frothingham, 3 Mass. R. 352; Angell on Watercourses, 6th ed. p. 52; On Tide Waters, 249; Phear, 43; Houck, 147.

[And, on the other hand, if the sea, or an arm of the sea, by gradual and imperceptible progress, encroach upon the land of a subject, the land thereby covered with water belongs to the Crown: *In re* Hull and Selby Railway, 5 M. & W. 327.]

(*v*) (If the manor includes the foreshore, the accretion to the foreshore will extend to the low-water mark; if it does not include the foreshore, then it will extend to the high-water mark only.—Ed.)

(5th. Of the foreshore when it is parcel of the manor. —ED.)

And by consequence, if either the demesnes, the copyhold, or waste, constitute the land immediately adjoining, the lord, as freeholder, will be entitled to the alluvion soil on the coast, as far as high-water mark. (And if the foreshore is parcel of the manor, the lord will be entitled to the alluvion growing to that foreshore to the low-water mark.—ED.) By the same rule, any owner of the *freehold* of the land immediately adjoining to and in boundary limited by the sea, will be entitled as far as high-water mark; and if the lord of the manor part with his freehold to another, in any spot of land adjoining to the coast, such person, it is conceived, acquires all "alluvion," properly so called, from the sea. (But if the foreshore be parcel of the manor and lie opposite the land of a freeholder, such foreshore not having been granted him as parcel of his freehold, the lord will gain the accretion to the foreshore, the freeholder, it is submitted, taking the accretion to his freehold above high-water mark.—ED.)

As to the demesnes, or lands in the lord's own hands, viz. which are neither copyhold nor waste, such land being his own absolute freehold, clearly entitles him to the adjoining alluvial land gained gradually and imperceptibly from the sea, as part of such demesnes; and on this point [113] no more need be said. But his freehold title in the copyhold tenements, and in the wastes, is subject to certain rights and interests, which require further consideration; and it may be contended,

As to the nature of the interest the lord of a manor gains in alluvion which attaches to a copyhold tenement, and the copyholder's interest therein.

1st. That if the adjoining land be a copyhold tenement, and its boundary is no otherwise limited than by the sea, then the copyholder acquires the same right to the alluvion as he had in the copyhold adjoining, and may claim to hold such new soil as copyhold, and part of his old tenement; and,

As to the right of the tenants, where such alluvion is part of the wastes.

2nd. That if the adjoining land be *waste* land of the manor, then all the copyholders have the same rights of common, &c. in the alluvion or new soil, that they had in such waste land adjoining, and as if it were part of such waste.

As to the copy-holder's right in respect of his tenement.

As to the first point, viz. the copyholder's right, it must be very much a question depending upon the description of the "tenement" in the court rolls of the manor. If the tenement, to which the copyholder has been admitted, extend, either expressly or by fair implication, to the sea, or expressly or by implication to high-water mark, then it may be contended that the new alluvial soil is part of the copyhold tenement adjoining; but if the boundary of the tenement be fixed, on the side of the sea, to a particular demarcation, *other* than that made by the water mark for the time being, and short of it, then all beyond that line of demarcation is clearly no part of his tenement, and must either be part of the demesnes or of the waste.

As to the lord's right as opposed to the copy-holder's.

If the lord set up a claim to the alluvion against the copyholder, when the adjoining land is copyhold, it must be in respect of his interest in the land adjoining, which is a *freehold* interest, subject to a *copyhold* interest. He cannot claim it as part of his own private demesnes, be-

[114]

cause he cannot show the adjoining land to be such, it being copyhold; nor can he claim it as part of the waste, because the adjoining land is copyhold, and not waste land.

As to the lord's claim when the alluvion is waste.

Next, suppose him to claim the alluvion as part of the adjoining waste, by the same reasoning as last used, the new soil being adjacent to the waste, is part of it, and subject to all the rights claimable in or out of the old waste, and by consequence to the local customs, commons, &c. (if any) alleged or prescribed for by the tenants in respect of such waste.

Having stated, that in regard to the new alluvial soil gradually heaped up and deposited at and above the edge of high-water mark, the lord, if possessed absolutely of the adjoining land, is entitled to such new soil, absolutely; but if only of the freehold of the copyhold tenement, then subject to such copyhold interest; and if only of the wastes, then subject to the customary rights of the tenants for commonage, &c. in such waste.—It may be further observed, that land gradually and *imperceptibly* left "PER "RECESSUM MARIS" is subject to the same kind of claim,

The same doctrine as to land imperceptibly derelict.

both in respect of the person, the form, and the substance, as the *alluvion* or soil heaped up "PER PROJECTIONEM "MARIS," and may, in like manner, assume the character of freehold demesnes, copyhold, or waste, according to the nature of the soil adjacent. (*w*)

The gradual and insensible *retreat* of the sea is, however, generally *the effect of its own action by the heaping up of alluvial soil, beach, or sand;* and the land thus acquired may rather be said to have been gained per alluvionem or projectionem, than per recessum or relictionem maris. Thus it is observed by Lord Hale, that "there is no alluvion "without some kind of reliction, for the sea shuts out itself." When, therefore we speak of land acquired "*per alluvi*-"*onem*," we may be understood to mean all *imperceptible* additions made by the sea to the adjacent soil; and when we speak of "*derelict*" land, we intend thereby land *suddenly*, and by *evident marks and bounds*, left and become dry land. There may indeed be some cases wherein it is matter of doubt whether the acquest ought to be deemed insensible and gradual, or sudden and manifest. Such cases must be left to the common sense and judgment of the jury, and the nature of the evidence, always remembering *prima facie* and *jure communi*, the land gained is the King's, since it was clearly his so long as it remained sea-bottom, and it is only *not* given to him, in the case in question, because of the difficulty of drawing the line, and the unwillingness of the common law (in respect of its own dignity and the liberty of the subject) to be too nice in trifles, "de minimis non curat lex."

The gradual retreat of the sea, generally the effect of alluvion, and more properly so called.

[115]

The word "derelict" is understood to import sudden and perceptible gains from the sea. Whether imperceptible or not must be left to the jury.

In marshy districts, however, a case might occur of some nicety; viz. where the sea gradually heaps up a bar to itself across a marshy arm or inlet of the sea; the communication between the sea and the inlet becoming gradually less, until at last the entrance is quite blocked up, and the inlet becomes a lake or pond, which also is capable of being drained, or gradually drains itself. Such an acquest from the sea may sometimes be of considerable extent and value. Now, if the lord of the adjoining manor can establish no

Large acquests from the sea in marshy districts, by gradual exclusion of the sea, forming marshes, lakes, ponds, &c.

(*w*) [See Phear, 43. Hunt. 24.]

title to the soil, as and when it was covered with water, the only question will be, whether it is a gradual and insensible or sudden and distinct acquest from the sea. On the part of the King it may be insisted that, until the sea was finally shut out, so much, at least, as was "aqua cooperta," continued part of the sea-bottom, and *as such* belonged to the King; and, consequently, that until the hour that the communication was shut out by the action of the last tide

[116] or storm, all the land covered with water was the King's; that the final exclusion of the sea was not a gradual but sudden effect, and that immediately thereupon the lake and its soil became, to the then edge of the still water, the King's own, and relieved from the common law rights of fishing, &c. That all subsequent diminution of the water by evaporation and drainage, natural or artificial, was for the benefit of the King, whether such drainage be gradual and imperceptible or not. It may also be insisted, that it is not the gradual or slow operation of nature in point of *time*, but the small and *imperceptible* nature of the daily addition of *soil* which governs the title in favour of the subject; and consequently, where the acquisition is not of that character, the reason for the rule against the King's right does not exist; and these, it is considered, are the grounds which would decide the case in favour of the Crown.

As to the King's right therein.

On the side of the owner of the adjoining soil, it may, however, be urged, that at least so much of the dry soil as had been added to his adjacent land, by the gradual and insensible decrease of the water, from the gradual closing of the communication with the sea and decrease of tide, becomes *de die in diem* his own "jure alluvionis," and that the King's claim can extend no farther than to that portion which is proved to have been subject to the tide at the time of the final exclusion of the sea. It may also be urged, with some plausibility, that the lake or pond which remains after the sea has shut out itself by a bar,—has become, in the eye of the law, "land,"—*i.e. in*-land, aqua cooperta; and that its gradual formation into a still water lake or pond, was tantamount to a gradual dereliction of so much land, *i.e.* an imperceptible addition, from time to time, of so

As to the claim of the owner of the adjacent soil therein.

much lake or pond of still water; and inasmuch as a lake or pond, surrounded by the land, is merely land in construction of law, so *this*, having become imperceptibly sur- [117] rounded by land, and cut off from the sea by its own action, has imperceptibly become so much additional soil to the adjacent old terra firma. But the answer to this is, that so long as any communication continues open with the sea and its tides, the whole soil which the water covers must have the same character in point of title, and be treated as "pars maris." Such peculiar cases as these must depend on the circumstances in evidence, and upon the point "an graduatim an non?" A question determinable only by evidence, and the judgment and common sense of the Judge and Jury. The inquiry is a question at common law, between the King and the subject, on a matter of *fact;* the law being already well known and established, and as the fact may be found, the land will be disposed of by the law; viz. if it be a gradual and imperceptible acquest, to the subject; if otherwise, then to the King. The evidence on both sides will be deduced from eyesight and hearsay testimony, natural or artificial land marks, perambulations, records, and written documents, tending to show whether the events and alterations which have happened are of a nature to be rightly deemed sudden and distinct, or gradual and too minute to be distinguished by ordinary observation.

It is not the gradual lapse of the time, but the imperceptible nature of the addition, which favours the subject.

It is not, indeed, either the *sudden* or the *gradual* nature of the *event* which governs the law, but the *perceptible* or *imperceptible* nature of the *acquisition;* and therefore the direction of the evidence will be to show the greater or less degree of distinctness and certainty with which the *quantum* of soil claimed can be ascertained to have accrued within time of memory. Whatever reason and common sense denominates imperceptible and indefinable, or which, even if perceptible and definable, is still too minute and valueless to appear worthy of legal dispute or separate ownership, will be deemed part of the adjoining soil, and, as it [118] were, to have grown out of it. In all other cases the King's right will attach. (*x*)

(*x*) (Att. *v.* Reeves, *ante*, p. 571.—Ed.) [See Houck, 154 *et seq.*]

Lord Hale observes that *custom* may, in the case of alluvion, "give the jus alluvionis to the land whereunto it "accrues." (*y*) But if the *jus alluvionis* be a general common law right, it does not appear how it can be given by "custom," unless the word be used in the sense of the "general custom of the realm," which is the common law. The following cases are quoted by him.

Abbot of Ramsey's case (ante, p. 158).

"Communia (*z*) Trin. 43 E. 3, Rot. 13, in Scaccario, which is that very record which is cited by Dyer, 326, out of the book of Ramsey. Process went out against the Abbot of Ramsey, ad ostendendam causam, quare 60 acræ marisci in manum Regis non debent sesiri, quas Abbas appropriavit sibi et domui suæ, sine licentia Regis, super quodam generali commissione de terris a Rege concelatis et detentis. Abbas respondit, quod ipse tenet manerium de Brancaster, quod *scituatur* est juxta mare, et quod est ibidem quidam mariscus, qui aliquando per influxus maris minoratur, aliquando per defluxus maris augetur, absque hoc quòd appropriavit sibi prout per præsentationem prædictam supponitur. And issue joined, and verdict given for the Abbot, by Nisi Prius, before one of the Barons. "Et judicium, quòd eat sine die, salvo semper jure Regis." The learned writer hereupon subjoins, "though there were "a verdict upon the issue, whether appropriavit an non, "yet it is plain that the title stood upon that which the "Abbot alleged by way of increment. And note, here is "*no custom* at all alleged; but it seems he relied upon the "*common right* of his case, as that he suffered the loss, so [119] "he should enjoy the benefit, *even by the bare common law*, "in case of alluvion." (*a*)

Abbot of Peterboro's case (ante, p. 157).

The next case is stated, by Lord Hale, as follows:— "M. 23, E. 3, B. R. Rot. 26. Lincolnia. The Abbot of Peter- "borough (*b*) was questioned at the King's suit for acquiring "30 acras marisci in Gosberkirk, licentiâ Regis non obtentâ.

(*y*) *Ante*, p. 395.

(*z*) The Abbot of Ramsey's case, *ante*, p 157, De Jure Maris, *ante*, p. 396.

(*a*) [See Woolrych, p. 445; Jerwood, 56. *Re* Hull and Selby Railway, 5 M. & W. 331.]

(*b*) Abbot of Peterborough's case, *ante*, p. 396.

"The Abbot pleaded, quòd per *consuetudinem patriæ* est, "et à tempore quo, &c., extitit ursurpatum, quòd omnes et "singuli domini, maneria terras seu tenementa super cos- "teram maris habentes, particulariter habebunt marettum "et sabulonem, per fluxus et refluxus maris, secundùm "majus et minus, prope tenementa sua projecta. Et dicit, "quòd ipse habet quoddam manerium in eâdem villâ, unde "plures terræ sunt adjacentes costeræ maris, et sic habet "per fluxus et refluxus maris circiter 300 acras maretti "terras suas adjacentes, et per temporis incrementum se- "cundùm *patriæ consuetudinem ;* et absque hoc quòd ipse "perquisivit, &c. And upon issue joined it depended many "years before the issue was tried. But afterwards, P. 41. "E. 3, B. R. Rot. 28, Lincolnia, Rex, viz. given, quòd se- "cùndum consuetudinem *patriæ*, domini maneriorum prope "mare adjacentium habebunt *marettum* et *sabulonem* per "fluxus et refluxus maris per *temporis incrementum* ad "terras suas costeræ adjacentes projecta, &c. Ideo Abbas "sine die." Lord Hale then proceeds to observe, "1st. "Here is *custom* laid, and he relies not barely upon the "case without it. 2d. In this case it was per incrementum "temporis et per mare projecta. It is not a sudden relic- "tion or recessus maris. And though there is no alluvio "without some kind of reliction, for the sea shuts out itself, "yet the denomination is taken from that which predomi- [120] "nates. It is an acquest per projectionem, not per reces- "sum or relictionem. 3d. That such an acquisition lies in "*custom and prescription*, and it hath a reasonable intend- "ment, because these secret and gradual increases of the "land adjoining cedunt solo tanquam majus principali ; and "so by custom it becomes a perquisite to the land, as it "does in all cases of this nature by the civil law."

It must be concluded that the "consuetudinem patriæ" is to be interpreted "the custom of the realm," which is the common law. It does not appear how a local custom of this kind can exist, as contradistinguished from the common right ; for, by common right, imperceptible alluvions or derelictions belong to the owner of the adjacent freehold, throughout the coasts of England.

(Ante, pp. 293, 299, 300.)

The words "secundum majus et minus," and "incremen-"tum temporis," put this case upon precisely the same ground as the former one. All other writers agree that such a right as the one claimed and established in both these cases, is a common law right, and if so, it cannot correctly be pleaded as a local custom; and at this day, beyond doubt, it is quite enough to rely *barely* upon the common law, acting upon the evidence of the gradual and insensible acquisition. The foregoing doctrine regarding "alluvion" was very fully argued and considered in the recent case of the King *v.* Lord Yarborough. (*c*)

The King *v.* Lord Yarborough.

This was a record transmitted from the petty bag office into the Court of King's Bench, which sets forth an inquisition taken at *Cleathorps*, in the county of *Lincoln*, on the 12th day of *November*, 1818, by which amongst other things, it was found that there is a certain piece of land [121] being salt marsh, lying near or adjoining to the parish or lordship of *North Cotes*, in the said county, which piece of land is bounded towards the south and south-west by the sea-wall or sea-bank of the said lordship of *North Cotes*, and towards the north-west by part of the sea-wall or sea-bank of certain lands in the lordship of *Titney*, and on all other parts by the sea, and contain by estimation 453 acres or thereabouts, and is of the annual value of 4*s*. an acre, and was in times past covered with the water of the sea, but is now and has been for several years past by the sea *left*, and is not covered with water except at *high* tides, when the sea doth flow to the said sea-walls or sea-banks; which said piece of land, from the time of such *dereliction*, hitherto has been and still is unoccupied, but the herbage thereof has been from time to time eaten and consumed by the cattle and sheep belonging to divers tenants or occupiers of lands situate within the said parish of *North Cotes*. And the inquisition then stated, that the said piece of land, together with other lands therein specified, the commis-

(*c*) 3 B. & C. 91 [in error 2 Bligh N. S. 147, S. C. 5 Bing. 163. See (*ante*, p. 454; Att. *v*. Reeve, *ante*, p. 871—ED.) Houck, 148; Jerwood, 90; Woolrych, 444; *In re* Hull and Selby Railway Co., 5 M. & W. 327.]

sioners had taken and caused to be seized into the hands of our said lord the King. To this inquisition the defendant filed a traverse, which (after craving oyer of the commissioners' return and inquisition, and admitting the boundaries, quantity, and value of the land in question, and that the same piece of land is now and has been for several years past not covered with water, except at high tides, when the sea doth flow to the said sea-wall or sea-bank) states, that "from time whereof the memory of man "runneth not to the contrary, there hath been and still is "a certain manor called or known by the name of the "manor of *North Thoresby* cum *North Cotes*, situate in the "parish of *North Cotes* aforesaid, in the said county of "*Lincoln*, and that the defendant, long before the respect- "ive days of issuing the commission and finding the inqui- "sition, to wit, on, &c., was seized in his demesne as of fee, [122]
"of and in the manor of *North Thorseby* cum *North Cotes*, "and the demesne lands thereof, and that the same piece "of land heretofore, to wit, on the 1st day of January, 1300, "and on divers other days and times between that day "and the day of the finding the inquisition, by *the slow*, "*gradual, and imperceptible projection, alluvion, subsidence*, "*and accretion of ooze, soil, sand, and matter, being slowly*, "*gradually, and by imperceptible increase in long time cast* "*up, deposited, and settled by and from the flux and reflux of* "*the tide and waves of the sea in, upon, and against the out-* "*side and extremity of the demesne lands of the same manor*, "hath been formed, and hath settled, grown, and accrued "upon and against and unto the said demesne lands of the "same manor, and the same and every portion thereof, "when and as the same hath so there been formed, settled, "grown, and accrued, hath thereupon and thereby at those "times respectively in that behalf above mentioned, forth- "with become and been, and from the same several times "respectively have and hath continued to be, and still are "and is part and parcel of the said demesne lands of the "same manor, and the several owners and proprietors of "the same manor for the time being during all the time "aforesaid, until the time of the seizin of the defendant as

The King *v.* Lord Yarborough.

"aforesaid, and defendant, during the time he hath been "so as aforesaid seized of and in the said manor, from the "time of the formation and accretion of the same piece of "land and every part thereof respectively, continually, "until the time of the finding of the inquisition respectively, "were and was seized in their and his demesne as of fee, "of and in the same piece of land and every part thereof, "when and as the same hath so been formed and accrued "as aforesaid, as and for part and parcel of the demesne "lands of the same manor. Without this, that the said
[123] "piece of land in the plea mentioned, and in the inquisi-"tion last above mentioned, or any part or parcel thereof, "was or now is by the sea *left*, in the manner and form as "in the inquisition is above supposed and found."—The replication of the Attorney General traversed part of the inducement to the defendant's traverse, as follows: "With-"out this, that the said piece of land in the inquisition "lastly mentioned, being the piece of land before described, "at the times in the said plea mentioned, by the slow, "gradual, and imperceptible projection, alluvion, subsi-"dence, and accretion of ooze, soil, sand, and other matter, "being slowly, gradually, and by imperceptible increase "in long time, cast up, deposited, and settled by and from "the flux and reflux of the tide, and waves of the sea in, "upon, and against the outside and extremity of the "demesne land of the same manor, hath been formed, and "hath settled, grown, and accrued upon and against and "unto the said demesne lands of the same manor, in "manner and form as the defendant hath above in his plea "in that behalf alleged;" and the defendant in his rejoinder took issue upon that fact.—The replication then took issue on the defendant's traverse, "that the said piece of land, in "the plea of defendant mentioned, was and now is by the "sea *left*, in manner and form as in the inquisition is above "supposed and found;" and thereupon also the defendant joined issue. These issues were tried at the then last assizes for the county of *Derby*, before *Park*, J., and a verdict found for the *defendant*. A rule *nisi* having been obtained to show cause why a new trial should not be had,

the Court directed, at the time of showing cause against the rule, that the facts proved at the trial should be stated in a special case for the opinion of the Court, and that if judgment should be given for the King upon such case, the verdict obtained for the defendant should be set aside and a new trial had; and if judgment should be given for the defendant upon such case judgment should be entered for the defendant upon the verdict. The case was as follows: [124]

The land in question consists of 450 acres of salt marsh called *fittees*, being the land covered with herbage, which, at the time of taking the inquisition set forth in the pleadings, lay between the sea-wall and the sea opposite to *North Cotes*, in the county of Lincoln. It was proved that this land had been formed in the course of time by means of ooze, warp, silt, sludge, and soil carried down by the *Humber*, and deposited and cast up by the flux and reflux of the sea, upon and against the adjacent land, whereby the land has been enlarged and increased, and the sea has receded. The matter thus deposited is at first soft and sludgy, but in the course of five or six years grows firm, and then produces herbage. With respect to the degree or rate of growth and increase of the land, the evidence produced on the part of the Crown was as follows:—The first witness proved that the sea had receded in parts 140 or 150 yards within twenty-six or twenty-seven years, and that within the last four years he could see that it had receded much in parts, but could not say how much; and in parts he believed that it had not receded at all. The alteration, he said, had been slow and gradual, and he could not perceive the growth as it went on, though he could see there had been an increase in twenty-six or twenty-seven years of 140 or 150 yards, and that it had certainly receded since he measured the land the year before. The second witness proved, that in fifteen years there had been an increase of the fittees on the outside of the sea-wall; in some parts from 100 to 150 yards; that it grows a little from year to year. That within the last five years there had been a visible increase in some parts during that period, of from thirty to fifty yards; that the gradual increase is not

[125] perceptible to the eye at the moment. The third witness said, there had been some small increase in every year ; and the fourth witness said, the swarth increased every year very gradually, and that perhaps it had gathered a quarter of a mile in breadth in some places within his recollection, or during the last fifty-four or fifty-five years, and in some places it had gathered nothing. It was proved that the ground between the sea-wall above mentioned and another sea-wall still more remote from the sea, appeared to have been covered over with the sea formerly.

The King v. Lord Yarborough.

Judgment of the Court.

The judgment of the Court was delivered by Lord Tenterden, after the Court had heard Counsel and taken time to consider. "Upon this case the only question for the "judgment of the Court is, whether the evidence given at "the trial was such as to justify the verdict of the jury "upon the issues joined. Whether the pleadings have been "correctly framed on either side, or what may be the legal "consequence and effect of the verdict, supposing it to "stand, are points now before us. I notice this, because "some part of the argument at the bar was more properly "applicable to a matter of law upon admitted facts, than "to the question whether particular issues are maintained "by the evidence ; or, in other words, whether particular "facts are found to exist.

Distinction between derelict land and alluvion.

"The second issue upon the record arises upon a traverse "of the matter found by the inquisition. The matter thus "found is, that the land now claimed by the Crown was in "times past covered with the water of the sea, but is now, "and has been for several years *left* by the sea. Now, the "distinction between land derelict, or left by the sea, "acquiring a new character in consequence of the mere "subsidence and absence of the salt water, and land gained "by alluvion or projection of extraneous matter, whereby "the sea is excluded and prevented from overflowing it, is
[126] "easily intelligible in fact, and recognised as law by all the "authorities on the subject. Upon the evidence it is very "plain that the land in question is of the latter description, and therefore the issue joined upon this point was "properly found for the defendant

"The principal question arose upon the first issue, and "it is, as I have before intimated, merely a question of "fact. The defendant has pleaded that the land in ques- "tion, by the *slow, gradual, and imperceptible projection,* "*alluvion, subsidence, and accretion of ooze, soil, sand, and* "*other matter, being slowly, gradually, and by imperceptible* "*increase, in long time cast up, deposited, and settled by and* "*from the flux and reflux of the tide and water of the sea,* "in, upon, and against the outside and extremity of the "demesne lands of the manor, hath been formed, and hath "been settled, grown, and accrued upon, against, and unto "the said demesne lands. This allegation has been denied "on the part of the Crown, and an issue taken upon it. "The allegation regards only the manner in which the "land has been formed: it contains nothing as to the "result of its formation, nothing as to the practicability of "ascertaining, after its formation, by any marks or limits, "or quantity previously existing and known, or by "measure to commence and be taken from such marks, or "with reference to such quantity, how much is now land "that once was sea. It is clear upon the evidence, that the "land has been formed slowly and gradually in the way "mentioned in the plea. The argument was upon the "word 'imperceptibly;' and for the Crown, two passages "were cited from *Sir Matthew Hale's* treatise, *De Jure* "*Maris*, wherein that very learned writer speaks of land "gained by *alluvion*, as belonging generally to the *Crown*, "unless the gain be *so insensible that it cannot be by any* "*means*, according to the words of one of the passages, or "*by any limits or marks*, according to the words of the [127] "other passage, found that the sea was there; idem est "non esse et non apparere. In these passages, however, "Sir Matthew Hale is speaking of the legal consequence "of such an accretion, and does not explain what ought to "be considered as accretion insensible or imperceptible in "itself, but considers that as being insensible, of which it "cannot be said with certainty that the sea ever was there. "An accretion extremely minute, so minute as to be im- "perceptible, even by known antecedent marks or limits,

The King *v.* Lord Yarborough.

" at the end of four or five years, may become, by gradual
" increase, perceptible by such marks or limits at the end
" of a century, or even of forty or fifty years. For it is to
" be remembered, that if the limit on one side be land, or
" something growing or placed thereon, as a tree, a house,
" or a bank, the limit on the other side will be the sea,
" which rises to a height varying almost at every tide, and
" of which the variations do not depend merely upon the
" ordinary course of nature, at fixed and ascertained
" periods, but in part also upon the strength and direction
" of the wind, which are different almost from day to day.
" And, therefore, these passages from the work of Sir
" Matthew Hale are not properly applicable to this ques-
" tion ; and considering the word 'imperceptible' in this
" issue as connected with the words 'slow and gradual,' we
" think it must be understood as expressive only of the
" manner of the accretion, as the other words undoubtedly
" are, and as meaning imperceptible in its progress, not
" imperceptible after a long lapse of time ; and taking this
" to be the meaning of the word 'imperceptible,' the only
" remaining point is, whether the accretion of this land
" might properly, upon the evidence, be considered by the
" jury as imperceptible. No one witness has said that it
" could be perceived, either in its progress or at the end of
[128] " a week or a month. One witness, who appears twice to
" have measured the land, says, that within the last four
" years he could see that the sea had receded, but he could
" not say how much ; the same witness said, that it cer-
" tainly had receded since he measured it last year, but he
" did not say how much ; and, according to his evidence,
" the gain in a period of twenty-six or twenty-seven years,
" was on the average about five yards and a half in a
" year. Another witness speaks of a gain of from 100 to
" 150 yards in fifteen years ; a much greater increase than
" that mentioned by the first witness ; and this second wit-
" ness adds, that during the last five years there had been
" a visible increase in some parts of from thirty to fifty
" yards. Upon the evidence of this witness, it is to be
" observed that he speaks very loosely, the difference

Meaning of the word "imperceptible;" it imports the *manner* of the accretion.

"between 100 and 150 in fifteen years, and between thirty "and fifty in five years, being very great. The third "witness said, there had been some small increase in every "year. The fourth witness said, the swarth increases every "year very gradually, and *perhaps* it had gathered a "quarter of a mile in breadth in some places within his "recollection, or during the last fifty-four or fifty-five "years, and in some places it had gathered nothing. And "this was the whole evidence on the subject. We think "the jury might, from this evidence, very reasonably find "that the increase had not only been slow and gradual, "but also imperceptible, according to the sense in which, "as I have before said, we think that word ought to be "understood; and, consequently, we are of opinion, that a "new trial ought not to be granted, and the rule, therefore, "must be discharged." *(d)*

It remains to be observed, that with regard to derelict [129] land left by any *sudden* and *violent* shrinking or retreat of the sea, whether upon the open coasts, or in creeks or arms or inlets of the sea, it *uniformly belongs to the King*, and may be claimed by him at any time within the period fixed by the statutes of limitation. *That*, also, must be regarded in the nature of derelict land, and as vesting in the Crown, which, although not *suddenly* left by or gained from the sea, is nevertheless, upon the evidence, perceptible in its acquisition and increase, in quantity and limits not to be mistaken by ordinary observation.

As to sudden violent derelictions of land.

In a note to Vaillant, ed. of Dyer, *(e)* p. 326 b, it is said, "the Prince [King] shall have all lands left by or gained "from the sea. I have seen and perused a treatise thereon "and therein many examples of Romney Marsh and "Bromhill, in Kent, of which there are farmers to the "King; and there is vouched a memorandum they came "to an agreement with the Lord the King. Trin. 43 Ed.

(d) A judgment of the House of Lords has since been reported [in the case of Gifford *v.* Lord Yarborough, 5 Bing. Rep. C. P. p. 163, by which this decision of the Court of K. B. has been confirmed, and see Ford *v.* Lacey, 7 H. & N. 151].

(e) Dyer, 326 b.

If the sea-marks of land covered by the sea can be ascertained, it remains to the original owner, or returns when the water is gone.

"3, Rot. 13, ex parte of the Treasurer's Remembrancer. "If the sea-marks are gone, so that it cannot be known if "ever there was land there, the land gained from the sea "belongs to the King. But if the sea cover the land at "flux of the sea, and retreat at the reflux so that the sea-"marks are known, if *such* land be gained from the sea, it "belongs to the owner." 8th Eliz., Corporation of Rumney's case. This is an addition to Dyer, by the Editor, from Dyer's own notes. So Lord Hale lays it down, (*f*) that "if "a subject hath land adjoining the sea, and the violence of "the sea swallow it up, but so that there be yet reasonable "marks to continue the notice of it, or though the marks "be defaced, yet if by situation and extent of quantity, and "bounding upon the firm land, the same can be known, "though the sea leave the land again, or it be by art and "industry regained, the subject doth not lose his property; "and accordingly it was held by Cooke and Foster, M. 7 "Jac. C. B. though the inundation continue forty years." For which he cites Dy. ub. sup. and "a notable case of an "overflowing by the Thames," Rot. Parl. 8 E. 2. M. 23. Burnell *v.* the Bishop of Bath and Wells. (*g*) Callis (*h*) also, in his book on sewers, puts this case: "The sea overflows a "field where divers men's grounds lie promiscuously, and "there continueth so long, that the same is accounted par-"cel of the sea; and then after many years the sea goes "back and leaves the same, but the grounds are so defaced "as the bounds thereof be clean extinct, and grown out of "knowledge, it may be that the King shall have those "grounds; yet in histories I find that *Nilus* every year so "overflows the grounds adjoining, that their bounds are de-"faced thereby, yet they are able to set them out by the art "of geometry." At this day it may be concluded that the former ownership may be identified by mensuration, so that if the sea suddenly swallow up ten acres, and after several

[130]

Recovery of ground once terra firma but since flooded.

(*f*) [*Ante*, p. 381, and *Re* Hull and Selby Railway Company, 5 M. & W. 331.]

(*g*) Vin. Abr. title Prerogative, B, a, 2. Com. Dig. title Prerogative, D. 62.

(*h*) Callis, p. 51.

years leave twenty acres dry, the ten acres may be reclaimed by admeasurement, but then the locality must be proved.

Sudden accession of land is not alluvion.

As soon as it is found by inquisition of office to be land *derelict*, the King's title attaches by the common law. "This "accession of land," says Lord Hale, (*i*) "in this eminent and "sudden manner, by the recess of the sea, doth not come "under the former title of *alluvio*, or increase *per projec-* "*tionem*; and therefore, if an information of an *intrusion* "be laid for so much land relict per mare, it is no good de- [131] "fence against the King to make title *per consuetudinem* "*patriæ* to the *marettum*, or *sabulonem per mare projectum*; "for it is an acquest of another nature." And this was accordingly adjudged, H. 12, Car. Rot. 48, in the case of the King against Oldsworth and others, for Sutton Marsh, in Scaccario. And in that case it was likewise held and adjudged that lands acquired *per relictionem maris* are not *prescribable as part of a manor*, or as belonging to the subject; for that were to prescribe, in effect, that the narrow seas to the coast of France or Denmark were part of a manor. In that case the information, plea, and judgment, were in substance as followeth: viz. "Quòd cum 7,000 acræ "marisci salsi vocati Sutton Marsh jacentes et existentes "juxta Sutton Long in comitatu prædicto, videlicet, inter "Sutton Long et mare ad refluxum ejusdem, fuissent parcella "littoris marini, ac ad refluxus maris naturales et ordinarios "aquis salsis et marinis inundatæ: cùmque eadem 7,000 "acræ marisci salsi nuper à mari undæ inundatæ fuissent, "fuissent relictæ." Then the information sets forth a grant by King James, under the great seal, to Peter Ashton and others, and a regrant by them by a deed inrolled to the King, and that Michael Oldsworth, &c. intruded. The defendant, Oldsworth, came in, and as to part, pleaded as tenant, viz. "Quòd bene et verum est, quòd prædictæ "7,000 acræ marisci salsi vocati Sutton Marsh, jacentes et "existentes juxta Sutton Long; viz. inter Sutton Long et "mare ad refluxum ejusdem, fuerunt parcellæ littoris marini, "et ad refluxus maris naturales et ordinarios aquis salis

Derelict soil does not lie in prescription.

(*i*) De Jure Maris, *ante*, p. 397; R. *v.* Lord Yarborough, 2 Bligh N. S. 162.

"inundatæ, et à mari relictæ prout per informationem. But "he further saith the King was seized, in right of the duchy "of the manor of Sutton, et quòd plures terræ dicti manerii "ante relictionem dictæ costeræ maris adjacebant; et quod "*consuetudo patriæ est* et à tempore quo, &c. quòd domini
[132] "maneriorum, terrarum, seu tenementorum super costeram "maris adjacentium, particulariter habebunt marettum et "sabulonem per fluxum et refluxum maris *secundum majus* "*et minus* prope terras seu tenementa sua projectum sive "relictum; quodque et prædictæ 7,000 acræ marisci salsi ad "terram prædictam parcellam manerii de Sutton adjacent, "et per fluxus et refluxus maris relictæ fuerunt à mari, "et projectæ ad terram prædictam parcellam manerii de "Sutton prædicti, ratione cujus relictionis prædictæ dominus "rex fuit seisitus, &c. de prædictis 7,000 acris in jure duca- "tus, &c." And then he entitles himself by a grant under the duchy seal, and traverseth what he had not confessed. Upon this there was a demurrer and judgment for the King, upon solemn argument, and principally upon this reason, that *custom cannot entitle the subject to relicted lands*, or *make it part of a manor*; (*k*) and it differed from the case of the Abbot of Peterborough before cited, for there it was only *project*, but here, *relict* is added to the plea, that it might answer the information; though the plea in the Abbot of Peterborough's case was the precedent by which the plea was drawn, and with which it agreed, saving the addition of relict.

Custom cannot entitle to derelict land.

"And yet the true reason of it is, *because the soil*

(*k*) This deserves notice. In a former page (759) we have seen, that Lord Hale considers prescription and usage time out of mind, to be sufficient to establish the ownership of the lord of a manor to the bed of the river Severn, as parcel thereof along a large extent of coast, and to the derelict land there, which, it seems, is often considerable. There is some discrepancy between the doctrine here laid down and that above alluded to. [See Hunt on Boundaries, 12, 25, *et ante*, p. 778.] (There is no discrepancy. Custom may not entitle, but prescription and usage time out of mind does. The case of Rex *v.* Oldsworth was on the open sea; that of the Severn *inter fauces terræ*, where the manor extended to the *filum aquæ*. Moreover, in Oldsworth's case, notwithstanding the judgment, the Crown did not get possession. See *ante*, pp. 304, 312, 314.—ED.)

"*under the water, must needs be of the same propriety as* "*it is when covered with the water.* If the soil of the sea, "while it is covered with water, be the King's, it cannot "become the subject's, because the water hath left it. "But in the case of *alluvio maris* it is otherwise, because "the accession and addition of the land by the sea to the [133] "dry land gradually, is a kind of perquisite, and an acces-"sion to the land; and therefore, in case of private rivers, "it *seems by the very course of the common law* such a "gradual increase, cedit solo adjacenti; and though it "may be doubtful whether it be so ex jure communi, in "case of the King, yet doubtless it gives a reasonableness "and facility for such right of alluvio to be acquired by "custom; for although in every acquest per alluvionem "there be a reliction, or rather exclusion of the sea, yet it "is not a recess of the sea, nor properly a reliction." Lord Hale then adds, "But this is to be carried along with us "in the case of recessus, or relictio maris, vel brachii "ejusdem; that where the land, as it stood covered with "water, did by particular *usage or prescription* (*l*) belong to "a subject, there the recessus maris, so far as the subject's "particular interest went while it was covered with water,— "so far the recessus maris vel brachii ejusdem belongs to "the same subject."

"The King of England hath the propriety as well as "jurisdiction of the narrow seas; for he is in a capacity of "acquiring the narrow and adjacent sea to his dominion, "by a kind of possession which is not compatible to a "subject, and accordingly regularly the King hath that "propriety in the sea, but a subject hath not, nor indeed "can have, that property in the sea, through a whole tract "of it, that the King hath; because, without a regular

(*l*) But, according to this doctrine, derelict land *may* be *virtually* prescribed for (a position denied, *ante*, p. 806).—For if a man may prescribe for 1,000 acres of sea and the soil under it, the soil, whether wet or dry, is equally prescribed for. Here also, there seems a discrepancy in his Lordship's doctrine. There seems no reason why portions of land under the sea may be prescribed for, and portions of land suddenly left dry, not.

"power, he cannot possibly possess it. But though a sub-
[134] "ject cannot acquire the interest of the narrow seas, yet he "may by *usage and prescription* acquire an interest in so "much of the sea as he may *reasonably possess;* viz. of a "districtus maris,(*m*) a place in the sea between such points, "or a particular part contiguous to the shore, or a port or "creek or arm of the sea. These may be possessed by a "subject, and *prescribed* in point of interest, both of the "water and *the soil itself*, covered with the water, within "such a precinct; for these are manoriable, and may be "entirely possessed by a subject." The learned writer then alludes to title by prescription:—

"The Civilians tell us truly, *nihil præscribitur nisi quod* "*possidetur.* The King may prescribe the property of the "narrow seas, because he may possess them by his navies "and power. A subject cannot; but a subject may possess a "navigable river or creek, or arm of the sea;—because these "may lie within the extent of his possession and acquest."

If an arm of the sea, or other tract covered with sea, be the property of the subject, it continues so, when the water is dried off.

"The consequence," says he, "of this is, that the soil "relinquished by such arms of the sea, ports, or creeks,— "nay, though they should be wholly dried or stopped up, "yet such soil would belong to the owner or proprietor of "that arm of the sea, or river, or creek, for here is not any "new acquest by the reliction, but the soil covered with "water was the subject's before, and also the water itself "that covered it; and it is so now that it is dried up, or [135]
"hath relinquished its channel, or part of it."(*n*)

(*m*) Along the coast, therefore, where none of these inlets or districts are found, the land under the water cannot, at all events, be prescribed for, being too open and indefinable, and, therefore, the shore, in such places, is not prescribable, even if a "districtus maris" may be, although neither the one nor the other would seem correctly to lie in prescription. It is difficult, also, to say what the quantity of sea is that a subject "may *reasonably* possess;" that which the King has actually granted, we may suppose the subject may reasonably possess; but what line shall be drawn as to the quantity or extent of sea a subject shall be allowed to claim by "prescription"?

(*n*) Callis, p. 51, seems to deny this doctrine, as if the *change* produced a change of title; but there can be no difficulty in agreeing with the doctrine laid down in the text, *supposing the title to the soil when covered with water to have been good.*

"And such an acquest of a propriety in an arm or creek "of the sea may be as well within the precincts of a port, "as without; and *that* though the King, or some subject "hath the port, in point of franchise or privilege.(*o*) For, "although the soil of all creeks and navigable rivers, *espe-* "*cially within ports*, do originally belong to the King, in "point of propriety, as well as in point of franchise, yet the "subject may have so great and clear a possession of the "soil lying under the water of that port, that it may belong "to a subject in point of interest or propriety of the soil, "though he have or have not the port in point of fran- "chise;(*p*) and consequently, if the sea should relinquish

As to the right to the soil in ports.

(*o*) If the port has never been out of the hands of the Crown, and is an ancient port, q. if it be possible for the subject to be owner of its soil? (Yes; and *de facto* it commonly and usually is, within the Editor's experience, in the Tyne, Colne, Thames, Medway, Humber, Orwell, Exe, Fal, and other rivers.—ED.)

(*p*) Also, since it is the King's undoubted right to originate new ports, and since he is also *prima facie* absolute owner of the sea-bottom and sea-shore, q. is it possible that the courts of law can allow a Lord of a Manor to make title to so essential a part of the new port as the soil (which may be of great extent), on mere prescriptive evidence? The shore within the precinct of ports often extends *several miles* along the coast. A title interfering with the prerogative of originating new ports ought not to be favoured. [As to the creation of new ports, see Nicholson *v.* Williams, L. R. 6 Q. B. 632, 40 L. J. N. S. M. C. 159 S. C.; Jenkins *v.* Harvey, 1 C. M. & R. 877; Exeter, Mayor of, *v.* Warren, 5 Q. B. 773, 8 Jur. 441 S. C.; 9 & 10 Vict. c. 102, s. 14; 16 & 17 Vict. c.. 107, s. 9; and Houck 185.] (The franchise of a port is a thing distinct from the ownership of the soil, and scarcely a case can be shewn where the soil of the port and the franchise are united in the same ownership. It is to be noted that there is a wide distinction between the local port, the franchise of which may have been granted to the subject, and the royal or fiscal port remaining in the Crown. The former are usually confined to the mouths of the rivers in which they are situate; the latter extend along the coast, and are varied in extent from time to time by royal commission to suit the necessities of the public service. The local port of Newcastle extends to Sparhawk at the mouth of the Tyne, the port of Ipswich to "Polleshed" at the mouth of the Orwell, the port of Colchester to the "metes" at the mouth of the Colne, the port of Exeter to the mouth of the Exe, the Water of Dart to the "Blackstóne" at the mouth of the Dart, the port of Plymouth to the "Mewstone" outside the breakwater; but the fiscal ports of all these places extend several miles along the coast outside the limits of the ancient local ports.—ED.)

" the channel, or creek, or arm of the sea within such a " port, it might and would belong to that subject who had " the propriety of the soil, and water before it were so " relicted."

" And this is an exception out of that generality, possi-
[136] " bly, that *terræ relictæ per mare* may not be prescribed. " But a certain creek, arm of the sea, *or districtus maris,* " *may be prescribed in point of interest;* and by way of " consequence or concomitance, the land relicted there, " according to the extent of such a precinct as was so pre- " scribed, will belong to the former owner of such *districtus* " *maris.* But otherwise it would be, if such *prescription,* " before the reliction, extended only to a liberty, or *profit* " *à prendre,* or jurisdiction only within that precinct; as " liberty of free fishing, admiralty jurisdiction, or the juris- " diction of a leet or hundred, or other court; for such may " extend to an arm of the sea, as appears by 8 E. 2, Co- " ronæ, for *these are not any acquests of the interest of the* " *water and soil, but leave it as it found it.*" (*q*)

" Therefore, the discovery of the extent of the prescrip- " tion or usage, whether it extend to the soil or not, rests " upon such evidence of facts as may justly satisfy the " court and jury concerning the interests of the soil." The learned author then proceeds to observe :—

1st. " That a subject may, by usage or *prescription,* be " owner or proprietor of such an arm of the sea, creek, or " particular portion of the sea contiguous to the shore, as *is* " *not a public port or haven,* and consequently if that part " be left dry, per recessum vel abstractionem maris, that

(*q*) This seems to contradict the doctrine of the same writer quoted and controverted in former pages of this tract. For if such rights, when prescribed for, leave the water and soil where they found them, and are not acquests of the water or soil, they ought not to be construed into evidence of title to such water or soil. (The Editor submits that there is no contradiction. Hale says distinctly and consistently that the *districtus maris* may be prescribed for, and consequently the relicted land, but he says *if* the prescription only goes to shew evidence of a liberty or jurisdiction exercisable without the ownership of the soil the case is the contrary, and such evidence affects not the title to the soil. See p. 811, note (*t*).—ED.)

"will belong to that subject that had such antecedent pro-
"priety when it was covered with water."

"This will appear by a review of those cases that are in "the precedent chapter concerning the right of fishing in "the sea, many of which instances make it appear that there "may be a right of propriety in the soil aquâ coopertâ, and "the right of fishing *resulting* not as a profit *à prendre*, but [137] "upon the very right of the soil itself. (And these "instances that follow in this chapter will further make out "the propriety of the soil of such places as those com- "patible to a subject.(*r*))"

A subject may have a port, and either with or without the soil.

2nd. "That a subject having a *port* of the sea may have, "and, indeed, in common experience and presumption hath, "the very soil covered with the water; for though it is true, "the franchise of a port is a different thing from the pro- "priety of the soil of a port, and so the franchise of a port "*may* be in a subject, and the propriety of the soil may be "in the King, or in some other, yet in *ordinary usage and* "*presumption* they go together."(*s*) (*t*)

q. Whether the grant of a "port," without more words, will carry the soil?

"If the King at this day grant *portum maris de S.*, the "King having the port in point of interest as well as in "point of franchise, it may be *doubtful* whether at this day "it carries the soil, or only the franchise, *because it is not to*

(*r*) (This passage from Hale's text is omitted by Hall.—ED.)

(*s*) It may be argued, that if the franchise of a port be prescribed for, and the port be dried up, and no longer a port, the prescription is lost, and consequently cannot exist to give title to the *soil* so left dry. See p. 748, *ante*. (This is absurd. Hale does not say that the soil is acquired by grant of the franchise, but that often the soil and franchise are united in one ownership. The loss of the franchise will not affect the ownership of the soil.—ED.)

(*t*) (Where the port has belonged to some ancient barony this is generally the case. The lord of the barony has been owner of the soil, and the franchise of the port with its dues has been added thereto. This is the case in the Water of Dart belonging to the Duchy of Cornwall; but where the franchise of the port has been granted to a corporation of a town or city we usually find that the soil of the foreshore and port is in the lords of the manors abutting upon it, as in the case of the Tyne, Exe, Orwell, Colne, Portsmouth, Medway, &c., the reason of this probably being that the foreshore and soil had been granted to the lords of the manors long before the grant of the franchise of the port to the corporation.—ED.)

"*be taken by implication*. But surely, if it were an ancient "grant, and *usage* had gone along with it, that the grantee "held also the soil, this grant might be effectual to pass "both, for both are included in it."

If a man have a port, by prescription, will that carry the soil?

The learned author then proceeds to say, "*and so* if by "prescription or custom, a man hath portum maris de S.; "in ordinary presumption he hath not only the franchise, "but the very water and soil within the port, for a '*portus* "'*maris*' is *quid aggregatum*, as a manor; and such a pre-"scription may carry the soil as well as the franchise; and "though this doth not always hold, yet most times it doth."

"Escaetria, 12 E. 1. n. l. Portus et piscaria et mariscus "de Topsham spectant ad Amiciam Comitissam Devon. "She had not only the franchise of the port, but the soil of "the port, and the fishing and salt marsh adjoining. And [138] "vide the case of the port of Plymouth,(*u*) parcel of the "manor of Trematon, wherein it will appear that a subject, "as he may be owner of a port in point of franchise, so he "*may be* owner of the very soil of the haven in point of pro-"priety. And so concerning the port of Poole: the Earl of "Surrey was owner of it in point of propriety, as well as fran-"chise, and had the anchorage of ships there, which seems "to be ordinarily a perquisite in respect to the soil."(*x*)

3rd. "That a man who is not owner of a port in point "of franchise, but the franchise of the port belonging to "the King, yet such a subject *may* by *usage* have the very "propriety of a creek or arm of the sea, parcel of that port, "and of the soil thereof; and may have, upon that account, "the increase of land that happens by the recess of the "water of that arm of the sea."

Case of the Prior of Christchurch, De Jure Maris, p. 402.

"Register, 252. The Prior of Christchurch Cantuariæ "petitions the King, quòd cum quædam antiqua trenchea, "quæ se ducit à brachio maris vocata A, versus villam de "B, *quæ est in solo* ipsorum Prioris et Conventùs, per sabu-"lones et arenam maris jam de novo taliter sit obstructa,

(*u*) [*Vide* Wightwick, p. 167, *ante*, p. 402; Jerwood, 61.]

(*x*) (But is not so always; it may be a port due, and so is in the case of Newcastle and of Sunderland. See *ante*, pp. 345, 346; Bishop of Durham *v.* Haselrig, p. 420; Att. *v.* Portsmouth, p. 555.—ED.)

"quòd naves per trencheam illam usque ad dictam villam "de B venire nequeunt ut solebant; et quædam alia "trenchea ducens ab eodem brachio maris usque ad eandem "villam de B jam vi maritimâ facta existet, per quam "naves et batelli a mari usque ad villam illam commodè "et sine impedimento poterunt transire. An 'ad quod "'damnum' issues to enquire, 'si sit ad damnum vel præ-"'judicium nostri aut aliorum, seu nocumentum dictæ villæ "'de B, si eis *licentiam concedamus* quòd ipsi dictam anti-"'quam trencheam omnino obstruere et commodum suum "'inde facere possint.'" Lord Hale then observes: "Here "the *common passage* for ships to a town *admitted* in point [139] "of *propriety* to belong to the Prior, and that they may "make profit of the soil being stopt up."

Comments.

This, however, it may be observed, does not seem to be a correct conclusion drawn from the case; the trenchea or common passage seems to have been *admitted* to belong to *the King*, whose *licence* was asked for the conversion of it to profit; there is no admission that the Prior could appropriate the soil of it without the King's licence. (*y*)

The learned author proceeds to inform us, "that though "the subject may have the propriety of a navigable river, "part of a port, yet these cautions are to be added, viz.:—

1st. "That the King hath yet a right of empire or "government over it, in reference to the safety of the "kingdom and to his customs, it being a member of a "port."(*z*)

(*y*) (On the contrary, the soil of the "trenchea" is admitted to be the Prior's subject to the right of navigation, and the *ad quod dampnum* was required to enable him to entirely stop the right of navigation which existed over his soil.—Ed.)

(*z*) An ancient survey of the King's ports is lodged in the Exchequer. Gilb. Evid. 69. The same, it is presumed, as that noticed by Selden, lib. 2, ch. 22, where he states that James 2d, in 1684, ordered 12 surveyors "rerum maritimarum callentissimis," to survey the coasts of England, and to fix on certain headlands, or points, by drawing straight lines from point to point, to fix the limits of the King's chambers, "regias cameras, et portus regios." This map, or chart, was drawn on a plate of brass, and published by the King's proclamation. (Procl. 1, martii 2, Jac. 2d, 1604, in Rot. Pat. part 32.) The spaces in the sea, enclosed within the straight lines, are 27. These

2nd. "That the people have a public interest, a jus publicum, of passage and repassage with their goods by water, and must not be obstructed by nuisances or impeached by exactions. For the *jus privatum* of the owner or proprietor is charged with and subject to that

[140] "*jus publicum* which belongs to the King's subjects, as the soil of an highway is; which, though in point of property it may be a private man's freehold, yet it is charged with a public interest of the people which may not be prejudiced or damnified." (*a*)

The learned writer then observes as to Islands:—

Islands, these belong to the Crown.

3rd. "As touching Islands arising in the sea, or in the arms, or creeks, or havens thereof, the same rule holds which is before observed touching acquests by the reliction or recess of the sea, or such arms or creeks thereof. "Of common right and *prima facie* it is true they belong "to the Crown; (*b*) but where the interest of such districtus maris, or arm of the sea, or creek, or haven, doth in point of propriety belong to a subject, either by charter or by *prescription*, the islands that happen within the precincts of such private propriety of a subject will belong to the subject according to the limits and extents of such propriety. And, therefore, if the west side of such an arm of the sea belong to a manor of the west

Unless formed out of a place the property of a subject.

"regias cameras," King's Chambers, are named as follows,—Holy Island, the Sowter, Whitby, Flamborough Head, the Sporne, Cromer, Winterton-nesse, Easter-nesse, Layestoff, Est-nesse, Orfort-nesse, the North-foreland, the South-foreland, Dungenesse, Beach, Dunenose, Portland, the Start, the Ramme, the Dudman, the Lizard, Lands-end, Milford, David's-head, Beardsie, Holyhead, and Mona-insula. [See Jerwood, p. 14, and *ante*, p. 404.] (This refers to the royal or fiscal ports, which are wholly distinct from private ports, being in the hands of subjects. These ports are variable in extent, and have been constantly set out as to their limits by royal commissions from the time of Elizabeth downwards. See 38th Report of the Deputy-Keeper of the Public Records, where a list of such commissions is set out.—ED.)

(*a*) [R. *v.* Tindall, 1 N. & P. 723; Williams *v.* Wilcox, 8 A. & E. 314, S. C. 3 N. & P. 616, *et ante*, p. 712; Mayor of Colchester *v.* Brooke, 7 Q. B. 339.]

(*b*) See accord. Callis, pp. 45, 47.

" side, and an island happen to arise on the west side of the " *filum aquæ* invironed with the water, the propriety of such " island will entirely belong to the lord of that manor of " the west side; and if the east side of such an arm of the " sea belong to a manor of the east side *usque filum aquæ*, " and an island happen between the east side of the river " and the *filum aquæ*, it will belong to the lord on the east " side; and if the *filum aquæ* divide itself, and one part " take the east and the other the west, and leave an island " in the middle between both the *fila*, the one half will " belong to the one lord and the other to the other. But " this is to be understood of islands that are *newly* made; for " if a part of an arm of the sea, by a new recess from his " ancient channel, incompass the land of another man, his " propriety continues unaltered. And with these diversities " agrees the law at this day. And Bracton, lib. 1, cap. 2, " and the very texts of the civil law,(*c*) vid. Digest, lib. 41, " de acquirendo rerum dominio legibus, 7, 12, 21, 29, 30, " 38, 50, 56, 65, et ibidem, lib. 43, tit. 12, de fluminibus l. 1 " and 6. Vide Bracton ubi supra, Habet etiam locum hæc " species accessionis in insulâ natâ in flumine, quæ, si " mediam partem fluminis teneat, communis eorum est qui " pro indiviso ab utrâque parte fluminis prope ripam prædia " possident, &c. For the propriety of such a new accrued " island follows the propriety of the soil before it came to " be produced." (*d*)

These will belong to the subject.

[141]

(*c*) But by the Civil Law, islands formed in the sea "dantur primo "occupanti." Just. Inst. [De rerum divisione, Britton, titulo Purchase, fol. 86 B.]

(*d*) [*Ante*, p. 404. Where a sand-bank has been formed in a tidal river, which at low water divided the river into two equal streams, a line drawn down the middle of the river at low water, taking the two channels together, is to be regarded as the limits of the respective rights: Wedderburn *v.* Paterson, 2 Scot. Sess. Cas. 3rd ser. 902, Scot. Jur. vol. xxxvi. p. 452, S. C. And if a shifting island springs up in the channel, so as to impede or embarrass the fishings of one of the proprietors, he must submit, and hope for a change; the law can give him no redress. But if the shifting island becomes fixedly annexed to, and incorporated with his bank, the permanent accretion will give rise to a new medium filum: Zetland, Earl, *v.* Glover; Incorporation of Perth, L. R. 2 Scot. App. 70. See also Hunt on Boundaries, p. 19;

Comments on the foregoing quotations from Lord Hale.

The foregoing pages of quotation from Lord Hale's treatise have been given at length, because they embrace all that is generally laid down as *good law* upon this part of [142] our subject, and also some other points, perhaps questionable. He first of all agrees with all other law authorities, that the *derelict* land belongs to the King. He further states it as law (and it is apprehended to be sound law), that *custom* or *prescription* cannot entitle the subject to *relict lands;* (*e*) (*f*) and that it was decided by a case he quotes, that lands acquired "per relictionem maris" are not prescribable as part of a manor, or as belonging to the subject, (*g*) (*h*) and we are also told "that the soil [which was] under the water, "must needs be of the same propriety [when left dry] as "when covered with water; (*i*) so that if, while it is covered "with water, it be the King's, it cannot become the subject's *because* the water hath left it." We are, however, soon after told (*k*) that the "subject may by *usage* and *prescription* acquire an interest in so much of the sea as he "may reasonably possess, as a districtus maris, a place in "the sea between two points, or in a particular part contiguous to the shore, or of a port or creek, or arm of the "sea. These," says he, "*may be prescribed* in point of "interest, both of the water, and the soil itself, covered with "the water." (*l*)

Custom cannot entitle a subject to relict land.

Soil which was covered with water does not change ownership by becoming dry.

Jerwood, p. 89; Phear, pp. 11 and 44; Schultes, 118. As to the law in America, see Middleton *v.* Pritchard, 3 Scam. (Ill.) 519, 522; Stuart *v.* Clark's Lessee, 2 Swan. 12; Jones *v.* Soulard, 24 Howard 64; People *v.* Canal Appraisers, 13 Wendell (N.Y.) Rep. 355; Hopkins Academy, Trustees of, *v.* Dickenson, 63 Mass. (9 Cush.) 548; Angell on Tide Waters, 267; Angell on Watercourses, 6th edit. p. 46 *et seq.*; Houck, 169.]

(*e*) See *ante*, pp. 806 and 808.

(*f*) (Hale says custom will not, but prescription and usage time out of mind will. See *ante*, pp. 351 and 704, note (*y*); and note (*l*) below. —Ed.)

(*g*) See accord. Dyer, 326.

(*h*) (It was decided that custom (not prescription) will not entitle.— Ed.)

(*i*) P. 807, *ante*. (*k*) P. 808, *ante*.

(*l*) (The arguments next following are wholly fallacious. They are built upon a misunderstanding of the word "prescription" as used by

According to this doctrine, land which when aqua cooperta *can* be prescribed for by the subject, *cannot* be prescribed for when relict by the sea. If the soil covered with water was the subject's before (and according to Lord Hale's doctrine it may be so by *prescription*, so long as it is covered with water), then, says he, such soil when dried up would belong to him who was such owner. But it may be asked, how does he prove himself to have been such owner when it was under water? The answer is, by *prescription;* and yet it is insisted that he cannot prescribe for derelict land at all! Surely this is *in effect* prescribing for the very same land. It may be fairly urged, that if land under the water may be prescribed for, against the King's *primâ facie* title, the *same* land when left dry may or rather must also be prescribed for,—because "it must needs be "of the same propriety as it was when covered with "water."

q. Whether a portion of land covered with sea, may be prescribed?

[143]

Suppose I have always claimed (but without having any actual *grant* to show) the ownership of a certain districtus maris, and have never had the title questioned, and it suddenly becomes dry land; can I *prescribe* that it was mine when under water, and thus acquire a title to it? If I can do so, this is virtually prescribing for the derelict land. The law of England, however, makes no distinction between land covered and land not covered with water; both are "*land*," technically speaking; and therefore, it seems a contradiction in terms to say that land covered with water can be prescribed for, and land relict cannot. Undoubtedly, if the subject had no legal ownership in the

Example.

Hale. Hale uses it to mean "long usage time out of mind," and, as has been shewn, distinctly lays it down that land can be prescribed for as well when covered with water as when left derelict—*i.e.*, title can be shewn to it by evidence of immemorial usage. Mr. Hall does not observe the distinction between Oldsworth's case and that of the Severn—that one is on the open sea, the other *inter fauces terræ*. The soil below low-water mark under the main sea may possibly not be prescribed for by evidence of user (but see Benest *v.* Pipon, *ante*, p. 460; Whitstable Fishers *v.* Gann, *ante*, p. 528); that *inter fauces terræ* may be shewn to be parcel of a manor which extends to mid-stream. See *ante*, pp. 153, 155, 285, 306, 352.—Ed.)

soil under the water, against the King's title, such subject can have no better title to it when it is relict and dry. This, however, does not explain why land covered with the sea may be prescribed for, and the same land left uncovered may not. Indeed, according to what has been before urged, neither the one nor the other can be made good, in point of title, by prescription; both being merely land, and therefore not lying in prescription.

q. Whether prescription for the franchise of a port, will carry the soil?

The doctrine that if, by prescription, a man "hath "portum maris de S. in ordinary presumption he hath not "only the franchise, but the very water and *soil* itself "within the port," rests also on doubtful ground, if the author's distinction be sound, viz. that the *port* or *franchise*, and the *soil*, do not *necessarily* go together: "the franchise "of a port," says he, "is a different thing from the pro- "priety of the soul, and so the franchise of a port may be
[144] "in a subject, and the soil in the King or some other."(*m*) Now, if this be the case, it does not appear why they should, in *ordinary* presumption, go together under one word, *portus*. The learned writer doubts(*n*) whether the *express* grant of a *port* would, at his time of day, without more words, carry the soil; but conceives that an *ancient* grant of the port, *coupled with ancient usage*, would carry the soil.(*o*) All grants of ports are now to be deemed

(*m*) See p. 809, *ante*.

(*n*) *Ibid.*

(*o*) (Here Hale is speaking from his large knowledge of facts, and, as is his practice, deducing his principles of law from existing facts. The historical fact undoubtedly is that ports are of more recent origin than grants of shore and soil. The lord or baron who got from the Conqueror his large barony received with it the river or arm of the sea lying within that barony and the soil thereof. He either held the whole of it, or granted parts away to his vassals, the lords of manors adjoining the river or arm of the sea, and with those manors he granted or did not grant his interest in th soil covered with water within those manors. He then got a grant of the franchise of a port over the whole river or arm of the sea. If he retained all the soil, then port and soil went together, as in the case of the Dart, and, to some extent, the case of Plymouth. Then, if he were challenged for the soil, he would shew his user, which would be user of the port and user of the soil intermixed, although it was user attributable to two ancient grants; no modern grants (at least including the soil) can be made: are we then to construe every ancient grant of a port, without more words, as giving inclusively a title to the soil? Undoubtedly, if the mere prescription for a port will carry not only the franchise, but the soil, by reason that "*portus*" is *quid aggregatum*,(*p*) like a manor, then indeed there can be no just reason why the word "portus," in a *grant*, should not also have the effect mentioned.

Whether the word "Portus" in a grant will pass the soil as well as franchise?

But, it may be asked, why in any case should the mere word "*Portus*" carry the soil, as well as the franchise, if the soil and the franchise are (as they are stated to be) separate ownerships, and capable of being possessed by different persons, and are sometimes so held? The franchise should rather be deemed an adjunct to the soil, than the soil to the franchise, and yet it is nowhere said that the ownership of the soil carries the franchise. It is not intended to be denied that one person *may* have *both;* but it may be doubted whether the word "*Portus*" will, in any case, carry more than the *franchise;* and consequently it is presumed that the grant must contain sufficient words of grant of the soil. It would be singular, in such a case, to allow the *soil* to be *prescribed* for, when the *port* only is actually *granted;* and if an express grant of the port, without more words, will not carry the soil, it is difficult to admit that the mere prescription for a *port* will give the [145]

titles, and not to one. This is what Hale refers to when he says that an ancient port coupled with ancient usage would carry the soil. The evidence might not be very accurately marshalled, but the result would be the same. The user would shew his title to the soil in conjunction with his title to the port, though, perhaps, in strictness not in *respect* of the port. It would simply raise the presumption that he had both soil and port. This, no doubt, was what Hale had in his mind, he evidently being aware that the Earls of Devon had the soil of the port of Topsham, and that the Duchy of Cornwall had the soil of the port of Plymouth as parcel of the barony of Trematon, and the Duchy has it still, except in such places as it had been granted away as in the case of Lopez *v.* Andrew, 3 M. & Ry. 329, where a grant was presumed, on evidence of user, to have been made to a subject previous to the creation of the Duchy.—Ed.)

(*p*) See p. 809, *ante.*

soil also. Prescription, or presumption, ought not to give more than the express grant (supposed to have had existence) would have given; especially against the Crown. (*q*) (*r*)

There can be no good reason of policy for thus construing the grant beyond its letter, or conferring the soil of a port on a subject by presumption or prescription. Where the port had better have been, the soil may as well remain. There can be no occasion to strain points of legal doctrine, the effect of which will be to deprive the King of that which was vested in him for the good of the public. The cases quoted by Lord Hale, in support of this doctrine, do not seem to warrant the conclusions drawn from them. Thus we find the words of the first case, "*Portus* et *piscaria* et mariscus de Toppesham spectant ad Comitissam "Devon," are deemed sufficient to prove that not only the *franchise* of the port, but the *soil* of the port also belonged to her. Now, the "piscaria" is not the soil of the port; nor is the "mariscus" *adjoining*, the soil of the port; and therefore all that the words *per se*, give, is the franchise of the port, the fishery, and the adjacent marsh; and the word "port," even in his own admission, may, or may not, carry the soil. Nothing appears to warrant a construction beyond the franchise, the fishery, and the adjacent marsh; yet, in a subsequent part of his work, (*s*) he draws similar conclusions more fully from this case; where, after quoting the case of the port of Toppesham in the same short form as above, he adds,—it appears,

"1st. That the Earls of Devon had the propriety of the "soil of the port by *prescription; for* they had all the "profits that arise by reason of the property of the soil;
[146] "viz. the *fishery* and the salt marsh, which possibly might "be an 'incrementum maritimum.' But upon this it may

(*q*) [Jerwood, p. 50.]

(*r*) (The utmost that Hale puts is that when a man has a port and shews usage of the soil therewith, such prescription may carry the soil as well as the franchise; and he distinctly adds, "*and though this* "*doth not always hold, yet most times it doth.*"—Ed.)

(*s*) [*Ante*, p. 402, and De Portibus, p. 55.]

"be observed, that the salt marsh was *adjoining*, and "might well pass *eo nomine;* and there is no more ground "for construing 'mariscus' into a grant of the soil of the "*port*, than for holding the grant of the 'portus' to be a "grant of the 'mariscus.' (*t*) As for the 'piscaria,' it seems "impossible to convert *that* into a grant of the soil itself, "for a piscaria, it is admitted on all hands, often exists "independent of the soil, where the soil is clearly in the "King, or another; this has been already shown. Besides, "the words 'spectant ad C, D,' prove nothing on the point "of *prescription*." But he proceeds,—

"2nd. They had also the franchise of the port, by pre-"scription, and all the incidents thereof, viz.

1. Applicatio navium,
2. Exoneratio navium,
3. Mercatum et venditio mercandisarum et per retail,
4. Victualling of mariners and ships,
5. Lodging and entertainment of mariners.

"All which are privileges in a special manner belonging "to ports, and cannot be had without that liberty legally "vested."—All which may be true enough, and yet not prove the *soil* to pass by the word "portus." (*u*)

The next case cited by the same learned writer is that of Plymouth and Sutton Pool. (*x*) "P. 10. Ed. 3, B. R. Rot. "73, dorso, it appears, that Willielmus De Warena Comes "Surrey, had the port of *Pool* and anchorage and other "duties belonging to it."

"It appeared among the charters of the Duchy of "Cornwall, the transcripts whereof remain in the receipt "of the Exchequer, that Rogerus de Valletort, gave to "Richard King of the Romans and Earl of Cornwall, and [147] "the heirs of his body, *Castrum* [castle] de Trematon, et 59

(*t*) (See p. 62, "mariscus" used to denote foreshore.—ED.)

(*u*) (Hale was no doubt well aware of what the title of the Earls of Devon was in the port of Topsham. There had been much litigation, as appears from the Public Records, both in his time and before it, respecting the Earls' rights at Topsham. The fishery was, and is, a fishery by weirs, which still exist, and the lords of the manor are still owners of the soil.—ED.)

(*x*) [De Portibus, p. 56; Jerwood, p. 63; *ante*, p. 402.]

"feoda militum, in Cornwall et Devon, ad idem *castrum* "pertin. ac etiam *manerium de Trematon*, et villam de esse, "CUM AQUA." (*y*)

"To this castle of Trematon belong a certain petty manor "called Sutton Vautort, and also the water and port of "Sutton; for so appears by the close roll, Claus. 17, E. 2, "m. 14, Sutton *cum aqua* et *portu* spectat ad castrum de "Trematon."

"By the death of Edmond, his son, without issue, the "earldom and this castle came to the Crown. Possibly "Richard, Earl of Cornwall, after issue had, made "some alienation before the statute of Westminster, 2d, "whereby the reversion to the heirs of Vautort was "barred."

"The earldom of Cornwall and this castle of Trematon "descended to King Edward the 3d. He, by *charter*, in "parliament, grants the earldom of Cornwall to his eldest "son, 'et castrum et manerium de Trematon, cum villa de "'Saltash, et parco ibidem cum aliis pertinentiis.' See the "Charter, 8 Rep. 8. The prince's case."

"By this grant," says Lord Hale, "without any special "mention of the *water* or *port* as belonging to it, the port "and water of Sutton, now Plymouth, was annexed to the "duchy of Cornwall, for though the charter grants 'prisas "'et custumas vinorum necdum proficua portuum nostro- "'rum, intra eundem Comitatum Cornub. simul cum
[148] "'wrecco maris, et balena, et sturgeono,' yet that did not "extend to the *water of Sutton*, which was in Devon, but

(*y*) Nothing passes by the word "aqua," save a fishery. "If," says Lord Coke, "a man grant aquam suam, the soil shall not pass, but "the piscary within the water passeth therewith." Co. Litt. 4 b. Plowd. 154, says, that by "aqua, a piscary shall pass;" and he adds, that "by a grant of a piscary, the soil shall pass;" by which it might be inferred that "aqua" will carry the soil. But in a former page it has been contended, under strong authority, that a grant of a "piscary" does not carry the soil. (But see Throckmorton *v.* Tracy, Plowden 155: *aqua et piscaria* carry the soil. Case of the "Aqua de Dart," by which the soil of the river has passed to the Duchy of Cornwall; "Castrum de Trematon *cum aqua*," under which the Duchy holds the soil of the port of Plymouth.—ED.)

"it [the water] passed by the strength of its being parcel "of, and appendant to the castle of Trematon."

"The *town of Plymouth*, which is indeed caput portus "from whence the port now takes its denomination, *was not* "*part of Trematon*, but built upon the *manor of Sutton* "*Prior*, and was incorporated, and its jurisdiction settled "by act of parliament. Rot. parl. 18 H. 6, n. 32, and con-"firmed by rot. parl. 3 E. 4, n. 45. But always in both, "whatever was *parcel of Trematon* was *excepted;* and con-"sequently the haven [portus] itself (which was parcel of "Trematon) was not annexed thereby to Plymouth, but "stood upon the same foot of interest as before."

"There lies adjacent to this town [of Plymouth], within "the barbican thereof, a space of about thirty acres, which is "covered *every* tide with the sea, and ships ride there, and "come to unlade at the keys of Plymouth, commonly called "*Sutton Poole;* for the interest of the soil of these thirty "acres, being parcel of the port, an information of *intrusion* "was, as directed out of the Exchequer chamber, preferred "against the Mayor and Commonalty of Plymouth. The "defendants pretended title to it as parcel of the town of "Plymouth, and showed *usage* to have had certain customs, "called land leave, terrage, &c. But these referred to the "*shore* rather than to the place in question. (*z*) They allege "that it was also within the limits of their charter, and that "they exercise *jurisdiction* of their courts there; both "which were admitted. But it was insisted upon, on the "other side, that the *soil itself was excepted*, as *parcel of the* "*castle of Trematon;* and it was showed that the King "had used to have in right of his duchy in the place in [149] "question, anchorage, basselage, fishing, and the rents of "fishers, and divers other port duties that savoured of the "soil; as appears by divers accounts of the duchy; divers "records mentioning Pola de Sutton was parcel of Tre-"maton; several leases made by the King's progenitors of

(*z*) Sed quære, if it was regularly covered by the ordinary tides, this place was also *shore?* (Sutton Pool is surrounded almost entirely by wharves built upon the shore; it is never dry at ordinary low water.—ED.)

"*aqua* et *Pola*(*a*) de Sutton; and some to the town itself, "or some in trust for them; and divers other weighty "evidences for the propriety of the soil of Sutton Pool; "being the very harbour itself, and belonging to Tre-"maton: and accordingly a verdict given for the King." The learned writer then adds, "I have mentioned this the "rather because,—

"1st. Here the very interest of the port, the water, and "*soil*, and port duties themselves, were claimed and re-"covered by the Crown, not upon any prerogative title; "for if it had been so, it would have passed to the town "of Plymouth, being within the precincts of their incorpo-"ration, and *grant;* and then the exception of Trematon "had not been available, but as parcel of and belonging to "a manor that was formerly a subject's."

"2nd. That the King, primâ facie, hath a right to ports "of a royal franchise, yet the accession of this manor to the "Crown did not sever the interest of the port from the
[150] "manor, no more than in case of a fair or market ap-"pendant by prescription; for if, by the accession to the "Crown, it had been divided from the castle, or manor, "it could not have passed, without special words, to the "Prince, as it plainly did here. As the *port* was *by pre-"scription* parcel of the manor of Trematon, so it con-"tinued parcel, notwithstanding the accession thereof to "the Crown, by the death of the Earl of Cornwall without "issue; and it passed, together *with the castle, by the general "grant of it*, as a leet or market, or any other parcel or

(*a*) Although, as before observed, "aqua" will not pass the soil (see note to p. 822, *ante*), yet the words "stagnum," or pola (forsan?), a pool,—"gurges," a deep pit of water,—"palus," and "mariscus," a marsh, will pass the soil, being *quid aggregatum*, see Co. Litt. 4 b. So a "boilourie of salt," and "salina," which signifies a salt pit. Co. Litt. *ib.* So also the word "*marettum*" signifies soil lying between the flux and reflux of the sea, and "you shall read," says Lord Coke, "that "such a man perquisivit trescent acr. maretti." Co. Litt. 5 a. So also the word "sea-grounds" will pass a portion of shore. Scratton *v.* Brown, 4 B. & C. 485. And since there are so many words and phrases, capable of passing the shore in any given spot, to say nothing of the word "shore" (littus) itself, there seems less reason for giving to other words a forced or far-fetched import.

"appendant; and so, not like those flowers of the Crown "which are rendered disappendant by the accession to the "Crown, as waifs, strays, &c."

Comments on the case of Plymouth and Sutton Pool.

With regard to this last cited case, the result undoubtedly was, that the King retained both the soil and the port of Sutton Vautort; but it does not seem so clear that he retained it as appendant by *prescription.*(*b*) As to the franchise of the port, it is not meant to deny that a franchise may *be appendant to a manor* by prescription; but the case by no means proves that the *soil* of the sea, or an arm, or port thereof, *may* be in like manner *appendant, by prescription, to a manor.* It is to be remembered that *the soil of the port* belonged to the King, before it was a port, and does not appear to have ever been divested from the Crown at all; (*c*) and even if his ancestors had granted it away as parcel of the land of the manor, yet when the whole fell again to Edward 3, he became possessed of the soil in his ancient title. (*d*) His descendant, King Charles 2 (for whom the verdict was given), (*e*) was, in the present case, entitled to it in a double right, if possible; for all that his ancestors [151] had once granted away with Trematon and the manor, fell to him again by descent; and if they had never granted the soil, then it was his *ab origine.* The town of Plymouth must have produced either the King's grant of the soil in question, or some tantamount evidence of right to it; and

(*b*) (He retained it as parcel by evidence of long usage.—ED.)

(*c*) The first grant quoted is that to the King of the Romans, and unless the soil in question was "*parcel of the castle* and manor of "Trematon," at the time of this grant, by metes and bounds,—(and nothing appears to shew whether it was or was not),—it was still in the Crown, for the words "*cum aqua*" did not pass more than a fishery. (On the contrary, the evidence shewed that the soil had passed to the Vautorts and was parcel of the manor of Trematon. That "aqua" may pass the soil, see case of the Aqua de Derte granted to the Duchy by the same charter, whereof the soil is vested in the Duchy by that charter.—ED.)

(*d*) (Not so; the soil was parcel of the manor, and, on the manor coming back to the Crown, it would not merge in the prerogative, but remain parcel of the manor in the hands of the Crown, and on the re-grant to the Duchy pass to the Duke as parcel, as was the fact.—ED.)

(*e*) Mich. 16 Ch. 2. in Scac.

as they failed to do so, even on the disputed ground of prescription, the *soil* necessarily remained to the King (as parcel of the manor), and the franchise of the *port* remained *appendant* to the manor. It does not appear that the evidence adduced on the King's side was necessary to his case, further than concerned the franchise, although it was also used to rebut the claim to the soil. The grant to the King of the Romans was of the castle and manor of Trematon, and the town *cum aquâ* [and "aqua" carried the fishery only], and the manor of Sutton Vautort, and also the *water* and *port* of Sutton Vautort, were admitted to belong to the *castle; i.e.* to be appendant to it. The castle, the manor, the town *cum aqua*, all fell to King Edward by descent, and he, by a somewhat different form, granted "castrum et manerium de Trematon cum villa de "Saltash et Parco ibidem cum *aliis pertinentiis*," without any mention of the *port* or *aqua* of Sutton Vautort. The town of Plymouth being built on another manor, viz. Sutton Prior, was no part either of the manor of Trematon or of the manor of Sutton Vautort; and the soil in question was clearly part of the port or pool of Sutton Vautort, which was parcel of the greater manor and castle of Trematon. (*f*) The *charter* of the town contained *an express exception of whatsoever was parcel* of the *castle and manor of Trematon;* and therefore, clearly Sutton Vautort, both pool and manor, were doubly excepted; first, if parcel of Trematon; and secondly, from being within a different
[152] manor from Sutton Prior, viz. Sutton Vautort, which, at all events, was not belonging to Plymouth. If the pool and soil of Sutton Vautort did not pass by the grant of King Edward, as a *less* within a *greater* manor, then it remained in King Edward, and subsequently, by succession, vested in King Charles; and if it *did* so pass to the Prince of Wales, then, through him, it came also to the Crown, and by the Crown it was *excepted* by the words of exception in the charter, so that quacunque, &c. the town

(*f*) By the name of *castle*, one or more manors may pass. Co. Litt. 5 a.

of Plymouth had no title. But surely this is no evidence that land covered with the sea may be *prescribed for.* (*g*) It was admitted on all sides that Sutton Vautort, (*h*) cum aqua et Portu, spectant ad [belong to] castrum de Trematon; and it was clear that Trematon was excluded, totidem verbis, from the Town Charter, and was vested in the King. The King, therefore, did not prescribe at all, for he produced written evidences of his title, and had his *original common law right besides.* In fact, all that did not pass from the Crown by the original grant to the King of the Romans, in the first instance, was the King's soil by common law; all that *did* pass by that grant came afterwards to King Edward by descent; and all that King Edward granted to the prince, and also all that did *not* pass in the grant to him, but was crown property *ab origine*, became ultimately vested in King Charles; so that in him, at the time of the dispute, all title centered, save what the town possessed by their charter, and there it was not to be found. (*i*) Lord Hale also cites in this place, in support of the same doctrine, the case of the Barons of Barclay (*k*) already quoted; but which case, if referred to, will not appear to establish the point, that he who prescribes for a *port* thereby also acquires the soil of it; for in that case the King was admitted to be owner of the franchises of the ports both of Bristol and Gloucester, within the precincts

(*g*) (The soil was not *prescribed* for; it was claimed as parcel of the manor of Trematon.—ED.)

(*h*) [See Jerwood, p. 63.]

(*i*) (It is true the Crown claimed under the prerogative title (*ante*, p. 314), but gave evidence and proved its case by the muniments of the Duchy, and succeeded, under the Duchy title, in shewing that the place was parcel of the manor of Trematon purchased of a subject. The title is still in the Duchy, which would not be the case if Mr. Hall's argument was sound, unless we presume a further grant to the Duchy since the case, which has never been made.—ED.)

(*k*) Barons of Barclay's case, pp. 306, 402, *ante*. (Lord Hale does not cite the case in support of this doctrine, nor does he anywhere say that he who prescribes for a port thereby also acquires the soil of it. He only says that ownership of a port, together with evidence of long usage of the soil, raises title in the owner thereof to the soil, and the case of Sutton Pool is distinctly in point.—ED.)

[153] of which the land claimed by the Barons was situate, and yet the land was adjudged to the Barons, whilst the ports remained in the King. The King was, prima facie, the lawful proprietor of the soil, and was also the owner of the port; and according to Lord Hale, the port and the soil ordinarily go together; and yet, it seems, these badges of ownership were not sufficient to outweigh the claims of the Barons, specially proved, to the land.

Distinction between "Portus" in a subject and in the Crown.

There seems to be this material difference when we speak of "Portus" in the crown,—and the same in a subject. In the crown, the soil and the port are ordinarily united, because the soil is the property of the crown by common law; but it is not so in the case of a subject, whose right to the soil is adverse to the ownership of the King. It is matter of course that the soil belongs to the King until the contrary be proved. So also the franchise of the port. But in the case of a subject, each of these distinct rights is set up against the King's prima facie acknowledged ownership, and it does not seem correct to take the one from the King by implication, because the other is substantiated against him. It is well known that the *portus* often extends over *several miles of shore*, on both sides of the actual harbour, as happened in the last cited Barclay case; and it would seem unreasonable to construe the word "Portus" into a title to such an extent of land, where the franchise alone will satisfy the word, and the franchise and land are fairly and technically distinguished from each other by the law itself. No other cases, save those quoted by the learned writer, present themselves to give colour to such construction: and with regard to the cases or records alluded to, it is not too much to say, that from the manner in which they are reported, it is not easy to collect out of the mass of evidence adduced, what was and what was not the true ground of the decision.(*l*)

(*l*) (This paragraph cannot be passed over without comment. In the first place, the soil and the port are very seldom united in the Crown, the whole of the foreshore within the port scarcely ever—portions of it may be. Mr. Hall does not seem to be aware of the distinction between royal and fiscal ports and the small ports or havens granted to the subject. These latter scarcely ever extend beyond the mouth of the river or creek on which the *caput portus* is situate.

The principal points of law discussed in the foregoing pages are these :—(the Editor has set out in the foot-notes the points on which he differs from the conclusions drawn by Mr. Hall.) [154]

1. That the dominion and ownership of the British Seas, and of the creeks, bays, arms, ports, and tide rivers thereof, are vested, by our law, in the Crown. (*m*)
2. That this ownership includes *aquam et solum*; both the water, its products and uses, and the land or soil under the water. (*n*)
3. That such ownership includes the shore, as far as the reach of the high-water mark of the [medium high tide between the springs and the neaps].
4. That the land subject to spring tides, and high spring tides, is no part of the sea, or sea-shore; but belongs to the title and ownership of the *terra firma*.
5. That by grant from the Crown, a subject may have a lawful ownership of a certain portion of the sea, its creeks, bays, arms, ports, or tide-rivers, and of the shores thereof, *tam aquæ quam soli*.

The former extend all round the coast, and are variable in extent at the pleasure of the Crown. This distinction between the royal and fiscal port and what might be called the "territorial port" must be borne in mind in perusing this treatise. An example of the territorial "portus," as the "Aqua de Darte," which extends from Totnes to a rock called the Blackstone at the mouth of Dartmouth harbour, whereas the port of Dartmouth extends from beyond Torquay on the east, to beyond Salcombe on the west. The fiscal port of Plymouth joins the fiscal port of Dartmouth on the east, and extends down into Cornwall, but there is no pretence that the "portus" belonging to Trematon Castle has or had any such limits. The case is the same in the Tyne, where the territorial port extends to a rock at the mouth of the Tyne, but the port of Newcastle extends over a large part of Northumberland, and so of the Orwell, Yarm, Colne, and other rivers. See note (*p*), *ante*, p. 809.—Ed.)

(*m*) (The dominion of the British seas, and the creeks, arms, bays, and tide rivers thereof within the limits laid down in Reg. *v.* Keyn, L. R. 2 Ex. D. 63, and the Territorial Waters Jurisdiction Act, 41 & 42 Vict. c. 73, is vested in the Crown under the *jus publicum*. The ownership of the soil of the sea, and the creeks, bays, arms, ports, and tide rivers thereof, is vested by law *primâ facie* in the Crown under the *jus privatum*, subject to the rights of the public to navigation, access, and fishery thereover under the *jus publicum*. But *de facto* such ownership has been granted out by the Crown over the greater part of the foreshore of such sea, creeks, bays, arms, and tide rivers, and the ownership of some portions of the bed and soil of the same, and such portions are vested in the grantees or their successors in title: *ante*, pp. 638 *et seqq.*—Ed.)

(*n*) (This ownership, whether vested in the Crown or in the subject, includes *aquam et solum*, both the water, its products and uses, and the land and soil under the water, subject always to the rights of the public thereover; but the ownership of the soil may be in the subject without the right of fishery over it.—Ed.)

6. But that such grants must have a date anterior to the statutes restraining the alienation of Crown lands. (*o*)
7. That no distinction exists at law, between the title or proofs of title to such land covered with water, and the title to *terra firma.* (*p*)
8. That where the ownership claimed by a subject in any such *districtus maris*, or tide-river, or shore cannot be proved by the production of the grant, such ownership can *no otherwise* be established than by adverse possession, under the Statutes of Limitation. (*q*)
9. That such ownership cannot be supported by "prescription," properly so called, against the King, and never could, at any period, be so supported under the feudal law. (*r*)
10. That the proofs of title, where the grant itself is not forthcoming, to such *districtus maris aut littoris* must be *paris materiæ* with those required to prove title to inland estates. (*s*)
11. That proof, by prescriptive evidence, of a right to a franchise, liberty, or easement in or out of the soil, is no sufficient evidence of title to the freehold and inheritance of the land itself, whether such land be *terra firma* or *pars maris.* (*t*)

(*o*) (Such grants must be ancient, the greater number of them being anterior to Domesday Book. See *ante*, pp. 614, 640.—ED.)

(*p*) (The distinction which exists at law between the title (or proof of title) to such land covered with water and the title to *terra firma* is as follows:—The title to the *terra firma* is capable of proof by evidence of absolutely exclusive ownership; the title to land covered with water of the sea is, and always was, incapable of such proof. The Crown originally had the absolute exclusive ownership of the *terra firma;* it never had more than a qualified and limited ownership of the land covered with water. Such ownership was qualified and limited by the rights of the public over it, and by the nature and situation of the land. By reason of both these circumstances, the Crown could never have had exclusive possession and ownership thereof; of the *terra firma* it could. As the Crown could not grant more than it had—viz., such qualified ownership—the grantee, on challenge of his title, cannot be called upon to shew more than such qualified and limited ownership as the Crown had: *ante*, pp. 627, 656; chapter xxii. p. 573; and p. 680, note (*j*), p. 702, note (*o*).—ED.)

(*q*) (Where the ownership claimed by a subject in any such *districtus maris* or tide river or shore cannot be proved by the production of the grant, such ownership can be established by the owner shewing evidence of such acts of ownership by long usage on such *districtus maris* as, from the nature, character, and situation thereof, may be reasonably and naturally exercised on such *districtus maris;* thus either shewing a title under the Statutes of Limitation, or raising the presumption in his favour of a lost grant from the Crown, or, by the same class of evidence, construing and explaining a grant in general terms so as to include the foreshore.—ED.)

(*r*) (Such ownership can be supported by evidence of such long usage, commonly called "prescription," against the Crown: *ante*, pp. 691, 693.—ED.)

(*s*) (The proofs of title where the grant itself is not forthcoming to such *districtus maris aut littoris* need not be, and in fact cannot be, *paris materiæ* with those required to prove title to inland estates, but should be proofs by such acts of ownership as, from the nature, character, and situation of such *districtus*, the Crown could have exercised had it remained in possession, and no more.—ED.)

(*t*) (Proof by prescriptive evidence of a right to a franchise, liberty, or easement in or out of the soil is *per se* no sufficient evidence of title to the freehold and inherit-

12. And consequently, that the ownership of a several fishery, or of the franchises of wreck, of flotsan, jetsan, and ligan, or of royal fish, or of ports, or the liberty of digging for sand, or shells, &c., will not be sufficient to establish an absolute ownership over the soil itself, where such rights are enjoyed against the Crown. (*u*)

13. And, therefore, neither the express *grant* of a franchise, or liberty, nor "prescription" for such (which supposes a grant) can be construed to include the soil, or freehold, against the Crown, by implication, or presumption. (*x*)

14. That "alluvion," properly so called, belongs to the ownership of [155] the freehold of the adjacent *terra firma*, subject to such interests in others as such ownership is liable to. (*y*)

15. That "derelict" land, properly so called, belongs to the Crown, as land suddenly and by manifest marks left by the sea. (*z*)

16. That islands produced out of the British Seas, and the creeks, bays, arms, ports, and tide-rivers thereof, belong, like derelict land, to the Crown.

ance of the land itself, whether such land be *terra firma* or *pars maris*, but proof by prescription or grant of the exercise of a franchise exercisable upon the soil or the water *infra manerium*, which cannot be exercised unless the soil lie within the manor, is proof presumptive that the soil is parcel of the manor or was parcel of the manor at the time of the grant; *e.g.*, a grant of free warren *in omnibus dominicis terris suis* implies that the lands were the demesne lands of the grantee. A grant of wreck, or perception of wreck, *infra manerium suum* implies that the foreshore is parcel of the manor.—ED.)

(*u*) (The ownership of a several fishery *not worked by fixed engines*, or the exercise of the franchises of wreck, of flotsom, jetsom, and ligan, or of royal fish, *not shewn to be either granted or exercised infra manerium*, or of the franchise of a port, will not alone be sufficient to establish an absolute ownership over the soil itself when such rights are enjoyed against the Crown; but the ownership of a several fishery worked by weirs and fixed engines, the exercise of the franchises of wreck, flotsom, &c., exercised *infra manerium*, or of the franchise of a territorial port, combined and coupled with exercise of other acts of ownership over the soil, as the digging of sand, shells, and taking seaweed, &c., are sufficient to establish an absolute ownership over the soil itself as against the claims of the Crown, on the principle of the presumption of a lost grant or the construction of a grant in general terms.—ED.)

(*x*) (The express grant of a franchise or liberty, or the prescriptive usage of such franchise or liberty, *infra manerium*, when such franchise or liberty can only be exercised upon the soil of the *districtus maris*, *coupled with other acts of ownership* upon the soil, such as the erection of weirs or fixed engines, the erection of piers or causeways, the inclosure of parts of the shore, the digging of sand, shells, or taking of seaweed, the digging of mines, will, and do, afford grounds for the presumption of a grant of the soil from the Crown, and will suffice to establish a title against the Crown.—ED.)

(*y*) (Alluvion properly so called belongs to the ownership of the freehold of the adjacent *terra firma* subject to such interests in others as such ownership is liable to; but the alluvion which accretes to the foreshore belongs to the owner thereof.—ED.)

(*z*) (Derelict land properly so called belongs to the Crown *primâ facie* as land suddenly and by manifest marks left by the sea; but when such land when covered by the sea was in the ownership of the subject, it remains in such ownership after the dereliction.—ED.)

17. Unless the soil under the water out of which such islands are produced, previously belong to a subject.
18. That the title of a subject to the soil of a *districtus maris*, viz. to the soil of any creek, bay, arm, port, or tide-river, or to the shore, in no substantial respect differs from a title to *terra firma*. (*a*)
19. That it is more for the public advantage that the ownership of subjects should be limited to the *terra firma;* and consequently, that by the rule of law, as well as of public policy, claims set up to tracts of sea, or of ports, or tide-rivers, or of the shore, ought not to be *favoured* against the Crown. (*b*)

(*a*) (The title of a subject to the soil of a *districtus maris* substantially differs from a title to *terra firma* in that only a qualified ownership can be shewn of a *districtus maris* whether it remains in the Crown or is granted to a subject.—ED.)

(*b*) (In dealing with a question of law with regard to the respective rights of the Crown and the subject, no consideration apart from the facts and evidence in the case ought to be permitted to weigh in the scales of justice; and although it may be for the pecuniary advantage of the public that the subject should be limited to the *terra firma* (where the public dare not attempt to confiscate his property), it consorts not with the honour and dignity of the Crown to question, by arbitrary, prolix, and expensive suits, ancient and valid titles of the subject in order to gain pecuniary benefits for the public, and therefore the very doubtful and shadowy claim of the *primâ facie* title of the Crown (now that its history is at last set forth) ought not to be favoured as against the ancient possession and beneficial enjoyment of the subject under grants from the Crown itself. The argument that it is likely to be more beneficial to the public if the shore is vested in the Crown for the protection of the exercise of its rights is plausible, but not sound. The subject can only hold the foreshore and soil of the sea subject to the *jus publicum*, and can be restrained from making any encroachment on the rights of the public by simple process by any one who is aggrieved by his proceedings. The Crown cannot be so restrained, and is practically free to sell and lease the foreshore at its pleasure, and without consulting the advantage or convenience or rights of the public in any way, and it does so readily whenever money is to be made (*ante*, chapter xxiii.). It grants exclusive fisheries (whether legally or not is to be doubted), closing ancient fishing grounds whereon poor fishermen have worked and got their living for centuries, for the advantage of limited companies and speculators (Herne Bay Fishery Company, Blackwater Fishery Company, and others). If the Crown chooses to erect wharves or buildings on a river which may hinder the navigation or cause expense in the dredging of it, what practical remedy have the Conservators? Against a subject they can get an injunction at once cheaply and speedily. It is submitted that the public is safer as to its rights if the subject is in possession. Him it can control, and he knows it, and will not transgress; the Crown it cannot practically control, and, if it acts detrimentally to the public, the mischief is done long before it can be checked, and, when done, who will dare to attack the Crown to get the mischief remedied? But, however plausible the argument may be, it is inconsistent with right and justice, and derogatory to the honour of the Crown, that such an argument should be put forward to throw prejudice upon a pure question of law and fact when litigation arises upon it between the Crown and the subject. The Crown cannot derogate from its grant. Is it right or honourable that it should endeavour to do so by putting forward a plea that its case is to be unduly favoured because it is plausibly alleged that it will be better for the public if its very shadowy claim shall be favoured by the Courts to the derogation of its own grants and the disherison of its grantees? See Introduction.—ED.)

SUPPLEMENTAL CHAPTER [156]

ON THE PUBLIC RIGHT TO USE THE SHORE FOR BATHING, AND FOR DIGGING AND TAKING SHELLS, SAND, ETC.

As to the Right to use the Shore for Bathing.

As to the right of bathing on the shore.

THE general right to frequent the shore for sea-bathing was made the subject of legal question, for the first time, in the case of Blundell *v.* Caterall. (*a*) The plaintiff, who resisted the right, " was the lord of the manor of Great " Crosby, which is bounded on the west by the river " Mersey, an arm of the sea." It is stated in the report of the case, " that as lord of the manor he was *owner* of the " *shore*, and had the exclusive right of *fishing* thereon *with* " *stake nets*. The defendant was the servant at an hotel " erected in 1815, upon land in Great Crosby, fronting the " shore, and bounded by the *high-water mark* of the river " Mersey, the proprietors of which hotel kept *Bathing* " *Machines* for the use of persons resorting thither, and " who were driven by defendant in machines across the [157] " shore into the sea for the purpose of bathing ; and the " defendant received a sum of money from the individuals " so bathing for the use of the machines and for his ser- " vice and assistance. No bathing machines were ever used " upon the shore of Great Crosby before the establishment " of this hotel ; *but it had been the custom for people to cross* " *it on foot for the purpose of bathing*. There was also a

(*a*) 5 Barn. & Ald. 268. [See Phear 47, and Mace *v.* Philcox, 15 C. B. N. S. 600 ; Angell on Tide Waters, 28.]

"common highway for carriages along the shore, and it "was proved that various articles for market were occa- "sionally carted across the shore, although the more common "mode of conveyance for such things was by a canal, made "about forty years ago. The defendant contended for a "*common law right* for all the King's subjects to bathe on "the sea-shore, and to pass over it for *that* purpose on foot "and with horses and carriages." It was decided by *three* of the learned judges against one, (*b*) that no such *general* right in the subject to frequent the shore, *for the purpose of bathing*, existed, whether on foot or in carriages.

Decided in Blundell *v.* Caterall, that the public have *no* common law right to bathe on the sea-shore.

Remarks on the case of Blundell *v.* Caterall.

This was the first case in which the public right to use the sea and sea-shore for bathing, was ever *judicially* either claimed or opposed, as was remarked by Mr. Justice Bayley. The case was very fully argued, and the judges gave their opinions at considerable length. The learned counsel who argued against the right, opposed it on *three* several grounds. "*First*, from the silence of the authorities. *Secondly*, "because such a right was contrary to analogies. *Thirdly*, "because it was contrary to acknowledged and established "rights;" and the three judges, by whom the case was decided, seem to have been governed, principally, by the *first* and *last* of these several grounds of argument.

Remarks continued.

It is to be observed, that the title of the lord of the manor to the absolute ownership of the shore itself was
[158] supposed to be proved; and not only the soil of the shore, but also "an exclusive right of fishing thereon with stake "nets," was taken for granted to be the private property of the lord; and, therefore, the particular question was *not* whether the shore was subject to such *general* customary right of bathing, but whether the *private ownership* of such shore, coupled with an exclusive private fishery with stake nets, was subject to such general customary right of bathing. The Court, however, did not confine themselves to the narrow ground of the incompatibility of the bathing with carriages, or on foot, in a place where a private fishery with stake nets existed; on the contrary, they decided upon the broad ground, that a general common law right did not

(*b*) Best, afterwards Lord Wynford.

exist at all, by ancient custom and usage, of frequenting the sea-shore for bathing. It was taken for granted, on all hands, that the original ownership of the shore is in the Crown; and that even the King's ownership was subject to the common law rights of fishing and navigation; and also, that the subject who became owner of the shore by the King's grant, was as liable as the King to those customary rights; but it was denied that either the King's or a subject's ownership of the shore was subject to a like general common law usage of bathing.

Silence of the books as to the right of bathing.

With regard to the *silence of the books*, the Court said, "that no trace of such a right was to be found in the "books." But it seems to have been admitted that "the "books" were not the *only* authorities for or against such right; for the Court also said, "that the existence or the "extent of the subject's right was to be collected in this, "as in other instances, from the *manner in which* the sea-"shores throughout the kingdom have been from time to "time immemorially used; as well as from legal authorities." Now the silence of the books may, in some cases, be alleged to testify the extreme certainty of, and general acquiescence in a right. The custom in question would seem to be a [159] right of all others the least likely to become the subject of legal dispute. The silence of the books in respect of a custom so natural and universal, may be thought to make as much *for* as *against* the usage: (*c*) nor can the mere silence of the

(*c*) It is admitted, that in some cases, "the silence of the books "may be eloquence," as Lord Ellenborough expressed it in Aubrey *v.* Fisher, 10 East 456. But *that* is where some singular custom differing from, or opposite to the general custom, is set up, and no mention or allusion made in the books to the opposite and particular custom. Thus in the case alluded to, the general custom of the *realm* was that trees under twenty years' growth were, if cut, to be deemed underwood and titheable, but trees of twenty years' growth and upwards were deemed *timber* trees, and not titheable. A custom was set up *in one county* that if the tree did not contain ten feet of solid timber, it was underwood; and his Lordship's remark was applied to this alleged custom, which was deemed not to be good accordingly. In the principal case the custom to bathe is general; and a custom set up, in one district, of limiting the bathing to one class of persons, or to persons of a certain age, or to a certain hour, would be a singular exception to

books be deemed a sufficient negative of a custom. If, indeed, the practice of bathing has generally prevailed, time out of mind, throughout the realm, the silence of the books gives consent rather than denial. The right in question was a case of *custom*, and by the *dicta* of the judges themselves, we are permitted, in the absence of all book authority, another distinct ground for decision, viz. "immemorial usage," which is the very essence of the common law itself.

Antiquity of the custom, and its universality.

It is not easy to point out a custom more universal, more natural, or more ancient on the sea-coasts not of England only, but of the whole world, than that of bathing. We know that the natives of the British Islands have been from time immemorial famous for their skill and intrepidity in the art of swimming. The most barbarous and the most
[160] civilized nations in all parts of the globe have equally practised bathing and swimming. So far from the silence of our books being a good authority for the non-existence of this right, it would have been the more singular circumstance of the two to have found the point in any way disputed. The constant enjoyment of this privilege for ages without dispute, would, it might be supposed, have proved sufficient to establish it as a common law right, similar to that of fishing in the sea. It is difficult, indeed, to imagine a general and public right of fishing in the sea, and on the shore, unaccompanied by a general right to bathe there.

Distinction between the custom as claimed in respect of the sea, &c. and inland waters.

It is true, that if the natural instinct or habit of man to bathe be *alone* sufficient to establish such right, it would confer a right to bathe in rivers, streams, lakes, &c., which not being subject to the tides, are no part of the sea. But it is not the inclination alone, but the universal and habitual practice which is necessary to establish such a right; due regard being also had to the nature of the ownership in the *locus in quo*. Rivers and lakes, &c. not subject to the tides, being no part of the sea, are no public highway,

a general rule; and if the books were silent about it, might well be denied. But it would be strange to construe the silence of the books into a denial of a custom *which has actually existed universally and immemorially*, and which, therefore, has always spoken for itself.

no "great waste," subject to public use for fishing, navigation, &c. They are, by our law, private property to all intents and purposes. The analogy, therefore, does not fully hold; but even in this case it may be doubted whether a custom, proved to have existed time out of mind, of bathing at a particular place, in any river or lake, by the inhabitants of the adjacent parish, town, or district, especially where a common of piscary exists, may not be reasonably supported as an easement or liberty, on the same principle as a right of way. However this may be, the nature and degree of these habits amongst a maritime people, dwelling on the sea-coasts, and addicted to navigation and fishing, are not to be considered on precisely the same footing as the habits of an inland people. We are, [161] nationally, a maritime people, and general customs should be tried by the national habits and pursuits of such a people.

The text of Bracton a favouring the right.

In the case before us it was argued, that although no express mention is made of bathing as a general common law right, yet the common right to frequent the shore (*littus*), without limitation of purpose (so that it be legal), is expressly asserted by Bracton. The learned judges, however, who decided the case, considered Bracton not only to have *quoted*, but to have *interpolated* this doctrine from the *Civil* law, and that the Civil law and our law do not agree. Mr. Justice Best (who dissented from the decision of the Court) replies to this reasoning, "that "Bracton has not *stated* this right as civil law; he has "made it part of his book '*de legibus et consuetudinibus* "'*Angliæ*.'" It appears, in fact, that the passage actually referred to and contradicted by the three learned judges, as being a mere transcript from the civil law, relates *not* to the *sea-shore*, but to the *banks of rivers*. There is a *separate* section in the Institutes relating to the sea-shore, which says, "LITTORUM *quoque usus publicus juris* "*gentium est, sicut et ipsius maris;*" (*d*) and *this* passage nearly in the same words, Bracton has also; (*e*) although

(*d*) Just. Inst. lib. ii. Tit. 1, sect. 5.
(*e*) Bracton, lib. i. ch. 12, sect. 5.

the learned judges commented on the text relating to *river banks*, viz. "*Riparum* etiam usus publicus est, jure gentium, sicut ipsius *fluminis*,"(*f*) which, at this day, is certainly not deemed, in its fullest extent, good law.(*g*) The reasoning, therefore, seems to have been this, Bracton is wrong in his law that "RIPARUM *usus communis est*," &c. therefore, "*littorum usus non est communis*." But this
[162] is certainly a "*non sequitur;*" and although the Court, from authorities, proved Bracton to be wrong, to a certain extent, in his law respecting particular uses made of banks of rivers (as for towage), yet no authorities were adduced showing that the "*communis usus*" of the *sea-shore* for bathing is not a good custom. It has been before shown that Bracton does not copy or follow the civil law in certain points relating to the sea and sea-shore. For whereas the language of the Institute(*h*) is, "*pro-*"*prietas autem eorum potest intelligi nullius esse*," the text of Bracton contains no such doctrine. Thus it is evident he did not merely copy the Institutes, since he has wholly omitted a most important sentence, which, as we have amply shown in former pages, is not law with us, whatever it might have been with the Romans.

Distinction between "ripa" and "littus."

The *ripa* or bank, and the *littus* or shore, are not one and the same. The *ripa* is *terra firma*, and generally cultivable, and therefore damageable in its crops and produce. But the *shore* is covered twice every twenty-four hours by the "tide," and partakes of the nature of sea-bottom, and is by Lord Hale himself distinguished from "*terra firma*," and classed rather with sea-bottom. In legal parlance, indeed, shore, sea-bottom, and *terra firma* are all technically *land;* still, however, with this further technical distinction, that a grant of so many acres of *land*, without more words, will include no more than the "ripam," and will not include the "littus," nor any portion of land covered with water, unless so specially described. Wherefore, it is evident that the two

(*f*) Bracton, lib. i. ch. 12, sect. 6.
(*g*) Ball *v.* Herbert, 3 T. R. 253. See *ante*, 717, and *post*, p. 851.
(*h*) Instit. lib. ii. tit. 1, sect. 5.

words, *ripam* and *littus*, are not quite identified with each other; nor does a negative applied to a right claimed in respect of the one, *necessarily* touch or disaffirm a right claimed as to the other. (*i*)

It may be safely admitted, that the banks of rivers not subject to the tides are not so open as *Bracton* represents, without admitting any mistake, to the same extent, as to the sea-shore. Few (if any) of our *old* law-writers are deemed better authority than Bracton; and if we are to assume, that because he is wrong in one case, and the law is since altered in another, therefore, in a third and different case he must also be wrong, what law-writer have we who can pass such an ordeal? Mr. Justice Buller, in the case of Ball *v.* Herbert(*k*) (which related to towage on the *banks* of a navigable river), (*l*) observes on the passage of Bracton, "riparum usus," &c.,—"It plainly appears to have "been taken from Justinian, and is only part of the Civil "law; and whether or not it has been adopted by the "Common law is to be seen by looking into our books, "and there it is not to be found."(*m*) But, it may be asked, what are "our books" if Bracton be not one? and [163]

The text of Bracton as it bears on this distinction.

(*i*) (But the grant of a manor or an undefined acreage of land may be shewn to include the shore.—ED.) [In the case of the Belfast Dock Act, 1 Ir. Eq. 139, the Master of the Rolls, in his judgment, says: "Counsel is perhaps right in stating that 'bank' more properly refers "to hard, dry land. This is so of the word 'ripa,' according to the "proposition in Hale's treatise; but the bank of the bay may include "a sand-bank or mud-bank, though alternately covered and uncovered "by the flux and reflux of the sea, and so be equivalent to 'shore.' "The American courts have held that a 'bank' of a river is that space "of rising ground above low-water mark, which is usually covered by "high water, and the term, when used to designate a precise line, "may be somewhat vague and indefinite:" Howard *v.* Ingersole, 17 Ala. U.S. 780, 13 How. (U.S.) 426, per Curtis, J.; Stone *v.* Augusta, 46 Maine 127, 137. See also Child *v.* Starr, 4 Hill 369, per Cowen, J., as to "Shore;" Angell on Watercourses, p. 32, 6th edit.] [163]

(*k*) 3 T. R. 253, *post*, 851, n.

(*l*) Quære, tide river?

(*m*) The judges, in the principal case, quoted the words of Judge Buller, as applicable to Bracton's doctrine relative to the sea-shore; although they were not so applied by Judge Buller himself, but to banks of rivers. (See cases as to Roman law, *ante*, p. 33.—ED.)

if Bracton be not contradicted by other authorities or customs, he is, *primâ facie*, an acknowledged law-writer of authority.

It does not necessarily follow that because Bracton's text is taken from the Civil law, that the doctrine may not be good at Common law.

Now, as the books are totally silent in regard to *bathing* (which is one part of the "communis usus littorum"), and [164] silent also as to several other common uses to which the shore may be applied, the authority of Bracton, as to the right of the public to *make use* of the sea-shore, might be deemed good authority for all such customary uses made of it as are uncontradicted by the books, and not incompatible with other unquestionable rights, or the known laws of the land. There is nothing singular in the laws of two different nations agreeing in their permission of a custom so natural as bathing. The habit of bathing is as natural to a native of Britain as to a Roman; much more so, indeed, if the effect of insular habits (and habit is second nature) be considered. It would have been more singular if the *Civil* and *British* laws had not agreed in throwing open the sea-shore for purposes of public use common to all mankind.(*n*)

The coincidence of phrase adopted in expressing such legal right, can be no sufficient ground for rejecting the law. The phrase may be borrowed, and yet speak the law of the land. If the law were as singular as the phrase, that might be a rational ground for doubting whether the law, as well as phrase, be not *foreign;* but in a case where it is so natural that all nations should think, and act, and legislate alike, it seems not reasonable to hold that the law is foreign because one of our jurists, writing in Latin, borrows a Latin phrase or sentence. Our early law writers wrote in the language of the Civil law, and not in their native tongue; the language of the Civil law was the language of our Courts in early times, though the law itself might differ; and many sentences in our early Latin writers might

(*n*) (To take sand, shells, and seaweed from the shore may have been lawful for the Roman and ancient Briton, as well as to bathe; but by our common law neither of these practices is legal. Yet the passage in Bracton would permit both practices, and, indeed, any use of the shore for which the public chose to use it.—ED.)

be pointed out, which lay down the undeniable Common law of England in the same words by which the Civil law expresses the same rule. Natural reason alone has made the Civil law and Common law to coincide in many points, without borrowing from each other; and if the Latin tongue be used to declare both codes, what wonder if the like [165] words and phrases of one and the same language be used to express similar laws.

The Roman law and our Common law agree in some points.

There are several points of the Roman law, delivered by Bracton in the language of the Institutes, which are allowed to be part of our Common law at this day, as Lord Hale himself admits. It is clear that our law has either *actually* adopted the Civil law in some points, or has, from the nature of things, coincided with it. The only true question is, whether the matter in dispute be or be not a part of *our* laws and customs? The Common law of England *may* adopt, and certainly has adopted, some detached portions of the Civil law; and it is not strange or difficult to suppose both these systems of law to have agreed in sanctioning a natural right and habit, coexistent with the earliest habits of the human race. Had the Roman law *first* declared that to bathe in the sea was *not* a common right, but must be asked or hired from the owner of the shore, and the English law had followed in the same words, it might then, indeed, be imagined that so strange a restraint in the law of England upon so natural a use of the sea-shore, expressed in the words of the Roman law, was interpolated from that law. But as regards the point in question, it is a custom common to all nations, and foreign to none.

The custom of bathing preceded the law both of England and Rome.

To say that the law was borrowed, is to infer that the custom did not exist before the time of borrowing. But will it be said that the shore was not as much frequented for bathing *before* that time as *after*? Men were used to bathe and swim long prior to the written codes of Rome or England. The *custom* preceded the *law*, and that which Roman law may have sanctioned by book, may have been already custom, *i.e.* Common law, in England. It must be admitted that our law and the Roman law do also *disagree* in *some* points respecting the use and property [166] of the sea-shore; this was, at some length, proved by Mr. Justice Holroyd; but this is no evidence that they do not *agree* in other points. They *do* agree in the common right of fishing; why may they not agree in the common right of bathing? In those points wherein they differ, our books and Common law cause the difference; but do our books and customs create any difference as to bathing? It is admitted that not one expression in our books is to be found *contradictory* to the common right to frequent the sea-shore for bathing; and that bathing is, and ever has been, a *general* custom and practice will hardly be denied; for the habit is coeval at least with fishing and navigation, two acknowledged "*communes usus*" of the sea-shore.

The words of Bracton not to be construed too largely,—by reasonable construction seem to be good law.

The Court seem to have construed the words of Bracton, "*communis usus*," in an extreme sense, viz. as denying *all* ownership over the shore, even in the King. But it does not appear that the words were intended by Bracton to be understood further than as importing common rights of *usage*, distinct from the "*jus proprietatis;*" nor is it *necessary* to interpret him to mean that the ownership of the soil was *not* (as now held to be) in the King. Indeed, we have just now shown that he wholly omits the doctrine of the Institutes, as regards the "*proprietas*." He must, therefore, be taken to have meant no more than that the shore was a public *common*, open to public resort, and convertible to various public uses, as is the sea. It is in every day's experience that the shore *is* open "to common use." It is difficult to say wh a other common uses the shore can be converted to by the public, besides those of a "highway for the exercise of "the fisheries and navigation," "digging of the soil for "manure, and for materials for building, ballast, &c.," and lastly, "bathing." The first three of these uses are confirmed by the law; and the digging and carrying away [167] sand, &c. is a right actually affirmed (*o*) by Statute law

(*o*) (Granted, not affirmed.—ED.)

to all the inhabitants of two of the largest maritime districts(*p*) in England, but has been disputed as a general right.(*q*)

Uses of the sea and sea-shore.

Thus the language of Bracton would seem to be warranted alike by law and practice in every use to which the *sea* can be applied; whilst one disputed instance (the digging of sand, &c.) will not apply to the *sea*, and therefore does not come strictly within his words, which are "*sicut et ipsius* "*maris*." The sea is a public highway,—so also is the shore. The sea is subject to the public right of fishing and navigation,—so also is the shore; and to what other purposes is the *sea* applied, by *common right*, to which the *shore* has not been at least *equally* applied by common *use*, digging for sand, &c. not excepted? So far, therefore, as relates to the "communis usus" (exclusive of the barren *ownership* of the soil) the text of Bracton is borne out by matter of fact.(*r*) Callis also, quoting from an old text-writer, says,

(*p*) Devon and Cornwall. See p. 768, *ante*. (The existence of this special and peculiar statute negatives any presumption as to the rest of the kingdom, and shews that the right was not a right at common law. The statute has been held to be *enacting*, and not *declaratory*. See also *ante*, p. 769; and Howe *v.* Stawell, 1 Alc. & Nap. 348, *ante*, p. 465; Macnamara *v.* Higgins, *ante*, p. 488; Hamilton *v.* Att. for Ireland, 5 L. R. Ir. 555, *ante*, p. 569.—Ed.)

(*q*) In Bagot *v.* Orr, 2 Bos. & Pul. 472.

(*r*) In the case, the King *v.* Commissioners of Sewers for Pagham, Sussex, 8 B. & C. 355, it is laid down by the Court, "that every land-"owner exposed to the inroads of the sea, has a right to protect him-"self, and is justified in erecting such *works* as are necessary for that "purpose." This was said in regard to *groynes*, a kind of work which takes permanent possession of the soil, and is only effectual when constructed upon the "shore." These groynes are piles of wood carried out from high-water mark, at right angles from the coast, towards the sea, across the "shore." The effect is to accumulate the beach and shingles on the one side into heaps, and which accumulation constitutes the protection sought for. The sea is thus made to shut out itself. This kind of work has, in many places on the coast, produced very extensive accumulations of beach, sand, &c., annexed to the adjoining land, and has thus not merely *protected* but *added to* the ownership of the land. How far the subject may assert a claim to the ownership of such soil, so recovered from the sea, may be judged from what has been already said, viz. that it will depend upon the gradual nature of the acquisition. But with regard to the right de-

[168] "*Rex habet proprietatem sed populus habet usum ibidem necessarium.*" (*s*) The practice of bathing and swimming may justly be termed "necessary" to a maritime people. It is true the shore may be converted to other uses than those

clared by the Court in the case above mentioned, it does not appear whether it was meant to be laid down as a general common law right,
[168] independent of the ownership of the "shore," or as a right inherent only in the ownership of the shore. Presuming the "shore" to belong to the Crown (as is to be presumed until the contrary be shown), the question is, whether all owners of lands on the coast have a right *so* to use the shore, such shore being the property of the King? or whether the Court intended to apply the doctrine only to *those* who were *owners* of both the land and the "shore"? Such works are, in fact, an *embanking* against the sea, and do not only protect the land from further inroads, but recover lost land from the sea. The question is of importance, as regards evidence of title to the "shore;" for if the right be *general*, and independent of the ownership of the shore, such acts cannot be evidence of *private* right to the shore. And if the ownership of the shore will alone give the right to do such acts, the ownership of the shore, in point of title, must have existed *before* any such act; and if so, then such act can only be proved *lawful* by proving a pre-existing title to the shore. If the title to the shore must be *first proved* to make any such act *lawful*, the title to the shore must be proved by evidence *dehors* the act itself. Presumption, in this case, is no good title against the Crown. (It is worthy of remark here, that the Anglo-Saxon grant of Pagham (Codex Dip. i. 82, *ante*, p. 2) shews that the shore was included in that manor.—ED.) Such acts as these, done by private individuals, are independent of acts done by Commissioners under the Statute of Sewers, 23 H. 8, ch. 5. It will hardly be held that the erection of *one* groyne, by the lord of the adjacent manor, will, after a lapse of twenty or more years, be *per se* sufficient evidence of title to the soil of the shore against the King. One or two groynes will often prove adequate to the protection of several miles of coast; and even occasion very considerable additions to such extent of coast. If, however, the right to erect such works upon the shore be held to be a general Common law right, it is no slight argument in favour of Bracton's doctrine. It may also be remarked, that if by the construction of such works such rapid *additions* are obtained from the sea as the law will *take notice of*, they will belong to the Crown, *unless* those additions have been taken possession of by sufficient acts of ownership for the period of time required by the Statutes of Limitation, to negative the King's title. See p. 795, *ante;* and 2 Anst. 614, Attor. Gen. *v.* Richards. [It is not competent for the proprietors of land on either side of a river to disturb the ordinary course of the stream to

(*s*) Callis, on Sewers, 54.

just mentioned, but not such as are in their nature *open* and [169] *common;* therefore, an *appropriation* or *in-taking* of it is not a "*communis usus.*" Now, in the case of a common within a manor, it is well known that the lord of the manor is owner of the soil of the common; but that the tenants have a certain "communis usus" of such common, so as to render the "soil" of comparatively trifling value to the lord. He cannot infringe upon the rights of the "commoners" by any in-taking or inclosure of the common. Why cannot this analogy serve for the sea-shore? The common uses to which it has *generally* and immemorially been applied by the public, might as reasonably be supported, as are similar uses of the soil of inland manors, so long as such uses are beneficial to the public; and the ownership of the soil might be available only in cases where the "common rights" are not injured. The soil of the shore would seem to deserve no better protection on behalf of private owners, than the soil of a common within a manor; on the contrary, a private ownership of the sea-shore, if asserted and acted upon, is very likely to prove a public nuisance; and therefore deserves no encouragement or support against any public uses which are laudable and beneficial, and have ancient usage in their favour. (*t*)

the prejudice of the opposite proprietor: Menzies *v.* Breadalbane, 3 Bli. N. S. 414, 3 W. & Shaw 235. In Rex *v.* Trafford, 1 B. & Ad. 888, [169] Lord Tenterden, distinguishing between a right to embank against the sea and against a river, says: "In the one case, if the works be successful, the water is prevented from coming where, within time of memory at least, it never had come; in the other it is prevented from passing in the way in which, when the occasion happened, it had been always accustomed to pass."

[It is no defence to an indictment for a nuisance for embanking in the water-way, that although the work be in some degree a hindrance to navigation, it is advantageous in a greater degree, to other uses of the port: R. *v.* Ward, 4 A. & E. 384, *ante*, p. 774; and *post*, p. 854.]

(*t*) (The analogy does serve in some respects. The owner of the shore may not inclose it against the public right of navigation or fishery without an *ad quod damnum*, unless he chooses to take the risk of proving that it is not *ad damnum*. Similarly the lord of a manor may inclose the waste so long as he leaves sufficient common for the tenants having *rights*, but he is not restrained as against the public. The tenants have a right to a profit out of the waste; the

As to the immemorial custom of bathing.

But the Court seem to have denied the *continued* and *immemorial* custom of bathing on the sea-shore. Lord Tenterden declared, "that if the right exist now, it must [170] "have existed at all times; but we *know*," he adds, "that "sea-bathing was, until a time comparatively modern, a "matter of *no frequent* occurrence;" and he adds, "that he "was not aware of any practice in this matter sufficiently "extensive or uniform to be the foundation of a judicial "decision." But with great deference, it seems singular to deny the uniformity, universality, and frequent occurrence of bathing and swimming in the sea; a practice known to exist habitually wherever man and sea-water are to be met with. There is not a village on the coast where the practice will not be found to have uniformly prevailed. Cleanliness, health, amusement, and utility have all operated to make the custom general on the sea-coast.(*u*)

Opinion of the Court as to bathing in "machines."

It is true that the *manner* of bathing in "machines" (as his Lordship remarked) may not be either *ancient* or extremely uniform; but the *right*, and the precise *manner* of exercising that right, are not the same questions. The right of bathing, and not the right of bathing in "*machines*," is the true question, and was, in fact, the question decided by the Court. It is another question whether the right of way to the sea be open for carriages in some *particular spot* of the *ripam* in regard to the private ownership there. If the public have a convenient approach to the shore, it is enough, without their being allowed to make as many ways as they please, and from mere caprice, over the grounds of others. That the public, in every parish, manor, &c. on the coasts, have a right to one or more convenient ways of approach to the shore, according to the wants, extent, and localities of the district, is not to be denied, since without this, fishing and navigation would be valueless. Nor is it sufficient that such way should be a mere foot-way; and if it be a way for horses and carriages, and I thus have a right
[171] to drive down to and along the shore in a machine or

public have no rights to such a profit, but only to an easement of navigation and fishery. See Introduction.—ED.)

(*u*) (Within the present century.—ED.)

carriage, to get into a boat to float on the sea, why may I not do so to get into the sea itself? The right of way to the sea was never yet contended to be a mere *footway;* the same mode of approach to and from the sea as is allowed for fishing or embarkation, is all that is desired on behalf of bathing. As to denying the right to bathe, on the ground that the "machines" are a "modern invention," it may be thought that they are rather a recommendation than otherwise in support of a custom, which, in its more ancient practice, was not so decent, or so well adapted to modern refinement.

As to bathing being a privilege inconsistent with private rights.

But it was further declared, by Mr. Justice Holroyd, that "such right of bathing is inconsistent with the nature of "permanent private property, as well as inconsistent with "the fishing on the sea-shore being also an exclusive right." Now, with regard to the sea-shore being private property, this does not seem to be a species of ownership worthy of being *favoured* either against the Crown or the public. It was also well and truly said, by the learned counsel for the defendant, "that no subject, claiming under the King, can claim a greater right than the King had in the shore;" and the true question all along is, whether the King's ownership in the shore is not itself subject to this usage? The ownership of the Crown in the shore has always been subject to the public right of using it as a road for fishing and navigation. It is evidently not the *sea* alone, but the *shore* also which is subject to these two Common law rights. Thus, the frequenting the shore is claimed and enjoyed as an accessory to these rights, which are the principals. It is like a grant by A, of a piece of ground to B, in the midst of the ground of A, which grant were useless unless B had a right of way over A's ground to the piece of ground granted to him; therefore, the law implies and gives to B a right of way over A's other ground. So the shore lies [172] between the fishery or navigation and the public, but the public have a right to the fishery and navigation, and a convenient way is presumed over the shore for carrying them on; such as for launching boats, carriage and footway for the conveyance of the fish, goods, &c. to and from the

The public have a right of way over and along the shore for fishing, navigation, &c.

boats, &c., and for exercising whatever other conveniences common sense and usage point out as *essential* to these rights; in short, whatever obstruction would render the fishery or navigation nugatory, must be deemed unlawful and incompatible with those rights. But to build houses or docks on the shore, or to form permanent quays or wharfs by the fishermen or traders themselves (not being owners of the soil), will be going beyond the essentials of their rights. All such permanent appropriations of the soil are no part of the public rights of fishery or navigation, and should therefore be matter of private bargain. The temporary purpose for which the shore is used must be essentially and necessarily subservient to the right claimed, and so far such temporary purpose, it is apprehended, is not inconsistent with private property in the shore. To this extent the Common law right to use the sea-shore, does, it is conceived, prevail throughout the coasts of England, whether such "*locus*" be a port, or not; or whether it be the King's property or the property of a subject.

A several fishery may exclude the right to bathe where the bathing would injure the fishery.

But if, in addition to his ownership of the soil of the shore, the subject claim a private fishery, such claim, if allowed, is paramount to the public fishery; and therefore no accessory to the public fishery (such as a right of way) can be allowed to injure the private right; for if the public fishery itself yield to the private, the incidents to such public fishery must yield also. Now, assuming the right to bathe to be coeval in antiquity of usage with the public right to fish (and there are some and the most
[173] ancient modes of fishing which require the fisher to immerse himself in the water), the same evidence which will support the private fishery against the public fishery, and its incidental right of way, will also support the private fishery against the "bathing" and its incidental right of way, so far as it may interfere with such private fishery; and if the bathing, in the case of Blundell *v.* Caterall, under consideration, did injury to the private fishery, and such private fishery was good in title, then the decision of the case was just, *quoad hoc.* Of two incompatible rights, if one be allowed to be good, the other cannot be so; but

then the case we have put is similar to the case of a private fishery, excluding the general and public fishery.

It was expressly allowed by the learned Judge, "that, as "incident to the fishery, the public *must* have the means of "getting to and upon the water for those purposes;" but he adds, "that it will appear, that it is by and from such "places only as necessity or usage have appropriated to such "purposes." Is it then meant to be laid down as law, that the "sea-shore" is only accessible for the purpose of fishing, in old fishing villages, or sea-ports? Suppose a village on the sea-coast, whose inhabitants never yet launched a boat, are the cottagers precluded from turning fishermen, and approaching and exercising on the shore their Common law right of fishery? It would seem that the whole sea-coast of the realm is the *place* appropriated by "usage and "necessity" to the public common of piscary. The right is attached to the person, to every individual of the public body. It is the birth-right of the subject, and he is not bound to exercise his right in one place more than another. All that he has to do is to pay regard to rights declared by the law paramount to his own; but the mere ownership of the soil is no such private right as can bar the *jus publicum* of the fishery. Even the King's ownership of the soil is subject to such right, and the ownership of individuals [174] derived from the Crown is not greater.

As to the right of way for fishing, &c., on the sea and shore.

It is said, by Mr. Justice Holroyd, "that it is not by the "Common law, nor by statute, lawful to come with, or land, "or ship customable goods in creeks or havens, or other places "out of ports, unless in cases of danger or necessity, nor fish, "or land other goods not customable, where the shore "or land adjoining is private property."(*x*) Undoubtedly,

As to the right to land from boats, &c., on the shore.

(*x*) "If one has piscary in any *water*, he has no power to land with-"out the assent of the tenants of the frank-tenement." Savil, xi. pl. 29, Inhabitants of Ipswich v. Brown, 23 Eliz. See Vin. Abr. title Piscary, D. But the fishery here meant is a *several* or *private* fishery. In Ward v. Cresswell, Willes 265, Vin. Abr. Piscary B,—Defendant in replevin, avows taking six boat oars (from boats hauled above high-water mark) as damage feasant, for that the *place where* was his freehold. Plaintiff pleads in bar of the avowry,—1. A common of

customable goods cannot lawfully be landed except in the ports assigned for their reception, and the payment of duties. The *jus regium* of the King, which entitles him to levy the customs, entitles him, as *custos portuum*, to appoint the places for the landing and shipping of customable goods; but it is difficult to consider the law as granting the public fishery, and yet denying the right to land the fish upon the *ripam*, as well as *shore*, so far as such *temporary* use of the *ripam* or of the shore is reasonably *necessary;* such fish to be forthwith removed, and not left or marketed there, to cause permanent or unreasonable obstruction to the ownership of the soil.

The public have a right to fish on the *shore*, as well as on the sea.

There can be no doubt whatever but that the public have a right to fish on the *shore*, although the soil thereof may happen to be private property. To exclude the public there [175] must be proved a *several* fishery, as well as an ownership of the soil. The public fishery extends over sea and shore, and there are many kinds of fish which can only be caught on the shore. The case of Bagot *v.* Orr, (*y*) has expressly decided that the public have a Common law right to take *shell fish* on the "shore," without reference to the person to whom the soil belongs; and, it is presumed, the "fishery" includes all kinds of fish (royal fish excepted) wherever their haunts may be, whether in the great waste of the sea, or upon the shore.

The public not compellable to land fish caught at sea at the port.

With regard to the fish taken at sea, it would be difficult to contend that it would be *necessary* to carry fish to a *port* before it is landed. The right to land the fish upon the strand nearest where it is caught, would seem to be an essential adjunct of the fishery; the fishery is for the sustenance of the fishermen, their families,

fishery in the sea there, *as appurtenant to certain tenements* there,—2. A liberty of landing and putting on shore their boats upon the place, for the use of the fishery. It was held that fishing in the sea, being matter of common right, a prescription for it, as appurtenant to a particular township, is void. Accord: the plea in bar was held to be ill. Here the landing and putting up their boats (which was the damage) seems to have been regarded as part of the public right of fishery. (Gray *v.* Bond, 5 Moore 527.—Ed.)

(*y*) Bagot *v.* Orr, 2 Bos. & Pul. 472. See this case more fully, *post*, p. 861.

and others dwelling on the spot whence they embark; and to require the fish to be landed at a port perhaps twenty miles off, with all the delays of winds, and tides, and office and land carriage, &c., is utterly destructive of the fishery. It must be presumed, that the Common law right of fishery includes the right to land the fish at the places where it may be most conveniently sold and used for food. Half the fisheries in the kingdom would be ruined if a contrary doctrine prevailed.

As to the right of way along the "ripa" above high-water mark.

It is difficult to regard the fishery as a *public* and *general* right, and the necessary way and passage for its exercise as a *local* and *partial* privilege. The public right to navigate the seas, and to fish therein, is not limited to particular places; it is not a local right, but pervades the whole coast of England. The right of way for the exercise of these public rights would seem to be commensurate. But the [176] fisherman or navigator must be ruled by the law, through the verdict of a jury, as to what shall be *sufficient* in the *locus in quo*. The law (for instance) will compel him to take the usual and public road down to the sea-side, if there be one within reasonable and convenient distance; but when there, how is he to reach his boat, which may be a mile off along the shore, at the time of *high water*, unless he can go along the edge of the coast on the *terra firma*, (z)

(z) Callis, p. 74, says, "I cannot more aptly compare a *bank* of the "sea, or of a navigable river, than to a high way;" and he extends this right of way to a right "to tow the boats to and fro." But more recent authority has decided that "towage along the banks of navi-"gable rivers is not a common right." Ball *v.* Herbert, 3 T. R. 253, *post*, p. 887. This would not seem to be a "necessarium usum" for navigation, properly so called. But for every "necessarium usum," affecting the public fishery and navigation, the bank would seem to be open to the public. Whether the fishermen and others have a *right* to drag up their vessels above the reach of the tides, upon the banks, for security and for repairs, as is the universal *practice*, does not seem ever to have been decided; this would appear to be *essential* to the protection of the fishery, and perhaps be supported. See note to p. 849, *ante*. So the practice of drying nets on the adjacent land, as well as on the shore, does not seem to have ever been sanctioned by a judicial decision, as a common right. Callis, however, states it as such, p. 73. It might be considered, perhaps, a practice of too vague

[177] to his boat? It would be a serious obstruction to the fishery if he must bring his boat where the old road runs into the sea, and nowhere else. So, when on the sea, if he desire to land his fish, his merchandise (not customable) or himself, at the time of high water, unless he is allowed a way along the *terra firma*, to the next public road, he cannot land at all; wherefore, in all such cases, at the time of high water, either there must be a Common law right of way, along the dry land to the nearest inland road, and consistent with the public right of fishing and navigation, or at the time of high water no man can embark or disembark at other places than where the inland road meets the sea. Such a rule, in regard to the fishery, and to all the boat and small craft navigation, would be very injurious to the common right, and prejudicial to the public.

The law does not compel goods not customable to be landed at a port.

The Common law does not seem to control, in such manner, the general rights of fishing in and navigating the seas. It does not compel the subject to embark or disembark his person or his goods (not customable) at one place more than another; and it is conceived, that in order to the full, complete, and unimpeded exercise of these great public rights, a right of way, above and along the edge of high-water mark, is involved in the existence of those other public rights, and annexed to them; but subject (for the due protection of *private* rights) to the control of a jury, as to what shall be deemed *sufficient*, in the place of exercise.

a character to be supported as a general right, or even local easement or liberty. In some places such a privilege might prevent the cultivation and usufruct of many acres of valuable ground. Nets are said often to extend more than a mile when spread out, belonging to one boat only. See what is said by Holroyd, J., in Blundell *v.* Caterall, 5 B. & Ald. pp. 295, 296, and cases cited there, which seem opposed to such privilege. [See Gray *v.* Bond, 2 B. & B. 667, 5 J. B. Moore 527 S. C. It was there held that it is not lawful for fishermen, merely as such, to dry their nets on a part of the shore which belongs to private persons, or to use such shore land for any purpose accessory to fishing; but the case shows that, by user, the owner of a fishery in a public navigable river may acquire a right to draw to land and land nets, used in the fishery, at certain places on the banks of a river, the property of private persons unconnected with the fishery. See also Hoyle *v.* McCunn, 31 Scot. Jur. 63; S. C. 10 Dec. 1858, 21 Court of Session Cases 96.]

The object of these remarks has been to shew, that if a right of common, or to a liberty, or easement be established, the essential means of enjoying that right are established with it. If there be a customary right to bathe in the sea, the use of the sea-shore, so far as such use is essential to the custom, must accompany it, but no further. The general doctrine of Bracton, that the sea-shore is "common for "use as the sea," is a legitimate argument in favour of the right of bathing, or any other common use of such shore, [178] until it be shewn that such general doctrine is contradicted by law, or custom, or both, as to that particular use of it; but no custom, no authority whatever has been adduced to *contradict* Bracton's general doctrine, so far as it is considered to include sea bathing.

As to the inconsistency of bathing with other private rights, and with private appropriations of the shore.

If this usage of bathing be rejected as not founded in law, it must be rejected by arguments grounded on "the "incompatibility with private rights, or with public con-"venience" of the custom. The Court, indeed, in their decision, seem to have addressed themselves most particularly to the points of the inconsistency of *this* right with *other* rights, and its public inconvenience. Its incompatibility with other rights was strongly insisted upon by all three of the learned judges. It was said by Mr. Justice Holroyd to be "inconsistent with the nature of permanent "private property." By Mr. Justice Bayley it was asked, "If the soil be vested in an individual, is he to be deprived "of the right of saying how that soil shall be used, and the "privilege of making any regulations he may think fit?" And by Lord Tenterden, "every public right to be exercised "over the land of an individual is, *pro tanto*, a diminution "of his private right:" and Mr. Justice Bayley and Lord Tenterden urged, that "it would prevent the owner of the "soil from building quays, wharfs, or private houses, as "well as from making embankments, &c.; for all such "would be obstructions to this public right of bathing (if "allowed), and, therefore, abateable as nuisances." (*a*)

(*a*) This argument, as well as that used by the Court, p. 847, *ante*, rests upon the assumption that the sea-shores throughout the kingdom are for the most part in the hands of private owners, and are *not* the property of the Crown. This, however, seems to be not only a gratui-

[179] But it is to be remembered, that any such appropriations of the shore, even by the owner, are liable to be abated as nuisances, if they interfere with the public rights of *fishing* and of *navigation*. Whether they are or are not nuisances is a question for the jury. Thus then the private property of the shore (such as it is) is already, in two material instances, under the check of a jury, by which the owner is plainly interdicted from doing with the shore "as he "pleases;" and why should it be thought *hard* to leave it to a jury to protect any other beneficial public custom (as bathing), by determining whether the obstruction be or be not, in reason and common sense, a public nuisance? that is,—such an obstruction of the bathing as ought to be put down. Quays, wharfs, and embankments in general, *below* high-water mark, convert that which was shore into *terra firma*, being, in fact, so much land gained from the sea, and therefore no longer shore. If any ground be left on the *other* side, towards the sea, that may be shore, and subject as before; but no one can suppose that an embankment by which the soil is rescued from the sea by the owner of the shore, would be abateable as a nuisance, in favour of bathing

As to its incompatibility with private rights.

Quays, wharfs, &c. on the shore.

tous presumption, but a presumption against the King's title. The true presumption is, that the shores of the kingdom are the property
[179] of the Crown, and that individual subjects have no right, except by ancient grant from the Crown, to build houses, or construct wharfs, &c. on the shore. It is not to be *assumed* that the Crown has granted away *all*, or the *principal* part of the shores of the kingdom. But if these private ownerships are only *partial*, and not *general*, it does not seem a legitimate ground of argument to object to a *general* custom, as such, *because* it might stand opposed, in a few places, to the *particular* ownerships of a *few* individuals. The question ought to be considered as one between the King's ownership in all the "shores" of the realm, and the uses claimed therein by his subjects, in diminution of such absolute ownership. The custom of bathing on the shores of the realm has always been as fully acquiesced in by the Crown as the fishery, and from times as remote and immemorial. (It appears to the Editor that Lord Tenterden and Mr. Justice Bayley spoke from wider experience of facts than Mr. Hall. It is not a *mere assumption* that the sea-shores throughout the kingdom are for the most part in the hands of private owners; it is the absolute fact: the assumption of fact lies with Mr. Hall, and not with those learned judges. Hence this argument is not of much weight.—ED.)

or fishing, whilst the shore, beyond and around, is still open to the public, and these rights may be enjoyed as easily as before. Nor was it ever contended that the supposed owner [180] of the soil of the shore has not a right to convert it into *terra firma*, at his own risk and expense, unless in so doing he created a public or local nuisance. (*b*)

Bathing not *necessarily* inconsistent with private rights.

There is no law which makes a conversion of the sea-shore into *terra firma*, *always* and *necessarily* a nuisance; it must be proved to be a nuisance in its consequences,—and if it prove so to the public, it is better put down. If a road have been used, time out of mind, in a particular direction down to the sea, and by my in-taking of the shore I interpose dry land between the water and the place where the water before met the road, where is the difficulty of prolonging the road down to the new-formed high-water mark? A road existed heretofore over the shore to the sea, and is not lost by the shore's being now dry land; the said land, when wholly dry, is not altered in title, but is still subject to the right of road to the sea. Why, therefore, are not these rights reconcileable with each other? Suppose the sea to have suddenly retired from a tract of land, and the old road, instead of ending in the sea, to be thrown back a mile from the water, will not the law carry it on into the water? And why not also if the land become *terra firma* by the act of the party? If I have a way to the shore, am I, when arrived there, to ask leave of the Crown, or other owner, to walk, or ride, or drive into the water? In launching boats, and disembarking when the tide is low, it is frequently necessary to wade some distance through the water,—and it is to be presumed that it is lawful so to do. When I have reached the shore, how can any line of road be prescribed to me which the next tide will not obliterate? The right of way on the sea-shore is bounded by the water's edge, which is never stationary between high-water and low-water mark. But if that which was shore be made dry land, one road may then be set out for general use over [181] it, in continuation of the road which before led to the shore, and so into the sea, or along the new shore. The right of

(*b*) [*Ante*, pp. 772, 843.]

bathing would seem to be nothing more than a right of way down to the shore, along the shore, and into the sea.

Right to bathe a right of way into the sea.

Every permanent occupation of the shore by exclusion of the sea is an embankment or in-taking; and every owner of the soil, whether the King or a subject, proving his ownership, has a right to appropriate such soil; but subject and without prejudice to existing rights of others. If the law of Bagot *v.* Orr (*c*) be good, and a general Common law right of fishing on the shore at ebb tide exist, then *any* exclusive appropriation of the soil of the shore is in derogation of the public common right of piscary, and abateable as a nuisance, *if a jury shall decide it to be so* in the disputed place. So any appropriation or obstruction of the shore, or of the customary public approaches to the shore, injurious to the public right of navigation, is abateable as a nuisance.

The right to bathe will not occasion other *more* beneficial uses to be put down as nuisances.

The learned Judges, however, doubted whether, if they admitted the use of the shore for *bathing* to be a public liberty or privilege, all useful appropriations of the shore would be prevented. But if the appropriation in any given case would be a nuisance not to the bathing only, but to the fishery and navigation also, the sooner it is abated the better, whether the bather, or the fisherman, or the navigator effect it; and if it be no obstruction, no nuisance, to navigation or fishing, but actually auxiliary and beneficial towards those national purposes, where is the probability that *such* an appropriation will, in its extent or locality, be adjudged a nuisance by a jury, on behalf of the bather alone? On the other hand, if the appropriation prove of [182] no advantage to fishing and navigation, whilst it materially interferes with the custom of bathing, a custom which may have become essential to the local interests of the place, the sooner such an appropriation is declared a nuisance the better.

National advantages resulting

The custom of bathing is not the less ancient or wholesome, because in the present age it has become a *fashion;*

(*c*) 2 Bos. & Pul. 472.

and it is now too late to deny that this fashionable custom, freely exercised, has caused a great resort of people to the sea-coasts, and has raised into existence many large and beautiful towns, and produced a spirit of industry and speculation, in furtherance of this bathing custom, which has added greatly to the wealth, population, and strength of the country. Millions of capital have been expended for the accommodation of those who frequent the shores of the realm, for the purpose of exercising their supposed right of bathing; and the fortunes of thousands are dependent on this "custom;" and yet, by the decision of the above case, it has been thought good to place all this great expenditure and risk of industry and capital at the mercy of a private owner of the sea-shore, out of regard to the barely possible case of a jury's interfering with the appropriation of such shore by the owner to the national purposes of fishing, navigation, and commerce, on the ground that it is *nevertheless* an obstruction to bathing. If the interests of these national purposes clash, it might be left to the Jury to decide which shall prevail.

from the present custom of bathing in the sea.

It is said by Mr. Justice Holroyd, that "where there is, "or has hitherto been, a necessity, or even urgency, for "such a right, there, as far as such necessity has existed, "some usage must have prevailed." This admits that there possibly *may* be a *local* usage or custom of bathing. Now every manor on the coast has its inhabitants, and it were an assertion easily disproved were it said, that bathing [183] in the sea is *not* customary with these inhabitants; and it would be impossible to arrive at the precise degree of necessity or urgency which introduced or continued the practice. Assuming that the inhabitants for the time being of the sea-coasts of England, are and have ever been accustomed to frequent the shore for bathing, it would be singular to denominate this a collection of *local* customs. The inhabitants of the sea-coast are, in fact, the only class of the community who *fish* in the sea, or on the sea-shore, and yet it is not a *local* but a public and *general* Common law right of fishing; and the custom of bathing is as general amongst the inhabitants of the sea-coast as fishing. It

The custom of bathing in the sea too general to be construed a local custom.

would be strange, therefore, to denominate the one custom a *general*, and the other custom (which is at least equally general amongst the same class of persons) a *local* custom. But if the right to frequent the shore for bathing by means of *carriages* be denied, then, indeed, every watering-place (as they are now called) in the kingdom may be wholly dependent upon the owner of the soil of the shore.

As to distinction taken by the court in Blundell *v.* Caterall, between bathing, and bathing in "machines."

Lord Tenterden observes, that the "machines are of "comparatively modern invention." It certainly is not handed down to us, by any records, by what various means our ancestors approached the sea for the purpose of bathing. But the question does not depend upon the inquiry as to what "machines" they employed to transport themselves *to* and *into* the sea;—but whether the sea-shore be, or be not, subject to a right of road or way for footmen, horses, and carriages to pass over and along it to the sea. Has not the subject a right of *carriage*, as well as *foot* way along the shore, to his fishing-boat, yacht, or trading vessel? And if he have, it would seem singular to deny his further right to drive or wade into the sea.

It is not meant to be said that a right of road will lie [184] over a man's *stake-nets*, wears, or private fishing-place; *that* is a case *sui generis*, and an exception to the general rule; but it is considered that no book, or authority, or custom whatsoever, denies the right of way *ad libitum*, over and along the "shore," so long as it is *shore*, whether the soil be the King's, or belong to a subject by grant from the Crown. Such right of way is allowed for fishing; and, when the case was *res integra*, it might have been expected that the Courts would have allowed the shore to be used as a highway as much for the one purpose as the other, instead of thus virtually declaring the same man a trespasser for bathing, who was no trespasser when up to his knees or neck in water, in search of a lobster, a crab, or a shrimp.

The right of way general over the shore, on foot and in carriages.

As to the profits arising to the persons who assist those who

It was further said by the Court, that in the exercise of this right (if allowed), "one man might make his own "special profit of conveying persons over the shore, the soil "of another; and that such man had no reason to complain "if the owner of the soil shall participate in the profit." (*d*) But the profit made by the bathing-assistant is upon the use of the "machine," and the labour of his driving it, and his attendance; and it might as well be urged, that if I am driven in a hired carriage across the soil of the lord of an inland manor, along a public parish road, the lord can, reasonably, stop the driver, and insist upon "participating "in his profit" or hire. According to this view of the case, the ownership of the sea-shore may, by a rapacious individual, be made, in many places of public resort, a most lucrative source of exaction. [185]

bathe, and the inconsistency of such profits with the rights of private owners.

The Court, moreover, decided against the liberty of bathing, not only from the silence of the books, and its supposed "inconsistency with certain private rights," but were also of opinion, that "in sea-bathing, as it now prevails, "particular regulations are desirable; and yet the existence of this common law right would be a great obstruction to any such regulation." But it can scarcely be deemed a public benefit to subject this right of bathing to the superintendence of the owner of the soil of the sea-shore, (*i.e.*) the lord of the manor, or his grantee, who may be a hundred miles off; and who is under no obligation, by law, to concern himself about it at all. It is to be remembered, too, that so far as *decency* is concerned, the public are perfectly able to protect themselves; for the *indecency* of bathing in too public places, and in too exposed a manner, is indictable as an offence, and punishable at common law, by the local magistrates, without paying any tax to the lords of the sea-shore. The idea of denying this ancient,

As to the supposed advantage of subjecting bathing to the regulation of the owners of the shore.

(*d*) This also seems to be an objection raised to a *general* custom, upon the ground of its interference with some *few partial* ownerships. But the ownership to which this general custom stands properly opposed, is the general ownership of the *Crown* in the sea-shores of the realm, and not to the ownerships of a few scattered individuals. It is not to be assumed, nor is it presumed by the law, that the subject has any right to the soil of the shore at all; and if no such presumption can be made, no argument can be founded on it. (But if the facts are to the contrary, as they certainly are, one may argue on the presumption of fact far more safely than on the presumption of a theory of law not warranted by the facts.—ED.)

universal, and heathful custom the support of the Courts of Law, *with a view* that the lord of the manor may superintend the bathing (not without charging his own price for it), or in order that "some contests" between the bathing men and women may be prevented thereby, seems singular. It is not probable that the owner of the soil will ever interfere in these matters, unless for the purpose of making a profit thereby. The public are not likely to be the gainers by his services, especially if they may be taxed for the use of the shore, at the will of the owner. The decision in the case of Blundell *v.* Caterall has, however, put it in the power of every owner of the soil of the sea-shore to levy a tax *ad libitum* upon the bathers, not only at fashionable watering-places, but throughout the coasts of England,
[186] *wherever such ownership of the shore can be proved.* If the public are laid open to such a tax, they will do well to try with a closer scrutiny the claims set up by lords of manors to the "sea-shore;" and not to take it for granted that, because A or B is lord of the manor *on the coast*, that he is *therefore* owner of the *shore*, now that such ownership involves a question most important to the property of thousands, the prosperity of numerous towns and districts on the coast, and the general health, convenience, and enjoyment of the public. (*e*)

(*e*) [See Angell on Tide Waters, 32. Where there is a local board, see as to Bathing 10 & 11 Vict. c. 89, s. 69; 21 & 22 Vict. c. 98, s. 44; and the Town Police Clauses Act, containing provisions as to bathing. Powers conferred upon local commissioners, or local boards of health under 10 & 11 Vict. cc. 34 and 89; or under any special Act, for the regulation of the mode of bathing on the sea-shore, and licensing bathing machines there, do not warrant the licensees of such machines in placing them on any part of the fore-shore which is private property: Mace *v.* Philcox, 15 C. B. N. S. 600, 33 L. J. N. S. C. P. 124.] (See also Lestrange *v.* Rowe, 4 F. & F. 1048.—Ed.)

As to the public right to dig for Sand, Shells, &c. on the Shore. (*f*)

Case of Bagot *v.* Orr, considered. 1. As to the public right to catch shell-fish on the shore. 2. As to the public right to dig for and use shells, sand, &c. on the shore. Case stated.

The case of Bagot *v.* Orr, 2 Bos. & Pul. 472, turned upon two points; 1st, whether the subjects of the realm had a general Common law right to catch and take *shell-fish* on the sea-shore, *between the flux and reflux of the tides?* [187] 2dly, Whether the subjects of the realm had a general Common law right of digging, collecting, and carrying away for use sea *shells*, and, by consequence, any other portion of the *soil* of the sea-shore? It was an action of trespass, brought by Bagot against the defendant Orr. The first count was, the breaking and entering the plaintiff's closes, called &c. [names] *and the sea-shore* in the parish of Keysham, and plaintiff's *shell-fish* and *shells* there finding, catching, taking and carrying away, and converting and disposing thereof to defendant's own use. The second count was for breaking and entering the same closes, and with defendant's feet, and the feet of his servants, in walking, treading up, trampling upon, subverting and spoiling plaintiff's soil, earth, and sand, and with the feet of cattle, and with the wheels of carriages, and the keels of boats treading up, trampling, &c.; and the plaintiff's *shell-fish* and *shells* breaking, crushing, and destroying, and with spades, &c. digging and making holes, pits, and turning up, &c. plaintiff's earth, soil, and sand, and digging up, raising up, and getting up divers large quantities of plaintiff's *shell-fish* and *shells*, and

(*f*) [It has been held in America that there is a public right to dig for shell-fish in a part of the shore which had become private property: Peck *v.* Lockwood, 5 Day (Conn.) R. 22. And there is a common right, in legal presumption, to take shell-fish on the shore between high and low water mark. Martin *v.* Waddell, 16 Peters (U.S.) R. 367; Arnold *v.* Munday, 1 Halst. (N.J.) R. 1; Fleet *v.* Hegeman, 14 Wend. (N.Y.) R. 42; Corfield *v.* Coryell, 4 Wash. (Cir. Co.) R. 371; Parker *v.* Cutler, Mill Dam Corp., 20 App. (Me.) R. 353; Hall *v.* Whillis, 14 Sc. Sess. Cas. 2nd ser. 324; Angell on Watercourses, p. 73; and Angell on Tide Waters, 135.]

carrying away the same, and converting and disposing thereof to defendant's own use. There were several other counts for breaking and entering plaintiff's *several fishery*, and his *free fishery;* on which issues in fact were joined. The defendant pleaded, 1st, the general issue. 2dly, as to the trespasses mentioned in the two first counts, that the closes therein severally mentioned were the same, and that the said closes in which, &c. at the said several times when, &c. were and still are, and from time immemorial have been, *parcel of a certain arm of the sea*, in which every subject of this realm, at the said several times when, &c. of right had, and of right ought to have had, and now hath, and of right ought to have, the liberty and privilege of *fishing*, and catching, digging for, raising, [188] getting, taking, and carrying away *shell-fish* and *shells* there, and therefore, defendant being a subject of this realm, at the said several times when, &c. entered into the said closes in which, &c. so being part and parcel of the said arm of the sea, to fish therein, and to catch, dig for, raise, get, take and carry away the *shell-fish* and *shells* there, and did then and there fish, and caught, took, and carried away the said *shell-fish* and *shells* in the second count lastly mentioned, as it was lawful for him to do, and for the digging up and carrying away of the said *shell-fish*, he entered the said closes in which, &c. by himself and with other persons, and with the said cattle, carts, waggons, and other carriages, and with the said boats, lighters, and other vessels, the same being reasonable, and proper, and necessary in that behalf, and in so doing, he necessarily, and unavoidably, with his feet, &c. in walking, a little trod up, &c. the earth and sand in the second count mentioned, and with the feet of the said cattle, &c. a little trod up, &c. other the soil of plaintiff's last-mentioned closes, and the said *shell-fish* and *shells*, in the second count first mentioned, necessarily and unavoidably a little broke, crushed, and destroyed, and with the said spades, &c. the same being useful, proper, and necessary in that behalf; and in digging up, raising, and getting the said *shell-fish* and *shells*, in the second count lastly men-

tioned, necessarily and unavoidably made the said holes, and pits, in plaintiff's said closes, and necessarily and unavoidably with the spades, &c. dug up, &c. a little of the earth, soil, and sand, in the said closes, doing as little damage on that occasion as he could, which are the same &c. whereof, &c. and this, &c. whereof, &c. Upon this the plaintiff new assigned, alleging that defendant, on the days in the first count mentioned, broke and entered plaintiff's closes in the first count mentioned, "being certain "closes lying *between the flux and reflux of the tides of the* "*sea*, in plaintiff's manor of Keysham, (*g*) and the said [189]
"*shell-fish* and *shells* there found, caught, took, and carried "away, and converted and disposed thereof when the same "closes in which, &c. were left dry, and not covered with "water." And also that defendant, on the days and in the manner in the second count mentioned, broke and entered into plaintiff's closes, being certain closes lying between the flux and reflux of the tides of the sea, within plaintiff's said manor of Keysham, and with his feet, &c. trod up, &c. the earth, soil, and sand in the second count mentioned, and with the feet of the said cattle, &c. trod up the said other soil in plaintiff's last-mentioned closes, in the said second count mentioned, and plaintiff's said other *shell-fish* and *shells*, in the second count mentioned, broke, crushed, &c. and with spades, &c. dug and made holes, &c. and raised up, and got up the said *shell-fish* and *shells*, &c. and took and carried away the same, and converted and disposed thereof, &c. when the said last-mentioned closes in which, &c. were left dry, and were not covered with water, as plaintiff in the first and second counts of the said declaration complained against him, which several trespasses so above new assigned are other and different trespasses, &c. wherefore, &c. To the new assignment the defendant pleaded, first, the general issue; secondly, that the said closes, first above newly assigned, and the several closes secondly above newly assigned are, and at the several times, &c. were the same closes, and not other or different closes, and are, and

(*g*) Thereby *claiming* the shore as parcel of the manor; but whether this claim was well founded, or not, was not in evidence, nor disputed.

at those times when, &c. *were certain rocks and sands of the sea;* lying within the *flux and reflux* of the tides of the sea; and that the said *shell-fish* and *shells* in the said closes, &c. were certain *shell-fish* and *fish-shells* which, at the said several times when, &c. were in and upon the said rocks [190] and sands of the sea, and which but a little before the said times when, &c. were by the ebbing of the tides of the sea, left there in and upon the said closes in which, &c. and that in the said closes in the said declaration mentioned, *every subject of this realm*, at the said several times when, &c. of right had, and of right ought, &c. the liberty and privilege of getting, taking, and carrying away the *shell-fish* and *fish-shells* left by the said ebbing of the tides of the sea, in and upon the said closes in which, &c. wherefore the defendant, being a subject of this realm, at the said several times when, &c. entered into the said closes in which, &c. to get, take, and carry away the *shell-fish* and *fish-shells* left by the ebbing of the tides of the sea, in and upon the said closes in which, &c. and then and there got, took, and carried away, the said *shell-fish* and *shells*, in the said first count mentioned, and also got, and for that purpose, with spades, &c. necessarily dug up and raised up, and took and carried away, the other *shell-fish* and *shells* in the second count lastly mentioned, and for the getting, taking and carrying away of the said *shell-fish* and *shells*, the defendant, at the said times when, &c. entered the said closes in which, &c. as it was lawful for him to do, by himself and with other persons, and with the said cattle, carts, &c. and the said boats, &c. the same being reasonable and proper and necessary in that behalf, and in so doing he necessarily and unavoidably, &c. broke, crushed, and destroyed, and with the said spades, &c. dug up, &c. a little of the said earth, soil, and sand, in the said closes, as it was lawful for him to do, for the causes aforesaid, doing as little damage on that occasion as he could, which are the same, &c. whereof, &c. and this, &c. wherefore, &c. To this plea there was a replication traversing the right of every subject to take *shell-fish* and *shells*, and a special demurrer thereto, because it traversed matter of law; but the Court seeming to think that the replication was clearly bad, it was abandoned by the plaintiff's counsel, who relied upon objections to the plea. [191]

It appears that the plaintiff asserted the said closes "were lying *within the flux and reflux of the sea*, WITHIN "the plaintiff's manor;" and his *ownership* of these closes (being part of the sea-shore) *was not disputed*. In virtue of this ownership, he (Bagot) denied the right of the defendant (Orr) to catch *shell-fish*, and also his right to carry away for use sea *shells*. The Report says, "the Court were "of opinion that, if the plaintiff had it in his power to "abridge the Common law right of the subject to the *shell-"fish*, he should have replied that matter specially; and "that not having done so, the defendant must succeed "upon his plea, as far as related to the taking of the *fish;* "but observed that, as no authority had been cited to sup-"port his claim to take *shells*, they should *pause* before they "established a general right of that kind."

Remarks upon the case of Bagot *v.* Orr.

Judgment of the Court.

It is to be regretted that a fuller report of the judgment in this case has not been given (if more was said); but it seems to be understood, that the Court affirmed the general Common law right of the subject to take or catch "*shell-"fish*," but doubted whether any such general Common law right existed for the subject to take *shells;* meaning, it is presumed, shells of fish destroyed by natural causes before capture, and not the shells of the shell-fish caught by the fishermen, otherwise the decision would have much of the character and effect of that recorded in the "Merchant of "Venice."

With regard to the catching of *shell-fish* on the sea-shore, it would seem to constitute an integral part of the public *common of piscary*, and to be subject only to the same occasional exclusion, by a prescriptive *several* fishery, as the public fishery in the sea itself, and creeks and arms thereof, or tide-rivers, is in some places liable to. The fishery for lobsters, crabs, prawns, shrimps, oysters, and various other [192] shell-fish, besides certain other kinds of fish, such as eels, &c. is carried on in every fishing village on the coast, and is one very useful and valuable branch of the fishing trade. The catch of these fish is, therefore, part of the public com-

The catching and taking shell-fish on the shore is of common right.

mon of piscary, however the fisheries may be regulated (as many are) by act of parliament. Acts of parliament for the regulation of the fisheries are very numerous, and would form a large volume in themselves; and they regulate, in many instances, private as well as public fisheries. But such acts of regulation do not concern the ownership of the soil. The *oyster* fisheries are especially subject to the most jealous enactments, and many of them belong to private owners, or to corporations. (*h*) But whether to one indi-
[193] vidual, or to a corporate body, it would seem that the title

(*h*) [In an action of trespass, quare clausum, &c., the defendant justified an entry for the purpose of taking oyster spawn in the locus in quo, being a public navigable river, the plea must shew that he took it under circumstances, that made the taking legal within the provisions of the several acts for its preservation: Maldon, Mayor of, *v.* Woolnet, 12 Ad. & E. 13. But the person who is entitled to fish for oysters is not now restricted from taking the spawn: see Bridger *v.* Richardson, 2 M. & S. 568. The statute therein cited has been repealed by 24 & 25 Vict. c. 109, sect. 39.

[By the Oyster and Mussel Fisheries Act, 29 & 30 Vict. c. 85, the Board of Trade may make a provisional order for an oyster fishery, on application by a memorial in that behalf, under certain conditions contained therein, but not for a longer period at once than sixty years; and where any portion of the sea-shore proposed to be comprised in the order belongs to the Crown, in right of the Crown, or forms part of the possessions of the Duchy of Lancaster or Cornwall, the consent, respectively, of the commissioners, the Chancellor of the Duchy of Lancaster, and the Duke of Cornwall, or other person empowered to dispose of the lands, must first be obtained. See also 30 Vict. c. 18; 31 & 32 Vict. c. 45; and 32 & 33 Vict. c. 31.

[The salmon fishings in the open sea around the coast of Scotland, unless parted with by grant, belong exclusively to the Crown, and form part of its hereditary revenue. This right of the Crown is not merely a right of fishing for salmon, but "a right to the salmon fishings "around the sea-coast of Scotland; it is not to be regarded simply as "an attribute of sovereignty, but rather as a patrimonium, a beneficial
[193] "interest constituting part of the regal hereditary property." Salmon fishings in the open sea around the coast of Scotland may not only become the subject of a royal grant, but they may be feudalized; the assertion that the sea is common to all, and that there can be no appropriation of it, except where it adjoins the shore, is an erroneous assertion: Gammell *v.* Commissioners Woods and Forests, 3 Macq. H. L. 419; see also the Salmon Fishery Acts.]

to such exclusive privilege must be supported, as against the *prima facie* public right, by the same kind of evidence as already mentioned in regard to a private fishery in the sea and tide rivers, viz.—grant from the Crown, or prescription. There is no distinction (in regard to the nature of evidence required to substantiate the right of a corporation) between a *separate fishery* claimed by a corporate body, or by one individual. The same remark applies to the ownership of the *soil* itself of the sea-shore in corporate bodies, or in individuals. It has already been contended, that the ownership of the soil of the shore does not necessarily confer a right to a several fishery, nor a right to a several fishery necessarily confer the ownership of the shore. Although, in regard to the latter, the cases incline to annex the soil to the ownership of a several fishery. But the *onus* of proof lies upon the individual, or corporate body, who would claim the exclusive right of fishery against the *general* Common law right of all the King's subjects to catch shell and other fish upon the sea-shore, as well as in the sea itself.

Now, if this be good law, and the King's subjects have a general Common law right of frequenting the shore (whether belonging to a lord of a manor or not, and so that there be no prescriptive several fishery) "on foot and with cattle, "carts, and carriages," for the purpose of catching these kinds of fish, there can be no doubt that the shore is a highway for fishing at least, as public as the sea itself. No part of the shore, from the extremest lines of the flood [194] and ebb tides, can be free from public use and resort for the fishery. The shore is, in this sense, part and parcel of the sea, and although an ownership is more frequently claimed in the shore by grant from the King, than in the sea itself; yet, as it was in the Crown as part of the sea, so it is granted to the subject as part of the sea, and therefore liable to the public common of piscary.

As to the public right to dig for shells, sand, &c. on the shore.

With regard to the question of right to dig for shells, &c., a technical distinction is to be noted between a mere right of egress and regress, or *way*, and a right to dig and take away the soil. The first is, in law, a mere *liberty*, or *ease-*

Distinction between easements and *profits-a-prendre.*

ment; but the carrying away the soil is called a *profit-a-prendre*, being the conversion of the soil into profit; the one takes more of the substance from the owner of soil than the other, and diminishes the value of the ownership of the soil in proportion. Blackstone, J., in his Commentaries, (*i*) after stating that "common" is "a profit which one man "hath in the land of another," and after describing the commons of pasture, piscary, and turbary, adds, "there is "also a common of digging for coals, minerals, stones, and "the like, all these bear a resemblance to common of pas- "ture in many respects; though in one point they go much "farther—common of pasture being only a right of feeding "on the *herbage* and *vesture* of the soil, which renews an- "nually; but common of turbary, and those afore men- "tioned are a right of carrying away the *very soil* itself." Nevertheless, a right to pasture cattle on the lord's common waste, and a right to dig turves or marl, are both *technically* the same, viz. *profits-a-prendre;* but a right of *way* over the soil is a mere *liberty* or *easement.* It is clear, however, that the subjects of the realm may enjoy
[195] a *profit-a-prendre* by general right, as well as an easement, because the public right of fishing is a profit-a-prendre. (*k*)

As to taking *profits-a-prendre* in the wastes of inland manors.

Now as the treatise ascribed to Lord Hale has compared the "great waste" of the sea (of which the shore is part) to the waste lands of a manor, it will be well to explain the point in question by shewing, that the wastes of a manor may be, and often are, subject to rights similar to that of digging and carrying away the materials of the "sea-shore;" and then to inquire how such right ought to be supported (if the point be not yet settled *contra*) in regard to the sea-shore, as well as inland manorial wastes. It must be remembered, however, that manorial customs are *local* and not *general* rights. Thus a copyhold tenant of an inland manor may dig for marl for manure, and for

(*i*) Vol. ii. p. 34.

(*k*) (On the ground that it is for the sustenance of man and the benefit of the commonweal, and not solely for the profit of the individal: see Mayor of Lynn *v.* Taylor, 3 Levinz 160.—ED.)

turf for fuel.(*l*) So he may dig for gravel and sand,(*m*) and notwithstanding these acts of the copyholder, the soil and freehold of the waste is in the lord of the manor. But these are local customs of the manor, and in some manors do not at all exist.

They are analogous to digging for shells, &c. on the shore.

The cases referred to in favour of taking sand and stones, &c. in an inland waste of a manor, which were expressly stated to be for building and repairs, and the case of taking marl for manure, are perfectly analogous to the uses to which the soil of the sea-shore is most capable of being applied, and which, together with the fishing and navigation, constitute its essential value. Since, then, the custom or usage to dig and carry away for use the materials of the soil of another in *inland* titles is (as a local custom) well known and admitted, the question remains, whether a custom to dig shells, or sand, or stones, &c. on the sea-shore, which shore is either owned by the King, or by the lord of the manor adjacent, can be claimed and [196] maintained as a *local* custom? or, if not, then whether as a *general* custom for all the subjects of the realm? (*n*)

As to the right of taking shells, &c. on the shore by *local* custom.

First, can it be claimed as a *local* custom or usage? for, if it can, *that* will be inconsistent with a *general* custom. As a local custom it must be claimed by the parties, either as *tenants* of the adjacent manor, under the manorial custom, and as if the *shore* were part and parcel of the *wastes* of the manor, and therefore within the manor; or it must

(*l*) Gilb. Ten. 327; 2 Atk. 189; [Hall's Profit à Prendre, p. 316.]

(*m*) Duberly *v.* Page, 2 T. R. 391; Shakspear *v.* Peppin, 6 T. R. 741. [See Hall's Profit à Prendre, p. 316.]

(*n*) (In considering these propositions, it must be recollected that the right of tenants of a manor to *profits à prendre* out of the wastes by custom is in all cases limited to this, that these profits are to be expended upon the tenement held of the manor, and that they arise out of contract and bargain between the tenant and the lord, and are for their mutual benefit. The public, between whom and the Crown, or between whom and the lord of the manor, no such relation exists, can have no such title to a *profit à prendre*, for the advantage would be all on one side and the loss all on the other, and manors the subject-matter of the profit would be liable to be absolutely destroyed: Race *v.* Ward, 4 E. & B 702.—ED.)

be claimed by them as "*inhabitants*" of the adjacent hamlet, town, parish, hundred, or county. If it be claimed in right of the manorial customs, the "sea-shore" of the *locus in quo* must be admitted or proved to be part and parcel of the waste lands of the manor. As waste of the manor, the shore, it is conceived, *may* be subject to such commons as waste lands in inland manors are usually subject to; and all that will be necessary in such case will be, to prove the usage or right of *common-à-prendre* by the usual evidence resorted to in the case of similar claims in inland manors. But if, from circumstances, the claimant cannot support such right by the custom of the manor, either because he is no tenant, or because the shore does not appear to be within the manor, in such case he must support his right as an "inhabitant" of the adjacent hamlet, vill, parish, hundred, or county, which is also a *local* claim; or, lastly, as a subject of the realm, which is a public and *general* claim. Neither the local claim, as "inhabitants of "the adjacent hamlet," &c., nor the general right make it *necessary* that the "shore" should be *extra manerium*. Whether it be or be not within the manor, it *may* yet be subject either to a *local* or to a *general* right. (*o*)

(*o*) [A custom for all the inhabitants of a parish to angle, and catch fish in the locus in quo is bad: Lloyd *v.* Jones, 6 C. B. 81, S. C. 17 L. J. C. P. 206; Bland *v.* Lipscomb, 24 L. J. Q. B. 155 n. And a similar
[197] custom to take shingle, &c. from the sea-shore above high-water mark is void, because it is a claim to take a profit in alieno solo: Pitts *v.* Kingsbridge Highway Board, 19 W. R. 884. See Constable *v.* Nicholson, 32 L. J. C. P. 240, S. C. 14 C. B. N. S. 230; Blewitt *v.* Tregoning, 3 A. & E. 554; Race *v.* Ward, 4 E. & B. 702; Post *v.* Pearsall, 22 Wend. (N.Y.) R. 425; Perley *v.* Langley, 7 N. Hamp. 233; Sale *v.* Pratt, 36 Mass. (Pick.) R. 191; Angell on Watercourses, p. 71; Angell on Tide Waters, 273. (Cases where a *profit à prendre* has been held bad for inhabitants or any uncertain class of persons:—Common of pasture: Grinstead *v.* Marlowe, 4 T. R. 717; Gateward's Case, 6 Rep. 59 b; Weekly *v.* Wildman, 1 Lord Raym. 405; Austin *v.* Amhurst, 7 Ch. D. 690. To cut boughs: Selby *v.* Robinson, 2 T. R 758; Chilton *v.* Corp. of London, 7 Ch. D. 735. To take litter in a forest: De la Warr *v.* Miles, 17 Ch. D. 535. To take fuel: Lord Rivers *v.* Adams, 3 Ex. D. 361. Tenants of manor to fish in water in the wastes: Allgood *v.* Gibson, 34 L. T. 883. To take

There is, however, a distinction taken at law, between "inhabitants" of a particular place or district, and "owners" of estates or tenements in such place or district, as to making title by prescription to these kind of [197] Distinction between prescription in the *que* estate,

seaweed: Howe *v.* Stawell, 1 Alc. & Nap. 348; Hamilton *v.* Att. for Ireland, 5 L. R. Ir. 555. To take sea-shells: Bagot *v.* Orr, 2 Bos. & Pul. 472. The only case of which the Editor is aware that seems to recognise any right in the public to take material from the shore is Corp. of Lynn *v.* Taylor, 3 Levinz 160, where a custom for freemen and proprietors of ships to take ballast on the common shore at Lynn was held good on the special ground that it was "for the maintenance "of navigation, and so *pro bono publico*, and custom is a *lex loci* and "inherent in the soil whereto it is fixed for the service of every one "that is qualified to use it." But even here it is distinctly limited to a class, and described as a *lex loci.*—Ed.)

[A profit à prendre in another's soil cannot be claimed by custom, however ancient, uniform, and clear the exercises of that custom may be; neither can a right to carry away the soil of another, without stint, be claimed by prescription, for a prescription to be good must both be reasonable and certain: Att.-Gen. *v.* Mathias, 27 L. J. Ch. 761, S. C. 6 W. R. 780, 4 K. & J. 579. The Court of Queen's Bench, in Rogers *v.* Brenton, 10 Q. B. Rep. 26, S. C. 17 L. J. Q. B. 34, expressed an extra-judicial opinion that the custom of tin bounding in Cornwall, which involves the taking of a profit in alieno solo, might have been good, if coupled with an obligation to work; but assuming, says Byles, J., in Att.-Gen. *v.* Mathias, *supra*, "that opinion to be correct, I "am not aware that it has ever been extended to any other case," and so difficult did the learned counsel for the plaintiff feel their position to be, that they desired to treat the custom which they were bound to support as the lex loci of a province. See Macnamara *v.* Higgins, 4 Ir. Com. Law R. 326.

[In Padwick *v.* Knight and others, 7 Ex. 854, it was held that a surveyor of highways cannot justify a trespass under a prescriptive right, or a custom to take stones from the waste, whether adjoining the seashore between high and low water mark, or otherwise, for the purpose of repairing the highways of the parish, but assuming such a prescription is good, it ought to be pleaded as an immemorial custom for the inhabitants of the parish to take stones from the waste for the purpose of repairing the highways, averring the surveyors were two of the inhabitants, as was done in Johnson *v.* Wyard, 2 Lutw. 1344. A person who pays highway-rate within a parish is not rendered a competent witness, by the 54 Geo. 3, c. 170, s. 9, upon the trial of an issue whether within that parish there is a custom, that all persons residing therein, whose duty it is to cause the highways within the parish to be repaired, may take shingle from the sea-beach for the purpose of such repair, [198] and as an "inhabitant."

customs. In the *latter* case, the custom is, as it were, attached to the *estate*, and the owner claims in respect
[198] of his estate; but in the *other* case it is merely *personal*, claimed in a personal character, as an "inhabitant." Lord Coke (*p*) lays it down, that a custom, such as gavel-kind or borough-english, cannot be alleged in an upland town, (*q*) but such town may allege a custom to have a way, or to well order commons, &c. "But," he adds, "in special cases, a custom may be alleged within a "hamlet, or town, or burgh, or city, manor, an honor, an "hundred, and a county." It is said, in Vin. Abr. tit. "prescription," (*r*) that "inhabitants, *unless incorporated*, "cannot prescribe to have any *profit* in the *soil* of another;
[199] "but in matters of *easement* only, as in a *way*, &c., but not

the custom not being a matter relating to ratio or cesses within the meaning of the Act: Oxenden *v.* Palmer, 2 B. & Ad. 236. See also remarks of Erle, C.J., in Le Strange *v.* Rowe, 4 F. & F. 1048.

[In the case of Constable *v.* Nicholson, 14 C. B. N. S. 230, the pleas claiming a right in the inhabitants to take the gravel, &c. to be used for the cultivation of their land, and in the parish officers for the necessary repairs of the highway, were all held bad; for that, so far as they were capable of being construed as justifying under such a custom, such custom would be void, being a claim of a profit à prendre in alieno solo, which can only exist by grant or prescription; and if the claim be founded on prescription it would be equally bad, inasmuch as it was a claim by persons who, not being a corporation, were incapable of taking by grant and not being claimed in a *que* estate. See also Dyce *v.* Lady James Hay, 1 McQueen H. L. 305.

[By sect. 52 of the Highway Act, 5 & 6 Wm. 4, c. 50, materials are not allowed to be taken away from the shore for the repair of highways, where any danger of an encroachment by the sea will be increased by such removal: see Pitts *v.* Kingsbridge Board, *supra*. As to the relief equity affords by injunction, see Clowes *v.* Beck, 13 Beav. 347; Chalk *v.* Wyatt, 3 Meriv. 688; Earl Cowper *v.* Baker, 17 Ves. 128; Youl on Waste, 186, 189.

[As to the removal of shingle from the shore or bank of a port or harbour, see Nicholson *v.* Williams, L. R. 6 Q. B. 632. It has been held that a grant by the Crown, to a class of persons previously unincorporated, of a profit à prendre to be taken out of the Crown's soil is valid: Willingale *v.* Maitland, L. R. 3 Eq. 103, S. C. 36 L. J. Ch. 64.]

(*p*) 1 Inst. 110 b.

(*q*) *i.e.* A town not having the privileges of a borough or corporation.

(*r*) Vin. Abr. tit. Prescription a.

"in matters of interest." Cro. Jac. 152, and Gateward's case (*s*) are cited.

This case is a leading case on the subject of pleading, alleging, or prescribing for customs. The point in the case was a common of pasture, claimed by the defendant in a close of land belonging to the plaintiff, as a customary right enjoyed time out of mind by the *inhabitants* dwelling and residing in an ancient messuage, in the ancient town of Stixwold, adjoining to the close. "It was resolved, that "the custom was against law, for several reasons. 1. There "are but four manner of commons, *i.e.* common appendant, "appurtenant, in gross, and by reason of vicinage: and this "common, *ratione commorant'*, and resident', is none of "them; and *argumentum a divisione est fortissimum in jure.* "2. What estate shall he who is 'inhabitant' have in the "common, when it appears he hath no estate or interest in "the house (but a mere habitation and dwelling), in respect "of which he ought to have his common? for none can have "interest in common in respect of a house in which he hath "no interest. 3. Such custom will be transitory, and alto- "gether uncertain; for it will follow the person, and for no "certain time or estate, but during his *inhabitancy*, and such "manner of interest the law will not suffer, for custom ought "to extend to that which hath certainty and continuance. "4. It will be against the nature and quality of a common, "for every common may be suspended or extinguished, but "such a common will be so incident to the person, that no "person certain can extinguish it, but as soon as he who "releases, &c. removes, the new inhabitant shall have it. "5. If the law should allow such common, the law would "give an action or remedy for it; but he who claims as an "'inhabitant' can have no action for it. 6. In these words "'inhabitants' and 'residents' are included tenant in fee [200] "simple, tenant for life, for years, tenant by elegit, &c. "tenant at will, &c., and he who hath no interest but only "his habitation and dwelling; and by the rule of all our "books, without question, tenant in fee-simple ought to

Gateward's case. Prescription for a *profit-a-prendre* by "inhabitants," not good.

By whom a *profit-a-prendre* may be prescribed for.

(*s*) 6 Rep. 59. [See Macnamara *v.* Higgins, 4 Ir. Com. Law R. 326, and Hall's Profit à Prendre, 162 *et seq.*]

Gateward's case.

"prescribe in his own name, tenant for life, years, by elegit, "&c., and at will, &c., in the name of him who hath the fee; "and as he who hath no interest can have no common, so "none that hath no interest, if he be but at will, ought to "have common, but by good pleading he may enjoy it. "7. No improvements can be made in any wastes, if such "common [custom] should be allowed; for the tenants for "life, for years, at will, tenant by elegit, statute staple, and "statute merchant of houses of the lord himself, would have "common in the wastes of the lord himself, if such prescrip- "tion should be allowed, which would be inconvenient. But "two differences were taken and agreed by the whole Court. "1. Between a charge in the soil of another, and a discharge "in his own soil. 2. Between an *interest* or *profit* to be taken "or had in another soil, and an *easement* in another's soil; "and, therefore, a custom that every inhabitant of a town "hath paid a *modus decimandi* to the parson in discharge of "their tithes, is good; for they claim not a charge or *profit-à-* "*prendre* in the soil of another, but a discharge in their own "land. So of a custom, that every inhabitant of such a town "shall have a *way* over such land, either to the church or "market, &c., *that* is good, for it is but an easement, and no "profit; and a way or passage may well follow the person, "and no such inconvenience as in the case at bar. 8. It was "resolved, that copyholders in fee, or for life, may, by custom "of the manor, have common in the demesnes [wastes] of the "lord of the manor, but then they ought to allege the custom "of the manor to be '*quod quilibet tenens customarius cujus-* "'*libet antiqui messuagii customar,*' &c., and not '*quod qui-*

[201] "'*libet inhabitans infra aliquod antiquum messuagium cus-* "'*tomar,*' &c. For a copyholder hath a customary interest "in the house, &c., and therefore he may have a customary "common in the lord's wastes; and in such case he cannot "prescribe in the name of the lord, for the lord cannot claim "common in his own soil, and, therefore, of necessity such "custom ought to be alleged. Vide 21 E. 3, 34, Foiston's "case, 4 Rep. 31, 32.(*t*) Another difference was taken and

But "inhabitants" may prescribe for easements.

(*t*) [See Dunstan *v.* Tresider, 5 T. R. 2, and Barwick *v.* Matthews, 5 Taunton 365.]

" agreed, between a *prescription*, which is always alleged in " the *person*, and a *custom*, which always ought to be alleged " in the land; for every prescription ought to have, by " common intendment, a lawful beginning, but otherwise it is " of a custom, for that ought to be reasonable, and *ex certâ* " *causâ rationabili* (as Littleton saith) *usitata*, but need not " be intended to have a lawful beginning, as custom to have " land devisable, or of the nature of gavel-kind, or borough-" english, &c. These, and the like customs, are reasonable, " but by common intendment they cannot have a lawful " beginning by grant, or act, or agreement, but only by " Parliament. See also, for this matter, Foiston's case. Also " it was agreed, that the custom of a manor that *dominus pro* " *tempore* shall grant lands customary, is good, and tenant at " will may do it; and so 20 H. 6, 8, b. by the custom of the " Court of Common Pleas, the Chief Justice grants divers " offices for life, and these customs are good; but, in such " cases, he who grants them hath an interest in the manor or " office, and their grant is made good by the custom; and " 19 R. 2, action sur le case, 52, a beadle of the hundred " shall have three flagons of beer of every brewer who sells " within the hundred, *causâ quâ supra*. But a custom, that " an *inhabitant* or 'resident' shall grant or take any profit, " is merely void. 9. It was resolved, that if the custom had " been alleged, that *quilibet paterfamilias infra aliquod anti-* [202] " *quum messuag'*, &c., it would also be insufficient for the " causes and reasons aforesaid; and if he hath any interest " he may be relieved as aforesaid. Vide reported by Spel-" man that such custom is not warranted by law, and so it " was adjudged in this Court. Trin. 33 Eliz. Rot. 422. " See the Book of Entries, Trespass, Common, 6. Vide 9 " H. 6, 62 b, 7 E. 6, Dyer, 70, Iseham's case."(*u*)

Grimstead *v.* Marlowe.

The case of Grimstead *v.* Marlowe(*x*) follows Gateward's case; and it is there laid down by Lord Kenyon, that a

(*u*) [See Lloyd *v.* Jones, 6 C. B. 81; Bland *v.* Lipscombe, 4 E. & B. 713 n.; Hudson *v.* McRae, 4 B. & S. 585; Att.-Gen. *v.* Mathias, 4 K. & J. 579, S. C. 27 L. J. Ch. 761; Waters *v.* Lilley, 21 Mass. (Pick.) R. 145.]

(*x*) 4 T. R. 717.

man must prescribe in a *que estate* for a *profit-a-prendre*, which a mere "inhabitant" or "resident" cannot do; and it seems settled, that where an *inhabitant of a town* would claim a *profit-a-prendre*, he must prescribe that "he and all "those whose *estate* he hath in his house have used to have "common," &c., as in Mellor *v.* Spateman, 1 Saund. 339, 343. (*y*)

Grimstead *v.* Marlowe. Mere "habitancy" not sufficient to support a plea for a *profit-a-prendre.*

The case of Grimstead *v.* Marlowe (*z*) was a right of common of pasture, claimed by an inhabitant of the parish of Leatherhead. It was pleaded in virtue of a custom, "that every 'inhabitant' occupying, residing, and dwelling "in any ancient messuage or tenement within the parish of "Leatherhead, for the time being, &c., had been used and "accustomed," &c. But the Court held that such plea was bad, because it was a *profit-a-prendre*, which could not be pleaded but in a *que estate*: here the plea was mere *habit-*
[203] *ancy*, or occupancy, not ownership; but the Court did not object to its being prescribed for by the party, "that he "and all those whose estate he hath, &c., in his house" had enjoyed such *profit-a-prendre*, and gave him leave to amend accordingly. Here it is to be observed that no distinction was taken that he could not (if he would) prescribe in a *que estate* in a parish or town, in contradistinction to a borough, or city, or county, inasmuch as the prescription, in such case, would be in respect of the *estate* he had in his tenement, and not in respect of its being in this or that place. It was immaterial where the *que estate* was situated, provided he could establish his prescription by the usual proofs, "that he and all those who owned, or had owned before "him that *estate*, had been used to have the *profit-a-prendre* "in question." (*a*)

How the custom to dig shells,

It would seem therefore that every one who would claim a *local* custom or usage to dig marl or sand, &c. in *inland*

(*y*) [See Lockwood *v.* Wood, 6 Q. B. 50; Post *v.* Pearsall, 22 Wend. (N.Y.) R. 425.]

(*z*) 4 T. R. 717. See also Weekly *v.* Wildman, 1 Ld. Raym. 405, and Selby *v.* Robinson, 2 T. R. 758; Rogers *v.* Brenton, 10 Q. B. 26.

(*a*) [McFarlin *v.* Essex County, 64 Mass. (Cush.) R. 310; Melvin *v.* Whiting, 24 Mass. (Pick.) R. 79, S. C. 30 Mass. (Pick.) R. 184.]

manors must (on account of its being a *profit-a-prendre*) plead in the *que estate*,(*b*) *i.e.* in respect of his interest in the tenement which he holds ; which prescription, however, must be laid in the person of him who is *seized in fee-simple*, and not in the person of one who holds any lesser interest ; who is not, in the eye of the law, owner of the estate. But tenant for life, for years, or at will, may prescribe in the name of the tenant in fee-simple. A copyholder is allowed to prescribe in his *own* estate for the reason given in Gateward's case. Thus far, however, seems clear, that by due form of pleading, in respect of his ancient tenement situate within a town, and by consequence, in other *loci* known to the law, as honors, manors (parishes), hundreds, boroughs, and counties, all these persons before named may, by [204] good evidence of immemorial usage, substantiate such *profits-a-prendre* as before mentioned. (*c*)

&c. must be prescribed for as a local custom.

Such being the law in regard to *profits-a-prendre* in *inland* titles, there would seem to be no objection in law to prevent the owners, or their lessees, of any ancient tenement in any such district or place before named, *situate on the coast* (as the defendant Orr in the case in question), from pleading in the *que estate*, and prescribing for a customary right or usage of taking shells, sand, or other portions of the soil of the *shore*, and if supported by the usual evidence, making good such local usage. There would seem to be no *technical* reason why this might not be done, in respect of the " great waste " of the sea-shore, where the party has an ancient tenement on the coast, as well as in respect of inland wastes.

Whether the Courts would permit any such customary

(*b*) [Waters *v.* Lilley, 21 Mass. (Pick.) R. 145; Perley *v.* Langley, 7 N. Hamp. R. 233; Sale *v.* Pratt, 36 Mass. (Pick.) R. 191.]

(*c*) (Provided they shew either a nexus of tenure between them and the owner of the waste, or a corporate capacity of such a nature that they could have been a corporation capable of taking a grant from a person capable of making it, or that the waste in question can be presumed to be held by the owner thereof subject to a trust for such a limited and ascertainable class as could have had an equitable interest in the profit : Chilton *v.* Corp. of London, L. R. 7 Ch. D. 735 ; Goodman *v.* Mayor of Saltash, 7 App. 633.—ED.)

Whether, as a local custom, the digging of shells, &c. can be prescribed for by "inhabitants." Quære?

profit, derivable from the *sea-shore*, to be pleaded as a *local* custom, *without* the *que estate*, *i.e.* as "easements" are pleaded, does not seem to have been ever mooted. The reasons given in Gateward's case would seem to preclude any such proposition; at least where the "shore" is part of the manor, and in the lord's ownership. Where the shore is not within the manor it is the property of the Crown, and whether, as such, it will admit of a different form of laying the local custom or profit in question, viz. in the *person* as "inhabitant," does not appear. It is concluded that it will not; but it is remarkable that the men of Devon and Cornwall have immemorially (*d*) enjoyed the custom of taking the *soil* of the shores of those counties for use, either in the character of "*dwellers*" and "*inhabitants*" *locally*, or else by the *general* Common law right, and not in the *que estate*. For this appears from the preamble of the statute, 7 Jac. 1, c. 18, reciting that, "whereas the *sea-*"*sand*, by long trial and experience, hath been found to be [205] "very profitable for the bettering of land, and especially "for the increase of corn and tillage within the counties of "Devon and Cornwall, where the most part of the *inha-*"*bitants* have not used any other worth for the bettering "of their arable grounds and pastures; notwithstanding, "divers having lands adjoining to the sea-coasts there, have "of late interrupted the *bargemen* and such others *as have* "*used of their free wills and pleasures* to fetch the said sea-"sand, to take the same *under the full sea-mark*, as they "have *heretofore* used to do;" the statute then goes on to confirm the right of "all persons whatsoever *resident* and "*dwelling* within the said counties of Devon and Cornwall, "to fetch and take sea-sand at all places under the full "sea-mark," &c.

Statute of 7 Jac. 1, c. 18, declaring the right in the "inhabitants" of Devon and Cornwall, to take sand on the shore.

Remarks on the statute.

Now this statute, it is to be observed, asserts a pre-existing(*e*) custom, commonly used by the *inhabitants*, at their free wills and pleasures, to take a *profit-a-prendre* upon the

(*d*) (See the Editor's remarks on Mr. Hall's reading of this statute *ante*, p. 769, note (*d*).—ED.)

(*e*) (Illegal practice.—ED.)

shores of the counties of Devon and Cornwall. (*f*) But if they were entitled to such custom as a local custom, *prior* to the statute, it must have been by "prescription," and a prescription *not* founded on the "*que estate*," but enjoyed as "inhabitants;" and if the "inhabitants" of the counties of Devon and Cornwall could have so claimed, at law, the profits in question, then the "inhabitants" of other countries, or districts, might set up a custom, *so pleaded*, to enjoy the like profit. It may be, and probably is the fact, that the inhabitants of other maritime counties have been used to take sand, shells, &c., for similar or equally useful purposes as those referred to in the statute of James; and yet it is evident, that unless the rule be relaxed so as to permit them to prescribe otherwise than in the *que estate*, they, the inhabitants of other counties, cannot maintain such custom [206] as a local custom, except by similar aid of Statute law, or as a general right, however it may have been heretofore acquiesced in by the King, or mesne lord of the soil, and is further recommended by its public utility. It is also manifest, that if those persons only who possess "ancient tenements" can maintain such right by pleading in the *que estate*, it will be confined to a comparatively limited number of persons, and very different from that enjoyed by the men of Devon and Cornwall. It must be allowed, however, that regarding Gateward's case as good law, it would seem to compel the Courts to put the claim to dig and use the soil, &c. of the sea-shore (if pleaded as a *local* custom) upon the same footing as an inland claim to dig, &c. in the waste of a manor, and to confine the right in question to those persons only who can plead in the *que estate*, *i.e.* who are owners of an ancient tenement on the coast. (*g*)

Whether the custom to dig for shells, &c. on the shore is of common right.

With regard to the custom as a *general right* in all the subjects of the realm, as pleaded in the principal case, it is obvious that if the Courts could support the right upon the

(*f*) (And makes that *practice* legal by force of the Act: Att. *v.* Hamilton, 5 L. R. Ir. 555; Macnamara *v.* Higgins, 4 Ir. C. L. 332, per Lefroy, C.J.—Ed.)

(*g*) [See Pitts *v.* Kingsbridge Highway Board, 19 W. R. 884.]

same footing as the public right to fish, no technical difficulties would arise as to the pleading. The defendant Orr, in the case referred to, seems to have felt the difficulty of pleading a local custom for a *profit-a-prendre* as an "inha-"bitant," and therefore grounded his case on the general right. As the Court *hesitated* before it decided on the general right, and did not use any very decisive language against it, there may perhaps be room for a further discussion of the question. The point, as regards the "sea-shore," and the public right so to use it, was *quæstio nova* in Bagot *v.* Orr.

The custom or practice is general throughout the maritime counties.

It certainly is not necessary to plead a *general* custom in the *que estate*, whether such custom be a *profit-a-prendre* or not. Looking at the general claim as *res integra*, it must [207] be admitted that there is reason to presume that the "inha-"bitants" of all the districts bordering on the sea-coasts of England, have *actually* (whether now allowed to be *lawfully* or not) been in the *habit* of resorting to the "shore" for the materials in question, for manure and other useful purposes, without asking the consent of the owner of the adjacent *terra firma;* and it would be difficult to find a cultivated and inhabited spot, on or within reasonable distance from the coast, where it has not been the practice of the inhabitants to resort to the shore for materials for manure, for ballast, for building, road mending, &c. It is the natural, if not the necessary result of their locality and wants. (*h*) It is not to be looked at as a want confined to those persons only who are *immediately* dwelling on the sea-side, but may be reasonably extended to all within convenient reach of it; to all such, in fact, as have, by a like immemorial usage, established a general right to fish. It may also be remarked, that where such general inducement exists everywhere along the coasts of England to use such materials, and yet no case is to be found *supporting* the practice as a

(*h*) Lord Hale mentions "ballastage" or a toll "for liberty to take up "ballast *out of the bottom of the port*," as a *port duty*, arising "from "the propriety of the soil," de Portibus maris, 74. Qy. As to any toll of the kind out of ports? (See Bishop of Durham *v.* Haselrig, *ante*, p. 420.—ED.)

local and limited custom, or *denying* it as a general right (if we except Bagot *v.* Orr), the presumption is in favour of it as a general custom.

In the case of Bagot *v.* Orr, after quoting the statute of James I., before noticed, the learned Counsel in favour of the right contended, (*i*) that "the statute was, in fact, a full "recognition of the right of the subject to use the shore of "the sea in every way in which it could be serviceable to "him." On the other side it was contended, that "it was "an enacting, and not a declaratory law; and that a pecu- "liar privilege is thereby granted to the men of Devon and "Cornwall, which peculiar privilege it would have been "absurd to have granted, if *all* the people of England had "been entitled thereto at Common law." The Court offered no argument upon this statute, or upon the reasoning on either side. Now, it may perhaps be insisted in favour of the public, that the statute is both a declaratory and an affirmative statute. It states a long existing usage, without throwing a doubt upon its legality, and affirms that such use shall be continued. It forbids the owner of the soil "adjoining the *coast*" to molest those who frequented the *shore* for the purposes of digging sand, &c. but allows such owners to take a reasonable toll, or composition, for the damage done, *not* to the *shore*, but to their "adjoining "grounds," and for casting sand there, and for way, passage, &c. in places where no general right of way existed to the shore. The toll was not for *digging* and *appropriating* sand, &c. *under the full sea-mark*.

Whether the statute of 7 James I., ch. 18, be declaratory of the common right or not.

[208]

There is not a word in the statute intimating a right in the owner of the land adjoining to a property in the sand, &c. itself, *under full sea-mark*. The words are, "paying "for the taking, casting out, and landing of every barge- "load of sand *upon the grounds of any man*, such duties, "&c., and for passage by and through such ways, &c., such "duties, &c. as had been used and accustomed."(*j*) There

(*i*) (See p. 769, note (*d*).—ED.) [Macnamara *v.* Higgins, 4 Ir. Com. Law, 332, per Lefroy, C.J.]

(*j*) Payments to the owner of the adjacent ground or bank, immediately above high-water mark, for *depositing* timber, stone, &c. there

[209] may have been abundance of the same materials worth taking *above* high-water mark, and the soil above high-water mark belonged to the adjoining land. The owners of the adjoining grounds, above the full sea-mark, appear to have also refused to permit sand to be heaped upon or carried over their land, which the statute, for the public good, compels them to allow ; but this does not show or prove a right in such persons to the *shore*, under the full sea-mark. The first section of the statute seems to be *declaratory* of the custom of the counties, viz. to dig and fetch away sand under full sea-mark. The second section is *remedial*, and mandatory, confirming and enforcing the *ancient custom*, and directing that the sand shall be unloaded and landed, &c. upon such adjoining places as have been used within fifty years, and be carried away by such ways as have been used within the last twenty years, saving to the owners of such places and ways, their reasonable right of toll and charge for such easements.

Here then is a customary right (*k*) of common, or *profit-a-prendre*, recognized and confirmed by statute law as belonging to all the inhabitants of Devon and Cornwall ;—not merely to the "owners of ancient tenements in their *que* "*estate*," but to all the "residents and dwellers" in those counties. It is manifest, therefore, that, according to the statute, a right of common *a-prendre* for digging sand existed, as an ancient custom, or usage, by *prescription* in two of the largest and most populous maritime counties of England. This custom *so* allowed would seem to be in opposition to the doctrine of Gateward's case, decided in the fourth year of the same reign, only three years prior to the statute, if it be regarded as a *local* custom. Therefore, in order to support the doctrine in Gateward's case,

are very common. But this is not for the *landing* the goods,—but for the use of the ground so appropriated. According to Lord Hale, de Portibus maris, 51, it was resolved, in a case he cites, that "though a "man may take amends for the *trespass* in unloading upon his ground, "yet he might not take it as a certain common toll." (Payments are equally common for using the foreshore, and the case cited by Hale appears to refer to that practice.—Ed.)

(*k*) (Practice.—Ed.)

it must be assumed (in opposition to the positive words of the statute) that no such *profit-a-prendre* existed in the in- [210] habitants of those counties prior to the statute, on the ground that such custom could not, according to law, be in "inhabitants," as such.

Gateward's case and the statute contrasted.

Yet the language of the statute certainly authorizes us to assume it to have been either a good general, or good local custom, independent of and prior to that statute; whilst Gateward's case decides that, considered merely as a *profit-a-prendre*, it could not have been a good *local* custom, *causa qua supra.* It would seem to follow, therefore, that if it could not be good as a *local* custom, it can be good *no otherwise* than as a *general* custom, in the same manner as the common of piscary in the sea and shore is a good custom (although a *profit-a-prendre*) as a general custom of the realm. That which is a good general custom of the realm, is good alike for Cornwall and Sussex, or any other maritime county. It cannot be supposed that such a custom, or such use of the shore, did not prevail as much in Dorset, Hants, or Sussex, and other maritime counties, as in Devon and Cornwall. All these were and are agricultural counties; and their farmers were then, and are now in the habit of manuring their lands, as well as the men of Devon and Cornwall; and it must be supposed knew as well the value and use of sand, or shells, or sea-weed, &c. for manure. There is every reason to believe that what the statute affirms to have been the old customary right of the Devonshire and Cornish men, was equally a practice in the other maritime counties. If so, the statute could not have set up a new, or merely local privilege.

The books are silent both ways.

But although the statute is not silent, the books certainly are; for the general right in question cannot be specifically traced in any of them, as a Common law privilege; neither is it *denied* by the books. In this view it resembles the question raised in the preceding case of Blundell *v.* Caterall, regarding the right to bathe in the sea. It also resembles [211] it, in that it is as difficult to say, that the practice of resorting to the sea-shore for materials, for the uses just mentioned, has *not* prevailed, time out of mind, throughout *all*

3 L 2

our maritime counties. In this respect, also, it resembles the public right to catch fish on the shore. In some places on the coast it would be impossible to prove that any one had *actually* been accustomed to catch shell-fish upon the "shore;" but this will not invalidate the general right. Common sense and experience entitle us to assume, that fishing on the shore is far *more* general than the *not* fishing there at all. Yet it would be difficult to say, that *shell-fish* fishing is a custom more frequent or general than the digging and taking materials from the shore for useful purposes. The presumption is in favour of *both*, as general and immemorial practices. It may reasonably be doubted, whether the men of Devon and Cornwall have not carried away from the shore as much shells, sand, &c., and from as many places, as they have carried away shell-fish. Nor would it be easy nor reasonable to contend, that the men of Dorset or Hants have not exercised, in an equal degree, these several privileges. If it be admitted that the *presumption* is in favour of it, as a general *practice*, and that the practice is a great public benefit to the agriculture of the kingdom, why should not that suffice to warrant it as a lawful public *custom?*—our *books* being *silent* alike as to the negative or affirmative of the point, but, *in general language*, favouring it.

Importance of the custom to agriculture and the general interests of the realm.

That it is a privilege very beneficial and important to the general advancement of agriculture and for other public purposes, cannot be denied: these are interests not *local* but *general.* Now it appears, that as a *local* custom it cannot be supported at law in favour of the "inhabitants" of the coasts of England; because there exists a legal technical objection (*l*) to its being so pleaded. In this respect
[212] it is in a worse situation than the right to *bathe;* for *that*, not being a *profit*, might, perhaps, be pleaded as a *local* custom by the "inhabitants," and as an "easement." But there is no mode by which the inhabitants of the maritime counties can maintain a right to manure their lands from the materials cast upon the shores of their coasts, except *that* which supports the public fishery, viz. the general cus-

(*l*) Gateward's case, 6 Co. Rep. 59 B.

tom of the realm. The men of Devon and Cornwall indeed may plead their statute, but the Statute law has done nothing for the other counties. This statute of James, however, can scarcely be construed into evidence that the general Common law right did *not* exist before; although such construction was attempted. If it *did* exist before, the statute certainly could not have abrogated it; for it is an affirmative and declaratory statute; and also in its operation *local.* No just or fair inference can be drawn from this partial statute to negative the right of other inhabitants of other maritime districts to a like privilege by common law. The statute did not confer this right as a *new* privilege, even upon these two counties, as appears by the very words of the statute itself. (*m*)

The custom coeval with the culture of land.

It will not be denied that agriculture is as ancient and as important a pursuit as fishing or navigation. The public interests are as much concerned in the one as in the other. It would also be difficult to contend, that the agricultural interests of *all* the maritime counties in the kingdom are *not* to be regarded as the general public interests of the realm. The right in question partakes of the character of the interests to which it is made subservient. It is subservient to the agricultural interests of all the maritime [213] counties of the realm; a range large enough to entitle it to be called a *general* public benefit, even as the fishery is a general right and benefit, although actually limited to the maritime districts. There seems no substantial reason why the one "*communis usus*" of the shore might not be supported by the Courts, on public grounds and general usage, as well as the other. The *practice* is in favour of it; the public interests are in favour of it; and the Statute law, as far as it goes, is in favour of it. The silence of the "books" is neutral. There was a time when the books were equally silent in regard to the fisheries; yet the fisheries subsisted at that time by the Common law.

And as general.

(*m*) If it be a fact, that in nine-tenths of the maritime districts, this privilege is, and has immemorially been exercised by all mankind who chose to do it, without toll or hindrance, it would seem to follow that, as "custom," it is no more "local" than the fishery.

At that time, also, agriculture subsisted in the same districts where the fisheries were carried on. Probably agriculture was the *most* ancient of the two pursuits ; and unless it be assumed that agriculture is a *modern* invention, as bathing was assumed to be, then, so far at least as regards the application of the several useful manures furnished *spontaneously* by the sea and sea-shore, the taking and using such manures must have prevailed in the very manner by law required to establish a general Common law custom, viz. immemorially and generally.

Antiquity of the practice of using marine manures in agriculture.

It is reasonable to conclude, that the use of these natural manures, so plentifully offered and so accessible, was more ancient than of those more artificial kinds which require greater science and skill than was anciently in vogue. (*n*) It may be supposed that some of these artificial kinds of [214] manure have superseded, in some places, the frequent use of the soil of the shore ; and perhaps it would appear that in other places the natural products of the shore have been more than ever resorted to for manures, where modern research has detected new soils, or new modes of combining such soils so as to increase the productive powers of land in tillage. In the same manner alterations and improvements have occurred in the fisheries. And when it is considered, that such common right to use the shore of the realm would include within its range not the open shores of the sea only, but the shores of all creeks and arms of the sea, and of tide-rivers, the value and utility of such a privilege to the public cannot be questioned. Every species

And its extent and utility.

(*n*) Agriculture, however, as an art, is of great antiquity in Britain. Julius Cæsar speaks of it as having been introduced into the *southern* parts of Britain from Gaul, a century before his invasion. Cæs. de Bell. Gall. lib. 5, ch. 12. By which it would seem that the *maritime* districts were the *first* to practise it as an *art*. It appears also, from Pliny, that we were *then* acquainted with *manures*, as he speaks of the wonderful effects of our *marl*-ing our fields. There is no doubt but that *lime* was also used both in Gaul and in Britain, in those early
[214] times ; and this is an artificial preparation of a manure to increase its powers. There is no doubt too but that the coming of the Romans into Britain introduced their improved modes of tillage ; and at that time, the Romans had studied agriculture as a science, and it was held in particular honour by that great and wise people.

of natural manure is to be found within this extensive range, as well as other products capable of conversion into rich manures by artificial processes. Some (such as chalk) are used both in the natural state, and also after being improved by artificial processes. (*o*)

In the case of Ball *v.* Herbert, (*p*) a right to use *towing-paths* along the *banks* of navigable rivers, was contended for, as a general public privilege for all the subjects of the realm. But it was decided by Lord Kenyon and other judges (and it is conceived most reasonably) that no such general custom existed at law. The naturally navigable rivers, subject to the tides, are so very *few* in these kingdoms, that the practice of towing could not be regarded as *general.* The character of the right partook of the limited nature of the custom. It was, accordingly, decided by the court, that as a *local* custom it might be good, but not as a general right. The public right to navigate the seas and tide rivers is a right of way, *not* upon the *terra firma,* but upon and over those seas and tide rivers.—Even granting a right to use the *ripam* along the coast so far as it is reasonably essential to fishing and navigation, still such right must be general in its quality, and such only as [215]

The right to towing-paths is not a general right along navigable rivers.

(*o*) In a book of agriculture of great authority (Sir John Sinclair's Code of Agriculture) it is said, p. 40, "an object deserving considera- "tion is the situation of the farm regarding manures; for an easy "access to lime, chalk, marl, seaweed, &c. is of essential advantage "to cultivation." In various parts of the same work, the manures furnished by the "shore" are spoken of in the highest terms. Thus in p. 242, "sea-ooze" is mentioned as "of a most enriching nature." In p. 243–4, seaweed is described as good for arable lands; and the late Duke of Richmond is stated to have used it in *Sussex.* Tangle, or drifted sea-ware, is extolled p. 243–4, as having "several advantages "over other sorts of manure." Sea-shells are said "to abound in various "parts of the British Isles," and these, together with sea-sand, are spoken of as excellent manures; and are stated to be in use, not in Devon and Cornwall only, but in the *North* and *East Ridings of Yorkshire,* and in *Scotland.* It is also remarked, that "farmers prefer [215] "taking it as near the low-water mark as possible," p. 238. Indeed, the books written upon this interesting subject of agriculture, uniformly allude to the use of sea-shore manures as quite common and universal throughout the kingdom.

(*p*) 3 T. R. 253.

is *necessary* to the fishing and navigation, as *generally* carried on. Towing, in fact, seems to begin where navigation, properly so called, ends. It is very limited both in place and practice, so far as tide rivers are concerned. (*q*)

Now, in this case, (*r*) Lord Kenyon, addressing himself to the question of general Common law rights, says, "Common law rights are either to be found in the opinions of "lawyers, delivered as axioms, or to be collected from the "universal and immemorial usage throughout the country." It seems, then, that *either* of these grounds will suffice. It [216] may, it is conceived, be "collected from universal and "immemorial usage," that the sea-shore has been resorted to for the purposes in question, not in a few places, or in two counties only, but *generally* throughout the realm. It is a custom quite in contrast with that of towage: it is, in fact, essentially, and in its nature *general;* as agriculture is general, and the manuring of lands general, and the products of the shore are also as generally applicable and available in one part of the kingdom as another.

The support of the custom desirable on grounds of public utility.

It is, therefore, on all accounts desirable, that the custom in question should be supported, if possible, as a general Common law right. As a *local* custom it is liable to be limited in extent and utility; the materials, in such case, cannot be legally carried away, used, or sold for use out of the precincts of the manor; besides, local customs may be *lost* by disuse, and cannot be revived. Ignorance, prejudice, want of capital, or of enterprise, or of means of conveyance, may, for a time, induce a neglect of the advantages afforded by the "sea-shore," in particular districts, until the right is lost by disuse, to the no small injury of the agriculture of those places. If the custom, as a local custom, cannot be proved to have existed within the memory of the inhabitants, it may be lost for ever; and however inclined, or capable, the next generation may be to use those advantages which their predecessors neglected, it is too late. It is well known, that in many places on the coast which had

(*q*) *Ante*, p. 851.

(*r*) Ball *v.* Herbert, 3 T. R. 261, Lord Kenyon's doctrine as to general Common law rights.

long been supposed destitute of good materials for manure, the finest manures have been ultimately found, either by accident, or scientific research. But the memory of man may not warrant its being taken, as a *local* privilege. So, the daily alterations which take place along the coast, by the action of storms and tides, will bring or lay open the finest manures, where there had been none for use before. But neither neglect, nor accident, can operate to destroy or prejudice a general Common law custom. It cannot be [217] lost by local disuse; and it may, at any time, be revived into use for the public good. Such is the case with the "fishery;" and, nationally speaking, so it should be with the custom in question.

REMARKS ON THE CASE OF DICKENS *V.* SHAW.

THIS case has decided, that a right to "wreck" will not Ante, p. 451. *alone* confer a title, by presumption or construction of law, to the ownership of the soil of the "shore," against the Crown. So far, therefore, the doctrine contended for in former pages has been judicially supported. But the learned judges did not explicitly state, what *other* additional or cumulative evidence might suffice to establish such ownership. (*s*) The exclusive right to take sand is alluded to, as *one* badge of ownership; and we are also told, that "the proper thing is to look to the exercise, and "see how the lord of the manor has, from time to time, "acted." There can be no doubt but that this must be the general rule, if *presumption of law* be allowed, at all, to confer a title to the "shore." Still, however, this case does not enable us to determine, out of all the badges of

(*s*) (This has been decided in Chad *v.* Tilsed, *ante*, p. 447; Calmady *v.* Rowe, *ante*, p. 472; Lestrange *v.* Rowe, *ante*, p. 542; Healy *v.* Thorn, *ante*, p. 552; and other cases. As to the *quantum* of user, see p. 656, and chapter xxii.—ED.)

ownership alluded to by Lord Hale, how many may, and how many may not, be dispensed with. Whether wreck and royal fish together will suffice? Whether wreck and an exclusive fishing, or an exclusive taking of sand, will suffice? Whether to these must be added jurisdiction of "purprestures?" or whether further acts of copyhold-grants,
[218] leasing and taking rent, embanking and in-taking from the sea, or some or one of these must also be brought into the scale? (*t*)

This case, however, furnishes a strong illustration of Bracton's doctrine regarding the *communis usus* of the sea-shore. For it appears that, in the shore of the manor of Brighton, between high and low-water mark, the public have immemorially exercised and enjoyed every useful privilege of which such shore seems capable. They have resorted to, and used it for the following purposes, viz. for the fisheries, for navigation, for free-way and passage, for bathing, for digging and taking sand, shell, stones, sea-weed, and other materials of the soil. And all this they have done, without restraint or hindrance from the Crown or the lord of the manor. These rights do not appear to have been confined or limited to the *tenants* of the manor, or to the *inhabitants* of the town; but have apparently been exercised by all men who dwelt within convenient reach of the shore. The franchise of wreck, or royal fish, could not be the subject of *common* use; but for all uses capable of *common* and general enjoyment, the whole shore seems to have been, immemorially, perfectly free and open.

If the manor of Brighton should be found to represent, in these respects, the prevailing practice in the *great majority* of the sea-coast manors of the kingdom, it would be difficult *à priori* to controvert Bracton's assertion, "that "the sea-shores are, *jure communi*, as open to common resort, "and common use, as the sea itself." (*u*) There are, no doubt, many exceptions grown up; some by actual grant from the Crown, and more by gradual encroachment; but, with these

(*t*) See Phear, p. 89. (*u*) P. 780, *ante*.

exceptions, the general rule and presumption seems to be, that the Crown has immemorially held its ownership of the shore, subject to these common uses, in like manner as its dominion over the seas is open to the common use of all [219] the subjects of the realm. It must be acknowledged, however, that such does not seem to be the prevailing doctrine of recent authorities, as regards the sea-shore. Yet the learned Judge, in the foregoing case, declared, that "the "right of the Crown is not, in general, for any beneficial "interest to the Crown itself, but for securing to the public "certain privileges in the spot between high and low-water "mark." And if this be so, it might, perhaps, be conceded, that all those common uses of the shore which have been immemorially acquiesced in by the Crown, and enjoyed by the public, are, by this time, established of common right, in the same manner as the public fisheries have been enjoyed and established. Nothing more is wanted for the public than those common uses of the shore, which, as it seems, have been immemorially enjoyed in the shore of the manor of Brighton.

It is a question of some interest and importance, how far the present state of the law, upon the subject of the foregoing pages, is susceptible of alteration and amendment. Possibly it may form one of the topics for the consideration of those to whom the reform of the "laws of real property" has been entrusted. The Crown, on behalf of the public, has an interest in the shores of every sea-coast manor within its dominions; and the public are still more directly and continually concerned in the clearness and certainty of this portion of our law. The only parties who profit by its existing uncertainty, are the lords of manors themselves, whose individual interests are, for the most part, opposed alike to the Crown and to the public. The prevailing mode of making title to the sea-shore, by *prescription* and *presumption of law*, has a tendency to favour "intrusions" and "encroachments" upon the ownership of the Crown, and the rights and privileges of the subject. It may be a question, whether it ought ever to have been in the power of the [220] Crown to alienate, by grants to individuals, any portions of the sea-shores of the realm; and it may be still more questionable, whether such alienation ought ever to have been *presumed* by a court of law, when no grant whatever could be produced. It may be thought, that prescription, or presumption of law, ought, in no case, to be allowed to prevail against the title of the Crown to so important a trust, confided, by the law, to its charge, for the good of the commonwealth. "If the King were to make the sea-shores of the "realm a source of private sale and profit, he would, according to what is said before by the Judges, be acting contrary "to the trust for which the ownership of the shore was vested "in the Crown by the Common law. Still less, therefore, "ought private individuals to be aided by presumption of "law, in their claims upon the shore, when the Crown and "public are both thereby greatly impoverished." (*x*) "Our "common law of England," says Callis, "doth much sur-"pass in reason, either the imperial or civil law; for, by "our law, it is said, *Rex habet proprietatem, sed Populus* "*habet usum ibidem necessarium.*" In the manor of Brighton, this doctrine seems to have been fully exemplified, and it may be doubted whether every judicial decision, which has diminished this *proprietatem* of the Crown, and narrowed this *usum necessarium* of the public, has not been a departure alike from the reason and the principles of the Common law.

(*x*) Jerwood, 125, 126.

APPENDICES.

APPENDIX I.

THE DECREE IN THE CASE OF ATTORNEY-GENERAL *v.* PHILPOTT, 8 MAY, 8 CHARLES I., A.D. 1632.

Adhuc termino Pasche anno viij° Regis Caroli Martis octavo die Maii.

MIDDLESEX: Whereas Sir Robert Heath, Knight, the Kings Majesties late Attorney Generall, did heretofore, in Michaelmas terme in the Fifth year of his Majesties raigne that now is, exhibit an Englishe Informacion into this Courte against Gregorie Phill-pott, John Taylor, Thomas Mace, Adry Mooter, widowe, John Houe, Thomas Cobb, John Coxe, Peter Mootham, and John Bradie, and diverse others defendants, shewinge thereby, amongst other things, that the Kings Majestie and his Progenitors tyme out of mynde were and had beene seized in right of the Crowne of England of and in the Porte and Haven of London, and of the River of Thames, beinge a royall and navigable River whereunto the sea did and had alwayes flowen and reflowen, which River had beene and was reputed to be an Arme of the Sea, and was and alwayes had beene the greate Porte of his Majestie and his Progenitors for the Cittie of London, Upon which River all manner of shippes and vessells, as well his Majesties and his subiects as the shippes of Forraine Princes and their Subiects, comynge to and from London, had tyme out of mynd freely sayled and passed upon the saide River, for their comynge to and from the saide Port of London for vendinge their goods and Comodities, By meanes whereof great traffique and store of shippinge alwaies had beene brought from Forraigne parts and divers places of this Kingdome to the Porte of London, whereby the Kings Majestie and his Progenitors, and the Cittizens of London, and others tradinge thither, had beene alwaies respectively more comodiously supplyed with all provisions as well for defence of this Realme as for the provision of his Majesties housholde and the

Exch. D. & O., series 3, vol. xii. 66b.

saide Cittie and other parts of this Realme, And that all shipps and Vessells had alwayes, at their comynge upp the saide River to the saide Porte of London, layen in Harbour at Anchor in and upon the saide River downewards from London Bridge Eastwards as farr as the remotest parts of the Towne of Wappinge, Shadwell, Ratcliffe, Lymehowse, and Blackwall, in the Countie of Middlesex, All which had beene parte of the saide Porte of London, And that the shipps and vessells there harbouringe were and had beene builte and repaired as occasion required in or neere the Cittie of London, and from thence had beene victualed and fraighted for their voyages into Forraigne parts, By meanes whereof great honor in all ages had arisen to the Kings and Queenes of this Realme, to the great increase of Navigacion and greate proffitt by their Customes and other Duties arisinge by goods exported and ymported to and from the saide Porte, And thereby the said Cittie of London was growne riche and famous both at home and abroade, All which was occasioned by the flowinge and reflowinge of the Sea to and from the saide Cittie and Porte of London, And further shewinge that the King's maiestie and his Progenitors for the tyme aforesaid had beene seized *of all the soyle of and under the saide River of Thames betweene the highe and lowe water marke, and all other places of the saide River*, and alsoe of all the walled bancks and Common Sewars leadinge alonge by the soyle of the saide River, from the Hermytage Wharfe, in the Countie of Middlesex, eastwards to a place called Dickeshore, at Lymehowse, in the saide Countie, and abuttinge and lyinge to the North of certaine marshes, lands, closes, and Tenements in or neare Wappinge, Shadwell, Ratcliffe, and Lymehowse, which River of Thames did and had alwayes flowen and reflowen into the said Common Sewars, and upp to the saide marsh lands aforesaide, where the highe water marke was and alwaies had beene untill of late before the exhibitinge of the saide Informacion, And the saide River soe flowinge and reflowinge, divers shipps and vessells from tyme to tyme did usuallie ride upon the same, from the Hermitage wharfe to Dickshore, and were tyed, anchored, and in harbour to, in, and upon the walles of the saide River leadinge from Hermitage Wharfe to Dickshoare aforesaide, att which tyme the saide River was large and broade from one side to the other, from Hermitage Wharfe to Dickshoare aforesaid, And many shipps and Vessells might then Anchor and Harbour safely without annoyance or offence one to another, and that the saide defendants Gregory Philpott, John Taylor, Thomas Mace, Adry Wooter, John Houe, Thomas Cobb, John Coxe, Peter Mootham, and John Brady, amongest others, not regardinge the publique weale and good of his Majestie, nor the welfare of this kingdome, nor his Majesties right to the said River, and the whole soyle thereof from the lowe to the highe water marke, for their owne private proffitt, had within the space of threescore yeares then at the tyme of the exhibiting of the saide Informacion last past intruded by a generall Combynacion betweene themselves against his majesties right, title, and interest, and incroached and entered into and uppon the soyle and wast of the saide River betweene the auncient highe and lowe water marke thereof upon the Northerne side thereof, and into and uppon the walles and Common Sewers lyinge on the north side of the saide River from Hermitage wharfe to Dickshore aforesaide, and within the saide tyme had made, enlardged, mayntayned, and Contynued upon the saide walles, bancks, Common Sewars, and soyle of the saide River soe intruded upon severall howses, Tenements, docks, and wharfes, and dwell in and upon the same, and had taken, made, contrived, and Claymed dyverse secrett estates in the whole and in severall parts of the premisses under severall persons, and by severall pretended tytles unknowne to his Majesties saide Attorney Generall, which the saide Defendants did refuse to discover, and haveinge gott into theire hands divers Deedes and other Evidences touchinge the premisses did refuse to discover and deliver the same to his Majesties saide Attorney Generall, and had possessed themselves of the severall howses, Tenements, wharffes, and Docks respectively made in and upon the saide walls, Common Sewers, banckes, shoares, and soyle of the said River, All which lye betweene the auncient highe and lowe water markes of the saide River, and the saide walles, Common Sewers, bancks, and shoares and soyle of the saide River at the tyme of the saide intrusions and the makeinge of howses, Tenements, Docks, and wharffes thereuppon as his maiesties saide Attorney Generall alleadged in his saide Informacion did belonge to the Crowne of Englande, And that by meanes of the saide Intrusion the saide River of Thames had for divers yeares then last past beene straightned, lessened, and stopped, the contynuance whereof was a purpresture of the highest nature, to the great hurte and prejudice of his Maiestie and his leige people passinge or anchoringe upon the saide Porte, and much derogatory to the honor and state of this nation; for reformacion whereof, and that his Majestie might be satisfied of such meane rates and proffittes of the saide howses, tenements, wharffes, and dockes made and builded upon the said walles, Common Seawers, bancks, shore, and soyle of the saide River intruded upon as aforesaid, which of right belongs to his Majestie, and that the purprestures made and Contynued uppon the Bancks, walles, and soyle of the saide River might bee abated, and to the end the saide Defendants might discover what estates, from whome, and by what title they clayme in the premisses, his maiesties said Attorney Generall prayed the proces of this Courte against the saide Defendants. Whereupon the said Defendants beinge served with proces, severally appeared and answeared. And the saide Gregory Philpott, for answeare to the saide Informacion, said that hee did hould a Capitall messuage or Tenement with a Backside and wharffe, comonly called the King's head Taverne, by lease from one Mr. Nicholls for about Nyne yeares then to come, which messuage or tenement are situat in Wappinge betweene Hermitage wharffe and Dickshore, and that about Twelve yeares since, his ould wharffe beeinge taken downe, hee caused the same to bee repaired and newe builte, And, by the lycence of the then Lord Admirall, sett the saide wharffe into the River of Thames about three foote further then the ould wharffe was, which he conceaved was noe annoyance to the River of Thames saveinge that the River, beinge by that meanes streightned, did yearelie overflowe and drowne his and many of his neighbours goods thereabouts; And the saide John Taylor likewise saide that hee did houlde one messuage or dwelling howse with two yards and a docke, situat in Wappinge, betweene Hermitage Wharffe and Dickshoare, by agreement betweene him and one Mrs. Mary Bourne, But what estate shee had in the same hee did not certainely knowe; and the saide other Defendants respectively saide that they did severallie and respectively holde the howses, tenements, wharffs, and dockes hereafter mencioned, viz. the saide Thomas Cobb twoe messuages or tenements, which hee had by lease from one Mr. Stepkyn for divers yeares then and yett to come, which messuages are situat in Wappinge, betweene the Hermitage and Dickshore aforesaide, And that the said Stepkin and his Auncestors had beene duringe his remembrance accompted the true Owners of the saide messuages and to have the inheritance thereof; And the saide John Houe one Messuage or Tenement by lease from Roger Stepkin for divers yeares then and yett to come, And alsoe one other Messuage or Tenement from the said Stepkin at will or sufferaunce, Which messuages or Tenements are situat in Wappinge, betweene the Hermitage wharffe and Dickshore aforesaide; And the said Peter Mootham one messuage and yarde, with the Backside situat upon Wappinge wall, betweene the Hermitage Wharffe and Dickshore aforesaide; And the saide Thomas Mace one messuage with one Wharffe adioyninge, beinge in Wappinge aforesaide, conteyninge in breadth about twelve foote, and in length betweene the streete and the River twoe and Fortie Foote, parcell of the premisses, as he conceaved, in the saide Informacion mencioned; And that all, or the most parte, of the saide messuage or Tenement were lately erected upon the soyle betweene the auncient highe and lowe water marke of the said River of Thames; And the saide Adrye Mooter, widowe, one howse or Tenement, with the appurtenances and the yarde or voyde grounde thereunto adioyninge, then late in the tenure or occupacion of Richard Pell Chaundler, and a shoppe and a yarde thereunto adioyninge in the occupacion of one Hopkins, situat upon the wall called Wappinge wall; And the saide John Cox did hould one messuage or Tenement, with a wharffe and Backside, beinge on the South side of the waye leadinge from Wappinge to Ratcliffe, which are situate betweene Hermitage Wharffe and Dickshore aforesaid; And the saide John Brady twoe messuages or tenements in the east end of Wappinge, with the Backsides and Wharffes by lease from one William Thilbelthorpe for about three and twentie yeares then to come, and one other howse or Tenement, with a yard, Wharffe, and Backside, in Wappinge aforesaide, by lease from one Peter Marshe, for about seaventeene yeares then to come, and alsoe one parcell of land, at twoe and thirtie shillings per annum, for about seaven and twentye yeares then to come, which saide Messuages and premisses the saide Defendant alleadged to bee situat in Wappinge betweene the Hermitage Wharffe and Dickshoare in the saide Informacion mencioned. And the said Defendants, and every of them severally, denyed the severall Incroachments and purprestures mencioned in the said Informacion to bee by them made or Contynued upon the saide River of Thames As by the saide Informacion and the severall answeares of the saide defendants, upon due relacion thereunto severally and respectively had, amongest other things more at lardge it doth and maye appeare. Whereuppon his Majesties saide Attorney Generall replyed, and the saide Defendants reioyned, and soe the cause discendinge to yssue divers witnesses were examined on both sides in the saide cause, whereupon publicacion beeinge graunted, the saide cause comeinge to hearinge in this Courte uppon thursdaye, the Fift daye of Maye, in Easter terme, in the seaventh yeare of his majesties raigne that nowe is, haveinge beene heard two whole dayes before, It was the same Day ordered by the right honorable the Lord Highe Treasurer of England, the Chauncellor, the Lord Cheif Baron, and the Barons of this Courte, that a Commission should be awarded out of this Court directed unto Sir Thomas Grymes, Sir William Pitt, Sir Robert Pye, Sir Henry Spiller, and Sir Thomas Fanshawe, Knights, thereby authorisinge them, or any three of them, to viewe the wharffes and buildings on the north side of the saide River of Thames from the saide place there called the Hermitage wharffe, unto the saide place called Dickshore eastwarde, and to survey, sett downe, and discribe where the auncient wall went which was aunciently called by the name of the Thames Wall or Wappinge Wall, and what howses, buildings, wharffs, and docks, or parts of howses, buildings, wharffs, and docks, had bynne, within the space of Fyftie yeares last past, builded, made, or erected on the south side of the saide wall, or on the South side of the place where the saide wall aunciently went, And that the saide Commissioners, or three of them, should sett the same downe, in writinge particularly and distinctly with as much certantie as conveniently they could, and certifie their doeings and proceedings therein before the second tuesdaye of the then next Trinitie terme, That thereupon this Courte might proceede further to doe and execute that which to the justice of this Courte should appertayne in that behalfe, as by the saide order at lardge appeareth, Accordinge to which order a Comission yssued fourth of this Courte directed to the saide Commissioners, which was by them executed and retorned into this Courte the saide Trinitie Terme, with their Certificate thereunto annexed, wherein the Commissioners did certefie what they conceaved touchinge the severall points mencioned in the saide last recited order, Whereupon upon wednesdaye the Nyne and twentieth daye of June, in the same terme, the Courte being informed by his Majesties saide Attorney Generall that, althoughe it did appeare by the saide Commissioners Certificate where the said wall went, and that there are many incroachments and purprestures on the south side of the said wall, yett it did not appeare in the saide Certificate in whose severall occupacions the howses, wharffs, and Docks then were which were Certified to be soe neewly erected and incroached upon the saide River of Thames, nor of what Content the same were the pretended Owners thereof, nor what or howe many houses, wharffs, or docks in certaine there were which was soe incroched, nor howe farr they extended from the saide wall Southward, It was, therefore, the same daye ordered by the Courte that the said Commission should bee renewed and directed to the said former Commissioners, authorisinge them, or any three of them, further to survey and viewe the premises, and to enquire of and certifie the particulers before mencioned, and such other circumstances touchinge the same as they should thinke fitt the better to enforme this Courte of the premisses, and to prepare the said Cause for a full hearinge, but noe person to bee bound thereby, as by the saide order amongest other things at lardge appeareth, accordinge to which saide order last recited a newe Commission was awarded to the saide former Commissioners, which was executed by Sir Thomas Grymes, Sir Henry Spiller, and Sir Thomas Fanshawe, Knights, three of the saide Commissioners, with their certificate thereunto annexed, wherein they certefie this Courte of their proceedings in the execucion of the said Commission, both which Commissions and Certificates and other proceedings thereupon are retorned into this Courte as aforesaide, and here remayne of Record in the Custodie of his Majesties Remembrancer, whereby the further proceedings of the saide Commissioners upon relacion thereunto had maye fully and at lardge appeare. And whereas also the saide cause came to further hearinge in this Courte, the twentieth daye of October, in Michaelmas terme last, uppon hearinge of his Majesties saide Attorney Generall and other learned Counsell on the behalfe of his Maiestie, and of the learned Counsell of fyve of the saide Defendants, viz. Gregory Philpott, John Taylor, John Houe, Thomas Cobb, and Peter Mootham, and upon readinge of the severall answeares of the other Fower Defendants, viz. Thomas Mace, Audry Wooter, widowe, John Coxe, and John

Brady, whoe made noe defence for themselves, and upon readinge of the deposicions of dyvers witnesses on his Majesties parte, the saide cause was appointed to bee further heard on that daye three weeks; which cause Comynge then to hearinge, beinge upon thursdaye, the tenth daye of November, after longe hearinge and debatinge thereof by the Councell learned on both sides, It was again appointed to bee heard on that daye senight, which cause comynge then likewise to bee heard and not fully ended, came againe to bee heard on Thursday, beeinge the fower and twentieth of November, and was then fully heard on both sides, yett, in regarde the saide cause was a cause of great weight and importance and verie muche concerned his Majestie, the Courte appointed Satterdaye, the sixe and twentieth of the saide moneth of November, to deliver their opynions therein, Whereupon it was the same daye, uppon full and mature deliberacion in that behalfe had, declared, adiudged, and decreed by this Court that the soyle and grounde situate or beeinge betweene the auncient wall commonly called Thames Wall or Wappinge Wall of the North, and the saide River of Thames upon the South, is and duringe all the tyme of memorie hath beene parcell of the saide Porte of London, and belonged and appertaynede to the Kings Majestie *as parcell of the same Porte and his Inheritance of the Crowne of England*, and that incroachments and purprestures made in and upon any Navigable River or Porte, much more in or uppon the Royall River of Thames and the Port of London, beinge the principall parte of this kingdome, ought to bee remooved and abated or otherwise arrented from the Crowne at his maiesties pleasure; And as touching the severall howses, wharffes, yards, and docks, and other buildings in the severall tenures or occupacions of the saide Nyne Defendants, or their Undertenants, It was likewise the saide sixe and twentieth of November last decreed by this Courte that soe many and soe muche of the saide howses, yards, wharffs, docks, and other buildings as should appeare to bee or to bee builte betweene the saide auncient wall called the Thames Wall or Wappinge Wall of the North, and the saide River of Thames of the South, are Incroachments and purprestures upon the saide River and Porte, and were to bee remooved and abated or otherwise arrented at his maiesties pleasure. But because it did not specially and precisely appeare to this Courte howe muche of the saide howses, yards, wharffs, and docks in the said severall tenures or occupacions of the saide Defendants, or of their Under-tenants, are builte or erected betweene the saide auncient wall of the North and the saide River of Thames upon the south, It was, therefore, likewise ordered by this Courte that a Commission should bee awarded, under the seale of this Courte, to Commissioners to bee named by this Courte, retornable att or before Hillary terme then next followinge, thereby authorisinge them, or any three or more of them, to survey and viewe the said howses, yards, wharffes, and docks, and other buildings in the severall tenures of the saide Defendants, or of their under-tenants, and of every or any of them, and as many or as muche of them, with the certaine and speciall contents and quanteties or extents thereof as shoulde appear unto them, uppon viewe thereof, to bee or to bee soe erected or builte as aforesaide in and upon the soyle or ground betweene the saide auncient wall called Thames Wall or Wappinge Wall upon the North, and the saide River of Thames upon the South; The which same auncient wall upon the North and the saide River was declared and adiudged by this Courte too bee and have beene of long and auncient tyme the highe water marke of the saide River in those parts, and the same to seize and take into his Maiesties hands as parcell of the said Porte of London and Inheritance of the Crowne, to bee abated or arrented at his Maiesties good pleasure, *for the increase of the Revenues of the Crowne.* And touchinge the saide wall called Thames Wall, the Courte did leave that undetermyned for his Maiesties saide Attorney Generall to take such further course therein as hee should think fitt. And whereas, accordinge to the saide decree, a Commission was made foorth under the seale of this Courte, and directed to the right honorable George Lord Goringe, Sir Thomas Edmonds, Knight, Sir Robert Killigrewe, Knight, Sir Sackvile Crowe, Baronett, Sir Richard Tichborne, knight, and Sir Nicholas Fortescue, knight, thereby authorisinge them, or any three of them, to survey and viewe the howses, yardes, docks, and wharffes, and other buildings in the decree mencioned in the severall tenures of the saide defendants or of their undertenants, and of every or any of them, and as many or as much of them, with the certaine and speciall contents and quanteties or extents thereof, as should appeare unto them, upon viewe thereof, to bee or to bee erected and builte in and upon the soyle or ground betweene the auncient wall called Thames Wall or Wapping wall upon the north and the saide River of Thames upon the south, to seize and take into his Maiesties hands, as parcell of the port of London and inheritance of the Crowne, to bee abated or arrented at his maiesties good will and pleasure, for the increase of the Revenues of the Crowne, Which saide Commission the saide Commissioners, all but the said Sir Richard Tichborne, did in Hillarie terme last retorne into this Courte, with their certificate of their doings therein, And thereupon, by order of the Courte, the xi[th] daye of February, the same terme, was given to the saide defendants to shewe cause whie the saide certificate should not bee decreed and an Iniunccion awarded to the Sheriffe of the Countie of Middlesex to putt his maiestie into possession thereof, which daye, upon hearinge of counsell of both sides, and upon readinge of the saide decree, Commission, and Certificate, for that the said Certificate was not possitive, but related only the opynions of the saide Commissioners and what they conceaved, the Courte did forbeare to make any order thereupon, But it was then ordered by the Courte that a newe Commission should bee made foorth, directed to the saide Commissioners, or any three of them, accordinge to the trewe effecte and true meanynge of the saide decree, Which Commission was executed by all the saide Commissioners, except the said Sir Richard Titchborne, and retorned into this Court, with their Certificate of their dooings therein to the same Commission annexed, The tenor of which certificate hereafter followeth, viz. Accordinge to his Maiesties Commission to us and Sir Richard Titchbourne, Knight, directed, Wee certifie unto this honorable Courte that the streete nowe called Wappinge streete is the verie place where the auncient wall called Wappinge Wall went, And that the howses, docks, yards, and wharffes in the severall tenures or occupacions of the nyne Defendants or their Undertenants mencioned in the decree doe all stand and are betweene the auncient walle or streete on the North and the River of Thames on the South, except fower foote of every of the saide howses next adjoyninge to the saide streete towards the Thames, and that all the saide howses, parts of howses, docks, yards, and wharffes which are beyonde those fower foote towards the Thames southward bee upon the soyle of the saide River of Thames, and have been incroached; And in pursuite of the saide decree we have seized into his Maiesties hands of the tenements, yards, and wharffes in the tenure of the Defendant Gregory Phillpott and his

Undertenants fiftie eight foote of Assize from the River on the south to Wappinge Wall on the north, and seaventie sixe foote of Assize from East to West, All which doe lye betwixt the saide River on the south and the saide wall on the north, and are incroached upon the soyle of the saide River of Thames, And wee have alsoe seized into his maiesties hands of the Tenements, yards, and docks, late in the tenure of the Defendant John Taylor, viz. of the said tenement and yarde fortie three foote of Assize from a longe yarde by the Thames side on the south to the saide wall on the north, and from east to west eleaven foote of Assize, and of the saide longe yarde fiftie foote of Assize from the River on the south to Wappinge Wall on the north at the west end of the same longe yard, and at the east end of the saide longe yard and docks one hundred and fyve foote of Assize from the saide River on the south to Wappinge Wall on the north, And from east to west by the side of the saide River twoe hundred and fowerteen foote of Assize, All which doe likewise lye betwixt the saide River on the south and the saide wall on the north, and are incroached upon the soyle of the said River of Thames; Wee have alsoe seized into his maiesties hands of the Tenement and wharffe in the tenure of the Defendant John Houe sixtie foote of Assize from the saide River of Thames on the south to the saide Wappinge Walle on the north, and from east to west thirteen foote of Assize, All which lye betwixte the saide River on the south and the said Wappinge Wall on the north, and are incroached upon the soyle of the said River of Thames; Wee have alsoe seized into his Maiesties hands of the Tenements, yards, and wharffes in the tenure of the Defendant John Coxe and his Undertenants seaventie three foote of Assize from the saide River on the south to the saide Wappinge Wall on the north, and from east to west fiftie twoe foote of Assize, All which doe alsoe lye betwixt the saide River on the south and Wappinge Wall on the north, and are incroached uppon the soyle of the saide River of Thames; Wee have likewise seized into his Maiesties hands of the Tenements, yards, and wharffes in the tenure of the Defendant John Brady and his undertenants sixtie nyne foote of Assize from the saide River on the south to the saide Wappinge Wall on the north, And from east to west thirtie foote of Assize, all which doe lye betwixt the saide River on the South, and Wappinge Wall on the North, and are incroached upon the soyl of the saide River of Thames; Wee have alsoe seized into his Maiesties hands of the Tenement and yarde in the tenure of the Defendant Thomas Cobb eightie twoe foote of Assize at the west end of the saide tenement and yarde from the saide River of Thames on the south to the saide wall on the north, and eightie fower foote of Assize from the saide River on the south to the saide wall on the north att the east parte or end of the saide yarde or Tenement, and seaventie twoe foote from east to west alonge by the saide Wappinge Wall or streete, All which doe lye betwixt the said River on the south and the saide wall on the north, and are incroached upon the soyle of the said River of Thames; Wee have likewise seized into his maiesties hands of the Tenement and yarde in the tenure of the Defendant Thomas Mace thirtie one foote of Assize from the saide River of Thames on the south to Wappinge Wall on the North, and from east to west thirteen foote of Assize, All which doe lye betwixt the saide River on the south and the saide Wapping Wall on the north, and are incroached from the soyle of the saide River of Thames; Wee have alsoe seized into his maiesties hands of the Tenement, wharffe, and docke in the tenure of the Defendant Peter Mootham sixtie three foote of Assize from the saide River of Thames on the south to the saide wall on the north, and one and thirtie foote of Assize from east to west, All which doe lye betwixt the saide River on the south and the saide Wappinge Wall on the North, and are incroached upon the soyle of the saide River of Thames; Wee have likewise seized into his Maiesties hands of the Tenements, yards, and wharffs in the tenure of the defendant Awdry Mooter or her undertenants thirtie eight foote of Assize at the west end of the saide Tenements from the said River of Thames on the south to the saide Wappinge Wall of the North, and at the east end of the said Tenements and yards Fortie eight foote of Assize from the saide River on the south to the saide wall on the north, and from east to west one hundred and eight foote of Assize, All which lye betweene the saide River on the south and the saide Wappinge Wall on the north, and are incroached upon the soil of the saide River of Thames; All of the aforesaid premises so seized as aforesaide to bee abated or arrented at his Maiesties good pleasure according to the said decree. All which wee humbly leave to the grave consideracion of this honorable Courte, The sixteenth of Aprill 1632. Goringe, T. Edmonds,

Robert Killigrewe, Sackvile Crowe, Nicholas Fortescue. After which Commission so retorned, severall dayes have beene given to the saide Defendants to shewe cause whie the saide Certificate should not be confirmed and established by decree of this Courte; Noue upon readinge of the saide Certificate and upon hearinge of his Maiesties Attorney Generall, Sir John Bankes, knight, the Princes Attorney, and Mr. Littleton, Recorder of the Cittie of London, on the behalfe of the Kings maiestie, and of Mr. Sergeant Bramston and others of Councell with the saide Defendants, The Courte doth confirme, establishe, and decree the saide Certificate and the Acts and doeings of the saide Commissioners therein mencioned.

PER CAPITALEM BARONEM.
BARONEM DENHAM.
BARONEM TREVOR.
BARONEM WESTON.

APPENDIX II.

Notes as to the Existence of Several Fisheries around the Coasts and in the Tidal and Non-tidal Rivers of the Kingdom.

As to the existence of a several fishery upon the sea-shore and in tidal rivers, Mr. Hall, *ante*, p. 716, in treating of the public right of fishing in the sea and tidal waters, says that the right is general, but that "there are also other excepted cases, viz. where private "individuals or corporate bodies claim and enjoy a separate "fishery in some particular places in derogation and exclusion "of the general right." He gives three instances only, and would seem to treat several fisheries as he does express grants of foreshore. He is evidently under the impression that cases of several fisheries in the hands of a subject are infrequent and exceptional. In this he is wholly mistaken. The true fact is, as can be shewn from the records, that all, or almost all, tidal rivers and estuaries were in ancient times, and where the right still remains valuable still are, covered by several fisheries in the hands of the subject. The River Tweed is entirely covered by them; the Tyne also from its mouth upwards; the Aln, the Coquet, the Wansbeck, the Wear, and the Tees are in the same case; many of the manors on the Humber have several fisheries appurtenant to them; the tidal waters of the Ouse, Derwent, Ayre, Calder, and Don were covered by several fisheries appurtenant to or parcel of the manors on the banks; the case is the same with respect to the Trent, Witham, the Welland, the Nene, the Ouse, the Cam, the Aire, the Waveney, the Stour, the Colne, the Blackwater, the Crouch, the Thames on the coast of Essex, the Swale, the Christchurch Avon, the Exe, the Teign, the Dart, the Tamar, the Fal, the Severn, the Wye, the Dee, the Mersey, the Ribble, the Lune, the Eden, the Derwent, and the Solway Frith. If reference were made to the grants and records relating to manors situate upon tidal rivers and estuaries there is no doubt that several fisheries would be found to be parcel of every one of them. With regard to fisheries upon the open sea-coast it is clear that they existed from the earliest time. Magna Charta, c. 23, which orders all kiddels to be destroyed throughout England, specially excepts those *per costeram maris;* and Hale remarks that "this exception of "weirs upon the sea-coast, and likewise frequent examples, make "it appear that there might be such private interests, not only in "point of liberty, but in point of propriety, on the sea-coast and "below the low-water mark, for such were regularly all weirs." The records shew that these several fisheries existed all round the coast, the lords of the manors having weirs placed upon the foreshore wherever the shore was suitable for that kind of fishery; kiddel fishing was universal throughout the open shore of the county of Essex. The Quo Warranto Rolls and the Hundred Rolls shew numerous instances of such fisheries in the counties of York, Lincoln, Norfolk, Suffolk, Kent, and elsewhere; the entries relating to them have not been set out in the previous treatise, but several have been incidentally noted (see pp. 48, 49, 50, 52, 53, 54, 55, 57, 58, 59, 60, 64, 65, 79, 88, 89, 102, 103, 104, 109, 145, 146, 153, 154, 156, 160, 163, 164, 167); in fact, there is practically no doubt that the whole foreshore of the kingdom wherever it was fit for fishing by weirs was covered by several fisheries. With regard to non-tidal waters there is no doubt whatever that in ancient times the whole of them were embraced in several fisheries as parcel of the manors which either abutted on or included the rivers.

Sir Henry Constable's case, ante, pp. 236, 239; also p. 230.

The following very imperfect list refers to places in which fisheries are shewn to have existed from notes of records in the Editor's collection. The list might be amplified if the inquisitions and extents of manors were inspected, the calendars of these documents not giving particulars as to fisheries. The Editor is fully conscious that this list is very imperfect, but it is here printed to shew that Mr. Hall's suggestion as to fisheries—viz., that they are rare and infrequent in the hands of a subject—is as unfounded as his assumption that the foreshore had only been granted but in very exceptional cases.

A

ABBOTSBURY, Kent—royal fish.
Abermo, Merioneth.
Abingdon, Berks, in Thames near.
Accrington, Lancaster.
Adderbury, Oxfordshire.
Alan, Cornwall.
Aldecote, Berks.
Aldencrawe, Northumberland.
Alne, River, Northumberland.
Alnwick, Northumberland.
Alveston, Warwick.
Ammeley, als. Elmely, Worcester.
Appleford, Berks.
Appleton, Berks.
Arlingham, Gloucester.
Armathwaite, Cumberland.
Arnot, River, Cumberland.
Arnside Bay, Cumberland.
Arundell, Sussex.
Aschelond, Warwick.
Ashby, Suffolk.
Ashford, West Devon.
Aston and Cote, Oxon.
Atlebrig, Norfolk.
Aure, Gloucester.
Auste, Gloucester.
Avene, Warwick.
Axe, Aqua de.
Aynstapeleth, Cumberland.

B

BAMPTON, Oxon.
Banne, Ulster.
Barling, Essex.
Barsham, Suffolk.
Bastenwater, Cumberland.
Baubend, Cumberland.
Bawtry, York—liberty of fishing in.
Baye, Lincoln.
Beaumond, Lancaster.
Beccles, Suffolk.
Bekerton, Norfolk.
Benfleet Ray, Essex.
Bennyngton, Lincoln.
Bensyngton, Oxon.
Berkeley, Gloucester.
Berton, Herts.
Berwick-on-Tweed.
Bikeresdik, Notts.
Bilawe, Norfolk.
Binzey, Oxon.
Birchemere, Hunts.
Bisham, Bucks.
Blaemyre, Le, Cumberland.
Blithe, Warwick.
Bontynghull, Sussex.
Botilbruge, Hunts.
Boveney, Bucks.
Bowness, Solway Frith.
Brade, Northumberland, fishery in Tweed called.
Bradwell, Essex.
Braham, Suffolk.
Bray, Berks.
Brecknock.
Brecon.
Brightlingsea, Essex.
Brightwell, Berks.
Broadwell, Oxon.
Brokewere, Glamorgan.
Bromehill, Kent.
Brythewell, Suffolk.
Buckland, Berks.
Buckland, Devon.
Bulshot, Northumberland.
Burcot, Oxon and Berks.
Burnham, Bucks.
Burnham, Essex.
Burton, Berks.
Burton, Notts.
Butterwich, East and West, Lincoln.
Buxton Marsh, Norfolk.
Bytham, Lincoln.
Bywell, Durham.

C

CALDECOTE, Bucks.
Calder, River, York.
Camer, Cornwall—fishing.
Canterbury, Kent—fishery.
Carlisle, Cumberland.
Carsington, Oxford.
Carswell, Berks.
Cartmel, Lancashire.
Cassington, Oxon.
Caversham, Oxon.
Chalkwell, Essex.
Charwell, River, Oxford.
Cherewell, Surrey.
Chestre, Durham.
Chilwell, Notts.
Cholsey, Berks.
Christchurch Twynham, Southampton.
Cleware, Berks.

Clewer, Berks.
Clifden Hampden, Berks.
Clopcote, Berks.
Coket, Northumberland.
Cokington, Devon.
Colewey, Notts.
Colne, River, Bucks and Middlesex (throughout).
Colne, River, Essex (throughout).
Colstocke, Cornwall.
Colverechirchestre, Somerset.
Conway, River, Carnarvon.
Cookham, Berks.
Copeland, Water of, Northumberland —fishing in.
Cossy, Norfolk.
Cowley, Oxon.
Craunkebiry, Kent.
Crawcrook on the Tyne.
Cromarty, Firth of—salmon fishery.
Crouch, River, Essex.
Crulle, York.
Crunwell, Notts.
Culham, Oxon and Berks.
Cumwhitton, Cumberland.
Cunmer, Berks.
Curry, North, Somerset.

D

DARWENT, WATER OF, Northumberland.
Darwent, York.
Datchet, Berks.
Deal Valley, Kent.
Dee, River.
Dengie Marsh, Kent and Sussex.
Denham Court, Bucks.
Denham Durdent, Bucks.
Dent, York.
Derwent, River, Cumberland.
Derwent, River, Yorkshire.
Deven, Leicester.
Dieping, Northumberland.
Dilston, Northumberland.
Dodbrook, Southampton.
Dodyngton, Leic.
Donyngton Castle, Leicester.
Dorchester, Oxon.
Dore, Water of, Snodhull, Hereford.
Dorney, Bucks.
Dowliswere, Kent.
Down Ampney, Wilts.
Draycott, Berks.
Draycott, Notts.
Drayton, Berks.
Drumburg, Cumberland.
Duneford, Wilts.
Dunham, Nottingham.
Dunston, Norfolk.
Durham.
Duxford, Berks.

E

EASTCHURCH, Kent.
Eaton Hastings, Berks.
Ebboth, Monmouth—fishing.
Eden, River, Cumberland.
Edwynistre, Northumberland.
Egre, Cumberland.
Elemersk, Lincoln—fishing.
Eltringham, Northumberland.
Emly, Kent.
Emsworth, Southampton.
Englewood, Cumberland.
Ensham, Oxon.
Eppeworth, Lincoln.
Erlesweye, Gloucester.
Erlingham, Gloucester.
Erme, Le, Devon.
Esh, River, Cumberland—salmon fishery.
Esk, Solway Frith, Cumberland.
Eston in Cleveland, York.
Eton, Bucks.
Ewdon, Bucks.
Exe, River, Devon.
Exiland, Devon.
Exmouth, Devon.
Eyre, Water of, Castleforde, York.
Eysworth, Northumberland.

F

FARINGDON, Berks.
Farnbridge, North Essex.
Farnbridge, South Essex.
Faversham, Kent.
Fawe, Water of, Cornwall.
Fawley, Bucks.
Fendick, Lincoln.
Fennihouse, Stafford.
Fifield, Berks.
Fikesburg, Lincoln.
Fishegarthe, Malton, York.
Fiskerton, Notts.
Force, Westmoreland.

Foulness, Essex.
Fowlestreme, Berwick.
Frampton-upon-Severn, Gloucester.
Frekenham, Suffolk.
Fremelond, Gloucester.
Freskeneye, Lincoln.
Fretherne, Gloucester.
Frome, Dorset.
Fulney, Water of, York.

G

GATHAMPTON, Oxon.
Gelham Nether, Essex.
Gelham Over, Essex.
Ghellinge, Notts.
Gilgarren, Pembroke.
Gillesland, Cumberland.
Glenye, Aqua de, Lincoln.
Glynneth, Gloucester.
Godstowe, Oxon.
Goldesclyve, Monmouth.
Goring, Oxon.
Greenlands, Bucks.
Gressemere, Westmoreland.
Gringeley, Notts.
Grobhardersferry, Norfolk.
Gulnethorp, Notts.

H

HACHAM, Lincoln.
Hadbroke, Leicester.
Hadley Ray, Essex.
Hagham, Lincoln.
Hailebrooke, River Ouse, Hunts.
Hambledon, Bucks.
Hamma, Gloucester.
Hampton Lucy, als. Bishop's Hampton, Warwick.
Hannington, Wilts.
Hardwick, Oxon.
Harewood, York.
Harleyford, Bucks.
Harpston, Oxon.
Hautboys Magna.
Haven, The, Essex.
Helpool, Norfolk.
Hengham, Essex.
Hengham, Norfolk.
Hengham Sibill, Essex.
Henley, Salop.
Henley on Thames, Oxon.
Hereford.
Hersepole, Gloucester.
Heysham, Lancaster—mussel fishery.
Hicfold Peverel, Essex.
Hikeley.
Hinton Waldridge, Berks.
Hinxsey, North and South, Berks.
Hitcham, Bucks.
Hoctun—fishery.
Holkham, Norfolk.
Holm Cultram, Cumberland.
Horneinge, Norfolk.
Hornsey, York.
Hoveton St. John, Norfolk.
Hovingham, Notts.
Hull, Gloucester.
Humber, River, York.
Hurley, Berks.

I

IFFLEY, Oxon.
Inglesham, Wilts.
Ingolmills, Lincoln.
Irte, Cumberland.
Irthnefeld.
Irwise, Notts.
Isall, Cumberland.
Iwade, Kent.
Ixninge, Suffolk.

K

KEBURG, Norfolk.
Kelmscott, Oxon.
Kempsford, Wilts.
Kempston, Bedford.
Ken, River, Westmoreland.
Kenilworth, Warwick.
Kennet, River, Berks.
Kennington, Berks.
Kent, Water of, Westmoreland.
Kildre, York.
Kilgarren, Pembroke.
Kilverdeston, Norfolk.
Kingesmede juxta Oseney, Oxford.
Kingeswere, Somerset.
Kingston Bagpuz, Berks.
King's Water, River Tweed, Northumberland.
Knayf, Notts.
Knotland, Cumberland.

L

LANDFORD, Notts.
Langenton, Essex.
Langer Marshes, Walton, Suffolk.
Langley Mareys, Bucks.
Langrake, York.
Lawe, Berwick-on-Tweed.
Lechlade, Wilts.
Ledeffe, Lincoln.
Lee, Water of, Cornwall.
Lene, Water of, Lancaster.
Leyfwy, River, Carnarvon.
Libstede, Berwick.
Limpeton.
Linburn, Southampton.
Liner, Cornwall.
Littlemore, Oxon.
Lodene, Berks.
Lodene, Water of, Wilts.
Lomley Magna, Durham.
Lone, Water of.
Long Parish, Southampton—right of fishing.
Longworth, Berks.
Lothingland, Suffolk—right of fishing.
Lound, Suffolk—right of fishing.
Lovent, Bucks.
Lugg, River, Hereford—right of fishing.
Lumley Magna, Chester, Durham.
Lydd, Kent.
Lydney, Gloucester.
Lympstone, Devon.
Lynwere, Glamorgan.

M

MANSFIELD, Notts.
Mapledurham, Oxon.
Mara, Hereford.
Marcheford, Cambridge.
Marcheton, Notts.
Marlow, Great, Bucks.
Marlow, Little, Bucks.
Marnham, Notts.
Marston, Kent.
Meales, The, Kent.
Medmenham, Bucks.
Medway, River, Penhurst, Kent.
Merchenfen, Lincoln.
Mersea, East and West, Essex.
Mersey, River.
Meys, Stafford.
Middleton, Lancashire.
Middleton Priory, Essex.
Midsomer Norton, Somerset.
Milton, Kent.
Minster, Kent.
Minsterworth, Gloucester.
Monkton, Devon.
Monmouth.
Moulsey, Surrey.
Moulsford, Berks.
Muschamp, North, Notts.
Mutford, Norfolk.
Mylton Keynes, Bucks.

N

NANTCONWAY, Carnarvon.
Neen, Water of, Tannessore, Northumberland.
Neuwenham, Cambridge.
Newark, Notts.
Newere, Gloucester.
Newe Water, Tweed.
Newnham, Oxon.
Norburg, Water of, Leicester.
Normanby, York.
Nortwell, Notts.

O

OREFORDE, Suffolk.
Orred, Northumberland.
Oswaldbeck, Nottingham.
Oswaldbeck, Yorks.
Ottermouth, Devon.
Ouse, Bedford.
Ouse, River, Yorks.
Overtun Burgenses, Wales.
Oxford.

P

PADSTOW, Cornwall.
Padworth, Berks.
Paglesham, Essex.
Pangbourne, Berks.
Pawley Stanks, Cumberland.
Paxtonford, Hunts.
Pettington, Essex.
Pideford, Isle of Wight.
Pitsey, Essex.
Plumstead Parva, Norfolk.
Polburghe, Cumberland.
Porteshede, Somerset.

Porthdulas, Anglesea.
Potterpole, Penwortham, Lancashire.
Prittlewell Priory, Essex.
Pudele, Dorset.

R

RADCLIFF, Notts.
Radcot, Oxon.
Radley, Berks.
Radley, Gloucester.
Rameton, Notts.
Reading, Berks.
Redeyagerna, Wilts.
Remenham, Berks.
Rhoder, River, Kent.
Ribbel, Lancashire.
Richemond, Lincoln.
Roach, River, Essex.
Roceholm, Yorks.
Roche, Cambridge.
Rodeley, Gloucester.
Rodmere, Gloucester.
Rogholme, Westmoreland.
Rosington, York.
Rothonfeld Gray, Oxford.

S

ST. BENNET OF HOLME, Norfolk.
St. John, Kent.
Salley, Notts.
Saltash, Cornwall—oyster fishery.
Sanford, Oxon.
Satwell, Berks.
Saundeye, Hunts.
Sawle, Gloucester.
Seton juxta Wodehorn, Northumberland.
Severn, River, Gloucester.
Sheldingthorp, Lincoln.
Shifford, Oxon.
Shiplake, Oxon.
Shoebury, North, Essex.
Shoebury, South, Essex.
Shotesham, Norfolk.
Shylyngford, Oxford.
Sidmouth, Devon.
Sidwell, Notts.
Sister Carilflet, Sandtoft Lincoln.
Skegness, Lincoln.
Skerne, York.
Slimbergh, Gloucester.
Smalney, River, Lincoln.
Snaith, York.
Snetesham, Norfolk.
Snodhull, Hereford.
Solway Frith.
Somerleyton, Suffolk.
Somerwater, Yorks.
Sonning, Berks.
Sore, River, Leicester.
Sore, River, Notts.
Southampton.
Southampton—right of fishing.
Southend, Essex.
Southhikham, Lincoln.
Speen, or Spene, Berks—fishing.
Stakingey, Salop.
Stamford, Lincoln.
Standlake, Oxon.
Stanleghe, Nottingham.
Stanton Harcourt, Oxon.
Stevyngton, Bedford.
Stockfield Hall, Northumberland.
Stockton-cum-Soca, Norfolk.
Stoke, Notts.
Stoke, Oxon.
Stowe, Norfolk.
Stowe Quye, Cambridge.
Streatley, Berks.
Sturmer, River, Suffolk.
Sudbury, Suffolk.
Sutton, Berks.
Sutton, Notts.
Sutton Courtney, Berks.
Swainssay, Hereford.
Swyllington, Yorks.

T

TAMAR, Cornwall.
Taplow, Bucks.
Taverham, Norfolk.
Taw, River, Devon.
Tawye, Water of, Hereford.
Tees, River, York (throughout).
Tempden, Salop.
Terste, Southampton.
Test, Southampton.
Teynbridge, Devon.
Teyng, Devon.
Thames, River.
Thetford, Norfolk.
Thomston, Norfolk.
Tillebury, Essex.
Tollesbury, Essex.
Tonge, Kent.

Topsham, Devon.
Torridge, Water of, Devon.
Tottenham Creek, Middlesex.
Tredeham, Gloucester.
Trengeham, Norfolk.
Trent, River, Northumberland.
Troutbeck Water, Westmoreland—fishing.
Tweed, River, Northumberland.
Tyne, River, Northumberland (throughout).
Tyte, Berwick-on-Tweed.

U

ULVERSTONE, Lancaster.
Upton, Bucks.
Upwell, Notts.

W

WADENHOE, Norfolk.
Wakering, Essex.
Waletkylch, Glamorgan.
Wallflete, Essex.
Wallingford, Berks.
Walton-on-Trent, Derby.
Wandesford, York.
Wansbeck, River, Northumberland.
Wareham, River, Dorset.
Wargrave, Berks.
Warkworth, Northumberland.
Watchet, Somerset.
Water Eaton, Wilts.
Waterflete Creek, Essex.
Waye, Water of, Hereford.
Waynflete, Lincoln.
Wear Giffard, Devon.
Wearmouth, Durham.
Webbe, Norfolk.
Weland, River, Lincoln.
Went, Water of, York.
Westallinge, Norfolk.
Weston, York.
Weybrigg, Norfolk.
Weylond, Lincoln.
Whiston, Bucks.
Whitchurch, Oxon.
Whitley, Berks.
Whittenham, Little, Berks.
Whittenham, Long, Berks.
Wiklesmar, Hunts.
Windermere, Westmoreland.
Windsor, Berks.
Wingfield or Winchfield, Berks.
Winne, River.
Wisbeach, Cambridge.
Wisbeche, High Fenn, Norfolk.
Witlesmere, Hunts.
Wittlesey, Cambridge.
Witton, Middlesex.
Woburn, Bucks.
Wodhull Parva, Bedford.
Wolvercote, Oxon.
Woodmill Bridge, Southampton.
Wraysbury, Bucks.
Wroxham, Norfolk.
Wye, River.
Wyston, Notts.
Wytegift.
Wytham, Berks.
Wytham, Lincoln.

Y

YARMOUTH, GREAT, Norfolk.
Yensfeld, Kent.
Yokflete Creek, Essex.

INDEX OF PLACES.

A

B

D

E

H

I

J

K

L

M

N

O

Y

GENERAL INDEX.

PRINTED BY BALLANTYNE, HANSON AND CO.
LONDON AND EDINBURGH

www.ingramcontent.com/pod-product-compliance
Ingram Content Group UK Ltd.
Pitfield, Milton Keynes, MK11 3LW, UK
UKHW041447071026
15587UKWH00010B/660

9 781584 775928